so me

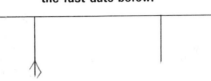
D0409394

**Books are to be returned on or before
the last date below.**

Advances in Consumer Research

Volume XXVIII

Mary C. Gilly

Joan Meyers-Levy

Editors

International Standard Book Number (ISBN): 0-915552-46-9

International Standard Serial Number (ISSN): 0098-9258

Mary C. Gilly and Joan Meyers-Levy, Editors

Advances in Consumer Research, Volume 28

(Valdosta, GA: Association for Consumer Research, 2001)

Preface

The thirty-first Annual Conference of the Association for Consumer Research (ACR) was held at the Little America Hotel and Towers in Salt Lake City, Utah, October 19-22, 2000. The Conference and this volume are dedicated to H. Keith Hunt upon his retirement as Executive Secretary of ACR, after an amazing 23 years of committed service. This volume is comprised of the presentations made at the meeting as well as the material presented at the luncheon honoring Keith.

The conference presentations consisted of a rich and diverse mix of consumer research topics, methods and philosophies. Participants could sample the traditional Special Sessions and Competitive Sessions, as well as the newer Working Paper Session and Roundtables. Attendance at all of the sessions was quite good, with standing room only in some sessions, animated one-on-one discussions at the Working Paper Session, and small groups getting to know one another and network at the Roundtables. It is safe to say that there was something of value for all attendees, and the unsolicited feedback we received from numerous attendees is that they felt that the sessions and papers presented at the 2000 conference were among the best ever! Conference attendance set a record high of 654 people, with many in attendance from outside the U.S. It was exciting to see and experience the vibrant and international flavor of the sessions.

Specifically, 93 competitive papers were presented in 31 sessions. As this is the second year in which the ACR Board of Directors decided to give authors the option of publishing an abstract or a full paper in these proceedings, this volume represents a mix of these. In 39 special sessions, 116 presentations were made. Abstracts of each session (and in many cases of each paper) also are contained in this volume. Forty-three working papers were presented as research posters. Titles of the working papers can be found in the conference program that is reproduced in the following pages. Eight roundtables were organized and led by enthusiastic chairs. We very much appreciate the effort made by all of our colleagues who submitted and presented their research, those who chaired sessions and acted as discussion leaders, as well as the conference attendees.

We also offer our heartfelt thanks to our colleagues who provided guidance in the difficult job of selecting competitive papers and special sessions. Fifty ACR members served on the Program Committee and provided helpful, constructive comments to us and to the people who submitted Special Session Proposals. Over 200 people, most of whom volunteered, did an outstanding job of reviewing an eclectic set of Competitive and Working Papers. Their names are also reproduced in the Program. We also extend our sincere thanks to Gerry Henderson for the exceptional job she did soliciting and putting together an interesting set of Roundtable sessions.

In addition to the help we received on the scholarly content of the conference, we must acknowledge the invaluable assistance we received on the many tasks required for the conference to run smoothly and be enjoyable. We simply do not know how conference chairs ever did this job without Kathy Brown, who made all of the hotel arrangements and was there to assist in any emergency before and during the conference. Jim Muncy has very ably filled Keith Hunt's very large shoes (metaphorically speaking!), and we thank him for training the volunteers for the registration desk, finding the artist, Ranena G. Beck, who did the cover design, coordinating awards' plaques, and all the other important tasks that he so ably did that are too many to mention. We also thank Jim and Steve Barnett for their work on producing this volume.

We also want to recognize Janeen Arnold Costa and her colleagues at the University of Utah for their help and suggestions with local arrangements. They not only brought to our attention but both handled arrangements and helped pay for some entertainment at the ACR Friday evening reception, a vibrant and colorful musical trio known as the Saliva Sisters. The volunteers for the registration desk performed admirably in getting everyone's conference off to a smooth start. We are grateful to the University of Utah students and staff who worked the registration desk: Rohit Varman, Tao Wu, Kim Dodson, Joel Watson, Anders Bengtsson, Hillary Leonard, Xin Zhao, Marie Hafey, Marlys Mason, Linda Briley, Todd Hayes, Michael Smalley, and Jana Pohlman. Hope Schau (now at Temple University) was an invaluable help to Mary, and Joan received top-notch help from doctoral students Juliet Zhu and Lan Nguyen at the University of Minnesota who also helped out at the registration desk. We are extremely grateful for their dedication and long hours.

The Saturday luncheon activities and ice cream social that were held in Keith Hunt's honor were fun, memorable, and heart-warming. We offer our sincerest thanks to our beloved friend and favorite target of teasing, Hal Kassarjian, who took on the onerous job of organizing the Saturday luncheon fete. Hollywood-bound Morris Holbrook served as an unforgettable emcee, and his appearance in cowboy togs singing his customized rendition of "The Ballad of H. Keith Hunt" was a highlight of the luncheon. The words to Morris' song are reproduced in this volume, and we have no doubt that it and Morris' entire performance will be forever remembered and cherished in the annals of ACR lore. We have also included in this volume Jerry Kernan's poem for Keith that Hal Kassarjian so ably read, and the many moving and witty comments that were delivered by Sid Levy, Gary McKinnon, and Tacy Wells. In the end, we laughed, we cried, and we stood in amazement at the dedication of the Hunt family. If you missed the tribute, don't miss that section of the Proceedings.

Finally, we would like to thank ACR President Marsha Richins for her confidence (probably viewed by many as questionably-placed) in our ability to pull this thing off. While we had our doubts along the way and fell victim to more snafus than we care to admit, the end result was a success, thanks in great measure to the help of so many fine and dedicated friends.

Joan Meyers-Levy, University of Minnesota
Mary C. Gilly, University of California, Irvine
2000 ACR Conference Co-Chairs/Proceedings Editors

Competitive and Working Paper Reviewers

Gwen Achenreiner
Praveen Aggarwal
Chris Allen
Mark I. Alpert
Søren Askegaard
Stacey Menzel Baker
Carlos Ballasteros
Gary Bamossy
James H. Barnes
Mike Barone
Mike Basil
Nada Nasr Bechwati
Karen L. Becker-Olsen
Suzanne C. Beckmann
George Belch
Michael Belch
Russell Belk
Matthew J. Bernthal
Abhijit Biswas
Paula Bone
Derrick S. Boone
Dominique Bouchet
Amanda B. Bower
Bridgette Braig
Karin Braunsberger
Terry Bristol
Susan Broniarczyk
Christie Brown
Anne M. Brumbaugh
Frederic F. Brunel
Steve Burgess
Jim Burroughs
Scot Burton
Meg Campbell
Les Carlson
Richard Celsi
Goutam Chakraborty
Dipankar Chakravarti
Pierre Chandon
Jennifer E. Chang
Patrali Chatterjee
Subimal Catterjee
Amitava Chattopadhyay
Ed Chung
Seh-Woong Chung
Claudia Clark
Larry Compeau
Margy Conchar
June Cotte
Robin Coulter
Deborah Cours
Jim Curran
Mary T. Curren
Darren Dahl
Vassilis Dalakas

Shai Danziger
Moshe Davidow
John Dawes
Stephanie Dellande
Ruby Dholakia
Aimee Drolet
Denver D'Rozario
Sandipa Dublish
Jennifer Edson Escalas
Steve Edwards
Richard Elliott
Basil G. Englis
Hooman Estelami
Richard Ettenson
Eileen Fischer
Mark Forehand
Susan Fournier
Susanne Friese
Terrance G. Gabel
Tao Gao
Ellen Garbarino
Meryl Gardner
Joan Giese
Ron Goodstein
Stephen Gould
John Gourville
Kjell Gronhaug
Ron Groves
John Hadjimarcou
Flemming Hansen
Manoj Hastak
Susan E. Heckler
Geraldine Henderson
Patrick Hetzel
Mark E. Hill
Elizabeth C. Hirschman
Margaret K. Hogg
Pamela M. Homer
Dan Horne
David Horne
H. Rika Houston
Chung-kue Hsu
Jim Hunt
Shailendra P. Jain
Chris Janiszewski
Bob Jewell
Christopher Joiner
Marilyn Y. Jones
Frank Kardes
Eric J. Karson
Harold H. Kassarjian
Steven Kates
Amna Kirmani
Lisa R. Klein

Noreen Klein
Susan Kleine
Scott Koslow
Robert V. Kozinets
Fredric Kropp
Barbara A. Lafferty
Frederick W. Langrehr
Sharmistha Law
Robert Lawson
Julie Lee
Brian Lofman
David Luna
Nicholas Lurie
Pauline Maclaran
Anne Weidemanis Magi
Ken Manning
Ingrid M. Martin
Michael S. McCarthy
John A. McCarty
Chuck McMellon
Havva J. Meric
Kathleen S. Micken
Anthony D. Miyazaki
Bruce Money
Melissa Moore
Robert Moore
Elizabeth Moore
Page Moreau
Marlene Morris
Ashesh Mukherjee
Jyotsna Mukherji
Albert M. Muniz Jr.
Sabrina M. Neeley
Keith E. Niedermeier
Steve Nowlis
Joe Nunes
Gillian Oakenfull
Sue O'Curry
Stephanie O'Donohoe
Thomas O'Guinn
Per Ostergaard
Kay Palan
H. G. Parsa
Connie Pechmann
Lars Perner
Simone Pettigrew
Barbara J. Phillips
Dianne M. Phillips
John W. Pracejus
Chris Pullig
Girish Punj
Priya Raghubir
Seshan Ramaswami
Rebecca Ratner

Nora J. Rifon
Scott Roberts
Bill Ross
Salvador Ruiz
Julie Ruth
Gad Saad
Sridhar Samu
Ozlem Sandikci
Shay Sayre
Robert Schindler
Bernd Schmitt
Jonathan Schroeder
Stewart Shapiro
Baba Shiv
Clifford J. Shultz
Itamar Simonson
Deepak Sirdeshmukh
Jan Slater
Amy K. Smith
N. Craig Smith
Karen H. Smith
Ruth Ann Smith
Jane Sojka
David E. Sprott
Donald E. Stem Jr.
Brian Sternthal
Lorna Stevens
Lisa Szykman
Siok Kuan Tambyah
Brian Tietje
Elizabeth Tissier-Desbordes
Sarah Todd
Darach Turley
Robert Underwood
Stijn van Osselaer
Marc Vanhuele
Madhu Viswanathan
Janet Wagner
Beth Walker
Anthony Ward
James Ward
Dan Wardlow
Bruce D. Weinberg
Klaus Wertenbroch
Tiffany White
Solveig Wikström
Robert Wilkes
Laura A. Williams
Patti Williams
Terry Witkowski
Charles M. Wood
David B. Wooten
Paschalina (Lilia) Ziamou
Rami Zwick

v

Table of Contents and Conference Program

ASSOCIATION FOR CONSUMER RESEARCH ANNUAL CONFERENCE

OCTOBER 19-22, 2000
SALT LAKE CITY, UTAH

THURSDAY, OCTOBER 19, 2000

ACR BOARD OF DIRECTORS MEETING
Noon - 5:00 pm

SCP EXECUTIVE COMMITTEE MEETING
2:00 pm - 5:30 pm

REGISTRATION FOR ACR DOCTORAL CONSORTIUM
2:30 pm - 3:00 pm

AMA MEETING
3:30 pm - 5:00 pm

FIRST ACR DOCTORAL CONSORTIUM
3:00 pm - 5:30 pm

BREAKOUT SESSIONS FOR DOCTORAL CONSORTIUM
4:30 pm - 5:30 pm

ACR REGISTRATION
4:00 pm - 7:30 pm

ACR WELCOMING RECEPTION
5:30 pm - 7:30 pm

DOCTORAL CONSORTIUM DINNER
7:30 pm - 9:30 pm

1.1 *Competitive Session*: **Consumers and Financial Matters**

Chair: Sue O'Curry, DePaul University
Discussion Leader: Michael Guiry, SUNY New Platz

1.2 *Special Session*: **Understanding the Adolescent's Consumption World: Shopping, Influencing, Deceiving**

Chair: Terry Bristol, Arizona State University West
Discussion Leader: Deborah Roedder John, University of Minnesota

1.3 *Competitive Session:* **The Impacts of Personality**

Chair: Yuping Liu, Rutgers University
Discussion Leader: Michael McCarthy, Miami University

1.4   *Competitive Session:* Consumers On-Line

Chair: Goutam Chakraborty, Oklahoma State University
Discussion Leader: Eric Shih, Wake Forest University

1.5   *Special Session:* A Fuller Understanding of Product and Brand Relationships: Antecedents, Dimensions, and Consequences

Chair: Julie R. Irwin, University of Texas at Austin
Discussion Leader: Susan Broniarczk, University of Texas at Austin

SPECIAL SESSION SUMMARY

Dimensioning Brand Relationships Using Brand Relationship Quality
    Susan Fournier, Harvard School of Business

Brand Relationships: The Influence of Relationship Type on Consumer Decision Making Strategies
    Pankaj Aggarwal, University of Chicago
    Ann L. McGill, University of Chicago

*If They Could See Us Now: A Look at How Consumers Relate to Their Products and How these Relationships
Explain Why Leading Brands Succeed or Fail*
    Peter Golder, New York University
    Julie Irwin, University of Texas at Austin

1.6   *Special Session:* The Instantiation, Shopping, and Handling of Consumer Displeasure (and Pleasure)

Chair: Michel Tuan Pham, Columbia University
Discussion Leader: Gerald Gorn, Hong Kong University of Science & Technology

SPECIAL SESSION SUMMARY

Who's to Blame? Consumers' Emotional Responses to Service Failures
    Kiersten Elliott, Duke University
    Julie Edell, Duke University

Contextually Shaping Customer Happiness
    Jennifer Ames, Columbia University
    Michel Tuan Pham, Columbia University

Problems, Emotional Responses to Redress, and Their Impact on Loyalty: What Real-World Data Tell Us
    Richard L. Oliver, Vanderbilt University
    John A. Goodman, TARP
    Marlene Yanovsky, TARP

1.7 *Special Session*: **Videography Versus Written Ethnography in Consumer Research**

Chair: Russell W. Belk, University of Utah
Discussion Leaders: Eric Arnould, University of Nebraska
                              Deborah Heisley, California State University, Northridge

1.8 *Roundtable*: **A Glimpse of Consumer Behavior in Vietnam: A Discussion of Gift-Giving**

Chairs: Francis Piron, Nanyang Technological University, Singapore
                              Mai Van Xuan, Hue University, Viet Nam
                              Wang Jian Feng, Nanyang Technological University, Singapore

---

FRIDAY, OCTOBER 20, 2000

SESSION 2
10:30 am - 12:00 noon

2.1 *Special Session:* **Consumer Confidence and Knowledge Calibration**

Chair: Christine Moorman, Duke University
                              Lyle Brenner, University of Florida
Discussion Leader: Wes Hutchinson, University of Pennsylvania

2.8   *Roundtable:* **Marketplace Diversity: Does Caveat Emptor Apply to "Vulnerable" Consumers?**

Chairs: Geraldine R. Henderson, Howard University
                           Pravat Choudhury, Howard University

---

FRIDAY, OCTOBER 20, 2000

LUNCHEON
ACR BUSINESS MEETING
12:00 noon – 1:50 pm

PRESIDENTIAL ADDRESS
Marsha L. Richins

AWARDS

FRIDAY, OCTOBER 20, 2000

SESSION 3
2:00 pm-3:30 pm

3.1   *Special Session:* **Experience-Based Processing and its Effects on Judgment, Decision Making, and Behavior**

Chairs: Laurette Dubé, McGill University
                           Ashesh Mukherjee, McGill University
Discussion Leader: Andrew Mitchell, University of Toronto

SPECIAL SESSION SUMMARY

The Influence of Cognitive Feelings on Judgments and Decisions
        Piotr Winkielman, University of Denver
        Norbert Schwarz, University of Michigan

Bodily States, Decision-Making, and the Somatic Marker Hypothesis
        Antoine Bechara, University of Iowa

Threat-Related Affective Feelings, Defense Mechanisms and the Behavioral Impact of Humor Appeal
        Laurette Dubé, McGill University
        Michael Conway, Concordia University
        Ashesh Mukherjee, McGill University

3.2   *Competitive Session:* **Implications of Gender**

Chair: Anne Brumbaugh, Case Western Reserve University
Discussion Leader: Deborah Cours, California State University, Northridge

3.3   *Competitive Session:* **Determinants and Effects of Mood**

Chair: Fredric Kropp, Monterey Institute of International Studies
Discussion Leader   Rajiv Vaidyanathan, University of Minnesota, Duluth

3.4   *Special Session:* **Rhetorics of Resistance, Discourses of Discontent**

Chair: Eileen Fischer, York University
Discussion Leader: Lisa Peñaloza, University of Colorado

SPECIAL SESSION SUMMARY

3.5   *Special Session:* **Consumer Preferences Towards Frequency Programs**

Chair: Ran Kivetz, Columbia University
Discussion Leader: Stephen J. Hoch, University of Pennsylvania

SPECIAL SESSION SUMMARY

3.6   *Special Session:* Strategic Behaviors in Competitive Games

Chairs: Wilfred Amaldoss, Purdue University
                                 Teck H. Ho, University of Pennsylvania
Discussion Leader: Colin Camerer, Caltech

3.7   *Competitive Session:* On-Line Information Sources

Chair: Peter Reingen, Arizona State University
Discussion Leader: Zeynep Gurhan-Canli, University of Michigan

3.8   *Roundtable:* Qualitative Data Analysis

Chairs: Eric Arnould, University of Nebraska
                                 Melanie Wallendorf, University of Arizona

FRIDAY, OCTOBER 20, 2000

WORKING PAPER SESSION
3:00 pm – 4:30 pm

4.1   *Special Session:* **Mysterious Sights: Consumption Creolization and Identity Construction in a Postmodern World**

Chairs: Ozlem Sandikci, Bilkent University
                               Güliz Ger, Bilkent University
Discussion Leader: Douglas B. Holt, University of Illinois

SPECIAL SESSION SUMMARY

American Expatriate Wives: Gender Class and Nationality in Transnational Suburbia
        Siok Kuan Tambyah, National University of Singapore
        Saroja Subrahmanyan, National University of Singapore

Where East Meets West and the Countermodern Meets Postmodern: Consumer Meanings in the Hybridized Cultural System of Natural Health
        Craig J. Thompson, University of Wisconsin
        Maura Troester, University of Wisconsin

4.2   *Special Session:* **When *Does* Culture Matter? The Transitory Nature of Cultural Differences in Judgments and Choices**

Chair: Donnel Briley, Hong Kong University
                               Jennifer Aaker, Stanford University
Discussion Leader: Robert Wyer, Hong Kong University of Science & Technology

SPECIAL SESSION SUMMARY

A Dynamic Perspective of Cultural Influence: Exploring the Role of Reasons
        Donnel Briley, Hong Kong University of Science & Technology
        Michael Morris, Stanford University

When Does Culture Matter: The Role of Accessibility
        Jennifer Aaker, Stanford University

Culture Matters When I'm Involved and Need Closure
        Lydia Price, Hong Kong University of Science & Technology
        Donnel Briley, Hong Kong University of Science & Technology

4.3 *Competitive Session*: **Cross-National Research on Price and Service Quality**

Chair: Richard Ettenson, Thunderbird
Discussion Leader: James H. Barnes, University of Mississippi

4.4 *Special Session*: **"Paradigms Regained": Humanities Theory and Empirical Research**

Chairs: Barbara Stern, Rutgers University
             Cristel Russell, San Diego State University
Discussion Leader: Bobby Calder, Northwestern University

SPECIAL SESSION SUMMARY

4.5 *Competitive Session:* **Brand Extensions and Associations**

Chair: Manoj Hastak, American University
Discussion Leader: Chris Pullig, University of Virginia

4.6 *Competitive Session:* **The Store-Consumer Interaction**

Chair: Marc Vanhuele, GROUPE HEC
Discussion Leader: Seh Wong Chung, INSEAD

4.7 *Special Session:* **The Impact of the Net: Strategies for Consumer Behavior Research Design in the 21ˢᵗ Century**

Chairs: Carolyn Folkman Curasi, Berry College
Pauline Maclaran, De Montfort University
Discussion Leader: Margaret K. Hogg, UMIST, UK

SPECIAL SESSION SUMMARY

A Critical Exploration of Internet & In-Person Depth Interviews-Customer Loyalty and the Internet: Benefits that Drive Loyalty on the Internet
    Carolyn Folkman Curasi, Berry College

Consumer Resistance and Resisting Consumers on the Web
    Pauline Maclaran, De Montfort University
    Miriam Catterall, The Queen's University, Belfast

Identity, Rituals and Role Transitions: Examining Empty Nesters as 'Liminal Consumers'
    Margaret K. Hogg, UMIST, UK
    Carolyn Folkman Curasi, Berry College
    Pauline Maclaran, De Montfort University

4.8 *Roundtable:* **Who Wants to be a Millionaire? That's Entertainment**

Chairs: Carol M. Motley, Howard University
Srinivas K. Reddy, University of Georgia

FRIDAY, OCTOBER 20, 2000

JCR EDITORIAL REVIEW BOARD MEETING
5:00 pm – 7:00 pm

RECEPTION
with live entertainment and music by the
Saliva Sisters
Co-sponsored by
ACR and the University of Utah Marketing Dept.
6:00 pm – 8:00 pm

```
┌─────────────────────────────────────────────────────┐
│                                                       │
│             SATURDAY, OCTOBER 21, 2000                │
│                                                       │
│               ACR NEWCOMERS' BREAKFAST                │
│                  7:00 am – 8:15 am                    │
│                                                       │
│              ACR CONTINENTAL BREAKFAST                │
│                  7:30 am – 8:30 am                    │
│                                                       │
│                  ACR REGISTRATION                     │
│                  8:00 am – 5:00 pm                    │
│                                                       │
│                 JCP BOARD MEETING                     │
│                  8:00 am – 9:00 am                    │
│                                                       │
└─────────────────────────────────────────────────────┘
```

```
┌─────────────────────────────────────────────────────┐
│                                                       │
│             SATURDAY, OCTOBER 21, 2000                │
│                                                       │
│                     SESSION 5                         │
│                 8:30 am – 10:00 am                    │
│                                                       │
└─────────────────────────────────────────────────────┘
```

5.0   Ferber Award Session

5.1   Special Session: The Retailer as a Master of Asymmetric Price Competition: Experimental, Empirical, and Simulation-Based Results

Chair: Timothy B. Heath, University of Pittsburgh
                                Joel Huber, Duke University
                                Xin He, University of Pittsburgh
Discussion Leader: J. Wesley Hutchinson, University of Pennsylvania

Product Assortment as a Source of Brand Choice, Brand Commitment, and Cross-Tier Switching
        Timothy B. Heath, University of Pittsburgh
        Xin He, University of Pittsburgh
        Subimal Chatterjee, Binghamton University

Developing Synergies Between Promotions and Brands in Different Price-Quality Tiers
        Katherine Lemon, Harvard University
        Stephen M. Nowlis, Arizona State University

The Role of Reference Dependence in Asymmetric Price and Attribute Change Effects
        Joel Huber, Duke University
        Alison Lo, Duke University

5.2   Competitive Session: Children as Consumers

Chair: Amitava Chattopadhyay, INSEAD
Discussion Leader: David Luna, Chapman University

5.3   *Competitive Session:* **The Feeling Consumer (Social Issues)**

Chair: Mike Barone, Iowa State University
Discussion Leader: Charles Wood, University of Tulsa

5.4   *Special Session:* **The Three Faces of E, commerce: Insight into Online Consumer Behavior Through the Interpretation of an Internet Consumer's Experience**

Chair: Wendy Schneier Siegal, Boston University
Discussion Leader: Bruce D. Weinberg, Bentley University

SPECIAL SESSION SUMMARY

DISCUSSANT'S COMMENTS

5.5   *Competitive Session:* **Aspects of Self**

Chair: Larry Compeau, Clarkson University
Discussion Leader: Stephen Brown, University of Ulster

5.6   *Competitive Session:* Inter-Consumer Influences

Chair: Kay Palen, Iowa State University
Discussion Leader: Fuat Firat, Arizona State University

5.7   *Special Session*: Creating Flow Experiences: The Influence of Individual Factors on the Antecedents of Flow

Chair: Lisa R. Klein, Rice University
Discussion Leader: Ann Schlosser, Vanderbilt University

5.8   *Roundtable:* The Impact of Homophily on Consumer Behavior

Chair: Oscar DeShields, California State University, Northridge

---

SATURDAY, OCTOBER 21, 2000

SESSION 6
10:30 am – 12:00 noon

6.1   *Special Session:* The Revival of Projective Techniques: Past, Present and Future Perspectives

Chair: Jennifer E. Chang, Penn State University
Discussion Leader: Sidney J. Levy, University of Arizona

6.2   *Special Session:* **The Role and Impact of External Recommendations in Decision Making**

Chair: Gavan J. Fitzsimons, University of Pennsylvania
Discussion Leader: Patricia West, Ohio State University

6.3   *Special Session:* **The Dual Role of Affect in Information Processing and Decision Making**

Chair: Yiorgos A. Bakamitsos, Dartmouth College
Discussion Leader: Alice Isen, Cornell University

6.4   *Special Session:* **New Insights about Consumers' Perception and Evaluation of Product Assortments**

Chairs: Erica van Herpen, Tilburg University
                          Brian Wansink, University of Illinois, Urbana-Champaign
Discussion Leader: Hans Baumgartner, Penn State University

6.5   *Competitive Session:* **Brand Images**

Chair: George Belch, San Diego State University
Discussion Leader: Chuck McMellon, Hofstra University

6.6   *Special Session:* **What is Your Goal? The Impact of Goals on Counterfactual Thinking, Attitude Formation, and Predictions of the Future**

Chairs: Jennifer L. Aaker, Stanford University
                      Angela Lee, Northwestern University
Discussion Leader: Rick Larrick, University of Chicago

6.7 *Special Session:* **Have-nots in a World of Haves: Disenfranchised Nations and Their Consumers in an Increasingly Affluent and Global World**

Chair: Clifford J. Shultz, II, Arizona State University
Discussion Leader: Don R. Rahtz, College of William and Mary

6.8 *Roundtable:* **Consumer Bargain Hunting: Among the Fleas, in the Mortar, on the Net, and on the Bay**

Chair: Lars Perner, George Washington University

6.9 **Meet the Editors**

SATURDAY, OCTOBER 21, 2000

TRIBUTE TO KEITH HUNT
Luncheon
12:00 noon – 1:45

SATURDAY, OCTOBER 21, 2000

SESSION 7
1:45 pm – 3:15 pm

7.1 *Competitive Session:* **Social Influences**

Chair: Jennifer Gregan-Paxton, University of Delaware
Discussion Leader: Connie Pechmann, University of California, Irvine

7.2   *Special Session:* **Individual Differences in Gender and Age: Theory Enhancement and Some Important Consequences**

Chair: Rui (Juliet) Zhu, University of Minnesota
                               Joan Meyers-Levy, University of Minnesota
Discussion Leader: Christie L. Nordhielm, Northwestern University

SPECIAL SESSION SUMMARY

Gender Differences in Processing Pictures in Verbal Messages: The Influence of Pictorial Ambiguity or Relational Coherence
    Joan Meyers-Levy, University of Minnesota
    Carolyn Yoon, University of Michigan
    Rui Zhu, University of Minnesota
    Michelle Lee, Singapore Management University

Reported Warnings About False Consumer Claims Can Make Them Seem True: A Paradoxical Age Difference
    Ian Skurnik, University of Toronto
    Norbert Schwarz, University of Michigan
    Denise Park, University of Michigan

The Effect of Aging on the Processing of Emotional and Non-Emotional Information
    Aimee Drolet, UCLA
    Patti Williams, University of Pennsylvania

7.3   *Competitive Session:* **Affect and Images**

Chair: Aparna Labroo, Cornell University
Discussion Leader: Barbara Phillips, University of Saskatchewan

7.4   *Special Session:* **Consumer Trust in an Internet Environment**

Chair: Marlene Morris, Georgetown University
Discussion Leader: Sumedha Gupta, MIT

SPECIAL SESSION SUMMARY

7.5   *Competitive Session:* **How Does Price Figure In?**

Chair:	Klaus Wertenbroch, INSEAD
Discussion Leader:	Noreen Klein, Virginia Tech University

7.6   *Special Session:* **Factors Affecting Consumer Choices Between Hedonic and Utilitarian Options**

Chair:	Michal Strahilevitz, University of Miami
	Ran Kivetz, Columbia University
Discussion Leader:	Drazen Prelec, MIT

SPECIAL SESSION SUMMARY

7.7 *Special Session:* **Qualitative Research Perspectives in Computer Mediated Environments**

Chair: Hope J. Schau, Temple University
Discussion Leader: Gary Ford, American University

7.8 *Roundtable:* **Toward an Agenda For Research on Family Consumption Behavior**

Chairs: Karin M. Ekström, Handelshögskolan vid Göteborgs universitet
                              Suraj Commuri, University of Nebraska

---

SATURDAY, OCTOBER 21, 2000

ICE CREAM SOCIAL
in honor of
H. KEITH HUNT
3:15 pm – 4:00 pm

SATURDAY, OCTOBER 21, 2000

SESSION 8
4:00 pm – 5:30 pm

8.1 *Special Session:* **New Perspectives on Consumer Evaluations of Experiences that Extend Over Time: Empirical Regularities, Integration Rules and Formal Modeling**

Chair: Gal Zauberman, The University of North Carolina at Chapel Hill
Discussion Leader: Drazen Prelec, Massachusetts Institute of Technology

8.8 *Roundtable:* **Consumer Behavior Research in Automaticity: Issues, Methods, and Directions**

Chairs: Suresh Ramanathan, New York University
Patti Williams, University of Pennsylvania

SATURDAY, OCTOBER 21, 2000

PROGRAM COMMITTEE MEETING FOR ACR 2001
5:00 pm – 6:00 pm

ACR RECEPTION
6:00 pm – 8:00 pm

SUNDAY, OCTOBER 22, 2000

JCR POLICY BOARD MEETING
7:30 am – 12:30 pm

ACR CONTINENTAL BREAKFAST
7:30 am – 8:30 am

ACR REGISTRATION
8:00 am – 10:00 am

SUNDAY, OCTOBER 22, 2000

SESSION 9
8:30 am – 10:00 am

9.1 *Special Session:* **Judgment Correction: Antecedents, Consequences, and Explanations**

Chair: Prashant Malaviya, INSEAD
Discussion Leader: C. Miguel Brendl, INSEAD

SPECIAL SESSION SUMMARY

9.5   *Competitive Session:* Motivation in Complex Consumption Environments

Chair: Jennifer Escalas, University of Arizona
Discussion Leader: Robert Jewell, Virginia Tech University

9.6   *Competitive Session:* Consideration Sets & Product Attributes

Chair: Bill Ross, Penn State University
Discussion Leader: Ingrid Martin, University of Colorado

**9.7   *Special Session:* Realer than Real: Retail Hyperreality and the Encoding of "Authentic" Cultural
Symbolism**

Chair: Michael R. Solomon, Auburn University
Discussion Leader: Christina L. Brown, University of Michigan

SPECIAL SESSION SUMMARY

10.1 *Competitive Session:* **Physiological Issues in Consumer Research**

Chair: Jill Klein, INSEAD
Discussion Leader: Jacques-Marie Auriefeille, The Reunion University

10.2 *Competitive Session:* **Consumerism & Moral Orientation**

Chair: Anthony Miyazaki, University of Miami
Discussion Leader: Mary Wolfinbarger, California State University, Long Beach

10.3 *Special Session:* **Discrete Emotions and Coping Strategies: Implications for Persuasion, Behavior, and Public Policy**

Chair: Mary Frances Luce, University of Pennsylvania
Discussion Leader: Julie Edell, Duke University

SPECIAL SESSION SUMMARY

How Consumers Cope with Negative Emotions
      Sungwan Yi, Pennsylvania State University
      Hans Baumgartner, Pennsylvania State University

Differentiated Fear Appeals
Kirsten Grasshoff, Pennsylvania State University
Mita Sujan, Pennsylvania State University

Emotional Antecedents of Protection Motivation
Punam Anand Keller, Dartmouth College
Ardis Olson, Dartmouth Hitchcock Medical Center
Deborah Shields, Dartmouth College

10.4   *Competitive Session:* **Communication, Recall and Persuasion**

Chair: Michael Belch, San Diego State University
Discussion Leader: Shay Sayre, California State University, Fullerton

10.5   *Competitive Session:* **Attribution and Categorization**

Chair: Jim Burroughs, Rutgers University
Discussion Leader: Stephen Brown, University of Ulster

10.6   *Special Session:* **Strategic Framing: The Art and Science of Influencing Others**

Chair: Rebecca W. Hamilton, University of Maryland
Discussion Leader: Peter Wright, University of Oregon

SPECIAL SESSION SUMMARY

Issue Framing, Value Tradeoffs, and Political Choice
Thomas E. Nelson, Ohio State University

Consumer Behavior As a Social Science

Marsha L. Richins, University of Missouri

I am going to use my president's address today to challenge you and, I hope, to make us all feel proud of our field and what it can be. I am frequently struck by how important a topic consumer behavior is. It is of compelling interest to society for many reasons. In my address today, I will attempt to describe some of these reasons, and at the same time convince some of you to change slightly your perspective on the scope of consumer behavior research.

THE SIGNIFICANCE OF CONSUMER BEHAVIOR

So, what is it about consumer behavior that makes it so compelling to everyone, not just consumer scholars?

First, as the Wall Street Journal and CNBC constantly remind us, consumption is important to economic performance. Consumption-related factors such as spending, saving, and consumer confidence have important impacts on cash flows, employment rates, and capital investments. Workers' desires to consume often increase their work motivation and employee productivity in the aggregate.

At a more individual level, consumption is necessary for our health and well-being. Many consumption experiences are associated with delight and joy, some with disappointment or anger. Consumption problems create frustration, stress, and ill-will. Deficits in individuals' ability to consume over a long period of time, or in a large portion of a population subgroup, are associated with property crime, hopelessness, and a general debilitation of the spirit.

Consumer behavior is important, also, because many pressing social problems are related to consumer behavior gone awry. Inappropriate consumption of drugs, alcohol, and firearms can have devastating impacts on individuals and families. Improper consumption of cellphones causes traffic accidents. A diet heavy in Twinkies and Jolt cola is hazardous to our health. Excessive consumption of all types creates pollution and endangers the planet and all its inhabitants.

Finally, casual observation reveals that consumption is an important topic in everyday interpersonal discourse. It influences what we talk about—as we describe our shopping experiences to co-workers, as we discuss the movie we just saw, the new restaurant we tried, and our hopes and dreams for the future.

Consumption influences how we interact with others—more frequently, perhaps, via email; more selectively, perhaps, when we tune out the world and into a Walkman. And consumption is a source of conflict—as when spouses disagree over what to buy and when children badger their parents for more things, more expensive things, or simply things their parents don't want them to have.

Consumption, simply, is about the way we live. When people, politicians, and pundits talk about the concerns of the day, the following issues come up again and again.

- How can people get close to one another?
- How can parents raise kids to be responsible and well-adjusted?
- How can people achieve happiness?
- How can we maintain good health and productivity?
- How can inequalities in the distribution of wealth and knowledge be reduced?

Every one of these questions is intimately associated with consumer behavior. These are big, important topics. Yet consumer researchers don't study them much. We have yielded these topics to scholars in other disciplines.

For example, an economist, Robert Frank (1999), in his book *Luxury Fever*, documents the rise in luxury consumption over the past two decades and assesses its impact on consumers' daily lives.

Sociologist John P. Robinson and Geoffrey Godbey (1997), in their book *Time for Life*, analyze how consumers use their time and find that our sense of "time famine" stems from our increased emphasis on the consumption of experiences.

An anthropologist, Katherine S. Newman (1993), has examined the effects of economic decline on consumption patterns, lifestyle, and family relationships.

BIG PICTURE RESEARCH

These are what I call "big picture" research. It is useful, I think, to consider what qualities these examples have in common. First, they take a macro perspective. The analyses are carried out at the social system level and look at multiple causes and multiple effects of actions and circumstances.

Second, they have had big impact. These books have been the subject of social and political discourse in the media and have provoked reflection and further research in several academic disciplines.

Third, they are the result of programmatic investigations that covered a period of several years. Newman's book, for example, is based on research that took her five years to complete.

Another characteristic is that their focus is on the substantive domain rather than the conceptual domain; that is, their research involves ongoing, real-world systems and has social, economic, technological, political, and moral content (see Brinberg and McGrath 1985).

And finally, this research takes a lot of pages to report. Such topics can't be effectively dealt with in a single journal article. Complex issues usually require a book-length effort to be covered appropriately.

THE NEGLECT OF BIG ISSUES IN CONSUMER RESEARCH

In consumer behavior, with few exceptions, we tend to look at focused issues—usually at the individual level—and not *big* issues. And we do this very well. We have well-trained scholars who publish well-crafted research in journals with rigorous standards. This is something that we as a discipline can be rightfully proud of. Yet this focus comes at a cost—the neglect of larger issues. We have ceded these larger issues to other social science disciplines less centrally concerned with consumption and with consumers.

Why has this happened? How has the consumer behavior discipline, for the large part, ended up with a micro focus rather than a broader view? It stems, I think, from an overly-narrow perspective on our discipline. Although we consumer scholars consider ourselves social scientists, in fact we have failed to treat consumer behavior as such. Social science is "the study of society and human relationships" (Concise Oxford Dictionary of Sociology, 1994) and deals with human behavior in its social and cultural aspects.

Nicosia and Mayer, in a seminal article in 1976, encouraged scholars to treat consumer behavior as a social science, particularly urging us to examine the influence of cultural values, institutions and their norms, and consumption activities as they relate to the network of social and cultural relationships. But as a discipline, we have failed to do this. Instead of looking at consumers in social systems and involved in social relationships, we have focused primarily on the individual. A review of articles published in the *Journal of Consumer Research* supports this conclusion.

Using the loosest possible definition of "social," I tallied the number of articles in *JCR* over the past 12 years that dealt with *anything* social. Any research that included social influence, norms, institutions, dyads of any sort, or social context, no matter how superficially, was counted as "social." I found that studies that include social variables comprise only about 20% of *JCR* articles, and that percentage is falling. The number of articles in which social variables feature prominently is even less, about 10% of the total. This is about two and one-half articles a year in *JCR*.

This journal represents the best research efforts in our field, yet few of the published articles in any one year deal with social or cultural relationships of any sort. Consumer behavior textbooks routinely acknowledge the importance of these topics, allocating large sections to them. But despite occasional pleas from consumer scholars to take a larger, more social view of consumer behavior (see Belk 1987; Lutz 1991; Zaltman 1991), we have failed to do so

REASONS FOR NEGLECT

After some thought, I have concluded that there are several reasons for our collective neglect of these issues in consumer behavior. First is socialization. Most consumer scholars are neither trained nor socialized to address big picture issues. We tend to do the kind of research our mentors have done, and a social perspective in consumer behavior simply has not evolved yet.

Second is institutional factors. Institutional constraints associated with tenure pressures and annual merit reviews encourage faculty to take a short-run perspective on publication. We are rewarded for pursuing relatively "safe" research projects of limited scope, which have a better chance of attaining the standards of rigor and control employed by our top journals.

Business school residency is another factor. Most ACR members reside in marketing departments in business schools. We teach business courses, sometimes to executives, and interact with colleagues in finance, accounting, management, and other business fields. We commingle with business people whom our deans hope will contribute to the b school's endowment. All this encourages a focus on business as the constituency for our research (see Holbrook 1985 for a fuller discussion). We concentrate on dependent variables like brand attitude and purchase intention. Certainly, these are important dependent variables, and doing research that is relevant to business and the effective functioning of the economy is meritorious.

But our discipline is larger than just business, and business is only *one* of our possible constituencies. By limiting our research to business-relevant topics, we are unnecessarily limiting our impact and our field of inquiry. For instance, our narrow focus has caused us to overlook interesting questions about the interaction between business and society and, especially, questions about how business practices influence social structure and social relations among consumers.

Finally, the discipline of consumer research in recent years has undergone some intense debate about the type of methods and the philosophical assumptions that should appropriately undergird consumer research. This debate has been a healthy and important

one. However, it has served to upstage the equally important issue of what types of research *topics* we as a discipline should choose to study. Although assumptions, methods, and research topic are intimately intertwined, the debate has focused on the first two of these—assumptions and methods—without explicitly addressing the questions of scope and emphasis in the discipline.

THE DIFFICULTIES

Perhaps the biggest inhibitor to big-picture research, however, is that it is hard to do well, and it is messy. How is it hard? Let me count the ways!

To illustrate, I will use a hypothesis that appeared several years ago in a Wall Street Journal article. A reporter noted that today's teens spend many hours in shopping malls, either working there or hanging out with friends. She speculated that this gives teens an unrealistic taste for goods that they can't satisfy once they become economically independent of their parents, and that this leads to unhappiness and disillusionment among young adults. That's an interesting question. Does hanging out at malls cause kids to be unhappy later on? Or, might it have the opposite effect of socializing young people to be savvier, more competent consumers? Any seasoned consumer researcher can immediately see some of the difficulties in trying to answer this question. These problems, some of which I will now describe, plague many big-picture consumer research topics.

An important impediment concerns theoretical framing of the problem. There aren't well-established literatures and theories in any one discipline that will help us get a handle on this problem. We would need to travel far and wide throughout the social sciences to find appropriate theoretical bases. We're talking about kids, so we'd need to look at developmental psychology. We can easily burn up a few months sorting through that literature. We can also look at learning theories, at sociology to understand how cultural expectations and norms develop, and while we're at it, some anthropologists have probably looked at similar issues in different cultural contexts. Then there's reference group theory and social comparison theory and yet more. Doing big picture research requires us to broaden our theoretical horizons—a time-consuming activity, but one that makes this type of research more rewarding.

One of the frustrating aspects of big-picture research is that it usually isn't amenable to traditional hypothesis testing approaches, and causal inference becomes ambiguous. For this reason, multiple studies using a variety of research approaches may be required. To answer the research question about teenagers and shopping malls, one might need to conduct longitudinal surveys, ethnographic research, and econometric analysis. Since no one scholar is likely to be well-versed in all these approaches, it may be necessary to gain new methodological skills or new colleagues. It may be necessary to use data sources that are unfamiliar to the researcher, such as archives of economic data on teen employment, expenditure patterns of teens and young adults, high school student tracking studies, and social survey data.

Yet finally, after all this work digging into new and diverse literatures, learning new methods and running lots of studies, the conclusions we draw would not be clear-cut. Our findings would be open to dispute, particularly if they cast a negative light on marketers, shopping malls, or parenting practices relating to those malls. Pundits and scholars would be quick to describe alternative explanations for our findings, as would journal reviewers.

These hindrances to big picture research loom large. They may seem insurmountable to some. And the risks are large. I suspect that at least 50% of the audience is mumbling—"They won't publish it in *JCR*." Perhaps it's time for us as *JCR* reviewers to have a more open mind to this kind of messy—but important—research.

THE PAYOFFS

Despite the difficulties, I urge ACR scholars to embrace a broader research perspective. In addition to our more typical research programs, each of us can and should think about some larger issue of interest to consumers themselves, to society, or to business in a long-term sort of way.

Why? you might ask. Big-picture research is labor-intensive and potentially risky—why do it? What's the payoff? I would argue that the payoffs are enormous.

First, it's fun. This kind of research is challenging, but for scholars, rising to a challenge and solving theoretical and methodological problems are fun. Discovering new, insightful literatures is fun. Learning new methods that allow new forms of discovery is fun. Meeting thoughtful scholars from other disciplines with different perspectives is stimulating and enjoyable.

Also, big picture research can make an important contribution to society. It can influence public policy decisions, child-rearing recommendations by "experts," and result in greater consumer satisfaction and well-being. It can also help companies, in the long run, better meet consumer and societal needs.

As a result of these contributions, this research can serve to enhance the stature of our discipline. Colleagues in other departments of our universities, decision-makers at grant-making institutions, the press, and perhaps even politicians will see that consumer behavior researchers are doing important work.

Many of us also will feel more pride in what we do as we plan our day's research activities, contemplate our accomplishments, or describe "what we do" to people we encounter.

SOME RESEARCH QUESTIONS

I would like, now, to take this opportunity to stimulate your thinking about some of the important issues that consumer scholars might pursue. The list I present contains topics that are personally interesting to me, but in no way represents the entire range of potential worthy topics. I offer them in the form of research questions that I hope will pique the interest of at least some of you here today.

• How does consumption bring people closer together?

Goods have important uses in interpersonal relationships, yet aside from some studies of gift exchange, we've neglected to examine how this is so. Some goods, like the gas grill on the patio or a game table, bring people together. Others—a Walkman or a Gameboy, for instance—can isolate their users. Yet we've done no systematic analysis of the interpersonal uses of consumption. We know little about how people use consumption rituals to reinforce relationships. What about shopping, for instance? How do people use shopping to enhance a sense of togetherness? When is the annual back-to-school family shopping rite a positive event for families and when is it stressful?

• How does consumption drive people apart?

In many cases, consumption can be a source of conflict. It can create family conflict, as when spouses disagree about consumption priorities or when parents and children disagree on the appropriate objects and limits of consumption. It can create tension among friends, as when one family displays photos of their trip to Disneyworld that their neighbors can't afford.

And it can create social class conflict. Disparities in consumption levels among social classes leads to dissatisfaction and envy and is implicated in criminal behavior as people try to get or destroy what they don't have. Such problems will only escalate as disparities among the social classes continue to increase. These

are some of the most compelling issues concerning consumer behavior, yet consumer scholars to date have essentially ignored them.

• How does consumption lead to happiness?

The consumer behavior discipline has been largely the study of choices, but we usually study only a small part of the choice process. We look at brand choice, but fail to look carefully at how consumers allocate resources across product classes. Fundamentally, people buy things to improve their happiness and their quality of life. Yet we don't know how consumers decide what will make them happy. For example, how do they choose whether to buy a home theater for the family or a new car for themselves? How do they decide whether to save for the future or to spend now on an exotic vacation, more fashionable new clothes, or extra Christmas presents for the kids?

We don't know how effective consumers are in making resource allocation decisions that will maximize their well-being. We don't know what consumption patterns are most likely to lead to happiness. These issues are at the core of consumer behavior, and we need to understand them better.

• What are the effects of consumption *un*happiness?

When does consumption and its pursuit make us miserable? We can all think of instances. The carefully tended lawn that is dead when you return from vacation. A celebration at an expensive restaurant ruined by a bad waiter. A travel agent who books you into a motel you'd like to forget. Door dings in your just-delivered new car. The excitement of your new gas grill suddenly dampened when you find that your co-worker just bought one that's even better. Rude salespeople. Ignorant salespeople. Bad haircuts....

Really, just how much consumption unhappiness is out there? How do these events influence people's moods and their relationships with others? What is the cumulative effect of all these dissatisfactions and what are their long-term implications? More generally, to what extent does the pursuit of consumption lead to time pressure and stress, family tensions, and general frustration?

• In what ways does marketing affect child socialization?

Consumer scholars have done quite a bit of research on the socialization of children as decision-makers (see John 1999 for a review). We know much less, however, about marketing's effects on other aspects of socialization. For instance, what is the personal and social impact on children of inviting shopping environments that entice kids to want? How does advertising influence the formation of values in children? Do certain family structures or particular social statuses make some children more susceptible to these influences?

• What effects does consumption itself have on children?

Goods and brand names have become increasingly central to children's lives—indeed, to the lives of all Americans—yet we know little about the effects of their consumption on children. When is consumption an aid to children's interpersonal relationships? When is it a hindrance?

How do products themselves affect our children? For instance, some children are heavy consumers of video games and associated products that simulate murder and mayhem. To what extent is marketing, versus other factors, responsible for the demand for these products? How are the peers of children who heavily consume these images and activities affected?

• How do marketing and product use affect family functioning?

The effects of marketing and consumption on family functioning is another area that has been largely neglected. To what extent does the consumption of convenience products create more time for high-quality parent-child interaction? What role does marketing and consumption play in the formation of family rituals, as when a family celebrates Friday evenings at the shopping mall or Saturday mornings with breakfast at McDonalds? How are products and gifts of products used in families disrupted by divorce to bring family members closer together or drive them apart?

• What are the effects of consumption patterns and marketing activities on society?

Critics have suggested that marketing selectively amplifies and reinforces some values, while ignoring or even denigrating others (see Pollay 1986). Is this true? If so, what are the long term effects on society at large?

We have devoted even less study to the impact of consumption patterns on the physical characteristics of a culture. Effects of consumption patterns on architecture and the aesthetics of roadways have been ignored by consumer scholars, as have effects on traffic patterns. What is the impact of e-commerce delivery trucks rumbling through quiet residential streets many times a day? Does it reduce crime? increase the number of children maimed in traffic accidents? increase or reduce air pollution and traffic congestion?

And what about the sensory over-stimulation resulting from marketing activities? We are flooded with visual stimuli whenever we enter a shopping environment or drive on city streets. The auditory environment is also overloaded. On one recent shopping trip I was simultaneously bombarded with Musak from store-wide loudspeakers, blaring rap lyrics from the electronics department, and a loud audiovisual presentation about how to apply wallpaper. Odor intrusion is increasingly an annoyance, as when the too-strong odor of Tommy Hilfiger cologne wafts from the pages of *Sports Illustrated*.

Does this incessant flood of stimuli have an effect on consumer well-being? Does it make us less able to hear the chirp of crickets on a quiet evening, less likely to savor the scent of fresh-mown grass? Or does the constant bombardment on our senses make people more likely to seek out opportunities for contemplation and reflection? And how does this unremitting assault on our senses influence our feelings of well-being, our relationships with others, and our general levels of irritability and civility?

• What is the proper relationship between marketing and the promotion of death and danger?

Advertisements encourage people to drink alcohol but are silent on the carnage caused by drunk drivers. Images of Double-deluxe Whoppers with cheese entice us into Burger King, but a steady diet of highly-advertised fatty products will eventually send many consumers to a cardiac care unit. During the summer months, my university's hospital has an organ transplant team on call around the clock to handle organ donations from jet ski and other boating accidents at the Lake of the Ozarks. As a discipline, we have failed to examine the extent to which marketing contributes to these tragedies. We have done little to investigate how consumption can be made safer or consumers be made wiser, or what marketing's responsibility should be in all of this.

CHOOSING A RESEARCH TOPIC

These are just a few of the questions consumer behavior scholars should rightfully be asking. Topics like these are truly exciting, and I hope every consumer scholar will devote at least some of his or her research efforts to issues that deal with consumption as part of a web of interpersonal relationships within society. I hope, that for at least a portion of their research activities, scholars will do the following three things.

First, when choosing a research topic, I hope that scholars will look to the world and their hearts. What about consumers, marketing, and society do you as a *person* truly care about? Where and how do consumption delights and consumption disasters occur? The things that most deeply affect us often provoke the most thoughtful research programs.

I hope also that on occasion scholars will look at phenomena first, then at theory. Theory has a high priority in our discipline, as well it should. But for at least part of our research, we should focus first on the substantive area of inquiry and cast theory in a supporting role. For part of our research, we should first ask what the phenomenon is that we want to understand. Perhaps what interests you is how consumers use products to build relationships. Perhaps you want to know how consumption conflicts are implicated in divorce. Or maybe you want to understand why on earth parents buy dangerous fireworks for their kids. The subject matter of most interest to consumer scholars, especially recently, has been purchase decisions. But that is only a tiny island in the world of consumer behavior, and it's time for us to do some exploring.

Third, we should occasionally ask the "who cares?" question. Before starting a line of research, we should at least sometimes ask "Would anyone besides me and three of my colleagues care about the outcome of this research? Does this research increase understanding about something of *direct* concern to consumers, policy makers, or business?"

THE TIME IS NOW

"Yes," you might say, "but I have to get tenure. Maybe I'll do some of this later." Yet we learn our research styles early in our careers, and it is difficult to break out of established patterns. Young scholars tend to have open minds and boundless enthusiasm. So the early part of one's career is a good time to begin thinking about big problems and to gain practice in struggling with research questions that cannot be answered with a one-shot survey or a 2 X 2 experimental design.

And the elders among us are not off the hook. Later career is also a good time to refocus on larger issues. Many senior scholars develop a sense of burnout or a sense that their research efforts have become somewhat repetitive or incremental. Turning to big picture topics can be refreshing and is perhaps an appropriate response to the considerable status and freedom that society gives to tenured professors.

SOME POSITIVE SIGNS

Fortunately, there are some positive trends in the discipline that make it easier for consumer scholars to pursue such topics and successfully publish them. First, the growth in interpretive research and its increasing acceptance in major journals is a positive sign. Study of many of the issues I've mentioned, and others like them, can profitably begin with interpretive approaches and perhaps be extended with more positivist research.

Also, there is an increasing number of publication outlets for this kind of research. The *JCR* Monograph series now provides an option for CB scholars to publish big-picture research in a prestigious setting. The *Journal of Macromarketing* and *Journal of Public Policy and Marketing* also provide publication outlets for system level research.

The Social Marketing Institute, recently founded and under the direction of Alan Andreasen, provides an excellent opportunity for scholars to apply their knowledge at a system level. Hopefully, academics working on SMI initiatives will also be moved to undertake basic research of relevance to social issues and social systems.

A CALL TO ACTION

In closing, I want to note that doctoral students are interested in the relationships between marketing, consumption, and society. A 1997 survey of student participants at the AMA doctoral consortium indicated that three-quarters of these students were moderately or highly interested in such issues (Wilkie and Moore-Shay 1997). It is the responsibility of more senior members of the discipline—faculty mentors, journal editors, and department chairs—to foster this interest.

I hope that some of you here today will be inspired to think again about the scope of consumer behavior research and take on some of the bigger issues that involve marketing and consumption. And perhaps, the next time you're at a university gathering talking to researchers who are working on cures for sickle cell anemia, trying to stop the transmission of AIDS, monitoring holes in the ozone layer, or studying political coups, you too will have something interesting to talk about. And when we're old and explaining our lives to our great grandchildren, perhaps we too can say we've had some small part in changing the world.

REFERENCES

Belk, Russell (1987), "ACR Presidential Address: Happy Thought," *Advances in Consumer Research*, Vol. 14, eds. Melanie Wallendorf and Paul Anderson, Provo, UT: Association for Consumer Research, 1-4.

Brinberg, David and Joseph E. McGrath (1985), *Validity and the Research Process*, Beverly Hills, CA: Sage.

Frank, Robert H. (1999), *Luxury Fever: Why Money Fails to Satisfy in an Era of Excess*, New York: Free Press.

Holbrook, Morris B. (1985), "Why Business is Bad for Consumer Research," *Advances in Consumer Research*, Vol. 12, eds. Elizabeth C. Hirschman and Morris B. Holbrook, Provo, UT: Association for Consumer Research, 145-146.

John, Deborah Roedder (1999), "Consumer Socialization of Children: A Retrospective Look at Twenty-Five Years of Research," *Journal of Consumer Research*, 26 (December), 183-213.

Lutz, Richard J. (1991), "Editorial," *Journal of Consumer Research*, 17 (March).

Marshall, Gordon, ed. (1994), *The Concise Oxford Dictionary of Sociology*, New York: Oxford University Press.

Newman, Katherine S. (1993), *Declining Fortunes: The Withering of the American Dream*, New York: Basic Books.

Nicosia, Francesco M. and Robert N. Mayer (1976), "Toward a Sociology of Consumption," *Journal of Consumer Research*, 3 (September), 65-75.

Pollay, Richard W. (1986). "The Distorted Mirror: Reflections on the Unintended Consequences of Advertising." *Journal of Marketing*, 50 (April), 18-36.

Robinson, John P. and Geoffrey Godbey (1997), *Time for Life: The Surprising Ways Americans Use Their Time*, University Park, PA: Pennsylvania State University Press.

Wilkie, William L. and Elizabeth S. Moore-Shay (1997), "Consortium Survey on Marketing and Society Issues: Summary and Results," *Journal of Macromarketing*, 17 (Fall), 89-95.

Zaltman, Gerald (1991), "One Mega and Seven Basic Principles for Consumer Research," *Advances in Consumer Research*, Vol. 18, eds. Rebecca H. Holman and Michael Solomon, Provo, UT: Association for Consumer Research, 8-10.

THE BALLAD OF H. KEITH HUNT

Morris B. Holbrook
Columbia University

*(Sung to the Tune of "I'm an Old Cow Hand,"
With Apologies to Johnny Mercer)*

I am H. Keith Hunt.
I'm from Brigham Young.
We don't drink or smoke,
But we still have fun
When we root real loud for the football team,
And we fight hard for the American Dream,
And we drown our sorrows in
    Russell's "Bear Claw" ice cream.
Yippy I O Ki Ay, Yippy I O Ki Ay.

I am Hunt, H. Keith;
And I'm really sweet
When old friends I greet
Or new folks I meet.
I have dabbled discreetly in politics.
I have gotten rich with my courtroom shticks.
I have taught my students some marketing tricks.
Yippy I O Ki Ay, Yippy I O Ki Ay.

Now I shall explore
What the "H" stands for.
It stands for a name
I don't use no more.
I have kept it secret for many a year.
When my friends ask, I pretend not to hear.
And I'm *not* telling you; so have no fear.
Yippy I O Ki Ay, Yippy I O Ki Ay.

You can call me Keith,
And Keith needs relief,
'Cause my job's too big —
Way beyond belief.
For the past two decades, I've been on top —
Running ACR like a traffic cop.
Now it's got gridlock; so I'm gonna stop.
Yippy I O Ki Ay, Yippy I O Ki Ay.

Since Nineteen-Eighty-Two,
I've been here for you,
Serving ACR,
With devotion true.
I've been calculating the annual dues
And writing blurbs for the *ACR News*.
When I think about it, I get the blues.
Yippy I O Ki Ay, Yippy I O Ki Ay.

Now I'm gonna quit,
'Cause I'm sick of it.
Someone else can be
The Executive Secretary.
I am tired of collecting the membership fees
And of licking stamps for
    eighteen hundred addressees.
So I'm now gonna do just what I please.
Yippy I O Ki Ay, Yippy I O Ki Ay.

So I say "Au Revoir"
To the ACR —
Where I've run the show,
Where I've been a star.
I'll learn blue-grass songs on my new banjo.
I'll get front-row seats at the rodeo.
And I'll grab my partner and do-si-do.
Yippy I O Ki Ay, Yippy I O Ki Ay.

With this chance I've got,
I'll travel 'round a lot.
And I'll always stay
At the Marriott.
I shall plumb the depths of the tourist action.
And with expertise based on long reflection,
I'll achieve full customer satisfaction.
Yippy I O Ki Ay, Yippy I O Ki Ay.

Touched By An Angel
(Being a Hagiography of H. Keith Hunt's Role in ACR's History on the Occasion of His Retirement as Its Executive Secretary)

Jerome B. Kernan
George Mason University
(presented, at the request of the absent author, by Harold H. Kassarjian)

Keith Hunt was born 3,250 weeks ago, on April 16, 1938, the direct result of events the day before. To reconstruct…

"Earth to God; Earth to God; Come in, God."

Yes, what is it? Another of your petty supplications?

"Sorry, God, but this is serious."

Listen, in case you hadn't noticed, I've got a worldwide depression on my hands. That Hitler guy is acting up again—could bust out into World War II any time. And Lucifer thinks he can unionize Hell now, just because your Congress passed that Wagner Act. So what have YOU got that's so serious?

"We realize all that stuff is terribly important, Lord, but…well, the Cardinals just traded Dizzy Dean to the Cubs for three no-name players and chump change."

Say what? Jerome Dean shipped off to Wrigley? Why Harry Carey isn't there yet. Neither is Ernie Banks. George W still needs to let loose of Sammy Sosa. And everybody knows, they NEVER win. Earth DOES have serious problems.

"Can you help us?"

Actually, the angel market is pretty tight these days. But maybe I could spare you a novice. You know, one without a Ph.D., who would have to be born and all that stuff. That's the best I can do.

"Wow! Thanks a lot, God, we'll be grateful for any help you can send. When might we expect this angel? And where should we look for him?" (You're not sending us … a girl angel, are you?)"

(I'll pretend I didn't hear that last crack.) Your angel will be there tomorrow and don't bother looking for him—he'll know how to take care of business.

KEITH !!! Get over here. They need you on Earth.

"Here I am, Lord. Did I understand You to say I was about to travel?"

Yes, Keith. And before you ask, that's my final answer.

"As You wish, but do You realize I don't yet have my wings? And I don't know whether I'm Cherubim, Seraphim, or one of those Guardian Angels who protects little girls and boys. [Editor's Note: In a recent poll, Keith was voted Cherubim—1,000 to 0.]

Oh ye of little faith! Report to the hangar for your wings. Tell them to fit you with one of those sets we've been holding for the Boeing 747—you'll be growing into a stout fellow. And don't worry about Cherus and Seras—I'm inventing a new category for you.

"But I have to be born, grow up, and all that stuff. How will I manage this? Do You have a cover story for me? And how do I go about bringing peace and common sense to the world? You know how much I like to make people happy."

Relax, Keith, I'm way ahead of you. I've decided to invent something called consumer behavior. You just report to Earth and work your way into consumer behavior.

"Very well, anything You say. But if I'm to work my way into consumer behavior, I'd better know what it is. Can you give me clue? Animal, vegetable, mineral? Is it bigger than a bread box?"

Not to worry, Keith. It will be a discipline. An interdisciplinary discipline. Look for a guy called Holbrook. He'll tell you—consumer behavior is anything and everything. Sleeping, listening to Mozart or Woody Guthrie, eating a Big Mac, getting tattooed, climbing mountains, having sex with that woman, Ms. Lewinsky, playing your banjo, anything. It's all consumer behavior.

"Gee. All that stuff is consumer behavior. But why do people do it?"

They're trying to find happiness.

"Really. Well, how do they know whether they're succeeding?"

Consumer researchers will tell them.

"Huh? What's a consumer researcher?"

Nobody really knows, but it helps to have a Ph.D.

"Let's see if I have this right. Persons with a Ph.D. can be consumer researchers and tell other persons whether they're happy. And I guess they can still be consumers, besides. But who tells THEM whether they're happy? I suppose other consumer researchers."

You're catching on fast, Keith. These consumer researchers will amuse themselves by talking and writing notes to one another at conferences. They'll paste their ideas into journals and this will create another special world of happiness for them. Each researcher will get to corner the market on a particular kind of happiness. Or maybe on a few catchwords or phrases—kind of like a brand name for each person's work.

"Now I understand. If I get a Ph.D., I can pose as a consumer researcher and do my good works from that cover."

Right on all counts, Keith. I just knew you were the one for this job. So don't forget about the Ph.D. See a guy called Levy. He'll be hanging out at Northwestern University by the time you're ready.

"I guess I shouldn't be getting ahead of myself, but I think the way to measure happiness is by whether people are satisfied or not."

Seems reasonable to me.

"So could my special happiness words be consumer satisfaction and dissatisfaction?"

Consider them yours, Keith. And when you grow up, you can even have your own journal. (Actually, more than one. But watch out for those advertising professors.)

"That's just wonderful. I'm very excited about my life ahead! Anything else before I get ready to go?"

As a matter of fact, yes, Keith. When you get to Earth, remain obscure—lead a normal, human existence. Grow up, marry, and have lots of children, because this organization of researchers—it will be called the Association for Consumer Research—will need all the help you can give. Build a big house for your family, because ACR will need a warehouse to hold all its stuff. And get your real life established, because all of a sudden you won't have time for a real life.

" I understand."

And so it came to pass that Keith arrived in 1938 and did as the Lord had instructed. In time, he found the Levy guy and got his Ph.D. We first encountered him that same year of 1972, when he sauntered into the Continuing Education Center at the University of Chicago and proceeded to wow the ACR academic and regulatory audience with his understanding of corrective advertising (which is taking back the lies you told consumers so they can be happy again).

The rest, as the saying goes, is history, so following are just some highlights of Keith's angelic beneficence, organized around a conceit of the seven deadly sins—around anger, avarice, envy, gluttony, lust, pride and sloth. But even these shards will demonstrate that Keith's association with ACR has been marked by a consistent thread of caring, fair play, and common sense. He has been called the soul of ACR and that is no hyperbole. Consider…

Anger, which is threatening our civilization. It's not something one associates with Keith. He does not lose his cool (as in rage) or try to get even (as in wrath), but that does not mean he never expresses displeasure. He gets very upset in the face of injustice, rudeness, or anything short of fair play, and he never hesitated to display his concern to us in the face of those things. However, he always stood as the great mediator, never thinking about wins or losses, only equity, when he found it necessary to remind a few of us—ever so gently—to behave like adults.

Avarice is a vice with which each of us must struggle, particularly as we are immersed in consumption. Keith, too. But his take on the temptation is so wonderful. Remember, this is the person who held all ACR's money. Unattended. Yet he never encouraged us to raise membership dues or conference fees, and every request

for funding was answered affirmatively. Recall any of his annual reports on the state of ACR's finances. "This past year we spent some money and we took in a little more. Our financial picture is fine." [Editor's Note: There is no evidence that actual numbers ever appeared in Keith's reports.] This shoebox mentality drove accountants crazy, but it exempted us for years from all concerns about money. Perhaps because Keith's methods had nothing to do with AICPA standards. His celestial bookkeeping seemed to be based loosely on the principles found in the parable of the loaves and fishes.

Envy runs rampant in our society and ACR has not been above it. We scratch and claw over intellectual property and invent metrics by which to assess status competition. (What else accounts for the tortured explanations of name ordering in author footnotes?) We fret over who gets credit for this and for that. Not Keith. A complete set of Advances in Consumer Research displayed on one's library shelf will reveal that one (and only one) of the volumes has a spine left blank. That volume is 5, edited by H. Keith Hunt. Keith replaced Kernan as ACR president (1979) and Kinnear as executive secretary (1982). After each job was finished, all he did was heap gratitude on the membership for allowing him to be a contributing part of ACR. Gratitude—from a person who ran ACR longer than FDR ran the USA.

Gluttony would seem almost trivial in our weight-obsessed culture—until we recall some of our conferees, who each year invade the banquet rooms for lunch before 11 AM, hoping to claim the perfect escape chair or to eat all the rolls at a satellite table. Of course, Keith's firm, no-badge-no-meal rule (meant only to protect us from ourselves) intercepted many of us attempting to storm these banquet rooms. But his consummate fat-fighter over the years was the chicken—Orem Borealis, I think he calls it—which was revealed initially in Kernan (1995). ACR lunches always featured chicken, because Keith was concerned that we might, well, put on a pound or two. So many years ago he discovered this faux chicken, which was served each year at the conference. (The same chicken. After the conference, the Hunt kids would gather it up and return it to Utah, where it was kept until the following year.) It was some space-age material, but looked just like real chicken. And perfectly harmless, because it couldn't be cut (we tried laser beams, hatchets, and Ginsu knives—all to no avail) and therefore couldn't be swallowed. People would just push it around on their plates, trying to act real adult about it, and experiencing terrific aerobics in the process. Conversing with our colleagues about important stuff distracted our attention from the chicken that wasn't, and we're all healthier today as a result. Thank you, Keith, for saving us from ourselves.

Lust is not something one imagines Keith being in charge of. But here's how it happened. And I'm not making this up. There was this thing called the ACR football game. Each year at the conference. Atlanta's Grant Park in 1976, Cincinnati's Nippert Stadium the year before. But now it was 1977 and we were at the O'Hare Hilton, with Keith as conference chair. Anyone who's seen that hotel understands that it is no exaggeration to say that certain adjustments needed to be made in order to produce a playing gridiron there. So while adjustments were being made, it seemed reasonable to add a few—like making the teams coed. Well, this really put Keith on the spot—until it occurred to him that these guys are intellectual before they're ludic. So without any hectoring he reminded them that ACR conferences are supposed to be about consuming and that while a football game surely qualifies as sports consumption, experiential consumption had not yet been invented, that Beth Hirschman and Morris Holbrook needed another five years to publish the papers that would introduce that topic to our canon.

Pride—in his family, in his association with ACR, and over accomplishments. Keith has self-respect in abundance. What he does not have is the ugly sort of pride we see in pretentiousness or superciliousness—vices that corrupt the soul and stand, as Thomas Aquinas saw it, at the root of evil. Here is a person who dodges recognition because he finds it embarrassing. (If humility has an avatar, surely it is Keith.) Yet Hal Kassarjian could confirm that H. KEITH HUNT constitutes a category unto itself in any content analysis of the Association for Consumer Research. Who among us is better known? (What was that story about King Solomon and the lilies of the field?)

Sloth or, in ACR parlance, "I'm too busy," is something Keith heard frequently from us during the many years of his service. Imagine how he must have felt—this professor, editor, husband, father, grandfather, religious and civic leader, who also found time to run ACR—when we begged off (or bagged) things that were to the organization's benefit. So he did those jobs himself, although it's difficult to understand why. Perhaps it was the huge salary we paid him. Or all the fringe benefits we provided. Or maybe he just saw a job that needed doing and did it, in his yeoman fashion. Shame on us.

If Keith Hunt seems larger than life it's because he is. No fancy packaging here and nothing to deconstruct—he is exactly what he seems to be. We in ACR are better people for having been touched by his presence. So thank you, Keith. And Carolyn. And all you Hunt kids. We owe this professional largesse to your quiet, unselfish, and rarely-recognized work over these many years.

To say that Keith will be remembered is quite insufficient. He will be missed. Godspeed, dear friend.

TRIBUTE TO H. KEITH HUNT

Sidney J. Levy
University of Arizona

I have known Keith Hunt since the late 1960's when he joined the doctoral progarm of the marketing department at Northwestern University. I had the pleasure of being Keith Hunt's dissertation committee chair, and have followed his career with admiration, with feelings of warmth and friendship. Keith impressed me at the outset with his sturdiness of mien and of character. Struck with his solidity of stance and purpose, one of his peers said that Keith would not be deterred by a tornado. His dissertation showed this ethical devotion. He studied whether advertising that included a corrective message was sufficient requirement to offset deceptive advertising. His turn with the Federal Trade Commission was congruent with this interest, as was his subsequent constructive career. We honor him today for his similar steadfast pursuit of the interests of the Association for Consumer Research. As an early mentor, I am proud of Keith's achievements, and appreciate this opportunity to tell him that.

Thank you, Keith.

Sidney

TRIBUTE TO H. KEITH HUNT

Gary F. McKinnon, Brigham Young University

I appreciate the opportunity of taking a few minutes to help you honor Keith Hunt.

Except for Carolyn, I have probably known Keith longer than any of you. Perhaps I can share a few things about Keith that you do not know.

Almost 40 years ago I was an undergraduate student at the University of Utah where Keith was an MBA student. After enrolling in an undergraduate marketing class I learned that a graduate student was also enrolled. Were really concerned that we had to compete with an MBA student, we weren't even sure he would speak us. Well, that MBA student was Keith Hunt, and we soon found that he was friendly and congenial to us, he was almost human. However, we were still concerned because Keith a high standard on the examinations.

About twelve years later I met with Keith at the AMA meetings in Chicago. I was trying to encourage him to leave the University Wyoming and join the faculty at BYU. We realized that we needed to hire faculty of Keith's ability if we were to become a better school.

At that time Keith had a full beard, neatly trimmed at about one or two inches. He looked almost like a mountain man. When he joined us at BYU he shaved his full beard. He looked very different, his children didn't recognize him, and for several days they were afraid of the stranger living in their house.

Many of you would guess that Keith is an excellent teacher. You're right! He has received numerous teaching awards. Keith taught our consumer behavior classes since coming to BYU in 1975, it has been a popular class for our students. You may not be aware that he has developed several classes in entreprenueship. He developed one class where he team teaches with Larry H. Miller. Larry is a local entrepreneur who owns about 30 auto dealerships in the western U.S., along with theaters, and restaurants. Larry is also the owner of the Utah Jazz NBA team and the Delta Center, the home of the Jazz. That entripeunial course is one of the most popular offered in our executive MBA program.

Keith has not only served the Association for Consumer Research; he has served his community in various ways.

As many of you know, Keith is a shaker and a mover. He gets things done. He chaired a committee that helped to create the Orem City Recreation Center with its accompanying open park areas. This is a large complex serving the residents of Orem and Provo.

Keith served for five years on the Orem City Board of Adjustments.

He was then twice elected to the Orem City Council he has been the chair of the Orem City Strategic Plan Advisory Commission since 1993.

Those of you who know Keith well would not be surprised to learn that he was kind of a maverick on the Board of Adjustments and on the city council. Keith is not like most politicians; he is more concerned about getting the right things done in the right way. He is less concerned about his popularity and appeasing special interest groups in order to obtain votes. He has given significant service to our community.

Keith has served as the department chairman at BYU and chaired several important committees. He has worked hard to move BYU toward becoming a better school. He is always anxious to help other faculty members. He is a great colleague.

Keith always leaves a lasting impression on his students.

A few years ago he was teaching a consumer behavior class. He was going to use some transparencies, so he turned his back to the class so he could reach up and pull down the screen. As he stretched to reach the cord, which was far above his head, his pants fell to his ankles. He pulled up his pants, turned to the class and said, "paraphrasing," now you know the type of underwear I wear." Then without a pause or missing a beat, Keith went on with his lecture. One of the best things that happened as a result of his experience is that all of the projection screens in the Marriott School are now motorized.

The faculty members in the Marriott School are pleased to join with you in honoring Keith Hunt for his splendid service to the ACR and for the influence, guidance, and vision that he has provided to us and to his students at BYU.

Thank you Keith and Carolyn. Congratulations.

TRIBUTE TO H. KEITH HUNT
Tacy Wells

Now you get to hear about Keith Hunt-the family man.

My dad tried to instill in his children a good work ethic. He used ACR as a main way to accomplish this. As we grew up, we all had the opportunity to do ACR work. Then, we kept growing and eventually most of us have married and moved out of my parents home. But, there were always those times throughout the year when we'd get a phone call from Mom or Dad saying "There's an ACR mailing to do—if you want to help, that would be great!" All of us kids and even our spouses have had the opportunity to work with ACR at some point. Whether by boxing books, opening mail, processing dues, keeping the computer files, preparing mailings, or even just delivering things to the Post Office.

There are many memories about our family and ACR. It's actually hard to remember life before ACR. I'd like to tell you about a few of these memories.

In the early years, we'd send the December newsletter out in November. My mom's threat to us kids was that we'd better have it all stuffed and out of the house by Thanksgiving...or else. Then, we became a little more sophisticated and put name labels on the dues notices and sent the December newsletter out with the dues notices. This was a very big event each December. We would have to find someplace in the house that could be the "work zone." It would be messy all month long, but not with Christmas decorations, with the ACR mailing.

Summer vacations always included a month or so of mailing out the yearly proceedings. When the truck arrived with the 6-8 palettes of books, the garage then became the "work zone."

Dad always liked doing things himself. In the early days, he would take the master copy of the directory to the printer who would print them and send them back to us collated. We would fold them in half and use Dad's saddle stapler to bind them. Then, we'd send them back to the printer to have them all trimmed evenly. And they'd come back to us and we would stuff and mail them. We did this every year...until the directory became so big that Dad's saddle stapler wouldn't bind them very well. Which actually was a relief to us kids, because then we could turn in the master copy of the directory to the printer and we would get back the final product, all ready to stuff and mail.

At the beginning of this year, as the 48' Yellow Freight Truck pulled out of Dad's driveway almost full of ACR books and records on it, I know it was a moment of reflection for Dad but I'm also sure he was thinking..."Well, it's been fun, but I'm glad it's Jim's turn now!!"

As Dad thought about retiring from ACR Executive Secretary, he really had a hard time making the decision. He told me many times that he would really miss the interaction with all of the members of ACR...many of whom (sadly) he only communicated with because of ACR and as life kept on, he would sincerely miss the phone calls, e-mails, letters, and personal notes written and sent on the annual dues notices.

When Hal Kassarjian called and asked me what I thought my Dad would like as a "gift" from ACR, I thought, "He would like to keep in contact with all of his ACR friends." So, I thought we could put together a memory book with member's thoughts and memories of ACR and my Dad. With Marsha Richins' help, I did this and want to present this to my Dad.

During all the years that I've worked with my Dad doing ACR things, I've seen and heard how much all of you mean to my Dad. This summer, as I received all of these letters and notes and photographs and drawings for my Dad, it was very rewarding to me, personally, to see how much my Dad means to all of you too.

Now, he'll have his own ACR book of memories to refer to and think fondly of all of you, who made this ACR adventure a ride worth taking!

Thank you.

Antecedents of Consumer Financing Decisions: A Mental Accounting Model of Revolving Credit Usage

Vanessa Gail Perry, University of North Carolina at Chapel Hill

ABSTRACT

Why do some consumer maintain outstanding balances on revolving credit cards while others do not? In this study, we examine whether mental accounting variables—mental budgeting, self-control, and short-term orientation—are significant predictors of revolving credit use and consumer price consciousness. We develop a multiple-item scale to measure mental budgeting, and use a structural equation modeling approach to test our hypotheses. Our findings generally support our mental accounting framework. In particular, we find that mental budgeting and short-term orientation are associated with higher revolving credit use. People with self-control, and people with low price-consciousness are less likely to use revolving credit.

Money, Money, Money! Not the Same by Another Name ... Shape ... or Form!

Priya Raghubir, University of California, Berkeley
Joydeep Srivastava, University of California, Berkeley[1]

ABSTRACT

The thesis of this paper is that people's valuation of money is subjective and contingent. To understand how people value, and spend money, it is important to examine the subjective value of money along with its actual economic value. Subjective monetary value is modeled as an anchoring and adjustment process where people anchor on the face value or *denomination* of an instrument and adjust by its intrinsic features (e.g., units of denomination and physical form such as coins, paper notes, gift certificates). In some instances, adjustment to the starting denomination anchor is inappropriate but performed due to preexisting schemas of value (e.g., *form* effects); in others, adjustment is required (e.g., foreign currency *units* need to be adjusted), but is inadequately performed. Using four experimental studies, we examine propositions relating to (i) anchoring on denomination (Studies 1 and 2); (ii) inappropriately adjusting for form (Studies 1 and 3); and (iii) inadequately adjusting for units (Study 4). The results show that subjective value of money systematically deviates from actual value. The primary theoretical implication of this research is that money is subjectively valued contingent on its intrinsic denomination, physical form, and unit of denomination. Managerial, public policy, and consumer welfare implications of the findings are discussed.

[1]The authors thank Jacob Cohen and the staff at Jimmy Bean's Caféfor their cooperation and assistance with Studies 1 and 2 and Ana Valenzuela for running the experiments. This research was partially funded by the Hellman Family grant awarded by the University of California, Berkeley to the first author. The authors, listed in alphabetical order, contributed equally to this article.

Sensitivity to Gains and Losses in Financial Decision Making: The Ubiquitous Influence of Promotion vs. Prevention Goals

Rongrong Zhou, Columbia University

ABSTRACT

Individual investors' financial decisions are largely influenced by pervasive, asset-specific, but mostly implicit goals. Extending Regulatory Focus Theory (Higgins, 1997) to the financial decision making domain, we propose that investors' relative concern for advancement and growth (promotion focus) versus safety and security (prevention focus) varies systematically across financial instruments. In particular, stock investments prime implicit goals that are primarily promotion-focused (i.e., gain seeking), whereas IRA fund investments prime implicit goals that are primarily prevention-focused (i.e., loss avoidance). These predictions were tested in a large-scale experiment among 198 real-world private investors. Consistent with the predictions, the results show that, in decisions involving stocks, investors show a disproportionate concern for potential gains and a relative disregard for potential losses. In contrast, in decisions involving IRA funds, investors show a disproportionate concern for potential losses and a relative disregard for potential gains.

Understanding the Adolescent's Consumption World: Shopping, Influencing, Deceiving

Terry Bristol, Arizona State University West

Adolescence is a particularly important time of life, representing the bridge from childhood to adulthood. The consumption habits and skills acquired during this time may carry over into later periods of a person's life. However, not only do adolescents represent "consumers-in-training," but they are important consumers in their own right. The purchasing power of teens has increased dramatically in recent years and teens represent a particularly large group of consumers. Thus, it is important for consumer researchers to understand adolescents and how they cope in the world of consumption–both inside and outside the context of the family. The general purpose of this session was to further our understanding of the consumption world of adolescents by focusing on their consumption behaviors and skills, and how these are learned or acquired.

The session was structured to fill distinct gaps in our knowledge of adolescent consumer behavior–inside the family and outside the family. The three papers presented during the session were devoted to exploring adolescents' shopping experiences and skills, how and why these consumers acquire and use purchase influence strategies, and the factors related to their tendency to deceive their parents about purchases. Lynnea Mallalieu's paper filled a gap in our understanding of the shopping skills of children. Her study explored teens' beliefs about "good" and "bad" shopping skills. While recent research has examined what influence strategies children use in the family, Kay Palan's paper investigated why adolescents choose to use particular influence strategies. Finally, although teen deception and parental monitoring of such behavior has been recently discussed in the popular press, no existing consumer research has examined teens' deception in purchasing. Tammy Mangleburg and Terry Bristol's paper filled that void, examining those factors that may be related to teens' propensity to use deception.

Discussion was lead by Deborah Roedder John. Upon reviewing Mallalieu's paper, John suggested that there has been little research concerning teenage shopping skills, and shopping skills in general. There appears to be a need for a taxonomy of shopping skills and linkage made between such skills and consumer development across the lifespan. For example, the development of negotiating skills within the family requires further exploration, particularly given that such skills and patterns may be carried to consumption settings outside of the family. John related these ideas to Palan's paper, noting that it went beyond basic teenage consumption patterns, skills, and strategies, to examine how parental styles and strategies impact teens' strategies in family purchase decisions. John suggested that the Mangleburg and Bristol paper looks at teens in a different way–traditionally children are thought of as victims in the children's consumption literature. Further, she noted that a wide range of "bad" behaviors engaged in by adolescents should be investigated, including theft, compulsive behaviors, and behaviors toward debt, particularly given that such behaviors may carry over into adulthood. The discussion ended with a call for more research into adolescents' consumption behavior, both inside and outside the family.

"My Mother Told Me You'd Better Shop Around: Exploring the Shopping Experiences of Teenagers"
Lynnea Mallalieu, Iowa State University

Researchers have explored a wide range of topics reflecting children's growing sophistication as consumers. Among children,

teenagers in particular are a highly sought after market segment. They have money to spend and seemingly have a keen awareness of brands, store images, and price-value concepts; however, little research exists that actually explores teenagers' shopping skills. Given the vast increase in marketing efforts directed at children over the last decade, it is important to ensure that children have the skills and knowledge needed to function as responsible consumers in the marketplace.

The aim of the present research is to explore teenagers' shopping experiences and examine their shopping skills and abilities. Shopping skills have referred to a wide array of abilities used for comparing product value prior to purchase. We have taken the liberty of extending this definition to include children's perceptions of what constitutes good and bad shopping habits. If children acquire shopping skills as they mature, then by the time they are teenagers they should have a fairly well developed set of shopping skills and have the ability to handle shopping encounters in a responsible fashion. There is, however, little empirical evidence to support this.

Given the dearth of research that examines teenagers shopping skills, some initial exploratory data was gathered on actual shopping experiences that teenagers have had and on their perceptions of what constitutes good shopping habits and bad shopping habits. The data was collected from a group of middle school students between the ages of 12 and 14. The author met with the students as a group once a week for about 90 minutes over a six week period. During the six sessions, several exploratory techniques were employed in an attempt to probe various aspects of the children's shopping skills and marketplace intelligence. Three of the techniques utilized and the resulting data were reported.

The first of the three techniques was designed to get the subjects to really think about the overall shopping experience. The initial task required them to generate 'love/hate' lists about shopping. This was designed to get them to think about the extremes of shopping in terms of what they really love about it and what they really hate about it. The second task required them to think about what they consider to be good shopping habits and what they consider to be bad shopping habits. This task was designed to begin to explore their awareness of different types of shopping behaviors. The third task required them to recount a specific shopping encounter that they had had recently. Using critical incident methodology, each teenager was asked to recall in as much detail as possible a recent shopping encounter that he or she had had. This task was designed to examine the specific types of shopping skills displayed by the teenagers.

Results indicate that the teenagers in the study have a fairly well developed set of shopping skills. The same themes consistently emerge from the data namely that the concepts of price-value, and of independent decision making are well developed. Teens seem to understand the purchase process, recognize good and bad shopping behaviors, and enjoy the end result of shopping–getting things. There is, however, some indication that teenagers are not yet at a stage where they are truly comfortable with all aspects of their shopping experiences. They appear to have a desire to feel power during their shopping experiences especially over the salesperson. This may be connected with the perception that the teen is not always treated with respect as a consumer in the marketplace and feels somewhat isolated and uncertain of how to respond to an adult salesperson.

"The Influence of Parental Style on Strategy Usage of Parents and Children in Family Decision Making"
Kay M. Palan, Iowa State University

The purpose of this research is to extend understanding of how and why adolescent children acquire and use strategies to influence purchase decisions within the context of the family. Since children primarily learn consumer behaviors from their parents, this study developed a conceptual model of children's influence strategy usage based on parental socialization style theory.

Socialization is an adult-initiated process by which children acquire habits and values congruent with their culture through insight, training, and imitation. That is, parents influence the development of children by purposely training, being role models, and providing opportunities to learn. Thus, a parent's general socialization orientation, or parental style, serves as a context that impacts how parents and children interact in purchase decisions.

The conceptual model is based on four proposed linkages. First, parents are expected to more frequently use influence strategies that reflect their parental style. Research supports this linkage. Two different paths are proposed to explain children's use of influence strategies: (1) through a direct relationship to the types of influence strategies used by parents; and (2) through a direct relationship to the effectiveness of children's strategies. A fourth linkage posits a direct relationship between parental strategies and children's strategy effectiveness. Finally, the model suggests the possibility that children's strategy effectiveness mediates the relationship between parental strategies and children's strategies.

Subjects were solicited through a school district in the midwestern U.S. The sample consisted of 74 mother-child dyads (40 mother-son dyads and 34 mother-daughter dyads); the adolescents were 7th and 8th graders (12-14 year olds). Both mothers and adolescents completed similar questionnaires, responding to questions about frequency and effectiveness of strategy use by adolescents and mothers for purchases "really important" to the adolescent; in addition, mothers completed questions that were used to determine their parental style. Using a procedure similar to that used in other studies, parents were categorized as neglecting (n=25), permissive (n=15), authoritarian (n=14), or authoritative (n=20).

To facilitate data analysis, parental and children's strategies were grouped into strategy groups via factor analysis. Three parental strategy groups were formed: discussion strategies (give opinions, invite opinions, need vs. want, alternative, reasoning, set parameters, and teach skills) bargaining strategies (money deals and other deals), and authority strategies (simple answer, can't afford it, and delay). Four children's strategy groups were formed: negative strategies (persistence, anger, pouting, whining, and manipulate), persuasion strategies (sweet talk, begging, and everyone else has it), reasoning strategies (reasoning, money deals, and other deals), and inform strategies (asking, telling, and opinionates). Groups of children's strategy effectiveness were formed to directly correspond to the children's strategy groups.

As predicted, the use of parental strategies was related to parental style. Permissive, authoritarian, and authoritative mothers used discussion strategies significantly more often than did neglecting mothers, while authoritarian and authoritative mothers used authority strategies more often than did permissive and neglecting mothers. With respect to explaining children's strategy use, mothers' use of bargaining strategies was significantly related to children's reasoning strategies, but other hypothesized relationships between mothers' and children's strategies were not found. However, all four children's strategy groups were significantly related to the effectiveness of the corresponding strategy groups; r-squares indicated that a large proportion of the variance in children's strategy use is explained by how effective a strategy has been in the past. There was a significant relationship between the effectiveness of children's reasoning and persuasion strategies and mother's bargaining strategies. Finally, significant mediation effects were found with respect to three of the four children's strategy groups, such that children's strategy effectiveness mediated the relationship between parental strategies and children's influence strategies. Taken overall, these results imply that parental style indirectly determines children's strategy use through both parental strategies and children's strategy effectiveness. In addition, the results indicate that it is possible that some influence strategies–parental bargaining strategies and adolescent persuasion strategies–are universally valued, regardless of parenting style.

"Not Telling the Whole Story: Teen Deception in Purchasing"
Tamara F. Mangleburg, Florida Atlantic University
Terry Bristol, Arizona State University West

Teenagers' consumption patterns have been studied from a number of different perspectives. One implicit assumption that many studies share is that parents are aware of how teens spend money. There is reason to believe, however, that teens are not always forthcoming with their parents and may even seek to hide or deceive parents about how they spend money. This research examined teens' tendency toward deception in purchasing. In particular, we conceptualized deception in purchasing as being related to parental socialization practices and teens' motivation, ability, or opportunity to be deceptive.

One aspect of parental socialization practices that is likely to be particularly relevant for deception is the nature of the family communication environment. With certain types of communication environments, teens may feel comfortable in discussing "controversial" products, whereas other types of environments may serve to stifle discussion of such issues. Socio-oriented communication stresses maintenance of harmonious social relations and deference to parental authority. Because socio-oriented communication stresses obedience and conformity, we would expect deception to be more likely here. In contrast, concept-oriented communication stresses acquisition of information and children's problem-solving abilities. Deception may be less likely in such an environment.

Another factor that is likely to affect teens' deception in purchasing is their desire to have certain products. When teens want products, and parents view these products as "undesirable," teens may be more motivated to engage in deceptive purchasing. Normative peer influence may motivate such desires. Peer groups may specify what are desirable and undesirable products. And to the degree that parents disapprove of or dislike these things, teens are likely to deceive parents in their purchase of such items. For similar reasons, we also expect that teens' extent of television viewing will be positively related to deception in purchasing. Ads on television may persuade teens that certain products are "cool" or more positively evaluated by popular groups. To the extent that parents disapprove of these products, teens may be more likely to engage in deception in purchasing them. Teens' level of materialism may be an important motivation to engage in deception. To the extent that teens are materialistic, they may desire to have popular products in and of themselves. This desire to acquire things and to value things heavily, in turn, may increase the tendency toward deception.

Teens' ability or opportunity to engage in deceptive purchasing is also likely to affect the extent to which they are deceptive. For instance, when teens shop with friends, they are able to buy any products that they and their friends like and can afford, without obtaining parents' approval. The source of teens' money is also likely to affect their degree of deception. If parents are giving an allowance, they may place stipulations on how the money is to be spent, inadvertently encouraging teen deception to avoid such constraints. When teens work and earn their own money, however, there may be less tendency to engage in deception. Parents may not feel that they should have much say in how teens spend job-related earnings.

The hypotheses were tested with data from a sample of students who attended a public high school in a city in the Southeast. The average age of respondents was 16 years and 56 percent were female. Results of the data analysis indicated that a socio-oriented communication environment, teens' susceptibility to normative peer influence, the extent teens shop with their friends, and teens' materialism are positively related to their tendency to engage in deception. And, as predicted, a concept-oriented communication environment is negatively related to deception. In sum, the data provide support for the conceptual model in which teens' deception in purchasing is associated with parental socialization practices and teens' motivation and ability to engage in deception.

An Examination of Demographic, Lifestyle and Personality Influences on Consumer Preferences for Participating in Promotional Games

Stephen R. McDaniel, University of Maryland

ABSTRACT

Although promotional contests and sweepstakes are popular marketing tools, only a handful of studies have been conducted on this subject over the past 15 years (cf. Browne, Kaldenberg and Brown 1993; Narayana and Raju, 1985; Ward, Hill and Gardner, 1988). Findings in this area suggest that demographics (Browne et al., 1993; Narayana and Raju, 1985) and gambling behaviors are both related to consumers' preferences for participating in promotional games. Moreover, it has been posited that people who like to take part in these forms of sales promotion have risk-taking (Narayana and Raju, 1985) and/or sensation-seeking personalities (Browne et al., 1993; Ward and Hill, 1991); although, this notion has yet to be examined.

A telephone survey methodology was employed here, to replicate and extend existing work in this area, by investigating the relationship between respondents' demographics, lifestyles and personalities and their reported preference for participating in promotional games (n=556). Data for this study were collected as part of a larger state-funded study on the commercial viability of certain gambling activities. A stratified random sampling technique was used to generate a list of names and telephone numbers for adults 18 years of age and older. The survey was conducted in the early fall of 1998, involving two top 25 Designated Market Areas (DMAs) in the eastern United States. The questionnaires were administered by a public opinion research facility using trained callers. Demographic questions were posed to respondents concerning their demographic characteristics, such as: gender, age, race, education level, household income and family status (cf. Browne et al., 1993; Narayana and Raju, 1985). They were also queried about their lifestyles, in terms of their level of interest in gambling, as well as if they had participated in certain forms of gaming during the past year (i.e., lotteries, racetrack betting, sports betting, video poker and slot machines). The personality trait of sensation seeking was measured using the 19-item Impulsive Sensation Seeking (ImpSS) scale (Zuckerman, 1994; 1996). Finally, preferences for promotional games were gauged based on the answer (yes/no) to the question: "Do you generally like to participate in promotional games, contests, or sweepstakes?". Data were analyzed using a multivariate logistic regression procedure.

Although no significant demographic influences were detected, results support the similarity between promotional game participants and gamblers (Browne et al., 1993; Ward and Hill, 1991). Mean levels of gambling interest, variety in gambling activities and sensation seeking were all found to be associated with respondents' reported preferences for participating in promotional games. Given that the more varied their gambling pursuits and the higher their levels of ImpSS, the greater their chances of reporting that they like to participate in contests or sweepstakes, it appears that such marketing activities may help to meet consumers' needs for varied, novel or stimulating experiences.

REFERENCES

Browne, B. A., Kaldenberg, Dennis and Brown, Daniel J. (1993), "Games People Play: A Comparative Study of Promotional Game Participants and Gamblers," *Journal of Applied Business Research*, 9(1), 93-99.

Narayana, Chem L. and Raju, P. S. (1985), "Gifts Versus Sweepstakes: Consumer Choices and Profiles," *Journal of Advertising*, 14(1), 50-53.

Ward, James C. and Hill, Ronald P. (1991), "Designing Effective Promotional Games: Opportunities and Problems," *Journal of Advertising*, 20(3), 69-81.

Ward, James C., Hill, Ronald P. and Gardner, Meryl P. (1988), "Promotional Games: The Effects of Participation on Mood, Attitude, and Information Processing," in Michael J. Houston, ed., *Advances in Consumer Research*, 15, 135-140.

Zuckerman, Marvin (1996), "Item Revisions in the Sensation Seeking Scale form V," *Personality & Individual Differences*, 20(4), 515.

Zuckerman, Marvin (1994), *Behavioral Expressions and Biosocial Bases of Sensation Seeking*. New York, NY: Cambridge University Press.

Truth, Lies and Videotape:
The Impact of Personality on the Memory for a Consumption Experience

Elizabeth Cowley, University of New South Wales
Marylouise Caldwell, University of New South Wales

Recently, evidence has been reported suggesting that consumers' memories for product experiences are not permanent, but that they can be affected by post-consumption information. The study reported here investigates whether personality variables help to explain when and how consumers, might be most susceptible to altering their memory and evaluation of a product or service with post-consumption information communicated through critical reviews.

INTRODUCTION

Direct experience with products is an important means by which consumers learn cognitive and affective responses to a product or brand (Hoch and Deighton 1989; Smith 1993). Consumers frequently use memories for direct experiences with products as a basis for their behaviour. For example, when deciding if a product is satisfactory, superior to other products, or performing as it usually does, consumers compare current performance to memories of previous performance. Depending on the frequency of consumption in the product category, some time may pass between the experience and the retrieval of the memory. Generally, in the marketing literature, memories of consumption experiences are assumed to be permanently retained (Burke and Srull 1988). Consequently, although consumers might acquire information about products after consumption, memories for 'own experience' would be stored separately from any new information about other consumers' experiences. This assumption is critical because it allows consumers to learn from others, while keeping their own highly valued 'own experience' memories unaltered.

A number of influences on memory have been considered in the marketing literature such as involvement (Berger and Mitchell 1989; Park and Hastak 1994), product knowledge (Mitchell and Dacin 1996), processing goals (Huffman and Houston 1994) and age (Law, Hawkins and Craik 1998) to name only a few. Personality variables, however, have not been used to explain differences in memory for consumption related experiences. In this paper we demonstrate that personality variables drawn from the Five Factor Model (Costa and McCrae 1992; Wiggins and Trapnell 1997) help to explain how post-consumption information impacts on memory for consumption experience. This is an important first step at trying to identify both how and when consumers' memory for consumption decisions are altered with post-experience information.

CONCEPTUAL DEVELOPMENT

Post-Event Information and Memory

Recently, the permanence of memory has been questioned as consumers have been demonstrated to allow post-consumption information in the form of advertising, to alter their perceptual memory (Braun 1999), and visual memory (Braun and Loftus 1998) for a product. This is consistent with findings reported in eyewitness testimony and false memory literatures, which are replete with examples of instances where post-experience descriptions of the event, communicated by others, are included in the witness's memory for an event (Loftus 1975; 1977; 1979). Information that is plausible and pertains to events for which little attention was paid during the original experience, is most commonly and confidently recognised as part of the original event (Migueles and Garcia-Bajos 1999).

Though often presented as a general phenomenon, there are conditions under which memory is most susceptible to post-consumption alteration. For instance, if some details of the experience were not processed deeply enough to retrieve later, and post-event information providing these details is processed, then when questioned about these details, the consumer may retrieve the post-consumption information. This *vacant slot* explanation assumes that only one memory trace is available in memory, because the information from the original experience was not encoded leaving a *vacant slot* that is filled in with post-event information (McCloskey and Zaragoza 1985). Imagine yourself having dinner in a restaurant with friends, great food, good conversation and good service. On the way home, one of your friends mentions that the best thing about the meal was the wine he selected for all to drink. You really can't remember much about the wine, but your friend describes it as having a complex and full-bodied flavour with a long finish. Later, if questioned about the wine, you might remember it as described by your friend.

Another condition under which a consumer might retrieve post-consumption information instead of memory for the original experience is when a consumer feels uncertain about their ability to retrieve 'our experience' information, but is certain that the source of post-event information can accurately remember the event. If the consumer is lacking confidence in their ability to remember the details of the original event, and they have information accessible in memory from a more reliable source, they may retrieve 'other's experience' information.

Finally, certain consumers may feel compelled to agree with the opinion and recollection of others. Instead of relying on accessible 'own experience' memories of a consumption episode, they choose to agree with the post-consumption information supplied to them by others. There is certainly plenty of evidence that the opinion of others affects an individual's judgement (Asch 1953; Bone 1995; Cohen and Golden 1972; Pincus and Waters 1975; Venkatesan 1966).

One individual difference variable that has not been used in the study of consumer memory is personality, even though evidence is emerging indicating an important relationship between personality and the malleability of memory (Bruck, Ceci & Melnyk 1997; Caruso & Spirrison 1996; Quas, Qin, Schaaf & Goodman 1997). The following brief review of personality literature is intended to focus on sub-facets of personality traits that might predict which consumers might find themselves in one of these three situations: 1] without memory for the experience, 2] lacking confidence in memory for the experience, or 3] agreeing with others about the memory for an experience.

Personality

Personality refers to an individual's relatively consistent responses to the environmental stimuli over time (Kassarjian and Sheffet 1991). Although various explanations of behavioural consistency associated with personality have been proposed, a trait based approach is currently most widely accepted (Ickes, Synder and Garcia, 1997). Trait theory sees humans behaving with comparative consistency over time as a result of stable behavioural traits. These traits contribute to relatively stable differential sensitivities to internal and external cues, which then lead to distinctive affective and cognitive states and behaviours (Revelle

1995). Traits are not good predictors of specific responses, rather they are useful in predicting types of behaviours given an understanding of perceptions of situational cues and psychological processes (Mischel and Shoda 1998; Revelle 1995). To add to this complexity, most behaviour is determined by the interaction of a number of traits rather than a single trait (Pervin 1985).

The Five Factor model provides a comprehensive and parsimonious trait based description of personality (Digman 1990; Ozer and Reise 1994; Wignell and Trapnell 1997), subsuming a wide range of well-established personality instruments (Digman 1996). There are five traits in the model; neuroticism, introversion/extroversion, agreeableness, openness to experience and conscientiousness, and each trait has six sub facets. Certain traits and sub facets of traits in the Five Factor Model of personality are of particular interest as we believe they relate to individual differences in suggestibility and false memory reports. For instance, whether an individual finds a situation threatening, interesting, or unusual, all of which affect encoding and retrieval (e.g. House 1975; Pickel 1998; Richards, French, Adams, Elderidge and Papadopolou 1999), depends on their sensitivities to external or internal cues which in turn are related to personality traits (Eysenck, Mogg, May and Richards 1991).

Personality and Memory

Although there has been little research into the impact of personality on the malleability of memory, the literature implicates at least three personality dimensions of the Five Factor Model. Anxiety, a sub-facet of neuroticism, has been identified as an influence on encoding, which ultimately affects memory. Competence, a sub-facet of conscientiousness, has been identified as a factor in suggestibility, and compliance, a sub-facet of agreeableness, has been identified as a determinant of response to a memory task. The following sections review the personality literature as it pertains to anxiety, compliance and competence.

Anxiety (a sub facet of Neuroticism). Dobson and Markham (1993) report that anxious subjects were less accurate in the recall of the central event in an episode, the *crime* in their study, than non-anxious subjects. They explain the results with a cognitive capacity argument which states that task-irrelevant worry limits working memory capacity for very anxious subjects. MacLeod and Donnelloni (1993) also demonstrate Eysenck's (1981) assertion that reduced working memory capacity explains the performance deficits found by anxious individuals. There are a number of inconsistencies in the literature, attributable in part to the different methods and scales for measuring anxiety. In general, the Yerkes-Dodson Law holds, anxiety improves performance on simple tasks demanding little cognitive capacity, but that anxiety appears to inhibit performance on cognitive demanding tasks (Eysenck 1981).

An individual high in trait anxiety may find it difficult to process the details of an event because of the expenditure on task irrelevant worry. However, if a consumer is able to process the post-experience information at their own pace, then the vacant slot may be filled with post-experience information.

Competence (a sub-facet of Conscientiousness). This sub-facet measures people's confidence in their own abilities and is strongly related to self-esteem and internal locus of control (Costa and McCrae 1992). High self-esteem individuals are resistant to suggestibility (Bruck, Ceci and Melnyk, 1997) while low self-esteem individuals are more susceptible to the effects of self-relevant stimuli in their environment (Brockner 1984): he labels this low self-esteem *plasticity*. Plasticity may occur because: (i) low self-esteem people have a more uncertain self-concept, they

are "more dependent on, susceptible to, and influenced by external self-relevant stimuli" (Campbell 1990, pp 539), (ii) the anxiety associated with low self-esteem hinders encoding or retrieval or (iii) self-esteem either negatively or positively impacts an individual's efforts to accurately recall an actual event (Bruck, Ceci and Melnyk 1997). The plasticity of an individual low in self-esteem may result in their retrieving the post-experience information because they have more confidence that it is correct.

Compliance (a sub facet of Agreeableness). In an extensive review of the literature on Agreeableness, Graziano and Eisenberg (1997), note that researchers often associate the trait with friendly compliance, dependency and a tendency to conform to others' wishes. Compliance, in a personality measure based on the Five-Factor Model, relates to these descriptions (Costa and McCrae 1992). Compliance has been found to be a significant indicator of whether post-event interrogation results in an individual changing their memory for an event (Gudjonsson 1991).

The willingness to comply and conform, with the wishes or opinions of others allows for a susceptibility to suggestion by others. Individuals with a high score on compliance defer to others. It follows that people high in compliance are more likely to access a memory trace that represents the event as others believe it to have occurred.

Post-event information

When evaluating a product from direct experience, it has long been understood that exposure to the opinions of others will affect an individual's overall evaluation, (Bone 1995; Cohen and Golden 1972; Pincus and Waters 1975; Venkatesan 1966). Consumers are exposed to a number of different types of information after consuming products, such as advertising, word-of-mouth and critic's reviews. We are particularly interested in indirect forms of word-of-mouth, in this case, critical reviews. Previous research indicates that consumers use critical reviews as an information source during the decision to attend a particular movie (Faber and O'Guinn 1984; Wyatt and Badger 1984). There are situations however, where consumers are not exposed to the review until after they have viewed the film. Is it possible the critic's words could influence consumers' memory for the film and overall evaluation of the film? A critic's review will be used here to test who is most likely to alter their memory for and evaluation of a movie on the basis of post-experience information.

HYPOTHESES

H_1: Individuals high in trait anxiety will find it difficult to retrieve 'own experience' information from memory. They will be most susceptible to the *vacant slot* situation. This will be evidenced by a lower hit rate, and a greater number of 'know' responses. High trait anxious individuals will also use the critic's information to 'fill in' the missing information when their anxiousness is combined with high trait compliance.

H_2: Individuals low in trait competence will retrieve post-experience information when asked to retrieve information about the original experience because they will be more confident using the memory reported by another, more competent source. In this case, two memory traces exist in memory, these individuals will be using what they believe to be most accurate, but not necessarily their own memory for the event. This will be evidenced by a greater number of false alarms accompanied by 'remember' responses for the information included in the critical review for low compared to high trait competent individuals. These individuals may also respond with 'know' when correctly identifying information from the film because they are uncertain of their own ability to retrieve information from memory.

H_3: Individuals high in trait compliance will retrieve information from the post-experience information when asked to retrieve information from the original experience because they tend to defer to others. They will not say they remember the information, but instead will tend to say they 'know' they saw it before when incorrectly identifying information from the critic's review as information seen in the film. In order to comply with the opinion of the critic, high trait compliance individuals will alter their overall evaluation for the event to be consistent with the critic, particularly when low in trait competence.

METHOD

To test whether post event information alters memory for, and overall evaluation of, a consumption experience, subjects viewed a 10-minute excerpt from a movie and were provided a critical review of the movie. The critical review included plausible misinformation. Later, subjects were asked to 'recognise' or identify the correct statements from a list of statements. The list is composed of plausible misinformation included in the review, plausible misinformation not in the review, and events from the film clip.

Subjects

Seventy-four commerce undergraduate students at a large Australian university volunteered to participate in the study. The age of the subjects varied between 18 and 33, with a mean age of 23 years old. Forty of the subjects were female, 34 were male.

Procedure

After a lecture on an unrelated topic, students were asked if they would be willing to participate in a research study on "movie-goers' preferences and market segmentation". Each participant was asked to answer 18 questions taken from the NEO-PI for the sub-facets of compliance, competence, and anxiety. Students then viewed a 10-minute excerpt from *Rosencrantz and Guildenstern are Dead*, a movie that had been released nine years earlier.

One week later, students were asked to read a critical review ostensibly taken from a local paper. Students were then asked to answer 21 questions about their movie attendance and the decision making process involved in attendance, and for their evaluation of the film clip. Students were asked to answer 40 multiple-choice questions. The 40 questions included 20 correct statements about the movie (target statements), 10 incorrect statements taken from the critical review (critic foils) and 10 incorrect statements that were not present in the review (misinformation foils). The instructions for the recognition questions were as follows: "Please indicate whether each of the statements describe the movie you saw one week ago by circling 'Yes'. Please indicate which statements do not describe something that you saw in the movie by circling 'No'. If you circle 'Yes' then please indicate whether you remember seeing the event in the movie or whether you know the event occurred. Circle 'Remember' if you can remember seeing the event, or if you remember something that you thought when you saw the event. Circle 'Know' if you believe that you did see the event in the movie, but do not have any clear memory of the event."[1] Students indicated their evaluation of the film clip on three eleven-point scale anchored with 'bad/good', 'unfavourable/

favourable' and 'desirable/undesirable'. Finally, subjects were asked if they had seen the film before, and if so, when.

Stimulus

The critical review was 320 words and was described as an excerpt of "a review published in a local Sydney paper in 1991, the year the film was released in Australia. The review has been edited to include the comments made by the reviewer about the portion of the film that you saw last week." The critique was either positive or negative and included both correct information from the movie and ten pieces of plausible misinformation. Thirty seven students saw the positive review and 37 students saw the negative review. The misinformation was the same in both versions. Examples of the misinformation are italicised in the following excerpt from the critique.

Playwright Tom Stoppard has scripted and directed a film about two minor characters in Shakespeare's Hamlet. *Rosencrantz & Guildenstern are Dead* tells the other side of the famous story. Two friends Rosencrantz (Gary Oldman) and Guildenstern (Tim Roth) find themselves in a most confusing situation. Hamlet's (Iain Glen) old friends *invite themselves* to Denmark to visit the Queen and new King, Hamlet's mother and uncle. The King and Queen encourage Hamlet's favourite confidantes to discover *how Hamlet feels about Ophelia*. The *King promises that he will pay them* handsomely for their effort.

Measures

Personality. Subjects were scored using the guidelines supplied with the NEO-Pi scale. Split medians are used on these scores to divide subjects into high and low groups for anxiety, compliance, and competence sub-facets of neuroticism, agreeableness and conscientiousness traits respectively. Though personality traits are generally reported to be uncorrelated, there are two significant correlations between the sub-facets in this dataset: compliance and competence are negatively correlated (-0.31, $p < 0.001$), as are competence and anxiety (-0.24, $p < 0.05$).

Recognition. On the recognition test subjects were asked to indicate whether or not they had seen the statement in the videotape. Suggestibility is tested using the subject's false alarm rate on misinformation foils compared to critic foils, and the hit rate for the target statements.

Evaluation. The three ratings provided by the subject were summed for the overall evaluation of the film clip.

RESULTS

All General Linear Models (GLMs) mentioned in this section are three-way GLMs with two levels of trait compliance, competence and anxiety. The first hypothesis states that high trait anxiety subjects will find retrieving 'own experience' memories very difficult because they do not have vivid memories of the consumption episode possibly due to the task-irrelevant worry that may have reduced their working memory capacity. Consequently, their hit rate should be lower than low trait anxiety subjects, and they should be more likely to respond 'know'.

The level of trait anxiety is a significant factor in the results ($F(1, 1472) = 21.05$, $p < 0.0001$). The hit rate for high trait anxious subjects was 0.47 which is not statistically different than chance. The hit rate for low trait anxious subjects was 0.60 which is

---

[1] These instructions are modelled after Roediger and McDermott (1995).

TABLE 1
Overall Rating of the Film Clip by Trait

		Competence	
		Low	High
Compliance	Low	Negative review = 10.0	Negative review = 14.4
		Positive review = 12.8	Positive review = 17.4
	High	Negative review = 12.3	Negative review = 13.1
		Positive review = 19.0**	Positive review = 17.3*

* weakly significantly different p < 0.10
**significantly different at p < 0.0005

significantly different than chance (p < .001)[2]. High trait anxious subjects responded 'know' more often than low trait anxious subjects ((F(1, 733) = 25.59, p < 0.0001), high = 46% 'know' responses, low = 24% 'know' responses). Contrary to our expectations, false alarm rates for high trait anxious subjects for the critic foils were not greater than for low trait anxious individuals nor were they different than for misinformation foils. It appears that high trait anxious subjects are most likely to find themselves without memory for the original experience, but were not necessarily more likely to use post-experience information.

The second hypothesis states that low trait competence subjects will retrieve the events as reported by another, more competent source. The critic, who may be considered a more competent source, provided the subject incorrect information in the form of a critical review of the film[3]. If low trait competence subjects use the critic's memory, their false alarms on the critic foil statements will be accompanied by 'remember' responses. If they are uncertain of their own responses, their correct identifications of target statements will be accompanied by 'know' responses. A GLM of responses for the critic foil statements reveals competence is a significant factor (F(1, 413) = 19.91, p < 0.0001), low trait competent people were more likely to respond 'remember' to information identified from the film that was actually from the critic's review (low = 64.1%, high = 40.4%). A GLM of responses for the target statements also reveals competence as a significant factor (F(1, 733) = 4.91, p < 0.05), low competence individuals were more likely to response 'know' than high trait competent individuals (low = 38.4%, high = 29.6%). Competence also predicts accuracy, the hit rate for high trait competent subjects was 0.60 compared to

the hit rate for low trait competent subjects 0.45[4]. The pattern of results is consistent with the hypotheses, it appears that low trait competence subjects find themselves willing to use a more competent source of information's recollection of the event over their own.

The third hypothesis states that high trait compliant subjects will be likely to have a high false alarm rate for the critic foils, particularly compared to the misinformation foils. A GLM run on the false alarm rate for critic foils reveals that compliance is the only significant factor (F(1, 727) = 4.8, p < 0.05). High trait compliant individuals did not claim to 'remember' the false information, they more often claimed that they 'knew' it to be true (F(1, 413) = 5.41, p < 0.05, low = 41.2% know, high 53.9% know). Not surprisingly, everyone was more likely to respond 'yes' to a critic foil, than they were to a misinformation foil (F(1, 1465) = 48.32, p < 0.0001), in particular, it was high in compliance / low in competence / low in anxiety subjects that remembered the information from the critic's review and falsely stated it was from the film clip (F(1, 1465) = 4.63, p < 0.05).

Hypothesis three also states that high trait compliant / low trait competent subjects will alter their overall evaluation for the event based on post-experience information. Here we would expect this group to rate the film clip more positively if they saw the positive review and more negatively if they saw the negative review. There was a general tendency amongst all subjects to agree with the critic's review of the film (F(1, 70) = 13.39, p < 0.005). However, the strongest effect is amongst those subjects high in trait compliance / low in trait competence (F(1, 70) = 4.51, p < 0.05). See Table 1 for cell means. It appears that high trait compliant / low trait competence subjects felt compelled to agree with the opinion and recollection of an event, even when the details may conflict with their 'own experience' memory.

DISCUSSION

In this paper we outlined some situations under which memory might be most susceptible to the influence of post-event information. We then used personality traits to predict who might be likely to find themselves in these situations. Although individual differences have been used to explain memory performance in a marketing context in the past, personality traits have not been among the selected differences.

Our results are consistent with Eysenck's (1981) claim that high trait anxiety may result in a working memory capacity deficit that limits the amount of processing that occurs during an experience. High trait anxious subjects were not as able to correctly identify the statements that accurately depict the facts seen in the

---

[2] Overall, high trait anxious subjects were not as accurate at differentiating between target and foil statements, this difference is directional only. The Luce's a statistic, which is similar to the d' measure, was 1.27 for high trait anxious subjects and 1.51 for low trait anxious subjects (higher a statistics reflect better recognition performance). Using signal detection theory, however, is problematic in this case. The intensity of the stimulus varies because critic foils were actually seen at some point, while misinformation foils were not. Essentially the question is not 'Did I see this before or not?', it is 'Did I see this in the movie, in the review, or not at all?'.

[3] Though competency of the critic was not tested specifically, there were questions in the filler task that relate to the issue. Subjects were asked to state their agreement with the following statement 'In general, critics are unbiased' on a scale ranging from strongly agree to strongly disagree. The scale was coded from +3 to –3. Although there was a general consensus among the sample that critics are unbiased, those low in competence were particularly likely to express confidence in the credibility of critical review (F(1, 73) = 4.03, p < 0.05).

[4] The Luce's a statistic also supports the hypothesis, more trait competent subjects were more accurate than less trait competent subjects (F(1, 79) = 3.77, p < 0.05).

film clip which is consistent with encoding deficits due to task irrelevant worry.

We also found evidence that low trait competence subjects are more likely to rely on the opinion of others as correct because competence is related to self-esteem and self-efficacy. This finding is in line with past research in eyewitness testimony revealing a relationship between self-efficacy and susceptibility to suggestion with leading questions (Mazzoni 1998). This is also important in this context because the subjects indicated that they believed the critic to be unbiased in his/her evaluation for the movie.

The data revealed that low trait competence / high trait compliance / low anxiety subjects were most likely to falsely recognise a fact from the critic's review as occurring in the film. Low trait competence and high trait compliance appears to affect the retrieval strategy used by the individual whether they are concerned with being accurate or consistent with others, while high trait anxiety affects encoding. We also found that these subjects displayed a general tendency to agree with the critic's review, whether positive or negative, which is consistent with past literature in both marketing and psychology. The most likely people to be affected by the opinions of others are high trait compliant/low trait competent. Consumer's decisions rely on memory for evaluations of past experiences for the same brand and other brands. Understanding how and when consumers' memories for consumption experiences can be altered by post-consumption information helps to explain the behaviour of consumers. The evidence reported here suggests that personality traits contribute to an understanding of when 'own experience' memory is most susceptible to alteration.

There are a number of different ways in which research could proceed in this area. First, human behaviour is considered by trait theorists to be comparatively consistent over time as a result of stable behavioural traits (Revelle 1985). A longitudinal study examining the behaviour of individuals over time within similar situations would allow for a test of whether the competence, compliance and anxiety traits explain memory for 'own experience' compared to 'others' experience'.

Second, trait theory, which is used here, is not the only paradigm in personality research; another group called the Interactionists has also contributed to the literature. At its most extreme interactionism asserts that individual differences in behaviour are a result of stable differences in situations rather than enduring personal dispositions (Magnusson and Torestad 1993; Rorer and Widiger 1983). The focus of research is on processing dynamics and mediating units such as perceptions, expectancies and goals (Mischel and Schoda 1998). Recently there has been some reconciliation between the trait theorists and the interactionists (Mathews and Deary 1998; Mischel and Shoda, 1998; Van Heck, Perugini, Caprara and Froger, 1994). Researchers now view a trait statement as "the conditional probability of a category of behaviours given a category of contexts" (Mathews and Deary, 1998; p. 43). A series of studies manipulating the situation and measuring for variation due to personality, situation, or the interaction of the two, would allow for a better understanding of what has driven the results in this study.

REFERENCES

Asch, S. E. (1953), "Effects of Group Pressure Upon the Modification and Distortion of Judgments", in *Group Dynamics*, eds. D. Cartwright and A. Zander. New York: Harper and Row.

Berger, Ida, E. and Andrew A. Mitchell (1989), "The Effect of Advertising on Attitude Accessibility, Attitude Confidence, and the Attitude-Behavior Relationship", *Journal of Consumer Research*, 16, 269-279.

Bone, Paula F. (1995), "Word-of-Mouth Effects on Short-term and Long-term Product Judgements," *Journal of Business Research*, Vol. 32, 213-223.

Braun, Kathryn A. (1999), "Postexperience Advertising Effects on Consumer Memory," *Journal of Consumer Research*, 25 (December), 319-344

_____ and Elizabeth F. Loftus (1998), "Advertising's Misinformation Effect, *Applied Cognitive Psychology*, Vol 12(6), 569-591.

Brockner, Joel (1984), "Low Self-Esteem and Behavioral Plasticity: Some Implications for Personality and Social Psychology," in *Review of Personality and Social Psychology, Volume 4*, ed. L.Wheeler, Beverley Hills, CA: Sage, 237-271.

Bruck, Maggie, Stephen J. Ceci, Laura Melnyk (1997), "External and Internal Sources of Variation in the Creation of False Reports in Children," *Learning and Individual Differences*, 9, 4, 289-316.

Burke, Raymond R. and Thomas K. Srull (1988), 'Competitive Interference and Consumer Memory for Advertising," *Journal of Consumer Research*, 15(1), 55-68.

Campbell, Jennifer D. (1990), "Self-Esteem and Clarity of the Self-Concept," *Journal of Personality and Social Psychology*, 59 (3), 538-549.

Caruso, John C. and Charles L. Spirrison (1996), "Reported Earliest Memory age: Relationships with Personality and Coping Variables," *Personality and Individual Differences*, 21 (1), 135-142.

Cohen, Joel B. and Ellen Golden (1972), "Informational Social Influence and Product Evaluation," *Journal of Applied Psychology*, 56 (1), 54-59.

Costa, Paul. T. Jr. and Robert R. McCrae (1992), *The Revised NEO Personality Inventory (NEO PI-R) Professional Manual*, Psychological Assessment Resources, U.S.A.

Digman John. M. (1990), "Personality Structure-Emergence of the 5 Factor Model", *Annual Review of Psychology*, 41, 417-40.

Digman John M. (1996), " The Curious History of the Five Factor Model" in The Five-Factor Model of Personality: Theoretical Perspectives ed. Jerry Wiggins, Guilford Press, U.S.A.

Dobson, Matthew and Roslyn Markham (1992), "Individual Differences in Anxiety Level and Eyewitness Testimony," *Journal of General Psychology*, 119 (4), 343-350.

_____, 1981), "Learning, Memory and Personality," in *A Model of Personality* ed. H. J. Eysenck, Springer Verlag, 169-209.

_____, Karin Mogg, Jon May and Anne Richards (1991), "Bias in Interpretation of Ambiguous Sentences Related to Threat in Anxiety," *Journal of Abnormal Psychology*, 100 (2), 144-150.

Faber, Ronald and Thomas O'Guinn (1984), "Effect of Media Advertising and Other Sources on Movie Selection," *Journalism Quarterly*, 61 (Summer), 371-77.

Graziano, William G. and Nancy Eisenberg (1997), "Agreeableness: A Dimension of Personality", *Handbook of Personality*, Academic Press, 795-824.

Gudjonsson, Gisli H. (1991), "The Effects of Intelligence and Memory on Group Differences in Suggestibility and Compliance," *Personality and Individual Differences*, 12(5), 503-505.

Hoch, Stephen J. and John Deighton (1989), "Managing What Consumers Learn from Experience," *Journal of Marketing*, 53(2), 1-20.

House, William C. (1975), "Repression-Sensitization and Response to the Implicit Cue Requirements of a Social Situation," *Journal of Clinical Psychology,* 31 (3), 505-509.

Huffman, Cynthia and Michael J. Houston (1993), "Goal-Oriented Experiences and the Development of Knowledge," *Journal of Consumer Research*, 20, 190-207.

Ickes, Wiliam, Mark Snyder and Stella Garcia (1997), "Personality Influences on the Choice of Situation", Chapter 7, *Handbook of Personality Psychology*, eds. Robert Hogan and Paul T. Trapnell, San Diego, CA: Academic Press.

Kassarjian, Harold H. and Mary Jane Sheffet (1991), "Personality and Consumer Behavior," in Perspectives in Consumer Behavior, 4th edition, eds. Harold H. Kassarjian and Thomas S. Robertson, Englewood Cliffs, NJ: Prentice Hall.

Law, Sharmistha, Scott A. Hawkins and Fergus I. M. Craik (1998), "Repetition-Induced Belief in the Elderly: Rehabilitating Age-Related Memory Deficits," *Journal of Consumer Research*, 25(2), 91-107.

Loftus, Elizabeth F. (1975), "Leading Questions and the Eyewitness Report," *Cognitive Psychology,* 7, 560-572.

_____ (1977), "Shifting Human Color Memory," *Memory and Cognition,* 5 (November), 696-699.

_____ (1979); *Eyewitness Testimony,* Cambridge, MA: Wiley.

MacLeod, Colin and Avonia M. Donnellan (1993), "Individual Differences in Anxiety and the Restriction of Working Memory Capacity," *Personality and Individual Differences,* 15(2), 163-173.

Mathews, Gerald and Ian J. Deary (1998), *Personality Traits,* Cambridge University Press.

Mazzoni, Giuliana (1998), "Memory Suggestibility and Metacognition in Child Eyewitness Testimony: The Roles of Source Monitoring and Self-Efficacy," *European Journal of Psychology of Education,* 13(1), 43-60.

McCloskey, Michael and Maria Zaragoza (1985), "Misleading Postevent Information and Memory for Events: Arguments and Evidence Against Memory Impairment Hypothesis," *Journal of Experimental Psychology: General,* 114(March), 1-16.

McCrae, Robert. R and Costa Paul. T. Jr (1989), "Reinterpreting the Myer-Briggs Type Indicator from the Perspective of the Five Factor Model of Personality," *Journal of Personality,* 57, 17-40.

Mischel, Walter and Yuichi Shoda (1998), "Reconciling Processing Dynamics and Personality Dispositions," *Annual Review of Psychology,* 49, 229-58.

Mitchell, Andrew A., and Peter F. Dacin (1996), "The Assessment of Alternative Measures of Consumer Expertise," *Journal of Consumer Research,* Vol 23 (3), 219-240.

Migueles, Malen and Elvira Garcia-Bajos (1999), 'Recall, Recognition, and Confidence Patterns in Eyewitness Testimony, *Applied Cognitive Psychology*, 13(3), 257-268.

Ozer, Daniel J. and Steven P. Reise (1994), "Personality Assessment," *Annual Review of Psychology,* 45, 357-388.

Park, Jong-Won and Manoj Hastak (1994), "Memory-Based Product Judgments: Effects of Involvement at Encoding and Retrieval," *Journal of Consumer Research,* 21 (3), 534-547.

Pervin Lawrence A. (1985), "Personality: Current Controversies, Issues and Directions," *Annual Review of Psychology*, 36, 83-114.

Pickel, Kerri L. (1999), "Unusualness and Threat as Possible Causes of Weapon Focus," *Memory,* 6 (3), 277-295.

Pincus, Stephen and L. K. Waters (1977), "Informational Social Influence and Product Quality Judgments," *Journal of Applied Psychology,* 62 (5), 615-619.

Quas, Jodi A., Jianjian Qin, Jennifer M. Schaaf and Gail S. Goodman (1997), "Individual Differences in Children's and Adults' Suggestibility and False Event Memory," *Learning and Individual Differences*, 9 (4), 359-90.

Revelle, William (1995), "Personality Processes," *Annual Review of Psychology*, 46, 295-328.

Richards, Anne, Chistopher C. French, Caroline Adams, Maria Eldridge and Elli Papadopolou (1999), "Implicit Memory and Anxiety: Perceptual Identification of Emotional Stimuli," *European Journal of Cognitive Psychology,* 11(1), 67-86.

Rorer, Leonard G. and Thomas A. Widiger (1983), "Personality Structure and Assessment," *Annual Review of Psychology*, 34, 431-63.

Smith, Robert E. (1993), "Integrating Information from Advertising and Trial: Processes and Effects on Consumer Response to Product Information," *Journal of Marketing Research,* 30 (May), 204-219.

Venkatesan, M. (1966), "Experimental Study of Consumer Behavior Conformity and Independence," *Journal of Marketing Research*, 3, 384-387.

Wiggins, Jerry S. and Paul D. Trapnell (1997), "Personality Structure: The Return of the Big Five", in *Handbook of Personality Psychology*, eds. Robert Hogan and Paul T. Trapnell, San Diego,CA: Academic Press.

Wyatt, Robert O. and David P. Badger (1984), "How Reviews Affect Interest in and Evaluation of Films," *Journalism Quarterly*, 61 (Winter), 874-78.

The Impacts of Personality Differences on Product Evaluations

Chingching Chang, National Chengchi University

ABSTRACT

This study suggests that subjects' personalities will affect product evaluations in two ways. First, subjects with certain personality traits are likely to evaluate products differently regardless of the advertising appeals employed. In addition, subjects' personalities will affect their product evaluations based on the discrepancies between their self-images and the advertised product's image. This study specifically examines subjects' personality differences on introversion/extroversion. Findings of this study showed that, overall, extroverted subjects evaluated products in more positive ways than introverted subjects. In addition, their evaluations of the advertised brand are more positive if the portrayed product image is more congruent with their real or ideal self-concepts. Most importantly, this study showed that subjects' sense of self-referencing and their ad-evoked negative emotional responses played mediating roles in the brand evaluation formation process.

Individual differences are important variables to consider when examining advertising effects. Several types of individual differences such as self-monitoring (e.g., Snyder & DeBono, 1985), need for cognition (e.g., Venkatraman, et al., 1990), involvement (e.g., Park & Young, 1986), and product knowledge (e.g., Maheswaran & Sternthal, 1990) have been explored in the past. With the increased importance of target segmentation, more researchers are paying attention to consumers' value and personality trait differences (e.g., O'Connor, 1997) and attempting to identify consumers with respect to these differences. However, instead of simply categorizing consumers into different groups, cognitive psychologists suggest that it is important to view personality differences as a part of self-knowledge and to explore these differences in terms of how they function as a framework that organizes and directs information processing (Fiske & Taylor, 1991). This study adopts this approach, viewing personality traits as important dimensions of self-concepts. Specifically, this study will explore the influence of individuals' introversion/extroversion, a trait that is well explored in past psychological literature, on advertising effects.

In treating personality traits as part of self-schemata, a logical question that follows then is, how does an individual's perception of him/herself as high or low on certain personality dimensions affect his/her responses to persuasion messages? This question has not drawn enough attention in past literature. Specifically, this study suggests that impacts of personality differences on advertising effectiveness can be inspected from two different perspectives. The first perspective explores how individuals' personality differences by themselves will influence the ways in which individuals respond to advertising messages in general. Past studies showed that subjects with different personality orientations tend to engage in different processing strategies, as a result they prefer different advertising appeals or imagery (e.g., LaBarbera, Weingard & Yorkston, 1998). Moreover, individuals with certain personality traits, as opposed to individuals with other personality traits, react to ads either more positively or negatively regardless of which appeals an ad applies (Mehta, 1999). Given that introverts, as opposed to extroverts, have been shown to react more negatively to their environment (Graziano, Rahe & Feldesman, 1985), it is important to explore whether introverts will evaluate ads or brands differently from extroverts even when imagery or appeals in ads are not necessarily directly tied to introversion or extroversion.

The second, and most popular approach to examining personality differences is to investigate the influence of congruency between self-concept and product image on product evaluations. Since advertising is an important vehicle to build up brand personalities (Kimani & Zeithamal, 1993), how ad messages are delivered is a crucial research question to explore. Past studies examining self-concept and brand image congruency effects reported positive and consistent results. That is, self-congruent brand images are perceived to be more positive (e.g., Sirgy, 1982) and ad messages that delineate users with a profile similar to subjects are more effective (e.g., Hong & Zinkhan, 1995). As discussed earlier, this study will treat personality attributes as part of an individual's self knowledge and test whether self-congruent personality appeals are more effective. Furthermore, what is not clear in past literature is the mechanism in the brand evaluation formation process. Therefore, this study tries to examine the mechanism involved in the process and specifically explores the mediating roles that self-referencing and ad-evoked emotions play.

THE CONCEPT OF SELF

Early psychologists were interested in identifying individuals with respect to certain dimensions of enduring characteristics (Cantor & Kihlstrom, 1981). With developments in cognitive psychology, scholars tend to see each individual as a cognitive being and the self as part of the information processing system (Kuiper & Derry, 1981). Individuals' knowledge of themselves is generally referred to as self-concepts or self-schemata. These are defined as "the person's mental representation of his or her own personality attributes, social roles, past experience, future goals, and the like" (Fiske & Taylor, 1991, pp.181-2). According to Markus and Smith (1981), each individual has a set of knowledge of who or what he/she is, with personality differences as some of the features contained in prototypes of the self. Self-concepts as a knowledge structure, like other cognitive systems, are functional (see Fiske & Taylor, 1991, for a review). They determine how we attend to, encode, and process incoming information about the self. An individual's prediction of his/her future behavioral orientation is also based on his/her self-concepts (Markus, et al., 1982). Finally, a unique and important function that self-concepts serve is affect regulation (Markus & Wurf, 1987).

Possible Selves

There are different possible perspectives that we can use to define ourselves (Markus & Nurius, 1986; Markus & Wurf, 1987). Among them are the real self, the ideal self (Higgins, 1987; Munson & Sirgy, 1980; Sirgy, 1985), the looking glass self (Munson & Spivey, 1980), and the ought self (Higgins, 1987), although most researchers identify just the real and ideal selves. Since a person's ideal self has been shown to be significantly correlated with his/her real self (Landon, 1974), even though some researchers argue that the ideal self is more salient in the purchase decision-making process, this study will examine both subjects' real selves and ideal selves.

Multi-dimensionality of Self

Self-concepts are multi-dimensional (e.g., Markus & Wurf, 1987). Individuals differ from each other not only in terms of how they define themselves on these various dimensions (Markus, et al., 1982), but also in terms of which dimensions are central. Personality traits are important dimensions in our self-knowledge structure and they have drawn more research attention than other self-relevant constructs. This study will focus on one enduring personality difference—introversion/extroversion—to investigate how subjects with different levels of introversion/extroversion respond to persuasive messages differently. The following literature review will first examine past studies on personality difference and then specifically focus on how introverts and extroverts are likely to respond to persuasive messages.

PERSONALITY DIFFERENCE AND PERSUASION

Individual differences in personalities have been shown to affect peoples' processing strategies. Holbrook (1986) developed scales to identify subjects with different personality orientations and showed that subjects' personality differences impacted their preferences for esthetic features of fashion designs. LaBarbera, Weingard and Yorkston (1998) suggested that individuals with different personality types reacted to and processed advertising imagery in different ways. Specifically, they examined the sensing/intuiting dimension of personality identified by Jung (1971). Their findings showed that the sensing type of subjects evaluated advertising images, as well as advertising as a whole, more positively when the ad contained more concrete visuals, whereas the intuitive type of subjects favored ad appeals that employed more abstract visuals.

In general, past findings showed that individuals with different personality traits tend to process information in different manners and, as a result, they favor certain types of imagery configurations. However, what has not been discussed is whether or not an individual's personality traits contribute to his/her evaluation of advertising messages regardless of which specific appeals are applied. When Mehta (1999) examined the effects of the convergence of consumer self-concept and the perceived brand image, results showed that the sensitive type of subjects, as opposed to adventurous and sensual types of subjects, rated commercials more negatively regardless of the appeals that were employed. This indicates that an individual's personality orientations might impact his/her view of things as well as his/her view of advertising. Thus to examine whether individuals' personalities will influence their responses to ads in general is one objective of this study.

INTROVERTS/EXTROVERTS AND PERSUASION

A person's introversion or extroversion is one of the most important personality dimensions that has been recognized and explored in past literature (e.g., Eysenck & Eysenck, 1976). Introverts and extroverts not only differ in terms of their behavior orientation (e.g., Eysenck, 1967), but also the values they hold (Furnham, 1984), and their attitudes toward their environments (Marjoribanks, 1989). In addition, introverts perform better under negative rather than positive reinforcement, whereas extroverts perform better under positive rather than negative reinforcement (Boddy, Carver & Rowley, 1986). Most importantly, introverts seem to systematically recall and expect more aversiveness in their social encounters with others than extroverts (Graziano, Rahe, & Feldesman, 1985). Eysenck (1977) proposed that introverts and extroverts have a different sense of the power they possess to control their behavior outcomes. Introverts are motivated toward avoiding costs whereas extroverts are oriented toward gaining awards. Due to the motivational differences, introverts tend to perceive things in a more negative light as a way to decrease the likely costs whereas extroverts tend to view things in more positive ways in order to enhance their sense of rewards. Since personality seems to be an underlying force that influences the way we interact with our environment, it is likely that introverts and extroverts will evaluate advertising differently regardless of ad message differences.

Hypothesis 1: Regardless of ad message differences, extrovert subjects will evaluate ads in more positive ways than introvert subjects.

Hypothesis 2: Regardless of ad message differences, extrovert subjects will evaluate brands in more positive ways than introvert subjects.

SELF-CONCEPT CONGRUENCY

Self-concept Congruency and Product Evaluation

What we possess reflects our identities (Belk, 1988). Our possessions help us present the self to others. Consumption, thus, is believed to be symbolic (Grubb & Grathwohl, 1967; Sirgy, 1982) and in service of the self (Shavitt & Brock, 1986). Given the symbolic self-defining functions that consumption or possession serve, it is not difficult to understand that individuals prefer products that are congruent with their real self-concept or ideal self-concept.

Indeed, an individual's evaluation of and intention to purchase a product has been shown to be determined by the interaction of his/her self-perception and the brand's personality (e.g., Grubb & Grathwohl, 1967; 1968; Sirgy, 1982). To the degree that they are congruent, an individual's responses to the product are more likely to be positive. This type of congruency effect was documented when both real self-concepts and ideal self-concepts were examined (e.g., Dolich, 1969; Sirgy, 1985).

In the 60s and 70s, the congruency between product image and self-image was extensively tested in consumer research. However, since it is generally accpted that advertising is one of the most important vehicles for imbuing a product with a specific personality and image (Kimani & Zeithamal, 1993), studies on self-concept congruency effects in the 90s were mainly conducted in the advertising processing context. This line of research will be reviewed in the following section.

Self-concept Congruency and the Effects of Different Advertising Appeals

Consumers who perceive themselves in opposing ways tend to respond to advertising messages differently. Since self-concept functions as a basic frame on which an individual's information processing and reference-making is based (Markus, et al., 1982), it is applied to situations in which advertising messages are processed. Past studies indicated that advertising messages that are congruent with an individual's self-concepts are more effective than advertising messages that are incongruent with an individual's self-concepts (e.g., Hong & Zinkhan, 1995; Wang & Mowen, 1997).

One of the reasons that self-concept congruent messages are more effective is that self-congruent messages are more likely to draw viewers' attentions and when advertising information is encoded with self-knowledge being activated, the enhanced linkages and associations make message recall more likely (e.g., Hong & Zinkhan, 1995). However, Hong and Zinkhan's (1995) studies have not empirically established the superior effects of memory due to message congruency. Instead, their study, as well as most other studies, demonstrated that self-concept congruent messages generate better ad attitude and brand evaluation, and higher purchase intention.

Ad messages that are congruent with or relevant to a person's self-concepts are usually evaluated more positively. For example, Wang and Mowen (1997) determined subject's orientations toward separatedness or connectedness then tested their responses to ads with a separate ad appeal or a connected ad appeal. The findings indicated that subjects preferred ads employing ad appeals that were congruent with their self-concepts. Leach and Liu (1998) found that ideocentric subjects rated in-group advertising message appeals more positively than out-group advertising appeals whereas allocentric subjects evaluated out-group message appeals in more positive ways. Dutta (1999) documented the same results when examining health campaign messages. He demonstrated that functional AIDS ad appeals are favored by ideocentric subjects, whereas social AIDS ad appeals are preferred by allocentric subjects when subjects are highly involved in processing ad messages. Emotional appeals have also been shown to work differently for individuals who have independent versus interdependent constructs of the self (Aaker & Williams, 1998). Aaker and Williams (1998) demonstrated that ego-focused emotional appeals generated more favorable evaluations for subjects in individualistic cultures, whereas other-focused emotional appeals elicited more positive evaluations for subjects in collectivist cultures.

Product evaluations also vary depending on how ad messages delineate product users. Hong and Zinkhan (1995) examined introverted and extroverted consumers and showed that consumers' evaluations of advertised brands were determined by the congruency between ad messages and self-concepts. Purchase intent has also been shown to increase when ad messages are congruent with subjects' self-concepts. For example, categorizing subjects into three groups: adventurous subjects, sensual subjects, and sensitive subjects, Mehta (1999) found that the higher the convergence of self-concept and brand image delineated in ads, the higher subjects' purchase intent. Therefore, this study suggests:

Hypothesis 3: Subjects favor brands with user portrayals that are congruent with their real selves.

Hypothesis 4: Subjects favor brands with user portrayals that are congruent with their ideal selves.

The Mediating Role of Self-referencing

Viewers may or may not refer messages to themselves when they are exposed to advertising. According to Burnkrant and Unnava (1995), self-referencing is regarded as the processing of information by relating it to the self-structure or aspects thereof. Early studies on self-referencing found that recall of words or phrases was greater when subjects were asked to relate words or phrases to themselves (e.g., Bower & Gilligan, 1979; Bellezza, 1984; Rogers, Kuiper, and Kirker, 1977). The greater recall resulting from self-referencing is attributed to subjects' more thorough elaboration (Burnkrant & Unnava, 1989; Burnkrant & Unnava, 1995). Since people's knowledge about the self is rich and plentiful, relating words to aspects of the self activates a well-connected cognitive structure. This activation makes more linkage points between incoming information and existing cognitive structures, thus making multiple retrieval routes available, and in turn enhancing recall (Burnkrant & Unnava, 1989; Burnkrant & Unnava, 1995).

The self-referencing effects on recall have been demonstrated in studies that explored advertising effects (e.g., Burnkrant & Unnava, 1989; Burnkrant & Unnava, 1995). Burnkrant and Unnava (1995) showed that self-referencing advertising messages encouraged subjects to engage in central route processing and led to more elaboration of messages. Under conditions in which messages prompting self-referencing were embedded in advertising copy, subjects rated a strong-argument message as significantly more effective than a weak-argument message. On the other hand, under

conditions in which self-referencing was not evoked, subjects did not rate messages with strong arguments and weak arguments differently.

The author argues that it is important to examine whether self-concept congruent ad messages encourage subjects to refer messages to themselves. Self-concept congruent messages in ads may activate subjects' self-schemata, which most people have available though they may not be activated at all times, and engage subjects in more self-referencing thinking. To the extent they feel engaged, they are likely to have positive attitude toward the advertised brand. In other words, their brand attitudes are determined by the level of self-referencing that ad messages evoke.

Hypothesis 5: Subjects' self-referencing mediates their evaluations of the advertised brand.

The Mediation of Subjects' Emotional Responses for Congruency Effects

Why do consumers favor self-concept congruent messages? It is suggested that inconsistency and dissonance have emotional consequences such as evoking tension, stress, and discomfort (see Higgins, 1987 for a review). Self-conflicts have also been shown to cause emotional problems (e.g., Rogers, 1961). Based on self-discrepancy theory, Higgins (1987) suggests that individuals are motivated to meet the expectations of others. He further proposes that discrepancies between a person's perceptions of his/her actual self and others' perceptions of what he or she should be will evoke a sense of dejection due to the anticipated loss of social affection or attractiveness.

As documented in past literature, media is said to set the standards and norms of our behaviors. It shows us what we should or ought to be in order to be socially attractive. By the same token, advertising can shape an image that we believe others will favor. Consumer researchers suggest that an individual's consumption is symbolic in that the individual is attempting to gain social recognition or self-image enhancement (e.g., Markus & Wurf, 1987; Sirgy, 1985; Zinkhan & Hong, 1991). To the extent that user images portrayed in advertising and consumers' real self-concepts are discrepant, consumers are likely to feel frustrated and sad. In turn, their emotional states may alter the way they feel toward the advertised brand due to mood congruency effects (Clore, Schwarz & Conway, 1994; Schwarz & Clore, 1996). Therefore, this study argues that the discrepancy between real self-concept and product image will elicit more negative emotions and less positive emotions. These emotional responses further mediate subjects' evaluations of the advertised brand.

Hypothesis 6: Subjects' emotional responses mediate their evaluations of the advertised brand.

METHODOLOGY

Subjects

Three hundred and ninety-six subjects were recruited for this study. Subjects were from the campus of a university in a metropolitan area and were paid for their participation. They were randomly assigned to one of two conditions (ads with introvert user portrayals vs. ads with extrovert user portrayals).

Procedures

Subjects were ushered into a classroom. After they were seated, the coordinator told them that the study was designed to examine the effects of various ad formats or techniques on viewers' information processing. This story was designed to discourage them from guessing at purposes of the study. Then subjects, at their own pace, read a filler ad followed by the stimuli ad and another filler ad. After reading the stimuli ad, they were asked to rate their affective states. Then after reading all ads, they rated their levels of self-referencing to the ad, after which they measured their perceptions of user images in ads. Following this they rated their ad attitudes and product attitudes. Finally, they rated their real selves and ideal selves on Eysenck et al's (1985) introversion/extroversion scale. After they finished the study, the coordinator provided a short debriefing.

Stimuli

Bottled water, a low-involving product identified in a pretest, was chosen as the advertised product because it is likely that risky or high-involving products will generate different responses from introverts, as opposed to extroverts, due to their orientation toward risk avoidance. Stimuli ads were created by professionals working at Ogilvy & Mather Ad Agency. Professional copywriters wrote ad messages to fit different personality portrayals and creative people provided visuals to fit message descriptions. Visuals and layouts were similar for ads with introvert user portrayals and ads with extrovert user portrayals in order to reduce any possible confounding effects. To improve external validity, the stimuli ad was inserted between two real filler ads.

Independent Variables

Real Self-image and Ideal Self-image on Introversion/Extroversion

Subjects rated their real selves and their ideal selves on Eysenck, Eysenck & Barrett's (1985) introvert/extrovert scale. This scale was composed of 12 items. Cronbach's reliability alpha was assessed to be satisfactory at .88 for the ratings of their real selves and at .82 for their ideal selves. For statistical analyses, subjects' responses to the 12 items were summed and averaged. A low figure indicates that the subject is more likely to be introverted, whereas a high figure indicates the subject is more likely to be extroverted.

Product User Image on Introversion/Extroversion

Subjects were exposed to ads containing messages delineating ad characters with either introvert characteristics or extrovert characteristics. Eysenck et al.'s (1985) introvert/extrovert scale was applied to measure subjects' perceptions of product users portrayed in ads. Cronbach's reliability alpha estimate for the scale is satisfactory at .98. A t-test analysis indicated that users portrayed in introvert ads did generate a significantly lower rating than ad characters in extrovert ads ($F(1, 391)=889.94$, $p<.01$, $M_{introvert}=2.79$, $M_{extrovert}=.5.71$).

Discrepancy of Self-image and Product Image

Subjects' ratings of ad users minus from their ratings of real selves formed a scale that captures the discrepancy between real self-image and product image. Similarly, subjects' ratings of ad users minus from their ratings of ideal selves formed a scale that captures the discrepancy between ideal self-image and product image. The discrepancy estimates will be used to test whether the larger the discrepancy, the more negative responses subjects generate toward brands.

Dependent Measures

Self-referencing

Subjects rated how well they could relate themselves to the users described in ads. The scale had four items "picture oneself in setting," "picture oneself in position of ad character," "similarity to life experience," and "similarity to ad character." This scale was adopted from Debevec & Iyengar (1988). The Cronbach's reliability estimate is satisfactory at .89.

Ad-evoked Emotion

Subjects rated their emotional states on a 20-item scale. These items were selected from Edell and Burke (1987). Factor analyses with varimax rotation generated three factors with eigen-values larger than one. The first factor includes seven items and is labeled "positive emotions." The second factor consists of six items and is labeled "negative emotions." The third factor has four items and is named "sentimental emotions." Three items had split loadings and were dropped from the analyses. Ad-evoked emotions were analyzed as if there were three sub-scales. Cronbach's reliability alphas for positive emotions, negative emotions and sentimental emotions are satisfactory at .91, .86, and .73 respectively.

Ad Attitude

A five-item seven-point semantic-differential scale was used to measure subjects' attitudes toward ads. The items were adopted from Madden, Allen, & Twible (1988). The five items include: "interesting-not interesting," "good-bad," "likable-not likable," "not irritating-irritating," and "pleasant-not pleasant." Factor analyses generated one factor with an eigen-value larger than one. Therefore, in all later analyses, ad attitudes will be examined by summing and averaging subjects' responses to the five items. Cronbach's reliability alpha is deemed satisfactory at .87.

Brand Attitude

Brand attitudes were measured with a five-item semantic-differential scale. The items were adopted from Mitchel and Olson (1981) and Holbrook and Batra (1987). The five items are "good-bad," "like-dislike," "pleasant-unpleasant," "positive-negative," and "high quality-low quality." Factor analyses generated one factor with an eigen-value larger than one. Therefore, in all later analyses, brand attitudes will be examined by summing and averaging subjects' responses to the five items. Cronbach's reliability alpha of this scale was deemed satisfactory at .93.

RESULTS AND ANALYSES

Subjects' introversion/extroversion was not measured in advance as a means of assignment to different experimental conditions. Instead, individual differences on introversion/extroversion were measured after subjects were exposed to advertising messages. Therefore, regression analyses rather than MANOVA or ANOVA were applied to test the hypotheses. Hypothesis one suggests that, regardless of ad type difference, extroverted subjects will evaluate ads in more positive ways than introverted subjects. Regression analyses indicated that, in addition to the variance explained by ad type difference, subjects' ratings of their real self-images did not contribute significantly more variance to ad liking (see Table 1). However, subjects' ratings of their ideal selves contributed significantly more variance to their attitudes toward ads other than what can be explained by ad type differences. Subjects who rated their ideal selves as more extroverted evaluated ads more positively than subjects who rated their ideal selves as less extroverted. Therefore, hypothesis one is supported when examining subjects' ideal selves but not their real selves.

Hypothesis two suggests that, regardless of ad message difference, extroverted subjects will evaluate brands in more positive ways than introverted subjects. Regression analyses indicated that, in addition to the variance explained by ad type difference, subjects' ratings of their real self-images did not contribute significantly more variance to brand liking (see Table 2). However, subjects' ratings of their ideal selves contributed significantly more variance to their attitudes toward ads other than what can be explained by ad type differences. Subjects who rated their ideal selves as more extrovert evaluated advertised brands more positively than subjects who rated their ideal selves as more introvert. Therefore, hypothesis

TABLE 1
The Impacts of Self-concept in Terms of Introversion and Extroversion on Ad Attitude

| | Attitude toward the ad | | | | | |
| | Real self | | | Ideal self | | |
	Beta	F	p	Beta	F	p
Ad type[a]	.01	.02	.99	.02	.02	.99
Extroversion	.02	.46	.65	.17	2.72	.01

[a] The extrovert ad was dummy coded as "1" whereas the introvert ad was dummy coded as "0".

TABLE 2
The Impacts of Self-concept in Terms of Introversion and Extroversion on Brand Evaluations

| | Attitude toward the brand | | | | | |
| | Real self | | | Ideal self | | |
	Beta	F	p	Beta	F	p
Ad type[a]	.34	2.96	.01	.34	3.01	.01
Extroversion	.06	1.15	.25	.15	2.37	.02

[a] The extrovert ad was dummy coded as "1" whereas the introvert ad was dummy coded as "0".

TABLE 3
The Impacts of Self-image and Product Image Discrepancy on Brand Evaluation

	Beta	t-statistic	p-value
Real self-image and product image discrepancy	-.07	-2.40	.02
Ideal self-image and product image discrepancy	-.09	-3.02	.01

two is supported when examining subjects' ideal selves but not their real selves.

Hypothesis three proposes that subjects favor brands with user portrayals that are more congruent with their real selves. The discrepancy between subjects' ratings of their real selves and the product users on introversion/extroversion was run as an independent variable on brand attitude in the regression analysis. Results indicated that the impact of the discrepancy between their real selves and product image was significant (see Table 3). The larger the discrepancy, the more negative the brand attitude. Therefore, hypothesis three is supported.

Hypothesis four suggests that subjects favor brands with user portrayals that are congruent with their ideal selves. The discrepancy between subjects' ratings of their ideal selves and product

image on introversion/extroversion was regressed on brand attitude. Results indicated that the impact of the discrepancy was significant (see Table 3). Subjects who perceive a large difference between their ideal selves and product users tend to evaluate the advertised brand in a more negative light. Therefore, hypothesis four is supported.

Hypothesis five proposes that subjects' levels of self-referencing mediate their evaluations of brand attitude. To test this hypothesis, a series of regression analyses were conducted (see Table 4). If the relationships among these variables could be demonstrated as specified by Baron and Kenny (1986), the mediating role of subjects' emotional responses can be established. Results indicated that the real self/product discrepancy had significant impacts on subjects' self-referencing (see equation 1). In addition, subjects'

TABLE 4

The Mediating Effect of Ad Evoked Emotion and Self-Referencing on Product Attitude when the Discrepancy between
the Real Self and Brand Image were Examined

	Beta	t-Statistic	p-Value
1. Self-referencing=$\beta_0 + \beta_1$ x Discrepancy	-.27	-6.67	.01
2. Positive emotion= $\beta_0 + \beta_1$ x Discrepancy	.02	.88	.38
3. Negative emotion= $\beta_0 + \beta_1$ x Discrepancy	.08	3.02	.01
4. Sentimental emotion= $\beta_0 + \beta_1$ x Discrepancy	-.21	-7.46	.01
5. Abr= $\beta_0 + \beta_1$ x Self-referencing	.17	5.61	.01
6. Abr= $\beta_0 + \beta_1$ x Positive emotion	.46	10.03	.01
7. Abr= $\beta_0 + \beta_1$ x Negative emotion	-.19	-3.90	.01
8. Abr= $\beta_0 + \beta_1$ x Sentimental emotion	.17	1.90	.06
9. Abr= $\beta_0 + \beta_1$ x Self-referencing	.17	5.47	.01
$\quad + \beta_2$ x Positive emotion	.46	9.72	.01
$\quad + \beta_3$ x Negative emotion	-.19	-3.69	.01
$\quad + \beta_4$ x Sentimental emotion	.07	1.74	.08
$\quad + \beta_5$ x Discrepancy	-.01	-.20	.39

n=396

TABLE 5

The Mediating Effect of Ad Evoked Emotion and Self-Referencing on Product Attitude when the Discrepancy between
the Ideal Self and Brand Image were Examined

	Beta	t-Statistic	p-Value
1. Self-referencing=$\beta_0 + \beta_1$ x Discrepancy	-.27	-6.67	.01
2. Positive emotion= $\beta_0 + \beta_1$ x Discrepancy	.01	.46	.64
3. Negative emotion= $\beta_0 + \beta_1$ x Discrepancy	.12	4.37	.01
4. Sentimental emotion= $\beta_0 + \beta_1$ x Discrepancy	-.27	-9.37	.01
5. Abr= $\beta_0 + \beta_1$ x Self-referencing	.17	5.16	.01
6. Abr= $\beta_0 + \beta_1$ x Positive emotion	.46	10.03	.01
7. Abr= $\beta_0 + \beta_1$ x Negative emotion	-.19	-3.90	.01
8. Abr= $\beta_0 + \beta_1$ x Sentimental emotion	.07	1.90	.06
9. Abr= $\beta_0 + \beta_1$ x Self-referencing	.17	5.51	.01
$\quad + \beta_2$ x Positive emotion	.46	9.60	.01
$\quad + \beta_3$ x Negative emotion	-.19	-3.63	.01
$\quad + \beta_4$ x Sentimental emotion	.07	1.62	.11
$\quad + \beta_5$ x Discrepancy	-.01	-.12	.91

n=396

self-referencing significantly contributed to brand evaluation variance (see equation 5). However, the impacts of discrepancy disappeared when subjects' self-referencing was in the equation (see equation 9). The same patterns of impacts were obtained for ideal self/product user discrepancy (see Table 5). The results indicated that subjects' self-referencing functions as the mediator in the brand evaluation formation process. Therefore, hypothesis 5 is supported.

Hypothesis six proposes that subjects' emotional responses mediate their evaluations of brand attitude. Results indicated that the real self/product user image discrepancy only had significant impacts on subjects' negative emotions and sentimental emotions but not on subjects' positive emotions (see Table 4, equations 3 & 4). Thus, positive emotion is not qualified to be the mediator. In addition, only subjects' negative emotions significantly contributed to brand evaluation variance (see equation 7). However, the impacts of discrepancy disappeared when subjects' negative emotion was in the equation (see equation 9). Sentimental emotion is not qualified to be the mediator here because its impact was not significant when discrepancy was also in the equation. The same patterns of impacts were obtained for the ideal self/product user discrepancy (see Table 5). The results indicated that, among three types of emotional responses, subjects' negative emotional responses are the only mediator in the brand evaluation formation process. Therefore, hypothesis six is supported for negative emotion.

DISCUSSION

Research on personality and consumer behavior is generally limited to examinations of the impacts of self-concept and brand image congruency on product evaluation. This study suggests that there are two different ways that subjects' personality orientations may interfere with their processing of advertising information. First, subjects of different personalities are likely to view their environment from different perspectives. Extroverts are attracted to rewards and tend to see their environment from a more positive perspective. On the other hand, introverts shun risks and pay more attention to negative aspects of their environment. As a result, extroverts tend to favor ads and products in general regardless of the degree of congruency between brand image and their self-concepts. However, we should note that only those who rated their ideal selves high on extroversion responded to the products and ads more positively. Those who rated their real selves high on extroversion did not evaluate the products or ads differently from those who rated their real selves low on extroversion. Future studies should try to explore the different impacts driven by consumers' real self-concepts and ideal self-concepts.

Second, subjects' perceptions of the discrepancies between their self-concepts and product images affect their product evaluations. Most importantly, this study further investigated the mechanism involved in the process that leads to subjects' preferences for product images similar to their self-concepts. Past research suggests that dissonance and discrepancy are causes of emotional discomfort. When advertising provides an image of whom a consumer should be, the consumer's perception of discrepancy has direct emotional consequences. As Higgins (1987) argues, discrepancies between what a person's perceptions of his/her actual self and others' perceptions of what he or she should be will evoke a sense of dejection due to the anticipated loss of social affection or attractiveness. Consistent with Higgins (1987), this study demonstrated that only negative emotion, as opposed to positive emotion or sentimental emotion, functions as the mediator in the brand evaluation formation process. Additionally, when subjects' self-concepts are congruent with a product's image, subjects are likely to refer ad messages to their own lives. The more they refer ad messages to themselves, the more positive responses they have toward the product.

The findings of this study not only contribute to our understanding of how and why consumers' personalities affect their product evaluations, they also have important implications for marketers. To develop appropriate advertising strategies appealing to their target segments, marketing managers should be aware of how target consumers' self-concepts affect their evaluations of advertised brands and what mechanism is involved in the process. On the other hand, to accurately estimate campaign effects, marketing managers should take into account their target audience's responses to advertising in general.

This study tests only one personality trait and examines only ads for bottled water. Since a person's self-concept is multidimensional, examining other personality traits is necessary for replications. As discussed briefly earlier, bottled water is a low-involving product. Extroverts and introverts are likely to respond differently to high-involving products due to their orientations toward risk. Further research involving other product types is warranted to provide a better view of the impacts of personality differences on product evaluations.

REFERENCES

Aaker, J. L., & Williams, P. (1998). Empathy versus pride: The influence of emotional appeals across cultures. *Journal of Consumer Research, 25,* 241-261.

Baron, R. M., & Kenny, D. A. (1986). The moderator-mediator variable distinction in social psychological research: Conceptual, strategic, and statistical considerations. *Journal of Personality and Social Psychology, 51,* 1173-1182.

Bellezza, F. S. (1984). The self as a mnemonic device: The role of internal cues. *Journal of Personality and Social Psychology, 47,* 506-516.

Belk, R. W. (1988). Possessions and the extended self. *Journal of Consumer Research, 15,* 139-168.

Boddy, J., Carver, a. & Rowley, K. (1986). Effects of positive and negative verbal reinforcement on performance as a function of extroversion-introversion: Some tests of Gray's theory. *Personality & Individual Differences, 7,* 81-88.

Bower, G. H., & Gilligan, S. G. (1979). Remembering information related to one's self. *Journal of Research in Personality, 13,* 420-432.

Burnkrant, R. E., & Unnava, H. R. (1989). Self-referencing: A strategy for increasing processing of message content. *Personality and Social Psychology Bulletin, 15,* 628-638.

Burnkrant, R. E., & Unnava, H. R. (1995). Effects of self-referencing on persuasion. *Journal of Consumer Research, 22,* 17-26.

Cantor, N., & Kihlstrom, J. F. (Eds.) (1981). *Personality, cognition, and social interaction.* Hillsdale, NJ: Erlbaum.

Debevec, K. & Iyer, E. (1988). Self-referencing as a mediator of the effectiveness of sex-role portrayals in advertising. *Psychology and Marketing, 5,* 71-84.

Dolitch, I. M. (1969). Congruence relation between self images and product brands. *Journal of Marketing Research, 6,* 80-84.

Dutta, M. J. (1999). *The effect of idiocentrism and involvement on attitude, cognition and behavioral intention with respect to AIDS appeal types.* Paper presented at the annual conference of AEJMC. New Orleans.

Edell, J. A., & Burke, M. C. (1987). The power of feelings in understanding advertising effects. *Journal of Consumer Research, 14,* 421-433.

Eysenck, H. J. (1967). *The biological basis of personality.* Springfield, IL: Charles C. Thomas.

Eysenck, H. J. (1977). *Human memory: Theory, research, and individual differences.* Oxford, England: Pergamon Press.

Eysenck, H. J., & Eysenck, S. B. G. (1976). *Psychoticism as a dimension of personality.* London: Hodder & Stoughton.

Fiske, S. T., & Taylor, S. E. (1991). *Social Cognition.* 2nd Ed. New York: McGraw Hill.

Furnham, A. (1984). Personality and values. *Personality and Individual Differences, 5,* 483-485.

Gaziano, W. G., Rahe, D. F., & Feldesman, A. B. (1985). Extraversion, social cognition, and the salience of aversiveness in social encounters. *Journal of Personality and Social Psychology, 49,* 941-980.

Grubb, E. L. & Grathwohl, H. L. (1967). Consumer self-concepts, symbolism and market behavior: A theoretical approach. *Journal of Marketing, 31*(Oct.), 22-27.

Higgins, E. T. (1987). Self-discrepancy: A theory relating self and affect. *Psychological Review, 94,* 319-340.

Holbrook, M. (1986). Aims, concepts, and methods for the representation of individual differences in esthetic responses to design features. *Journal of Consumer Research, 13,* 337-347.

Holbrook, M. B., & Batra, R. (1987). Assessing the role of emotions as mediators of consumer responses to advertising. *Journal of Consumer Research, 14,* 404-420.

Hong, J. W., & Zinkhan, G. M. (1995). Self-concept and advertising effectiveness; the influence of congruency, conspicuousness, and response mode. *Psychology and Marketing, 12,* 53-77.

Kihlstrom, J. F., & Cantor, N. (1984). Mental representations of the self. In L. Berkowitz (Ed.), *Advances in Experimental Social Psychology, 17,* 2-48. New York: Academic Press.

Kirmani, A., & Zeithaml, V. (1993). Advertising, perceived quality, and brand image. In D. A. Aaker & A. L. Biel (Eds.) *Brand equity and advertising* (pp. 143-162). Hilldale, NJ: Erlbaum.

Kuiper, N. A., & Derry, P. (1981). The self as a cognitive prototype: An application to person perception and depression. In N. Canter & J. F. Kihlstrom (Eds.), *Personality, cognition, and social interaction* (pp. 217-232). Hillsdale, NJ: Erlbaum.

Landon, E. L. (1974). Self concept, ideal self concept, and consumer purchase intentions. *Journal of Consumer Research, 1,* 44-51.

LaBarbera, P. A., Weingard, P., & Yorkston, E. A. (1998). Matching the message to the mind: Advertising imagery and consumer processing styles. *Journal of Advertising Research, 38*(5), 29-43.

Leach, M. P., & Liu, A. H. (1998). The use of culturally relevant stimuli in international advertising. *Psychology & Marketing, 15,* 523-546.

Madden, T. J., Allen, C. T., & Twible, J. L. (1988). Attitude toward the ad: An assessment of diverse measurement indices under different processing "sets". *Journal of Marketing Research, 25,* 242-252.

Marjoribanks, K. (1989). Attitudes and environments: Personality group differences. *Psychological Reports, 64,* 99-103.

Markus, H., Crane, M., Bernstein, S., & Siladi, M. (1982). Self-schemas and gender. *Journal of Personality and Social Psychology, 42,* 38-50.

Markus, H., & Nurius, P. (1986). Possible selves. *American Psychologist, 41,* 954-969.

Markus, H., & Smith, J. (1981). The influence of self-schemata on the perception of others. In N. Canter & J. F. Kihlstrom (Eds.), *Personality, cognition, and social interaction* (pp. 233-262). Hillsdale, NJ: Erlbaum.

Markus, H., & Wurf, E. (1987). The dynamic self-concept: A social psychological perspective. *Annual Review of Psychology, 38,* 299-377.

Maheswaran, D., & Sternthal, B. (1990). The effects of knowledge, motivation, and type of messages on ad processing and product judgments. *Journal of Consumer Research, 17,* 66-73.

Mehta, A. (1999). Using self-concept to assess advertising effectiveness. *Journal of Advertising Research,39*(1), 81-89.

Mischel, A. A., & Olson, J. C. (1981). Are product attribute beliefs the only mediator of advertising effects on brand attitudes? *Journal of Marketing Research, 18,* 318-332.

Munson, J. M., & Spivey, W. A. (1980). Assessing self concept. *Advances in Consumer Research, 7,* 598-603.

Park, C. W., & Young, M. (1986). Consumer response to television commercials: The impact of involvement and background music on brand attitude formation. *Journal of marketing research, 23,* 11-24.

Rogers, T. B., Kuiper, N. A., & Kirker, W. S. (1977). Self-reference and the encoding of personal information. *Journal of Personality and Social Psychology, 35,* 677-688.

Sirgy, M. J. (1982). Self-concept in consumer behavior: A critical review. *Journal of Consumer Research, 9,* 287-299.

Sirgy, M. J. (1985). Using self-congruity and ideal congruity to predict purchase motivation. *Journal of Business Research, 13,* 195-206.

Snyder, M., & DeBono, K. G. (1985). Appeals to image and claims about quality: Understanding the psychology of advertising. *Journal of Personality and Social Psychology, 49,* 586-597.

Thibout, J., & Kelley, H. H. (1959). *The social psychology of groups.* New York: Wiley.

Venkatraman, M. P., Marlino, D., Kardes, F. R., & Sklar, K. B. (1990). The interactive effects of message appeal and individual differences on information processing and persuasion. *Psychology & Marketing, 7,* 85-96.

Wang, C. L., & Mowen, J. C. (1997). The separateness-connectedness self-schema: Scale development and application to message construction. *Psychology and Marketing, 14,* 185-207.

Zinkhan, G. M., & Hong, J. W. (1991). Self concept and advertising effectiveness: A conceptual model of congruency, conspicuousness, and response mode. *Advances in Consumer Research, 18,* 348-354.

.Com Satisfaction and .Com Dissatisfaction: One or Two Constructs?

Qimei Chen, University of Minnesota
William D. Wells, University of Minnesota

ABSTRACT

In the study of consumer satisfaction (CS), there is a long running controversy about whether satisfaction and dissatisfaction are equal and opposite constructs or to some degree independent. Parallel to the exponential growth of e-commerce, this issue needs to be revisited with respect to the Internet due to its uniqueness compared with traditional retailing channels. This study employs depth-interviews with Web developers to address this issue. The findings suggest that .com satisfaction and .com dissatisfaction are partially, but not completely independent; just as they are partially, but not completely equal and opposite. This finding provides communication between Web professionals and their customers and further supports e-businesses in planning their marketing strategies.

The exponential development of the Internet creates magic. These days, a domain name ending with ".com" is a symbol of corporate progressiveness and leading-edge image (Cross 1998). But of course, establishment and maintenance of a corporate Web site is expensive, and once a Web site has been created, its sponsor needs to know whether it is functioning as intended. Web user satisfaction is one such evaluation mechanism.

The purpose of the present project is to understand how Web site developers think about online consumer satisfaction, how they position the relationship between online satisfaction and dissatisfaction, which factors they believe contribute to satisfaction and dissatisfaction, and their beliefs about the importance of satisfaction and dissatisfaction to e-business.

LITERATURE REVIEW

Though satisfaction has been an important concept in several disciplines, little research has focused on satisfaction within the domain of e-commerce.

In study of consumer satisfaction (CS), there is a long running controversy about whether satisfaction and dissatisfaction are equal and opposite constructs or to some degree independent. In industrial psychology as well as in marketing, the traditional view has been that satisfaction and dissatisfaction are points on a single dimension such that the presence of one implies the lack of the other (Howard and Sheth 1969, p. 145; Nicosia 1966, p. 186). However, more recent research on job satisfaction has suggested that satisfaction and dissatisfaction may be at least partially distinctive variables (Herzberg, Mausner, and Snyderman 1959; SRA 1951).

Herzberg et al. (1959) were among the first to adopt a two-dimensional view of job satisfaction. Employing a critical incident or "sequence of events" methodology, they found that one set of factors characterized satisfying job incidents and a different set characterized dissatisfying incidents. The first set, named "motivators," includes intrinsic factors such as "…achievement, recognition, advancement, possibility of growth, responsibility and work itself." The second set, named "hygienes" (dissatisfiers or extrinsic factors), on the other hand, includes "salary; interpersonal relations with superiors, subordinates and peers; technical supervision; company policy and administration; personal life; working conditions; status; and job security" (Wood and LeBold 1970). Herzberg, therefore, argued that

"Since separate factors need to be considered, depending upon whether job satisfaction or job dissatisfaction is being examined, it follows that these two feelings are not opposites of each other. The opposite of job satisfaction is not job dissatisfaction but, rather no job satisfaction; and similarly, the opposite of job dissatisfaction is not job satisfaction but no job dissatisfaction" (Herzberg, Mausner and Snyderman 1959, pp. 107-109).

Recent research in marketing resonates this view (Aaker and Day 1971; Buskirk and Rothe 1970; Leavitt 1977). In discussing conceptual issues related to consumer satisfaction, Czepiel and Rosenberg (1973) proposed that consumer satisfaction and dissatisfaction should be considered as parallel evaluative scales.

"Since most behavior has multiple motivations, it might be more accurate to consider that some degree of satisfaction or dissatisfaction would accrue to each motivation. This is more in agreement with common usage as when someone says: 'it gives me great satisfaction, except for the color.' Considering satisfaction-dissatisfaction as parallel evaluative scales, however, does not permit the prediction of one from the other…" (p. 6).

These authors also discussed the necessity of adopting a two-dimensional approach to consumer satisfaction by embracing Herzberg's position fully (Leavitt 1977):

"For any level of satisfaction, these facets may be of two types: maintainers, which must exist in order for dissatisfaction to be avoided, and satisfiers, which truly motivate and contribute to satisfaction" (Czepiel, Rosenberg and Akerele 1974, p. 5).

Although the appropriateness of a two-factor model is still debatable, this issue needs to be considered with respect to the Internet. Compared with traditional retailing, the Internet offers surfers more abundant choices and more convenient exits from one e-tailer to another; therefore, there are reasons to believe that online satisfaction and dissatisfaction are not equal and opposite— that the facets of dissatisfaction are not necessarily the obverse of the facets of satisfaction. A two-factor model, therefore, might bring new light to understanding online consumer behavior. In addition, we will also look at whether consequences of dissatisfaction are the obverse of the consequences of satisfaction.

METHOD

One obvious way to investigate this issue would be to look at online consumer responses. However, in the present study, we take an alternative route: We employ depth-interviews with Web developers. We choose Web developers for the following reasons: 1) Web developers pay close attention to consumer satisfaction issues. Therefore, knowing their opinions and practices helps the development of a .com satisfaction|dissatisfaction framework. 2) Web users' evaluations of Web sites have been examined in previous studies (e.g. Chen and Wells 1999), while Web developers, who may offer different a point of view, have been avoided. 3) Web developers usually get feedback from Web users. Therefore,

FIGURE 1
Two Factor Model of .com Satisfaction/Disatisfaction

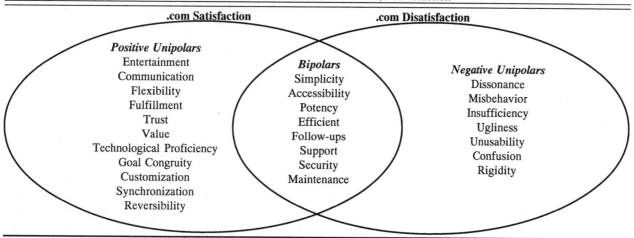

Web developers' viewpoints might constitute a condensation and integration of reactions of Web users.

The developers interviewed in the present investigation are from 25 top Web design firms. On the average, they have 4.5 years of Web Site development experience. They all hold crucial positions in planning their companies' e-commerce activity. They are Web designers, creative directors, producers, and senior art directors. They commonly hold a BA/BS degrees in communication, computer science, or English. Some of them also earned their MA and Ph.D. degrees. They are predominantly male, and they are all active Internet surfers and e-commerce patrons. The companies they work with vary greatly in revenue, size, function and marketing niche. They provide a rough picture of typical Web professionals.

In-depth interviews employed the critical incident technique (Grigaliunas and Herzberg 1971), which requires individuals to describe instances in which they felt particularly satisfied or particularly dissatisfied about a Web experience and the consequences of the experience. The purpose of this step was to identify the possible components and consequences of satisfaction and dissatisfaction (Grigaliunas and Herzberg 1971). Interviewees were asked to relate and describe their responses to these incidents.

Fourteen in-depth interviews were completed. This cutting point was chosen because responses in the later interviews basically repeated responses in the earlier ones. Interviewees were asked open-ended questions such as: What about a Web site results in a satisfied online consumer and what are the consequences? What efforts have you made on the Web sites you've developed to ensure consumer online satisfactions. What is it about a Web site that results in a dissatisfied online consumer and what are the consequences? What efforts have you made to decrease consumer online dissatisfaction?

FINDINGS

Sixteen-hours of interview responses were transcribed from audio tapes to text files. The files were then coded and content analyzed. Preliminary findings are as follows:

Web developers regard .com satisfaction and dissatisfaction as very important in e-business. In average, they gave a mean score of 9.4 on a scale from 1 to 10 (with 10 the highest). Most Web developers regard .com satisfaction and .com dissatisfaction as partially independent constructs. They believe that, in many cases, the opposite of .com satisfaction is the lack of .com satisfaction and

the opposite of .com dissatisfaction is the lack of .com dissatisfaction. Designer W related the following experience:

W is a busy professional. As his girlfriend's birthday approached, he became anxious about the selection of an appropriate gift. He finally figured that ordering a gift online might be a wise way to save the hassle. He used a search engine to help identify some virtual sources. Then he visited each shop to take a brief survey. The first e-shop he visited had several broken links. He therefore quickly exited. The second e-shop actually had some items that looked pretty good, and the price seemed fair, but the product images were too blurry for him to make a decision. He had to exit again. The third e-shop obviously wanted to provide high-resolution pictures for the Web page, but took more than 3 minutes to be fully downloaded. W got impatient and stopped the downloading process. The forth shop he went to had a nice design and offered many options. He checked some gifts and liked them. However, he felt that the price of the gift was higher than his budget, so he left this shop. The fifth shop he went to was quite pleasant and very organized. He quickly found a watch that he thought was quite cool. The thumbnail picture offered the link that he could click to see an enlarged image. He was also pleased to find that he also had the option to view images taken from different angles. He ordered the watch, and spent a sweet night with his girlfriend on her birthday. He felt very satisfied with his experience with the fifth e-shop. When he was asked his evaluation of his experience with the other four e-shops, he expressed high dissatisfaction toward the first three sites. He emphasized, however, even if these three sites fixed their broken links, set up some clear images, and made their files smaller for downloading, he would not necessarily feel satisfied with them. About the forth site, he said that he found it was OK and he did not feel dissatisfied with it. But he lacked satisfaction with it.

The above example shows that with respect to e-commerce, the opposite of satisfaction may be lack of satisfaction rather than dissatisfaction (as in W's evaluation of the forth e-shop) and the opposite of dissatisfaction may be lack of dissatisfaction rather than satisfaction (as in W's evaluation of the first three e-shops).

This issue impacts e-commerce practice significantly. If satisfaction and dissatisfaction are simple obverses of each other, the often-stated goal of maximizing consumer satisfaction is appropriate. However, if it turns out that satisfaction and dissatisfaction are at least partially independent concepts, the practitioner is faced with a more complex situation. If practices that lead most directly to maximization of satisfaction do not necessarily lead most directly to minimization of dissatisfaction, these two goals must be pursued separately and simultaneously with different actions (Stokes 1974, p.2).

By analyzing the depth interviews, we delineate a tentative framework in explaining the conceptual domain of .com satisfaction|dissatisfaction (see Figure 1). This framework maintains that .com satisfaction and dissatisfaction are partially independent constructs.

These interviews suggest that at least three kinds of facets helps describe, explain and predict .com satisfaction and dissatisfaction. The first kind portrays .com dissatisfaction as the bipolar opposite of .com satisfaction. We call these facets *bipolars*. These facets include Simplicity, Accessibility, Potency, Efficient, Follow-Ups , Support, Security and Maintenance. In Table 1, at least two statements were used to describe each facet. Web developers indicate that these *bipolars* are the barometers used to evaluate Web sites. A very positive evaluation would evoke satisfaction while a very negative evaluation would evoke dissatisfaction. For instance, a Web site offering very convenient, one-step checkout would evoke consumer satisfaction. By contrast, if checking out from a Web site requires a very complex, painstaking ordeal, site users might feel increasingly dissatisfied. Some Web developers indicate that they have been noticing this realation:

When you are in this business for a while, you sort of gain the sense automatically what you should demonstrate to make them [the consumers] happy…Checkouts have to be simple, no way a very complicated checkout won't annoy your customers. Just think about this standing in their shoes for a while, you would know that what they really want is a straight forward, one step checkout. Bingo! (Smile) (Mr. D, project manager with 4-year and 8-month experiences)

We tentatively group the *bipolars* in Table 1. A semantic 7-point Likert scale describes each bipolar for future quantitative measurement.

The second kind of facet solely describes, explains or predicts dissatisfaction. We call these facets *Negative Unipolars*. These facets include Dissonance, Misbehavior, Insufficiency, Ugliness, Unusability, Confusion, and Rigidity. They show that the opposite of .com dissatisfaction is not necessarily satisfaction, but rather lack of .com dissatisfaction. Web developers indicate that these *negative unipolars* are the norms used to critique the performance of Web sites. On *negative unipolar* facets, evaluations could range from zero to very negative. The more negative the evaluation becomes, the more dissatisfaction will be evoked. However, fixing these points does not guarantee satisfaction. One example would be a Web site that forces whoever happens to visit there to sign on for a membership. Some of consumers may only visit for a casual look-around. This enforcement, therefore, is very annoying and increases consumers' dissatisfaction. On the other hand, no membership enforcement does not guarantee satisfaction to be evoked. Some Web developers illustrate this point in a more colorful way:

There are bunch of sites that designed in a very inappropriate way. I've been to some Web sites where you have no way to click through something looks like a button. In this business, there are some tacit norms. For example, if you decide to put

a button on your site, it must be clickable. So we call that "something looks like a button should better act like a button." Otherwise, you gonna piss off your customers. Imagine how frustrated they will be after click all your button-like stuff, nothing happens…Well, of course it does not mean that a clickable button will make then love you, it only mean that you play the game according to the norm. (Mr. E, Art Director and Principal with 5-year experience)

We tentatively group the *negative unipolars* in Table 2. At least two statements are used to describe each facet. A binary (agree; disagree) or 7-point Likert scale (range from completely agree to completely disagree) could be employed here for future quantitative measurement.

The third kind of facet solely describes, explains or predicts satisfaction. We call these facets *Positive Unipolars*. These facets include Entertainment, Communication, Flexibility, Fulfillment, Trust, Value, Technological Proficiency, Goal Congruity, Customization, Synchronization and Reversibility. These facets show that the opposite of .com satisfaction is not necessarily dissatisfaction, but rather lack of .com satisfaction. Web developers indicate that these *positive unipolars* are additional values used to appraise the performance of Web sites. On *positive unipolars*, evaluations range from very positive to zero. The more positive the evaluation becomes, the more satisfaction will be evoked. However, not having these features does not necessarily generate dissatisfaction. For instance, a Web site that offers consumers a sense of belonging would likely gain more satisfaction from consumers. On the other hand, no sense of belonging does not necessarily generate dissatisfaction. Web developers make this point quite clear:

Web sites that could truly excel are those provide additional values to their customers. For instance, some sites keep their consumers' record and very considerately make their check-out process more pleasant…Ever been to Amazon? If you buy things from them for more than once, you will notice when you check out your item, they've already memorized your address, preference and even your friends' name and address if you'd ever sent gifts to them via Amazon. All you have to do is to select the desirable address instead of typing your address again tediously as you usually have to do in other sites. From the standpoint of a consumer, he will say, "Hi, it's really neat. I'm pleasantly impressed." (Ms. K, Producer with 1-year experience)

We tentatively group the *positive unipolars* in Table 3. At least two statements are used to describe each facet. A binary (agree; disagree) or 7-point Likert scale (completely agree to completely disagree) could be employed here for future quantitative measurement.

Previous studies of consumer satisfaction (Leavitt 1977) suggest that the one-factor approach does not explain the phenomenon fully, nor does the two-factor model. Resolution of this problem calls for more complex, finer textured models. The findings in this study meet this challenge. We find that .com satisfaction and .com dissatisfaction are partially, but not completely independent; just as they are partially, but not completely equal and opposite. We also provide detailed facets that describe, explain and predict satisfaction|dissatisfaction online.

IMPLICATIONS AND FUTURE RESEARCH

"The satisfaction literature has not yet, explicitly or implicitly, established a generally accepted definition of satisfaction." (Giese

TABLE 1
Bipolars in .com Satisfaction/Dissatisfaction Model

Bipolars

Facet: Simplicity

◆ The presentation of the information is

Clear	1	2	3	4	5	6	7	Overwhelming

◆ The checkout has

One-step checkout	1	2	3	4	5	6	7	Too many checkout steps

◆ The order form is

Simple	1	2	3	4	5	6	7	Complicated

◆ The whole purchase process is

Simple	1	2	3	4	5	6	7	Complicated

Facet: Accessibility

◆ The Web site is

Completely constructed	1	2	3	4	5	6	7	Has broken links

◆ The Web site is

Well-organized	1	2	3	4	5	6	7	Poorly organized

◆ The Web site offers

Good navigation aids	1	2	3	4	5	6	7	Poor navigation aids

◆ The interface of this Web site is

Friendly	1	2	3	4	5	6	7	Unfriendly

◆ Locating desirable product/information in this Web site is

Easy	1	2	3	4	5	6	7	Difficult

◆ The URL of this Web site is

Easy to remember	1	2	3	4	5	6	7	Difficult to remember

Facet: Potency

◆ The information in this Web site is

Accurate	1	2	3	4	5	6	7	Inaccurate

◆ This Web site has

High technological competency	1	2	3	4	5	6	7	Low technological competency

Facet: Efficiency

◆ This Web site provides

Prompt shipments	1	2	3	4	5	6	7	Delayed shipments

◆ This Web site provides

Timely feedback	1	2	3	4	5	6	7	Slow feedback

◆ This Web site loads

Quickly	1	2	3	4	5	6	7	Slowly

Facet: Follow-ups

◆ This Web site provides

Complete order confirmation confirmation	1	2	3	4	5	6	7	Incomplete order confirmation

◆ This Web site provides

Good after sale service	1	2	3	4	5	6	7	Poor after sale service

◆ This Web site follows through the offer

Very Well	1	2	3	4	5	6	7	Very Poorly

Facet: Support

◆ The service provided by this Web site meets consumer needs

Very well	1	2	3	4	5	6	7	Very Poorly

◆ The products offered by this Web site

Exceed consumer expectations	1	2	3	4	5	6	7	Fail to meet consumer expectations

Facet: Security

◆ This Web site provides

Secure surfing environment	1	2	3	4	5	6	7	Insecure surfing environment

◆ This Web site

Ensures privacy	1	2	3	4	5	6	7	Violates Privacy

Facet: Maintenance

◆ This Web site is

Frequently updated	1	2	3	4	5	6	7	Out-of-date

◆ The information content offered on this Web site is

Most recent	1	2	3	4	5	6	7	Very old

TABLE 2
Negative Unipolars in .com Satisfaction/Dissatisfaction Model

Negative Unipolars

Facet: Dissonance
This Web site
◆ disobeys conventional design norm
◆ does not employ industry standards
◆ does not employ standard navigation rules

Facet: Misbehavior
This Web site is
◆ rude
◆ intruding
◆ meaningless

Facet: Insufficiency
This Web site offers
◆ insufficient information
◆ insufficient inventory
◆ no hyperlinks to relevant information
◆ insufficient technical support

Facet: Ugliness
This Web site has
◆ bad color
◆ cheap look
◆ poor branding strategy

Facet: Unusability
This Web site
◆ is alienating
◆ has no usability
◆ has no search function

Facet: Confusion
This Web site
◆ provides no abstract for large pieces of information
◆ has overwhelming number of links
◆ has too much animation
◆ is confusing
◆ pops out too many additional windows

Facet: Rigidity
This Web site
◆ forces consumers to join its membership
◆ offers no packing choices
◆ offers no shipment option
◆ fails to work properly in unconventional browsers

and Cote 2000) There are even fewer attempts to clarify satisfaction|dissatisfaction online. This study revisits the two-factor model employed in the consumer satisfaction and job satisfaction literature and proposes a working framework to identify the components of .com satisfaction|dissatisfaction.

This study suggests that .com Satisfaction and .com Dissatisfaction are partially, but not completely independent; just as they are partially, but not completely equal and opposite. To further validate and improve this view, data from online consumers need to be collected.

This study has the following implications: First, by revisiting the issue of dimensionality of consumer satisfaction|dissatisfaction in the special domain of e-commerce, it supports e-businesses' decision-making in terms of designing marketing strategies. If .com satisfaction and .com dissatisfaction are at least partially independent concepts, e-commerce managers need to pursue two goals simultaneously: i.e., maximization of satisfaction and minimization of dissatisfaction. The *negative unipolars* that contribute to .com dissatisfaction offer insights to prevent problems or correct problems at early stages. Reliable information on these issues will help businesses gain new customers and retain existing customers by improving the quality of their service (Fornell and Wernerfelt's 1987).

Second, by reporting the viewpoints of Web developers, this study provides communication between Web professionals and their customers. This is a critical issue because Web developers must understand what leads to .com satisfaction and dissatisfaction. Increases in this understanding will contribute to development of new theories of how consumers react to Internet presentations. Obviously, increases in this understanding will also have

significant managerial implications in helping e-businesses' practices.

REFERENCES

Aaker, David A. and George S. Day (1971) *Consumerism: Search for the Consumer Interest,* New York: The Free Press.

Buskirk, Richard H. and James T. Rothe (1970) "Consumerism—An Interpretation," *Journal of Marketing,* 34 (October), pp. 61-65.

Chen, Qimei and William D. Wells (1999) "Attitude toward the Site" *Journal of Advertising Research,* Vol. 39, No. 5, Sept./Oct. pp. 27-38.

Cross, Lisa (1998) "Printer Use Net, a Survey Reveals," *Graphic Arts Monthly,* July, p. 78.

Czepiel, John A., and Larry J. Rosenberg (1973) "Consumer Satisfaction: Concept and Measurement," working paper, New York University Graduate School of Business Administration.

Czepiel, John A., Larry J. Rosenberg and Adebayo Akerele (1974) "Perspectives on Consumer Satisfaction," *Proceedings,* Fall Conference, American Marketing Association.

Fornell, Claes and Birger Wernerfelt (1987) "Defensive Marketing Strategy by Customer Complaint Management: A Theoretical Analysis," *Journal of Marketing Research,* 24 (November), pp. 337-346.

Giese, Joan L. and Joseph A. Cote (2000) "Defining Consumer Satisfaction." Academy of Marketing Science Review [online] 00(01). *Http://www.amsreview.org/amsrev/theory/giese00-01.html*

Grigaliunas, Benedict S., and Herzberg, Frederick (1971) "Relevancy in the Test of Motivator-Hygiene Theory," *Journal of Applied Psychology,* 53, pp. 79-89.

TABLE 3
Positive Unipolars in .com Satisfaction|Dissatisfaction Model

Positive Unipolars

Facet: Entertainment

This Web site is
◆ fresh
◆ visually appealing
◆ attractive
◆ fun
◆ trendy
◆ beautifully designed

Facet: Communication

This Web site provides
◆ viable contact to human customer care staff
◆ other contact channels
◆ feedback to consumers' complaints

Facet: Flexibility

This Web site
◆ has abundant selection of products/information
◆ gives options for comparing products
◆ gives consumer choices of printer friendly version
◆ offers search options

Facet: Fulfillment

This Web site
◆ delivers on its promises
◆ provides fulfillment
◆ offers better prices

Facet: Value

This Web site
◆ gives consumers a sense of being cared about
◆ is considerate
◆ is thoughtful
◆ actively finds out what consumers want
◆ tracks consumers' preferences
◆ gives consumers a sense of community
◆ gives consumers a sense of belonging

Facet: Technological Proficiency

This Web site has
◆ outstanding features
◆ innovative features
◆ technological expertise

Facet: Trustworthiness

This Web site
◆ gives a sense of trust
◆ ensures transparency in business procedure
◆ does not demand information

Facet: Goal Congruity

This Web site
◆ meets consumers' purposive surfing tasks
◆ provide relevant information
◆ meets the mindset of the consumer
◆ provides goal-relevant suggestions

Facet: Customization

This Web site
◆ provides information tailored to target consumers
◆ lets consumers personalize the presentation
◆ offers options of skipping animations
◆ offers options according to consumers' preferences

Facet: Synchronization

This Web site synchronizes
◆ with its real store
◆ offline services with online promises
◆ its image with its branding strategy
◆ with its foreign language version

Facet: Reversibility

This Web site
◆ allows reversibility of steps (for instance, consumers will be able to go back to correct the errors they made in previous steps)
◆ is forgiving of errors made by consumers

Herzberg, Frederick, Bernard Mausner and Barbara B. Snyderman (1959) *The Motivation to Work,* 2nd edition (New York: John Wiley & Sons, 1959).

Howard, John A. and Jagdish N. Sheth (1969) *The Theory of Buyer Behavior,* New York: John Wiley & Sons.

Leavitt, Clark (1977), "Consumer Satisfaction and Dissatisfaction: Bi-polar or Independent?" *Conceptualization and Measurement of Consumer Satisfaction and Dissatisfaction,* in Keith Hunt, ed. Cambridge, MA: Marketing Science Institute.

Nicosia, Francesco M. (1966) *Consumer Decision Processes,* (Englewood Cliffs, N. J.: Prentice-Hall)

S. R. A. (1951) *Employee Inventory,* Chicago: Science Research Associates.

Stein, Tom (1998), "Service on the Net," *Information Week,* December 21-28, p. 76-80.

Wood, Donald A. and William K. LeBold (1970) "The Multivariate Nature of Job Satisfaction," *Personal Psychology,* 23 (Summer), pp. 173-89.

An Empirical Study of Online Atmospherics and Shopper Responses

Sevgin A. Eroglu, Georgia State University
Karen A. Machleit, University of Cincinnati
Lenita M. Davis, University of Cincinnati

ABSTRACT

This study presents an empirical testing of a model of online atmospherics (Eroglu, Machleit and Davis, 2001). Central to the model is the notion that online retailers, just like their brick-and-mortar counterparts, provide a "store" atmosphere via their website, which affects shoppers' image of, experience with and responses to the virtual store. The model, which is based on the Stimulus-Organism-Response framework, proposes a classification of online atmospheric cues, and hypothesizes relationships between these stimuli and shopper responses. This study presents the results of two pretests followed by an experiment to empirically test the model. The results substantiate the theoretical model. We find that increasing the atmospheric qualities of the online store site increases the level of pleasure felt by the shopper which, then, affects attitude toward, satisfaction with and approach/avoidance behaviors with respect to online shopping. Importantly, the findings show that the relationship between site atmospherics and shoppers' affective and cognitive states is moderated by at least two personality characteristics, namely, involvement and atmospheric responsiveness.

Toward Understanding Individual Differences in Web Usage: The Case for Timestyle

Lisa Ricci, University of Connecticut
June Cotte, University of South Carolina

ABSTRACT

Recent research on Web usage experiences and behaviors has stressed the role of constructs such as flow, telepresence, and time distortion. Yet, little research has been done to examine the locus of individual differences in how consumers experience the Web. Neither has much research been done on the role of specific individual-difference variables in how consumers behave online and the underlying motives that drive these behaviors. We focus here on the role of individual differences in *timestyle*. Specifically, we investigate how the social, planning, and polychronic dimensions of timestyle influence several facets of Web usage experiences, behaviors, and motives. We distinguish between utilitarian and hedonic motives for Web usage and suggest how the various dimensions of timestyle are likely to impact differentially on these motives. We also postulate that the three timestyle dimensions are likely to influence the frequency of exploratory behavior, information search behavior, entertainment behavior, and electronic shopping behavior on the Web, with the two types of motives acting as mediating variables. We examine these predictions with data from a survey of 216 respondents and conclude with a discussion of the implications of our research for the practice of interactive marketing.

A Fuller Understanding of Product and Brand Relationships: Antecedents, Dimensions, and Consequences

Julie R. Irwin, University of Texas at Austin

"Dimensioning Brand Relationships Using Brand Relationship Quality"

Susan Fournier, Harvard School of Business

In this presentation, Dr. Fournier presented results of the validation of a scale to measure Brand Relationship Quality (BRQ) –a construct inducted in Fournier (1998) to capture the cognitive, affective, and behavioral dimensions along which consumer-brand relationships vary. Differential effects of six BRQ facets (intimacy, commitment, partner quality, interdependence, love, identity attachment) on a range of relationship outcomes (e.g., tolerance, top-of-mind saliency, resistance, trial of extensions, persistence) were explored, as were the predictive capacity of BRQ in general. The BRQ explains differences in relationship outcomes that are not captured in traditional loyalty or satisfaction measures. Facet profiles were also articulated that capture different relationship "types," thereby advancing knowledge of the differential successes of varying consumer-brand relationship classes.

"Brand Relationships: The Influence of Relationship Type on Consumer Decision Making Strategies"

Pankaj Aggarwal, University of Chicago
Ann L. McGill, University of Chicago

The authors extended prior work on brand relationships that draws a parallel between how people form relationships with each other in social situations and how they form relationships with brands in a consumption situation. In this presentation, they focused on differences in information processing strategies depending on the type of relationship the customer has with the brand. They looked at two types of relationships, adopting a distinction that has been developed in the social psychology literature between communal relationships, in which concern for a partner's need is paramount; and exchange relationships, in which a matched benefit is expected back from the partner. The central thesis of the research is that characteristics of brands and brand communication may trigger different relationship types and norms of behavior. They found that these characteristics predict both the type of cognitive processing (e.g., overall effort exerted, the degree of abstractness of considered features, the use of compensatory vs. noncompensatory decision rules) and the degree of negative affect experienced while choosing between brands.

"If They Could See Us Now: A Look at How Consumers Relate to Their Products and How these Relationships Explain Why Leading Brands Succeed or Fail"

Peter Golder, New York University
Julie Irwin, University of Texas at Austin

The presenters focused on the ability of leading brands to maintain strong relationships with consumers. They addressed two questions: which consumer-brand relationships are enduring and which are fleeting? And, how do we explain these differences? They built on the product and brand relationship literature by proposing a multi-item scale that measures how consumers relate to their products. Then, they extended studies evaluating long-term brand leadership with an extensive data set of brand leaders from the 1920s until today in over 100 categories. They presented findings on the rate of leadership persistence over time. Also, they used their new measures to explain differences in leadership persistence.

Discussion

Susan Broniarczk, University of Texas at Austin

The discussion, led by Dr. Broniarczyk, focused on integrating the three papers, with a special emphasis on the ways in which brand relationships may drive category relationships, and vice versa.

The Instantiation, Shaping, and Handling of Consumer Displeasure (And Pleasure)

Michel Tuan Pham, Columbia University

As the concept of relationship is replacing the concept of value as the dominant metaphor guiding marketing practice in Western economies, the one area of consumer research that will most certainly not lose any of its relevance is the one that focuses on the judgmental reactions that consumers have to marketers' product/service deliveries—an area loosely called "consumer satisfaction." This area is not only managerially relevant. It is theoretically meaningful: It is one of the few areas that we, consumer researchers, can truly call "our own."

As all of us know, many important contributions have been made in this area by people like Valerie Folkes, Valarie Zeithaml, Leonard Berry, and Richard L. Oliver (just to name a few). It would therefore be tempting to feel that "we know it all." Yet, do we really? Consider, for instance, a type of satisfaction response that we, consumer researchers and marketing teachers, really should be expert at: student satisfaction. All of us realize how intricate it is to keep our student "customers" satisfied, class after class, semester after semester, year after year. This should remind us that we clearly do not "know it all" about satisfaction.

It is in the spirit of going past this feeling of knowing it all about customer satisfaction that this session was assembled. The three papers in the session collectively addressed the following issues. How does consumer displeasure (and pleasure) arise? When do different forms of pleasure (e.g., satisfaction vs. happiness) and displeasure (e.g., regret vs. disappointment) arise? Can consumer displeasure be altered by simple contextual cues? What are these contextual cues? Once displeasure has arisen, how can it best be addressed? How do marketers' attempts to address consumer displeasure mitigate its effects on loyalty? Are there any differences across industries?

The first presentation by Kirsten Elliott (in collaboration with Julie Edell and Kay Lemon), focused on the instantiation of consumer pleasure-displeasure and on the emotional responses that comprise it. Drawing on recent work on regret, counterfactual thinking and attribution theory, they argue that consumer pleasure-displeasure arises in different forms (e.g., satisfaction vs. happiness, regret vs. disappointment). They hypothesize that an important determinant of the form that pleasure-displeasure takes is the focus of the consumer's emotional response to the service encounter (outcome, self or provider). This in turn influences consumers' willingness to pursue the relationship with the provider. They reported the results of an experiment that strongly supported their predictions.

The second presentation by Michel Pham (in collaboration with Jennifer Ames) focused on ways of "shaping" (i.e. altering) consumer pleasure-displeasure *independently* of the delivery itself. They argue that consumer pleasure-displeasure can be shaped by simple contextual cues that raise the consumer's self-awareness (i.e., self-focused attention), such as the presence of a mirror or filling out a self-disclosing questionnaire. Such cues can modify consumers' happiness with any outcome by shifting the attribution locus toward the customer and away from the provider. They reported two experiments showing that, when the outcome of a service interaction is negative, heightened self-awareness will increase satisfaction with the provider, as customers accept a greater share of the responsibility (i.e., blame) for the negative outcome. However, when the outcome of the interaction is positive,

heightened self-awareness will decrease satisfaction with the provider, as customers will take a greater share of the responsibility (i.e., credit for the positive outcome). Mediational analyses show that these effects are indeed mediated by a relative shift of the attribution locus under high self-awareness.

In the third presentation, Richard L. Oliver (in collaboration with John Goodman and Marlene Yanovsky) presented the results of large-scale field studies conducted by e-Satisfy.com (formerly known as TARP) a consulting firm specializing in customer relationship management. The studies, which covered a wide spectrum of industries, focused on the handling of consumer displeasure after it has arisen. They examined how consumer dissatisfaction affects subsequent loyalty and how displeased consumers respond to redress attempts by marketers. The results suggest that these responses are, in part, moderated by "price-satisfaction," a unit-cost weighted index of satisfaction. The results also show that emotional responses to redress have stable effects on loyalty across industries. In all cases, fully satisfying redress results in greater loyalty intentions than "mollification" (somewhat satisfying redress) which, in turn, dominates dissatisfying redress. Additionally, it is frequently observed that mollification results in greater loyalty than that exhibited by dissatisfied consumers who do not complain.

Gerald Gorn led the discussion and made insightful comments about each presentation. He noted, for instance, that the new economy calls for a reconsideration of the notion of satisfaction as consumers are increasingly involved in the co-production of services. Interested readers are invited to contact the speakers directly.

Videography Versus Written Ethnography in Consumer Research

Russell W. Belk, University of Utah

The possibility of using broadcast quality video in conducting and presenting consumer research has grown rapidly in the past several years. Not only has such equipment become affordable for many consumer researchers, but the possibilities for distributing finished videos are expanding as well through media such as the Internet, video CDs, and DVDs. However, the fact that something *can* be done, does not necessarily mean that it *should* be done. This session examined the advantages and disadvantages of doing videography versus more traditional written ethnography. Not everyone has the skill to produce compelling visual research. However, as everyone who has done editorial reviewing can attest, not everyone has the skill to produce compelling written accounts either. Yet both are skills that can be learned and improved upon. And both are skills likely to be expected of the consumer ethnographer in the future.

Rob Kozinets and I first put our written ethnographies on the web for discussants and others to read. In addition to the abstracts below, see: http:www.kellogg.nwu.edu/faculty/kozinets/htm/research/BurningMan/ritual/htm and http:www.business.utah.edu/~mktrwb/zimelite.htm .

At the session the two 20-25 minute videos from these studies were screened. Eric Arnould and Deborah Heisley then critiqued and lead the discussions of two paired projects. Their critique raised largely pragmatic questions including whether the audience for videographies can develop critical visual literacy, whether a peer review process can be employed for videos, and whether university promotion and tenure committees will be able to evaluate such work. They noted that videography has the opportunity to reach a far broader audience than written papers. Possibilities of collaborative research, as with the Belk video, were acknowledged as a way to overcome the neo-colonialist videographer as "voice of God." Deb noted that the Society for Visual Anthropology is developing guidelines to help in tenure decisions. Deb's comments follow.

Audience discussion demonstratively overcame passive "television audience" illiteracy, asking questions such as what were the biases of the videographers and what was not shown in the edited videos. High session attendance and spirited discussion suggest that the session stimulated critical awareness of emerging issues in videographic consumer research.

ABSTRACTS

"'Ritual Without Dogma': Liberating, Purifying, and Primalizing Consumption at the Burning Man Project"
Robert V. Kozinets, Northwestern University

The Burning Man festival is an unfettered celebratory event held for one week every year in Nevada's barren Black Rock Desert. Through videography and written ethnography, this research explores the consumption meanings, themes, and experiences presented at Burning Man's live and virtual communities. The research presents the rules, performances and rituals that are enacted by participants in order to psychically distance consumption from the sphere of the commonplace, and to re-enchant it into a transformative experience. Theoretical implications draw from the postmodern thought and include enhancing consumer research understandings of gifts, art, resistance, primitivism and high technology.

"Consumption Lifestyles of the New Elite in Zimbabwe"
Russell W. Belk, University of Utah

Since Zimbabwean independence in 1980, a small percentage of blacks have become wealthy. This video and paper explore their consumption patterns based on a collaboration with graduate students at Africa University. We find that the consumption patterns of these nouveaux riches largely emulate those of the former colonialists as well as consumption images of the West. One cost of these new consumption lifestyles is neglect of traditional African obligations to care for extended family. Issues are also raised concerning Zimbabwean culture, environmental sustainability, and Third World development.

Visual Research: Current Bias and Future Direction

Deborah D. Heisley, CSUN

INTRODUCTION

One could easily advise a doctoral student that if they want to be taken seriously, they should not play with pictures. Luckily, thirteen years ago, under the guidance of Sidney Levy, Howard Becker, and John Sherry, at Northwestern University, I never received such advice, but instead received support and encouragement in the area of visual research. Out of my interest in visual research came the Autodriving article with Sidney Levy (1991), the photoessay of the Farmers' Market with Mary Ann McGrath and John Sherry (1991), and involvement with the Odyssey video with Russell Belk, Melanie Wallendorf and John Sherry (1988). There are now quite a few consumer behavior ethnographers who regularly use photography in their work. Russell Belk and Robert Kozinets continue to add breadth and strength to the, dare I call it, "visual movement" in consumer behavior with their videographies.

CRITICISMS OF VISUAL WORK

I could play Devil's advocate. It is easy enough to criticize visual work. I could refer to the camera as a weapon that creates a barrier to engagement a la Susan Sontag. I could discuss photography and film production, and consumption, as voyeurism a la "CBS's Summer 2000 hit program "Survivor," which had 51.7 million people tuned into the two hour finale (Flint 2000). In a day where "dialogue" is valued in ethnography above all else, "taking" a photo or video can be construed to be an evil process.

Historically, there was more to criticize. "Natives" and "objects" from "exotic cultures" were put on display, either literally or with photos or films. The films and photos were often created in a "short-term invasion" or "expedition" into the culture of interest. Around World War I: Malinowski's work in Trobriand Islands was crucial in launching the movement towards joining life and coming to understand it through participant observation. This required sustained fieldwork and collaboration between the ethnographer and the members of the culture of interest. (This paragraph draws heavily from Peacock 2000).

Howard Becker understood what this meant for visual research 13 years ago when he instructed us not to "take pictures," but to "make photographs." It is important to understand that an ethnographer today must engage the members of the culture of interest as consultants in gaining an understanding of the culture. The photographs or film are not "taken of" the consultants, but are "made with" the consultants.

Like all other methodologies, visual research does have its attendant challenges. And like all other methodologies, a well-trained researcher is aware of and attempts to mitigate the shortcomings inherent in the method. Finally, like all other methodologies, we use it in spite of its flaws because we are able, in fact, to gain and disseminate knowledge with it.

THE VIEW THAT TEXTUAL IS SUPERIOR TO VISUAL

There is a long-standing academic bias against visual work. Mary Strong's announcement in the March 2000 Anthropology News from Mary Strong is illustrative of this bias.

"SVA [Society for Visual Anthropology] is planning a position statement whereby visual materials such as film and video be considered legitimate scholarly work applicable to tenure and promotion decisions. Statement will appear in a future column. Debate on this subject is welcome." (p. 76).

Why wouldn't visual work be considered legitimate scholarly work? Because, as Peacock writes in the March 2000 Anthropology News, after the shift from interrogation and display to participant observation and dialogue, the work of anthropology shifted from "eye to ear." As Peacock notes, today "To look is voyeurism, to touch is harassment, while to listen is to be properly engaged" (p. 6).

What makes a product scholarly work? Legitimate scholarly work is theoretically informed and theoretically informative work that is based on the systematic gathering and analysis of data in ways that are consistent with the understandings of a community of scholars. Does visual research fit this definition? Almost. Importantly, to date, while visual work in print form has benefited from peer review, video output in consumer behavior lacks the peer review process.

WHY IS THE ACADEMY RESISTENT?

There seems to be a need to impose hierarchy on entire bodies of knowledge or legitimate methodologies. We know from our information processing colleagues that visual information is cognitively most complex. We also know from our information processing colleagues that learning occurs more easily when information is presented across multiple modalities. Thus, a product that combines the visual with the textual, as these Belk and Kozinets videos do, should be considered superior in disseminating knowledge. However, the academy seems to downgrade, rather then upgrade, a piece of work that embraces the visual. I am optimistic that this very modern notion of textual work being somehow more serious than visual work will soon be discredited. It seems obvious that both are equally valuable. The best method or output should be chosen to address the question at hand or to communicate the message at hand.

Strength comes from diversity. This was not understood even 20 years ago. I hope that scholars become more accepting of the strength that comes from diversity of perspective, diversity of methods, diversity of questions, and diversity of output (film, Internet site, photographs, journal article, books, plays, or poems). Each of these brings richness to our understanding.

WHY DO SCHOLARS RESIST THE VISUAL?

Why do scholars resist the visual? Visual media is the only way to disseminate the complexity of visual information.

1. As per the discussion above, scholars feel visual work may be seen as less serious by the academy.
2. Visual understanding is accessible. It allows the "reader," or in this case "viewer," a lot of interpretation. This loss of control can feel uncomfortable and threatening for a scholar.
3. Consumer behavior scholars may lack familiarity with high quality, academic, video product.
4. Scholars are influenced by the general population's bias toward viewing the written word as being more intellectual than the visual.
5. There is no peer review process in place to legitimize the work.
6. The work is not included in the traditional journal, so it

Advances in Consumer Research
Volume 28, © 2001

does not benefit from the signaling of quality that a respected journal can confer.

7. It is a lot of work.

Businesses are actively sending researchers out into the world of consumers and cultures with cameras and video cameras in hand in pursuit of understanding (for profits). They are ahead of us in the sense that they understand the value of visual data. However, they are behind us in the sense that the methods they are using are often reflective of the invasion tactics used by anthropologists long ago and since discredited. Meanwhile, we lag behind, punishing valuable visual scholarship, which is done properly, by not recognizing it as a legitimate pursuit. We need to support this work and disseminate both the substantive and methodological findings from it.

A FUNDAMENTAL TECHNOLOGY AND CULTURAL SHIFT

What I don't like about videotape:

1. Videotape is bulky and doesn't fit in my file cabinet very well.
2. I can't underline it.
3. My yellow highlighter doesn't work on it.
4. I can't write notes in the margin.
5. I can't easily access a specific part of it.
6. Post it notes are tough.
7. There is no peer review and revision.
8. It does not get into journals.

These issues have been barriers to the use of video in scholarly pursuits.

The situation I just described has profoundly changed, and will continue to do so. The barriers to utilizing visual information are falling. While making, revising (editing), distributing, storing and accessing films used to be prohibitively complicated to do, this is no longer the case. Technology, particularly digital video cameras and the Internet have changed all of this. Visual information is stored digitally on CD's, DVD's, and the Internet. Authors/producers (what will they be called?) are able to display textual transcripts or include voiceovers *with* video, clips from video, or photographs. With a profound improvement in ease of editing, we must put a peer review process into place. With journals moving to the Internet, if visual scholars put peer review into place, visual work can become commonplace. Viewers/readers are able to underline, paste in notes, and search for and access a specific segment of the video. As the technology continues to develop, all of this will only become easier.

Watching my 11 year old daughter, Taylor, put together a report is, I believe, informative of what the future holds. For her, a report is not complete until she has downloaded at least one visual element from the Internet. Will this generation grow up and abandon the visual? I think not. I hope not. The visual will not be seen as "augmentation" to the textual, but as an integral part of a product. I suppose that it will become standard to produce academic product that is not paper or video per se, but a marriage of the two. The pure textual or pure visual will only be endpoints on a hybrid continuum. The videographies that you saw here today were such hybrids. The major ideas in the papers were communicated with visual information, voiceovers, and by superimposing text over the video. The videos also contained an abundance of visual information that the text could not convey. I believe that in the not too distant future, our current debates on whether video product should be considered for promotion and tenure will seem quaint indeed.

REFERENCES:

Flint, Joe (2000), "CBS's Hit Show 'Survivor' Ends Summer Run With Huge Ratings," *Wall Street Journal*, August 25, p. B7

Heisley, Deborah D. and Sidney J. Levy (1991), "Autodriving: A Photoelicitation Technique," *Journal of Consumer Research*, 18 (December), 257-272.

Heisley, Deborah D., Mary Ann McGrath and John F. Sherry, Jr. (1991), "'To Everything There is A Season:' A Photoessay of a Farmers' Market," *Journal of American Culture*, 14 (fall), 53-79. Reprinted in *Highways and Buyways: Naturalistic Research From the Consumer Behavior Odyssey* (1991), ed. Russell W. Belk, Provo, UT: Association for Consumer Research, 141-166.

McGrath, Mary Ann, John F. Sherry, Jr. and Deborah D. Heisley (1993), "An Ethnographic Study of an Urban Periodic Marketplace: Lessons from the Midville Farmers' Market," *Journal of Retailing*, Vol. 63, No. 3 (fall), 280-319.

Peacock, James (2000) "Eye to Ear and Mouth to Hand," *AnthropologyNews*, March, 5-6.

Strong, Mary (2000) "Society for Visual Anthropology," *Anthropology News*, March, p. 76.

Video

"Deep Meaning in Possessions: Qualitative Research from the Consumer Behavior Odyssey," (1988) Written and directed by Melanie R. Wallendorf and Russell W. Belk, Produced by Melanie R. Wallendorf, Russell W. Belk, Thomas C. O'Guinn, Deborah D. Heisley and Scott Roberts, Marketing Science Institute, Cambridge Massachusetts, 38:00.

Consumer Confidence and Knowledge Calibration
Christine Moorman, Duke University

The papers in this session illustrate three approaches to consumer confidence: (1) as an estimation of what a consumer thinks she knows (Moorman et al.); (2) as subjective probabilities associated with predictions (Brenner et al.) and (3) as an enduring trait reflecting a consumer's perceived ability to generate positive marketplace experiences (Bearden et al.).

In "Random Support Theory: A Flexible Approach to Modeling the Calibration of Subjective Probabilities," Brenner, Koehler, and Griffin presented a random support model of the calibration of subjective probabilities. In this model, subjective probabilities are based on the distributions of support–or strengh of evidence—for true and false hypotheses. Using this approach, they examined the degree to which people take into account evidence about the particular *case* and evidence about the *class* of events from which the current case is a member when generating probability judgments. Interpreting support as "strength of evidence" about the case at hand leads to the prediction that case data will primarily drive probability judgments, while class data will be underweighted. This prediction was supported in several studies of consumer judgments of the likelihood of stock price increases. Random support theory can represent the underweighting of class data in terms of insensitivity of its parameters to changes in outcome base rate (e.g., whether it is overall a bull or bear market) and cue diagnosticity (whether the evidence predicting price increases is of high or low validity).

In "Consumer Self-Confidence: Refinements in Conceptualization and Measurement," Bearden, Hardesty, and Rose develop and validate a scale to measure multiple dimensions of self-confidence. The result is a six-factor correlated model comprised of confidence in information acquisition, consideration set formation, personal outcomes and social outcomes decision-making, persuasion knowledge, and marketplace interfaces. A series of studies demonstrate the psychometric properties of the measures, their discriminant validity with respect to related constructs, and their construct validity. In one application, they predict that is reasonable for a consumer to avoid relying on price (P) as a cue to quality if he or she is confident and believes strongly that price is not related to quality (Q). Thus, consumer self-confidence is expected to moderate the relationship between the strength of consumers' PQ-schema and their choice of a higher priced product. Results support this idea by finding that confidence increases the likelihood of choosing the higher priced product when PQ-schema is strong and decreases the likelihood of choosing the higher-priced product when the PQ-schema is weak.

Finally, in "Knowledge Calibration and Knowledge-related Goals," Moorman, Brinberg, Diehl, and Kidwell focus on the interplay of objective (accurate, stored expertise) and subjective (confidence in that expertise) knowledge. We propose that the impact of *internal calibration* (the match between objective knowledge [OK] and subjective knowledge [SK]) depends upon the level of *external calibration* (the match between knowledge and the goals used in choice). We measure OK (nutrition), manipulate SK (nutrition) by giving false feedback to subjects about their performance on the OK test, and manipulate goals (with a moderate goal–choose a healthy diet and no goal–choose whatever you like). Subjects made two days of food choices in a computerized supermarket. We find, as we predict, that low SK-low OK consumers have significantly less fat in their choices in the no goal situation indicating that the moderate goal overwhelmed them. Likewise, the high SK-high OK consumers did worse in the presence of a moderate goal presumably because they automatically evoke more challenging goals. Finally, the high SK-low OK consumers perform better in the goal situation than in the no goal situation describing one condition under which SK facilitates better decision making.

Wes Hutchinson lead a discussion of the issues involved in studying consumer confidence.

Advances in Consumer Research
Volume 28, © 2001

"Just Do It!"
The Influence of Brand Names on Children's Lives

Deborah Roedder John, University of Minnesota

Understanding how consumers relate to brand names has been an important topic in consumer research for the past decade. Surprisingly, none of the published research to date has examined similar branding issues with children. We know that children have a growing awareness of brand names as they grow older, which results in greater preference and requests for branded items. Beyond these observations, we know virtually nothing about how children of different ages relate to brand names, what types of associations and meanings they attach to brand names, and how they use brand names as cues in evaluating products and forming their own identities as consumers. The purpose of this session was to showcase emerging research addressing these issues.

The first paper, presented by Gwen Bachmann Achenreiner, explored the emergence of brand names as an important cue in children's consumer judgments in an experimental setting with 8, 12, and 16 year-olds. In this study, children evaluated an advertised product (e.g., athletic shoes) with a familiar brand name that was either popular (e.g., Nike) or unpopular (e.g., Kmart). Children also evaluated owners of the popular and unpopular branded items (e.g., "cool-nerdy") and hypothetical brand extensions of the popular brand. The results indicated that, by age 12, children use brand names as an important cue in making these judgments.

The second paper, presented by Shi Zhang and Sanjay Sood, followed up on the topic of brand extension evaluations with several studies conducted with 12 year-olds and adults. Across three studies, the authors reported that 12 year-olds, relative to adult consumers, tend to evaluate brand extensions by relying less on the fit between the parent brand and the extension category (category similarity) and more on linguistic factors related to the name of the parent brand. For example, in the first experiment, adults rated near brand extensions more favorably than far brand extensions, while children rated them equivalently. Although children were capable of using category similarity in their evaluations when prompted (Experiment 2), children were more likely to rely on linguistic surface features (e.g., rhyming names) when evaluating brand extensions (Experiment 3).

The third paper, presented by Lan T. Nguyen and Deborah Roedder John, continued the theme of examining the importance of brand names to children, but explored the topic in terms of how children use brands to define their self images. Using several qualitative tasks with children 8 to 17 years of age, the authors examined how children define their self-concepts at different ages, looking at when brands become a defining feature of one's self concept. Results indicated that the number of self-brand connections, used as a measure of the extent to which children define their self-images in terms of brand names, increased with age.

Leading a discussion of these papers, Kevin Keller noted the need to look more thoroughly at the way children evaluate brand extensions, especially with regard to determining the age at which children evaluate extensions in a similar manner as adults. Also discussed were issues related to methodologies for studying branding issues with children, particularly the types of procedures, brand names, and age groups included in studies with children.

Getting to the Heart of the Consumer: The Role of Emotions and Cognition (or the Lack Thereof) in Consumer Decision Making

Suresh Ramanathan, New York University
Baba Shiv, University of Iowa

INTRODUCTION

Much research on consumer decision making has regarded consumers as dispassionate, logical thinkers, adopting a rational orientation to the various tasks they engage in. Not much attention has been paid to the role of the "heart," i.e., feelings and emotions, a lacuna that has been widely criticized by eminent researchers such as Bettman (1993), Hoch and Loewenstein (1991), Holbrook and Hirschman (1982), Loewenstein (1996), Mellers et al. (1997) and Olshavsky and Granbois (1979). Fortunately, serious efforts have been made by consumer researchers in recent years to redress this imbalance (see, e.g., Garbarino and Edell 1997; Hoch and Loewenstein 1991; Kahn and Isen 1993; Luce 1998; Luce, Bettman, and Payne 1997). The broad purpose of this session was to present work that adds to this growing body of research, and to delineate conditions under which the heart dominates the mind. In doing so, we wished to show that the traditional view of humankind as rational and cognitive decision-makers needs considerable revision. Specifically we aimed to show that there are at least some consumer decisions that are ruled primarily by emotions, whether they are "low-road" spontaneous emotions or "high-road" controlled emotions (Shiv and Fedorikhin's paper), or characterized by lack of cognition (Ramanathan's paper) or disregard for costs (Hsee's paper).

The specific purposes of the proposed session were three-fold: a) to outline the theoretical basis of the processes that underlie emotional decisions; b) to determine the conditions that facilitate and impede these processes and to understand the boundary conditions thereof; and c) to explore these effects in different domains and across multiple research paradigms.

SESSION OBJECTIVE AND OVERVIEW

Descriptions of consumer behavior in marketing literature have followed a path of reason and consciousness. Ajzen's (1991) Theory of Planned Behavior epitomizes this view. Theories of rationality and bounded rationality build on this view of people as cognitive decision-makers. While irrationality has been documented extensively, no major role has been ascribed to emotions as the basis for such decisions. Most accounts of irrationality have been descriptive and not explanatory. In contrast, social cognition literature is replete with instances where people act automatically on the basis of perceptual, affect-driven or motivational processes (see Bargh and Chartrand 1999 for a review). Unfortunately, consumer researchers in the past have been loath to examine conditions under which consumer behavior can proceed under the guidance of automatic or lower-order processes (for an exception, see Fitzsimons and Williams 1999). As we showed in this session, there are several decision domains in which cognition either plays a marginal role or does not have a role at all in explaining behavior. For instance, Shiv and Fedorikhin's paper demonstrated that constraints placed on capacity by manipulating decision time and concurrent cognitive activity lead to a greater reliance on affect and evoked emotions as the basis for the decision, even if the consequences of engaging in such an action are potentially deleterious. Ramanathan argued that the pursuit of the affect resulting from such actions becomes a goal in itself that can be activated automatically by environmental stimuli. Hsee made the case that people often have affection for

objects that directs behavior in a way that is not predicted by standard choice theories. In all three of these papers, the common theme was the role of emotions and/or the limited role of cognition/reason as a determinant of consumer behavior.

The focus of the first paper by Baba Shiv and Alexander Fedorikhin was on how choice behavior can be influenced by emotions that arise both spontaneously ("low-road" emotions) and in a controlled fashion ("high-road" emotions). They presented a conceptual model that is based on recent evidence obtained from brain-scan and chemical tracing techniques (LeDoux 1987, 1995, 1996). The model elucidated the conditions under which low and high road emotions are likely to arise and influence choice behavior. They then presented the results of two studies in support of this model, one where subjects chose between chocolate cake and fruit-salad, and the other where subjects chose between pizza and soup.

The second paper by Suresh Ramanathan took a different route to show that the pursuit of gratification is endemic in some individuals to the point that the behaviors associated with the realization of the goal of gratification are represented as action scripts that get automatically activated. His research focused on the role of goal-dependent automaticity in impulsive decisions. Across two experiments, he showed that impulsive behavior, where people choose items that are hedonically valenced, can be influenced by merely activating gratification goals through a priming task. Further, he showed that the goal of gratification is chronically accessible in impulsive people and does not need to be activated explicitly. In a second experiment, he showed the motivational properties of the goal of gratification by demonstrating an increase in impulsive behavior after a delay among impulsive people, while the same delay led to a decrease in the tendency to act impulsively among non-impulsive people.

In the third paper, Chris Hsee and Howard Kunreuther argued that individuals develop affection toward products and services just as they do toward other individuals or toward their pets. They presented extensive evidence suggesting that this affection can lead to behavior that violates standard rational choice theories. For example, imagine that the consumer has the choice between two medicines of *identical* efficacy, but substantially different costs for her ailing pet. As per rational choice theories, the consumer ought to choose the cheaper option, irrespective of how fond they are of their pets—after all both the medicines are identical in efficacy. Chris and Howard presented evidence running contrary to decision theory, suggesting that consumers are more likely to choose the expensive medicine when they have higher affection for their pets than when they do not.

These three papers provided for a healthy debate on the role of emotions in consumer decision-making. Besides contributing to the theory of such decision processes, they brought in new perspectives from neuropsychology (Shiv and Fedorikhin), conditional automaticity (Ramanathan) and behavioral decision theory (Hsee and Kunreuther). They addressed important issues hitherto not examined in extant literature and brought together a seamless understanding of how consumers make certain decisions.

Dr. Antoine Bechara acted as our discussant. Dr. Bechara is widely acknowledged as one of the leading contemporary neuroscientists and has published several papers on the neurological foundations of emotions together with another renowned neuroscientist, Dr. Antonio Damasio. Dr. Bechara presented additional neurological evidence of the nature of emotions and cognition. In a fascinating presentation, Dr. Bechara outlined how the amygdala and the hypothalamus are implicated differently in different situations and how affective and cognitive processes play out in the human brain.

Gender Role Incongruency and Memorable Gift Exchange Experiences

Kay M. Palan, Iowa State University
Charles S. Areni, James Cook University
Pamela Kiecker, Virginia Commonwealth Univeristy

ABSTRACT

Men are typically thought to dislike being involved in gift giving. The results of this study, however, show that men's involvement in gift exchange is sometimes incongruent with society's gender role expectations. Using written narratives of memorable gift exchange experiences, we find that men are far more likely than women to recall gift giving experiences and that men with feminine gender identities are more person-focused than object-focused in their gift giving orientation. Based on the results, directions for future research are discussed.

Gift exchange is an activity familiar to both men and women—as both gift givers and gift recipients. In fact, the ritual of gift exchange suggests that individuals are compelled to give, to receive, and to reciprocate (Gouldner 1960). Yet, most studies show that women, relative to men, are the primary gift givers (Cheal 1987; Fischer and Arnold 1990). Two possible arguments have been used to explain this finding. First, women are socialized to be shoppers to a much greater extent than are men (Scanzoni 1977) and, thus, may accept gift shopping as work women do, whereas men, who have not been socialized to shop, do not think of gift shopping as part of their household responsibilities. Second, the giving of a gift often communicates love and affection (Belk 1979), and women are more concerned than men with showing love (Cheal 1987).

Femininity, typically associated with being female, is defined as focusing on relational personality traits such as caring, considerateness, and sensitivity (Cross and Markus 1993). In contrast, masculinity, typically connected with being male, is associated with separating the self from others (Gill, Stockard, Johnson, and Williams 1987) and characterized by independence, assertiveness, instrumentality, and competitiveness (Cross and Markus 1993). Consequently, biological sex significantly impacts socialization processes and is, therefore, an important indicator of the kinds of consumer activities a person will engage in.

However, with respect to gift exchange, men's behaviors have not always been congruent with the socially expected masculine gender role. Fischer and Arnold (1990) reported that men who held egalitarian role attitudes were more involved in Christmas gift shopping than were men with traditional role attitudes; to a lesser extent, men with feminine gender identities were also more involved in gift shopping. Recent studies report that gay men were more involved in gift giving activities relative to heterosexual men (Newman and Nelson 1996; Rucker, Freitas, and Huidor 1996). Gender identity theory asserts that men and women learn to be masculine or feminine through socialization (Bem 1981), and, moreover, that an individual's gender identity—how s/he identifies with gendered personality traits—is not always congruent with his/her biological sex. This incongruency may be more apparent as cultural representations of masculinity and femininity are transformed (Craig 1992). Together, these findings suggest that how a man identifies with femininity and masculinity may result in gift giving behaviors incongruent with gender role expectations.

Consequently, the purpose of this study is to examine a possible influence of gender identity in gift exchange. Specifically, gender identity is examined for its effect on the relationships among biological sex and gift exchange roles and gift exchange focus. These gift exchange variables are important for what they reveal about the task of gift giving and gift receiving (roles) and gift exchange involvement (focus). Since the concepts of masculinity and femininity are directly related to biological sex and form the basis of gender identity conceptualization and measurement, these concepts are discussed first.

MASCULINITY AND FEMININITY

Social scientists have noted for many years that men are more oriented toward impersonal or individualistic goals than women, while women are more oriented to social integration than men (Gill et al. 1987). Masculinity, an instrumental orientation, is defined as "concern with the attainment of goals external to the interaction process" (Gill et al. 1987, p. 379). Involving the manipulation of objects, the environment, and people to accomplish tasks, a masculine orientation often uses formal authority and technical control; it is centered toward objective ends and supported by impersonal attitudes such as approval, esteem, and respect. A feminine orientation, also referred to as an expressive orientation, however, "gives primacy to facilitating the interaction process itself" (Gill et al. 1987, p. 380). A feminine orientation involves understanding and dealing with emotions in self and others, although it is not "being emotional"; rather, it concerns being actively interdependent and relational. Thus, expressiveness, in contrast to instrumentality, is often rewarded with more personal attitudes like love and friendship. The assumption is frequently made that males endorse a masculine orientation and females endorse a feminine orientation.

Themes linking males to masculinity and females to femininity have emerged in gift exchange research. For example, Goodwin, Smith, and Spiggle (1990) found that females were more likely to mention the needs of the receiver when discussing gift giving (expressiveness), compared to males who tended to list guiding principles (instrumentality). While both men and women are gift givers, women have been described as the primary gift givers in American culture (Otnes, Ruth, and Milbourne 1994). Otnes and McGrath (1994) also found gift buying/exchange to be a feminine activity among their sample of informants as young as three years of age, suggesting an early gender socialization process related to gift exchange. These studies are supported by McGrath (1995) who found that females were more likely to discuss gift giving across a variety of recipients, whereas males were more likely to link gift giving with romantic relationships. Moreover, while women are accustomed to receiving gifts, males appear to have less experience as receivers. Thus, the literature suggests that women are more involved than men in gift exchange, and, in particular, in gift giving.

H1: Females are more likely to recall gift giving experiences than are men.

Related to the distinction between instrumentality and expressiveness is whether males and females devote more attention to the gift itself (i.e., object-focus) or to the other person involved (i.e., person-focus) when describing gift exchanges—in other words, the focus of an individual's involvement in the gift exchange process. Consistent with the theoretical definitions of femininity and masculinity, a significant body of evidence suggests that females are likely to adopt a person-focus, whereas males are likely to adopt an object-focus. As week-old infants, females exhibit a greater propensity to attend to the people around them; by contrast, male infants are just as likely to attend to objects as to people (McGuiness 1985). Other researchers observing the play patterns of preschool children have noted that boys' play tends to involve the manipulation of toys (e.g., building blocks, toy vehicles, etc.), whereas girls engage in games involving role playing, often in mock family settings (Harris 1981). Within the context of gift exchange, Fischer and Arnold (1990) described male Christmas shoppers as children looking for the most popular toys, an object-focus. For women, on the other hand, gifts serve to establish, maintain, or even repair personal relationships (Otnes, Lowrey, and Kim 1993), an indication that they are person-focused in gift exchange. These findings suggest the following hypothesis:

H2: Females are more likely than males to be person-focused in descriptions of gift exchange, whereas males are more likely than females to be object-focused in descriptions of gift exchange.

GENDER IDENTITY

Whereas the previous discussion implies that men are masculine and women are feminine, there is considerable evidence that an individual's gender identity, i.e., the degree to which an individual endorses masculinity or femininity, is not necessarily consistent with one's biological sex (see, e.g., Bem 1974). In fact, researchers do not consider masculinity and femininity as opposites; rather, they are conceptualized as two separate, orthogonal dimensions, coexisting in varying degrees within an individual (Gill et al. 1987). Consequently, an individual is sex-typed when his/her gender identity matches his/her biological sex; cross-sex-typed when his/her gender identity is opposite to biological sex; androgynous when s/he endorses both masculinity and femininity to a high degree; and undifferentiated when s/he endorses both masculinity and femininity to a low degree (Bem, Martyna, and Watson 1976).

Since biological sex and gender identity are not necessarily congruent, gender identity has often been used to explain within-sex differences with respect to consumer behaviors. For example, response to the contemporary representations of women in ads are more favorable for females who endorse masculinity than for females who endorse femininity (Jaffe 1991). In another advertising study, Gentry and Haley (1984) reported that masculine females recalled and sequenced ads for masculine products more easily than did feminine females. Within the gift exchange literature, gender identity has explained differences among males. For example, males have been reported to have higher involvement in gift giving when scoring high on femininity relative to masculinity (Fischer and Arnold 1990, 1994).

This discussion suggests that gender identity moderates the effect of biological sex on the gift exchange variables examined in this study.

H3: Feminine individuals are more likely to recall gift giving experiences than will masculine individuals.

H4: Feminine individuals are more likely to be person-focused than are masculine individuals, whereas masculine individuals are more likely to be object-focused than are feminine individuals in descriptions of gift exchange.

METHOD

To examine the relationships between biological sex, gender identity, and the gift exchange variables, a critical incident method was adopted (Mick and DeMoss 1990). In the study, 115 college students (51 female and 64 male) from a major, state-funded university in the Southwest were asked to describe in writing a particularly memorable occasion when they were either the giver or the receiver of a special gift. They were encouraged to provide detailed information regarding the occasion for the gift exchange (including their age at the time), their relationship with the giver or receiver, and the gift itself. After the narrative was completed, informants completed the Bem Sex Role Inventory (Bem 1974) and provided answers to demographic questions.

Consistent with the techniques employed by Mick and DeMoss (1990) with similar qualitative data, multiple judges blind to the purpose of the study classified each narrative using formal definitions provided to them in the instructions; the formal definitions of object-/person-focus were furnished. Each narrative was coded as being primarily person-focused (0) or object-focused (1). The writer of each narrative was coded as either the gift giver (0) or gift receiver (1). Disagreements in coding were resolved during a coder debriefing session. Overall interrater reliability was .87, exceeding the threshold of .85 for content analyses (Kassarjian 1977).

Bem Sex Role Inventory

The Bem Sex Role Inventory (BSRI) was used to measure gender identity in this study. The BSRI incorporates the multidimensional conceptualization of gender identity, i.e., that masculinity and femininity coexist in varying degrees within an individual (Bem 1974). The original development of the BSRI was based on college students' assessments of stereotypically desirable masculine and feminine personality traits. Thus, Bem classified 20 traits as reflecting masculinity since they were judged as significantly more desirable for a man than for a woman; the Bem masculinity scale includes traits such as "aggressive," "self-sufficient," and "willing to take risks." In a similar classification manner, 20 traits were chosen to reflect femininity, including "cheerful," "flatterable," and "gullible." Bem (1981) purports that the masculinity and femininity scales on the BSRI are diagnostic and predictive of broad gender-related constructs, including gender role identity and gender schema. Consequently, an individual's classification on the BSRI should be linked to a wide range of gender-related attitudes, attributes, and behaviors.

Both long and short forms of the BSRI have been used in research. The long (and original) form of the BSRI (Bem 1974) consists of twenty masculine and twenty feminine characteristics; in addition, twenty neutral characteristics considered neither masculine nor feminine are included. After researchers began reporting factor solutions containing more than three factors (e.g., Feather 1978), Bem (1979) developed a short version of the BSRI consisting of ten masculine and ten feminine items, all of which were considered more desirable for a given sex. Based on their own factor analysis, Stern, Barak, and Gould (1987) developed another short version of the BSRI, consisting of ten masculine and ten feminine items. A two-factor solution with Bem's short BSRI has been reported (Martin and Ramanaiah 1988). However, in another study using both short versions, Bem's (1979) version produced a four-factor solution while the Stern et al. (1987) version produced a two-factor solution (Palan 1994). Based on these results, the short version of the BSRI developed by Stern et al. (1987) was used in this study.

In this study, informants indicated how well each of the 10 masculine and 10 feminine characteristics described them, with 1 indicating "never or almost never true" and 7 indicating "always or almost always true." Responses to the masculine and feminine items were summed and averaged, separately, to determine the masculinity and femininity scores. Factor analysis (principal

TABLE 1
BSRI Scale Items

Scale Items	Factor Loading
Masculine Items	
Have leadership abilities	.77
Assertive	.70
Willing to take a stand	.67
Ambitious	.63
Competitive	.51
Dominant	.79
A strong personality	.62
Forceful	.71
Act like a leader	.88
Aggressive	.76
Feminine Items	
Affectionate	.71
Tender	.88
Sensitive to others' needs	.77
Sympathetic	.82
Warm	.86
Eager to soothe hurt feelings	.81
Understanding	.83
Gentle	.84
Compassionate	.90

components with varimax rotation) of the twenty items resulted in a three-factor solution—nine feminine traits loaded on the first factor, ten masculine traits on the second factor, and one feminine trait (loyal) on the third factor. Elimination of the feminine trait, loyalty, resulted in a two-factor solution; the femininity scale thus consisted of nine traits and the masculinity scale consisted of 10 traits. Coefficient alphas for the masculinity scale were .90 and .89, with alphas reported separately for males and females, respectively. Likewise, coefficient alphas were .94 and .88 for the femininity scale.

Consistent with previous use of the BSRI, median splits of the masculine and feminine scales were calculated using the total sample; informants were categorized according to Bem's original four-way classification. Thus, those informants scoring high on the masculine scale and low on the feminine scale were classified as "masculine" (26 males and 10 females); informants scoring high on the feminine scale and low on the masculine scale were classified as "feminine" (12 males and 22 females; informants scoring above the medians of both the masculine and feminine scales were classified as "androgynous" (10 males and 12 females); and informants scoring below the medians of both the masculine and feminine scales were classified as "undifferentiated" (16 males and 7 females). Since the moderation hypotheses state expectations only with respect to masculine and feminine gender identities, only these two classifications are included in the analyses. The scale items and their factor loadings are listed in Table 1.

Biological Sex

An independent variable, biological sex is a dichotomous variable coded "0" for male informants and "1" for female informants.

RESULTS

Hypothesis tests were examined by constructing a 2 x 2 frequency table and using the Pearson chi-square statistic.

Gift Giving

Given a choice between recalling a gift giving vs. a gift reception experience, H1 posited that more women than men would recall gift giving experiences. The results, in Table 2, show that biological sex (χ^2_1=19.48, p<.001) was a significant predictor of the gift giving role, although the result was counter to expectations—men were more likely than women to recall gift giving experiences (45% of men versus 8% of women).

Although gender identity significantly moderated the relationship between biological sex and gift giving (H3) (χ^2_1=5.64, p<.025), the results were opposite than predicted. That is, masculine individuals were more likely than feminine individuals to recall gift giving experiences (36% vs.12%). Moreover, the results of H3, in Table 3, are fully attributed to males, since there were no feminine or masculine females who described gift giving experiences.

Gift Focus

Women were significantly more person-focused and men more object-focused, as predicted in H2 (χ^2_1=6.10, p<.05). As can be seen in Table 4, 47% of women were person-focused, compared to only 25% of men. In contrast, 75% of men were object-focused versus just 53% of women. Gender identity was found to significantly moderate the relationship between biological sex and gift exchange focus (H4). The results, in Table 5, show that more feminine individuals (41%) than masculine individuals (19%) were person-focused, while more masculine (81%) than feminine (59%)

TABLE 2
Recall of Gift Exchange Role

	Gift Giver	Gift Receiver	Total
Males	29 (45%)	35 (55%)	64
Females	4 (8%)	47 (82%)	51
Total	33	82	115

NOTE: Numbers in parentheses indicate the cell percentage based on the row total.

TABLE 3
Relationship of Gender Identity to Gift Exchange Roles

Gender Identity	Gift Giver	Gift Receiver	Total
Masculine	13 (36%)	23 (64%)	36
Male	13 (50%)	13 (50%)	
Female	0 (0%)	10 (100%)	
Feminine	4 (12%)	30 (88%)	34
Male	4 (33%)	8 (67%)	
Female	0 (0%)	22 (100%)	
Total	17	53	70

NOTE: Numbers in parentheses indicate the cell percentage based on the row total.

individuals were object-focused (χ^2_1=3.93, p<.05). An examination of males separate from females reveals results in the predicted direction for both groups, though significance was not reached. Specifically, feminine females were more likely than masculine females to be person-focused (45% vs. 20%), whereas masculine females were more likely to be object-focused than were feminine females (80% vs. 55%) (Fisher's Exact Test , p=0.16).[1] Similarly, feminine males were more likely to be person-focused than were masculine males (33% vs. 19%), and masculine males were more likely than feminine females to be object-focused (81% vs. 67%) (Fisher's Exact Test, p=0.29).

SUMMARY

Using narrative descriptions of memorable gift exchange experiences, this study reports findings that challenge commonly-held assumptions about the participation of men in gift exchange. First, despite the commonly reported finding that women are more likely to be gift-givers than are men, the men in this study were far more likely to recall gift-giving memories than were the women. Furthermore, masculine males were more likely to recall gift giving experiences than were feminine males. These findings, incongruent with male role expectations, suggest that while it may not be "masculine" to give gifts, it may be very "masculine" to talk about

[1]Low cell frequencies occurred when males and females were examined separately. Consequently, because the chi-square statistic may not be valid when cell frequencies are low, Fisher's exact test was used, since this test is appropriate with small cell sizes and when n<40 (Cochran 1952).

TABLE 4
Gift Exchange Focus

	Person-Focus	Object-Focus	Total
Males	16 (25%)	48 (75%)	64
Females	24 (47%)	27 (53%)	51
Total	40	75	115

NOTE: Numbers in parentheses indicate the cell percentage based on the row total.

TABLE 5
Relationship of Gender Identity to Gift Exchange Focus

Gender Identity	Person-Focus	Object Focus	Total
Masculine	7 (19%)	29 (81%)	36
Male	5 (19%)	21 (81%)	
Female	2 (20%)	8 (80%)	
Feminine	14 (41%)	20 (59%)	34
Male	4 (33%)	8 (67%)	
Female	10 (45%)	12 (55%)	
Total	21	49	70

NOTE: Numbers in parentheses indicate the cell percentage based on the row total.

a single experience of gift giving, memorable perhaps because considerable time and effort were involved. This interpretation is consistent with the argument that men take a reciprocal approach to gift giving—that is, they give in order to receive something in return (Gilligan 1982). Thus, it might not be surprising that masculine men are more likely to vividly recall gift-giving experiences than feminine males.

Second, whereas men have traditionally been expected to be very goal-oriented in their gift-giving activities, in this study, men with feminine gender identities were very person-oriented in their gift giving. In other words, they seemed to take a relational approach to gift giving, in which the concern centers on communicating and expressing affection for others—an approach to gift giving expected of females (Gilligan 1982). The clear message is that many men behave similarly to women when it comes to gift giving—they give gifts throughout the year, to a

variety of recipients, for a variety of reasons. The fact that men with feminine gender identities focus more on the recipient than the gift in gift exchange implies that these men will be very involved in the gift giving process; they will invest a lot of time searching for a gift that they know will especially please the recipient. This defies the notion that men just buy gifts because they "have to."

Limitations of this study point to opportunities in future research. For example, a potential limitation of this study is the fact that males and females have different communication styles (Gilligan 1982), and informants communicated gift exchange memories in a narrative format. At issue is whether or not the data reflect differences in communication styles rather than differences in gift exchange behaviors. However, two aspects of this study lead us to conclude that male and female communication styles did not bias our results. First, as education increases, communication differences between males and females are expected to decrease (Gilligan 1982); because the sample in this study was well-educated (college juniors and seniors), the emergence of communication style differences is unlikely. Second, one indication of communication style differences is narrative length; males are expected to write shorter narratives since their goal is to succinctly complete the task rather than to elaborate on the task. Yet, the average length of male and female narratives was equally long (1.8 and 1.6 pages, respectively) despite the fact that informants were not instructed on page expectations. Consequently, it seems likely that the data were a reflection of differences in gift exchange behavior.

Other possible limitations are related to the nature of the data collection method. For example, instructing informants to recall "memorable" gift exchange experiences may have created a demand effect, resulting in so few females recalling gift giving experiences. Indeed, the lopsided nature of reported gift giving experiences from males and females suggests that the results should be cautiously interpreted and that steps should be taken in future research to control for this effect. Other avenues for future research include examining person- vs. object-focus in a variety of gift exchange situations and examining gift exchange as a transactional/relational continuum in relation to "masculine" and "feminine" gift giving in men and women. Future research should also include more variation in the sample with respect to age, education, and location. An interesting avenue of study would be to examine the research questions across cultural contexts.

REFERENCES

Belk, Russell W. (1979), "Gift Giving Behavior," in *Research in Marketing*, Vol. 2, ed. Jagdip Sheth, Greenwich, CT: JAI Press, 95-126.

Bem, Sandra L. (1974), "The Measurement of Psychological Androgyny," *Journal of Consulting and Clinical Psychology*, 42, 155-162.

Bem, Sandra L. (1979), "Theory and Measurement of Androgyny: A Reply to the Pedhazur-Tetenbaum and Locksley-Colten Critiques," *Journal of Personality and Social Psychology*, 37, 1047-1054.

Bem, Sandra L. (1981), "Gender Schema Theory: A Cognitive Account of Sex Typing," *Psychological Review*, 88, 354-364.

Bem, Sandra L., Wendy Martyna and Carol Watson (1976), "Sex Typing and Androgyny: Further Explorations of the Expressive Domain," *Journal of Personality and Social Psychology*, 34, 1016-1023

Cheal, David J. (1987), "Showing Them You Love Them: Gift Giving and the Dialectic of Intimacy,"*The Sociological Review*, 35, 150-169.

Cochran, W G. (1952), "The c^2 Test of Goodness of Fit," *Annals of Mathematical Statistics*, 23, 315-345.

Craig, Steve, ed. (1992), *Men, Masculinities and the Media*, London:Sage.

Cross, Susan E.and Hazel R. Markus (1993), "Gender in Thought, Belief, and Action: A Cognitive Approach," in *The Psychology of Gender*, eds. Anne E. Beall and Robert J. Sternberg, New York: Guilford Press, 55-98.

Feather, N. T. (1978), "Factor Structure of the Bem Sex-Role Inventory: Implications for the Study of Masculinity, Femininity, and Androgyny," *Australian Journal of Psychology*, 30, 241-254.

Fischer, Eileen and Stephen J. Arnold (1990), "More Than a Labor of Love: Gender Roles and Christmas Gift Shopping," *Journal of Consumer Research*, 17, 333-345.

Fischer, Eileen and Stephen J. Arnold (1994), "Sex, Gender Identity, Gender Role Attitudes, and Consumer Behavior," *Psychology & Marketing*, 11, 163-182.

Gentry, James W., and Debra A. Haley (1984), "Gender Schema Theory as a Predictor of Ad Recall," in *Advances in Consumer Research*, Vol. 11, ed. Thomas C. Kinnear, Ann Arbor, MI: Association for Consumer Research, 259-264.

Gill, Sandra, Jean Stockard, Miriam Johnson, and Suzanne Williams (1987), "Measuring Gender Differences: The Expressive Dimension and Critique of Androgyny Scales," *Sex Roles*, 17, 375-400.

Gilligan, Carol (1982), *In a Different Voice: Psychological Theory and Women's Development.*, Cambridge, MA: Harvard University Press.

Goodwin, Cathy, Kelly L. Smith and Susan Spiggle (1990), "Gift Giving: Consumer Motivation and the Gift Purchase Process," in *Advances in Consumer Research*, Vol. 17, eds. Rebecca. H. Holman and M. R. Solomon, Provo, UT: Association for Consumer Research, 690-698.

Gouldner, Alvin (1960), "The Norm of Reciprocity: A Preliminary Statement," *American Sociological Review*, 25, 176-177.

Harris, L. J. (1981), "Sex Related Variations in Spatial Skill," in *Spatial Representation and Behavior Across the Life Span*, eds. L. S. Liben et al., New York: Academic Press, 83-117.

Jaffe, Lynn J. (1991), "Impact of Positioning and Sex-Role Identity on Women's Responses to Advertising," *Journal of Advertising Research*, (June/July), 57-64.

Kassarjian, Harold H. (1977), "Content Analysis in Consumer Research, *Journal of Consumer Research*, 4, 8-18.

Martin, H. and Ramanaiah, N. (1988), "Confirmatory Factor Analysis of the Bem Sex Role Inventory," *Psychological Reports*, 62, 343-350.

McGrath, Mary Ann (1995), "Gender Differences in Gift Exchanges: New Directions From Projections," *Psychology and Marketing*, 12, 371-393.

McGuiness, Diane (1985), *When Children Don't Learn*, New York: Basic Books.

Mick, David G. and Michelle DeMoss (1990), "Self-Gifts: Phenomenological Insights From Four Contexts," *Journal of Consumer Research*, 17, 322-332.

Newman, Peter J., and Michelle R. Nelson (1996), "Mainstream Legitimization of Homosexual Men Through Valentine's Day Gift-giving and Consumption Rituals," in *Gays, Lesbians, and Consumer Behavior: Theory, Practice, and Research Issues in Marketing*, ed. Daniel L. Wardlow, New York: Harrington Park Press, 57-69.

Otnes, Cele, Tina M. Lowrey, and Young Chan Kim (1993), "Gift Selection for Easy and Difficult Recipients: A Social Roles Interpretation," *Journal of Consumer Research*, 20, 229-244.

Otnes, Cele, and Mary Ann McGrath (1994), "Ritual Socialization and the Children's Birthday Party: The Early Emergence of Gender Differences," *Journal of Ritual Studies*, 8, 73-93.

Otnes, Cele, Ruth, J. A., & Milbourne, C. C. (1994), "The Pleasure and Pain of Being Close: Men's Mixed Feelings About Participation in Valentine's Day Gift Exchange," in *Advances in Consumer Research*, Vol. 21, eds. Chris T. Allen and Deborah Roedder John, Provo, UT: Association for Consumer Research, 159-164.

Palan, Kay M. (1994), *Family Decision Making: A Study of Parent-Adolescent Interactions in the Purchase Decision Making Process*, unpublished Doctoral Dissertation, Texas Tech University, Lubbock, Texas.

Rucker, Margaret, Anthony Freitas, and Oscar Hidor (1996), "Gift-Giving Among Gay Men: The Reification of Social Relations," in *Gays, Lesbians, and Consumer Behavior: Theory, Practice, and Research Issues in Marketing*, ed. Daniel L. Wardlow, New York: Harrington Park Press, 43-56.

Scanzoni, John (1977), "Changing Sex Roles and Emerging Directions in Family Decision Making," *Journal of Consumer Research*, 4, 185-188.

Stern, Barbara B., Benny Barak and Stephen J. Gould (1987), "Sexual Identity Scale: A New Self-Assessment Measure, *Sex Roles*, 17, 503-519.

Faring One Thousand Miles to Give Goose Feathers:
Gift Giving in the People's Republic of China

Jianfeng Wang, Nanyang Technological University
Francis Piron, Nanyang Technological University
Mai Van Xuan, Nanyang Technological University

INTRODUCTION

Gift giving is important to consumer behavior and has generated a significant flow of research. The phenomenon is rich as it investigates consumers, their motives, the social interactions that accompany the giving of a gift, and the reformulation of consumers' relationships once the gift has been given and received (Hoyer and MacInnis 1997; Ruth, Otnes and Brunel 1999). In the Western world, where most of the research effort has focused, gift giving and its complexities are becoming increasingly understood. However, this not so in most parts of Asia, the most populated continent, where gift-giving is often used as a complex medium for social interaction and personal expression. This paper is a stepping stone as it offers a seminal, descriptive research on the giving of gifts in the People's Republic of China (PRC). To ensure a proper grounding in the study of the behavior in the PRC, we largely duplicated Beatty et al's (1991) study, allowing for necessary adaptations to the particularities of the PRC environment.

Gift giving is a pervasive and universal phenomenon that has stirred research interests from disciplines such as anthropology, sociology and psychology (Levi-Strauss 1965; Mauss 1954; Schwartz 1967). In consumer behavior research, Sherry's (1983) comprehensive model of gift-giving serves as the foundation for knowledge development: gift search and acquisition have been extensively researched over the past fifteen years (Beatty, Kahle, Homer and Misra 1986; Fischer and Arnold 1990; McGrath 1989; Otnes, Lowrey and Kim 1993; Sherry and McGrath 1989).

From an Asian perspective, and most particularly with a focus on China, little is known. With its long history and complexity, Chinese culture stands alone and it is fair to assume that what is known of Western gift giving is not necessarily transferable to Chinese consumers. Yau, Chan and Lau (1999) offer a model of gift-giving in Hong Kong: while now a part of the PRC, Hong Kong, with its blend of Western and Chinese cultures and often affluent lifestyles, does not represent consumers from the PRC. These distinctions are important since gift giving is strongly bound by culture (Hill and Rom 1996; Park 1998), and by the social fabric of societies. So, for example, what may be observed in a culture that fosters individualism (e.g., Western countries, Hong Kong) may be different from cultures that support collectivism, such as the PRC (Belk 1984). In summary, this research brings a distinct contribution as it starts up the process of understanding gift giving in the PRC from a consumer behavior perspective.

SCOPE OF THE STUDY

Hill and Romm (1996) observe that, in the PRC, gift giving helps reinforce one's self-concept in a society that is fundamentally group-based (e.g., contemporary factory workers are housed and fed in factory-sponsored dormitories and canteens). In addition, traditional values, based on Confucianism, stress the importance of family security and affiliation, and compliance to social norms over individual recognition and achievement. Yet, when one's achievements are recognized, benefits and other positive outcomes are expected to contribute to the group's welfare. The group may be one's family, work unit, village, or any other appropriate form of socio-professional affiliation.

As a rapidly developing nation, the PRC is experiencing significant movements of rural masses to the industrialized centers. Landry's (1998) suggestion that urban consumers are more sophisticated and influenced by Western cultures than their rural counterparts, supported by casual observations of the PRC environment, is assessed in this research. We compare two samples of PRC consumers in their gift-giving behavior: migrant rural workers in newly developed industrial centers and white-collar consumers in Beijing.

The study also focuses on potential, gender-based differences. Cheal (1988) and Romm and Hill (1996) suggest that women are more generous gift givers than men are. In spite of publicized statements and education of gender equality, along with the late Chairman Mao's statement that half of the sky is held up by women, the reality is that, within the PRC society, women still hold a position second to men. In turn, and as briefly mentioned earlier under the group-based self-concept, such differences may be actualized in distinct gift giving behaviors between male and females subjects.

MEASURE DEVELOPMENT

This study adapts Beatty et al.'s (1991) research on "personal values and gift-giving behaviors" to a PRC environment. Again, since little is known about personal values and the behavior itself within the country, it follows that basing this research on a format adopted in published research would increase the value of this effort.

Kahle, Beatty and Homer (1986) developed the "List of Values" (LOV) used in the survey. It consists of 9 items, and taps attitudes toward gift giving, as well as gift purchasing behavior. We are not aware that the LOV has been used in non-Western cultures. Such cultures may share fundamental values with traditional European-North American cultures, such as personal (e.g., birthday celebrations), social (e.g., mothers' day) or religious events (e.g., Christmas). Yet, they also retain certain peculiarities that may not be captured by the LOV itself. Later, Beatty et al. (1991) report that two of the LOV items were collapsed into one and another item was altogether eliminated from their survey. Our version of the LOV contains eight items: we reincorporated the discarded item, as, in our best judgment, "being well respected" is an important characteristic of the Chinese culture, and adapted two items as follows. A panel of seven PRC consumers were given the eight LOV items, translated into Mandarin and asked to reflect on the meaning of each item within the context of gift giving. Three items required adaptation to better fit within the PRC's cultural environment: the items related to "Sense of Belonging," " Self Fulfillment," and "Security."

"Sense of Belonging" was worded in Kahle (1986) as "to be accepted by your family, friends, and community." The panel was of the opinion that no PRC respondent would answer such question truthfully: a negative answer would be an acknowledgment of loss of face, particularly the part of the question dealing with being accepted. Panel members were asked to word a statement that would measure a construct as similar as possible to the one tapping the "Sense of Belonging." Eventually, a unanimous decision was

Advances in Consumer Research
Volume 28, © 2001

TABLE 1
List of Values (LOV)

Dimension	LOV Original Wording	Our Wording
Sense of Belonging	To be accepted and needed by your family, friends, and community	"You believe that your loved ones need your gifts."
Excitement	To experience stimulation and thrills	"Gift giving is exciting to you."
Warm Relationships with Others	To have close companionships and intimate friendships	"Giving gifts to your loved ones builds closeness."
Self Fulfillment	To find peace of mind and to make the best use of your talents	"To you, giving gifts to your loved ones is a way to get peace of mind."
Being Well-Respected	To be admired by others and to receive recognition	"Gift giving is a way to earn recognition from your loved ones."
Security	To be safe and protected from misfortune and attack	"You think it obliged to give gifts to your loved ones."
Self Respect	To be proud of yourself and confident with who you are	"You feel proud of yourself with the gifts you give to your loved ones."
A Sense of Accomplishment	To succeed at what you want to do	"By giving gifts to your loved ones, you can show them that you are successful."

reached with "You believe that your loved ones need your gifts." While it is not possible to capture the exact essence of the statement in English, the Mandarin version was a considerately worded statement hinting at the relationship between the giver and the gift.

Secondly, the "Self Fulfillment" item , "to find peace of mind and to make the best use of your talent" was also found to be unclear in its Mandarin translation. Specifically, the panel could not understand the relationship between "peace of mind" and "to make the best use of [one's] talent." Also, the second part of the statement seemed too similar to the item tapping the "Sense of Accomplishment" ("By giving gifts to your loved ones, you can show them that you are successful.") A decision was then made to limit the wording to solely capture the "peace of mind" construct.

Thirdly, the item tapping the "Security" dimension of the LOV scale asked whether gift giving was done "to be safe and protected from misfortune and attack." The panel thought that good luck and good fortune were already intrinsically attached to giving gifts. However, the item would tap a similar construct if it were worded to convey some form of obligation to give gift. In other words, when asking whether one felt obliged to give gifts to loved ones, the answer would have to be positive as it would be a socially acceptable expression of affection, and thereby producing or maintaining security within the relationship.

In sum, we adapted the wording of three of the eight LOV items to more accurately capture the intended dimension of those items. While, from a non-Chinese perspective, the words may convey different meanings, from the respondents' perspective, the indirect link was the proper medium to use when asking about private matters, such as expressions of love and affection. To exemplify, Chinese lovers would admire the full moon and describe it such a way that are understood to be descriptive of the relationship, rather than the moon itself.

To better account for the "Chineseness" of gift giving, we incorporated in the questionnaire three dimensions that are more specific to "Chinese cultural values […] that relate more directly to gift giving" (Yau et al. 1999, p. 101). Yau (1988, 1994) identifies three concepts that, while present in most cultures under different forms, have uniquely Chinese "twists": the concepts of Face, GuanXi, and Reciprocity. The concept of Face is two-pronged, and implies that a consumer will lose peers' confidence when offering a gift that is a poor match to the recipient's and/or the presenter's standing in life (du lien) or prestige (mien tsu). The concept of GuanXi refers to the incremental building of relationships, an intrinsically two-way process that cements individuals throughout their professional and public lives. Finally, the concept of Reciprocity refers to the mechanism permitting GuanXi to evolve: a person will purposefully time the giving (the returned favor is not expected until a later, appropriate time) of an item of a value at least equal to what is expected in return. [For a more complete discussion on these fascinating topics, readers may wan to refer to Gouldner (1960), Kipnis (1997), Lebra (1976), and Malinowski (1959)].

A focus group discussion with manual laborers helped us identify additional dimensions or expressions of gift giving that were deemed appropriate to migrant rural workers. These items reflect the importance to the giver of maintaining a sense of connection with loved ones who s/he may see but once a year or less, due to the expatriation to urban industrial magnets.

In sum, the instrument developed for this study is hybrid, incorporating eight items from the LOV scale, three items from Yau's (1988, 1994) discussion, and six items to more precisely capture the essence of rural migrants' need to express and assure the maintenance of connections with far-away loved ones.

In addition to the scale-related items discussed above, five questions were asked to assess whether the respondent enjoyed

TABLE 2
Chinese Value Items

Dimension	Our Wording
Face Saving	"You can gain face by giving gifts to your loved ones."
GuanXi (Relationship)	"Gift giving is a way to earn recognition* from your loved ones."
Reciprocity	"After you give gifts to your loved ones, you wish them to reciprocate."

*In the Chinese text, we use the term Guan Xi which does not need to be clarified to PRC readers.

giving gifts, how often, when and to whom gifts were given. Another question tapped gift attributes, such as price, uniqueness, style, etc. that were important to the presenter

The questionnaire went through several stages of translation to increase its validity. The LOV items were translated into Mandarin and back. The items identified in the focus group discussion with migrant workers were circulated among Mandarin speakers to reach a consensus on exact wording[1]. Finally, the concepts used by Yau (1988, 1994) were incorporated in Mandarin sentences. Finally, respondents were asked personal questions to record demographic characteristics, such as gender, age, income, education, and marital status.

METHOD

Data collection was done two weeks prior to the Chinese New Year (February 5, 2000) in two locations in the PRC. Migrant rural workers to urban centers were surveyed in the cities of Gaoming (90 respondents) and Dongguan (36 respondents), and 133 middle-class consumers were interviewed in Beijing. Migrant workers were asked to participate in the survey while on a break from work, at their work site, and Beijing residents were interviewed using a traditional mall-intercept technique. All questionnaires were self-administered. Due to the conciseness of the Chinese language, the questionnaire was printed on both sides of a single sheet.

RESULTS

A total of 259 questionnaires were collected for this study, almost evenly split between rural migrant and urban consumers (126 vs. 133). Seven of the questionnaires administered to the rural migrant workers and 12 of those administered to the urban consumers were unusable. Fifty-four (43% of the rural sample) of the migrant workers and 57 (43% of the urban sample) of the urban respondents were female.

Migrant and urban consumers answered evenly the first question about whether they enjoyed giving gifts (40% vs. 42%) or not (15% vs. 17%). The second question asked how often and to who gifts were given. Using a Chi-square procedure, we compared answers across genders and residencies and identified significant differences (a=. 05) in the frequency of spousal gift giving: more urban husbands (16 vs. 5) treat their wives on a monthly basis than rural consumers (some of the rural workers migrated to the cities with their families) . Rural females (a=.05) and young (21-30 y.o.) rural adults (a=.10) are less generous with their supervisors than urban residents. Younger married, as well as single (21-30 y.o.) urban consumers offer gifts more frequently (a=.01) to their spouses or girl/boyfriends than their rural counterparts. A similar effect is noted with middle-aged urban parents who reward their sons more frequently (a=.01).

Respondents were then asked to identify the first, second and third persons to whom they would choose to give a gift. No statistically significant differences (a=.05) were noted for the first gift recipients of choice. However, significant differences (a=.05) were noted between urban female respondents who selected their spouses/boyfriends as second choice over rural women who had chosen their parents.

The next question attempted to identify differences in behavior according to the time of gift giving. Respondents were asked to identify the first, second, and third holiday (Chinese New Year, Mid-Autumn festival) or social events (birthdays, weddings) when they would give gifts. No meaningful differences were found between either sample for the first and third choices. However, young (21-30 y.o.) urban residents celebrated anniversaries and the Western New Year while none of their rural counterparts did. Throughout, Chinese New Year and birthdays were ranked first and second, respectively.

The last question of the initial section of the questionnaire asked respondents to choose from a list (price, durability, quality, brand, uniqueness, style, and practicality) the three most important factors to them in selecting a gift. The practical aspect of the gift, its price and quality were ranked in similar order and proportions in both samples.

The next section of the instrument assessed respondents' answers on the eight LOV items. Only one of the income levels showed to be a potential discriminant for statistically significant differences (a=.05), but the differences were not meaningful. In other words, neither residential origins (urban vs. rural), nor genders, nor achieved educational levels, nor marital status, nor income (except for the highest level) caused respondents' perceptions of gift-giving to differ.

However, we observe that three out of four (76.7%) respondents agreed that they thought they were obliged to give gifts to loved ones and a slightly larger number (84%) found gift giving to be exciting. Also, responses are almost evenly distributed across the three levels of agreement (Strongly Agree-Agree-Moderately Agree). The magnitude of agreement was almost identical when asked whether giving gifts to loved ones is a way to get peace of mind (78% agreed) or build closeness with them (85% agreed). Respondents also agreed, overall, that they believed that loved ones needed their gifts (63%), and that they earned recognition from loved ones by giving gifts (66%). Finally, respondents agreed (57%) that they felt proud with themselves for the gifts, but

[1]Chinese is a very precise, but concise, language. While most Western languages may allow for lengthy explanations of concepts and ideas, Chinese speakers are more accustomed to simple, direct and precise (combination of) characters. Only two characters describe for instance the concept of GuanXi discussed above, while the same effort may require several paragraphs in English.

a smaller part of the respondents (28%) agreed that they would be able to show their loved ones how successful they were by giving gifts. Actually, almost the majority (46%) moderately disagreed with that statement.

Three questions tapped respondents (dis)agreement to the three Chinese values referred to by Yau (1988, 1994). As with the LOV items, there were no significant differences (a=.05) between respondents in their perceptions of the three items referring to the Chinese values using any of the demographic variables available in this survey. While one third of the respondents agreed that one could gain face by giving gifts to loved ones, a larger proportion (43%) moderately disagreed. More importantly, only 19% agreed with the Concept of reciprocity, while 73% also agreed with the Concept of GuanXi.

Finally, six items were developed from focus group interviews. From these, we learned that over 75% of the respondents perceived themselves as generous gift givers (evenly spread over the 3 options on the agree dimension). Also, 55 % agreed or strongly agreed that gift giving is important to them. Almost 90% agreed in some form that they thought it over before giving gifts, and 71% agreed that they always made an effort to find the right gift. The behavior was perceived as an important means of expressing affection in spite of physical/geographical separation by 93% of the respondents who also overwhelmingly agreed (72%) that it was important to them that the recipient liked the gift.

Initially, these results appear somewhat puzzling as they tend not to support what has been conventionally accepted as Chinese cultural values. The implications derived from the analysis of the data are discussed in the following section.

DISCUSSION

This research had several objectives. First we wanted to know whether and which were the differences in gift giving between urban, somewhat Westernized, consumers and newly-migrated consumers from the rural areas who are expected to have had less contact with values brought in by the Western culture and its media. Second, we were interested in discovering elements of PRC consumers' gift giving behavior. As noted earlier, little is known about this phenomenon from a consumer behavior perspective.

Altogether, the behavior of rural migrants was not strikingly different from that of the urban sample. This apparent homogeneity is breached in some instances as rural husbands, as well as singles, seem less apt to buy frequent gifts for their wives or closed ones than urbanites. This is understandable as the rural migrants we interviewed may be living far away for months at a time. While some may have migrated with their families, their income is usually significant lower than hat of the settled urbanites. An interesting difference is noted as the rural migrants' gifts to supervisors are not as frequent as those from urban residents. This finding is somewhat counterintuitive as we would have expected that someone who is displaced, albeit temporarily, may find it beneficial to ingratiate him/herself with a supervisor, an expression of the Concept of GuanXi .

The PRC has had a one-child policy for decades. As a result, and in line with the cultural importance of lineage, sons are known to be more cherished than daughters are. This widely accepted observation is supported by our findings that show parents as giving gifts more often to sons than to daughters. Urban residents who have higher financial means than the migrants can afford to dote on their sons even more.

With respect to the time when gifts are given, we observe an interesting development as young PRC urbanites celebrate Western holidays, such as New Year's Eve. While this may be partially explained by the publicity the new millennium received, it is still an encroachment of Western values that has no place in traditional Chinese culture which has its own calendar. The Western calendar is widely used in the business and government circles which do not recognize the Judeo-Christian and do not support its holidays. Clearly, the more traditional rural population has not yet taken in that element of Western enculturation.

Similarly, the celebration of anniversaries is a new Western value with no history in the traditional Chinese culture. For instance, older generations are not known to celebrate wedding anniversaries or other yearly memorable events, outside of birthdays which are very important reasons for immediate family gatherings. The celebration of meeting or other anniversaries is another form of urbanites' western enculturation through gift giving.

Analysis of respondents' answers to the LOV items clearly indicates the normative aspect of the behavior, as eight out of ten consumers feel obliged to give gifts. However, the perceived obligation of gift giving is not solely normative, as the behavior brings good luck to the giver. More importantly, open displays and statements of affection are not customary within the Chinese cultural environment, as opposed to Western societies. There, such statements are now openly encouraged as means of self-esteem development (e.g., parents regularly tell their children how much they are loved to enhance the children's self-esteem). However, in the PRC, gift giving, instead of words and gestures, is used as a tangible statement of love and affection, which may explain that most Chinese feel obliged to give gifts since there are few other outlets for expression of love. In other words, giving gift provides some form of security. The perceived obligation to give gifts is matched in number and distribution across the 3 options on the "agree" side by those respondents who see themselves as being generous, and those consumers who perceive their gift giving as building closeness.

Most of the surveyed PRC consumers (90%) are involved in their gift giving, putting thought into the process of selecting a gift for a loved one. This is supported by the 71% of respondents who make effort to find the right gift. Earlier, we discussed the meaningfulness of gift giving to loved ones in the PRC as an expression of love and affection. Apparently, PRC consumers, in a large majority, take time and effort into expressing their feelings to someone for whom they care through their gift giving. Still, as gift giving is not as frequent as it may be in the West, probably due to lesser economic wealth, PRC consumers take pride (57% agreed) in their decision, considering its importance as a message that cannot be frequently expressed.

Consumers' responses to the Chinese culture-related items appear somewhat in contradiction with findings from previous research or treaties (Yau et al. 1999). Again, Yau and co-authors (1999) describe the three Concepts of Face, GuanXi and reciprocity. Our findings find no discrimination between rural migrant and urban consumers, thus supporting the homogeneity perception of Chinese people. What is interesting, though, is that a small proportion (1/3) of respondents agree, and a larger number (43%) disagree that one can gain face by offering presents to loved ones. Also, only one in five consumer agreed with the concept of Reciprocity, while three out of four agreed with the Concept of GuanXi. This is stark contradiction with what has been mentioned in the literature. A careful inspection of research findings on these issues indicate that no distinction is made between gift giving to loved ones and to relatives, friends, and acquaintances. While giving presents surely cements relationships (GuanXi), it does not necessarily improve prestige or calls for later gifts in return when dealing with loved ones. A distinction may then be necessary between the types of gifts' recipients, be they proximate or remote.

This finding blends well with perceptions of a traditional Chinese family as a very close hierarchical unit in its immediacy, associated by blood relations with relatives and by GuanXi with non immediate relatives and acquaintances. In other words, the immediate, closely-knit, family does not rest on Concepts of Reciprocity and Face for its up building. Surveyed consumers clearly differentiated in their responses between questions relating to their "loved ones" and questions related to others, such as friends, supervisors, etc.

Of equal importance is the overall finding that consumers did not respond as strongly as expected in directions supporting the uniqueness of Chinese culture. This may be attributed to two factors that merit further investigation: the enculturation through acquisition of Western values of PRC citizens and the recently proposed concept that Asian values may not be so uniquely Asian after all (Wolf 1999). As the PRC has opened its doors to foreign investments and marketing of foreign brands and products, its citizens take in, at different paces, certain Western values (e.g., holidays), social behaviors (e.g., disco dancing), consumer behaviors (e.g., fried chicken, hamburgers) that alter the previously, outwardly monolithic Chinese culture. This research has identified such changes as when young urbanites purchase presents for anniversaries or for the calendar New Year.

Wolf (1999)[3] discusses Asian values and reports on his own findings, comparing Asian and Western values. He offers that "values cherished by Asia's various peoples, nations and cultures are very diverse and much of what is valued highly in Asia is markedly similar to what is highly valued in the West." He further reports on a survey conducted in six Asian capitals, including Beijing, four Western European countries and in the United States on nine attributes, including two attributes of relevance to this study: family relationships and having good relationships with others. Only two significant differences were identified: Asians "place somewhat greater importance on family relationships, while Westerners accord somewhat greater importance to leisure activity." Also, he noted that Asians " varied more widely among themselves in the importance assigned to good relations with "others," as distinct from relatives [...] than did Westerners. Wolf (1999) then concludes that "Asian values are decidedly more similar to Western values than is presumably assumed."

In summary, this research is important as it is, to our knowledge, the first investigation of gift giving behavior in the PRC. It identifies the importance of specific aspects and motivations for offering presents. Contrary to what was expected from introspection and casual observation, rural migrants did not differ significantly, in general, from the more sophisticated urbanites. This study also contributes to a better understanding of the age-long debate on Asian values. Yau et al.'s (1999) indication of the fundamental importance of the Concepts of Face, GuanXi and Reciprocity was not observed to such extent in our research. Particularly, it may be worthwhile to note how the three Concepts vary in their application between relatives and non relatives, a phenomenon that seems corroborated by Wolf's (1999) findings. Finally, along with Wolf (1999), we observe that PRC consumers' (gift giving) behavior may not be all that different from that of Western consumers, adding weight to the concept that consumers, throughout the world have similar needs, and that it is how those needs are satisfied that may differ across cultures.

Still, the area of gift giving in the PRC is important as it is a medium to express love and affection, two feelings for which publicly display is not culturally acceptable. Our findings are limited by the PRC consumers' attitude toward surveying. Consumer enquiries are novel phenomena in the PRC's urban centers and may be even more alien to rural migrants. Also, for historical and cultural reasons, PRC citizens have a known reluctance to answer any form of inquiries, and prefer not to participate in such public statements of opinion, albeit related to consumer issues.

REFERENCES

Beatty, Sharon. E., Lynn R. Kahle, Pamela Homer, Misra (1985), "Alternative Measurement Approaches to Consumer Values: The List of Values and the Rokeach Value Survey," *Psychology & Marketing*, 2 (3), 181-200.

Beatty, Sharon. E., Lynn R. Kahle and Pamela Homer (1991), " Personal values and Gift-giving Behaviors: A Study Across Cultures," *Journal Of Business Research*, 22: 149-157.

Belk, Russell W. (1976), "It's the Thought that Counts: A Signed Digraph Analysis of Gift-Giving," *Journal of Consumer Research*, 3 (3), 155-162.

_____ (1979), "Gift-Giving Behavior," *in Research in Marketing*, ed. Jadish N. Sheth, Greenwich, CT: JAI Press, 95-126.

_____ (1984), "Cultural and Historical Difference in Concepts of Self and Their Effects on Attitudes Toward Having and Giving," *Advances in Consumer Research,* Vol. 11, 753-760.

_____ and Gregory S. Coon (1991), "Can't Buy Me Love: Dating, Money and Gift," *Advances in Consumer Research*, Vol. 18 ed. Rebecca H. Holman and Michael S. Solomon, Provo, UT: Association for Consumer Research, 521-527.

_____ and Gregory S. Coon (1993), "Gift Giving as Agapic Love: An Alternative to the Exchange Paradigm Based on Dating Experiences," *Journal of Consumer Research*, 20 (December), 393-417.

Caplow, T. (1982), "Christmas Gifts and Kin Networks," *American Sociological Review*, 47 (June), 383-392.

Cheal, David. (1988), *The Gift Economy*, London and New York: Routledge.

Ching, Julia. (1977), *Confucianism and Christianity : A Comparative Study*. Tokyo ; New York : Kodansha International.

Ching, Julia. (1992), *Discovering China : European interpretations in the Enlightenment* / edited by Julia Ching and Willard G. Oxtoby. Rochester, N.Y., USA : University of Rochester Press.

Dentsu Institute for Human Studies (1999), *"Beyond the Crisis: Asia's Challenge for Recovery"*.

Euromonitor 1999

Fischer, Eileen. and Stephen J. Arnold (1990), "More than a Labor of Love: Gender Roles and Christmas Gift Shopping," *Journal of Consumer Research*, 17: 333-345.

Hill, Constance and Celia T. Romm (1996), "The Role of Mothers as Gift Givers: A Comparison Across Three Cultures," *Advances in Consumer Research*, 23, 21-27.

Hoyer, Wayne D. and Deborah J. MacInnis (1997), *Consumer Behavior*, Houghton Mifflin Co, Boston, MA, USA.

Garner, Thesia I. and Janet Wagner (1991), "Economic Dimension of House Gift Giving," *Journal of Consumer Research*, 18 (December), 368-379.

---

[3] Charles Wolf Jr. is a senior economic advisor at Rand and a research fellow at the Hoover institution, Stanford University. The academic/scientific version of his findings was not available at the time of writing of this research. Comments about Wolf's (1999) findings and quotes are from a newspaper article recently published in Singapore's Strait Times (11.11.99).

Goodwin, Cathy, Kelly L. Smith and Susan Spiggle (1990), "Gift-giving: Consumer Motivation and the Gift Purchase Process. In M. E. Goldberg, et al. (eds.) *Advances in Consumer Research*, Vol. 18, Provo, UT: *Association for Consumer Research*, 690-698.

Gouldner, A. (1960), "The norm of reciprocity: A preliminary statement," *American sociological Review*, 25, pp. 1976-1977.

Kahle, Lynn R., Sharon E. Beatty, and Pamela Homer (1986), Alternative Measurement Approaches to Consumer Values: The List of Values (LOV) and Values and Life Style (VALS). *Journal of Consumer Research*, 13:405-409.

Kipnis, A. R. (1997), *Producing Guanxi*, Durham: Duke University Press.

Landry, John. T., "Emerging Markets: Are Chinese Consumers Coming of Age?" *Harvard Business Review*; Boston; May/ Jun 1998.

Lebra, T. S. (1976), *Japanese Patterns of Behavior*, Honolulu: University of Hawaii Press.

Lee, W., and David K. Tse (1994), "Becoming Canadian: Understanding How Hong Kong Immigrants Change Their Consumption", *Pacific Affairs*, 67(1), 70-96.

Leung, J.P. (1991), "Smoking Cessation by Auricular Acupuncture and Behavioral Therapy", *Psychologia*, 34, 177-187

Levi-Straus, Claude (1965), The Principle of Reciprocity, in *Sociological Theory*. L.A. Coser and B. Rosenberg, eds., Macmillan, New York.

Mainowski, B. (1959), *Crime and Custom in Savage Society*, Paterson, N. J.: Littlefield.

Mauss, Marcel (1954), *The Gift*, London: Cohen & West.

McGrath, Mary Ann (1989), "An Ethnography of a Gift Store: Wrappings, Trappings, and Rapture." *Journal of Retailing*, 65(Winter), 421-441.

Mick, David Glen, and Michelle DeMoss (1990), "Self-Gift: Phenomenological Insight From Four Contexts", *Journal of Consumer Research*, 17 (December), 322-332.

Otnes, Cele, Tina M. Lowrey and Young Chan Kim (1993), "Gift Selection for 'Easy' and 'Difficult' Recipients: A Social Roles Interpretation," *Journal of Consumer Research*, 20 (September), 229-244.

Park, S.Y. (1998), " A Comparison of Korean and American Gift-giving Behaviors," *Psychology & Marketing*, 15: 577-593.

Ruth, Julia A., Cele C. Otnes, and Frederic F. Brunel (1999), "Gift Receipt and the Reformulation of Interpersonal Relationships," *Journal of Consumer Research*, 25:385-402.

Schieffelin, Edward (1980), "Reciprocity and the Construction of Reality," *Man*, 15(3), 502-517.

Schwartz, Barry (1967), "The Social Psychology of the Gift," *American Journal of Sociology*, 73 (July), 1-11.

Sherry, John. F. (1983), "Gift-giving in an Anthropological Perspective," *Journal of Consume Research*, 10: 157-168.

Sherry, John. F. and Mary Ann. McGrath (1989), "Unpacking the Holiday Presence: A Comparative Ethnography of Two Gift Stores," in *Interpretive Consumer Research*, ed. Elizabeth C. Hirschman, Provo, UT: Association for Consumer Research, 148-167.

Sherry, John. F., Mary Ann McGrath, and Sidney J. Levy (1993), "The Dark Side of the Gift," *Journal of Business Research*, 28 (November), 225-244.

Shurmer, Pamela (1971), "The Gift Game, New society," 18 (482), 1242-1244.

Sun, L.J. (1990), *The Deep Structure of the Chinese Culture* (revised edition) [in Chinese], Taipei: Tong Shan Publishing Company.

The Strait Times. (2000), "*Chinese Culture is Dead*", May 14, 2000.

Tse, David. (1996), *The Handbook of Chinese Psychology*, edited by Michael Bond, Hong Kong ; New York : Oxford University Press.

Vietnam Culture & Tourism (1995), Nguyen Tu (Ed.) Vietnam Exhibition – Fair Center.

Wolf, Charles. JR., "Asian Values Markedly Similar to Those of the West," *The Strait Times*, Nov 11, 1999

Yang, K. S. (1993), "Can traditional and modern values coexist?" [in Chinese]. In K. S. Yang (Ed.), *Chines Value: A Social Science Viewpoint* (pp. 65-120). Taipei: Kwai Kuan.

Yau, Oliver. H. M. (1988), "The Chinese Cultural Values: Its Dimensions and Marketing Implications," *European Journal of Marketing*, 22(5), 44-57.

Yau, Oliver. H. M. (1994*), Consumer Behavior in China: Customer satisfaction and Cultural Values*, Routledge, London & New York, 68-93.

Yau, Oliver. H. M.; T. S. Chan and K. F. Lau (1999), " Influence of Chinese Cultural Values on Consumer Behavior: A Proposed Model of Gift-purchasing Behavior in Hong Kong," *Journal of International Consumer marketing*, 11: 97-116.

Zheng, D.L. (1992), *The Hong Kong Miracle: Economic Success as A Cultural Motivation*[in Chinese], Hong Kong: Commercial Press.

Gift-Giving as a Metaphor for Understanding New Products that Delight

Jeffrey F. Durgee, Rensselaer Polytechnic Institute
Trina Sego, Rensselaer at Hartford

ABSTRACT

This paper explores skills and knowledge that providers use to produce offerings (products and services) which delight consumers. Gift-giving within intimate relationships is used as a metaphor to understand producer-consumer relationships. Ten couples were interviewed about their gift-giving and gift-receiving experiences. Results suggest that givers find novel combinations of valued gift attributes and select gifts that reflect life orientations of receivers. Successful givers also know how to look for gifts that reflect valued products meanings to receivers. Implications for understanding delightful new product designs are discussed.

INTRODUCTION

Academic researchers (Kumar and Olshavsky 1997; Oliver, Rust and Varki 1997; Williams and Anderson 1999) and marketers of new products and services (Coyne 1989) are looking at the concept of "delight." The researchers' goal is to understand consumer delight, while the marketers' goal is to introduce new products that go beyond basic need satisfaction. All are interested in new products that generate a special level of excitement such as the sport utility vehicle and the laptop computer.

There is not a lot of agreement, however, about what "delight" means. A recent definition by Oliver, Rust and Varki (1997) suggests that delight consists of three components: positive affect, arousal, and surprise. A standard definition from expectancy-confirmation theory suggests that delight occurs whenever perceived deliverables exceed expectations (Kumar and Olshavsky 1997). The latter definition is useful for much new product research and development, but it restricts innovation to simply moving farther and farther along known dimensions. Cars become more powerful, houses get bigger, and food portions at restaurants become more massive.

To the extent that models of satisfaction are features-based, market research efforts aimed at finding opportunities to delight consumers will be aimed at identifying key features. However, as Fournier and Mick (1999) point out, satisfaction is highly complex. Models of satisfaction—and delight—should address different ways that satisfaction might be achieved. Furthermore, such models should address how products relate to daily life and to associated meanings and feelings.

Marketers might learn how to identify opportunities for breakthrough products by exploring the exchange of delightful gifts. A delightful gift is defined here as a gift that both pleases and surprises the recipient. Whether it is called hitting a hot button or striking a responsive chord, a delightful gift, like a great new product, involves an intimate understanding of the recipient and creative anticipation of the intense reaction that a gift might generate.

In this paper, we describe results of an exploratory study in which men and women in ten couples are asked about gifts that they found delightful. By interviewing people in intimate relationships, we address provider or giver models of satisfaction which reflect the complexity of the satisfaction response as described by Fournier and Mick (1999). People in intimate relationships know each others' needs not only in terms of desired product features (e.g., "she likes fast cars"), but also in terms of the others' personalities and daily life situations (e.g., "she likes to be 'hot stuff,' always driving the 'hottest' car").

The following section summarizes research questions and examines parallels between new product development and gift-giving. Subsequent sections review the results from an exploratory study of gift-giving between men and women in ten couples and provide implications for identifying needs for new products that delight.

RESEARCH QUESTIONS

The central question driving this research is how do providers know how to surprise and please receivers? What tacit skills and knowledge of receivers do they use? To suggest some answers, we considered delightful gift-giving in intimate relationships, and explored the following questions:

1. What types of gifts generate delight? What do delightful gifts have in common?
2. What does the delight experience consist of in receiving special gifts? What role do delightful gifts play in peoples' lives?
3. What happens when a giver selects the perfect gift? Why are some people particularly adept at understanding overt and latent needs of other people, and using this understanding to select gifts that delight these people? What is the nature of their understanding of these people? How much creativity is involved? Can that creativity be understood?

Simply put, how does one person understand another so well that he or she can select a gift that delights that person? And what are the implications of gift-giving in intimate relationships for new product development?

GIFT-GIVING AND NEW PRODUCT DEVELOPMENT

Given the size of the gift industry, the lack of popular literature on gift-giving is surprising. Baldridge (1978) notes the importance of considering receiver needs and hobbies, and Nelson (1987) recommends positive gifts such as good wine for people one wants to welcome into an extended family, and neutral gifts such as items from art museums to people one does not know very well. An owner of a large gift shop (Hoffman 2000) advises gift shoppers to make the gifts as personal as possible, and to add an element of surprise. Hoffman presented an example of a man who gave his wife a music box that played music from her favorite musical, and put inside the box two tickets to the musical. She also recommends gifts that commemorate shared histories and tap special memories (e.g., anniversary gifts) and items that might become family heirlooms.

Otnes, Lowrey and Kim (1993) found that gift-hunters use a number of different strategies: 1) "sleuthing" or testing reactions to possible gift ideas; 2) "treasure hunting" in unusual places (e.g., antique shops) for things that would have special meanings to receivers; 3) "latching on" or sticking to "whatever gift made them happy last year;" and 4) "compensating" or giving an item that replaces something the receiver recently lost. Ruth, Otnes and Brunel (1999) note the importance of empathy in the giver's ability to "see inside the recipient and know just what he or she needs the most" (p 390). Fischer and Arnold (1990) argue that this quality is

Advances in Consumer Research
Volume 28, © 2001

found more often in women than in men "because [women] have greater familiarity with the tastes, wants and needs of recipients" (p.336).

Selecting successful gifts, like developing successful new products, appears to involve two steps: 1) a need or opportunity in the target is identified, and 2) the giver comes up with a creative solution to fill that need. Both steps involve insight and creativity. For example, a male respondent in this study learned that his new girlfriend was very interested in Gothic movies, Edgar Allen Poe stories, and arts of the Renaissance. He could have given her a book or a videotape on any of these subjects, but instead he gave her a set of Renaissance swords, which surprised and pleased her. The swords were a creative expression of Gothic themes and Renaissance art.

Successful gift-givers, like successful product designers, work hard to produce the right offering. In *Never Leave Well Enough Alone* (1951), designer Raymond Loewy tells other designers to constantly look out for ways to improve their designs. Similarly, respondents in this study often took extra steps to find the perfect gift. For example, it was not enough that a woman respondent gave her fiancé—who loved Mark Twain—an old set of Mark Twain books; she gave him a set of *autographed* Mark Twain books.

Marketers today are pushed to develop close "relationships with their buyers" and to "know them in depth." Could they know their buyers as well as spouses know each other? Could they please them as well as spouses please each other? General Electric (GE) tries to communicate positive concern and intentions toward consumers through advertising claiming that GE brings "good things to life." But do such companies really exercise such a level of concern?

Pollay (1987) refers to the concept of the "Acme Delivery" in which a very thoughtful gift or gesture comes suddenly out of nowhere and touches people deeply. Could manufacturers learn how to make Acme Deliveries? Could they at least get closer to the Acme philosophy? In their discussion of provider-consumer relationships in the context of services marketing, Price and Arnould (1999) describe how popular hairstylists consider not only features such as head shape when creating a new hairstyle, but also clients' personalities, anxieties and life events.

AN EXPLORATORY STUDY OF GIFT-GIVING

To explore gift-giving in close relationships, in-depth interviews were conducted with a convenience sample of ten couples. Six couples had been married for 20 years or more, and two couples had been married for ten years. One couple was engaged, and one was still dating although the relationship was very close. Each respondent was interviewed individually.

The focus of this research is on how these individuals understand each other and use this understanding to identify creative gifts that will please and surprise. Most gift research has focused on how gift-giving defines or redefines giver-receiver relationships (e.g., Fischer and Arnold 1990); however, we do not examine the relationships per se, but rather the tacit and creative skills givers might be using to delight receivers.

During the interview, each respondent was asked to think of and describe gifts that he/she had given in the last ten years to one's spouse (or fiancé or partner) that both pleased and surprised the receiver. Respondents were also asked to think of gifts that they had received from their partners that caused them to feel pleasure and surprise.

All gifts mentioned are considered in this study. Gifts were classified as "hit" gifts (to borrow a term from the game *Battleship*) if they were mentioned by givers and receivers; that is, hit gifts were ones that the giver thought the receiver would feel was a special gift, and then the receiver in fact named that gift as a special gift from the giver.

Other gifts were classified as: 1) "misses"—gifts which givers hoped would please and surprise but which did not, and 2) "accidental hits,"—gifts which recipients felt were pleasing and surprising yet were not mentioned by givers. (On the last note, this often happens in new product marketing. A new product is a big success but no one knows why!) Respondents were asked how they selected gifts and what they expected to receive. They also discussed their spouses (or partners), the duration of the relationships, shared lifestyles, and shared interests.

Previous research on gift-giving has been criticized for focusing mainly on gift-givers rather than receivers (Otnes, Lowrey and Kim 1993) and few studies focus on both. Given recent emphasis on the creation and maintenance of marketing relationships (e.g., Fournier 1998) as well as more traditional research on buyer-seller dyads in industrial marketing (Schurr and Ozanne 1985), it is surprising that so few studies consider gift-giving from the perspectives of the giver and of the receiver. Because we interviewed both givers and receivers, our approach offers a more balanced view of giver-receiver understandings and interactions.

RESULTS

Most of the married couples said they do not give surprise gifts, and two older males said they did not even like to receive gifts. At holidays and special occasions, respondents reported that they simply tell each other what they would like or give each other lists. With dual careers and pressures from home, many are too busy to invest much time in shopping for gifts. One male said he "doesn't like surprises." Also, in many cases of high pleasure and high surprise, the surprise was because the gift was expensive and the receiver "never thought he would spend that much money." Some gifts were felt to be surprises merely because they were received outside of the normal gift-giving occasions (holidays, etc.).

We found a number of successful gift-givers, people whose gifts satisfied the high-pleasure, high-surprise criteria. Respondents generally had an easy time remembering gifts they gave and those they received, and tended to focus on gifts given and received in the last three years. All gifts are listed in Table 1.

The Gifts

Respondents named 49 gifts. Approximately half were hits, 20 percent were accidental hits, and the remainder were misses. In spite of pressures from marketers to give more services (e.g., gift of a day at a health spa, Broadway show tickets), people tend to think of products (rings, books) rather than services when they think of special gifts (Table 1).

Not surprisingly, common among the hit gifts were indulgent, luxury items: limousine rides, bracelets, massages. Also among the hits mentioned are commemorative gifts such as anniversary jewelry and special birthday dinners. These gifts all represent delightful departures from daily life and everyday consumption experiences. Givers present such items as special treats to receivers—and receivers appreciate them as such. If designers of everyday functional products wanted to incorporate more "delight" attributes into their products, perhaps they should consider indulgent products.

The "accidental hits"—gifts which delighted even though givers did not expect them to delight—tended to include everyday functional items: a videocassette recorder, a color printer, a jacket, and tools. In some cases, it was possible to re-interview givers and ask them about these gifts. Givers said things like, "Oh, yes, I forgot

TABLE 1
Gifts Given By Males to Females, and by Females to Males

Couple	Male to Female	Female to Male
1	**Renaissance swords** Fushigi Yougi video (anime')*	Chinese calligraphy set Susan Cooper book set Tickets to Scarlet Pimpernell*
2	**Omega watch** **Baccarat vase** **Shearling coat**	Binoculars
3	**Engagement ring** **Indian ankle bracelet** Color printer*	**Mark Twain autographed books** **Watch**
4	**Limo for birthday dinner** Gold watch	Figurine of father-son* Golfing items "Picture of me as a baby" Clown nurse for birthday party*
5	**SLR camera** Zoom lens **Gift certificate for massage** Bracelet*	Nautica jacket* Plaque signed by Brett Favre* Black and Decker Wizard tool Business card holder
6	Flowers Bracelet Books Videocassette Recorder*	Set of drills Leather jacket
7	**Anniversary ring** **Mother's Day ring**	Woodworking tools*
8	**Curio cabinet** **30-year anniversary ring**	**Golf clubs** **Dept. 56 Christmas Village items**
9	**Dress suits** One rose in a vase*	**Limo for anniversary dinner** **Sexy nightie**
10	**Pearls** **White kitchen baskets** **Egyptian necklace**	**Cigar humidor** **Tall brandy decanter**

Gifts in **boldface** are "hits" (gifts mentioned as pleasing and surprising by both givers and receivers).
Gifts with asterisks (*) are accidental hits (mentioned as pleasing and surprising only by receivers).

about that..." and "Oh yeah, I figured he could use that." In many of these cases, it appeared that givers simply got lucky. They hit a nerve or gave something that was needed by the receiver at that moment (e.g., a color printer needed to print a dissertation, or a videocassette recorder for a new apartment). One woman said, "I was really pregnant and I was feeling terrible...My husband gave me a single rose in a vase which was the perfect thing to give me at that time."

The most misses were found in two couples, one a commuter marriage, the other experiencing the usual crush of mid-stage marriages: two careers, children, business trips, etc. It is simply harder for these couples to devote the time and attention to finding special gifts. In contrast, just like successful marketers who are very close to their customers, newlyweds, dating couples and spouses who are very close seem to come up with the most hits and accidental hits. Moreover, people in these couples often put themselves—symbolically or literally—*in* the gifts (Belk and Coon 1993). The sexy nightie presented to male 9 was worn by the woman giver. An ankle bracelet from India was given by an Indian male early in couple 3's relationship. The bracelet very likely represented the giver's immigrant identity (Mehta and Belk 1991) and the significance of his ethnicity in a relationship with a non-Indian woman.

Many of the gifts—including hits as well as accidental hits—are unique, even obscure items. While there are many books among the gifts, receivers note special titles of the most liked gifts: "Susan Cooper set" or "autographed Mark Twain set." Other unique items include a Department 56 Christmas Village Christmas set, a set of white kitchen baskets, an Egyptian necklace, a five-stone Mother's Day ring (one star for each child), a single rose in a vase, a curio cabinet, a Baccarat vase, and the aforementioned Indian ankle bracelet.

The uniqueness of these items highlights their personalness. By being unique, they have a "just for you" quality for the receivers. Receivers are able to describe the uniqueness in detail: For example, woman 4 reported that "the watch had interwoven gold and white gold threads…" Receivers feel touched that givers know them so well that they could come up with gifts which were so personal and unique (Belk 1996).

Gifts from men to women include flowers, rings, and expensive watches. Some of the gifts from women to men seem more utilitarian: tools, binoculars, and clothes. Perhaps because of this, the women were more likely to be recipients of hit gifts. Many of the wives and girlfriends, however, seemed very surprised to receive these gifts because the husbands seldom gave them. Fischer and Arnold (1990) found in their research that women are more successful gift-givers than men, where success is defined in terms of percentage of gifts not returned to the store. Our research would suggest, however, that men are better at pleasing and surprising women. However, this finding might be attributable to the poorer memories for gifts among men as well as the surprises women feel when they receive gifts.

In sum, our results support findings of earlier work by Belk (1996), and Rucker, Freitas and Kangas (1996). In these papers, the perfect gift was described as representing the following criteria: 1) there is sacrifice on the part of the giver; 2) the giver's sole wish is to please the receiver; 3) the gift is a luxury; 4) the gift is something uniquely appropriate to the receiver; 5) the receiver is surprised by the gift; and 6) the receiver is pleased by gift.

Receiver Reactions

Particularly with the hits in Table 1 (i.e., gifts intended to please and surprise that were actually experienced as such), the response by recipients is one of joy and, in many cases, disbelief. Receivers say the gifts seem "unreal" and "impossible." The man who received the autographed Mark Twain books called this "the mother of all gifts." The woman who received the shearling coat said she could hardly believe that one could ever be found it in her size, and the man who received the Scarlet Pimpernell tickets for the Broadway show said he could not believe his wife could get the tickets. To repeat a point made earlier, receivers feel that these gifts are unique or "just for me." They feel that someone knows them very well, and selected a gift for them which is "perfect."

Women receivers seemed more surprised and appreciative than men with their gifts. Many of them gave detailed, excited descriptions of the gifts. Men seemed to take longer to think of special gifts they had received, and had more trouble explaining why they were special. Are women generally easier to "delight?" To repeat an issue raised earlier, how much of the excitement is due to the gift and how much to the relationship?

How Givers Identify Special Gifts

Several strategies givers use to understand receivers have been noted in the literature:

Receiver interests

As indicated earlier, the most basic knowledge is of receiver hobbies and interests. An old gift-giving strategy is simply to find something that relates to a hobby. Woman 8 collected miniatures, so her husband surprised her with a nice cabinet for them. With collections, there are always more objects to acquire.

Bring a feeling of closure

Wherever interests can be represented as sets of items, successful givers often use this knowledge to find novel items that can bring psychological closure to that set. The idea of adding to receiver collections has already been noted. Receivers are excited when they feel, "that is the last thing I needed! Where did you find

it?" Marketers know that they can market items to the extent that they can claim, "This is the last item you need for your kitchen (or bath, or tool box, or cosmetics drawer…)" To the extent that there are product constellations or socially agreed-upon sets of items needed for certain social roles or identities (e.g., attorneys, doctors; Solomon and Assael 1987), givers can use this knowledge to find gifts which complete these sets. Man 10 knew that his wife had many of the amenities appropriate to an upper-middle class woman, except pearls, so he gave her a strand of pearls.

Receiver hints

Another tactic successful givers use is to be very attentive to receiver foreshadowing. Givers say they shop with receivers and watch their eyes as they examine items on store shelves. Receivers might even be unaware of what is happening, but givers notice moments when receivers give a little more attention to one thing over another, and signal special interests in particular items (Sherry 1983).

At the same time, the results of this study suggest several additional ways givers anticipate needs of receivers and how to delight them:

Hypothetico-deductive models

Several givers noted using simple deductive models. The man who bought his wife the white kitchen baskets (couple 10) reasoned: a) she likes to organize things; b) she recently redecorated the kitchen in black, white and green; and c) she has a closet she wants to use to store cans and bottles; therefore, d) she would like white steel mesh baskets that fit into cabinet shelves. This strategy is intriguing insofar as it can incorporate creativity and generate surprise. If the elements a, b, and c are individually liked by the receiver, but are seldom associated together, a gift which incorporates all of them could bring surprise and pleasure.

Surprise and pleasure in the reaction of the receiver of the Mark Twain books may be because the receiver would like to have a) Mark Twain's autograph; as well as b) some nice Mark Twain books. So the combination, a set of autographed Mark Twain books, was to him unbelievable. Hypothetico-deductive models might extend to product design as well. For a long time, consumers valued the power of big, clunky desktop computers, but also the lightness and portability of a small portable typewriter—hence, the delight associated with new, powerful laptops.

Core meaning

Many gifts were successful because the giver, consciously or unconsciously, understands the core meaning of a product category to the receiver, and used this knowledge to identify a purest expression of that meaning in a potential gift. Anniversary dinners could potentially represent a wide variety of possible meanings: commemoration of a marriage, return to a restaurant where a couple had their first date, sharing a special type of food. In the cases of successful dinner gifts, however, what made them successful was the special thrill or extraordinariness of the evening. This being the case, what might maximize that meaning is a ride in a limousine (couple 9).

The reaction to these gifts might be described as a shock of recognition. Receivers might be expecting an item in a given category, but are shocked when they see a personally-relevant exemplar from that category which is extreme in terms of some quality they highly value. A Mother's Day ring is a nice ring, but is special because it has five stones, each representing a child in the "yours, mine and ours" marriage (couple 7). A woman who wants to learn more about photography might expect a camera from her boyfriend, but is surprised to see that his Christmas gift to her represents the highest level of photographic knowledge and expertise: an SLR camera (couple 5).

Receiver Orientation to World

The most interesting approaches, however, involve giver insights about how the receivers orient themselves to the world, or what Fournier (1998) would refer to as life context. For example, as indicated above, woman 10 loves to organize things. She is an accountant, has a lot of energy, and loves to plan and arrange things. Any product that facilitates these tasks will be very satisfying for her. She likes calendars and telephone answering machines. The white steel baskets for organizing her kitchen cabinets were a perfect gift.

A second woman sees the world mainly in terms of her children. She has five children and constantly monitors their every move. A Mother's Day ring with five stones was the perfect gift for her (couple 7). A third woman, who received the Renaissance swords, sees the world as a source of romance and adventure (couple 1). In each case, the gift becomes an extension of the receiver's values (Belk 1988).

A few consumer products companies understand this strategy and use it to design products. General Motors (GM) knows that their upscale buyers value being higher than or "above" the world. In spite of all the negatives associated with sport utility vehicles (SUVs), consumers buy them because they like the elevated driving position. In fact, designers at the GM Design Center use the metaphor of riding a horse with an English saddle to capture the orientation of drivers of SUVs to the world around them. SUV drivers like the feeling of being above the world as well as the creaking leather seats and slow, deliberate movements of these vehicles (Lystad 2000).

SUMMARY AND DIRECTIONS FOR FUTURE RESEARCH

This research examined three types of gifts which are exchanged between couples: a) hits, gifts which the givers thought would please and surprise receivers and which receivers mentioned as having their intended effect; 2) accidental hits, gifts which receivers found pleasing and surprising, but givers did not mention; and 3) misses, gifts which givers thought would please and surprise, but which receivers did not mention. The goal of the research was to explore how successful givers understand receivers, and use this understanding to infer what makes delightful new products so successful.

Findings from the research as well as recent literature indicate that givers use a number of strategies to identify high-delight gift opportunities. Givers:

1. Consider current receiver hobbies and interests;
2. "Sleuth out" receiver hints and reactions to possible gift ideas;
3. "Compensate" or give receivers something they recently lost;
4. Give receivers something that symbolizes the self or the relationship (e.g., is hand-made, reflects shared interests);
5. Give luxury and unique gifts to emphasize specialness and personalness;
6. Give things that bring closure, for example, an item that completes a collection or project;
7. Identify previously uncombined receiver wants or values, and find a gift which combines these wants in a unique way;
8. Identify a core receiver want or value, and find a gift which is a pure expression of that want or value; or
9. Find a gift that reflects how the receiver orients himself or herself to the world in general.

All of these strategies are applicable to new product development as well as to gift-giving.

Like most research, the present study suffers from limitations. First, the sample for this exploratory study is small, as is the number of gifts. Second, respondents may have said that they liked some gifts not because of the gifts themselves but because they came from loved ones. One's attitude toward a gift is likely to be bound up with affect associated with a relationship to the gift giver. This issue has been noted in many studies of gift-giving (e.g., Ruth, Otnes and Brunel 1999; Belk and Coon 1993), and represents a limitations of the analogy between gift-giving in intimate relationships and designing new products.

A gift might also be cherished because the giver and receiver simply like the same things (Belk 1976). In the interviews conducted here, successful givers sometimes said things like "I give him things that *I* like because we both like the same things." This might suggest that one way to assess needs and wants of target segments in marketing might be to interview people in intimate relationships with target consumers

Future research might consider gift-giving strategies from parents to children, since parents presumably follow their children and their wants very carefully. Future research might also involve interviews with superstar gift-givers, individuals who are reputed among friends and colleagues to have special powers of intuition and are able to identify the most exciting gift opportunities. Sociometric methods might be used to identify such gift-givers.

REFERENCES

Baldridge, Letitia. (1978), *Amy Vanderbilt's Everyday Etiquette*, New York: Bantam Books.

Belk, Russell (1976), "It's the Thought that Counts: A Signed Digraph Analysis of Gift-giving," *Journal of Consumer Research*, 3, 155-162.

Belk, Russell (1988), "Possessions and the Extended Self," *Journal of Consumer Research*, 15, 139-168.

Belk, Russell (1996), "The Perfect Gift," In *Gift giving: A research anthology*, ed. Cele Otnes and Richard F. Beltramini, Bowling Green, OH: Bowling Green State University press, 59-84.

Belk, Russell and Gregory S. Coon (1993), "Gift Giving as Agapic Love: An Alternative to the Exchange Paradigm Based on Dating Experiences," *Journal of Consumer Research*, 20, 393-417.

Coyne, K. (1989), "Beyond Service fads—Meaningful Strategies for the Real World," *Sloan Management Review*, Summer, 69-89.

Fischer, Eileen and Stephen J. Arnold (1990), "More than a Labor of Love: Gender Roles and Christmas Gift Shopping," *Journal of Consumer Research*, 17, 333-345.

Fournier, Susan (1998), "Consumers and their Brands: Developing Relationship Theory in Consumer Research," *Journal of Consumer Research*, 24, 343-373.

Fournier, Susan and David Glen Mick (1999), "Rediscovering Satisfaction," *Journal of Marketing*, 63, 5-23.

Hoffman, S. (2000). Personal interview with store owner.

Kumar, Anand and Richard Olshavsky (1997), "Distinguishing Satisfaction from Delight: An Appraisal Approach," Paper presented at The Annual Conference of the Association for Consumer Research, Tucson, AZ, October.

Loewy, Raymond (1951), *Never Leave Well Enough Alone*, New York: Simon and Schuster.

Lystad, D. (2000), Personal interview with design engineer.

Mehta, Raj and Russell W. Belk (1991), "Artifacts, Identity, and Transition: Favorite Possessions of Indians and Indian Immigrants to the United States," *Journal of Consumer Research*, 17, 398-411.

Nelson, P. (1987), "Present and Accounted For," *Harper's Bazaar*, December, 127.

Oliver, Richard L., Roland T. Rust and Sajeev Varki (1997), "Customer Delight: Foundations, Findings, and Managerial Insight," *Journal of Retailing*, 73, 311-336.

Otnes, Cele, Tina M. Lowrey and Young Chan Kim (1993), "Gift Selection for Easy and Difficult Recipients: A Social Roles Interpretation," *Journal of Consumer Research*, 20, 229-244.

Pollay, Richard (1987), "The History of Advertising Archives: Confessions of a Professional Pac-rat," In *Advances in Consumer Research*, Vol. 14, ed. Melanie Wallendorf and Paul Anderson, Provo, UT: Association for Consumer Research, 136-139.

Price, Linda L. and Eric J. Arnould (1999), "Commercial Friendships and Service Provider-Client Relationships in Context," *Journal of Marketing*, 63, 38-56.

Rucker, Margaret, Anthony Freitas and April Kangas (1996), "The Role of Ethnic Identity in Gift Giving," In *Gift giving: A research anthology*, ed. Cele Otnes and Richard F. Beltramini, Bowling Green, OH: Bowling Green State University press, 143-162.

Ruth, Julie A., Cele C. Otnes and Frederic F. Brunel (1999), "Gift Receipt and the Reformulation of Interpersonal Relationships," *Journal of Consumer Research*, 25, 385-402.

Schurr, Paul H. and Julie L. Ozanne (1985), "Influences on Exchange Processes: Buyers' Preconceptions of a Seller's Trustworthiness and Bargaining Toughness," *Journal of Consumer Research*, 11, 939-953.

Sherry, John F. (1983), "Gift Giving in Anthropological Perspective," *Journal of Consumer Research*, 10, 157-168.

Solomon, Michael R. and Henry Assael (1987), "The Forest or the Trees: A Gestalt Approach to Symbolic Consumption," In *Semiotics: New directions in the study of signs for sale*, ed. Jean Umiker-Sebeck, Berlin: Mouton de Gruyter, 189-218..

Williams, Jacqueline A. and Helen H. Anderson (1999), "Customer Delight: The Beat of a Different Drummer," *Journal of Customer Satisfaction, Dissatisfaction and Complaining Behavior*, 12, 44-52.

Mental Accounting: Flexible Accounts, Order Effects and Incommensurable Entries

Joseph C. Nunes, University of Southern California

This session explored some of the boundaries and limitations of Mental Accounting. Mental Accounting describes the cognitive processes utilized by individual decision-makers to keep track of their assets. This involves the perception of inputs and outcomes, the categorization of funds and the timing of how accounts are balanced (Thaler 1999).

The first paper by Dilip Soman and Amar Cheema, "Malleable Mental Accounting," (MMA) challenged some of the rules of Mental Accounting by incorporating motivational reasons for people's behavior. Research in mental accounting assumes that consumers form and operate on mental accounts on the basis of a set of relatively unambiguous rules. However, the authors argued that if there is flexibility or ambiguity in accounting, consumers manipulate the accounts to *justify whatever they want to do* (either purchase or consumption decisions). More formally, their malleable mental accounting (MMA) hypothesis states: "Consumers will manipulate their mental accounts in order to justify choosing desirable options and reject undesirable ones in situations where there is flexibility." They provided evidence for the MMA hypothesis in four experiments with hypothetical and real choices. Their results and proposed theoretical framework joins the growing literature that speaks to the importance of motivation in consumer decision making. It also adds to the mental accounting literature by talking about factors that influence the formation and interpretation of mental accounts. MMA also explains the simultaneous self-control and temptation in the presence of commitment devices like spending categories.

The second paper by Haipeng (Allan) Chen Akshay R. Rao, "Close Encounters of Two Kinds," challenged certain predictions from Mental Accounting and Prospect Theory regarding the evaluation of neutral outcomes, based on the order of outcomes. According to prospect theory's value function, a loss always looms larger than a gain. Following this principle, the combined utility of a loss and an equivalent gain is negative if they are segregated and the utility is zero if they are integrated (Kahneman & Tversky 1979; Thaler 1985). The authors predicted, however, that the order of the two events matters: a negative event followed by an equivalent positive event makes people happier and a positive event followed by an equivalent negative event makes people less happy, compared with a zero outcome. The authors posit that this order effect is caused by an imperfect shift of the reference point after the first event occurs. In a series of studies they demonstrated this order effect for absolute and relative framing (Heath et al. 1995), for both large and small outcomes, and in monetary as well as academic and social situations (Linville and Fischer 1991). They also demonstrated in a separate study that this order effect is due to an imperfect movement of the reference point. A final study demonstrated the marketing implications.

Finally, the third paper by Joseph C. Nunes and C.W. Park, on "Non-Cash Incentives," explores how the "rules" of mental accounting apply, or don't apply, when transactions include non-monetary factors. Changes in monetary magnitude often are based not on their absolute level, but rather on their deviation from some reference level, or "frame." The pricing literature is replete with research focusing on how consumers respond to changes in price (i.e., sales), when both the reference level and change are expressed in monetary measures. Often times, however, a promotion is presented in non-monetary terms (e.g., a premium). This research demonstrated how people do not exhibit the same diminishing sensitivity to additional costs or benefits when they are accrued in a currency other than the referent currency (e.g., receive a free razor with a can of shaving cream versus receiving 20% more shaving cream free). The results suggest that it is more difficult for the individual to transform the value of benefits provided in different currencies onto the same value function. Consequently, the benefit or marginal value of a non-monetary premium may not be evaluated in relation to the same reference point as the focal product (i.e., relativistic processing); hence its value is less likely than a "sale" (e.g., $5 off a $45 item) to be diminished as an incremental gain. The results contribute to a richer understanding of how and when certain "rules" of mental accounting apply and help explain how managers might benefit from the strategic use of non-monetary promotions and free add-ons rather than "more of the same" for free.

Changing Faces in Services Relationships:
Customers' Roles During Dissatisfactory Service Encounters

Mark Ligas, Fairfield University
Robin A. Coulter, University of Connecticut

ABSTRACT

In this paper, we draw upon Erving Goffman's role-playing work and conduct narrative analyses of three women's descriptions of their deteriorating service relationships. The informants describe the nature of their long-term relationships with a hair stylist, a telecommunications company, and a physician. Our analyses focus on understanding how their roles are shaped in service relationships during which they have had some dissatisfactory experiences. Four customer roles emerge from our data: the contented customer, the helping customer, the discontented customer, and the disgusted customer. We discuss customers' anticipated (back-stage) roles prior to their service encounters and their actual (front-stage) roles enacted during the service encounters. Further, we comment on the multiple roles customers take on during the course of their encounters and the consistency between their roles and cognitions. Finally, we consider how characteristics of the services involved and the service provider interactions may impact the faces customers bring to their service encounters.

In 1985, Solomon et al. suggested that customers and service providers play specific roles in order to achieve satisfying relationships. As they point out, the interaction process is reciprocal rather than linear. Because the interactions are purposive, ritualized behavior patterns evolve that assist both the customer and the service provider in achieving their goals. In the past 15 years, services marketing has focused on understanding the relationships that develop between the customer and the service provider (Bendapudi and Berry 1997; Liljander and Strandvik 1995; Mittal and Lassar 1996; Price and Arnould 1999), what causes breaks in relationships and eventual failures (Bitner, Booms, and Tetreault 1990; Taylor 1994), and how customers react to such failures (Bolton 1998; Keaveney 1995; Roos and Strandvik 1997). While this research has provided much knowledge about the workings of service relationships, little attention has focused on achieving a better understanding of the roles that customers and service providers take on during their service relationships.

Our purpose is to again draw attention to the idea that customers take on various roles with regard to their service relationships. A focus on customers as role-playing individuals within the services context introduces the dramaturgical metaphor into the research domain (Goffman 1959, 1967; Grove and Fisk 1983). Goffman (1959) distinguishes between the front-stage, where a performance takes place, and the back-stage where the individual contemplates and prepares for the performance. Grove, Fisk, and John (2000) explicitly discuss *services as theater* and apply Goffman's terminology to both services personnel (*actors*) and customers (*audience*). With a focus on the customer in a service relationship, we suggest that the back-stage is the time prior to the service encounter when the customer determines which role he will take on during the encounter, and the front-stage, the actual service encounter, is where the customer engages in a particular role, and possibly changes roles.

In this paper, we draw upon Goffman's work and conduct exploratory narrative analyses of three women's descriptions of their deteriorating service relationships. The informants describe the nature of their long-term relationships with a hair stylist, a telecommunications company, and a physician. Our analyses

focus on understanding how their roles are shaped in service relationships during which they have had some dissatisfactory experiences. Our specific intent is to understand customers' roles and how they change during the course of service relationships, with a focus on examining how negative encounters might cause customers to take on different roles in order to create more satisfying, or balanced relationships.

We present our research as follows. First, we consider Goffman's theories on role-playing and incorporate them into the services context. Next, we present the results obtained from data with each of our three informants, and we discuss our results in terms of how customers' roles emerge and change over the course of their relationships. In the concluding section, we identify the shortcomings of this work and suggest ideas for future work.

ROLE PLAYING IN SERVICES RELATIONSHIPS

In order to study customer roles, specifically as they occur when customers deal with dissatisfactory service experiences, we draw upon the works of Erving Goffman (1959, 1967). We ground our work in a theory of role-playing, and apply it to the services domain with a view of the service customer as a role-playing individual (Grove and Fisk 1983; Grove, Fisk, and John 2000; Solomon et al. 1985).

Goffman's Theories on Role-Playing

Goffman's theoretical perspective couches human action in a theatrical context. Interaction occurring between two or more parties encompasses ritualized and scripted behavior, where the expectation exists that each party member, i.e., character, will act out a specific response or scripted role performance. The individual, i.e., the actor, usually carries out this scripted performance with the intention of achieving a specific goal (Schank and Abelson 1977). In order to understand these performances (and the motivations that create them), Goffman identifies two areas where action takes place. The *front-stage* is where the actual performance takes place, and the *back-stage* is where the individual contemplates his performance and prepares to perform again. While role performances may be scripted back-stage, once action commences, the players, based on the interaction on the front-stage, may change roles.

Scripted role performances involve *rules of conduct* that the actors follow (Goffman 1967). Even if one party engages in actions that are not scripted, the other party may show respect or *deference* (Goffman 1967). Goffman comments on two acts of deference, *avoidance rituals* and *presentation rituals*. The former pertains to the actor feeling inadequate and as a result leaving the performance without warning, whereas the latter involves the actor behaving in a ritualistic and socially acceptable way.

Role-Playing in Services Contexts

Applying these ideas to the customer-service provider relationship setting, the back-stage represents the customer's interests and efforts to develop and maintain a working relationship with the service provider *prior* to actual interaction with that service provider (e.g., taking guidance from the service provider, being supportive of the service provider's acts). The front-stage encompasses the interactions between the customer and the service provider, as well as both parties' thoughts about the success or failure of the interaction. In the front-stage, the customer and service provider present specific roles that attempt to follow scripted behavior as closely as possible in order to achieve the successful delivery of the service (Solomon et al. 1985).

However, it is not always the case that the interaction with the service provider will meet the customer's *scripted* expectations (Schank and Abelson 1977; Smith and Houston 1983, 1985). If the customer's expectations are not met, he may be dissatisfied with the service provider (Bitner, Booms, and Tetreault 1990; Oliver 1997) and engage in a number of possible behaviors. Following on Goffman's perspective, the dissatisfied customer may choose to avoid the situation and leave the encounter. Alternatively, he may continue interacting without questioning the service provider, essentially being dissatisfied, but *presenting* a satisfied front.

Another possibility is that the customer changes from the scripted behavior and takes on a different role, in order to help rectify the situation. This front-stage role, i.e., his public self, may or may not reflect the customer's true thoughts and feelings, i.e., his private self (Schlenker 1980). Hence, there may be a discrepancy between one's prepared role back-stage and actual performance in the front-stage.

Clearly, the provider's level of attention, perception, and responsiveness to the interaction will directly affect the customer's satisfaction (de Ruyter and Wetzels 2000); thus others' acts in the situation directly affect the customer's response. It may be the case that the customer either wants to get along with the service provider or create a confrontation (Grove and Fisk 1997).

In the next sections, we turn to our data to explore the existence of roles in services relationships. Using Goffman's theories as "lenses" for looking at customer-service provider interactions, we perform narrative analyses on depth interviews collected from three informants. We uncover emergent roles as they take shape in the context of customers dealing with their service providers after having negative experiences.

METHODOLOGY

The scope of our research was exploratory, with the objective being to identify various roles that dissatisfied service customers might undertake when interacting with their providers. Hence, we purposively sampled via personal contacts (Fournier 1998; Mick and Buhl 1992) three women who had experienced dissatisfactory relationships with service providers within the last six months. Our informants were a 29 year old woman who was dealing with a telecommunications firm, a 52 year old woman who was dealing with a hairdresser, and a 54 year old woman who was dealing with a physician.

One researcher conducted one-on-one depth interviews (McCracken 1988; Mishler 1986) with each informant. Each interview lasted approximately one and one-half hours. Each interview began with the informant identifying the service provider and reviewing her experiences while in the service relationship. The intention of the interview was to identify and understand the informant's changing reactions as the interaction with the service provider occurred around a particular event, i.e., a negative service experience. Therefore, the interviews were relatively unstructured, allowing the informants to freely discuss their own interpretations of and reactions to the relationships (Thompson, Locander, and Pollio 1989). The informants' *thick descriptions* of their encounters yielded rich data about their changing roles as the encounters progressed (Geertz 1973).

We adopted a narrative analysis approach to examine the data and structure our findings (Stern 1995; Stern, Thompson, and Arnould 1998; Wallendorf and Arnould 1991). This approach

enabled us to focus on the consumer's perspective, to realize her view of the consumption experience, and to identify her changing relationship with the service provider and the reasons for it (Stern, Thompson, and Arnould 1998). Analysis of the data occurred in two stages, with both researchers engaged in reading and interpreting the texts and coming to consensus about the data. First, each interview was read a number of times to gain a perspective of that particular woman's changing thoughts and behaviors as she dealt with the service provider. Our intention was to understand each woman's story, entirely from her perspective (Riessman 1993; Stern 1995; Thompson 1997). Once this was accomplished, we took a more holistic perspective by looking for commonalties among all three informants.

EMERGENT CUSTOMER ROLES

Based on narratives offered by three informants who experienced some dissatisfaction with their service relationships, four front-stage customer roles emerge. They are: *the contented customer, the helpful customer, the discontented customer*, and the *disgusted customer*. The contented customer, regardless of level of satisfaction with the provider and the relationship, presents a "happy, content face" during encounters that indicates satisfaction to the service provider. Our data suggest that the contented customer indeed may be a reflection of a very satisfied customer or it may be a façade that hides some level of dissatisfaction. In the helpful customer role, the customer attempts to assist the service provider in creating, rectifying or developing the service. The helpful customer may present a "friendly, helpful face," or a "perturbed, helpful face;" the former has a more pleasant demeanor and the latter a more agitated style. Regardless of the face, the customer communicates with the provider in an attempt to help rectify or resolve the source of her dissatisfaction. In the discontented customer role, the customer expresses her dissatisfaction to the service provider; such communication may come in the form of negative non-verbal communication (e.g., tapping one's foot, wincing), or more directly as the customer tells the provider her concerns. The discontented customer does not hold back her irritation/frustration; however, it may or may not be vocalized. The final role that emerged in these data is the disgusted customer. The disgusted customer communicates her dissatisfaction, and perhaps anger, directly to the service provider; she is very vocal and her communication may be of a threatening nature.

Next, we present three informants' "stories," making note of their thoughts and behaviors that occur both back- and front-stage, as well as their front-stage roles.

Narrative 1: Judy

Judy discussed her relationship with a long-distance telecommunications firm. She switched to this company three and a half years ago, and at that time she believed that it was the best alternative. Judy was pleased with her decision (back-stage thoughts).

> It was really nice and professional, and from time to time, they would call me and tell me about better rates…so I thought they had a good data system because they are tracking wherever I am calling. And whenever it is a Canadian call, they call me and tell me there is a better plan…So I would switch plans and always save money, and my bills were going down and down and down…

This level of superior service delivery lasted for a few years, until one month when Judy realized that her bills were going up. She started to investigate her bill more closely (back-stage action) and became irritated (back-stage thoughts) when she realized that she was being charged random rates. Judy suppressed her irritation, however, and instead took on the role of a *helpful customer* who wanted to rectify the problem. She contacted a customer service representative to make the problem known and to seek assistance (front-stage action).

> So I call them and they were very professional. And I said, 'Listen, there is something wrong.' They said, 'Yes, your rates seem to be fluctuating.' I was mad because I did not know how long it had been going on...I don't keep the bills once they are paid...They said 'No problem.' They apologized profusely and said they would credit my account on next month's bill.

When the next bill came, Judy was credited for the previous month's errors, but she was charged random rates again. She became angrier, but still hoped that the problem could be resolved (back-stage thoughts). In her next interaction with the service provider, Judy assumed the role of a *discontented customer*, expressing her irritation by threatening to discontinue the relationship (front-stage actions).

> I called and said, 'The bill's wrong again'...I said, 'Listen, this happens next month, I'm switching'...It is time out of my day, I have to calculate my bill and this is ridiculous. So they said, 'We are sorry, it won't happen again.' The same thing they said last time, although this guy seemed to take it more seriously.

The next month saw the same problem, and Judy was angry. She immediately called the company and conveyed her intentions to terminate the relationship (front-stage action). She took on the role of a *disgusted customer*; she took control and gave the service provider an ultimatum.

> The customer service representative comes back on the line and says, 'I can't find the supervisor.' I know this is crap, and I said, 'Ok, somebody has 24 hours to call me about this. Someone in management, or else I am switching.' 'Oh, don't do that.' I said, 'No, no, you have 24 hours or I'm switching.' I gave them 24 hours. I mean I am very vindictive when I want to be, and I called exactly 24 hours later and switched...and I got a call from the manager four days later, and they were wondering why I had switched!

In Judy's narrative, we are able to identify four different roles that she takes on when dealing with her service provider. First, Judy who at the outset of the relationships is extremely happy with the level of professionalism she was experiencing with her service provider, presents a *contented customer* role. When something goes wrong, Judy becomes the *helpful customer* in order to try to rectify the negative experience. Unfortunately, when the outcome is not as she expects, Judy's irritation becomes much more noticeable as she takes on the role of a *discontented customer*. And finally, when she can no longer tolerate the repeated mistakes by the service provider, Judy becomes a *disgusted customer* who "calls the shots" in the relationship.

Narrative 2: Sarah
Sarah discussed her relationship with her hairdresser, Gail. She was a client of Gail's for five years. During their acquaintance, Gail moved to a new salon. Sarah was so happy with Gail's work that she followed her. She made appointments with Gail to

coincide with her regular shopping trips. Thus, she was not only pleased with Gail's work but also with the convenience of her service (back-stage thoughts). Sarah was a *contented customer*.

> I decided that I would just go to MaryAnn's studio, and my first appointment was with Gail. It was just by chance that I liked her and the way she cut my hair...She was a very nice person...And she was there for about a year and then she told me that she was moving to a shop out near the airport which also happens to be near Walmart, and that was when I became a once-a-month Walmart shopper.

After approximately four years, Sarah became disenchanted with how Gail was cutting her hair (back-stage thoughts).

> I could not see the back, and so I didn't realize that she was sort of building a shelf there. And every-now-and-then, I would look at the back, and I would think, 'I wish it would come down.'

Sarah took on the *helpful customer* role by trying to describe to Gail how she wanted her hair to look (front-stage actions). She even thought about bringing in pictures to illustrate to Gail how the cut should look (back-stage thoughts).

> I tried to communicate with her about [how I wanted my hair cut], but it didn't seem to work. It was like I couldn't explain. Maybe if I had found a picture or something...

After several more dissatisfying encounters with Gail, Sarah decided not to keep her next appointment (avoidance ritual).

> I called Gail and left a message...I created a white lie. Instead of saying, 'I don't want to come, I don't want to have you cut my hair anymore,' I decided that I would call her and tell her that I was canceling my appointment because I had stayed in Virginia longer than I had planned, and I had gotten my hair cut down there. She knew that every-now-and-then I just had to have it cut...

Realizing that she could not be helpful, Sarah became a *discontented customer* and did not show up for her rescheduled appointment (discontent led to cancellation of the performance).

> I don't know when I rescheduled, but it was one that I simply just did not go to...part of it was my difficulty coping with what I was going to do about extricating myself and still having a nice ending.

Sarah found another hairdresser, Lisa (back-stage actions); however, even though she liked the cut, Sarah was not happy with Lisa's in-home shop (back-stage thoughts). As a consequence, Sarah contacted Gail again, and asked her to copy Lisa's cut. Because Gail was unable to do so, Sarah decided to find another hairstylist. Sarah, taking on the role of the *contented customer* in a letter, attempted to explain to Gail her reasons for seeking another hairstylist.

> ...Within the next couple of weeks I wrote her a note and told her how much I had always enjoyed seeing her and that I had just decided to do something different. I just wanted a change and I thought I would be back, and I had always enjoyed her very much.

Sarah's narrative exhibits the uncertainty that many customers face when trying to extricate themselves from a relationship. It is clear that for several years, Sarah was a *contented customer*; she enjoyed her relationship with Gail, from both a personal and a business perspective. When Sarah became dissatisfied with the service, she took on the *helpful customer* role. Unfortunately, she was unable to effectively communicate a solution to her dissatisfaction to Gail. As a result, Sarah became a *discontented customer* who carries out an avoidance ritual and cancels the performance rather than making her anger and irritation known during the performance. Sarah then rethinks her actions toward Gail and reverts back to a *contented customer* role, sending her a letter thanking her for her service and friendship.

Narrative 3: Rhonda

Rhonda's narrative focused around her dealings with her physician of seven years. Her primary criteria for choosing the doctor included his being competent and having access to a particular hospital (back-stage thoughts). In terms of the doctor's access, Rhonda was pleased.

> I really wanted to find a physician fairly close by who had privileges at Rockville, because I…had gone to Rockville and had received wonderful care.

Additionally, Rhonda was satisfied with his competence and pleased with the relationship. She stated that, "He was very competent" (front- and back-stage thoughts). Unfortunately, when it came to being personable with patients, this physician was unable to live up to Rhonda's expectations (front-stage thoughts).

> …It is very important that the staff be friendly and concerned and understanding and helpful…The doctor himself is very competent, but we never clicked on a personal level. I mean…you would like to feel some kind of connection, and I thought he was always pleasant, but…

Although Rhonda was somewhat unsettled having to deal with a physician who was not personable, she continued to portray a *contented customer* during the service encounters (front-stage actions). At times, Rhonda thought about how the relationship almost seemed more personal when the physician thought that she might have some major medical problem (front-stage thoughts).

> There was one instance where I really had a problem and it was almost like he was delighted. I know it sounds terrible, but I realized that there was a mindset that…that I would really like to have something wrong!

Regardless of her continued nagging desire for a more compassionate relationship, Rhonda appreciated his competence and the fact that the physician knew her well enough to make prescriptions over the phone. As a consequence, during her appointments, she never communicated her dissatisfaction with his style, and always presented a very *contented* face.

Throughout the relationship with her physician, Rhonda portrayed a *contented customer* during their service encounters. Regardless of the extent to which she wanted a more personal doctor-patient relationship, she did not communicate her need to her physician. Instead, Rhonda focused on other aspects of the relationship that continued to please her and maintained her *contented customer* role, even when she was dissatisfied.

CHANGING FACES IN SERVICE ENCOUNTERS

Based on our narrative analyses, we have identified four roles that customers might take on during encounters with their service providers, specifically in the context of somewhat dissatisfying relationships. We now examine: 1) some of the motivations that might give rise to the customers' roles, 2) the various roles in our informants' relationships, 3) the consistency between informants' public selves (i.e., their role presentation) and their private selves (thoughts about the provider and the relationship), and 4) the nature of the service and its implications for taking on specific roles.

Our data suggest that customers may take on particular roles depending on their goals for the service relationship. For example, Judy's goal early in her relationship with the telecommunications provider was to maintain a good relationship. She began in the *contented customer* role, but when her goal changed to rectify some billing errors, she evolved into the *helping customer* and the *discontented customer*. When Judy continued to encounter billing problems, she turned into *the disgusted customer*; her goal being to get the problem resolved once and for all or to move on to another provider. Similarly, Sarah's initial goal for her relationship was to maintain a good relationship with her hairstylist. As she experienced some dissatisfaction with her haircuts, her goal changed to better communicating her haircut needs to Gail; thus, she (like Judy) changed roles to the *helping customer*. When Gail was unable to give Sarah the cut she wanted, Sarah took on the *discontented customer* role, canceling and not showing up for appointments. As Sarah terminated her relationship with Gail, her goal was to maintain a personal friendship, and the possibility of using her services at some later date. Thus, Sarah took on the *contented customer* role and sent a letter to Gail indicating that she was going to try another hairstylist because she needed a change in her life.

Both Judy and Sarah changed roles in an attempt to resolve their service-related problems. For Judy, each changing role signifies less tolerance for the service provider's acts and a need to exert her beliefs about the experience. Sarah comes across as less direct and aggressive; though she is dissatisfied, her emotional and behavioral reactions are more in line with a complacent personality, one who does not like to "rock the boat" unless absolutely necessary.

Rhonda offers yet another perspective on customers' roles. She maintained the *contented customer* role throughout her less than satisfying relationship with her physician. Although Rhonda would have liked to feel a more personal connection with the physician, she was motivated to keep the relationship because she valued the fact that he was competent, more personal during serious illnesses, and practiced at a hospital that she preferred. Further, it might be Rhonda's personality not to be aggressive in general, or in the presence of someone who is providing good care. Neither Sarah nor Rhonda was completely honest with her feelings and thoughts, but instead both presented happy faces to disguise their discontent (Hochschild 1983).

Because our data are stories about our informants' evolving relationships with their providers, we are able to follow the progression of their roles over time. Indeed, Judy's roles proceeded from the very positive, *contented customer* role to the very negative *disgusted customer*. In contrast, Sarah changed from being a *contented customer* to a *helping customer* to a *discontented customer* and back to a *contented customer*, and Rhonda portrayed a *contented customer* throughout. Thus, at least in somewhat dissatisfying relationships, it appears that both customer motivation and personality are more likely to drive the role performances than customers following some linear progression from a happy camper to a disgruntled, exiting consumer.

Additionally, our data show that a customer's thoughts and behaviors may or may not be consistent with the role that she enacts. In Judy's case, her ever-increasing irritation and anger consistently matched her front-stage roles. In each role, she was less accommodating of the service provider and more direct about what she needed from the company to stay as a customer. In contrast, Sarah's and Rhonda's thoughts and actions were at times quite inconsistent; in other words there was a disconnect between their public and private selves. Although Sarah exited her relationship with her hairstylist because she was unhappy with the cut, her letter made it sound as if she was just looking for a change, rather than expressing her discontent. And, although Rhonda continued to be unhappy with the impersonal nature of her relationship with her doctor, she continued to be pleasant around him. The data generated from both Sarah's and Rhonda's narratives indicate the discrepancy between one's thoughts and outward behaviors and feelings. Thus, it may not always be the case that one's motives (which are often put into action through scripted behavior) exclusively drive how one reacts in service situations; individual personality may also account for the changing face of the customer, especially in dissatisfactory situations.

Our data suggest that the type of service might influence the development and enactment of roles. Both Sarah and Rhonda talk about highly relational services (i.e., hairstylist and physician), relationships where the customer is likely to develop a personal attachment to the service provider (Bendapudi and Berry 1997; Mittal and Lassar 1996). In contrast, Judy discusses her interactions with the long-distance firm, and her conversations with a different customer service representative every time she calls the company. Recall that only Judy took on the role of the *disgusted customer*. One might speculate that because she dealt with a different customer representative about her problems, someone who she did not really "know," it was easier for her to take on a more openly irritated, *discontented customer* role or a threatening and controlling *disgusted customer* role. Additionally, our informants may have had differing levels of concern about their ability to find satisfactory alternative service providers given the services in question. For example, Judy believed that she could get better service going to another telecommunications firm. In contrast, in the more personal services (hairstylist and physician), Sarah and Rhonda seemed somewhat more apprehensive about their ability to find another, more satisfactory provider. Thus, in an attempt to not completely sever their relationships, they chose not to take on the *disgusted customer* role.

CONCLUSIONS AND FUTURE RESEARCH

The objective of this exploratory research was to examine customers in dissatisfactory service relationships and attempt to understand their roles, and how those roles might change as a consequence of negative service encounters. Because the consumption of a service is a process that is both created and maintained by the customer and the service provider (Shostack 1977), a clear understanding of how successful services thrive can come about only when research can understand the specific roles that each party undertakes. By applying role theory (Goffman 1959, 1967; Grove and Fisk 1983; Solomon et al. 1985) to the services domain, we explore how roles arise and change in service situations. Clearly, the impression management literature contributes to the perspective that customers don't always behave in manners consistent with their thoughts and feelings.

Our investigation relied on the retrospective accounts of three women and their dissatisfactory service relationships. We con-

ducted narrative analyses to help identify customer roles in these circumstances. Future research might help to address some of the limitations of this investigation. First, further research targeted to understand customer roles might employ a larger sample and multiple methods to more closely examine the effects of particular types of negative encounters (e.g., service encounter failures or core service failures) on customers' roles. Additionally, our informants were women; further study might examine the similarities and differences among men and women and the roles they take. Clearly, an area ripe for research is that of better linking customer goals and the roles they play. Also, our focus centered on roles that arise as customers attempt to deal with and remedy dissatisfactory service experiences; future work might consider roles undertaken in satisfactory service relationships. Finally, our study focused solely on customer roles. Understanding service providers' roles and the consistency between the roles they play, which one might argue have more defined rules of conduct, and their thoughts and feelings would be of great interest in developing a more comprehensive look at role-playing in the services context.

REFERENCES

Bendapudi, Neeli and Leonard L. Berry (1997), "Customers' Motivations for Maintaining Relationships With Service Providers," *Journal of Retailing,* 73 (1), 15-37.

Bitner, Mary Jo, Bernard H. Booms, and Mary Stanfield Tetreault (1990), "The Service Encounter: Diagnosing Favorable and Unfavorable Incidents," *Journal of Marketing,* 54 (January), 71-84.

Bolton, Ruth N. (1998), "A Dynamic Model of the Duration of the Customer's Relationship with a Continuous Service Provider: The Role of Satisfaction," *Marketing Science,* 17 (1), 45-65.

de Ruyter, Ko and Martin G. M. Wetzels (2000), "The Impact of Perceived Listening Behavior in Voice-to-Voice Service Encounters," *Journal of Service Research,* 2 (3), 276-284.

Firat, A. Fuat (1994), "Gender and Consumption: Transcending the Feminine?," in *Gender Issues and Consumer Behavior,* J. A. Costa (ed.), Thousand Oaks, CA: Sage Publications, 205-228.

Fournier, Susan (1998), "Consumers and Their Brands: Developing Relationship Theory in Consumer Research," *Journal of Consumer Research,* 24 (March), 343-373.

Geertz, Clifford (1973), *The Interpretation of Cultures*, New York: Basic Books.

Goffman, Erving (1959), *The Presentation of Self in Everyday Life*, New York: Doubleday.

Goffman, Erving (1967), *Interaction Rituals: Essays on Face-to-Face Behavior*, New York: Pantheon Books.

Grove, Stephen J. and Raymond P. Fisk (1983), "The Dramaturgy of Services Exchange: An Analytical Framework for Services Marketing," in *Emerging Perspectives on Services Marketing,* L. L. Berry, G. L. Shostack, and G. D. Upah (eds.), Chicago, IL: American Marketing Association, 45-49.

Grove, Stephen J. and Raymond P. Fisk (1997), "The Impact of Other Customers on Service Experiences: A Critical Incident Examination of "Getting Along," *Journal of Retailing,* 73 (1), 63-85.

Grove, Stephen J., Raymond P. Fisk, and Joby John (2000), "Services as Theater: Guidelines and Implications," in *Handbook of Services Marketing and Management*, T. A. Swartz and D. Iacobucci (eds.), Thousand Oaks, CA: Sage Publications, Inc., 21-35.

Hochschild, Arlie Russell (1983), *The Managed Heart*, University of California Press.

Keaveney, Susan M. (1995), "Customer Switching Behavior in Service Industries: An Exploratory Study," *Journal of Marketing,* 59 (April), 71-82.

Liljander, Veronica and Tore Strandvik (1995), "The Nature of Customer Relationships in Services," in *Advances in Services Marketing and Management,* Vol. 4, T. A. Swartz, D. E. Bowen, and S. W. Brown (eds.), Greenwich, CT: JAI Press, 141-167.

McCracken, Grant (1988), *The Long Interview,* Newbury Park, CA: Wadsworth.

Mick, David Glen and Claus Buhl (1992), "A Meaning-Based Model of Advertising Experiences," *Journal of Consumer Research,* 19 (December), 317-338.

Mishler, Elliot G. (1986), *Research Interviewing: Context and Narrative,* Cambridge, MA: Harvard University Press.

Mittal, Banwari and Walfried M. Lassar (1996), "The Role of Personalization in Service Encounters," *Journal of Retailing,* 72 (1), 95-109.

Oliver, Richard L. (1997), *Satisfaction: A Behavioral Perspective of the Consumer,* New York: McGraw-Hill Companies, Inc.

Price, Linda L. and Eric J. Arnould (1999), "Commercial Friendships: Service Provider-Client Relationships in Context," *Journal of Marketing,* 63 (4), 38-56.

Riessman, Catherine K. (1993), *Narrative Analysis,* Newbury Park, CA: Sage Publications.

Roos, Inger and Tore Strandvik (1997), "Diagnosing the Termination of Customer Relationships," Relationship Marketing Conference, Dublin, Ireland: American Marketing Association, 617-631.

Schank, Roger C. and Robert P. Abelson (1977), *Scripts, Plans, Goals, and Understanding: An Inquiry into Human Knowledge Structures,* Hillsdale, NJ: Lawrence Erlbaum Associates.

Schlenker, Barry R. (1980), *Impression Management: The Self-Concept, Social Identity and Interpersonal Relations,* Monterey, CA: Brooks/Cole.

Shostack, G. Lynn (1977), "Breaking Free from Product Marketing," *Journal of Marketing,* 41 (April), 73-80.

Smith, Ruth A and Michael J. Houston (1983), "Script-Based Evaluations of Satisfaction with Services," in *Emerging Perspectives on Services Marketing,* L. L. Berry, G. L. Shostack, and G. D. Upah (eds.), Chicago, IL: American Marketing Association, 59-62.

Smith, Ruth Ann and Michael J. Houston (1985), "A Psychometric Assessment of Measures of Scripts in Consumer Memory," *Journal of Consumer Research,* 12 (September), 214-224).

Solomon, Michael R., Carol Surprenant, John A. Czepiel, and Evelyn G. Gutman (1985), "A Role Theory Perspective on Dyadic Interactions: The Service Encounter," *Journal of Marketing,* 49 (Winter), 99-111.

Stern, Barbara B. (1995), "Consumer Myths: Frye's Taxonomy and the Structural Analysis of Consumption Text," *Journal of Consumer Research,* 22 (September), 165-185.

Stern, Barbara B., Craig J. Thompson, and Eric J. Arnould (1998), "Narrative Analysis of a Marketing Relationship: The Consumer's Perspective," *Psychology and Marketing,* 15 (3), 195-214.

Surprenant, Carol F. and Michael R. Solomon (1987), "Predictability and Personalization in the Service Encounter," *Journal of Marketing,* 51 (April), 86-96.

Taylor, Shirley (1994), "Waiting for Service: The Relationship Between Delays and Evaluations of Service," *Journal of Marketing,* 58 (April), 56-69.

Thompson, Craig (1997), "Interpreting Consumers: A Hermeneutical Framework for Deriving Marketing Insights from the Texts of Consumers' Consumption Stories," *Journal of Marketing Research,* 34 (November), 438-455.

Thompson, Craig J., William B. Locander, and Howard R. Pollio (1989). "Putting Consumer Experience Back into Consumer Research: The Philosophy and Method of Existential-Phenomenology," *Journal of Consumer Research,* 16 (September), 133-147.

Wallendorf, Melanie and Eric J. Arnould (1991), "We Gather Together': The Consumption Rituals of Thanksgiving Day," *Journal of Consumer Research,* 19 (June) 13-31.

Stick Around . . . You Won't Regret it: An Exploration of Future Regret Avoidance on the Service Retention Decision

Katherine N. Lemon, Boston College
Tiffany Barnett White, University of Illinois
Russell Winer, University of California at Berkeley

ABSTRACT

The trend in marketing towards building relationships with customers continues to grow and marketers have become increasingly interested in *retaining* customers over the long-term. Not surprisingly, many practical and theoretical models of customer retention have explored satisfaction as a key determinant in customers' decisions to keep or drop (i.e., discontinue) a given product or service relationship (Bolton 1998, Boulding et al. 1999, Rust et al. 1999). Indeed, satisfaction measures have accounted for up to 40% of the variance in models of customer retention (Reichheld 1996).

Though robust, we argue that the findings regarding the role of customer satisfaction, traditionally conceptualized as a mental integration of customers' expected and experienced (i.e., *past and current*) level of utility from a given product or service experience, can be augmented by incorporating *future* utility considerations as well. Specifically, we advance the notion that, when deciding whether or not to continue a service relationship, consumers not only consider current and past evaluations of the firm's performance (e.g., overall satisfaction, service quality or perceived quality), they also incorporate *future* considerations regarding the service. Accordingly, we examine one anticipated future state–the anticipation of future regret–and demonstrate the impact of this factor, over and above satisfaction, on consumers' keep/drop decisions.

In this paper, we review literature that motivates the inclusion of future considerations into models predicting consumers' keep/drop decision. Drawing from the consumer decision-making literature, we explore the impact of the mental simulation of future outcomes on consumers' decisions to remain-in versus end service relationships. Next, we discuss the proposed effects of anticipated regret, on consumers' decisions to keep or drop a given service. Particular emphasis is placed on the manner in which the anticipation of regret moderates the impact of satisfaction on this decision. In addition, we conceptually distinguish the decision to continue or discontinue an on-going service relationship from the decision to re-purchase (or re-visit) a given service or establishment (i.e., from a more transaction-based service), highlighting the differential impact of anticipated regret on these disparate service types.

The results of this study show support for the predicted influence of anticipated regret on the consumer's keep/drop decision. When asked *merely to consider* the regret they might experience from dropping (or discontinuing) a given service in error, consumers appeared to be more likely to continue consuming (or re-patronizing) the service–even when current levels of satisfaction are relatively low.

The results also show that the effects of priming anticipated regret seem stronger for those consumers in on-going relative to transaction-based services. Those consumers in on-going services, those in which dropping the service required a deviation from the status quo, were even more hesitant to drop the service relationship than those who were deciding whether to re-purchase or re-use the more transaction-based service. These results provide compelling preliminary support for the conceptual distinction drawn between the two service types.

Taken together, the findings support our assertion that consumers are forward-looking with respect to the decision to remain in versus leave service relationships. In addition to speculating about a given firm's past and current level of performance, we show that consumers also take into account their own future-oriented behaviors and outcomes. In this research we focus on the extent to which consumers may be motivated to reduce the possibility that they experience regret in the future as a result of continuing or discontinuing a given service in "error." Understanding that customers take future considerations into account when making decisions about the firm should influence customer acquisition and retention strategies, and all elements of the marketing mix.

REREFENCES

Bolton, R. (1998), "A Dynamic Model of the Duration of the Customer's Relationship with a Continuous Service Provider: The Role of Satisfaction," *Marketing Science*, 17 (1), 45-65.

Boulding, B., A. Kalra and R. Staelin (1999), "The Quality Double Whammy," *Marketing Science*, 18 (4), 463-484.

Reichheld, Frederick (1996), *Loyalty Effect: The Hidden Force Behind Growth, Profits and Lasting Value*, The Harvard Business School Press: Cambridge, MA.

Rust, Roland, J. Jeffrey Inman, Jianmin Jia and Anthony Zahorik (1999), "What You Don't Know About Customer-perceived Quality: The Role of Customer Expectation Distributions," *Marketing Science*, 18(1), 77-92.

How Should One be Told to Hold?

France Leclerc, University of Chicago

ABSTRACT

Please hold, all our agents are presently busy helping other customers! Every one of us has had to listen to this or a similar message while trying to get through to airlines, phone-ordering companies or utilities. In fact, it is common to hear such messages more than once in a single phone call since often the same message is repeated at regular intervals while the caller is waiting for the service provider to answer.

Presumably, one of the objectives of the service provider for using such tactics is to affect how people experience the waiting time. Not surprisingly, the amount of time spent waiting for a service appears to be negatively correlated with customer satisfaction (Clemmer and Schneider 1989). Since reducing waiting time is not always possible (or profitable), managers may opt to rely on tactics that can affect subjective waiting time. As suggested by Maister (1985), if customers are kept busy, the wait should feel shorter. This view would suggest that the more messages heard during the waiting period, the shorter the wait will feel.

Theories of time perception suggest that whether this assumption holds is a function of whether consumers are indeed trying to evaluate the waiting time while they hold. More generally, it has been proposed that when people are told ahead of time to evaluate the length of a time period (prospective judgment), more "events" occurring during this period make the period seem shorter. On the other hand, when people are asked about the length of the time period only after having experienced it (retrospective judgments), the more events, the longer the time period appears. Said differently, when under a prospective mode, consumers seem to process according to an attentional model. The attentional model holds that judged duration is a direct function of the amount of attention paid to the passage of time. The less attention spent focusing on waiting because of distractions the shorter the wait will feel. On the other hand, under a retrospective mode, since there is no memory trace of time, the judgments have to be reconstructed and duration estimations are based on encoded information available in memory. At the time the duration is judged, the person retrieves stimulus information and estimates duration based on the amount of information that was retrieved. Therefore, when a time interval is filled with more events, more information, more complex information, or when the interval is more segmented or altered in any other way that would increase the amount of information available in memory, the perceived duration is greater.

Predictions derived from these theories were tested in a laboratory study. Subjects were asked to evaluate a new "phone-ordering" system that was entirely computerized (no human interaction). They were told that they would have to order a good using the new system and would be asked afterwards to evaluate their interaction with the system on a number of dimensions. After having dialed the service, subjects were put on hold for 4 minutes. The temporal paradigm (i.e., whether or not they were explicitly told to attend to the wait per se) was manipulated as well as the messages the subjects heard while waiting. At the end of the wait, subjects were asked how long they had waited.

The pattern of results obtained supports the predictions fully, but only for the female subjects. An additional condition was added to this experiment to contrast the two underlying models (attentional and memory) by independently manipulating the number of messages and the amount of time devoted to messages. In the prospective condition, the amount of time spent listening to the messages affected female subjects' evaluation of how long the wait was whereas the number of messages did not. As expected, this pattern of results supports the attentional model. In the retrospective condition, however, female subjects' evaluation of the time waited was affected by the number of messages listened to, but not by the amount of time spent listening to them, supporting the memory model, as predicted.

This research suggests that the tactic of keeping someone busy while waiting will not necessarily lead to consumers remembering the waiting period as shorter. Clearly, a number of other factors have to be considered. This research highlights the challenge of defining optimal managerial practices in this domain.

Consumption Ecology: The Role of Time & Space in the Adoption, Integration and Consumption of Technology Products in Everyday Life

Susan M. Lloyd, University of Illinois, Urbana-Champaign

ABSTRACT

This pilot study explores the adoption and consumption of technology products as two complementary parts of a single, ongoing process. Semi-structured, phenomenological interviews are used to develop an ecology metaphor that explains the complexity of consumer-technology product relationships. The metaphor is comprised of four key components–selective impacts, spatial behaviors, dynamic variability, and stability/resilience–and provides a base for theory development. Implications and future research directions are discussed.

INTRODUCTION

Touch-tone telephone. Cordless telephone. Cellular phone. Videophone. Email. Pager. Answering machine. All of these products represent technologies that allow us to communicate with other persons. Virtually all of us own at least one of these products–and some of us own most (or even all) of them.

Technological products increasingly pervade our lives and shape our interactions with others. In fact, as the example above suggests, technology provides us with myriad choices of how we perform various functions, such as communicating with others. Originally, personal visits and written notes were the only ways of communicating with others. In the mid-18th century, the telegraph provided a new means of communicating urgent information. In the 1880s, the telephone was invented, and eventually served as the first purely mechanical means of communication readily available to the masses. Gradually, the telephone moved into the home, becoming a personal communications device. And more recently, we have experienced an explosion of personal communications technologies, including cordless phones (for mobile communications), cellular phones (for transportable communications), pagers (for immediate notification of attempts to communicate), answering machines and email (for leaving messages), and videophones (for audio-visual communications).

Such a group of products forms a "technology cluster." More formally, a technology cluster is defined as a group of products that use different technologies to satisfy a core (or basic) consumer need. Thus, a technology cluster is broader than a product class, but more specific than a product family. For purposes of this paper, "technology" is defined as the processes, mechanisms, or other components of a device that allow it to function. Products may be arrayed on a technology continuum ranging from "low-tech" (i.e., non-electronic products that are perceived by consumers to operate via mechanical action) to "high-tech" (i.e., electronic products that are perceived by consumers to "think" for themselves by use of embedded knowledge, generally in the form of a programmed computer chip).

When a new product is introduced into a technology cluster, these products sometimes *replace* existing products, which are now obsolete. For example, touch-tone telephones replaced rotary dial telephones. In other cases, however, new products *supplement* existing products, such that the overarching function (e.g., "interpersonal communications") is sub-divided into more refined "micro functions." For example, the introduction of the cordless phone in the 1980s was associated with a new micro-function, "mobile communications," that in turn, filled an emerging consumer need. This suggests that the introduction of new products into a technology cluster can lead to greater complexity in both the adoption and

consumption processes resulting in ongoing decisions about how new products will be used and how they will be integrated with existing products.

The complexity of adoption has been explored to some extent (e.g., Hirschman 1987; Oropesa 1993), as has consumption (e.g., Holt 1995; Holbrook, Chestnut, Oliva, and Greenleaf 1984), although most of the latter tends to focus on satisfaction (e.g., Oliver 1992) rather than on the actual *process* of consumption, per se. The purpose of this pilot study is to explore the post-adoption consumption process of products in a technology cluster. Such an approach will help highlight the evolutionary nature of consumer-technology product relationships. The study focuses on high-technology products because they tend to be complex and fairly expensive, thus making them more salient for consumers. Based on semi-structured, phenomenological interviews, a metaphor that explains the complexity of consumer-technology product relationships will be developed and supported. This metaphor can serve as a first step in developing a theory of post-adoption consumer-technology product relationships as they evolve over time.

THEORETICAL BACKGROUND

Traditionally, the marketing literature separates the processes of product purchase (including new product adoption) and product use (or consumption) into two distinct research streams. More recent research is beginning to cross-cut these two domains, implicitly *and* explicitly. For example, using a longitudinal approach Mick and Fournier (1998) explore the paradoxes inherent in high-tech consumer products and the coping strategies used during adoption and consumption. While these authors examine consumer interactions with *individual* high-tech products, the current research will explore consumer interactions with products in a technology cluster.

At an aggregate level, two models (or typologies) of the relationship between consumers and individual products already exist. Both models–the product life cycle and Roger's (1995) adopter categorization–are generally depicted as continuous, normally distributed curves and focus on a single product. Together, they suggest that the stages through which the product progresses from the time it is first introduced to the market until the time it is "retired" (and therefore, no longer available for purchase) temporally correspond to consumer groups organized on the basis of innovativeness–the "degree to which individuals ... [are] relatively earlier in adopting new ideas than other members of a social system" (Rogers 1995). Thus, when a product is in the "introductory" stage of the life cycle, people classified as "innovators" will be the first consumers to purchase the product.

Three specific points can be made about the product life cycle (PLC). First, while it is readily acknowledged that the PLC does not always follow a normal distribution (see Figure 1, A-D), the *key determinant* of these alternate shapes is the characteristics of the *product*, rather than the characteristics of the *consumer* (Berkowitz, Kerin, Hartley, and Rudelius, 1997). For example, a "high-learning product" has a life cycle with a long introductory period because these products (e.g., personal computers) are complex and require a lengthy period of customer education prior to purchase (Berkowitz et al, 1997).

Second, PLC curves represent product sales. However, these sales may be to a first-time buyer or to a repeat buyer. Moreover,

Advances in Consumer Research
Volume 28, © 2001

FIGURE 1
Alternative Product Life Cycles

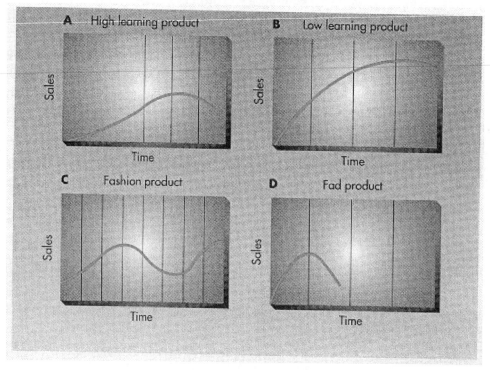

Source: Berkowitz, Eric N., Roger A. Kerin, Steven W. Hartley, and William Rudelius (1997), *Marketing*, Boston: MA: Irwin McGraw-Hill. Reproduced with permission.

underlying these sales are various motivations and consumption processes. The point is this: although the PLC *implicitly* integrates consumers and products, it does not *explicitly* explore the consumption activities that instigate or follow the purchase transaction.

Third, while some of the alternative PLC curves (notably that for fashion products) indicate that purchases may be cyclical, it is important to remember that these curves are *aggregate* in nature and focus on a single product. Thus, they demonstrate *overall market trends* related to 35mm cameras, for example, suggesting what all–or most–consumers are doing at a given time, but reflect neither the puchase motivations nor the consumption patterns of *individual consumers*.

In a similar manner, the adoptor categorization curve also presents aggregate information at the sacrifice of understanding and acknowledging the purchase motivations and consumption behaviors of individual consumers. This curve implies rigidity; i.e., once a product is adopted by a consumer, it remains adopted and can not be "dis-adopted" or adapted. Moreover, the curve implies that a successful new product is *eventually* adopted by all consumers–it is "just a matter of time." Finally, the curve, because it is focused on a single product, leaves little room for understanding if and how the adoption of new products is integrated with the consumption of existing products in a technology cluster, or alternatively, whether it represents a "one-time" purchase that is later dis-adopted or resisted. The point is this: while the product life cycle and the adopter categorization models provide useful, overall frameworks, they do not adequately address the ongoing post-adoption decisions that characterize consumer-product relationships.

METHOD

Overview

To *understand* the dynamic relationship between consumers and technology products from the time of adoption through consumption, integration, and re-purchase, a semi-structured phenomenological inquiry was conducted. This approach is particularly suitable because "phenomenological research is the study of lived experience … [it] aims at gaining a deeper understanding of the nature or meaning of our everyday experiences. [It] asks, 'What is this or that kind of experience like?'" (Van Manen, 1990). Depth interviews regarding technology purchases and consumption experiences were conducted with three respondents.

Interviewee Selection and Profiles

Three consumers were interviewed for this pilot study. Two interviews approximately 60-90 minutes in length were conducted with each during the period November 1998 to January 1999. In keeping with the pilot nature of the study, a convenience sample was used. In addition, an effort was made to select a set of interviewees who were fairly diverse in terms of age, occupation, gender, and household composition. These variables were selected because they reflect inherent differences in technology comfort, familiarity, and usage. Brief profiles of the respondents are provided in Table 1.

It should be noted that the interviewees are fairly similar in terms of educational background and orientation–all of them have advanced degrees in business. This is important because educa-

TABLE 1
Brief Profiles of the Interviewees

Name & Basic Demographics	Additional Information
"Dick" Late 40's Married, no children MBA, MS (Pol. Sci.)	• Self employed as a marketing and strategy consultant. Has had an eclectic work history with positions in government, public relations, theater marketing, theater management, cable TV programming, and market research • Has lived in Alaska, Michigan, California, Illinois, Connecticut, NY, and London, England
"Jane" Late 30's Married 3 children aged 8-15 MBA	• Currently works part-time coordinating the activities of teaching assistants in the business administration department of a large university. Previously worked as a loan officer for a bank in a large Mid-Western city. • Has interspersed full- and part-time employment with child rearing. • Admitted that she sometimes has difficulty learning new technologies.
"Sally" Early 30's Single, 1 child age 9 MS (Finance)	• Currently enrolled as a business student at a large Mid-Western University. • Little professional work experience; formerly a customer service representative. • Moved to the Mid-West from Texas; raised in Southern California. • Describes her parents as "former 1960's hippies."

tional attainment and social status are two of the most important characteristics of early adopters of new products and technologies (Midgley 1987, Im, Bayus, and Mason 1998).

Interview Method and Materials

The semi-structured interview protocol was organized around four sets of household products, representing communications technologies, kitchen technologies, entertainment technologies, and computing technologies. Each set contained 5-6 products that can be used for the same basic function. These sets–or technology clusters–were developed prior to conducting the interviews. Although this type of structure conflicts with the general tenets of phenomenological inquiry, this modification was made for two reasons: (1) the time constraints inherent in a pilot study and (2) the newness of the "technology cluster" construct. However, in the spirit of phenomenology, the interviewer did not explicitly label the technology clusters when presenting them to interviewees; in addition, she solicited ideas from them regarding how each group might be labeled and whether products should be removed from it or added to it.

At the start of the interview, respondents were asked to select two of the four groups of products: that which represents the *most* technology products they (or their household) has ever owned and that which represents the *fewest*. Starting with the "most technologies" group, the interviewee was asked to place individual cards (each imprinted with a picture of one of the products from the group) on a board set up in Table 2, indicating their *own* purchase and use.

Interviewees were given three other stacks of cards (with the same products) and asked to organize the products in terms of purchase history (earliest purchase to most recent purchase), current frequency of use (most often to least often/never), and technology perceptions (low-tech to high-tech). Using these product arrangements as a framework, the respondents were asked a series of interrelated questions about the circumstances leading to purchase, initial consumption, changes in consumption, how products were integrated with one another following the purchase of new products within the group, etc. This approach allowed a cohesive and comprehensive picture of each interviewee's experience/relationship with technology products to emerge. In addition, as relevant,

interviewees discussed the role of these products in terms of broader household dynamics; i.e., how other members of the household use the products, and in so doing, how they interact with the respondent.

Analytical Approach

Interviews were transcribed and read in their entirety. An analytic memo was developed outlining four key concepts: (1) circumstances for selecting and using technology products, (2) trade-offs made in technology purchase and consumption, (3) factors influencing consumers' technology saturation point, and (4) linkage of behaviors to perceptions and definitions of household technologies. Using these as very general categories, line-by-line coding was done for all transcripts, yielding a comprehensive coding outline. (The coded interviews and coding outline were reviewed and critiqued by four persons trained in qualitative research, but not actively engaged in the current study.) Following a re-reading of all transcripts in their entirety, the coding outline was re-organized into a coding matrix, with "major categories" listed in the columns and "sub-categories," in the rows. The major categories represent "stages" (or decision points) in the technology adoption-consumption process. The sub-categories represent consumer issues, perceptions, and experiences related to technology products that are present at one or more "stages" of the adoption-consumption process. An excerpt from the coding matrix is shown as Table 3.

Using the coding matrix as a guide, analytic memos were written for each interview transcript. Each memo highlighted and reflexively explored a relevant sub-set of key items from the coding matrix. These memos were pre-cursors to the development of a single emergent theme. This theme focused on the complexity of consumption as an ongoing intertwining between consumers and products that may be modeled as an evolutionary process characterized by stability *and* change. Elements from the individual analytical memos that helped form this emergent theme include, for example, the role of products in establishing boundaries for personal privacy, consumer-product "negotiations" and "re-negotiations," the multiple roles of time in consumer-product relationships, and the inter-generational aspects of consumer's tendencies to adopt (or resist) new technologies.

TABLE 2
Board Used by Interviewees to Organize Products in a Technology Cluster

Purchased, Use Frequently	Purchased, Use Rarely
Never Purchased, Use (frequently or rarely)	Never Purchased, Never Used

TABLE 3
Excerpt from the Coding Matrix

	Purchase	Integration	Adaptation	Use	Resistance	Controversies
Confidentiality/ Security Concerns	X	X		X		X
Control	X	X		X	X	
Direct Family Influence	X					X
Life Stage	X	X		X		
Product Characteristics/ Proliferation	X	X	X	X		X
Time		X		X	X	
ETC.	…	…	…	…	…	…

The Role and Meaning of Metaphor

As discussed above, analysis and interpretation of the data suggests that the relationship between consumers and technology products is both *complex* and *dynamic*. The relationship clearly extends beyond the actual purchase transaction and, through consumption, shifts, expands, shrinks, and re-forms as both the consumer (and his or her needs) and the product change. While we all *experience* these changes in some form, they can be difficult to describe. And that is why I chose to frame the analysis in terms of a metaphor.

According to Richardson (1990), "Metaphor is the backbone of social science writing, and like a true spine, it bears weight, permits movement, links parts together into a functional, coherent whole–and is not immediately visible." In keeping with this description, a metaphor was created from the interview data that would not only help *explain* consumer-technology product relationships, but could also serve as a useful first step in theory development. Such a theory could build upon the work of Mick and Fournier (1998) who explore consumer-product relationships for individual technologies, using a framework of paradox and coping.

Initially, a dance metaphor was considered, but discarded due to too many dissimilarities. In an effort to overcome these issues, an ecology metaphor was developed.[1]

THE ECOLOGY/ECOSYSTEM METAPHOR

Introduction to Ecology and its Link to Consumption

Ecology provides an apt metaphor for consumer-technology product relationships. Fundamentally, ecology is defined as "the scientific study of the relationship between organisms and their environment" (Smith and Smith, 1998). In fact, as originally coined by Haekel in 1866, ecology is based on the same Greek root as the word economics; thus, it may be considered "'the body of knowledge concerning the economy of nature" (Kormondy 1996). The primary unit of study in ecology is the ecosystem, defined by Tansley in 1935 as "'…the whole system, including not only the organism-complex, but also the whole complex of physical factors we call the environment" (Kormondy 1996).

Ecosystems and consumer-technology product relationships have several characteristics in common. First, both ecosystems and consumer-technology product relationships involve an *interdependence* between two entities, one animate (i.e., organisms or consumers) and one inanimate (i.e., the environment or products).[2] This interdependence occurs over both *time* and *space*, the two most

---

[1]A dance, while dynamic, fluid, and ongoing, is performed between two "like" entities (i.e., two people), whereas consumer-technology product relationships represent two "unlike" entities. In addition, many dances tend to be formally scripted (or choreographed); have clearly defined beginning and end points; and usually require that one entity lead, while the other follows. These characteristics are not clearly analogous to consumer-technology product relationships.

[2]In his article on the extended self, Belk (1988) discusses the important role of consumer-object-consumer interactions during the consumption process–a type of interdependence–in the development of the personal meaning of things.

critical dimensions in ecology and ecosystems (Capra 1996). Second, both ecosystems and consumer-technology product relationships are *interactive* (not static) and characterized by *non-linear feedback* loops and self-regulation (Capra 1996). For consumer products, such relationships have been found by Bell and Tasaki (1992) who demonstrate that the level of attachment associated with 10 common household products follows a flattened bell-shaped curve (or "consumption life cycle") from pre-acquisition through disposal. This suggests that over time, product use encourages reflexive feedback that impacts, in turn, how the consumer will perceive and use the product in the future. Third, both ecosystems and consumer-technology product relationships become more complex when *external actions* are taken into account. In ecosystems, these external (or "third-party") actions are typically initiated by humans and are distinct from naturally occurring activities. Such third-party actions can cause unexpected (and sometimes, irreversible) change in the ecosystem, facilitating the emergence of ecosystem management (Dickinson and Murphy 1997) and more recently, ecological economics (Van den Bergh and Van der Straaten 1997) to help limit/control potential disruptions caused by development.

> Throughout the long history of Man, people have altered the environment on which we all continue to depend. Generally, this alteration was undertaken in order to make the environment … a better place to live in–more productive of food, shelter, water, mineral resources, or other useful products. Such alteration is now commonly termed 'development.' (Hollings, 1978).

Similarly, companies that manufacture and sell technology products function as a "third-party" in consumer-technology product relationships. Companies are essentially research and development engines: they monitor, fill, and influence consumer needs; and then develop and modify the requisite new products. Such activities can disrupt the routines and relationships consumers have with existing products.

Properties of Ecosystem Change–A Framework for Consumer-Technology Product Relationships

Whether internally or externally driven, ecosystems (and the consumer-technology product relationship) ultimately are characterized by change. According to Hollings (1978), ecosystem change is based on four properties that relate to the critical ecological dimensions of time and space: (1) selective impact within ecosystems, (2) spatial behavior, (3) dynamic variability, and (4) "stability" and resilience. Using these properties as a framework, I will develop a tentative theory of consumer-technology product relationships.

1. Selective Interconnections & Impacts within Ecosystems (time and space dimensions)

Viewed as a whole, ecosystems form an intricately interconnected web. This can occur on a variety of levels; at the most aggregate level, the Gaia hypothesis contends that all ecological systems on earth are interlinked and self-regulating (Dickinson and Murphy 1997). However, not all interconnections are equally strong or equally important. Moreover, each species does not have the same number of links with other species or with elements of the physical environment. Thus, when viewed closely, "the parts of an ecological system are connected to each other in a *selective* way… everything is *not* strongly connected to everything else" (Holling, 1978), a fact that becomes apparent only over time. An example of this is fish in the North Sea. Certain species live in the upper layers of water and others, in the lower layers. When fish in the upper layer declined through over-fishing, those in the lower layer unexpect-

edly increased. Since the territories of the two fish were completely separate, scientists reasoned that a change in one population would not affect the other population. However, the decline of the fish that traditionally inhabited the upper layer created an opportunity for fish that can inhabit *both* layers to enter the North Sea habitat. The new species, in turn, brought more food and other resources to fish in the lower layer. These few changes were the only ones that occurred in the ecosystem. This single specific link represents a limited, localized impact that selectively affected only *part* of the total ecosystem (Holling 1978).

Turning to the family–a type of consumer ecosystem–prior research (see Rogers 1995, p. 269-279 for a summary) suggests that adult children whose socioeconomic status, occupation, and years of formal education are similar to or higher than their parents would tend to classify themselves as being similar to, or perhaps more innovative than, their parents vis-à-vis Roger's adopter categorization curve. However, the interviews from this study indicate that the relationship is much more complex, such that children are *selectively* influenced by their parent's attitudes and tendencies toward high-technology products–factors which appear to be more important than simple demographic or economic variables. These attitudes are most clearly reflected in the purchase stage of the relationship where they play a selective role in adoption decisions and subsequent behaviors.

> …My parents like to have a lot of appliances–the latest 'whatever … I'm like my mom in that I am able to sit down and figure [technological] things out, although that's not my forte … she's more experimental than I am (Jane, age 39).

> My parents were kind of early adopters of television … hi-fi systems … the VCR … and cable TV. It's a kind of recurrent pattern that they would get new, uh, gizmos, kind of early and then not really keep up with wanting the latest and greatest thing. They would just sort of get one and use it forever until it wore out. To the extent their approach to it was influential [is] the idea that not every new things that comes along you necessarily need … I think if anything I am maybe less likely to be an early adopter than they were in the sense of getting a TV or stereo system earlier than most of their peers (Dick, age 49).

> I remember my parents … we had a beta, not the laser disc, but the old disc where you *shoved* it into the machine and pulled it back out. It was the *new wave*. And it didn't last that long. So now, they're stuck with these things and nobody knows how to fix these huge discs … It was like 20 years ago. And then [after the disc], beta was 'it'. And then they came out with the VHS. So now in the garage, my parents have a videodisc player and a beta. And I guess because of all that and because of other purchases they've made … Growing up with all this stuff, I wait until something has been around … When somebody tells me this is the "new wave," I wait a little bit (Sally, age 32).

Of the three, Jane feels she is most like her parents, while Sally adamantly chooses to be the least like her parents. Thus, like the population of fish in the "lower" North Sea who are selectively impacted by time-based changes in the fish population of the "upper" North Sea, the interviewees were selectively impacted by their parents' attitudes and behaviors regarding new technology products. While the respondents have been clearly influenced by their parents, the impact is limited, rather than all-encompassing. Of particular interest is that while all three interviewees are well-educated, holding at least one Master's degree, they all admit being *less innovative* than their parents. This is a curious finding since most research on early adopters indicate that younger and more educated consumers have a greater tendency to be innovative than do older and less educated ones (Gatignon and Robertson, 1985).

2. Spatial Behavior (space dimension)

Typically, ecological impacts are gradually diluted over space and follow a bell-shaped curve. The end-points of the curve represent boundaries. For example, animals are linked with specific habitats. In the Sierra Nevada Mountains four species of chipmunk are each associated with a specific territory denoted by vegetation zone/elevation. Within each zone, the population of a specific species of chipmunk can be expected to be most dense near the center, and least dense near the "edges" (i.e., where one form of vegetation begins to give way to another (Smith and Smith 1998). Such boundaries are also present when the ecosystem is disturbed. For example, soil pollution tends to be highest at the point where the pollutants were released, and the effects diminish the farther one move (in any direction) from this place.

In some cases, however, the strength and intensity of ecological impacts may not follow a simple dilution pattern, resulting in boundaries that are less clear-cut (Holling 1978). Consider the 1994 Northridge earthquake in Southern California. The impact of this quake was felt much more strongly in Santa Monica than in Beverly Hills, although the two cities are about equidistant from the epicenter (about 15 miles). This differential impact is explained by the topography of the region whereby the tremors emanating from this hidden fault flowed more readily through the mountains separating Northridge and Santa Monica than through the flatter lands lying between Northridge and LA.

In consumer-technology product relationships, spatial behavior can be observed by how three technology products–the boombox (a large, portable radio/cassette/CD system with–usually–superior sound quality), the CD player, and the cordless phone are used and integrated into daily life. In particular, we will examine (1) how these three products impact privacy considerations as an aspect of personal space, and (2) how these spatial configurations are either orderly and conventional or more erratic and unconventional.

> Some of [the boomboxes'] use has been replaced by a portable CD player. 'Cause that's something else that's like an individual thing, except that it's even better ... because it has the headphones that don't make any noise for anybody else to deal with. (Dick)

> If I didn't want to be where the noise was downstairs, I just wanted to relax, I'd go upstairs. And I'd sit and I'd play a soft song or something. So I wanted something upstairs other than just my clock radio. So I went looking and I found a good [CD player] on sale. It was my Christmas present to myself. So that's its purpose–when I want to get away. And my daughter doesn't use [it]. It's *mine. It's in my bedroom.* If she wants, she can take the boombox to her bedroom. (Sally)

In both vignettes, music technologies allow a personal space to be created–they are used to create and reinforce boundaries that follow an orderly pattern. This is most apparent for Sally: the CD player denotes *her* territory and the boombox, *her daughter's* territory. In both examples, the technology products clearly fill an individual, rather than a group (or social) role. Dick frames his discussion of privacy in terms of how the boombox helps him to *avoid* annoying others in the household. Sally, meanwhile, discusses her use of the CD player as creating a haven, a personal space that others in the household are wary to violate. Unlike Dick, she is not concerned with annoying *others*, but is more concerned with others annoying *her*.

Jane's experience, meanwhile, illustrates a different dimension on how technology products create (or in this case, violate) personal space:

> I'm a little more aware now, too, that my conversations [on the cordless phone] can be picked up by other people. In the beginning, I don't think I ever really realized that. When I picked up my neighbor's [conversation], actually, I was walking to her house. Her husband called me because he couldn't get through on her line ... and suddenly, her conversation was superimposed on *our* conversation. It was very strange. But it did make me realize the security [risks] (Jane).

In this vignette, Jane is concerned about privacy in terms of potential security violations. She is worried that the space she assumed was personal (i.e., that between her voice and the person's ear on the other end of the phone connection) may be accessible to other unintended ears as a result of anomalies in the physical and transmission environments. Thus, in this instance, the spatial relationship between Jane and her cell phone yields irregular and uncertain boundaries, as contrasted with the more conventional and clear-cut boundaries illustrated by the music technology vignettes.

3. Dynamic Variability (time and space dimensions)

Traditionally, ecologists believed that stability was a desired– and "natural"–characteristic of ecosystems. It is now clear, however, that the spatio-temporal dimensions of ecosystems are much more complex (Pahl-Wostl 1998). In fact, scientists believe that ultimately, the survival of ecosystems is based on change, rather than on stability. Ecosystems are fluid, reacting and adapting to disturbances that may be caused by natural phenomenon (e.g., hurricanes and other storms) or by the presence and activities of Man (e.g., pollution, de-forestation). Thus, "variability, not constancy, is a feature of ecological systems that contributes to their persistence and to their self-monitoring and self-correcting capacities ... environmental quality is not achieved by eliminating [naturally occurring] change" (Holling, 1978). For example, it is now widely acknowledged that forest fires play a productive role in the renewal of certain natural spaces, serving to fertilize the area and to propagate tree species whose seed is released only at extremely high temperatures. And as a result of the destruction, some animal species temporarily leave the area, while others move in. This type of dynamic change is part of the evolutionary process, leading to an orderly succession of flora and fauna that may occur over decades or centuries.

The consumer-technology product relationship is characterized by a similar evolution. For each technology and for each consumer, the evolutionary process proceeds at a different rate. However, both entities–the consumer and the technology products– undergo change, sometimes sequentially and sometimes simultaneously. As consumer needs shift, and as products improve and change, new relationships and new opportunities emerge. Change is most evident when a "disturbance" occurs–e.g., when consumers adopt new technology products and need to integrate them into their lives or when dramatic events (births or weddings) impact established routines. Such changes often instigate a search for optimum way(s) to use the product, and can be particularly challenging for gifts that the consumer did not specifically request or anticipate.

> You know, it's like I felt that everyone has a microwave, so we needed to have one. So I took it even though [my parents] were getting rid of it probably because of the same reason I had concerns about it [– that it would take up too much counter

space]. [I used it initially] mostly to warm up hot water for tea. Or hot chocolate, or something. In the beginning, I didn't use it very much. And then I eventually used it warm up baby food a little bit. And that was about it. We use it more [now]–a lot more. Because there are more people in my family. We have a lot of dinners that need to be warmed up. Or I get dinner ready and not everybody is there, so we wait for everyone to come and then we need to throw the potatoes in the microwave and heat them up. So we definitely use it a lot more, because we're bigger and busier. (Jane)

In this vignette, Jane tells an evolutionary story of how the microwave came to play a central role in her family's life. Much of the transition from non-use to partial-use to full-use was spurred by lifestage changes, specifically, the birth of her first child and the subsequent growth of her family, which encouraged her to cook at home more often, rather than eat out. The microwave becomes especially handy when family schedules become uncoordinated.

I have a computer that's less than a year old. A PC. So [receiving a laptop for my birthday] was a complete surprise and I thought, 'this *could* work.' It was mostly a toy [at that point]. I played with it … It was only after the initial 'little kid in a candy store' reaction … and having it for awhile and actually using it that I could see 'well, it *could* have this use, too.' And so, gradually, I'm thinking of other uses that would allow it to fit into my life. But right now … I guess I'm not used to having a laptop. I see everybody in the library, and they have theirs plugged in. But I go and make my copies and then I go home and I type something up [on my desktop computer]. (Sally)

In this story, Sally, like Jane, is searching for a way to use an unexpected gift. However, the evolution is at an early stage and it is not entirely clear how the product may be integrated into her life. While she *envisions* how the technology might be used, she has not been successful in implementing any of her ideas. She readily admits that she reverts back to her "old" way of collecting data for papers, for example, suggesting that for Sally the laptop may become extinct and not, in fact, become integrated into her life at all.

4. "Stability" and Resilience (time and space dimensions)

Despite the fact that true stability does not exist in ecosystems, scientists acknowledge that ecological change does seem to move toward a natural end point or climax where the ecosystem is "capable of self-perpetuation under prevailing environmental circumstances" (Smith and Smith 1998). Such "stability" is embedded within a specific context and does not represent equilibrium since change continues to occur selectively and at a low level. For example, in "old growth" forests, new trees take root as older ones die.

When an ecosystem is impacted by a disturbance (such as those described in section 3 above), one of two things will occur: the ecosystem will move back toward its original climax point or it will shift to a new climax point. Ecosystems tend to be surprisingly resilient (i.e., able to 'bounce back" to their original climax point) (Kormondy 1996). However, the "stability" of a ecosystem is bounded by thresholds which, once breached, are difficult to re-enter, leading to dramatic and–to humans–unexpected changes in the ecosystem that effectively result in a establishment of a new climax point (Holling, 1978). For example, in the Great Lakes, the numbers of some of the fish caught for commercial purposes suddenly declined sharply after many years of slight fluctuations in size. When over-fishing was curtailed, the fish population did not revert back to its original size. Apparently, a critical threshold had

been breached, leading to an irreversible impact on the fish population and a new "stability" level (Holling, 1978).

"Natural" climax points, as well as the shifting climax points and resilience that occur as a result of disturbance can also characterize consumer-technology product relationships. Sometimes, as the following vignette illustrates, a "natural" climax point–and maximum effectiveness–is reached when new technology products are supplemented by old technology products:

Maybe ten years ago … we got a cordless phone … And we did away with all the regular phones. Then over time, I realized that when the electricity went out that I had no communication when the cordless phones weren't working. So, after about, probably about seven years or whatever, I went out and bought one with a cord, just *specifically* [for this emergency] … Secondarily, I thought it would be nice to have in case we [my husband and I] have conversations that I don't want overheard. (Jane)

An example of shifting climax points may be seen in Jane's earlier vignette (section 3) about the microwave oven. In this vignette, Jane's usage of the microwave moved from its original climax point–where it was used for heating water and baby food–to a new climax point–where it was used for a variety of heating, re-heating, and cooking tasks. This shift in climax points occurred when a "disturbance," namely, the growth of her three children and their subsequent involvement in multiple activities–moved the use of the microwave beyond the earlier threshold (heating of water and baby food).

Finally, Dick's story about outdoor grill provides an example of resilience.

The gas grill to me is an idiotic product, because the whole point of having a grill in the first place is to have that wonderful charcoal flavor when you grill something … It's not as good as what it supposedly replaces–although it is more convenient, I guess, and less messy. To me, the charcoal grill is the perfect example of appropriate technology … it's fun to use because it's so simple and so basic. When I grill sometimes, I think about the fact that thousands of years ago people were essentially doing the same thing–cooking over fire–and enjoying the same taste experiences that I'm enjoying from this food. Sot it has kind of a romantic low-tech quality. (Dick)

Faced with a disturbance–i.e., the introduction of gas grills to the marketplace–Dick considers the new technology, but moves back toward his original climax point that was established with charcoal grills. It is important to distinguish Dick's resistance of gas grills from his attitude toward technology in general. He does not actively resist all new technology products–in fact, when asked if he would adopt a grill product that is more high-tech than the gas grill, he readily agreed *as long as the distinctive charcoal flavor is preserved*.

ISSUES & QUESTIONS FOR FURTHER RESEARCH

In this pilot project, an ecological metaphor was developed to help explain consumers' relationships with technology products. The metaphor is comprised of four components–selective impacts, spatial behaviors, dynamic variability, and stability/resilience–and provides a first step for developing a full-blown theory of consumer-technology product relationships. In developing such a theory, three broad questions, stimulated by the pilot project, might be addressed.

First, *is more technology necessarily better?* An implicit assumption of the pilot study was that in society today there is a prevailing attitude (verging on "peer pressure") that owning, being aware of and/or knowing how to use new technologies is inherently "good." In the research presented above, however, this assumption is not necessarily always upheld. For example, the three respondents readily admit that they are less innovative and thus, more reticent about adopting new technology products than are their parents. Moreover, some respondents, such as Dick, actively resist new technologies he feels are inferior. To what extent do these attitudes and behaviors generalizable?

Second, *what happens to one's "sense of self" as the consumer-technology product relationship evolves?* Clearly, the technology products a person owns and uses–like most products–reflect his/her personal self–that is, the overall sense of who he/she is and the type of person he/she wishes to become (Belk 1988). In fact, this may be at the heart of the consumers' search for integrating gifts into their lives. What is not so clear, however, is how the sense of self evolves as the consumer adopts and integrates new technologies into his or her life. Dick provides a few insights through his discussion of the grill technologies and all three interviewees hint at the important role technology products play in privacy considerations.

Third, *consumer-technology product relationships appear to be re-negotiated over time. But what, precisely, does this mean?* Clearly, the pilot research shows that consumer-product relationships are not static–they change over time in predictable as well as less obvious ways. These shifts suggest that negotiation and re-negotiation occur between the consumer and the product as both evolve. These negotiations may include (but are not limited to) re-evaluating the need for a technology product, reconsidering how the product may be integrated with existing products to fit into one's life, recognizing the limitations of the product (by comparing new versions of the product to old versions or to earlier technologies), and recognizing one's "new maturity" as a technological consumer.

REFERENCES

Berkowitz, Eric N., Roger A. Kerin, Steven W. Hartley, and William Rudelius (1997), *Marketing*, Boston, MA: Irwin McGraw-Hill.

Belk, Russell W. (1988), "Possessions and the Extended Self," *Journal of Consumer Research*, 15 (September), 139-168.

Capra, Fritjof (1996), *The Web of Life*, New York: Anchor Books Doubleday.

Dickinson, Gordon and Kevin Murphy (1998), *Ecosystems: A Functional Approach*, New York: Routledge

Gatignon, Hubert and Thomas S. Robertson (1985), "A Propositional Inventory for New Diffusion Research," *Journal of Consumer Research* (March), 849–867.

Hirschman, Elizabeth C. (1987), "Adoption of an Incredibly Complex Innovation: Propositions from a Humanistic Vantage Point," in *Advances in Consumer Research*, Vol. 14, eds. Melanie Wallandorf and Paul Anderson, Provo, UT: Association for Consumer Research, 57-60.

Holling, C.S. (1978), *Adaptive Environmental Assessment and Management*, New York: John Wiley & Sons.

Holbrook, Morris B., Robert W. chestnut, Terence A. Oliva, and Eric A. Greenleaf (1984), "Play as a Consumption Experience: The Roles of Emotions, Performance, and Personality in the Enjoyment of Games," *Journal of Consumer Research*, 11 (September), 728-739.

Holt, Douglas B. (1995), "How Consumers Consume: A Typology of Consumption Practices," *Journal of Consumer Research*, 22 (June), 1-16.

Im, Subin, Barry L. Bayus, and Charlotte Mason (1998), "Personal Characteristics, Consumer Innovativeness and Innovative Behavior," Working Paper, Kenan-Flagler Business School, University of North Carolina.

Kormondy, Edward J. (1996), *Concepts of Ecology (fourth edition)*, NJ: Prentice-Hall.

Mick, David Glen and Susan Fournier (1998), "Paradoxes of Technology: Consumer Cognizance, Emotions, and Coping Strategies," *Journal of Consumer Research*, 25 (September), 123-143.

Midgley, David F. (1987), "A Meta-Analysis of the Diffusion of Innovations Literature," in *Advances in Consumer Research*, Vol. 14, eds., Melanie Wallendorf and Paul Anderson, Provo, UT: Association for Consumer Research, 204-207.

Oliver, Richard L. (1992), "An Investigation of the Attribute Basis of Emotion and Related Affect in Consumption: Suggestions for a Stage-Specific Satisfaction Framework," in *Advances in Consumer Research*, Vol. 19, eds. John F. Sherry and Brian Sternthal, Provo, UT: Association for Consumer Research, 237-244.

Oropesa, R.S. (1993), "Female Labor Force Participation and Time-saving Household Technology: A Case Study of the Microwave from 1978 to 1989," *Journal of Consumer Research* (March), 567-78

Pahl-Wostl, Claudia (1998), "Ecosystem Organization Across A Continuum of Scales: A Comparative Analysis of Lakes and Rivers," in *Ecological Scale: Theory and Applications*, eds., David L. Peterson and V. Thomas Parker, NY: Columbia University Press.

Richardson, Laurel (1990), *Writing Strategies: Reaching Diverse Audiences*, Thousand Oaks: Sage Publications.

Rogers, Everett M. (1995), *Diffusion of Innovations*, NY: The Free Press.

Smith, Robert Leo and Thomas M. Smith (1998), *Elements of Ecology (fourth edition)*, Menlo Park, CA: The Benjamin/ Cummings Publishing Co., Ltd.

Van den Bergh, Jeroen C.J.M. and Jan Van der Straaten, eds. (1997), *Economy and Ecosystems in Change: Analytical and Historical Approaches*, Cheltenham, UK: Edward Elgar Publishing, Ltd.

Van Manen, Max (1990), *Researching Lived Experience: Human Science for an Action Sensitive Pedagogy*, NY: State University of New York Press.

Do-It-Yourself Investing: Exploring the Ethos of Online Trading

Michael S. Mulvey, Rutgers University
Carl Stech, Rutgers University

ABSTRACT

The exploding phenomenon of online trading has given rise to a new model of investing. Rather than paying for the financial advice of professional stockbrokers, many investors are opting for do-it-yourself, point-and-click trading. In this paper, we examine the ethos of do-it-yourself (D-I-Y) investing through the lens of advertising. Our concern is with how advertising, through repetition of common themes, functions as a form of meta-communication that structures reality within a culture. We analyze a sample of 118 magazine ads to develop a better understanding of the appeal and popularity of D-I-Y investing. Finally, we discuss the broader implications of consumers' propensity to "do-it-themselves" rather than hiring a professional, and we detail directions for future research.

The Home of the Future: An Ethnographic Study of New Information Technologies in the Home

Alladi Venkatesh, University of California, Irvine[1]
Norman Stolzoff, King, Brown Partners
Eric Shih, Wake Forest University
Sanjoy Mazumdar, University of California, Irvine

ABSTRACT

This paper explores the "Home of the Future" from the ethnographic perspective. It conceptualizes the home as a constellation of physical, technical, and social and cultural spaces, and asks the question of how these new information technologies fit into the household. Findings from the present research suggests that there is incomplete domestication of information technologies into the household, and that emerging technologies should pay close attention to the family's requirements for everyday living.

1. INTRODUCTION

This research is based on a project whose focus is the "Home of the Future." Within the academy, industry, and government there is burgeoning interest in the "home" as a site of accelerated technological innovation (Kraut, et. al 1998). Yet, how do we make sense of these developments and what will be the impacts of the new information and technologies for the home of the future? And, what are the implications of these developments for the society and economy as a whole? To address these issues adequately requires a systemic investigation of the present use of information technologies in the home, from which we can draw insights into the future developments of home-based technologies.

Our current project examines the adoption, use, and impact of New Media and Information Technologies (ITs) in the home and how prepared these consumers are to accept "Smart Home" technologies that will be on the market in the next 3-7 years. It adopts an ethnographic methodology as a complement to previous researches that used survey and time diary techniques (e.g., Kraut et al. 1998). As part of this ethnographic study, which commenced in 1999, we recruited 50 families living in the Orange County and Los Angeles areas who have personal computers (PCs) with Internet access in their homes. Newspaper advertisements were used to recruit the families. The study extends over a period of one year and the participating families were interviewed twice during the study period at roughly six-month intervals.

The interviews consisted of one to three hour semi-structured interviews in the homes of the participating households. The interviews focused on 1) how PCs and the Internet are currently being used in the home, 2) how life in the home is being impacted by these information technologies, and 3) the attitudes and potential interest that members of the households have about "Smart Home" appliances that will be on the market in the next few years.

In addition to conducting depth interviews in the participating households, we also engaged in the anthropological method known as participant-observation in order to investigate 1) the physical placement of PCs in the living space and their relation to other ITs in the home, 2) the use patterns of the computer, and 3) how family members (especially parents and children) interact with each other

and their computers (i.e. human computer interactions). In terms of our research into the smart home in particular, we showed pictures of futuristic homes and their networked appliances to elicit responses to them. Finally, we took digital photographs of the technological environments in the home for further analysis.

2. THE ETHNOGRAPHIC METHOD

Ethnographic methods (developed primarily within the field of anthropology), based on fieldwork, participant-observation, and the comparative perspective, bring a unique took kit to the study of information technologies in the home. Ethnographic fieldwork provides a practical means of getting at the consumer's (i.e. the user's) point of view, that is, the cognitive, social, and cultural processes, that inform an individual's understanding of the role of information technology in the home. By allowing the informant to communicate their own perspective and to observe their actions in a natural setting over an extended period of time, the ethnographer is equipped to take individual, social, and cultural differences seriously and, thus, to make interpretations that account for, rather than ignore, these particularities. When combined with survey techniques, time diaries, and focus groups—as we are currently doing—ethnography serves to enhance our analysis of the quantitative data and vice-versa. In this sense, ethnography aims to bring a holistic perspective to the study of information technologies (Van Maanen 1988).

In our study ethnographic method has offered concrete advantages (and real payoffs) in the study of information technology in the home. First, it provided access to a rich dialogic context. By this we mean that unlike surveys which yield discrete kinds of information in a non-interactive fashion, the interviewer can easily ask for clarification of answers that he or she thinks needs further elaboration or clarification, and can even test tentative interpretations with the consumer in the course of the interview. Second, by visiting the residence of the consumer, we have been able to observe the home and its technological environment. This has provided a rich context for asking questions and for understanding the role of IT in the household. Third, observation (and limited participation) in the consumer's household provided us with insight on how ITs are actually being used by family members. This is especially illuminating with respect to children's use of PCs, because they are relatively willing and unselfconscious about being observed. This is an opportunity that is not attainable by any other research method. Lastly, a successful ethnographic method creates rapport and trust between the researcher and the family. This allows for the possibility of follow-up research and for deeper insight into home life.

3. THE LIVING SPACE MODEL

Our current theoretical approach to the study of the home of the future is informed by what we are calling the "Living Space Model," (Figure 1) which conceptualizes the home as a constellation of three overlapping spheres: 1) the physical/architectural space 2) the social and cultural space and, 3) the technological space. Examining the home in these terms of the interactions between these spaces allows us to ask new questions and gives us a structure

---

[1]Acknowledgement: We gratefully acknowledge the financial support received from the National Science Foundation (Project No IRI 9619695), Microsoft Corporation, Canon Information Systems, and Nortel, Canada).

FIGURE 1
Home As Living Space

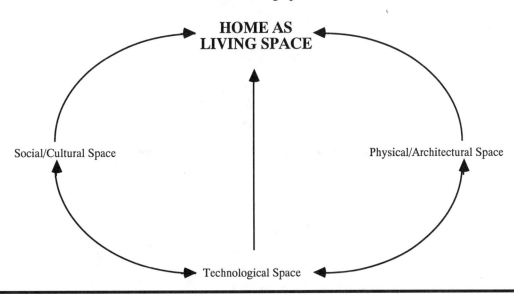

for analyzing our observations about ITs in the home (Venkatesh 1996, Venkatesh and Mazumdar 1999).

The application of our model encourages us to start off by asking: What is a "home"? That is, how has the incorporation and use of new ITs changed the implicit meanings and metaphors (i.e. the cultural concepts), the explicit physical designs and boundaries of the home, and the social and cultural dynamics associated with life in the home?

We have observed that the home is indeed a locus of several re-formulations. For example, as a result of recent IT innovations (e.g. the Internet and mobile communications), the traditional boundaries between the home as private sphere and the society as a public sphere have dramatically shifted in the following ways. First, work and domestic life are increasingly interpenetrating each other reversing a trend that Rybczynski (1987) identifies as central to the modernization of the home. In the postmodern home, people are able to work from home as well as to carry out household and personal activities from the workplace. Second, there has been a blending of home and retail shopping. E-shopping has brought the retail space into the home in an unprecedented way, and reciprocally home-based shopping has now influenced the way consumer's shop in brick and mortar retail stores (Gilly and Wolfinbarger Forthcoming, 2001). Third, the Internet homepage and mobile communications technologies have given the "home" a nomadic quality (Turkle 1995; Markham 1998). That is, home is no longer fixed in space; we can access it or be accessed wherever we happen to be. The arrival of smart home technologies that allow us to interact with the home from remote locals will only intensify this phenomenon.

Concomitant with these changes, the home has become a contact zone where the tensions associated with rapid technological change are being played out. Now that the home has become a center for both productive and family life, rooms in the house are used in increasingly the multi-functional ways, and the nature of "privacy" at home is being redefined, it is not surprising that households express a wide-range of attitudes about the desirability of these innovations from enthusiastic support to disparaging critiques. Because technological change will continue to impact the home, we anticipate that these attitudes will remain quite fluid and will thus continue to change as well.

4. THE PRELIMINARY FINDINGS

The preliminary findings are based on 25 selected households from the total study sample of 50. The analysis that follows proceeds in terms of the living space model outlined above.

4.1 Physical/Architectural Space

The home as a physical/architectural space has not undergone much in the way of infrastructural modification for new information technologies (ITs). None of the homes in our sample had been structurally altered for ITs. Additionally, the basic blue print of the suburban home in the study area is relatively stable as is evidenced by new home building which is only minimally changing its basic design for ITs. For example, we visited the Ladera Ranch, a new housing scheme under construction in Southern Orange County, which is being marketed as a "technologically revolutionary" new community. Each of the homes in the 4,000 acre development will be wired with fiber-optic cable for easy high speed access to the Internet and the community's own Intranet. Despite these cutting edge accommodations, the interior spaces of these homes were only minimally designed for intensive IT use. The photograph below (Figure 2) of a work-space nook taken from a model home in the Ladera Ranch shows a space that is poorly designed for the PC and its peripherals.

While the architectural infrastructure has remained fairly static, the internal space of the home has been modified to a greater extent. This was observed in the various ways that the internal space was accommodated to IT use through furnishings and changing use patterns of rooms. To the degree that these modifications have been successfully integrated ITs into the home, we see this as a process of "domestication" of the technological space. Our latest survey data (Venkatesh 1999) shows that home computer users are increasingly using their computers in several different living areas. They are not, however, generally spending a lot of money to equip these user stations with special furniture (desks, chairs, lighting etc). These spaces are basically "make-do" set-ups, unless the computer station is used primarily as a home office for telecommuting. On the whole, chairs and desks are not being bought specially for children's use.

The most common modification of the interior space we observed involves accommodating ITs to the existing furniture.

FIGURE 2

FIGURE 3

These consist of make-do set-ups, which often produce a cluttered and inefficient IT environment (Figure 3). We characterize these arrangements as exhibiting low domestication.

Less common is the purchasing of furniture to accommodate the introduction of new ITs into the home. These configurations allow for more flexible use of space. For example, Figure 4 shows how armoire-styled computer furniture is used in the kitchen, which gives the parents the ability to supervise their three-year-old son while doing meal preparation, while at the same time when not in use it can be closed up to fit into the overall decor of the space. Set-ups like this demonstrate a much higher degree of domestication than in the previous example.

The third, and least prevalent, modification of the interior space for ITs involves building customized furnishings. In these configurations the household users have taken an active role in domesticating the space to their needs. Figure 5 demonstrates how under severe space constraints a small bedroom was modified to double as a home office.

The previous three scenarios illustrate varying degrees of domestication of IT to the home's interior space. We believe the reasons for the incomplete domestication are as follows. Under the present condition of rapid product development many consumers are reluctant or not able to invest in special modifications (e.g. purchasing furniture) because they are unsure about their future needs. As a result, the ITs are treated something like "visitors" rather than a permanent part of the household landscape. Because PCs are frequently replaced by upgraded equipment and an ever changing array of peripherals (e.g. zip drives, digital cameras, scanners etc.) the IT ensemble is perceived as a temporary part of

the home. It is thus not treated as a permanent appliance (i.e. a fridge) or as furniture (i.e. a sofa). Money is put into upgrading hardware rather than domesticating the space to accommodate the machinery. Not surprisingly, the appearance of the PC and peripherals was of very little importance to these users. Also, as the PC moves out of the confines of the home office or den, users are unsure how to integrate it into the unfamiliar surroundings.

4.2 The Social and Cultural Space

Our analysis of the social and cultural space examines the patterns of adoption and use as well as the impacts of ITs in the home. The households in our preliminary sample were generally optimistic about their adoption of ITs in the home. The two most prominent reasons for adoption were related to work and children's education (Venkatesh and Vitalari 1992).

Pragmatism and price sensitivity characterize their technology purchasing decisions. Users of home-based computers and related technologies are savvy consumers and we found an attitude that we could call an "appropriateness ethic" with respect to adoption of new technologies. They weigh their purchases against several factors, including price, intrusiveness, whether it fills a perceived need, and the desire to stay current with the latest innovations. Overall, these users were not lead adopters. Rather they were fairly risk adverse preferring to "let the bugs shake out." Also, they show a low level of brand loyalty being more sensitive to price than make of their equipment.

In contrast to research findings from the 1980s (Venkatesh and Vitalari 1990), women and children are becoming increasingly important "change agents" (those who introduce new ITs into the

FIGURE 4

FIGURE 5

home and generally disseminate information about them) (Lindlof 1992). Women are just as likely to have knowledge of computers as men, and in of the homes we have studied they have been the adopters and teachers of computer skills at a roughly equal rate to men. Additionally, children are using their computer knowledge and skills they have acquired at school or through friends back to the home and influencing their parents IT related decisions.

The use of ITs in the home on the whole is increasing by all household members. To meet this demand families are resorting to scheduling computer time and purchasing additional machines. The advent of Internet has had a revolutionary impact on PC use making it "virtually essential to family life." While the PC is not yet as ubiquitous as the TV or as central to family life, interestingly the PC is generally seen as more positive, productive, and educational in nature (Orleans and Laney 2000).

Current uses of the PC are not only increasing, but also expanding into new areas (especially those opened up by the Internet and the World Wide Web). The PC and the Internet are on the whole seen as easy to use, fun, and creativity enhancing. A relatively high degree of frustration persists with software difficul-

ties and hardware glitches, however (Norman 1998). There is a lingering perception that PCs easily malfunction and among new users there is a fear that "pressing the wrong button" will cause the computer to be destroyed or all the data will instantly vanish. For both children and adults, playing games is a way to get familiar with the computer and to overcome any sense that it is fragile or unforgiving of any mistakes.

Enthusiasm for the Internet is very high. It is seen as a revolutionary information tool with an awesome power to access information and news. As an educational medium, parents perceive the Internet as crucial for their children's future (Lindlof 1990; Papert 1996). The convenience and cost saving attributes of Internet communications (primarily e-mail, but also home pages, user groups, instant messaging, and chatting) are also extremely popular with users. The entertainment dimensions of the Internet are not yet as critical as the above functions, but users spoke of it having a promising future.

Even though interest for the Internet is high, there are still a number of frustrations and concerns associated with its use. First among these is speed and reliability of the Internet connection.

Nearly every household expressed frustration with the slowness of their dial-in access (only one of the ten households had a cable connection). Second, users were concerned with the access to "objectionable" content, especially as it impacts young users without the ability to discern what reliable information is or who seek out pornographic or violent web sites. Third, consumers expressed worries about the security of web-based transactions, primarily those involving credit card purchases. Fourth, and this closely related to the previous case, there is strong feeling among households that Internet use is compromising their families' privacy. Fifth, a few families talked about the potential or actual problems associated with over-use, even addiction to the Internet. In this regard, most users felt that the danger of addiction generally declined once the novelty of the Internet wore off. Six, families members had concerns that the Internet could disrupt family life. Because the PC is most often not in a communal space but in a home office, den, or bedroom, users talked about how extended Internet use isolates the user from the rest of the family. A few of the families intentionally placed the PC in the living room or kitchen to avoid this problem.

At present there is only moderate interest in E-Shopping. Families anticipate a growth in their interest, especially because of its perceived convenience. The reasons for current reticence include: lack of price competitiveness, fears about credit card security, loss of ability to touch and inspect products, a resentment of the dot-com mania, and an attachment to the ritual of retail shopping (e.g. a chance for the family to spend time together on a regular basis).

The use of IT in the home affects, and is affected by, the families social structure and culture. In terms of gender roles, there is a marked difference between the general orientation of women and men (Turkle 1984). On the one hand, women have what we are calling a "tool/task orientation," which is characterized by a "I just want it to work" mentality, a lack of concern for what is "under the hood," a preference for user-friendly features (like the AOL user interface), and low interest in the style of their equipment. On the other hand, men have what we are calling an "object/pleasure orientation," which is characterized by a fascination with hardware "innards" (i.e. processor speed, memory, and the latest components), they are in their own words often "gadget freaks," see that having a powerful machine is a status symbol, and have almost no interest whatever in the style of their equipment.

When it comes to the generational differences within families, we found that children and adults are practicing different learning styles in their acquisition of computer proficiency. According to their parents, children tend to learn more intuitively than they do by "pressing buttons" in a trial-and-error fashion. Their children's facility with computers and the Internet amazes parents, and reinforces their feelings that the computer is important to children's education. In contrast, parents rely on a wider range of learning techniques (formal and informal instruction, reading manuals, and the trial-and error method) and experience a more difficult time gaining comfort with ITs. While there were no seniors in this restricted sample, respondents voiced their concerns about older users being left behind by the PC/Internet revolution.

Much of the observation time in the respective homes focused on children's use of ITs. As stated above, the educational needs of children were a primary reason for households to adopt ITs. Computers are seen as necessary for education and there was a strong feeling that homes without PCs would hinder their children's education and employment in the future. A number of families have used the metaphor of the "library" to discuss the truly awesome access to information that the World Wide Web provides. They are generally encouraged by this availability and are especially opti-mistic about the opportunities it provides their children for learning and school projects. In general, the use of the PC by young children is highly mediated by their parents (especially going on the Web), while older children and teenagers gain progressively more autonomy in their use as they get older.

Parental concern about IT use is focused on gaming, Internet content, and the potential anti-social aspects of overuse. With respect to games, parents universally expressed a preference for educational over entertainment oriented programs. They were especially worried about the violence of many games designed for boys. Lastly, they expressed mild concern that too much time on the PC might have negative implications for their child's social development and should be balanced out by a well-rounded schedule of activities.

4.3 The Technological Space

Our analysis of restricted sample does not permit a detailed report on the technological space. We can summarize our finding as follows. Overall, households have a generally positive outlook on computers and the Internet, but they have concerns and fears about some of the potentially negative consequences on their families and the society at-large. We have found a strongly developed sense of what role IT should play in their homes and the ability to reflect on the potential anti-social influences these products may have on society, especially on young children's access to inappropriate Internet content and the loss of face-to-face social skills. Users grapple with their desire for new forms of access and control versus their worries about losing traditional forms of control, such as the privacy of the home. For the most part, progress is seen as inevitable and there is thus a need to stay current with the latest IT innovations (Pfaffendberger 1992). Along with this need to keep up with latest developments is a pragmatic questioning of the necessity of every new product that reaches the market (Coyne 1995). On the whole, families are searching for balance in these times of rapid change.

With respect to children's use of PCs, we identified an area of special concern that needs to be discussed. Namely, our observations of how children and parents interact with while playing together on the computer and the Internet. From our field research it became apparent that the PC remains only partially adapted and integrated to the special needs of families and home-based users. That is, the PC has not been fully domesticated for family usability.

While many computer manufacturers share the goal of moving the PC into the mainstream of family life, the legacy of the desktop user interface (UI) has proved in many ways a difficult obstacle to surmount. One of the persistent shortcomings of the desktop UI is its single-user orientation. Even though many software products (primarily in the areas of education and gaming) support multiple users, the typical configuration of the PC in the home (i.e. the single keyboard, mouse, monitor set-up) does not optimally facilitate these interactions. And, while this problem area was not always immediately apparent to the parents during our interviews, it did become obvious to them once we pointed it out to them. In turn, they responded that the PC is really designed as a "one person at a time thing." Beyond this, we believe that it is awkward, and even dangerous (especially small children), and ultimately inefficient for multiple-user interactions (see Figure 6).

The following product scenarios seek to offer potential solutions to these problems. Once identified, we envisioned three new Family and Multi-User Interfaces which could potentially alleviate many of the above inefficiencies. The first is the Remote Access Monitor, a handheld device that gives each user their own display terminal. The second is the Split Screen Monitor, which accommodates two or more users simultaneously. And the third is the Parent-Child Tandem User Interface, which uses specially designed seating and

FIGURE 6

FIGURE 7
Remote Access Monitor

peripherals for parent and child use. We more fully elaborate these in the document that presents our new product scenarios.

4.4 Remote Access Monitor

The first of these concepts is the Remote Access Monitor (RAM), which are handheld displays linked to a central PC (Figure 7). They share the same "vision" as the main monitor, and can alleviate the uncomfortable user configurations depicted in the pictures on the previous page. Instead of being confined to the immediate area around the computer's main monitor, each user is provided with his or her own Remote Access Monitor so the activity can be viewed anywhere in the room. This RAM feature can prove to be useful in home and conference room environments where there is only one computer, but multiple users.

The RAM can also be used for security purposes. By carrying a RAM, a user can monitor his or her computer terminal when he or she is away. Another scenario involves the family. A parent can keep track of his or her kids' computer activities from afar via the RAM. If a child is web surfing and wanders into an objectionable website, the parent will know, and he or she has the option of shutting down the PC remotely.

4.5 Split Screen Monitors

The Split Screen Monitor will work like any other monitor, except the view space will be wider. The wide-screen will be especially effective when watching wide-screen format CD-Rom or DVD-Rom movies (Figure 8). The monitor splits into two halves. If a user wanted to run two applications simultaneously, he can devote one screen to each application. A ball joint behind each half connects each half-monitor to the main stock. The Split Screen Monitor enters private mode when both half-monitors are tilted back in a 45-degree angle, away from each other. Designed with dual users in mind, we realized that some people would rather work

4.6 Parent-Child Tandem Interface

This concept is developed for the parent-child computer interactions (Figure 9). Frequently, parents assist their younger children when they use the computer. Young children usually need help surfing the Web, typing, or operating applications, yet the typical seating and UI arrangement for the parent and child(ren) is often less than ideal. The parent has to straddle the child, or the child has to stand besides or behind the parent. The Tandem User Interface provides an ergonomic alternative to these scenarios. The

FIGURE 8
Split Screen Monitor

FIGURE 9
Parent-Child Tandem User Interface

Tandem User Interface is an ergonomic Tandem chair, which features a frontal segment that seats a small child. The parent and child no longer have to share the same seat cushion. When the front segment is not in use, it can be detached, or it can fold down and act as a footrest.

5. SMART HOME TECHNOLOGIES

The final section of this report examines how prepared households are to accept "Smart Home" technologies that will be on the market in the next 3-7 years. We attempted to gain insight into the attitudes and potential interest that members of the households have about the home of the future by eliciting responses from a series of photographs and illustrations of smart homes and appliances (e.g. Figure 10). The general tenor of their reactions were markedly different than our discussion of technologies now present on the market. Most of the adults' responses were inflected by an aura of detachment, humor, awe, and mild repulsion. Because the interviewees had not interacted with these technologies there was

some reluctance to offer detailed opinions. The most frequent response alluded to the Jetsons cartoon. The children who we spoke with, however, had been exposed to the idea of the home of the future through films, such as Disney's "Smart Home," and they felt that it was "cool."

Currently, adults in the households we interviewed were highly attracted to the potential overall convenience that the home of the future promises to offer. In terms of particular features of the smart home, highest interest was for the ability to monitor and remotely control the temperature/climate, lighting, and for the area of home security. There is a medium-level of interest in having the home's computers connected by a Local Area Network (LAN) and for the integration of all information and communication devices. There is low interest in the Internet refrigerator and for robotic intelligent devices.

Concerns about the impact of the smart home on families were quite extensive. Nearly every respondent expressed worries about the loss of control that these technologies might pose. They wondered

FIGURE 10
Smart Homes and Appliances

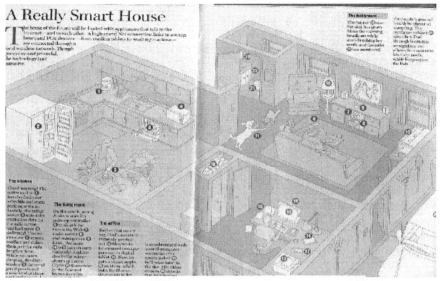

if there would be sufficient ability to manually override the smart home automation. They also talked about not wanting to be replaced by automation. In specific, they said that they fear becoming dependent of these machines and had doubts if "convenience" in every aspect of life was good for the health of families and society at-large. Expressions of their hesitancy are reflected in common refrains such as these: "What will I do with myself?", "I like challenge in my life", or "Have we gone too far?". Other areas of skepticism about the smart home related to its affordability and whether this would become an exclusively elite technology which would cause a deeper "digital divide."

The attraction and repulsion—namely, ambivalence—to the smart home is discussed in an excerpt from an interview with the following upper middle-class man in his late 40s, who is married and a father of two teenage girls:

Q: Does anything scare you about more automation in the home?

A: No. The only thing that—and I don't want to sound paranoid, but it does concern me a little bit if the information that I'm sharing on the Internet in the computer, if somebody has access to that. You know, I don't—I've a little bit of a big brother kind of a feeling. If that stuff is actually being captured someplace and kept on file. Just because I feel, you know, your own private life is your own private life. You shouldn't have to be worried about that. *It's kind of a two-edged sword* (our emphasis), I mean, you can't get there without, you know, being on there. So that worries me a little bit. It's not like I lay awake at night and think about it. It doesn't keep me from using it. But no, I don't worry about, you know, other technology and stuff like that. It's proven to be pretty dependable. We've had, you know, a lot of computers in our cars for a long time. Shoot, you don't see cars sitting on the side of the freeways because the computers went out. It's usually a flat tires, or out of gas, or like.

Or the following example, from a husband (H) and wife (W) in the their late-twenties with a nine-year-old daughter:

Q: So do you think there's a possibility that the smart home has an anti-social potentials?

H: Yes. It's surprising that I would say that. We've coped with having the net, having cable, having a lot of stereo equipment. We've found ourselves reading books and just being a very close-knit, *non-electronic family* (our emphasis). But I can see, I don't think with us, but I think if we'd all grown up with this sort of thing, it would be easy to be detached. Very electronic. But it also does look a lot more convenient.

W: I'm reading this. This is very good. The kitchen thing is great.

Q: Like they're talking like these refrigerators would have a computer screen built into the door.

W: And you could tell when the milk is expired and stuff.

Q: A complete inventory of your kitchen. Because everything would have like a zebra code and you could just read it into the door, or actually even the more advanced, the transponder you drive on the freeway. It could just read everything as you put it in.

W: It would help in shopping. There's a good and bad....

H: I still think there would be more good than bad. It should be tempered but I'm more for it. It looks great.

6. CONCLUSION

This research presents findings from ethnographic fieldwork on computer use in the home and home of the future. We found that home is a site of technological innovation and rapid change. However, despite the influx and diffusion of technologies into various activity spaces in the home, we observed that many of the technologies are incompletely integrated into the domestic life of the household. Specifically, the single-user desktop interface, and the solo nature of computers in general, are inadequate for typical family use. The current home PC configuration causes substantial frustration among users and such problems need to be resolved before further domestication can take place. Here we presented some preliminary product scenarios and concepts as a starting point for some of the needed potential design solutions.

In designing the home of the future, product developers and marketers need to pay particular attention to the concerns and requirements for everyday living in the home. Some of the ambivalence expressed by our interviewees regarding these smart home technologies may be roadblocks to their successful diffusion and integration. Future research should be sensitive to these issues and explore them in greater detail.

Summary and Conclusions

1. Concept of "home" changing quite dramatically.
   - Varying degrees of computer domestication
   - Computers are being integrated into the home but the integration is not complete.
   - Ubiquity of computers spatially.
   - Ad hoc designs of space.
2. Current Uses
   - Uses not only increasing but expanding.
   - Computers generally seen as easy to use, fun, creativity enhancing.
   - Frustration with software difficulty and hardware glitches.
3. Enthusiasm for the Internet
   - Revolutionary information/communication tool.
   - Educational medium - crucial for children.
   - Communication center - cost savings and convenience.
   - Information Center - Extremely important.
   - Entertainment center - moderately enthusiastic.
   - Shopping Center - Moderate interest.
4. Frustration about Internet
   - Speed
   - Content
   - Security
   - Privacy
   - Addiction
5. Gender Differences
   - Women (tool and task orientation).
     - "I just want to work."
     - Not concerned with what is under the hood.
     - Attracted to user friendly features.
     - Low interest in style
   - Male (object/pleasure orientation)
     - Fascination with innards (speed, power, latest components)
     - Gadget orientation
     - Status symbol
     - Not interested in style
6. Generational Differences
   - Children are learning intuitively.
   - Adults are relying on instructions (formal and informal. e.g. manuals, seeking help).
   - High degree of parental mediation.
7. Children's use
   - A primary reason to adopt
   - Necessary for education
   - Concerns about gaming
   - Knowledge not entertainment view
   - Violence/pornography
   - Addiction/anti-social impact.
8. Class issues
   - Working class families receiving computers as gifts
   - Computers have an aura of precious commodity.
   - Limited working knowledge
   - See IT as means for children's mobility.
9. Impacts
   - Access to new forms of control vs. loss of old.
   - Progress seen as inevitable.
   - Need to stay current.
   - Pragmatic questioning.
   - Searching for balance.
10. Smart Home
    - High interest in remote monitoring of temperature, lighting and security.
    - Medium interest in LAN.
    - Low interest in smart appliances (e.g. Screen Fridge)
    - Concern that smart homes may mean loss of control.
    - Is manual override possible?
    - Are we going too far with the idea of automation?"
    - Attraction-Repulsion syndrome.

REFERENCES

Coyne, R. (1995), *Designing Information Technology in the Postmodern Age: From Method to Metaphor*, Cambridge, MA: MIT Press.

Escobar, A. (1994), Welcome to Cyberia: Notes on the Anthropology of Cyberculture," *Current Anthropology*, 35(3), 211-231.

Gilly, M. and Wolfinbarger, M. (Forthcoming, 2001), A Comparison of Consumer Experiences With Online and Offline Shopping, *Consumption, Markets and Culture*, Volume 4, No. 2.

Kraut, R., . Mukhopadhyay, J. Szczypula, S. Kiesler, B. Scherlis (1998), "Communication and Information: Alternative uses of the Internet in the Households," *Conference Proceedings on Human Factors in Computing Systems*, 368-375.

Lindlof, T. R. (1990), "New Communications Media and the Family: Practices, Function, and Effects," in *Progress in Communication Sciences, Volume 10*, B. Dervin (Ed.), Norwood, NJ: Ablex, 103-141.

Lindlof, T. R. (1992), "Computing Tales: Parents' Discourse About Technology and Family," *Social Science Computer Review*, 10(3), 291-309.

Markham, Annette N. (1998), *Life Online: Researching Real Experience in Virtual Space*, Walnut Creek, CA: AltaMira Press.

Norman, D. A. (1998), *The Invisible Computer*, Cambridge, MA: MIT Press.

Orleans, M. and M. C. Laney (2000), *"Children's Computer Use in the Home: Isolation or Socialization?"* Social Science Computer Review, *18(1), 56-72.*

Papert, S. (1996), *The Connected Family*, Marietta, GA: Longstreet Press Inc.

Pfaffenberger, B. (1992), "Social Anthropology of Technology," *Annual Review of Anthropology*, 21, 491-516.

Rybczynski, W. (1987), *Home: A Short History of an Idea*, New York, NY: Penguin Books.

Turkle, S. (1984), *The Second Self: Computers and the Human Spirit*, NY: Simon & Schuster.

Turkle, S. (1995), *Life on the Screen*, New York, NY: Simon & Schuster.

Van Maanen, J. (1988), *Tales of the Field: On Writing Ethnography*, U of Chicago Press.

Venkatesh, A. (1996), "Computers and Other Interactive Technologies for the Home," *Communications of the ACM*, 39(12), 47-54.

Venkatesh, A (1999), "Project NOAH II–Preliminary Results," http://www.crito.uci.edu/noah

Venkatesh, A and N. Vitalari (1990) Project NOAH I, A Longitudinal Analysis of Computing in the Home," *NSF Report*, http://www.crito.uci.edu/noah

Venkatesh, A and N. Vitalari (1992), "Emerging Distributed Work Arrangement: An Investigation of Computer-Based Supplemental Work at Home," *Management Science*, Vol. 38, No 12, December, 1687-1706.

Venkatesh, A. and S. Mazumdar (1999), ""New Information Technologies in the Home: A Study of Uses, Impacts, and Design Strategies," *EDRA Conference Proceedings*.

Experience-Based Processing and its Effects on Judgment, Decision Making, and Behavior

Laurette Dubé, McGill University
Ashesh Mukherjee, McGill University

Consumer and decision making research have traditionally focused on the rational side of human beings, viewing judgment and behavior as the outcome of rational processing. Rational processing assumes that individuals have a conceptual understanding of the object in question, and consciously use information in the environment to make judgments about the object. Unlike rational processing which operates solely at the conscious level, experience-based processing is driven by subjective feeling states that may operate at both conscious and non-conscious levels. Further, the experiential system— in comparison to rational processing–is said to be more closely tied to immediate affective experience, is less well differentiated, more action oriented and less reflective, and often based on gut feelings, favoring judgments and behaviors that "feels right." Although there is mounting evidence in diverse research domains such as psychology and neuroscience on the pervasiveness and importance of experience processing, there has been little research in consumer behavior on this topic. Hence the goal of this special session was to gain a better understanding of the underlying mechanisms of experiential processing, using the latest research findings in psychology, neuroscience and consumer behavior.

It has been suggested that experience-based processing may rely on *cognitive feelings*, *affective feelings* and *bodily states* to guide judgment, decision making, and behavior in different ways. The first paper, by Piotr Winkelman and Norbert Schwarz) pertained to *cognitive feelings*, that is feelings generated in the course of information processing. Such feelings include the experience of processing ease or difficulty and the experience of recall ease or difficulty. In their paper, the authors show that the outcome of various judgments (e.g., risk perception, subjective report of attitude strength, judgments of truth) is significantly influenced by the experience of cognitive feelings, over and above the traditionally examined effects of attribute belief and evaluation. The second paper, by Antoine Bechara, examined the impact of *bodily states* on decision making, using a new theoretical framework called the Somatic Marker Hypothesis. The key idea of this hypothesis is that decision-making is influenced by marker signals that arise in bio-regulatory processes, including those that express themselves in emotions and feelings. Using a gambling task, the author shows that somatic signals are indispensable for effective decision making, and that the role of somatic or bodily signals may be outside of our consciousness. Finally, Laurette Dubé, Micheal Conway, and Asheeh Mukherjee focused on threat-related *affective feelings*. Their work shows that the use of humor appeal may favor the adoption of threat-prevention behavior by making individuals who tend to react to threat by pre-conscious defensive reactions, namely high-masculinity individuals), better able to experience threat-related negative feelings. Theoretical and applied contributions of the three papers were discussed by Andrew Mitchell.

Gender Differences in the Risk Perceptions and Effectiveness of Risk Reducers in Online Purchasing

Ellen Garbarino, Case Western Reserve University
Michal Strahilevitz, University of Arizona

ABSTRACT

This paper examines how men and women differ in both their perceptions of the risks associated with shopping online and the effectiveness of various risk reducers. The first study examines how gender affects the perceptions of the probability of negative outcomes and the severity of such negative outcomes should they occur for five risks associated with buying online (i.e., credit card misuse, fraudulent sites, loss of privacy, shipping problems, and product failure).

The second study examines gender differences in the effectiveness of 33 risk reducers. The third study experimentally tests whether women's willingness to purchase online is more strongly affected by recommendations from friends than men's. The results suggest that, even when controlling for differences in Internet usage, women perceive a higher level of risk in online purchasing than men do. In addition, having a site recommended by a friend leads to a stronger increase in willingness to buy online among women than among men.

Relationship Marketing, Gender, and Culture: Implications for Consumer Behavior

Kara A. Arnold, Queen's University
Constanza Bianchi, Queen's University

ABSTRACT

This paper presents a conceptual framework that proposes gender identity and culture as variables that impact on the success of a relationship marketing strategy when dealing with business-to-consumer relations. A number of authors have suggested that firms should adopt both transactional and relational strategies for different customers (Berry 1995; Anderson and Narus 1991). This approach would indicate segmentation based on a relational/transactional continuum. How would a firm determine which customers are more relational (and hence presumably more positively inclined towards engaging in relationships) than others? The framework presented suggests that two variables that have an important influence and have not been examined in the literature are gender and culture. Propositions for future research are suggested.

INTRODUCTION

Ongoing relationships between firms and their customers are receiving renewed interest in marketing (Sheth and Parvatiyar 1995). These relationships are discussed under the paradigm of relationship marketing which refers to "all the marketing activities directed toward establishing, developing and maintaining successful relational exchanges" (Morgan and Hunt 1994 p.22). Specifically relationship marketing in the consumer market is defined as attracting, maintaining, and enhancing consumer relationships in order to meet the objectives of both parties involved (Berry 1995).

Marketing research has shown that building strong customer relationships is a means for gaining a competitive advantage for firms (McKenna 1991; Reichheld 1993), and has benefits for consumers as well (Gwinner, Gremler and Bitner 1998). But in what circumstances is this most likely to be a viable form of advantage? What consumers would be more likely to want to engage in a relationship with a marketer? What are the boundaries beyond which relationship marketing and the increased investment necessary are not likely to be profitable? Under what circumstances is a transactional strategy more appropriate?

Certain consumers are likely to be more relational and hence more interested in engaging in relationships with the firm, the service provider, and the product/program or brand. For example, Anderson and Narus (1991) present the argument that in business-to-business situations firms should analyze their customers on a continuum from transactional to relational and adopt strategies for each respective segment. While this idea is accepted (Berry 1995), there have been few attempts to delineate, either conceptually or empirically, the factors that would differentiate these two types of consumers in the business-to-consumer relationship marketing literature.

Fournier, Dobscha, and Mick (1998 p.44) suggest that "relationship marketing is powerful in theory but troubled in practice", due to the fact that firms are attempting relational initiatives with all customers, without regard to the customers' relational orientations. They argue that consumers who prefer discrete transactions feel stressed and manipulated by firms that attempt to engage them in relationships. This is because companies may not be targeting the right consumer (Reichheld 1993), or not evaluating the consumer's relational orientation (Fournier et al., 1998).

Garbarino and Johnson (1999) empirically segmented the customers of a theater company (high and low relational) and test whether they differ in their evaluations of future intentions to attend subscribe and donate. Their focus was on what different role satisfaction, trust, and commitment played for high relational and low relational customers. Antecedent variables determining which consumers were high versus low relational were not addressed.

Sheth and Parvatiyar (1995) present a conceptual framework discussing the antecedents of the relational consumer. These authors suggest a variety of cognitive, sociological and institutional factors that may be influential on consumer partnering with firms. This paper builds on Sheth and Partivayar's (1995) framework by proposing that the relational behavior of consumers is also affected by gender and culture.

Gender and culture are introduced as key considerations when segmenting consumers along the transactional/relational continuum. Theories and ideas that have been developed in using primarily western male subjects cannot necessarily be applied to all persons or all cultures (for an example see Gilligan 1982a). We argue that research focusing on business-to-business relationships is likely to be male dominated and deal with male-male relationships. As such it may not apply equally to other types of relationships (female-male or female-female). Similarly, most research in consumer relationship marketing is based on theoretical frameworks developed in western cultures, primarily the U.S. It is quite possible that the benefits received, or their importance, in firm-consumer relationships may be very different when considered in other cultural contexts. This paper fills a gap in the current thinking about how to identify consumers who are more likely to engage in relational behavior by considering these missing links.

The first contribution of this paper is that it builds on the existing consumer relationship marketing literature by providing insight into the characteristics of relational consumers, an issue requiring further research suggested by Berry (1995). Second, a conceptual framework with several propositions for future testing is proposed. Finally, by linking gender and cultural variables to relational marketing, this paper adds to the existing theory on relationship marketing.

RELATIONSHIP MARKETING

Relationship marketing is a term that has been defined in various ways by various authors. Morgan and Hunt (1994 p.22), dealing with interfirm and intrafirm relationships propose that it "refers to all marketing activities directed toward establishing, developing, and maintaining successful relational exchanges". This definition appears to be overly broad (Peterson 1995). Sheth and Parvatiyar (1995 p. 256) look at consumer goods markets and state that "relationship marketing connotes an ongoing cooperative market behavior between the marketer and consumer". Peterson (1995 p. 279) suggests that thought "should be given to a definition of relationship marketing that stresses the development, maintenance, and even dissolution of relationships between marketing entities, such as firms and consumers". In discussing two definitions of relationship marketing, Peterson (1995 p.278) pulls out common threads of the idea of "individual customer-seller relationship, that both parties in the relationship benefit, ... that the relationship is longitudinal in nature ... [and that] the focus ... is on retaining customers".

While definitions differ with respect to scope and specifics, some common ideas persist. To state the obvious relationship marketing involves relationships. The parties involved may be firms and consumers (business-to-consumer), or firms and other firms (business-to-business), firms and suppliers, firms and distributors, or different departments within a firm or various potential others (Frenzen and Davis 1990). For a relationship to be successful, the customer must be prone to engage in a relationship, which means that he/she must have a relational orientation.

Relationship marketing can be thought of as a strategy used to gain a competitive advantage and stands in contrast to a transactional strategy. Discrete transactions have a "distinct beginning, short duration, and sharp ending by performance", while relational exchanges are "longer in duration, reflecting an ongoing process" (Dwyer, Schurr, and Oh 1987 p.13). The use of the term relationship implies more than a discrete transaction. It implies a long-term focus. The implication is that both parties benefit in some way from the association over a period of time. On this basis we make the following propositions:

P1: Relationship marketing will be a more effective strategy when consumers have a relational orientation.

P2: The more relational a consumer is, the more interested he/she will be in participating in a relationship with the firm, product/program or brand.

LEVELS OF RELATIONSHIP MARKETING

Important distinctions need to be made between the relationships a consumer has with the firm or corporate entity, the person who provides the service (in case of services), the product or program (for example frequent flier miles), and the brand (for a discussion of relationship with a brand see Fournier 1998). Different types of relationships and their relative importance and influence may differ depending on the situation. For example, in the banking industry the relationship that a consumer has with the actual person who provides the service may be most important. The relationships the consumer has with either the corporate entity (for example Citibank), or the product (for example their checking account), are probably secondary concerns in this example. Depending on the type of product or service and also on the type of individual, different relationship partners may potentially become more salient.

Berry (1995) delineates three levels of relationship marketing. They are financial, social, and structural. With the financial level, the reliance is on pricing to secure customer loyalty (e.g., American Airlines Advantage program). The second level of relationship marketing is the social level. Customers are offered social bonds as a means to secure loyalty (e.g., Harley-Davidson's Harley Owners' Group). The third level is structural, which is most similar to the firm/corporate level. At this level structural solutions to customer problems are used to create loyalty instead of - or in addition to – an individual service provider (e.g., Federal Express' Powership Program). Thus, there are numerous 'levels' or types of relationship in consumer markets and there are also different parties that consumers can form relationships with. Both of these dimensions need to be considered when conducting research.

On the basis of the preceding discussion we propose the following:

P3: In consumer product markets, the consumer will develop the strongest and most significant relationship with the product/program or brand.

P4: In service industries the consumer will develop the strongest and most significant relationship with the actual service provider, unless the firm undertakes measures to implement a relationship marketing pro-

gram that creates dependence on the brand/firm, in which case the relationship with the firm will be most salient.

SEX, GENDER IDENTITY, AND RELATIONAL ORIENTATION

Given the literature on sex differences in relationships, both academic (for example Chodorow 1978; Gilligan 1982a), and in the popular press (for example Gray 1997), sex and/or gender identity are potential individual difference variables that may impact on the extent to which a relationship marketing effort will be successful. In fact "consumer behavior is one area in which the differences in behavior between men and women, and often the hierarchical implications of those differences, are evident" (Costa 1994 p.2).

Bristor and Fischer (1993 p.525) suggest that "feminism based on women's voice/experience can suggest additional consumer problematics that, because they arise from women's experiences, have been largely ignored". One such suggestion they discuss is the implications for consumer behavior of the idea that women are more focused on relationships than are men. In the consumer behavior literature only a small amount of research has directly explored the implications of this "importance (to women) of relationship building and maintenance" (Bristor and Fischer 1993 p. 526).

Chodorow (1978) argued that women are more "relationship focused" than men. She discussed how this tendency develops from a psychoanalytic viewpoint. Because women have been primary caregivers the childhood of girls differs fundamentally from that of boys. Girls identify personally with their mothers who are around a lot. Boys are encouraged to identify with their fathers who are not available as much and hence tend to identify with the 'position' of father versus personally. This difference between "positional identification" of boys and "personal identification" of girls is the key to what makes women more open to relationship formation (Bristor and Fischer 1993).

Gilligan (1982a; 1982b) studied the difference between men and women on conceptions of self and morality in the context of conflict and choice. Her work suggests that theories of human development (based on research using male subjects) are sex-biased. A theme in her research is that women are more concerned with relationships and the responsibility of caring for others. For women, "identity is defined in a context of relationship and judged by a standard of responsibility and care" whereas the male 'I' is defined in separation (Gilligan 1982a p.160-161). The male self is "defined through separation" and the female self is one "delineated through connection" (Gilligan 1982a p.35).

Fournier (1998) used female informants exclusively in her study of brand relationships. She based this decision on previous research that suggested women "exhibit more and stronger interpersonal relationships and brand involvement" (Fournier 1998 p.347).

This research separates men and women based on biological sex and proceeds to create generalizations on that basis. The discussion until now has focused on previous work showing that women are more relational than men, concentrating on biological sex as the differentiating variable. Gender identity is another important distinction.

Other streams of research suggest differences between femininity and masculinity – the idea of gender versus biological sex – are more important. In developing her sex-role inventory, Bem (1974 p.156) states that in general "masculinity has been associated with an instrumental orientation, a cognitive focus on 'getting the job done'; and femininity has been associated with an expressive orientation, an affective concern for the welfare of others". A "feminine gender identity is guided by a communal (other) orientation, whereas a masculine gender identity is guided by an agentic (self) orientation" (Gainer 1993 p.269).

Overall, the research looking at biological sex has shown that, in general, women more often than men define themselves in terms of their relationships with others and are more 'relationship focused'. It is important to note that this is a general statement. Gilligan (1982a) suggests that there will be some within group variation. The interpretations given should not necessarily be taken to "represent a generalization about either sex" (Gilligan 1982a p.2). There will be individual differences among each sex and there will also be overlap between the two distributions (Settle and Alreck 1987). In terms of the research on masculinity and femininity, "feminine gender identity is often associated with biological sex" and in fact women tend to have higher feminine gender identities (Gainer 1993 p.270). Yet it also has been shown to be valuable as an independent predictor of consumer behavior in certain cases (Fischer and Arnold 1994).

The foregoing literature review suggests:

P5:   Women are more relational than men and will therefore be more likely to engage in relational market behavior with firms, products or brands.

If an association is shown to exist between the effectiveness of a relationship marketing effort and biological sex (women) then attention should turn to understanding why this association exists. It is in this understanding that practical and theoretical implications become salient. To say that a firm will be more successful using a relationship marketing strategy with women may be helpful but does not give the firm any grounding in how to approach increasing their effectiveness. The question that is important to answer is why is there this association?

BIOLOGICAL SEX OR GENDER IDENTITY?

The distinction between sex, gender identity, and gender role attitudes is an important one to make that has implications for consumer behavior. Fischer and Arnold (1990; 1994) identify the differences between these three concepts. Often consumer behavior research assumes there are differences between men and women with respect to things like the products they buy or responses to advertising. This research, however, has been unclear in its distinctions between these three concepts. This distinction is important because the concepts may have different impacts on consumer behavior. In a given circumstance one or the other may have greater explanatory and predictive power.

According to Fischer and Arnold (1994), sex refers to biologically based categories of male and female. Gender is used to describe the psychological features associated with sex. Gender identity refers to the personality traits of masculinity and femininity and gender role attitude refers to attitudinal differences about the roles, rights and responsibilities of women and men.

Which variable will have more predictive power in the case of wanting to engage in relationship with a marketer? There are no clear answers to this question. A contingent approach is probably called for. Stern (1988) reviewed literature on sex-role self-concept measures and consumer behavior and found that biological sex was as good a predictor as psychological sex traits with respect to various aspects of consumer behavior. Fischer and Arnold (1990) in their literature review discuss the fact that research in consumer behavior has shown that gender identity has only a small

impact. However, they found that people who were more feminine in terms of gender identity were more involved in Christmas shopping. A person's biological sex does not mean that their behavior is predetermined. However, biological sex does have a large impact on socialization and hence on the "consumer activities that an individual will be involved in and learn" (Fischer and Arnold 1990 p.335). There is also some evidence that each variable has differential explanatory power (For example Gainer 1993). The proposed framework will use both biological sex and gender identity as explanatory individual antecedents to the propensity to engage in marketing relationships. Empirical testing will be necessary to determine the stronger influence. Hence the sixth proposition is:

P6:   Persons with a feminine gender identity will be more likely to engage in relational market behavior with firms, products or brands.

Gainer (1993) argues that certain products are 'gendered". While some products are linked to biological sex (for example feminine hygiene products), others have a feminine or masculine image that is not necessarily connected to biological sex (for example hand lotion has a feminine image). Gainer's (1993) work suggests that for products perceived as feminine, persons with higher feminine identities will be more involved. We argue that not only are women and persons with a feminine gender identity more likely to be relational, they will also be more involved with products that are linked to biological sex and feminine gender respectively. The more involved a person is with a product the more likely they are to be open to engaging in a relationship with the firm that sells the product, or the product itself, or a particular brand of that product. Hence our final propositions dealing with gender are:

P7:   Females will be more involved and more relational with respect to firms or products linked to biological sex.
P8:   Persons with feminine or masculine gender identities will be more involved and more relational with respect to firms or products of the corresponding gender.

CULTURE AND RELATIONAL ORIENTATION

One of the most important social influences which has a profound impact on the way consumers perceive and behave is culture (Clark 1990). Culture is defined as a pattern of assumptions, values, and beliefs whose shared meaning is acquired by members of a group (Hofstede 1991). Attitudes, beliefs, intentions, norms, roles, and values are aspects of the self. The self affects the way people process and assess information and promotes differential processing and evaluation of information from the environment (Triandis 1989). The self is shaped through interactions with groups, and leads to differences in social behavior (Triandis 1989). Some aspects of the self may be universal and have the same meaning across time and geography and other elements may be extremely culture specific (Hofstede 1991).

It is generally accepted that Asian and Latin nations are very different from the U.S. and Canada. Most research in consumer relationship marketing is based on theoretical frameworks developed in western cultures, primarily in the U.S. It is quite possible that the benefits received, or their importance, in business-to-consumer relationships may be very different when considered in other cultural contexts. The knowledge that all people are culturally conditioned (e.g. Hofstede 1991) and that culture affects how consumers respond to marketing efforts suggests that knowledge of the cultural similarities and dissimilarities across cultures provides an awareness of where marketing practices can be effectively transferred.

Cross-cultural research has found that cultural differences can affect consumer information processing (Aaker & Williams 1998), decision-making (Tse et. al. 1988), and quality expectations (Donthu & Yoo 1998). In addition, some studies have shown that variables important to the understanding of marketing relationships can be affected by cultural differences. For example, Japanese firms were found to use more referrals and engage in more network activity than U.S. firms (Money, Gilly and Graham 1998), and Bianchi, et. al. (2000) suggest that cultural differences affect the development of trust and commitment in exchange relationships. However, little research has looked at the specific effect of culture on business-to-consumer relationship marketing.

Hofstede (1991) offers perhaps the seminal work in operationalizing national culture. By examining between-country differences in values and perceptions through factor analysis and other statistical methods, Hofstede (1991) identified four independent dimensions of national culture. These dimensions are: power distance, uncertainty avoidance, individualism/collectivism, and masculinity/femininity.

Indices of Hofstede's four cultural dimensions show meaningful relationships with demographic, geographic, economic, and political characteristics, and have been frequently used in international management research (Sondergaard 1994). We propose that these differences in cultural dimensions will lead to differences in relational orientation. For example, according to Hofstede (1991), Canada, the U.S., and the U.K., have high scores in individualism and masculinity, and low scores in power distance and uncertainty avoidance, therefore these countries may be less likely to engage in relational behavior. On the other hand, many Latin American countries such as Brazil, Chile, Venezuela and Mexico show low scores of individualism and masculinity and high scores of power distance, and will be more likely to engage in relationships with firms, products and brands. We will discuss the predicted effect of each dimension and the resulting implications for relationship marketing.

INDIVIDUALISM / COLLECTIVISM

Individualism pertains to societies in which the ties between individuals are loose and everyone is expected to look after himself or herself and his or her immediate family (Hofstede 1991). In individualistic societies, people from birth onwards are integrated into strong, cohesive groups, which throughout people's lifetime continue to protect them in exchange for unquestioning loyalty (Hofstede 1991). Meanwhile, in societies that are collectivist, identity tends to be much more connected to the social network. This orientation leads to valuing membership and identification with the group to which one belongs.

Members of individualistic nations such as Canada, the U.S., Australia, and Great Britain, will tend to hold an independent view of the self that emphasizes separateness, internal attributes, and the uniqueness of individuals. In contrast, collectivist South American countries will tend to hold an interdependent view of the self that emphasizes connectedness, social context, and relationships (Singelis 1994, Triandis 1989). This implies that members of individualistic cultures will probably hold more favorable attitudes towards differentiation and uniqueness, while members of collectivist cultures will hold more favorable attitudes towards building relationships and maintaining connections. Thus, behavior of members of individualistic cultures will be motivated by personal preferences, while behavior of members of collectivist

cultures will be more influenced by preferences and needs of close others. Hence we propose:

P9:   Consumers belonging to collectivist societies are more likely to engage in relational market behavior with firms, products, or brands, than consumers from individualistic societies.

POWER DISTANCE

Power distance refers to the extent to which the less powerful members of institutions and organizations within a country expect and accept that power is distributed unequally (Hofstede 1991). In societies with high power distance, individuals tend to be more submissive toward their superiors and prefer a more autocratic/paternalistic superior (Hofstede 1991). In low power distance countries, individuals value equality and democracy, and view superiors as being accessible and similar to them (Hofstede 1991). Power distance will therefore affect the role of each partner in an exchange relationship. In terms of style, sellers will probably have to be respectful and subservient to their buyers in high-power distance societies.

Another manifestation of power distance is the willingness to trust other people (Hofstede 1991). High power distance countries (e.g., Mexico and Venezuela) will view others as a threat and, therefore, show less inclination to trust others. Conversely, people in low power distance countries (e.g., Austria, Denmark, and Norway) will feel less threatened by others and tend to trust them more. Thus, the following is proposed:

P10:   Consumers belonging to low power distance societies are more likely to engage in relational market behavior with firms, products, or brands, than consumers from high power distance societies.

UNCERTAINTY AVOIDANCE

Uncertainty avoidance refers to the extent to which members of a culture feel threatened by uncertain or unknown situations and the degree of ambiguity and change that can be tolerated (Hofstede 1991). Societies with greater uncertainty avoidance tend to feel threatened by ambiguity and uncertainty, and try to reduce it through stability and by establishing formal rules (Hofstede 1991). Consequently, such societies emphasize the strong need to control environment, events, and situations. Thus, consumers from high uncertainty avoidance societies such as Japan would show relatively greater preference for established brand name, superior warranty, money-back guarantee, security, and resistance to change, and may prefer a more traditional style of interaction.

In societies with low uncertainty avoidance, ambiguity is more tolerated and individuals accept and handle uncertainty without much discomfort. Members of these societies tend to prefer fewer controls, thereby providing them with greater flexibility in determining how to accomplish goals. They tend to accept each day as it comes, take risks rather easily, and show a relatively greater tolerance for opinions and behaviors different from their own.

P11:   Consumers belonging to high uncertainty avoidance societies are more likely to engage in relational market behavior with firms, products, or brands.

MASCULINITY/FEMININITY

This dimension represents the "dominant gender role pattern related to behaviors and values" (Hofstede 1991, and 1998). It expresses the extent to which the dominant values in a society are masculine or feminine. Masculinity pertains to societies in which social gender roles are clearly distinct (i.e. men are supposed to be assertive, tough, and focused on material success, whereas women are supposed to be more modest, tender, and concerned with the quality of life). Societies with high masculinity tend to admire qualities such as ambitiousness, achievement, and assertiveness, with an understanding that performance is the means to gain wealth and admiration (Hofstede 1991). In these societies, one might expect individuals to strive aggressively to advance their careers, both by performing well and by gaining recognition from their superiors.

Female societies value nurturance, quality of life, service, and interdependence (Hofstede 1998). These societies are associated with patience. Motivation comes from a desire to serve and work is viewed as a necessity for living rather than the focus of life (Hofstede 1991). In feminine countries like Chile, Portugal, and Thailand, since decision-making is participative and compromises the watchword for maintaining friendly working conditions, it is suggested that they are more prone to relationship formation. Thus, we propose:

P12: Consumers belonging to feminine societies are more likely than consumers belonging to masculine societies to engage in relational market behavior with firms, products, or brands.

PROPOSED FRAMEWORK FOR ENGAGING IN RELATIONAL MARKET BEHAVIOR

The statement that relationship marketing is effective in all situations and applies equally well to all products and all businesses is too simplistic. Research needs to concentrate on delineating the boundary conditions under which this strategy will be most effective. Firms need to know what variables to segment on if they want to pursue different strategies for relational versus transactional consumers. In fact, the distinction between relational and transactional consumers may vary depending on the product or service.

The propositions suggested can augment Sheth and Parvatiyar's (1995) framework. In their framework they offer personal, social, and institutional influences, drawn from consumer behavior research, as reasons that consumers engage in relational market behavior. The personal influences that they offer as reasons are drawn mainly from the information processing and cognitive psychology domains. The proposed framework adds two important variables to the framework: gender and culture. If consumers are more interested in a relationship with a marketer, the tactics of the firm along these lines will be more effective.

IMPLICATIONS AND CONCLUSIONS

This paper has proposed to direct relationship marketing tactics to customers on the basis of how likely they are to be relational. How relational they are will depend on their biological sex and/or their gender and also on their cultural orientation. The proposed relationships discuss the theory behind the possible associations that seem reasonable given previous research. Areas for future research include empirical testing of our propositions as well as a delineation of when each of these influences will be operative. For example will gender be the overriding factor determining relational orientation or will culture? Will there be an interaction between these factors? Which cultural dimensions will have a greater impact on relational behavior? If a person with a feminine gender identity is from a masculine culture which will dominate?

There are numerous practical implications to these additional factors. If these associations were shown to hold, a firm would have some guidelines to use to assess what customers and nations they should target for relationship marketing efforts and what products/programs would be most suitable for this type of strategy.

The arguments presented suggest some avenues for future research into relationship marketing effectiveness and the personal and social influences that impact on consumers' propensity to engage in relational market behavior. The proposed framework adds two important antecedent variables to those previously suggested. The variables of sex/gender and culture are proposed to influence propensity to engage in relational market behavior. The variables of sex/gender and culture have some potentially large impacts on the effectiveness of relationship marketing strategy and international marketing and as such are worthy of future attention.

REFERENCES

Aaker, Jennifer and Patti Williams (1998), "Empathy versus Pride: The Influence of Emotional Appeals across Cultures", *Journal of Consumer Research*, Vol. 25, 241-61.

Anderson, James C. and James A. Narus (1991), "Partnering as a Focused Market Strategy," *California Management Review*, 33 (Spring), 95-113.

Bem, Sandra L. (1974), "The Measurement of Psychological Androgyny," *Journal of Consulting and Clinical Psychology*, 42 (2), 155-162.

Berry, Leonard L. (1995), "Relationship Marketing of Services - Growing Interest, Emerging Perspectives," *Journal of the Academy of Marketing Science*, 23(4), 236-245.

Bianchi, Constanza; Peggy Cunningham, and Shirley Taylor (2000), "The Effect of Cultural Differences on the Development of Trust and Commitment in International Agency Relationships: Some Propositions", *Academy of Marketing Science Conference Proceedings*, Montreal.

Bristor, Julia M. and Eileen Fischer (1993), "Feminist Thought: Implications for Consumer Research," *Journal of Consumer Research*, 19 (March), 518-536.

Chodorow, Nancy (1978), *The Reproduction of Mothering: Psychoanalysis and the Sociology of Gender*, Berkeley: University of California Press.

Clark Terry (1990), "International Marketing and National Character; a Review and Proposal for an Integrative Theory," *Journal of Marketing*, Vol. 54, 66-79.

Costa, Janeen Arnold (ed) (1994), *Gender Issues and Consumer Behavior*, London: Sage Publications.

Donthu, Naveen and Boonghee Yoo (1998), "Cultural Influences on Service Quality Expectations", *Journal of Service Research*, Vol. 1, (2), 178-186.

Dwyer, Robert F., Paul H. Schurr, and Sejo Oh (1987), "Developing Buyer – Seller Relationships," *Journal of Marketing*, 51 (April), 11-27.

Fischer, Eileen and Stephen J. Arnold (1990), "More Than a Labor of Love: Gender Roles and Christmas Gift Shopping," *Journal of Consumer Research*, 17, 333-345.

Fischer, Eileen and Stephen J. Arnold (1994), "Sex, Gender Identity, Gender Role Attitudes, and Consumer Behavior," *Psychology & Marketing*, 11(2), 163-182.

Frenzen, Jonathan K. and Harry L. Davis (1990), "Purchasing Behavior In Embedded Markets", *Journal of Consumer Research*, Vol. 17 (1), 1-12.

Fournier, Susan (1998), "Consumers and Their Brands: Developing Relationship Theory in Consumer Research," *Journal of Consumer Research*, 24 (March), 343-373.

Fournier, Susan; Susan Dobscha and David Glen Mick (1998), "Preventing the Premature Death of Relationship Marketing, *Harvard Business Review*, 76 (Jan/Feb), 42-51.

Gainer, Brenda (1993), "An Empirical Investigation of the Role of Involvement with a Gendered Product," *Psychology & Marketing*, 10(4), 265-283.

Garbarino, Ellen and Mark S. Johnson (1999), "The Different Roles of Satisfaction, Trust, and Commitment in Customer Relationships," *Journal of Marketing*, 63 (April), 70-87.

Gilligan, Carol (1982a), *In a Different Voice: Psychological Theory and Women's Development*, Cambridge, Massachusetts: Harvard University Press.

Gilligan, Carol (1982b), "Why Should a Woman be More Like a Man?" *Psychology Today*, June, 68-75.

Gray, John (1997), *Mars and Venus on a Date*, New York: Harper Collins.

Gwinner, Kevin P., Dwayne D. Gremler and Mary Jo Bitner (1998), "Relational Benefits in Service Industries: The Customer's Perspective", *Journal of the Academy of Marketing Science*, Vol. 26,101-114.

Hostfede, Geert (1991) *"Cultures and Organizations- Software of the Mind"*, London: McGraw-Hill.

Hofstede, Geert (1998), *Masculinity and Femininity: The Taboo Dimension of National Cultures*, London: Sage Publications.

McKenna, Regis (1991), *"Relationship Marketing: Successful Strategies for the Age of the Customer"*, Reading MA: Addison-Wesley.

Money, R. Bruce, Mary C. Gilly, and Graham, John L. (1998), "Explorations of National Culture and Word of Mouth Referral Behavior in the Purchase of Industrial Services in the United States and Japan", *Journal of Marketing*, Vol. 62, 76-87.

Morgan, Robert M. and Shelby D. Hunt (1994), "The Commitment – Trust Theory of Relationship Marketing," *Journal of Marketing*, (July), 20-38.

Peterson, Robert A. (1995), "Relationship Marketing and the Consumer," *Journal of the Academy of Marketing Science*, 23(4), 278-281.

Reichheld, Frederick F. (1993), "Loyalty-Based Management", *Harvard Business Review*; March/April.

Settle, Robert B. and Pamela L. Alreck (1987), "Buying Behavior: Distinctly Female," *Marketing Communications*, 12 (9), 24-30.

Sheth, Jagdish N. and Atul Parvatiyar (1995), "Relationship Marketing in Consumer Markets: Antecedents and Consequences," *Journal of the Academy of Marketing Science*, 23(4) 255-271.

Singelis, Theodore M. (1994), "The Measurement of Independent and Interdependent Self-Construal", *Journal of Personality and Social Psychology*, Vol. 20(5), 580-591.

Sondergaard, Mikael (1994), "Hofstede's consequences: A study of Reviews and Citations", *Organization Studies*, Vol. 15, (3) 447.

Stern, Barbara B. (1988), "Sex – Role Self – Concept Measures and Marketing: A Research Note," *Psychology & Marketing*, 5(1), 85-99.

Triandis, H.C. (1989), "The Self and Social Behavior in Differing Cultural Contexts", *Psychological Review*, Vol. 96, 506-520.

Tse, D., K. Lee, I. Vertinisky, D. A. Wehrung (1988), "Does Culture Matter? A Cross-Cultural Study of Executives' Choice, Decisiveness, and Risk Adjustment in International Marketing", Journal of Marketing, Vol. 52(4), 81-95.

The New Woman and the New *Byt*: Women and Consumer Politics in Soviet Russia

Natasha Tolstikova, University of Illinois at Urbana-Champaign
Linda Scott, University of Illinois at Urbana-Champaign

Feminist theory first appeared in the *Journal of Consumer Research* in 1993 (Hirschman 1993, Bristor and Fischer 1993, Stern 1993). These three articles held in common that a feminist theoretical and methodological orientation would have benefits for research on consumer behavior, but did not focus upon the phenomenon of consumption itself as a site of gender politics. In other venues within consumer behavior, however, such examination did occur. For instance, a biannual ACR conference on gender and consumer behavior, first held in 1991, has become a regular event, stimulating research and resulting in several books and articles, in the marketing literature and beyond (Costa 1994; Stern 1999; Catterall, McLaran, and Stevens, 2000). This literature borrows much from late twentieth century feminist criticism, including a tendency to focus upon the American or western European experiences and a heavy reliance upon Marxist theory. As a result, consumption is often treated as a phenomenon peculiar to postindustrial capitalism—as are many marketing practices, such as advertising. Therefore, in our own literature as in the broader literature of cultural studies, the gender ideologies manifest in material culture are sometimes too easily attributed to the particular economic system of the postindustrial Western world.

Yet gender oppression has occurred under every economic system heretofore devised (Chafetz and Dworkin 1986, Rubin 1975) and, as consumer researchers, we recognize that consumption occurs under all economic and historical circumstances, not just under late twentieth century capitalism. Therefore, to the degree that gender ideology would be manifest in material practice, we should expect to find gendered, politicized consumption under any and all conditions in human historical experience. So, a truly feminist perspective would look to theorize consumption even under Marxist and non-industrial economies, expecting the politics of gender to occur in material culture everywhere. This paper examines the attempts made in the early years of the world's largest and longest-running Marxist regime to eliminate both gender oppression and consumer desires at the same time.

THE NEW WOMAN OF THE OCTOBER REVOLUTION

Before industrialization and the October Revolution that followed, Russia was a farming nation whose population was more than four-fifths rural peasants (Clements 1982). As in the West, women had little status and virtually no political or economic rights. The specific articulations of gender ideology paralleled those in, for instance, the United States: women were the mothers, the nurturers, the church-goers, and the consumers. Their sexual behavior was regulated by an uncompromising double standard. They had little choice but to marry and seldom married their choice. Women were denigrated as less intelligent, less trustworthy, and less rational than men, but more emotional, more acquisitive, and more socially ambitious. Women were valued primarily for their looks, particularly in the upper levels of society; among the peasants, physical strength and stamina could also be a plus. In agricultural work, the women did traditional farm labor; as industrialization burgeoned, they were relegated to gender-specific jobs in factories. Opportunities, especially for education, were reserved for boys. Women, therefore, were by and large illiterate, unskilled, and economically vulnerable, as compared to men. All these ideas, prejudices, and disadvantages were carried into the post-Revolutionary world, just as they were carried through industrialization into modernity in the West.

The last days of the monarchy in Russia were a struggle among factions with different ideas about how the society needed to change. One faction was a group of feminists who, in an alliance with intellectuals, actually won the first stage of the revolution, which occurred in February 1917. However, in the more famous moment of October 1917, the Bolsheviks came to power, displacing their rivals in revolution, including the feminists. The Bolsheviks adamantly insisted that the path of freedom for women laid through alliance with the workers. They were scrupulous in avoiding any notion that might suggest women organize in their own behalf or that women's oppression was peculiarly their own. Therefore, their ideology was explicitly anti-feminist in the sense that we now use that term. Nevertheless, the Bolsheviks did attempt to institute a number of reforms that were similar to those advocated by feminists in the West.

In the new order proposed by the Bolsheviks, women were to be the equals of men in both the workplace and the political arena. The revolutionaries saw that the household duties and sexual vulnerability of women hindered them from advancing to this role. So, they brought about a number of changes in law and municipal management that were intended to redress the imbalance. Communal housing, for instance, was supposed to allow for the collective raising of children and the sharing of homemaking duties, thus freeing women to work and attend Party meetings. Birth control was made available, abortion made legal, and divorce made easy (Fuqua 1996). These legal and infrastructural changes were not enough, however, to change centuries of gender enculturation. The problem had to be addressed on the ideological front as well.

A cadre of Bolsheviks was assigned to "reeducate" the female peasantry. Called *Zhenotdel*—in English, the "Women's Section"—this group was formed entirely of highly-educated middle and upper class women. The Zhenotdel membership was, therefore, substantially different from the typical Russian woman, much as early feminists in the United States and Great Britain were better educated and more privileged than the average woman in those countries. The women of Zhenotdel undertook to change the beliefs and practices of their countrywomen through a variety of means. Various events were planned and communiqués issued. Mechanisms devised to convert the female population to the thinking of the rulers are hauntingly similar to those used in capitalist countries, particularly the publication of women's magazines (Tolstikova, 2000). For instance, Zhenotdel published *Rabotnitsa* (translates as "Woman Worker"), a vehicle that was, in many ways, the *Ladies' Home Journal* of Soviet culture. *Rabotnitsa* became the leading women's magazine in Russia and was published continuously during Soviet rule. Every page of it was controlled by the Party, first by Zhenotdel and then, when Stalin eliminated the "Women's Section," by the leaders of the Party themselves. (Over the course of the Soviet regime, control of the press was always centralized within the top levels of the Party and tightly managed.) Additional mechanisms included special events, like International Women's Day, and other, less popular magazines, such as *Krestianka* ("Peasant Woman") and *Kommunistka* ("Communist Woman"). Eventually, the Soviets would even publish a fashion magazine aimed at the "correct" education of women.

Using this highly controlled and fully integrated ideological apparatus, the Communist Party of the early Soviet Union tried to compel its citizens to give up the notions of gender they had held for centuries. Always, however, the position was pointedly Marxist, rather than feminist. For instance, in the first issue of Rabotnitsa (1914), a story called "Natasha's Dreams" appears. It tells of a woman worker fired right before the New Year holiday. Depressed, Natasha went home, took a nap, and had three dreams. The first two dreams presented her with solutions to her real life problems, including marriage. On awakening each time, she realized that her life would be a misery under the conditions of the dream. With the third dream, however, Natasha learned that happiness was really possible if only she would join her brothers and sisters who struggled for the people's equality.

The integration of the press under the guidance of the Central Party allowed a kind of ideological "cross-ruffing." For example, another early short story, "A Newspaper Girl" (No. 4, April 19, 1914) told about a young woman who lost her husband and had to sell commercial newspapers to support herself. She met a boy who convinced her to read and sell *Pravda* instead. It changed her life: even her dark and cold environment became sunny and warm. Suddenly, she had a purpose. Thus, much as feminists in the West sometimes argue that the ideology of capitalism is seamless and unavoidable in its cultural artifacts, we find a relentless continuity in the works of the Soviet regime.

Capitalist imagery is given almost magical power by Western feminists. Its alleged tendency to distort reality, to heroize a narrow set of ideals, to psychologically manipulate viewers has been criticized a great length, particularly where advertising is concerned. Yet Soviet art has been similarly criticized. From Socialist Realism to Constructivism, the styles approved by the regime were used to propagandize its policies, to glamorize its view of daily life, and to present its ideals of women (Bonnell 1991, Groys 1990). In short, the images of the Bolsheviks were consciously used as a tool in "forming the psychology of the new Soviet person" (Groys 1990, p. 139). Images of women were employed in the same unabashed way that fiction was used to propagandize for the regime. For instance, the cover of the 1923 *Rabotnitsa* looks much like a Soviet poster: the image of a woman worker unfurling a protective banner over the countryside (Figure 1).

This grand image of a working woman is one of many manifestations of the Revolutionary ideal woman. It its first days, one of Zhenotdel's main goals was the creation of the "New Woman." Like the New Woman of the American feminists of the same period, this new ideal was to be active and independent, transformed into a fully-functioning, productive person (Clements 1992). In the Soviet version, however, the identification with the proletariat revolution was an essential element. This tough equal of men was even expected to look like a soldier of revolution. Usually young and militant, she was often dressed in a leather army jacket and pants, topped by a big furry hat and a Browning slung on her hip (Stites 1978). This suspicious narrowed eyes of the state milita member in Figure 2 epitomizes the type—she appeared in *Rabotnitsa* in 1924. Another frequent incarnation is that of the dedicated worker, like the one on the cover of the August 1924 (Figure 3).

The desired change in gender relations was often articulated in material terms through the New Woman. As a member of the ideal revolutionary force, the New Woman was expected to be a kind of nomad, a person whose belongings could fit into a suitcase, whose room was furnished like a monk's (Boym 1996). All personal life was subjugated to the needs of the regime. Beauty, for instance, was defined by Zhenotdel by a paraphrase from Lenin as "everything that complies with the interests of proletariat struggling for socialism" (December 1927, p. 15). *Rabotnitsa* emphasized that good looks came from physical fitness and should not be enhanced with "unnatural" means like jewelry and cosmetics. Yet the New Woman, like the supermodel of the postmodern capitalism, was typically quite thin. Her slenderness was supposed to be a strike against the overeating that characterized the bourgeoisie, but Naiman comments that the New Woman ideal promoted anorexia (much like Western consumer culture today) (1993).

Many people, whether revolutionaries or not, were getting thin under the Bolsheviks. The first few years of the new regime were marked by famine, general economic scarcity, political instability, and war. The regime showed remarkable insensitivity to its starving citizenry, choosing to feed itself by sending militia into the countryside and forcing peasants to give up grain at gunpoint. Many peasants resisted and some were shot. The government tried to solve shortages by centralizing distribution of consumer goods to the working population. Rationing was rigid—citizens attempting to get more food were summarily executed. Almost all industries were nationalized and private trade was declared illegal (Nove 1992). Economic hardships were, therefore, accompanied by an extreme concentration of political authority and the violent crush of daily life. .

From its brutal first years, the Soviet regime was quite unsympathetic to the problem of providing goods to ordinary folks. Throughout the life of the Soviet government, centralized economic plans would focus primarily on heavy industry and defense production, rather than consumer goods. As a result, consumer choice was always extremely limited, even in times (such as the late Stalin years and the Krushchev reign) when the government at least gave lip service to providing more material comforts for its citizens. Furthermore, the consumer information and distribution systems that became so sophisticated in the West were never developed in Soviet Russia. Consequently, supply was always unstable and goods procurement always problematic for the ordinary family, particularly the women.

Some historians focusing of the experience of Russian women (Clements 1982, 1992, 1997; Gorsuch 1992, 1996; Koenker 1995; Fuqua 1996; Stites 1978, Wood 1997), argue that the inattention to consumer goods in the early years of the Party was one reason that women did not achieve the goals of equality advocated by the Bolsheviks. While middle class housewives in the capitalist countries were able to take advantage of the labor-saving devices of consumer culture to work for women's rights (Chafetz and Dworkin 1986), Russian women found that their household duties only became more onerous under the Bolsheviks. The focus on heavy industry and defense production meant than none of the labor-saving inventions brought to women in the West during this period made their appearance in Russia. Instead, women there continued to produce clothing and prepare food according to labor-intensive methods that had kept them at home for centuries. Shortages and general economic instability meant that women, as the primary consumers, had to spend more time procuring goods for their families than before and had to pay more attention to budget-stretching and creative solutions typical of women in times of scarcity. Far from being liberated to participate in Party politics, women had to spend more time finding food and other provisions for their families than they had before.

The insensitivity of the regime to the economic problems of its citizenry meant that little aid was available from the state, throwing women back into patterns of familial dependence. Thus, family ties in some ways actually strengthened under a regime determined to

FIGURE 1

loosen the effect of kinship on women. Some historians argue that a resurgence of patriarchal behavior during this period was a way of enforcing stability on a society increasingly characterized by chaos (Clements 1982). And, as a practical matter, a conservative reaction among men seems to have resulted in increased demands that daughters, as well as wives and mothers, stay home to attend to family life rather than go to political meetings. At the grassroots level, women who did manage to attend Party meetings were often relegated to housekeeping duties (making Revolutionary decorations, sweeping the floors) anyway.

Not all women were in equally bad shape. A system of privileges that would persist throughout the life of the Soviet Union took root in the first years of famine and civil war. Initially, the Party rationalized that the top echelon serving the needs of the Party (and,

FIGURE 2

FIGURE 3

presumably, the people) had to be supplied with basic goods so that they would not waste valuable time searching for necessities. Thus, special rations were accorded to members and their families. Bolshevik women therefore "enjoyed material benefits—the best food, clothes, housing, and transportation available" (Clements 1982: 234). Thus, the distance between Zhenotdel and the average Russian female grew wider, contributing to the sense of separation between the inner Party and the populace, rather than furthering a feeling of solidarity.

The history of women in Russia—as the history of women everywhere—is also a history of everyday life. The absence of attention paid by the ruling regime to the needs of everyday life—for food, for clothing, for acceptable shelter—fell most heavily on women, forcing them to use most of their energies to provide basic necessities for themselves and their families. In the end, their

encumbrance by the needs of the home were no less than in the United States—and their participation in the political system no more. Ultimately, the agenda of political equality was undermined at least in part by the government's failure to recognize women as the consumers of the society. This, of course, is a situation directly counter to that of the United States, in which the attempts of corporations to "turn women into consumers" has repeatedly been cited as a cause for their oppression (for instance, Garvey 1996, McCracken 1993, Scanlon 1995). Yet the Soviet pattern demonstrates the opposite effect—as well as the continued oppression of women in a supposedly non-consumer society.

NEP AND THE NEW *BYT*

As central to Russian culture as the oppositions of gender is the binary between the material and spiritual. From folklore to propaganda, the dangers of the material and the banality of everyday life, or *byt,* are contrasted to the virtues of the spirit and the world of the mind, or *bytie* (Boym 1996). The word *byt* is so heavily fringed with distinctively Russian connotations and cultural associations that many scholars have claimed it cannot be translated into English, much as they also say that the word "privacy" cannot be translated from English into Russian (ibid). For our purposes the contrast is instructive: in the English-speaking world and many other cultures, the "private sphere" of home, women, and consumption was less valued in Russia than the "public sphere" of politics, men, and production (see Costa 1994). Because of its location in the private sphere, the word *byt* is associated with family life and is a feminine term. And it is at the cross-section of privacy, gender, and everyday life that the new Communist ideology of consumption was built.

Given the inattention to consumption needs and the negative effects of material shortages on the political agenda in the early years, it is interesting that the next few decades in Soviet history are marked by an obsession with the politics of material culture. Succumbing to the dissatisfactions of the populace, the Party instituted a new economic strategy in 1921. Initiated by Lenin, the "New Economic Policy" (or "NEP") was intended to restore the state economy, to ease pressure on the peasants, and to allow the overstrained population a break from rationing and shortages, primarily by allowing the reinstitution of private production and trade (Ball 1991). Though touted as a softer transition to a communist utopia, many "true revolutionaries" saw in the NEP a dangerous opportunity for backsliding into capitalism and its "bourgeois" preoccupation with material comforts. Such interest in material goods was seen by the revolutionary radicals as a contradiction of Bolshevik values. In 1922 Alexandra Kollontai, a famous woman Bolshevik, wrote an article called "The New Threat" against the NEP. Her largest concern was that NEP were forcing out women from the productive sphere back to the home which would again make her dependent on men, a "doll-parasite." When such a woman became a *"NEPmansha"*—the wife or a mistress of an entrepreneur made newly rich by NEP—she became a a symbol of his wealth, displaying too high heels, too red lips, and too much fur bought with "ill-gotten income" (Kollontai cited in Wood 1997: 176-177).

Party hard-liners rushed to stigmatize specific consumption behaviors as frivolous, individualistic, and *petit-bourgeois*. Beginning in the early 1920s, therefore, Party communications evidenced the emergence of an elaborate ideology of goods, which came to be known as the campaign for the "new *byt*." Interestingly, the word *byt*, though in colloquial and literary use before 1900 appears in no dictionaries published prior to the Revolution of 1917. By 1927, however, this one entry took up six full pages in the Soviet Encyclopedia. The growth in the relative importance of the concept in the minds of the keepers of information reflects the ideological initiative.

In its expanded usage, *byt* implicitly recognizes the broader cultural, governmental, and ideological dimensions of daily life. The term, for instance, was often used in Russian anthropological writing to refer to the everyday culture of other populations and appears in set phrases like *"byt* and customs" or *"byt* and culture." This word thus refers generally to the way things are done, to the assumptions of culture as they are manifest in practice. It is *byt* that gives life in a certain place its particular organization and character. Though *byt* refers specifically to the arena of private affairs, those supposedly not regulated by the state, it also refers to the infrastructure that daily routines support. It is, therefore, a word that implicitly recognizes the separation between private and public as illusory. Further, the usage of *byt* covers daily social interactions, including shopping, interpersonal messages, and, importantly for our purposes, communications with the state (Fitzpatrick 1999).

Thus, *byt* is also a word that recognizes the reach of material culture into ideology.

The campaign for the new *byt* that began in the 1920s shows the Soviet government had come to see that a key to the success of its social reforms and ideological initiatives was to change the material objects and practical routines that embody and act out—in every culture—a society's politics. Through the Lenin and, especially, the Stalin years, the politics of object ownership would become exquisitely politicized. Over the next three decades, the Party's vigilance in the politics of everyday objects would reach levels that are truly absurd: material symbols of decadence or capitalism or counterrevolutionary thought were vigorously erased from paintings, removed from homes, and used as evidence against enemies of the state. The very presence of simple objects like a rubber plant or a porcelain elephant could be mute testimony to the presumed Western sympathy, counterrevolutionary politics, even fleeting doubt of the owner. Doubt or dissidence thus expressed could result in suspicion and, ultimately, arrest and death. In fact, it was the concept of the new *byt* that put down the basis for the Soviet secret police house searches that became a daily terror under Stalin—the ultimate breakdown between public and private. Thus, from being disavowed by the early Bolsheviks to being the blunt instrument of Stalin's police, the ideology of consumption went from periphery to center stage. In the process, controlling the habits of *byt* became the practical edge of Marxist theory.

Since *byt* was associated with the private sphere (and thus with women), the official campaign for the new *byt* was undertaken by Zhenotdel. There were several areas pinpointed for combating the bourgeois influence of "domestic trash": (1) family (since the private familial sphere was seen as a spontaneous generator of middle-class values, as well as a space that preserved religion), (2) domestic realm (elimination of housework; widespread attraction of women into the labor force) and (3) further extension of the "New Woman." As the creators of daily life, women were key to the success of the new *byt*. Nevertheless, women were also seen by the Bolsheviks as the most vulnerable to succumbing to the temptations of NEP.

The iconography of the new byt was thought out to the last detail—down to the buttons on one's clothing some have said. But probably the most lasting, insidious, and representative of the new byt initiatives was communal housing. As a microcosm of the socialist city, the "house-commune" was "not just a retreat for the individual, a place marked by personal traces and memories; rather, it was a public and therefore ideologically charged site" (Boym 1997: 163). The plan for communal housing, initiated by Lenin, implied a different kind of person, someone not entitled to a room or private space, but to a certain square footage. As a result, a large home would be carved up "mathematically and bureaucratically, as if it were not a 'living' space, a real home once inhabited by real people, but some topological abstraction. As a result, countless apartments in major cities were partitioned in the most bizarre manner, creating unlivable spaces, long winding corridors, back entrances, and labyrinthine interior yards" (ibid: 168). The destroyed sense of privacy was pathetically reconstructed by people who hung doorbells outside their rooms or strung up a sheet so that they might have sex in private. The fulcrum of the communal housing ideology was the kitchen. Communal kitchens were supposed to free women from the toils of cooking for their families. Instead, kitchens became the site of jealous guarding of utensils, foodstuffs, and fuel, as well as bickering and criticism.

Historians and social scientists studying life under the Soviets blame communal housing for widespread disfunctions in Soviet life ranging from sexual impotence to alcoholism to deep-seated resentments and irrational fear of embarrassment. On women particularly, the invasion of the private was a devastating blow. Without a commensurate accommodation in the public sphere, the private sphere of women was systematically destroyed. From child-rearing to courting to cooking, the practices of women's daily lives were forever interrupted. But in the ideology of the new *byt*, "anything private was denigrated as politically dangerous, literally de-prived of social utility and significance (Boym 1997: 167). As the sphere of women, the site of daily life, therefore, the private sphere, the home space, was systematically devalued by the new byt.

The pages of *Rabotnitsa* promoted Party values in grimly austere consumer advice columns. Under the regular heading "For the help of a working woman," there could be found instructions on how to build a device from the wooden planks that allows to cook food without somebody being present: "A cold box for the preparation of food" (January 1924). On the same page, a reader could find advice aimed at the consumption of found objects: on cleaning spots out of old fabric, as well as instructions how to make a crib out of a barrel. A few months later, there were instructions on how to make toys from refuse (No. 4, February 1924). Though such advice may appear appealingly similar to the "voluntary simplicity" of contemporary culture, it must be remembered that the real fact of continued shortages is reflected here—in actual terms, there was little that was voluntary about such "simplicity."

Though the ideal New Woman promoted by the Party had rejected traditional values in the concrete forms of consumption—pretty dresses, cozy apartments, gramophones (Naiman 1993), real women were still seen as prone to domesticity, "female" interests, and petty values. And, indeed, in her study of the print shop culture of the 1920s, Diane Koenker finds that young working women greatly cared about dressing well and dancing; they plucked their eyebrows, used cosmetics, and dyed their hair (1995). Young party activists working in a factory of the same period reported cases of several young women workers who literally starved because they spent all their wages on silk stockings, make-up, manicures, fashionable low-cut dresses and narrow-toed shoes (Gorsuch 1992).

Rabotnitsa responded to the conflict between ideology and reality by propagandizing stories of women workers who made different choices, such as one group who decided never again use facial powder and cosmetics (No. 2, January 1927: 13). In October 1924, E. Kantorovich reported on a retreat for members of the trade union in the Soviet Republic of Belorussia. Women there made a group decision to get rid of their jewelry, even wedding rings. Because earrings were only for bourgeois women and barbarians, a modestly dressed office worker proudly took off her single decoration—small white earrings. "This was the power of the new thinking, a new daily life," crowed the author"(25).

Despite their firm goal of resisting the imagery of capitalism and femininity, Party publications often contradicted their own messages. Dress styles similar to the infamous "flapper" of capitalist culture were fashionable among NEPmanshi—patterns were presented by the April 1926 *Rabotnitsa*. The dresses, with their typical lowered waistlines, are also accessorized with cloche hats and pointed shoes. Their intricately patterned fabrics, decorated with ruffles and bows are the height of the feminine (Figure 4). In an ad appearing in *Rabotnitsa* in July 1927 a dark, smiling beauty announced that "There is no gray hair anymore" and listed products that achieve this condition: natural hair dyes Henna and Basma (Figure 5). Despite the editorial attacks on cosmetics, ads for the State Fats Trust appeared on the pages of *Rabotnitsa*. Because this government agency was responsible for the production of cosmetics and soaps, the ads tout powder boxes, perfumes, and cosmetics, in addition to fine toilet soaps—and the imagery is highly stylized (Figure 6). For women who were not related to NEPman or members of the Party, products such as these were often inaccessible. Furthermore, though the regime forbade certain goods, over

time it had its own favorites (particularly for the elite), the display of which spoke of the owner's political correctness—pink lampshades in the Stalin years, for instance. During periods when competition with the West put pressure on the Soviets to develop consumer culture—as in the Krushchev era—the machine flipped around to focus on encouraging women to decorate their homes and covet appliances. The approved status of such goods were announced, along with the gender politics of the moment, in the women's magazines published by the Party.

The gender ideology, like the preferred *byt*, also shows contradictions. In Stalin's time, for instance, there is a strong emphasis on women workers, just as in the early years of the Bolsheviks; however, we also see a marked shift of emphasis toward family and maternity. Policy changes of the day show the same shift: birth control and marital policies of the Bolshevik period were abruptly reversed in the 1930s. As in the late 'teens, the facts behind the ideological shift were brutal: twenty million men were killed in the purges and wars that occurred under Stalin's rule. Yet the Soviet leader clung to his strategy of winning global dominance through heavy industry. So, to keep up industrial productivity, women were encouraged to take factory jobs. At the same time, however, the need to replenish the decimated population caused the Party also to emphasize the traditional "feminine" side—motherhood, family, home-making. Thus, in a situation not dissimilar to the "super-woman" role criticized by late 20th century feminists, the Russian woman under Stalin found herself the head of the household, the major breadwinner (under great pressure to increase productivity), and the primary caregiver and home-maker. Stalin himself had a very low opinion of women and the return to domesticity evident in the propaganda of the time reflects this personal prejudice as well.

Western feminists often seem to have adopted the same kind of male-oriented "production" versus "consumption" values in their tendency to blindly valorize increased labor participation as a victory for women. One of the few statistics that suggests feminist success under the Soviet regime is that nearly half of the female population was employed by mid-century. Such "gains" occurred at great physical and emotional cost to Russian women—and developed in the shadow of massive murderousness. All the while, the status of women remained chained to the traditional gender roles the Soviets had inherited from the rural economy that preceded them. The problematic nature of the situation for women was justified, glamorized, glossed over, and generally "mystified" by the ideological apparatus of the Party, especially the women's magazines. Therefore, the women's magazines show the same kinds of "contradictions" feminists have found in Western ideological artifacts. And, in this case, the explanation also consistently lies in the political agenda of the ruling elite.

CONCLUSION

As a concept that bridges everyday life, social organization, and ideology, *byt* allows us to see the seamlessness between politics and consumption, however they are organized. It is a commonplace in cultural criticism to note that the growth of the Western-style capitalist economies depended upon consumption and, particularly, the enculturation of women to the role of consumers. But since, as we have noted, consumption occurs in all human societies, it is probably more precise to say that the growth of capitalist economies depended upon *certain styles* of consumption, *certain roles* for consumers, and *certain systems* for disseminating consumer goods and cultural information about them. Thus, the emergence of certain phenomena in the early twentieth century, such as color-coordinating objects and ensemble purchases led to increasing levels of consumption. In other words, the growth of capitalism depended on a certain *byt*.

FIGURE 4

FIGURE 5

The growth of the Soviet state also depended upon *certain styles, certain roles, and certain systems* of consumption. Because the Party's agenda focused on heavy industry and military development instead of consumer goods, however, the prevailing ideology had to devalue private purchase in order to minimize the growth of consumption, rather than maximize it as in the West. Throughout the life of the Soviet regime, the supply of consumer goods remained relatively constrained and the choices limited. Therefore, the systems for consumption were considerably more rigid and consumer behaviors more regimented than in the West. Political imperatives were expressed in ideological messages that encouraged or discouraged certain *byt*. The Communist ideology that preached against individualistic consumption, indulgence in luxury, and the like was clearly attempting control consumer desire in order that the production goals of the state could proceed unimpeded. And, though the notion of the New Woman has many parallels to the same figure in Western feminism, Russian feminists today suggest that the ideals of the Bolsheviks did not really promote freedom for women, but instead promoted Party politics: "For the majority of women, the 'liberation' offered by *zhenotdely* was not freedom, but

political mobilization which created additional burdens in a realm where women had little authority" (Fuqua 1996, p. 48). However, because there were, even under this totalitarian government, resistance and desire among the populace, there were times when it was more politic to play to the need for private goods. And there were, even among the Soviets, "liberalizing" forces that sometimes resulted in a temporary softening of the stance. Further, there were times in which the state needed to stimulate demand for certain classes of goods. And, as in other forms of government, provisions were made that allowed elites to circumvent the official system, resulting in obvious consumption inequalities. Thus, there are, just as in capitalist systems, contradictions in the artifacts—magazines, advertisements, film, and the like—that carry the ideology. The ideals for women disseminated through the regime's ideology machine were, in many way, as demeaning as any the American soaps and women's magazines offered and were no less obviously hitched to the agendas of those in power.

Without exception, this literature puts the blame on capitalism's consumer culture, as if consumption ideology could not serve a different, but equally gendered, economic system.

REFERENCES

Ball, Alan (1991). "Private Trade and Traders During NEP," *in Russia in the Era of NEP: Exploration in Soviet Society and Culture*, ed. by Sheila Fitzpatrick et al, Indiana University Press.

Bonnell, Victoria (1991) "The Representation of Women in Early Soviet Political Art," *The Russian Review*, 50, 267-288.

Boym, Svetlana (1996) "Everyday Culture," *in Russian Culture at the Crossroads: Paradoxes in Postcommunist Consciousness*, ed. Dmitri Shalin, Westview Press.

Bristor , Julia M. and Eileen Fischer (1993), "Feminist Thought: Implications for Consumer Research," *Journal of Consumer Research*, 18 (March), 518-536.

Catterall, Miriam, Pauline McLaran, Loraine Stevens (2000), *Marketing and Feminism*, London: Routledge.

Chafetz, Janet Saltzman and Andrea Dworkin (1986), *Female Revolt: Women's Movements in World and Historical Perspective*, Totowa, N.J.: Rowman & Allanheld.

Clements, Barbara Evans (1997) *Bolshevik Women*, Cambridge: Cambridge University Press.

Clements, Barbara Evans (1992) "The Utopianism of the Zhenotdel," *Slavic Review* 51, 2, 485-496.

Clements, Barbara Evans(1982) "Working-Class and Peasant Women in the Russian Revolution, 1917-1923," *Journal of Women in Culture and Society*, 8, 21, 215-235.

Costa, Janeen Arnold (1994), *Gender Issues and Consumer Behavior*, Sage: London, New Delhi.

Fitzpatrick, Sheila (1999), *Everyday Stalinism* (New York: Oxford, 1999).

Garvey, Ellen Gruber (1996), *The Adman in the Parlor: Magazines and the Gendering of Consumer Culture, 1880s to 1910s*, New York: Oxford University Press.

Gorsuch, Anne E. (1996) "'A Woman Is Not a Man': The Culture of Gender and Generation in Soviet Russia, 1921-1928," *Slavic Review*, 55, 3, 636-660.

Gorsuch, Anne E. (1992) "Soviet Youth and the Politics of Popular Culture During NEP," *Historie Sociale/Social History*, 17, 2, 189-201.

Groys, Boris (1990) "The Birth of Socialist Realism from the Spirit of the Russian Avant-Garde," in *The Culture of Stalin Period* ed. By Hans Gunter, New York: St. Martins Press.

Fuqua, Michelle (1996), *The Politics of the Domestic Sphere: The Zhenotdely, Women's Liberation, and the Search for a Novyi Byt in the Early Soviet Russia*, The Henry M. Jackson School of International Studies, University of Washington.

Hirschman, Elizabeth (1993), "Ideology in Consumer Research, 1980 and 1990: A Marxist and Feminist Critique," *Journal of Consumer Research*, 19 (March), 537-553.

Koenker, Diane (1995) "Men Against Women on the Shop Floor in Early Soviet Russia: Gender and Class in the Socialist Workplace," *American Historical Review*, December, 1438-64.

McCracken, Ellen (1993), *Decoding Women's Magazines from Mademoiselle to Ms.* , New York: St. Martin's Press.

Naiman, Eric (1993) "Revolutionary Anorexia (NEP as Female Complaint)," *Slavic and East European Journal*, 37, 3, 305-325.

Nove, Alec (1992), *An Economic History of the USSR 1917-1991*, New York: Penguin Books.

Rubin, Gayle (1975), "The Traffic in Women," *Toward an Anthropology of Women*, Rayna Reiter, ed., New York: Monthly Review Press, 157-210.

Scanlon, Jennifer (1995), *Inarticulate Longings: The Ladies' Home Journal, Gender, and the Promises of Consumer Culture*, New York: Routledge, 1995.

Schudson, Michael (1984), *Advertising, the Uneasy Persuasion*, New York: Basic.

Stern, Barbara B., ed (1999), Special Issue, *Journal of Advertising*. 28 (Summer), 33-49.

Stern, Barbara B. (1993), "Feminist Literary Criticism and the Deconstruction of Ads," *Journal of Consumer Research*, 19 (March).

Stites, Richard (1978), *The Women's Liberation Movement in Russia: Feminism, Nihilism, and Bolshevism 1860-1930*, Princeton University Press, NJ.

Tolstikova, Natalia (2000), "Reading *Rabotnitsa*," Catterall, Miriam, Pauline McLaran, Loraine Stevens, editors, *Marketing and Feminism*, London: Routledge (forthcoming).

West, Sally (1995) "Constructing Consumer Culture: Advertising in Imperial Russia to 1914," PhD Dissertation, University of Illinois at Urbana-Champaign.

Wood, Elizabeth (1997), *The Baba and the Comrade: Gender and Politics in Revolutionary Russia*, Bloomington: Indiana University Press.

Walking the Tightrope between Feeling Good and Being Accurate: Mood-as-a-Resource in Processing Persuasive Messages

Raj Raghunathan, New York University
Yaacov Trope, New York University

ABSTRACT

This paper examines the role of mood in processing self-relevant information. We argue that positive mood acts as a resource, enabling people to better cope with negative, but useful, information. In contrast, negative mood makes the goal of terminating the aversive mood-state more important, thus leading people to focus more on positive information. Consistent with this prediction, when asked to read an essay on caffeine consumption, negative mood subjects focused more on positive (vs. negative) effects of caffeine, while those in positive moods showed no such bias. We discuss the theoretical contributions of this research and derive some important marketing implications.

The Effect of Mood on Self-Referencing in a Persuasion Context

Anick Bosmans, Ghent University
Patrick Van Kenhove, Ghent University
Peter Vlerick, Ghent University
Hendrik Hendrickx, Ghent University

The present study investigates the influence of mood on self-referencing. Two alternative explanations regarding self-referencing effects are contrasted. On the one hand, it can be hypothesized that self-referencing is a data-driven, high elaboration, bottom-up process, manifested under conditions of high motivation (e.g. when mood is negative). Alternatively, it can also be hypothesized that self-referencing is a schema-based top-down process, manifested under conditions of low motivation (e.g. when mood is positive). A 2 (positive versus negative mood) by 2 (self-referencing versus not self-referencing) design shows that self-referencing effects increase under conditions of negative mood, suggesting that self-referencing is a data-driven bottom-up process.

Advertisers often try to persuade consumers by encouraging them to relate the information presented in the ad to aspects of oneself (e.g. one's own personal experiences). This information processing strategy, known as self-referencing, can be induced by a variety of techniques: Photo's are presented that visually place consumers in the position of the scene actor or participant (instead in that of an uninvolved onlooker), or relatively personal second-person wording is used ('You are going to a party') as opposed to rather removed third-person wording ('He/She is going to a party'). Self-referencing has been described in the literature as a cognitive process whereby individuals associate self-relevant incoming information with information previously stored in memory (one's self-concept) in order to give the new information meaning (e.g. Kuiper and Rogers 1979; Markus 1980).

Research suggests that self-referencing has a considerable impact on recall of information (e.g. Baumgartner, Sujan and Bettman 1992; Sujan, Bettman and Baumgartner 1993), as well as on product evaluations (e.g. Baumgartner et al. 1992; Sujan et al. 1993; Meyers-Levy and Peracchio 1996; Sujan et al. 1993). However, the results obtained from the different studies are not at all unequivocal. Although most studies show enhanced memory and evaluation effects as a result of self-referencing, others show detrimental effects (for a meta-analyses see Symons and Johnson 1997).

The self-reference effect is thought to occur because knowledge of oneself is rich and plentiful, containing many associations that can be related to the incoming information. The self is described in the literature as an elaborate and organized network of associations (e.g. Markus 1980). Consequently, it affects elaboration of relevant stimulus information and also individuals' evaluative judgments in a persuasion context.

Research (Burnkrant and Unnava 1995; Meyers-Levy and Peracchio 1996) reveals that both elaborations and evaluations may be more favorable when people engage in moderate rather than extremely high or low levels of self-referencing (Anand and Sternthal 1990). Referencing, or thinking about, the self is an attention-consuming task; as self-focus increases, attention to the environment decreases, and there may be interference with the encoding of new information. This is because people only have a limited processing capacity (Kardes 1998). Baumgartner for example (Baumgartner et al. 1992; Sujan et al. 1993) found that as retrieval of autobiographical memories (i.e. a form of self-referencing) increases, thoughts are more focused on the autobiographical episode, and thoughts about, and memory for, product features become less accessible. This has serious implications for

evaluations: when self-referencing is high, evaluations will be based less on arguments presented in the message. When the self-related knowledge structure (e.g. an autobiographical memory) has strong positive affect, this affect will transfer to the product attitudes resulting in favorable product evaluations. On the other hand, when the self-related knowledge structure has negative affect, the affect transfer will result in less favorable evaluations.

One of the unresolved issues about the self-reference effect in the literature concerns the plausible factors that moderate self-reference effects on persuasion. The purpose of the present research is twofold. First, we investigate the moderating influence of one of these plausible factors, namely the influence of mood, on self-referencing. Secondly, we attempt to, through the use of mood as plausible moderator, clarify the mechanisms underlying self-referencing. Two alternative explanations concerning self-referencing effects are contrasted. We will first however, review some effects of mood on elaboration and evaluation.

MOOD

Recent research has shown that mood states have a considerable impact on people's processing strategies as well as on their evaluation of the attitude object. It is found that happy moods are associated with heuristic processing strategies, whereas sad moods are associated with systematic elaboration of information (e.g. Bless, Clore, Schwarz, Golisano, Rabe and Wölk 1996; Sinclair and Mark 1995). With regard to evaluations, it is observed that when people in different moods make evaluations, the typical result is that those in positive moods render more favorable evaluations than those in negative moods (e.g. Mayer, McCormick and Strong 1995; Sedikides 1992).

Several explanations have been formulated to account for these mood effects. According to memory-based models (e.g. Bower 1981; Isen 1984), mood influences evaluations by increasing the accessibility of mood-congruent information. According to Mackie and Worth (1991) for example, being in a positive mood causes people to bring more positive information to mind than does being in a negative mood. According to this affect priming principle (Isen 1987; Mackie and Worth 1989), being in a good mood limits processing capacity because of the activation of a large amount of interconnected positive material stored in memory. Hence, individuals in a good mood may not have the cognitive resources required by systematic processing strategies and may therefore default to less taxing heuristic strategies.

Alternatively, according to the affect-as-information view (Schwarz and Clore 1983), negative affect signals that the environment poses a problem, whereas positive affect signals that the environment is benign. As a result, negative affective cues may motivate detail-oriented, systematic processing, which is usually adaptive in handling problematic situations. In contrast, positive affective states, by themselves, signal no particular action requirement, and happy individuals may hence not be motivated to expend cognitive effort unless called for by other goals. In accordance with this affect-as-information hypothesis, Bless (Bless et al. 1996) found that happy moods increase, whereas sad moods decrease the reliance on general knowledge structures. Similarly, Bodenhausen (1993) argues that happy mood participants make more use of stereotypic information when making a judgment.

Recently however, it has been argued that effects of mood on the persuasion process follow a dual process (e.g. Forgas 1995), dependent upon different conditions (e.g. involvement). Petty (Petty, Cacioppo, Strathman and Schumann 1992) indeed found evidence for affective priming when elaboration likelihood was high (indirect effect of mood on persuasion through valenced thoughts) while evidence for the affect-as-information hypothesis was found when elaboration likelihood was low (direct effect of mood on persuasion).

THE RELATIONSHIP BETWEEN MOOD AND SELF-REFERENCING

Our main research question concerns the influence of mood on self-referencing. We argue that insight into the plausible moderating influence of mood on self-referencing can help us to clarify the mechanisms underlying self-referencing effects and gives us more insight into the self-concept in general. We furthermore argue that through the manipulation of mood under different self-reference conditions, more theoretical insight can be obtained concerning mechanisms responsible for observed mood effects in the persuasion literature. In the next sections, these contributions will be explained in more detail.

According to the mood-as-information theory, being in a positive mood (compared to being in a negative mood) signals that the situation is characterized as benign, resulting in a greater reliance on general knowledge structures (see Bless et al. 1996; Bodenhausen 1993). Because the self-schema is such a well-organized cognitive schema, it can be expected that self-referencing prompts will be more effective for persuasion under conditions of positive mood: the self-reference prompt activates the self, and because people are in a good mood (and experience the situation as benign) they will rely on their self-concept when making evaluations. Note that in this case, we hypothesize that self-referencing is a top-down or schema-based process (Schank and Abelson 1977).

On the other hand however it is argued that self-referencing will only manifest itself if respondents are sufficiently motivated to process the information presented in the ad, making them responsive to the self-reference prompts (Meyers-Levy and Peracchio 1996). This reasoning is based on evidence that when processing motivation is limited, ad recipients tend not to respond to nonsalient cues such as the self-reference prompts in question (Meyers-Levy and Maheswaran 1991; Meyers-Levy and Sternthal 1991). It has been shown that individuals who favor such perfunctory processing typically base their evaluations on simple heuristic cues, such as the affect they associate with the product category, the enjoyment they derive from the ad photo or the ad copy's writing style, and the like (e.g. Alba and Hutchinson 1987; Mick 1992). Consequently, since negative affect has been found to be an effective motivator to process information in a more detailed and systematic manner than does positive affect (Bodenhausen 1993; Petty et al. 1993), it can be expected that self-referencing prompts will only be used by respondents under conditions of negative mood. Note that in this case, we hypothesize that self-referencing is a bottom-up or stimulus based process (Schank and Abelson 1977).

The main objective of this research is to distinguish between these two alternative self-referencing explanations.

HYPOTHESES

Effects of Self-Referencing and Mood on Product Evaluations

Because the present study does not deal with mental schema's associated with negative emotions (such as fear or guilt), it can be expected that self-referencing will lead to more positive product evaluations. Consistent with results obtained by studies dealing with the effect of self-referencing on persuasion, it can be expected that:

H1a: Product evaluations will be more positive in self-referencing conditions compared to no self-referencing conditions.

We can furthermore expect that if self-referencing is a top-down process (see above), and is the result of a reliance on general knowledge structures (the self-concept in this case), product evaluations will be more positive under conditions of positive mood:

H1b: If self-referencing can be considered as a top-down process, it can be expected that under conditions of self-referencing, product evaluations will be more positive when subjects are in a positive, compared to a negative mood.[1]

If however, self-referencing can be considered as a bottom-up process (see above), and will only manifest itself when subjects are sufficiently motivated to process, product evaluations will be more positive under conditions of negative mood:

H1c: If self-referencing can be considered as a bottom-up process, it can be expected that under conditions of self-referencing, product evaluations will be more positive when subjects are in a negative, compared to a positive mood.

Moreover, it can be expected that under low elaboration likelihood (e.g. Petty et al. 1993) mood can be taken as an affective cue when making evaluations (see earlier, affect-as-information hypothesis). So, for the no self-referencing condition, the following hypothesis concerning the effects of mood on evaluations can be formulated:

H1d: In the no self-referencing condition, product evaluations will be more positive when subjects are in a positive, compared to a negative mood.

Hence, if self-referencing can be seen as a schema-based top-down process, we expect a main effect of self-referencing (H1a) and a main effect of mood (H1b and H1d) on product evaluations. If however, self-referencing is more like a bottom up process, a main effect of self-referencing (H1a) and an interaction effect of mood and self-referencing (H1c and H1d) on product evaluations can be expected.

Effects of Self-Referencing and Mood on Positivity of Thoughts

Self-referencing is also thought to have an effect on the valenced thoughts subjects have (Anand and Sternthal 1990; Burnkrant and Unnava 1995; Meyers-Levy and Peracchio 1996). This is because as elaboration rises (as is the case for self-referencing), people have a greater opportunity to recognize, appreciate, and reflect on the cogency of a message and the favorable information that the persuasive message mostly conveys (Meyers-Levy and Peracchio 1996). As a result, respondents generate predominantly favorable thoughts. Another explanation is that self-referencing leads to the activation of the self-concept that

---

[1] For reasons of simplicity, we chose to contrast hypothesis b and c in the next sections to indicate contrasting explanations.

is in most cases (except in cases of depression) a positively valenced mental knowledge structure (e.g. Alloy, Abramson, Murray, Whitehouse and Hogan 1997). Through the principle of affect transfer (Baumgartner et al. 1992; Sujan et al. 1993) thoughts about the product and the ad also become more positive. At this point however, distinguishing between these two explanations is not crucial.

H2a: In general, self-referencing will lead to a greater positivity of thoughts (number of positive thoughts compared the total number of thoughts) compared to when there is no self-referencing.

Furthermore, we can hypothesize that in the case self-referencing is a top-down process:

H2b: If self-referencing can be considered as a top-down process, it can be expected that in the self-referencing condition positive mood will lead to a greater positivity of thoughts compared to negative mood.

In contrast, when self-referencing is a bottom-up process:

H2c: If self-referencing can be considered as a bottom-up process, it can be expected that in the self-referencing condition negative mood will lead to a greater positivity of thoughts compared to positive mood.

Effects of Self-Referencing and Mood on Purchase Intentions

Because self-referencing has generally been found to enhance advertising effectiveness (Baumgartner et al. 1992; Burnkrant and Unnava 1995), it can be expected that self-referencing will lead to increased purchase intentions (e.g. Krishnamurthy and Sujan 1999):

H3a: Overall, self-referencing will lead to higher purchase intentions compared to no self-referencing.

Also, when self-referencing can be considered as a top-down process:

H3b: If self-referencing can be considered as a top-down process, it can be expected that in the self-referencing condition purchase intentions will be higher when mood is positive compared to when mood is negative

In contrast, when self-referencing is a bottom-up process:

H3c: If self-referencing can be considered as a bottom-up process, it can be expected that in the self-referencing condition purchase intentions will be higher when mood is negative compared to when mood is positive

Effects of Self-Referencing and Mood on Recall of Product Features

It should be noted that the literature is not very clear upon what can be expected concerning the effects of self-referencing on the recall of product features.

On the one hand, it has been extensively shown that self-referencing enhances message recall (for a review see Symons and Johnson 1997). Because the self is a complex, well organized knowledge structure, its activation provides more potential linkages between new information and information that is already stored (memory structures). Because of these linkages, elaboration

of the incoming information is facilitated (Anderson and Reder 1979).

On the other hand, detrimental effects of self-referencing on recall have been reported in the literature (e.g. Sujan et al. 1992). Referencing the self is an attention-consuming task, and as this referencing increases, attention to the environment diminishes (Carver and Scheier 1981) and there may be interference with the encoding of new information. Baumgartner (Baumgartner et al. 1992) showed that increased retrieval of autobiographical memories (a form of self-referencing) results in more thoughts about the autobiographical episode, and less thoughts about the product features.

Given these different research findings, we argue that it is not very opportune to formulate specific hypotheses regarding the effect of self-referencing and mood on the recall of product features. Therefore we consider our recall variable, although previously investigated in the literature, as exploratory.

METHOD

Participants and Design

Participants were 83 undergraduate university students. They participated on a volunteer basis.

Participants were randomly assigned to the conditions of a 2 (Mood: positive versus negative) X 2 (Self-referencing: self-referencing versus not) full factorial between-subjects design. Participants were received in groups up to 4 by the experimenters, who briefly explained that participants would be completing some independent tasks that had been combined into one session. These tasks (described below) included (a) the mood induction, (b) presentation of the ad (for a fictitious brand of orange juice), and (c) measurement of the dependent variables related to the ad: product evaluations, positivity of thoughts, purchase intentions, and recall of product attributes.

For the mood induction task, participants were asked to provide a vivid written report of either a happy or a sad life event, purportedly to help with the construction of a "Life Event Inventory" (as done by Bless et al. 1996). Subjects were led to believe that this Life Inventory Task was unrelated to the remaining of the tasks. Reporting a happy event was intended to induce a happy mood, whereas focusing on an experienced sad event was intended to induce a sad mood. Participants were given 12 minutes to complete their reports. They were then asked several questions about the task. Embedded among these questions was a manipulation check question that read "How do you feel right now?". Consequently 6 9-point semantic differential items (ranging from −3 over 0 to 3) were presented. These items were derived from the Mehrabian and Russell (1974) Pleasure scale (happy/ unhappy, pleased/ annoyed, satisfied/ unsatisfied, contended/ melancholic, hopeful/ despairing, relaxed/ bored). Subjects were asked to indicate to what extent these items described their feelings at the moment.

Self-referencing was manipulated by systematically varying the introductory paragraph of the ad. In the high self-referencing condition, the messages addressed subjects directly by using very personal second person wording (e.g. "Citrus Orange and your breakfast is complete ... You love a good breakfast? ..."). In the low self-referencing condition, the message was written in the third person (e.g. "Citrus Orange and his breakfast is complete ... He loves a good breakfast ..."). Similar self-referencing techniques have been described in the literature (e.g. Burnkrant and Unnava 1995; Meyers-Levy and Peracchio 1996). After the presentation of the ad, subjects were asked to answer a series of questions designed to provide a check on the validity of the self-referencing

TABLE 1
Means and Standard Deviations as a Function of Mood and Self-Referencing

Effect	Product Evaluation		Positivity of Thoughts		Purchase Intentions		Recall of Features	
	M	(SD)	M	(SD)	M	(SD)	M	(SD)
Self-Referencing								
High	3.32	(1.14)	46.16	(31.06)	3.14	(1.63)	2.00	(1.56)
Low	2.77	(1.17)	36.24	(26.66)	2.15	(1.30)	1.80	(1.75)
Mood								
Positive	3.06	(1.20)	37.21	(29.53)	2.63	(1.54)	1.98	(1.71)
Negative	3.04	(1.18)	45.61	(28.63)	2.68	(1.58)	1.83	(1.60)
High Self-Referencing								
Positive Mood	2.99	(1.34)	35.99	(28.83)	2.82	(1.59)	2.41	(1.74)
Negative Mood	3.68	(.76)	57.36	(30.20)	3.50	(1.64)	1.55	(1.23)
Low Self-Referencing								
Positive Mood	3.13	(1.06)	38.49	(30.90)	2.43	(1.50)	1.52	(1.60)
Negative Mood	2.40	(1.19)	33.87	(21.91)	1.85	(.99)	2.10	(1.89)

manipulation. The questions asked about the extent subjects believed the ad was meant for them, they were personally involved by the ad, the ad was written with them in mind, the ad was relevant for them, they felt personally attracted to the ad, the ad related to them personally, and the degree they thought about their own experiences with orange juice (inspired on Burnkrant and Unnava 1995). For each of these seven questions, they indicated their agreement on a 7-point scale (strongly disagree to strongly agree).

PROCEDURE

Subjects were first asked to help the department of Psychology of the university with the collection of sad and happy life events (see earlier). Afterwards, they were presented the critical ad (either containing a self-referent prompt or not) in a standardized way. Participants were told that it was a pretest ad. The ad depicted a fictitious brand for orange juice (Citrus Orange), together with a picture of a breakfast situation and some text describing the new brand. Afterwards, subjects were asked to fill in a questionnaire containing measures about the dependent variables.

DEPENDENT VARIABLES

The questionnaire began with the measurement of the validity of the self-referencing manipulation (see earlier). After this manipulation check, subjects were given a three-minute cognitive response task in which subjects were asked to list all the thoughts they had when they read the orange juice ad. After they had listed all their thoughts, subjects were asked to code each thought as positive, negative, or neutral in terms of its implications for the orange juice. Instructions on the thought-listing and coding task followed Cacioppo and Petty (1981). These valenced thoughts were used to calculate the positivity of thoughts index: (number of positive thoughts / total number of thoughts) X 100.

After this thought-listing procedure, attitudes towards Citrus Orange orange juice were measured on 4 7-point semantic differential items: positive/negative, love/hate, good/bad, desirable/undesirable (Simons and Carey, 1998). These product evaluation items were averaged for analysis (alpha = 0.90).

Behavioral intention was measured by asking subjects about their purchase intentions on one 7-point item: "How likely is that you will actually buy Citrus Orange when it is for sale?" (e.g. Krishnamurthy and Sujan 1999). Answers had to be given from very unlikely to very likely.

The questionnaire concluded with a recall question, in which subjects were asked to write down as much as they could remember about the orange juice ad. We subsequently scored each subjects' recall protocol by counting the number of arguments from the ad that were recalled (maximum 6).

RESULTS AND DISCUSSION

A MANOVA analysis was performed on our dependent variables product evaluation, positivity of thoughts, purchase intentions and recall of product attributes. Overall, this analysis shows a significant main effect of self-referencing: $F(4, 76) = 2.80$, $p < .05$ (power = .74), as well as a significant interaction effect of self-referencing and mood: $F(4, 76) = 3.21$, $p < .05$ (power = .81). The main effect of mood was not significant ($F < 1$). Table 1 gives the means and standard deviations as a function of mood and self-referencing for each dependent variable. In the remaining, we will report separate univariate tests for each variable. First however we will discuss the validity of our manipulations.

MANIPULATION CHECKS

Participants' ratings of how happy and sad they felt after the mood induction task indicated that the mood manipulation had been successful. Mean scores on the mood items (alpha = .80) were higher for participants who had described a positive life event compared to subjects who had described a negative life event (M = 2.18 vs. M = 1.62), $t(81) = 2.30$, $p < .05$[2].

With regard to self-referencing, a significant effect of second- versus third-person wording was found after averaging our manipulation check items (alpha = .91): $t(81) = 2.27$, $p < .05$ (M = 3.08 vs. M = 2.52). As intended, subjects felt that the ad related more to themselves when second-person wording was used compared to

---

[2] Note that both scores are at the positive end of the mood scale. We argue that this has no further implications for our research. In a pilot study we found that both positive and negative mood manipulation conditions differed significantly (both in the expected direction) from a neutral condition, where people were asked to describe the room they were in. Instead of talking about 'more than usual positive' or 'more than usual negative' (which is actually the case in the present study), it seems more opportune to talk about *positive* and *negative* moods.

when third-person wording was used, suggesting that our self-referencing manipulation was successful.

PRODUCT EVALUATIONS

ANOVA shows a significant main effect of self-referencing on subjects' attitudes towards the advertised orange juice ($F(1, 79)$ = 5.36, $p < .05$), as well as a significant interaction effect ($F(1, 79)$ = 8.04, $p < .01$). No main effect of mood on product evaluations was found.

Consistent with hypothesis H1a it was found that in general, self-referencing has a significant effect on product evaluations: subjects' attitudes in the self-referencing condition were more positive compared to attitudes of subjects in the no self-referencing condition ($M = 3.32$ vs. $M = 2.77$). This finding is consistent with existing literature showing that self-referencing is beneficial for product evaluations. It should be noted however, that the mental knowledge structure called for by the ad is a positive one (drinking orange juice in a breakfast situation), such that the possibility remains that, because of affect transfer (e.g. Baumgartner et al. 1992, Sujan et al. 1993), self-referencing has detrimental effects on product evaluations when negatively valenced knowledge structures are used (see our discussion earlier).

More importantly however, as our interaction effect already indicated, planned comparisons show more positive product evaluations when mood is positive ($M = 3.13$) compared to when mood is negative ($M = 2.40$) when self-reference prompts are absent: $F(1, 79) = 4.42$, $p < .05$. This finding is consistent with our hypothesis H1d. On the contrary, when the self has been prompted, product evaluations are more positive when mood is negative ($M = 3.68$) compared to when mood is positive ($M = 2.99$): $F(1, 79) = 3.40$, $p < .05$. Hence, support was found for our hypothesis H1c, suggesting that self-referencing indeed needs a certain level of motivation (by the induction of negative mood) to become effective and can be considered as an active bottom-up process. No evidence was found that self-referencing will result in a reliance on general knowledge structures when subjects are in a positive mood.

POSITIVITY OF THOUGHTS

ANOVA shows a near to significant main effect of self-referencing on the positivity of thoughts: $F(1, 79) = 2.86$, $p < .10$ and also a significant interaction effect of self-referencing and mood: $F(1, 79) = 4.39$, $p < .05$. No main effect of mood on positivity of thoughts was found ($p > .10$).

Consistent with our hypothesis H2a, it was found (although marginally significant) that thoughts were more positive when a self-reference prompt was given compared to when this prompt was absent ($M = 46.16$ vs. $M = 36.24$), suggesting that self-referencing leads to a higher positivity of thoughts (at least when positively valenced mental knowledge structures are activated by the ad).

Moreover, planned comparisons show that, consistent with hypothesis H2c, when personal second-person wording is used (self-referencing condition), more positive thoughts are generated when mood is negative, compared to when mood is positive ($M = 57.36$ vs. $M = 35.98$) ($F(1, 79) = 6.00$, $p < .05$). As for product evaluations, this suggests that self-referencing is a bottom-up process. No evidence for H2b was found.

In the no self-referencing condition, no effects of mood were found on positivity of thoughts ($M = 38.49$ vs. $M = 33.87$) ($F < 1$). This is not so surprising, since in this condition little message elaboration is expected to occur, and subjects will base their judgment more on peripheral cues (such as felt affect during ad presentation) instead of on extensive elaborations.

PURCHASE INTENTIONS

In line with our hypothesis H3a, ANOVA revealed a significant main effect of self-referencing on subjects' purchase intentions: $F(1, 79) = 10.13$, $p < .01$. In general, subjects had higher intentions to buy the advertised orange juice in the future when they were exposed to the self-referencing condition compared to subjects in the no self-referencing condition ($M = 3.14$ vs. $M = 2.15$). This suggests that self-referencing enhances advertising effectiveness. No main effect of mood on purchase intentions was found ($F < 1$).

Again, as for our product evaluation and positivity of thoughts results, superior self-referencing effects were found when mood was negative compared to when mood was positive: a significant interaction effect of self-referencing and mood was found on purchase intentions $F(1, 79) = 3.87$, $p = .05$. This interaction effect shows a slight increase in purchase intentions in the self-referencing condition as mood becomes more negative ($M = 2.82$ vs. $M = 3.5$), and a slight decrease in purchase intentions in the no self-referencing condition as mood becomes more negative ($M = 2.43$ vs. $M = 1.85$). However, these effects could not be supported for by our planned comparison analysis.

RECALL OF PRODUCT ATTRIBUTES

Nor a significant main effect of self-referencing ($F < 1$), nor a main effect of mood ($F < 1$) was found on the recall of product attributes presented in the ad. In contrast, we did find a significant interaction effect: $F(1, 79) = 3.99$, $p < .05$. In our self-referencing condition, a decrease in recall was observed as mood became more negative ($M = 2.41$ vs. $M = 1.55$) ($F(1, 79) = 2.89$, $p < .10$), while no significant effect of mood was observed in our no self-referencing condition ($M = 1.52$ vs. $M = 2.1$) ($p > .10$).

These recall results support the findings of studies on the effects of autobiographical memories (e.g. Baumgartner et al. 1992; Sujan et al. 1993) suggesting that as self-referencing increases (as in our negative mood manipulation), thoughts become more focused on the autobiographical episode, and thoughts about, and memory for, product features become less accessible.

CONCLUSION

The present study was able to gain more insight into the underlying mechanisms of self-referencing. By investigating the moderating effect of mood on self-referencing, it was found that enhanced self-referencing effects were observed under conditions of negative mood. Under self-referencing conditions, product evaluations were more positive, purchase intentions higher, and positivity of thoughts greater when mood was negative compared to when mood was positive. These findings suggest that self-referencing cues are only picked up by respondents when they are sufficiently motivated to process the information that is presented to them. As a consequence, self-referencing can be seen as an active, data-driven bottom-up process.

As a reviewer correctly stated, one can argue that, because individuals in a positive mood will be less likely to process information in a detailed manner, they may have 'missed' the self-reference prompt. So, if subjects in the positive mood condition did not completely process the self-reference prompt, it is not possible to make the above inferences concerning bottom-up processing. However, a t-test between our two mood conditions with regard to the self-referencing manipulation check revealed no significant differences between these two conditions, suggesting that positive mood respondents did pick up the self-reference prompt. This finding makes it more likely to assume that self-referencing is a bottom-up process.

Note that our results are not consistent with the hypothesis that self-referencing is the result of a reliance in general knowledge structures (such as the self), because being in a positive mood – usually thought to increase a reliance in knowledge structures (e.g. Bless et al. 1996) – did not lead to increased self-referencing results. In contrast, opposite results were found. At first, this finding seems in contradiction with research concerning the automatic activation of the self-concept (e.g. Bosmans, Vlerick, Van Kenhove, Hendrickx 2000), that shows an increased reliance on general knowledge structures when the self-concept is confronted with information relevant for it (e.g. a self-relevant personality trait). We would like to argue however, that automatic activation and self-referencing are two distinct mechanisms, both operating under different conditions: the first mechanism being an automatic process, the second a conscious control process. Further research however is needed to gain more insight into the similarities of and differences between automatic activation effects and self-referencing.

It should furthermore be noted that our results indicate that further research into mood effects is needed. Consistent with the mood literature, mood-congruent product evaluations were observed in our low elaboration, no self-referencing condition. At the same time, no mood effects were found on the positivity of thoughts in this condition. Both observations are consistent with dual theories (e.g. Forgas 1995; Petty et al. 1992) stating that under low elaboration conditions, mood is considered by subjects as an affective cue (heuristic process), and leads (without affecting the valence of generated thoughts) to mood congruent judgments (see the affect-as-information hypothesis, Schwarz & Clore 1983). This line of theorizing however, also predicts that under conditions of high elaboration (like in our self-referencing condition), because of the spread of activation, positive mood leads to more positive thoughts and to more positive product evaluations (see the affective priming hypothesis, Mackie and Worth 1991). In contrast, the results obtained on our study revealed the opposite pattern. Hence, it was found that under conditions of low elaboration, (positive) mood functioned as an affective cue, while under conditions of high elaboration, (negative) mood functioned as a motivator to process such that relevant cues (like self-reference prompts) could be picked up. Further research is necessary in order to clear out these mood effects under different forms of elaboration.

REFERENCES

Alba, Joseph W. and J. Wesley Hutchinson (1987), "Dimensions of Consumer Expertise," *Journal of Consumer Research,* 13 (March), 411-454.

Alloy, Lauren B., Lyn Y. Abramson, Laura A. Murray, Wayne G. Whitehouse and Michael E. Hogan (1997), "Self-referent Information-processing in Individuals at High and Low Cognitive Risk for Depression", *Cognition and Emotion,* 11(5/6), 539-568.

Anand, Punam and Brian Sternthal (1990), "Ease of Message Processing as a Moderator of Repetition Effects in Advertising," *Journal of Marketing Research,* 27 (August), 345-353.

Anderson, John R. and Lynne M. Reder (1979), "An Elaborative Processing Explanation of Depth of Processing," in *Levels of Processing in Human Memory,* ed. Laird S. Cermak and Fergus I.M. Craik, Hillsdalen NJ: Erlbaum.

Baumgartner, Hans, Mita Sujan and James R. Bettman (1992), "Autobiographical Memories, Affect, and Consumer Information Processing," *Journal of Consumer Psychology,* 1(1), 53-82.

Bless, Herbert, Gerald L. Clore, Norbert Schwarz, Verena Golisano, Christina Rabe and Marcus Wölk (1996), "Mood and the Use of Scripts: Does a Happy Mood Really Lead to Mindlessness?," *Journal of Personality and Social Psychology*, 71(4), 665-679.

Bodenhausen, Galen V. (1993), "Emotion, Arousal, ans Stereotypic Judgments: A Heuristic Model of Affect and Stereotyping," In D.M. Mackie and D.L. Hamilton, *Affect, Cognition, and Stereotyping: Interactive Processes in Group Perception* (pp. 13-37). San Diego, CA: Academic Press.

Bosmans, Anick, Peter Vlerick, Patrick Van Kenhove and Hendrik Hendrickx (2000), "Automatic Activation of the Self in a Persuasion Context," *Advances in Consumer Research*, vol. 27, 274-278.

Bower, Gordon H. (1981), "Mood and Memory," *American Psychologist*, 36(2), 129-148.

Burnkrant, Robert E. and H. Rao Unnava (1995), "Effects of Self-Referencing on Persuasion," *Journal of Consumer Research*, 22 (June), 17-26.

Cacioppo, John T. and Richard E. Petty (1981), "Social Psychological Procedures for Cognitive Response Assesment: The Thought Listening Technique," In T.U. Merluzzi, C.R. Glass and M. Genest (Eds.), *Cognitive Assessment* (pp. 309-342). NY: The Guilford Press.

Carver, Charles S. and Michael F. Scheier (1981), *Attention and Self-Regulation: A Control-Theory Approach to Human Behavior.* New York: Springer-Verlag.

Forgas, Joseph P. (1995), "Mood and Judgment: The Affect Infusion Model (AIM)," *Psychological Bulletin*, 117(1), 39-66.

Isen, Alice M. (1984), "Towards Understanding the Role of Affect in Cognition," In Robert Wyer, Thomas Srull, and Alice Isen (Eds.), *Handbook of Social Cognition* (vol.3). Hillsdale, NJ: Lawrence Erlbaum, 179-236.

_____ (1987), "Positive affect, Cognitive Processes, and Social Behavior," In L. Berkowitz (Ed.), *Advances in Experimental Social Psychology* (vol. 20, pp. 203-253). San Diego,CA: Academic Press.

Kardes, Frank R. (1998), *Consumer Behavior and Managerial Decision Making,* Addison – Wesley.

Krishnamurthy, Parthasarathy and Mita Sujan (1999), "Retrospection versus Anticipation: The Role of the Ad under Retrospective and Anticipatory Self-Referencing," *Journal of Consumer Research*, 26 (June), 55-69.

Kuiper, N. A. and T. B. Rogers (1979), "Encoding of Personal Information: Self – Other Differences," *Journal of Personality and Social Psychology*, 37 (April), 499-512.

Mackie, Diane M. and Leila T. Worth (1989), "Processing Deficits and the Mediation of Positive Affect in Persuasion," *Journal of Personality and Social Psychology*, 57(1), 27-40.

_____ and Leila T. Worth (1991), "Feeling Good, but not Thinking Straight: The Impact of Positive Mood on Persuasion," In Joseph P. Forgas (Ed.), *Emotion and Social Judgments* (pp 201-219). Oxford, UK: Pergamon Press.

Markus, Hazel (1980), "The Self in Thought and Memory," In D.M. Wegner and R.R. Vallacher (eds.), *The Self in Social Psychology*, New York: Oxford Press.

Mayer, John D., Laura J. McCormick, Sara E. Strong (1995), "Mood-Congruent Memory and Natural Mood: New Evidence," *Personality and Social Psychology Bulletin*, 21(7), 736-746.

Mehrabian, Albert and James Russell (1974), *An Approach to Environmental Psychology*, Cambridge, MA: The MIT Press.

Meyers – Levy, Joan and Duraraij Maheswaran (1991), "Exploring Males' and Females' Processing Strategies: When and Why Do Differences Occur in Consumers' Processing of Ad Claims?," *Journal of Consumer Research,* 18 (June), 63-70.

_____ and Laura A. Peracchio (1996), "Moderators on the Impact of Self-Reference on Persuasion," *Journal of Consumer Research*, vol. 22 (March), 408-423.

_____ and Brian Sternthal (1991), "Gender Differences in the Use of Message Cues and Judgments," *Journal of Marketing Research*, 28 (February), 84-96.

Mick, David Glen (1992), "Levels of Subjective Comprehension in Advertising Processing and Their Relations to Ad Perceptions, Attitudes, and Memory," *Journal of Consumer Research,* 18 (March), 411-424.

Petty, Richard E., David W. Schumann, Steven A. Richman and Alan J. Strathman (1993), "Positive Mood and Persuasion: Different Roles for Affect Under High- and Low-Elaboration Conditions," *Journal of Personality and Social Psychology,* 64(1), 5-20.

Schank, Roger C. and Robert P. Abelson (1977), *Scripts, Plans, Goals, and Understanding: An Inquiry into Human Knowledge Structures*, Hillsdale, NJ: Erlbaum.

Schwarz, Norbert and Gerald L. Clore (1983), "Mood, Misattribution, and Judgments of Well-Being: Informative and Directive Functions of Affective States," *Journal of Personality and Social Psychology,* 45(3), 513-523.

Sedikides, Constantine (1992), "Mood as a Determinant of Attentional Focus," *Cognition and Emotion*, 6(2), 129-148.

Simons, Jeffrey and Kate B. Carey (1998), "A Structural Analysis of Attitudes Toward Alcohol and Marijuana Use," *Personality and Social Psychology Bulletin,* 24(7), 727-735.

Sinclair, Robert C. and Melvin M. Mark (1995), "The Effects of Mood State on Judgemental Accuracy: Processing Strategy as a Mechanism," *Cognition and Emotion,* 9(5), 417-438.

Sujan, Mita, James R. Bettman and Hans Baumgartner (1993), "Influencing Consumer Judgments Using Autobiographical Memories: A Self-Referencing Perspective," *Journal of Marketing Research,* 30(4), 422-436.

Symons, Cynthia S. and Blair T. Johnson (1997), "The Self-Reference Effect in Memory: A Meta-Analysis," *Psychological Bulletin*, 121(3), 371-394.

Does It Make Sense to Use Scents to Enhance Brand Memory?

Maureen Morrin, University of Pittsburgh
S. Ratneshwar, University of Connecticut

ABSTRACT

Two studies are reported which investigate the impact of ambient scent on consumer memory for brand information. Both studies demonstrate that ambient scent can improve the recall and recognition of brand-related information. The results suggest that cognitive, rather than affective, mechanisms are responsible for the observed effects. In the first study, subjects were exposed to full color package shots of familiar and unfamiliar brands of toiletry/household cleaning products on a computer screen. Subjects evaluated these products in a congruently scented, incongruently scented, or unscented environment. Twenty-four hours later, in the same scented condition, their memory for brand-related information was tested. In this study, the presence of either a congruent or incongruent ambient scent increased the amount of attention paid to brand stimuli, but only the presence of a congruent ambient scent significantly improved brand recognition and recall. Thus, semantic matching appears to play a role in scent's impact on memory performance. The second study used a 2 x 2 design to manipulate the presence or absence of scent at both the time of encoding and time of retrieval. Analyses indicate that the presence of ambient scent at the time of retrieval had no discernable impact on memory performance. Thus, contextual reinstatement does not appear to play a role in scent's impact on memory. Instead, ambient scents that semantically match the items to be remembered enhance memory performance by increasing the amount of attention paid to stimuli at the time of encoding. Implications, limitations, and areas for future research are discussed.

Rhetorics of Resistance, Discourses of Discontent
Eileen Fischer, York University

With notable exceptions (e.g. Firat and Venkatesh 1995; Hermann 1982,1993; Murray and Ozanne 1991; Ozanne and Murray 1995; Peñaloza and Price 1993), the consumer behavior literature has been more concerned to understand what makes people happy shoppers, buyers and owners than to understand what makes them try resist the siren songs of the market. And although more consumer researchers are likely to be attuned to consumer resistance in the wake of such phenomena as the "Battle of Seattle," where protestors effectively shut down talks organized by the World Trade Organization, this session was not simply a topical look at a timely issue. Rather, the premise of this session was that we cannot consider consumer resistance as an interesting phenomenon marginal to our real concern of understanding those who want to consume. Rather, as the papers in this session show, we must understand consumption and resistance as co-constituting discourses that are inextricably linked: to understand one, we *must* understand discursive practices associated with the other.

The session's purpose, then, was to deepen our understanding of some of the emerging or escalating practices of consumer resistance by focusing on how those practices are rhetorically constructed and re-constructed in dynamic tension with consumption. The first paper (Handelman) took an institutional perspective to examine the tactics that boycotters and activists use to subvert marketing practices, showing how consumer activists may appropriate marketers' tools and tactics in order to redefine them (cf Peñaloza and Price 1993).

The second paper (Fischer) placed contemporary forms of resistance in historical context as emergent collective action frames that are informed by past activist traditions. Drawing on social movement and evolutionary theory, the paper focused on the dynamics of problem definition, solution identification, and mobilization of action.

The third paper (Holt) examined critically the rhetorics of consumer resistance that have been generated in the academy and mass media and considered the social effects of these rhetorics in relation to the interests of capital. The session discussant, Lisa Peñaloza, drew on her conceptual model of consumer resistance (Peñaloza and Price 1993) to situate the papers and identify their contributions to our understanding of both resistance and consumption.

The papers were relevant to a broad spectrum of those whose interests range from consumer activism, to public policy and from branding to symbolic consumption.

ABSTRACTS

"Changing the Rules: An Institutional Perspective on the Rhetorics of Consumer Activism"
Jay Handelman

This research studies the rhetorics of resistance used by Nike boycotter and Media Foundation culture jammers to subvert marketing images and norms. The researchers used a three-year ethnographic study of boycotters and culture jammers that included archival research, semistructured interviews, and participant-observation at a boycotting event. The findings were examined from a perspective drawn from institutional theory. Four aspects of the rhetorics of consumer resistance were identified: defining a higher purpose, exposing the boundaries between organization and environment, recoupling the negative actions of the corporations with

their brands, and linking consumer resistance to legitimate norms and institutions.

"Evolution in Rhetorics of Resistance: An Analysis of the Emergence of the Anti-Brand Movement"
Eileen Fischer

This paper draws on recent developments in the literature on social movements and institutional evolution to investigate the emergence of the collective action frames embodied in the current "no-logo" campaign. Drawing on a variety of textual materials generated by leaders in the movements, current action frames for consumer resistance are shown to be rooted in, and a reaction to, the problems analysed and solutions identified in earlier movements. Implications of this historically situated analysis for understanding the dynamics of contemporary consumer resistance movements are discussed, as are the implications for understanding collective consumer behavior of other types.

"Deconstructing Consumer Resistance: How the Reification of Commodified Cultural Sovereignty is Entailed in the Parasitic Postmodern Market"
Douglas B. Holt

How does the cultural organization of consumption—consumer culture–aid the market? Consumer culture is usually represented using the metaphor of *cultural authority*: the idea that consumers grant the market tastemaking power to orchestrate consumption meanings and practices. I use case analyses of long interviews to argue against this rhetoric. Rather than cultural authority, postmodern consumer culture is premised upon taken-for-granted acceptance that one pursues cultural sovereignty as a consumer. The market today thrives on people who pursue individuating identity projects through nonconformist, local, producerly consumption practices. Postmodern marketing, operating within this new consumer culture, increasingly acts as a parasitic cultural machine that constantly pilfers from public culture to cycle through commodities a massive and dynamic universe of meanings, sensibilities, and pleasures.

REFERENCES
Firat, A. Fuat and Alladi Venkatesh (1995), "Liberatory Postmodernism and the Reenchantment of Consumption," *JCR* 22 (December), 239-267.
Herrmann, Robert O. (1982), "The Consumer Movement in Historial Perspective," in *Consumerism: The Search for the Consumer Interest*, 4th edition, David Aaker and George Day, New York NY: Free Press, 23-32.
Herrmann, Robert O. (1993), "The Tactics of Consumer Resistance: Group Action and Marketplace Exit," in *Advances in Consumer Research*, Volume 20, ed. Leigh McAlister and Michael L. Rothschild, Provo, UT: Association for Consumer Research, 130-134.
Murray, Jeff B. and Julie L. Ozanne (1991), "The Critical Imagination: Emancipatory Interests in Consumer Research," *Journal of Consumer Research*, 18(September), 129-144.
Ozanne, Julie and Jeff Murray (1995), "Uniting Critical Theory and Public Policy to Create the Reflexively Defiant Consumer," *American Behavioral Scientist*, 38(February), 516-525.

Advances in Consumer Research
Volume 28, © 2001

Penaloza, Lisa and Linda L. Price (1993), "Consumer Resistance: A Conceptual Overview," in *Advances in Consumer Research*, Volume 20, ed. Leigh McAlister and Michael L. Rothschild, Provo, UT: Association for Consumer Research, 123-128.

Consumer Preferences Towards Frequency Programs

Ran Kivetz, Columbia University

Frequency (loyalty) programs that recognize and reward frequent customers have become one of the most commonly used marketing tools for retaining customers and stimulating product or service usage. Nevertheless, we still know very little about the factors that influence consumer perception of and response to such programs and why some programs are highly successful whereas other programs fail. Thus, the main goal of this session was to improve our understanding of consumer preference towards frequency programs (FPs) and, more generally, towards streams of efforts that lead to future rewards (e.g., publishing to get tenure and dieting to get thin). The papers in this session addressed a broad range of questions regarding how consumers construct their preference towards FPs. In the process of examining these questions, the session participants and the discussion leader, Steve Hoch, provided insights into important topics in consumer research, such as intertemporal choice, consumer motivation, mental accounting, and reinforcement schedules and conditioning.

First, Hsee demonstrates that the presence of a "medium" can increase people's willingness to exert effort. Medium is defined here as currency (e.g., points) that is obtained for exerting effort and that can be traded for rewards. Why, then, would points increase consumers' tendency to engage in the required effort? Hsee proposes that the medium can make an otherwise concave effort-reward relationship look linear and/or make an otherwise ambiguous effort-reward relationship look clear.

Second, Kivetz and Simonson show that, under certain conditions, increasing the program requirements (e.g., twenty vs. ten gasoline purchases)–while holding the reward constant–enhances the likelihood of joining the program and the willingness to pay membership fees. They explain the results based on the notion of *idiosyncratic fit*, whereby in certain cases, consumers construe their effort as being lower than a reference effort (e.g., the typical effort of others). That is, when consumers have an idiosyncratic fit with a program (e.g., they live especially close to a gas station offering a FP), they derive additional transaction utility (Thaler 1985), which can increase with greater program requirements.

Third, van Osselaer and Alba employ two simulated buying experiments to show that consumers' choices are influenced by the way loyalty programs allocate points to purchases, even when the number of purchases needed for a reward is held constant. In particular, options with flat reward schedules (200 points per purchase) are chosen more often than increasing (100 points for first, 200 for second, for 300 third purchase) and step-descending (400, 100, 100) but not more than linear-descending (300, 200, 100) schedules. The results are consistent with a tendency to meliorate that is only weakly counteracted by a tendency to stick with one option in order to minimize losses due to point expiration.

Finally, Steve Hoch led a discussion on the papers presented in the session and on FPs in general. Steve integrated the three papers and proposed some underlying principles that could account for the performance of various FPs (e.g., highly successfull frequent flyer programs). Furthermore, Steve proposed several intriguing directions for future research, such as investigating the intertemporal aspects of FPs, the impact of different reward currencies, and more.

Strategic Behaviors in Competitive Games

Wilfred Amaldoss, Purdue University
Teck H. Ho, University of Pennsylvania

"Network versus Network: Theory and Experimental Evidence"

Wilfred Amaldoss and Amnon Rapoport

Collaborations are becoming increasingly popular. By being part of a network, a firm is likely to gain access to a larger resource base (e.g., Mahoney and Pandian 1992, Kraatz and Zajac 1999). Yet the conventional wisdom is that larger networks are more likely to fail (Gomes-Casseras 1994, p 9). There is a basis for this wisdom: As the number of partners in a network increases, its partners will commit fewer resources for the joint endeavor. In agreement with the conventional wisdom, the large Mips network, in contrast to the smaller PowerPc network, is a failure in the microprocessor business. On the other hand, the Visa network with over 23,000 member banks is thriving in the face of competition from American Express, a fully integrated firm. Similarly, the Star Alliance, a nine-member airline network established in 1997, is growing stronger in the competitive airline business. In light of this contradictory evidence what is the effect of number of partners in a network on fostering collaboration? The answer is not clear. There may be circumstances when the positive effect of network size may even override the free-riding problems, making it optimal for firms to forge larger networks.

It is possible that the type of investments required for the joint effort may moderate the effect of network size. Contrary to intuition, our game-theoretic model predicts that, if the investments are recoverable, the joint investment increases as the size of network increases. This is because the incremental investment from the new partners more than compensates for the total loss in investment due to under investment by current partners. However, if the investments are nonrecoverable, our model predicts that the joint investment does not depend on the network size. This is because the total decrement in investment, on account of the under-investment by current network partners, is precisely offset by the incremental investment made by new members.

We report the results of a series of 12 experiments designed to examine the effect of type of investment and network size on fostering innovation. When the investments were recoverable, our results show that individual network partners invested less as the network size increased. Yet, in keeping with the model prediction, the joint investment of the network increased as the network size increased. When the investments are nonrecoverable, theory predicts that the joint investment should not be affected by network size. In reality, the joint investment increased as the network size increased. This is because network partners made less than predicted reductions in investments, as the network size increased.

On the average, our subjects invested more that the equilibrium predictions. What could have caused such a behavioral deviation from the theoretical norm? We examine the implications of three competing explanations for the deviation: *risk attitude*, *warm glow*, and *altruism*. On generalizing our model to accommodate different risk attitudes in addition to risk neutrality, we observe that risk-seeking behavior on the part of all the members increases joint investment, while risk-aversion has the opposite effect. Allowing for warm glow preferences increase the mean joint investment. However, it doesn't cause the joint investment to vary with network size, if the investments are nonrecoverable. On the other hand, altruism causes the joint investment to vary with network size, besides increasing the mean joint investment, even if the investments are nonrecoverable.

There is evidence of altruism in the investment decisions of our subjects. This suggests that a supply-side externality is at play in larger networks–partners in larger networks may well invest more in their joint endeavor merely out of altruistic regard for their partners. The altruistic regard increases as the network size increases, and, in part, helps to reduce the desire to free ride on the efforts of partners.

Later with the aid of the Experience Weighted Attraction (EWA) Learning model (Camerer and Ho 1999), we attempt to discern the *adaptive learning mechanism* that can account for the investment behavior of our subjects. Our analysis suggests that the investment decisions were not exclusively guided by forming beliefs about other players. Rather, our subject's strategy choices were guided by reinforcement-based learning, either completely or predominantly.

"Are Posted Prices 'Fair'? An Experimental Analysis of Dynamic Buyer-Seller Interactions"

Darryl Banks, J.Wesley Hutchinson, and Robert J. Meyer

This paper examines "fairness effects" in posted-price markets. Two explanations for the phenomena have been offered. By way of an experimental investigation we seek evidence of the empirical validity of these explanations. The persistent observation of "fairness effects" in posted-price markets is strong evidence that the classic economic model, in which buyers are price-takers and sellers choose prices to maximize profits against the distribution of reservation values, given that buyers are price-takers, is incomplete.

The dominant explanation for these effects posits that the perceived fairness of a prospective transaction affects the buyer's assessment of the transaction's utility, and that sellers take this into account when setting prices. Fairness is related to the division of gains from trade, a 50/50 split being the fairest of them all. Consequently, the perceived fairness of a posted price is a function of the perception of the seller's cost, as, for any given price, the lower is the seller's cost the smaller is the buyer's share of the gains. This explanation is consistent with a great deal of existing evidence that shows that buyers are more resistant to high prices when they believe sellers' costs are low, and sellers try to justify high prices with claims of high costs.

In a recent paper Banks et al propose a different explanation for "fairness effects," arguing that they are "rational" behaviors of forward-looking buyers and sellers. They argue that the phenomena are due to the parties' intertemporal incentives and to the existence of private information on both sides–only buyers know their reservation values and only sellers know their costs. A buyer's willingness to reject prices that are no higher than his/her reservation value is a strategy designed to make the seller post low prices now and/or in the future. This strategy can be effective only if the seller is uncertain about the buyer's reservation value. The seller anticipates this and posts prices that, if accepted, reveal the truth about the buyer.

Banks et al's results are consistent with the existing empirical evidence but yield a striking prediction about the effects of the parties' initial beliefs. They predict that a buyer's initial beliefs about a seller's cost will *not* affect his/her responses to the seller's prices but *will* affect the prices that the seller posts. Moreover, while the buyer's own initial beliefs will not affect his/her responses to the seller's prices, the *seller's* initial beliefs will affect the buyer's responses to the posted prices. This prediction differs sharply with what we would expect to observe if perceived fairness is an argument in the utility function, providing a basis for a test of the two theories. We find evidence supporting the Banks et al result.

"An Experimental Study of Several Electronic Market Institutions"
Teck H. Ho and Steve Hoch

The internet has opened up a whole host of opportunities for sellers and buyers to experiment with different market institutions. Some experts believe, for example, that the future of business-to-business and business-to-customer e-commerce will be dominated by auctions (InfoWorld, 1998) and the stock market success of several new market makers (e.g., ebay.com and priceline.com) demonstrates investors' beliefs that these innovative market institutions will significantly increase in revenue in the future. Thus the study of different internet market institutions has tremendous practical relevance.

It is also intellectually challenging to study electronic market institutions. Most market institutions outside of the well-developed financial markets and a limited number of auction markets rely almost exclusively on posted prices by a limited number of sellers. With significant reductions in e-search and transactions, the internet already has spurred the development of numerous new market institutions where not only sellers post prices (amazon.com) but so do buyers, both statically (priceline.com) and interactively (ebay.com). Enthusiasts of e-commerce argue that these new market mechanisms can dramatically increase efficiency by appropriately matching buyers' willingness-to-pay with sellers' willingness-to-sell.

There are 3 critical dimensions along which one can evaluate a market institution:

- Which market institution has the highest average price of transaction?
- Which market institution generates the most social surplus?
- Which market institution has the most equitable way of dividing the social surplus between the buyers and sellers?

We reported experimental results from two commonly used electronic market institutions and evaluate them along the 3 dimensions mentioned above.

Dipankar Chakravarti was the discussant for this special session.

An Investigation of Agent Assisted Consumer Information Search: Are Consumers Better Off?

Robert Moore, Mississippi State University
Girish Punj, University of Connecticut

ABSTRACT

Over the past few years, the World Wide Web has quickly become part of the consumers' information arsenal. However, few researchers have examined the impact of consumer use of this electronic medium in the decision process; especially under different task conditions. With this focus, we address the issue of the amount of external information search that is conducted in a Web environment versus a traditional print environment. Specifically, in an experiment consisting of a 2 (environment) X 2 (time pressure) X 2 (number of alternatives) design, we examine differences between Web-based and traditional decision environment with respect to external information search activities. The study examines aspects of information search that the Web purportedly will affect the most, the ability to filter large amounts of data based on individual preferences. Dependent measures of interest include; the amount of search a consumer engages in, satisfaction with search, and decision confidence as a result of search activities. Findings indicate that the amount of information that is searched is indeed higher in a traditional environment, however the amount of search was not seen to affect information search outcomes such as satisfaction.

Online Reviews: Do Consumers Use Them?
Patrali Chatterjee, Rutgers University

ABSTRACT

The use of the WWW as a venue for voicing opinions, complaints and recommendations on products and firms has been widely reported in the popular media. However little is known how consumers use these reviews and if they subsequently have any influence on evaluations and purchase intentions of products and retailers. This study examines the effect of negative reviews on retailer evaluation and patronage intention given that the consumer has already made a product/brand decision. Our results indicate that the extent of WOM search depends on the consumer's reasons for choosing an online retailer. Further the influence of negative WOM information on perceived reliability of retailer and purchase intentions is determined largely by familiarity with the retailer and differs based on whether the retailer is a pure-Internet or clicks-and-mortar firm. Managerial implications for positioning strategies to minimize the effect of negative word-of-mouth have been discussed.

Research on word of mouth (WOM) effects provides plenty of evidence that a satisfied customer may tell some people about his experience with a company, but a dissatisfied one will tell everybody he meets. Virtual communities with active members who provide evaluations and opinions on products and firms now provide a venue to tell the world and represent one of the fastest growing phenomena on the Web (Armstrong and Hagel 1996). It is not surprising therefore, that providing consumers a venue to voice their opinions, recommendations and complaints and monitoring this word-of-mouth activity has become a business and some firms pay (in cash, points, recognition) consumers for their contributions (Tedeschi 1999) since they can be used as instruments to compete for consumer attention and visits (e.g., eBay, Oxygen Media). While some reports in the popular media provide anecdotal evidence that companies are listening, little is known if complaints and reviews posted at Web sites are instrumental in changing purchase decisions of consumers who read them. In this research we investigate if negative WOM information or reviews of online retailers affect evaluations and patronage intentions.

Online Consumer Reviews as Word-of-Mouth Information

Online word of mouth activity differs from those in the real world in many aspects. In the marketing literature WOM communication is "oral, person-to-person communication between a receiver and a communicator whom the receiver perceives as noncommercial, regarding a brand, a product, a service or a provider" (Arndt 1967, p. 5). Adapting this definition to be relevant to the online medium requires reference to online communication modes (e-mail and hypertext), the existence of remote many-to-many communication (most WOM information are from strangers who have never met or will in the future, e.g. epinions.com). The non-commercial focus may not be certain. Most of these online forums point out that while they do not edit consumer comments, some get paid for referrals or purchases and/or get advertising income from target firms. Further, word-of-mouth information available online is far more voluminous in quantity compared to information obtained from traditional contacts in the offline world and includes several units of positive and negative information presented together from multiple sources at the same time as opposed to a single piece of information that is either positive or negative in valence.

The underlying benefit consumers derive from availability of other consumers' evaluations in online virtual communities is the scale advantages they experience in going through their purchase decision making. Word of mouth information on the Internet exists in various forms that differ in accessibility, scope and source. Despite popular wisdom that all content on the Web is accessible, the immense volume and variety of information available online and time constraints faced by the consumer provide opportunities for manufacturers and retailers to make some word-of mouth information more easily accessible compared to others by placing them close to purchase information. Reviews (actual user comments) or ratings (on a scale) of product or retailers conveniently provided along with purchase information at online stores and comparison shopping agents represent the most accessible and prevalent form. In contrast, USENET groups exist independently from purchase information, are relatively less under marketer control but require prior knowledge of their existence and conscious effort by the consumer (e.g., deja.com).

Consumer evaluations may differ in scope by pertaining to either products or retailers. While most online retailers feature evaluations of products, reviews of online and offline retailers are generally provided by comparison shopping services (e.g., www.mysimon.com) and e-business rating services (e.g., www.bizrate.com). While some offline sources of product comparison information (e.g., Consumer Reports) are popular, similar information and reviews of retailers are practically unavailable (Sinha 2000). Hence, online sources of retailer information are widely used for both offline and online purchases and the topic of investigation in this research.

Effects of Product Reviews on Purchase Decisions

Research in marketing literature points out that WOM information plays an important role in hybrid decision processes or recommendation-based heuristics in which the decision maker obtains recommendations for the purpose of reducing the uncertainty and amount of information that must be processed to make a decision (Olshavsky and Granbois 1979). The consequences of WOM communication occur in the behavior of those who receive it – their awareness, beliefs, attitudes and actual decisions. Research on the potency of WOM information indicates that the inferences people draw are contingent upon their receptivity to the WOM information (Wilson and Peterson 1989). A substantial literature documents the mediating influence of the receiver's predisposition towards the target of WOM communication on receptivity to and interpretation of new information. The stronger an individual's feelings or confidence in choice prior to exposure to WOM information, the more the feelings will dominate the interpretation and use of WOM information. Hence criteria used by consumers in product decision or choice drivers play an important part in determining if and how much of WOM information is obtained and the influence of the WOM information on product evaluation and purchase decision.

WOM sources usually studied in the marketing literature are predominantly, though not exclusively, personal sources of information (Stewart et al. 1985) and may be strong and weak tie depending on the closeness of relationship between the decision maker and the recommendation source (Brown and Reingen 1987). In the online medium however, the "tie strength" is always very weak because recommendations are from total strangers. Unlike the

FIGURE 1
Online WOM Information Effects

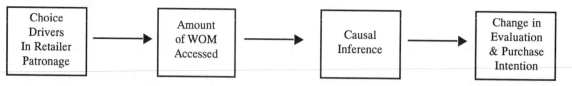

case of WOM from interpersonal sources, the online recipient cannot use source similarity, expertise and accessibility to determine the credibility of information in Internet forums. Thus the theoretical framework of attribution theory (Kelly 1967) can be used to investigate the inferences consumers draw from WOM activity of weak tie sources. The direct and indirect (through influence on person perception) effects of causal inference on product perception and purchase intention are a function of the generalizability (or consensus) of the cause across people, and the stability (or recurrence) of the cause. Figure 1 shows the processes involved when consumers access WOM information or reviews online.

PROPOSITIONS

The first research objective is to predict the extent of WOM information search during an online purchase occasion based on choice drivers behind the retailer choice decision. Next we examine the impact of negative WOM information on purchase intentions by examining the joint influence of an individual's reasons for patronizing a firm and inferences consumers draw from the negative WOM information on retailer evaluation and purchase intention.

Choice Drivers and Extent of WOM Information Search

The online shopping medium facilitates comparison shopping by consumers, and most shopping engines permit easy searching on the basis of price. A common problem consumers face while shopping online is choosing between a familiar retail firm that appears to be an expensive but safe choice (either a well-known online/ offline retailer or a firm they have prior experience with) and a cheaper alternative whose reliability is unknown to the consumer. Adapting the research on uncertainty in decision-making in brand choice to the online medium would suggest that consumers choosing an unfamiliar retailer are more likely to search for information on the retailer to reduce their uncertainty compared to consumers choosing a familiar option (Biswas 1992). This is especially relevant for the online retail channel because of security and risk concerns and the fact that transactions are conducted remotely.

P1:   Consumers whose decision to patronize a firm is driven by their familiarity with the firm are less likely to search for WOM information voluntarily than those who decide to buy from a retailer based on price.

The volume of WOM information available online is far greater (some products and firms have more than 40-50 postings by consumer reviewers) than those available through traditional contacts in the offline world. Exposure to online WOM information is totally under consumer control and is only limited by the time and cognitive constraints of the information-seeker. The regret literature suggests that actions that deviate from the norm (choosing unfamiliar retailer) involves greater attribution of responsibility for the negative consequences that follow. This implies

that consumers who choose an unfamiliar retailer are more likely to attribute responsibility for negative future consequences to themselves compared to consumers who patronize a familiar retailer (Simonson 1992). This anticipation of regret is expected to make consumers choosing an unfamiliar retailer search and access more WOM information compared to consumers choosing a familiar retailer. Hence,

P2.   Consumers whose decision to patronize a firm is based on familiarity with the firm will search for less negative WOM information compared to those who decide to buy based on price.

Generalizability and Stability of Negative WOM Information

Research in the marketing literature has been fairly consistent in assigning high credibility to WOM information in general and negative WOM in particular, because WOM sources have nothing to gain. In a study of unfavorable product ratings, Mizerski (1982) shows that when information about an object or firm comes through the opinions or recommendations of another person, negative information may be more credible and generalizable than positive information. However, consumer perception of credibility and hence generalizability of both positive and negative WOM information available online is suspect because of the lack of personal knowledge about the motivations of unseen strangers offering recommendations and the possibility that the commercial interests of the Web site or online forum are involved. Even in the case of independent online forums like USENET groups, reports in the popular media of firms systematically infiltrating online forums and paying students and consumers to "spread bad word" and to deflate popularity ratings of firms and products lead to cynicism about the veracity of the WOM information. Wilson and Peterson (1989) show that evaluative predispositions toward products and firms effectively acted as filters through which word-of-mouth information flowed. Consumers who decide to patronize a retailer based on familiarity have stronger positive feelings and are less likely to trust negative WOM information regarding the firm compared to consumers who choose retailers based on price.

P3.   Consumers who choose to patronize a retailer based on familiarity will be less likely to perceive negative WOM information as credible compared to consumers who choose a retailer on the basis of price.

Past studies provide evidence to the notion that consumers' reactions to WOM communications varied by their familiarity with the target company, product or brand (Mowen 1980). Hence, consumers who decide to patronize a retailer based on familiarity are more likely to attribute the cause of negative retailer reviews or WOM information to situational or temporary factors (i.e., holiday rush of orders affecting service, or local server/technical failure). These factors are perceived less likely to recur and hence less severe compared to stable causes.

P4.   Consumers who choose to patronize a retailer based on familiarity will be more likely to perceive the cause of negative WOM information as unstable compared to consumers who choose on the basis of price.

Effect on Purchase Intention

There is a sizable body of evidence which suggests that the influence of negative WOM information is more potent compared to positive WOM information in influencing purchase intentions of potential buyers (Brown and Reingen 1987; Weinberger, Allen and Dillon 1980). However, since the salience of negative WOM information on purchase intention will depend on consumer's perception of the generalizability and likelihood of recurrence of service failure and hence on the reasons for patronizing a firm we expect differential effects of WOM information on purchase information.

P5.   Consumers who choose a retailer based on familiarity will be less likely to change their purchase intention in response to negative information compared to those who decide to buy from a retailer based on price.

METHOD

In this research, we consider online WOM information in the form of retailer reviews provided by comparison shopping engines along with purchase information. To control for the confounding effect of brand features and other marketing mix factors that are difficult to capture in an experimental study and maintain participants' involvement we confine ourselves to exploring the effect of negative reviews on decision to patronize the retailer given that a particular product (the recommended course textbook) will be bought.

Sample. Data for this study was collected from undergraduate marketing (314) and physics (105) students in two northeastern universities, with about equal number of males and females. After the first day of class in a computer lab students were asked to shop for their course textbook online using links to comparison-shopping search engines provided from the course Web page. Participation was requested for 45 minutes on a voluntary basis. 38 students did not complete the entire study so their responses were discarded.

Questionnaire Stimuli. The comparison-shopping pages had pre-programmed information on price of the textbook and shipping charges. Delivery time and buy back policy were maintained same across retailers. To test for possible differences in familiarity/price effects across pure-play Internet and click-and-mortar retailers, students were divided into 2 groups. For each group of students two retailers were offered for consideration, actual prices were listed $2 and $20 (after shipping and handling charges) lower than the campus bookstore (priced at $89.99). For the pure-Internet group the "familiar" retailer (A) had the highest price, while the unknown online retailer (B) had the lower price. This was done to ensure that respondents who typically shop on the basis of price will be in the unfamiliar condition (but we cannot infer price-effects). Similarly, for the clicks-and-mortar group, the "familiar" retailer (C) had the highest price, while unknown retailer (D) had the lower price. We did not consider the high familiarity - low price and low familiarity - high price situations because experiments in an earlier separate study revealed that all subjects chose the former option. A radio button next to the link – "Get retailer reviews" was provided for each retailer (the page linked to it indicated no reviews were available at the present time – so WOM information would not affect initial choice) and student clicks were recorded. On the next page students selected their chosen retailer, and the

reasons behind their choice. Initial purchase intention was recorded in terms of how likely they were to buy from the retailer on a 5-point scale (1-most likely not buy, 5-most likely buy). Responses to the open-ended question on retailer choice drivers was followed by asking students to select the most important reason for their choice.

On the next page all subjects (including those who had not clicked on get retailer reviews) were informed that an independent online forum had agreed to make consumer reviews for their chosen retailer available. They were given the option to browse through as many or few reviews and could use as much or little time as needed and take a final decision at the end of the session. Subjects who did not want to browse through the reviews were asked to fill out their "final decision" and leave.

Selection of WOM information. Selection of multiple units of WOM information was made while controlling for effects that are not the focus of study. The retailer review pages were identical for all retailers except for the change in name (based on the respondent's choice) and pre-programmed using actual consumer negative reviews from online forums at www.deja.com, www. thirdvoice.com and www.buyerpower.com. Since prior research indicates that weak-tie sources are more important for evaluation of instrumental (rather than affective) cues (Brown and Reingen 1987), and to control for differences in salience of WOM information on different attributes, we confined ourselves to comments on the retailer's order processing issues (e.g., order form on Web site gave errors, e-mail confirmation not sent etc.) available as a link. This section had an index page with one-line links to 30 reviews. The one-line description had the contributor's screen name or e-mail address, and the first 3 letters of the message as in actual review sites. Respondents had to click on the link to access the actual message. At the end of each message respondents had to judge if the message was believable (1-not believable at all, 5-totally believable) and stable (1-not likely to happen to me, 5- most likely to happen to me) on a 5-point scale.

On each page students had the option to end their WOM search and "take the final decision" by clicking on a link. On the "final decision" page subjects responded to three items. First item measured if they would use online consumer reviews in their purchase decision making in the future on a 5-point scale (1-most likely not use, 5-most likely use). The second question measured change in purchase intention compared to initial decision on a 5-point scale (1- certainly less likely to buy now, 3- as likely to buy as before, 5-certainly more likely to buy now). The third item recorded how reliable their retailer is on a reverse-coded 5-point scale (1-very reliable, 5-not reliable at all). Subjects were debriefed at the end of the session and thanked for their participation.

Manipulation Checks: In the later part of the questionnaire, students were asked to indicate their level of familiarity with retailers A, B, C and D using a 9-point scale where 1=not familiar and 9=very familiar. An analysis of variance test indicated significant differences for both pure-Internet and clicks-and-mortar groups (F=123.4, p=.0001; F=106.9, p=.0001) between unfamiliar (x=1.74, x=2.23) and familiar (x=7.81, x=8.64) treatments, suggesting that brand familiarity was effectively manipulated.

RESULTS

To evaluate the impact of choice drivers, responses for the most important reason for choosing a retailer were categorized into those based on familiarity (e.g., prior buying experience online or offline, well-known) and price-related factors. To test our propositions we combine the familiarity treatments for both groups. As can be seen in Table 1, more subjects selected a retailer based on price than familiarity. This may be particularly true of online purchases of textbooks that are standardized products, and consum-

TABLE 1
Choice Drivers And Propensity To Voluntarily Access WOM Information

Most important reason for choosing retailer	Number of Respondents	Respondents Voluntarily Accessed Retailer Reviews (P1)*	Respondents Agreeing to Search Reviews
Familiarity	144 (38%)	23 (16%)	86 (59%)
Price	237 (62%)	59 (25%)	119 (50%)
Total number of respondents	381	72	205

TABLE 2
Choice Drivers And Propensity To Access WOM Information

Choice Drivers	(Standard Deviations In Parentheses)		
	Non-voluntary Access of Retailer Reviews		
Most important reason for choosing retailer	Mean No. of Reviews accessed (P2*)	Credibility of -ve Reviews (P3)	Perceived Stability of -ve Reviews (P4*)
Familiarity	6.27 (1.5)	3.16 (1.06)	1.6 (1.27)
Price	8.04 (1.94)	2.06 (1.92)	2.4 (2.13)
All respondents	7.24 (1.79)	2.99 (1.65)	2.04 (1.79)

TABLE 3
Effect Of WOM Information On Purchase Intention

Most important reason for choosing retailer	(Standard deviations in parentheses)		
	Use Online Reviews in future	Change in Purchase Intention (P5**)	Reliability of Retailer
Familiarity	3.16 (0.84)	3.93 (0.59)	3.85 (0.46)
Price	3.7 (2.57)	3.4 (1.04)	4.1 (0.8)
All respondents	3.46 (1.99)	3.74 (0.97)	3.96 (0.63)

* Tests significant at 0.001 level.
** Tests significant at 0.01 level.

ers do not have an option of choosing among brands of products. Further significantly more subjects (25%, z=2.43, p>0.01) who selected their retailer on the basis of price tried to access retailer reviews on their own during their decision-making process compared to 16% of subjects who selected a retailer they were familiar with, thus supporting P1.

When subjects were informed about the availability of retailer reviews 205 (54% of total participants) subjects chose to access the recommendation section before taking their final decision. An equal proportion of participants from both familiar (59%) and price (50%) groups wanted to access the reviews. We found consumers who selected their retailer on the basis of price browsed through significantly (t=6.02, p< 0.001) more negative reviews overall compared to those who selected their retailer on the basis of familiarity thus supporting P2. Contrary to our expectations, Table 2 indicates that the perception of credibility of negative WOM information did not differ across consumers who chose their retailer on the basis of price or familiarity (t=1.37, p>0.10) hence P3 is not supported. However consumers who chose their retailer on the basis of familiarity are more likely to attribute temporary causes to the service failures reported in reviews that will not affect their experience with the retailer compared to those who chose a retailer based on price. Hence our proposition regarding the perceived stability or likelihood of recurrence (P4) is supported (t=3.24, p<0.001).

As expected, consumers who selected their retailer on the basis of familiarity are less likely to change their purchase intention

(t=2.26, p<0.01) on exposure to negative WOM information compared to subjects who selected the retailer offering the best price, providing support for P5. Though we do not specify any hypothesis for reliability of retailer after exposure to negative WOM we find that consumers choosing a familiar retailer are less likely to be negatively affected compared to those who choose a retailer based on price (t=2.87, p<0.001). In contrast, however there is no significant difference among consumers in their desire to use online reviews in the future.

Analyzing data for pure Internet and click-and-mortar retailers separately we find some differences in results. Similar to overall findings, consumers choosing a clicks-and-mortar retailer based on familiarity display significant differences from those choosing on the basis of price in seeking less negative WOM nonvoluntarily (P2 supported), and perceive problems to be less stable (P4 supported). However, contrary to overall findings, these consumers are less likely to seek negative WOM voluntarily (P1 not supported) , and do not differ significantly in changing their purchase intention. In contrast, consumers choosing among pure-Internet retailers are more susceptible to negative WOM (P1, P2, P3 and P5 supported) if they choose an umfamiliar retailer.

DISCUSSION AND CONCLUSION

The present findings suggest that for Internet retailers in general and click-and-mortar and pure Internet retailers, the deleterious impact of negative consumer reviews on perceived reliability of retailer and purchase intention is mitigated by consumer's familiarity with the retailer. Further, consumers patronizing a familiar retailer are less receptive to negative WOM information and seek less information. Consumers choosing an unfamiliar retailer because of a lower price seek more negative WOM information, and are more likely to believe that the problems may recur compared to consumers patronizing a firm they are familiar with.

These results have implications for consumer service and positioning strategies of online retailers. Firms positioning themselves as offering "the absolutely lowest price" are more susceptible to negative WOM activity because consumers find negative WOM to be more credible and likely to recur in their case.

This is particularly true for pure-Internet retailers than for click-and-mortar firms. Click-and-mortar firms are less susceptible to negative WOM even if they are unknown. For pure-Internet retailers providing superior service experience and establishing an image of reliability through advertising provides better protection against negative WOM information.

REFERENCES

Armstrong, Arthur R. and John Hagel III (1996), "The Real Value of On-Line Communities", *Harvard Business Review*, 74, 134-141.

Arndt, Johann (1967), "Role of Product-Related Conversations in the Diffusion of a New Product," *Journal of Marketing Research*, 4 (August), 291-295.

Brown, Jacqueline Johnson and Peter H. Reingen (1987), "Social Ties and Word-of-Mouth Referral Behavior," *Journal of Consumer Research*, 14 (December), 350-362.

Biswas, Abhijit (1992), "The Moderating Role of Brand familiarity in Reference Price Perceptions," *Journal of Business Research*, 15, 251-262.

Olshavky, Richard W. and Donald H. Granbois (1979), "Consumer Decision Making: Fact or Fiction?" *Journal of Consumer Research*, 6 (September), 93-100.

Richins, Marsha L. (1983), "Negative Word-of Mouth by Dissatisfied Consumers: A Pilot Study," *Journal of Marketing Research*, 47 (Winter), 68-78.

Simonson, Itamar (1992), "The Influence of Anticipating Regret & Responsibility on Purchase Decisions," *Journal of Consumer Research*, 19, 105-118.

Sinha, Indrajit (2000), "Cost Transparency: The Net's Real Threat to Prices and Brands, Harvard Business Review, March-April, 3-8.

Stewart, David W., Greald B. Hickson, Srinivasan Ratneshwar, Cornelia Pechmann and William Altemeier (1985), "Information Search and Decision Strategies Among Health Care Consumers," *Advances in Consumer Research*, Vol. 12, ed., Ann Arbor, MI:Association for Consumer Research,252-257.

Tedeschi, Bob (1999), "Consumer Products and Firms are Being Reviewed on more Web Sites, Some Featuring Comments from Anyone with an Opinion," *New York Times*, Oct. 25. New York.

Weinberger, Marc G. , Chris T. Allen and William R. Dillon (1980), "Negative Information: Perspectives and Research Directions," *Advances in Consumer Research*, Vol. 8, ed., Kent Monroe, Ann Arbor, MI:Association for Consumer Research, 398-404.

Wilson, William R. and Robert A. Peterson (1989), "Some Limits on the Potency of Word-of-Mouth Information," *Advances in Consumer Research*, Vol. 16, ed.,Thomas Srull, Ann Arbor, MI:Association for Consumer Research, 23-29.

Internet Forums as Influential Sources of Consumer Information

Barbara Bickart, Rutgers University
Robert Schindler, Rutgers University

ABSTRACT

We report the results of an experiment in which consumers were instructed to gather online information about one of five specific product topics by accessing either online discussions (i.e., Internet forums or bulletin boards) or marketer-generated online information (i.e., corporate web pages). At the end of a 12-week period, the consumers who gathered information from online discussions reported greater interest in the product topic than did those consumers who acquired information from the marketer-generated sources. We discuss the study's implications for better understanding word-of-mouth communication and for developing more successful consumer web sites.

WORKING PAPER SESSION

The Role of Price in Choice of Brands: A New Conjoint Approach

Ron Ventura, Lancaster University
Susan Auty, Lancaster University

The proposed research concerns the role of price in determining consumer choice between brands. Pricing decisions are considered to be the most difficult and sensitive in planning the marketing mix. The difficulty of pricing arises from its different cost and quality effects on consumer perceptions and its impact on other elements of the marketing mix. The conjoint model is unique in its specification of response to price of competing brands, integrated with latent class segmentation. The research aims to contribute by offering a model that will help managers to make more effective pricing and brand management decisions

Constructing an Interpersonal Influence Attempt: An Examination of Influence Strategy Choice and the Effects of Strategy Sequencing

Lynnea Mallalieu, Iowa State University

This research examines the construction of consumption-related influence attempts and the importance of influence strategy sequencing. Study 1 focuses on examining how influence strategies are sequenced within an influence attempt. Existing research indicates that individuals tend to rely on a relatively small set of influence strategies that they combine in some way to attempt influence. The purpose of Study 1 is to examine in detail how influence attempts are constructed. Study 2 examines the importance of strategy sequencing in terms of social acceptability and compliance gaining. Study 2 seeks to ascertain if individuals perceive that influence attempts should be constructed in a certain way and whether or not the sequencing of strategies in a particular way is likely to affect compliance.

A Theoretical Framework for Measuring Within-Micro-Culture-Market Differences

Denver D'Rozario, Howard University

First, the importance of understanding what the key differences are between individuals in a micro-culture market is highlighted. Next, the concept of assimilation is introduced as a construct by which these differences may be accounted for. Following this, the literature on the measurement of differences within micro-culture markets is surveyed and classified in light of the assimilation construct and a set of conclusions based on this survey are drawn up. Finally, based on these conclusions, a set of recommendations is developed to guide marketers in the future who might wish to rigorously measure the major differences within any micro-culture market.

When "Eureka" Fades Into "You're Nuts!"...

Terrance G. Gabel, California State University, Northridge

This paper extends previous disciplinary discussions of the scholarly review process via consideration of heretofore neglected obstacles to publication uniquely faced by authors of research deemed controversial on topical grounds. Our discussion of these obstacles suggests the possible existence of a growing conflict of interest which threatens to (continue to) significantly stifle the discipline's contribution to the understanding of important social phenomena. Implications of the perspective developed are addressed in the context of what might be done to facilitate the improvement of the scholarly review process in marketing and consumer research.

The Greatly Exaggerated Globalization-Driven Death of Consumer Nationalism?: The Ironic Case of Burton Helms and the Globalization of Nationalism in Mexico

Terrence G. Gabel, California State University, Northridge
Gregory W. Boller, University of Memphis

It has been asserted that a major misconception about globalization is that the process has rendered nationalism amongst the world's consumers a virtual relic of the distant past. The present inquiry empirically supports and extends this critical contention via in situ interpretive analysis of television advertising—and consumer reaction to it—airing in the context of the 1997 privatization of Mexico's long-distance telecommunications industry. Data suggest, overall, that although nationalism remains alive and well in Mexico its character has been changed significantly by the powerful forces of globalization.

How Does Prior Knowledge Influence Consumer Learning? A Study of Analogy & Categorization Effects

Jennifer Gregan-Paxton, University of Delaware

The purpose of this research is to broaden and refine our understanding of knowledge transfer in a consumer context by comparing and contrasting the impact of analogy and categorization on consumer memory. Consistent with the main assertion of this research, our findings suggest that analogy leads to more restrictive processing of new product information than categorization. The results also shed light on the interaction of the two processes, suggesting that analogy overwhelms categorization when they occur within the same learning episode. Discussion centers on possible explanations for this interaction effect.

Dimensional Range Overlap Model for Explanation of Contextual Priming Effects

Yi-Wen Chien, Purdue University
Chung-Chiang Hsiao, Purdue University

By proposing the dimensional range overlap model, this study attempts to provide a more complete theory to explain the underlying process for contextual priming effects. This model suggests that the overlap likelihood between target range and prime range on the judgment dimension can determine the occurrence of assimilation and contrast effects. Derived from this key postulate, the dimensional range overlap model further proposes that the interaction effects of three factors, target range width, prime range width, and the relative distance between target and prime, can influence the overlap likelihood so as to influence the occurrence of assimilation and contrast effects.

Correction for Multiple Biasing Factors in Product Judgments

Yi-Wen Chien, Purdue University
Chung-Chiang Hsiao, Purdue University

Consumers' judgments can be biased by many factors. Some biasing factors may make judgments more favorable than they actually would be, while other biasing factors may make judgments less favorable than they actually would be. This study attempts to examine how consumers correct biases in their judgments, especially when they encounter multiple biasing factors that produce the opposite biasing effects. It is proposed that consumers are more likely to correct only the biasing factors that can be identified, and they will correct these identified biasing factors in a direction opposite to their perceived biasing effects.

Aging and Consumer Responses: Opportunities, Evaluation and a New Research Focus

Yany Grégoire, University of Western Ontario

The purpose of this paper is to critically review what is known about the influence of age on consumer responses, and to point out the major contributions and gaps. In order to organize the literature, we propose a framework with two components: age-related changes (e.g., psychological, social and biological changes) and consumer responses (e.g., cognition, affect and behavior). Finally, a new research focus is offered to help to overcome some challenges associated with the existing literature. This research focus is characterized by the development of integrative theory that takes into account several age-related changes.

A Cross-National Examination of Horizontal and Vertical Individualism and Collectivism Measurement and Impact on Consumer Decision-Making

Eugene Sivadas, Rutgers University
Norman T. Bruvold, University of Cincinnati
Michelle R. Nelson, University of Wisconsin-Madison
Sharon Shavitt, University of Illinois at Urbana-Champaign

This study examines the cultural values of horizontal and vertical individualism and collectivism proposed by Triandis and colleagues (1995, Triandis & Gelfand, 1998). We investigate the dimensionality of the 32-item measure of horizontal and vertical individualism and collectivism developed by Singelis et al (1995), in two cultures: China and the United States. Results indicate that a reduced 16-item measure may be more robust. Logistic regression indicates that HI, HC, VI, and VC can predict country of the respondents. Finally, the impact of individual cultural characteristics on product evaluations and purchase intentions is explored, looking at the impact of information about others' product attitudes on the judgments of HI, HC, Vi, and VC participants. Results suggest that horizontal collectivists' product judgments could be favorably influenced by learning of a strong social consensus in favor of the product. In contrast, both horizontal and vertical individualists could be unfavorably influenced by a strong social consensus.

Globalization and the Consumer in Emerging Markets: 'India Will Survive'

Giana Eckhardt, University of Minnesota
Humaira Mahi, University of Minnesota

There exist multiple points of view within academic disciplines as to how much multinationals and the specter of globalization in general harms or helps the development—culturally and economically—of emerging markets. The role of the consumer has been largely left out of this discussion. By using historical and modern analyses of acceptance and rejection of foreign influences in India we argue that consumers "...may appropriate consumer goods to enhance rather than erode their previous cultural imperatives" (Miller, 1996). By examining the consumer's role, we contribute to the globalization debate in demonstrating that the consumer can transform the meaning of the `foreign' offerings to fit in to traditional meaning systems. We find that this process of transformation may involve the consumer rejecting offerings that do not fit into the existing cultural milieu. Consumer behavior literature has not empirically examined this issue, and our analysis suggests a direction for future research that gives the consumer art active role in the globalization debate.

The Effect of Warning Labels on Consumers' Evaluations of War Toys
John C. Kozup, University of Arkansas
Elizabeth H. Creyer, University of Arkansas

Many argue that today's children are desensitized to violence through constant exposure to violent acts on television, in the movies, in videogames, and through toys. The state of Hawaii recently attempted to mandate that a warning label be included on any toys that may be considered "war toys." An experiment consisting of a 2 (Australian versus American consumers) X 2 (warning label versus no warning label) X 2 (the price of the war toy was the same as or less than the other toy) X 2 (prior knowledge or no knowledge of product preference) between subjects design was conducted to assess the effects of a warning label and price manipulations on consumers moral judgments and beliefs, attitudes toward the product, purchase intention, and choice process satisfaction. Results indicate war toys, presented in conjunction with a warning label exhibit lower perceived levels of product quality, attitude toward the product, and purchase intention. In addition, warning labels also lead to decreased levels of choice process satisfaction and increased levels of choice deferral. Implications for policy makers, study limitations and additional research opportunities are also discussed.

The Real Thing: Conceptualizing Authenticity in a Commodity Culture
Dan Fisher, University of Arkansas
Jeff B. Murray, University of Arkansas

This paper examines the important role authenticity plays in our lives and the manner in which authenticity inevitably becomes problematic in a commodity culture. Personal and product identities are established in very similar ways. Often personal identity is constructed through the careful choice of products that have certain associations belonging to them. The system of commodity signs invites us to establish our individuality through acquisition, yet it seems fundamentally inauthentic to buy one's authenticity. There seems to be no escape. Those who remain outside, or desire exclusion from, the commodity system are targeted as potential sources for authenticity. Incorporation paradoxically leads to a greater sense of alienation. Authenticity becomes a struggle to get beyond the commodity system, but a new set of signs and objects in opposition to the system become prime resources for advertisers and marketers to use to differentiate and authenticate their products in the marketplace.

Information Sequence and Decision Quality
Dan Ariely, MIT
Sridhar Moorthy, University of Toronto
Ashesh Mukherjee, McGill University

The Internet is opening up the possibility of tailoring information to individual tastes. In this context, an issue arises as to whether the sequence in which information is presented affects the way it is used, with potential consequences for decision quality. Of particular interest is the interaction between information sequence and exposure time the time to which a consumer is exposed to each piece of information.

In a 3-by-2 between-subjects full-factorial experiment, we asked subjects to use the information in a brand-by-attribute matrix to choose the best brand for a principal. Two independent variables were manipulated: information sequence and exposure time. The three levels of information sequence were: simultaneous presentation of all attributes (i.e., no sequence), attribute-by-attribute in increasing order of importance, and attribute-by-attribute in decreasing order of importance. The two exposure time conditions were: low (1.7 seconds per cell) and high (3.4 seconds per cell).

Our results show that, between the two information sequences, decision quality (relative to the simultaneous presentation case) is best when attributes are presented in decreasing order of importance. Further, the lower the exposure time the worse the performance of the increasing-attributes sequence. These results support our theory that in memory-taxing information-processing environments, subjects process information as it comes, making interim judgments as they go along, and adjusting these interim judgments for new data, instead of trying to assemble the entire matrix of information first before beginning the processing. Their final judgments are, therefore, susceptible to primacy effects, favouring the brand that performs best on the first attribute presented.

The Impact of Perceived Control, Counterfactual Thoughts, and Regret on Product Returns: The Case of E Commerce
Carolyn Bonifield, University of Iowa
Catherine A. Cole, University of Iowa

What causes a consumer to return a product that he/she apparently liked well enough to purchase in the first place? Is it a result of a failure to provide the promised benefits, a consumer's reconsideration of his needs, or something as mundane as a shipping delay (in the case of a catalogue or Web-based order). Clearly, a multitude of possible reasons exist. This paper examines the impact of perceived control on affect, counterfactual thinking, regret and disappointment, and ultimately, on product returns. Specifically, it is postulated that when individuals' perceived situational control increases, that positive affect increases, and counterfactual thoughts decrease. Once the consumer knows the outcome of the purchase, if perceived situational control was high, the consumer experiences more regret (and less disappointment), which results in an increased likelihood of product returns, but also an increased likelihood of returning to that retailer. This research utilizes a Web-based electronic shopping simulation to manipulate varying levels of perceived control, and demonstrate a broader phenomenon that should have theoretical and managerial applications to both traditional and non-traditional shopping experiences.

Consumption and the Urbanised Self: Consumption Experience of a Group of Provincial Students Studying in the Cosmopolitan Bangkok

Kritsadarat Wattanasuwan, University of Oxford
Richard Elliott, University of Exeter

This study explores how a group of students from provincial areas exercise everyday consumption to urbanise their sense of selves when they come to study in Bangkok. An interpretive approach via ethnographic fieldwork is employed to achieve an in-depth understanding of the relationship between the self and consumption practices in the consumer acculturation processes. The findings reveal the complexly dynamic and paradoxical selves of these informants. Although they aspire to urbanise their selves in order to assimilate properly into the new social environment, they still wish to persevere their ties with the provincial roots.

The Worldminded Consumer: An Emic Exploration

Suzanne C. Beckmann, Copenhagen Business School
Günther Botschen, Copenhagen Business School
Martina Botschen, Copenhagen Business School
Susan P. Douglas, Copenhagen Business School
Susanne Friese, Copenhagen Business School
Ed Nijssen, Copenhagen Business School

In many cross-national consumer studies, a scale developed in one country or context, often the US, is translated and used in another country or context, assuming that it is equally applicable or relevant. This gives rise to a number of issues relating to construct equivalence and bias. The present study adopts a "decentred, convergent" approach to explicate the concept of worldmindedness, and to develop operational definitions and measures of the construct in different countries and linguistic contexts. The paper reports findings from the first stage of this project, probing the concept of "worldmindedness" in three countries, namely Austria, Denmark and the US.

Images of Integrated Symbols: Consumer Negotiation of Brand Meanings

Anders Bengtsson, Lund University

The occurrence of integrated symbols through affinity partnerships like co-branding and joint promotion raises the question: How do consumers interpret and give meanings to consumer goods that feature several brand names? The creation of brand meanings is here considered as a process of negotiation between several contexts. When two or more brand names appear together in an ad or on a package there may come up additional meanings that consumers use for negotiating brand meanings. The figure/ground metaphor is used to illustrate what consumers perceive when negotiating meanings for integrated symbols.

Consuming Matsuri: The Legacy of Religion in Japanese Consumer Culture

Rika Houston, California State University, Los Angeles

This cross-cultural conceptual paper explores the notion of religion as a cultural institution and the legacy of religion as a shaping force in contemporary Japanese consumer culture. After first presenting a historical overview of the evolution of religion in Japan as well as its contemporary manifestation, the author explores the heightened level of enthusiasm and consumption that takes place in the context of such religious fetes. Conclusions are drawn in the form of questions for future research and challenges associated with misinterpretation of religion and religious constructs in different cultural settings.

Personality Processing Traits and Shopping Behavior

Jane Sojka, Ohio University

This paper explores differences in shopping behaviors based on two personality processing traits—need for cognition and need for affect—which have been useful in previous consumer research. Using a grounded theory approach, preliminary results suggest individuals with different traits report different shopping patterns. In comparison to the other groups, Thinkers (high NFC, low NFA) recalled and compared prices, Feelers (high NFA, low NFC) reported more impulsive purchases and brand commitment, while Combiners (high NFC and high NFA) compared prices, compared brands and were most likely to evaluate sales representatives. Exploratory results suggest that linking personality processing traits with specific shopping patterns warrants further investigation.

In The Shadow of Doubt: Advertiser Deception and the Defensive Consumer

Robin Ritche, University of British Columbia
Peter R. Darke, University of British Columbia

Despite the prevalence of deceptive and misleading advertising, little is understood about the consequences of deception on consumer response to subsequently presented ad claims. We conducted an experiment to examine these effects, and to determine whether they would generalize to claims made by a different advertiser. Using the heuristic-systematic model as our conceptual framework, we hypothesized that consumers would exhibit negative bias regardless of the source, but that processing would be systematic in the case of the deceptive retailer and heuristic in the case of other retailers. Our experiment confirmed these predictions. Theoretical and practical implications are discussed.

The Effect of Brand Name on Consumers' Evaluation of Price Discounts and Tie-In Product Promotions

Rajesh Manchanda, *University of Manitoba*
Rajneesh Suri, *Drexel University*
Kent B. Moore, *University of Illinois*

The focus of this research was to examine the effect of brand name on the evaluation and preference for price discounts versus tie-in product promotions. Findings of an experimental study suggest that for reputable or strong brands (e.g., Sony) price discounts enhance the value of the promotional offer and are preferred to tie-in product promotions. However, for less reputable or weak brands, consumers' perceptions of value are enhanced by high quality tie-in product promotions, which are preferred to price discounts. The price-quality-value literature and thought measures of participants provide reasons for this finding. Implications for managers are offered and discussed.

The Red-Faced Customer: Investigating Embarrassment in the Context of Consumer Purchase

Darren W, Dahl, *University of Manitoba*
Rajesh V. Manchanda, *University of Manitoba*
Jennifer Argo, *University of Manitoba*

While it has been documented in the marketing trade literature that certain products can cause embarrassment when they are purchased (e.g., adult diapers, hemorrhoid creams), relatively little is known regarding when and why embarrassment occurs in consumer purchasing situations. An empirical study seeks to identify when embarrassment occurs in purchase, and to investigate some of the theoretical reasons for purchase embarrassment. This study utilizes a field experiment conducted in a real-world context. Drawing from established psychological theory relating to the causes of embarrassment, a conceptual framework is developed and tested. In this study, previous purchase experience, social presence at the time of purchase, and individual characteristics of the consumer are shown to impact purchase embarrassment.

"Oh!...Wow!" How Surprise Enhances Satisfaction

Joëlle Vanhamme, *Université Catholique de Louvain*
Dirk Snelders, *Delft University of Technology*

Empirical findings suggest that surprise plays an important role in consumer satisfaction, but there is a lack of theory to explain why this is so. The present paper provides possible explanations for the process through which surprise may influence consumer satisfaction. A first explanation is that the arousal that is part of the surprise reaction contaminates subsequent positive affective reactions or emotions about the product or service. An alternative explanation is that the surprise reaction allows for a strong focus on a single product or service aspect. This will create more accessible knowledge that will have a disproportionate effect on memory-based satisfaction judgements.

Day-of-the-Week Biases in Tracking Surveys

Lance-Michael Erickson, *NewYork University*
Vicki G. Morwitz, *New York University*

This paper examines whether the results of tracking surveys vary systematically with the day-of-the-week the survey was conducted. Responses to surveys conducted daily during the 1996 and 1992 U.S. Presidential elections, and the 1996 Congressional election conducted by CNN, USA Today, and Gallup are analyzed. The results suggest that surveys conducted during weekdays overstate support for the Republican candidate relative to the results of surveys conducted during weekends. This paper reports the difference in results of tracking surveys by day-of-the-week, suggests why such differences may occur, and discusses the implications of the results for survey research practice.

If it's a Question of Life and Death Does "How Often" Matter? Frequency Judgments in Affectively Valenced Messages

Sucharita Chandran, *New York University*

Research has shown that with respect to day-to-day affective behavior, a shorter reference period (implying more frequently performed behavior) implies lower intensity of the affective behavior. The current study attempts to reverse that result in the context of behavior that has severe affective consequences in domains such as personal safety and heath. Consumers are often confronted with affectively valenced messages on life threatening or life saving issues. In order to create a maximal impact, these messages usually carry statistics on lives lost or lives saved, represented in some reference period e.g., per day or per year. In this context this study tests the hypothesis that when differential reference periods of the same event are embedded in affectively valenced messages, the shorter reference period elicits the greater event likelihood and intensity of occurrence. The results of the first study provide support for this hypothesis.

Are You a Lark or an Owl? The Effects of Time of Day and Circadian Type on Consumer Information Processing
Suresh Ramanathan, New York University

This paper examines the effect of varying energy levels resulting out of biological rhythms on the type of processing strategies used by consumers: We demonstrate that people adopt a peripheral mode of processing under non-optimal conditions, where their own biological rhythm does not match with the time of day. On the other hand, people find the subjective resources to elaborate on information when their biological rhythm matches the time of day. A key implication of these findings is that the same individual, with a stable level of involvement, can process information differently depending on what time of day the information is presented. These states of mind act in the same manner as constraints placed on cognitive resources, but are more systematic than temporary cognitive loads. These findings are discussed within the framework of the Elaboration-Likelihood Model.

A Model for Consumer Devotion: What We Can Learn From Football Fans
Ronald W. Pimentel, University of Central Florida
Kristy Reynolds, University of Central Florid

We present a model of the consumer devotion process, based on findings from qualitative research. We propose that the process begins with several antecedent factors, which then may motivate the consumer to develop either calculative or normative commitment. Consumers who move through a "transition" phase may then progress to affective commitment. Several important outcomes then result. We illustrate our findings in a football context, offering rich examples from the data. Managerial implications are offered, as well as future research directions.

An Emergent Model of Intra-Household Resource Allocation
Suraj Commuri, University of Nebraska

Several household structures are dominant today prominent among them is the dual income family. In addition, it is estimated that one in three working wives earns more than her husband. Yet, this emerging household form has not been researched. The current understanding of the household in marketing rests on research conducted on the "traditional" household structure and many assumptions are contained within resource theory. This paper presents data that suggest that resource theoretic assumptions about family consumption behavior may need revision. A revised resource theory model is presented that reveals more than one pool of resources in dual income families.

Beyond Reference Price: The Role of Unmet Price Expectations in Consumers' Perceptions of Value
Joan Lindsey-Mullikin, Babson College

This manuscript posits a new approach for understanding the reference price phenomenon. It is proposed here that Festinger's (1957) theory of dissonance reduction provides a practical framework for studying situations in which consumers' encountered prices are significantly different from their expectations. The three modes of dissonance reduction initially proposed by Festinger (to change one's attitude or cognition, to seek consonant information, or to trivialize some element of the dissonant relationship) are experimentally manipulated. These three modes of dissonance reduction are then evaluated for their impact on consumers' perceptions of value and consumers' purchase intentions. A computer-controlled shopping experiment is utilized to test the hypotheses.

Effects of Product Congruency on Dimensions of Endorser Expertise
Scott Smith, University of Arkansas
Jennifer Christie, University of Arkansas
Thomas Jensen, University of Arkansas

This research investigated the effects of product/endorser congruency and endorser familiarity on perceptions of endorser credibility and attitudes. Another purpose of this study was to extend and revise Ohanian's (1990) scale to measure endorser credibility, distinguishing between product and expertise and professional-related expertise. Subjects were able to make the distinction. Product congruency affected both expertise and credibility. Endorsers were perceived as more credible when advertising a product congruent with their area of expertise. Endorser/product congruency also resulted in more favorable attitudes toward the brand, the ad, and purchase intentions.

Hospice Voices: Attitudes About Physician Assisted Suicide
Kathleen S. Micken, Roger Williams University
Jamie Goldstein-Shirley, University of Washington

Physician assisted suicide is one of the more contentious health care issues in our society. The opinions of physicians, nurses, pharmacists, and of the general public have been assessed. The opinions of hospice professionals, those on the front line of the assisted suicide issue, have so far gone unreported. This paper helps to rectify that omission. It presents the results of an initial investigation of hospice professionals' comments on a survey about physician assisted suicide. While the comments generally echo the positions articulated in the media, they also present very personal pictures of the debate—and thereby expand its consideration away from the polar extremes.

Comparison of the Popularity of 9-Ending Prices in the U.S. and Poland

Rajneesh Suri, Drexel University
Ralph E. Anderson, Drexel University
Vassili Kotlov, Drexel University

American multinationals, when deciding pricing strategies for their culturally diverse foreign markets, usually have to debate whether to change or to keep the pricing strategy that they have been using at home. The recent move towards standardization in global markets has only raised the importance of this issue. This research addresses this issue by comparing the effectiveness of 9-ending prices or just below prices in the US and in an eastern bloc country like Poland. A conceptual framework was developed to predict why there might be differences in preference for such 9-ending prices in Poland and US. Result from the first study shows that 9-ending prices, which are popular in the US market, are not well received in the Polish market. The second study provided further insights by determining reasons for differences in perception and preference for such prices in the two countries.

The Effect of Uncertainty Avoidance on Information Search, Planning and Purchases of International Vacation Travel Services

R. Bruce Money, University of South Carolina
John C. Crotts, College of Charleston

Academics and marketers know relatively little about haw national culture affects the way people plan and spend in the $448 billion international travel and tourism economy. From a patched sample of 1,213 German, Japanese, and Taiwanese visitors to the U.S., this research explores the relationship between the cultural dimension of uncertainty (or risk) avoidance with information search, trip planning time horizons, travel party characteristics (e.g., size of group) and trip characteristics (e.g., length of stay). Results show that consumers from national cultures characterized by higher levels of uncertainty avoidance use information sources that are related to the channel (e.g., travel agent), instead of personal, destination marketing-related, or mass media sources; they also more frequently purchase prepackaged tours, travel in larger groups, and stay on average a shorter time and visit fewer number of destinations. Contrary to expectations, they do not spend more time making the decision to travel or making their airline reservations. Implications for future research and marketing practice (e.g., segmentation and standardization) are also discussed.

Expanding the Boundaries of Self-Prophecy: The Use of Prediction Requests in Advertising

Bianca Grohmann, Washington State University
Eric R. Spangenberg, Washington State University
David E. Sprott, Washington State University

Based on research surrounding the self-prophecy phenomenon (whereby the prediction of one's own behavior elicits future actions consistent with the prediction), we explore whether the inclusion of a prediction request in an advertisement affects recycling behavior. A pretest, field study, and a laboratory experiment indicate an advertisement with prediction request ("Ask yourself...will you recycle?") can enhance recycling behavior. The current research provides optimism for the wide-scale use of self-prophecy to affect behaviors in a socially beneficial manner. Implications for social marketing, business and research are provided.

The Search for Information: Multiple Measures of Search & Interdependency of Search Activities

Jinkook Lee, University of Tennessee
Jeanne M. Hogarth, Program Manager, Federal Reserve Board

The difficulty of measuring consumer's information search behavior has long been acknowledged and continuously discussed in the literature. We investigate consumers' information search patterns using multiple measures and the potential interdependencies among search activities. Using the 1997 University of Michigan Survey of Consumers, we find consumers have diverse patterns of information search that cannot be captured by a macro-measure or a few single measures of search. In addition, strong interdependencies exist among search activities.

Composite Products as Conceptual Combinations: Combinatorial Processes and Brand Evaluative Effects

Tripat Gill, McGill University
Laurette Dubé, McGill University

Composite products are new products that are combinations of multiple existing product concepts (e.g., Web-TV or Sports-Utility Vehicles). We view composite products as a conceptual combination (e.g., Web, as modifier and TV, as header). In this paper, we build on the most recent developments in this literature to develop a set of research propositions on consumer perception and evaluation of composite products. Following Wisniewski's theorizing, we propose that composite products are formed by one of three processes: mapping of the modifier's property on that of the header (e.g., digital camera); linking the header and modifier with a plausible relation (e.g., underwater camera); hybridization with mapping of central properties of the modifier on central properties of the header (e.g. watch camera). We identify moderators of these processes (headermodifier similarity, visual imagery instructions, momentary mood), and specify how brand effects on consumer evaluation of composite products may vary as a function of the underlying combinatorial process.

Can Product Attributes be Reduced to Affective and Cognitive Dimensions in Measuring Attitude Bases? A Cross-Cultural Confirmatory Factor Analysis

Marie Cecile Cervellon, McGill University

Laurette Dubé, McGill University

Han Jingyuan, Hebei University of Science and Technology

This paper reports a multi-sample confirmatory factor analysis to test the theoretical structure of a multi-item scale developed to capture the affective and cognitive basis of product (food) attitude. 329 participants (divided in 3 samples, 118 French from France, 100 Chinese from People Republic of China, and 111 Chinese from Canada) completed the measurement scale. Results of multi-sample confirmatory factor analyses show that across samples, reducing the product attributes scales to the two basic affective and cognitive dimensions did not provide an acceptable structure. Superior fit was obtained for a four-attribute model, encompassing emotional, sensorial, health and convenience, and for a second-order model preserving a hierarchical structure between the two basic dimensions and their corresponding product attributes. The degree of fit did not differ between these two models. The implication of the results for product attitude measurement is discussed

Consumer Perceptions of and Attitudes Toward Brand Names: The Effect of Morphemic Familiarity

Dawn Lerman, Fordham University

A morpheme is the smallest unit of language that carries information about meaning or function (O'Grady, Dobrovolsky, and Aronof, 1989). English contains more than 6,000 morphemes ranging from full words (free morphemes) such as "man" to small parts of words that cannot stand alone (bound morphemes) such as "-ly." These 6000+ morphemes can and have been combined to form the tens of thousands of words found in today's English language dictionaries. Similarly, managers create new morphemic combinations to be used as brand names. This paper discusses two types of names generated by this morphemic approach and examine their influence on consumer perceptions and attitudes. More specifically, this paper argues that no one name type is consistently superior in eliciting positive consumer perceptions thus making explicit some of the tradeoffs involved in brand naming.

Consistency in Consumer Preferences: Connecting Perceptions of the Product, the Person, and the Situation in Preference Schemas

Inge Brechan, Norwegian School of Management

Even J. Lanseng, Agricultural University of Norway

The purpose of this paper is to examine the extent to which we may enhance the prediction of actual purchase by conceptualizing personal and situational variables in terms of schema theory. It is argued that consumers combine features from products with situational and personality elements to form preference, and that the resulting preference appears at a different level of aggregation than features related to nominal product categories. To come up with such a conceptualization of preference we emphasizes literature on social cognition and categorization theory. Based on a review of this literature, we derive to propositions concerning the efficiency of such preference schema. The paper also outlines two studies that may be conducted to examine theses propositions.

Is There A "Golden" Ad? The Effect of Ad Shape and Spatial Layout of Ad Elements on Ad Preference

Johan de Heer, Tilburg University

Esther Noble, Tilburg University

The focus of the present study is on the effects of advertisement spatial layout on ad preference. In an experimental study we manipulated ad shape (external layout) and the spatially arrangement of the ad elements (internal layout): headline, body-text, picture, and logo. We found that ad shapes conform to a complex height/width ratio, and in which the ad elements were spatially arranged according to a simple ratio, were preferred over other ads. Content analyses, based on 1356 ads, revealed that a complex height/width ratio is applied frequently in real ads. A theoretical rationale was found in the most recent developments in neurobiology on the subject of aesthetic preferences. We conclude this paper by some theoretical, methodological and practical implications for consumer and advertising research.

Information? Yes! Processing? No! Consumers' Use of Ethical Product Labeling

Soren Askegaard, SDU Odense University

Dannie Kjeldgaard, SDU Odense University

Reflecting an increasing interest from consumer policy agencies to provide information about such issues as "ethically correct products" on top of the existing product information on various types of labeling, this work-in-progress paper summarizes the present results and conclusions of an ongoing investigation of consumers' uses of product labeling, with specific focus on labeling for ethical issues. The study uses a variety of methods, but the focus in this paper is mainly on results from the depth interviews with families. A second round of interviews using also experimental designs for conjoint analysis are scheduled for this spring and results of these experiments as well as label tests made with the interviewed families will be shown at the poster presentation. The study is sponsored by the Danish State Consumer Policy Board.

Mysterious Sights: Consumption Creolization and Identity Construction in a Postmodern World

Ozlem Sandikci, Bilkent University

As a result of increasing flows of goods, money, people, technology and information across borders, cultures are encountering more of each other today, outcome of which is the creation of new globalized and hybridized forms of consumer cultures and consumption strategies and practices. In line with this development, the issue of identity construction through consumption in a globalizing world has started to receive an increasing research attention (e.g., Costa and Bamossy 1995; Ger and Belk 1996; Peñaloza 1994). This session contributes to this field of inquiry by examining identity negotiation and consumption experiences of three different consumer subcultures in three different parts of the world.

The highlighting of the tensions between West/global/centre and East/local/peripheral, as they are experienced within the domain of consumption, underlie the integrative rationale of the session. The modernist accounts of culture view cultural forms as exhibiting a functionally integrated and internally consistent order (Luke 1996), and regards hybridization resulting from contacts with exogenous cultural images, meanings, and consumption practices as the contamination of authentic cultural forms (Friedman 1995). In contrast, a postmodernist reading of culture challenges the dichotomic understanding of local versus global, East versus West, and traditional versus contemporary, and adapts a critical stance that emphasizes culture and consumption as a dynamic constellation of diverse practices and transnational flows of meanings, styles, conventions, etc. (Appadurai 1990; Firat and Venkatesh 1995). In this view the essentialist and modernist conceptions of culture are displaced by notions such as creolization and hybridization which enable exploration of how goods and meanings are appropriated and reconfigured, sometimes in paradoxical ways, to help people to negotiate their identities and consumption experiences.

The three papers offer perspectives from various consumption subcultures in Singapore, Turkey and the United States, and discuss how multiple tensions get played out in the consumption domain as consumers negotiate and craft identities in fluid contexts that are informed by the complex dynamics of the authentic/traditional/local and the new/contemporary/global. Tambyah and Subrahmanyan explore the experiences of American expatriate wives living in Singapore by analyzing their perceptions of their identities as expatriate wives and the consumption practices they engage in while managing conflicting emotions resulting from their foreign and privileged status. The results of in-depth interviews reveal a wide spectrum of consumption strategies at work, and suggest that an expatriate wife is a unique social construction that is infused with multiple tensions between the local and the global. Thompson and Troester explore the natural health consumer subculture in the United States and discuss two key forms of hybridization that they have identified as operating in consumers' narratives. The first concerns the syncretic mixing of postmodern and countermodernist cultural outlooks; the second involves an attempt to synthesize Eastern thought and cosmologies with a more goal-directed and pragmatic Western outlook. The in-depth interviews reveal that consumers' motivations and goals are uniquely constructed in specific hybridized contexts and exhibit distinct constellations of meanings, ideals, tensions and symbolic connections to specific consumption practices. Finally, Sandikci

and Ger investigate the hybrid fashion style that has recently emerged among a sub-group of young, educated and urban religious women in Turkey, which mixes Islamic dressing codes with Western clothing patterns. They discuss the dynamics of the fusion of Western and Islamic fashion styles vis-a-vie the notions of identity, fashion and consumption politics through analyses of daily practices and the marketing context that institutionalizes and legitimizes these practices through retail outlets, fashion shows, catalogues and advertisements.

The session elaborates on the heterogenous and heterogenizing aspects of cultural life in a global world. Each manuscript relates to how a subculture experiences the wide reaching phenomenon of globalization. The diversity of the subcultures investigated offers opportunities for noticing any similarities and differences in the consumers' experience of global and local forces/tensions. The papers motivate a discussion on the notions of culture, subculture and identity politics at the intersection of the local and the global, and offer insights into how consumer research theories can be adapted to better address the socio-cultural transformations precipitated by cultural and economic globalization.

REFERENCES
Appadurai, Arjun (1990), "Disjuncture and Difference in the Global Cultural Economy," *Theory, Culture and Society*, 7(3), 295-310.

Costa, Janeen A. and Gary J. Bamossy, eds. (1995), *Marketing in a Multicultural World: Ethnicity, Nationalism, and Cultural Identity*, Thousand Oaks, CA: Sage.

Firat, A. Fuat and Alladi Venkatesh (1995) "Liberatory Postmodernism and the

Reenchantment of Consumption," *Journal of Consumer Research*, 22(3), 239-267.

Friedman, Jonathan (1995), "Global System, Globalization, and the Parameters of

Modernity," in *Global Modernities*, ed. M. Featherstone, S. Lash and R. Roberston, London: Sage, 69-90.

Ger, Guliz and Russel W. Belk (1996), "I'd Like to Buy the World a Coke:

Consumptionscapes of the 'Less Affluent World'," *Journal of Consumer Policy*, 19, 271-304.

Luke, Timothy (196), "Identity, Modernity, Globalization and Detraditionalization in Postmodern Time-Space Compression," in *Detraditionalization*, eds. P. Heelas, S. Lash, P. Morris, London: Blackwell, 109-133.

Peñaloza, Lisa N. (1994), "Atravesando Fronteras/Border Crossings: A Critical Ethnographic Exploration of the Consumer Acculturation of Mexican Immigrants," *Journal of Consumer Research*, 21 (June), 35-54.

"American Expatriate Wives: Gender, Class and Nationality in Transnational Suburbia"
Siok Kuan Tambyah and Saroja Subrahmanyan, National University of Singapore

To date, most research on expatriates, especially in international human resource management, have focused on facilitating and managing cross-cultural adjustment (e.g., Black et al 1991).

Studies have shown that the satisfaction of spouses (mainly wives) is one of the most crucial factors influencing the success of an expatriate assignment. However, the voices of these women have remained largely muted. In this paper, through in-depth interviews with 12 American expatriate wives, we highlight the lived experiences of these women as they partake of the opportunities available to them in a globalized world. Specifically, we examine their perceptions of their identities as expatriate wives, and how they manage possibly conflicting emotions with regard to their foreign and privileged status through consumption choices and practices. The paper extends Thompson and Tambyah's (1999) work on the narratives of dwelling by exploring the more feminized aspects of transnational experiences in terms of how American expatriate wives embrace or reject specific consumption practices in crafting their identities.

The term "expatriate wife" embodies an array of gendered, classed and nationalistic ideologies. Expatriate wives in Singapore are often cast as rich, privileged, foreign women (primarily Caucasian) who accompany their husbands on their overseas assignments. They are perceived as spending their time and money shopping and having afternoon tea with women friends who are in similar situations, and also indulging in conspicuous consumption (e.g., Asian artifacts and travel to exotic destinations). These stereotypical images hark from a colonialist era where expatriates enjoyed handsome compensation packages in return for their expertise and willingness to work in "hardship" conditions. Although compensation packages are not as generous as in the past, expatriate families presently in Singapore can usually afford to live on the husband's salary while the wife stays at home.

In consumer research, various consumption-related phenomena have been explored with regard to transnational movements of people. For example, there has been some interest in consumer learning or consumer acculturation across cultural divides (Peñaloza 1994). Studies on the meanings of things have also yielded insights into how possessions are significant containers and conduits of personal and cultural meanings for people on the move (Mehta and Belk 1991; Gilly 1995). In addition to finding out what possessions expatriates brought over, we also examined the meanings of possessions acquired here. This proved to be a fruitful venture as there are many retailers and also specific retail locations in Singapore that catered to expatriates. The participants' narratives revealed a localized form of "expatriate consumption", especially in the consumption of furniture and furnishings. The women experimented with blending both American and Asian furniture and styles in their current homes in Singapore. They also exhibited a future orientation in deciding what to purchase, often planning how to incorporate Asian furniture into their homes when they eventually return to America.

Our participants' narratives also revealed a wide spectrum of strategies in managing their transient status as expatriate wives. For some, there was an underlying tension between living the privileged expatriate lifestyle and what they were used to doing back home in suburban America. Although most of the expatriate wives we interviewed had maids, there were heroic attempts to re-enact their juggling lifestyles (Thompson 1996), that is, to continue to maintain their cultural ideal of the "suburban mum". This desire to take charge of their lives was fraught with difficulties in a different cultural and consumer context. Although most of the women interviewed had been in Singapore for at least a year, they still experienced frustration at not being able to do things the American way, that is, "get everything in one store" or "do everything in 15 minutes". This frustration was compounded by language barriers, logistical hurdles, unfulfilled expectations of customer service, etc.

More extreme forms of resistance such as the refusal to employ a maid were also manifested in our participants' narratives.

Alternatively, there were some women who saw their sojourn in Singapore as an opportunity to experience a more comfortable and cosmopolitan lifestyle that was not possible back home in the United States. They attempted to learn more about the Asian culture, and they enjoyed another form of "freedom"—the choice to stay at home and look after the children. Others relished their participation in what they viewed as exotic consumption behaviors such as purchasing Asian artifacts (e.g., carpets, teak furniture, and antiques) and shopping and recreational trips around the region. These consumption activities were viewed as "compensation" for the inconveniences they had to endure as part of their cross-cultural displacement. Their purchases were also used to authenticate their experiences in Asia and to serve as conversation pieces back home in America. However, this eager anticipation of sharing their experiences in Asia was somewhat dampened by the concern that some of their American friends might not be "cosmopolitan" enough to appreciate their stories.

Interestingly, there was also a distinction among American expatriate wives themselves. Some clearly did not associate themselves with those who left the household chores and care of the children to their maids while they engaged in their own hobbies, parties and travels. Some were careful to emphasize that their spending patterns were not as materialistic or conspicuous as the other expatriate wives who bought expensive carpets and teak furniture, and went to 5-star resorts at exotic vacation spots. They also did not want to be perceived as "*tais-tais*", the local equivalent of rich, female socialites.

Being an expatriate wife is an uneasy and potentially identity-threatening role for which no amount of cross-cultural training would be deemed sufficient. An expatriate wife is also a unique social construction that is infused with multiple tensions between the local and the foreign. For the women in our paper, it meant coming to terms with a largely distorted and transient reality that challenged their long-standing assumptions and treasured beliefs relating to gender, class and nationality.

REFERENCES

Black, J. Stewart, Mark Mendenhall and Gary Oddou (1991), "Toward a Comprehensive Model of International Adjustment: An Integration of Multiple Theoretical Perspectives," *Academy of Management Review*, 16, 2, 291-317.

Gilly, Mary C. (1995), "The Consumer Acculturation of Expatriate Americans," *Advances in Consumer Research*, eds. Frank R. Kardes and Mita Sujan, Vol. 22, p.506-510.

Mehta, Raj and Russell W. Belk (1991), "Artifacts, Identity, and Transition: Favorite Possessions of Indians and Indian Immigrants to the United States," *Journal of Consumer Research*, 17 (March), 398-411.

Peñaloza, Lisa N. (1994), "Atravesando Fronteras/Border Crossings: A Critical Ethnographic Exploration of the Consumer Acculturation of Mexican Immigrants," *Journal of Consumer Research*, 21 (June), 35-54.

Thompson, Craig J. (1996), "Caring Consumers: Gendered Consumption Meanings and the Juggling Lifestyle," *Journal of Consumer Research*, 22 (March), 388-407.

Thompson, Craig J. and Siok Kuan Tambyah, (1999), "Trying to be Cosmopolitan," *Journal of Consumer Research*, 26 (December), 214-241.

"Where East meets West and the Countermodern meets the Postmodern: Consumer Meanings in the Hybridized Cultural System of Natural Health"

Craig J. Thompson and Maura Troester, University of Wisconsin

Thompson and Troester present interpretivist results from depth interviews with thirty-three natural health consumers. Their paper focuses on two key forms of hybridization that operate within these consumer narratives. The first concerns the syncretic mixing of postmodern and countermodernist cultural outlooks. Drawing from the work of anthropologist Emily Martin (1994), they argue that natural health discourses and practices offer a prominent marketplace manifestation of a postmodern ethos emphasizing the cultural ideals of adaptability, complexity, and systemic interconnectedness. They show that these postmodern ideals function as an overarching microcultural frame-of-reference that incorporates and revitalizes a nexus of countermodernist discourses. This latter family of discourses have long opposed the modernist valorization of science and technology by proclaiming the inherent primacy of art, nature, and spiritual mystery in human experience (Lears 1994). This postmodern-countermodernist fusion provides a robust network of collective meanings from which natural health consumers can understand their health conditions, their power relations to the medical establishment, their identities, and their abilities to cope with the existential dilemmas posed by conditions of postmodern life (e.g., Giddens 1991).

The second form of hybridization involves an attempt to synthesize Eastern thought and cosmologies with a more goal-directed and pragmatic Western outlook. Unlike the postmodern-countermodern hybridization, this juxtaposition of Eastern and Western traditions encodes salient points of contradiction that consumers try to negotiate through four major emic themes or strategies, which Thompson and Troester discuss and illustrate.

They conclude by making the theoretical case that, in the age of postmodernity, consumer motivations can no longer be effectively conceptualized as general, psychological states. Rather, postmodern motivations and goals are uniquely constructed in specific hybridized, consumer micro-cultural contexts and exhibit distinct constellations of meanings, ideals, tensions, and symbolic connections to specific consumption practices. Accordingly, these pivotal consumer research constructs need to be theorized in culturally nuanced terms that address the dialogical interplays between consumers' personal histories and the micro-cultures of consumption relevant to their identities.

REFERENCES

Giddens, Anthony (1991), *Modernity and Self-Identity: Self and Society in the Late Modern Age*, Stanford, CA: Stanford University Press.

Lears, T.J. Jackson (1994), *No Place of Grace: Antimodernism and the Transformation of American Culture*, 2nd Edition, Chicago, Ill: University of Chicago Press.

Martin, Emily (1994) *Flexible Bodies: The Role of Immunity in American Culture from the Days of Polio to the Age of Aids*, Boston, MA: Beacon.

Fundamental Fashions: The Cultural Politics of the Turban and the Levi's

Ozlem Sandikci, Bilkent University
Güliz Ger, Bilkent University

ABSTRACT

In the last decade an Islamic consumptionscape competing against the secular consumptionscape in every domain of life emerged in Turkey. Summer resorts, fashion shows, fitness and beauty centers, popular culture and entertainment products targeted specifically at the Islamists became common place. In this paper we explore one of the most visible sites of the Islamic consumption culture, Islamic fashion, and discuss the newly-emerged fashion style which mixes Islamic dressing codes with Western clothing patterns as an example of consumption fusion. We argue that today's Islamic consumptionscape is characterized by pluralism and difference, and cannot be explained as either rejection of consumerism, capitalism and globalization or resistance to modernity. Constructing a modern Islamic identity within the local power network involves simultaneously negotiating multiple tensions both between the local and global and within the local itself, and increasingly finds its symbolic expression in the domain of consumption.

The December 2, 1999 issue of the *Washington Post* newspaper included an article with the following headline: "Spreading Faith Through Fashion: Turkish Chain Promotes Islamic Clothing." The article reports a Turkish company which built a lucrative business in the last decade by marketing Islamic fashion: "Mustafa Karaduman is a profoundly pious Muslim who says he is spreading the faith through fashion. Karaduman owns Turkey's largest Islamic-style clothing chain, Tekbir Giyim, which means "Allah is Great apparel." Stroking his neatly trimmed beard with one hand and fingering a string of worry beads with another, Karaduman explained during a recent interview at his flagship store here [Istanbul] that he is serving God by encouraging 'my sisters to dress in accordance with the teachings of the holy Koran. In so doing, Karaduman has built a multimillion-dollar clothing empire, with 600 outlets across Turkey and as far away as Sarajevo, Bosnia and Sydney" (Zaman 1999).

In the last decade Islamic-style clothing stores, Islamic fashion shows and Islamic fashion at large have become mainstream news in Turkey. Imitators of the Tekbir style have mushroomed, with 200 Islamic fashion companies now competing in an ever-expanding market to serve women who want to look fashionable yet fulfill the requirements of Islam. For many analysts, the emergence of fashion consciousness in the fundamentalist Islamic subculture along with the proliferation of hotels and summer resorts, fitness and beauty centers, popular culture and entertainment products such as books, newspapers, radio and television channels that specifically target at the religious people are the indicators of a rapidly developing Islamic market and consumption culture within a predominantly Muslim but officially secular country (Bilici 2000; Bulut 1995; Özdür 1994). In this paper we discuss Islamic fashion as an example of consumption *fusion* by exploring the daily practices as well as the underlying marketing context, and review the theoretical challenges they introduce into the existing notions of fashion, consumption and identity politics at the intersection of the local and the global.

POLITICAL ISLAM AND FAITHFUL CONSUMPTION

After the establishment of the republic in 1923, Turkey became the only predominantly Muslim yet secular state in the world. At the core of the republican revolution was a change of values, which articulated itself through the conceptual opposition between "republican" (=modern, urban, secular, European) and "Islamic" (=backward, rural, religious, Ottoman). As Yalman notes "an entire generation was educated thinking religion to be some evil and irrational force of mere orthodoxy and blind tradition" (1969, p.47). Although the republican ideology aspired to create a civic religion through a variety of public rituals, it failed to attract especially the rural population and could not offer an alternative to Islam in providing identity and organizing principles of life (Tapper 1991). The introduction of multi-party politics in 1946, and first genuinely free elections in 1950, in which the right-wing Democrat Party gained governmental control, marked the beginnings of fundamental changes in regard to the place of Islam in Turkey. By the end of 1950s, under the pressure of severe economic problems, Democrat Party had taken a clearly religious character. Religious courses were brought back into education, government support for the Hajj was restored, shrines were reopened and training for religious officials was restarted. Large-scale migrations of 1960s and 1970s brought the geographically and socially peripheral Islamic revivalism into the center, into the heart of the big cities. After the military intervention of 1980, government attitudes toward Islam changed. A departure from strict traditional secularism was supported by the newly active *tarikats* (religious orders) and substantial Islamic funding from abroad, which was used to set up educational facilities as well as Islamic companies. The 1980s and 1990s witnessed the politicization of Islam and the increasing polarization between the Islamists and the secularists. For the secularists, the emergence of fundamentalist Islamic Party as the winner of the 1994 municipal elections was the first sign of a much-feared possibility of an Islamic revolution in Turkey.

By the 1990s the turban has already become the symbol of political Islam as the distinction between traditional Islam and political Islam was revolving mainly around the issue of women's head covering. Turkish military and the military-backed government perceived the turban as an indisputable symbol of religious militancy and strictly enforced the ban on religious-inspired clothing in schools and state offices. The frequent clashes between the turbaned women, protesting in front of the universities and state offices, and the police were extensively reported and debated in the media. The distinction between traditional and political Islam, which found its expression in the style of headdress, was representative of the contrasting background, education, public participation and militancy of the women who cover their hair. While many rural, elderly and traditional Muslim women covered their heads using a *ba?örtüsü* (a scarf that covers only the head not the neck), it was primarily the young, urban and educated women who wore the turban and the complementary long overcoat regardless of seasonal change.

The turban was not only the symbol of the political Islam; it also became the symbol of the cultural "Other" in Turkey. For the secular women, the turbaned woman was the threatening and frightening Other who sought to undermine the modern, urban and Western lifestyle, and hence, had to be resisted. The secular resistance, similarly, took a symbolic form. While the turbaned students were protesting in front of the universities, the secular women, wearing short skirts, bodies and tank-tops with Atatürk (the founder of the republic) brooches pinned on their collars have been organizing expeditions to Atatürk's mausoleum in Ankara. Indeed, commodification has a central role in the shaping of both Islamic and secular identities in Turkey and transforming identity politics into a war over symbols. As Navaro-Yashin (forthcoming) comments Islamists and secularists alike differentiate their identities from each other by appropriating and consuming distinct objects and by creating particular consumption styles. Given the close association between identity and consumption, "the rise of Islamist movement in popularity and power is indissoluble from the development of specialized businesses for 'Islamic goods' and the formation of market networks for believers" (Navaro-Yashin forthcoming).

The emerging Islamic market and consumption styles became increasing visible in the 1990s. Many factors contributed to such a development. The 1980s and 1990s witnessed rapid urbanization as well as a large-scale globalization and privatization of the Turkish economy. Multinational companies entered to the Turkish market, making available many goods that were previously foreign to Turks; shopping malls carrying global brands, entertainment centers, five-star hotels, foreign cuisine and fast food restaurants, bars and cafes quickly became commonplace. As television was privatized, new television channels flourished, changing the objective of broadcasting from education to entertainment. The advertising industry took a new shape, fully utilizing the new sources of publicity to increase the allure of the new products. An imminent result of these was the development of young urban professionals, highly Westernized in their values and perceiving consumption as a measure of happiness and success. However, it was not only the secular urbanites whose lives have changed. The government equally supported the small companies of the religious cities of Anatolia, motivating them to develop their businesses in order to compete with the secular bourgeoisie. Backed with the foreign capital, coming mainly from other Muslim countries as well as from Turkish workers living in various European countries, Islamic businesses were soon able to compete in almost all the sectors of the economy. The religious and conservative small scale, rural businesses grew into bigger companies in the cities by following the logic of contemporary capitalism and marketing. These businesses built an alternative market for those who were religious and felt alienated from the westernized goods that dominated the consumption domain. As wealth accumulated among particular sections of the religious population, a bourgeoisie, conservative in values but avant-garde in consumption practices, started to emerge. As much as secular upper classes have developed a taste for bourgeois consumption, so have the religious upper classes.

In 1996 a summer resort—Caprice Hotel—located in the Aegean coast was opened. The hotel catered to religious people who felt uncomfortable in resorts to which secularists and tourists attended. Caprice Hotel quickly became, in the words of its owner, "the name of the alternative vacation." Separate swimming pools and beaches, and separate entertainment and leisure activities for men and women offered a safe heaven for religious upper classes who wanted to enjoy the summer yet remain true to the requirements of Islam. The responses to Caprice hotel, however, were mixed. Some Islamists condemned the hotel as they perceived it as a sign of degeneration and capitalization of Islam. Others defended the right of religious people to enjoy leisure activities as long as they are in line with the teachings of the Koran and the prophet.

A new style of consumption rapidly emerged in every domain of life. Today, surfing the Islamic web sites and chatting on the internet, kids of the Islamists listen to Turkish pop music, that "everyone else listens to" as one Islamist explains, and even heavy metal. But, unlike most secularists' kids, they also listen to "Islamic pop" (popularized hymns, part hymn part pop modern arrangements

played with Turkish and Western instruments) although it is less popular now than it was ten years ago. They shop with their parents in malls as well as in department stores built inside mosques and in flourishing marketplaces set up on mosque grounds. Such marketplaces, which are known by the name of the mosque that they are located next to, sell Korans, prayer beads and religious books as well as sacralized profane goods such as Islamic pop music tapes, CDs and romance novels, bright colored clocks with lights and a picture of Kaba in Mecca, landscape paintings or impressionistic reproductions framed with Koranic calligraphy, and many other items including stickers, posters, key-chains, coloring books, calenders, greeting cards, decorative items in brass, copper, silver, ceramic, wood, all decorated with Islamic symbols, pictures, or calligraphy. Next to a stall selling pictures of Kaba surrounded by pilgrims one can find a stall of natural products—herbs, herbal teas, shampoos, soaps, herbal medicine, natural foods—that would be typically sold in organic/natural/health stores in Europe. Islamic moderns appear to claim both the natural and the traditional: cuisine, home made objects, an almost lost ancient form of art, *ebru* (marbling), Ottoman culture and history, social practices such as taking home made food to sick neighbors and friends, going to *kaplica* (health spas associated with old/local culture) and alternative tourism (going to the mountains). Even at the Caprice hotel, the café serves herbal teas made from actual leaves rather than the more common teabags.

While interested in reviving the traditional, the Islamist moderns are not traditional at all. Consider, for instance, the consumption practices of a 32 years old turbaned female, wife of a member of the parliament from the Islamist Party, who had lived in Jeddah for 9 years:

> I recently bought a microwave, an Imperial from Miele. I liked its functions, it is beautiful and the manual is good. [when inquired about a Turkish brand, Arçelik] It is good maybe, but I am not used to it. Arçelik's quality is getting better than before. Before it was not nice, I did not like it. … [talking about appliances] I prefer first general Electric then Miele then Bosch. … I could not find Turkish coffee in Jeddah so I started to drink Nescafe in the morning. Also my husband. Normally everyone drinks tea [in Turkey] in the morning but in our home we drink Nescafe, orange juice, tea or milk. We don't drink tea every morning. … I am used to buying foreign clothes. For my children I always bought from Mother Care. Marks and Spencer. I prefer to buy from England or Germany, because I use it for a long time. But we also have good brands, I can buy from here, my son wears Waikiki, a French brand, made in Turkey. My scarves, those I usually use at night or when I go outside, are Hermes. … For underwear, I first go to Marks and Spencer then I look at other places. … European clothes are classic, in Turkey fashion changes more quickly. Fashion is very important here, but not for me. … I buy jewelry and gold when I have a chance to go to Italy or Jeddah. Because it is different.

Many such turbaned women are seen in tennis courts, on the ski slopes, playing volleyball or doing aerobics, or heard talking about dieting. Increasing numbers of them have professional careers and drive to work in their own cars. To be able to work in public offices or attend universities, some wear a wig, made by hairdressers specialized in making customized turban-covering wigs. Some go on a holiday with their female friends leaving children at home with their husbands. They dress in their stylish clothes as they go out together with their female friends to have fun, dancing to Shakira, Ricky Martin and Jennifer Lopez, or belly dancing to popular Turkish songs.

The embourgeoisement of the Islamists becomes particularly vocal in the domain of fashion. As the Turkish textile industry developed rapidly in the 1980s, clothing businesses also grew in the Islamic sector. The rise of political Islam fostered the demand for headscarves, overcoats and other clothing items. The initial uniformity in Islamic attire, which was characterized by the turban and the accompanying loose-fitting long overcoat, gradually transformed into heterogeneity in the dressing style, signaling the raising fashion consciousness especially among the upper class, urban, well-educated, young religious women. In *Unkapani* district of Istanbul, an entire shopping center, catering only to the covered women emerged. Many of these shops, which are known as *tesettür* (dress that complies with Islam) stores, have brand names that evoke Islam, such as "Tevhid" (unity under one God), "Ihvan" (Muslim brotherhood," and "Hak" (one of the names of God).

The most famous and controversial of these shops is "Tekbir Giyim," which translates as the "Allah is Great Apparel." Since opening its first shop in 1983, Tekbir Giyim developed into a multinational company, transforming its brand name into "The World's Trademark in Covered Women's Clothing."[1] It gradually expanded from supplying clothing to *tarikat* members to providing fashionable Islamic clothing to people who can afford to pay the high price. Cleverly enough, Tekbir Giyim targeted the upper class religious women, who were active in professional life and developing a taste for fashion and brand names as much as like their secular counterparts. The company's motto was to make covering beautiful, and change the image of Islamic style dressing as unappealing and uniform. So did it. Mixing Islamic aspirations with a capitalist ambition, Tekbir Giyim utilizes all the tools of fashion marketing to reach to its target segment. To get inspirations for new designs, Tekbir stylists follows the fashion trends of Turkey and of the West. They develop models named after famous covered Turkish women. They aggressively publicize their clothing line through fashion shows, catalogues and newspaper advertisements. Fashion shows, which draw significant media attention on the part of both secularists and Islamists, feature famous Turkish models who present the company's attire in a podium animated by artificially produced clouds, projecting lights and music. Models, whose only made-up faces are uncovered, sell covered women's clothes as beautifully and eloquently as they do so when they normally exhibit underwear, bathing suits and westernized clothes to the secular upper classes (for a detailed description of a Tekbir fashion show, see Navaro-Yashin forthcoming).

FASHIONABLE YET FAITHFUL

While Tekbir Giyim promotes itself as the "fashion source of the Islamic high-society" (Kas 1999), many Islamist moderns find its designs to be too dressy and ornate, and prefer more "modern," "sporty," "youthful," and "tasteful" clothes. They shop in "normal" stores where secularist moderns shop, ranging from mid-priced to exclusive designer stores. They window shop to familiarize themselves with the latest fashion trends even though they cannot buy many of these items because they are too tight, too open, too short, too transparent—simply not appropriate. If they cannot find a suitable outfit, they go to a tailor. A major complaint is the difficulty of finding clothes that they both like and can wear: modern, casual, fashionable yet sensitive to Islam. For example, a 35 year old woman, not able to find a suitable two-piece suit, described to us how she spent days searching for pieces that would

[1]Company logo.

make a matching set. In another instance we observed a turbaned woman in her mid twenties shopping with her friend in a clothing store. She adored a mustard colored sleeveless top that came with a button down fishnet sweater. As she sighed desperately thinking that she cannot wear it, her friend suggested that if she bought a long sleeved blouse of the same color, she could. She found a tight t-shirt of the same color and ended up purchasing both the sweater and the t-shirt.

For many Islamist women forming an ensemble of clothes and accessories is indeed a very laborious act. The most arduous search is for scarves, as these women own 30, 40, or even 100 scarves. All women complain about the difficulty of finding scarves that are harmonious with the colors and styles of their clothes. The upscale prefer Hermes, Dior, Gucci, Vakko (a prestigious Turkish brand), or Aker (a prestigious Turkish Islamist brand). The advertisements of Aker and numerous other *tesettür* brands often portray unturbaned models with fashionable dresses. The styles promoted through Islamic fashion shows, company catalogues, and television and newspaper advertisements for *tesettür* brands as well as clothes worn by anchorwomen of the Islamist television channels provide inspiration to the turbaned women for the clothes they wear daily on the city streets, resorts, and offices. But that inspiration is not always easy to act upon. For Islamist moderns, the search is for clothes that are loose enough not to show the contours of the body but not too loose to be shapeless and outdated: religiously acceptable and modest yet tasteful, stylish and modern. What they aspire to have is a look that is aesthetically pleasing and refined yet does not draw carnal attention.

In contrast to 1980s' uniform style, 1990s are characterized by variety in Islamic style dressing with more elegant, stylish and trendy clothes becoming increasingly visible. The standard long overcoat of the 1980s is now perceived by the Islamist moderns as the tasteless "grandmother's overcoat." The normative long, dark colored overcoat and large scarves, covering the head, the neck, the shoulders and the bosom, yielded to colorful, stylized pants and long jackets, skirts and blazers, long vests, above-the-knee coats, and smaller more tightly tied scarves placed inside the jacket. Denim jackets, vests, skirts, shirts, overcoats as well as jeans are commonly worn. More casual, modern, distinctive, and youthful designs are sought and purchased both by the young and the middle-aged women. As these women turn away from the long overcoat to designer brands and stylish cuts, to compliment their overall modern look, they also switch from the locally produced "faithful" perfumes—perfumes that do not contain alcohol and have religiously inspired brand names such as "Friday Wind"—to imported foreign brands of perfumes.

Clothes worn at home and outside vary. Shorts, mini skirts, tight tops, sexy lingerie are regarded to be appropriate to wear in the private space. Yet, in the public spaces, one can easily come across to turbaned women wearing tight long skirts with slits up to the thighs, very tight tops under transparent shirts or jackets, sexy high-heels or trendy platform shoes accompanied by high-fashion handbags. Shoes—trendy sandals worn on bare feet or fashionable and sexy high-heels worn under the long overcoats—are very perceptible to the eyes. In the all-female swimming pool at the Caprice Hotel, we observed women flaunting their fashionable bikinis—some of them with the trendy little wraps around the waist—while a few were sunbathing in swimsuits worn over knee-length tights and one in a *ha?ema* (a two-piece swimming outfit that fully covers the body). To much of our surprise, there were even a few topless sunbathers.

However, not all Islamists enjoy the stylish clothes, Islamic fashion shows, beauty and fitness centers, and five-star hotels, and complain about the lack of Islamic fashion magazines, designers, and attractive clothes that comply with the Islamic codes. Some Islamists condemn these developments, arguing that they indicate the lack of a thorough internalization of Islam and, hence, the lack of true faith. For instance, observing that heavily made-up models who are famous for displaying sexy lingerie or swimsuits also display *tesettür* clothes, a female Islamist sociologist comments that Islamic fashion shows do not Islamicize fashion, but rather turn Islam into a show (Yeni ?afak 1999, p.8). According to a columnist writing in an Islamic newspaper, *Vakit*, the fashion shows are approved by Muslims "who [have] submitted to the hegemony of capitalist relations of business" and "if you were to knock the consumerist practice of fashion shows over, the capitalist building would be destroyed" (Özdür 1994, p.4).

In the 1980s, the Islamists sought to differentiate themselves from the secularists by adopting a uniform Islamic dressing style and making it increasingly visible in the public domain. At the core of the distinction was, and still is, the opposition between religious sensitivity and secularist immodesty. Now, however, the initially homogeneous Islamic identity appears to be fragmented, as various segments of the Islamists attempt to differentiate themselves from each other. Symbolically enough, the struggle for difference finds its loudest expression in the creative and eclectic world of fashion. Some Islamists dress in a "modern" and "urban" style, and try to distance themselves from the conventional "rural" image of Islamic attire. Others perceive the long, loose overcoat accompanied by a large turban covering the shoulders and the bosom as "tasteless," "unnecessarily conservative," and "passé" and, instead, seek a "tasteful," "casual," and "youthful" style. They want to be "just like the rest of us [secularists]" but with "religious sensitivity". They repeatedly comment that except for the turban and less revealing cuts, they wear whatever the secularists wear. The Islamist newly rich, on the other hand, wear stylish turbans and lavish designer clothes to set themselves apart from the poorer faithful. Yet, others consider the Islamist newly-riches' interest in international brands such as Gucci and Versace and their gaudy styles as flaunting and exaggerated, and favor unpretentious refinement and simplicity as opposed to their pretentious style.

THEORIZING THE FAITHFUL CHIC

The rise of Islam is generally seen as an opposition to globalization and Western consumerism (Barber 1996; Göle 1996; Witkowski 1999). For instance, in his book *Orientalism, Postmodernism and Globalism*, Brian Turner devotes an entire chapter to convince his readers that "consumerism offers or promises a range of possible lifestyles which compete with, and in many cases, contradict the uniform lifestyle demanded by Islamic fundamentalism" (1994, p.90). According to Turner the cultural, aesthetic and stylistic pluralism fostered by postmodernism and the spread of global system of consumption contradicts with the fundamentalist commitment to a unified world organized around incontrovertibly true values and beliefs. While "the consumer market threatens to break out into a new stage of fragmented postmodernity in late capitalism," fundamentalism "acts as a brake on the historical development of world capitalism" (Turner 1994, p.80). From a different perspective, but in a similar vein, Bocock (1993) suggests that religion can provide an alternative to overcome the consumerist ideology.

However, Islam, at least in the context of Turkey, does not seem to oppose consumption or offer an alternative to consumerism. The more ascetic and orthodox Muslims do restrict their consumption, but most do not—they actively engage in consumption albeit in an Islamic way. As the Turkish case demonstrates consumption patterns can be and are appropriated into religiously

acceptable styles without undermining consumption itself. This is more so in the case of Islam for which hedonism is an accepted way to life and is less of a sin than Christianity. Islam permits the pursuit of desires as long as they are integrated with moral principles such as generosity, sharing, giving to the poor, and fairness, and one is not enslaved by passionate attachment (Belk, Ger and Askegaard forthcoming). Islam accepts that material things are important in life. However, it requires that acquisitiveness and competition are balanced by fair play and compassion. That is, material goods are to be distributed and wealth is to be shared among all in a just manner. Being honest, fulfilling commitments, seeking virtue, providing for dependents generously, and being socially conscious legitimize consumption. Historically, religious (and secular) ethics in Turkey, in line with the teachings of Islam, have reinforced consumption for pleasure, practiced along with the principles of generosity and fairness (Ülgener 1981).

As much as the consumption practices of the Islamists challenge the conventional view of Islam as a value system that categorically opposes consumerism and Westernism, the fashion practices of Islamist women contradict the common conceptions of female body and identity within Islam. The discourse of colonial feminism views Islam as innately oppressive to women. The turban and the covering of women's bodies represent the seclusion and segregation of women, and women's subordination to the masculine power. This discourse places an unwarranted significance on the "modern" outlook of women while constructing the covered woman as a symbol of backwardness and as an obstacle to civilization. In this Orientalist narrative, the turbaned woman epitomizes the exotic as well as the threatening Other of the West. Internalizing the oriental discourse, the Turkish republican ideology similarly perceives the turbaned women as a threat to modernity and Western lifestyle (Witkowski 1999).

The diverse fashion practices of urban turbaned women in contemporary Turkey imply highly complex and multi-layered identity dynamics and politics that go well beyond a dichotomous Orientalist reading. The newly emergent urban, middle-class turbaned women do not simply differentiate themselves from the Westernized, secular Turkish women; they equally distance themselves from the traditional Islamic women who wear a headscarf out of habit in rural areas and small towns and from the newly-rich Islamists. They reject both the image of covering as a sign of cultural backwardness and as a sign of extravagance and flaunting. At a broader level, the Islamist consumptionscape evinces the emergence of an Islamic elite seeking to ascertain itself as an alternative to the secular elite that has traditionally been dominant in the public space. Drawing both from Islam and local cultural resources, this elite crafts new consumption practices—modern, casual and trendy clothes, natural goods, traditional cuisine, Ottoman culture and artifacts, alternative vacation and traveling, books, intellectual debates, educational programs and documentaries on Islamic television channels—and attempts to differentiate itself from the secularist moderns, the Islamist newly-rich and the habitually religious lower classes.

Today's Islamist consumptionscape is characterized by pluralism and difference, and cannot be explained as either rejection of consumerism, capitalism and globalization or resistance to modernity. Struggle over identity between secularists and Islamists as well as among different groups of Islamists is strongly implicated in the domain of consumption and is constantly transformed as a result of various local and global dynamics and forces. Similar to their secular counterparts, different groups of Islamists, located in various *habituses*, seek to construct distinct identities for themselves by adopting or rejecting particular consumption practices. Although the resultant consumption practices resonate the processes of "creolization" or "hybridization" we believe neither terms sufficiently explain them.

Creolization refers to the meeting and mingling of meanings and meaningful forms from disparate sources—old and new, foreign/ global and local—and reflects the dialectics of adoption and resistance (Ger and Belk 1996, Hannerz 1992, Howes 1996). Ger and Belk (1996) report that consumptionscapes of less affluent societies, including Turkey, are characterized by creolized consumption more than other alternatives, such as emulation of the West, return to roots, resistance to the West, or recontextualization. They argue that creolization incorporates the other alternatives and offer a new synthesis which help individuals to differentiate themselves in the social hierarchy.

Similar to creolization, hybridity rejects the notion of total domination (i.e., the West dominating the East) and, instead, emphasizes the interaction between different parties. According to Homi Bhabha, in contrast to Said's static dichotomy between the Occident and the Orient, Western culture never totally dominates other cultures because resistance through "translation" operates at the intersection of two. "Cultural translation" occurs when one "statement" travels from one specific cultural context to another, creating "a new statement", or "the difference of the same" (Bhabha 1994, p.22). Translation creates a hybrid identity as the eastern and western cultures transgress each other's boundaries and constantly negotiate the borderline cultures where plural voices speak out.

While creolization and hybridization emphasize the complex and dynamic interaction between opposing cultural resources— Western and Eastern, global and local, old and new, traditional and contemporary—and avoid binary explanations, they both fail to acknowledge the creation of multiple internal Others as a side-effect. Identity is always relational and cannot be totally indeterminate if it exists as a part of the symbolic order whose purpose is to fix some meaning. The creolized or hybrid identity also needs its own Other(s) as its boundary-marker, and in doing so, attempts to secure its distance from elements differing in terms of social class, cultural capital, political beliefs, etc. What we observe in the Islamic consumptionscape cannot be viewed only as mixing or transformation of the local with the global elements. New consumption patterns emerge as consumers negotiate various tensions both between the local and the global and within the local itself. Constructing a "modern" Islamic identity within the local power network involves simultaneously negotiating multiple tensions—the tensions between the West and the East, the secular and the religious, the urban and the rural, the elite religious and the lower class or newly-rich religious, the urban religious and the rural religious—and distancing itself from various internal Others.

Multi-layered and multi-tensional meaning transformations and translations go well beyond a mere mixing of existing forms, a mere pastiche devoid of identity politics. Endlessly reformulated, transformed, inverted, subverted, diverted, rejected, domesticated, exoticized, and reinvented grammars, scripts, settings, objects, and meanings blend into new ensembles. Rather than an "Escher etching"[2] this fused ensemble is an Escher*esque* social practice whose full meaning emerges from its union "with actors and audience *at a given moment in a group's ongoing social process*" (Turner 1986, 24, italics ours). We propose the term *fusion* to refer to the reconciliation of diverse dialectical forms and tensions, and to the resultant transformed forms in new social formations. We believe that Escher*esque* fusions, in fashion and consumption, characterize the Turkish Islamist modernity. With various

oppositions taming and transforming each other, the "faithful chic" paradoxically upholds the ideals about modern identity albeit its postmodern plurality, and opens up a theoretical space for the consumer behavior researchers to explore.

REFERENCES

Belk, Russell W., Güliz Ger, and Søren Askegaard (forthcoming) "The Missing Streetcar Named Desire," in: S. Ratneshwar, David Glen Mick, and Cynthia Huffman (eds.), *The Why of Consumption*, London: Routledge.

Barber, Benjamin R. (1996) *Jihad vs. McWorld: How Globalism and Tribalism are Reshaping the World,* New York: Ballantine Books.

Bhabha, Homi (1994) *The Location of Culture*, New York: Routledge.

Bilici, Ebru Nida (2000) "İslami Gençlik Kabuk Degistiriyor," *Aksiyon*, March 18, No.276, 32-39.

Bulut, Faik (1995) *Tarikat Sermayesinin Yükselisi*, Istanbul: Öteki Yayıncılık.

Bocock, Robert (1993) *Consumption*, London: Routledge.

Ger, Güliz and Russell W. Belk (1996) "I'd Like to Buy the World a Coke: Consumptionscapes of the 'Less Affluent World'," *Journal of Consumer Policy*, 19(3), 1-34.

Göle, Nilüfer (1996) *The Forbidden Modern: Civilization and Veiling*, Ann Arbor: The University of Michigan Press.

Hannerz, Ulf (1992) *Cultural Complexity: Studies in the Organization of Meaning*, New York: Columbia University Press.

Howes, David, ed. (1996) *Cross-Cultural Consumption*, London: Routledge.

Kadıoglu, Ayse (1994) "Women's Subordination in Turkey: Is Islam Really the Villain?" *Middle East Journal*, 48:4, 645-660

Kas, Nilüfer (1999) "Testtürde Aç-Kapa Nesrin Modası," *Tempo*, October 21-27, No.619, 54-56.

Navaro-Yashin, Yael (forthcoming) "The Market for Identities: Secularism, Islamism, Goods," in Deniz Kandiyoti and Ayse Saktanber, ed. *Fragments of Culture: The Everyday of Modern Turkey*, I. B. Tauris and University of California Press.

Özdür, Atilla (1994) "Birbirimize İslam Satacagız," *Vakit*, November 11, p.4.

Tapper, Richard (1991) *Islam in Modern Turkey,* London: I. B. Tauris and Co. Ltd.

Turner, Brian (1994) *Orientalism, Postmodernism and Globalism*, London and New York: Routledge.

Turner, Victor (1986) *The Anthropology of Performance*, New York: PAJ Publications.

Ülgener, Sabri (1981) *Zihniyet ve Din: Islam, Tasavvuf ve Çözülme Devri Iktisadi*, Istanbul: Der Yayinlari.

Yalman, Nur (1969) "Islamic Reform and the Mystic Tradition in Eastern Turkey," *Archives Europeennes de Sociologie*, 10.

"Herkes Tesettür Defilesinde," *Yeni Safak*, 3 July 1999, p. 8.

Witkowski, Terrence H. (1999) "Religiosity and Social Meaning in Wearing Islamic Dress," paper presented at the 7th Cross Cultural Research Conference, Cancun, Mexico, December 12-15, 1999.

Zaman, Amberin (1999) "Spreading Faith Through Fashion: Turkish Chain Promotes Islamic Clothing," *Washington Post*, December 2, p. A32.

---

[2]Howes' analogy; 1996, p.6.

When *Does* Culture Matter? The Transitory Nature of Cultural Differences in Judgments and Choices

Donnel Briley, Hong Kong University
Jennifer Aaker, Stanford University

Consumer behavior literature examining cultural differences has expanded dramatically in the past several years, yielding important insights about how cultures differ. But this body of work has not yet incorporated important social cognitive concepts showing that individual's cognitions, attitudes and behaviors can change depending on situational and contextual factors (see Wyer and Srull 1989 for a review). Such concepts, when applied to the cross-cultural realm, suggest that cultural inclinations may vary in strength based on the context in which judgments and decisions are made (Hong, Chiu and Kung 1997; Oishi, Wyer and Colcombe 2000). For example, Hong et al. (2000) show that subjects' patterns of social attributions change when they are exposed to pictures of Chinese vs. American cultural icons prior to the attribution task. For both Hong Kong Chinese and Asian-American subjects, exposure to the Chinese icons resulted in a more Chinese mode of thinking (attributing cause to groups), while exposure to American icons resulted in a more Western mode of thinking (attributing cause to individuals).

Examinations of cross-cultural values and attitude constructs, the presumed drivers of cultural differences in behaviors, provide further evidence suggesting the need to explore the stability of cultural inclinations. These examinations have questioned the stable nature of values and attitude constructs (e.g., Heine et al. 1999; Peng, Nisbett and Wong 1997) and, further, using priming mechanisms have shown evidence that values can be shifted in predictable ways by situational forces (Briley and Wyer 2000; Lee, Aaker and Gardner 2000).

The aforementioned findings suggest that consumer behavior researchers should include in their thinking the possibility that culture-related behavioral inclinations are not ever-present, but are transitory. In the proposed session, we examine the malleability of consumer judgments and choices in a cross-cultural setting in order to answer the question, 'When does culture matter?' The session has two primary objectives: (1) raise awareness of the potential transitory nature of culture-related cognitions and behaviors, and (2) suggest specific moderating variables that indicate conditions under which cultural leanings are either 'in force' or dormant.

The session's three papers present evidence suggesting that culture-specific patterns of behavior can be present in some situations but weak or absent in others. Each of the three deals with a different consumer behavior phenomenon and offers a distinct moderating variable to explain the effect. Briley, Morris and Simonson (2000) suggest that cultural leanings 'come forward' to influence choices when cultural knowledge is activated, though such leanings may be dormant under other conditions. In particular, it is suggested that deliberating on reasons prior to making choices brings cultural knowledge to the fore of the mind. Prompting decision makers to provide reasons for selections causes them to search for 'plausible' reasons (Wilson and Schooler 1991) and, it is argued, to recruit rules and principles that derive from cultural knowledge. Thus, culturally-conferred decision rules should be drawn upon when individuals seek rationales for their decisions, but not on many other occasions. The paper finds support for this proposition, which represents a dynamic rather than dispositional view of cultural influence, in a set of studies of consumer decisions that involve a tradeoff between diverging attributes, such as low

price and high quality. Differences between East Asians and Americans in the tendency to select compromise options (Simonson 1989) emerged only when subjects were asked to explain their selections.

By manipulating the level of accessibility in the associations embedded in marketing communications, Aaker provides evidence indicating that cultural preferences, often assumed to be relatively stable and driven by culture-based norms and traditions, may in fact be relatively malleable. For example, when North American participants were exposed to a brand associated with "Peacefulness" associations (e.g., peaceful, mild, shy), significantly less favorable attitudes were found as compared with those of Japanese individuals. The converse pattern was found with a set of "Ruggedness" associations embedded in the appeals. More importantly, however, when the level of accessibility of the associations was increased (e.g., when cognitive elaboration was heightened through multiple exposures to the appeal), both culture-based differences were eliminated. Mediation analyses indicated that participants in the non-target culture elaborated on the relatively novel, yet positively-valenced appeal to a greater degree in the high vs. low elaboration conditions, a process that yielded increasingly positive thoughts which subsequently affected attitudes. In contrast, the increased elaboration by participants in the target culture generated increasingly negative associations toward the appeal. These results, which were replicated across three experiments using distinct operationalizations of the culture variable, provide additional support to a growing stream of research that suggests that culture-driven preferences are more malleable than previously thought.

In Price and Briley (2000) involvement and need-for-cognitive-closure are explored as moderators of cultural differences in responses to persuasion attempts, particularly in the context of deceptive advertising. Prior research has shown that cross-cultural differences in advertising outcomes are more pronounced under conditions of intensive processing. For example, Aaker and Maheswaran (1997) showed that members of Chinese cultures are generally more sensitive than those from North American cultures to consensus information as an input to product judgments, but the effect is most pronounced under high involvement conditions. Similarly, Chiu et al. (1994) found that differences in Chinese and American attributional reasoning are enhanced when the need for cognitive closure is high. It appears that cognitive pressures exerted by high involvement and high need-for-closure conditions lead consumers to rely more heavily on their natural cultural tendencies than they do in low involvement and low need-for-closure settings. Price and Briley examine the differential effect of cognitive pressure on the responses of Americans and Chinese to deceptive persuasion messages. Consistent with the above findings, they predict and confirm that these cultural groups have opposite responses to the involvement manipulation. While Americans have been found to be *more* susceptible to deception under high pressure conditions, Chinese individuals were *less* susceptible to deception under high pressure conditions.

Together, the papers demonstrate the malleability of cultural inclinations in different domains (consumer choice, attitude formation, and susceptibility to advertising) and show three distinct moderating factors that account for the effects (need to provide reasons, accessibility of associations, and cognitive pressures).

Thus, converging evidence is offered to support the assertion that cross-cultural differences in behaviors and judgments can be transitory. This result, which is found in three distinct settings, sheds new light on current findings in the cross-cultural consumer behavior literature, which as discussed by Robert Wyer, conceptualizes culture as a more stable or chronic force. Further, insights into the types of factors that raise and attenuate cultural differences are offered. Thus, it is expected that the proposed session will be of interest to a wide audience, including researchers interested in cultural influence, consumer choice and persuasion.

The Formality Dimension of Service Quality in Thailand and Japan

Terrence H. Witkowski, California State University, Long Beach
Mary F. Wolfinbarger, California State University, Long Beach[1]

ABSTRACT

Service firms expanding globally must address cultural differences both in the desired dimensions of service quality and in the behaviors that represent these dimensions. This paper investigates formality and its relation to other dimensions of service quality in Thailand and Japan. Based on a survey (N = 400) using Servqual and related scales, factor, correlational, and regression analyses all indicate the existence of a separate formality dimension in both bank and restaurant service settings. This finding has implications for international service studies.

INTRODUCTION

A decade ago, Michael Porter (1990) predicted the emergence of a new breed of larger, internationally competitive, service companies. Recent cross-border mergers, acquisitions, and start-ups in retailing, banking, telecommunications, entertainment, and other service businesses appear to validate his forecast. For example, America's Wal-Mart has entered markets in Latin American, Asia, and Europe where it purchased two German chains, Spar and Wertkauf, in 1998 and the British Asda group in 1999 (Williams 1999). France's Carrefour, Holland's Ahold, and Sweden's Ikea also have expanded, among other places, in the formerly communist countries of central and eastern Europe. On the web, Amazon.com has duplicated its e-commerce model overseas through subsidiary websites in Britain and Germany.

When companies enter foreign consumer markets, they frequently introduce practices that change and even improve upon local service delivery. In a fascinating series of essays based on ethnographic research, Watson and his colleagues (1997) describe how McDonald's has introduced orderly queuing, self-provisioning (napkins, utensils, drinks), and self-seating, not to mention more hygienic food preparation and cleaner toilets, in several East Asian markets. Inexorably, such foreign competition forces domestic service firms to upgrade the quality of their own offerings. Local fast food chains in Beijing now regularly employ workers to mop floors and wash windows all day long and often in entryways where their performances can be seen by prospective customers (Watson, 1997, p. 34).

In many cases, however, service marketers must be much more accommodating to local service cultures. The quality of a service interaction often depends upon the provider's skill in expressing socially desirable emotions and behaviors in a manner credible to customers (Ashforth and Humphrey 1993). American service personnel are known for their chirpiness and ability to keep their problems at home. Many Europeans, on the other hand, find role-playing behavior to be superficial. They see no reason to disguise their true feelings and differentiate their private and public selves (Murphy 1994). In Germany, customers have come to expect frowns, glares, or a bored look of compulsory compliance from store, bank, and service desk employees (Lord 1994; Stern 1996). Thus, Wal-Mart has been very cautious in introducing chatty American-style greeters in its newly acquired German stores (Williams 1999).

Achieving global service standards is problematic because consumers in different countries disagree over both the appropriate *dimensions of service quality* and the *behaviors that represent these dimensions*. Most Americans value their time and generally

expect a swift response to questions, complaints, and purchase orders. In developing countries, where people are less driven by the clock, the concept of "promptness" is more flexible (Riddle 1986) and customer satisfaction can result from simply getting a response (Malhotra *et. al.*, 1994). Some cultures, such as the Arabian Gulf States, define service quality in terms of personal attention and pampering (Kassem 1989), whereas others may have a more "do-it-yourself" attitude and may not object to interacting with machines such as automated telephone answering services. The perishability of services sometimes requires the shifting of demand, but not all cultures may have the same waiting line behavior or willingness to defer consumption. Interestingly, a recent study showed that Japanese and Americans cannot even agree on the emotions represented by facial expressions. Whereas 91.1 percent of American respondents concurred that a model's face showed sadness, only 37.4 percent of the Japanese subjects so agreed (Emmons 1997). Across cultures, non-verbal cues are typically difficult to read and easy to misinterpret (Ferraro 1998), but they have much to say about the relationships between service providers and customers (Gilly and Graham 1996).

The objective of this research is to study whether formality constitutes an independent dimension of service quality in two Asian cultures: Thailand and Japan. Formality has received some attention from the services marketing field (Goodwin and Frame 1989; Goodwin and Smith 1990; Winsted 1997), but little research has been conducted outside the U.S. even though the international business literature suggests that formality is an important characteristic of many cultures (Gesteland 1999; Hall and Hall 1990). This proposition is investigated through surveys of consumer service expectations and outcomes, and overall service satisfaction, in bank and restaurant settings. The conclusion considers some limitations of the research and offers some implications for theory and service studies.

FORMALITY IN SERVICE CULTURE

Formality is defined herein as interpersonal communications, both verbal and nonverbal, that express courtesy and proper etiquette and maintain social distance. Formality represents the "highest" and most traditional social standards. This approach coincides with Goodwin and Frame (1989) and Goodwin and Smith (1990), who investigated addressing service patrons by their first names, and Winsted (1997), whose Japanese sample were concerned with nice dress and proper language. Formality is not the same as service "formalization," which Suprenant and Solomon (1987) defined as "high standardization, routinization, or codification with limited opportunity for option personalization" (p. 88). Personalized services can be offered with or without high levels of civility and deference.

Cultures can be differentiated according to their level of formality, ranging from those that are relatively informal to those that are relatively formal. While the U.S., Canada, Australia, New Zealand, and the Scandinavian countries typify informal cultures,

---

[1]The authors wish to thank Panwadee Chantori and Hideyuki Hirakawa for their valuable assistance in translation, data collection, and data entry.

most of the rest of the world is characterized by more formal cultures (Gesteland 1999). The former tend to value egalitarian organizations and relatively small status and power distinctions, whereas the latter have steep hierarchies reflecting major differences in status and power. A culture's level of formality is not immutable. America was arguably a more formal culture 100 years ago and, today, it appears that much of the world is gradually drifting toward greater informality.

Language constitutes an important element of culture and a variety of linguistic practices express formality. For example, many languages distinguish between the formal "you," the Chinese *Nin*, French *Vous*, Spanish *Usted*, and German *Sie*, invoked to maintain social distance and the informal *ni*, *tu*, or *du* used with children, family, and close friends. The English "you" makes no such distinction. English speakers introduce formality by addressing people by their title and surname. More formal German speakers precede the surname with two or more titles such as in "Professor Doktor Schmidt." Moreover, Australians and American frequently address others by their first name, even before meeting them, a practice most Europeans, among others, deplore (Hall and Hall 1990).

Nonverbal communication also expresses degrees of formality. Americans, for instance, convey a relaxed, informal attitude by leaning back in their chairs and putting their feet on their desks. More formal cultures would consider such body posture rude (Ferraro 1998). The choice of clothing for a particular situation also communicates degrees of formality. Americans appear to be moving away from business attire and are more frequently wearing casual clothes in the office. In South and Southeast Asia, "Wearing a suit and tie to meetings during the hot season sends a positive signal of respect, and keeping one's jacket on in a non-air conditioned office signals even greater respect" (Gesteland 1999, p. 49). Communicating formality non-verbally should be especially important in high-context cultures, where language is less precise and direct and meaning is transmitted more through restricted codes and contextual cues (Ferraro 1998).

Formality appears to have a connection with two of the Hofstede (1997) values: "power distance," the extent to which people accept an unequal distribution of power, and "uncertainty avoidance," the extent to which people feel threatened by uncertain or unknown situations. Formality is an important means of conveying and reinforcing disparities in social rank and authority (Gesteland 1999). By preferring more formal rather than more spontaneous verbal and non-verbal communication, members of a culture high on uncertainty avoidance can reduce the anxieties and ambiguities of interpersonal relations. The U.S., Canada, Australia, New Zealand, and the Scandinavian countries all score fairly low on both the power distance and the uncertainty avoidance indexes.

Whatever the overall level of formality, it undoubtedly varies *within* cultures according to the specific social context (Ferraro 1998). For example, age and status differences generally elicit more formal communication. Younger people typically use less slang and more polite language when speaking to their elders. Employees use more deferential speech with senior executives, patients with their physicians, and the religious with their clergy. Dress and other nonverbal communication often convey impressions more forcefully than language. "Clothes serve as a strong cue to the degree of formality in a situation and help shape how individuals interact" (Kaiser 1997, p. 337).

According to Goodwin and Smith (1990), the intimacy generated by "high-touch" services, such as hair styling and sports instruction, increases first name usage and other elements of informality between providers and clients. In contrast, seriously upmarket restaurants and hotels will insist that waiters and the front desk practice verbal politeness, maintain decorum, and wear classy, even "formal" attire as part of their performance. Across many service settings, personnel making customer contact dress and behave more formally than those who are out of sight (Goffman 1959). Dress and health codes ("No shoes, no shirt, no service!") impose more formal comportment upon customers.

Interestingly, neither the path-breaking conceptual work of Parasuraman, Zeithaml, and Berry (1985) nor their later empirical work (Parasuraman, Zeithaml and Berry 1988) identified formality as a separate dimension although the original model included a courtesy criterion (politeness, respect, clean and neat appearance) which has some elements of formality. The reason may be because this research was carried out in the highly informal American context.

SERVICE CULTURE IN THAILAND AND JAPAN

The quality of customer service in Thailand is frequently hampered by infrastructure deficiencies, including onerous government intervention and poorly educated service workers, typical of a "middle-income" developing country. However, some liberalization of financial markets, growing inbound tourism, foreign competition, and imported technological and managerial know-how have raised service standards (Ratanakomut 1995).

Thai cultural practices affect service performance. Thailand is typically referred to as the "Land of Smiles" because this facial expression is so often visible. Rather than indicating an inner state of mind, Thai smiles convey both positive and negative messages and provide a way of lubricating difficult or embarrassing social interactions such as when a request is being denied (Hendon 1999). Showing consideration for the needs and feelings of others, known as *kreng jai*, all too often means a tendency to say yes to or agree with a customer even when the sales person knows it is not possible to fulfill the promise (Niratpattanasai 2000). Because Thais are trained to avoid conflict, customers seldom complain to shop owners who have, therefore, little motivation to improve service.

Thai business communication tends to be very reserved and business dress is usually extremely neat and formal (Gesteland 1999; Global Road Warrior 1999b; Hendon 1999). Thais also emphasize the use of titles and have a very hierarchical business culture that stresses deference to rank and authority (Hendon 1999). Thailand scores somewhat high on Hofstede's (1997) power distance index (22nd out of 53 countries and regions) and slightly below average on uncertainty avoidance (30th out of 53).

Being a highly developed country, Japan is in the position to deliver a superior level of service quality and, indeed, the Japanese expect and receive a great deal of customer attention (Hall and Hall 1987; Schlossberg 1990) and deference from sellers (Gesteland 1999; Graham and Sano 1989). White-gloved young women greet department store customers and thank them for coming in (Schlossberg 1990) and Japanese salesmen serve their good customers in any way they can in order to build long-term relationships (Hall and Hall 1987). Personal attention is so ingrained that self-service fuel pumps were not introduced in Japan until April 1, 1998 (Reitman 1998). As the Japanese put it: "The customer is God." Overseas, the Japanese report lower levels of satisfaction with all aspects of in-flight service than airline passengers from other countries (Gilly and Graham 1996) and have been disappointed with the treatment they receive from shop clerks in Great Britain (*International Herald Tribune* 1992). Airlines, hotels, restaurants, and retail stores in the U.S. have learned to cater to finicky Japanese tourists and business travelers (Witkowski and Yamamoto 1991).

Japan is a relatively formal culture (Holroyd and Coates 1999). Japanese communication with strangers tends to be ritualized and reserved. Barnlund (1989) attributes this to a Japanese need to "reduce the unpredictability and emotional intensity of personal encounters" (p. 33). Japan scored seventh highest out of 50 countries and three regions on Hofstede's (1997) uncertainty avoidance index. Although Japan scores in the middle on the power distance index (33rd highest out of 53), it has a vertically organized social structure and people either know or find out who is above and who is below them while conversing (Barnlund 1989). The Japanese also exhibit formality in their non-verbal communication. Bowing and ritualized presentation of business cards (*meishi*) are two such cultural practices (Holroyd and Coates 1999). Japanese business attire is often conservative with finely tailored dark suits and expensive but understated accessories common for both men and women (Global Road Warrior 1999a). Although long in decline, the institution of the *geisha*, with its traditional costumes and elaborately scripted tea ceremonies, epitomizes formality in Japanese service culture (Hoh 1998).

Winsted (1997) found that formality-related behaviors (nice dress, proper language) formed a separate dimension for the Japanese, but did not show up among the American respondents; whereas authenticity (genuineness of behavior) was a separate factor for the Americans, but not for the Japanese. Her data also indicated that these different dimensions overlap in the minds of the consumers. These findings inspired the present research which seeks to replicate and elaborate upon the import of formality within Japan and a second, comparative Asian culture — Thailand.

RESEARCH METHODS

A five-page, self-administered questionnaire was developed in English. It consisted of 22 original Servqual items measuring service expectations and outcomes, three Servpref scales (Cronin and Taylor 1992) assessing overall service quality, and some standard demographic questions about respondent age, sex, education, and income. The instrument also added six items to tap three of the dimensions Winsted (1997) discovered in her Japanese sample: *conversation* ("Employees at this bank [restaurant] have a sense of humor" and "Employees at this bank [restaurant] like to talk to me"), *formality* ("This bank [restaurant] insists that its employees use proper language" and "This bank [restaurant] insists that its employees were appropriate clothing"), and *civility* ("At this bank [restaurant], employees are never arrogant" and "Employees at this bank [restaurant] have a good attitude"). These items all appeared relevant to an informality — formality continuum.

Slightly different versions of the questionnaire were created for bank and restaurant service settings. The translations proceeded in two stages: (1) preliminary translations were made by the Thai and Japanese graduate students who were to collect the data and (2) two additional auditors for each language reviewed their work and suggested changes. In effect, by having translation "committees," this approach was deemed equivalent to back translation, parallel blind, or other techniques.

During the summer of 1998, two hundred usable questionnaires were completed in Thailand (100 for bank and 100 for restaurant settings) and another 200 in Japan, (again 100 for bank and 100 for restaurant settings). The Thai data were collected in Bangkok and the Japanese data were collected in Kitakuyushu, a city of one million on the island of Kyushu. In both places, the graduate students used opportunistic or "snow-ball" techniques to recruit participants. No unusual problems were reported from the field although some Japanese respondents did not understand the concept of "household" income and reported personal income instead.

Although efforts were made to obtain more or less representative and comparable samples from the two countries, there were some differences. The average age of the Thai respondents was 33.0, while that of the Japanese was 39.7. The Thai sample was 41.0% female and 59.0% male; the Japanese sample was 57.0% female and 43.0% male. Finally, while 81% of the Thais were in the top two out of five educational categories (college graduate and some graduate work or degree), only 25% of the Japanese were so well educated. Thus, the Thai sample was younger, more male, and better educated than its Japanese counterpart. Thailand does have a much younger population than Japan. In Thailand, 27% are under age 15 and only 5% are over 65. In Japan, just 15% are under 15, while 16% are over 65 (Population Reference Bureau 1999).

RESEARCH FINDINGS

Checking Convergent and Discriminant Validity of Formality: Factor Analyses

The 22 original items from Servqual, along with Winsted's (1997) suggested items for conversation, formality and civility, were submitted to principal components factor analysis using Equimax rotation because this method of analysis produces a factor structure that is the most interpretable as well as being the most consistent with the original Servqual analyses (Parasuraman, Zeithaml and Berry 1988; 1991). Nevertheless, four items from the original Servqual crossloaded on multiple factors and were removed from analysis as they did not achieve sufficient discriminant analysis for this Asian sample. The four items came from different Servqual dimensions and three of the four crossloaded on the new factor, formality. The four removed items and the associated factor from Servqual are listed at the bottom of Table 1.

Additionally, the Servqual items intended to load separately on assurance and responsiveness instead loaded together on one factor. In order to further probe this finding, a separate factor analysis was performed utilizing only the original Servqual assurance and responsiveness items (including the two items later removed from analysis for crossloading). The items were submitted with instructions to extract two factors, but all assurance and responsiveness items, except for one, still loaded on a single factor, with the remaining item being "forced" on a separate construct. Inconsistent factor structures have been a feature of Servqual analyses (see Parasuraman, Zeithaml and Berry 1994 for a detailed analysis and review of Servqual properties). Part of the inconsistency in factor structure is likely due to insufficient variance in the underlying sample which prevents factor analyses from differentiating successfully between variables, especially when those variables tend to be correlated. It is unclear whether insufficient variance or cultural factors are the explanation for assurance and responsiveness items loading together. It may be that our Asian subsamples do not perceive assurance and responsiveness to be separate dimensions of the service experience.

Once the four crossloading items are removed from analysis, a five factor solution results explaining 72% of variance, with four dimensions consisting of the original Servqual factors (with responsiveness and assurance being *one* rather than *two* factors) and a new factor, formality, which includes the civility items and clearly constitutes a separate factor with high discriminant and convergent validity (Churchill 1979) (see Table 1). In addition to the four formality and civility items suggested by Winsted (1997), one item associated by Servqual with assurance—courteousness— loaded more strongly with formality than assurance in our analysis.

TABLE 1
Asian Servqual Factor Analysis

Item	Component				
	Formality α=.91	Responsive/ Assurance α=.93	Empathy α=.89	Reliability α=..86	Tangibles α=.80
Q55 At this bank, employees are never arrogant. (New)	**.822**	.266	.179	.127	.123
Q54 This bank insists that its employees wear appropriate clothing. (New)	**.807**	.120	.136	.141	.223
Q56 Employees at this bank have a good attitude. (New)	**.796**	.205	.250	.187	.006
Q53 This bank insists that its employees use proper language. (New)	**.769**	.218	.257	.181	.150
Q44 Employees at my bank are consistently courteous with you. (Note:an Assurance item in Servqual)	**.594**	.488	.120	.261	.224
Q42 The behavior of employees at my bank instills confidence in customers.	.259	**.702**	.315	.320	.190
Q41 Employees at my bank are never too busy to respond to your requests.	.259	**.689**	.222	.328	.137
Q40 Employees at my bank are always willing to help you.	.202	**.684**	.336	.369	.184
Q43 You feel safe in your transactions at my bank.	.276	**.682**	.172	.175	.332
Q39 Employees at my bank give you prompt service.	.355	**.559**	.170	.415	.176
Q51 Employees at this bank have a sense of humor. (New)	.190	.003	**.762**	.260	.115
Q48 My bank has employees who give you personal attention.	.168	.280	**.731**	.006	.272
Q52 Employees at this bank like to talk to me. (New)	.177	.125	**.702**	.316	.136
Q49 My bank has your best interests at heart.	.254	.371	**.684**	.181	.244
Q50 Employees at my bank understand your specific needs.	.188	.383	**.681**	.202	.271
Q33 When my bank promises to do something by a certain time, it does so.	.109	.122	.158	**.782**	.297
Q36 My bank provides its services at the time it promises to do so.	.178	.284	.201	**.725**	.178
Q34 When you have a problem, my bank shows a sincere interest in solving it.	.110	.414	.316	**.629**	.137
Q35 My bank performs the service right the first time.	.312	.398	.167	**.620**	.259
Q38 Employees at my bank tell you exactly when services will be performed.	.193	.269	.386	**.512**	.004
Q30 My bank's physical facilities are visually appealing.	.006	.157	.01	.142	**.880**
Q29 My bank has modern-looking equipment.	.004	.201	.140	.002	**.862**
Q32 Materials associated with the service (such as pamphlets or statements) are visually appealing at my bank.	.260	-.007	.185	.317	**.640**

Extraction Method: Principal Component Analysis.
Rotation Method: Equamax with Kaiser Normalization.

*Crossloading items removed from analysis: Q31: My bank's employees are neat-appearing. (Tangibles) Q37: My bank insists on error-free records. (Reliability) Q45: Employees at my bank have the knowledge to answer your questions. (Assurance) Q46: My bank gives you individual attention. (Empathy)

Interestingly, the two conversation items suggested by Winsted's research to constitute an additional factor nevertheless clearly load with the original empathy items from Servqual.

Correlations: Another check of Discriminant Validity

An additional test of discriminant validity is to perform correlations between formality and all other Servqual factors. The correlation matrix appears in Table 2. Formality is moderately to strongly related to other Servqual factors, with correlations between .40 and .69, suggesting that formality retains some uniqueness from the other factors. In fact, two pre-existing sets of factors of Servqual, responsiveness/assurance and reliability and respon-

siveness/ assurance and empathy, are more strongly correlated to each other than to formality. Interestingly, all correlations in the Asian data set are higher than those reported in the original Servqual analyses, in which inter-factor correlations are between .23 and .35 (Parasurman, Zeithaml and Berry 1988). Perhaps the correlations would be less with a larger sample size and a larger variety of service settings.

Is Formality Relevant and does it have Diagnostic Validity?

One way of evaluating the validity and relevance of formality as a service quality dimension is to assess consumer's expectations for formality, especially as compared to the other Servqual factors

TABLE 2
Correlations Between Servqual Factors

(all correlations significant at p<.01)

	Tangibles	Reliability	Responsive/ Assurance	Empathy	Formality	**Service Quality**
Tangibles	1.0	.48	.48	.50	.40	**.46**
Reliability		1.0	.77	.69	.59	**.59**
Responsive/ Assurance			1.0	.72	.69	**.67**
Empathy				1.0	.61	**.60**
Formality					1.0	**.59**

TABLE 3
Average Expectations and Outcomes for Servqual Factors

(Max=7, All factor items added and divided by number of items)

Thailand	**Expectations Bank**	**Outcomes Bank**	**GAP**	**%**	**Expectations Restaurant**	**Outcomes Restaurant**	**GAP**	**%**
Tangibles	5.15	4.79	.36	-5%	4.92	4.66	.26	-4%
Reliability	6.55	4.94	1.61	-23%	6.31	4.82	1.49	-21%
Responsive/ Assurance	6.44	5.03	1.41	-20%	6.31	5.04	1.27	-18%
Empathy	5.37	4.12	1.25	-18%	5.12	3.96	1.16	-17%
Formality	6.49	4.89	1.60	-23%	6.48	5.20	1.28	-18%
Japan	**Expectations Bank**	**Outcomes Bank**	**GAP**	**%**	**Expectations Restaurant**	**Outcomes Restaurant**	**GAP**	**%**
Tangibles	4.35	3.74	.61	-9%	4.53	4.36	.17	-2%
Reliability	5.91	4.30	1.61	-23%	5.53	4.12	1.41	-20
Responsive/ Assurance	5.77	4.36	1.41	-20%	5.92	4.45	1.47	-21%
Empathy	4.71	3.77	.94	-13%	4.77	3.55	1.22	-17%
Formality	5.77	5.12	.65	-9%	5.99	4.94	1.05	-15%

(Table 3). Of the five dimensions across all four settings, the Asian respondents had the highest or second highest expectations for formality, suggesting that the factor has high relevance. These expectations ratings change somewhat by service setting, with both the Thai and Japanese samples particularly emphasizing high expectations of formality in the restaurant service setting, with formality coming in second to reliability for both samples in the bank setting. Following the reasoning of Perreault (1992), Parasuraman, Zeithaml, and Berry (1994) suggest that diagnosticity or impact on interpretation (not just predictive power) is an important measure of the validity in including a dimension in Servqual. This research measured outcomes and expectations and can thus diagnose gaps between what consumers expect and what they actually receive. Interestingly, both Thai consumers experience relatively large differences between the formality they wish to receive compared to hat they actually receive. Smaller gaps existed for formality in both Japanese settings. These "gaps" suggest managerially actionable areas concerning formality; thus the formality dimension results in diagnosticity.

Nomological Validity of Formality: How well does Formality Predict Service Quality?

Cronin and Taylor (1992) suggest and Parasuraman, Zeithaml, and Berry (1994) concede that Servqual *outcome* measures do a better job predicting service quality than do measures based on

differences between outcomes and expectations, although the difference measures may have superior diagnosticity. Thus, to test nomological, predictive or "construct" validity (Carmines and Zeller 1979; Churchill 1979), regression analyses were performed with the factor scores for the five outcome dimensions as independent variables and overall service quality as the dependent variable. For Thai restaurant consumers, formality is the most strongly related to service quality of the five dimensions; in fact, the relationship (partial beta) between formality and service quality is quite strong (β=.56), while the next strongest relationship is with responsiveness at (β=.38). Interestingly, formality is much less important (although statistically significant) to Thais in the bank setting (β=.19). In the Japanese sample, formality, responsiveness and empathy are all strong predictors of service quality for both the restaurant and bank settings. As in the Thai sample, formality is more strongly related to service quality ratings for restaurants than for banks. These findings increase diagnosticity as well; for instance, formality is very important to Thai restaurant consumers, and yet, the gap between formality desired and received is 18%; together these findings suggest the importance of improving formality before concentrating on other elements of the restaurant experience.

An incremental F-test was conducted to assess whether or not the inclusion of formality in the set of predictors increases explanatory power significantly (Pedhazur 1982). The F-test is significant

TABLE 4
Explained Variance in Overall Service Quality

Thailand	Bank	Restaurant
Reliability	.32*	.30*
Empathy	.18**	.25*
Responsiveness	.45*	.38*
Tangibles	.34*	.26*
Formality	.19**	.56*
Total Variance Explained	**49%**	**65%**
Variance Explained w/o Formality	*46%*	*35%*
Incremental Variance Explained — F test	*3.94, p<.05*	*84.00, p<.01*
Japan		
Reliability	.30*	.09
Empathy	.44*	.33*
Responsiveness	.42*	.37*
Tangibles	.11	.15***
Formality	.29*	.41*
Total Variance Explained	**61%**	**42%**
Variance Explained w/o Formality	*53%*	*27%*
Incremental Variance Explained — F Test	*20.10, p<.01*	*25.34, p<.01*

* p<.001, **p<.05, ***p<.10

for all four settings (Table 4), indicating that formality should be included with the other Servqual factors. The variance in service quality explained when formality is included increases mildly — 3% and 8% — for the bank settings, but is quite dramatic — 15% and 30% respectively — for the Thai and Japanese restaurant samples.

In sum, the factor analyses and correlations between factors suggest that formality is a discriminable factor with high convergent validity for our Asian samples. As well, the analyses of expectations show that Asian consumers have high expectations for formality, again suggesting the factor's validity for diagnosis of service quality in Asian settings. Last, formality has strong predictive validity, as it is strongly associated with service quality in Thai and Japanese restaurant settings, and moderately but significantly related to service quality in bank settings in both countries. Perhaps most importantly, the incremental variance in service quality ratings increased significantly in all four settings, and dramatically in restaurant settings.

IMPLICATIONS AND RESEARCH LIMITATIONS

Because this study employed a non-probability sampling method, the findings should be further validated by other studies. Although sampling issues are less important for scale development and theoretical research (Calder, Phillips and Tybout 1981; Cook and Campbell 1979), which is the focus in this paper, descriptive and diagnostic findings associated with service quality require greater generalizability than is achieved with the present sample.

Moreover, the research does not assess the effect of survey biases that may be introduced by a tendency to react to surveys in a culturally systematic fashion. Particularly when assessments of customer satisfaction use subjective reports, the findings may reflect substantive differences in perceived service quality across countries, but possibly culturally determined response biases as well. Asians in general, and Thais in particular, have been know to exhibit a "courtesy bias" on survey questionnaires because of their desire to please the interviewer (Onkvisit and Shaw 1993, p. 286). Nevertheless, predictive modeling, comparisons between

Servqual factors, and differences between outcomes and expectations within a culture should be unaffected by any biases.

While services research conducted in the U.S. has established a relationship between service quality, behavioral intentions, and overall profitability (Zeithaml, Berry and Parasuranam 1996; Reichheld and Sasser 1990), the present study does not establish such a link. Despite this shortcoming, the findings suggest the importance of including the formality dimension in international service studies, and the continued importance of considering other dimensions that might be relevant to non-American cultures. Above all, there is a need for new research concepts to identify and measure variations in cross-national service quality. There are likely to be additional dimensions of importance in international contexts that researchers have not yet systematically conceptualized, identified, and measured. As these concepts are uncovered and investigated, they are likely to not only shed light upon different service cultures, but may also increase understanding and conceptualization of service quality within domestic settings as well. For instance, while formality may be unimportant to some Americans in some contexts, there may be service settings and provider age and status characteristics in which formality is quite relevant to consumers. Thus, more work is necessary not only in conceptualizing service quality in different cultures, but in developing theories which explain and aid in understanding differences across services settings and between participants *within* a culture.

REFERENCES

Ashforth, Blake E. and Ronald H. Humphrey (1993), "Emotional Labor in Service Roles: The Influence of Identity," *Academy of Management Review*, 18 (January), 88-115.

Barnlund, Dean C. (1989), "Public and Private Self in Communicating with Japan," *Business Horizons*, 32 (March-April), 32-40.

Calder, Bobby J., Lynn W. Phillips and Alice M. Tybout (1981), "Designing Research for Applications," *Journal of Consumer Research*, 8 (September), 197-207.

Carmines, Edward G. and Richard A. Zeller (1979), "Reliability and Validity Assessment," Sage Publication Series Number 07-017. Newbury Park, CA: Sage Publications, Inc.

Churchill, Gilbert A., Jr. (1979), "A Paradigm for Developing Better Measures of Marketing Constructs," *Journal of Marketing Research*, 16 (February), 64-73.

Cook, Thomas D., and Donald T. Campbell (1979), *Quasi-Experimentation: Design and Analysis Issues for Field Settings*, Chicago: Rand McNally College Publishing Company.

Cronin, J. Joseph and Steven A. Taylor (1992), "Measuring Service Quality: A Reexamination and Extension," *Journal of Marketing*, 56 (July), 55-68.

Emmons, Steve (1997), "Emotions at Face Value," *Los Angeles Times* (December 5), E1, E8.

Ferraro, Gary P. (1998), *The Cultural Dimension of International Business*, Third Edition, Upper Saddle River, NJ: Prentice Hall.

Gesteland, Richard R. (1999), *Cross-Cultural Business Behavior: Marketing, Negotiating and Managing Across Cultures*, Copenhagen: Copenhagen Business School Press.

Gilly, Mary C. and John L. Graham (1996), "International Services Marketing," in *Services Marketing*, Valerie A. Zeithaml and Mary Jo Bitner, authors, New York: McGraw-Hill, pp. 414-445.

Global Road Warrior (1999a), "Japan - Business Culture," World Trade Press (*www.wellsfargo.com/inatl/grw/japan/busculture/*), accessed February 25, 2000.

Global Road Warrior (1999b), "Thailand - Business Culture," World Trade Press (*www.wellsfargo.com/inatl/grw/thailand/busculture/*), accessed February 25, 2000.

Goffman, Erving (1959), *The Presentation of Self in Everyday Life*, Garden City, NY: Doubleday Anchor Books.

Goodwin, Cathy and Charles D. Frame (1989), "Social Distance Within the Service Encounter: Does the Consumer Want to be your Friend?," in *Advances in Consumer Research*, 16, Thomas K. Srull, ed., Provo, UT: Brigham Young University, pp. 64-71.

_____ and Kelly L. Smith (1990), "Courtesy and Friendliness: Conflicting Goals for the Service Provider?," *Journal of Services Marketing*, 4 (Winter), 5-20.

Graham, John L. and Yoshihiro Sano (1989), *Smart Bargaining: Doing Business with the Japanese*, New York: Harper & Row.

Hall, Edward T. and Mildred Reed Hall (1987), *Hidden Differences: Doing Business With the Japanese*, Garden City, NY: Anchor Press/Doubleday.

_____ and _____ (1990), *Understanding Cultural Differences*, Yarmouth, ME: Intercultural Press, Inc.

Hendon, Donald W. (1999), "How to Negotiate with Thai Executives," in *Proceedings of the Seventh Cross-Cultural Research Conference*, Scott M. Smith, ed., Provo, UT: Brigham Young University (CD-ROM, no page numbers).

Hofstede, Geert R. (1997), *Cultures and Organizations: Software of the Mind*, New York: McGraw-Hill.

Hoh, Erling (1998), "Memory and Desire," *Far Eastern Economic Review*, 161 (November 19), 46-48.

Holroyd, Carin and Ken Coates (1999), *Culture Shock! Success Secrets to Maximize Business in Japan*, Portland, OR: Graphic Arts Center Publishing Company.

International Herald Tribune (1992), "Japanese Put Tourism on a Higher Plane," (February 3), 8.

Kaiser, Susan B. (1997), *The Social Psychology of Clothing: Symbolic Appearances in Context*, Second Edition Revised, New York: Fairchild Publications.

Kassem, M. Sami (1989), "Services Marketing: The Arabian Gulf Experience," *The Journal of Services Marketing*, 3 (Summer), 61-71.

Lord, Richard (1996), *Culture Shock! Germany: A Guide to Customs and Etiquette*, Portland, OR: Graphic Arts Center Publishing Company.

Malhotra, Naresh K., Francis M. Ulgado, James Agarwal, and Imad B. Baalbaki (1994), "International Services Marketing: A Comparative Evaluation of the Dimensions of Service Quality Between Developed and Developing Countries," *International Marketing Review*, 11 (2), 5-15.

Murphy, Dean E. (1994), "New East Europe Retailers Told to Put on a Happy Face," *Los Angeles Times* (November 26), A1, A18.

Niratpattanasai, Kriengsak (2000), "Promises, promises and *Kreng Jai . . . ,*" *Thailand Tales: Doing Business in Thailand*, Asian Pacific Management Forum (*www.apmforum.com/columns/thai27.htm*), accessed February 25, 2000.

Onkvisit, Sak and John J. Shaw (1993), *International Marketing: Analysis and Strategy*, Second Edition, New York: Macmillan Publishing Company.

Parasuraman, A., Valarie A. Zeithaml and Leonard L. Berry (1985), "A Conceptual Model of Service Quality and Its Implications for Future Research," *Journal of Marketing*, 49 (October), 41-50.

_____, _____, and _____ (1988), "SERVQUAL: A Multiple-item Scale for Measuring Customer Perceptions of Service Quality," *Journal of Retailing*, 64 (Spring), 12-40.

_____, _____, and _____ (1994), "Reassessment of Expectations as a Comparison Standard in Measuring Service Quality: Implications for Further Research," *Journal of Marketing*, 58 (January), 111-124.

Pedhazur, Elazar J. (1982), *Multiple Regression in Behavioral Research: Explanation and Prediction*, New York: CBS College Publishing.

Porter, Michael E. (1990), *The Competitive Advantage of Nations*, New York: The Free Press

Population Reference Bureau (1999), "1999 World Population Data Sheet," (www.prb.org/pubs/wpds99.htm), accessed March 9, 2000.

Riddle, Dorothy I. (1986), *Service-Led Growth: The Role of the Service Sector in World Development*, New York: Praeger Publishers.

Ratanakomut, Somchai (1995), "Industrializing the Service Sector, with Special Emphasis on Tourism," in *Thailand's Industrialization and Its Consequences*, Medhi Krongkaew, ed., New York: St. Martin's Press, pp. 85-98.

Reichheld, Frederick and W. Earl Sasser, Jr. (1990), "Zero Defections: Quality Comes to Services," *Harvard Business Review*, 68 (September/October), 105-111.

Schlossberg, Howard (1990), "U.S. Firms Must Contend with Japanese-style Service," *Marketing News*, 24 (May 28), 1-2.

Suprenant, Carol F. and Michael R. Solomon (1987), "Predictability and Personalization in the Service Encounter," *Journal of Marketing*, 51 (April), 86-96.

Stern, Susan (1994), *These Strange German Ways: The New Book*, Bonn, Germany: Atlantik-Bruecke e.V.

Watson, John L. ed. (1997), *Golden Arches East: McDonald's in East Asia*, Stanford University Press, Stanford, CA.

Williams, Carol J. (1999), "Not All Ways Wal-Mart as Chain Takes on Germany," *Los Angeles Times*, (August 15), C1, C4.

Winsted, Kathryn Frazer (1997), "The Service Experience in Two Cultures: A Behavioral Perspective," *Journal of Retailing*, 73 (3), 337-360.

Witkowski, Terrence H. and Yoshito Yamamoto, (1991), "*Omiyage* Gift Purchasing by Japanese Travelers in the U.S.," in *Advances in Consumer Research*, v. 18, Rebecca H. Holman and Michael R. Solomon, eds., Provo, UT: Association for Consumer Research, pp. 123-128.

Zeithaml, Valarie A., Leonard L. Berry, and A. Parasuraman (1996), "The Behavioral Consequences of Service Quality," *Journal of Marketing*, 60 (April), 31-46.

Price Perceptions: A Cross-National Study between American and Chinese Young Consumers

Zheng Zhou, Virginia Polytechnic Institute and State University
Kent Nakamoto, Virginia Polytechnic Institute and State University

ABSTRACT

This paper examines the influence of cultural factors (i.e., face consideration and risk aversion) and marketing environments upon price perceptions and compares price perceptions between American and Chinese young consumers empirically. The cross-national measurement validity is assessed to make the comparison meaningful. The findings show that, contrast to the common notions about Chinese traditionalism, Chinese young consumers perceive a weaker price-quality relationship than American young, and they are more prestige sensitive, less price conscious, and less coupon prone than their US counterparts, but they are as value conscious as American young consumers.

INTRODUCTION

With its substantial population and fast growing economy, China has become one of the most fascinating markets to Western companies. However, due to its high-context culture, difficult language and different political system, China is also confusing and frustrating to foreigners (Tse, Belk, and Zhou 1989). As Ram (1994) notes, surprisingly, Chinese consumers' demands for luxury products extend beyond watches and cognac to include a wide range of high price tag consumer items even before they have secured adequate food, clothing, and shelter.

Unfortunately, academic research on Chinese market and consumers is still limited. Another critical issue of cross-national research is the lack of validity assessment in applying measurement models developed in one country to other countries and cultures (c.f., Steenkamp and Baumgartner 1998). The current study intends to shed some light on these issues by comparing price perceptions between American and Chinese young consumers (aged from 16 to 35). Price perceptions, which emphasize on consumers' negative perceptions of price (e.g., economic sacrifice) as well as the positive perceptions of price such as perceived quality and prestige (Zeithaml 1988), are found to have a strong predictive validity of consumers' marketplace responses and behaviors (Lichtenstein, Ridgway and Netemeyer 1993). The reasons why the young are especially studied are (1) young consumers are recognized as a specialized global market segment for a variety of goods and services (Moschis and Moore 1979). (2) In China, compared with the older, the younger have more appetites for and consuming experience with Western products, and are more likely to be the potential consumers for Western companies (Anderson and He 1998). To make the comparison valid, the cross-national applicability of price perception measures is assessed through the model comparison procedures proposed by Steenkamp and Baumgartner (1998).

PRICE PERCEPTIONS

Price, one of the most important marketplace cues, is the pivotal factor in consumption values due to its prevalence in every purchasing situation (Monroe 1979). Price is perceived as a multidimensional stimulus to consumers in that it affects consumers' purchasing intentions both positively and negatively (Dodds, Monroe and Grewal 1991). On one hand, a higher price increases the perceived economic sacrifice and thus decreases the consumer's willingness to buy. On the other hand, a higher price may lead to a higher perceived quality or prestige and consequently increase

one's intention to buy (Zeithaml 1988).

In order to investigate the "positive role" and "negative role" of price, Lichtenstein, Ridgway and Netemeyer (1993) put forward seven constructs to conceptualize price perceptions. Two of them, price-quality schema and prestige sensitivity, are believed to impact consumers' willingness to buy positively. The other five, value consciousness, price consciousness, coupon proneness, sale proneness, and price mavenism,[1] are viewed to play a negative role in affecting consumers' purchase intentions.

Price-quality schema refers to the generalized belief that the price cue is related positively to the quality level of the product. Prestige sensitivity means the favorable perceptions of the price cue based on purchaser's feelings of prominence and status brought by higher prices. Value consciousness emphasizes the consumers' concern about the ratio of quality received to price paid in a transaction. In other words, value conscious consumers are trying to maximize the product quality from the money they spend. Price consciousness focuses on the degree to which the consumer focuses exclusively on paying low prices. Coupon/sale proneness refer to consumers' propensity to respond to a purchase offer because the coupon/sale promotion positively affects their purchase evaluations (for a detailed discussion, see Lichtenstein, Ridgway and Netemeyer 1993).

FACTORS SHAPING PRICE PERCEPTIONS

Level of economic development is undoubtedly a very important factor that influences price perceptions (Tse, Belk, and Zhou 1989). Rostow (1952) suggests that in a less developed economy, consumers pay more attention to the basic necessities such as food and shelter. As the economy develops, consumers will express higher and social needs such as prestige and self-actualization (Maslow 1954). According to this logic, it is natural to predict consumers in a less developed economy (China) are more likely to have negative price perceptions, and consumers in a more developed economy (the US) tend to perceive price positively.

However, the Maslow's hierarchical needs, as a theory developed in Western society, may not apply in Chinese cultures (Tse, Belk, and Zhou 1989). As described by Belk (1988), Chinese consumers are acquiring the higher needs of consumption values such as social status and prestige in a different way and much more rapidly than Western consumers. In an international context, cultures and marketing environments are the important factors in shaping price perceptions (Belk 1988; Hofstete 1980; Triandis 1995).

Individualistic and Collectivistic Culture

American culture is characterized as highly individualistic, while Chinese culture is a typical collectivistic one (Triandis 1995). The basic difference between individualistic and collectivistic cultures is that, an individualistic culture emphasizes "I-identity" and personal self-esteem enhancement, but a collectivistic

---

[1] Price mavenism is not a theoretical predictor of the market place responses/behaviors (Lichtenstein, Ridgway and Netemeyer 1993), and it may be interpreted differently in the US and China, so we don't study this construct here.

one pays more attention to "We-identity" and social group-esteem maintenance (Hofstede and Bond 1984). More specifically, Chinese consumers differ from American consumers in their face consideration (Ho 1976; Ting-Toomey and Kurogi 1998) and risk aversion (Hosfstede and Bond 1984; Gao 1998).

Face is defined as a claimed sense of favorable social self-worth that a person wants others to have of him or her in a relational and network context (Ting-Toomey and Kurogi 1998). Face consideration, accordingly, refers to one's desire to enhance, maintain, and avoid losing face in social activities. In China, one's needs for self-face, as well as concerns for others-face, influence people's everyday life (Gao 1998; Ho 1976). Because of face consideration, consumption in China has a strong social trend and serves every aspect from physiological need to self-actualization need. The social needs, consequently, make Chinese consumers pay more attention to the "extrinsic" rather than "intrinsic" attributes of a product due to their desires to express their images, positions, or feelings toward group members (Belk 1988).

On the contrary, in an individualistic culture like the US, an individual is an independent entity with free will, emotions and personalities (Markus & Kitayama 1991). Decisions are encouraged to be made individually (Reykowski 1994). Therefore, the consumption of American young is more likely to reflect their own wills.

Risk aversion is defined as "the extent to which people feel threatened by ambiguous situations, and have created beliefs and institutions that try to avoid these." (Hofstede and Bond 1984, p. 419). Partly because of face effects, i.e., people are afraid of losing face in public, and also because of other factors such as the influence of the long history of an agriculture-dominated economy, Chinese people are highly risk averse (Gao 1998). On the other side, American people are encouraged to be adventurous (Triandis 1995). As argued by Shimp and Bearden (1982), risk aversion strongly affects consumers' decision makings. Therefore, the different attitudes towards risk could result in various price perceptions of Chinese and American consumers.

Market Environments

Compared with the US, the marketing environments in China are deficient in terms of market regulation and market competition (Fan and Xiao 1998; Nee 1992). In the US, extensive regulations and ready access to litigation prevent fake products from entering the market. American companies also tend to use various sale and promotion campaigns in order to attract consumers (Mela, Gupta, and Lehmann 1997). The intense competition makes abundant and comparable goods available to every consumer. As a result, American consumers become used to comparing various brands and stores when they purchase a product (Lal and Rao 1997).

In the transition process from a planned central economy to a market economy, the Chinese market is characterized by lack of coherent business regulation and legislation (Nee 1992). Deceptive advertising (exaggerated and fraudulent advertising), trademark violation (counterfeit goods with poor quality but always under the names of popular brands), and unethical business practices (e.g., selling poor-quality products at very high prices) are prevalent and arouse a particular concern in China (Fan and Xiao 1998; Ho and Sin 1988). Therefore, Chinese consumers have to be very cautious about the information in the ad and have to distinguish fake products by themselves (Ho and Sin 1988). In addition, competition in China is relatively low. Consequently, Chinese consumers are more concerned with the availability and/or the quality instead of the price of a product (Fan and Xiao 1998).

As a summary, these two societies differ widely with respects to cultural and market environments. American young consumers are more self-concerned and adventurous in a more refined market, and Chinese young are more face-concerned and risk-averse in a developing market. These differences form the base for why and how American and Chinese consumers differ in their price perceptions.

HYPOTHESES

Price-quality Schema

As we discussed before, the market in China is far from the refined market in the US. Less intensive competition and incomplete regulation lead to a less fair pricing system in China. Some name brand products are overpriced, yet some general products are under-priced due to the poor marketing administration (Fan and Xiao 1998). In addition, weak regulation allows large numbers of fake products to enter the market. Fake products charge consumers much more than their own values, and sometimes are unsafe and even fatal to use (e.g., food and electronic products) (Ho and Sin 1988). But in the US, the intense market competition and strong regulation make price a relatively good indicator of product quality. Therefore, we predict Chinese young consumers are more likely to doubt the credibility of price in indicating product quality than American young.

H1: Chinese young consumers perceive a weaker price-quality relationship than American young consumers.

Prestige Sensitivity

A traditional Chinese virtue is saving money, while American consumers are used to consuming in advance. Further, the income level of China is much lower than that of the US. Thus, it sounds reasonable to expect that American consumers might be more prestige sensitive than Chinese consumers. However, face consideration makes Chinese young consumers pay much attention to the social functions of a product. The purchase or use of a prestigious product becomes a symbol for people to show their face (Belk 1988). In the US, though the consumption behaviors of American youth are also influenced by others, the extent of the influence is not as strong as that in such a face-considerate culture like China (Tse 1996). Moreover, in China, group interest is the priority over individual interest. It leads to face loss if one does not conform within a group or distinguish from other groups (Gao 1998). While in the US, individual interest ranks first. One will lose nothing and can maintain his/her prestige without conformity (Ting-Toomey and Kurogi 1998). Since losing something is much more painful than not gaining something (Heath, Chatterjee, and France 1995), Chinese consumers sometimes have to be prestige sensitive. For these arguments, we hypothesize,

H2: Chinese young consumers are more prestige sensitive than American young consumers.

Value Consciousness and Price Consciousness

In a less refined market, Chinese young are more concerned about quality rather than price. In order to get the authentic or high-quality product, they are willing to pay a higher price. On the contrary, the intense competition and strict regulation make American young accustomed to comparing various brands and stores even for a specific product, and consequently, becoming more and more price sensitive (Lal and Rao 1997; Mela, Gupta, and Lehmann 1997). Therefore,

H3: Chinese young consumers are less price conscious than American young consumers.

Highly risk-averse consumers tend to pay more for a product as a means of reducing the risk of purchasing one of inferior quality (Rao and Bergen 1992). This might imply that Chinese consumers may be less value conscious than American young. On the other hand, in such an immature market, Chinese youth must carefully judge the benefits in relation to price in purchase decision makings because they are highly risk-averse. As such, we may imply that Chinese young are more value conscious than their American counterparts. In balance, we predict,

H4: Chinese young consumers are as value conscious as American young consumers.

Sale Proneness and Coupon Proneness

In America, sale and coupon promotions are two of the most widely used marketing strategies (Lal and Rao 1997). According to acquisition-transaction utility theory (Thaler 1985), purchase with a coupon or a price discount represents a "good deal" by increasing consumers' transaction utility through decreasing the purchasing price (Zeithaml 1988). Therefore, it is natural for American young to purchase a product on sale or with a coupon. However, the situation in China is quite different. First, the poor regulation of the market and deceptive advertising make consumers doubt the credibility of a sale or coupon. In addition, in a high-context culture, people think more for what is not being said than what is being said, such as "is there anything wrong with the product" (Anderson and He 1998, p. 154). For example, an ad like "$19.95, was $29.95", which is normal in America, will be easily interpreted as "was $16.95, now labeled $19.95" by Chinese consumers. Thus, Chinese consumers tend to perceive sale or coupon promotions as efforts to get rid of inventory that is below average in quality. Being highly risk-averse, Chinese consumers are not likely to be sale-prone or coupon-prone. These arguments suggest,

H5: Chinese young consumers are less coupon-prone than American young consumers.

H6: Chinese young consumers are less sale-prone than American young consumers.

METHODOLOGY

Sampling

A survey study was constructed to collect data regarding young consumer's price perceptions in both the US and China. No attempt was made to select the sample on a purely random basis. Rather, convenient college student samples were used in both the US and China because college student was a typical representative of the target population (young consumers). To insure time comparability, both data sets were collected during the Fall semester of 1999. Altogether 226 usable questionnaires were obtained, in which 120 collected from a university in Beijing, China and 106 from a large southern state university in the US. The demographic characteristics of the sample were similar in these two data sets. For example, all the American subjects were undergraduate students, 72.9% were Junior, and they aged from 19 to 27 with a mean as 21.1. All the Chinese subjects were also undergraduate students, 48.7% were Junior, and they were between 18 and 25 years old with a mean age as 20.4.

The questionnaire was translated into Chinese by a doctoral student from China who was studying business administration at a Western university. The translated questionnaire was then back translated into English by another Chinese student. The translation

was modified several times in order to make it accurate and consistent.

Measures

Price perceptions were measured with thirty-six seven-point Likert scale items ranging from 1 "strongly agree" and 7 "strongly disagree" (adapted from Lichtenstein, Ridgway, and Netemeyer 1993). An exploratory factor analysis and a reliability analysis were conducted to refine the measures. After dropping ten items possessing either low item-total correlations or high cross loadings, we got a six-factor measure with twenty-six items which were consistent in both data sets (see Appendix).

Assessing Measurement Invariance. Measurement invariance refers to whether or not the measurement operations yield measures of the same attribute under different cultures or countries. If a measure is not cross-nationally invariant, conclusions based on that scale are "at best ambiguous and at worst erroneous" (Steenkamp and Baumgartner 1998, p. 78). For example, if we compare directly price perceptions between American and Chinese young without assessing the measurement invariance and find some difference, we won't tell whether the difference comes from consumers' price perceptions or just due to their semantic interpretations of the questionnaire. In order to compare means across counties, metric and scalar invariance for at least two items per construct is required. Following the procedures proposed by Steenkamp and Baumgartner (1998), we tested the price perception measurement invariance via Amos 4 with maximum likelihood as the estimation method (Arbuckle and Wothke 1999).

Price-Quality Schema. The first step was to test of the equality of covariances and means of the four indicators of this measure. The test results were: χ^2 (14) = 69.53, p < .001; comparative fit index (CFI) = .98, Tucker-Lewis Index (TLI) = 0.96; root mean square error of approximation (RMSEA) = .133, Akaike information criterion (AIC) = 97.53. The significance of chi-square and the relatively large RMSEA and AIC indicated the lack of invariance of covariance matrices and mean vectors across the US and China.

Thus we turned to test the configural invariance, which means indicators should load on the factor in a similar pattern across countries. This model was the baseline model against which further models could be compared. The results (χ^2 (4) = 9.63, p = 0.047; CFI = 0.97, TLI = 0.91; RMSEA = 0.079, AIC = 41.63) indicated a good fit of the model. All factor loadings were highly significant in both countries (p < 0.01), and standardized factor loadings ranged between .50 and .82. Therefore, it could be concluded that the price-quality schema was configurally invariant across the US and China samples.

Next, we tested the metric invariance which means the matrix of factor loadings was invariant across countries. Results (χ^2 (7) = 12.55, p = 0.084; CFI = 0.97, TLI = 0.95; RMSEA = 0.059, AIC = 38.55) showed that the increase in chi-square was not significant ($\Delta\chi^2$ (3) = 2.92, p = .40) and CFI, TLI , RMSEA, and AIC actually improved. Thus, the price-quality schema was also fully metric invariant across the US and China samples.

Finally, the scalar invariance was tested. The intercepts of the four indicators were set to be invariant across countries. Such a model resulted in an acceptable fit (χ^2 (11) = 22.01, p = 0.024; CFI = 1.00, TLI = 0.99; RMSEA = 0.067, AIC = 56.01). The increase of chi-square over the full configural invariance model was not significant ($\Delta\chi^2$ (7) = 12.38, p = .089); CFI, TLI, RMSEA, and AIC also exhibited a good fit. Thus full scalar invariance was supported.

The previous procedure was run for each of the six price perception constructs. Note that if the full metric or scalar invariance model was not adequate, then constraints on certain indicators

TABLE 1
Assessment of Measurement Invariance

Model	χ^2	df	p-value	CFI	TLI	RMSEA	AIC	Relaxed Constraint [a]
Price-Quality Schema								
Equality of Covariances and Means	69.529	14	.000	.978	.969	.133	97.529	—
Configural Invariance	9.626	4	.047	.969	.908	.079	41.626	—
Full Metric Invariance	12.547	7	.084	.970	.948	.059	38.547	—
Final Partial Metric Invariance	—	—	—	—	—	—	—	—
Initial Partial Scalar Invariance	22.006	11	.024	.996	.992	.067	56.006	—
Final Partial Scalar Invariance	—	—	—	—	—	—	—	—
Prestige Sensitivity								
Equality of Covariances and Means	62.796	19	.000	.985	.977	.101	104.796	—
Configural Invariance	17.531	10	.063	.984	.967	.058	57.531	—
Full Metric Invariance	20.211	14	.124	.986	.981	.045	52.211	—
Final Partial Metric Invariance	—	—	—	—	—	—	—	—
Initial Partial Scalar Invariance	63.640	19	.000	.985	.976	.102	105.640	—
Final Partial Scalar Invariance	28.072	17	.044	.996	.993	.054	74.072	PS2, PS9
Value Consciousness								
Equality of Covariances and Means	18.694	10	.044	.997	.992	.062	78.694	—
Configural Invariance	—	—	—	—	—	—	—	—
Full Metric Invariance	—	—	—	—	—	—	—	—
Final Partial Metric Invariance	—	—	—	—	—	—	—	—
Initial Partial Scalar Invariance	—	—	—	—	—	—	—	—
Final Partial Scalar Invariance	—	—	—	—	—	—	—	—
Price Consciousness								
Equality of Covariances and Means	131.069	14	.000	.947	.925	.193	159.069	—
Configural Invariance	0.557	4	.968	1.000	1.000	.000	32.557	—
Full Metric Invariance	5.650	7	.981	1.000	1.000	.000	31.650	—
Final Partial Metric Invariance	—	—	—	—	—	—	—	—
Initial Partial Scalar Invariance	109.712	11	.000	.956	.919	.200	143.712	—
Final Partial Scalar Invariance	32.493	9	.000	.989	.977	.108	70.493	PC1, PC3
Coupon Proneness								
Equality of Covariances and Means	80.449	14	.000	.967	.952	.146	108.449	—
Configural Invariance	6.670	4	.154	.992	.977	.055	38.670	—
Full Metric Invariance	9.500	7	.219	.993	.988	.040	35.500	—
Final Partial Metric Invariance	—	—	—	—	—	—	—	—
Initial Partial Scalar Invariance	67.951	11	.000	.971	.948	.152	101.951	—
Final Partial Scalar Invariance	13.313	9	.149	.998	.995	.081	51.313	CP4, CP5
Sale Proneness								
Equality of Covariances and Means	84.572	14	.000	.970	.957	.150	112.572	—
Configural Invariance	9.986	4	.041	.975	.920	.082	41.986	—
Full Metric Invariance	18.453	7	.010	.953	.920	.085	44.453	—
Final Partial Metric Invariance	—	—	—	—	—	—	—	—
Initial Partial Scalar Invariance	74.621	11	.000	.973	.950	.161	108.621	—
Final Partial Scalar Invariance	45.097	9	.000	.984	.985	.134	83.097	SP3, SP4

[a] See Appendix for details on the scale items.

(as revealed by Modification Index [MI]) were relaxed to get an acceptable partial invariance model. Details of construct invariance assessment were listed in Table 1.

The results of Table 1 showed that the measure of prestige sensitivity was configural invariant, full metric invariant, and partial scalar invariant (the scalar invariance constraints on indicator PS2 and PS9 were relaxed). Table 1 also showed the support to the covariance and means equality model of the measure of value consciousness. Thus, the measure model satisfied full metric and scalar invariance automatically (Steenkamp and Baumgartner 1998). Measures of price consciousness, coupon proneness, and sale proneness were also found to be configural invariant and full metric invariant. But we only got acceptable partial scalar invariance models for price consciousness and coupon proneness measures.

TABLE 2

Correlations, Means, Standard Deviations, and Reliabilities

	US				
	1	2	3	4	5
1. Price-Quality Schema	1.000				
2. Prestige Sensitivity	.481*	1.000			
3. Value Consciousness	.153	-.121	1.000		
4. Price Consciousness	-.044	-.287*	.582*	1.000	
5. Coupon Proneness	-.172	-.036	.351*	.282*	1.000
Mean*	5.024	4.228	5.185	4.915	3.868
Standard Deviation	1.005	1.273	1.104	1.122	1.212
Coefficient reliability	.819	.886	.789	.786	.883

	China				
	1	2	3	4	5
1. Price-Quality Schema	1.000				
2. Prestige Sensitivity	.416*	1.000			
3. Value Consciousness	.322*	.169	1.000		
4. Price Consciousness	-.084	-.203*	.406*	1.000	
5. Coupon Proneness	.105	.216*	.090	-.060	1.000
Mean*	4.677	4.767	5.053	3.908	3.521
Standard Deviation	.927	1.143	1.002	1.098	1.145
Coefficient reliability	.573	.802	.706	.681	.775

* Significant at the 0.05 level (2-tailed)
** Averaged and reverse coded

The best partial scalar invariance model for sale proneness obtained after relaxing the constraints on the intercept invariance of SP3 and SP4 didn't show adequate fit; therefore, the measure of sale proneness is not cross-nationally invariant.

In summary, five measures of price perceptions (except sale proneness) were full metric invariant and either full or partial scalar invariant; therefore, these five measures were cross-nationally invariant and their means could be compared meaningfully (Steenkamp and Baumgartner 1998).[2] To make the comparison more intuitive, construct means are averaged and reverse coded. Table 2 reports the means, standard deviations, correlations, and coefficient reliabilities of these five measures (price-quality schema, prestige sensitivity, value consciousness, price consciousness, and coupon proneness).

RESULTS

We tested the hypotheses with structural equation method, which was considered advantageous to the traditional ANOVA/MANOVA approach by incorporating errors in construct measurement (Durvasula et. al. 1993). Following Steenkamp and Baumgartner (1998), we constructed a model (M1) that fixed the factor means as zero in the US data set and constrained one intercept per factor to be invariant across the two data sets. The factor means in Chinese sample were then estimated relative to the means in the US sample. If model M1 fit the data well, the p-value of relative factor means in Chinese sample would show whether the mean difference was significant or not. If M1 didn't fit the data adequately, then a further restriction which constrained the construct means in Chinese sample to be zero was imposed on the model (M2). A significant chi-square change (M2-M1) indicated the non-equality of the means. The results of hypotheses testing were reported in Table 3.

H1 argues that Chinese young consumers perceive a weaker price-quality relationship than American young. The results in Table 3 show that M1 fits data satisfactorily (χ^2 (4) = 9.63, p =.047; CFI = 1.00, TLI = .99; RMSEA = .008). The mean value of Chinese sample (4.68) is significantly less than that of American sample (5.02, p < .01). Further, a comparison between M1 and M2 ($\Delta\chi^2$(1) = 8.70, p < .01) also indicates the non-equality of the price-quality schema between American and Chinese young consumers. Therefore, these findings lend support to H1.

H2 deals with the comparison of prestige sensitivity. Table 3 shows M1 fits data acceptably (χ^2 (10) = 17.53, p = .063; CFI = 1.00, TLI = .99; RMSEA = .058) and Chinese young consumers are more prestige sensitive (μ = 4.77) than American young (μ = 4.23, p < .001). In addition, a comparison between M1 and M2 ($\Delta\chi^2$(1) = 18.925, p < .001) also indicates that American and Chinese young differ in their prestige sensitivity. Thus, H2 is supported.

H3 to H6 deal with the negative role of price. Consistent with our predictions in H3 and H5, the results show that Chinese young are less price conscious (μ = 3.91) than American young (μ = 4.92, p < .001), and Chinese young are not as coupon-prone (μ = 3.52) as American young (μ = 3.89, p < .05). From the results of M1 and model comparison (M2 – M1), we also get supports for H4, i.e., Chinese young are as value conscious (μ = 5.05) as American's (μ = 5.19, p > .10). As indicated earlier, sale proneness measure is not cross-nationally invariant. We cannot test H6 since we do not know whether the mean difference of sale proneness comes from consumers' price perception or semantic interpretation. So H6 is left undetermined.

---

[2]An optimal approach would be assessing the measurement invariance for the full measurement model. But in this study, given the number of items, it is unrealistic to test the full model with the relatively small sample size.

TABLE 3
Results of Hypotheses Testing

	Mean			Model Fit	(M2-M1)
	US	China	Difference	(M1)	$\Delta\chi^2(1)$
Price-Quality Schema	5.024	4.677	0.347**	$\chi^2(4) = 9.63$, $p = 0.047$; CFI = 1.00, TLI = 0.99; RMSEA = 0.008	8.703 [b]
Prestige Sensitivity	4.228	4.767	-0.540***	$\chi^2(10) = 17.53$, $p = 0.063$; CFI = 1.00, TLI = 0.99; RMSEA = 0.058	18.925 [a]
Value Consciousness	5.185	5.053	0.132	$\chi^2(10) = 8.70$, $p = 0.561$; CFI = 1.00, TLI = 1.00; RMSEA = 0.000	0.399
Price Consciousness	4.915	3.908	1.007***	$\chi^2(4) = .56$, $p = 0.968$; CFI = 1.00, TLI = 1.00; RMSEA = 0.000	21.612 [a]
Coupon Proneness	3.868	3.521	0.347*	$\chi^2(4) = 6.67$, $p = 0.154$; CFI = 1.00, TLI = .99; RMSEA = 0.055	3.667 [c]
Sale Proneness	4.618	3.925	—	—	—

***- $p < .001$ (1-tailed)   **- $p < .01$ (1-tailed)   *- $p < .05$ (1-tailed)
[a] - $p < .001$ [b] - $p < .01$ [c] - $p < .10$

DISCUSSIONS

Our findings show that, Chinese young consumers behave quite differently from the common notions about Chinese traditionalism and their price perceptions may seem strange to foreigners. Constrained by immature market system, and motivated by face consideration, Chinese young consumers perceive a weaker price-quality relationship, and are more prestige sensitive, less price conscious, and less coupon prone than their US counterparts. But they are as value conscious as American young consumers.

These findings are very encouraging for Western companies seeking business opportunities in China, especially for American companies. The US represents the most advanced technology in the world and American products are perceived as highly prestigious by Chinese young consumers (Anderson and He 1998). American companies thus can get a premium simply because of being from the US. This provides important implications for these Western companies in making their pricing strategy. Our study can also guide companies toward effective advertising and promotion. High product quality and distinguished product social status should be emphasized and sale or coupon promotion may be improper. Maintaining a steady price or even raising the price may be perceived as signaling more prestige for Chinese young consumers. But since Chinese consumers perceive a weak price-quality relationship, other market cues such as store and brand name must be provided to assure the product quality and prevent the impairment of fake brands. For example, a company can choose marketing channel seriously so as to assure the product quality through the retailer's reputation.

However, the results do not imply Chinese young have a higher purchasing power than American young. In a developing economy, Chinese young do not purchase frequently or impul-

sively (they are as value conscious as American young), although Chinese young are more sensitive to prestige. "Buy nothing, or buy something prestigious" is a good saying to reflect their consumer behaviors precisely.

This paper also provides important implications for future research. First, face is such an important factor in Chinese society (Gao 1998) that its conceptualization and operationalization will greatly help us better understand Chinese consumers and predict their consuming behaviors. Then, the predictive power of face consideration could be investigated within a model which links face consideration to price perceptions, and price perceptions to shopping behaviors in an international context. Third, this paper also emphasizes the importance of validity assessment of models developed in one country (mostly the US) must be examined in other countries before we use them to examine consumer behaviors cross-nationally. For example, in this study, sale proneness is found lack of invariance. Table 2 shows the coefficient reliabilities in American sample (ranging from .79 to .89) are generally higher than those in Chinese sample (ranging from .57 to .80). This suggests that the measurements adapted from one culture may not capture variance in another culture very well. And consistent with the results exhibited by Lichtenstein and his colleagues (1993), the correlations for American sample show the price-related constructs can be meaningfully categorized as "positive" and "negative" in the predicted direction. But for Chinese sample, value consciousness is positively related to price-quality schema and prestige sensitivity, which again suggests measurement validity should be first assessed for a cross-cultural study.

Future research is also encouraged to overcome the limitations of this paper. First, samples from other consumer segments are needed in order to generalize the findings. Second, in this study, the sample size is relatively small. So we cannot investigate the invariance of the full measurement model of price perceptions. As discussed earlier, the underlying dimensions of these six constructs in China may be not the same as proposed by Lichtenstein, Ridgway and Netemeyer (1993). Future research with a larger sample is needed in order to examine this point. Finally, this study only compares price perceptions between American and Chinese young. Given that face consideration plays an important role in collectivistic cultures (Ting-Toomey and Kurogi 1998), and over two thirds of the population in the world live in collectivistic cultures (Triandis 1995), it would be worthwhile to conduct further studies in a worldwide context.

REFERENCES

Anderson, Patricia M. and Xiaohong He (1998), "Price Influence and Age Segments of Beijing Consumers," *Journal of Consumer Marketing*, 15 (2), 152-169.

Arbuchle, James L. and Werner Wothke (1999), *Amos 4.0 User's Guide*, SmallWaters Corporation.

Belk (1988), "Third World Consumer Culture," *Marketing and Developments*, eds. Erdogan Kumcu and A. Fuat Firat, Greenwich, CT: JAI, 103-127.

Dodds, William B., Kent B. Monroe, and Dhruv Grewal (1991), "Effects of Price, Brand, and Store Information on Buyers' Product Evaluations," *Journal of Marketing Research*, 28, 307-19.

Durvasula, Srinivas, J. Craig Andrews, Steven Lysonski, and Richard G. Netemeyer (1993), "Assessing the Cross-National Applicability of Consumer Behavior Models: A Model of Attitude toward Advertising in General," *Journal of Consumer Research*, 19 (March), 626-636.

Fan, Jessie X. and Jing J. Xiao (1998), "Consumer Decision-Making Styles of Young-Adult Chinese," *The Journal of Consumer Affairs*, 32(2), 275-294.

Gao, Ge (1998), "An Initial Analysis of the Effects of Face and Concern for "Other" in Chinese Interpersonal Communication," *International Journal of Intercultural Relation*, 22, 467-82.

Heath, Timothy B., Subimal Chatterjee, and Karen R. France (1995), "Mental Accounting and Changes in Price: The Frame Dependence of Reference Dependence", *Journal of Consumer Research*, 22 (June), 90-97.

Ho, DYF. (1976), "On the Concept of Face," *American Journal of Psychology*, 81, 867-84.

Ho, Suk-ching and Yat-ming Sin (1988), "Consmer Protection in China: The Current State of the Art," *European Journal of Marketing*, 22 (1), 41-57.

Hofstede, Geert (1980), *Culture's Consequences: International Differences in Work-related Value*, Beverly Hills, CA: Sage.
_____ and Michael H. Bond (1984), "Hofstede's Culture Dimensions," *Journal of Cross-Cultural Psychology*, 15 (4), 417-433.

Lal, Rajiv and Ram Rao (1997), "Supermarket Competition: The Case of Every Day Low Pricing," *Marketing Science*, 16(1), 60-80.

Lichtenstein, Donald R., Nancy M. Ridgway, and Richard G. Netemeyer (1993), "Price Perceptions and Consumer Shopping Behavior: A Field Study," *Journal of Marketing Research*, 30 (May), 234-245.

Markus, H. and Kitayama, S. (1991), "Culture and the Self: Implications for cognition, Emotion, and Motivation," *Psychological Review*, 2, 224-253

Maslow, Abraham (1954), *Motivation and Personality*, New York: Harper.

Mela, Carl F., Sunil Gupta, and Donald R. Lehmann (1997), "The Long-Term Impact of Promotion and Advertising on Consumer Brand Choice," *Journal of Marketing Research*, 34 (May), 248-61.

Moschis, George P. and Roy L. Moore (1979), "Decision Making among the Young: A Socialization Perspective," *Journal of Consumer Research*, 6 (September), 101-12.

Monroe, Kent B. (1979), *Pricing: Making Profitable Decisions*. New York: McGraw-Hill Book Company.

Nee, V. (1992), "Organizational Dynamics of Marketing Transition: Hybrid Firms, Property Right, and Mixed Economy in China," *Administrative Science Quarterly*, 31 (March), 1-27.

Ram, Jane (1994), "Luxury Goods Firms Find A Haven in Asia," *Asian Business*, 30 (July), 52-53.

Rao, Akshay R. and Mark E. Bergen (1992), "Price Premium Variations as a Consequence of Buyers' Lack of Information," *Journal of Consumer Research*, 19 (Dec), 412-23.

Reykowski, J. (1994), "Collectivism and Individualism as Dimensions of Social Change," *Individualism and Collectivism: Theory, Method, and Applications*. Newbury Park: CA: Sage, 276-292.

Rostow, Walt w. (1952), *The Process of Economic Growth*, New York: Free Press.

Shimp, Terrence A. and William O. Bearden (1982), "Warranty and Other Extrinsic Cue Effects on Consumers' Risk Perceptions," *Journal of Consumer Research*, 9 (June), 38-46.

Steenkamp, Jan-Benedict E. M. and Hans Baumgartner (1998), "Assessing Measurement Invariance in Cross-National Consumer Research," *Journal of Consumer Research*, 25 (June), 78-90.

Thaler, Richard (1985), "Mental Accounting and Consumer Choice," *Marketing Science*, 4 (Summer), 199-214.

Ting-Toomey, Stella and Atsuko Kurogi (1998), "Facework Competence in Intercultural Conflict: An updated Face-Negotiation Theory," *International Journal of Intercultural Relation*, Vol. 22, 187-225.

Tse, David K. (1996), "Understanding Chinese People as Consumers: Past Findings and Future Propositions," In *The Handbook of Chinese Psychology*, Oxford University Press (China), Hong Kong.
_____, Russell W. Belk, and Nan Zhou (1989), "Becoming a Consumer Society: A Longitudinal and Cross-Cultural Content Analysis of Print Ads from Hong Kong, the People's Republic of China, and Taiwan," *Journal of Consumer Research*, 15 (March), 457-72.

Triandis, Harry C. (1995), *Individualism and Collectivism*, Boulder, CO: Westview Press.

Zeithaml, Valarie A. (1988), "Consumer Perceptions of Price, Quality, and Value: A Means-End Model and Synthesis of Evidence," *Journal of Marketing*, 52 (July), 2-22.

MEASUREMENT APPENDIX
(Adapted from Lichtenstein, Ridgway and Netemeyer 1993)

Price-quality schema
PQ1. Generally speaking, the higher the price of a product, the higher the quality.
PQ2. The old saying "you get what you pay for" is generally true.
PQ3. The price of a product is a good indicator of its quality.
PQ4. You always have to pay a bit more for the best.

Prestige Sensitivity
PS1. People notice when you buy the most expensive brand of a product.*
PS2. Buying a high priced brand makes me feel good about myself.
PS3. Buying the most expensive brand of a product makes me feel classy.
PS4. I enjoy the prestige of buying a high priced brand.
PS5. It says something to people when you buy the high priced version of a product.
PS6. Your friends will think you are cheap if you consistently buy the lowest priced version of a product.*
PS7. I have purchased the most expensive brand of a product just because I knew other people would notice.*
PS8. I think others make judgments about me by the kinds of products and brands I buy.*
PS9. Even for a relatively inexpensive product, I think that buying a costly brand is impressive.

Value consciousness
VC1. I am very concerned about low prices, but I am equally concerned about product quality.
VC2. When grocery shopping, I compare the prices of different brands to be sure I get the best value for the money.*
VC3. When purchasing a product, I always try to maximize the quality I get for the money I spend.
VC4. When I buy products, I like to be sure that I am getting my money's worth.*
VC5. I generally shop around for lower prices on products, but they still must meet certain quality requirements before I buy them.
VC6. When I shop, I usually compare the "price per ounce" information for brands I normally buy.
VC7. I always check prices at the grocery store to be sure I get the best value for the money I spend.

Price consciousness
PC1. I am not willing to go to extra effort to find lower prices.
PC2. I will grocery shop at more than one store to take advantage of low prices.*
PC3. The money saved by finding low prices is usually not worth the time and effort.
PC4. I would never shop at more than one store to find low prices.
PC5. The time it takes to find low prices is usually not worth the effort.

Coupon proneness
CP1. Redeeming coupons makes me feel good.
CP2. I enjoy clipping coupons out of the newspapers.
CP3. When I use coupons, I feel that I am getting a good deal.*
CP4. I enjoy using coupons, regardless of the amount I save by doing so.
CP5. Beyond the money I save, redeeming coupons gives me a sense of joy.

Sale proneness
SP1. If a product is on sale, that can be a reason for me to buy it.*
SP2. When I buy a brand that's on sale, I feel that I am getting a good deal.*
SP3. I have favorite brands, but most of the time I buy the brand that's on sale.
SP4. One should try to buy the brand that's on sale.
SP5. I am more likely to buy brands that are on sale.
SP6. Compared to most people, I am more likely to buy brands that are on special.

All the items are anchored from "1" (strongly agree) to "7" (strongly disagree).
* Items that were deleted from further analysis.

An Evaluation of the Retail Service Quality Scale for U.S. and Korean Customers of Discount Stores

Soyoung Kim, University of Georgia
Byoungho Jin, Yonsei University

The objective of this study is to examine if the Retail Service Quality Scale could successfully capture customers' perceptions of service quality in discount stores across cultures. The U.S. and South Korea are selected as they reflect two different discount retail environments and cultural backgrounds. Behavioral intentions and satisfaction are also examined in relation to customer perceptions of service quality. Data are collected from two convenience samples of U.S. and Korean college students and analyzed using factor and regression analyses. The results suggest that the dimensionality of service quality is not universal across countries.

INTRODUCTION

Faced with increasing competition and limited opportunities for growth in their home markets, a growing number of retailers are expanding globally. The top 100 global retailers represent one-fifth of the world's retail market and continue to take market shares from their smaller local competitors (Carr, Hostrop, and O'Connor 1998). Leading discounters, such as Wal-Mart in the U.S. and Carrefour in France, are among the most successful global retailers, aggressively moving into foreign markets including many Asian countries. While discount retailing holds a dominant position in the retail industry in many western countries such as the U.S. (*Chain Store Age* 1999), it is a relatively new concept in Asia where most consumers shop at supermarkets and small neighborhood stores (*Korea Herald* 1999; Murphy 1999). Global discounters have long been aware that their success overseas depends largely upon their ability to adapt to the local market. A sound understanding of the foreign market becomes even more important to those looking for opportunities in Asia, given the differences in the retail environment and cultural background.

An examination of customers' retail store experiences provides insight into how retailers can modify their goods and services to satisfy their customers. While much retail research has focused on customers' evaluations of physical goods and overall store image (e.g., Hansen and Deutscher, 1977-78; Lindquist 1974-75; Reardon, Miller, and Coe 1995), few researchers have attempted to fully understand customers' service-related retail store experiences (e.g., Parasuraman, Zeithmal, and Berry 1985; Parasuraman, Zeithmal, and Berry 1988). Providing high quality service is essential in the retail industry as it increases customers' purchase intentions, store loyalty, and favorable word-of-mouth communication (McAlexander, Kaldenburg, and Koenig 1994; Zeithaml, Berry, and Parasuraman 1996). By satisfying customers through high quality service, business firms not only retain their current customers, but also increase their market share. Ultimately, it leads to the enhancement of their overall financial performance (Finn and Lamb 1991; Sirohi, McLaughlin, and Wittink 1998).

While considerable efforts have been directed to developing and validating research instruments for measuring service quality in the service sector, (e.g., Hurley and Estelami 1998; Parasuraman et al. 1985; Parasuraman et al. 1988; Yükel and Rimmington 1998), little research has considered service quality in the retail sector (Dabholkar Thorpe and Rentz 1996). A recent exception is a study by Dabholkar et al. (1996), who proposed the Retail Service Quality Scale (RSQS), an instrument for measuring service quality

in a retail environment. In their study, the validity of the scale was supported for U.S. customers of department stores. We do not know if the RSQS instrument is applicable to non-U.S. cultures and to retail formats other than department stores. The generalizability of a measure is important because "constructing a new measure for each specific situation is both wasteful and expensive" (Reardon et al. 1995, p. 86).

The objective of this study is to examine the generalizability of the RSQS instrument in different research settings. In order to explore whether consumers' perceptions of service quality in discount stores differ from culture to culture, we selected the United States and South Korea (hereafter Korea) because these two countries reflect two different discount retail environments as well as dissimilar cultural backgrounds. Korea represents the collectivist culture with a high tolerance of power differences whereas the United States is classified as the individualistic culture with a low tolerance of power differences (Hofstede 1980). In addition, compared to the United States, Korea has a relatively short history of discount retailing. It is important to know whether cultural and retail environmental differences would bring customers different service-related retail store experiences.

It is also of interest to examine the applicability of the RSQS instrument to discount retail settings. Traditionally, discount stores have offered relatively limited customer service to keep their prices down. In today's highly competitive market, however, discounters have come to realize that price is no longer the great differentiator (*Discount Store News* 1996b). Now discounters are offering more and more value-added services in order to differentiate themselves from their competitors and also to satisfy customers who are becoming increasingly sensitive to service (Schwartz 1997). Their improvements in customer service are evidenced by a recent consumer survey that found discount and department stores tied in rankings of customer service (Paajanen 1997). Wal-Mart, the most successful discounter in the United States, is now known not only for low prices but also for "warm-sell" service (*Discount Store News* 1996a). If the RSQS instrument is to be a valid tool for measuring retail service quality, it should successfully capture customers' perceptions of service quality in discount stores across cultures. This study would contribute to the extant literature in service quality by examining whether an instrument developed in the United States can be replicated in another culture and applied to a different research setting. Furthermore, this study has a practical implication in that its empirical results may be used to help multinational and domestic discounters operating in the United States or Korea better understand their target market.

DISCOUNT RETAILING IN THE U.S. AND KOREA

Korea is the 11th largest economy in the world with a population of 47 million people (*Discount Store News* 1999). The first discount store in Korea, E-Mart, was introduced in 1993 by a leading Korean retailer. Since then, sales of the Korean discount store market increased 2000 times (*Dong-A Il Bo* 1998), reaching 2.49 trillion won ($2.08 billion) in the first half of 1998 (*Korea Herald* 1998). Since the Korean retail sector was fully liberalized in 1996, three global retailers, Carrefour, Costco, and Wal-Mart, have expanded into Korea, intensifying the competition. These global discounters currently hold a market share of 18.7% in Korea

(*Korea Herald* 1998). As the ninth largest trading partner of the United States (USITC 2000), Korea possesses a great potential for U.S. discounters wishing to expand their market. Wal-Mart, the biggest U.S.-based discount retailer, moved into Korea in 1998 and, as of 1999, it operates five superstores in Korea (*Discount Store News* 1999). Joe Hatfield, president of Wal-Mart Asia, commented that "Wal-Mart is committed to the Korean market for the long-term" (*Discount Store News* 1999, p. 93). Among 87 discount retailers operating in Korea, two U.S.-based discounters, Wal-Mart and Costco (Price Club), respectively, achieved the seventh and the tenth highest sales in 1999. E-Mart, a Korean discounter, took the top position by reporting sales of 695.2 billion won ($579 million) in the first half of 1999, while Carrefour of France took the third position with sales of 298.1 billion won ($248 million) (*Korea Economic Daily* 1999).

In the United States, full-line discount retailing has over 40 years of history. The U.S. discount-store sector of the retail industry has grown from about $2 billion in sales in 1960 to more than $175 billion in 1999 (*Chain Store Age* 1999). This sector retains the largest market share of many product categories, such as table linen and kitchen textile products (Gunin 1999), menswear, boyswear, girlswear, and bath products (*Chain Store Age* 1999). Many successful discounters, such as Wal-Mart and Kmart, are among the fastest-growing retailers in the U.S.

DEVELOPMENT OF A SERVICE QUALITY MEASUREMENT

Many business organizations have felt the critical need to develop a reliable and valid tool for evaluating service quality so that they can properly assess and improve their service performance. Using in-depth interviews with executives from service firms as well as focus group interviews, Parasuraman and his colleagues (1988) developed the SERVQUAL scale, which has become the most widely known research instrument for measuring service quality. SERVQUAL measures a gap between customers' original expectations and the actual service they receive. Parasuraman et al. (1988) argued that, regardless of the type of service, consumers evaluate service quality using similar criteria, which can be grouped into five dimensions: tangibles, reliability, responsiveness, assurance, and empathy.

Since the original work of Parasuraman et al. in 1988, SERVQUAL has attracted numerous studies by both academics and practicing managers. It has been replicated in many different pure service settings as well as retail store environments. Despite its wide usage and the fact that it has proven to be a reliable scale in several studies for assessing pure service organizations, SERVQUAL has been criticized by many marketing researchers. In fact, the definition and operationalization of SERVQUAL have emerged as major debate topics among researchers in service quality for the past decade. Some of the widespread concerns are the five-dimension structure of the scale, the appropriateness of operationalizing service quality as the expectations-performances gap score, and the scale's applicability to a retail setting (Babakus and Boller 1992; Finn and Lamb 1991; Gagliano and Hathcote 1994; Winsted 1997).

Several researchers (e.g., Babakus and Boller 1992) argued that people tend to indicate consistently high expectation ratings and that their perception scores rarely exceed their expectations. Therefore, including expectation scores on an instrument may be inefficient and unnecessary. Cronin and Taylor (1992), who questioned the relevance of the perceptions-expectations gap conceptualization, suggested that their performance-only SERVPERF scale is superior to SERVQUAL in terms of construct validity and operational efficacy. Researchers also found that

performance-only measures better predict customer satisfaction than the gap expectation-perception score (Yüksel and Rimmington 1998). These studies provide support for the decision to use performance-only measures in this study.

SERVICE QUALITY IN A RETAIL STORE ENVIRONMENT

Parasuraman et al. (1991) argued that SERVQUAL can be applied to a wide range of industries. However, many researchers (e.g., Babakus and Boller 1991; Dabholka et al. 1996; Finn and Lamb 1991) have suggested the need to design measures for specific industries. For example, Dabholka et al. (1996) recently developed the RSQS instrument, a hierarchical model of retail service quality, suggesting that the dimensionality of service quality in a retail setting may not be similar to that of service quality in pure service industries. This model includes five dimensions of retail service quality: physical aspects; reliability; personal interaction; problem solving; and store policies. Dabholka et al. used only performance-based measures and found that their scale possessed strong validity and reliability, adequately capturing customers' perceptions of retail service quality. In their study, the five-factor structure model was tested with U.S. customers of department stores. To our knowledge, the present study is the first attempt to test Dabholka et al.'s hierarchical model, using data obtained from customers of discount stores.

Given the differences in the cultural background and the discount retail environment, we do not expect the service quality of discount stores in the United States and Korea to have the same five-factor structure identified by Dabholka et al. Although there exist only a few comparative studies that explored differences in service quality perceptions between countries, they agree that different cultures evaluate service differently (Malhotra, Ulgado, Agarwal, and Baalbaki 1994; Winsted 1997). In their conceptual paper, for example, Malhotra et al. (1994) proposed that environmental, economic, and sociocultural factors influence service quality determinants and that multinational firms should not adopt a standardized marketing approach. Winsted (1997), who examined customers' service experiences in restaurants in the United States and Japan, also commented that "studies examining service encounters need to be sensitive to differences in culture and, perhaps, to industry differences" (p. 355).

METHOD

Samples

Data for this study were collected using a self-administered questionnaire given to two convenience samples of U.S. and Korean college students who had recently shopped at a discount store. The questionnaire was completed by 214 U.S. students at a western university in the United States and 217 Korean students at two universities in Seoul, Korea. In preparation, the questionnaire was originally written in English and translated into Korean by one of the researchers. Two different bilingual interpreters (native Koreans who were fluent in English) then translated the results back into English. Based on a comparison between the original English version and the back-translated version, some modifications were made.

The respondents were predominantly female for both samples (89.7% for the U.S. sample and 82.5% for the Korean sample). This was because the questionnaire was given to students enrolled in several courses in apparel merchandising in both countries. U.S. respondents ranged in age from 19 to 30 with an average age of 20 years and Korean respondents from 18 to 38 with an average age of 22 years. According to a recent survey, the most common

TABLE 1
Factor Analysis of Perceptions of Service Quality (U.S.)

Factor Title and Items	Factor Loadings	Alpha
Factor 1 (53.0%) - Personal Attention		0.97
Employees give you prompt service.	0.92	
Employees are able to handle customers complaints directly and immediately.	0.90	
Employees are always willing to help customers.	0.90	
Employees are never too busy to respond to your request.	0.89	
Employees understand customers' specific needs.	0.87	
Employees are consistently courteous with you.	0.87	
The behavior of employees instill confidence in customers.	0.84	
This store has employees who give you personal attention.	0.82	
This store gives you individual attention.	0.80	
When a customer has a problem, this store shows a sincere interest in solving it.	0.78	
This store has your best interests at heart.	0.75	
Employees have the knowledge to answer customers' questions.	0.75	
Employees in this store are neat-appearing.	0.74	
This store provides its services at the time it promises to do so.	0.60	
Factor 2 (7.8%) - Reliability		0.83
When this store promises to do something by a certain time, it does so.	0.80	
This store insists on error-free records.	0.77	
Employees tell customers exactly when services will be performed.	0.76	
Factor 3 (5.6%) - Convenience		0.66
The store layout makes it easy for customers to move around.	0.71	
Customers feel safe in their transaction with this store.	0.65	
This store has operating hours convenient to all its customers.	0.58	
The store layout makes it easy for customers to find what they need.	0.50	
Factor 4 (4.6%) - Credit Card Policy		0.57
This store accepts most major credit cards.	0.70	
This store offers its own credit card.	0.63	

shoppers at large discount stores in Korea are young females 20 to 30 years old (*Korea Herald* 1999). Similarly, young women are the core shoppers of discount department stores in the U.S. (Duff 1999). This justifies, to some degree, the use of predominantly female college students in this study. About 45% of the U.S. respondents reported they shopped at a discount store once a week or more. On the other hand, only 12.9% of the Korean respondents shopped once a week or more.

Measures

The questionnaire consisted of four sections. The first section asked the respondents to indicate the discount store where they had shopped most often in the past year and how often they shopped at that store. A discount store was defined as "a general merchandise retailer that offers a wide variety of merchandise, limited service, and low prices" (Levy and Weltz, p. 41). In the second section, respondents were asked to rate their most preferred store on various aspects of service quality. To measure the service quality of discount stores, Dabholkar et al.'s (1996) multi-item scale was adopted. This scale consists of 33 items that measure the five dimensions of customer perceptions of service quality for a retail store. Dabholka et al. used perception measures instead of the gap between perceptions and expectations because the evidence demonstrated that perception measures have a stronger predictive power than the gab score (e.g., Cronin and Taylor 1992; McAlexander et al. 1994). The scale was measured on a 7-point Likert scale from 1 (strongly disagree) to 7 (strongly agree). The third section was designed to measure respondents' behavioral

intentions toward the store as well as their satisfaction with the store. The final section solicited demographic information such as age and gender.

ANALYSIS AND RESULTS

The data were analyzed in two stages. First, the dimensionality of each of the measures in each sample was examined using principal component analysis with an oblique rotation. The factor structure identified through this exploratory factor analysis was then validated by confirmatory factor analysis via LISREL 8 (Jöreskog and Sörbom 1996). The second stage involved using regression analyses to assess the relationship between service quality, behavioral intentions, and satisfaction.

Factor analyses

Principal component analysis with an oblique rotation was first performed on the retail service quality measure to examine the underlying dimensions of the construct. Factor analysis for the U.S. sample produced four dimensions with eigenvalues greater than one (Table 1). The items loaded on the first factor appeared to be a mixture of items that related to two of the five dimensions of the RSQS instrument: personal interaction and problem solving. This factor was entitled *personal attention*. The second factor contained three items that reflected the store's ability to perform service dependably and consistently, and was named *reliability*. The next factor, *convenience*, included four items that related to making customers' purchase processes efficient and convenient. The last factor, labeled *credit card policy*, contained two credit

TABLE 2
Factor Analysis of Perceptions of Service Quality (Korean)

Factor Title and Items	Factor Loadings	Alpha
Factor 1 (37.0%) - Tangibles		0.81
The store layout makes it easy for customers to move around.	0.82	
This store has modern-looking equipment and fixtures.	0.79	
The store layout makes it easy for customers to find what they need.	0.77	
This store has clean, attractive, and convenient public areas.	0.58	
Employees are neat-appearing.	0.51	
Factor 2 (7.2%) - Empathy		0.72
This store has employees who give you personal attention.	0.68	
This store gives you individual attention.	0.56	
Factor 3 (6.2%) - Responsiveness		0.80
This store has your best interests at heart.	0.81	
Employees give you prompt service.	0.78	
Employees are able to handle customers complaints directly and immediately.	0.61	
This store willingly handles returns and exchanges.	0.59	
Employees are always willing to help customers.	0.55	
Factor 4 (6.1%) - Store Policy		0.43
This store insists on error-free records.	0.81	
This store offers its own credit card.	0.70	

card-related items such as *accepting most major credit cards* and *offering its own credit card*. Cronbach's alpha coefficient was used to examine the reliabilities among the items within each factor. It was decided to accept an alpha coefficient higher than .60 as indicating reliability. The coefficients of the first four factors revealed acceptable internal consistency. The last factor, *credit card policy*, however, indicated a low reliability (α=.57), and was excluded from further analyses. The first three factors, *personal attention, reliability*, and *convenience*, correspond to those identified by Gagliano and Hathcote (1994) in a study of apparel specialty stores. This suggests that perhaps U.S. customers of discount stores and apparel specialty stores may perceive service quality in a similar manner. Confirmatory factor analysis provided moderate support for the three conceptualizations (χ^2=597.69, df=186, p<.001; RMR=.06; GFI=.80; AFGI=.75; CFI=.90). The correlations among the factors were also examined. Positive correlations existed among the three factors (ϕ=.56 between *personal attention* and *reliability*; ϕ=.68 between *personal attention* and *convenience*; ϕ=.34 between *reliability* and *convenience*). This suggests that customers who hold favorable perceptions of one dimension of service quality also tend to perceive other dimensions of service quality favorably.

In the Korean sample, the 33 items loaded on four factors (Table 2). The items loaded on the first factor, *tangibles*, involved physical aspects of the store and its staff. The second factor, *empathy*, included two items about giving customers personal and individual attention. The third factor captured the store's willingness to provide prompt service, and was labeled *responsiveness*. The last factor included two items, "This store insists on error-free records" and "This store offers its own credit card," and was named *store policy*. The alpha coefficients for the first three factors were .81, .72, and .80, respectively, indicating a high level of internal consistency. The smallest alpha coefficient found was .43 for *store policy* and we decided that it should be excluded from further analyses. Confirmatory factor analysis indicated an adequate, although not excellent, fit for the three-factor solution (χ^2=140.18, df=51, p<.001; RMR=.06; GFI=.89; AFGI=.83; CFI=.89). As in

the U.S. sample, there were positive correlations among all three factors (ϕ=.50 between *tangibles* and *empathy*; ϕ=.78 between *tangibles* and *responsiveness*; ϕ=.60 between *empathy* and *responsiveness*).

The 14 behavioral-intention items were also factor analyzed separately for U.S. and Korean samples. Factor analysis for the U.S. respondents identified four factors (Table 3). The first factor contained five positively worded intention items that reflected the customer's loyalty. Thus, it was named *loyalty* (α=.87). On the other hand, the second factor, *switch*, included three negatively worded items that indicated the customer's intention to switch (α=.66). The third factor contained only one item, "I will do less business with this store." This single-item factor was deleted from all subsequent analyses as one item might undermine its meaningfulness (Zeithaml et al. 1996). The last factor, labeled *complaint*, included two items related to making a complaint to external agencies and to the store's employees (α=.66). The first three factors entered into confirmatory model revealed a good fit to the data (χ^2=86.51, df=32, p<.001; RMR=.07; GFI=.93; AFGI=.88; CFI=.93). *Loyalty* had no significant correlation with either *switch* or *complaint*. On the other hand, *switch* was positively associated with *complaint* (ϕ=.45).

As for the Korean respondents, three factors emerged that were comparable to those obtained for U.S. respondents (Table 4). The first factor was named *loyalty* (α=.83). The second factor, *switch*, was identical to the second factor found for the U.S. respondents (α=.64). In addition, surprisingly the single item loaded on the last factor for the Korean respondents was the same statement that loaded on the last factor for the U.S. respondents. Again, this single-item factor was eliminated. A two-factor confirmatory model of behavioral intentions provides a reasonable fit to the data (χ^2=90.04, df=26, p<.001; RMR=.08; GFI=.90; AFGI=.83; CFI=.88). There was no significant association between *loyalty* and *switch*. In both samples, the six-factor solution was not supported; however, the consistency between the two samples suggested that the dimensionality of behavioral intentions may be determined by the store type.

TABLE 3
Factor Analysis of Behavioral Measures (U.S.)

Factor Title and Items	Factor Loadings	*Alpha*
Factor 1 (32.2%) - Loyalty		0.87
Will recommend this store to someone who seeks your advice.	0.90	
Encourage friends and relatives to do business with this store.	0.89	
Will do more business with this store in the next few years.	0.83	
Will continue to do business with this store if its prices increases somewhat.	0.72	
Say positive things about this store to other people.	0.70	
Factor 2 (19.1%) - Switch		0.66
Will switch if you experience a problem with its service.	0.78	
Take some of your business to a competitor that offers better prices.	0.76	
Will complaint to others if you experience a problem with its service.	0.74	
Factor 3 (10.9%)		
Will do less business with this store in the next few years.	0.92	
Factor 4 (9.3%) - Complaint		0.66
Will complaint to external agencies if you experience a problem with its service.	0.92	
Will complaint to its employees if you experience a problem with its service.	0.76	

TABLE 4
Factor Analysis of Behavioral Measures (Korean)

Factor Title and Items	Factor Loadings	*Alpha*
Factor 1 (31.8%) - Loyalty		0.83
Will recommend this store to someone who seeks your advice.	0.81	
Encourage friends and relatives to do business with this store.	0.79	
Will continue to do business with this store if its prices increases somewhat.	0.78	
Will do more business with this store in the next few years.	0.76	
Will pay a higher price than competitors charge for the benefits you currently receive from this store.	0.69	
Say positive things about this store to other people.	0.56	
Factor 2 (17.5%) - Switch		0.64
Take some of your business to a competitor that offers better prices.	0.79	
Will switch if you experience a problem with its service.	0.72	
Will complaint to others if you experience a problem with its service.	0.70	
Factor 3 (11.1%)		
Do less business with this store in the next few years.	0.82	

Cronbach's alpha coefficient for customer satisfaction was high at .81 for the U.S. sample and at .84 for the Korean sample. Factor items for all the measures in this study were summed into multi-item scales. The means of the resulting scales were examined to compare the perceptions and attitudes between the two samples. In the eyes of U.S. customers, the most favorably perceived dimensions of service quality were *convenience* (mean=5.72), *personal attention* (5.28), and *reliability* (4.94), in order. On the other hand, Korean customers perceived *tangibles* (4.29) most favorably, followed by *responsiveness* (3.91) and *empathy* (3.20). Overall, U.S. consumers rated their discount stores more favorably than did Korean consumers. In addition, U.S. respondents exhibited stronger *loyalty* (5.68) toward their favorite discount store and higher level of satisfaction (5.61) than Korean respondents (3.99 for *loyalty* and 3.99 for satisfaction). Both samples, however, expressed a somewhat high degree of intention to switch if they experience a problem with the service (5.12 for U.S. and 5.16 for Korean sample). This suggests that their continued patronage of a discount store is strongly based on their satisfaction with its service.

Regression analyses

In order to determine the best predictors of behavioral intentions, regression analyses were then used, separately, for U.S. and Korean respondents. The multi-item scales of service quality dimensions were entered into regression as the independent variables, while the behavioral-intention factors and customer satisfaction were used as the dependent variables.

As for U.S. respondents, two of the three service quality factors, i.e., *personal attention* (β=.64) and *convenience* (β=.18), were significantly associated with *loyalty*. *Reliability* was not significant in predicting *loyalty*. Coefficient of determination (R^2) for this model was 55% and the model was significant at the .001 level. The same set of the three service quality factors explained only 2% of variance in *switch* and 1% of variance in *complaint*. These two models were not significant at the .01 level. None of the

TABLE 5

Comparison of the Service Quality Dimensionality

SERVQUAL	RSQS (1996)	Present Study	
		U.S.	Korea
Tangibles	Physical aspects	Personal attention	Tangibles
Reliability	Reliability	Reliability	Empathy
Responsiveness	Personal interaction	Convenience	Responsiveness
Assurance	Problem solving	Credit card policy	Store policy
Empathy	Store policies		

TABLE 6

Comparison of the Behavioral Intention Dimensionality

Zeithaml et al. (1996)	Present Study	
	U.S.	Korea
Loyalty	Loyalty	Loyalty
Switch	Switch	Switch
Pay more	Complaint	
External response		
Internal response		

three service quality factors predicted *switch* and *complaint*, while all the factors significantly predicted satisfaction. The satisfaction model was highly significant at the .001 level (β=.54 for *personal attention*; β=.20 for *reliability*; β=.13 for *convenience*) and the R^2 was 55%. Overall service quality appeared to be a significant predictor of only one dimension of the behavioral-intention measure, i.e., *loyalty*. Its predictive powers for *loyalty* and customer satisfaction were equally strong. Among the three service quality factors, *personal attention* seemed to be the best predictor of the two dependent variables mentioned above.

As for Korean respondents, only *tangibles* (β=.22) and *responsiveness* (β=.28) were significantly associated with *loyalty*. This model was significant at the .001 level and the R^2 was 27%. None of the service quality factors was significant in predicting *switch* (R^2=1%). but all of them were significant in predicting customer satisfaction (β = .37 for *tangibles*; β = .13 for *empathy*; β=.19 for *responsiveness*) (R^2=33%). As for the Korean sample, *empathy* seemed to be the least important in predicting the dependent variables. *Responsiveness* was the best predictor of *loyalty* while *tangibles* was the strongest predictor of customer satisfaction. Overall, service quality appeared to better predict customer satisfaction than *loyalty*.

DISCUSSION

The purpose of this study was to examine whether the RSQS instrument developed by Dabholkar et al. (1996) could capture both U.S. and Korean customer perceptions of service quality in discount stores. We believe that the understanding of the dimensionality of service quality is critical not only for measurement purposes but also for providing greater insights into customers' perceptions and shopping behavior. Overall, the factor-loading patterns identified through factor analysis did not appear as expected from Dabholkar et al.'s study and, therefore, failed to support their conceptualization of retail service quality (Table 5).

In both U.S. and Korean samples, a four-factor solution resulted from the principal component analyses; however, the items that factored together were not identical. This suggests that customers' perceptions of service quality in discount retailing

differ from culture to culture. The *personal attention* factor that contained staff quality items relating to giving customers personal attention emerged as the most important dimension of service quality in the U.S. sample. In the Korean sample, however, many of the same items split into two factors (i.e., *empathy* and *responsiveness*). Just as Dabholkar et al. found in their study of U.S. customers of department stores, the U.S. respondents in this study did not differentiate *empathy* items from *responsiveness* items. However, in the mind of Korean customers, *empathy* and *responsiveness* were two distinct dimensions of service quality.

Tangibles was the most important factor in the Korean sample, but this factor was not identified in the U.S. sample, although some of the physical-aspects items loaded on the *convenience* dimension. According to Malhotra et al. (1994), service providers in developing countries put a greater emphasis on the tangible core service whereas in developed countries intangible benefits are more important. Using Maslow's needs hierarchy, Malhotra et al. explained that physical aspects of service are of a lower order and the lower-level needs should be satisfied before higher-level needs are addressed. Service providers in developing countries have yet to satisfy fully such lower-level needs, whereas those in developed countries put a greater emphasis on extended benefits beyond the physical and functional. These extended benefits tend to be more intangible. In Korea, discount retailing has recently been introduced and, therefore, customers and discount retailers still may be preoccupied with the tangible service. On the other hand, U.S. customers may be more interested in intangible benefits such as personal attention. Also, in their minds, physical aspects of service were not a distinct factor.

Except the last factor that appeared not to be reliable, all the factors were subjected to confirmatory factor analysis in both samples to confirm the factor structure identified through principal component analysis. In both samples, confirmatory factor analysis provided a moderate support for the factor structure. Taken together, these results indicate that the factor structure, reported by Dabholka et al., was not present in this study of discount store customers. In addition, the factor structures found in the two samples were not identical. Perhaps the discount retail sector and the department store retail sector do not view service quality in a similar manner, nor do U.S. and Korean customers of discount stores. In other words, the dimensionality of service quality is not universal across industries nor across countries.

Although factor analysis of behavioral intentions did not confirm Zeithaml et al.'s (1996) five-factor structure in both samples, the emergence of the two largest factors, *loyalty* and *switch*, in both the U.S. and Korean samples indicated that these are two distinctive dimensions of behavioral intentions toward discount stores in two countries (Table 6). However, given that all *loyalty* factor items were positively worded and all *switch* items were negatively worded, it is possible that these two factors emerged because of this wording variation.

In general, the U.S. respondents perceived service quality in discount stores more favorably than did the Korean respondents. They also expressed more favorable behavioral intentions toward discount stores and greater satisfaction than their counterparts. These results probably suggest that Korean consumers have not yet established their trust and patronage toward discount stores, which makes sense considering the relatively recent introduction of this sector in this country. We also observed that, overall, the Korean respondents tend to shop at a discount store less often than the U.S. respondents. This finding can be misleading, falsely suggesting that there is not much potential for discount stores in Korea. According to a recent survey, Korean consumers tend to go to large discount stores less often than the two major traditional distribution channels in Korea, supermarkets and small neighborhood stores; however, on average, consumers spend the same amount of money at large discounters as at the other two distribution channels. In other words, Korean consumers make fewer trips to discount stores but make larger purchases per trip (*Korea Herald* 1999). It would be interesting to investigate the amount of purchases both U.S. and Korean consumers make at discount stores as well as their purchasing patterns.

A major limitation of this study was the use of predominantly female college students as a sample. College students have more limited resources than other consumer groups and thus may favor discount stores mainly for their low prices. On the other hand, consumers of higher income, who can afford to shop at department or specialty stores, which offer better customer service, may be less tolerant of the low-quality service provided by discount stores. In a more affluent consumer sample, there might be a stronger association between service quality and behavioral intentions. The use of students enrolled in merchandising courses also limits the generalizability of the results, as they are more likely to be better informed about the retail industry. Therefore, future studies should examine a nationwide sample of discount store customers in all age groups. In addition, studies that include other variables would be an important extension of this study.

REFERENCES

Babakus, Emin and Gregory W. Boller (1992), "An Empirical Assessment of the SERVQUAL Scale," *Journal of Business Research*, 24(May), 253-268.

Carr, Mark, Arlene Hostrop, and Daniel O'Connor (1998), *"The New Era of Global Retailing,"* The Journal of Business Strategy, *19(May/June), 11-15.*

Chain Store Age (1999), "Discounters Survive Volatile Year," 75(August), 19A-20A.

Cronin, J. Joseph and Steven A. Taylor (1992), "Measuring Service Quality: A Reexamination and Extension," *Journal of Marketing*, 56(July), 55-68.

Dabholkar, Pratibha A., Dayle I. Thorpe, and Joseph O. Rentz (1996), "A Measure of Service Quality for Retail Stores: Scale Development and Validation," *Journal of the Academy of Marketing Science*, 24(Spring), 3-16.

Discount Store News (1999), "A Rocky But Rewarding Opportunity," 38(October), 93.

Discount Store News (1996a), "Friendly Service Has Its Rewards," 35(May), 64-65.

Discount Store News (1996b), "Value-Added Services Breed Loyal Shoppers," 35(May), 56-57.

Dong-A Il Bo (1998), "Discount Stores Are Growing," (December 18), B3.

Duff, Mike (1999), "In Mom We Trust: Kmart Makes Core Customer Its Top Priority," *Discount Store News*, 38(March), 67-68.

Finn, David W. and Charles W. Lamb (1991), "An Evaluation of the SERVQUAL Scales in a Retailing Setting," in *Advances in Consumer Research*, Rebecca H. Holman and Michael R. Solomon, eds. Provo, UT: Association for Consumer Research, 483-490.

Gagliano, Kathryn B. and Jan Hathcote (1994), "Customer Expectations and Perceptions of Service Quality in Retail Apparel Specialty Stores," *Journal of Service Marketing*, 8, 60-69.

Gunin, Joan (1999), "Discounters Dominate the Category," *Home Textiles Today*, 19(March), 952-953.

Hansen, Robert A. and Terry Deutscher (1977-78), "An Empirical Investigation of Attributes Importance in Retail Store Selection," *Journal of Retailing*, 53 (Winter), 58-72.

Hofstede, Geert (1980), *Culture's Consequences: International Differences in Work-Related Values*. Beverly Hills: Sage.

Hurley, Robert F. and Hooman Estelami (1998). "Alternative Indexes for Monitoring Customer Perceptions of Service Quality: A Comparative Evaluation in a Retail Context," *Journal of the Academy of Marketing Science*, 26(Fall), 209-221.

Jöreskog, Karl G. and David W. Sörbom (1996), *LISREL 8 User's Reference Guide*. Chicago: Scientific Software International, Inc.

Korea Economic Daily (1999), "E-Mart Tops in Discount Store Sales," (August 12), 1.

Korea Herald (1998), "Discount Retailing: A New Experience for Sellers, Consumers in IMF Era," (November 3), 1.

Korea Herald (1999), "New Purchasing Pattern for Daily Necessities," (July 28), 1.

Levy, Michael and Barton A. Weitz (1998), *Retailing Management*. New York: McGraw-Hill.

Lindquist, Jay D. (1974-75), "Meaning of Image: A Survey of Empirical and Hypothetical Evidence," *Journal of Retailing*, 50(Winter), 29-38.

Malhotra, Naresh K., Francis M. Ulgado, James Agarwal, and Imad B. Baalbaki (1994). "International Services Marketing: A Comparative Evaluation of the Dimensions of Service Quality between Developed and Developing Countries," *International Marketing Review*, 11(Summer), 5-15.

McAlexander, James H., Dennis O. Kaldenburg, and Harold F. Koenig (1994), "Service Quality Measurement," *Marketing Health Services*, 14(Fall), 34-40.

Murphy, Claire (1999), "Tesco Braves the Dangers of Taking Brands Abroad," *Marketing*, (April 22), 19.

Paajanen, George (1997), "Customer Service: Training, Sound Practices and the Right Employee," *Discount Store News*, 36(September), 20.

Parasuraman, A., Leonard L. Berry, and Valarie A. Zeithaml (1991), "Refinement and Reassessment of the SERVQUAL scale," *Journal of Retailing*, 67(Winter), 420-50.

_____, Valarie A. Zeithaml, and Leonard L. Berry (1988), "SERVQUAL: A Multiple-Item Scale for Measuring Consumer Perceptions of Service Quality," *Journal of Retailing*, 64(Spring), 12-40.

_____, _____ and _____ (1985), "A Conceptual Model of Service Quality and Its Implications for Future Research," *Journal of Marketing*, 49(Fall), 41-50.

Reardon, James, Chip E. Miller, and Barbara Coe (1995), "Applied Scale Development: Measurement of Store Image," *Journal of Applied Business Research*, 11(Winter), 85-93.

Sirohi, Niren, Edward W. McLaughlin, and Dick R. Wittink (1998), "A Model of Consumer Perceptions and Store Loyalty Intentions for a Supermarket Retailer," *Journal of Retailing*, 74(Summer), 223-45.

Schwartz, Ela (1997), "Helping Customers Help Themselves," *Discount Merchandiser*, 37(January), 105.

U.S. International Trade Commission (2000), "U.S. Trade Balance by Partners, 1998," Online: http://dataweb.usitc.gov/scripts/cy_m3.asp

Winsted, Kathryn F. (1997), "The Service Experience in Two Cultures: A Behavioral Perspective," *Journal of Retailing*, 73(Fall), 337-360.

Yüksel, Atila and Mike Rimmington (1998), "Customer-Satisfaction Measurement: Performance Counts," *Cornell Hotel and Restaurant Administration Quarterly*, 39(December), 60-70.

Zeithaml, Valarie A., Leonard L. Berry, and A. Parasuraman (1996), "The Behavioral Consequences of Service Quality," *Journal of Marketing*, 60(April), 31-46.

"Paradigms Regained": Humanities Theory and Empirical Research

Barbara Stern, Rutgers, The State University of New Jersey
Cristel Russell, San Diego State University

There is no reason that the conceptualizations of interpretive knowledge cannot be submitted to sophisticated falsificationist methodology; they may, in fact, be a good source of scientifically testable hypotheses. (Calder and Tybout 1987, p. 139).

This session aimed at demonstrating (rather than discussing) the role of the humanities as a source of theory and testable hypotheses. Three presentations provided instances of knowledge transfer from arts theory (literature, theology, painting) to consumer research and the reverse.

The papers' core assumption is that pluralistic research projects drawing from different paradigmatic strengths (Kuhn 1962; Laudan 1984) contribute to knowledge exchange (Lakatos 1978). The "show us the money" presentations provided evidence of value added to consumer research by means of synergy between humanities theory and scientific method (Geertz 1988; Holbrook 1987). Synergy was achieved in the presentations by the strategic decision to maximize the long suit of each knowledge domain. That is, arts theory was invoked in analysis of stimulus objects (art products) and scientific methods in the measurement of responses (human reactions to objects).

Russell and Stern's presentation, "From Art to Science: Literary Theory in the Laboratory," was content-oriented, using literary theory to generate testable hypotheses and laboratory experimentation to test them. They analyzed consumer responses to product placement in a television sitcom by means of hypotheses derived from literary theory (genre, persona, male/female reading styles) and tested them using traditional experimental procedures. The results support the turn to literary theory to generate more finely tuned hypotheses derived from the stimulus side.

Iacobucci's presentation investigated several issues within theological texts. She demonstrated hypothesis testing on words and paragraphs embedded in modern day scripture. Texts are qualitative, but their study is illuminated through the use of techniques that are analogous to statistical (quantitative) methods. She closed with a substantive conclusion (regarding the study of the Sacred in consumer behavior) and a philosophical one, namely, that we should consider the relationship between different paradigmatic data (quantitative vs. qualitative) and research philosophies (positivist/postmodern) as independent.

Apostolova-Blossom and Wallendorf's presentation, "The Role of Marketing Research in Consumer-Market Relationships: A Case Study of "The People's Choice" Exhibit by Komar and Melamid," was epistemologically oriented, discussing the use of techniques from market research to produce an art exhibit. They critiqued the marketing/consumer research methods used to create the paintings, as well as the paintings that were the product of this process. More broadly, they addressed the application of social science methods to creating art as well as a wider range of aesthetic products. Their paper examined the cultural priority granted to scientific research in producing market-driven products in late capitalism, and evaluated the knowledge that artists and other product-producers gain by using marketing research techniques to determine product attributes and features that consumers will favor.

The session's goal was the practical one of showing how the development of better questions can lead to better answers. Its justification was that the process of generating sophisticated and theoretically grounded hypotheses and of testing them empirically is likely to yield findings that are valid, reliable, and acceptable to the consumer research community.

REFERENCES

Calder, Bobby J. and Tybout, Alice M. (1987), "What Consumer Research Is..." *Journal of Consumer Research*, 14 (June), 136-140.

Geertz, Clifford (1988), *Work and Lives: The Anthropologist as Author*, Stanford, California, Stanford University Press.

Holbrook, Morris B. (1987), "What Is Consumer Research?" *Journal of Consumer Research,* 14 (June), 128-132.

Kuhn, Thomas S. (1962), *The Structure of Scientific Revolutions*, Chicago: University of Chicago Press.

Lakatos, Imre (1978), *The Methodology of Scientific Research Programs*, Cambridge, England: Cambridge University Press.

Laudan, Larry (1984), *Science and Values*, Berkeley: University of California Press.

The Effects of Brand Expansions and Ingredient Branding Strategies on Host Brand Extendibility

Kalpesh Kaushik Desai, State University of New York at Buffalo
Kevin Lane Keller, Dartmouth College

ABSTRACT

A new product decision of increasing importance is how ingredient attributes that make up a new product should be labeled or branded, if at all. This research conducted a laboratory experiment to consider how ingredient branding affected consumer acceptance of an initial novel line extension (i.e., not introduced before), as well as the ability of the brand to introduce future category extensions. Two particular types of novel line extensions or brand expansions were studied: 1) *Slot filler expansions*, where the level of one existing product attribute changed (e.g., a new to the laundry detergent category scent in Tide detergent) and 2) *new attribute expansions*, where an entirely new attribute or characteristic was added to the product (e.g., cough relief liquid added to Life Savers candy). Two types of ingredient branding strategies were examined by branding the target attribute ingredient for the brand expansion with either a new name as a *self-branded ingredient* (e.g., Tide with its own EverFresh scented bath soap) or an established, well-respected name as a *co-branded ingredient* (e.g., Tide with Irish Spring scented bath soap). The results indicated that with slot filler expansions, a co-branded ingredient facilitated initial expansion acceptance, but a self-branded ingredient led to more favorable subsequent category extension evaluations. With more dissimilar new attribute expansions, however, a co-branded ingredient led to more favorable evaluations of both the initial expansion and the subsequent category extension.

Advances in Consumer Research
Volume 28, © 2001

Role of Consumer Relationships with a Brand in Brand Extensions:
Some Exploratory Findings

Jong-Won Park, Korea University
Kyeong-Heui Kim, University of Minnesota[1]

ABSTRACT

Prior research on brand extensions has shown that an extension's success depends on the perceived quality of the original brand and the extension's similarity to its original brand. The present research attempts to extend this literature by proposing and demonstrating that consumer-brand relationships are also important for an extension's success. The general proposition is that consumers having a strong relationship with a brand might react to its extensions more positively than those lacking such a relationship, and that this effect is above and beyond the effect that the perceived quality might have on judgments about the extension. To test this possibility, a survey about five national brands and their potential extensions was conducted with a sample of 430 adult consumers. Findings from causal path analyses indicated that brand relationships directly influenced purchase intentions of the extensions regardless of the extension's similarity to the original brand. In addition, brand relationships indirectly influenced purchase intentions via affecting the perceived quality of the extension. However, this effect was pronounced only when the extensions were dissimilar rather than when similar to the original brand category. Theoretical and managerial implications of these findings are discussed.

BACKGROUND

It is now well documented in the literature that the effectiveness of a brand extension depends on at least two factors: the perceived quality of the original brand and the similarity between the extension and the original brand category. A number of empirical papers have shown that although a higher quality brand can produce a more successful extension, it is likely to be the case only when the extension is similar to the original brand (Aaker and Keller 1990; Broniarczyk and Alba 1994; Park, Milberg, and Lawson 1991). One direct implication of these findings is clear: "Do not extend to a dissimilar category." But, it is not difficult to observe successful extensions to dissimilar categories in the real world. This seemingly contradictory phenomenon can be better understood when one considers additional factors, which might contribute to the success of extensions. In this paper we show that a consumer's existing relationship with a brand plays an important role in the brand extension's success, on top of the role played by the perceived quality of the original brand.

Brand Extension Literature

A number of factors have been proposed to influence consumers' acceptance of proposed extensions, including brand characteristics, extension characteristics, strategic characteristics, and firm characteristics. Much focus has been on how extension judgments might be shaped by attitudes toward or other associations with the original brand that consumers currently hold (e.g., MacInnis and Nakamoto 1991), congruity or similarity between the extension and the original brand category (e.g., Aaker and Keller 1990; Park et al. 1991), and the interaction between these two (Aaker and Keller

---

[1]We would like to thank Professors Bob Wyer and Jin Yong Lee, and members of the Korea University B.E.S.T. Marketing Group for their helpful comments on earlier drafts of this paper, and Younghan Cho and President Han at M&C, Inc. for their assistance in data collection.

1990; Keller and Aaker 1992). Strong evidence has been found for these determinants of evaluations of extensions.

There is ample empirical evidence that strong brands benefit extensions more than weak brands. For example, Smith and Park (1992) argued that stronger brands might have a greater ability to reduce perceived risk than weaker ones and showed a positive and significant relationship between brand strength and the brand extension's market share. In addition, it has been experimentally demonstrated that the perceived quality of a parent brand is likely to be transferred to its extensions. In this experimental research, brand strength is often conceptualized in terms of consumers' attitudes or judgments of quality associated with the brand (Aaker and Keller 1990; Smith and Park 1992). Finally, the similarity between an extension and the original brand category moderates the transfer of attitude or affect. Substantial evidence has implicated category similarity in brand extension evaluations (Aaker and Keller 1990; Boush and Loken 1991; Keller and Aaker 1992).

Perhaps the most useful conceptual framework that can be used to account for these results might be the dual processing formulations of person impression formation postulated by social cognition researchers (e.g., Brewer 1988; Fiske 1982; Fiske and Pavelchak 1986). These formulations are based on the distinction between the category-based processing and the piecemeal processing (for a recent review, see Fiske, Lin and Neuberg 1998; Fiske and Neuberg 1990). Briefly, upon exposure to an evaluation object, perceivers first attempt to categorize that object on the basis of salient cues. These cues can take the form of physical characteristics, such as skin color or body shape, or a verbally transmitted categorical label such as race or gender. Upon receiving additional features or individuating information, perceivers may engage in a confirmatory categorization process to preserve the initial categorization, but this additional process is largely dependent upon the level of personal relevance of the evaluation object for the perceivers. Whether or not the initial categorization is maintained is a function of the degree of congruence between the features of the stimulus object and the features of the category prototype (e.g., Loken and Ward 1991). If the categorization is successful, the evaluation of the object is likely to be based on the affect associated with the category. If the categorization is not successful, however, subtyping or piecemeal integration of various features may serve as basis for forming an evaluation (e.g., Bodenhausen and Wyer 1985).

Similar category-based processes have been observed in the context of forming product judgments (e.g., Meyers-Levy and Tybout 1989; Rao and Monroe 1988; Sujan 1985; Sujan and Dekleva 1987). Further, it has been shown that a brand name can serve as a category label and thus lead to a category-based evaluation (e.g., Chaiken and Maheswaran 1994; Hong and Wyer 1989; Maheswaran, Mackie and Chaiken 1992). In line with these findings, the evaluations of an extension that are contingent upon its similarity to the original brand category have been conceptualized as a category-based processing phenomenon (e.g., Boush and Loken 1991; Meyers-Levy, Louie, and Curren 1994; Milberg, Park, and McCarthy 1997). That is, the level of congruity with a previously defined category (i.e., brand) is viewed as varied by the similarity between the original brand and its extension. Therefore, when a brand extension is perceived as similar to the original brand and thus, identified as belonging to the brand category, the affect

179

Advances in Consumer Research
Volume 28, © 2001

or perceived quality associated with that category is likely to be transferred to that extension.

More recently, research has shown that brand extensions can be successful even when the product-level similarity is low, if the extension possesses a concept consistent with that of the original brand or if it effectively utilizes the strong specific associations of the original brand. For example, Park et al. (1991) reported that perceptions of the extension's fit depended not only on product-level similarity, such as features or attributes, but also on the consistency of the extension with a parent brand's concept. Broniarczyk and Alba (1994) found that a brand's specific association made a greater contribution to the evaluation of brand extensions when it was "relevant" in the extension category than when it was not. Although different in more specific aspects, the above studies strongly suggest that similarity or fit between a parent brand and its extension moderates the effects of brand associations such as brand affect, brand concept, and specific features. Finally, people experiencing a positive mood might accept an incongruent extension quite well, and sometimes even better than a quite similar extension (Barone et al. 2000). However, all of these effects are likely to operate only when the extension's incongruity is relatively moderate. When it is rather extreme, an extension is doomed to failure. In this paper, however, we propose that there might be conditions under which extensions into quite dissimilar categories can be successful. Specifically, it is proposed that an extension in a dissimilar category can be successful if the parent brand has developed a strong relationship with consumers. This proposition is explained next.

Brand Relationships

Research on interpersonal relationships has attempted to identify key determinants of the stability of close relationships as well as the processes underlying them (see Bersheid and Reis 1998 for a review). One conclusion from this literature is that a relationship, once developed, tends to stabilize at a particular level of intimacy or closeness. According to the investment model of close relationships (Rusbult 1983), individuals become increasingly dependent on their relationships to the degree that (a) satisfaction level is high, (b) quality of alternatives is poor, and (c) investment size is high. As a result, they become increasingly "committed" to the relationships. Here, commitment represents long term orientations toward the relationships, including psychological attachment and intent to persist the relationship, thus including cognitive, conative, and affective components. It has been demonstrated that commitment is the critical determinant of relationship stability.

The investment model further suggests that, once a relationship reaches a satisfactory level, it is likely to be maintained at that level. Commitment reliably promotes persistence in a relationship. There is good empirical support for this in the literature (for a review, see Rusbult and Van Lange 1996). Moreover, commitment also promotes so-called pro-relationship behaviors. Specifically, commitment encourages willingness to sacrifice or tendencies to forego desired activities for the good of the relationship (Van Lange et al. 1997). Further it promotes accommodative behaviors or tendencies to accommodate rather than retaliate when a partner engages in a potentially destructive behavior. Thus, although a partner's destructive behavior may be harmful or seem unjustifiable, the person in a satisfying relationship may exhibit a high level of affect and submission, and react constructively. For example, Rusbult et al. (1991) found that students who were more satisfied with their relationships exhibited greater accommodation such as

loyalty (e.g., "I give my partner the benefit of the doubt and forget about it") than did those in less satisfying relationships.

The above commitment processes are largely motivational. However, commitment also influences cognitive processes and thus creates cognitive biases such as positive illusion or tendencies toward excessively favorable evaluations of one's partner or relationship. According to this cognitive perspective interpersonal interactions and on-going relationships result from cognitive processes around self-partner schemas. This schema has been posited and empirically proven to often guide the individual's behavior in social interactions and in the development and *maintenance* of relationships (e.g., Baldwin 1992; Bersheid and Reis 1998; Bradbury and Fincham 1990). Specifically, schemas about the self-partner relationship (also called "relational schema") often lead to top-down processes in new instances, thus creating interpretation biases, as well as attributions that cast the partner's behavior in a positive or negative light depending on the quality of the relationship. For example, Murray, Holmes, and Griffin (1996) have shown that individuals' impressions of their partners were more a mirror of their self-images and ideals than a reflection of their partners' self-reported attributes. These impressions were more positive than their partners' self-reports, reflecting positive illusion.

Do consumers engage in a relationship with a brand as they do with a person? Further, will they exhibit the sort of commitment processes described above? An affirmative answer is available in the recent research by Fournier (1994, 1998). In this research, she has documented compelling evidence for the existence of consumer-brand relationships and further proposed a relationship quality framework in consumer-brand contexts. According to the framework, consumer and brand actions determine the brand relationship quality. This relationship quality is then assumed to be associated with the intermediate process of developing and maintaining the relationship as well as with ultimate consequences such as relationship stability and satisfaction.

This consumer-brand relationship perspective along with the research on interpersonal relationships discussed above seems to provide an implication for brand extensions. That is, an extension into a dissimilar category may be viewed as a brand's "deviant" behavior and perhaps as an unjustifiable act. However, if consumers have established good relationships with the original brand and thus feel strongly committed to their relationships, they might exhibit pro-relationship behaviors to a great extent. For example, they may interpret the dissimilar extension in light of the existing relationship schema, which is positive in nature (e.g., perceiving the extension as an "adventurous" rather than as a "reckless" act; c.f., Higgins, Rholes, and Jones 1977). Or they may see the possibility of its success rather than its failure via positive illusion processes. These processes are likely to lead to a more favorable perception of the extension's quality, which in turn would increase the purchase intention of the extension. In addition, consumers in a good relationship with the original brand may just accommodate the dissimilar extension as it is or at least, be willing to try it. As a consequence, their purchase intension for the extension might increase, while their perceptions of the extension's quality being unaffected.

In sum, it was expected that brand relationships might play an important role in brand extensions that is above and beyond the role by original brand quality. Specifically, independent of the original brand quality, the brand relationship quality might influence purchase intentions of brand extensions through first affecting perceived quality of the extensions. In addition, the brand relationships might directly influence the purchase intensions.

TABLE 1
Extension Product Categories

Brand	Original category	Similar extension	Dissimilar extension
Pulmuone (brand concept: healthy food)	Grocery food	Ready-to-eat healthy lunch	Fitness center
Ace (brand concept: scientifically designed and good for health)	Bed-set	Sofa	Kitchen sink
Anycall (brand concept: electric sound technology)	Cellular phone	Audio response system	Printer
Birak (brand concept: smooth taste)	Canned juice	Canned tea	Tea cup set
Hite (brand concept: good taste)	Beer	Wine	Water purifier

METHOD

Focal Brand and Extension Categories

Characteristics of focal brand. A total of five brands were used as the focal brands for extensions in the present study. All five were national brands in Korea and currently the market leaders in their product categories. Specifically, they consisted of one grocery food brand (*Pulmuone*), one bed-set brand (*Ace*), one cellular phone brand (*Anycall*), one nonalcoholic drink brand (*Birak*), and one beer brand (*Hite*). This choice was made based on two considerations: (1) they must represent diverse product categories including both durable and non-durable products and (2) must be well known to consumers.

Two potential extension categories. For each focal brand, two product categories were chosen as potential extension categories. This choice was made to create two different levels of similarity (similar vs. dissimilar) between the original brand and the extensions. That is, one of them was quite similar to the original brand and the other was dissimilar in terms of the key brand concept and/ or the product class type. For example, the extension categories considered for the grocery food brand (*Pulmuone*) were related to the key concept of the original brand, healthfulness ("ready-to-eat a healthy lunch" and "fitness center"). However, the first one pertained to the same food category, whereas the other pertained to a totally different category. In this sense, the first extension was considered to be similar to the original brand, but the second was not. Table 1 shows two extension categories for each focal brand in the descending order of similarity.

Subjects

A total sample of 430 adults living in Seoul, the capital of South Korea, participated in the survey. A quota sampling procedure was used with consideration of the age and sex distributions of the sampling population. The sample's ages ranged from 20 to 54 years old. Among them, 50.1% were females.

Survey Procedure

The survey was administered by a professional survey organization. The data were collected through face-to-face interviews along with a structured questionnaire. All interviewers were female and well experienced. About an hour long orientation was given to these interviewers regarding the purpose of the survey and the contents of the questionnaire prior to the survey. The data were collected over approximately a two-week period of time.

Measures

The original survey administered has diverse objectives and covers more issues than those relevant for the present paper. Below, we describe only the relevant measures, which consist of two parts. The first part examines the respondents' judgments about the focal brands per se, and the second part examines judgments about the extensions of these brands.

Assessment of focal brands. First, cognitive evaluations of the focal brands were measured. Two 7-point semantic differential scales were used: ('1'- poor quality, '7'- good quality) and ('1'- bad product, '7'- good product). These scales are most frequently employed in the previous brand extension research to measure the strength or quality of the original brand (Aaker and Keller 1990; Smith and Park 1992). Since the two scale items were highly correlated, they were averaged into a composite quality index of the original brand for later analyses (hereafter, BQ, Cronbach a=.86). Second, the nature of respondents' relationships with each brand was measured along various dimensions. Respondents were first instructed to indicate the degree to which they agreed or disagreed on several statements along 7-point scale ('1'- absolutely disagree, '7'- absolutely agree). Then, four statements tapping various aspects of consumer-brand relationships were presented. These were: "This brand and I have very similar personalities," "I strongly prefer this brand to others in this product category," "I know a lot about this brand," and "I have been committed to this brand and will continue to be so in future." These statements were thought to reflect brand-self concept association, satisfaction, brand knowledge, and commitment, respectively (c.f., Fournier 1998). These were followed by two items measuring consumer feelings of psychological attachment to the brand. Respondents were asked to indicate how they would feel if they encountered the brand on two 7-point scales: ('1'- very displeased, '7'- very pleased) and ('1'- feel bad, '7'- feel good). Although much

TABLE 2

Mean Judgments about Brand Extensions As a Function of Similarity

Focal brand	(1) Purchase Intention			(2) Perceived Quality		
	Similar extension		Dissimilar extension	Similar extension		Dissimilar extension
Pulmuone	4.78	>>*	4.02	4.87	>>	4.24
Ace	4.54	>>	4.21	4.78	>>	4.26
Anycall	4.31	>	4.09	4.88	>>	4.46
Birak	4.22	>>	3.64	4.53	>>	3.96
Hite	4.21	>	3.94	4.49	>>	4.14

Note. '>' and '>>' mean a statistically significant difference at p=.05 and p=.01, respectively.

simpler, these measures altogether correspond well to recent conceptualizations and measures of brand relationship quality (Fournier 1994, 1998). Since all six items above were highly correlated, they were averaged into a composite brand relationship quality index for later analyses (hereafter, RQ, Cronbach a=.88).

Assessment of brand extensions. The second part of the measures concerned the effectiveness of brand extensions. In general, a very lengthy questionnaire might cause respondents to be fatigued and bored, which potentially can result in response bias. To minimize this problem, respondents were asked to assess brand extensions of only two (out of five) focal brands. One of them was the grocery food brand (*Pulmuone*) for all respondents. The other was one of the remaining four focal brands and was counterbalanced across respondents. Thus, the number of respondents for each of the four focal brands was approximately the same (i.e., a quarter of the sample each).

Effectiveness of brand extensions was assessed in terms of purchase intention and perceived quality. Respondents were first instructed to assume that they were about to make a purchase decision in a given product category. Then, they were provided with an extension and asked to indicate the likelihood that they would seriously consider the extension if it was available in the market ('1'- very unlikely, '7'- very likely). This purchase intention will be denoted by PI, hereafter. Next was the assessment of their perceived quality of that extension. Respondents indicated their judgments about the extension on two 7-point scales: ('1'- poor quality, '7'- good quality) and ('1'- bad product, '7'- good product). These two items were highly correlated, thus were averaged into a composite quality index for later analyses (hereafter, QUAL, Cronbach a=.88).

To control possible order effects in administering these items, four different question orders were created by counterbalancing the order of two focal brands and the order of two extensions (similar vs. dissimilar) within each focal brand. That is, half of the respondents answered the questions for extensions of the grocery brand, *Pulmuone* first, whereas the other half answered the questions for the other focal brand first. Crossed with this counterbalancing, half of the respondents answered the questions for the similar extension first, whereas the other half answered questions for the dissimilar extension first.

RESULTS

Effects of Similarity

We first compared purchase intentions and perceived quality of brand extensions as a function of similarity between the original

brand and the proposed extensions. Consistent with the previous research, we expected that judgments about extensions would be more favorable when the extensions were similar than when they were dissimilar to the original brand. This in fact was the case. As shown in Table 2, in all five focal brand cases both purchase intentions and perceived quality of extensions were consistently more favorable in the similar extension than in the dissimilar extension conditions. This tendency also appeared to be relatively stronger on perceived quality than on purchase intentions.

Effects of Perceived Brand Quality (BQ) and Brand Relationship Quality (RQ)

Causal path analyses. It was expected that brand relationships might play an important role in brand extensions on top of the role played by original brand quality. Specifically, independent of the original brand quality (BQ), the brand relationship quality (RQ) was expected to influence purchase intentions of brand extensions (PI) through first affecting perceived quality of the extensions (QUAL). In addition, the brand relationships might directly influence the purchase intentions. However, the magnitude of direct and indirect effects was likely to depend on the degree of similarity of the extensions to the original brand. To investigate these possibilities the following causal path model was developed and tested.

In the path model tested, BQ was hypothesized to influence QUAL, which in turn would influence PI. That is, BQ was expected to have only indirect effects on PI. By contrast, RQ was hypothesized to have both direct effects (RQ -> PI) and indirect (RQ -> QUAL -> PI). Figure 1 shows these hypothetical paths between the constructs in the model.

The validity of this model was assessed using LISREL 8 (Jöreskog and Sörbom 1993) in each of similarity (similar vs. dissimilar extensions) by focal brand (grocery food brand/four focal brands combined) combinations. Four conventional model-fit indicators were used: the chi-square statistics, the goodness-of-fit index (GFI), the root mean square residual (RMR), and normed fit index (NFI). In addition, a beta coefficient was estimated for each path in the model.

Results. Reports of results from these analyses will be organized as following. Note that all respondents judged the extensions of the grocery food brand (*Pulmuone*) and the extensions of only one of the remaining four focal brands. We first analyzed judgments (PI and QUAL) about the extensions of the grocery food brand. Some important results were obtained (they will be reported below). We then analyzed PI and QUAL of each of the remaining four focal brands' extensions separately to see if

FIGURE 1
Results from Path Analyses as a Function of Similarity

(1) Similar Extension

1) Grocery food brand

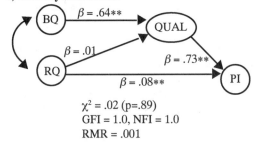

$\chi^2 = .02$ (p=.89)
GFI = 1.0, NFI = 1.0
RMR = .001

2) Four focal brands combined

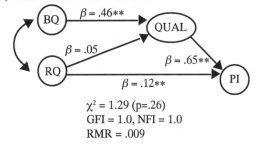

$\chi^2 = 1.29$ (p=.26)
GFI = 1.0, NFI = 1.0
RMR = .009

(2) Dissimilar Extension

1) Grocery food brand

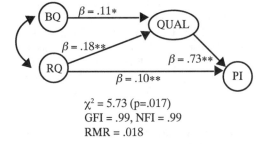

$\chi^2 = 5.73$ (p=.017)
GFI = .99, NFI = .99
RMR = .018

2) Four focal brands combined

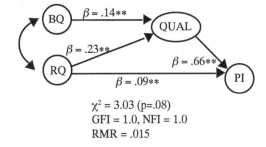

$\chi^2 = 3.03$ (p=.08)
GFI = 1.0, NFI = 1.0
RMR = .015

Note. *p<.10, **p<.05, BQ: Original brand quality, RQ: brand relationship quality, PI: Purchase intention of extensions, QUAL: Perceived quality of extensions.

the results from the grocery food data were replicated. That was in fact the case. Since the separate analyses produced virtually the similar pattern of results regardless of which of the four brands was concerned, we combined the data across the four brands for final analyses in order to increase the sample size and the power of analyses, and thus present those results only.

In terms of overall validity of the path model, it was apparent that the model fit the data pretty well in all four cases (see Figure 1). GFI, NFI, and RMR indices indicated an almost perfect fit of the model regardless of similarity levels and regardless of which focal brand was concerned. χ^2 statistics supported the model in three out of the four cases. Even for the one unsupported case (in the case of the dissimilar extension of the grocery food brand), the absolute χ^2 value was quite small. In sum, the causal path model well accounted for the data, suggesting that brand relationships significantly influenced judgments about the extensions independently of the original brand quality.

Next, beta coefficients for causal paths strongly suggested that BQ and RQ had different roles in brand extensions, depending on the similarity level. Specifically, effects of BQ on QUAL were consistently greater in the similar extension conditions (β=.64 and .46, in the grocery food brand and in the other brand cases, respectively) than in the dissimilar extension conditions (β=.11 and .14). This is consistent with the past findings that the affect or evaluation associated with the parent brand is transferred to the extension only when it is similar to the parent brand category. Different results emerged for the effect of RQ. Specifically, RQ had virtually no effect on QUAL in the similar extension condi-

tions (β=.01 and .05, in the grocery food brand and in the other brand cases, respectively), but exerted a significant influence on QUAL in the dissimilar extension conditions (β=.18 and .24). Finally, RQ had a significant direct effect on PI in both similar and dissimilar extension conditions. This was true regardless of which focal brand was concerned.

DISCUSSION

The brand extension literature has emphasized the strength of the original brand and the similarity between the original brand and the extensions. Thus, a brand extension is expected to be potentially successful only when consumers perceive the original brand as strong in quality as well as the extension as similar to the original brand. On the other hand, the relationship literature suggests that a strong brand relationship may help overcome the obstacles that otherwise, dissimilar extensions might face. This possibility was supported in the present study.

Overall, the brand relationship quality significantly influenced judgments about the extensions and particularly the purchase intentions, even after the effects due to the original brand quality were controlled. This effect was obtained both in the grocery food brand case and in the four other (combined) cases. Specifically, the brand relationship had direct effects on purchase intentions about the extensions regardless of whether the extensions were similar or dissimilar to the original brands. In addition, the relationship further influenced purchase intentions via affecting the perceived quality of the extensions when the extensions were dissimilar.

It is intriguing that as the extensions became dissimilar, the effect of the relationship quality on perceptions of extension quality increased, whereas the effect of the original brand quality decreased. Parallel with the previous findings (e.g., Aaker and Keller 1990), this research demonstrated that the effect of original brand quality on evaluations of the extension was limited to the situation in which there was congruence between the extension and the original brand category. The effect was very strong in similar extension conditions, but negligible in dissimilar conditions. On the other hand, the effect of the relationship quality on evaluations was not pronounced in the former conditions, but was significant in the latter. One possibility is that consumers might be motivated to bolster the efficacy of their partner's act (i.e., the brand extension), but do so only when they feel it is necessary (i.e., when the extension is dissimilar). In such case, the extent to which the bolstering occurs is likely to be a function of the strength of the relationship quality. Another possibility is that cognitive biases such as positive illusion, thus more favorable evaluations of extensions are subject to the ambiguity of the target object (e.g., Herr, Sherman, and Fazio 1983, Stapel, Koomen, and Van D. Plight 1997). Thus, when the implication of an extension is clear (e.g., when it is very similar to the original brand), there might be no room for consumers' relationship schema to operate in determining the extension's quality.

This research makes a contribution to the current literature. On one hand, it increases our understanding of the brand extension phenomenon by providing an explanation about how dissimilar extensions might be successful. On the other hand, it contributes to the brand relationship research in that this study provides a concrete evidence for the importance of brand relationships. A managerial implication of this seems straightforward. Brand managers are better off when they manage their brands from the perspective of relationships with consumers, not just based on consumers' cognitive evaluations of the brands.

Several limitations of the present study should be noted for future research directions. First, our measures of brand relationships are rather crude. Future research needs to investigate if the results obtained here will be replicated when a more refined measurement scheme is employed for the consumer-brand relationship construct. In this regard, Fournier's (1994) measurement scheme seems to be a good starting point. Second, the explanations we provided concerning the pattern of the relationship quality effects observed in this study are rather speculative in nature. More precise mechanisms need to be outlined and put on empirical tests. Finally, the present research did not address how to develop and strengthen a relationship with brand. Undoubtedly, future research addressing these issues would be of great importance.

REFERENCES

Aaker, David A. and Kevin Lane Keller (1990), "Consumer Evaluations of Brand Extensions", *Journal of Marketing*, 54 (January), 27-41.

Baldwin, Mark W. (1992), "Relational Schemas and the Processing of Social Information," *Psychological Bulletin*, 112 (3), 461-484.

Barone, Michael J., Paul W. Miniard, and Jean B. Romeo (2000), "The Influence of Positive Mood on Brand Extension Evaluations," *Journal of Consumer Research*, 26 (March), 386-400.

Bersheid, Ellen (1985), "Interpersonal Attraction," In *Handbook of Social Psychology*, 3rd, ed. G. Lindzey and E. Aronson, New York: Random House, 413-484.

_____ (1994), "Interpersonal Relationships," *Annual Review of Psychology*, 45, 79-129.

_____ and Harry T. Reis (1998), "Attraction and Close Relationships," in *The Handbook of Social Psychology*, 4ed, ed. Daniel T. Gilbert, Susan T. Fiske, and Gardner Lindzey, Boston, MA: The McGraw-Hill Companies, Inc., 193-281.

Bodenhausen, Galen and Robert S. Wyer (1985), "Effects of Stereotypes in Decision and Information-Processing Strategies," *Journal of Personality and Social Psychology*, 48 (2), 267-282.

Boush, David M. and Barbara Loken (1991), "A Process-Tracing Study of Brand Extension Evaluation," *Journal of Marketing Research*, 28 (February), 16-28.

Bradbury, Thomas N. and Frank D. Fincham (1990), "Attributions in Marriage: Review and Critique," *Psychological Bulletin*, 107 (1), 3-33.

Brewer, Marilyn (1988), "A Dual Process Model of Impression Formation," in *Advances in Social Cognition, Volume I: A Dual-Process Model of Impression Formation*, ed. Thomas K. Srull and Robert S. Wyer, Hillsdale, NJ: Lawrence Erlabum.

Broniarczyk, Susan M. and Joseph W. Alba (1994), "The Importance of the Brand in Brand Extension," *Journal of Marketing Research*, 31 (May), 214-228.

Chaiken, Shelly and Durairaj Maheswaran (1994), "Heuristic Processing Can Bias Systematic Processing: Effects of Source Credibility, Argument Ambiguity, and Task Importance in Attribute Judgment," *Journal of Personality and Social Psychology*, 66 (3), 460-473.

Fiske, Susan T. (1982), "Schema-Triggered Affect: Applications to Social Perception," in *Affect and Cognition: The 17th Annual Carnegie Symposium on Cognition*, ed. M. S. Clark and S. T. Fiske, Hillsdale, NJ:Erlbaum, 55-78.

_____ and Steven L. Neuberg (1990), "A Continuum of Impression formation, from Category-Based to Individuating Processes: Influences of Information and Motivation on Attention and Interpretation," in *Advances in Experimental Social Psychology*, Vol. 23, ed. M. P. Zanna, 1-74.

_____, Monica Lin, and Steven L. Neuberg (1999), "The Continuum Model: Ten Years Later," in *Dual-Process Theories in Social Psychology*, ed. Shelly Chaiken and Yaacov Trope, New York, NY: The Guilford Press, 231-254.

_____ and Mark A. Pavelchak (1986), "Category-based versus Piecemeal-based Affective Responses: Developments in Schema-triggered Affect," in *Handbook of Motivation and Cognition: Foundations of Social Behavior*, ed. Richard M. Sorrentino, Edward Tory Higgins, et al., New York, NY: Guilford Press, 167-203.

Fournier, Susan (1994), A Consumer-Brand Relationship Framework for Strategic Brand Management, unpublished doctoral dissertation, University of Florida.

_____ (1998), "Consumers and Their Brands: Developing Relationship Theory in Consumer Research," *Journal of Consumer Research*, 34 (March), 343-373.

Higgins, E. Torry, William S. Rholes, and Carl R. Jones (1977), "Category Accessibility and Impression Formation," *Journal of Experimental Social Psychology*, 13 (March), 141-154.

Herr, Paul M., Steven J. Sherman, and Russell H. Fazio (1983), "On the Consequences of Priming: Assimilation and Contrast Effects," *Journal of Experimental Social Psychology*, 19 (July), 323-340.

Hong, Sung-Tai and Robert S. Wyer (1989), "Effects of Country-of-Origin and Product-Attribute Information on Product Evaluation: An Information Processing Perspective," *Journal of Consumer Research*, 16 (September), 175-187.

Jöreskog Karl G. and Dag Sörbom (1993), *Structural Equation Modeling with the SIMPLIS Command Language*, Hillsdale, NJ:Erlbaum

Keller, Kevin Lane and David A. Aaker (1992), "The Effects of Sequential Introduction of Brand Extensions," *Journal of Marketing Research*, 29 (February), 35-50.

Loken, Barbara and James Ward (1990), "Alternative Approaches to Understanding the Determinants of Typicality," *Journal of Consumer Research*, 17 (September), 111-126.

Maheswaran, Durairaj, Dianne M Mackie, and Shelly Chaiken (1992), "Brand Name as a Heuristic Cue: The Effects of Task Importance and Expectancy Confirmation on Consumer Judgments," *Journal of Consumer Psychology*, 1 (4), 317-336.

Meyers-Levy, Joan and Alice M. Tybout (1989), "Schema Congruity as a Basis for Product Evaluation," *Journal of Consumer Research*, 16 (June), 39-54.

_____, Therese A. Louie, and Mary T. Curren (1994), "How Does the Congruity of Brand Names Affect Evaluations of Brand Name Extensions?" *Journal of Applied Psychology*, 79 (February), 46-53.

Milberg, Sandra J, C. Whan Park, and Michael S. McCarthy (1997), "Managing Negative Feedback Effects Associated with Brand Extensions: The Impact of Alternative Branding Strategies," *Journal of Consumer Psychology*, 6 (2), 119-140.

Murray, Sandra L., John G. Holmes, and Dale W. Griffin (1996), "The Benefits of Positive Illusions: Idealization and the Construction of Satisfaction in Close Relationships," *Journal of Personality and Social Psychology*, 70 (1), 79-98.

Park, C. Whan, Sandra Milberg, and Robert Lawson (1991), "Evaluation of Brand Extensions: The Role of Product Feature similarity and Brand Concept Consistency," *Journal of Consumer Research*, 18 (September), 185-193.

Peracchio, Laura A. and Alice M. Tybout (1996), "The Moderating Role of Prior Knowledge in Schema-Based Product Evaluation," *Journal of Consumer Research*, 23 (December), 177-192.

Rao, Akshay and Kent B. Monroe (1988), "The Moderating Effect of Prior Knowledge on Cue Utilization in Product Evaluations," *Journal of Consumer Research*, 15 (September), 253-264.

Rusbult, Caryl E. (1983), "A Longitudinal Test of the Investment Model: The Development and Deterioration of Satisfaction and Commitment in Heterosexual Involvement," *Journal of Personality and Social Psychology*, 45, 101-117.

_____, D. J. Johnson, and G. D. Morrow (1986), "Impact of Couple of Patterns of Problem Solving on Distress and Nondistress in Dating Relationships," *Journal of Personality and Social Psychology*, 50, 744-753.

_____ and P. A. M. Van Lange (1996), "Interdependence Processes," in *Social Psychology: Handbook of Basic Principles*, ed. E. Torry Higgins and Arie Kruglanski, New York: Guilford, 564-596.

_____, Julie Verette, Gregory A. Whitney, Linda F. Slovik, and Isaac Lipkus (1991), "Accommodation Processes in Close Relationships: Theory and Preliminary Empirical Evidence," *Journal of Personality and Social Psychology*, 60 (1), 53-78.

Smith, Daniel C. and C. Whan Park (1992), "The Effects of Brand Extensions on Market Share and Advertising Efficiency," *Journal of Marketing Research*, 29 (August), 296-313.

Stapel, Diederik A., Willem Koomen, and Joop Van Der Plight (1997), "Categories of Category Accessibility: The Impact of Trait Concept versus Exemplar Priming on Person Judgments," *Journal of Experimental Social Psychology*, 33, 47-76.

Sujan, Mita (1985), "Consumer Knowledge: Effect on Evaluation Processes Mediating Consumer Judgments," *Journal of Consumer Research*, 12 (June), 31-46.

_____ and Christine Dekleva (1987), "Product Categorization and Inference Making: Some Implications for Comparative Advertising," *Journal of Consumer Research*, 14 (December), 372-378.

Van Lange, P. A. M., Caryl E. Rusbult, S. M. Drigotas, X. B., Arriaga, B. S., Witcher, and C. L. Cox (1997), "Willingness to Sacrifice in Close Relationships," *Journal of Personality and Social Psychology*, 72, 1373-1395.

Wieselquist, Jennifer, Caryl E. Rusbult, Craig A. Foster, and Christopher R. Agnew (1999), "Commitment, Pro-Relationship Behavior, and Trust in Close Relationships," *Journal of Personality and Social Psychology*, 77 (5), 942-966.

The Effects of Strengthening Category-Brand Associations on Consideration Set Composition and Purchase Intent in Memory-Based Choice

Steven S. Posavac, University of Rochester
David M. Sanbonmatsu, University of Utah
Maria L. Cronley, University of Cincinnati
Frank R. Kardes, University of Cincinnati

ABSTRACT

An experiment was conducted to explore the effects of strengthening the association between particular brands and a superordinate choice category on the likelihood of those brands being included in the consideration set, and chosen in a memory-based choice context. Results showed that a brand was more likely to be present in the consideration set, and indicated as an intended choice, if the association between the brand and the choice category was strengthened vs. not strengthened. Attitudinal data suggest that the positive effects of a brand being strongly associated with the choice category operate independently of attitude toward the brand.

INTRODUCTION

In recent years researchers have become increasingly interested in the processes by which choice options come to receive consideration, and the consequences of consideration effects in decision-making. Some researchers have developed models of the consideration process itself (Ratneshwar and Shocker 1991; Kardes, Kalyanaram, Chandrashekaren and Dornoff 1993; Payne, Bettman and Johnson 1993). Kardes et al., for example, reported the advantages enjoyed by a pioneering brand as the universal set (all brands that may satisfy a consumer need), is pared to the retrieval set (the set of brands a consumer is aware of at the time of decision making), which in turn is pared to the consideration set (set of brands that receive careful consideration prior to choice), and ultimately to choice. Other research has focused on determinants of the composition of the retrieval set (Posavac, Sanbonmatsu and Fazio, 1997) and the consideration set (Lehman and Pan 1994; Shapiro, MacInnis and Heckler 1997). Implicitly, most decision making research in marketing and psychology concerns how individuals make decisions from a consideration set. That is, research on attitudes and persuasion, multiattribute studies, and so on, typically explore the determinants of choice from a specified set of alternatives.

The importance of each stage of the consideration process may depend on the level of specification of alternatives in the decision context (Nedungadi 1990). In stimulus-based choice, alternatives are specified in the decision context. For example, the decision of which soft drink to purchase at the grocery store is a stimulus-based choice because all of the options are clearly displayed on the grocer's shelves. Memory-based choice contexts, in contrast, do not contain specified alternatives. Trying to decide on a restaurant after having started the car is a memory-based choice because the recognition that one is hungry suggests only that a restaurant should be sought, but does not specify which alternatives should be considered.

The selection of a particular brand of soft drink, and other stimulus-based consumer choices in which alternatives are highly salient in context, requires the assessment of the options that are present and the choice of a preferred brand. Choosing a restaurant for lunch, and other memory-based decisions, requires the additional step of generating alternatives from memory prior to assessment of the alternatives, and subsequent choice. Figure 1 presents the essential difference between choice contexts that contain vs. do not contain specified alternatives. In memory-based choice, alternatives must be generated from memory prior to the assessment of alternatives and decision making.

When alternatives are not specified in the choice context the likelihood of a particular brand being chosen has been shown to depend on how strongly associated the brand is with the superordinate choice category (Posavac et al. 1997). To the extent that a brand is strongly associated with the choice category, it is likely to be generated upon consideration of the category, and to be present in consumers' consideration sets. Of course, in memory-based choice only those options that are recalled from memory and identified as options may ultimately be chosen. In stimulus-based choice the category-brand association is less relevant because options are present at the time of decision-making, and accordingly do not need to be generated from memory.

Although prior research has shown that brands strongly associated with the choice category are at an advantage in memory-based choice, this research is correlational, and to date no studies have explored the utility of manipulating the category-brand association in the promotion of particular brands. That is, prior research has related measured associative strength to decision making, but has not manipulated the associative strength of the category-brand association for particular brands. In this study we sought to provide direct evidence that manipulating associative strength may influence consumers' decision making. More specifically, we explored the possibility that strengthening the association between brands and the choice category would increase the likelihood of those brands being included in the consideration set, and ultimately being chosen, when decision making is memory based.

The effects of manipulating the strength of brand-category associations on choice may operate independently of attitudes toward the brand. Prior research has established reliable choice effects that result from differential likelihood of competing brands being considered prior to choice (Nedungadi 1990). In the present research, we expected that a brand would be at an advantage to the extent that it was manipulated to be strongly associated with the category, but that such a manipulation would not have consequences for attitudes.

Overview of the Research

An experiment was conducted to explore the potential of strengthening the association between particular brands and the choice category on the likelihood that those brands would be present in consumers' consideration sets, and ultimately chosen. The experiment took place in two sessions, which were separated by a week. In the first experimental session participants engaged in a rehearsal task that strengthened the association between some (rehearsal group), but not other (control group), alternatives and the superordinate choice category to which the alternatives belonged. In the second session participants were asked to indicate choice intentions. They were also asked to report the other options that they seriously considered prior to indicating their choice

FIGURE 1
Tasks Requisite to Choice in Stimulus-Based and Memory-Based Decision Contexts

intentions (i.e., options in their consideration sets in addition to their choice). Choices were always completely memory-based. Specifically, participants indicated their choice intentions, as well as the other alternatives in their consideration sets, on a blank sheet of paper that did not contain the names of any choice options.

We predicted that alternatives that were manipulated to be strongly associated with the choice category (i.e., alternatives in the rehearsal group) would be more likely to be generated from memory than alternatives not rehearsed (i.e., those in the control group). Accordingly, we anticipated that rehearsal group alternatives would be more likely than control group alternatives to be present in participants' consideration sets. Moreover, we also expected that alternatives in the rehearsal group would be more likely to be chosen than options in the control group. This reasoning suggests the following two hypotheses;

H1: Rehearsal group brands will be more likely than control group brands to be present in participants' consideration sets.

H2: Rehearsal group brands will be more likely to be chosen than control group brands.

Consistent with reasoning delineated in Nedungadi (1990), Kardes et al. (1993), and Posavac et al. (1997) we expected that these consideration processes would operate independently of attitudes. Accordingly, we predicted that the rehearsal task would not influence attitudes towards the alternatives.

H3: The rehearsal manipulation will not affect attitudes. That is, average attitude toward rehearsal brands will not be different than average attitude toward brands in the control group.

METHOD

Participants

106 university students participated in the experiment in exchange for extra course credit. Students participated individually.

Procedure

First experimental session. Participants recruited for an experiment described as an investigation of cognitive skills were asked to perform several cognitive tasks. After engaging in several distractor activities, participants engaged in a categorization task designed to strengthen the association between some brands and the superordinate choice category to which they belonged (see Posavac et al. 1997 for a similar procedure). Participants were

given a list of objects that each belonged to one of four categories, and were asked to place a letter next to each object according to its category membership. For example, participants were instructed to place an "s" next to each object on the list that was a brand of athletic shoe. In an earlier pilot study we identified well-known examples of local Chinese restaurants, local auto service shops that provided oil changes, local pizza restaurants that delivered, as well as shoe brands. Equal numbers of exemplars within each category were randomly assigned to either Group A or Group B. Participants were randomly assigned to rehearse the category membership of exemplars belonging to either Group A or B. Thus, each participant rehearsed the category membership of half of the alternatives within each category. Exemplars appeared six times on the lists. After completing the rehearsal task, participants scheduled a second experimental session and were excused.

Second experimental session. Upon arrival to the second experimental session, participants completed three distractor tasks that supported the cover story. The purpose of the second session was to measure participants' choice intentions, as well as the composition of their consideration sets. Participants were asked to assume that they were going to make a purchase within each of several categories, and to indicate which brand or store they would choose. They were then asked to list up to two additional brands or stores that they seriously considered prior to stating their choice intent. Participants recorded their choice intentions and other consideration set items on a blank sheet that did not list the names of any choice options. To evaluate H3 without bias, participants were randomly assigned to state a choice intention and indicate their consideration sets for only two out of the four categories that were included in the rehearsal task. H3 explored the potential of the rehearsal task to influence attitudes, and we were concerned that making a choice from a category might influence subsequently measured attitudes. Accordingly, by not having participants state choice intent and consideration set composition for two categories, the attitudes stated toward items within these categories would be uncontaminated by the choice task. Participants were asked to state choice intentions and other considered options for eight distractor categories in addition to the two choice categories of interest. The two relevant choice categories were randomly chosen from the four categories in the rehearsal task, as was the order of the choices.

After the choice intent and consideration set measures, participants' attitudes towards all of the exemplars of each of the categories were measured. The order of exemplars on the attitude rating sheets was random, and accordingly Group A and Group B items were interspersed. The order of presentation of the catego-

TABLE 1
Consideration Set Composition and Choice Incidence as a Function of Rehearsal Condition

	rehearsal group	control group
consideration set	130	97
choice	108	81

Note: The consideration set data here excludes the chosen brands.

TABLE 2
Average Attitude Toward Exemplars of Each Choice Category as a Function of Rehearsal Condition

	rehearsal group	control group
pizza delivery services	5.3	5.4
Chinese restaurants	5.3	5.5
oil change shops	3.8	4.1
shoe brands	5.3	5.7

Note: Lower numbers indicate greater positivity of average attitudes.

ries was also randomized. Participants were asked to rank order their attitudes toward the exemplars belonging to each category.

Following completion of the choice intention and consideration set questionnaire, participants were given extra credit, debriefed, and excused.

RESULTS

Table 1 presents consideration set and choice data. Because there were 106 participants, and choices were made from two categories, there were 212 possible choices. In addition to the choice from each category, participants were asked to list up to 2 additional options that were seriously considered but not chosen. Accordingly, in sum participants could have listed 424 options that were present in the consideration set but not chosen. In some cases participants did not make any choices from a category (e.g., "I change my own oil, so I wouldn't go to any shop"), or failed to list 2 options that were considered but not chosen. As a result, in total there were 189 choices made, and 227 consideration set options listed (excluding the chosen option).

H1 was evaluated by comparing the number of options in the consideration set from the rehearsal group with the number of options in the consideration set from the control group. The first analysis considered options that were present in the consideration set, but were not chosen. H1 was supported as there were more items in participants' consideration sets from the rehearsal group than from the control group, $\chi^2(1) = 4.797, p < .03$. Consistent with this result, when the data for the complete consideration set were analyzed (i.e., the complete consideration set includes choices and unchosen items that received consideration), more items from the rehearsal group were present than from the control group, $\chi^2(1) = 8.654, p < .003$.

H2 was evaluated by comparing the number of choices from the rehearsal group with the number of choices from the control group. The data show that options from the rehearsal group were more likely to be chosen than options from the control group, $\chi^2(1) = 3.857, p < .05$. Accordingly, rehearsing the association between a particular brand and the relevant superordinate choice category increased the likelihood that the brand would be chosen.

H3 would be supported by a finding of no difference in average attitude as a function of whether the category membership of exemplars was rehearsed vs. not rehearsed (see Table 2). To test H3 we computed within-subject t-tests comparing average attitude toward exemplars in the rehearsal vs. control group. Because we were concerned that stating a choice intention from a category might influence subsequently measured attitudes, these tests only included data for the two categories from which a participant did not make a choice. There was no evidence that the rehearsal task influenced attitudes as p values for each of the four product categories were all $\geq .2$.

DISCUSSION

The results of the experiment clearly show that manipulating the strength of association between brands and the choice category can have significant effects on subsequent memory-based consumer decision making. An alternative was much more likely to be present in consumers' consideration sets if its category membership was rehearsed. Brands with experimentally strengthened associations to the choice category were also more likely to be chosen than control brands. This second finding is perhaps unsurprising given the first. In memory based choice, in which alternatives must be generated from memory prior to decision making, a brand cannot be chosen unless it is first identified as an alternative and included in the consideration set.

Consistent with earlier research, this study demonstrates that consideration effects in consumer decision making may operate independent of attitudes (cf. Nedungadi 1990). In this experiment, rehearsal of an alternative increased the probability that the alternative would be present in the consideration set and chosen, but not did influence attitudes.

The finding that rehearsal did not influence attitudes is important because it rules out a mere exposure account of the results. Research has shown that in some cases simply being exposed to stimuli increases individuals' liking of the stimuli. If attitudes toward rehearsal set options were more favorable than attitudes toward control set options, one could argue that rehearsal led to attitude change, which in turn was reflected in decision making. The data, however, demonstrate that rehearsal did not influence liking of the choice options. Accordingly, it is implausible that mere exposure drove the findings.

This experiment, in conjunction with prior work (e.g., Kardes, et al. 1993; Nedungadi 1990; Posavac et al. 1997), demonstrates the importance of considering what is considered in consumer choice. Until recently, researchers in marketing and psychology generally explored decisions from constrained sets to the exclusion of contexts in which options must be generated from memory prior to choice. This research clearly demonstrates that manipulating a determinant of the likelihood that a brand will receive consideration (i.e., the strength of the brand-category association) may also influence the choice that is made when alternatives are not specified in context.

The managerial implications of this study are relatively straightforward. In line with prior research, we suggest that marketers should consider whether the brand being promoted belongs to a category relevant to decision contexts that contain vs. do not contain specified alternatives. In either case it is important to develop and maintain strong positive attitudes towards the target brand. If the brand to be promoted is typically chosen or not chosen in a memory-based context, an important second goal of promotion should be to develop and maintain a strong association between the brand and the relevant superordinate category. To the extent that the association is strong, the target brand is likely to be generated from memory upon consideration of the category, and accordingly will be eligible to be ultimately chosen.

Given the competitive advantage in memory-based choice engendered by a strong brand-category association, it is important to consider how this association may be strengthened. Generally, any intervention that results in consumers rehearsing the association between the target brand and the relevant category may increase the strength of the association. This experiment employed a simple rote rehearsal task. There are multiple methods of encouraging rehearsal available to practitioners. In a study of television ads Fazio, Powell, and Herr (1992) demonstrated that "mystery" television ads, in which the brand and product category are not revealed until the end of the ad, contribute to strong category-brand associations. Fazio et al. suggest that the mystery format leads viewers to be cognitively ready to categorize the product when it finally appears, and this readiness leads to more elaborative rehearsal of the brand-category association. Other methods that may encourage category membership rehearsal include simply repeating the brand and the category in advertising, buying high advertising volume, creating a memorable tag line or jingle that mentions brand and category, and the dissemination of branded merchandise.

Caveats and Some Future Directions

The rehearsal task in this study was designed to increase the likelihood that target brands would be recalled upon consideration of the superordinate choice category. Farquhar and Herr (1993) termed the likelihood that a product category will evoke a particular brand the category dominance of the brand. These authors have made the extremely important, but somewhat under appreciated, distinction between category dominance and instance dominance. Instance dominance refers to the strength of the directional association from a brand to a particular product category. That is, given contact with a brand, how likely is it that a particular category will be evoked? Although both category and instance dominance are aspects of the representation of categories and brands in memory, category dominance is the more important determinant of a brand's accession to the consideration set in memory-based choice. If a

social influence attempt increases instance dominance instead of category dominance, the target brand would not likely enjoy the advantages of a strong category-brand association evident in this experiment. Future research on consideration effects in consumer choice should take account of this distinction.

We have suggested that strong category-brand associations may be particularly beneficial when alternatives are unspecified vs. specified in context. However, the benefits of a brand being strongly associated with the category may extend to stimulus-based choice contexts as well. In some instances individuals may form a choice intention for a product belonging to a stimulus-based category away from the point of purchase. For example, while constructing a shopping list a consumer may think of specific brands while noting the product categories he or she is in need of. A brand strongly associated with the category may pop into the consumer's mind at this early stage of decision-making, and thereby be at an advantage when the consumer makes the stimulus-based choice. Future research is needed to delineate the circumstances in which strong brand-category associations are beneficial in stimulus-based choice.

REFERENCES

Farquhar, Peter H. and Paul M. Herr (1993), "The Dual Structure of Brand Associations," in *Brand Equity & Advertising*, ed. David A. Aaker and Alexander L. Biel, Hillsdale, NJ: Lawrence Erlbaum Associates, 263-277.

Fazio, Russell H., Paul M. Herr and Martha C. Powell (1992), "On the Development and Strength of Category-Brand Associations in Memory: The Case of Mystery Ads," *Journal of Consumer Psychology*, 1, 1-13.

Kardes, Frank R., Gurumurthy Kalyanaram, Murali Chandrashekaren and Ronald J. Dornoff (1993), "Brand Retrieval, Consideration Set Composition, Consumer Choice, and the Pioneering Advantage," *Journal of Consumer Research*, 20 (June), 62-75.

Lehman, Donald R. and Yigang Pan (1994), "Context Effects, New Brand Entry, and Consideration Sets," *Journal of Marketing Research*, 31 (August), 364-374.

Lynch, John G., Howard Marmorstein and Michael F. Weigold (1988), "Choices from Sets Including Remembered Brands: Use of Recalled Attributes and Prior Overall Evaluations," *Journal of Consumer Research*, 15 (September), 169-184.

Nedungadi, Prakash (1990), "Recall and Consumer Consideration Sets: Influencing Choice Without Altering Brand Evaluations," *Journal of Consumer Research*, 17 (December), 263-276.

Payne, John W., James R. Bettman and Eric J. Johnson (1993), *The Adaptive Decision Maker*. New York: Cambridge University Press.

Posavac, Steven S., David M. Sanbonmatsu and Russell H. Fazio (1997), "Considering the Best Choice: Effects of the Salience and Accessibility of Alternatives on Attitude-Decision Consistency," *Journal of Personality and Social Psychology*, 72 (February), 253-261.

Ratneshwar, S. and Allan D. Shocker (1991), "Substitution in Use and the Role of Usage Context in Product Category Structures," *Journal of Marketing Research*, 28 (August), 281-295.

Shapiro, Stewart, Deborah J. MacInnis and Susan E. Heckler (1997), "The Effects of Incidental Ad Exposure on the Formation of Consideration Sets," *Journal of Consumer Research*, 24 (June), 94-104.

The Effects of Store Environment on Shopping Behaviors: A Critical Review

Shun Yin Lam, City University of Hong Kong

ABSTRACT

This paper reviews previous studies about the store environmental effects on shopping behaviors with an aim of identifying issues for future research. A conceptual framework which integrates various environmental effects is first constructed. Using the framework, I analyze previous findings about environmental effects and posit several propositions for future investigation. These propositions concern the multiple effects of individual environmental elements/factors, congruence among these elements/factors, congruence between these elements/factors and a store's merchandise, the moderating role of consumer characteristics, and the lagged effects of store environment.

Many retailers acknowledge the importance of store environment as a tool for market differentiation (Levy and Weitz 1995). Store environment, the physical surroundings of a store, is made up of many elements, including music, lighting, layout, directional signage and human elements, and can also be divided into external environment and internal environment (that is, exterior and interior of a store). The effects of store environmental elements could be complex. While many of these elements influence shoppers' behavior through their effects on shoppers' emotion, cognition and physiological state, some of these elements could elicit more direct response from shoppers with very little impact on their thinking, feeling or body comfort . Despite numerous studies on store environment, their findings are not enough to provide a detailed understanding of the store environmental effects.

By reviewing previous studies on store environment, this article attempts to identify research issues inadequately explored or with conflicting findings, and to posit several propositions for future investigation. In this review, I include studies that report empirical results or discuss (review) empirical results of other studies. I used the ProQuest Direct database to search for relevant articles, employing concepts such as store environment and store design, and environmental elements such as music, color and scent, as keywords for the search. The search mainly covers major marketing journals in the 1989-1999 period as the articles published in this period would reflect the current, more systematic approach to store environment research. The journals selected for review mainly include the top ten marketing journals based on the survey by Hult, Neese and Bashaw (1997). These include *Journal of Marketing, Journal of Marketing Research, Journal of Consumer Research, Journal of Retailing, Journal of the Academy of Marketing Science, Marketing Science, Harvard Business Review, Journal of Business Research, Journal of Advertising*, and *Journal of Advertising Research*. As some articles selected from these journals also cite other articles from other sources (such as *Advances in Consumer Research*) or before the 1989-99 period, I also include in the review some of these articles, considering their contribution to store environment research. In addition, I also looked into the retail patronage and service quality literature for relevant articles as physical facility is often cited as a factor affecting patronage and service quality evaluation.

To achieve the review's objectives, I first construct a framework that integrates the various effects of store environment, and describe the methodology of store environment research, based on a synthesis of numerous studies about store environment. With the help of the framework, I summarize and discuss previous findings about the store environmental effects, identifying "gaps" not well addressed by previous studies. Based on these gaps, I posit a number of propositions for future research.

AN INTEGRATIVE FRAMEWORK

The framework proposed here takes account of the multiple effects that store environment could have on shopping behaviors and shopping outcomes (see Figure 1). Store environment may be studied at different levels of aggregation. At an elementary level, one may examine individual environmental elements, such as music, noise, color, odor and furnishing. At a more aggregated level, the factor level, one may study these elements as groups (factors) – for example, the ambient, design and social factors defined by Baker (1986). The ambient factor refers to background characteristics, such as temperature, lighting, noise, music and ambient scent; the design factor includes stimuli that exist at the forefront of our awareness, such as architecture, color and materials; and the social factor refers to social conditions represented by the number, type and behavior of customers and employees (Baker 1986; Bitner 1992). At the factor level of analysis, researchers manipulate several elements belonging to the same factor to project a particular store image (Baker, Levy and Grewal 1992; Baker, Grewal and Parasuraman 1994). For instance, Baker et al. (1992) in their experiment defined a high image by background classical music and soft lighting, and a low image by foreground music and bright lighting. At an even more aggregated level of analysis, the global level, researchers use the environments of different stores as manipulations. Their focal interest is on the relationship between emotions induced by a particular environment and behaviors in this environment, rather than how the emotions or behaviors are related to the characteristics of the environment (Donovan and Rossiter 1982; Donovan, Rossiter, Marcoolyn and Nesdale 1994).

Store environment could affect shoppers' behaviors in several ways (see Figure 1). Certain response of human being to environment may be conditioned or hard-wired in the human brain. For example, for a store layout in a racetrack form, shoppers may follow the path defined by the layout with little thought or emotion aroused by the layout (Levy and Weitz 1997). In the environmental psychology literature, Mehrabian and Russell (1974) showed that in a variety of settings (schools, hospitals, homes, etc.), the emotions affected by the environment can be fully described by three states, pleasure, arousal and dominance (PAD). The majority of studies on emotional response to store environment adopt the PAD paradigm, and provide evidence that shoppers' emotional states can be largely represented by the PAD dimensions (Donovan and Rossiter 1982; Bellizzi and Hite 1992; Babin and Darden 1995). These studies also show that the emotional response leads to a variety of behaviors and outcomes, such as how long the shoppers stay and how much money they spend inside a store. Some other studies use other scales that include some emotion measures (Bellizzi et al. 1983; Crowley 1993). However, many of these measures are similar to the measures found in the PAD dimensions.

Store environment also influences various stages of shoppers' cognitive process inside a store, including attention, perception, categorization and information processing. For example, it has been shown that perceived waiting time varies with the valence of music and consumers' categorization of a restaurant as a fast food outlet depends largely on the external appearance of the store (Hui, Chebat and Chebat 1997; Ward, Bitner and Barnes 1992). The influence of store environment on these cognitive stages would

FIGURE 1
An Integrative Framework of Store Environmental Effects

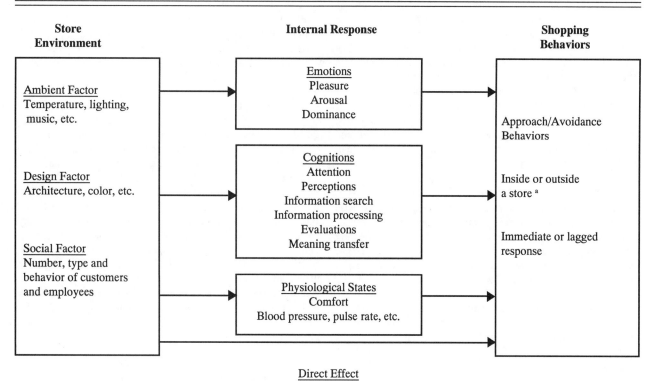

N.B. a. For example, a shopper walking along the front of a store may be attracted by the shop-window display to enter the store.

subsequently affect evaluations of the store, its merchandise and service, and hence on the shopping behaviors or outcomes (Hui et al. 1997; Ward et al. 1992). Furthermore, store environment may influence these evaluations directly by providing consumers with a peripheral cue or a tangible evidence for assessing the service and merchandise quality of a store, or by transfer of meanings from the environment (Parasuraman, Zeithaml and Berry 1988; Bitner 1992).

While the foregoing discussion is mainly concerned about the immediate effects of store environment, store environment may also have lagged or carryover effects on shopping behaviors. For example, consumers' impression of store environment can influence their retail patronage decision (store choice or choice of a shopping area for visit) over a period of time. Store environment can provide shoppers with various kinds of shopping value (such as convenience in locating products and recreation), and hence shoppers' impression of a store's environment in terms of shopping value that the environment delivers may affect their likelihood of choosing the store for shopping (Darden, Erdem and Darden 1983; Babin, Darden and Griffin 1994).

Bitner (1992) postulates that environmental conditions, such as noise, temperature and air quality, affect people's physiological state (such as comfort) and hence influence whether people stay in or enjoy a particular environment. Griffitt (1970) demonstrated in a lab setting that attraction and affective feelings towards strangers are negatively related to the effective temperature of the surroundings. Birren (1997) reported that red color increased blood pressure and pulse rate of participants in a lab setting.

METHODOLOGY

Baker et al. (1992) describe several methods of testing the effects of store environment: using a prototype store, asking participants to respond to verbal descriptions of a store, or creating a simulated store environment. Retail chains, such as the Limited, first develop a prototype store and determine customer acceptance before adopting the new design throughout the chains. This approach incurs high cost and may not be feasible for small retailers. An alternative technique is to ask subjects to respond to verbal descriptions of a store. Gardner and Siomkos (1985) found that such descriptions systematically affect consumer perceptions of physical sensations. However, Baker et al. (1992) comment that although this technique is good for laboratory testing, it is limited in external validity because verbal descriptions can be value-laden. Other studies have used slides or videotapes to provide a simulated store environment. Ecological validity of this simulation method is supported by Bosselman and Craik (1987), and Bateson and Hui (1992). Furthermore, the method enables researchers to keep all irrelevant cues constant across subjects. In addition to the foregoing methods, qualitative methodology has also been used by researchers. For example, using the methods of in-depth interview with shoppers and participant observation, McGrath (1989) recorded shoppers' response to the atmospherics of a gift store.

In terms of setting, store environment research has been done in both laboratories and the field. In a laboratory setting, subjects may be asked to imagine themselves in hypothetical situations and to respond accordingly, or be required to respond as they believe others would in these situations. Gardner and Siomkos (1985) found that assessments of atmosphere effects are not biased by the use of role playing or third party. For studies based on the laboratory setting, researchers can randomly assign subjects to different treatment conditions and balance the number of subjects in different treatment conditions. Most field studies do not have these advantages although they may have higher external validity. The correlation between explanatory variables and the unbalanced design commonly found in field studies reduce the power of hypothesis testing and hence the statistical conclusion validity of the findings. For example, Donovan et al. (1994), failed to find conclusive evidence for the interaction effect between pleasure and arousal on shopping behaviors, and attributed the lack of strong evidence to the unbalanced design of their field study.

DISCUSSION OF PREVIOUS FINDINGS

Previous findings are summarized in Table 1. Consistent with the integrative framework, I classify the findings into three categories: elementary level, factor level and global level. By reviewing these findings critically, I identify several issues which have not been researched into or have not been studied adequately, and also posit several propositions for future research.

Multiple Effects of Store Environment

As Table 1 shows, previous studies provide evidence at the elementary, factor and global levels that store environment affects cognition (Findings 2, 3, 7, 8, 10, 17, 19 and 27), emotions (Findings 3, 4, 5, 10, 15 and 21) and behaviors (Findings 1, 6, 9, 11 and 16). Furthermore, previous research provides support for the mediating role of cognition and emotions in the relationship between store environment and shopping behaviors (Findings 11, 16, 18, 21 and 27). However, no study has investigated the direct effect of store environment and the mediating role of physiological states in the relationship between store environment and shopping behaviors. Also, no study has empirically examined the consequences of meaning transfer from store environment to a store's merchandise.

With the exception of Donovan et al. (1994), no study has investigated the multiple effects of store environment simultaneously, and thus our understanding about the unique contribution of each kind of effects is very limited. Some environmental elements may have multiple impacts on shopping behaviors. Lighting, for example, could affect visual acuity of objects in display and arousal experienced by shoppers (Areni and Kim 1993). It may also have a direct effect on consumer movement inside a store as human being may have an innate response towards contrast between light and dark. In contrast, some elements may primarily affect shopping behaviors through a particular route – for example, background color may mainly affect shopping behaviors through the "emotions" route shown in Figure 1. It is worth studying the multiple effects of store environment simultaneously. This investigation can indicate which routes are particularly important for a particular element or factor, and hence enable us to differentiate the elements or factors from each other. Thus, the following propositions are posited.

P1: Individual environmental elements or factors can have multiple effects on shopping behaviors, and these effects vary from one element/factor to another. In particular, the following propositions about specific elements and effects would be worth investigating:

P1a: Through the process of meaning transfer, product display affects the cognitions and emotions of shoppers in a store environment.

P1b: A store layout can affect shoppers' behavior inside a store without significant impact on their emotions, cognitions or physiological state.

P1c: Lighting condition of a store can affect shoppers' emotions, attention towards and evaluation of the store's merchandise, and hence their behaviors inside the store. However, it can also elicit direct response from shoppers in certain circumstances.

Congruence Issues

The congruence between environmental elements/factors may greatly facilitate consumers' categorization of a retail outlet. For example, when both the ambient and design conditions project a prestige image, consumers may readily accept that the outlet is a high-class store. Since categorization and evaluation are often intertwined, the congruence may thus magnify the effect of these factors on product evaluation (Cohen and Basu 1987; Grewal and Baker 1994). This magnifying effect may also manifest itself as a positive interaction effect between the elements/factors on shopping behaviors or the internal response variables – emotions and cognition. However, only two studies investigated this congruence issue (Baker et al. 1992; Grewal and Baker 1994). They reported conflicting results (compare Findings 15 and 19, Table 1). In view of the contradictory findings and the small number of studies conducted, more research would be needed to test the congruence proposition.

P2: If store environmental elements/factors are congruent with each other, their effects on emotions, cognition and shopping behaviors will be magnified. For example, when both the ambient and design factors project a prestige image, their resultant impact on shoppers' evaluation of the store and its merchandise will be greater than the sum of their individual impacts.

The congruence between environmental elements/factors and product category has also raised some concerns. The study by Mitchell, Kahn and Knasko (1994) on ambient scent indicates that the congruence between a store's merchandise and environment could affect shoppers' information search and processing (refer to Finding 7). While Mitchell et al. focus on the odors of a product category, one may extend their research to other characteristics of a category. For instance, one may look into the congruence between the image of a product category and the image of store environment. Some categories, notably apparel, watches and jewelry, may have specific images associated with them, such as "casual", "formal", "lively" and "prestige". Through careful selection and combination of certain design elements (music, lighting, decorations, etc.), a store environment may project an image similar to that of the merchandise. One may study whether this congruence in image substantially affects consumer response, particularly information search and processing inside a store. Likewise, the effects on shopping behaviors due to the congruence in shopping value between a product category and the type of store design could be examined. For example, Floch (1988) found that consumers tend to emphasize the utilitarian value (such as convenience) when they shop for household and some grocery items, but to focus on hedonic value (such as fun) when they shop for books, perfumes and fashion. Thus, a grid layout that works well for a household section may not be suitable for an apparel section in a store. Furthermore, ethnic products (such as sushi) may be matched by environmental stimuli having the same origin (such as Japanese music). The match in the cultural dimension may help shoppers retrieve from their

TABLE 1
Summary of Previous Findings

Topic	Findings	Studies
Elementary level		
Effects of music	1. Shopping behaviors and outcomes, including time of stay, pace of movement, store sales, consumption of beverages in a restaurant, are related to volume and tempo of store music. 2. Evaluation of a store and shopping behavior, including likelihood of making a purchase and money spent, varies with music type (background music versus foreground music). Furthermore, this variation changes with department (men's department versus women's department in an apparel store) and age. 3. The presence of classical music makes consumers feel more positive towards the environment of a bank setting (less stressful, tense or rushed). Compared with music disliked by consumers, music liked by consumers increased perceived waiting duration in the setting.	Hui, Dube and Chebat 1997; Milliman 1982; Milliman 1986; Smith and Curnow 1966; Yalch and Spangenberg 1990; Yalch and Spangenberg 1993
Effects of color	4. Compared with warm-color (red or yellow) background, cool-color (violet or blue) background is generally reported by respondents to be more pleasant. 5. Colors at both ends of the visible spectrum, that is, red and violet, seem to be more stimulating than colors at the middle of the spectrum (yellow or green). 6. Cool-color background is generally associated with purchase outcomes favored by retailers, such as higher chance of making purchases by subjects. Warm-color background seems to be more capable of eliciting attention and attracting people to approach a store.	Bellizzi, Crowley and Hasty 1983; Bellizzi and Hite 1992; Crowley 1993
Effects of ambient scent/odor	7. When odor in the air is congruent with the product class being examined, consumers spend more time on processing product information, are more holistic in their processing and more variety-seeking compared to when the odor is incongruent with the product class. 8. When an inoffensive scent is present in a store environment, shoppers evaluate the store and its merchandise more positively, perceive less time spent inside the store, and are more inclined to visit the store, compared to when no scent is present.	Mitchell, Kahn and Knasko 1995; Spangenberg, Crowley and Henderson 1996
Effects of lighting	9. Shoppers examine and handle more merchandise in a wine cellar inside a restaurant when the lighting is brighter.	Areni and Kim 1994
Effects of visual information rate[a]	10. Consumers in a bank setting experience more pleasure and perceive a longer waiting time when the visual information rate is high compared to when the rate is low.	Chebat, Chebat and Filiatrault 1993
Effects of consumer density	11. Consumer density (density of people inside a store or a shopping area) directly increases consumers' perceived crowding, which in turn reduces pleasure and hence approach behaviors. 12. Consumer density also affects consumers' perceived control which decreases perceived control. The relationship between consumer density and perceived control depends on the situational goals of consumers.	Eroglu and Machleit 1990; Hui and Bateson 1991

TABLE 1
Summary of Previous Findings (CONTINUED)

Topic	Findings	Studies
Effects of consumer density, cont'd.	13. Under a high density condition, task-oriented shoppers experience more crowding and less satis faction with the store environment. No such difference is found under a low density condition. 14. Under a high density condition, perceived purchase risk and time pressure intensify perceived crowding. No such relationship is found under a low density condition.	
Factor level Main effect and interaction effect of ambient, social and design factors	15. Under a low social condition, shoppers experience higher pleasure when the environment projects a high ambient image. However, under a high-social condition, pleasure is unrelated to ambient image. 16. The effect of the ambient and social factors on shoppers' willingness to buy is mediated by the pleasure and arousal variables. 17. Ambient and social factors affect evaluations of product and service quality but the design factor does not. A prestige image in the ambient and social dimensions leads to better evaluations of product and service quality compared to a discount image. 18. Evaluations of product and service quality mediate the relationship between store environmental factors and overall image of a store. 19. Shoppers consider the price of an item more acceptable in a high-social environment compared to a low-social environment. Price acceptability is positively related to the ambience factor in a high-design environment but unrelated to the ambient factor in a low-design environment.	Baker, Levy and Grewal 1992; Baker, Grewal and Parasuraman 1994; Grewal and Baker 1994
Global Level Identification of emotions and their relationship with shopping behaviors	20. Shoppers emotions can be largely represented by the pleasure and arousal factors. The dominance factor appears to be important for certain types of shoppers and retail settings. 21. Pleasure, arousal and dominance affects a variety of shopping behaviors and outcomes, including extra time spent in a store and actual incremental spending. 22. The relationship between arousal and shopping behavior is moderated by pleasure.	Babin and Darden 1995; Donovan and Rossiter 1982; Donovan, Rossiter, Marcoolyn and Nesdale 1994; Foxall and Greenley 1999
Moderating role of consumer characteristics	23. The effects of store environment on shopping behaviors are moderated by consumers' age, environmental dispositions and self-regulation.	Babin and Darden 1995; Grossbart, Hampton, Rammohan and Lapidus 1990
Relationship between store environment and retail patronage	24. Although store environment affects retail patronage, it is less important than other determinants (such as merchandise and price).	Arnold, Oum and Tigert 1983; Gentry and Burns 1977-78; Malhotra 1983
Importance of store environment as a service quality dimension	25. The tangible dimension of the SERVQUAL scale, which reflects store environment, is considered by consumers as the least important dimension. 26. The tangible dimension do not affect several criterion variables, such as overall service quality rating and whether a customer would recommend a service firm to a friend.	Parasuraman, Berry and Zeithaml 1991; Parasuraman, Berry and Zeithaml 1991

TABLE 1
Summary of Previous Findings (CONTINUED)

Topic	Findings	Studies
Relationship between store environment and perceived prototypicality of a store	27. External environment strongly affect consumers' perceived protypicality, which in turn affects their attitude towards the store and their decision regarding whether to visit the store.	Ward, Bitner and Barnes 1992

N. B. a. Amount of visual stimuli to which a consumer is exposed in a time period.

memory information about these products, thus facilitating them to make their purchase decisions.

P3: The congruence between store environment and a store's merchandise affects shoppers' information search and processing, and hence their shopping behaviors. For example, shoppers' retrieval of purchase needs or other information about a product category from their memory is facilitated when a store environment matches the image of the category.

Moderating Role of Consumer Characteristics

Previous studies provide evidence that the effects of store environment on emotions, cognition and behaviors are moderated by several consumer variables, including age, environmental dispositions, self-regulation and task-orientation, and several situational variables, such as purchase risk and time pressure (Findings 2, 12, 13, 14 and 23). However, consumer differences due to countries' conditions are yet to be examined. Consumers in different societies may show different preferences regarding environmental elements because these elements may produce different connotations in different cultures. For example, people in different cultures prefer particular colors because of the meaning that they attach to these colors. Thus, the effects of store décor or store music on shopping behaviors may depend on whether the color(s) of the décor matches the prevailing preference in a culture. In addition, consumers in different countries may adapt to different levels of retail density (Eroglu and Harrell 1986). Thus, shoppers' sensitivity to a change in retail density and hence their response to the change may vary across countries. The moderating role of culture and adaptation level on consumer response to store environment is to be explored.

P4: The effects of store environment on emotions, cognition and shopping behaviors differ across countries owing to differences in culture and adaptation level of environmental stimuli.

The service quality literature suggests that store environment (indicated by the tangible dimension of the SERVQUAL scale) has weak influence on overall service quality assessment and customers' recommendation of a store to a friend (Findings 25 and 26). Nevertheless, the importance of store environment may actually vary with consumers' shopping experience with the store. Compared to regular customers, new customers of a store may rely more heavily on the tangible cues provided by a store environment in evaluating the service and the merchandise of the store as the new customers may have little knowledge or experience about the other

attributes of the store. Thus, response to store environment may differ by shopping experience.

P5: The effects of store environment on service quality assessment and shopping behaviors vary with consumers' shopping experience with a store.

Immediate and Lagged Effects of Store Environment

Most of previous studies on store environment focus on the immediate effects, particularly on how consumers react to store environment when they are inside a store. The lagged effects of store environment on patronage decision are examined in the retail patronage literature. Overall, this literature shows that store environment is a weak predictor of patronage. However, anecdotal evidence suggests that renovation of a store often leads to subsequent change in shoppers' evaluation of the store and shopping behaviors (e.g., *Discount Store News*, February 21, 1994; *Chain Store Age*, October 1995). Thus, the magnitude of the lagged effects needs to be re-examined.

P6: Change of store environment can have substantial lagged effects on shopping behaviors, particularly consumers' patronage behaviors.

The low level of importance of store environment reported by the patronage literature may be related to the methodology used by previous patronage studies. These studies typically ask consumers to evaluate store environment based on their previous shopping experience in the studied stores. As Donovan and Rossiter (1982) caution that emotional responses by consumers are transient and not always readily recallable, the evaluation based on recall of shopping experience may have weak predictive validity. Perhaps other methodology could better unveil the lagged effects of store environment. For example, an intervention analysis based on time-series behavioral data may capture these effects more precisely.

REFERENCES

Areni, Charles S. and David Kim (1993), "The Influence of In-store Lighting on Consumers' Examination of Merchandise in a Wine Store," *International Journal of Research in Marketing*, 11, 117-125.

Arnold, Stephen J., Tael H. Oum and Douglas J. Tigert (1983), "Determinant Attributes in Retail Patronage: Seasonal, Temporal, Regional, and International Comparisons," *Journal of Marketing Research*, 20 (May), 149-57.

Babin, Barry J., William R. Darden, and Mitch Griffin (1994), "Work and/or Fun: Measuring Hedonic and Utilitarian Shopping Value," *Journal of Consumer Research*, 20 (March), 644-56.

_____ and William R. Darden (1995), "Consumer Self-Regulation in a Retail Environment," *Journal of Retailing*, 71 (1), 47-70.

Baker, Julie (1986), "The Role of the Environment in Marketing Services: The Consumer Perspective, " in John A. Czepeil, Carlole A. Congram and James Shanahan (eds.), *The Service Challenge: Integrating for Competitive Advantage*, Chicago, IL: American Marketing Association, 79-84.

_____, Dhruv Grewal, and A. Parasuraman (1994), "The Influence of Store Environment on Quality Inferences and Store Image," *Journal of Academy of Marketing Science*, 22 (4), 328-39.

Baker, Julie, Michael Levy, and Dhruv Grewal (1992), "An Experimental Approach to Making Retail Store Environmental Decisions," *Journal of Retailing*, 68 (4), 445-60.

Bellizzi, Joseph, A., Ayn E. Crowley, and Ronald W. Hasty (1983), "The Effects of Color in Store Design," *Journal of Retailing*, 59 (Spring), 21-45.

_____ and Robert E. Hite (1992), "Environment Color, Consumer Feelings, and Purchase Likelihood," *Psychology and Marketing*, 9 (September/October), 347-363.

Birren, Faber (1997), *The Power of Color: How It Can Reduce Fatigue, Relieve Monotony, Enhance Sexuality, and More*, Secaucus, New Jersey: Carol Publishing Group.

Bitner, Mary J. (1992), "Servicescapes: The Impact of Physical Surroundings on Customer and Employees," *Journal of Marketing*, 56 (April), 57-71.

Chain Store Age, October (1995), "Bob's Rolls Out New Signage Package," 71 (10), 90.

Chebat, Jean-Charles, Claire Gelinas-Chebat, and Pierre Filiatrault (1993), "Interactive Effects of Musical and Visual Cues on Time Perception: An Application to Waiting Lines in Banks," *Perceptual and Motor Skills*, 77 (3), 995-1020.

Cohen, Joel B. and Kunal Basu (1987), "Alternative Models of Categorization: Toward a Contingent Processing Framework," *Journal of Consumer Research*, 13 (March), 455-72.

Darden, William R., Orhan Erdem, and Donna K. Darden (1983), "A Comparison And Test of Three Causal Models of Patronage Intentions," in William R. Darden and Robert F. Lusch, eds., *Patronage Behavior and Retail Management*, New York, NY: North-Holland.

_____ and Barry J. Babin (1994), "Exploring the Concept of Affective Quality: Expanding the Concept of Retail Personality," *Journal of Business Research*, 29 (February), 101-10.

Discount Store News, February 21 (1994), "HB & C Section Puts on a Good Face," 33 (4), 79.

Donovan, Robert J. and John R. Rossiter (1982), "Store Atmosphere: An Environmental Psychology Approach," *Journal of Retailing*, 58 (1), 34-57.

_____, John R. Rossiter, Gilian Marcoolyn, and Andrew Nesdale (1994), "Store Atmosphere and Purchasing Behavior," *Journal of Retailing*, 70 (3), 283-94.

Eroglu, Sevgin and Gilbert D. Harrell (1986), "Retail Crowding: Theoretical and Strategic Implications," *Journal of Retailing*, 62 (4), 346-63.

_____ and Karen A. Machleit (1990), "An Empirical Study of Retail Crowding: Antecedents and Consequences," *Journal of Retailing*, 66 (2), 201-21.

Floch, Jean-Marie (1988), "The Contribution of a Structural Semiotics to the Design of a Hypermarket," *International Journal of Research in Marketing*, 4 (3), 233-52.

Foxall, Gordon R. and Gordon E. Greenley (1999), "Consumers' Emotional Responses to Service Environments," *Journal of Business Research*, 46, 149-58.

Gardner, Meryl P. and George J. Siomkos (1985), "Toward a Methodology for Assessing the Effects of In-Store Atmospherics," in Richard Lutz (ed.), *Advances in Consumer Research*, Chicago, IL: Association for Consumer Research.

Gentry, James W. and Alvin C. Burns (1977-78), "How 'Important' Are Evaluative Criteria in Shopping Center Patronage," *Journal of Retailing*, 4 (Winter), p. 73-85.

Grewal, Dhruv and Julie Baker (1994), "Do Retail Environmental Factors Affect Consumers' Price Acceptability? An Empirical Examination," *International Journal of Research in Marketing*, 11 (2), 107-115.

Griffitt, William (1970), "Environmental Effects on Interpersonal Affective Behavior: Ambient Temperature and Attraction," *Journal of Personality and Social Psychology*, 15 (3), 240-44.

Grossbart, Sanford, Ronald Hampton, B. Rammohan, and Richard S. Lapidus (1990), "Environmental Dispositions and Customer Response to Store Atmospherics," *Journal of Business Research*, 21 (3), 225-41.

Hui, Michael K. and John E. G. Bateson (1991), "Perceived Control and the Effects of Crowding and Consumer Choice on the Service Experiences," *Journal of Consumer Research*, 25 (September), 175-86.

_____, L. Dube and J. Chebat (1997), "The Impact of Music on Consumers' Reactions to Waiting for Services," *Journal of Retailing*, 73 (1), 87-104.

Hult, G. Tomas M., William T. Neese, and R. Edward Bashaw (1997), "Faculty Perceptions of Marketing Journals," *Journal of Marketing Education*, 19 (1), 37-52.

Levy, Michael and Barton A. Weitz (1998), *Retailing Management*, 3rd ed., Chicago: Irwin NcGraw-Hill, Chapter 18, 540-69.

Malhotra, Naresh K. (1983), "A Threshold Model of Store Choice," *Journal of Retailing*, 59 (2), 3-21.

Milliman, Ronald E. (1982), "Using Background Music to Affect the Behavior of Supermarket Shoppers," *Journal of Marketing*, 46 (2), 86-91.

_____ (1986), "The Influence of Background Music on the Behavior of Restaurant Patrons," *Journal of Consumer Research*, 13 (September), 286-89.

Mitchell, Deborah J., Barbara E. Kahn, and Susan C. Knasko (1995), "There's Something in the Air: Effects of Ambient Odor on Consumer Decision Making," *Journal of Consumer Research*, 22 (September), 229-38.

Parasuraman, A., Leonard L. Berry, and Valerie A. Zeithaml, (1991), "Refinement and Reassessment of the SERVQUAL Scale," *Journal of Retailing*, 67 (4), 420-50.

_____, Valerie A. Zeithaml, and Leonard L. Berry (1988), "SERVQUAL: A Multiple-Item Scale for Measuring Consumer Perceptions of Service Quality," *Journal of Retailing*, 64 (1), 12-46.

Smith, Patricia and Ross Curnow (1966), "'Arousal Hypothesis' and the Effects of Music on Purchasing Behavior," *Journal of Applied Psychology*, 50 (June), 255-56.

Spangenberg, Eric R., Ayn E. Crowley, and Pamela W. Henderson (1996), "Improving the Store Environment: Do Olfactory Cues Affect Evaluations and Behaviors," *Journal of Marketing*, 60 (April), 67-80.

Ward, James C., Mary Jo Bitner, and John Barnes (1992), "Measuring the Prototypicality and Meaning of Retail Environments," *Journal of Retailing*, 68 (2), 194-220.

Yalch, Richard F. and Eric Spangenberg (1990), "Effects of Store Music on Shopping Behavior," *Journal of Consumer Marketing*, 7 (Spring), 55-63.

_____ and Eric Spangenberg (1993), "Using Store Music for Retail Zoning: A Field Experiment," in *Advances in Consumer Research*, Vol. 20, Leigh McAlister and Michael L. Rothschild, eds., Provo, UT: Association for Consumer Research, 632-36.

Shopping as a Jungle Trip

Yaolung James Hsieh, National Chengchi University
Janeen Arnold Costa, University of Utah

ABSTRACT

This paper employs projective techniques premised upon anthropomorphism and totemism to explore shoppers' inner world and how consumers' shopping perceptions vary between Taiwanese and American cultures. The data indicate that more similarities than distinctions exist in comparing the two societies. Informants in both cultures focus on shopping strategy and shopping partners' loyalty and overall helpfulness; informants also responded similarly to queries concerning "good" and "bad" salespeople. Nevertheless, while the Taiwanese data suggest a pro-social orientation consistent with Taiwanese cultural values of "face," group and harmony, the American data often suggest an individualistic point of reference and experience.

INTRODUCTION AND LITERATURE REVIEW

Many scholars have examined factors that affect shoppers' consumer behavior, including temporal aspects (Bergadaa 1990; Taylor 1994), physical and social surroundings (Hirsch 1995; Solomon, Zaichkowsky and Polegato 1999), and individual cognition, emotion and mood (e.g., Dube and Schmitt 1991). Social characteristics such as gender, class and ethnicity contribute to variations in shopping behavior and experiences (e.g., Belk and Costa 1990; Costa 1995; Fischer and Arnould 1990; Fischer and Gainer 1991; McGrath 1996; Otnes, Kim and Lowrey 1992; Sherry and McGrath 1989). According to Babin, Darden and Griffin (1994), humans engage in shopping for either utilitarian or hedonic reasons. While some or all of these findings may be generalizable to other societies, it is important to recognize that the majority of these and other studies concerning shopping have been conducted in the U.S.

We would anticipate both cross-cultural and contextual variation in the extent to which the above-mentioned factors and social characteristics and conditions influence consumers' shopping experiences and behavior. Similarly, if we place Babin et al's (1994) shopping purposes at opposite ends of a continuum, we would expect the degree to which individuals in a given society pursue utilitarianism vs. hedonism to vary cross-culturally and also on the basis of a given shopping experience. In the research presented here, the data indicate both important differences *and* similarities in the shopping experiences of informants from two distinct societies, Taiwan and the United States.

In order to achieve a greater understanding of how consumers in these two societies feel about their shopping experiences in general, we chose to utilize projective techniques, described in greater detail below. In addition to looking broadly at consumers' feelings about shopping, however, we were also interested in their specific comprehension of themselves in terms of positive, negative, and social dimensions of shopping. Thus, we inquired about how our informants felt after they had purchased something they liked, what their descriptions of their regular shopping 'partners' would be, and their understandings of 'good' and 'bad' service people. While we were attempting through these latter queries to discern aspects of the entire shopping process, the data also provided extensive information about shoppers' strategy or style. An emergent finding of this study, then, is that shopping strategy or style is a particularly important part of the way in which consumers understand their shopping experiences, including their

own moods, emotions and self-perceptions, shopping with relevant social others, and encounters with salespersons.

Taken as a whole, the body of data indicates that shopping is a *process* wherein an individual's judgements and perceptions of self and others may alter during the course of a shopping experience. In turn, these alterations affect the shopper's mood, which in and of itself may have a strong impact on which products are purchased and how they are evaluated (Dube and Schmitt 1991). For the purposes of this paper, however, we focus upon an analysis of the cultural similarities and differences in the shopping experiences as expressed by our Taiwanese and U.S. informants. We leave an exploration and explication of the shopping process as a whole, with its mood-altering elements and implications, for later, expanded research.

SHOPPING BEHAVIOR IN TAIWAN

Studies of shopping behavior in Taiwan are limited. However, according to Hsieh's (1997) work, Taiwanese consumers' shopping motives can be classified into two categories: Personal motives and social motives. Personal motives include physical (e.g., tasting good food and taking exercises), economic (e.g., paying less during on sale and being able to shop for better prices), psychological (e.g., releasing personal stress, being fashionable in order to be compatible with one's friends, and enjoying spending money), and emotional motivations (e.g., showing care for his/her family or girl/boy friends). Alternatively, Hsieh indicates that social motives involve understanding social others and sharing good times with friends, a sense of belonging (being accepted by one's friends), purchasing gifts for friends, negotiating as a fun thing to do, and gaining respect by playing the role of an opinion leader. Based on these descriptions, it appears that shopping behavior may be much more of a social than an individual activity for many Taiwanese consumers.

METHOD

Projective techniques permit the consumer to describe and/or analyze him/herself, others, and given situations freely and imaginatively. The "projective hypothesis" also suggests that the use of projective techniques allows informants to reveal "personality styles as well as clues about specific conflicts and problem areas" (Rabin and Zlotogorski, 1981, p. 127). In consumer research, it is clear that researchers have used projective techniques primarily to aid consumers to access more easily their feelings and thoughts about various consumption situations (Belk, Ger and Askegaard 1997; Bamossy and Costa 1997; McGrath, Sherry and Levy 1993; Sherry, McGrath and Levy 1992, 1993; Zaltman and Coultier 1995). Some evidence exists that such techniques also provide for less ethnocentric cross-cultural research, as long as the researchers are willing to recognize that wording and concepts still must be adjusted on the basis of cultural and linguistic considerations (see Belk, Ger and Askegaard 1997; Bamossy and Costa 1997).

It is critical to base projective queries on comparisons that facilitate, rather than hinder, the human imagination. Some theorists have suggested that consumers' "inner worlds" may be accessed more easily through research premised upon either anthropomorphism—whereby human attributes are ascribed to non-humans, or totemism — the assignation to humans of animal or other emblematic qualities (Belk 1988; Hirschman 1994). In both U.S. and Taiwanese/Chinese societies, self-identification or, at the very least, a sense of affinity, with animals, is a cultural feature. In the U.S., for example, animals may be seen as an extension of self, as friends, children or child substitutes (e.g., Beck and Katcher 1983; Belk 1988; Feldman 1979; Hirschman 1994; Robins, Sanders and Cahill 1991; Sanders 1990; Serpell 1986; Savishingsky 1986). American totems include the politically-affiliated donkey and elephant, as well as the boom and bust stock market bull and bear, for instance (Daniels 1995). Among the Chinese, a particularly important example of totemism is found in the zodiac calendar, where 12 animals (mouse, cow, tiger, rabbit, dragon, snake, horse, sheep, monkey, chicken, dog, and pig) represent 12 types of animal qualities *as well as* the people who are born in a particular animal year. These "totemic qualities" are enhanced for individuals each time the year in which they were born comes around on the calendar: "So here we go, into the Year of the Tiger, and here I go— as a tiger myself, I am of course feeling courageous, determined, alert, restless, spendthrift, independent and argumentative" (Checketts 1998, p. 7). Because our intent was to investigate cultural aspects of consumers' shopping perceptions, and because we were aware of the ease with which both U.S. and Taiwanese informants access comparisons of themselves with animals, we chose projective techniques based on 'animal terms.'

In this project, we sought to investigate the shopping process through consumer perceptions of themselves and others during and immediately after shopping. Thus, projective inquiries were designed to elicit information about the informant's descriptions of him/herself during shopping and after he/she had purchased something particularly desirable, and of others with whom the informant typically shopped. In addition, we elicited consumers' projective portrayals of service people in terms of their behavior and attitudes toward consumers. In each query, we asked informants to provide the name of an animal that seemed to describe best the type of individual given, as well as to suggest reasons why that particular animal seemed appropriate. Using student researchers trained in qualitative research methods, we collected projective data on 26 Americans, aged 22-28, 7 females and 19 males, residing in a large metropolitan city in the western United States, and on 31 Taiwanese, aged 17-40, 20 females and 11 males, residing in Taipei, Taiwan.

The data were first coded according to animal type and were then analyzed for content and themes. Following this, the emergent patterns were contextualized within the individual culture/society in which the data were collected. Finally, the data were compared across the two cultures/societies. In this paper, we provide our conclusions both on the cultural contextualizations and on the cross-cultural comparisons and contrasts.

One of the authors is Taiwanese, while the other is American (United States). Both authors were involved in analysis and contextualization. While each individual author may be considered an "analytical informant" (Barrett 1984) with respect to his/her culture and the contextualization of responses within that cultural milieu, the authors also relied on the work of other theorists who have evaluated the respective cultures. In addition, one of the authors is an anthropologist (PhD) and is well trained in the area of culture and its effects. Both authors also have substantial training in marketing (Postdoc and PhD). The authors utilized an iterative process of inquiry of tacking between the data and pertinent scholarly works, both on cultural perspectives and on other relevant intellectual considerations. The trustworthiness of the data obtained in this study is ensured primarily through researcher and data triangulation (see Erlandson et al 1993). In addition, member checks were utilized in the American sample, as was peer debriefing. An audit trail exists for the entire study. Finally, the Taiwanese answers were translated into English by the Taiwanese author and by a research assistant, who then consulted with one another for accuracy.

PRESENTATION AND ANALYSIS OF DATA

As might be expected, some differences exist between the Taiwanese and the American data. However, the authors were surprised to find that the similarities may be more prevalent than the distinctions. In the first part of this section, we present and analyze those data that are comparable across the two societies. We then describe the data that seem to suggest important, but sometimes subtle, differences between the two cultures and the experiences of the informants in those cultures.

Similarities: Concern with Strategy and Style

Concerning the animals they described themselves to be while shopping, both Taiwanese and American informants focused on their own shopping strategy and style. Their answers suggest such tactical and experiential approaches may be a very basic part of consumers' approach to shopping. Furthermore, both American and Taiwanese responses indicate that shopping style and strategy are perceived primarily in terms of pace and attitude. Their answers also suggest that the ways in which informants look at products, seek bargains or information, and deal with other shoppers and with salespeople, as well as informants' intentions in terms of purchase, are significant parts of shopping strategy. In describing themselves while shopping, informants indicated: [I would describe myself as a(n)]

Taiwan:
…turtle. Because I usually stay longer than other people for window-shopping. If I really want to buy something, I will shop one store after another and take a slow and careful look at the products. I usually walk slowly and feel like I am blocking other people's way, or there will always be someone who overpasses me (TF#11,19).
…crocodile. Crocodiles move toward their prey quickly, and I am the same. When I see something I like, I will go for it (TM#27,21).

U.S.:
…shark. When I decide I want something, I'm aggressive in getting it; sharks I perceive as aggressive (USM#1,25).
…Tiger (because I've very predatory. When I shop I am on the hung and finding a great deal on something fabulous is like making the kill). Also, I feel that my senses are at a heightened level. My eyes are scoping the area, my ears are perked up and my energy level is peaking (USF#25,24)

As with the projective queries concerning the informants themselves as shoppers, answers concerning shopping partners frequently mentioned shopping strategy, again with an emphasis on pace, compatibility and other aspects of strategy and style: [Shopping partners are]

Taiwan:
…lions, tigers and leopards. Because only friends with such shopping speed can keep pace with me and buy all the products we need (TM#27,21).
…a herd of deer (good partners). If I shop with partners that I like, I feel that I am with a herd of deer. They give me the feeling of harmony (TF#7,22).

U.S.:

...hummingbirds. Flitting around from rack to rack–sometimes together, sometimes apart. Seeking each other out to test finds or to share discoveries with (USF#20,25).

...a pair of crocs. We just sit around allowing the flow [to] take us & when we see something, we grab it and won't let the other have it (USM#19,26).

Another commonality between the Taiwanese and American data in the shopping partner projectives is the emphasis on partners' "loyalty," willingness to shop with the informant, and overall helpfulness: [Shopping partners are]

Taiwan:

...wolfhound. They are very loyal to me, just like wolfhounds are loyal to their masters (TM#30,26).

...dogs. Because I feel they are very loyal. They shop with me, chat with me, and if I need their opinions, they will provide (TF#13,19).

U.S.:

...dog. Because there is a lot o "barking" (talking) among friends. A lot of loyalty to each other as a dog is to their owner (USM#8,27).

...flock of birds. We always stick together and ask each other's opinion (USF#23,22).

Alternatively, a shopping partner who was not compatible with the informant in terms of strategy was portrayed as annoying and an overall hindrance to shopping activity. Such partners shopped together primarily by virtue of other aspects of their relationship that drive their choice to shop together, rather than their similarities in shopping strategy or mutual enjoyment of the experience:

Taiwan:

...louse (girlfriend who shops with me). She is like a louse attaching to my body. She does not have special requests, but will spend all the money I have. I think that is like a louse sucking all the blood in my body (TM#28,19).

...Lion. Because he shops all the time and always shows his arrogance. He never listens to opinions of salespeople or anyone else...(TF#4,20).

U.S.:

...sloth...Sometimes they don't want to be there, so you have to drag them everywhere (USF#21,22).

...elephant. Elephants are considered giant rats in Africa because they're a nuisance. My friends are annoying to shop with because they take forever and stop at every store (USM#16,23).

Similarities: Encounters with Salespersons

Finally, the Taiwanese and American informants responded in similar ways to projective queries concerning salespersons with "good" or "bad" attitudes. While the specific animals chosen were not the same in the Taiwan and U.S. samples, the underlying reasons for choosing that animal were comparable in the two data sets.

In general, for retail service providers who were seen as pleasant or having a "good attitude," informants chose an animal that represented the salesperson's orientation toward the customer in terms of helpfulness, lack of "pressure," or overall amount/

degree of interest in the consumer. These projectives typically described friendly, loyal animals: [Salespersons are]

Taiwan:

...small pets. Because some people have very good attitudes, they [are] like lovely small pets. They always smile and make me feel good. With them around, I can shop without any pressure (TF#2,22).

...dogs. Because they make you feel warm and free of pressure. They are like lovely dogs, which please me a lot (TM#26,19).

U.S.:

...dog. They are cheerful, nice and willing to help. A good store clerk doesn't have any ulterior motives (USF#23,22).

...an able owl. Wise, knows about its surroundings (store, products, etc.) can answer questions. Able to go swiftly to check out something or find something (USM#18,24).

With respect to unpleasant salespersons or those described as having a "bad attitude," both Taiwanese and American informants chose animals that seemed remarkably vile or vicious. This was the case when the underlying reason for choosing the particular animal emphasized the perceived "greed" of the salesperson:

Taiwan:

...wolf...Because they always watch you with bad intention. They will try their best to hunt for your money (TF#7,22).

...spiders...They are like spiders. Before the sale, they induce [entice] you to their "nets" [webs] to buy their products. However, after you purchase the product, they, after sucking all of your money, kind of hang you there and ignore you (TF#18,22).

U.S.:

...vulture. Stands over you, won't leave you alone, unfriendly. Just wants to take your money. If they think you don't have money, won't bother with you (USF#21,22).

...a reticulating python. Because they are really aggressive, mean, moody snakes (US#14,23).

Sometimes, the animals chosen in response to this projective query were described as annoying or pestering, without specific mention of any perceived underlying money-making motive of such salespersons:

Taiwan:

...never dead cockroaches, flies and earthworms. Although I have no intention to buy, they still keep selling. I just cannot keep them away. They are like cockroaches and flies. They are so disgusting, but it is difficult to get rid of them. And some of them are very arrogant; that makes me angry even more. They are like earthworms. I hate earthworms very much (TF#10,20).

...hens...Because they will keep giving you their opinions or push you to make a quick decision...(TM#26,19).

U.S.:

...a hyena. Annoying, always pestering (USM#11,26).

...dog–poorly trained. Hang around too close when you don't want them. Follow you, you can't lose them, breathing down your neck. Trying *too* hard to please. Won't back off. Tries to be your best 'unwanted' friend (USF#20,25).

Finally, both Taiwanese and U.S. informants sometimes chose a projective that portrayed a salesperson as apathetic and unhelpful in general. The animals chosen in these responses were typically described as lazy or self-centered:

Taiwan:
...cats...These service people do not pay any respect to their jobs and customers. When I ask them some questions, they do not really like to respond to me. This attitude really disgusts me. I think they provide very poor services. They are just like cats. Cats are difficult to understand and to stay close. Although you want to play with cats, they will play with you only when they have [are in a] good mood...(TM#26,19).
...cockroaches—annoying service people. One type of service people is that they ignore you right from the beginning [when] you enter the store...(TF#19,20).

U.S.:
...a sloth. Slow and quiet, doing nothing for anyone (USM#13,mid-20s).
...pig. Unattentive [sic], unhelpful, cares about only themselves and their own pleasures (USM#10,28).

Contrasts: Social Display vs. Individualism

The data from the Taiwanese informants typically are suggestive of the underlying pro-social orientation of Taiwanese culture. Rather than suggesting self-orientation, the data seem to indicate that behaviors and attitudes are often directed toward the social other. In this way, some of the Taiwanese answers contrast markedly with the individualistic orientation of many of the American (U.S.) informants. We present and analyze examples of the Taiwanese data, theorizing that the informant answers are overwhelmingly consistent with the Chinese cultural values of "face," social group considerations, and harmony (see Hsieh 1994, 1999; Hsieh and Scammon 1993). We then distinguish these from the examples in the U.S. data, where individualistic concerns are manifest much more often than in the Taiwanese data.

In answering the projective query concerning self during shopping, Taiwanese informants often suggested the importance of social display for the approval and observation of others:

Taiwan:
...poodle. Because they are always dressed beautifully...Besides, they usually walk confidently and proudly. And they are also very attractive. I dress like that too when I go shopping. I like to attract other peoples' attention (TF#2,22).
...peacock (wearing beautiful clothes to shop). Because peacocks are very beautiful, especially with their tails wide open. Wearing beautiful clothes makes me feel like peacocks. The purpose for me to dress up on the street is to show my clothes to other people (TF#14,20).

Similarly, in describing themselves when they have purchased something they "like very much," Taiwanese informants reflected the desire to exhibit themselves to others, as well as the "happiness" they feel in being able to do so:

Taiwan:
...mermaid. Because I will demonstrate the products I bought to everyone I know. Mermaid is a rare animal and everyone will pay attention to me (TF#3,40).
...peacock. Because when I buy something new, I like to show it to everybody. I want to show the best part of me (TM#24, 17).

The notion of display for others, the presentation of self as beautiful while shopping, also appears in queries concerning animal representations of informants' shopping partners:

Taiwan:
...butterfly (girlfriend who shops with me). She looks like a butterfly, because girls like to dress beautifully when shopping. Being beautiful can attract other people's attentions, just like butterflies, which are so colorful and beautiful (TM#21,24).
...poodle. Because they also like to dress up before shopping. I think all girls like to dress themselves beautifully...(TF#2,22).

Finally, we see a similar notion of social exhibition in some of the projective responses concerning salespersons, with an emphasis placed on their beauty and elegance. In some cases, the informants indicated this was especially true in certain shopping districts or in shops/departments selling certain types of products:

Taiwan:
...peacocks (service people in high class stores). They are very elegant and stylish. Mermaid (service people in the cosmetics counters)...they are well trained, and have beautiful shapes and faces (TF#18,22).
...cats...service people in East District of Taipei. They are elegant, wear beautifully and have high dignity (TF#19,20).

In sum, Taiwanese apparently conceptualize shopping primarily as a social or group experience. As a final example of this, the data suggest that shopping is frequently perceived not only in terms of exhibition or presentation of self to others, but also in terms of the experience of a marketplace swarming with other humans. Thus, Taiwanese often see themselves as visiting shops in a crowd, where they are simply one of many shoppers:

Taiwan:
...earthworm. Because there are always many people crowded together when shopping (TF#7,22).
...ant. I usually shop on holidays, so I am always trapped in a lot of crowded people. This is especially true when there is a sale. These people are like ants looking for something, and I am no exception (TM#23,21).

The Taiwanese clearly indicated a pro-social orientation more often than did the U.S. informants. Conversely, the American data often suggest an individualistic point of reference or experience; such self-orientation was notably lacking in the Taiwan data. U.S. informants provided answers to several of the projective queries in a manner that indicated they prefer to shop alone and/or to avoid the perspectives, opinions and experiences of others, including shopping companions or salespersons:

U.S.:
...a bear. I go it alone through the wilderness...I rarely go shopping, and when I do, it's by myself (USM#3,24).
...panther. Slipping quietly around the store, hunting for bargains or unusual items that there are only a few of. Ignoring displays with lots of the same items, going for the things standing alone (USF#20,25).
...unicorn. Because a unicorn doesn't exist, and neither does the concept of "shopping with friends," for me. I want as little distraction as possible when I'm shopping (USM#6,mid-20s).

Again placing these responses in a cultural context, Americans often accentuate individualism, while Taiwanese prioritize social group over individual concerns. The American cultural emphasis on the individual pervades the social fabric of the United States. Individualism is manifest in competitive urges and behaviors observed throughout the social and economic systems, as well as in the primacy of individual interests even within the context of marriages or the family, for example (see Althen 1988; Harris 1981).

CONCLUSION

The projective-based investigation of consumers' shopping perceptions and experiences accesses their inner worlds and enhances our overall understanding of their behaviors. Applying the same basic techniques in collecting data in Taiwan and the United States, we found both similarities and differences among our informants.

Our data indicate that shoppers in Taiwan and the United States approach and perceive their own shopping behaviors in remarkably similar ways, citing shopping style and strategy in particular. Taiwanese and Americans also provided analogous descriptions of desirable shopping partners as loyal, willing and helpful and of less desirable partners as those whose shopping strategies were unlike those of the informant. Finally, informants in both societies agree that "good" and "bad" salespersons affect shopping experiences through the clerks' attitudes toward the shopper and toward profit in the shopping transaction.

The underlying reason for similarities in the two societies is unclear. It is possible that some aspects of shopping are "universal;" i.e., found in all or in many societies based on correspondence in the structure of the experience, the nature of transactions within a market system, etc. Alternatively, it is quite possible that, given global diffusion of U.S. consumer culture, aspects of engaging in that consumer culture through shopping have diffused as well. Further investigation may reveal the principal bases for the similarities we found in our data.

On the other hand, some apparent differences among Taiwanese and U.S. shoppers exist and are manifest primarily through orientation toward social other versus toward self. This discrepancy is validated through cultural contextualization. Thus, we better understand our Taiwanese shoppers by situating their answers within the Taiwanese cultural values of social harmony, group considerations and "face." Conversely, the cultural emphases on individualism, competition, and "going it alone" dominate many aspects of U.S. society and provide a broader framework with which we can interpret our U.S. informants' responses.

We utilized projective techniques based on comparisons of self and others to animals in our investigation of consumers' perceptions of shopping in Taiwan and the United States. While the specific choice of animals varied in the different cultural contexts, we found that the application and interpretation of those animal qualities to the shopping context provided ample basis for comparison between the two societies. In summary, our comparison of Taiwanese and American (U.S.) consumers' answers to projective queries concerning their shopping expands our overall understanding of consumer behavior.

REFERENCES

Althen, Gary (1988), *American Ways*, Yarmouth, Maine: Intercultural Press, Inc.

Babin, Barry J., William R. Darden and Mitch Griffin (1994), "Work and/or Fun: Measuring Hedonic and Utilitarian Shopping Value," *Journal of Consumer Research*, 20, 644-656.

Bamossy, Gary J. and Janeen Arnold Costa (1997), "Consuming Paradise: A Cultural Construction," *European Advances in Consumer Research*, Basil G. Englis and Anna Olofsson, eds., 3, 146.

Barrett, Richard A. (1984), *Culture and Conduct*, Belmont, CA: Wadsworth Publishing Co.

Beck, Alan and Aaron Katcher (1983), *Between Pets and People: The Importance of Animal Companionship*, New York: Putnam.

Belk, Russell W. (1988), "Possessions and the Extended Self," *Journal of Consumer Research*, 15, 139-168.

_____ and Janeen Arnold Costa (1990), "Nouveaux Riches as Quintessential Americans: Case Studies in an Extended Family," *Advances in Non-Profit Marketing*, Russell W. Belk, ed., Greenwich, CT: JAI Press, Inc., 3, 83-140.

_____, Guliz Ger and Soren Askegaard (1997), "Consumer Desire in Three Cultures: Results from Projective Research," *Advances in Consumer Research*, Merrie Brucks and Debbie MacInnis, eds., 24, 24-28.

Bergadaa, Michelle M. (1990), "The Role of Time in the Action of the Consumer," *Journal of Consumer Research*, 17, 289-302.

Checketts, Susanna (1998), "Tiger, Tiger, Burning Bright!," *New Straits Times*, January 20, 7.

Costa, Janeen Arnold (1995), "The Social Organization of Consumer Behavior," *Contemporary Marketing and Consumer Behavior: An Anthropological Sourcebook*, John F. Sherry, Jr., ed., Newbury Park, CA: Sage Publications, Inc., 213-244.

Daniels, Mary Alice (1995), "Packwood Carried Patterning too Far," *Kansas City Star*, September 27, 27.

Dube, Laurette and Bernd H. Schmitt (1991), "The Processing of Emotional and Cognitive Aspects of Product Usage in Satisfaction Judgements," *Advances in Consumer Research*, Rebecca H. Holman and Michael R. Solomon eds., 18, 52-56.

Erlandson, David A., et al. (1993) *Doing Naturalistic Inquiry*, Newbury Park, CA: Sage Publications, Inc.

Feldmann, Bruce Max (1979), "Why People Own Pets," *The Handbook of Animal Welfare*, Robert D. Allen and William H. Westbrook, eds., New York: Garland STPM, 15-24.

Fischer, Eileen and Stephen J. Arnold (1990), "More than a Labor of Love: Gender Roles and Christmas Gift Shopping," *Journal of Consumer Research*, 17, 333-345.

_____ and Brenda Gainer (1991), "I Shop Therefore I am: The Role of Shopping in the Social Construction of Women's Identities," *Gender and Consumer Behavior,* Janeen Arnold Costa, ed., Salt Lake City, UT: University of Utah Printing Service, 350-357.

Harris, Marvin (1981), *America Now*, New York: Simon and Schuster.

Hirsch, Alan R. (1995), "Effects of Ambient Odors on Slot Machine Usage in a Las Vegas Casino," *Psychology & Marketing*, 12, 585-594.

Hirschman, Elizabeth C. (1994), "Consumers and Their Animal Companions," *Journal of Consumer Research*, 20, 616-632.

Hsieh, Yaolung J. (1994) "Personal Relationship and Its Influence on Export Behavior: An Empirical Study," *Enhancing Knowledge Development in Marketing*, Ravi Achrol and Andrew Mitchell, eds., 5, 368-373.

_____ (1997), *Customer Satisfaction*, Hwa-Tai Publishing Co., Taipei, Taiwan (in Chinese).

_____ (1999), "Relationship Marketing Strategies of Life Insurance Firms in Taiwan and Their Association with Marketing Performance," *Sun Yat-Sen Management Review*, 7, 821-846 (in Chinese).

_____ and Debra L. Scammon (1993), "Cultural and Economic Antecedents to Evolving Consumer Concerns in Taiwan," *Journal of Consumer Policy*, 16, 61-78.

McGrath, Mary Ann (1996), "Gendered Perceptions of Ideal Retail Service Venues," *Gender, Marketing and Consumer Behavior*, Janeen A. Costa, ed., Salt Lake City, UT: University of Utah Printing Service, 172-175.

_____, John F. Sherry, Jr., and Sidney J. Levy (1993), "Giving Voice to the Gift: The Use of Projective Techniques to Recover Lost Meanings," *Journal of Consumer Psychology*, 2, 171-191.

Otnes, Cele, Young Kim and Tina Lowrey (1992), "Christmas Shopping for 'Easy' and 'Difficult' Recipients: A Social Roles Interpretation," *Journal of Consumer Research*, 15, 422-433.

Rabin, A. I. and Zoli Zlotogorski (1981), "Completion Methods: Word Association, Sentence and Story Completion," *Assessment with Projective Techniques*, New York: Springer Publishing Co., 121-149.

Robins, Douglas M., Clinton R. Sanders, and Spencer E. Cahill (1991), "Dogs and Their People," *Journal of Contemporary Ethnography*, 20, 3-25.

Sanders, Clinton R. (1990), "Excusing Tactics: Social Responses to the Public Misbehavior of Companion Animals," *Anthrozoos*, 4, 90-92.

Savishinsky, Joel S. (1986), "Pet Ideas: The Domestication of Animals, Human Behavior and Human Emotions," *New Perspectives in Our Lives with Companion Animals*, Aaron Katcher and Alan M. Beck, eds, Philadelphia: University of Pennsylvania Press, 112-131.

Serpell, James (1986), *In the Company of Animals: A Study of Human-Animal Relationships*, New York: Basil Blackwell.

Sherry, John F. Jr. and Mary Ann McGrath (1989), "Unpacking the Holiday Presence: A Comparative Ethnography of Two Gift Stores," *Interpretive Consumer Research*, Elizabeth Hirschman, ed., Provo, UT: Association for Consumer Research, 148-167.

_____, Mary Ann McGrath, and Sidney J. Levy (1992), "The Disposition of the Gift and Many Unhappy Returns," *Journal of Retailing*, 68, 40-65.

_____, Mary Ann McGrath, and Sidney J. Levy (1993), "The Dark Side of the Gift," *Journal of Business Research*, 28, 225-244.

Solomon, Michael R., Judith L. Zaichkowsky, and Rosemary Polegato (1999), *Consumer Behavior—Buying, Having, and Being*, Canadian edition, Prentice-Hall Canada Inc.

Taylor, Shirley (1994), "Waiting for Service: The Relationship between Delays and Evaluations of Service," *Journal of Marketing*, 58, 56-69.

Exclusive or Intensive Distribution? The Signaling Role of Channel Intensity in Consumer Information Processing

Scarlett Li Lam, University of California at Berkeley

ABSTRACT

One of the firm's strategic goals in restricting product availability is to signal quality and market demand. Such signals sometimes backfire when consumers consider them incongruous with product merits. We examine three conditions under which backfiring is likely to occur: (1) high processing motivation, (2) strong need for cognition, and (3) moderate product familiarity. We discover two hierarchical processes by which the consumer's inferential beliefs may mediate the effect of distribution intensity signals on purchase intention. One process treats distribution exclusivity as a signal that facilitates purchases by providing diagnostic information on product target and quality. Another process treats exclusivity as a restriction that inhibits demand by increasing search cost and inducing unfavorable attribution to the firm. These two processes differentially respond to high and low distribution intensity signals.

SPECIAL SESSION SUMMARY

The Impact of the Net: Strategies for Consumer Behavior Research Design in the 21st Century

Carolyn Folkman Curasi, Berry College
Margaret K. Hogg, UMIST.
Pauline Maclaran, De Montfort University

"A Critical Exploration of Internet and In-Person Depth Interviews~Customer Loyalty and the Internet: Benefits that Drive Loyalty on the Internet"
Carolyn Folkman Curasi

This paper compared two different interpretive data collection techniques: semi-structured depth interviews conducted over the Internet with semi-structured, depth interviews conducted in person. After a literature review of research on electronic data collection, the advantages and disadvantages of on-line data collection were examined. Major points were illustrated from a project on Internet shopping loyalty in which data was collected using both techniques. Strategies for successfully collecting on-line data were discussed, as well as its potential for combining different data collection sites for the purposes of triangulation and achieving greater levels of trustworthiness in interpretive research designs.

"Consuming Resistance and Resisting Consumers on the Web"
Pauline Maclaran and Miriam Catterall

We examined methodological issues linked to consumer resistance at two levels. Firstly, we took a netnographic approach to explore Internet communities that use their dislike or boycott of a particular brand as the basis for their interaction (e.g. Anti-Amway and Boycott Best Buy Webrings). Secondly, we considered consumer resistance to the research process itself within the context of the Internet. The web's interconnectedness meant that resistance to marketing research was no longer necessarily experienced at a fragmented and individual level (where consumers have problems expressing their voice), but was often, on the Internet, experienced within a community environment where consumers found it easier to express their resistance.

"Identity, Rituals and Role Transitions: Examining Empty-nesters as 'Liminal Consumers'"
Margaret K. Hogg, Carolyn Folkman Curasi and Pauline Maclaran

In this study we identified and examined the informal rituals which consumers used to negotiate their role transition to an empty nest. We collected data in two stages, adopting a 'mixed method' approach. Firstly we used in-depth interviews in 'real life settings' to explore how women experienced consumption rituals and 'communitas' in their life journeys from a full to empty nest. Secondly, we used two e-based methods (netnography and email interviews) in cyber space to explore how women discussed their experiences of consumption rituals and virtual communities in this role transition. The data was analysed to identify themes associated with (re)-negotiating identity in periods of role transition.

"Consumer Behavior Research in Real and Virtual Environments"
Margaret K. Hogg

The goals of this session were, firstly, to illustrate and examine different strategies for using the web in consumer behavior research design; and secondly, to evaluate and conceptualise how R-Life [Real Life][1] and e-based research methods might be used, combined and applied in designing interpretive studies of consumer behavior. Three studies were used to present different perspectives on the impact of the net in consumer behavior research. The authors illustrated how different mixed method approaches were adopted to explore consumer behaviour in real and virtual research settings. A conceptual framework was developed for evaluating strategies for mixed method approaches to consumer behavior research design in actual and cyberspace.

---

[1]Real Life (RL) has been distinguished from computer-based virtual lives (Turkle (1995), cited in Kozinets 1998:366).

The Retailer as Master of Asymmetric Price Competition: Experimental, Empirical, and Simulation-Based Results

Timothy B. Heath, University of Pittsburgh
Joel Huber, Duke University
Xin He, University of Pittsburgh

Empirical models of purchase data show that consumers switch to discounted higher-quality brands more than discounted lower-quality brands (*asymmetric price competition*). Only recently, however, have researchers like those in this session begun to isolate the causes of this asymmetry.

Our first study reports two experiments demonstrating that product assortments influence brand choice, commitment to the brand chosen, and switching tendencies (Heath, He, and Chatterjee). As we move from assortments that have more lower-quality brands to those with more higher-quality brands, choice of, and commitment to, higher-quality brands increases steadily. These effects then partially drive competitive asymmetries, but only partially since statistical controls for commitment fail to eliminate asymmetries. Also contributing was the dominance that sometimes arises when brands discount. If, for example, multiple brands within a tier have similar prices and features, a discounting brand is likely to dominate (be superior on at least one dimension but inferior on none) one or more brands within that tier. Two laboratory experiments report that discounts that effect such within-tier dominance do, in fact, tend to produce more switching, where asymmetries arise more commonly when such dominance arises. The fact that national brands can produce within-tier dominance with price discount more readily than can store brands (since the latter are often the lowest quality brands available) implicates within-tier dominance as a contributor to the asymmetric price competition commonly reported in the marketplace.

Lemon and Nowlis extend asymmetry management into a rich set of promotional tactics. Using multiple methods that include a scanner study, a paper-and-pencil experiment, and an internet-based experiment, the authors show that feature advertising and end-of-aisle displays benefit higher-quality brands more than lower-quality brands. However, the difference across quality tiers in price response is mitigated by marketing tactics that impair direct comparisons between competing brands (e.g., end-of-aisle displays that segregate the discounted brands). In fact, while asymmetries favor higher-quality brands when tactics are used alone, combining tactics reverses the asymmetry which comes to favor lower-quality brands. Again, while store brands often suffer at the hands of competitive asymmetries, retailers can mitigate this suffering by applying marketing tactics that bolster brand perceptions and reduce head-to-head comparisons.

Huber and Lo are the first researchers (we know of) to apply conjoint analysis to the study of competitive asymmetries. Based on a study of over 1,400 consumers, the authors used part-worth utilities in simulations of different market structures to predict consumer responses to changes in competitors' prices and product features. These tests assess the ability of consumer heterogeneity to account for asymmetric competition. Asymmetric price competition, for example, might arise because consumers of lower quality brands are generally more responsive to price reductions than are consumers of higher quality. The simulations also tested for effects of loss aversion. In general, the results show that consumer heterogeneity is capable of accounting for asymmetries in both price and quality competition (the latter favoring lower-quality brands), suggesting that appeals to more involved psychological mechanisms such as loss aversion may not be needed.

Children's Perceived Truthfulness of Television Advertising and Parental Influence:
A Hong Kong Study

Kara Chan, Hong Kong Baptist University

ABSTRACT

This study examines Chinese children's perceived truthfulness, liking and attention of television advertising in Hong Kong. A quota sample of four hundred and forty-eight children (ages 5 to 12) was personal-interviewed in May 1998. Results indicated that nearly equal proportions of children perceived that television advertising was mostly true and mostly not true. The judgment was mainly derived from their perception of the advertising content. The bases for skepticism about advertising varied by age. Older children depended more on personal user experience and younger children relied on others' comments. Hong Kong children liked television advertising and watched commercials sometimes. Like children in the West, perceived truthfulness and liking of commercials decreased with age. Perceived truthfulness of television advertising was positively related with liking and attention. Hong Kong children reported that their parents often used commercials to teach them about good citizenship and bad products to avoid.

INTRODUCTION

Advertisers target at children because of their high disposable income, their early establishment of loyalty to certain brands and a conventional wisdom that young adults buy products on impulse (Fox 1996). Many parents and critics fear that children are susceptible to commercial appeals because young viewers lack the necessary cognitive skills to process the highly persuasive messages and make appropriate judgements about them (Choate 1975). Educators and researchers have attempted to design programs that will teach children about the intent of advertisements and help children construct defenses from commercial messages (Pecora 1995).

Twenty-five years of consumer socialization research have yield impressive findings on the developmental sequence characterizing the growth of consumer knowledge, skills, and values as children mature throughout childhood and adolescence. Many evidence shows that as children grow in cognitive and social terms, there is growth in knowledge of products, brands, advertising, parental influence strategies, and consumption motives and values (John 1999). Although the issue of children and advertising is a largely explored issue in the U.S.A., there has been limited investigation on children's receptivity to advertising in Asian cultures.

Children in Hong Kong are exposed to a large amount of advertising, especially through television advertising. According to a weekly AC Nielsen's television rating report, the average rating of TVB-Jade, the dominant Chinese channel, from 7 a.m. to 12:00 mid-night on a school day in May 1999 for children 4 to 14 was 11 rating points (equivalent to an audience size of 95,000). Children watched a lot more television during school holidays. The average rating of TVB-Jade on an Easter holiday was 16 rating points (40 percent more audience than on a typical school day). A child that spends four hours per day watching television may be exposed to 15,000 commercials every year. Hong Kong parents were concerned about the impact of advertising on children. A survey of Hong Kong adults indicated a majority accused television advertising of having adverse effects on children. They reported television advertising leads children to pester their parents (Chan and Ruidl 1996).

There are stringent regulations that govern television advertising to children in Hong Kong. The basic principle is that television commercials should not take advantage of the natural credulity and sense of loyalty of children. The presentation of commercial information must not result in physical, mental or moral harm to children. Commercials that are frightening, anxiety provoking or which contain violent, dangerous or anti-social behaviours can not be directed toward children. Children in commercials also need to display good manners and behaviour. If there is a reference to a competition in an advertisement aimed at children, the value of prizes and the chances of a child winning one must not be exaggerated. The true size of the product advertised and any free gift for children should be made easy to judge (Hong Kong Broadcast Authority 1993).

With all the efforts to control the advertising presentation, what is the overall attitude of Hong Kong children toward television advertising? Do they perceive commercials to be truthful and how do they make such judgments? How do Hong Kong parents communicate with their children about television advertising? This study attempts to examine children's attitudes toward television advertising. The study adopts Piaget's (1970) theory of cognitive development. The theory identifies distinct stages of cognitive development and postulates that children would manifest differences in the ways they select, evaluate, and use information. Children's attitudes toward television advertising will therefore be analyzed by school year.

The objectives of the current study are:

a) to study children's perceived truthfulness of television advertising and how they judge whether commercials were true or not;

b) to examine children's attention to and attitudes toward television advertising;

c) to investigate whether attention and attitudes toward television advertising are related to perceived truthfulness; and

d) to investigate children's perceived parental guidance on their exposure to TV advertising.

The study is of major interest to both marketers and to public policy makers. Marketers are keen to know if their target audiences are attending to the commercials and children's general attitude toward television advertising. Policy makers are concerned whether existing regulations are effective to protect the interests of the children. The study has much to contribute as there is a paucity of empirical information on the topic in Asian cultures.

LITERATURE REVIEW

Studies about children and advertising often refer to Piaget's (1970) theory of cognitive development due to the consistent age differences in the way children understand and respond to commercials (Cosley and Brucks 1986; Wartella 1980). In Piaget's theory, children pass through four stages of cognitive development: (1) sensorimotor thought from ages 0 to 2; (2) preoperational thought from ages 2 to 7; (3) concrete operational thought from ages 7 to 12; and (4) formal operational thought after age 12. During sensorimotor thought, children represent information with their bodies. During preoperational thought, children begin to use symbols and representational thinking. Because of the cognitive limitations that are age-related, children have difficulty in distin-

Advances in Consumer Research
Volume 28, © 2001

guishing fantasy from reality (Wartella and Ettema 1974) and understanding commercial intent (Macklin 1987). During concrete operational thought, children begin to think logically, but concrete experiences continue to set boundaries on their thinking. At this stage, children are able to understand the difference between commercials and programs and between imaginary and real experience. Finally, children at formal operational thought exhibit abstract thinking and are able to differentiate between image portrayed in advertising and reality.

Previous study findings indicate that comprehension of commercial intent is related to age. Children younger than 7 or 8 years old show little awareness of what a commercial is and its persuasive intent and appear unable to deal with commercials appropriately (Blosser and Roberts 1985; Ward and Wackman 1973). As children get older, they increasingly understand that the underlying motive in commercial advertising is to persuade them to buy things. Children begin to understand persuasive intent at about 7 to 8 years of age, and most children master this concept by about 10 or 11 years (Comstock and Paik 1991; Van Evra 1990; Young 1990). Researchers using non-verbal measures found that some children at younger age from 5 to 8 also understand advertising intent (Macklin 1987).

While understanding of the purpose of advertising improves with age, belief in the truthfulness of advertising tends to decline over age. With comprehension of persuasive intent comes cynicism and distrust about the advertised product (Rossiter 1980). Distrust begins to emerge by the second grade and is evident for most sixth graders (Gaines and Esserman 1981; Rossiter 1980). Ward, Wackman and Wartella (1977) reported that the percentage of kindergartners, third graders, and sixth graders believing that advertising never or only sometimes tells the truth increased from 50 percent to 88 percent to 97 percent, respectively. Children also developed a better understanding of why commercials were sometimes untruthful and how to distinguish truthful from untruthful ads. For example, kindergartners could not state the reason for why commercials lie while older children connected lying to persuasive intent (Ward, Wackman and Wartella 1977).

A national survey of over 500 British children aged 4 to 13 found that only six percent thought that commercials 'always' tell the truth, while 15 percent thought they 'quite often' are truthful. Most (60 percent) reported that commercials 'sometimes' tell the truth. The remaining 20 percent perceived commercials 'rarely or never' tell the truth (Greenberg, Fazal and Wober 1986). Perceived truthfulness of advertising was not found to differ according to the gender or social class of the children, but age did make a difference. The youngest children were most likely to believe that commercials told the truth, while older children were more skeptical (Greenberg, Fazal and Wober, 1986).

The same survey indicated that attention to commercials varied among children. Thirty percent said that they watch all commercials and 37 percent said they watch most. Fifteen percent reported that they watch around half and fifteen percent watch a few. None of the children said that they did not watch commercials at all. Attention did not differ by age or social class, but did differ by gender. Girls reported greater attention to commercials than boys. Furthermore, attention was positively related to the perceived truthfulness of advertising. Those who paid more attention to advertising were more likely to perceive that commercials were truthful (Greenberg, Fazal and Wober 1986).

Despite their skepticism, children had favorable attitudes towards certain type of commercials. A survey on children aged 9 to 10 in Belfast, Northern Ireland found that two-thirds believed that advertisers only sometimes tell the truth. Despite the doubt toward commercials, most of the children said they enjoyed par-

ticular commercials, especially the ones featuring humor (Collins 1990).

Review of the literature indicates there are two under-researched areas that need further study. There is a lack of studies that investigate how children viewers make judgment on whether commercials were truthful or not. There is also limited research on how parents use the commercials to teach children in Asia. The current study will attempt to fill these gaps.

METHOD

Six advertising and public relations undergraduate students of Hong Kong Baptist University interviewed four hundred and forty-eight Hong Kong Chinese children from five to twelve years old recruited through personal sources. The children were from a quota sample of equal number of boys and girls for each school year from kindergarten through grade six. Interviewers were trained on the purpose of the study, the structure of the interview and the skills in soliciting responses. Interviews were conducted at public libraries, churches, restaurants and parks near school areas in May 1998. Efforts were made to minimize interruptions and intrusions by other family members or friends present. In order to minimize potential problems and facilitate children's efforts, respondents were told that 'when we are watching television, sometimes the program stops and there is other message coming up. These messages are called the commercials'. The interviews then went on to ask three closed-ended questions about how often they watched the commercials, whether they liked them or not, and whether these commercials were mostly true or not. Two open-ended questions were asked about how they know commercials are true or not, and what their parents asked them to learn and not to learn from television advertising. The interviews were recorded, transcribed and later coded by a research assistant. A coding menu was developed for the open-ended questions after reviewing all the responses, and one tenth of the questionnaires were counter-checked. The inter-coder reliability coefficients for open-ended responses were over 85 percent.

FINDINGS

Perceived truthfulness of television advertising. Table 1 summarizes Hong Kong children's perception about the truthfulness of television advertising. Nearly equal proportions of children perceived that commercials were mostly true (forty two percent) and mostly not true (forty percent). Fourteen percent of respondents perceived that commercials were partly true. Result for children in kindergartens and grade one was bi-modal. They either perceived commercials to be 'mostly true' or 'mostly not true' and very few of them considered commercials 'partly true'. Perceived truthfulness of television advertising differed according to gender and school year. On the whole, a higher proportion of younger children perceived commercials to be mostly true than older children (Chi-square value=16.6, significance<0.005). When analyzed by gender and by school year, results indicated that difference in perceived truthfulness of television advertising according to school year was significant for boys but not for girls. Boys had increased skepticism of commercials with school year, but not girls. The percentage of boys in kindergartners and first graders, second and third graders, and fourth to six graders believing that advertising is mostly true dropped from 58 percent to 41 percent to 33 percent respectively. The drop for girls was from 48 percent to 41 percent to 38 percent respectively.

Table 2 summarizes how children know whether TV advertising is true or not. A majority of the children's judgments were based on perception of advertising content as well as intrusive feelings. Thirty nine percent of children said they perceived

TABLE 1
Children's Perceived Truthfulness of TV Advertising

	Year	(%)		
	Kindergarten,G1	G2-3	G4-6	Total
	n=128	128	192	448
Television advertising is	%	%	%	%
Mostly true	53	41	35	42
Partly true	6	15	18	14
Mostly not true	32	41	45	40
Don't know	9	3	2	4
Total	100	100	100	100

chi-square value for the sample = 16.6 (<0.005)
chi-square value for boys = 18.9 (<0.005)
chi-square value for girls = 10.1 (N.S.)

TABLE 2
How Children Know Whether Television Advertising is True or Not True

		Year			
		Kindergarten, G1	G2-3	G4-6	Total
	Ad is				
	True(T)	n=55	50	69	174
Reason*	Not-true(NT)	n=43	69	114	226
The content seems so/	T(%)	33	38	43	39
I feel that it is	NT(%)	49	61	56	56
Other people tell me	T(%)	31	12	7	16
	NT(%)	35	20	10	18
Having/Having not	T(%)	20	32	26	26
seen the product	NT(%)	0	3	4	3
Having tried the product	T(%)	15	14	20	17
	NT(%)	14	10	26	19
The product is just like/	T(%)	0	0	0	0
not like the advertising	NT(%)	2	3	4	3
Others	T(%)	2	3	3	0
	NT(%)	0	3	1	1

* coded from open-ended responses
Chi-square value for those considered advertising is mostly true = 15.7 (N.S.)
Chi-square value for those considered advertising is mostly not true =22.6 (<0.05)

commercials mostly true because the content seemed so or they felt so. Fifty-six percent of children said they perceived commercials mostly not true because the content seemed so or they felt so. Other frequently mentioned reasons for perceiving commercials true were through encountering the product (seeing the product: 26 percent; trying the product: 17 percent) and from word-of-mouth (16 percent). Other frequently mentioned reasons for perceiving commercials not true were having tried the product (19 percent) and from word-of-mouth (18 percent). Chi-square test results indicated that the reasons given by those perceiving commercials mostly true were similar for children of different school years. However, the reasons given for suspicion were different according to school year. Skepticism about advertising for the youngest children came mainly from others' opinions while that for the older children came mainly from their personal experience. Bases for judgments did not differ by gender.

Attention to television advertising. Table 3 summarizes Hong Kong children's self-report of their attention to TV advertising.

This only measures children's perceptions of their attentiveness to commercials. Children's actual visual attention to the television screen was not measured in the current study. Only three percent of children said that they did not watch TV commercials at all. Fifty-two percent of children said they 'sometimes' watched TV advertising. Twenty-nine percent said they watched often and sixteen percent watched nearly every time. Comparing with the results of a survey on British children, Hong Kong children were less attentive to TV advertising. However, when compared with results from a survey on Hong Kong adults, Hong Kong children paid more attention to TV advertising than adults. Two-way ANOVA result indicated that attention did not differ either by school age or by gender.

Attitudes toward TV advertising. Table 4 summarizes children's attitudes toward TV advertising. Results indicated that children liked TV advertising. Fifty-six percent of respondents expressed liking while seventeen percent expressed disliking of commercials. Result for children in kindergartens and grade one

TABLE 3
Children's Attention to TV Advertising

	Year Kindergarten, G1 n=125	(%) G2-3 128	G4-6 192	Total 445	British Children 4-13* National sample of over 500	HK adults# 691
Don't watch at all	3	2	3	3	0(did not watch any)	2
Watch sometimes	46	57	53	52	33(watch a few/around half)	76
Watch often	28	27	32	29	37(watch most)	20
Watch every time	23	13	13	16	31(watch them all)	2
Total	100	100	100	100	100	100

chi-square = 8.7 (N.S.)

* Greenberg, Fazal and Wober (1986), original wordings of answers in bracket
\# Chan and Ruidl (1996), wordings of questions and answers are the same as the current study

TABLE 4
Children's Attitudes Toward TV Advertising

	Kindergarten,G1 n= 128	Year G2-3 128	(%) G4-6 192	Total 448	HK adults# 691
Dislike very much	2	4	2	2	1
Dislike	20	16	11	15	7
Neutral	12	27	37	27	34
Like	61	49	46	51	49
Like very much	6	4	4	5	10
Total	100	100	100	100	100

chi-square = 28.9 (<0.0001)

\# Chan and Ruidl (1996), wordings of questions and answers are the same as the current study

TABLE 5
Attention to TV Advertising and Perceived Truthfulness of TV Advertising

	TV advertising is	
Attention to TV advertising	Mostly true (%)	Mostly not true (%)
Don't watch at all	3	4
Watch sometimes	44	57
Watch often	32	26
Watch every time	21	13
Total	100	100

chi-square = 8.3 (<0.05)

was bi-modal. They either 'like' them or 'dislike', and very few of them reported a neutral answer. Chi-square test results indicated that attitudes differed by school year for boys as well as girls. Younger children liked TV advertising while older children took neutral position. Older girls reported a greater drop in liking of commercials than older boys did.

Table 5 shows the relationship between children's perceived truthfulness of TV advertising and attention to TV advertising. Attention to commercials was positively related to the perceived truthfulness of TV advertising. Those who perceived commercials 'mostly true' paid more attention to commercials than those who perceived commercials 'mostly not true'.

Table 6 shows the relationship between children's perceived truthfulness of TV advertising and attitudes toward TV advertising. Attitude toward commercials was positively related to the perceived truthfulness of TV advertising. Those who perceived commercials 'mostly true' were 50 percent more likely to say they like them than those who perceived commercials 'mostly not true'.

Table 7 summarizes the children's perception of the parental influence on what to learn and what not to learn from commercials. The actual parental influence was not measured in the current study as parents were not asked directly. Children reported more don'ts than do's. Children perceived that their parents were concerned about the consumption of 'bad' products including drugs, ciga-

TABLE 6
Attitudes Towards TV Advertising and Perceived Truthfulness of TV Advertising

| | TV advertising is | |
	Mostly true	Mostly not true
Attitudes toward TV advertising	(%)	(%)
Dislike very much	2	4
Dislike	10	18
Neutral	21	32
Like	60	44
Like very much	9	3
Total	100	100

Chi-square=20.2 (<0.0001)

TABLE 7
Children's Perception of Parental Influence on What to Learn from Television Advertising

	No.	Total
Don'ts*		*124 (73%)*
don't take illegal drugs	38	
don't copy violent behaviour	33	
don't copy incorrect behaviours (tell lies, watch bad movies and read bad books, etc)	13	
don't steal/corrupt	11	
don't smoke	9	
don't copy dangerous action	9	
don't imitate a specific cartoon figure	8	
don't drink alcohol	3	
Do's*		*45 (27%)*
study hard	13	
keep good health	8	
be good to parents	3	
be a good child	9	
keep Hong Kong clean/conserve	7	
others	3	
Total mentions		*169 (100%)*

* coded from open-ended responses

rettes and liquor. Hong Kong children also reported that their parents asked them not to imitate violent and dangerous actions. Some children reported that their parents were concerned about illegal behaviours (e.g. stealing) and incorrect behaviours (e.g. telling lies). Children reported that parents use commercials to teach them to study hard and be good children. They also reported that parents used commercials to teach them about keeping good health and a tidy environment.

DISCUSSION AND CONCLUSION

The current study indicates belief in the truthfulness of commercials and liking of television advertising tend to decline over age. This is in line with previous findings in Western societies. However, children's attention to television advertising did not decline over age.

Chinese children were not totally susceptible to advertising appeals. Even children in kindergarten and grade 1 cast doubt about the truthfulness of commercials. It was interesting to find children's bases for skepticism about advertising vary by age. Younger children relied mainly on the advertising content or had been told to cast doubt on advertising. This study is limited in that most of the interviewers did not follow up on children's sources of information about the truthfulness of commercials. Younger

children probably learned to defend themselves against the persuasive messages from their parents, siblings, teachers or other adults. Older children had more consumer experience and were more likely to draw upon them to cast doubt on the commercials. One fifth of those who perceived commercials were mostly not true because they had tried the product. According to findings in Western societies, belief in the truthfulness of television advertising declines with age. This is consistent with Piaget's (1970) theory of cognitive development. As the children entered the concrete operational stage, they were better able to differentiate between imaginary portrayals in the commercials and real-life experiences. Children, as consumers, were better able to compare user experience with advertising promises.

As most of the children relied on the commercial content to make judgments about its trustworthiness, existing regulations on message presentation should be maintained.

Another interesting finding is the difference in skepticism of television advertising with age for boys and girls. A high percentage of boys in kindergartens and grade 1 believed that commercials were mostly true while boys in grades 4 to 6 no longer believed so. Skepticism toward commercials was moderately high for girls in kindergartens and grade 1. The drop in perceived truthfulness with age was not significant for girls. The results seem to suggest boys and girls have different pace of cognitive development. Girls seem to be more mature in early age and read commercials more critically than boys. However, boys read commercials more critically than girls in older age. Further research is needed to explain such difference.

Despite children's skepticism of television advertising, most of the respondents expressed their liking of commercials. The results indicated that those who put perceived commercials 'mostly true' were also more likely to enjoy commercials and paid more attention to them. Perhaps this represents the group of children most easily persuaded by selling messages. Media education on critical reading and viewing of persuasive messages is mostly needed for this audience segment.

Hong Kong children reported that their parents used commercials as teaching aids. The emphasis was on topics related to health, safety and proper behaviours of children. Children seldom reported that their parents use commercials to teach them about consumerism and purchasing decision making. Although Hong Kong parents perceived that television advertising took advantage of children (Chan and Ruidl 1996), children did not perceive that their parents helped them to become competent consumers. Surprisingly, children's rights as consumers are not fully respected. Fostering a consumer culture empowering consumers to be conscious of their rights and obligations is one of the main areas of work of the Hong Kong Consumer Council (Hong Kong Consumer Council 1998). Over the past decades, the Consumer Council has launched several campaigns to encourage dissatisfied consumers to lodge complaints with them. However, none of these campaigns are targeted at children. Publicity campaigns on children's consumer rights and ways to collect consumer complaints from children should be developed. Perhaps consumer education should start with the parents, teachers, community leaders and administrators. Parents and teachers should discuss with children their consumer rights and support them to express their dissatisfaction, if any. Hong Kong is certainly in need of a media literacy program to teach people how to read advertising messages critically.

To conclude, Hong Kong children did cast doubt about television advertising. Perceived truthfulness of commercials decreased with age. Hong Kong children also enjoyed television advertising and paid a lot of attention to it. Perceived truthfulness of television advertising had positive association with children's liking and attention to these messages. Hong Kong children reported that their parents were more concerned about the influence of commercials on their health and moral standards. Commercials were perceived as teaching aids for becoming good citizens and avoiding hazardous product categories. As a result of the study, continuing consumer education and media literacy programs for children and adults should be encouraged.

REFERENCES

Blosser, B.J. and Roberts, D.F. (1985) "Age Differences in Children's Perceptions of Message Intent: Responses to TV News, Commercials, Educational Spots and Public Service Announcements", *Communication Research*, 12, 455-484.

Chan, K. and Ruidl, R. (1996) "Predicting Attitudes Toward Television Advertising: The View from Hong Kong", Paper presented at the 20th International Association of Mass Communication Research Scientific Conference and General Assembly, August 18-22, Sydney, Australia.

Choate, R.B. (1975) Petition of the Council on Children, Media and Merchandising to issue a trade regulation rule governing the private regulation of children's television advertising. Filed before the Federation Trade Commission, Washington DC, March.

Collins, J. (1990) "Television and primary school children in Northern Ireland, The impact of advertising", *Journal of Educational Television*, 16, 31-39.

Comstock, G. and Paik, H. (1991) *Television and the American Child*. San Diego, CA: Academic Press.

Cosley, R.S. and Brucks, M. (1986) "Product Knowledge as an Explanation for Age-related Differences in Children's Cognitive Responses to Advertising", *Advances in Consumer Research*, 14, 288-292.

Gaines, L. and Esserman, J.F. (1981) "A Quantitative Study of Young Children's Comprehension of Television Programmes and Commercials", pp. 95-105 in J.F. Esserman (ed.), *Television Advertising and Children*, New York: Child Research Service.

Greenberg, B.S., Fazal, S. and Wober, M. (1986) *Children's Views on Advertising*, London: Independent Broadcasting Authority, Research Report, February.

Fox, R.F. (1996) *Harvesting Minds: How TV Commercials Control Kids*, CT: Praeger Publishers.

Hong Kong Broadcasting Authority (1993) *Television Code of Practice on Advertising Standards*, Hong Kong: Government Printer.

Hong Kong Consumer Council (1998) *Annual Report 1997-98*, Hong Kong: Consumer Council.

John, D.R. (1999) "Consumer socialization of children: A retrospective look at twenty-five years of research", *Journal of Consumer Research*, 26, 183-213.

Macklin, N.C. (1987) "Preschoolers' Understanding of the Information Function of Television Advertising", *Journal of Consumer Research*, 14, 229-239.

Pecora, N. (1995). "Children and Television Advertising from a Social Science Perspective", *Critical Studies in Mass Communication* 12, 354-364.

Piaget, J. (1970) "The Stages of the Intellectual Development of the Child", pp.291-298 in P.H. Mussen, J.J. Conger and J. Kagan (eds.) *Readings in Child Development and Personality*. New York: Harper and Row.

Rossiter, J.R. (1980) "The Effects of Volume and Repetition of Television Commercials", pp.153-184 in R.P. Adler, G.S. Lesser, L.K. Meringoff, T.S. Roberson, J.R. Rossiter and S. Ward (Eds.), *The Effects of Television Advertising on Children: Review and Recommendations*. Lexington, MA: Lexington Books.

Van Evra, J.P. (1990) *Television and child development*. Hillsdale, NJ: L. Erlbaum.

Ward, S. and Wackman, D. (1973) "Children's Information Processing of Television Advertising", pp.119-146 in F.G. Kline and P. Clarke (eds.) *New Models for Mass Communication Research*, Sage Annual Reviews of Communication Volume 2, Beverly Hills, CA: Sage.

Ward, S., Wackman, D., and Wartella, E. (1977) *How Children Learn to Buy*, Beverly Hills, CA: Sage.

Wartella, E. (1980) "Individual Differences in Children's Responses to Television Advertising", in E.L. Palmer and A. Dorr (eds.) *Children and the Faces of Television*, New York: Academic Press.

Wartella, E. and Ettema, J. (1974) "A Cognitive Developmental Study of Children's Attention to Television Commercials", *Communication Research*, 1, 46-69.

Young, B. (1990) *Television and Children*, Oxford: Clarendon Press.

Child-Brand Relationships: A Conceptual Framework

Mindy F. Ji, Texas A&M University

ABSTRACT

This paper presents a conceptual framework for understanding the formation of child-brand relationships. It first reviews evidence that supports the existence of child-brand relationships and then examines children's *potential* to enter such a relationship. This potential is suggested to be a function of children's *motivation*, *opportunity*, and *ability* (MOA) to form and maintain relationships with brands. Research propositions are posited to explain how children's age, gender, and social environmental factors (i.e., parents and peers) affect their potential to enter into the relationships. Finally, the paper provides suggestions on how to nurture successful child-brand relationships and discusses some managerial implications.

An Examination of Urban Chinese Children's Relative Influence in Family Decision-Making

Laura A. Williams, Louisiana Tech University
Ann Veeck, Western Michigan University
Naihua Jiang, Yangzhou University

ABSTRACT

In the People's Republic of China, strict population control measures and the movement toward a more open economy have combined to create a unique environment in which to study the influence of children in family decision-making. The objectives of this study are to examine the relative influence of family members in purchase decision-making and to explore demographic factors thought to explain variation observed across family members. A survey of 286 urban Chinese families was examined, with the parent-child pair constituting the unit of analysis. The analysis found that the influence of family members varied by product category and by the character of the purchase decision. An additional finding was that, in contrast to American children, Chinese children attributed less purchase influence to themselves than did their parents. The findings offer insight into how the purchase influence of children varies according to cultural and economic conditions.

Advances in Consumer Research
Volume 28, © 2001

Spending Time: Caregiving Consumption in the Context of AIDS/HIV

Steven M. Kates, Monash University

ABSTRACT

The AIDS pandemic has resulted in profound social changes within and outside gay men's communities, providing an interesting and unique context for caring consumption that emphasizes patient-centered care and empowered health consumers, persons living with AIDS (PLWAs) and their families. This article reports the findings of a study of the psychological and social dynamics involved with the caregiving practices associated with the dying and death of someone with AIDS. Twenty informants were interviewed about the circumstances involved in the palliative care, the difficulties encountered with service providers, doctors, and other caregivers, and about how they dealt with grief after death. Findings include an unpacking of the meanings of consumers' time in the context of caregiving practices.

Guilt Appeals: The Effects of Responsibility and Altruistic Norms

Debra Z. Basil, University of Lethbridge
Nancy M. Ridgway, University of Colorado
Michael D. Basil, University of Lethbridge

ABSTRACT

Guilt appeals are commonly used by charities to motivate prosocial behavior (Huhmann & Brotherton, 1997). A modest amount of research has examined the relationship between guilt appeals and charitable donations (e.g. Bozinoff & Ghingold, 1983; Regan, 1971), but many questions remain. As noted by O'Keefe (1998), previous research regarding guilt appeals has focused primarily on the explicitness of the guilt appeal (e.g. Coulter & Pinto, 1995; Ruth & Faber, 1988). One major unanswered question relates to the process through which guilt appeals operate. This research seeks to begin clarifying the process through which guilt appeals lead to charitable donations.

The means through which guilt facilitates helping behavior is of particular interest. Miceli (1992) proposed three essential ingredients for guilt induction. The first is responsibility. One will not feel guilty about something for which he or she does not feel in some way responsible. Responsibility may stem from causing something to occur, or from failing to avoid the onset of some occurrence. An individual may feel guilty about failing to avert some negative situation for others if he or she does not make the needed financial contribution. The second requisite for guilt is that the action or lack thereof causes harm. Failing to make a charitable donation may lead to a lack of food or other necessities for other people, which would cause harm. The third requisite for guilt is that one's personal moral standards are violated.

Miceli (1992), and Miceli and Castelfranchi (1998) focused on interpersonal guilt induction in their proposed guilt framework (i.e., one on one interactions). The present research adapts their framework to guilt appeals for charitable donations. Based on their propositions, if one feels guilty, then he or she must feel some sense of responsibility for the situation (responsibility either to act or not to act in some manner). It would seem, then, that successful guilt appeals should operate by inducing a sense of responsibility to help. A sense of responsibility, in turn, should lead to larger charitable donations.

Two laboratory experiments were conducted to test this. Study one demonstrated that guilt appeals engender a relatively stronger sense of responsibility to help the less fortunate, compared to a control appeal. This study also demonstrated that a stronger sense of responsibility increases an individual's intention to make a charitable donation. A variety of guilt advertisements (nine) were used in this study, to assure that the results were not dependent upon the wording of a specific advertisement. These results should therefore be generalizable to a wide variety of guilt advertisements for charity.

The results of study two demonstrated that the effect of guilt appeals on charitable donations depends upon both a sense of responsibility and the activation of altruistic norms. When others are present, altruistic norms are activated to a greater extent, and individuals have a stronger desire to act altruistically (compared to when others are not present). The presence of others also interacts with a strong sense of responsibility such that when both are present individuals give even larger charitable donations.

The results of these studies provide initial insight into the process through which guilt appeals generate donations. An important element in generating charitable donations through the use of guilt appeals appears to be instilling a sense of responsibility to help. These results suggest that advertisers who choose to use guilt appeals should test not just the level of guilt that the appeal induces, but also the level of responsibility the appeal instills. Additionally, these results demonstrated that activation of altruistic norms can be an important factor in the functioning of guilt appeals. As such, guilt advertisements that successfully induce a sense of responsibility and activate altruistic norms should be more effective than those that do not.

REFERENCES

Bozinoff, Lorne and Morry Ghingold (1983). Evaluating Guilt Arousing Marketing Communications. *Journal of Business Research*, 11, 243-255.

Coulter, Robin H. and Mary B. Pinto (1995), "Guilt Appeals in Advertising: What Are Their Effects?" *Journal of Applied Psychology*, 80(6), 697-705.

Huhmann, Bruce A. and Timothy P. Brotherton (1997), "A Content Analysis of Guilt Appeals in Popular Magazine Advertisements," *The Journal of Advertising*, 26(2), 35-45.

Miceli, Maria (1992), "How To Make Someone Feel Guilty: Strategies of Guilt Inducement and Their Goals," *Journal for the Theory of Social Behavior*, 22(1), 81-104.

Miceli, Maria and Cristiano Castelfranchi (1998), "How to Silence One's Conscience: Cognitive Defenses Against the Feeling of Guilt," *Journal for the Theory of Social Behavior*, 28, 287-318.

O'Keefe, Daniel J. (2000), "Guilt and Social Influence," in M.E. Roloff (ed.) *Communication Yearbook*, 23, Thousand Oaks, CA: Sage.

Regan, Judith W. (1971), "Guilt, Perceived Injustice, and Altruistic Behavior," *Journal of Personality and Social Psychology*, 18 (April), 124-132.

Ruth, Julie A. and Ronald J. Faber (1988), "Guilt: An Overlooked Advertising Appeal," *Proceedings of the 1988 Conference of the American Academy of Advertising*, John D. Leckenby, ed., Austin, TX: American Academy of Advertising, 83-89.

Consuming to Achieve Affective Goals: A Framework for Analysis with Application

W. Edward Roth, Penn State University

ABSTRACT

A framework for analyzing how people use consumer objects to achieve affective goals is developed. The term *affective consumption* refers to the use of a good to achieve an affective goal of either entering a positively valenced affective state, or leaving a negatively valenced one. Affective goals may be achieved using either an instant gratification strategy or a delayed gratification strategy. The two dimensions of goal and strategy are crossed to form a two-by-two framework delineating four types of affective consumption: sensation, relief, recovery, and fulfillment. This framework is then applied to interview data gathered from ten users of health and fitness centers, and is found to be useful in analyzing and categorizing affective goals involved in the use of these centers. Implications for consumer research are discussed, as are directions for future research.

The Three Faces of E, commerce: Insight into Online Consumer Behavior Through the Interpretation of an Internet Consumer's Experiences

Bruce D. Weinberg, Bentley College

Chair:
Nancy Puccinelli, Harvard Business School

Presentations:
The Psychology Of An Online Shopping Pioneer
Sidney J. Levy, University of Arizona

He Says, She Says: Two Versions of a 24/7 E-consumption Life
Frederic Brunel, Boston University

Interpreting the Interpreter: The (Mis)Adventures of a True Techy in E-Love
Susan Dobscha, Bentley College

Research In Exploring The Online Consumer Experience
Bruce D. Weinberg, Bentley College

Bruce Weinberg, as part of his Internet Shopping 24/7 Project, set out to do all of his retail shopping exclusively online (and to not enter any retail stores, excluding restaurants and services) from September 15, 1999 to September 26, 2000. He chronicled his shopping experiences in an online diary (i.e., text) at www.InternetShopping247.com (when he initiated the project, the site people.bu.edu/celtics was used).

In this session, three researchers presented their interpretations of his Internet Shopping 24/7 Project experience and Weinberg served as the discussant. Both Sidney Levy and Susan Dobscha based their interpretations solely on the text. Fred Brunel's interpretation was based primarily on depth interviews with Bruce and Amy, his wife.

Sidney Levy's manuscript, detailing his interpretation, is listed in full here. Synopses of the interpretations presented by Brunel and Dobscha are also detailed. Finally, a manuscript by Weinberg is included.

"He Says, She Says: Two Versions of a 24/7 E-consumption Life"
Frederic F. Brunel, Boston University

This interpretation focused on the following research questions:

- How does e-consumption adoption take place?
- How is e-consumption affecting consumption for one person (Bruce) but also for the family unit?
- How is everyday consumption changed?
- What are the adaptations that take place?
- What types of challenges have to be negotiated?
- What are the outcomes of this experience?

The methods used were depth interviews with both husband (Bruce) and wife (Amy) and a content analysis and interpretation of Bruce's first person account of his experience and Amy's third person account of her observations of Bruce's experience. One major challenge in this analysis was in identifying the behaviors of Bruce as a researcher and Bruce as a consumer; could the two be untangled? Would the analysis be based on a sample size of one or two? An effort was made to differentiate, when possible, Bruce as researcher and Bruce as consumer.

ADOPTION FACTORS

As a researcher

The Internet Shopping 24/7 Project was the product of a crisis and three catalysts. The crisis was a tenure case that was denied. Bruce initiated the formal tenure application process at Boston University in the spring of 1997 and a final decision to deny tenure was made on his case in the fall of 1998. During both the time period that his case was under review and the time period that followed the announcement of the final decision, it was a time of great introspection for Bruce—approximately two years. Part of this process resulted in his serving as a visiting professor of marketing at Northwestern University's Kellogg Graduate School of Management—where he was exposed to researchers who influenced his conceptualization of the Internet Shopping 24/7 Project.

At Kellogg, he had frequent exposure to Mohan Sawhney and he was impressed with Mohan's knowledge about and understanding of ecommerce. Bruce saw Mohan as a "player" in this space and he wanted to realize a similar level of understanding in the area as he felt it would help advance his research. Bruce says about Kellogg and Mohan "I went visit at Kellogg, I spent time with Mohan. It was fascinating. That guy was up on everything; he had a website where he was doing his thing; reading and evaluating books… He was engaged in it… It was the real thing, not just reading about it [the Internet] … I had to figure out what my thing was… What do I love? What do I know that can be mine?"

He also was exposed to Sidney Levy while at Kellogg. Sidney made a presentation to the marketing department about his research. Bruce was impressed and quite taken by Sidney, his research and the potential value of using qualitative research methods. Bruce states, "When I was there [Kellogg], Sid gave a talk and I felt wow! It was incredible. His presentation was not about the Internet, but about qualitative research methods and some of his research experiences. I thought that it was a great approach, and because the Internet was unknown, I had to live it."

Bruce's experience and research in both the general and online automobile industry also served as a spark for initiating the Internet Shopping 24/7 Project. During one trip to California he interviewed senior executives at Autobytel.com, CarsDirect.com and Edmunds.com; he came away curious (and impressed) that some consumers would purchase online a new automobile without visiting a dealership or, in some cases, without taking a test drive.

As a consumer

Several aspects of Bruce's personal background influenced his adoption of online shopping. Bruce has a BA in computer science and he is very proud of this; he worked in the high tech industry full time for a couple of years as part of a startup software group for a small company that was, before he left it, purchased by a large high tech company; he has maintained and used his computer skills in his research. He will tell you that "I am a computer scientist." He has a clear affinity of technology.

Bruce is also cheap. When he shops, he is in search of the "best deal." The "deals" available on the Internet during his Internet Shopping 24/7 Project experience were amazing and he reveled in finding those which he could use. Bruce comments, "I have always loved reading the Sunday circulars since I was a teenager. I like finding the best deal and being a smart shopper. When I was shopping in stores, I liked Costco because I could buy in bulk and pay a lower price per unit. For example, I typically bought two giant things of toilet paper. I got a lot of it because I knew I was saving money…Also I liked to figure out when things would go on deal in stores and the deal patterns at stores. For example, there was a time when I knew that Tropicana orange juice would go on deal every four to six weeks, so I would purchase a four to six week supply every time it was on sale."

Amy, Bruce's wife, confirms his love for the deal; she believes that "Bruce is an aggressive shopper. He likes to conquest and find the best deals. He checks out the ads, the circulars, and researches the competition. He used to drive around a lot and search for the best value… he is price conscious. I am the opposite. Price is not as much of a concern for me."

Though Bruce sought out great deals, he also could not stand poor service. Amy informs that "Bruce enjoyed shopping in stores, but also he used to complain that people that work in the stores were not social or nice enough. He hated standing in lines to pay and get out of the store."

Bruce was also clear about his service preferences, "If I want help, I want help, not just a clueless sales person. For example one of my last purchases in a store was at KB-Toys. I did not get the attention from the teenage store personnel [at the cash register]. She did not even acknowledge my presence. I was waiting to pay, and I wanted to move. I don't need a friend, but I want to tell her, stop chatting with your buddy here and pay some attention to me. A computer program is reliable, not like a robot clerk talking with her robot teenage friend."

And so the project began in September, 1999. Bruce says, "I was going to shop online for some time. At first it was supposed to be for three and a half months. I was going to make my own site. Mohan [had his site and] wrote about books. I was going to [have my own site and] write about shopping. I liked this. I could be proactive.

DIVISION OF SHOPPING

To understand some of the family dynamics, investigation of the division of shopping was assessed. The experience clearly had an impact not only in the context of shopping, but also on running the household. Amy comments on their shopping responsibilities during the Project, "Because Bruce stopped going into stores, I felt a bigger burden to run the household. I had to make sure to get items. I had to give him a list to shop on line and order. I could not just ask Bruce to pick up something at the last minute on his way home from work. It was hard for me. Much more planning was involved…Also, Bruce would want to shop online in the evening. At 11pm my brain is fried. I can't think what to order, so I would tell Bruce get whatever you want. He would buy staples, but [he] did not put menus together. I ended up going to stores more. I did a lot of small trips. Bruce got a lot of big items -like diapers."

Amy feels that the Project experience created more work for her. Prior to the Internet Shopping 24/7 Project, there was more sharing of the shopping responsibilities. Bruce says, "Before, I went to the supermarket a fair amount. Amy would go to Bread and Circus [an upscale supermarket owned by Whole Foods]. She did a lot. I did a fair amount. I would do 65 or 70% of the supermarket shopping. She would create the shopping list, but I would go out and buy everything. Also I would go to Costco, or be involved in any big ticket item purchase."

Amy recalled Bruce's greater assistance with shopping prior to the Project experience, however, she did not perceive the division of labor in quite the same way, "I did most of the shopping, about 60% of it. Bruce shared and went to stores, but I did most [of the shopping]. I had the most responsibility. I planned menus and lists. Yet, Bruce was happy to go to the store… I did the day to day shopping, he did the bulk. I did most of the immediate shopping, for example, buying presents or going to the drugstore."

There is evidence of a foundation of shared responsibility in this household prior to the Internet Shopping 24/7 Project experience and there is evidence that this was preserved through the art of compromise. Amy recalls, "When Bruce decided to extend the duration of his experiment [from the originally planned three and one half months], he told me that I could use Streamline [an online grocer that was preferred by Amy and charged a monthly fee, unlike the "no fee" grocery service provider preferred by Bruce]. I really liked Streamline. I had to do it once a week only–every Wednesday. It made me more organized, with once a week ordering only. So I ordered on Streamline and Bruce ordered on Homeruns [Bruce's preferred online grocer]."

Another compromise situation involved the purchase of beds for their two young boys (ages 3 and 2 at the time of the purchase). Amy, who was pregnant at the time and expecting to give birth within two to three weeks—as one can imagine, she was a busy mother—wanted beds for both boys as part of the process of getting the household ready for the new baby. She felt that she would have no time to do this later. Bruce recalls, "We wanted to buy beds for the guys. I wanted to buy them on line; Amy wanted to go to a store. I kept on insisting that we had to buy them online. It was like saying "Amy can't stop me!" I kept on pushing deadlines and negotiated…One day, I came home and the baby sitter was there and then I just knew she had gone to store to buy the beds… She let me buy the mattresses on line."

ONLINE SHOPPING ISSUES

Control

Bruce felt that he was in greater control during the online shopping process. He refers to store shopping experiences where he felt that his preferred mode of shopping or shopping decisions were impeded. "When I would go to a store," Bruce commented, "I just wanted people to let me browse by myself. Let me focus, be by myself. I just wanted to be left alone. On the Internet. I am by myself. I am in control of what I do." It is important to consider whether Bruce, and any other consumer, is truly in greater control when shopping online. Perceived control may be quite different from the actual degree of control.

The Value of Time

One of the often pronounced benefits of online shopping is time savings (e.g., shopping can be done in minutes as opposed to hours). Amy found that for some tasks, utilizing the Internet actually increased the overall amount of time needed. For example, she found it faster to place an order over the telephone with Hanna Anderson, rather than logging into their website, placing desired items into a shopping cart and clicking through the checkout process. Also, she had concerns about waiting time for delivery. She found it more convenient to go to CVS—less than one mile away—and get something immediately, rather than wait for it to arrive a few days later.

Bruce seemed to place little value on his time (either before or during the Project experiment). Yet, his attitude toward the value of time may have changed as a direct result of his online shopping experience. He highlights, "I was worse before. Now, I am better. I have realized that I was burning a lot of time. I have to let go [and realize] you don't always have to be perfect [and] get the absolute best deal. … I realized that it is great to save time and that it could be worth paying more in return for this some time."

In the Flow

Bruce could be described as being in the flow with respect to his research and shopping behavior. He moved easily and quickly from site to site in search of better deals. He was frequently up late, e.g., until 3:00am, surfing around. His experience was arguably of one who was a consumer, obsessed and addicted. Amy's characterization of Bruce when he completed his data collection (i.e., stopped his run of exclusive online shopping) was telling, "When he stopped, he got depressed and withdrawn. Something important was ending… He was going to have to go back into stores."

A Religious Conversion

When Bruce talked about his experience, it sounded as if he had gone through a religious conversion and that he wanted to help others convert as well. He talks about "taking a *leap of faith*" and doing his online shopping for the cause. In some instances, he talked about the importance in "believing that it will work out fine;" for example, when he decided to order online a Honda Odyssey—a motor vehicle with a list price in excess of $26,000—from an automobile dealership in Connecticut that was over 130 miles away from his home (and willing to deliver it to his house). In discussing this experience and others he comments "If I do not do it, who will? Who will establish that this can or can not be done, or how it could be done well?"

This begs the question, who might care? Aren't some of the online shopping experiences absurd? Bruce may have created a dogma, and, as a result, refuses to look at evidence that might clearly contradict the beauty and splendor of online shopping. He talks about those in and not in the faith. When he refers to online shopping, he uses the word "I', and when he discusses bricks & mortar shopping he uses the pronoun "they" and refers to these shopping environments as the "dirt" world, which is in marked contrast to the pure, clean world of online shopping.

He exhibited evangelical behavior in how he thought about, talked about and utilized online shopping. He worshipped the online shopping scripture that he perceived (and perhaps partially created, at least in his own mind). And his cause begot global interest from the media, executives, academics and other online shoppers. He took on a new public persona. He was ordained as "The Netty Professor" by Inc. Magazine in its lengthy article (October 2000) about his Internet Shopping 24/7 Project experience He took on a new public persona that was enthusiastic about exploring online shopping; Bruce wanted to persuade others, to convert the world.

MAJOR CONCLUSIONS

- Consumers seem to need special incentives or combination of circumstances to make the switch–but which ones?
- New burdens and benefits can be found in e-consumption– but what are the big trade offs?
- Fanatic behavior can emerge–Can the fanatics convert others?

- Through carefully negotiated compromises and changes to daily life, 24/7 e-shopping can work.
- Understanding consumers' time orientation and value for time are of central importance.
- Issues of flow and control seem to be at the core of e-shopping enjoyment.

"Interpreting the Interpreter: The (Mis)Adventures of a True Techy in E-Love"
Susan Dobscha, Bentley College

This presentation discussed interpretations of the text based on both astrological and feminist perspectives. This presentation, like the others, was hilarious and thought provoking. Her introductory comments were of surprise as she thought that her presentation would be the only one laced with a healthy dose of tongue in cheek and an abundance of humor.

ASTROLOGICAL INTERPRETATION

An initial thought was that Bruce is definitely a Leo. A Leo is governed by the credo "I will," has the confidence to lecture others, takes charge of his own life, wants to protect others, and knows (or *believes* that he knows) all the answers. Bruce had exhibited each of these characteristics, as described in his text, in both action and words. Yet, in the final analysis, she did not believe that he was a Leo.

Then, Susan was convinced that Bruce had to be a Virgo. Virgo's are ruled by the credo "I analyze," believe that learning to compete is very important, compete fiercely (e.g., his being the first all e-shopper), and achieve scholastic excellence. Given that the first personality trait of a Virgo is *practicality*, however, this sign was ruled out as a possibility. Other signs ruled out were Libra— who are much more balanced—and Sagittarius—who are highly people focused.

Prior to asking Bruce for his birthdate, Susan concluded that he must be a Capricorn. A Capricorn is ruled by the credo "I use," "longs to abandon duty but is resigned to the knowledge that spontaneous enthusiasm can never replace experience," reveres achievements (e.g., the creation and administration of The Brucie Awards), and recognizes the dangers of impulsive actions (n.b., using eBay was the one exception for him).

Bruce was born under the sign of Aquarius. Aquarians are forward-thinkers who see the big picture. They are unpredictable, original and idealistic. Aquarians rule the future, universal communication and worthy causes.

DIFFERENCE IN PERSPECTIVES

Amy and Bruce had a number of different perspectives about the experience. Bruce thought that online shopping was terrific and that everyone should do it. He felt that it was convenient, made life easier, made obtaining products effortless, saved him time and provided him with a higher degree of control over the shopping experience (vis a vis bricks and mortar shopping).

Amy felt that he was "going overboard" with the experience and that he was online "more than usual," thereby not saving time at all. She would on occasion issue "computer time-outs" so that he would spend more time interacting directly with the family. In addition, she did not believe that the experience made life easier for her; she found herself taking on more work. Bruce writes that "there were moments when she wanted someone to go out and get something for her."

BEHAVIORAL ISSUES

Competition versus Collaboration

Shopping is thought of as a social collaborative exercise by many consumers, The text reveals a consumer who is engaged in competition rather than collaboration during a number of consumption experiences. When discussing eBay, Bruce writes "I won an eBay auction," "spotted an auction…and what do you know…I won," and when referring to the fact that he was finally using an online grocer—something that his mother had already been doing—he writes "take that mom, I'm catching up."

The Foil of Human Contact

At first glance, one could believe that Bruce immersed himself in online shopping in an effort to get further away from human contact—at least with respect to shopping. Describing an online car shopping experience, he declared that "buying a car online is great except for the part that includes humans." In another shopping situation, he rails that "the human ruined the experience." One time when he was purchasing gasoline, the pump malfunctioned and would not allow him to pay at the pump—this was after he pumped the gas; when forced to engage the attendant and pay him directly "inside," Bruce wanted to believe that this was not really happening "I'm not really here, I thought. There's no place like online; there's no place like online; there's no place like online, I repeated to myself as I clicked my heels together. I wish that I could say that I woke up and realized that it was a dream (and you were there, and you were there, and you were there too…it was terrible Auntie Emm…)."

As one reads further through the text, however, one realizes a consumer who does indeed enjoy human interaction and seeks it out in shopping experiences. For example, he "fires up" Lands' End Live [a live chat for assistance when navigating the Lands' End Website] and enjoys interacting with the online assistants. He refers to them by name, e.g., Susan and Sarah, and when he requests a Lands' End Live session and one of them is not assigned to help him, he tells other Lands' End Live assistants to say hello to them for him. He also makes comments about people that are part of the "physical" part of the shopping process, e.g., "the delivery driver was pleasant."

Unpaid or Extra labor

In a number of shopping experiences, Bruce performs tasks that require extra labor for which he is not compensated—or so it would appear. For example, a friend asked Bruce if he wanted to erect a sukkah for the Jewish holiday Sukkot. After agreeing, the friend discovered that the price for a sukkah "kit" at the nearby Israeli bookstore was $350—unreasonable to both the friend and Bruce. He writes "Were I able to visit Home Depot, I would have purchased the necessary items and been 'good to go' for less than $34.99. Given the timing, a delivery would have been too late; and I can't go to stores (smile). What's a sukkah builder to do? Good old fashioned ingenuity (and a little bit of sweat) was a cure for this problem. Some home construction had been going on at another neighbor's house; some fallen trees were still sitting in the rear of their backyard (and they were happy when I took them away). I cut up these trees and made a wonderful sukkah frame. Some friends came over and a good time was had by all." Dumpster diving, it is assumed, is not typical of Bruce's shopping behavior in general, let alone for religious celebrations; yet, he engaged this laborious activity because he was not willing to enter a store.

Theory of Trying

Bruce wanted to make online shopping work and he went to many extremes to prove this out. He put forth great effort in this endeavor. This is not pronounced as a flaw, rather, as something important to know when interpreting the data. A number of factors, as outlined in Solomon (1999) detail the factors which came into play when he made an effort to carry out a certain behavior. For example, he had no doubts that he could get online whatever he wanted (e.g., "I will buy black shoes") and he made great efforts to dominate the online world and exert his control of the domain in satisfying a need, no matter what was required.

CONCLUSIONS

- E-suming (i.e., online consuming) would require a major shift in lifestyles. How many people would likely make the necessary changes? How long would it take? What would the path to adoption look like?
- The concept of involvement is overturned in the environment and conditions in which Bruce operated as much psychic energy and attention was paid to most purchases.
- Online shopping requires one to realize more unpaid labor.
- What effect would race, class or gender have on the likelihood of success of this experience?

The Psychology of an Online Shopping Pioneer

Sidney J. Levy, University of Arizona

On July 19, in the year 1660, Samuel Pepys wrote the following entry in his famous diary.

"I did lie late a-bed. I and my wife [went] by water, landed her at Whitefriars with her boy with an iron of our new range which is already broke and my wife will have changed, and many other things she has to buy with the help of my father today...afterwards, to the Dog Tavern, where I did give [guests] a dish of anchovies and olives and paid for all..."

In the year 2000, also on July 19, I prepared for this conference of the Association for Consumer Research the following entry in my diary.

"July 19, 2000. I did not lie late a-bed. Early to the office and immediately to the computer where I transcribed the above quotation for July 19 from Samuel Pepys's diary 340 years earlier.

Then to the Web where I read the following entry from the Diary of Bruce Weinberg.

"July 19 "I was going to order from Batteries.com, however, I decided to give Amazon.com a look. I was surprised and delighted to see that Amazon offered the same Energizer rechargeable products sold by Batteries.com (in their Electronics section); even better, both the charger and batteries were on sale and priced significantly less than at Batteries.com. The Amazon price for the needed items was $36 without shipping. I estimated a shipping charge of around $5-$6. I decided to place my order with Amazon.com. (By the way, the information about the items at Amazon.com was terrific. The customer reviews helped a lot.) "I decided to shop around and see if there was anything else I wanted to get while I was at Amazon. Incidentally, part of my thinking this way was because with any order—I believe—one is already incurring the base shipping charge (i.e., what Amazon terms the "Per Shipment" shipping charge), so why not order something else now rather than later (assuming one has a good idea that one will want to get something else soon) as the incremental shipping cost will be only for each item."

Making use of a sample of one person is an old tradition. Individuals may be used as respondents who tell about themselves and as informants about other people as well. Samuel Pepys's diary tells us a lot about himself and about life in England in the middle of the 17th century, and Bruce Weinberg's diary tells us a lot about himself and modern life, as you can see from the example of his ruminative report and the rest of his diary at his Web site. Bruce vowed to avoid retail stores since September, 1999, and instead to do all his shopping on the Internet. I printed out the record he posted on the Web (Weinberg 2000), of his experience from September through August, 2000. I then treated that record as a year-long longitudinal interview of around 365 pages, as if he were responding to the prompt, "Tell me about it." I went through the protocol the way I treat an interview with the first respondent of any qualitative project I might undertake, reading it closely to see what insight, understanding, and hypotheses I could generate. Introspectionists are often accused of being self-indulgent, as if it

were a bad thing to gratify one's own desires. But that seems just an envious or puritanical view. Weinberg indulged himself; and I surely indulged him as well by reading his shopping autobiography of some 365 pages. That length also raises the issue of parsimony; that is, how much is enough? After wading through several months of data, I found the general incremental gain to become less and less, although Bruce became more self-expressive and gave more details. Some self-indulgent entries were not about online purchasing at all. For example, he gives several pages of NCAA tourney March Madness results, names Ryder Cup players, and on May 1, Bruce lists 38 big shots with whom he mingled at The CEO Summit Conference, La Quinta Resort, Palm Desert, California. And his tracking of the RBI's by someone named Luis Castillo left me totally blank.

My analysis will sum up who Bruce Weinberg seems to be from the protocol, as I do not otherwise know him personally. Then I will talk about his experience shopping on the Internet and what comes across to me about that, especially compared to shopping in other ways.

THE RESPONDENT AND INFORMANT

Dr. Weinberg is a professor of marketing at Boston University. He is proud that he has a Ph.D. from MIT and generally that he knows his stuff; and he is anticipating his move to Bentley College because of its orientation to technology. Some people objected to me that he is not a typical consumer, that his shopping on the Internet would be unique, an individualistic activity, just an idle curiosity, and therefore not generalizable. Also, his self-consciousness about what he is doing, being not just a shopper, but also engaged in a research study, adds a complexity that I have to take account of. Nevertheless, as a pioneer online shopper he describes events likely to be encountered by other venturesome individuals. He does represent various consumer segments in our society, sociologically and psychologically, so that his experience is of general interest.

Although he reports mainly his experience in shopping online, he makes numerous references to his family, his students, and a variety of his everyday life circumstances and events. From the description of his education, his occupation, his home, his cars, his aspirations, and his purchases, he is clearly an upper middle class man, generally secure in that social status and comfortable in the activities and behavior that go with it. He respects family traditions, liking the vision of himself as a *paterfamilias* taking his family for a drive in an heirloom Rolls Royce.

"September 15
"I am looking to buy a Rolls Royce silver cloud...Amy's grandfather, Richard Mermis, bought a 1958 Rolls Royce Silver Cloud I in 1958. When the mood struck him to get one, he walked into a dealer and said, in essence, "I want to buy Rolls Royce...now." When he passed on, Amy's grandmother, Kate, continued to operate the Rolls, and drove it, typically, on Sundays. Well, Amy's grandmother passed on recently and the fate of the car is uncertain. Anyways, I would like to carry on the family tradition of driving a Rolls Royce Silver Cloud on Sundays, with family in tow, of course."

Bruce shows his participation in conventional American culture in many ways. He observes some Jewish customs such as building

Advances in Consumer Research
Volume 28, © 2001

a sukkah to celebrate the Jewish harvest festival. As non-Orthodox, and an assimilated American, he includes the reading of *How the Grinch Stole Christmas*, sending a holiday greeting to the tune of *Christmas Snowmen Wish*, and eating lobster. He is an ardent sports fan, attends ball games, tracks some batting averages, and once ran the Boston Marathon. Despite his higher status orientation to names such as Rolls Royce, Lexus, Volvo, Tiffany, and Polo Cologne, Bruce's purchasing has a strong conventional core that includes Disney and McDonalds. He collects Toy Story 2 and Batman figures and animation sericels; and he buys videos for the kids that include The Lion King, Aladdin, and Rudolph the Red Nosed Reindeer. The list of brands he buys sounds like a roster for the All-American team, including Charmin, Pampers, Diet Coke, Pepperidge Farm, Hershey's, Ben and Jerry's, Wheaties, Perdue, Tropicana, Finesse, Energizer, Mott's, Frito-Lay, etc.

As a man with a family of three young children, much of his life goes on around his home, being a responsible son, husband, and father. He talks often about his wife, his children, his mother, and his mother-in-law, expressing his devotion to them with warmth, affection, and an eagerness to please. He shares information and is vigorous in acquiring it. He is a positive relative, friend, colleague, and teacher. His personal qualities are notable. He is intelligent and lively-minded. He is alert and quick, good-natured and witty. He is highly articulate and apparently able to type a blue streak. He has a remarkable ability to get on top of a great volume of detail. He enjoys expressing himself as well as observing himself doing so ("I'm not the shy type", he says). Although not quite up to Samuel Pepys who cheated on his wife and told about it in French, Bruce has an outgoing, exhibitionistic streak, manifest in his telling all, so to speak, on the Web, in his enthusiastic exclamations, and in his entertaining songs and parodies along the way. He comments that his "heart is warmed by the eBay transaction praise left online by ToyKlectrr for all the world to see." He is firm-minded, self-confident, and willing to assert criticism. When sufficiently frustrated, he has a small tantrum, is sarcastic, or severely rebukes the persons vexing him. He sometimes justifies this as for their own good, he being a marketing professor who is qualified to improve them. In one instance, he shouted in print at a recalcitrant vendor by insisting

"THAT IS NOT THE QUESTION I AM ASKING.
THAT IS NOT THE QUESTION I AM ASKING.
THAT IS NOT THE QUESTION I AM ASKING.
THAT IS NOT THE QUESTION I AM ASKING.
THAT IS NOT THE QUESTION I AM ASKING."

But more generally he seems amiable and ameliorative in his approach, admonishing offenders toward improvement. He makes many side comments about his own remarks, finds himself amusing and is willing to question his conclusions, to qualify, consider alternative possibilities, and to offer constructive suggestions.

SHOPPING ON THE INTERNET

A Dedicated Internet Shopper

Bruce plays several roles in this project. A main goal is to dedicate himself to shopping online. He works hard to keep his vow to do that, and carries out a vigorous search for the products and services he and his family require. He shops for and/or buys food and clothing, furniture, books, toys, and hardware, cars, batteries, computer equipment, a hot water heater, videos, diapers, cologne, dry cleaning, travel tickets, etc. He realistically shows how one might learn to acquire these products, starting with a few familiar sites. However, before long we hear of Shoplink, Mercata, MicronPC,

Costco, Peapod, OfficeMax, Staples, AcmeAnimation, eToys, KBKids, OnlineShoes, Onvia, Gomez, eCost, tirerack, Computers4Sure, Onsale, bizrate, Buy, CDWorld, Zoots, HomeWarehouse, Cooking, Williams-Sonoma, Kitchen, toysmart, ibaby, Send, CambridgeSoundworks, Hifi, LinkExchange, Outpost, Network Solutions, Register, Midwest Express, Ashford, ibeauty, Blue Mountain Arts, dogpile, CVS, Drugstore, TX, PlanetRx, DrugEmporium, Automotive, and numerous other automobile sites. Like most shoppers, he tends to settle to doing business with some main sites: eBay, Land's End, Amazon, and ToysRus, with Streamline and Homeruns for groceries, and Kozmo for convenience items.

Bruce's searching serves to find suitable sites for specific products. He thus illustrates the benefits of shopping on the Internet by tapping into a variety of possible outlets for what he needs. He believes that he is therefore able to be a superior shopper. He compares what is available, what it costs, and when it will be delivered. His extended scrutiny of the details he is comparing often seems excessive, obsessive, or ridiculous, as he recognizes, in these examples.

"January 6
"CVS.com, you fascinate me. On December 30, 1999, I placed three separate orders, within the span of three minutes, for several Misfit beanbag toys from CVS.com. When I placed the orders, I was curious as to whether they would be handled separately or would be combined and processed together (believing that CVS may notice that each order came from the same person within a short time interval)...On January 4, 2000, I received three emails from CVS indicating that my orders had shipped. The first email had a time stamp of 17:42:19 GMT (i.e., 42 minutes and 19 seconds past five in the afternoon, Greenwich Mean Time); the second email had a time stamp of 17:42:20; and the time stamp on the third email was 17:42:42. Unfortunately, the order numbers were not included in the body of emails. Therefore, I do not know which email was associated with each order. Given the proximity in which the shipping confirmation emails arrived, I thought that perhaps they did bundle the orders together into one large box or, if not, that they would all arrive simultaneously. I now know that each order was shipped separately as the second order arrived today...The other orders were nowhere to be found. Fascinating. Three orders placed at nearly identical times, shipping confirmation emails received at nearly identical times, and, yet, the orders did not arrive at nearly identical times. I love it. Anyone who enjoys counting the number of sand granules on the beach would probably enjoy figuring this one out."

"February 21
"The shipping charge was $6.00. Therefore, the total bill came to $14.74. Does it bother me that the charge for shipping was nearly the same as the total price for the items? No. Well, actually, there is a story here. Originally, I was just going to get the two containers of seasoning for $4.96. The shipping charge for this would have been $5.75—more than the items. Now that, I didn't like. So, my remedy was to order something else so that the shipping charge would be less than the price of all the items being ordered. Logical, right? Hey, who cares? I'll be a very happy camper when that seasoning arrives and my broiled scrod or salmon will taste like heaven."

"December 16
"In case you are wondering, the full retail price for Tara Road

is $24.95. Kozmo.com's price or the book is $17.47 ($12.47 with a $5 off coupon); their price with one hour shipping is $17.47 ($12.47 with a $5 off coupon). Buy.com's price for the book is $12.48; their price with regular shipping is $16.43, with 2nd day air shipping is $20.43, and with next day air shipping is $23.43 (by the way, Buy.com specifies that next day air does not necessarily mean that the product will arrive the next day; it means that when they finally put the order together for shipping—could be 1-2 days—it will arrive the next day after it is shipped). Decisions, decisions."

This intent approach is partly due to Bruce's desire to communicate explicitly about his thinking, but more generally because he is interested, because he wants to demonstrate that one can shop exclusively on the Internet, and that one can get good deals that way. It is also evident that he thinks in this detailed and focused way, that he is a quant jock who is capable of making and weighing all the calculations necessary to figuring out the best deal. He realizes that he overdoes in this vein, leading his forbearing wife, Amy, at times to say, "You should hear yourself."

As Bruce tends to buy well-known brands, he does not settle for merely cheap stuff, but rather works hard to get good values and good deals. He is alert to avoid shipping costs, and to derive various financial benefits. Some of the discounts and incentives he encounters may be due to these being early days of Internet marketing and a lot of these marketers are losing money; such advantages might decrease when Bruce's vision of total online shopping arrives and there is less wooing and subsidizing.

In addition to the cost savings that Bruce claimed to derive (there being no true total comparison with what a savvy bricks-and-mortar shopper would have paid), there are other benefits. The issues of time, convenience, and enjoyment are more complicated. Bruce spends so much time at the computer doing his shopping that it is hard to imagine other shoppers doing that outside of the most hard-boiled computer buffs or the huge pornography crowd of ordinary guys buying their kicks, perverts, and masquerading FBI agents. Some of Bruce's time must be attributed to his professorial activities, and to his insistent desire to demonstrate that he can do it. And, of course, a lot of time is accounted for by making the detailed record of his experience. Nevertheless, he seems to spend an inordinate amount of time to accomplish rather trivial purchases. Also, while it is impressive when Kozmo.com makes deliveries within an hour, many products did not arrive for several days. Bruce ordered a computer online and it was delivered 12 days later. (I went to Costco, bought a computer with a big rebate, and a man delivered it and installed it the same afternoon.) He started shopping for an HP printer on November 4, and received it on November 17. He waited 8 days to get his Polo cologne and eleven days to receive a refrigerator bulb from HomeWarehouse.com. A stroller took more than two weeks to arrive from babycatalog. He does brood some about the utility of time saved versus greater cost. The closest to a hassle Bruce reported between him and his wife, Amy, was about new beds for their boys: he wanted to order them online and she refused to wait 6-8 weeks for delivery, saying, "I'm not waiting for these beds. I'm just going to go get them." She did; and Bruce reconciled himself to it, by deciding that it was worth the $200 more they paid the dirt store to have the earlier delivery and to placate his wife.

More generally, Bruce justifies waiting for packages to be delivered by making it an asset, saying, "I loved the excitement of getting the item in the mail." Throughout, he emphasizes that placing orders on the Internet takes only a few seconds (except for those irksome occasions when it does not work out that way), that

he can do other things while he waits for responses, and that going to the store to shop would have taken a lot more time and expense. His experience suggests that one must engage in a fair amount of planning ahead and be quite patient. Thus, he is calm about things that would drive me crazy, such as waiting so long for a refrigerator bulb, not being able to pick out his own produce, arranging suitable delivery times, never browsing in the supermarket and the mall, not being able to watch people as they shop, and having to be disappointed and send back unsatisfactory goods.

A Robust Consumer

The Weinbergs are substantial upper middle class consumers. They have a lot of material desires and the means to satisfy them. Although the focus of the data is on shopping, there is a lot of information about consuming as well. Their shopping is in the service of achieving and maintaining a high level of consumption. They buy all the products they find necessary to furnish a comfortable home, and to accommodate their growing family. They have a second refrigerator in the basement to hold food from Streamline.com. They enjoy an ample diet, with lots of treats. Bruce says he loves to eat certain foods so much that he is willing to consume a steady diet of Maalox to ease his gastric pain. The family also fairly devotedly collect items from the world of sports and entertainment such as figures, cels, and videos.

In an earlier paper on "The Discretionary Society," (Levy 1970), I described consumers as either sufficing, replete, or omnivorous; the Weinbergs appear to be the latter, working hard at participating in the acquisitive segment of American society, fulfilling their wants in generous and often luxurious ways. I also characterized various attitudes toward shopping. Here is one description: "Some shoppers act almost 'pseudopodically,' wanting to take in all they can, putting out many arms to sweep in a lot, unloading proudly all the substance at the checkout counter (p.324)." Bruce may represent this kind of shopper psychology in an Internet version, perhaps with a grander element of being able to conjure up resources from across the universe, commanding goods to come in from the vast realm of cyberspace. Instead of the labor of self-service in the store, electronic orders go out and the obsequious, fawning tribes of Amazon, Kozmo, and Homeruns send tribute, to be unloaded on the kitchen counter.

A Marketing Professor and Researcher

Being a professor and a marcologist accounts for Bruce's determination to discover if it is feasible to survive via the 'Net, to test the hypothesis that the "dirt-store-less" future could be said to be here in a rudimentary but sufficient sense. Bruce's experience shows that it is possible to survive as a consumer for the most part by shopping online and avoiding the stores he defines as brick and mortar. His definition of brick-and-mortar stores and his derogatory attitude toward them as "dirt" stores, is self-serving, as if avoiding retail stores were the goal, rather than finding one's most beneficial shopping pattern. In fact, all of the commercial purchases that Bruce does make outside his home indicate that he would not be a happy consumer if he stayed home and survived on what he could order only via his computer. As a marketing professor, he knows (or should) that McDonalds is a retail store that sells prepared food, and there is no reason to violate his oath of research by allowing himself to go into restaurants, ballparks, and hotels, which he does when he wants a product, service, or experience that he cannot have online. Except, of course, that he recognizes his unwillingness to substitute the Internet when he acknowledges that he could follow a ball game on his screen. Also, when he has to buy a bicycle tire or gasoline at a gas station, what real difference does it make whether he pays outside or goes into the store? It just shows that buying gasoline online would be a problem. In addition, much of what he does could be done by mail, telephone, and fax rather than the Internet; and he makes use of them as well, presumably because they are electric companions to the Internet and not dirt stores.

Bruce's anti-brick-and-mortar vow is an amusing way of setting up his project, and as a consumer, he is entitled to his enthusiasm for shopping on the Internet. However, as a research scientist he seems too devoted to his hypothesis, reminding me of the time I wrote a spoof on doing research and said, "My hypotheses were borne out; I know, because I bore them out myself." He exaggerates, saying that visiting bricks-and-mortar retail stores is "living in the dark ages." He tolerates many negative experiences. His insistent determination to find the superiority of Internet shopping tends to arouse counter-argument. Although the assets of shopping on the Internet are apparent, and I have used Amazon.com, Travelocity, Iomega, and eBay, I found myself defending going out to shop, and when I describe his project to other people, they tend to do that, too. One person said, "Only a technical man would do that," and even people who normally gripe about shopping immediately started describing the many pleasures of going shopping in retail stores and malls when faced with the possibility of never doing it at all.

Some of Bruce's enthusiasms are ineffable or indescribable; he several times says something or other is fascinating without explaining why. He sometimes criticizes Web sites without specifying what is wrong with them. However, as he goes along, his energy for the project and recording of his experience is unflagging. The entries get longer and more detailed. His project grows as he gains skill, and he does not merely shop but issues Noosies and Brucies to indicate his displeasure or appreciation. He is candid in exposing his thoughts and self-evaluations, although he sometimes goes awry. On April 27 he says, "This was not the standard level of Kozmo service. I am surprised to hear myself make a comment like this as I usually am not one for service; has online shopping changed my attitudes toward the importance, meaning, and expectations of service?" However, despite this denial he has obviously been evaluating service all along, as he judges response times, observes whether or not customer service representatives are gracious, and describe his reactions to how he is being treated.

SUMMING UP

From the foregoing, I conclude the following.

Bruce Weinberg is convinced that he showed the superiority of online shopping in savings of time, money, and in providing a variety of other consumer satisfactions. He does so by playing up the advantages of avoiding retail stores and minimizing the disadvantages of shopping online. The Weinberg experiment with shopping online was not controlled by tight or systematic comparisons with shopping at brick and mortar stores.

The venture is unnatural, as maintaining a Web site record of one's search and purchasing behavior is like living in a fish bowl. Weinberg has an audience who pay attention, who send examples of their own experiences and approving email. They come from the media and other organizations to hold interviews and invite talks, and they include research analysts in the wings. All this is exciting and adds a show business flavor to the enterprise. Bruce revels in all this as a performer as well as a shopper, conveying the tone of playing a game in which he is Master of the Universe, lordly dispensing his Brucies and Noosies of approval and chastisement. All this presumably helps to foster his motivation and sustain his perseverance in the face of an accumulation of frustrating experiences with extended searches and poorly designed Web sites. Bruce

encounters unresponsive vendors, stupid personnel, unsatisfactory products, omissions, inordinate delays, and mistakes. But, after all, we can get all that at dirt stores, too.

Focusing on successful sites will be essential. By now, HomeWarehouse and PlanetRx, are gone. Gary Putka (2000), in the *Wall Street Journal*, comments that "At midsummer 2000, the bloom is off the Internet rose. A lengthening list of e-tailers–Beauty Scene, RedRocket, Toysmart, Value American, Boo.com, to name a few–have gone out of business, sold out under duress, or face financial crises. Many Internet stocks are down 50% or more from their highs, and the initial public offering market for an online company is no longer a rocket ride (p. R52)." The wonderful service that Kozmo.com has provided Bruce may not continue; in the month of August the Kozmo.com online delivery service laid off 275 workers.

Bruce Weinberg shows us that it is possible to shop online for almost everything, and he offers us a glimpse of what the cyberfuture might be like. Other data (*WSJ 2000*) demonstrate that some products and services are doing increasingly well on the Internet. The projected shares of market penetration for the year 2000 are already estimated to be as high as 29% for financial brokerage; 23% for computer hardware and software; 11% for books; and 10% for music and video, and other substantial shares for travel, event tickets, collectibles, consumer electronics, and toys. In general, the sites that do better are ones that also have the advantage of multi-channels (retail stores, catalogs) due to their convenience, established imagery, and marketing experience.

The online shoppers are all kinds of individuals who shop for particular kinds of goods. They are willing to tolerate the shortcomings of doing so and can be satisfied with reading about products or just seeing them. But Steve Nowlis (2000) shows the importance to some people of the ability to physically inspect and touch merchandise. (A good recent example is the man who devoted himself to crushing bread and cookies.) Those who make greater use of the Internet and shop more across the board are similar to Bruce in their ready access to computers, their facility with computers, their higher social status, and relative affluence. According to Jeffery D. Zbar (2000), the average affluent household owns two PCs; 46% of the affluent use their PCs for investment management (wired millionaires are 79% more likely to trade stocks online than a non-affluent counterpart), and when shopping online, they are more likely to buy across almost all product categories from books to clothing, hotel reservations to sporting goods. Sites they browsed a lot this year are epicurious.com, nordstrom.com, ashford.com, and omahasteaks.com.

Currently, online companies face more competition from offline rivals, low employee morale, consumer reluctance to change buying patterns, and wary investors demanding that these businesses boost profits. But there is little doubt that access to computers will spread, the competition and skill of vendors will increase, and consumers will gain greater familiarity and comfort with shopping online. Doing so will continue to spread and to grow, just as shopping by catalog and telephone did despite the widespread irritation with "junk mail" and telemarketing's maddening dinnertime calls. Some devoted customers might try to do it all online, as Bruce Weinberg has been doing, vividly and with panache. But most people will add the Internet to their several customary shopping channels, just as I suspect Bruce will do when he frees himself from his vow.

REFERENCES

Bayne, K.M., (2000), *The Internet Marketing Plan*, New York, NY: John Wiley & Sons.

Bulkeley, W.M., (2000), "A Step Back," *Wall Street Journal*, July 17, p. R4.

Frost, R. D., and J. Strauss, (2000), *The Internet: A New Marketing tool*, Upper Saddle River, NJ.: Prentice Hall.

Levy, S. J., (1970). "The Discretionary Society." in Levy, S.J. (1999), *Brands, Consumers, Symbols, and Research*, Thousand Oaks, CA: Sage Publications, Inc., 319-328.

McLaren, C. H., and B. J. McLaren, (2000), *E-commerce: Business on the Internet*, Cincinnati, OH: South-Western Educational Publishing.

Nowlis, Steve, (2000), "Online vs. Offline Consumer Decision-Making: The Effect of the Ability to Physically Inspect Merchandise," (research in progress, Arizona State University).

Pepys, S., (1660), *The Diary of Samuel Pepys*, Heritage Club Edition.

Putka, G., (2000), "The E-Commerce Battleground," *Wall Street Journal*, July 17, p. R52.

Zbar, J. D., (2000), "E-tailing Fits in Upscale Niche," *Advertising Age*, August 14, p. s12.

Weinberg, Bruce D., *24/7 Internet Shopping Diary*, www.internetshopping247.com, Sept., '99-Aug., '00.

Research In Exploring The Online Consumer Experience

Bruce D. Weinberg, Bentley College

In this paper, I discuss important areas for research in the realm of online consumer behavior based on my experiences in the Internet Shopping 24/7 Project. First, however, I focus on a couple of my own interpretations which were arrived at post hoc the presentations in the special session "The Three Faces of E, commerce: Insight into Online Consumer Behavior Through the Interpretation of an Internet Consumer's Experiences." These presentations helped me perceive some underlying aspects of this experience which may have gone unnoticed otherwise.

REACTION TO THE INTERPRETATIONS PRESENTED

I believe that most of the interpretations about my behavior and musings as an online consumer during the Internet Shopping 24/7 Project experience were — pardon me while I take a deep breath — either accurate or plausible. Throughout each presentation, I frequently found myself either nodding in agreement or ruminating about the many thought provoking interpretative statements — with many instances of hearty laughter along the way as this was a fun special session. Any clarifications that I could offer are somewhat minor. For example, Brunel states that I am cheap, whereas I believe that I am frugal; and the interpreters (and others) refer to this research as an "experiment" (and, then based on this assumption, argue for deficiencies such as "control") whereas I *never* said or wrote at all that the Internet Shopping 24/7 Project was an experiment.

MY POST HOC REALIZATIONS AND INTERPRETATIONS

The presentations were thought provoking; having been removed from my year of exclusive online shopping for less than a month, the presentations helped me gain some perspective on the Internet Shopping 24/7 Project experience. I discuss some of my own post hoc realizations and interpretations that were stimulated by the three interpreters.

CEO of a dotcom

In my "About Me" section of the Internet Shopping 24/7 Project website, I state:

"The Internet Shopping 24/7 Project was partly an outgrowth of my autonet research, and my desire to immerse myself in and learn about the nature of e-shopping. Through CarsDirect.com, a company started by Bill Gross of idealab! and Scott Painter, consumers can shop for and buy a new automobile entirely online; the car can even be delivered directly to your door. Initially, I thought that this concept was crazy as it excludes visiting a dealer for the time honored traditions of tire kicking and test driving. Later, I realized that tire kicking in this day and age is absurd; and a five minute spin on a smooth surfaced highway doesn't really provide much value, and is nothing more than a part of a dealership's manipulative sales script. I reasoned that if visiting a dealership is unnecessary for a significant purchase like an automobile, then visiting a retail outlet may be unnecessary for lesser purchases; I shall see..."

I never state in the Internet Shopping 24/7 Project website (http://www.InternetShopping247.com) that I was in Southern California during the late spring of 1999, interviewing executives from Edmunds.com, Autobytel.com and CarsDirect.com about the autonet industry (Weinberg 1999) and car buyer behavior. In addition, I do not mention that after I had completed my research interviews with the Vice President of Marketing and the CEO of CarsDirect.com, they surprised me by offering me the position of Director of Marketing Research, with all the usual dotcom temptations (e.g., 50,000+ stock options, which they kept saying to just add two zeroes to the end in order to estimate their near future value, i.e., shazam, I was going to become a millionaire — I kept thinking, yeah right, it's probably more like just multiply by zero, and besides I do things more out of love than for money, but I kept my mouth shut).

I was initially excited about the opportunity — recall, that ecommerce hype was at or near its high at this time — as it would enable me to learn more about "real" ecommerce through immersion from the "inside" and it fit perfectly with some of my passions (i.e., cars) and past research experiences (e.g., I developed a computer based automobile shopping system as part of my "information acceleration" dissertation — Weinberg 1993 — and one of my publications in the *Journal of Marketing* described the information acceleration forecasting methodology and an application of it for an electric vehicle by General Motors, the currently available EV1 — see Urban, Weinberg and Hauser 1996).

Amy and I seriously considered the CarsDirect.com offer and moving from Boston to Los Angeles. I spoke with individuals who I felt understood well the dotcom experience and industry, and could offer me valuable input in evaluating this job offer (e.g., Mohan Sawhney). One of the individuals with whom I spoke about this job offer was a venture capitalist that I had met while serving as a visiting professor at Northwestern University. In summary, he made statements to the effect "you've got to do it, these are rare times, the learning will be tremendous, you'll never have a greater time, the dotcom experience is incredible." In the end, after careful consideration about my family situation and what I wanted to discover in my research, as well as my academic leanings, I declined the offer from CarsDirect.com.

The enthusiastic statements made by the venture capitalist, however, kept ringing in my ear. I had felt some of the dotcom "rush" and I had decided to "get in the game." In addition, it was my perception that Mohan Sawhney's high degree of understanding about ecommerce was partly due to his involvement with firms engaged in this practice. I wanted to be part of the great potential learning experience that was at hand and I believed that immersion, in some way, in "real" ecommerce would be a worthwhile approach for realizing this potential. To make a long story short — as I can hear Sidney saying, he is "able to type a blue streak" (Levy 2001) — I perceived the Internet Shopping 24/7 Project as a "real" engagement in an area of ecommerce that both interested me and had many questions unanswered (e.g., in light of the hype about ecommerce, why were so few consumers satisfied enough with online shopping to try it and why were so few dotcoms firms profitable?).

So, why mention all of this? I believe that it can help explain some of the interpretations of my behavior. For example, Levy commented, "He tolerates many negative experiences" and that I have an "insistent determination to find the superiority of Internet shopping...." In addition, Brunel notes that I am "evangelical" and I state that "one must believe" in the process, "for if I do not do this,

Advances in Consumer Research
Volume 28, © 2001

who will?" I do not take issue with these statements. In fact, they helped me realize that my stated reasons for undertaking this research—to develop hypotheses about the online consumer buyer decision process — may have been partly a scientific veil for an entrepreneurial part of me that was determined to "figure it all out" and then, as a result be able to help make ecommerce work. (And why I felt this need is potential fodder for additional interpretation which I will likely engage in another publication forum.)

Perhaps, I was behaving not only as a researcher investigating ecommerce, but also as a CEO of a dotcom who was immersed in ecommerce. A dotcom whose mission it may have been—and how this happened is a question that may be worthy of exploration at a later time — not only to search for principles for success based on both positive and negative experiences, but also to engage others in the experience of online shopping and to get them to contribute their wisdom to understanding better and improving ecommerce. As the CEO, I had to motivate the troops and keep the spirits up. Yes, I tolerated some negative experiences, however, I believed that this would result in important discovery which could, in turn, be used to improve the online shopping experience (I believe that in some situations, failure can be a great teacher). I was indeed immersed in ecommerce; this was one of the reasons that I had selected the ethnographic methodology. A priori, I believed that this immersion would enable me to "get inside" the phenomenon that I was studying, ecommerce (as has been done before, e.g., see Schouten and McAlexander 1995).

The rebellious 1960s

I believe also that I may have been evangelical about online shopping because I came to perceive it as a *gateway* to engaging the Internet; and I believed that the Internet, because it did so for me and — in my estimation — others, could assist one in identifying and pursuing one's passions and in realizing greater equality (e.g., with the powerful forces of Big Business, Lobbyists or "The Man"). I hold some beliefs which, perhaps — were I older at the time — would have made me a good candidate to be a rebellious "flower power" teenager or twenty-something who held certain (altruistic?) ideals during the 1960s in the United States. For example, I believe that anything is possible; I have some intolerance for authority that uses its shear muscle to get things done in a less than optimal way (and because it is "its" way and implicitly designed more for its own betterment); and I like to assist consumers who are at a lesser advantage, for whatever reason (e.g., less knowledge or understanding), not get "taken" by others (e.g., "slick" sales people)—I believe in fairness and equality.

Many dotcom organizations, perhaps the majority, were founded and led by either teenagers or twenty-somethings. In the 1990's, rather than have love-ins, lots of sex, Woodstock, Rock 'n roll and Vietnam War protests — the acts of rebellion and protest during the 1960s in the US (as opposed to conforming along with Ozzie and Harriet Nelson and Ward and June Cleaver by not questioning authority and serving loyally the corporation) — the dotcom "youth of America" may have been protesting conformance to Corporate America and its rules of business by creating their own companies (based on technology they either created or better understood how to use), doing things their own way and proving that they were adults with valuable opinions and skills.

I felt as part of this alleged revolution. A part of me felt like telling Corporate America to stuff it and that "we" — the consumers (?), the employees (?), the techy geeks (?), the people (?) — do not have to take it anymore; no more boring and meaningless jobs; no more forcing us to take products on terms that are not agreeable. (Via the Internet, the Web and other current technologies that "we"

created) we could reach everyone else now too and we could make, buy and sell what we wanted. We were going to create and advance a new playing field for business where anyone could participate and have greater access to success and control of their own destiny. We were going to come of age and build something better.

IMPORTANT RESEARCH DOMAINS (I.E., FUTURE RESEARCH)

The Internet Shopping 24/7 Project enabled me to participate in a large variety and number of online shopping experiences, and to interact with a large variety and number of people (e.g., consumers, students, CEOs, members of the media). Based on these rich experiences and interactions, I believe that I have identified several important areas to both researchers and practitioners.

Control

I believe that the issue of control is very important with respect to examining and understanding online consumer behavior (or if you prefer to say, consumers' behavior online or consumer behaviors that are related to online phenomena). In many respects, I felt that I was in greater control when interacting with an online environment than with an offline environment; yet, as Brunel said to me during a debriefing after our final post depth-interview, my actual control may have been diminished when moving from a predominantly offline experience to a highly online experience (e.g., online retailers had information pertaining to when I arrived, what I viewed, when I left, etc.). This stimulates much curiosity about the definition of control in a marketing context and its antecedents from both consumer and service provider perspectives.

Independent of this, I had identified control as an important issue. I perceived myself (as well as other consumers online) as having greater control online in many of my shopping experiences when compared to offline experiences. For example, I was able to shop at any time of the day; the store was open when *I* wanted to shop, not just when the *store management* wanted to be open. Any online retail store was, in spirit, available to me in every city or town that *I* visited — assuming that I had access to a computer; whereas, bricks & mortar stores were, for the most part (e.g., excluding telephone ordering) available to me in only the cities in which the parent *firm* elected to operate a store. I was able to shop alone when desired (e.g., sales clerks on commission were not hounding or pushing product on me) and I could obtain assistance when I desired it (e.g., live sales help available through instant chat sessions such as Lands' End Live).

In a general sense, I define online consumer control as: 1) consuming or getting an item a) that (i.e., what) one wants, b) when one wants it, c) where one wants it, d) how one wants it, e) from whom one wants it, and 2) the ability to a) obtain desired information (which implicitly includes aspects of source, timing, complexity, breadth, depth, etc.), b) retain selected information (e.g., birth date, social security number), c) distribute selected information, d) interact with other consumers, e) collaborate with other consumers (which includes aspects such as organizing, aggregating, sharing, and building), and f) interact and collaborate with suppliers, manufacturers, intermediaries and stakeholders of these organizations. Inherent in this is an ability to bring about desired results both physical and psychological.

Extending the buyer decision process to incorporate the importance of "selling" behavior

I found access to easy tools for experiencing not only buying behaviors (e.g., information search, purchase), but also selling behaviors (e.g., advertising, listing products as available for sale).

FIGURE 1
The Evolution of the Internet Consumer

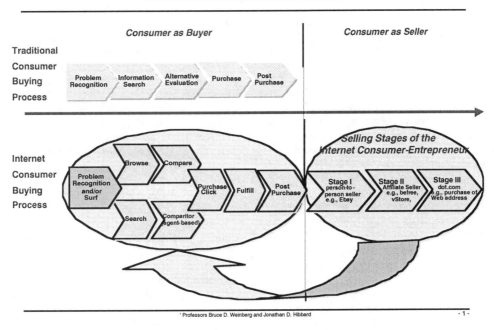

' Professors Bruce D. Weinberg and Jonathan D. Hibbard   - 1 -

For example, I sold a board game in an eBay auction and I sold some books as an Amazon.com associate (for which I earned a commission on the sale). Millions of other consumers participate as sellers in much the same way.

As the project evolved, I believe that my selling behaviors became more involving (e.g., I eventually evolved to a point where I was buying website addresses and creating websites — my products were primarily content) and that my selling activities informed my buying behavior. I felt engaged in ecommerce not only as a buyer, but also as a seller. I considered myself, at times, to be an Internet Consumer Entrepreneur (iCE) — see, Weinberg and Hibbard (2000).

I believe that a "feedback loop" exists in that as iCEs gain online *selling knowledge and experience*, it influences their online *buying behavior* (see Figure 1). iCEs, are more aware of marketing processes because of their selling behavior, and, as a result, are more sophisticated and more demanding than "buy only" consumers. Marketers need to update their fundamental view of online consumer behavior by recognizing this distinction and developing more sophisticated marketing strategies and tactics to acquire and satisfy iCEs.

Weinberg and Hibbard (2000) observed that online consumers who evolve toward iCEs, and in essence are opening their own "virtual lemonade stands" move through a series of "selling stages" that become increasingly challenging and complex. Stage I selling involves the use of consumer-to-consumer (C2C) trading sites such as eBay and Yahoo! Auction because of their ease-of-use and low resource requirements. Stage II selling involves the utilization of affiliate-related programs where affiliate members (e.g., iCEs) earn a "referral" commission on qualified purchases made by a shopper. Stage III selling includes more sophisticated and deliberate activities such as Web address purchase, site creation and management.

24/7/360°

A significant part of the excitement and perceived potential about ecommerce was the ability to shop anytime — "24/7" (i.e.,

24 hours per day, 7 days a week). With no constraints in the *time* dimension, it was believed that this increased (and theoretically always open) access to shopping would reward significantly retailers with an online presence. As is now well known post the "dotcom bubble" burst, creating an online 24/7 shopping environment was no guarantee of profitability.

I believe that researchers and practitioners have overlooked another important dimension with respect to Internet access and developing ecommerce — *space*. At the present time, the most widely used technologies, which enable access to the Internet, tether consumers to a fixed physical location (e.g., in a home, at the office, wherever a data port is available). Consumers, however, stroll the earth *untethered* from the confines of their base location (of Internet access), and encounter "needs" and access to means for satisfying these needs while "away from the desk"; needs can arise *anywhere*.

It is important for researchers and practitioners to study environments where both Internet access is available and one can shop anytime and *anywhere*. I characterize these types of scenarios as "24/7/360°" where "360°" represents the concept of access anywhere — the full span of the globe. Mcommerce (mobile commerce) technologies have already, to some extent, made these environments a reality. A significant impact can still be made in this burgeoning area.

The concept of 24/7/360° can be valuable to consumers in environments where shopping is defined along the dimensions of ubiquity and seamlessness. Consider some hypothetical scenarios which suggest the potential value of a 24/7/360°:

- A consumer walking by Macy's Department Store, on the way to lunch with a friend, glances at a sofa being displayed in the window that arouses interest. Information about this sofa is being transmitted and can be received with a portable device. The consumer may either peruse information about the sofa immediately or record the location of this information for later review (e.g., over lunch with the friend). In addition, the consumer may enter the store to learn more or, if certain enough about purchasing it, could even put in an order while on the way to lunch.

- While walking through a park, a consumer admires the detail and juxtaposition of a lamp post and bench; he sits on the bench and enjoys the sparkle of light coming from the lamp post. He would like to purchase these products and construct the same juxtaposition in his back yard. Utilizing a portable device that can receive a transmission of information that is always available about these products, the consumer reviews the reputation of the manufacturer and the product prices and then decides to put in an order while sitting on the very type of park bench being ordered.
- On the way to a friend's house on the Upper East Side of New York City, a consumer decides to get a toy for her friend's daughter. Unfamiliar with the area, the consumer uses a portable device to contact her credit card company, who can either inform her of where to purchase a toy in the area or can have the desired toy delivered to her, where she stands, by a local merchant who sells toys.

Trust

The Internet enables not only a different medium for communication, but also the preservation and public posting of experiences. For example, participants of Edmunds.com's Townhall post about their experiences with automobile manufacturers and dealerships. These comments are easily accessible and remain posted (presumably for as long as Edmunds.com maintains the Townhall).

Given the potential availability of information to all consumers about any individual's exchange experience with a merchant, it becomes important for a merchant to be honest, as its exchange experiences with all consumers could very well be posted and become known to all current and potential customers–i.e., as in a small community, there are no secrets. Consumers would likely notice and reward consistent integrity, conversely merchants who, often enough, try to or do succeed in "pulling a fast one" on a consumer should not assume that the case would likely go no further than "you said vs. she said." The evidence of "you said versus *they* said" will be available and harder to sniggle out of.

I believe that it is important to define and assess trust with respect to online consumers and relevant environments. What are the components of trust? How do online consumers assess the trustworthiness of a merchant, manufacturer or peer? What are the cues of trust? What are trust busters? When do consumers devote significant effort in assessing trust? When is trust assumed? When is trust most important?

Consumers are more than click-streams

I purchased a Weber charcoal chimney starter from Amazon.com; in a visit to Amazon shortly after this purchase, it recommended, *especially for me*, the Leatherman multitool product. I have no interest in the Leatherman multitool at the moment and this experience lead me to believe that Amazon does not know me very well. Amazon's Leatherman recommendation was partially based on their quantitative analysis of my prior click-stream data (e.g., webpages visited, when items were placed in a shopping cart, items purchased); a method used by many firms for gaining an understanding about their online consumers. These data are used to estimate preference functions in an effort to create *true* "one-to-one" relationships with consumers. While these data can inform about a customer, I do not believe that they provide enough insight to establish and maintain a rich one-to-one relationship.

To do this, researchers and practitioners could utilize qualitative methods (e.g., online chat, email, actual in-person or "voice-to-voice" interviews or visits) and visit environments where consumers express themselves. These environments could be the consumers' 1) own websites — e.g., see http://www.homestead.com/dpbuck/index.html to learn about DP, currently a computer science student at Stanford University who dislikes sushi, prefers Coca Cola over Pepsi, roots for the Detroit Red Wing, drives a Suzuki Esteem, and hails from Las Vegas., or 2) online communities — e.g., see http://townhall-talk2.edmunds.com/WebX?14@163.n7dlaXWCikV^7@.ee93ec6/88 where Trevor, a Honda vehicle accessories salesperson, provides valuable and detailed information about — surprise, surprise — Honda vehicles and accessories; he gets to know the members of this Honda Odyssey online community by reading their posts, providing useful responses to a broad range of community member posts, and by emailing with them outside of the forum.

Culture, deep rooted beliefs, trial and adoption

Online shopping is not the "be all and end all," yet many consumers reject it or do not try it when it could be a better shopping alternative in many situations. Some of the reasons have face validity (e.g., limited access to a computer with an Internet connection, limited technical proficiency — though I question this as Weinberg (1993) found that consumers with limited or no computer experience found his "information acceleration" computer based "point and click" automobile shopping system easy to navigate and use) while others do not.

For example, many consumers who have rejected trial of online grocery services have told me that their primary reasons were that they a) "like" shopping and b) "prefer" to hand pick their own produce or meats. On average, I do not believe that these are the primary reasons (I acknowledge, however, that some people "like" to grocery shop in certain situations and some might "like" to grocery shop under all conditions, of course). These fairly consistent knee-jerk responses have aroused my curiosity as grocery shopping consists of many less than desirable aspects, which happen to be eliminated when using an online grocery service (e.g., physical lugging of heavy items, getting dings and dents on one's car while parked at the supermarket, using time that could be put toward other activities). I do not suggest that tradeoffs are not made when using an online grocery service (e.g., getting products immediately vs. waiting until the next day, sku selection), however, consumers are not so quick to raise issues beyond "liking" and "picking produce" when explaining their rejections of online grocery shopping services (at least in my experiences).

I believe that the true nature of the rejection lies deeper below the surface and has a strong cultural component that harkens back to the long history and importance of the relationship among man, woman, family, hunting, food, eating, meals and the inside of one's body (and the placement of objects — physical, psychological and spiritual — inside it). Given the ubiquity, frequency and the seemingly visceral attachment to in-store grocery shopping among consumers, then exploration and discovery in online grocery shopping may inform on important lessons for not only grocery shopping, but also many other online shopping domains.

Some specific questions that I have are:

- What are the benefits of grocery shopping? What is the perceived purpose of grocery shopping? (e.g., Caring for the self? Caring for the Family? Hunting? Carrying on tradition? Socialization?)
- What is being adopted when using an online grocery service? (e.g., Technology? A new way of life? The Internet

lifestyle? Freedom? Time to engage more preferred activities? Revolution?)

- What is being rejected when consumers do not adopt online grocery shopping? (e.g., Technology? Something untraditional? Inexperienced "upstarts?," Assignment of responsibility to a "stranger?," All of the reported fears of the Internet such as privacy and security? Radicalism?)
- Do consumers reject the entire online grocery shopping process or just certain aspects of it?
- What actions might compensate for the rejected aspects?
- For which products and why is hand selection preferred when grocery shopping?
- Have these types of consumers felt discomfort when any other individual has done the grocery shopping for them? Why or why not?
- What are their attitudes toward technology? Internet?
- Which food preparation or food delivery services have been successful and why (e.g., takeout food, takeout food delivery services, Harry & David). Could these reveal clues for success in the online grocery service business?

Online grocery shopping services may be facing a problem that is similar in nature to that confronted by Betty Crocker when it first launched its instant cake mix in the 1950s — all one had to do was add water to the mix and put it in the oven. Product acceptance was poor; analysis of focus group data concluded that homemakers associated baking with the birthing process and that they did not feel that simply adding water to a mix made them feel that they were taking good care of their family. In response to the focus group findings, the recipe was modified to include "adding one egg." In concert with the "Bake Someone Happy" campaign, the reformulated Betty Crocker cake mix flew off the shelves. Perhaps online grocery services would take off if they could identify their "egg" and make it part of their service?

The Five Senses and Technology

Consumers require certain types of information to reduce uncertainty in order to proceed with a purchase. Consumers have become accustomed to utilizing many of their senses when processing this information. At the present time, the technology which is widely used for engaging the Internet limits the extent to which consumers can utilize their senses. An important challenge to consider is the technology necessary for increasing the potential value of the online consumer experience.

For example: developing body scanners that can be used to inform precise body measurements, which in turn can be used to either order the correct predetermined/manufactured size or manufacture a custom fit size article of clothing (e.g., shirts, slacks, dress, shoes, etc.); building sensors that enable one to feel a product "in use" (e.g., do these clothes feel comfortable, does this camera feel good in my hands, etc.).

It is important to identify the shopping processes and the information used by consumers and to simulate online these processes. Or, assuming either an inability to or significant prohibitions in simulating these processes, to identify alternative or new online processes and information (i.e., not direct translations of existing nononline shopping processes and information) that could more readily be delivered and would provide similar utility or reduce a similar level of uncertainty?

Sample Size of One

Levy (2001) acknowledges an issue that has been raised by some colleagues as to the generalizability of my experiences as I am a "sample size of one." I recognize this issue as well, however, I

provide some evidence that my experiences are indeed representative of what a large part of the population could experience in the future and that these experiences could provide significant insight into understanding the behavior of a significant proportion of the online consumer population.

Many of the observations, interpretations and findings reported in Wolfinbarger and Gilly (2001), which involved interviews with 60 online consumers, were similar to many of those presented in this special session (i.e., The Three Faces of E, commerce...) which were based on my experiences and detailed in the Internet Shopping 24/7 Project website (e.g., the importance of control, accessibility, convenience, selection, information availability, social interaction, sales staff avoidance, shopping motives).

According to the Gartner Group, as reported by Mahoney (2000), "The average American who logs on [to the Internet] is 41 years old with an average income of $65,000 (US$), married with 2.81 children and uses a PC at work." During the data collection phase of the Internet Shopping 24/7 Project, I was an American, 41 years of age, married with 3 children, used a PC at work, and had an income that was somewhat close to $65,000. According to the Gartner Group, I would be considered the average American Internet user.

Levy (2001) states (page 1) "He does represent various consumer segments in our society, sociologically and psychologically, so that his experience is of general interest." Dobscha suggests in her astrological analysis that I exhibit the characteristics of a cross section of astrological sign types (e.g., Leo, Virgo, Capricorn). When members of the audience were asked to guess my "sign," other signs mentioned were Gemini and Taurus. My sign, however, is Aquarius.

I do not believe that my experiences are representative of the entire population, however, I do believe that my background and passions (e.g., computer science, computer mediated environments, marketing, shopping, consumer advocate, consultant, blue collar, white collar) gave me significant command in the online shopping domain and the ability to experience and evaluate the environment with depth from diverse perspectives. I believe that my experiences as a computer scientist and as a consumer advocate (as well as other experiences) enabled me to consider the circumstances and consequences of online shopping from not only my own perspective, but also that of others.

Social Dynamics

Many consumers that I have interviewed about shopping mention the social element of the experience (e.g., "shopping is social," "it is something that one does with friends"). Many of these same consumers mention the relative dearth of socialness in the online shopping experience. How can the effect (i.e., utility) of social dynamics be realized in the online shopping experience. What technologies could enable more of a social feeling to online consumer behavior? Will cobrowsing (i.e., the ability for more than one person to interact with the same website simultaneously) partially do this?

REFERENCES

Levy, Sidney J. (2001), "The Psychology Of An Online Shopping Pioneer," in *Advances in Consumer Research*, Volume 28, Mary Gilly and Joan Myers-Levy (Editors), Provo, Utah: Association of Consumer Research, forthcoming.

Mahoney, Michael (2000), "Study: Net Users Now Older, Wiser," *E-Commerce Times*, http://www.ecommercetimes.com/news/articles2000/001031-4.shtml, October 31, 2000

Schouten, John W., and James H. McAlexander (1995), "Subculture of Consumption: An Ethnography of the New Bikers," *Journal of Consumer Research,* 22 (June), 43-61.

Urban, Glen L., Bruce D. Weinberg and John R. Hauser (1996), "Premarket Forecasting of Really-New Products," *Journal of Marketing,* 60 (January), 47-60.

Weinberg, Bruce D. (1993), "An Information-Acceleration-Based Methodology for Developing Preproduction Forecasts for Durable Goods: Design, Development, and Initial Validation," Unpublished PhD Dissertation, MIT Sloan School of Management, Cambridge, Massachusetts.

Weinberg, Bruce D. (1999), "Click and Drive, The Emerging AutoNet Industry," *The Manager*, 4 (Fall), 23-24

Weinberg, Bruce D. and Jonathan Hibbard (2000), "Virtual Lemonade Stands: The Emerging Internet Consumer-Entrepreneur," *The Manager*, 1 (Spring), 23-24.

Wolfinbarger, Mary and Mary C. Gilly (2001), "Nibbling on the Net: Are We Having Fun Yet?," in *Advances in Consumer Research*, Volume 28, Mary Gilly and Joan Myers-Levy (Editors), Provo, Utah: Association of Consumer Research, forthcoming.

O Self, Are Thou One or Many? An Empirical Study of How Consumers Construct and Perceive the Self

Stephen J. Gould, Baruch College, The City University of New York

Concern with the self is a major element of consumer behavior in terms of constructing one's identity and embodying and/or signifying it through the use of goods. Moreover, it has been widely recognized in this regard and investigated by numerous consumer researchers (e.g., Belk 1988; Sirgy 1982). That said, major issues surrounding the self and such related concepts as identity and self-concept remain abundant and open. One major issue involves the very definition of that self and how the perspective taken on it informs consumer behavior. Much of the current controversy is driven by postmodern thought which suggests that even the 'inner' self and its conceptualization are under assault by the disintermediation and shattering of social structures. These disintermediating forces it is argued render the self as fragmented, transitory, or even as non-existent (Giddens 1991; Hall 1992). Yet, contradictory perspectives from other disciplines or conceptualizations, seem to indicate that there is something labeled "self" which can be viewed as central, cohesive and well recognized in its various aspects by everyday individuals (Hall 1992).

Surprisingly, there has been little empirical study in consumer research (or apparently anywhere else) to back up the various postmodern (perhaps superficial) theoretical claims made about the self (cf. Kellner 1995). Postmodern thought in that regard is often just that, thought, however informed it might be by the brilliance of the thinker and infused with the situating of his or her understanding. Indeed, a leading postmodern critic of the academic perspective on the everyday, Maffesoli (1996), suggests that there is an elitism among intellectuals that tends to either ignore or judgmentally disfigure the perspectives of ordinary people. This seems to create a potential gap between theoretical and empirically-driven accounts of the self that needs to be considered and which this paper will address.

METHOD

To conduct this study, an open-ended protocol applying written responses was used to provide revelatory consumer narratives (Gould 1997; Helgeson 1994; Holbrook 1987; Hunter 1983; Rook 1987). There were 20 participants in the study, ranging in age from 20 to 34. They were drawn from an undergraduate marketing class at a large Northeastern U.S. university. Fourteen were female and 6 were male. They were asked to write their responses to three questions within a period of two weeks and were given classroom credit. The questions focus on (1) defining the self in the informants own words, (2) considering whether there is "one central self, many selves, no one self, or even any self at all," and (3) indicating whether the self stays the same or changes.

THEMATIC RESULTS

The foregoing questions served as *a priori* themes which are considered below. Additional emergent aspects were uncovered in the interpretive process.

Definitions of the Self

In summary and conclusion, the informants tended to define the self in commonly recognized terms, suggesting that longstanding or modernist accounts of the self are embedded in their collective consciousness.

One or Many Selves?

The main theoretical issue in this paper concerns how consumers perceive the self in terms of its various proposed characterizations as being unified, manifold or even non-existent. Most tended to focus on one self. Beyond these general polarized views, the self-narratives revealed on an emergent basis more information related to the central-multiple self issue than the simple dichotomy between the two can account for.

Mixed View: Distinctions Concerning Aspects of Self. Some informants managed to view the self as some sort of admixture of both one and multiple aspects.

Appearances. The self as an intangible must in the view of a number of informants be expressed, manifested or given certain types of appearances. However, such appearances may belie something else that is hidden, i.e., they are suggestive of the concepts of the private or inner self and the public self (Triandis 1989).

Self as Difference. There was also some evidence in the narratives supportive of the idea of a unique self. Such a self is perhaps a central idea in various domains of research, ranging from psychology with its focus on individual differences to various phenomenological and interpretive approaches that to various degrees privilege idiosyncrasies. For example, Hallowell (1955) suggested that people viewed the self as representing something different from the self of others. Given this history, this element would also seem to be a more longstanding one.

Does the Self Change or Stay the Same?

The informants in this study strongly recognize the force of the evolution of the self. Moreover, while their perspectives serve to reinforce the answers given to the other questions in this study, they also add an emergent element that is revealing about what we may call *consumer self processes.* These processes are conveyed as lay psychological theories about the self and its workings. In summarizing the opinions of the informants on the self and change, the self evidently changes. But what is it that changes? Is it a central self or many selves? The answer would seem to be for most is that the central self changes and yet somehow endures.

DISCUSSION

This paper has not answered nor has it sought to fully consider the philosophical, metaphysical or spiritual issues surrounding the self, at least *per se.* Moreover, there are a number of inherent limitations in the study, including the sample, the particular questions asked, and the definitional-theoretical aspects of the self considered. Nonetheless, several conclusions stand out. First, while the self is stretched through all sorts of turgid gyrations in postmodern thought, it is seen in far more familiar, everyday, and perhaps more 'coherent' terms by everyday consumers. Second, there are many perspectives which provide insight into the construction of the self. The present study is suggestive of them but further theoretical development and empirical research is badly needed, especially in terms of the following two areas: (1) the discourse of the self—however, the self is described, it remains a central element of the lives and discourse of the informants in this study and (2) distinctions concerning the self—the self may or may not be multiple, but it also appears to be *multidimensional* in its construction as indicated by the informants in this study. They did not use that term but did speak of the "inner self" (as opposed to the outer or public self), "many sides," or "facets."

Third, the results of this study indicate some variance from *etic* theories of the postmodern. While the extent and nature of this variance are open to discussion, it does drive a major concern to consider when formulating theories and inscribing them in our consumer research narrative. It may indicate that we have an *imposed etic theory* which simply means that we have applied a misconstrued theory and taken it as supported (Yang and Bond 1990), i.e., a theory of the self rooted in sectors of academe which is at odds with one derived from everyday consumer culture. Therefore, we also need to consider the *emic* perspectives of consumers when investigating theorized postmodern phenomena. Fourth, the immediate implications for postmodern theory suggest that we consider the basis of the postmodern versus longstanding-modernist contesting of the metanarrative of the self (Gould and Lerman 1998; Thompson and Hirschman 1995) in terms of what Derrida (1988) calls undecidability. Thus, while most of the informants indicated they thought there was one central self, they still differed in emphasis from one another, and moreover, the narratives of those who suggested there were multiple selves or some mixed views even more strongly suggest this undecidability.

CONCLUSION

This study has identified some issues in the study and conception of the self that consumer researchers need to consider further. Most notably, they need to rethink how their *etic* metanarratives may not stand up under the deconstructive scrutiny of *emic* considerations, especially where postmodern thought is concerned. While there are probably as many discourses of the self as there are individuals, there does appear to something called the "self" that many, if not most consumers reify and hold as central.

(Note: references for the citations in this text as well as the full list of references are provided in the full paper which is available from the author)

Being Like or Being Liked: Identity vs. Approval in a Social Context

Susan Auty, Lancaster University Management School
Richard Elliott, Exeter University

This study adopts a sociological approach to adolescent consumer behaviour to examine normative influence on fashion brand choice. Bearden's social influence scale (1989) is applied to the choice of sports footwear brands by teenagers. The informational factor is found to be hardly relevant, and the normative factor divides into two components—identity and compliance. Modifying the concept of compliance to the rather softer notion of 'approval' results in a scale (based on Bearden's original) that significantly discriminates between fashion brand buyers and others. The need to be liked by one's peers appears to be a more important driver of choice than the need to express one's identity with them.

INTRODUCTION

Researchers into the psychology of consumer behaviour generally agree that for products with a high degree of shared product meanings, product choice depends largely on the consumer's desire to be associated with those meanings (Douglas and Isherwood 1979; Bourdieu, 1984; Mayer and Belk 1985; McCracken and Roth 1989; Dittmar 1992). Differences among individuals are expressed by alignment with particular images. Recent research has emphasised the identity-construction role of fashion: 'People buy goods solely to be different from others' (Gabriel and Lang 1995). Thompson and Haytko (1997) state that 'through this logic of self-identity construction, the sense of 'who I am' is constantly defined and redefined through perceived contrasts to others.' Bauman (1990) introduced the notion of 'neo-tribes' to characterise the changing nature of social groups which in contemporary society are based on 'individual acts of self-identification. . . . Tribes exist solely by individual decisions to sport the symbolic traits of tribal allegiance.' The emphasis therefore is on individual 'self-construction efforts'. But do these self-constructions at the individual level depend on self-definition through likeness to some and difference from others or on the need for social approval? Bauman (1991) acknowledges that the 'postmodern celebration of difference and contingency has not displaced the modern lust for uniformity and certainty.' As Elliott (1998) notes, 'the development of individual self-identity is inseparable from the parallel development of collective social identity' and 'self-identity must be validated through social interaction'. The distinction between identity construction and the validation process appears to be an important one, especially in the case of adolescent fashion products, where the need to define an identity is not necessarily the same as the need for social approval.

Translated into the scheme of consumption values devised by Sheth, Newman and Gross (1991), the distinction is between social values, where association with a specific social group drives the choice, and emotional values, where one is satisfying the feeling of security or happiness in being positively perceived by others. Although much research has focused on identity-seeking as an explanation of choice behaviour, approval-seeking has recently been subsumed into discussions on identity: 'Identity then does not mean the creation and projection of any image, but of one that commands respect and self-respect' (Gabriel and Lang 1995). The distinction made by Kelman (1961) between identification and compliance has effectively been lost, yet their goal orientations are quite different (self-maintenance or enrichment vs. external reward): 'Compliance can be said to occur when an individual accepts influence from another person or from a group because he hopes to achieve a favorable reaction from the other.' Warde (1997) notes that 'preoccupation with identity value acquired through the purchase of commodities' has 'arguably . . . been emphasized unduly, thereby encouraging the view that consumer behaviour has primarily been driven by processes of individualization and stylization.'

Identification (according to Burnkrant and Cousineau 1975) is unrelated to the 'visibility' of a conforming behaviour in contrast to compliance, where 'the individual in a product evaluation situation would be expected to comply with the prior evaluations of others only where his evaluation is visible to others who are perceived by him as mediators of significant rewards or punishments.' Hence conformity to prevailing fashion is most likely motivated by compliance rather than identity-seeking. Among adolescents especially compliance takes precedence over identity. According to Erikson (1965) 'the growing and developing youths, faced with this physiological revolution within them, . . . are now primarily concerned with what they appear to be in the eyes of others as compared with what they feel they are'. Psychologists agree that 'the conformist stage normally emerges during early adolescence and may be retained through late adolescent and adult life' (Kroger 1996).

If we widen the context of consumer behaviour from the psychological level to encompass more social and cultural perspectives then it becomes evident that recent developments in social theory have moved from conceptualising consumption as a prime force for individualisation towards its playing a more social role. Poststructuralist cultural theory has conceptualised consumption as culturally dependent, that is, consumer choice depends on contextualised characteristics rather than on cognitive traits (Holt 1997), and in opposition to the use of fashion for self-identity construction, it is also used for purposes of the construction of social affiliation and 'to foster an affirming sense of social belonging' (Thompson and Haytko 1997). Anthropological approaches to consumer behaviour are also beginning to highlight its pro-social functions, where the purchasing of goods is almost always linked to other social relationships (Miller 1998). Maffesoli (1996) focuses on consumption as playing a prime role in building social cohesion, suggesting that we live in 'the time of the tribes', new social collectivities which attempt to counter the rise of 'identity politics' and 'lifestyle cultures', while Cova (1997) identifies the 'linking value' which supports the social link between persons. This is largely a rediscovery of earlier theoretical approaches to consumption; the role of fashion as not only 'differentiating' but also 'socialising' was pointed out nearly a hundred years ago by Simmel (1904).

Firat (1992) observes that 'consumers of postmodernity [seem to be] no longer seeking centered, unified characters, but increasingly seeking to 'feel good' in separate, different moments by acquiring self images that make them marketable, likable and/or desirable in each moment', implying that identity-seeking has become secondary to approval-seeking in consumption behaviour. Indeed, for Firat and Venkatesh (1993) consumers do not have an identity, but rather 'assume different images and personalities in different situations to make themselves acceptable in each case'. In this view, identity-seeking has become subsumed in approval-seeking rather than the other way round.

CONCEPTUAL AND MEASUREMENT ISSUES

Social psychologists have long distinguished between informative and normative influences on purchase behaviour, and in the 1970s Burnkrant and Cousineau (1975) looked specifically at reference group influence on brand choices and concluded that 'after observing others evaluating a product favorably, people perceive the product more favorably themselves than they would have in the absence of this observation. . . .People may frequently buy products that others in their groups buy, not to establish some self fulfilling role relationship to the others nor to obtain some reward or avoid some punishment mediated by the others, but rather to acquire what they perceive as a good product.' They suggest, indeed, that the main influence is informational rather than normative.

A separate stream of research began to try to identify personality differences that make certain people more susceptible to normative influence than others. Snyder's Self Monitoring Scale (1974) grew out of this research; this attempted to distinguish people on the basis of adaptive behaviour in social situations. Self-monitoring was found to have a modest correlation with purchase behaviour (Auty and Elliott 1998, 1999). Bearden and Etzel (1982) pursued the original motivations of Deutsch and Gerard (1955) as explanatory variables of behaviour. These in turn had been modified by Stafford (1966), who identified knowledge, affectivity (identity) and sanctions (rewards). In devising a scale to measure Consumer Susceptibility to Interpersonal Influence (SII), Bearden, Netemeyer and Teel (1989) started out with the intention of developing a three-factor instrument in keeping with the distinction between 'value expressive' (identity-seeking) and 'utilitarian' (compliance) behaviour, in addition to information-seeking behaviour. Their analysis of the data indicated a very high intercorrelation of the value expressive and utilitarian factors, leading them to combine the two into a single 'normative' factor. However, in the postmodern/poststructuralist cultural context, a 3-factor scale may be more appropriate, with the factors preserving both an identity element and a social approval element. Defining the normative factor more accurately allows marketers to understand what is actually driving the choice in products with shared symbolic meanings. Indeed, practitioners concerned with modelling the emotional attributes of brands (Morgan, 1998) have identified three components of brand affinity: the first (less relevant here) is Authority, which refers to the heritage and trust associated with the brand; the second and third are Identification and Approval, which clearly discriminate between the private meaning and the public prestige of the brand. According to Morgan (1998), the approval element is particularly important 'in market sectors where the visible consumption of a brand is "saying something" about the chooser.' As Netemeyer, Bearden and Teel (1992) note, susceptibility to interpersonal influence 'is enhanced when individuals are highly concerned with the inferences others make or may make regarding their behavior' or, in other words, the compliance factor may be more important in consumption behaviour than identity-seeking is.

The present research is designed to explore the distinction in today's society and to understand current purchase motivations of adolescent consumers of symbolic products. In an attempt to discriminate between the motivations of top brand vs. lesser or store brand buyers, the SII Scale was administered together with questions on recent purchases of sports footwear and the associated meanings of the top brands.

HYPOTHESES

The following hypotheses represent expected findings in keeping with previous research into social influence.

H1   The stronger the desire to identify with one's peer group the more likely one is to purchase one of the top three brands in a fashion category.

H2   The stronger the tendency to comply with group norms the more likely one is to purchase one of the top three fashion brands.

H3   The stronger the tendency to seek information from peer groups, the more likely one is to purchase one of the top three fashion brands.

The next two hypotheses are designed to explore demographic differences with regard to social influence. Previous studies have indicated that females are orientated towards 'an affiliation with disparate parties and attachment of self and other' (Meyers-Levy and Sternthal 1991) suggesting that girls will be more susceptible to influence than boys. This is also the conclusion of a meta-analysis which showed that "women are somewhat more easily influenced than men, particularly in situations where other group members exert pressure on women to change their minds" (Matlin 1987), although the actual size of the sex difference was small. In keeping with Erikson's (1965) research into the developing adolescent, it is suggested that even in the narrow age band of middle to late adolescence, a difference in susceptibility will be noticeable.

H4   Girls are more likely than boys to be influenced by peer groups in choosing fashion brands.

H5   High school age adolescents are more likely than college age adolescents to be influenced by peer groups in choosing fashion brands.

A proposition has been put forward to reflect the expectation that in today's society, the approval of peer groups (which have the sanction of ridicule at their disposal) is a more salient motivation than shaping an identity is.

P1   A unidimensional scale measuring tendency to seek approval of peer groups is more closely associated with brand purchase than the existing two dimensional scale measuring normative and informational influences.

METHODOLOGY

After a series of focus groups at local schools and with university students to determine usage patterns of trainers and brand attitudes, a survey was designed to allow quantitative analysis. Adolescents aged between 15 and 19 were interviewed in dispersed shopping precincts in the United Kingdom, resulting in a convenience sample of 555 young men and women who responded to the full questionnaire. The survey asked for information on sports played and sports trainers owned. Information was elicited on the usage of particular brands for particular sports and for general street wear. Criteria for choosing brands were established with a series of itemised-scale ratings, and attitudes to the three largest-selling brands (Nike, Adidas and Reebok) were obtained with Likert scale statements for each. Open-ended questions asked for 'one word that comes to mind' for each of the three brands. Finally, respondents were handed Bearden's Susceptibility to Interpersonal Influence (SII) Scale (using 5 scale points) for self-completion. Three additional questions were included to ascertain the influence of films, sports stars and top bands on brand choice, but these have been excluded from the current analysis.

TABLE 1
Rotated Component Matrix (Loadings over .2)

		Component Identity	Compliance	Informational
Scale 2	If I want to be like someone, I often try to buy the same brands that they buy	**.736**		
Scale 12	I get a sense of belonging by buying the same products and brands that others do	**.720**	.299	
Scale 6	I often identify with other people by buying the same products and brands they do	**.702**	.222	
Scale 11	If other people can see me using the product, I often buy the brand they expect me to buy	**.700**	.301	
Scale 5	I rarely buy the latest fashion styles until I am sure my friends approve of them	**.605**	.285	
Scale 8	When buying things, I generally buy brands that I think others will approve of	.257	**.801**	
Scale 3	It is important that others like the products and brands that I buy	.273	**.746**	
Scale 9	I like to know what brands and products make good impressions on others		**.724**	
Scale 4	To make sure I buy the right product or brand, I often observe what others are buying and using	.360	**.510**	.236
Scale 7	If I don't have much experience with a product, I often ask my friends about it		.275	**.814**
Scale 10	I frequently get information from friends or family about a product before I buy	.276		**.811**
Scale 1	I often consult other people to help me choose the best brand of a particular product	.412		.460
	Eigenvalues	4.64	1.32	1.09
	% of Variance	38.7	11.0	9.1

Extraction Method: Principal Component Analysis. Rotation Method: Varimax with Kaiser Normalization. Rotation converged in 5 iterations.

THE SAMPLE

55% of the sample of British adolescents were between 15-17 years old (secondary school age) and the remainder were 18-19 (tertiary education age). 50% were male. The modal figure for number of pairs of trainers worn regularly was two, while the range of the pairs owned was from 1-15. The median cost of the most recently purchased pair was £43 in a range from £5-£120. 33% had purchased Nike, 22% Adidas and 16% Reebok. The latest quoted market shares for the UK and Europe are 35% Nike, 24% Adidas and 14% Reebok (*Marketing* 22 April 1999). Market shares for the specific age range were not available, but a split sample analysis of the ownership variables showed no significant differences, giving confidence in the results.

ANALYSIS

The survey was analysed using SPSS, and included factor analysis of the SII scale and analysis of variance of brand attitudes, behavioural and demographic characteristics. The behavioural predictors were the number of pairs of sports trainers owned, and the brand and cost of the most recent pair purchased. Brands were grouped for ease of interpretation into the 'top three' (Nike, Adidas and Reebok); 'lesser brands' (eg. Fila, Ellesse) and 'unfashionable' (eg. store brands). Cost of last pair was divided into two groups by the median expenditure (£45). Recency of last purchase was classified according to purchase within the past month, past year or earlier. Respondents were assigned to three groups based on their

scores on the relevant items of the SII scale; thus for each manipulation, there were three groups representing high, medium and low scores on a particular factor. The effect of age was considered by dividing the sample into high school and post high school age (15-17 and 18-19). One-way analysis of variance was performed using these groups and the behavioural predictors.

THE FINDINGS

Factor Analysis

Factor analysis of the SII scale with a varimax rotation indicated a three-factor solution, where eigenvalues over 1 is the criterion. A scree-test pointed to a four factor solution, a not unexpected difference between the two extraction criteria (Hair, et al 1998), but this was rejected upon examination of the results, which split one of the items normally associated with information-seeking into its own factor. The three components may be interpreted as being related to identity-seeking, compliance-seeking and informational/consultative (see Table 1). The first factor (identity-seeking) accounted for the highest percentage of variance (39%), and total variance explained was 59%. Individual items, however, did not always fall into the expected category, and item 4 ('To make sure I buy the right product or brand, I often observe what others are buying and using'), suffers from multiple loadings, although the original scale has it clearly in the informational camp. In the current study, this item loads over .5 only in the 'compliance-seeking'

TABLE 2
Pattern Matrix (Oblimin Rotation with 2 components extracted; loadings over .2)

		Component Normative	Informational
Scale 12	I get a sense of belonging by buying the same products and brands that others do	.775	
Scale 11	If other people can see me using the product, I often buy the brand they expect me to buy	.739	
Scale 8	When buying things, I generally buy brands that I think others will approve of	.722	
Scale 3	It is important that others like the products and brands that I buy	.708	
Scale 6	I often identify with other people by buying the same products and brands they do	.685	
Scale 5	I rarely buy the latest fashion styles until I am sure my friends approve of them	.651	
Scale 2	If I want to be like someone, I often try to buy the same brands that they buy	.636	
Scale 9	I like to know what brands and products make good impressions on others	.585	.324
Scale 4	To make sure I buy the right product or brand, I often observe what others are buying and using	.577	
Scale 7	If I don't have much experience with a product, I often ask my friends about it	.851	
Scale 10	I frequently get information from friends or family about a product before I buy	.817	
Scale 1	I often consult other people to help me choose the best brand of a particular product	.340	.412
	Eigenvalues	4.64	1.32
	% of Variance	38.7	11.0

Extraction Method: Principal Components Analysis. Rotation Method: Oblimin with Kaiser Normalization. Rotation converged in 4 iterations.

TABLE 3
Reliability Comparisons of SII Factors (Cronbach's alpha)

	Normative	Informational
Bearden (1989) N=141	.88	.82
Shroeder (1996) N=477	.89	.77
Current Survey (1999) N=555	.84	.63

factor. Even more messily, item 5 ('I rarely purchase the latest fashion styles until I am sure my friends approve of them') loads clearly into the 'identity-seeking' category, rather than the expected compliance category, while item 1 ('I often consult other people to help me choose the best brand of a particular product') loads almost equally on informational and identity-seeking, and below .5 in both cases.

Replication using the oblimin rotation (as performed in the two earlier studies) indicates that neither items 1 and 4 load above .5 on any category in the 3-factor solution. Correlation between the two normative components was .47, much lower than the 0.92 initially found by Bearden. When analysis was restricted to extracting two components, as in the earlier studies (see Table 2), item 1 remained highly ambiguous, loading almost equally on both factors. Item 4 is firmly in the normative category, rather than the expected informational. Correlation between the two factors was .34, the same as that found by Shroeder in his 1996 replication of Bearden's work (.44 in Bearden's study). Removal of items 1 and 4 result in greater clarity whatever method is used, and should perhaps be considered by future researchers.

Analysis of the younger (15-16 year olds) and oldest (19 year olds) was performed separately to see if older adolescents were perhaps more secure in their identity and therefore more likely to make a distinction between identity and compliance. The only difference, however, was found in Item 1 (an informational item), which is more clearly associated with the Identity component among the older age group. The variance extracted for the two normative components was virtually identical for both age groups.

Scale Reliability

Overall, the scale achieves an alpha of .85. The three components achieve .80, .77 and .61. When the items were analysed in their original categories, comparison with Bearden's components shows that reliability of the informational factor is still quite low at .63, especially relative to previous applications (see Table 3). Our sample was younger in age and British, either of which may have affected results, but it does suggest that the informational factor is not robust across experimental conditions. In contrast, the normative factor seems stable as well as reliable. However, the question remains about how effective it is for explaining brand-buying behaviour.

One-way analysis of variance

One-way analysis of variance of the behavioural variables indicated that social influence is closely associated with ownership of the top brands, although the informational factor was not signifi-

TABLE 4
F-Statistic (p<) of Behavioural Variables with SII Variables

	Identity	Compliance	Informational	SII	Normative	'Approval'
Top Brands Owned	**5.3**	**4.5**	1.8	**4.2**	**9.0**	**10.2**
	(.005)	**(.011)**	(.166)	**(.015)**	**(.000)**	**(.000)**
Cost of Last Pair	2.5	2.6	0.6	1.2	3.5	**4.5**
(< or >than £45)	(.112)	(.108)	(.452)	(.281)	(.061)	**(.035)**
Bought within	0.8	0.3	1.3	1.9	0.9	1.1
past year	(.465)	(.727)	(.286)	(.148)	(.421)	(.337)
No. of pairs owned	0.2	0.7	0.3	0.0	0.2	0.9
	(.692)	(.419)	(.577)	(.991)	(.667)	(.341)

TABLE 5
F-Statistic (p<) of Demographic Variables with SII Variables

	Identity	Compliance	Informational	SII	Normative	'Approval'
Sex	0.4	2.3	**8.4**	0.0	1.9	2.2
	(.514)	(.127)	**(.004)**	(.871)	(.169)	(.136)
Age	**25.2**	**23.4**	1.8	**23.7**	**28.7**	**30.1**
	(.000)	**(.000)**	(.178)	**(.000)**	**(.000)**	**(.000)**

TABLE 6
F-Statistic (p<) of Demographic Variables with Behavioural Variables

	Brands Purchased	No. of Pairs Owned	Recency of Last Purchase	Cost of Last Pair
Sex	1.2	**17.1**	**9.8**	**22.2**
	(.282)	**(.000)**	**(.002)**	**(.000)**
Age	**3.7**	1.0	**6.7**	1.3
	(.055)	(.327)	**(.010)**	(.251)

cant at the 95% confidence level (see Table 4). Thus, H1 and H2 are supported, but H3 is not. In order to more clearly isolate the compliance factor from the identity factor, a new scale of seven items (Cronbach's alpha = 80) comprising those items in which the wording refers to peer approval was tested. The items were 3,4,5,8,9,11,12. These were mostly drawn from the original normative factor, but excluded the two items that refer specifically to identity, items 2 and 6, and included the informational item (4) about observing others to buy the 'right' brand. Only this 'approval' factor was aligned with the cost of the last pair (p<.035), with those most seeking approval being more likely to spend more than the median amount. As might be expected, the number of pairs owned and recency of last purchase were not associated with social influence.

The same analysis of sex and age groups by different factors of social influence indicate that the sex is only significant for information-seeking (see Table 5): girls tend to seek information more than boys do. With regard to age, however, the story is reversed. Younger (high school age compared with college age) adolescents are more susceptible to normative social influence, regardless of whether one is looking specifically at identity-seeking or approval-seeking. However, they are not significantly more likely to seek information than older adolescents. Thus H4 is only

partially supported and H5 is supported, with the proviso that information-seeking does not play a large role in influencing them.

In assessing the effects of social influence, it is important to rule out an association between demographics and brands purchased. The analysis using sex and age and all the behavioural variables was carried out to see if other explanations than social influence were associated with purchases (see Table 6). Looking at the relationship between sex and brands purchased, one finds no significant relationship. However, there is a significant relationship between sex and number of pairs owned, recency of last purchase and price paid for last pair, with boys owning more pairs, buying more frequently and spending significantly more than girls. The nature of the product suggests that this finding cannot be generalised beyond sports trainers: boys are more likely to take sports seriously and to require specialist trainers than girls are. Indeed, inspection of the brands owned for sports rather than street wear shows that a large number of boys own Adidas trainers exclusively for sports (much more so than girls own Reeboks just for sports). With regard to age, younger adolescents are barely significantly more likely to buy fashionable brands than older ones are, and are more likely to buy frequently than older—perhaps because their feet are still growing! There was no significant interaction between age and sex with regard to number of pairs owned. None of the demographic findings argue against the interpretations of the social influence factors.

DISCUSSION

Bearden's scale is a useful construct for its intended purpose, but when looking specifically at adolescent conformity in fashion consumption, it would appear that only half the scale is required. The 'approval' subscale seems to predict actual behaviour better than the full SII scale, as measured by choice of brand in most recent purchase of a visible fashion item (sports footwear). There was a highly significant association ($p< .000$) between a high score on these items and choice of the top three brands. In contrast, the informational element of the scale was not at all associated with brand choice, in that those scoring high on the need to consult were not more likely to choose the top three brands than others were.

The normative factor of Bearden's social influence scale divides into two components, identity and compliance, which have become blurred in recent research into consumer behaviour. Modifying the concept of compliance, with its connotations of reward and punishment, to a less disciplinarian concept of 'approval', seems to define the motivation even more meaningfully and to result in a more significant discrimination between fashion brand buyers and others. Scores on an 'approval-seeking' scale showed more association with actual purchase behaviour (brand last bought and cost) than did the identity-seeking scale, although this modified scale admittedly includes some items that load strongly on identity-seeking in the three factor solution of the SII scale.

The distinction first made from a sociological perspective by Mead in 1934 has most relevance here: the 'me' aspect of identity ('the self's image of the others' image of itself' in Bauman's (1990) words) is predominant among adolescents in choosing fashion brands over the 'I' aspect (the self's 'inner core'). McCracken's (1986) emphasis on the transfer of symbolic meanings, the 'systematic appropriation of the meaningful properties of goods', from the group to the self, which has been embraced by Dittmar (1992), does not explain adolescent brand behaviour so much as the human need for social approval does: teenagers are not trying to be *like* other people so much as trying to be *liked* by them. Dittmar acknowledges this when she says that: 'Many aspects of self-definition become associated with people's possessions because they reflexively evaluate themselves on the basis of how others perceive them and respond to them in terms of material symbols.' That identity and compliance motives often coalesce is not surprising, given that the apparently simplest way to gain approval is to be like the people one chooses to be liked by. It is important, however, not to lose the approval motivation in elucidating the identity-seeking motivation.

IMPLICATIONS FOR FUTURE RESEARCH

This study has attempted to broaden the context of consumer behaviour from the individual towards a more socially-situated person, but this is only a first step towards locating choice behaviour in a truly cultural context. Although the conceptualisation of consumer behaviour as being driven by individual preferences has dominated the field since its inception, recent radical reframings of consumer choice suggest that rather than choice being a psychological variable it should be thought of as a cultural variable; 'the basic choice that a rational individual has to make is the choice about what kind of society to live in. According to that choice, the rest follows' (Douglas 1996). This extends the social affiliation role of brands to one of the symbolic expression of a basic cultural value system and points us away from simple preferences and towards the negative pole of 'hostility'. Rather than focus simply on what people want, it may be more informative to ask what they do not want, as people do not only seek social approval from some social groups, they also want to express hostility to other groups. We therefore need to enrich our conceptualisation of the symbolic meaning of brand choice as not just a badge of allegiance but also as an act of rejection and hostility. 'To understand shopping practices we need to trace standardised hates, which are much more constant and more revealing than desires' (Douglas 1996). The work on anti-choice behaviour (e.g. Hogg, 1998) has made a start in re-contextualising consumer choice, but despite being based on Bourdieu's (1984) sociological theory of 'refusal of taste' it has not embraced the cultural perspective taken by Douglas and remains focused on individuation. Future research should explore the extent to which affiliation, the building and maintenance of social relationships and the expression of cultural values are key factors in understanding brand choice.

REFERENCES

Auty, S and R Elliott (1998) "Fashion Involvement, Self-Monitoring and the Meaning of Brands," *Journal of Product and Brand Management*, 7, 109-121.

Auty, S and R Elliott (1999) ' "Reading" Advertising and "Writing" Identity' in *Advances in Consumer Research*, ed. E Arnould and L Scott, 26, pp. 439-444.

Bauman, Z (1990) *Thinking Sociologically*. Oxford: Basil Blackwell.

Bauman, Z (1991) *Modernity and Ambivalence*. Cambridge: Polity Press.

Bearden, W and M Etzel (1982) 'Reference Group Influence on Product and Brand Purchase Decisions', *Journal of Consumer Research*, 9, pp. 183-194.

Bearden, W, R Netemeyer and J Teel (1989) "Measurement of Consumer Susceptibility to Interpersonal Influence," *Journal of Consumer Research*, 15, pp. 473-481.

Bourdieu, P. (1984) *Distinction: A Social Critique of the Judgement of Taste*. London: Routledge.

Burnkrant, R and A Cousineau (1975) 'Informational and Normative Social Influence in Buyer Behavior, *Journal of Consumer Research*, 2, 206-215.

Cova, B (1997) 'Community and Consumption: Towards a Definition of the "Linking Value" of Products or Services', *European Journal of Marketing*, 31, pp. 297-316.

Deutsch, M and H Gerard (1955) 'A Study of Normative and Informational Social Influences Upon Individual Judgment', *Journal of Abnormal and Social Psychology*, 51, pp. 624-636.

Dittmar, H (1992) *The Social Psychology of Material Possessions*. Hemel Hempstead: Harvester Wheatsheaf.

Douglas, M. (1996), *Thought styles: Critical Essays on Good Taste*. London: Sage Publications

Douglas M and B Isherwood (1979) *The World of Goods*, London: Allen Lane.

Elliott, R (1998) 'A Model of Emotion-Driven Choice', *Journal of Marketing Management*, 14, pp. 95-108.

Erikson, E (1965) *Childhood and Society*, Harmondsworth: Penguin Books.

Firat, A F (1992) 'Fragmentations in the Postmodern' in *Advances in Consumer Research*, ed. J Sherry and B Sternthal, 19, pp. 203-205.

Firat, A F and Venkatesh (1993) 'Postmodernity: the Age of Marketing' *International Journal of Research in Marketing*, 10, pp. 227-249.

Gabriel, Y and T Lang (1995) *The Unmanageable Consumer: Contemporary Consumption and its Fragmentation*, London: Sage Publications.

Hair, J, R Anderson, R Tatham and W Black (1998) *Multivariate Data Analysis*, 5th ed. London: Prentice Hall International.

Hogg, M (1998), Anti-constellations: Conceptualisation and Critique. In B. Engel and A. Oloffson (eds.) *European Advances in Consumer Research*, 3, pp. 44-49.

Holt, D (1997), 'Poststructuralist Lifestyle Analysis: Conceptualising the Social Patterning of Consumption in Postmodernity', *Journal of Consumer Research,* 23, pp.326-350.

Kelman, H (1961) 'Processes of Opinion Change' *Public Opinion Quarterly*, 25, pp. 57-78.

Kroger, J (1996) *Identity in Adolescence: The Balance Between Self and Other*, 2nd ed. London: Routledge.

Maffesoli, M (1996), *The Time of the Tribes: The Decline of Individualism in Mass Society*. trans. D. Smith, London: Sage Publications.

Matlin, M (1987), *The Psychology of Women*. New York: Holt, Rinehart and Winston.

Mayer, R and R Belk (1985) 'Fashion and Impression Formation Among Children' in *The Psychology of Fashion*, ed. M. Solomon, Lexington MA: Lexington Books, pp. 293-307.

McCracken, G (1986) 'Culture and Consumption: A Theoretical Account of the Structure and Meaning of Consumer Goods,' *Journal of Consumer Research*, 13, pp. 71-84.

McCracken, G and V Roth (1989) 'Does Clothing Have a Code? Empirical Findings and Theoretical Implications in the Study of Clothing as a Means of Communication,' *International Journal of Research in Marketing*, 6, pp. 13-33.

Mead, G (1934) *Mind, Self and Society*. Chicago: Chicago University Press.

Meyers-Levy J and B Sternthal (1991) 'Gender Difference in the Use of Message Cues and Judgments, *Journal of Marketing Research*, 28, pp. 84-96.

Miller, D. (1998), *A Theory of Shopping*. Cambridge: Polity Press

Morgan, R (1998) 'Linking Brand Imagery with Preference' in *Brand Choice Modelling*, ed. I Greig, ESOMAR, pp.63-84.

Netemeyer, R, W Bearden and J Teel (1992) 'Consumer Susceptibility to Interpersonal Influence and Attributional Sensitivity' *Psychology and Marketing*, 9, pp. 379-394.

Cova, B. (1997) "Community and consumption: Towards a definition of the "linking value" of products or services", *European Journal of Marketing*, 31, 3/4, 297-316.

Simmel, G. (1904), "Fashion" Reprinted in *American Journal of Sociology*, 62 (May 1957), 541-548.

Douglas, M. (1996), *Thought styles: Critical Essays on Good Taste*. London: Sage publications

Miller, D. (1998), *A Theory of Shopping*. Cambridge: Polity Press

Bourdieu, P. (1984), *Distinction: A social critique of the judgement of taste*. London: Routledge.

Sheth, J, B Newman and B Gross (1991) 'Why We Buy What We Buy: A Theory of Consumption Values' in *Journal of Business Research*, 22, pp. 159-170.

Schroeder, J (1996) 'An Analysis of the Consumer Susceptibility to Interpersonal Influence Scale', *Journal of Social Behavior and Personality*, 11, pp. 585-599.

Simmel, G (1904), 'Fashion' Reprinted in *American Journal of Sociology*, 62 (May 1957), pp. 541-548.

Snyder, M (1974) "Self-Monitoring of Expressive Behavior," *Journal of Personality and Social Psychology*, 30, pp. 526-537.

Stafford, J (1966) 'Effects of Group Influence on Consumer Brand Choice Preference, *Journal of Marketing Research*, 3, pp. 68-75.

Thompson, C and D Haytko (1997) 'Speaking of Fashion: Consumers' Uses of Fashion Discourses and the Appropriation of Countervailing Cultural Meanings' *Journal of Consumer Research*, 24 (June), pp 15-42.

Warde, A (1997) *Consumption, Food and Taste*, London: Sage Publications.

Mapping the Negative Self:
From 'So Not Me'…to 'Just Not Me'

Emma N. Banister, Manchester School of Management, UMIST

Margaret K. Hogg, Manchester School of Management, UMIST

ABSTRACT

This paper examines how consumers create and interpret meaning from the *negative aspects* of their self concept via symbolic consumption. This approach is in contrast to earlier studies of symbolic consumption and self-congruency which have traditionally focused on understanding how consumers use and interpret the *positive* meanings associated with their consumption decisions. In this paper we conceptualise and explore the relationships between dislikes, distastes and the negative self. Mini group discussions, friendship pairs and projective techniques were used to elicit qualitative data. A number of different consumer views of the 'negative self' (undesired and avoidance) emerged linked to various degrees of dislikes and distastes embodied by the 'refusal of tastes'. This major finding indicated the importance of appreciating the *multifaceted* nature of the negative self, which has hitherto been treated largely as a homogeneous entity within the self-concept.

LITERATURE REVIEW

Understanding how individuals define themselves through consumption is a central concern of consumer research (Arnould and Price 1993; Celsi, Rose and Leigh 1993; Levy 1959; Schouten and McAlexander 1995; Thompson and Hirschman 1995). However, the role of *different negative* (or unwelcome) aspects of the self in consumption (and the associated rejection of products) has received scant attention in consumer research compared with extensive research into positive aspects of the self (e.g. actual, ideal). This relative neglect of negative selves represents a significant gap in our understanding of consumers' self-concepts. In this paper we examine, firstly, how consumers create and interpret meaning about the *negative aspects* of their self concept via symbolic consumption. Secondly, we explore the rejection of product or brand images within the context of negative possible selves (Markus and Nurius 1986).

Possible selves are presented as *a set of* imagined roles or states of being and can be either positive or negative (Markus and Nurius 1986). Negative possible selves function as incentives for future behavior, representing selves to be rejected or avoided (Markus and Nurius 1986). The undesired self (Ogilvie 1987) has been identified as one aspect of the negative self, and the *push* (of the undesired self) has been found to be more effective than the *pull* (of the ideal self) in terms of the standard for measuring one's present place in life (Ogilvie 1987). This undesired self seems to be linked to feelings of repulsion, revulsion (Rozin and Fallon 1987) and rejection. Various aspects of the negative self, and specifically the undesired self, can be considered to be important reference points or 'implicit standards' which individuals will use to assess how close or distant they are from being like their most negative images of themselves (Ogilvie 1987, Eisenstadt and Leippe 1994). It is proposed that what a person is afraid of becoming, or more specifically an individual's undesired or un-ideal self, is of particular relevance when they imbue products with negative meanings.

Operating within the context of the possible self-concept would suggest that a multitude of negative selves exist. Mapping these different facets of negative possible selves is important in any drive to understand negative symbolic consumption. The Undesired Self – identified by Ogilvie (1987) - is often manifested via the

refusal of tastes (Bourdieu 1984). In fact a small yet growing body of literature (e.g. Wilk 1994, 1995, 1997; Freitas et al 1997) has suggested that *what we choose not to consume* is an important aspect of both individual and group identity (or identities). It could be that distastes or the 'refusal of tastes' says as much about us personally and socially as that which we opt to consume.

Tastes often carry positive connotations, yet it is significant that tastes are predominantly asserted in negative terms through the "refusal" of other tastes (Bourdieu 1984:56). Consumers often have less difficulty articulating their distastes and dislikes than they do their desires (Wilk 1997), and also in articulating the negative product user stereotypes and the negative inferences that can be associated with product cues.

CONCEPTUAL FRAMEWORK

On the basis of the literature, a framework was constructed which seeks to identify the means by which consumers attach undesirable qualities to items (Figure 1). This is in direct contrast with the work of Grubb and Grathwohl (1967) who looked at product and brand purchases as a means of self-enhancement. Unlike McCracken's (1986) account of the transfer of the movement of cultural meaning of consumer goods, the framework seeks to understand how *individual* consumers use the consumption process as a vehicle for creating meaning.

The framework depicts the means by which product and brand meanings are interpreted by consumers in the context of (negative) possible selves and the product and brand user imagery that they bring into play. The spheres on the left and the broken arrows depict the probable influences on individual consumers' (negative) possible selves and the stereotypes that are important to them.

RESEARCH DESIGN AND METHODS

This was an exploratory study of a neglected construct in consumer behavior research: the 'negative self', so the research design used qualitatively-based methods for data collection to facilitate understanding. The objectives of the empirical study were to examine firstly, the negative self-concept and, secondly, the rejection of products.

Clothing was selected as a category for which both product symbolism and the theory of congruency is highly relevant (Belk et al 1982; Holman 1980; Freitas et al 1997; Feinberg et al 1992; Kaiser 1997). The study concentrated on the impact of consumer stereotyping on product/brand imagery in the category of clothing, and the implications of negative associations in the interpretation of product/brand-user imagery. The research specifically explored the extent to which consumers are able to construct product user stereotypes (Sirgy 1982), and the extent to which these were used by consumers when discussing their consumption choices.

As this was an exploratory study, we were not concerned with making "sample to population" statements (Firestone 1993, cited in Miles and Huberman 1994:28). The sampling was theoretically driven, as earlier studies (e.g. Holman 1980; Belk et al 1982; Belk et al 1984; Freitas et al 1997) had indicated the relevance of exploring symbolic consumption via clothing and younger consumers. A combination of purposive and convenience sampling was used, aimed at involving what Patton (1990) terms "informa-

Advances in Consumer Research
Volume 28, © 2001

FIGURE 1.

Conceptual framework: consumers' interpretation of (negative) product and brand meanings

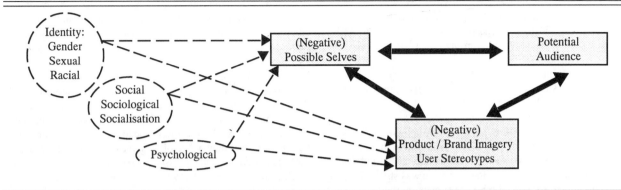

tion rich cases". Thirty participants were recruited, reflecting strategies adopted in other areas of consumer research (Thompson and Haytko 1997; Kimle and Damhorst 1997). Although no incentive was used, food and drink was provided for the participants. An equal number of male and female informants were recruited, as gender has been seen as an important variable for fashion meanings (Kaiser et al 1993; Kaiser 1997) although it was attempted to achieve a fairly even spread of ages within the selected age category. Other effects of consumer socialization were deliberately limited through keeping class differences to a minimum.

In the first phase, two mini discussion groups – each with four participants of the same gender - were conducted which provided an opportunity to explore the main issues and different lines of questioning, and to pilot the projective technique.

In the second phase, a series of semi-structured interviews were held using single sex 'friendship pairs' (ten interviews were held in all). Three main issues were explored in the interviews: firstly, attitudes to clothing styles and outfits; secondly attitudes to brands; and thirdly attitudes to fashion retail outlets. Although a number of set themes were covered, the discussion within these friendship pairs was fairly unstructured, following the flow of the conversation (Kvale 1996).

To promote discussion about clothing and fashion, ten photographs of same-sex models (which were considered by three independent judges to reflect a range of consumer images) were used as stimuli material.

To explore attitudes to brands and fashion retail outlets, a projective exercise was carried out individually, which involved the construction of collages, and participants' self-analyses of their collages. The projective technique required participants to map firstly, sports (trainer) brands and, secondly, clothing retailers' logos in relation to the three different views of themselves (actual, ideal and undesired). These collages, and the 'participant self-analyses' that followed, proved an effective means of eliciting firstly, self and brand / retailer connections; secondly, negative stereotypes of the rejected brands and retailers; and, thirdly the participants' negative attitudes about the rejected brands and retailers.

FINDINGS AND DISCUSSION

All the discussions were taped and transcribed. The qualitative data and projective material were analysed by an iterative process of searching for instances and themes (Miles and Huberman 1994). To clarify the presentation of the findings from the qualitative data, the key differentiation between aspects of the negative self can be summarized into *undesired* (So not me!) and *avoidance* (Just not me!).

The Undesired Self "So Not Me!"

The *Undesired Self* was the most extreme view of the negative self, compared with the *avoidance self*. Participants had little difficulty in articulating dislikes (see Wilk 1997), responding with clear distaste and the 'active rejection' (Schouten 1991) of outfits, brands and retailers that they considered to represent images that are 'not me'. Participants had clear views of the type of people that would wear the outfits, brands or retailers that they were describing, supporting Ogilvie's (1987) argument that the undesired self is less abstract than the ideal self.

Stereotypes

Participants made a host of (negative) assumptions predominantly on the basis of clothing. Negative stereotypes or portraits of negative 'typical' consumers, which emerged from the discussions, provided support for the use of negative product-user stereotypes as a means by which to understand and explore the negative aspects of symbolic consumption and the 'undesired self', thus extending earlier research into product-user stereotypes (Sirgy et al 1997).

Female participants, who themselves had fairly dissimilar self-images, provided illustrations of the undesired self that were remarkably similar. One stereotype was viewed particularly negatively by women.

"....wearing like a little white skirt with white stilettos and American tan tights ... you know what I mean ... and things like that with like a curly perm" (Lisa, 24, Doctoral Student).

"...I don't want people thinking I'm a slapper[1] ... white short skirt and white stilettos" (Karen, 26, Project Officer)

Many of these more extreme images – representing the 'undesired self' – were spontaneously labelled by participants. Often accompanying these 'labels' were ideas and assumptions concerning the behavior and attitudes of the consumers, in line with Sirgy et al's (1997) notion of product user stereotypes. Two women respondents, for instance, described what they considered to be undesirable images, and gave them labels – "Sharon and Tracy" - which they saw as describing behavior as well as dress sense. These 'avoidance groups' were assumed to involve goals that were rejected by the participants, confirming earlier research (Englis and Solomon 1995; Freitas et al 1997).

---

[1] English slang for appearing 'like a tart' or 'loose' usually used for young women and having negative connotations regarding appearance and morals. Derived from early 20th Century slang term 'slap' for make-up.

"The typical Sharon is… that girl, she had this tiny little dress on and she was absolutely hammered[2] with her mate and she was trying to chat up this group of lads… because she had obviously decided that everybody else wore the short strappy little dresses, and that was what she was wearing… She looked dreadful…" (Adele, 27, Telecom Manager)

"I always think of Sharon and Tracys as wearing cheap clothes. That sounds awful doesn't it, but sort of cheap fashion clothes." (Liz, 27, Marketing Executive)

The male participants, in contrast, were not so specific as the women, perhaps because they are not socialized in the same way (Miller 1997) or because their 'clothing vocabulary' is not so vast (Kimle and Damhorst 1997). However there was still an identifiable tendency to stereotype other consumers on the basis of the clothing that they wore. The two youngest male participants (both undergraduate students aged 19), for instance, labelled one product-user stereotype as "Essex boys" when talking about white trousers. The term "Essex boys" was an interesting one particularly as the participants themselves lived in Greater London, very near Essex[3].

Simon: "They ['Essex Boys'] go clubbing every night and you know, just general sort of things..."
Steve: "They have got earrings in both ears"
Simon: "XR2i[4] and...."
Steve: "White socks"
Simon: "They are on the pull, every second of every day they are on the pull, they have a shower four times a day you know and usually have short gelled hair"
Steve: "And mobile phones"

In effect the description accompanying "Essex boys" appeared to be the male equivalent of "Sharon" (when used by women), with a set of behaviors and (similar) lifestyle assumptions accompanying the terms. Eisentadt and Leippe (612:1994) suggest that these kinds of clear views of negative selves are important in achieving a level of satisfaction; "The actual self – thankfully devoid of an undesirable quality – looks good 'by comparison' with the rejected self".

Behavioral Assumptions Accompanying the Undesired Self

The main difference that existed between the *undesired self* and the *avoidance self* was the notion that specific 'undesirable' qualities accompanied the undesired self. In certain cases this affected individuals' behavior towards others (see Feinberg et al 1992).

"It is quite possible for someone to be wearing something which totally puts you off them from the start" (Peter, 27, Art Dealer)

---

2 English slang for drunk
3 It is difficult to describe the connotations that surround the term 'Essex' when used as an adjective by English people. Originally describing a county in the South East of England next to London, it has assumed pejorative overtones in English culture and tends now to be used in a derogatory sense often when denigrating someone or something in terms of 'having too much money and no taste, culture or breeding about how to spend that money'.
4 XR2i is a sports model of a small Ford car

Both male and female participants expressed greater degrees of distaste for certain images, asserting that the image would *never* be one that they might embrace. This is in contrast to the *avoidance* selves which could become relevant if the individual's situation changed – for example as they got older or changed their occupation.

Personality Assumptions Accompanying the Undesired Self

Sometimes participants commented on individuals' personality or character, which suggested that not just complete images, but even small details of a person's dress, could communicate fairly specific messages. Where these negative comments concerned personality traits, they would often serve to ensure that the discussant would never consider dressing in a similar way, illustrating the 'push factor' of Ogilvie's (1987) argument.

"… so if they [teachers] look scruffy, they [school children] will consider them scatty and unorganised..." (Josie, 29, Teacher)

"…I know it is a real stereotype, but someone who wears kind of street-wear … you look at them and you think 'they've got a bit of an attitude'…." (Jayne, 25, Marketing Manager)

"…I think you ought to be able to see a cuff in a suit or you look untrustworthy if you can't..." (Craig, 29, Solicitor)

Experience Related

Ogilvie (1987) argued that the undesired self is more experience based and less conceptual than the ideal self. The findings supported this, with negative images emerging regarding clothing that were often formed on the basis of previous experience. This previous experience related either to [usually disliked] others, or it might be defined by an image that individuals used to have – often dictated by their parents. Sometimes this 'past experience' meant not making previous mistakes again.

"I think I have been stung before, and got stuff and thought that looks great and worn it once and never again" (Stuart aged 25, Business Advisor)

Dislikes could also be informed by links with the past:

"My parents always tried to get me to buy C&A …so it's probably one of the reasons why I don't even look in there any more" (Wayne aged 22, Production / Sales Manager)

"I have a life long aversion towards Indian fringed skirts…I think because when I was about fourteen I thought it was very easy kind of hippie chic thing. I don't know, I have always associated it with pretentiousness basically, I still do... if somebody, even now, I mean obviously they are not around as much any more, is wearing an Indian fringed skirt I would regard them with suspicion." (Deirdre aged 26, Features Writer)

Links with disliked individuals were also made:

"…there is this woman at work that I don't really like very much. She's very fashionable but she's got a certain look, and I will go shopping … I quite like what this girl wears but she is a bit … I am probably quite jealous of her actually, she has got a very good figure and she is very blonde and girlie and I think …Maybe it is not stuff that I would buy anyway, but it

is just names come into your head while you are going round Top Shop[5] and you just think 'ooh maybe they are not the clothes for me'" (Joanna aged 26, Buyer Services)
"...It is like when you talk about what you would call your kids if you ever have them and you say well I would never call them say Megan, because it would remind me of Megan Childs or something... it is a bit like that. It is like I couldn't buy that because it would remind me of so and so." (Deirdre aged 26, Features Writer)

Avoidance Self "Just Not Me!"

The *Avoidance Self* can be contrasted with *the Undesired Self* because the undesired self is *always* viewed negatively – whether in relation to the individual or in relation to someone else. The 'avoidance self' is viewed negatively in relation to the individual, but might well be viewed positively on someone else. A different set of criteria were found to be significant when looking at the avoidance self – specifically age, body image, character / personality, situation – and many of these are less permanent characteristics than those that are associated with the undesired self.

"See like the dress Caroline wore on Saturday night, I really like it, but it *just isn't me* I would look totally out of character. I personally really really like it. But ...maybe it is the pattern... refined isn't the right word because that isn't Caroline either... I would feel out of place, I would feel like it was above me ... in a different situation maybe I would have carried it off, but I just don't think I could have mingled very well in it" (Suzanne, 25, Journalist)

Age Related

The age dimension was one of the clearest ways in which the negative aspects of the avoidance self emerged. Clothes were often used to indicate the age of the wearer. If clothing was worn that was not considered appropriate for the individual's age, it would be interpreted as 'bad taste'. The age dimension functioned in both directions – the wearing of clothes that were too young for an individual and the wearing of clothes that were considered to be too old.

Particularly for females – perhaps as a result of societal norms and pressures – a *faux pas* was the danger of wearing something that was considered to be 'too young' for the individual.

"... sometimes they [late teens] can be less inhibited, because I probably wouldn't wear something like that, not just because of what it is saying about you but also my body is a lot older whereas a seventeen year old you know ... can strut her stuff quite easily and people think it is OK and she probably looks pretty good for it" (Pippa, 30, Housing Policy Officer)

"...if I saw my Granny wearing a mini skirt, I would say that was really tasteless..." (Peter, 26, Art Dealer)

"people who try and look younger than they are is not to be encouraged, that is very tasteless" (Guy aged 28)

"I don't mind sandals, [but] I think they look stupid on middle aged men. I think you should wear them if you are young enough and can get away with it, but middle aged men look

completely daft and usually wear them with socks as well..." (Adam, 27, IT Project Manager)

The greatest potential danger seemed to be associated with wearing clothes that were more appropriate for an older age group – perhaps this was a reflection of their age – i.e. as young adults and supported the findings of Freitas et al (1997). The impression was given that certain 'looks' would be acceptable for someone older, but that if a young person dressed in a similar manner they would be classed as dowdy.

"Oh I hope that is not me! I'd say that is a thirty something...fuddy duddy person. That would be more like my mum would dress" (Pippa, 30, Housing Policy Officer)

The impression was given that as a young person, you had almost a 'responsibility' to dress in a certain way, a 'choice' that disappears as you get older – particularly for women.

"There are a lot of stylish clothes around, and I think if you are young and reasonable looking you might as well wear something that is stylish and quite good because when you are old you haven't got as many choices so you might as well make the most of it when you are young. It is a bit sad to be wearing clothes that you are likely to wear when you are sixty when you are thirty.." (Guy, 28, Travel Consultant)

At the centre of the relevance of age to clothing choices lies the question of the 'inevitableness' or otherwise of the progression into wearing clothes that for these young adults represented an avoidable self. One participant, Adele, rather than accept this 'slide', indicated that she would hope to fight against it, citing the example of her step mother who she says *"would never be seen dead"* in certain things. Others – for example Liz – claimed that it is almost a natural 'progression' *"you just start wearing more sober clothes"*.

Body image

In some instances, linked to the age of participants, clothing choices (and the associated avoidance of products) were associated with body image. It was important to wear clothes that were flattering to their body shape; as well as appropriate.

"Women wear a lot more revealing clothes... bikinis and mini skirts and things, women reveal a lot more flesh than men in general, so if that flesh is all wrinkly and horrible, it is better to cover it up...Men develop beer bellies and so on which means tight tee-shirts don't look so good..." (Guy, 28, Travel Consultant)

"I think they [men] lose their acute sense of worry about clothes at a younger age probably" (Peter, 26, Art Dealer)

"....maybe I would think I would really like to wear stuff like that but I would have to buy something in a [size] fourteen." (Joanna, 26, Buyer Services)

Character / personality

Participants acknowledged the need for clothing to be congruent with the character or the personality of a person. It was perhaps the major way in which clothing could still be considered negatively, in spite of its recognition as a positive image on someone else.

---

5 Top Shop is a British fashion chain store, predominantly targeted at teenage girls and young women stocking fairly inexpensive clothing.

"You see people and they can be wearing clothes that I wouldn't dream of wearing, but you can still look and think they have got good taste in clothes because it suits that individual but it wouldn't necessarily suit me, but that doesn't mean that I think he has got bad taste in clothes, I can still think he has got good taste. I think a certain type of clothes can suit certain types of individuals ..." (Andy, 26, Telecom Manager)

"... you know what suits you, you know what you are comfortable in and anytime I have bought something that feels slightly outside of those boundaries, no matter what it was then it will sit in the cupboard and never be worn again, ... You wouldn't buy something similar to that again." (Paul, 27, Telecom Manager)

Individuals need to be aware of what their image is and the type of dress that they can 'get away with' and linked to this, the 'limitations' that exist for them. Therefore some items / images may be rejected for symbolic reasons but without the negative connotations attached to the clothing.

"I don't think of myself as somebody who is particularly fashionable and naturally stylish" (Deirdre, 26, Features Writer)

"... you can go into a pub and you will see someone and you will think 'they look really stunning in that' you might say 'oh I couldn't wear it' but you might comment that they look really nice" (Adele, 27, Telecom Manager)

Situational

Often clothing will reflect an individual's life situation – which could be partly dictated by occupation, life stage, age or simply their priorities at a particular point in time (Martineau 1957). Often it would be a reflection of an individual's very specific ideas about what represents 'me' and therefore by contrast 'what is not me'. At times, 'situational not mes' became relevant, with job interviews and certain functions, providing examples of situations when participants 'played' roles that were different from their usual ones.

"it depends on the location because you can get away with a quite skimpy dress in a night club because it is dark whereas you wouldn't wear a skimpy dress to work because it would be the wrong occasion for it" (Melissa, 25, Marketing Executive)

"I went to a wedding at the weekend, and I was wearing this dress from French Connection and some high shoes and had done my hair nicely and was wearing make up and contact lenses....people kept coming up to me and saying 'bloody hell you don't look like you' and stuff ...." (Deirdre, 26, Feature Writer)

"I wear a track suit and t-shirt or shorts and a rugby shirt or whatever if I was sat at home just because it would be comfortable, yet if I was going out I would straight away put a pair of jeans on or whatever just so you are giving the same sort image as what everybody else ... you don't want people to stop and stare at you." (Wayne, 22, Production / Sales Manager)

The work environment was particularly relevant for decisions about what to wear, and it was felt to be imperative that the correct signals were communicated at work.

"I can't be a real scruff, like turning up to work with holes in jeans and all the rest of it, because it gives the wrong image to everybody else. You can't take somebody seriously" (Dave, 27, Telecom Technician)

For women, the 'correct' work signals meant restraining from communicating sexual signs.

"I have got a couple of tops that I wouldn't wear to work just because they are black and tight or something.... if I went to clubs then I would probably wear something I wouldn't wear at work I think, like high heels if I am feeling a bit saucy!" (Joanna, 26, Buyer Services)

This contextual nature of clothing and identity creation complements the arguments of Davis (1985) who saw the relevance of wearer, occasion, place and company to the meanings that clothing communicates.

GENERAL DISCUSSION

A review of the literature indicated the multi-faceted nature of positive possible selves (see Markus and Nurius 1986). The negative self-concept effectively operates within the scope of possible selves and the findings suggest it to be equally multi-faceted.

Different aspects of the negative self were clearly identified and could be classified under two headings. The Undesired Self ('so not me') embodied the most extreme notions of what is 'not me' and could be linked to feelings of repulsion (Rozin and Fallon 1987) in the *rejection* of products/brands and product/brand-user stereotypes. The Avoidance Self ('just not me'), in comparison, embodied less strong views about 'not me' and could be linked to feelings of aversion and the *avoidance* of products/brands and product/brand-user stereotypes. What clearly differentiated the Undesired from the Avoidance self was that the latter incorporated images that were negative when individuals applied the images to themselves but these images could be viewed positively on someone else.

Limitations

This was a small-scale study with the emphasis on exploration rather than developing hypotheses for testing. The presentation of visual stimuli provided an effective means through which to explore the way that individuals interpret the clothing worn by others. However the social interaction, although it promoted discussion, could also potentially have had the disadvantage of encouraging careful self-presentation and impression management when discussing negative stereotypes in detail.

Future Directions

Considerable work remains to be done to clarify the relationship between the undesired and avoidance self; to explore other aspects of the negative self (e.g. social and ideal social aspects); and to extend understanding of the negative self beyond the product category of clothing. It would be interesting to develop a more longitudinal approach to the study of the negative self concept, exploring its evolution and the effects of different forms of socialization and psychological or developmental influences on both the undesired self and the acquisition of negative stereotypes. In addition a study which involved a broader sample would be likely to expand the range of discoveries.

CONCLUSION

Our examination of negative aspects of the self and symbolic consumption stands in marked contrast to earlier studies of symbolic consumption and self-congruency which have traditionally focused on understanding how consumers use and interpret the *positive* meanings associated with their consumption decisions. In this paper we have sought to extend and challenge traditional thinking about how individuals strive to manage the inferences which others make about their consumption decisions. Through an exploration of the negative self-concept we examined whether and how individuals try to support their self concept through the avoidance of certain products which have negative images. This represented an extension of current work on self-image / product-image congruency (Erickson and Sirgy 1992; Kleine et al 1993; Grubb and Grathwohl 1967). Secondly, the paper sought to challenge the current homogeneous view of the negative self by mapping different possible negative selves. Thirdly, we discussed the potential links amongst the different aspects of the negative self which emerged from the empirical study to propose a conceptualization of the multifaceted negative self around the dimensions of 'undesired' and 'avoidance'.

REFERENCES

Arnould, E. J. and Price, L. L (1993) "River Magic: Extraordinary Experience and the Extended Service Encounter" *Journal of Consumer Research,* June, 20, 24-45

Belk, R.W, Bahn, K.D. and Mayer, R.N. (1982) "Developmental recognition of Consumption Symbolism" *Journal of Consumer Research* 9 (June) 4-17

Belk, R, Mayer, R and Driscoll, A (1984) "Children's recognition of Consumption Symbolism in Children's Products" *Journal of Consumer Research* 10 (March) 386-397

Bourdieu, P (1984) *Distinction* Routledge, Kegan and Paul, London

Davis, F (1985) "Clothing and Fashion as Communication" P15-27 in *The Psychology of Fashion* ed by M R Solomon, Lexington Books

Celsi, R.L, Rose, R.L. and Leigh, T.W. (1993) "An Exploration of High-Risk Leisure Consumption through Skydiving" *Journal of Consumer Research,* June, 20, 1-23

Eisenstadt, D. and Leippe, M.R. (1994) "The Self-Comparison and Self-Discrepant Feedback: Consequences of Learning You Are What You Thought You Were Not" *Journal of Personality and Social Psychology* 67, 4, 611-626

Englis, B.G. and Solomon, M. (1995) "To be and not to be: lifestyle imagery, reference groups, and the clustering of America" *Journal of Advertising* 24, 1, 13-29

Erickson, M.K. and Sirgy, M.J. (1992) "Employed Females' Clothing Preference, Self-Image Congruence, and Career Anchorage" *Journal of Applied Social Psychology* 22, 5, 408-422

Feinberg, R.A, Mataro, L. and Burroughs, W.J (1992) "Clothing and Social Identity *Clothing and Textiles Research Journal* 11,1, 18-23

Freitas A, Davis, C H and Kim, J W (1997) "Appearance Management as Border Construction: Least Favorite Clothing, Group Distancing and Identity … Not!" *Sociological Inquiry* 67, 3, 323-335

Grubb, E.L. and Grathwohl, H.L. (1967) "Consumer Self-Concept, Symbolism and Market Behavior: A Theoretical Approach" *Journal of Marketing*, 31, 22-27

Holman, R.H (1980) "Apparel as Communication" in *Symbolic Consumer behavior. Proceedings of the Conference on Consumer Ethics and Symbolic Consumption* ed Elizabeth C. Hirschman and Morris B. Holbrook. Sponsored by Association for Consumer Research and Institute of Retail Management, New York University

Kaiser, S.B. (1997) *The Social Psychology of Clothing* Second Edition Revised, Fairchild Publications, New York

Kaiser, S.B., C.M. Freeman and J.L. Chandler (1993) "Favourite Clothes and Gendered Subjectivities: Multiple Readings" *Studies in Symbolic Interaction* 15, 27-50

Kimle, P.A. and Damhorst, M.L. (1997) "A Grounded Theory Model of the Ideal Business Image for Women" *Symbolic Interaction* 20 (1) 45-68

Kleine, R.E, Kleine, S.S. and Kernan, J.B. (1993) "Mundane Consumption and the Self: A Social-Identity Perspective" *Journal of Consumer Psychology* 2, 3 209-235

Kvale, S. (1996) *An Introduction to Interviewing* Sage, Thousand Oaks

Levy, S. J. (1959) "Symbols for Sale", *Harvard Business Review 37(4), 117-124.*

Markus, H. and Nurius, P. (1986) "Possible Selves" *American Psychologist* 41, 9, 954-69

Martineau, P. (1957) *Motivation in Advertising: Motives that make people buy* McGraw-Hill Book Company, Inc, New York

McCracken, G (1986) "Culture and Consumption: A Theoretical Account of the Structure and Movement of the Cultural Meaning of Consumer Goods" *Journal of Consumer Research* 13, (June) 71-82

Miles, Matthew B. and Huberman, A. Michael (1994) *An Expanded Sourcebook Qualitative Data Analysis*, Second Edition, Sage Publications, London

Miller, K A (1997) "Dress: Private and Secret Self-Expression" *Clothing and Textiles Research Journal* 15, 4

Ogilvie, D.M. (1987) "The Undesired Self: A Neglected Variable in Personality Research" *Journal of Personality and Social Psychology* 52, 2, 379-385

Patton, M.Q. (1990) *Qualitative Evaluation and Research Methods* second edition, Sage Publications, London

Rozin, P. and Fallon, A. (1987) "A Perspective on Disgust" *Psychological Review* 94, 1, 23-41

Schouten, J.W. (1991) "Selves in Transition: Symbolic Consumption in Personal Rites of Passage and Identity Reconstruction" *Journal of Consumer Research* 17, March, 412-425

Schouten, J.W. and McAlexander (1995) "Subcultures of Consumption: An Ethnography of the New Bikers" *Journal of Consumer Research* 22 (June) 43-61

Sirgy, M.J. (1982) "Self-Concept in Consumer Behavior: A Critical Review" *Journal of Consumer Research* 9, Dec, 287-300

Sirgy, M.J, Grewal, D, Mangkeburg, T.F, Park, J, Chon, K, Claiborne, C.B, Johar, J.S and Berkman, H (1997) "Assessing the Predictive Validity of Two Methods of measuring Self-Image Congruence" *Journal of the Academy of Marketing Science* 25, 3 229-241

Thompson, C.J. and Haytko, D.L. (1997) "Speaking of fashion: consumers' uses of fashion discourses and the appropriation of countervailing cultural meanings" *Journal of Consumer Research* June, 24, 1, 15 (28)

Thompson, C.J. and Hirschman, E.C (1995) "Understanding the Socialized Body: A Poststructuralist Analysis of Consumers' Self-Conceptions, Body Images, and Self-Care Practices" *Journal of Consumer Research* 22 September 139-153

Wilk, R. (1994) "'I Hate Pizza' Distaste and Dislike in the Consuming Lives of Belizeans" Presented at the Annual Meeting of the American Anthropology Association, Atlanta

Wilk, R. (1995) "Learning Distaste The Social Importance of Not Wanting" prepared for the conference Learning to Consume, Lund University, August 18-20

Wilk, R.R (1997) "A Critique of Desire: Distaste and Dislike in Consumer Behavior" *Consumption, Markets and Culture*, 1, 2, 175-196

The Effect of Co-Consumer Age and Service Context on Service-Related Attitudes

M. V.Thakor, Concordia University
Katayoun Saleh, Concordia University

ABSTRACT

Although services are often delivered in settings where many consumers are present at the same time, the issue of how co-consumers affect service perceptions has received little attention. In the present study we manipulate co-consumer age and service setting in an experimental context, using settings selected to make salient either physical or personal-expressive person attributes. We find that younger consumers do regard older consumers significantly more negatively compared to those who are their own age, and this affects their patronage intentions. Perceptions of co-consumer sociability are not affected by age.

The Impact of Other's Opinions on Decision-Making: Role of Extreme Prediction Rate

Ashesh Mukherjee, McGill University
Andrew Gershoft, Columbia University

ABSTRACT

Past research indicates that individuals often use the overall prediction rate, or the overall match percentage between past opinions of the source and target consumer, to assess the usefulness of the source's future opinions. In this paper, we identify extreme prediction rate, or the match between the source and target on extremely evaluated items only, as an important additional factor in the acceptance of external source opinions. Specifically, we show that extreme prediction rate has a significant effect on source opinion acceptance when individuals have a consummatory motive, and when opinion information is presented in a low complexity format. In conclusion, the paper discusses marketing implications of these findings especially for Internet retailers such as Amazon.com, and also identifies promising avenues for future research.

The Role of Collaboration in Consumers' In-Store Decisions

Robert J. Fisher, University of Western Ontario

ABSTRACT

Despite the frequency and importance of joint consumption decisions, most consumer research focuses on decision-making by individuals. The research that does examine joint decision-making tends to assume that such interactions are a bargaining process where one individual can only "win" at the expense of the other. In contrast, the present research develops and tests a model of how consumers collaborate within a traditional "bricks and mortar" retail environment. The hypothesized model posits that in-store collaboration between pairs of retail shoppers is facilitated by aspects of their relationship (shared goals, pre-visit planning, and power symmetry), and influenced by retail (the degree to which the salesperson uses coercive influence and the retail ambiance) as well as situational factors (time pressure and budget constraints). In turn, collaboration is thought to lead to higher decision quality and smaller deviations between consumers' planned and actual expenditures. The results have important implications for the quality of in-store decisions, and the methods used by retailers to affect in-store purchase behaviors.

Creating Flow Experiences: The Influence of Individual Factors on the Antecedents of Flow

Lisa Klein, Rice University

Since the flow model was first introduced into the marketing literature as a framework for understanding consumer response to the new interactive media (Hoffman and Novak 1996), a stream of research has emerged that focuses on investigating the antecedents and consequences of flow. Understanding the construct of flow is a critical step in understanding how consumer behavior differs in interactive media. With respect to the antecedents of flow, much of the research to date has focused on the task and context factors that influence the consumer experiences of flow. Task factors have included the impact of goal-related versus experiential behaviors (Hoffman and Novak 1997, Novak, Hoffman and Yung 2000), while context factors studied have included user control (Klein 1999, Schlosser and Kanfer 1999) and media richness (Klein 1999). In contrast, this session focuses on the *individual* factors that influence the flow experience in interactive environments. Identifying critical individual differences in the tendency to experience flow will help us further isolate the construct from related ones and help marketing practitioners fully exploit the opportunities offered by customization.

Csikszentmihalyi (1990) first defined flow as "the process of optimal experience" and identified one of its critical antecedents as the fit between the perceived challenge and perceived expertise. When the level of perceived challenge and expertise are comparable and above an individual's mean level, the individual feels stimulated, involved, and less conscious of outside environments and time. In the model proposed by Hoffman and Novak (1996), the key antecedents are: skill/challenge, arousal, attention focus, and telepresence. Each of the three papers explores the individual factors that may influence one of these antecedent; together, they provide a multi-method approach, using both surveys and experiments, to explore the flow model.

The three papers proposed for this session address the importance of locus of control (paper #1), processing style (paper #2), and expertise (paper#3) on the consumer flow experience in Web shopping environments. The first paper explores the influence of locus of control (LOC) on user satisfaction, goal-directed and experiential usage of the Internet, and use of the Web as a substitute for other activities. Earlier research has shown control to be a critical construct in the flow paradigm (Hoffman and Novak 1996, 1997)

Here, the authors conduct a large scale survey focusing on the different usage patterns and experiences of those with an internal LOC versus an external LOC. The second paper investigates the role of processing style on enjoyment of the Web experience (challenge/arousal) and ultimately on flow overall.. The third paper focuses on the influence of expertise on telepresence, another antecedent to flow, elucidated in Hoffman and Novak's model. The primary goals in this experimental study are: (1) to understand the criticality of telepresence to the response to the product and the advertisement and (2) to evaluate the impact of expertise on the process.

Overall, these papers work together to enrich our understanding of the form and boundaries of the Hoffman and Novak model (1996) of flow and its relationship to consumer experiences on the Web.

The Revival of Projective Techniques: Past, Present, and Future Perspectives

Jennifer E. Chang, Penn State University

SESSION OVERVIEW

Derived from clinical psychology, projective techniques have been used in consumer research over the past 50 years in order to understand consumers' inner thoughts and feelings about products, services, people, behaviors and situations. Projectives elicit what consumers often cannot or will not verbalize in more direct, verbal measures such as interviews and surveys.

The session's paper contributors–Dennis Rook, Jerry Olson, Jerry Zaltman and Jennifer Chang–each brought to bear a historical, present and/or future look at projectives and their implications for consumer research. Sidney Levy provided both a retrospective and introspective discussion of projectives.

ABSTRACTS

"Typology of Projective Research Techniques"
Dennis W. Rook, University of Southern California

Projective research techniques have enjoyed a highly visible revival in recent years. This methodological family has grown considerably and, arguably, is the most diverse among the main types of qualitative research. Previous efforts at classifying these highly varying techniques are limited by their analytic scope, and by their clinical psychological priorities. This discussion offers a framework that examines particular projective techniques in terms of four key properties: (1) the focal behavior(s), (2) elicited content, (3) task structure, and (4) research process elements. Better understanding of these important differentiating features should help researchers make more informed and effective projective technique choices.

"Using Projective Methods in ZMET to Elicit Deep Meanings"
Jerry Olson, Penn State University
Gerald Zaltman, Harvard University

We describe two projective tasks—"Expand the Frame" and "Create a Movie/Story"—that are steps in the Zaltman Metaphor Elicitation Technique (ZMET). These methods are designed to "dig deeper" than traditional measures to elicit the fundamental orienting concepts (metaphors) that structure people's thoughts, emotional responses, and behaviors. We review the theoretical foundations of each procedure and describe the interpretation process in some detail. Next, we provide examples of the kinds of insights each method can produce. Finally, we briefly discuss the future of projective methods in general.

"Tapping the Untapped Consumer: Personally-Relevant Elicited Projectives (PREP)"
Jennifer E. Chang, Penn State University

This research introduces a new projective technique, Personally-Relevant Elicited Projectives (PREP). The PREP method has been designed to tap into the thoughts and feelings of a particular subset of consumers, those who exhibit a resistance to projective tasks. The use of PREP facilitates self-expression by utilizing projective probes not only relevant to the informant's everyday life but also created by the informant. In particular, the method attempts to alleviate issues of non-response bias. In addition to discussing the value of PREP, supported by examples, we address the process of implementing the technique, and its implications for consumer research.

DISCUSSION

Sidney J. Levy, University of Arizona

As Dennis Rook pointed out in his remarks, I have been welcoming the revival of projective techniques at intervals for the past 50 years. In the late 1940s I studied them at the University of Chicago as part of my psychological training for the Ph.D. with the Committee on Human Development. A great variety of techniques were in common use at that time. The Thematic Apperception Technique, and numerous adaptations of it, and the Rorschach Test were the most outstanding, but several others had their devotees. In 1951, Harold H. Anderson and Gladys L. Anderson edited a volume, *An Introduction to Projective Techniques* (Prentice-Hall), that discussed the merits and drawbacks of such methods, including chapters on The Rorschach Test, the TAT, word association, sentence completion, The Rosenzweig Picture-Frustration Study, The Bender Visual Motor Gestalt Test, Drawings of the Human Figure, Graphology, Expressive movement, The Szondi Test, Puppetry, and Psychodrama. In 1965, Bernard I. Murstein edited a volume, *Handbook of Projective Techniques* (Basic Books), in which he said that more than a half century had passed since projective techniques formally became part of the clinical armamentarium. Clearly, our topic has a lot of background.

It becomes apparent that all behavior is projective when it is taken as indicative of something about the actor. We commonly take each other's simplest words and movements as having implications and are casually confident about our inferences. At least, the question may arise, as in the joke about the psychoanalyst who was greeted with "Good morning" by another psychoanalyst and thereupon thought, "I wonder what he meant by that."

The presentations this morning show us the contemporary diversity of usage of projective techniques. Jerry Olson illustrated how a visualization and montage task, organized by Jerry Zaltman as the ZMET method, provides insight into both consumers and their conceptualization of their experience with objects in the marketplace. Jennifer Chang did the same thing using another approach, termed PREP, wherein she focused on eliciting an extended somewhat ethnographic awareness of the consumers' detailed experience to better understand the sources of their marketplace behavior. Both techniques fulfill the specific goals of projective methods that distinguish them from direct questioning: that is, to learn what consumers' ideas, feelings, and attitudes are when they are not able to articulate them, even to be aware of them, or deny them.

To illustrate this denial, as well as the framing process that Jerry mentioned, I recall an instance in my experience when an outstanding creative person at the J. Walter Thompson advertising agency prepared two ads for Cracker Barrel Cheese. One had no people in it, but showed brown bread, mugs, and some game equipment, with a wedge of the cheese standing on its smallest edge. The other showed flowers and teacups, with the cheese wedge lying on a long side. Consumers projected men into the first scene and joked about the erect posture of the cheese, and envisioned women in the second scene with the cheese lying down. When I confronted the agency art director with her great Freudian skill, she was amazed and denied any deliberation, saying it had just seemed more natural to do it that way.

The fundamental use of metaphor is widely known, of course, and studied in various disciplines. Here, marketing study is making explicit use of the metaphorical character of projection. Freud compared the processes and mechanisms of the human mind to military operations when he noted that regression is like an army falling back to better- defended positions. He used hydraulics in talking about the damming up of psychic energy. And he moved into electricity as it became more prevalent, in saying that the cathexis of some object was like a positive electrical charge. In our times, we use the computer to create new metaphors: falling back on some stereotype might be called the default—itself a metaphor about lack or failure.

Dennis Rook gave us a splendid overview. His paper is an excellent contribution to thinking about projective methods in an organized way, laying out ideas about their varying character and offering practical guidance to thinking about how and when to use them. The three papers provided a well integrated workshop, combining a good orientation with satisfying specific detail, and should encourage continued creative use of our projective abilities.

SPECIAL SESSION SUMMARY

The Role and Impact of External Recommendations in Decision Making

Gavan J. Fitzsimons, University of Pennsylvania

People commonly use recommendations as a decision aid when choosing between multiple options in a choice set. Prior to the advent of the Internet recommendations mainly came from personal connections, from an employee at a physical store, or perhaps from an expert rating agency such as *Consumer Reports*. Regardless of the source of the recommendation, many consumers use them to help reduce the uncertainty surrounding a choice between similarly valued options. While recommendations clearly play an important role in many decision processes, previous research in the area has not adequately addressed many of the issues that present themselves in today's consumer environment in which recommendations are incredibly prevalent (e.g., *Wine Spectator* ratings of wine displayed at your local wine retailer, book suggestions from *Amazon* when purchasing a book online, etc.). Recent research in the area answers interesting new questions, and has substantial import from theoretical, managerial and societal perspectives.

In the first paper presented, Diehl and Lynch explored aspects of the role of recommendations in online environments. While traditional wisdom would argue that online shopping provides benefits to consumers through a substantial expansion of choices, they argued that this enhanced assortment would only benefit consumers when accompanied by a particular form of recommendation. Specifically, they argued that the benefits of size and variety in an online assortment are a function of the correlation between the consumer's utility function and the ordinal position in a list of alternatives recommended to the consumer. The second paper, presented by Zhou and Lehmann, looked at the role of unintended recommendations heard by overhearing another conversation. This idle chatter under certain conditions led to substantial changes in choice of the most desirable product in a category. They also demonstrated that idle chatter matters even in the face of fairly unambiguous attribute information. Finally, the third paper, by Fitzsimons and Lehmann, examined the unexpected impact of recommendations on choice in situations in which consumers actually demonstrate a backlash against the provided recommendation. In situations where experts recommend against an option that consumers believe should be a good one, choice of the option receiving the negative recommendation actually increased.

The Dual Role of Affect in Information Processing and Decision Making

Yiorgos A. Bakamitsos, Dartmouth College

Researchers in both psychology and marketing have long been interested in the effect that affect has on the ability to process information and make decisions. Two streams of literature have evolved independently in an attempt to identify different ways in which affect can affect information processing and consumer behavior. One stream of research postulates that affect can be used as a cue that people may use in rendering judgments (e.g. Schwarz and Clore, 1988; Pham, 1998). The second stream of research posits that affect influences information processing by enhancing relational elaboration (e.g., Isen, Daubman and Nowicki, 1987; Lee and Sternthal, 1999).

These two streams of research seem to coexist independently, as extant literature is silent on the conditions under which these two roles of affect operate in information processing and decision making. The objective of this session was to provide an answer to the question under which conditions mood will act as a cue and under which conditions it will act as a process moderator.

The first paper by Bakamitsos set up the research problem of interest. In three studies, the dual role that positive affect plays was explained and the conditions under which positive affect adopts each role were identified. Bakamitsos' findings indicated that consumers relied on mood as a contextual cue in rendering a judgment when the information presented to them was difficult to process. However, when participants were motivated to hold accurate beliefs, they corrected for the effect of their mood on their judgment. In the third study, the findings reported earlier were replicated and mood was also shown to serve as a process moderator. Under certain conditions positive mood facilitated relational elaboration, which in turn had a positive effect on respondents' judgment. These findings indicate that the use of mood as a contextual cue is the least effortful way of completing an evaluation. Nevertheless, when people are in a positive mood and are presented with information that is easy to process and relevant to the target of the evaluation, they will incorporate this information in their judgment.

In the second paper, Keller aimed at shedding more light on the effect of affect on relational elaboration. Her research indicates that individuals in a happy mood had a greater need to feel they had control over their long-term mood (health) than individuals in a sad mood, whereas individuals in a sad mood seemed to be more concerned with managing short-term mood (anxiety) than individuals in a happy mood. This view is supported by her findings that the loss frame resulted in higher perceived control over long-term health and higher intentions to get a mammogram than the gain frame among those in a happy mood. By contrast, the gain frame produced higher intentions to get a mammogram for those in a sad mood because it evoked less anxiety than the loss frame. Together her findings indicate that contrary to the hedonic contingency model, people in a positive mood do not attend to the immediate hedonic consequences of their actions if the perceived loss is consequential. Furthermore, individuals in a sad mood may be as responsive to the hedonic consequences of their actions as individuals in a positive mood.

Finally in the third paper, Pham, Cohen and Pracejus further elaborated on the role of monitoring one's feelings as a judgment and decision making heuristic. Challenging the widespread notion that feelings and emotions are necessarily detrimental to judgment and decision making, they argue that feelings have distinct judgmental properties. They document these properties in a series of four studies (involving over 670 participants) comparing feeling-monitoring and "cold" reason-based evaluation responses to both static and dynamic stimuli. Their findings indicate first, that even when monitored consciously, feeling responses are registered faster and are adjusted more rapidly than reason-based evaluation responses. Second, contrary to popular wisdom, respondents agree more on their feeling responses than on their reason-based-evaluation responses. Third, feeling-monitoring responses are significantly more predictive of people's spontaneous thoughts than reason-based evaluation responses are. These results explain why affect monitoring provides a potent valuation heuristic in judgment and decision making.

SELECTED BIBLIOGRAPHY

Isen, A. M., Daubman, K. A. & Nowicki, G. P. (1987). "Positive Affect Facilitates Creative Problem Solving," *Journal of Personality and Social Psychology*, Vol. 52, No. 6, 1122-1131.

Lee, A. Y. & Sternthal, B. (1999). "The Effect of Positive Mood on Memory", *Journal of Consumer Research*, Vol. 26, No. 2, 115-127.

Pham, Michel Tuan (1998), "Representativeness, Relevance, and the Use of Feelings in Decision Making," *Journal of Consumer Research*, Vol. 25 (September), 144-159.

Schwarz, N. & Clore, G. L. (1988). "How Do I Feel About It? The Informative Function of Affective States," in Fiedler, K. & Forgas, J. (Eds.) *Affect, Cognition and Social Behavior*, Toronto: Hogrefe, 44-62.

New Insights about Consumers' Perception and Evaluation of Product Assortments

Erica van Herpen, Tilburg University

Brian Wansink, University of Illinois at Urbana-Champaign

Assortment management is one of the key issues for improving store performance (Raftery 1993), and retailers are recognizing that understanding consumer perceptions is the core of a good assortment management program. Yet, whereas research concerning the evaluation of a single product has a long history, product assortments have only recently received attention (e.g. Kahn & Lehmann 1991; Broniarczyk, Hoyer & McAlister 1998; Hoch, Bradlow & Wansink 1999; Van Herpen & Pieters 2000). This literature is only now approaching the issues of perception and evaluation in large assortments (Kahn 1999).

Perceptions of size and variety are important, and are not necessarily equal to the actual size and variety of an assortment; they may be biased by category space or presentation format (Broniarcayk et al. 1998; Hoch et al. 1999). Although research on product assortments has demonstrated that perceived assortment size and variety are not equal to actual assortment size and variety, it has neglected the underlying perceptual processes. In addition, the effect of assortment size and content on evaluations of the assortment, such as choice accuracy and effort, have not been systematically examined. The papers in this session offer new insights into these important emerging issues.

The first paper, by Madhu Vishwanathan and Brian Wansink, focuses on consumers' perceptions of assortment size. This paper proposes that consumers do not see numbers in a linear manner, but use a general categorization above a certain point, counting '1, 2, 3, sufficient, excessive'. The implication is that consumers' perception of assortment size is not a simple function of the number of products in the assortment, as has generally been assumed. The paper examines this effect both for grocery store assortments and for household inventories.

In the second paper, Alan Cooke and Claude Pecheux explore consumers' perception of assortment variety. Their study focuses on assortments that are bought by consumers at one point in time. Consumers have the choice between buying duplicates of one product, and buying mixed assortments with diverse products. Cooke and Pecheux show that perceptions of assortment variety depend on the number of products, the topic of the first paper, and on the proportion in which different types of products are available. Next, they examine why consumers prefer varied assortments.

Van Herpen and Pieters investigate consumers' expected choice success (likelihood that the assortment has a desired product) and expected choice effort. Specifically, effects of assortment size, number of attribute levels, dispersion across attribute levels, and dissociation between attributes are examined. Two studies show that increasing the expected choice success does not always mean an increase in the expected effort.

As the papers show, assortment research is of great importance to understanding and managing store assortments, to the assortments or bundles of products that are bought by consumers, and to the pantry stocks at consumers' home. The implications are across a broad range of research areas, including store assortment research, variety seeking, consumer stockpiling, and perceptual processes.

REFERENCES

Broniarczyk, Susan M., Wayne D. Hoyer, and Leigh McAlister, 1998, "Consumers' Perceptions of the Assortment Offered in a Grocery Category: The Impact of Item Reduction", *Journal of Marketing Research*, 35 (May), 166-176.

Hoch, Stephen J., Eric T. Bradlow, and Brian Wansink, 1999, "The Variety of an Assortment", *Marketing Science*, 18, 527-546.

Kahn, Barbara E., 1999, "Introduction to the Special Issue: Assortment Planning", *Journal of Retailing*, 75, 289-293.

Kahn, Barbara E., and Donald R. Lehmann, 1991, "Modeling Choice Among Assortments", *Journal of Retailing*, 67, 274-299.

Raftery, Dan, 1993, "Trim the Dead Wood", *Progressive Grocer*, 42 (September), 42-43.

Van Herpen, Erica, and Rik Pieters, 2000, "Assortment Variety: Attribute- versus Product-Based", working paper, Tilburg University.

How Now Ralph Lauren? The Separation of Brand and Product in a *Counterfeit Culture*

James W. Gentry, University of Nebraska-Lincoln
Sanjay Putrevu, Brock University
Clifford Shultz II, Arizona State University–East
Suraj Commuri, University of Nebraska-Lincoln[1]

ABSTRACT

In discourses on search in marketing and consumer behavior, we assume that consumers search for brands within a product. Research among consumers in markets where counterfeit goods abound reveals that consumers also search for "products" within a brand. In other words, even after consumers make a brand choice in a purchase context, search may ensue and further evaluation takes places between a genuine article and various counterfeits. This indicates that when brand equity begins to symbolize strongly an image rather than more tangible product attributes, consumers may begin to regard the brand and the product as different entities serving different purposes. This notion has the potential to explain the complex search and decision-making process involved in the volitional purchase of counterfeits.

INTRODUCTION

Product quality variance has reduced greatly in North America (Carsky, Dickinson, and Canady 1998), and brand name has become an exceptionally strong cue for quality. The consumer search literature has strong roots in economics. It is interesting to note that early economic models assumed that consumers had or could easily obtain perfect information and, therefore, knew the most efficient brands and stores (Goldman and Johansson 1978; Stigler 1961). While such unrealistic assumptions have been discarded for more complex and realistic models, the consumer search process is essentially assumed to be one involving two steps: (1) the determination of the preferred brand(s) through some kind of evaluation process that compares the various brands across the salient attributes and (2) the systematic search for the lowest price on the identified brand across stores based on a cost/benefit tradeoff (cf., Putrevu and Ratchford 1997). The order of the two steps is unclear; i.e., some consumers might first select the store and then search across brands. What is important is that such a perspective concentrates primarily upon pre-purchase search, a notion that has been questioned frequently (Bloch, Sherrell, and Ridgway 1987). As an example, Bloch et al.'s (1987) ongoing search construct acknowledges that those with enduring involvement may search all the time, and not just when a need to purchase has been recognized. However, most search literature still focuses on comparisons across brands, with little emphasis on search within brands—not so much in the price/quality tradeoffs made within a brand's product line, but rather the search for quality within one model of the brand. Whereas most Western consumers would assume little variation to exist within a model, the existence of counterfeit goods makes this process far less than a given. Figure 1 depicts the typical search behavior that is examined in marketing and consumer behavior.

The assumption here is that once a consumer makes a product decision, then the search is restricted to brands in terms of brand equity, quality, and price. However, when counterfeits are available, even after consumers make a brand model choice, they may search among the genuine product and the counterfeits. This may be

with regard to distinguishing the genuine item from the counterfeit or differentiating among counterfeits. The purpose of this paper is to investigate consumer search within the brand model in market conditions where fakes are plentiful. The intent here is not to discuss the ethical issues involved in counterfeiting [which have been discussed systematically in Gutterman and Anderson 1997; Jain 1996; Nill and Shultz 1997; Shultz and Saporito 1996] nor to attempt to understand the cultural bases facilitating counterfeiting (see Mittelstaedt and Mittelstaedt 1997 for a systematic discussion). Instead, we accept the reality of counterfeits and investigate consumers' lived experiences with the phenomenon.

THE GROWTH OF COUNTERFEITS

Globally, the sales of counterfeit products are estimated to be about $299 billion (Chakraborty et al. 1997). The International Chamber of Commerce estimates that counterfeit products account for 8% of world trade (Freedman 1999). Though currently a topic of keen global interest, this phenomenon is not new. For example, counterfeit paintings became so common in late Ming China that only one in ten paintings was estimated to be genuine (Clunas 1991).

Most Westerners (and most people in general) attribute the purchase of counterfeits to "others." For example, even informants in countries where counterfeits are rampant claim that the majority of purchases are by tourists (Gentry, Putrevu, and Schultz 2000). While notions such as a $10 Rolex, a $5 Swiss Army knife, and a $3 bottle of Napoleon brandy may not be unfamiliar to Western consumers, the general belief is that such items are only available in urban areas from street vendors or from people selling from the trunks of their cars. However, *Business Week* (1999) recently noted that billions of dollars worth of golf equipment sold in the US are counterfeits imported from Asia, including a version of the $500 Great Big Bertha driver from Calloway Golf. Even more recently, US customs officials seized more than $20 million worth of counterfeit Pokeman products in the last six months of 1999. Nintendo, which owns the marketing license for Pokemon goods, is training customs officials and police officers in New York City and Honolulu how to tell the difference between real and fake Pokemon cards (*Lincoln Journal Star* 1999). We argue that we are seeing just the tip of the iceberg, as the prospect for counterfeiting is enormous with the advent of e-commerce. Startup firms offering great prices may or may not be selling the genuine brands. The credibility justifiably earned by many mail-order operations and by e-commerce leaders such as Amazon.com may reduce consumer skepticism in the short run. However, the lack of Western consumer expertise in identifying counterfeit items may provide opportunities for those with access to "quality" counterfeit goods.

Traditionally consumers in environments flooded with fake branded goods have used non-product cues such as price or the type of outlet selling the item to identify counterfeits. The perception that there is a simple dichotomy (authentic brand vs. obvious fake) is questionable in today's global economy. The outsourcing of production to developing economies has provided these countries an access to improved manufacturing processes and access (and familiarity) to the Western brands themselves. Further, technology

---

[1]The authors would like to thank Roger Dickinson for his comments on an earlier version of this paper.

FIGURE 1
Typical Search Behavior

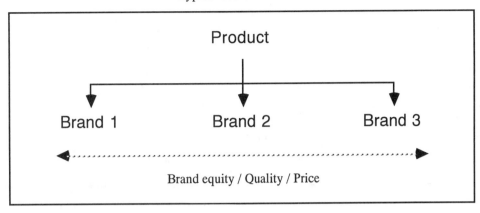

advances have decreased the startup costs for counterfeiters greatly. Given the costs associated with establishing brand equity, borrowing others' equity apparently is an attractive alternative.

THE STUDY

Over 100 students at an Australian research university conducted interviews with international students. The students were trained in data collection through interviews by one of the researchers and were required to collect the data reported here as part of a course requirement. The focus of the interviews was on discussing the existence of counterfeit items in the home countries of informants, the level of sophistication in terms of being able to identify counterfeits, and the rationale for purchasing counterfeits deliberately. Table 1 provides a list of the countries represented in the study. The nature of the sample reflects Perth's relatively close location to Singapore, Malaysia, and Indonesia. Further, nearly all of the informants from these three countries were members of the Chinese subcultures there, and not members of the more populous Malay subcultures found in Malaysia and Indonesia.

By reviewing the text of the interviews, emergent themes were gleaned (e.g., Lincoln and Guba 1985). Though the vignettes shared here might be categorized as less than "thick descriptions," collectively they provide rather vivid portrayals of consumer perceptions vis-à-vis quality issues concerning counterfeit items. The home countries of the informants are used to identify the quotations used in this paper.

As noted by a reviewer, it might well be better in future research to collect data focusing less on opinions about getting counterfeit goods in general than on specific instances (e.g., critical incidents) when consumers actually bought a counterfeit versus an authentic version of a brand.

INTERPRETATION AND ANALYSIS

The Volitional Choice for Counterfeits

Though there appeared to be a certain caution against being deceived into buying a counterfeit, some respondents also expressed a rational choice in favor of counterfeits. In cases where the display of a brand insignia was an important part of consumption of a product, consumers appear to be paying attention to the brand insignia and less importance to the more tangible product attributes. Under such circumstances, a less expensive and inferior quality counterfeit that bore the insignia appeared to be preferred over the more expensive original.

Singapore is a very materialistic country where people are judged solely on what they drive and wear. This has led to many Singaporeans buying counterfeit goods so that it is very hard to tell a counterfeit shirt from an original unless you look at the label which is the reason why a lot of money is spent on counterfeit goods by the residents. On the streets, a typical Singaporean will not care if the clothes look good or not as long as the right designer brand is on the garment. [Singaporean]

As the branded goods in Singapore are highly priced, not many of them [consumers] can afford the genuine stuff. Thus, they go for the next alternative, which are counterfeit products that are so much cheaper. They do not go for the quality but it is the name that they are after, this is why it doesn't really matter whether the good is genuine or fake. As long as people are able to see them possessing the 'branded' goods, they are satisfied. They may even go to an extent of telling others that the counterfeit good is real stuff, not admitting they bought a fake one at a cheaper price. It is also very common nowadays that when Singaporeans go traveling, they will buy back lots of imitation goods. Such places like Hong Kong and Bangkok are very popular with counterfeit goods and it may be the main reason why they go there in the first place. [Singaporean]

In other cases, the volitional purchase of a counterfeit appeared to serve other purposes. Consumers also appeared to view the purchase of a counterfeit as a less risky trial or prelude to the purchase of the more expensive original or simply as a less expensive alternative to the more expensive original.

Frequently the product is not expected to be used for a long period of time. For example, in terms of counterfeit accessories such as bags, the fashions change so frequently and the price is sufficiently negligent that it is OK to buy numerous counterfeits. [French]

The adoption of 'Why pay more ...much more ... when you can purchase a counterfeit which is extremely similar to the original brand?' is prevalent among the locals. [Hong Kong]

If you want to collect CDs or VCDs, you buy the cheap pirated one first and then, if you like it (music/movie), buy the original. [Malaysian]

TABLE 1
Informants' Cultures of Origin

Country / Region	Number	Country / Region	Number
Singapore	31	USA	3
Malaysia	30	Eastern Europe (Romania, Yugoslavia)	2
Indonesia	8		
Western Europe (Italy 3, France, England, Austria)	6	Papua New Guinea	2
		Taiwan	2
Hong Kong	5	PRC	2
Brunei	4	South Africa	1
Thailand	4	New Zealand	1
Egypt	1		

Sometimes, the goods are so cheap (inexpensive) that they do not see it as counterfeits but just another product to buy and use. Once it is broken or ruined, it is replaced. [Malaysian]

In other cases, in addition to being less expensive, counterfeits also appeared to offer "more product for the buck" as compared to the genuine item.

Counterfeits may be actually better. They provide more value for the money. For example, there are more songs in a compilation CD. [Singaporean]

In Malaysia, the authentic ones may not even match the quality of the fake one. [Malaysian]

Two other factors that appeared to facilitate a conscious choice of a counterfeit over a genuine item appeared to be the growing acceptance of counterfeits among members of the cohort and adjusted criteria for evaluating counterfeits. As the purchase of counterfeits rose among peers, a decision to purchase a counterfeit appeared to be a sensible and guilt-free alternative.

For goods like VCDs, CDs, and Playstation games, Hong Kongers would rather pay less because, first, they are much cheaper and second, because everyone is doing the same thing too. [Hong Kong]

Counterfeits are very popular among customers who have low purchasing power and yet yearn for the status and class of branded goods. [Singaporean]

As the purchase of counterfeits became more common, consumers appeared to develop relevant parameters for the evaluation of counterfeits. Unlike evaluating the purchase of a counterfeit as being a compromise or the result of being deceived, many consumers appear to evaluate the value-for-money of a counterfeit vis-a-vis the reduced value (durability and reliability) against the reduced price of a counterfeit. The avoidance of the consideration of the genuine item appeared to aid a conscious decision to purchase a counterfeit.

Customers are fully aware that they are buying imitations because nobody could get such good bargains for the real stuff anywhere. Their expectations on their purchases are also directly related to the prices they pay. Thus, they will not expect these products to match up to the authentic versions. [Thai]

Thus, there appears to be, often times, a conscious comparison of a counterfeit with a genuine item. The predominantly western notion that the genuine article is the norm and the counterfeit is deception may not be valid in a marketplace where counterfeits abound and where consumers have begun to build norms for comparison of counterfeits with genuine items.

In fact, in such markets, consumers demonstrated high levels of confidence in their ability to distinguish a counterfeit from an original. While (lower) price and (non-conventional) location were some ways in which consumers could tell whether an item was genuine or a counterfeit, far more intricate ways to differentiate were also common.

I can recognize these counterfeit goods upon inspection since they are usually made of low-grade materials. Moreover, the labeling and brand names are usually slightly different from the genuine products. For instance, real branded wallets are usually made of genuine leather while counterfeit wallets are usually made of PVC leather. [Malaysian]

From my experiences, counterfeit products are usually of a lower quality with logos lacking minor details or with slight amendments. Take for example, Prada handbags. The counterfeit ones usually come with logos that are not as well defined as the originals, or with certain minor details missing though they are not easily noticeable to someone who is unfamiliar with the brand. [PRC]

It is possible to detect the piracy goods. For instance, material used to make a particular product (e.g. handbags) can be different in terms of quality. More specific details like the brand's logo must be symmetrical to each other at all angles and whether this product is truly designed by a particular brand designer, only loyal or brand conscious customers can pick out these differences from a counterfeit product. [Singaporean]

The ability to differentiate a counterfeit from a genuine item also appeared to vary from one product to the other (and certainly across consumers). Some products appeared to lend themselves to easy detection because of the difference in quality of the packaging/ instruction manual and the actual product (packaging and other peripherals being of inferior quality).

I am able to recognize counterfeit software and VCDs at one glance because they usually have inferior packaging. [Malaysian]

FIGURE 2
Tiers of Search

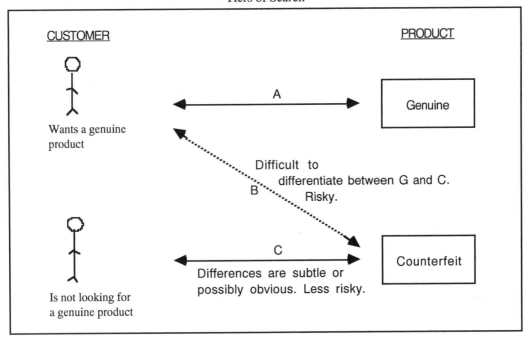

Video CDs are obviously counterfeit from the packaging which are often in plastic sleeves rather than proper clear plastic boxes. The boxes provided are also of a cheap plastic quality and totally black in color. [Malaysian]

Consumers are wise in judging which is counterfeit by the packaging and the method in which the products are displayed. Tags on clothing will be the easiest to determine quality. [Brunei]

In the case of products that were not individually packaged or did not carry instructions (e.g. clothing), the more obvious cues offered by the packaging were absent and detection was more difficult.

With regards to poor quality stitching, the judgment of the brand quality could be found in the time factor (in terms of product durability). Often counterfeit goods would be worn off after a few washings but the genuine product would have a much longer period of durability. [Brunei]

Even for famous products, although the counterfeit's price is still high, it has differences with the real one. If we look closely, the stitches or pirated design are quite different from the real one. It is hard to identify the differences, but for people who are used to encountering the real one, they will realize the difference immediately. [Indonesian]

Thus, there appear to be three possible consumer-product relationships in markets where counterfeits are plentiful and they are depicted in Figure 2. Relationship A is what is commonly studied in marketing and consumer behavior. Consumers in a market do not expect to buy anything other than the genuine item and that is what is commonly offered in the marketplace. Product

search and evaluation behavior follows the typical pattern discussed in Figure 1 earlier. Consumers make a product decision and then search for brands within the product model. The polar opposite (the existence of the extremely obvious counterfeit) will also be included in this category (as it too ignores the possibility of intervening levels of quality). One difference is that the purchase of the novel fake item (most often by tourists) represents the playfulness dimension discussed by Holt (1995). Relationship B is the case where consumers unwittingly purchase a counterfeit because they are led by sellers into believing that the item is a genuine one. What is typically examined under research on counterfeits is the deception involved. Here the assumption about consumer search is that consumers are searching for a brand under a product model but are offered a counterfeit brand. The fact that a counterfeit is offered in the marketplace is not expected to alter consumer search or evaluation as the consumer is not expected to possess the knowledge that s/he purchased one.

What also emerges from the data is the presence of product-customer relation C (Figure 2)—a case where consumers seek counterfeits and there is little deceit involved. This means that consumers are not simply searching for a brand within a product, but also for further "products" within the brand model. In other words, what our data reveal is that after making a product choice, consumers make a brand choice as in the case of any other search behavior. However, after making the brand decision, consumers may be now faced with another choice, whether to purchase a genuine item or a counterfeit. Figure 3 illustrates this second tier search for products. Several informants discussed the results of the Asian meltdown; prior to that event, they had developed preferences for a certain brand (see Wong and Ahuvia (1998) for a discussion of the relationship between economic progress of a nation and the consumption of luxury brands in Eastern cultures). After the meltdown, they could no longer afford the brand, but could buy a counterfeit version.

FIGURE 3
Post Brand Search

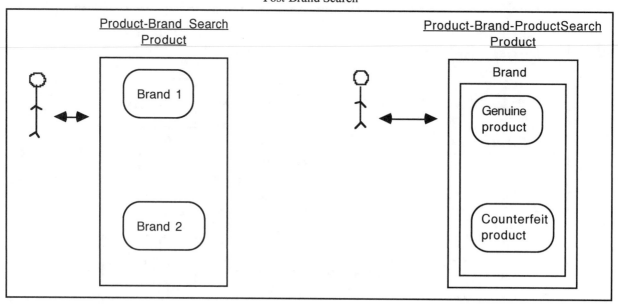

FIGURE 4
Genuine-Counterfeit Continuum

Genuine item	Second	Overrun	Legitimate copycat	High quality counterfeit	Low quality counterfeit
Original product with full warranty	Manufacturer authorised products with defects or out of date	Manufacturer unauthorised locally produced to original standards	Retailers such as the Limited copy designs from fashion houses	Not produced to original standards yet similar on key attributes	Significantly different from original on several key attributes

Quality Comparisons Across Counterfeits

Consumers also appeared to search among counterfeits. The difference between counterfeits and genuine articles did not appear to be dichotomous but a more continuous one that was made up of various levels depicted in Figure 4. In other words, consumers perceived differences in quality among genuine items, seconds, and various counterfeits. Our data collection focused mainly on the extreme phenomena listed in the Figure. This is an interesting notion that reveals that there are different levels of counterfeits ranging from those that are closer in quality to the genuine to those that are easily distinguishable as counterfeits because of their inferior quality.

The more fashion and status-oriented of course will buy only those of higher quality and refined imitation from overseas when compared to those available cheaply at local weekend markets. In Hong Kong, for example, one now has the choice of buying different grades of counterfeit goods for different products. [Singaporean]

There are two classes of counterfeits in these countries. First is the "same-name-but-different-style-positive-feel-bag." Sure it has the word Prada written, but the material of the counterfeit bag is weak, easily torn, and zippers don't work. Even in the extreme case, Prada is spelt differently. Hence, very cheap. The second class is "up class fake bag." It is 95% the exact replica of the original Prada, material and color is closer than far from the first class counterfeit, and probably the only difference from the real thing is the price and where it is made. Plus it doesn't come from Italy and contain an authentic Prada card inside. Now that is the true-blue thing. [Hong Kong]

The best indicator to judge the quality of the counterfeits would be price. Many consumers would not mind paying for it if the quality is good and it is value for money. [Singaporean]

Many are willing to pay for better quality counterfeit products. This is especially true for products such as sunglasses and clothing. [Malaysian]

At times the difference in quality of counterfeits appeared to vary from truly inferior to one that cannot be distinguished from that of the genuine item.

> For VCDs, the counterfeit ones are easy to recognize. The filming quality is so poor you know that someone has just decided to bring his or her own video camera into the theater and film it while he or she is watching. At times you see the shadows of a patron who stood up and walk out in the middle of the screening. [Malaysian]

> When you watch the movies (VCD), you will be shocked to know that the quality is almost the same as the original. [Malaysian]

> One can get a Prada handbag at as low as HK$120 but it would be for a poorly produced imitation. However, there are some consumers who are willing to pay more than HK$1000 for an imitation, which has the quality and design of the genuine one. [Hong Kong]

These quotes provide strong evidence that intense "hands-on" product evaluations can distinguish varying levels of quality, and that such search processes are indeed a reality. Many marketers have attributed the slow acceptance of direct marketing approaches in Southeast Asia to the fact that consumers are high-context and need to see and touch the products before purchase. An expanded explanation would include the presence of counterfeits. If there is any skepticism of the provider's ability to provide genuine items, the need to investigate systematically the item to be purchased is understandable. And, given the obviously high frequency of encountering counterfeits in these environments and the varying qualities of counterfeits, skepticism is to be expected.

In addition to careful examination of the quality of counterfeits, consumers also developed several heuristics to differentiate the quality of a counterfeit. Country of origin and type of retail outlet appeared to be two such heuristics.

> Counterfeits from Hong Kong are the best, and more expensive. Counterfeits from PRC are cheaper but less quality. [Indonesian]

> Korea is known to be the best at producing exquisite imitation goods. Hong Kong comes in second then followed by Thailand. [Singaporean]

> The clothing everywhere is fake. I will not buy any article of clothing in Brunei as it generally appears fake, and I know the quality is lower. [Brunei]

The type of retail outlet appeared to offer an indirect cue of the quality of the counterfeit. There appeared to be a perception that counterfeits were usually sold in street markets and smaller stores in markets known for selling only counterfeits and not in larger stores.

> Counterfeit goods are typically sold in open air markets, street stalls and small shops in both cities and small villages around the country. [French]

> In Malaysia, counterfeits are so predominant that it is generally accepted as the culture there. Petaling Street and Sultan Street, both situated in Kuala Lumpur, are the equivalent of Temple Street in Hong Kong (famous for counterfeit products at a low price). [Malaysian]

> In the US, you can get counterfeits on the streets. Jeans are the largest items on the streets in Seattle, almost always being sold out of the back of vans or at a street vendor's. [American]

However, there also appeared to be the knowledge that some larger stores did sell counterfeits along with genuine items. But the confidence to shop at these larger stores appeared to be drawn from presumptions that the counterfeits in these stores would be closer in quality if not akin to the genuine items, that the difference will be very difficult to distinguish, and that these retail stores offered competitive prices appeared to be an additional incentive that overrode any ambiguity.

> Stores even place the real and the counterfeit products in the same stores, same shelves, and charge the same price. It is a real cheat to customers even though the quality difference is so little that people who are not used to encountering the real products would not know if they end up buying the fake one. In this case, customers buy counterfeit products unwillingly. [Malaysian]

> Consumers purchase these counterfeit products, sometimes even unknowingly (they think it's original). They are usually of high quality, at times higher quality than originals, and priced below the original's price tag. As it is almost impossible to tell the difference between counterfeits and originals, all consumers tend to buy the counterfeits when available on the market, simply because they are cheaper. [Italian]

Thus, in addition to the volitional purchase of counterfeits, in markets where counterfeits abound, there also appears to be a search for the desired quality of a counterfeit. After making a decision to purchase a counterfeit or a genuine item, consumers appear to be searching for information on quality of counterfeits and are left with the decision of the level of counterfeit that they are willing to purchase.

Counterfeits and Price Bargaining

A final stage of search appears to be a search for the right price within the product-brand-"level of counterfeit" schema. After identifying the level of counterfeit that they are willing to buy, consumers enter the—often lengthy—process of bargaining for the right price. Bargaining for a price appeared to be common in shopping for counterfeits and the asking price appeared to have been seldom accepted by consumers.

> The price would be a lot cheaper, say for a Rolex for example. The seller may initially put the price high for about $1000, but when the customer is really interested, the final bargaining can make the watch reach to $50. [Malaysian]

> For as little as RM$10 (about US$3.00), one can purchase a full version of Microsoft Windows 98, as well as many of the latest software that may not even be available in legal market yet. [Malaysian]

Thus, though consumers who consciously seek counterfeits behave like other consumers in seeking the lowest price, its place in search and evaluation appears to be different than in the case of what we understand in the West as search and evaluation in the case of genuine products (the latter schema is depicted in Figure 1). More specifically, it appears to be within the chosen alternative and not across a set of alternatives as in the case of what is understood as search and evaluation behaviors in the case of the purchase of genuine items.

FIGURE 5
Revised Search Model

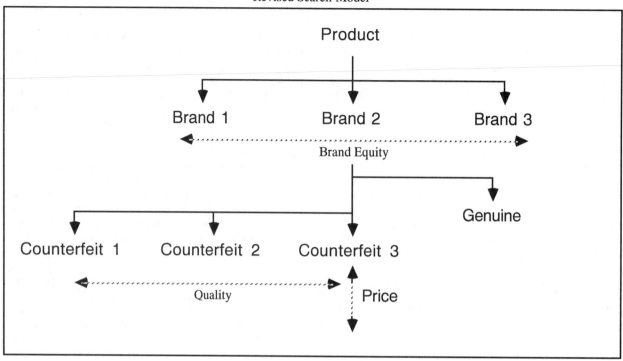

CONCLUSIONS AND DISCUSSION

Counterfeiting is a global phenomenon, though its presence is more common in some parts of the world than others. Our findings indicate that there are obvious cues (informal retail setting, unbelievably low price—after negotiation, and poor packaging and labeling) that help identify counterfeits (cf. Cordell, Wongtada, and Dieschnick 1996). However, the quality of counterfeits has improved greatly, especially as manufacturing technology has been outsourced and new technology such as cheap, high quality color printers and copiers, and cheap CD burners and recording equipment have become more common. The sophistication needed to discern quality counterfeits from authentic items has increased.

Ethical issues aside, manufacturers no doubt are in a quandary as to the real cost of counterfeits. Large manufacturers spend millions of dollars tracking consumer tastes, designing hot new products, distributing them efficiently, and creating demand through impressive advertising campaigns. Also it would seem clear that counterfeits reduce the brand equity so established, especially if the purchase of shoddy merchandise is made unwittingly. On the other hand, what brand would have any equity if it were not worth counterfeiting? Ironically in some cases companies actually may view being counterfeited as a boon to their efforts to build brand awareness (cf. Freedman 1999; Shultz and Saporito 1996). Regardless, we argue that one needs to look at the issue from the consumer's perspective and, more specifically, from one's tendency to search. One view is that obvious knockoffs are easily identified and that consumers (tourists) buy them only for novelty purposes. In fact, a trial judge in Hong Kong, while sentencing a wholesale counterfeiter, noted that "no one (Dunhill, D&G, Polo, or Ralph Lauren)–ever lost a sale to this sort of activity... No one would be fooled" (*Strait Times* 1999). On the other hand, evidence suggests that the quality of some counterfeits can approach or even match that of the authentic items, making the cost of search much higher.

Our findings indicate that there may be other explanations here. First, counterfeits allow consumers to try a low-grade version with the intent of purchasing the authentic item if the trial is successful. Second, counterfeits also appear to offer lesser value for lesser cost, an acceptable compromise and at times a desirable one given the initial outlay of expenditures required. However, what may be most critical for owners of brands to consider is the extent to which counterfeits allow consumers to delink the brand and the product. Counterfeits are only good as long as they are counterfeits *of* some brand. Thus, the reason why consumers buy a counterfeit is because it represents—albeit to varying degrees—the brand it is supposed to be copying. In cases where consumers are deceived into purchasing a counterfeit, it can be argued that the consumers may have been under the assumption that s/he may be buying the genuine product. However, our data reveal that consumers often purchase counterfeits out of conscious choice. Under such circumstances, consumers are reaching for a specific brand and willing to compromise on the product. A counterfeit appears to offer consumers a chance to separate the brand from the product. While the purchase of a counterfeit represents the consumption of the brand (brand decision), it does not appear to represent a "product" decision. Consumers have yet to choose among the various counterfeits of the brand and yet to agree on the price of the product. In other words, the consumer purchase decision in the case of counterfeits appears to follow the schema represented in Figure 5, rather than the conventional model in Figure 1.

Informants from developed countries acknowledged that counterfeiting exists there, but only in street markets. A certain degree of insulation from such activities was obvious. As e-commerce grows though, the developed world may see vastly increased numbers of counterfeits circulating. Some marketers have questioned why fixed-format retailers would compete against themselves by creating web sites. This paper indicates an obvious reason: the store's equity will assure the buyer of obtaining an authentic item, whereas skepticism will exist for lower-priced competitors.

Another insight from our findings is the mirror-image of a point raised frequently by Belk (1999) and others: people in transition economies are willing to pay disproportionate parts of their income for symbolic Western products. Our data reveal that such desires are also fulfilled through the possession of the brand and not necessarily of the product. There is evidence that well-resourced tourists also seek to acquire symbolism, but in the form of obviously counterfeit goods. The novelty and the tangible symbol of one's travel experiences merit more investigation, especially given tourism's role as the largest industry in the world.

A final insight is one that contradicts the guidelines of most international marketing textbooks, that consumers in developing countries are extremely price conscious and that the price for one's product should be kept as low as possible. Our findings indicate that a very low-priced Western good may be seen as a counterfeit, rather than as a good buy. If there is a degree of brand equity involved, we would admonish the manufacturer to distribute the product to "upscale" stores (though, admittedly, this emic may vary greatly across cultures) and avoid being extremely competitive in terms of price. An extension of this implication is that manufacturers may want to be very careful when introducing a modified product into a market flooded with fakes, as it may well be seen as a counterfeit. Care needs to be made that those subtle cues used to judge authenticity are still evident in the modified product.

REFERENCES

Belk, Russell W. (1999), "Leaping Luxuries and Transitional Consumers," in Rajeev Batra (Ed.), *Marketing Issues in Transition Economies*, Boston: Kluwer Academic Press, 41-54.

Bloch, Peter H., Daniel L. Sherrell, and Nancy M. Ridgway (1986), "Consumer Search: An Extended Framework," *Journal of Consumer Research*, 13 (June), 119-126.

Business Week (1999), "Taking a Swing at Phony Clubs," February 22, p. 8.

Carsky, Mary L., Roger Dickinson, and Charles L. Canady III (1998), "The Evolution of Quality in Consumer Goods," *Journal of Macromarketing*, 18 (Fall), 132-144.

Chakraborty, Goutam, Anthony Allred, Ajay Singh Sukhdial, and Terry Bristol (1997), "Use of Negative Cues to Reduce Demand for Counterfeit Products," *Advances in Consumer Research*, 24, 345-349.

Clunas, Craig (1991), *Superfluous Things: Material Culture and Social Status in Early Modern China*, Urbana, IL: University of Illinois Press.

Cordell, Victor, Nittaya Wongtada, and Robert L. Dieschnick (1996): "Counterfeit Purchase Intentions: The Role of Lawfulness Attitudes and Product Traits as Determinants," *Journal of Business Research,* 35 (January), 41-53.

Freedman, David H. (1999), "Faker's Paradise," *Forbes ASAP*, April 5, 49-54.

Gentry, James W., Sanjay Putrevu, Clifford Shulltz II (2000), "Cross-Cultural and Home-Country Perspectives of IPR Infringements," in *Marketing Contributions to Democratization and Socioeconomic Development*, eds. Clifford Shultz II and Bruno Grbac, Macromarketing Conference, Lovran, Croatia.

Goldman, Arieh and Johny K. Johansson (1978), "Determinants of Search for Lower Prices: An Empirical Assessment of the Economics of Information Theory," *Journal of Consumer Research*, 5 (December), 176-186.

Gutterman, Alan and Bentley Anderson (1997): *Intellectual Property in Global Markets.* London: Klumer Law International.

Holt, Douglas (1995), "How Consumers Consume: A Typology of Consumption Processes," *Journal of Consumer Research*, 22 (June), 1-16.

Jain, Subhash (1996): "Problems in International Protection of Intellectual Property Rights," *Journal of International Marketing*, 4 (1), 9-32.

Lincoln, Y and E. Guba (1985), *Naturalistic Inquiry*, Newbury Park, CA: Sage.

Lincoln Journal Star (1999), "Poke-Con: Trading Cards Latest Target of Counterfeiters," December 15, p. 6A.

Mittelstaedt, J. and R. Mittelstaedt (1997): "The Protection of Intellectual Property: Issues of Origination and Ownership," *Journal of Public Policy & Marketing.* 16 (1), 14-25.

Nill, Alexander and Clifford J. Shultz II (1997), "The Scourge of Global Counterfeiting," *Business Horizons*, 39 (November-December), 37-42.

Putrevu, Sanjay and Brian T. Ratchford (1997), "A Model of Search Behavior with an Application to Grocery Shopping," *Journal of Retailing*, 73 (No. 4), 463-486.

Shultz, C. and Bill Saporito (1996), "Protecting Intellectual Property: Strategies and Recommendations to Deter Counterfeiting and Brand Piracy in Global Markets," *Columbia Journal of World Business*, 31 (Spring), 18-28.

Stigler, George (1961), "The Economics of Information," *Journal of Political Economy*, 69 (No. 3), 213-225.

The Straits Times, (1999), "First Time HK Court Jails Fake-Goods Seller," October 9.

Wong, Nancy Y. and Aaron C. Ahuvia (1998), "Personal Taste and Family Face: Luxury Consumption in Confucian and Western Societies," *Psychology and Marketing*, 15 (August), 423-441.

Passionate Surfers in Image-Driven Consumer Culture: Fashion-Conscious, Appearance-Savvy People and Their Way of Life

Fang Wan, University of Minnesota
Seounmi Youn, University of Minnesota
Tammy Fang, University of Minnesota

ABSTRACT

Benefiting from a nationally sampled database, the study explores the relationship between fashion consciousness and its relevant constructs. Dissatisfied with the fragmented linkage between fashion consciousness, the psychological mechanism underlying the construct, and the behavioral implications in the previous study, this study attempts to adopt an integrative frame to bridge the separate linkages of the concept in the literature. Factor analysis, regression analysis, and correlation analysis yield supporting evidence that fashion-consciousness is a multi-dimensional construct, predicted by a host of demographic variables and psychological measures. Fashion conscious people also reveal a special style of socializing and consuming in the consumer culture. The importance of the study is discussed in the conclusion.

With the evolution of Hollywood movie-making techniques, contemporary consumer culture is more and more defined and expressed by images. It seems that culture itself is built upon its ability to fabricate images and meanings and distribute them en mass (Ewen & Ewen, 1992). With the power to access mass audience, commercial media disseminate and promote images, thus, make the commercial traffics in images, each with a sale to make, become a central force of culture, delineating the ideals and norms of behaviors and social life. Images diffuse throughout modern consumer culture and shape the experiences, motivations, lifestyles, self-concepts and consumer values (Thompson & Hirschman, 1995). The impact of image on social life lies in the fact that people socialize and interact based on their impressions of each other, which in turn are formed based on the images portrayed by individuals themselves.

In material terms, clothing, fashion, or adornment has become an essential part of conspicuous and material embodiment of the image which one wishes to express. They also constitute an important arena of popular expression—often a self-defined voice. As William James once wrote, "The old saying that the human person is composed of three parts—soul, body, and clothes—is more than a joke" (James, 1890, p.292). He considered clothing to be a vital component of the "material self", which constituted a major part of the self. It seems that what we choose to wear and possess is the extended forms of our self-expression.

However, each individual may place different emphasis on "material" and "immaterial" self, or interpret and interact with the popular images differently based on their psychological or sociological make-up. In this sense, this study takes the perspective of consumers to explore how their psychological constructs influence their way of participating in consumer culture. Instead of adopting critical and interpretive orientation, which is considered as a common practice of researchers who study cultural and phenomenon, this study tends to employ a micro-level or individual-level analysis to identify the psychological mechanism of those appearance-savvy consumers. This study attempts to understand how the psychological constructs of fashion are related to people's socializing and consuming behaviors.

To deal with such a task, we try to identify the key psychological constructs in the previous literature to understand what psychological characteristics make consumers sensitive to images and physical appearances, and how these psychological aspects make them become allegiant and avid consumers in a modern consumer culture.

LITERATURE REVIEW

A voluminous literature describes that fashion consciousness is an important construct to define those avid consumers who are sensitive to the images, and their physical attractiveness. The literature of fashion theory tried to explore why and how fashion-related behaviors or preferences are related to self-concept and psychological traits. Researchers explored fashion-related trait, consumption or behavior in several ways. The first approach emphasizes psychological processes of fashion diffusion (e.g., Schrank, 1973; Goldsmith & Stith, 1990; Stanforth, 1995). These researchers examined who the fashion or trend setters were and how others followed and adopted fashion. For example, Schrank (1973) found that opinion leadership and innovativeness are two important variables to predict fashion adoption. Goldsmith and Stith (1990) reported that fashion innovators are younger and place greater importance on the social values such as being respected, excitement, and fun/enjoyment aspect of life than non-innovators. Stranforth (1995) found that fashion innovators are more related to traits such as sensation seeking, adventure seeking, boredom, susceptibility and clothing individuality.

Researchers (e.g., Gould & Stern, 1989; Gurel & Gurel, 1979; Summers, 1970; Demby, 1972; Crask & Reynold, 1978) from the second approach take both social and psychological aspects into consideration when examining fashion-related concept. Specifically, fashion-conscious consumers are related to traits such as self-assertive, competitive, venturesome, attention seeking, self-confident (Summers, 1970); creative, upwardly mobile, innovative, and sociable (Demby, 1972); they are slightly younger, better educated, have higher income, are much more active at travel and sports and entertained frequently (Crask & Reynold, 1978).

Other traits such as self-esteem, clothing interests, innovativeness, vanity, public or private self-consciousness are related to fashion-consciousness. For example, Kwon (1997) investigated the relationship between perceived facial attractiveness, social self-esteem, and interest in clothing. His findings show that one's interest in clothing might be interpreted as a form of social skill which is associated with one's social self-esteem and one's facial attractiveness. Both studies of Kwon (1997) and Gould & Stern (1989) show that there is a gender difference in fashion consciousness. Women, compared to men, indicate greater interest in clothing (Kwon, 1997). Moreover, fashion conscious women pay more attention to external appearance while men more private, or internalized self-identity and maleness.

The final approach is to relate fashion concepts to outcome variables such as shopping activities and shopping preferences (e.g., Bloch & Richins, 1992; Netemeyer, Burton & Litchtenstein, 1995). For example, Bloch and Richins (1992) found that when using adornments, a person may feel more attractive, and thus experience greater self-esteem, or a more positive mood. Such effect is also found to be true in both clothing and cosmetics (e.g., Cash & Cash, 1982). The increased level of feeling attractive will also improve user's satisfaction because the reactions of others to

FIGURE 1

An integrative framework of studying fashion-consciousness

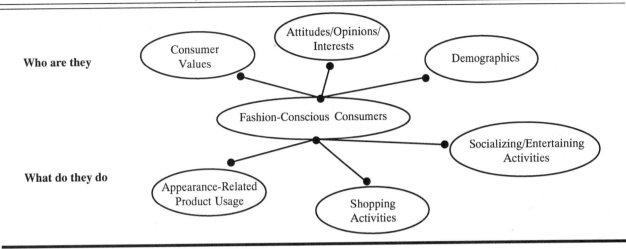

the self are enhanced (Bloch & Richins, 1992). Solomon (1985, 1992) also found that fashion conscious people are more ready to use appearance-related products to enhance their self-concept.

Previous studies provide different linkages among fashion consciousness, psychological constructs, and the subsequent behaviors. However, the linkages and connections are remaining separate and fragmented. Also, measuring fashion-consciousness by a particular scale (e.g., clothing interest scale), researchers in the past assume unidimensionality of fashion-consciousness. There is a need, first, to conceptualize fashion-consciousness as a multi-dimensional concept which is not only limited to clothing consciousness. Also, it is important to disentangle how psychological constructs are involved differently in the appearance-related consumption and how they are linked to other fashion-related behaviors. Fragmented linkage between fashion and other related concepts fails to provide comprehensive framework to study fashion consciousness. The current study adopts an integrative framework, examining who those fashion-conscious people are in terms of demographics, their attitudes, interest, and opinions (AIO), and consumer values. Furthermore, this study explores how fashion conscious people consume appearance-related products and are engaged in entertaining and socializing activities. The integrative framework is outlined in Figure 1.

METHODOLOGY

Data. The data used in this study came from the 1997 DDB Needham Life Style Study. This is an annual consumer mail survey that assesses attitudes, interests, opinions, personality traits, activities, and product consumption. Approximately 5,000 adult Americans were selected by quota sampling based on national census data. In 1997, 1,591 males and 1,871 female provided usable data, and the response rate is 69.3%.

Measures. To examine a comprehensive theoretical framework of fashion consumption, a wide range of measures were selected from the Life Style Questionnaire that assess psychological constructs, attitudes, interests, opinions, usage of products, and activities.

Fashion Consciousness. One of our interests is to explore the structure of "fashion" as a multi-dimensional construct, not a unidimensional construct. For this, fifteen items were identified as potential indicators of fashion consciousness or behavior from

AIO section. They were measured by a six-point scale ranging from "definitely disagree" to "definitely agree." This study applied Principal Components analysis to these items, rotating to a Varimax solution. This analysis yielded a four-factor structure that accounted for 52.8% of the variance, with factor loading ranging from .43 to .78. Table 1 presents these four factors and illustrative items.

The first factor, which accounted for 27.9% of the variance, was comprised of items that indicated interest in clothing or dressing. This was labeled "Dressing Style." The second factor was composed of items reflecting materialistic value in fashion consumption, with the variance of 9.7%. We labeled it "Materialism." The third factor, which explained 7.8% of the variance, included items concerning young and gook-looking appearance or indicating experimentation with appearance (i.e., plastic surgery). This factor was named "Physical Appearance." The fourth factor included items reflecting enhancement of uniqueness, unconformity, or distinctness. This factor explained 7.4% of the variance, and was labeled "Individuality."

Three factors produced Cronbach's alphas ranging from .58 to .72, and these were considered to have achieved an acceptable level of reliability (Nunnally 1978). Individuality had an alpha of .52. While this was considered rather low, this factor was retained because of its perceived theoretical interest. In fact, given that the exploratory nature of the secondary data analysis, this factor was deemed somewhat reliable. For subsequent analysis, individual items were aggregated for each factor as index for individual sub-factors. The scores of the items were also summed across four factors to create an index for the overall factor.

Notably, the four-factor structure provides us an empirical support for argument that the all-encompassing fashion concept can be broken down into more narrowly defined constituent concepts. Furthermore, this framework makes it possible to speculate that each sub-concept is differently related to fashion-related constructs including AIO and consumer values.

Psychological Discrimination Measures. It is of particular interest to determine what constructs are related to both the four sub-factors and overall fashion factor. To identify a wide range of discrimination measures, this study selected approximately fifty-seven items that reflect any of the constructs expected to potentially relate to fashion and consumption. These items were also chosen from attitudes, interests, and opinion section in the Life

TABLE 1
Factor Structure of Fashion Consciousness

	Pct of Var	Alpha	Factor loading
Factor 1: Dressing Style	27.9	.72	
I enjoy getting dressed up.			.76
Dressing well is an important part of my life.			.69
I enjoy looking through fashion magazines.			.68
I have more stylish clothes than most of my friends.			.43
Factor 2: Materialism	9.7	.58	
The car I drive is a reflection of who I am.			.78
People recognize that I buy only the best.			.73
The clothes I wear reflect who I am as a person.			.52
Factor 3: Physical Appearance	7.8	.64	
I strongly consider consulting with a dermatologist or plastic surgeon to deal with the signs of aging.			.75
It is worth to pay for cosmetic dentistry solely to improve my appearance.			.75
It is important to have my hair cut in the latest style.			.49
I work at trying to maintain a youthful appearance.			.43
Factor 4: Individuality	7.4	.52	
I like sports cars.			.67
I like to feel attractive to members of the opposite sex.			.62
I have much better taste than most people.			.57
I want to look a little different from others.			.55
Cumulative percent of variance	52.8		

Note.
An alpha score of overall Fashion Consciousness factor is .80.

Style Questionnaire, and were measured by a six-point scale, "definitely disagree" to "definitely agree."

The fashion-related AIO constructs were "healthy eating," "financial concerns," "price consciousness," "brand consciousness," "self-confidence," "risk-avoiding," and "innovativeness." The fashion-related consumer values were "attitude toward technology," "attitude toward sexual issues," "advertising skepticism," and "environmental concerns." Benefiting from the original data set, we included some constructs such as brand consciousness, attitude toward sexual issues, or environmental concerns, which the previous studies never dealt with, in our analysis to explore new facets of fashion-consciousness construct.

Fifty-seven items potentially related to fashion were also subjected to a Principal Components analysis, with a Varimax rotation and eigenvalues over 1.0. This analysis produced eleven interpretable factors that generally conformed to the expected pattern of constructs, accounting for 50.2% of the total variance. Table 2 shows these factors, with illustrative items.

Negatively loaded items were reverse-coded and a Cronbach's alpha was calculated for each factor. Eleven factors yielded alpha ranging from .58 to .87. They were then included as independent variables and regressed on the four sub-factors as well as overall factor. In the further analysis, index for each factor was constructed by summing scores of all items in that factor.

Behavioral Discrimination Measures. As literature shows, fashion consciousness is expected to link to behavioral measures such as shopping activities, consumption of fashion-related products, entertaining activities, and socializing activities (e.g., Netemeyer, Burton & Litchtenstein, 1995). To illustrate the relationship, this study selected a variety of items that, from earlier work, would show meaningful patterns from activities and products/services usage section in the questionnaire. Items of fashion-related activities were all asked on a seven-point scale, from "none in past year" to "more than 52 times in past year," except the online shopping, which was measured dichotomously. Regarding the consumption of fashion-related products, this study selected personal products items such as skin care products, hair-styling products, and cosmetics (only for women). They were measured by a seven-point scale, "don't use" through "once a day or more." Demographic variables such as gender, age, education, and income were included.

For the sake of data reduction, we factor analyzed items reflecting shopping activities, socializing behaviors, and consumption of skin care products, using Principal Components, with a Varimax rotation and eigenvalues over 1.0. Factor scores for each factor were saved and used for correlation analyses with each of the sub-factors and the overall factor of fashion consciousness. Some behavioral measures (such as on-line shopping) were composed of single item.

TABLE 2
Factor Loadings and Internal Consistency Coefficients for Major Constructs

Factors	Pct. of variance	Alpha	Factor loading
Factor 1: Healthy Eating (10 items)	12.4	.87	
I try to avoid foods that are high in fat.			.78
I try to avoid foods that are high in cholesterol.			.78
I use a lot of low calorie or calorie reduced products.			.69
I am concerned about how much sugar I eat.			.69
I am careful about what I eat in order to keep my weight under control.			.68
I try to avoid foods with a high salt content.			.67
I make a special effort to get enough fiber in my diet.			.64
I try to select foods that are fortified with vitamins and minerals.			.59
I am concerned about getting enough calcium in my diet.			.53
I try to avoid foods that have additives in them.			.47
Factor 2: Financial Problem (7 items)	7.6	.82	
Our family is too heavily in debt.			.79
Credit cards have gotten me into too much debt.			.76
No matter how fast our income goes up we never seem to get ahead.			.75
I am not very good at saving money.			.67
I frequently buy things when I can't afford them.			.64
Saving for the future is a luxury I can't afford right now.			.62
I pretty much spend for today and let tomorrow bring what it will.			.58
Factor 3: Attitude Toward Technology (5 items)	6.7	.73	
Surfing the internet is more interesting than watching television.			.75
The internet is the best place to get information about products.			.73
I don't have a clue what the internet is and what it can do for me. (r)			.68
I am usually among the first to try new technologies.			.63
We'd be better off without computers. (r)			.57
Factor 4: Advertising Skepticism (5 items)	4.6	.74	
I avoid buying products advertised on violent TV programs.			.71
TV commercials place too much emphasis on sex.			.66
Advertising for beer and wine should be taken off TV.			.57
Advertising directed to children should be taken off television.			.55
I avoid buying products advertised on shows with too much sex.			.52
Factor 5: Attitude Toward Sexual Issues (4 items)	3.9	.75	
I am in favor of legalized abortions.			.74
Public high schools should be allowed to distribute condoms to students.			.73
I am in favor of legalizing same sex marriages.			.69
Couples should live together before getting married.			.66
Factor 6: Price Consciousness (5 items)	3.2	.64	
I always check prices even on small items.			.66
I shop a lot for specials.			.66
I only buy a new product if I have a coupon or if it's on sale.			.58
I shop around a lot or look up lots of information before a purchase.			.53
Before shopping, I sit down and make out a complete shopping list.			.50
Factor 7: Brand Consciousness (4 items)	2.9	.65	
I try to stick to well-known brand names.			.75
A nationally advertised brand is a better buy than a generic brand.			.73
I would buy a brand name prescription drug than a generic one.			.69
When I have a favorite brand I buy it - no matter what else is on sale.			.58
Factor 8: Self-Confidence (3 items)	2.6	.63	
I like to be considered a leader.			.73
I have more self-confidence than most of my friends.			.71

TABLE 2

Factor Loadings and Internal Consistency Coefficients for Major Constructs (CONTINUED)

Factors	Pct. of variance	Alpha	Factor loading
I am the kind of person who knows what I want to accomplish in life and how to achieve it.			.65
Factor 9: Environmental Concerns (5 items)	2.2	.59	
I would be willing to accept a lower standard of living to conserve energy.			.64
I worry a lot about the effects of environmental pollution on my family's health.			.59
I support pollution standards if means shutting down some factories.			.58
I make a strong effort to recycle everything I possibly can.			.51
I make a special effort to look for products that are energy efficient.			.42
Factor 10: Innovativeness (4 items)	2.1		.58
I spend a lot of time visiting friends.			.63
My friends and neighbors com to me for advice about products.			.63
I am usually among the first to try new products.			.55
I am influential in my neighborhood.			.50
Factor 11: Risk-Avoiding (5 items)	2.0	.54	
When making investments maximum safety is more important than high interest rates.			.71
Investing in the stock market is too risky for me.			.60
On a job, security is more important than money.			.51
I don't like to take chances.			.48
I would feel lost if I were alone in a foreign country.			.41
Cumulative Percent of Variance	**50.2**		

ANALYSIS AND RESULTS

Identification of Interrelationship Between Fashion Constructs

The primary goal of our study is to explore the multifacet nature of fashion-consciousness as a construct. To investigate this, this study conducted a correlation analysis to the overall factor of Fashion Consciousness and its sub-factors (see Table 3).

Interestingly, the overall factor of Fashion Consciousness was most strongly correlated with Dressing Style (r=.80, p<.001) and Physical Appearance (r=.77, p<.001) sub-factors, followed by Individuality (r=.71, p<.001) and Materialism (r=.63, p<.001).

For the interrelationship among four sub-scales, Dressing Style sub-factor was highly associated with Physical Appearance sub-factor (r=.52, p<.001), and rather moderately related with Individuality (r=.39, p<.001) and Materialism (r=.33, p<.001) sub-factors. Individuality and Materialism sub-factors revealed relatively moderate relationship with other constituent sub-factors, indicating somewhat less of interrelationships each other.

Psychological Characteristics of Fashion Conscious Consumers

As we conceptualized in Figure 1, one of our goals is to explore the relationship of psychological constructs to the overall and sub-factors of Fashion Consciousness. We expect that, in addition to demographic variables, psychological constructs (e.g., AIO) and consumer values would be important determinants of fashion consciousness or behavior. For this, different hierarchical multiple regression models were performed on both the overall factor of fashion consciousness and its four sub-factors.

A total of fifteen independent variables, grouped in three separate blocks, were included in this analysis. Demographic variables such as gender, age, education, and income were entered in the first block. The AIO variables including healthy eating concerns, financial concerns, price consciousness, self-confidence, brand consciousness, risk-avoiding, and innovativeness were entered in the second block. Finally, consumer values such as attitudes toward advertising, technology, sexual issues, and environmental concerns were included as the last block. Overall and sub-factors of fashion were treated as dependent variables separately. We adopted this analytic approach because this study attempted to determine whether the psychological constructs including the AIO constructs and consumer values will contribute to the Fashion Consciousness in addition to demographic variables. The results are shown in Table 4.

As the results in Table 4 show, the independent variables explained 37% of the total variance of the overall factor of Fashion Consciousness. Among them, the AIO variables and consumer values are important predictors of the overall factor even after demographic variables had been controlled.

First, demographic variables, as a block, explained 6% of the total variance. Gender and age were significant predictors of overall Fashion Consciousness factor. Women showed greater level of fashion consciousness than men (β=13, p<.001), and younger consumers were more concerned about their fashion styles than older consumers (β=-.09, p<.001). The education and income variables did not emerge as significant predictors in this study.

The AIO variables added another 29% to the explained variance, after controlling for the demographic variables. Innovativeness was clearly the strongest predictor of Fashion Consciousness among these variables (β=.30, p<.001), supporting the findings of the previous studies (Goldsmith and Stith 1992;

TABLE 3

Correlations of Overall and Sub-factors of Fashion Conciousness

	Overall	Sub-factors			
	Fashion Conscious.	Dressing Style	Materialism	Physical Appearance	Individuality
Sub-factors					
Dressing Style	.80				
Materialism	.63	.33			
Physical Appearance	.77	.52	.29		
Individuality	.71	.39	.32	.37	

Note.
Correlation coefficients were all significant at the level of p<.001.

TABLE 4

Hierarchical Multiple Regression Explaining Fashion Consciousness[a]

	Overall Fashion	Dressing Style	Materia lism	Physical appearance	Individuality
	Final Beta[c]	Final Beta	Final Beta	Final Beta	Final Beta
Demographics					
Female[b]	.13***	.29***	-.04*	.12***	-.03
Age	-.09***	-.08***	.02	.01	-.20***
Education	.02	.01	.02	-.01	.03
Income	.02	-.02	.07***	.05**	-.02
ΔR^2	.06***	.12***	.02***	.04***	.11***
Activities, Interests, & Opinions					
Healthy Eating	.23***	.25***	.07**	.24***	.08***
Financial Concerns	.11***	.07***	.03	.10***	.14***
Price Consciousness	.04*	.02	.02	.04*	.04
Self Confidence	.14***	.12***	.11***	.01	.17***
Brand Consciousness	.19***	.12***	.18***	.16***	.09***
Risk-Avoiding	.03	.02	.06**	.04*	-.04**
Innovativeness	.30***	.24***	.20***	.25***	.18***
ΔR^2	.29***	.19***	.14***	.19***	.16***
Consumer Values					
Att. Toward Technology	.07***	.03	.07**	.06**	.08***
Advertising Skepticism	-.11***	-.09***	-.04*	-.07**	-.12***
Att. Toward Sexual Issues	.05**	.02	.02	.05*	.08***
Green Consciousness	-.00	-.04*	.01	-.01	.05*
ΔR^2	.02***	.01***	.01***	.01***	.03***
Total Adjusted R²	**.37***	**.31***	**.15***	**.24***	**.29***

Note.
a. Higher scores indicated a greater level of fashion consciousness.
b. Dummy variable was created for sex (female = 1 and male = 0).
c. Beta reported here was from the final equation.
*** p<.001, ** p<.01, * p<.05

Tatzel 1982). Interestingly, healthy eating was also strongly and positively associated with fashion consciousness (β=.23, p<.001), indicating that health conscious consumers are greatly concerned about their external appearance or fashion style. Brand consciousness emerged as a positive predictor of fashion consciousness (β=.19, p<.001), and self-confident consumers were more likely to be involved in fashion-oriented behaviors (β=.14, p<.001). Financial concerns turned out to be a significant but moderate predictor of fashion behavior (β=.11, p<.01), implying that consumers who

don't hesitate to buy are more likely to be concerned about their fashionable appearance. Notably, price consciousness and risk-avoiding constructs showed weak relationship with the overall Fashion Consciousness.

Consumer values explained additional 2% of the total variance after controlling for demographics and AIO variables. Attitude toward technology appeared to be a positive contributor of overall fashion consciousness (β=.07, p<.001), which implies that consumers who hold more positive attitudes toward Internet or computer usage are more likely to be attentive to fashionable appearance. Liberal attitude toward controversial sex issues was moderately associated with fashion consciousness (β=.05, p<.001). Consumers with more liberal value about socially sensitive sexual issues (e.g., same sex marriages, sex education for adolescents, and abortion) tend to be more concerned about fashion and their external appearance.

Advertising skepticism was a negative predictor of fashion consciousness (β=-.11, p<.001). Consumers more tolerant with advertising issues (e.g., children ads, sex in ads, and liquor ads) tend to be more concerned about their fashionable appearance. Green consciousness (concerning energy efficiency and environment protection) was not a significant predictor of fashion consciousness factor (β=-.00, ns).

When individual sub-factors were entered as the dependent variable, each model performed well, explaining 24% to 31% of total variance, except "Materialism" sub-factor. In the case of "Materialism", the regression model only accounted for 15% of total variance.

Regarding "Dressing Style" sub-factor, demographic variables explained 12% of the variance. Women and younger consumers were more likely to have a greater level of interest in clothes (β=.29, p<.001 for women; β=-.08, p<.001 for age). The AIO variables contributed additional 19% of the variance after controlling demographics. More health conscious (β=.25, p<.001), more innovative (β=.24, p<.001), more self-confident (β=.12, p<.001), and more brand conscious people (β=.12, p<.001) tended to pay more attention to what they wear and how they dress. Among consumer values, advertising skepticism appeared to be a significant but negative predictor (β=-.09, p<.001), and green consciousness was moderately associated with interest in dressing up (β=-.04, p<.05). Unlike in the regression model of the overall factor, attitude toward technology turned out to be an insignificant factor to predict "Dressing Style" sub-factor.

When "Physical Appearance" sub-factor served as the dependent variable, the demographic variables explained 4% of the variance. Consistent with other analyses, women showed higher level of interest in physical appearance. Interestingly, age didn't appear as a significant determinant (β=.01, ns), while income variable turned out to be moderately significant predictor of this sub-factor (β=.05, p<.01). Higher income consumers tend to show a great willingness to keep young and good-looking appearance. For "Physical Appearance," the AIO variables explained 19% of the variance after controlling for demographics. More health conscious (β=.24, p<.001), more innovative (β=.25, p<.001), and more brand conscious (β=.16, p<.001) were more interested in improving their external appearance. Interestingly, self-confidence trait didn't emerge as a significant predictor, indicating that people who are self-confident may not be willing to take the risk of undertaking cosmetic surgery to improve their appearance. Consumer values explained only additional 1% of the total variance. Attitudes toward technology (β=.06, p<.001 and sexual issues (β=.05, p<.05) appeared to be positive predictors, while advertising skepticism appeared to be a negative predictor (β=-.07, p<.001).

When "Individuality" sub-factor was entered as the dependent variable, the results demonstrated a different pattern. Demographic variables accounted for 11% of the variance. Different with other models, only age appeared to be a powerful, but negative predictor of "Individuality" (β=-.20, p<.001). Younger consumers tend to be more concerned about demonstrating their uniqueness or distinctiveness. The AIO variables explained another 16% of the variance. More innovative (β=.18, p<.001) and more self-confident (β=.17, p<.001) consumers thought they were unique. Unlike other mod-

els, health conscious (β=.08, p<.001) and brand conscious (β=.09, p<.001) traits are significant and positive, but not strong predictors of Individuality sub-factor. Financial concern was moderately associated with Individuality sub-factor (β=.14, p<.001). Notably, risk-avoiding construct turned out to be a significant and negative predictor (β=-.04, p<.01), indicating that more risk taking consumers were interested in developing their individuality. Consumer values accounted for additional 3% of the variance. Open-minded to technology (β=.08, p<.001) and liberal attitudes toward sexual issues (β=.08, p<.001) appeared as important predictors, compared to other models. Also, advertising skepticism was negatively associated with this sub-factor(β=-.12, p<.001), suggesting that consumers with more positive attitude toward advertising tended to show higher level of individuality.

When "Materialism" sub-factor served as the dependent variable, this model showed different pattern. Demographic variables explained only 2% of variance. Unlike other models, income variable appeared to be the most important predictor of "Materialism" sub-factor (β=.07, p<.001). Among the AIO variables, which explained additional 14% of the variance, innovativeness (β=.20, p<.001) and brand consciousness (β=.18, p<.001) were dominant predictors of "Materialism." Self-confidence trait was also moderately associated with "Materialism" sub-factor (β=.11, p<.001). Like "Individuality" sub-factor, healthy eating variable appeared as a significant, positive, but not a strong predictor of "Materialism" sub-factor (β=.07, p<.001). Surprisingly, risk-avoiding turned out to be a positive determinant of this sub-factor (β=.06, p<.001). Among consumer values, which explained only 1% of the variance, attitude toward technology turned out to be an important predictor of this sub-factor (β=.07, p<.001), meaning that people who held more positive attitude toward technology tended to be more conscious of how the things they buy are the expressions of themselves.

These findings suggest that sub-factors of Fashion Consciousness showed slightly different relationships with demographic, AIO, and consumer values. These findings lent support to our previous argument that Fashion Consciousness construct should be considered as a multi-dimensional, not a uni-dimensional one.

Behavioral Characteristics of Fashion Conscious Consumers

As demonstrated by the correlations among overall factor and the sub factors, fashion conscious people are highly aware of their appearance, of how they dress and of how the things they possess are the extended forms of their self-identity. Taken together all these characteristics, we expect that these people are avid consumers, or passionate surfers in the consumer culture and highly involved in any appearance-related consumption and activities. But it is interesting to see which facet of their fashion awareness is related to what specific consumption activities. To investigate this, we chose a range of items measuring fashion-related products consumption, shopping activities, entertaining and socializing activities and correlated them with fashion consciousness factors. The results are shown in Table 5.

Regarding shopping styles, fashion conscious consumers tend to shop at the high-quality stores and be engaged in home shopping activities such as informercial or mail order. They are less likely to go to the convenience store, which is in line with the results of other studies that fashion conscious consumers tend to shop in traditional department stores, rather than national chain or discount department stores (Hirschman, 1979). Interestingly, those who are more conscious of showing individuality are more likely to be involved in on-line shopping activities.

In terms of appearance-related activities, highly fashion conscious people are more likely to spend money on clothing, to be on

TABLE 5.

Correlations Between Fashion Consciousness, Consumption Activities, and Appearance-Related Product Usage

	Overall Fashion	Dressing Style	Materialism	Physical Appearance	Individuality
Consumption Style					
Frequently used stores					
Appliance store	-.01	-.09***	.04*	-.04*	.08***
Low-price store	.04*	.09***	-.01	.05*	-.01
Home shopping	.11***	.07***	.04*	.13***	.07***
Convenience store	-.01	-.09***	-.01	-.04*	.14***
High-quality store	.24***	.24***	.15***	.16***	.13***
Mail shopping	.08***	.10***	.03	.05***	.03
On-line shopping	.03	.00	.02	-.01	.08***
Appearance-related consumption					
Clothing expenditure	.34***	.32***	.22***	.23**	.20***
Weight-reducing diet	.15***	.15***	.04*	.15**	.08***
Buying from hair saloon	.22***	.21***	.09***	.22**	.10***
Went to hair saloon	.24***	.27***	.10***	.25**	.03
Entertaining consumption					
Art gallery or museum	.12***	.10***	.04*	.09***	.11***
Pop or rock concert	.13***	.07***	.09***	.05***	.17***
Country music concert	.06***	.04*	.05**	.04*	.03
Classical concert	.08***	.08***	.05***	.05***	.03
Movies	.20***	.16***	.07***	.12***	.18***
Socializing activities					
Sent cards to strengthen interpersonal ties	.17***	.24***	.05***	.16***	-.01
Party giving, social gathering	.10***	.11***	.02	.07***	.08***
Appearance-related Product Usage					
Special hair care product	.31***	.35***	.09***	.28***	.14***
Cosmetics (Female only)	.39***	.37***	.14***	.33***	.26***
Special facial care products	.31***	.32***	.10***	.29***	.16***
Sun tan products	.14***	.12***	.06***	.14***	.09***
Normal moisturizer	.09***	.21***	-.03	.13***	-.08***

Note.
*** p<.001, ** p<.01, * p<.05

diet, or to go to hair saloon more frequently and get some special hair care products from saloon. The table also shows that "Dressing Style" and "Physical Appearance" are two facets highly correlated with appearance-related consumption. For example, those who would undertake cosmetic surgery to enhance one's looking will definitely be willing to spend money on clothing, be on diet, and take good care of their hairstyle.

In addition, highly fashion conscious people have colorful entertaining activities. They are more likely to go to concerts and movies. Compared to other facets of fashion-consciousness, individuality is more correlated with activities such as going to pop or rock concert and movies. This can be explained by the previous finding that these groups of people are usually young.

In terms of socializing activities, highly fashion-conscious people love social gatherings, and they send cards on different occasions to strengthen their personal ties with friends and family. The last aspect of the finding is that fashion conscious people are avid consumers in terms of their product usage patterns. They are more willing to use special hair care, skin care products, suntan

products to enhance their looking. For women, most heavy cosmetic users are highly fashion conscious people.

CONCLUSIONS AND DISCUSSIONS

The major purpose of this study is to adopt an integrative framework to test the linkages between fashion consciousness, the related constructs, and consumption patterns. Benefiting from rich measures of a nationally selected sample data, we were able to use new variables, which have not been tested in the past studies, in our analysis to test new constructs relevant to fashion-consciousness. Specifically, they were brand consciousness, healthy eating concerns, attitude toward technology and socially sensitive sexual issues, and advertising skepticism. They all turned out to be important predictors of fashion consciousness. The study broke some new testing grounds of the research on fashion consciousness.

However, one limitation of the study is that large sample size helped make small coefficient significant, as one reviewer pointed out. Therefore, we need to make cautious generalizations of the statistically significant yet weak relationships found in the study.

Also, the study is exploratory in nature in terms of exploring the underlying components of fashion consciousness and the relationship between fashion consciousness, as a global trait, or psychological construct, and the attitudinal, behavioral variables. We are not interested in using fashion consciousness as an independent variable to predict the behavioral or attitudinal outcomes. Therefore, correlation analysis serves the purpose well.

We explored fashion conscious because fashion conscious people are a very interesting group in modern consumer culture. Paying greater attention to their external appearance, preoccupied with how they consume will reflect who they are, this group of people are avid and passionate surfers in the image-driven consumer cultures. They absorb the images and fashion styles in advertising. They value the brand names of the products they consume because the things they possess are deemed to reflect their self-identity. They are willing to spend money on clothing, on appearance-related products, which will enhance their self-concept and make them feel, look, and smell good. They set the fashion trend, monitor the latest style and serve as opinion leaders to guide people around them to consume. They are innovative, self-confident and upbeat people, who are the allegiant participators in the consumer culture. All these characteristics deserve more attention from scholars in their future research on fashion culture and consumption in the image-constructed society.

REFERENCES

Bloch, P.H. & Richins, M.L.(1992). You look "Marvelous": The pursuit of beauty and the marketing concept. *Psychology and Marketing, 9*:3-15.

Cash, T.F., & Cash, D.W.(1982). Women's use of cosmetics: Psychosocial correlates and consequences. *International Journal of Cosmetic Science, 4*:1-14.

Crask, M.R. & Reynold, F.D. (1978). An in-depth profile of the department store shopper. *Journal of Retailing, 54*:23-32.

Ewen, S. & Ewen,E. (1992). *Channels of Desire: Mass Images and the Shaping of American Consciousness.* Minneapolis: University of Minnesota Press.

Hirschman, E.C.(1979). Intratype competition among department stores. *Journal of Retailing, 55*:20-34.

Goldsmith, R.E. & Stith, M.T. (1990). The social values of fashion innovators. *Journal of Applied Business. 9*: 10-15.

Gould, S.J. & Stern, B.B. (1989). Gender Schema and Fashion Consciousness. *Psychology and Marketing. 6*:129-145.

Gurel, L.M. & Gurel, L. (1979). Clothing interest: Conceptualization and measurement. *Home Economics Research Journal, 7*:274-282.

James, W. (1890). *Principles of Psychology.* Vol.1. New York: Henry Holt.

Kwon, Y.H. (1997). Sex, sex-role, facial attractiveness, social self-esteem and interest in clothing. *Perceptual and Motor Skills, 84*:899-907.

Nunnally, J. C. (1978). *Psychometric Theory.* New York: McGraw-Hill Inc.

Solomon, M.R. (1985). *The Psychology of Fashion.* Lexington, MA: Health.

_____, (1992). *Consumer Behavior: Buying, Having and Being.* Needham Heights, MA: Allyn & Bacon.

Schrank, H.L.(1973). Correlates to fashion leadership: Implications for fashion process theory. *The Sociological Quarterly 14*:534-543.

Stanforth, N (1995). Fashion innovators, sensation seekers, and clothing individualists. *Perceptual and Motor Skills, 81*:1203-1210.

Summers, J.O. (1970). The identity of women's clothing fashion opinion leaders. *Journal of Marketing Research, 7*:178-185.

Tatzel, M. (1982). Skill and motivation in clothes shopping: Fashion-conscious, independent, anxious, and apathetic consumers. *Journal of Retailing, 58*:90-97.

Thompson, C.J & Hirschman, E.C. (1995). Understanding the socialized body: A poststructrualist analysis of consumers' self-conceptions, body image and self-care practices. *Journal of Consumer Research, 22*:139-153.

Netemeyer, R.G., Burton, S. & Litchtenstein, D.R. (1995). Trait Aspects of Vanity: Measurement and Relevance to Consumer Behavior. *Journal of Consumer Research, 21*: 612-626.

An Experimental Investigation of the Processes Underlying the Interpretation of Nonverbal Signs and Metaphors in Advertising

Eric DeRosia, University of Michigan

ABSTRACT

This paper investigates nonverbal symbolic signs and metaphors in advertisements and the processes which consumers use to interpret such advertisement elements. As a result of interpretation, consumers infer complex meanings such as brand personality beliefs. Further, motivation to devote cognitive resources to the interpretation process plays a role. Under low motivation, consumers exert insufficient cognitive effort to interpret such advertising elements. Under moderate motivation, such elements lead to brand personality beliefs. Under high motivation, consumers interpret such elements but reject the implied brand personality beliefs as nonsensical. Advertising stimuli with such elements are proposed and tested, and the results of a experiment which tests the hypotheses are reported.

SPECIAL SESSION SUMMARY

What is Your Goal? The Impact of Goals on Counterfactual Thinking, Attitude Formation, and Predictions of the Future

Jennifer L. Aaker, Stanford University
Angela Lee, Northwestern University

Consumer researchers have long recognized that consumer preferences and choices are often influenced by the goals that a consumer holds. Considerable research, with its theoretical underpinnings in categorization theory (Barsalou 1986; Rosch, Simpson and Miller 1976), has focused on examining the types of attributes possessed by a target product that best fulfill one's consumption goal (e.g., Ratneshwar, Pechmann and Shocker 1996), what types of benefits underlie those attributes (e.g., Huffman and Houston 1993), and what alternative consumption products one could buy instead of the target product (e.g., Johnson 1989). In this stream of research, the goal is often defined explicitly and is functional in nature, such as "buying a car" or "shopping for a gift".

A distinct stream of research has arisen recently that investigates how consumer decision making involving functional goals may be affected by strategies and behaviors that are motivated by higher level goals. For instance, when trying to decide what brand of fruit juice to purchase (i.e., functional goal), consumers may be more attracted to advertising appeals that focus on positive outcomes such as energy creation (i.e., promotion goal). Alternatively, they may be more persuaded by appeals that focus on negative outcomes like unclogging arteries (i.e., prevention goal). These higher level goals often influence how consumers approach functional goals. Unlike functional goals that may be more transient and disappear once they are satisfied, these higher level goals tend to be chronically accessible, either out of habit (e.g., smoking) or due to dispositional or cultural inclination.

The objective of this session is to introduce the notion of higher level goals and demonstrate how they may influence the consumer's cognitive processes, attitudes and predictions of future behavior in the pursuit of lower level functional goals. All three papers focus on how higher level goals affect the consumer's approach toward fulfilling certain functional goals. Each paper, however, examines a different aspect of how cognitive and affective responses related to the past (counterfactual thinking; Pennington), present (attitude formation; Aaker and Lee) and future (choice related to future consumption; Brendl and Markman) consumption goals are influenced by the higher level goals.

In the first paper, Pennington discusses how higher level goals influence individuals' cognitive responses to the nonfulfillment of functional goals. Individuals often express regrets and generate counterfactual thoughts (i.e., thoughts about what might have been) when they experience a product failure. In four studies, Pennington identifies the subtypes of counterfactual thoughts that result from the nonfulfillment of a functional goal. When a promotion (i.e., gain focused) goal is thwarted, individuals tend to generate counterfactual alternatives that specify the hypothetical inclusion of some previously omitted action (e.g., "Had I bought Brand X instead..."). When a prevention (i.e., loss focused) goal is not met, however, individuals are more likely to generate counterfactuals that remove, or subtract, a past action or event (e.g., "Had I not purchased Model Y..."). These findings suggest that when consumers are disappointed with products or services, those with a prevention focus are likely to react to failure by generating subtractive counterfactual thoughts. In contrast, consumers with a promotion focus are likely to react to failure by generating additive counterfactual thoughts that involve potential alternative actions.

In the second paper, Aaker and Lee discuss how these higher level goals influence individuals' attitudes, and how this process is influenced by one's view of the self. They draw on prior research showing that individuals with an accessible independent self view are likely to have promotion goals that focus on approaching positive outcomes, whereas individuals with an accessible interdependent self view are likely to have prevention goals that focus on avoiding negative outcomes. The authors posit that the activation of a particular goal and the subsequent exposure to persuasion information that is compatible with that goal should lead to more favorable attitudes. In four studies, they manipulate goal compatibility by exposing participants with a promotion versus prevention goal to product information that focuses on positive consequences (e.g., creating energy) versus negative consequences (e.g., preventing heart disease). Their results show that under conditions of goal compatibility versus incompatibility, a) information is better recalled, b) strong vs. weak arguments are better discerned, and c) attitudes towards websites, advertisements and brands are more favorable.

In the third paper, Brendl and Markman present results showing that consumer's choice decisions pertaining to a functional goal (e.g., purchase of a lottery ticket) that benefits future consumption are based on some higher level promotion goals that are currently active (e.g., desire to smoke). The authors suggest that when people are faced with options about consumption preferences in the future, their higher level goal that is currently active often presides over their choice of how to best fulfill the functional consumption goal. People assume that their future goals will be similar to, if not the same as, their current goals. For example, smokers bought more lottery tickets that could win cigarettes instead of cash five minutes before smoking a cigarette, even though they were fully aware that the prize drawing would occur two weeks later. In contrast, 5 minutes after smoking a cigarette, a second group of habitual smokers exhibited the reverse pattern of choices, purchasing more tickets for a lottery to win cash than for a lottery to win cigarettes. These findings demonstrate how consumer choice decisions are dependent upon the absence or presence of a higher level goal (promotion or prevention-based).

The three papers integrate research from multiple disciplines (marketing, psychology and organizational behavior), and present a coherent picture of how individuals' cognitive processes, attitudes, and predictions of future behavior are affected by higher level goals that underlie currently activated functional goals. Further, together the papers aim to broaden our current understanding of goals in two ways. First, from a conceptual perspective, we distinguish between lower level goals that tend to be more functional in nature and higher level goals that guide attitude and behaviors relating to the functional goals. Our particular focus is on identifying these higher level goals by addressing the following questions: What are the antecedents to these goals? When and how do they guide thoughts, attitudes and behavior? Second, from a substantive perspective, we hope to demonstrate how examining the individual's underlying motivational states may help to explain his/her counterfactual thoughts, attitudes and behavior relating to the (non)fulfillment of past, present and future consumption.

Have-not's in a World of Haves: Disenfranchised Nations and Their Consumers in an Increasingly Affluent and Global World

Clifford J. Shultz, II, Arizona State University

The study of consumer behavior has been largely a study of the world of "haves"; that is, a study of consumers who live in socioeconomic conditions above the poverty line and that afford considerable consumer choice in buying and consumption behavior. In short, the discipline overwhelmingly tends to study consumers who have many choices vis-à-vis consumer products and consumption experiences and have disposable income to enable those choices. Notable exceptions are found in the literature (e.g., Belk 1988; Hill and Stamey 1990; Shultz, Belk and Ger 1994). However, given that generally accepted measures of poverty or consumer well being, as reported by the likes of United Nations Development Programs and the World Health Organization, would require us to place approximately 3 *billion* of the world's population into the category of "have-nots," the participants of this special session feel it is important to share results from some of their longitudinal work on an eclectic sample of these consumers. The participants thus hope to raise consumer-researcher consciousness and ultimately to mobilize further research to enhance consumer well being among the have-nots, who tend to reside in nations relatively unfamiliar to most ACR attendees.

Toward that end this special session assembled scholars with extensive scholarly experience in three particular countries of focus: Cambodia, Kazakstan, and Zimbabwe. Though these countries evince complex and diverse systemic forces that affect consumers, two interactive factors are evident in each of them: (1) the pervasiveness of have-nots and (2) the extent to which endemic forces will make difficult various intervention policies designed to transform the particular country into an environment in which haves will emerge and flourish. Consider, for example, that Cambodians still reel from one of the most horrific social experiments in the history of humanity, in which the intelligentsia was eradicated and the infrastructure decimated; Kazaks struggle to find their way in the wake of 70 years of Soviet domination and the current and startling "bombardment" of globalization; a new elite in Zimbabwe strives to carve a niche among the remnants of British colonialism. Furthermore, each country maintains socio-political systems or influential factions that do not fully embrace the consumer society and Western conceptions of social, spiritual and material well-being, which raises questions about the desirability of joining the world of haves, as Americans might typically envision that world.

Each participant was asked to frame and to analyze his/her country and consumers of discussion, with respect to some of the most salient systemic forces in that country. They include natural forces, economic forces, political forces, socio-cultural forces and the various national administrative systems implemented to affect consumer behavior and well being (cf. Shultz and Pecotich 1997). This more macro approach to consumption and consumer behavior is rather atypical of the consumer behavior literature, but each participant believes–and their experience indicates–that such a systemic analysis is imperative if intervention programs are to be implemented that can effect changes to enhance consumer well-being.

As a final preamble, an impetus for this special session was the participants' belief that globalization will force all of us to understand and to interact more closely with these disenfranchised nations and consumers. Consider that each of these countries is "wired" to the Internet; each has access to satellite TV-transmissions and each is moving, however slowly in some cases, toward the consumer society. Precisely what the end game of those societies can or will look like, can be and should be affected by consumer researchers. Moreover, a disproportionately large amount of multilateral aid to Cambodia is funded by the US (and thus is funded by tax-paying American consumers); Kazakstan, a newly independent state is a population of consumers who are virtually *tabula rasa* and are just now forming Western product category and brand hierarchies and are trying to make sense of their evolving consumer society; Zimbabwe has an emerging elite that tends to replicate consumption patterns and tendencies seen among haves. Globalization, coupled with the finite resources of our planet, will require increased interaction with have-nots. Indeed, one can plausibly argue that the sustainability of our status as haves may be driven by our co-dependence on the world of have-nots and our humanity to bring them under the umbrella of well-being enjoyed by the world of haves. As consumer research scholars, therefore, we would be remiss if we failed to understand them and the systems that shape them.

Cliff Shultz served as Chair, Don Rahtz as discussion leader. What follows are synopses of the presentations.

"Local and Global Models of Consumption and Their Appeal to Consumers in Zimbabwe"
Russell W. Belk, University of Utah

This video-aided presentation investigated the following tendencies, based on a year's fieldwork in Zimbabwe during 1998-99. Maslow's need hierarchy suggests that consumers will adequately satisfy "lower order" needs for food, clothing, and shelter before turning to goods that serve "higher order" needs for prestige, entertainment, and enlightenment. Nevertheless, consumers in many Third World nations often "leapfrog" to purchase televisions, stereos, Nike athletic shoes, Coca-Cola, and other seeming luxuries while sacrificing such presumed necessities as nutrition and health care. Ostensibly, one of the reasons for such consumption tendencies is the allure of world brands in the increasingly visible global community. Depth interviews with both rich and poor Zimbabweans as well as television and magazine advertisements were analyzed and used to present a portrait of the appeal of both local and global consumption patterns in Zimbabwe. Are these consumers more influenced by the consumption of local Zimbabweans (white or black) or by the imagined consumption of distant others in foreign countries? The answer is that both referents are important and that it is sometimes difficult to untangle these influences since local consumption models are themselves influenced by images of global consumption.

The strongest foreign influences in Zimbabwe, for several reasons and partly depending on the type of consumer good, are Great Britain, the United States, and South Africa. Zimbabwean consumer desires must be contextualized within the current Zimbabwean political environment, which regularly attacks Western nations and world institutions such as the IMF and world bank for creating the difficult economic conditions presently facing Zimbabwe. Global referents apparently can be loved on some grounds at the same time that they are hated on others. Furthermore, global brands often specifically attempt to localize their image. At the same time, severe economic problems are rapidly widening the already huge gaps between haves and have-nots within Zimbabwe and between Zimbabwe and the more affluent world. All of this makes a simple distinction between global and local consumer goods problematic. The presentation used interviews against a backdrop of advertisements in order to detail the nature of the consumption dilemma of being poor in a visibly affluent world.

"Beer versus Vodka: Becoming Citizens and Consumers in Kazakstan"
Güliz Ger, Bilkent University

In this presentation, Güliz Ger discussed the ambivalence of experienced modernity—the past versus the present, Islam, the availability of goods versus their high prices and/or bad quality, the newfound national independence and freedom versus uncertainties, poverty, and unemployment–in Kazakstan. Kazakstan is an oil, gas, and mineral-rich Central Asian country, which attracts the attention of many MNCs. Similarly to other Central Asian republics, it experienced an externally imposed communism for over 70 years. This period entailed Soviet modernization along with efforts to break Central Asians' links to their own, allegedly inferior, past. The widespread and good Soviet education and health systems bolstered Sovietization of structures and ways of life. In this fastest marketizing country in the region, renamed Soviet structures still prevail and cultural and psychological ties to Russia, seen to be the closest ally and the main reference, remain strong.

Yet modernity is now assembled to be anything that is non Soviet. National pride is linked to the recent break with the Soviets. Breaking away from a Soviet identity, constructions of Islam, local/ national culture, and Western things/ways are resources people draw from to build their new social selves. In that pursuit, photos and paraphernalia of Amaco baseball teams come to be displayed in the National Museum in Almaty. However, many consumers are pessimistic that capitalism will make life better and long for the certainty of communist times when "there was no unemployment." Human Development Index dropped since 1992 and, in 1997, only 20% of Kazakstani citizens received wages on time.

Consumers, with an immense lack of trust and a sense of being lost, have taken up advertising as a reading interest in its own right. People buy magazines and newspapers for the adverts in this country where there were no advertisements before 1994. Consumers are drawn to novel, high-tech and high quality goods, with the newest features, yet most can only afford the "poor and cheap" Chinese products or fakes of prestigious brands.

Consumers integrate foreign products into their lives by mixing the local and global, the old and the new. For example, a "typically Kazak" dinner included a bazaar-bought Korean salad accompanying home-made dishes, a Western cake served along with a traditional desert, and Coke, vodka, champagne (and/or wine and/or cognac), beer, homemade cherry juice, and tea. The buffet, across from the dining table covered with these dishes and drinks, displayed a decorative copper plate with carved Arabic calligraphy from Kuran, a collection of French perfume bottles, and plastic Smurf characters in front of Russian literature books. Analysis and discussion will focus on creolized consumption entities such as respectability, investment/security, gift-giving/social ties, and aesthetics.

The creolization/hybridization observed in the ever-more-important consumption in Kazakstan makes lucid the in-between and localized nature of consumer culture. It also indicates the confluence of consumption and social identity. Whether globalization and the increased inter-penetration between the affluent and less-affluent societies will enhance consumer well-being in countries like Kazakstan or not depends on how accessible the economic

and cultural resources are in the rural-urban, ethnic, gender, age, and other social classifications.

"From Killing Fields to Consumer Society: a Consumer Gap-Analysis in Cambodia"
Clifford J. Shultz, II, Arizona State University

The purpose of this presentation was to introduce session-attendees to the evolving conditions in which Cambodian consumers live, make purchase choices and ultimately consume, and to share policy recommendations to assist Cambodia's hopeful transition to the world of haves. It was noted that, in the collective wake of the killing fields, the UNTAC-brokered elections, and the volatile political period currently being administered by Hun Sen and Prince Ranariddh, the primary focus of scholarly analysis continues to be policy-oriented, with a growing emphasis on economic conditions and trends. Only now are we beginning to have a glimpse of the consumption environment in Cambodia (see Shultz and Tith 1998). Thus, findings from over 5 years of the author's active fieldwork in Cambodia were shared, with a principal focus on evolving consumption trends in Phnom Penh and Siem Reap.

The presentation focused on the gap between idealized outcomes planned by various change-agents—such as private and public sector programs, multilateral aid programs and direct foreign investment–and the tangible outcomes experienced by the majority of Cambodian citizens. Though it was not the purpose of this presentation to discuss the killing fields per se, attendees were reminded that after the Khmer Rouge marched into Phnom Penh on April 17, 1975, a chain of crimes-against-humanity was perpetrated on the Cambodian people that resulted in the death or departure of the intelligentsia, the bourgeoisie, and any detractor to Pol Pot's vision of an agrarian utopia. Some estimates indicate more than 2 million people (more than one third of the population) were killed or fled the country.

To some extent Cambodia and its people have scratched and clawed their way back from the brink of annihilation. Direct foreign investment and multilateral aid, for example, are evident in the forms of new products, some manufacturing start-ups, trade and export development, infrastructure, new people and new ideas. Many consumer goods and information technologies familiar to Western consumers are available in urban centers. Thanks to unique archaeological resources, the Angkor temples and other touristic destinations, for example, the tourism sector continues to grow. There is cause for very cautious optimism in Cambodia. Nevertheless, the net socioeconomic result of Pol Pot's vision was a virtual scorched-earth consumption environment of subsistence living that still permeates every aspect of daily life for Cambodian consumers. A decimated infrastructure, illiteracy, massive public health challenges, the prevalence of unexploded ordnance, prostitution, repression and corruption all impede Cambodians' struggle to join the world of haves.

The presentation concluded with integrative consumer-policy recommendations intended not only to abet Cambodian transition and Cambodia's consumers, but also to serve as a template for other war-ravaged transition economies.

REFERENCES

Belk, R. (1988), Third World Consumer Culture," in *Marketing and Development: Toward Broader Dimensions*, E. Kumcu and A.F. Firat, eds. Greenwich, CT: JAI Press.

Hill, R. and M. Stamey (1990), "The Homeless in America: An Examination of Possessions and Consumption Behaviors," *Journal of Consumer Research*, 17 (December), 303-321.

Shultz, C., R. Belk and G. Ger (1994), *Research in Consumer Behavior: Consumption in Marketizing Economies*, Greenwich, CT: JAI Press.

Shultz, C. and A. Pecotich (1997), "Marketing and Development in the Transition Economies of Southeast Asia: Policy Explication, Assessment and Implications," *Journal of Public Policy & Marketing*, 16 (1), 55-68.

Shultz, C. and Naranhkiri Tith (1998), "Cambodia: Transition and the Consequences for Future Consumption and Marketing," in *Marketing and Consumer Behavior in East and Southeast Asia*, A. Pecotich and C. Shultz, eds. Sydney: McGraw Hill.

Differences in Normative and Informational Social Influence

Kenneth R. Lord, Mercer University
Myung-Soo Lee, City University of New York
Peggy Choong, Niagara University

ABSTRACT

In an investigation of the distinctive characteristics of normative and informational social influence, a survey probed purchase decision, individual difference, and consumer-referent relationship characteristics associated with recent purchase episodes involving advice from others. Levels of involvement and complexity were shown to be greater in informational influence situations than in normative. Conspicuousness, contact and advice solicitation frequency, and consumer-referent homophily with respect to the value attached to warm relationships were greater when normative influence was involved.

INTRODUCTION

Despite a recognition that social influence in the marketplace may be either normative (motivated by social norms/rewards) or informational (based on perceived referent expertise), little attention has been paid to differences between the two. The intent of this research effort is to explain and empirically demonstrate the distinctive characteristics of normative and informational social influence with respect to decision, individual difference, and consumer-referent relationship variables.

LITERATURE REVIEW

"One of the most pervasive determinants of an individual's behavior is the influence of those around him," observed Burnkrant and Cousineau (1975) in their pioneering work on social influence in consumer behavior (p. 206). "It seems necessary," they suggest, "if we are to gain insight into the determinants of buyer product evaluation, to come to grips with the role or roles played by the evaluation of relevant others in affecting the individual's product evaluation."

Following early conceptual work by Deutsch and Gerard (1955) and Kelman (1961), researchers in this area have identified three forms of social influence — informational, normative and value expressive. Informational influence refers to the provision of credible evidence of reality (Burnkrant and Cousineau 1975). It is important when consumers feel the need to make informed choices. They perceive the opinions or usage of products by those who are seen as credible as proof of a product's quality or characteristics. Normative social influence relates to conformity with the expectations of other persons or groups to achieve rewards or avoid punishment (Homans 1961). The greatest normative influence is usually exerted within primary reference groups such as the immediate family (Cooley 1962). Recognizing the prevalence of normative social influence in many decision situations, Fishbein and Ajzen (1975) incorporated "subjective norm" into their "Theory of Reasoned Action," developing and validating a measurement approach for this normative construct as an integral component of their behavioral intention model. Value-expressive influence is characterized by a need for psychological association with a group through the acceptance of its norms, values and behavior. The individual likes or admires the reference group and attempts to mimic it.

Although normative and value-expressive influence are conceptually different, they have been found to be quite similar and have proven difficult to distinguish empirically (Burnkrant and Cousineau 1975; Bearden, Netemeyer and Teel 1989). This is perhaps because they are likely to coexist in the same sources; e.g., family members and friends both establish a value system (value expressive) and mediate rewards/punishments for compliance/noncompliance with its norms and values (normative). Like the studies cited above, and more recently Mascarenhas and Higby (1993), the present research treats social influence dichotomously, comparing informational with a combined normative/value-expressive construct.

The prior two decades have seen sporadic research efforts aimed at further clarifying the nature of social influence in a consumer decision context. Some have explored referent or product effects on social influence without regard to influence type (informational or normative). Brown and Reingen (1987) demonstrated that strong primary ties (e.g., close friends) are more likely than weak secondary ties (e.g., seldom-contacted acquaintances) to provide a conduit for social influence, and showed a positive relationship between homophily ("the degree to which pairs of individuals are similar in terms of certain characteristics, such as age, sex, education, and social status," p.354) and social tie activation. In a modified replication of Bearden and Etzel's (1982) study of reference-group influence, Childers and Rao (1992) observed that "the degree to which the product is a *luxury* appears to be the driving force behind the manifestation of peer influence" (p. 205), while intergenerational familial influence (in the United States) was stronger for necessities than for luxuries; their work did not distinguish between informational and normative influence.

A few studies have sought to clarify normative influence mechanisms and outcomes. Brinberg and Plimpton (1986) found a relationship between consumption and conspicuousness and value-expressive influence. Bearden and Rose (1990) provided evidence that "attention to social comparison information" (ATSCI) — a measure of a general tendency to conform (Lennox and Wolfe 1984) — moderates the influence of normative consequences on behavioral intention. Testing a model of the role of social context in early adoption behavior, Fisher and Price (1992) showed that "perceived visibility of consumption" (conspicuousness) affects consumer predictions of social approval from referents.

The informational-normative distinction has been an explicit focus of a few studies in the last decade. LaTour and Manrai (1989) hypothesized and showed support for a synergistic interaction between normative and informational social influence attempts, such that combined normative-informational strategy yielded results superior to those observed for either approach employed in isolation. Bearden, Netemeyer and Teel (1989) developed and validated a scale for measuring consumer susceptibility to informational and normative interpersonal influence; they found that Lennox and Wolfe's (1984) ATSCI scale and the "motivation to comply" construct (Ajzen and Fishbein 1980) exhibited correlations with susceptibility to normative influence which were relatively strong and significantly greater than correlation coefficients associated with informational influence. More recently, Mascarenhas and Higby (1993) found that informational influence exceeded normative in the area of teen apparel shopping, although teen boys were more susceptible to normative influence than were girls; further, family size was positively related to the level of social influence, while the amount of gift money received and age were negatively related.

While extant literature establishes the existence and some characteristics of normative and informational social influence, more research is needed. From a strategic perspective, the effective management of social influence requires an understanding of the type of social influence likely to prevail under different purchase decisions or situational conditions and the identification of individuals best positioned to exert such an influence. Research is thus needed to establish the distinctive antecedents of the two types of social influence and differences between them with respect to the nature of the relationship between influence wielders and recipients.

HYPOTHESES

The motivational differences that define the distinction between normative and informational social influence provide an appropriate starting point for an inquiry into their antecedents and relationship characteristics. Fundamental to the distinct nature of the two influence types is the issue of whether the consumer's overriding concern is with the achievement of desired product/service-relevant (informational) or relationship (normative) outcomes. Drawing upon those motivations and relevant prior research, hypotheses are proposed that employ type of influence as the independent variable, examining differences in several decision-characteristic, individual-difference and consumer/referent-relationship variables. (While the impracticality of a longitudinal design precluded measurement of the constructs before the social-influence incidents they affected, these variables are assumed to be sufficiently stable to allow an inference that hypothesis-consistent results indicate their existence antecedent to that influence.)

Mascarenhas and Higby (1993) suggest that "susceptibility to interpersonal influences could be proportional to one's involvement with the products/services that one plans to purchase" (p. 57). Involvement (or degree of personal relevance) has been shown to be positively related to external search and cognitive processing of decision-relevant stimuli, apparently motivated by an attempt to increase the effectiveness of alternative evaluation (cf. Beatty and Smith 1987; Celsi and Olson 1988). Such an objective is seemingly more consistent with informational social influence than with a normative focus on social rewards or conformity. Accordingly, it is hypothesized that:

H1: Purchase situations involving informational social influence will be characterized by higher levels of involvement in the product or service decision than those involving normative influence.

Effects similar to those predicted for involvement have been ascribed to product or decision complexity; e.g., the more evaluative criteria employed in alternative evaluation the more time spent in search (cf. Assael 1987). The decision uncertainty occasioned by complexity would potentially activate a motivation to seek input from those perceived as possessing expertise relevant to the salient attributes of the desired product or service. Complexity, like involvement, is thus expected to relate positively to informational, but not to normative, social influence.

H2: Purchase situations involving informational social influence will be characterized by higher levels of decision complexity than those involving normative influence.

A popular conceptualization of reference group influence views that form of social influence as being most pervasive for "public" as opposed to "private" goods (Bearden and Etzel 1982), but does not differentiate between informational and normative influence. What appears in large measure to discriminate between public and private goods is their level of conspicuousness, a factor which would appear to be more relevant to the motives identified earlier as being associated with normative than with informational influence. While the relevance of conspicuousness to normative considerations has already been demonstrated (Brinberg and Plimpton 1986, Fisher and Price 1992), an objective of this study is to establish whether it differs between informational and normative influence situations. In most purchase categories, the extent to which the purchase and/or usage of a product or service is seen by others does not relate directly to the functional benefits it delivers to the user, but may elicit judgments on the part of social observers. Conspicuousness, therefore, is expected to be associated more with normative than with informational social influence.

H3: Purchase situations involving normative social influence will be characterized by higher levels of product or service conspicuousness than those involving informational influence.

As noted earlier, Bearden and Rose (1990) established the validity of the Lennox and Wolfe (1984) Attention to Social Comparison Information (ATSCI) scale, designed to capture "consumers' predisposition to act on the social cues available at the time a purchase or consumption decision is being made" (p. 461). These researchers did not concern themselves explicitly with the distinction between normative and informational social influence. However, the very nature of the scale items (concerned with behavior which "makes me fit in" or may elicit "disapproval") and the assumption that sensitivity to social comparison information is "motivated by such factors as a fear of negative social evaluation" point to normative as the type of social influence that would be driven primarily by this individual-difference factor. This leads to the following prediction:

H4: Consumers soliciting referent advice for normative reasons will be characterized by higher levels of attention to social comparison information than those reporting informational influence.

With respect to the question of the types of individuals whose advice is sought in normative and informational influence conditions, the issue of homophily becomes relevant. A homophilous tie is one in which the consumer and the referent possess shared characteristics with respect to values, lifestyles, demographics, etc. Alternatively, a heterophilous tie is one in which the two individuals manifest substantial differences on such relevant dimensions. The work of Brown and Reingen (1987), cited earlier, established that "of an individual's potential personal sources of information, the more homophilous the tie, the more likely it is activated for the flow of referral" (p.354), but did not address the issue of potential differences between normative and informational influence. Social networks are known to be populated primarily by individuals characterized by homophilous ties, and it is within those networks that social norms and their corresponding rewards or punishments are manifest. Alternatively, there is no reason to expect any consistent or systematic social/demographic similarity among consumers and those referents sought out because of their superior knowledge, experience or expertise. In-

TABLE 1
Summary of Hypotheses

	Social Influence Type	
	Normative	Informational
Antecedents	Conspicuousness Attention to Social Comparison Information	Involvement Complexity
Consumer-Referent Relationship	Homophilous Frequent Contact/ Influence	Heterophilous Infrequent Contact/ Influence

deed, a consumer's need to access purchase-relevant expertise that s/he does not personally possess would potentially lead to the solicitation of information and advice from persons not only different from the consumer her/himself, but different from referents contacted for other purchases (e.g., legal and landscaping expertise may reside in substantially different individuals). This reasoning leads to the following prediction:

H5: Homophilous ties are more characteristic of normative social influence, with heterophilous ties more prevalent in informational social influence situations.

In addition to the role of similarity between consumer and referent, the frequency of contact has been shown to relate to social influence. Brown and Reingen (1987) found that "strong ties," defined in part as those characterized by high contact frequency, are more likely than weak ties to serve as a conduit for the transfer of purchase-relevant information. Contrary to their expectations, however, they also discovered that weak ties were more likely to be actively sought out explicitly for such information. The normative-informational distinction may account for these contrasting findings. Frequent contact (strong tie) allows extensive opportunity for information transfer via casual conversation. However, whether the active solicitation of such information takes place among those with whom a consumer has frequent or infrequent contact may depend upon whether the objectives of such solicitation are normative or informational. A consumer seeking normative rewards will likely seek out the mediators of such rewards, commonly members of peer, reference, or other associational groups with whom s/he has regular contact. If the objective is to obtain the information most pertinent to the functional or performance aspects of a purchase decision, there is no reason to expect a systematic bias towards frequently contacted or strong-tie referents. The latter would seem to be the situation Brown and Reingen's respondents faced as they decided upon a piano teacher. Consistent with the expected difference in the frequency of prior contact between normative and informational referents, one might expect influencers accessed for normative purposes to play a referent role in more purchase situations than informational sources. These expectations lead to the following hypothesis:

H6: Relative to referents solicited for informational purposes, normative referents will be characterized by:
a. Greater frequency of contact;
b. Greater regularity of providing purchase-relevant advice.

The six hypotheses are summarized in Table 1.

METHOD

A survey approach was employed to investigate these issues. Forty students in an evening MBA program were asked to provide information about two recent purchase decisions involving social influence. The resulting data set contained 74 incidents of social influence (a few respondents reported only one purchase situation).

Respondents completed the ATSCI scale (Cronbach a reliability coefficient .90). Each respondent was then asked to identify two purchase decisions, occurring within the most recent three months, in which information or advice was sought from another person or persons. Respondents completed the following hypothesis-relevant measures separately for each of the two decisions: why the particular individual was approached for advice or information (open ended), frequency of contact with the referent prior to the decision (six-point scale ranging from once or twice a year to daily), the number of occasions on which the respondent had sought advice or information from the referent (six-point scale ranging from once to more than seven times), product/service conspicuousness (six-point scale: observed by the general public, observed by many people, observed by several people, observed by several people you know, observed by one or a few people you know, unobserved by others), decision complexity (number of attributes considered in making the decision, measured on a six-point scale from one to more than five), involvement in the decision (20-item Personal Involvement Inventory, Zaichkowsky 1985, $\alpha = .91$; the mean of the twenty items serves as the decision involvement index for subsequent analysis). A battery of questions addressing the characteristics of the referent followed, including gender, age, education, marital status, ethnic background, income, occupation, political and religious affiliation, and value priorities (using the University of Michigan Survey Research Center's nine-item List of Values scale; Kahle, Beatty and Homer 1986). Having completed the latter battery of questions for each referent, the respondent completed the same psychographic and demographic measures relative to himself or herself.

RESULTS

For purposes of hypothesis testing, the type of influence exerted served as a blocking variable (to capture normative and informational social influence), with means for the variables addressed by the hypotheses compared across groups. In coding the questions addressing respondent's reasons for consulting a particular referent, it became obvious that multiple decisions included a combination of normative and informational objectives on the part of respondents. Hence the type of influence was treated as a three-level variable (normative, informational, both), based on the coding of two independent judges. The judges agreed in 88

TABLE 2
Results

| | | Influence Category | | |
		Normative	Informational	Both
Decision Characteristics	Involvement (H1)**	5.17[a] (.79)	5.76[b] (.68)	5.65[b] (.76)
	Complexity (H2)*	1.50[a] (.90)	2.36[b] (1.21)	2.50[b] (1.50)
	Conspicuousness (H3)*	3.67[a] (2.31)	2.13[b] (1.69)	3.75[a] (1.65)
Individual Difference Characteristics	ATSCI (H4)	2.35[a] (.60)	2.79[a] (.81)	2.78[a] (.70)
Consumer-Referent Relationship	Shared Importance of "Warm Relationships" (H5)*	0.83[ab] (.72)	1.10[a] (1.03)	0.50[b] (.61)
	Frequency of Contact (H6a)**	4.08[a] (1.08)	3.14[b] (1.52)	3.80[a] (1.24)
	Prior Advice (H6b)*	4.33[a] (1.07)	3.29[b] (1.80)	4.30[a] (1.08)

Note: The top cell values represent the mean; values in parentheses are standard deviations. For a given variable (row), contrast results reflect significant differences (p < .05) between those social influence categories that do not share a common superscript.
* Superscripted differences significant at p< .05
** Normative-informational difference significant at p < .05; other difference(s) at p < .10

percent of the cases, and differences were resolved by discussion. Coded in this fashion, the data contained 12 instances of normative social influence, 42 of informational, and 20 characterized by both influence types.

The first hypothesis related to consumers' involvement in the product or service involved in the decision. As predicted, involvement differed significantly between the three categories ($F_{2,71} = 3.16$, p < .05, $\eta^2 = .08$), with the mean involvement level higher in informational social influence contexts (5.76) than in normative (5.17). Situations involving both normative and informational social influence were characterized by a mean involvement level comparable to that of the informational group and significantly higher than the normative (5.65). The means, standard deviations and contrast results associated with this and the other hypothesis tests are reported in Table 2.

Support for hypothesis 2 is marginally significant ($F_{2,71} = 270$, p < .10, $\eta^2 = .07$). Product complexity in informational social influence scenarios (and those involving both informational and normative) exceeded that observed in decisions involving exclusively normative influence (2.36, 2.50 and 1.50, respectively).

The conspicuousness hypothesis (3) obtained support ($F_{2,71} = 6.31$, p < .01, $\eta^2 = .15$). Higher levels of that construct were associated with normative and combined influence situations (3.67 and 3.75, respectively) than with purchases involving only informational influence (2.13).

The ATSCI scale index (mean of the scale's thirteen items) failed to yield the hypothesized significant differences between groups ($F_{2,71} = 1.58$, p > .10, $\eta^2 = .21$). Thus hypothesis 4 finds no support in the data.

With respect to the hypothesis that consumer-referent relationships are characterized by homophily in normative influence situations and heterophily in informational (H5), little support emerged. Analyses of reported differences between the two parties with respect to the demographic and psychographic variables

identified in the earlier description of the measurement instrument yielded only one significant difference in means or proportions between social influence categories ($F_{2,71} = 3.06$, p < .05, $\eta^2 = .08$). One item in the LOV scale, the perceived importance of "warm relationships with others," was characterized by the highest level of respondent-referent dissimilarity when social influence was informational (mean difference of 1.10), with the difference in the normative category only directionally lower (.83) and that in the combined category significantly lower (.50). There is thus little evidence in this data set of differences in homophily/heterophily between normative and social influence.

Hypothesis 6 addressed the strength of the consumer-referent relationship from the perspective of frequency of contact (H56a) and incidence of prior advice solicitation (H6b). With respect to the former perspective, the test of differences between category means ($F_{2,71} = 2.89$, p < .10, $\eta^2 = .08$) showed lower respondent-referent contact frequency in informational (3.14) than in normative or combined situations (4.08 and 3.80, respectively). A comparable pattern emerged, but at a higher level of significance, when prior advice solicitation served as the dependent variable (F = 4.06, p < .05, $\eta^2 = .10$); again normative and combined (4.33 and 4.30, respectively) exceeded informational (3.29). The pattern of results emerging from these tests is thus consistent with H6.

DISCUSSION

The contribution of this research lies not in the demonstration that the variables measured and analyzed herein relate to social influence, but in isolating the type of social influence activity most likely associated with them. The implication is that projecting the likelihood of social influence *per se* is inadequate for a marketer attempting to inject his or her product/service into this communication realm. Effective management of the social influence process requires an understanding of consumers' objectives in exposing themselves to such influences and the distinctive characteristics of such objectives as they relate to properties of the product/service decision and the relationship between consumer and referent.

The foregoing analysis suggests that higher levels of involvement and product/service complexity are associated with purchase decisions involving informational influence than with those involving normative, while the opposite is true of the conspicuousness of the purchase and/or consumption of the product or service. Thus the objectives for seeking information from social referents (to enhance one's decision-making ability through the acquisition of product-relevant information from a more knowledgeable source or to attain or reinforce normative rewards or avoid punishments) will be partially a function of the levels of involvement, complexity and conspicuousness. Marketers adopting such common strategies as the targeting of opinion leaders and promotions to reference groups may enhance the efficiency of such efforts by designing the communication elements of such a strategy around the informational or normative (or combined) motivations that prevail in their target markets. The observation that in many instances consumers jointly pursue both normative and informational objectives in exposing themselves to such sources is also a message that should not be lost on the marketer.

The examination of consumer-referent relationships extends and to some extent clarifies earlier research on strong and weak ties as they relate to social influence (Brown and Reingen 1987). Frequency of contact and prior advice solicitation were clearly greater in normative than in informational influence situations. This implies that normative rewards typically flow through "strong tie" relationships, while informational benefits may accrue from any known party possessing the required knowledge and expertise, regardless of tie strength.

Some limitations exist in the research reported herein. The inconclusiveness of the homophily test, and perhaps also of the ATSCI findings, may be partially attributable to the constrained demographic and psychographic variability that is inherent in the use of a student sample. To the extent that the evening MBA students participating in this study differed systematically in their choice of or opportunity for social contacts across a broader cross-section of society, results may be distorted. Since, however, the major effect of such a bias would presumably be to mask actual differences between social influence categories because of constrained variance, it seems unlikely that such a bias could provide a plausible alternative explanation for the significant results obtained in support of the other hypotheses. Another limitation of this survey is the dependence upon respondents' ability and willingness accurately to report their objectives in soliciting information. A self-report bias may exist in favor of informational social influence, given a possible reluctance to admit normative motivations (hopefully minimized by the assurance of anonymity), that would result in the miscategorization of some purchase episodes. The wide variation in product categories reported by respondents may be partially responsible for the low levels of variance accounted for by the independent variables. The fact that such implicit heterogeneity of variance did not attenuate the significance of the differences between the three social influence categories, however, speaks to the reality of the observed differences. Tests of homophily and heterophily are constrained by the lack of objective observation or reporting of referent characteristics. Since the variable for which significant respondent-referent differences emerged dealt with subjective value perceptions, a determination of whether differences in heterophily/homophily are real or only perceived must await further research.

While this effort represents an initial step in the examination of the characteristics of normative and social influence, much work

remains to be done in this under-researched area. As a starting point, it would be appropriate to replicate this study, using a larger and more representative sample. There is a need to test the unsupported homophily and ATSCI predictions under more powerful conditions before rejecting them out of hand, and to identify any other individual-difference characteristics that may play a role in normative and informational social influence. In addition to individual differences, situational factors (e.g., the presence or absence of referents at the time of decision making and their relationship to the decision maker) may dramatically affect the extent and type of social influence that occurs – a possibility that could be examined experimentally. To avoid self-report bias, to enhance internal validity and to reduce heterogeneity of variance, a follow-up study could productively adopt an experimental approach, in which subjects role play decisions, product categories are held constant across subjects, and relevant independent variables (e.g., homophily) are experimentally manipulated. Another issue warranting investigation is the extent to which the two types of social influence differ in the propensity for a particular referent's influence to be exerted for a single product or service, related products only, or across product categories (monomorphism versus polymorphism). Both marketers and consumers alike stand to benefit from a more complete understanding of social influence motivations, their facilitating conditions, and susceptibility to influence strategies.

REFERENCES

Ajzen, Icek and Martin Fishbein (1980), *Understanding Attitudes and Predicting Social Behavior*, Englewood Cliffs, NJ: Prentice-Hall.

Assael, Henry (1987), *Consumer Behavior and Marketing Action*, Boston: Kent.

Bauer, Raymond A. (1960), "Consumer Behavior as Risk Taking," in *Dynamic Marketing for a Changing World*, ed. Robert S. Hancock, Chicago, IL: American Marketing Association, 389-398.

Beatty, Sharon E. and Scott M. Smith (1987), "External Search Effort: An Investigation Across Several Product Categories," *Journal of Consumer Research*, 14 (June), 83-95.

Bearden, William O. and Michael J. Etzel (1982), "Reference Group Influence on Product and Brand Decisions," *Journal of Consumer Research*, 9 (September), 183-194.

_____, Richard G. Netemeyer, and Jesse E. Teel (1989), "Measurement of Consumer Susceptibility to Interpersonal Influence," *Journal of Consumer Research*, 15 (March), 473-482.

_____ and Randall L. Rose (1990), "Attention to Social Comparison Information: An Individual Difference Factor Affecting Consumer Conformity," *Journal of Consumer Research*, 16 (March), 461-471.

Brinberg, David and Linda Plimpton (1986), "Self-Monitoring and Product Conspicuousness on Reference Group Influence," in *Advances in Consumer Research*, Vol. 13, ed. Richard J. Lutz, Provo, UT: Association for Consumer Research, 297-300.

Brown, Jacqueline Johnson and Peter H. Reingen (1987), "Social Times and Word-of-Mouth Referral Behavior," *Journal of Consumer Research*, 14 (December), 350-362.

Burnkrant, Robert E. and Alain Cousineau (1975), "Informational and Normative Social Influence in Buyer Behavior," *Journal of Consumer Research*, 2 (December), 206-215.

Celsi, Richard L. and Jerry C. Olson (1988), "The Role of Involvement in Attention and Comprehension Processes," *Journal of Consumer Research*, 15 (September), 210-224.

Childers, Terry L. and Akshay R. Rao (1992), "The Influence of Familial and Peer-based Reference Groups on Consumer Decisions," *Journal of Consumer Research*, 19 (September), 198-211.

Cooley, Charles H. (1962), *Social Organization*, New York: Schoken.

Deutsch, M and H.B. Gerard (1955), "A Study of Normative and Informational Social Influence Upon Individual Judgment," *Journal of Abnormal and Social Psychology*, 51, 629-636.

Fishbein, Martin and Icek Ajzen (1975), *Belief, Attitude, Intention and Behavior: An Introduction to Theory and Research*, Reading, MA: Addison-Wesley.

Fisher, Robert J. and Linda L. Price (1992), "An Investigation into the Social Context of Early Adoption Behavior," *Journal of Consumer Research*, 19 (December), 477-486.

Homans, George (1961), *Social Behavior: Its Elemental Forms*, New York: Harcourt.

Kahle, Lynn R., Sharon E. Beatty, and Pamela Homer (1986), "Alternative Measurement Approaches to Consumer Values: The List of Values (LOV) and Values and Life Styles (VALS)," *Journal of Consumer Research*, 13 (December), 405-409.

Kelman, Herbert C. (1961), "Processes of Opinion Change," *Public Opinion Quarterly*, 25 (Spring), 57-78.

LaTour, Stephen A. and Ajay K. Manrai (1989), "Interactive Impact of Informational and Normative Influence on Donations," *Journal of Marketing Research*, 26 (August), 327-335.

Lennox, Richard D. and Raymond N. Wolfe (1984), "Revision of Self-Monitoring Scale," *Journal of Personality and Social Psychology*, 46 (6), 1349-1369.

Lutz, Richard J. and Patrick J. Reilly (1974), "An Exploration of the Effect of Perceived Social and Performance Risk on Consumer Information Acquisition," in *Advances in Consumer Research*, Vol. 1, eds. Scott Ward and Peter Wright, Chicago, IL:Association for Consumer Research, 393-405.

Mascarenhas, Oswald A.J. and Mary A. Higby (1993), "Peer, Parent, and Media Influences in Teen Apparel Shopping," *Journal of the Academy of Marketing Science*, 21 (Winter), 53-58.

Taylor, James W. (1974), "The Role of Risk in Consumer Behavior," *Journal of Marketing*, 38 (April), 54-60.

Zaichkowsky, Judith Lynne (1985), "Measuring the Involvement Construct," *Journal of Consumer Research*, 12 (December), 341-352.

Socialization in Context: The Differential Effects of Family, Peers, and Market Communications

Jyotsna Mukherji, Texas A&M International University
Dan L. Sherrell, University of Memphis

ABSTRACT

In this paper the socialization influence of family, peers, and market communications is discussed from the perspective of socialization theory. The results show that family influence and influence of television and direct mail is important in impacting young adults' financial attitudes. Social network influence from peers was found to be non-significant. This is an interesting finding. One explanation is that peers are important when it comes to items such as clothes, but in important issues such as savings and financial planning, the family is significant. Finally, this research shows that television and direct mail have an important influence on financial socialization.

Lighting The Torch: How Do Intergenerational Influences Develop?

Elizabeth S. Moore, University of Notre Dame
William L. Wilkie, University of Notre Dame
Julie A. Alder, Hershey Foods

ABSTRACT

Intergenerational inquiry focuses on the transmission of information, attitudes and skills between generations within families. In consumer research, primary emphasis thus far has been given to determining whether the intergenerational phenomenon exists, and the forms it may take. This paper shifts attention to the primary influences in the formation of these effects during childhood. Here, we report the findings of an interpretive study conducted with twenty-five young adult women, using three depth interviews with each informant - one at home, one while shopping in-store, and one discussing a pantry check. A rich set of insights emerged: nineteen formative factors are identified and discussed.

INTRODUCTION

Traditional theories of socialization suggest that childhood learning is so prolonged and powerful that the beliefs and attitudes formed within the family persist well into adulthood. This premise is supported by research in psychology, political science, sociology and to a lesser extent, consumer behavior (e.g., Carlson et al. 1994; Glass, Bengston and Dunham 1986; Miller and Glass 1989). Within consumer behavior, researchers have shown that brand and product preferences as well as significant aspects of consumer buying styles may be transferred from one generation to the next within families (e.g., Arndt 1971; Hill 1970; Moore and Lutz 1988; Olsen 1995). These effects are interesting and potentially important in the marketplace. However, intergenerational research is in many ways still an underdeveloped research area. Emphasis thus far has primarily been placed on testing to determine if the phenomenon exists, and the forms it may take. Given this body of evidence, the present paper shifts focus to the *formation* of intergenerational effects within households, drawing on findings from an interpretive study conducted with young adult women.

BACKGROUND

Childhood Socialization

The term "intergenerational influences" (hereafter "IG") refers to the within family transmission of information, beliefs and resources from one generation to the next.[1] Its conceptual basis rests within socialization theory, particularly childhood socialization. Socialization has been described as the process through which individuals develop specific patterns of socially relevant behavior (Ziegler and Child 1969), or the process by which individuals learn social roles and behaviors needed to participate effectively in society (Brim 1966). It helps individuals to develop their personal identities, and to assume new roles as they move through the life cycle. Although socialization is a life-long process, childhood and adolescence are particularly crucial periods. During childhood, the socialization process focuses on the present as well as roles and behaviors that will be needed in the future (McNeal 1987).

Childhood socialization is guided by such sources as relatives, peers, the educational system, religious institutions, and the mass media (see e.g., Faber and O'Guinn 1988; Moschis 1987). The family is the first and typically most powerful source. No other agent of socialization enjoys such a cumulative edge in exposure, communication, and receptivity. Parents and other family members serve as important channels of information and sources of

social pressure, as well as support for one another. As a family develops, it creates a distinct lifestyle, pattern of decision making, and interaction style (Sillars 1995). Children have countless opportunities to observe, then internalize their parents' beliefs, preferences and values, accepting these as a natural norm.

Consumer socialization represents one aspect of this broader process. It has been defined as "the processes by which young people acquire skills, knowledge and attitudes relevant to their functioning in the marketplace" (Ward 1974). A number of interesting topics have been studied within consumer socialization, including the scope of parental influence (e.g., Churchill and Moschis 1979), effects of parenting style (e.g., Carlson and Grossbart 1988), and how parents and children interact in making purchase decisions (e.g., Beatty and Talpade 1994; Foxman, Tansuhaj and Ekstrom 1989; Palan and Wilkes 1997). While parents do not typically set out to "teach" their children how to be consumers, they often are concerned that their children learn to shop for quality products, and learn to manage money (Ward, Wackman and Wartella 1977). How these goals are realized, however, is often a function of subtle interpersonal processes.[2] Collectively, this research highlights the important role that parents play in the consumer socialization of their children. It also recognizes that children influence their parents, particularly as they mature: this effect has been labeled "reciprocal socialization."

The Broad Range of Intergenerational Influences

Prior research in other disciplines has shown that intergenerational influences are active in a wide variety of spheres, including political party affiliation, candidate preferences, achievement orientation, religious values, as well as gender and racial attitudes (Beck and Jennings 1991; Cashmore and Goodnow 1985; Jennings and Niemi 1974; Whitbeck and Gecas 1988). Strength of such influence can vary considerably, likely to be strongest within religious and political arenas, and weakest on certain lifestyle dimensions (Troll and Bengston 1979). It is also more substantial for concepts that have concrete referents and long-term visibility within the family (Acock 1984). Children are most likely to imitate, model or identify with those attributes of their parents that are most consistent and reinforced (Beck and Jennings 1991).

Socialization theory would suggest that intergenerational effects are likely to diminish over time. Proponents of developmental

---

[1] Within the social sciences, the term "generation" is employed in multiple ways (Bengston and Cutler 1976). It is often used to refer to a cohort, or a group of people born at the same time, who by virtue of having come of age under the same historical circumstances are likely to share important characteristics that mark them as a social aggregate (e.g., "Baby Boomers"). In contrast, generational research that focuses on lineage effects, as in this paper, emphasizes individuals, and the transmission of private culture within families.

[2] This is consistent with findings in political socialization. Research there has shown that parents do little to actively direct the development of their children's political ideas, and often do not accurately perceive their children's attitudes (e.g., Jennings and Niemi 1974).

aging or status inheritance models argue, on the other hand, that parents and children may actually converge over time as children assume adult status, role demands and responsibilities (e.g., Glass et al. 1986). Though few studies have addressed this issue empirically, the findings are quite interesting. While there are indications that parent-child attitude similarity does decline over time, vestiges of parental influence remain even for individuals who are well into middle-age. The greatest erosion seems to occur during the first few years after the young adult leaves home, with a leveling off by the late 20s or early 30s, and then stabilization over time (see e.g., Beck and Jennings 1991; Niemi and Jennings 1991; Whitbeck and Glass 1988). Thus IG impacts can endure well into adulthood.

Intergenerational Effects in Consumer Behavior

Despite longstanding interest in this topic, consumer researchers have only begun to investigate the beliefs and attitudes that are transferred intergenerationally, and how they come to develop within households. Early research in consumer behavior tended to focus on intergenerational similarities in consumer buying styles (e.g., Arndt 1971, 1972; Hill 1970). For example, Hill's (1970) longitudinal analysis showed that financial planning skills were transmitted across three generations (particularly among families who were poor financial managers, and who tended to spend impulsively). Other aspects of consumer buying styles have been investigated as well, sometimes with mixed results. For example, Arndt (1971) reported significant agreement between college students and their parents on opinion leadership, innovativeness, and store preferences but not on product importance, brand variation or loyalty proneness. Further, Moore and Lutz (1988) revealed some commonalities in family members' choice rules and marketplace beliefs which have been further extended by Carlson et al. (1994).

Beyond these broader aspects of consumer buying styles, researchers have examined whether, and to what extent, specific brand preferences and loyalties are transmitted across generations. While largely exploratory, the evidence does suggest that intergenerational influences occur at the level of brand choice, but that important differences may exist across product categories, and across families. For example, Moore and Lutz (1988) compared mothers' and daughters' brand preferences for eight common supermarket items, and noted significant yet varying levels of agreement across categories. Support for the basic proposition was also noted by Heckler, Childers and Arunchalam (1989) who found that both middle-aged and young adults report that they prefer many of the same brands as their parents, and that this is particularly true for packaged goods (versus shopping goods). Perhaps reflecting the upward potential of intergenerational effects, Woodson, Childers and Winn (1976) indicated that 62% of men in their 20's reported that their auto insurance carrier also supplied coverage to their fathers. Even at age 50, almost 20% of the sample met this criterion (note, however the special exchange characteristics of this product category). Most recently, Olsen (1993, 1995), introduced interpretivist research methods to this area to investigate the transfer of brand loyalty across three generations. She notes that similar brand loyalties may sometimes emerge as an expression of affection and respect, thus operating at a basic level as a reinforcer of familial bonds. However, it should also be noted that observed intergenerational impacts on consumers' preferences for products/brands are likely reduced by factors such as age, marriage, greater distance from parents and culture (Childers and Rao 1992; Heckler et al.1989; Shah and Mittal 1997).

In summary, past research indicates that intergenerational effects are a likely source of influence in the marketplace. How these patterns develop in consumers' lives, however, has not yet been closely examined. Given the ability of interpretivist methods to capture richer elements of phenomena, we used a discovery-oriented approach to delve more deeply into this issue.

METHOD

Research Design and Sample

Multi-phased depth interviews were conducted with 25 young adult women. All informants were students living in off-campus housing, and each shopped for groceries on a regular basis. Each informant was interviewed for a total of 3-4 hours in three phases, at home, in-store, and at home again. Loosely structured, the initial interviews were designed to gather information about shopping patterns, personal shopping styles, brand preferences and family histories. Then, on a different day (typically within one week of the first interview) one of the researchers accompanied the informant on a grocery shopping trip. Informants were encouraged to "think out loud" during the shopping trip: these conversations centered around the purchases made that day, as well as preference histories. Immediately following the shopping trip, the researcher and informant returned home, put the groceries away and continued the interview. During this final phase of the interview process, kitchen cabinets were opened and informants encouraged to "tell the story" behind the brands there, as well as those just purchased. Life-history information, particularly as related to mother-daughter relationships, was gathered during this closing interview.

Informants were purposely selected to maximize potential insight into intergenerational phenomena, an appropriate goal at this stage of the research (Lincoln and Guba 1985). Poised at the threshold of independence from parents, this population is a particularly interesting one to study. While the brand portfolios used at home remain salient, independent purchasing enables the trial of new brands, products and shopping approaches. The women interviewed had been independent shoppers for as little as two months and as long as two and a half years, thus providing some range of experience.

Analysis

Verbatim transcripts served as the primary data from which conceptual categories and relationships were identified, using a relatively structured process following the discovery-oriented aims and procedures of grounded theory (Glaser and Strauss 1967). Each interview was read and independently coded by the first two authors. Emergent categories were compared and discussed in detail for the first few interviews. These initial categories served as a structural basis for coding the remaining interviews, with enrichments incorporated as necessitated by the data. All interviews were independently coded by the first two authors and comparisons were evaluated on a line by line basis for each interview. Discrepancies were few in number, and resolved through discussion. Data relevant to each emerging category were then sorted, compiled, and assessed for conceptual fit: a total of 19 categories were created, and are reported below.

RESULTS: FORMATIVE FACTORS EMERGING IN OUR STUDY

The emergent categories constitute a broad range of interesting insights into how intergenerational influences came to develop in our informants' lives as consumers.[3] For purposes of presentation, we have arranged these into three sets of insights. First are those relating to *Households* as the fundamental unit within which IG beliefs, attitudes, and behaviors are developed. Included here are categories relating to the structure of the household, the lifestyle of the household, and the personal characteristics of particular family members, all serving as factors that influence the formation of specific IG influences. Second, a number of categories reflect the

FIGURE 1
IG Influencers within the Household

- Impacts of a Family's Structure and Lifestyle
- It's a Mother's Domain
- The Influencers Beyond Mom
- Altogether, A Rich Information Environment
- Parental Roles: Guidance and Adaptation
- Heterogeneity Across Households is the Rule

Substantive Development of IG influences. Focus here shifts to the children – their learning processes, family interactions, and specific activities that contribute to IG effect creation. Finally, our third set of insights explicitly accounts for *IG Development Across Time.* Attention here is given to the fact that these processes occur in a continuous fashion over many years, and that several structural elements are significant to understanding this progression over time.

Intergenerational Influencers Within the Household

As noted in Figure 1, six categories of formative factors reflect the fact that a child's family household is both the location and context within which IG influences are formed. First, it was apparent that both *structural and lifestyle considerations* played key roles in the specific IG effects learned by children — daughters raised in households that differed on these dimensions frequently reflected these differences in the knowledge and preferences they carried forward into their adult lives (e.g., high or low income, vegetarian diet, outdoor athletics, etc.). In addition, it became quite clear that the specific family form could have striking and lasting impacts. This was particularly apparent in some cases of blended families and families in transition:

"I don't see my real Dad that often and if I do see him we're not in a home situation. He's at a hotel or—you know? So, I'm not really sure if he goes grocery shopping or if his wife does, but I'm pretty sure he doesn't. As for my Stepdad, he really isn't at home that much and when he is he likes to relax and I think it would really annoy him if he had to go grocery shopping." (21a3)[4]

"My grandmother came to live with us (after death of mother) and my dad was working. He's an attorney. He was working full time, really busy. So, my grandmother came to live with us and she took care of me and my brother and my sister. I suppose she raised me, but my Dad was there too. And then after he remarried, my Stepmom came in. I don't really know if I would say that she really raised me, but I'm sure she would like to say that." (1a2)

In these instances shifts had occurred as the major sources of influence changed within the daughter's household, and this was clearly reported as a major life event, long-remembered, and with continuing consequence.

Our second category reflects that, across the range of household forms and lifestyles, the *mother generally emerged as the primary influence agent.* Her particular expertise in supervising household activities was readily acknowledged and appreciated, and continuing references back to her as different products, brands, and memories were discussed was the norm for these interviews. Also, depending on the household, *other family members* also emerged as having exercised significant influence - this included fathers, siblings, grandparents and aunts.

"My Mom does all the shopping and cooking. Of course, my Dad likes to cook and there are special things that he makes, but typically like six days out of the week, it's my Mom that does it." (17a1)

"That's why he never goes grocery shopping. That's why my Mom never really sent him, or let him go grocery shopping, because he would buy all the wrong things. I mean he doesn't look at price at all, like my Mom does. She cuts coupons, and she compares prices." (2b7)

"My grandmother used to make me bread and swiss cheese with mustard on it. It was the best sandwich in the world. I still make that. The other thing that my grandmother used to do that everyone makes fun of me for is... and this is kind of funny, my grandmother made pasta with butter and ketchup, it's a really strange thing." (9b8)

"For salads I like Seven Seas—but when I make pasta salad it has to be the Kraft Zesty Italian. I don't know why that is either. I think it's because the first time I ever had pasta salad it was made with that and my Aunt had made it." (13a12)

When multiple influencers were at work, moreover, their multiplicity of preferences and recommendations created a sometimes confused *rich information environment* in which adaptations and compromises were necessary. Our informants were well-aware of the parameters in which their households seemed to operate, and easily accommodated to them. Evidence of such adjustments were readily apparent. For example,

"When my Dad would go grocery shopping we would have the bare essentials. We would have corn flakes. When my Stepmother would go shopping we would have no essentials, but we would have Lucky Charms, and Trix, and Fruit Loops, and Captain Crunch and we would have Hostess, and we would have Doritos, and we would have some more Hostess. It just depended on who did the shopping." (1a13)

"I'll specify the brands. My Mom knows what I use. But in case my Dad would do the shopping—oh God...I'm sure he'd come up with something off the wall. I always try to be

---

[3] These dimensions are also listed as part of the findings of a larger project on the role of intergenerational influences in the creation and maintenance of brand equity (Moore, Wilkie and Lutz 2001). They are not explored in any detail there, however. The present paper is the only outlet for discussion of these results on the formation of IG effects.

[4] Informants are identified by a number (1-25), the interview (a=first interview conducted in home, or b=second interview conducted in store and completed in informant's home) and page number in the interview transcript.

FIGURE 2

The Substantive Formation of IG Influences

- Governed by Children's Learning Processes
- Shopping Participation Plays a Huge Role
- Observational Learning Also Contributes
- Shopping Lists, Rules, and Limits as Control Devices
- Allowing for Personal Tastes
- Children's Influence Attempts as Participant Learning
- Coherence Helps: Resolving Inconsistent Messages
- Parents are Evaluated Too

specific in case my Dad does the shopping for some weird reason. Cause my Mom knows me backwards and forwards and she knows exactly what I use, exactly what I like—what size I want, everything. But my Dad does not." (15a8)

In numerous cases, the parents (particularly mothers in our study) were reported to have taken on *multiple parental roles that helped to guide these adaptive processes* within the household. Perhaps most basic and significant was the mother's nurturing role. These young women readily described the care and concern their mothers dedicated to meeting the needs of individual family members. Sometimes this was apparent simply by her willingness to consider multiple wants, and her often unselfish and extensive efforts to accommodate all. High levels of trust were also implicit in our informants' commentaries. Not only did these young women trust in the fact that their mothers' were highly aware of their wants and needs but that she would do her best to fulfill them. Also, functionally, mothers often took on the role of family purchasing agent. Thus, in many ways mothers tended to bring family members together, by blending multiple wants, by fostering cooperation, and by supporting household operations. Finally, mothers also played a supervisory role, guiding their daughters' development of consumer skills. Evidence of this included the "rule-based" nature of some IG impacts, such as mother's "tests" that had to be passed before children were allowed to shop on their own (i.e., where participation depended on acceptance of the family norm).

"My Mom is not a very selfish person at all. She's not a person who really wants anything for herself. She's a person that is more concerned with what I want, or my Dad or my brother. She kind of goes along with what we want." (8b17)

"My Mom would do a lot of it (grocery shopping) and I would sort of just take whatever was in the house that I wanted to eat. And sometimes tell her what I wanted, but generally—she knew and she'd get it." (12a5)

"When we were younger, Mom would never take us because we'd want the sugar cereal or something like that. But when we got older she sent us shopping on our own because we knew what kind of lunch food that we could buy. We didn't want the sugar cereals anymore, and we could shop smart." (7a8)

Finally, we would explicitly note that, while structural elements across households were common, heterogeneity was also evident: we observed many instances of a *household's characteristics providing idiosyncratic influences*:

"To tell you the truth we never really went shopping like a family. It was because my little brother was really sick for the

first three or four years of his life, and he would cry non-stop. So, if we ever went out as a family it was usually to church or to family gatherings. But, we never really went to the stores all together because it was really hard at first. So, I guess that's why my father always went grocery shopping—because my father didn't work and my Mom worked." (19a2)

"My Mom quit her job to raise me. So, I mean she was always home. I always had a home cooked dinner when I came home. And, even in high school, you know I would come home from basketball practice and she'd have dinner ready. I mean, I never had to make my own dinner because she always had it ready. She's always, she'll cook cookies or something." (16a2)

The Substantive Formation of Intergenerational Influences

Our second set of insights shifts focus to the children themselves, and highlights the substantive development of IG influences. As noted in Figure 2, the eight formative factors here focus on what is learned, and how such learning occurs for the consumer world. The first entry in Figure 2 reflects that IG effects are a natural subset of what is learned as a child matures, and are governed by *children's broader learning processes* (e.g., John 1999; Moschis 1987; Ward 1974). (We shall return to this point in the paper's conclusion). The second entry points out that, for consumer behavior, *participating in household shopping* emerged as a central force in forming IG effects. Many informants recalled these shopping trips as an agreeable, ongoing feature of their everyday lives.

For some, these excursions became a pleasant mother-daughter ritual, offering repetitive opportunities for observation and directed learning. Joint shopping also offered chances to influence purchases and obtain special favorites. When life circumstances began to alter these rituals, both mothers and daughters seemed to miss them:

"It would be every Thursday. And I would go with her. We'd always go at noon. Her and me, yeah I'd always hit her with the cart at her ankles (laughs)—I remember that. On Thursdays, I don't know why. And we'd have the same route. We'd always hit the store in a certain route.... I remember I started to get older and I stopped going with her and it was kind of a...she'd be like, "You're not coming?" (16a6)

"It was fun. I could get what I wanted. You know, "Hey Mom, let's get that" and my brothers weren't there so they couldn't get extra stuff. I did, they didn't. That's how you grow up, you go shopping with your mother...... They (her brothers) didn't understand my obsession. I still like to grocery shopping with her. (3a16)

Given the packaged goods context in which this research was conducted, it is not surprising that the *observation of product use* and brand packaging in the home emerged as having a memorable impact on future purchases. Notably, both successes and failures in the marketplace were instructive. Also, some mothers used *public family lists, rules, and purchase limitations,* and these also proved to be influential factors in helping IG effects to develop.

"Especially the (bologna) with the little paper on the side, that you have to peel off. I hate it. It's gross, I think it's disgusting... My Mom bought it 'cause it was on sale. I learned from her mistake. Oscar Meyer on sale, you should just get that." (3a13)

"Something not on sale, more expensive kind of stuff. Like, I'd always ask for Sara Lee Butter Pecan Coffee Cake because that's my favorite thing. It is. And she'd be like, "Unless I have a coupon for it, I'm not going to get it."" (14a5)

"She makes a list, a big long detailed list. I remember when we were at home..., she'd be like, "What do you need from the store? If you don't tell me—you're not going to get it" and I had to think of everything I needed, otherwise I didn't get it." (11a10)

"In my family—if we need to go grocery shopping for anything somebody will start a list. Any one of the four of us will start a list with things that we need, then everybody adds to the list so ... it's got all four of our handwriting on it. And whoever does the grocery shopping, usually my Mom, will just get them." (15a7)

As opposed to simply fitting in, our interviews also provided numerous reports of children's efforts to modify processes as they were occurring, so as to *satisfy their personal tastes.* In this sense, IG preferences seemed to transfer more readily when children felt that their personal desires were being represented in the household's purchase decisions. Examples of *in-store purchase influence attempts,* both successful and not, also reflected this phenomenon. Clear knowledge of parental boundaries was apparent, yet children also attempted to take advantage of lax styles where possible, such that the exercise of power in these interactions flowed not only from parent to child, but also from child to parent (many informants freely acknowledged that complaints, sulking or even tantrums were ready strategies in their arsenal of influence tactics). For example,

"When I was little for the most part I can remember my mother taking us grocery shopping and on occasion if our Dad did take us grocery shopping, we got anything we wanted. Because he didn't want a tantrum. And, in public he doesn't want his kids to look bad. If we started crying or screaming, he didn't want any part of it. He just wanted to go to the store, get this done, have it look like we're fine. So, if we were like "we want chocolate, we want cake"—he'd get anything just to shut us up, so we could get out of there. But, my Mom would leave us in the aisle crying. She did not care. She'd be like "See you later I'm leaving." She would just start walking away. (18a3)

"The only kind of croutons we'll eat in my house is Pepperidge Farm Seasoned Croutons. I think that at one point I didn't like

the brand that my Dad got and I made such a fuss over it that he never attempted to buy them again." (9a6)

"My Mom did all the shopping I would make requests, but everything I requested was always too expensive and I was the only one in the house who ate it. So, I had to eat what everybody else ate. I wasn't real happy with that.....She would always buy Ruffles because that's what my Dad likes. But, if my brother had his way he would want Frito-Lay or something. She would tend to buy what her and my Dad like as opposed to what we would choose. (6a5)

In this regard, daughters also spoke more broadly of themselves and other family members having to *reconcile conflicting preferences*: households with more coherence here also seemed to yield more robust IG product and brand preferences. For example,

"My Dad likes Jif Chunky and I can't stand chunky peanutbutter. And every time he'd come home and buy that, I'd send my Mom out for another jar of peanut butter so that I would have something to eat. And I liked Skippy better. We always had a big fight about that. It was like, we had two things of peanut butter in our house." (9a5)

"No, we weren't picky on brands... pretty much we'll all eat the same, like we're all used to the same brand—so it just was kind of the same what we bought." (13a8)

"I mean she bought the same things for like eighteen years." (3a12)

"We usually got that egg brand—you know Eggos, Mrs. D's Potatoes, Heinz Ketchup, Bulls-eye Barbecue Sauce, Open-Pit Barbecue Sauce, Claussen's Pickle Relish. We get the same kind of mustard, Morton's Salt...we always buy the same stuff." (10a8)

As a final entry, numerous daughters reported *evaluating – both positively and negatively – one or both parents* on many consumership dimensions, such as shopping styles, diet, choices, spending, and planning or lack thereof (when direct comparisons were made, usually it was the father who came out on the short end of the judgments). For example,

"He would buy all junk food—he would waste our money. You should see what he would buy. Like he'd buy all crap, he'd buy like all these chips and Hostess cupcakes and Twinkies and all this ice cream. And its not even good food that I like. It's gross, I don't even like it. I mean he'll buy all this fat and meat and stuff... he doesn't buy the right stuff. And he spends too much money.... My mom gets mad 'cause he spends so much money and you don't need all this junk food." (2a9)

"She's not as picky about Tide.... I think I'm maybe more into brands then she is. It ticked me off because she would go get the cheaper one, even though we all liked something better, she'd still get the cheaper sometimes and it really ticked us off." (3a14)

Overall, the substantive dimensions of IG formation encapsulated much higher levels of activity, evaluation, adaptation, and

FIGURE 3
IG Development Across Time

- A Continuous Process Across the Years
- Some IG Effects are Age-Specific
- Preference Stability a Plus for IG Growth
- Impacts of Structural and Lifestyle Changes on IG
- As Life Cycle Moves Along, Shifts in IG and Acceleration of Reverse IG

negotiation than might be expected initially. Clearly, however, much of this is due to the extensive time span involved — all of childhood.

Intergenerational Influences' Development Across Time

Our final category includes five further insights reflecting on intergenerational influences' development across time. Here we explicitly recognize some larger dynamics of this influence process. First, it in reality *operates in a continuous fashion* for many years, until the child leaves the family home. It thus incorporates millions of episodes that can leave impacts, and is in this sense difficult to measure and describe. However, some useful further insights did arise from our interviews. For example, certain of children's key experiences are *embedded within a particular life stage* (e.g., children's cereals, early teen cosmetics), and that IG influences here will not persist over time (however, as noted earlier, some may reappear when these daughters raise their own children in the future). Further, it is natural that within this extended time frame, some intergenerational influences will develop, then be replaced as the marketplace shifts or the household revises its preferences and behavior.

Further, *changes in a family's structure or lifestyle* appear to have particularly powerful impacts, often to disrupt previously developed intergenerational preferences and behaviors as particular family members leave, join, or change their behavior within the child's household. The impact of *life cycle progression* was also apparent in a number of ways, such as mothers returning to work outside the home as children age, shifts in the handling of older children's influence attempts, increases in influence from peers (a clear rival to intergenerational influence effects), and teens assuming more responsibility for the family's shopping and purchase decisions when they begin to drive. Not surprisingly, the incidence of *reverse intergenerational flows also accelerates* at this time (however, it was also clear that mothers remained an influential source of expertise as the daughters left home). Overall, this segment of our framework reminds us that a careful look across time is necessary to understand how intergenerational influences develop.

"When I was really little my Mom only had one job and she went every Saturday morning at seven o' clock to the grocery. And, she bought all of our groceries for that whole week. And now—(laughs) we don't ever have any groceries...when we got older she started giving us money and we would just go to the store and get groceries for the family." (7a8)

"Ever since I could drive, when I turned sixteen. Yeah— because my Dad worked these obnoxious hours. By the time I had turned sixteen she had been working, and she was obviously more busy... And she'd just give me her debit card. She would hand me the list from the counter and I would just go get it. And I would add my own stuff to it, that I wanted." (15a9)

"The last time I went shopping with my Mom before I left, she really did explain the meat a lot. She really did explain the meat more. 'Cause you know, she would always just get it. But I was like, "How do you know which stuff to get Mom?" I just never knew what kind she bought, I just knew it wasn't the cheapest kind." (10b17)

CONCLUSIONS

This exploratory study was successful in presenting a rich set of 19 factors related to the formation of intergenerational effects in consumer behavior. Our assessment identifies three underlying categories for these factors: (1) the household structure and context in which family interactions take place; (2) the processes involved in the substantive development of these effects; and (3) the extended time period across which these processes are occurring on a daily basis. Our results are, of course, subject to the limitations of this study's scope, sample, and method. Nonetheless, they are informative and should be useful for future research.

More generally, this study's findings underscore the fact that the intergenerational transfer of marketplace learning occurs naturally, within the repetitive rhythms and rituals of everyday life. It involves much activity, negotiation and evaluation on the part of both parents and children. While there is personal adaptation, families also seem to develop their own stable and coherent patterns that help them to function as a unit with ease and comfort. Theoretically, there was ample evidence that the three major childhood learning processes previously identified in the literature were at work here (e.g., Moschis 1987; Ward et al. 1977). Many instances of *observational learning* about brands, packaging and parents' shopping strategies were apparent, as noted earlier. Multiple manifestations of *experiential learning* were also evident, particularly via participation in household shopping, and in the trial and use of products within the home. *Direct communication* also clearly occurred on an ongoing basis (interestingly, many daughters also reported that, upon discovering gaps in their knowledge as they prepared to leave home, they had actively sought out their mother's remedial advice).

Overall, this study and its findings confirm that the intergenerational research area is interesting, important in the marketplace, and a worthwhile venue for further study. Perhaps because of our shift in emphasis toward the formation of IG effects (rather than the substance of these effects in adulthood), the close linkage of this area to children's learning, socialization, and family research were reinforced for us, indicating positive potential for future advances.

REFERENCES

Acock, Alan C. (1984), "Parents and Their Children: The Study of Inter-generational Influence," *Sociology and Social Research*, 68 (2), 151-171.

Arndt, Johan (1971), "A Research Note on Intergenerational Overlap of Selected Consumer Variables," Markeds Kommunikasjon, 8 (3), 1-8.

_____ (1972), "Intrafamilial Homogeneity for Perceived Risk and Opinion Leadership," *Journal of Advertising*, 1 (1), 40-47.

Beatty, Sharon E. and Salil Talpade (1994), "Adolescent Influence in Family Decision Making: A Replication with Extension," *Journal of Consumer Research*, 21 (September), 332-341.

Beck, Paul Allen and M. Kent Jennings (1991), "Family Traditions, Political Periods, and the Development of Partisan Orientations," *Journal of Politics*, 53 (August), 742-763.

Bengtson, Vern L. and Neal E. Cutler (1976), "Generations and Intergenerational Relations: Perspectives on Age Groups and Social Change," in *Handbook of Aging and the Social Sciences*, eds. R.H. Binstock and E Shanas, Van Nostrand Reinhold, 130-159.

Carlson, Les and Sanford Grossbart (1988), "Parental Style and Consumer Socialization of Children," *Journal of Consumer Research*, 15 (June), 77-94.

Carlson, Les, Ann Walsh, Russell N. Laczniak, and Sanford Grossbart (1994), "Family Communication Patterns and Marketplace Motivations, Attitudes, and Behaviors of Children and Mothers," *The Journal of Consumer Affairs*, 28(1), 25-53.

Cashmore, Judith E. and Jacqueline J. Goodnow (1985), "Agreement between Generations: A Two- Process Approach," *Child Development*, 56, 493-501.

Childers, Terry L. and Akshay R. Rao (1992), "The Influence of Familial and Peer-based Reference Groups on Consumer Decisions," *Journal of Consumer Research*, 19 (September), 198-211.

Churchill, Gilbert A., Jr. and George P. Moschis (1979), "Television and Interpersonal Influences on Adolescent Consumer Learning," *Journal of Consumer Research*, 6 (June), 23-35.

Faber, Ronald J., and Thomas C. O'Guinn (1988) "Expanding the View of Consumer Socialization: A Nonutilitarian Mass-Mediated Perspective," in *Research in Consumer Behavior*, Vol. 3, JAI Press Inc., 49-77.

Foxman, Ellen R., Patriya S. Tansuhaj, and Karin M. Ekstrom (1989), "Family Members' Perceptions of Adolescents' Influence in Family Decision Making," *Journal of Consumer Research*, 15 (March), 482-491.

Glaser, Barney G. and Anselm L. Strauss (1967), *The Discovery of Grounded Theory: Strategies for Qualitative Research*, Chicago, IL: Aldine.

Glass, Jennifer, Vern L. Bengston and Charlotte Chorn Dunham (1986), "Attitude Similarity in Three-Generation Families: Socialization, Status Inheritance, or Reciprocal Influence?," *American Sociological Review*, 51 (October), 685-698.

Heckler, Susan E., Terry L. Childers and Ramesh Arunchalam (1989), "Intergenerational Influences in Adult Buying Behaviors: An Examination of Moderating Factors," in *Advances in Consumer Research*, Vol. 16, ed. Thomas K. Srull, Provo, UT: Association for Consumer Research, 276-284.

Hill, Reuben (1970), *Family Development in Three Generations*, Cambridge, MA: Schenkman.

Jennings, M. Kent and Richard G. Niemi (1974), *The Political Character of Adolescence*, Princeton, NJ: Princeton University Press.

John, Deborah Roedder (1999), "Consumer Socialization of Children: A Retrospective Look at Twenty-Five Years of Research," *Journal of Consumer Research*, 26 (December), 183-213.

Lincoln, Yvonna S. and Egon G. Guba (1985), *Naturalistic Inquiry*, Beverly Hills, CA: Sage.

McNeal, James U. (1987), *Children as Consumers*, Lexington, MA: D. C. Heath.

Miller, Richard B. and Jennifer Glass (1989), "Parent-Child Attitude Similarity Across the Life Course," *Journal of Marriage and the Family*, 51 (November), 991-997.

Moore, Elizabeth S. and Richard J. Lutz (1988), "Intergenerational Influences in the Formation of Consumer Attitudes and Beliefs About the Marketplace: Mothers and Daughters," in *Advances in Consumer Research*, Vol. 15, M.J. Houston (ed.), Provo, UT: Association for Consumer Research, 461-467.

_____ William L. Wilkie and Richard J. Lutz (2001), "Passing the Torch: Intergenerational Influences as a Source of Brand Equity," working paper, Graduate School of Business, University of Notre Dame.

Moschis, George P. (1987), *Consumer Socialization*, Lexington, MA: Lexington Books.

Niemi, Richard G. and M. Kent Jennings (1991), "Issues and Inheritance in the Formation of Party Identification," *American Journal of Political Science*, 35 (November), 970-988.

Olsen, Barbara (1993), "Brand Loyalty and Lineage: Exploring New Dimensions for Research," in *Advances in Consumer Research*, Vol. 20, Eds. L. McAlister and M.L. Rothschild, Provo, UT: Association for Consumer Research, 276-284.

_____ (1995), "Brand Loyalty and Consumption Patterns: The Lineage Factor," in *Contemporary Marketing and Consumer Behavior: An Autobiographical Sourcebook*, ed. John F. Sherry, Jr., Thousand Oaks, CA: Sage, 245-281.

Palan, Kay M. and Robert E. Wilkes (1997), "Adolescent- Parent Interaction in Family Decision Making," *Journal of Consumer Research*, 24 (September), 159-169.

Shah, Reshma H. and Banwari Mittal (1997), "Toward a Theory of Intergenerational Influence in Consumer Behavior: An Exploratory Essay," in *Advances in Consumer Research*, Vol. 24, ed. Merrie Brucks and Deborah J. MacInnis, Provo, UT: Association for Consumer Research, 55-60.

Sillars, Alan L. (1995), "Communication and Family Culture," in *Explaining Family Interactions*, eds. Mary Anne Fitzpatrick and Anita L. Vangelisti, Thousand Oaks, CA: Sage, 375-399.

Troll, Lillian and Vern Benston (1979), "Generations in the Family," in Contemporary Theories about the Family, Vol. 1, eds. Wesley R. Burr, Reuben Hill, F.I. Nye, and I.L. Reiss, New York, NY: Free Press, 127-161.

Ward, Scott (1974), "Consumer Socialization," *Journal of Consumer Research*, 1 (Sept), 1-14.

_____ Daniel B. Wackman and Ellen Wartella (1977), *How Children Learn to Buy: The Development of Consumer Information Processing Skills*, Beverly Hills, CA: Sage.

Whitbeck, Les B. and Viktor Gecas (1988), "Value Attributions and Value Transmission between Parents and Children," *Journal of Marriage and the Family*, 50(August), 829-840.

Woodson, Larry G., Terry L. Childers and Paul R. Winn (1976), "Intergenerational Influences in the Purchase of Auto Insurance," in *Marketing Looking Outward: 1976 Business Proceedings*, ed. William B. Locander, Chicago, IL: American Marketing Association, 43-49.

Ziegler, Edward and Irvin L. Child (1969), *Socialization and Personality Development*, Reading, MA: Addison-Wesley.

Individual Differences in Gender and Age: Theory Enhancement and Some Important Consequences

Rui Zhu, University of Minnesota

Joan Meyers-Levy, University of Minnesota

The objective of this session is to further our understanding about individual differences, particularly gender and age, and how they affect consumers' processing of information, perception, and judgments. The session consists of three papers.

First, Joan Meyers-Levy, Carolyn Yoon, Rui Zhu and Michelle Lee examine gender differences in processing pictorial data that vary in relational coherence. They posited that because males' processing tends to focus on salient cues or singular subsets of highly available information, they may be inclined to neglect and respond relatively unfavorably to ad pictures that are low in relational coherence, with males instead directing their processing to the clearer, factual verbal claims. By contrast, because females tend to process information more elaborately, they should process the pictorial ad information extensively regardless of the picture's degree of relational coherence and whether such picture processing subsumes resources otherwise devoted to accompanying verbal claims. As such, females' extensive and likely extra-stimulus processing of the low relationally coherent ad pictures may lead females to produce impaired recall of the accompanying verbal ad data, high levels of both valid and false intrusions in picture recall, and relatively favorable thoughts and judgments about the advertised product. A study assesses these predictions for several products and generally finds support for the theorizing.

Second, Ian Skurnik, Norbert Schwarz, and Denise Park explore age differences in the "illusion of truth" effect, a memory distortion whereby people think that vaguely familiar information is probably true, even when it was originally identified as false. Based on the distinction between two types or uses of memories, namely recollection, which involves detailed memory for a claim and its context at the time of acquisition, versus familiarity, which entails a vague, context-free trace for a claim, they hypothesize and find that when people are exposed either once or repeatedly to health and medical claims that are identified explicitly at exposure as true or false, younger people tend to misremember false claims as true after three days but not immediately. In addition, repeated claim exposure helps younger adults correct their false memories at both time periods. By contrast, older individuals tend to misremember false claims as true both immediately and after a delay. Moreover, while repeated warnings about false claims enable older adults to correct their erroneous memories immediately, such repetition does not do so after a delay. In fact, paradoxically, repetition tends to *increase* the illusion of truth effect among older adults after a three-day delay.

Third, Aimee Drolet and Patti Williams also explore age differences by examining why older individuals tend to focus more on emotional than non-emotional information. While some researchers have suggested that this focus on emotional data is attributable to older individuals' declining cognition and thus presumed reliance on peripheral, emotional information, the research in this presentation investigates a different possibility. Specifically, older individuals' increased attention to emotional information may reflect the increased diagnosticity or relevance of such emotional data as opposed to a decline in older people's cognition. That is, because older individuals are likely to anticipate and/or experience emotion-laden changes such as their own or

peer's declining health and approaching death, emotional data may take on greater significance or precedence compared to other, less affective information. Three experiments are reported that test and find some support for this theorizing.

Finally, Christie Nordhielm synthesized the three pieces of research and highlighted topics within individual differences that merit further investigation.

Measuring Ad-Evoked Love

Ming-Hui Huang, National Chung Cheng University

ABSTRACT

A 12-item measure for one of the most important human emotions, love, is developed by bringing together the three basic components of love: platonic love, sex, and companionate love (more commonly labeled as warmth). A second-order confirmatory factor analysis is specified using four love-centered perfume ads as stimuli to validate the ad-evoked love scale. Results support the plausibility of the proposed measure in representing two categories of love: romantic love (including platonic love and passionate love) and companionate love. The measure fills a current need by providing an appropriate measure for ad-evoked love.

INTRODUCTION

The theme of love is commonly used in advertising, reflecting its importance in consumers' lives. Lazarus and Lazarus (1994, p. 107) said that when people are asked to name the most important human emotions, love is usually the most important. However, our understanding of the role that love plays in advertising is hindered because various subtypes of love can be evoked by ads, and because current measures lack the specificity to tap into these subtypes of love. We have platonic and passionate love for our partners; however we have companionate love for parents, children, friends, and mankind in general. The soap opera type campaign for Taster's Choice instant coffee which portrayed an ongoing romance between two neighbors presented the platonic version of love, with the coffee playing a background role (Belch and Belch 1998, p. 273; Shimp 1997, pp. 270-272). A recent ad for the Peugeot 306 automobile, which depicted the wife of a young married-with-children family lovingly looking on as her husband washed the car, and then the couple passionately making love, presents the passionate version of love. The AT&T campaign which showed images of family, love, hope and trust as facilitated by AT&T's communication technologies (Cleland and Gleason 1997), is likely to produce the companionate version of love (Belch and Belch 1998, p. 269).

These subtypes of love differ in nature. However, the current measurements of ad-evoked love tend to treat the construct of love at too broad a level. For example Aaker, Stayman, and Hagerty's (1986) warmth monitor used love and tenderness as two major anchor points. To identify feelings elicited by advertising, Aaker, Stayman, and Vezina (1988) clustered together feelings of love, affection, compassion, romance, warmth, tenderness, and warmheartedness. Edell and Burke (1987) and Burke and Edell (1989) identified warm feelings as one of the three ad feeling dimensions. This dimension included feeling affectionate, calm, concerned, contemplative, emotional, hopeful, kind, moved, peaceful, pensive, sentimental, touched, and warmhearted.

Love in advertising and in consumers' lives is interwoven with other emotions and can seldom be examined systematically as a distinct emotion. Without isolating love from other emotions, this lack of specificity renders love as a response to a very wide range of stimuli and situations, with consequent difficulty in using the construct for specific strategic purposes. Based on the distinction into two broad categories of love: romantic and companionate love, and by further defining the category of romantic love into platonic and passionate subtypes, this study provides a definition of each subtype and explores their relationship. The purpose of the study reported here is to develop a measure for ad-evoked love, taking its subtypes into account.

THE CONSTRUCT OF LOVE: ROMANTIC AND COMPANIONATE LOVE

Love is a pleasant emotion accompanied by varying degrees of sexual attraction, and is experienced in various relationships. As a higher order construct, love is comprised of a number of variants. The most important and interesting contrast is that between romantic and companionate love (Lazarus and Lazarus 1994, p. 109). Romantic love includes platonic and passionate subtypes, both of which are experienced in romantic relationships with the passionate subtype including strong sexual implications. Companionate love is experienced in various relationships, and excludes the possibility of sexual implications. The following delineates the four love-related components using two differentiators: the degree of sexual implications and the nature of the relationships where the love is embedded. Figure 1 illustrates the relationship of the four related constructs.

Romantic Love: Platonic and Passionate Love

Romantic love is a pleasant emotion that is experienced in romantic relationships. Sex or the possibility of sex is one of the important characteristics of romantic love (Hendrick and Hendrick 1992, p. 24; Shaver and Hazan 1988). However, not all forms of romantic love that are experienced in a romantic relationship are sexual in origin or purpose. The platonic version of romantic love does not involve explicit sexual implications, whereas the passionate version of romantic love does.

Platonic Love. Romantic love can exist without sexual involvement or passion (Lazarus and Lazarus 1994, p. 108). Originally defined by Plato, this subtype of love can be considered as the soul's dynamic attempt to achieve oneness with the source of its being, whereas sex is but a means of propagating the race and little more (Murstein 1988, p. 22). The campaign for Taster's Choice instant coffee serves as an example of platonic love, where a romance between the two partners develops by the aid of coffee with only a very limited amount of sexual implication involved.

Sex. Sex is an innate human drive evolved from reproductive requirements (Tompkins 1984, pp. 164-164). Sexual desires are among the strongest motivators of human behavior (Shaver, Hazan, and Bradshaw 1988) and sexual infatuation can result from passionate arousal in the absence of the intimacy and commitment components of love (Sternberg 1988). Ads for Travel Fox sports shoes serve as examples of sexual appeals. The ads showed, from the chest down, two adults engaged in sexual intercourse, completely naked except for the advertised sports shoes and matching socks (Severn, Belch, and Belch 1990).

Passionate Love. Evidence of passionate love involving explicit sexual implications can be shown from the following studies. Branden (1988) stated that people who are happily in love are inclined to experience sexual intimacy as an important vehicle of contact and expression. In developing scales for consumption-related emotions, Richins (1997) measured romantic love using the items sexy, romantic love, and passionate, suggesting sex as a component of passionate love. The ad for the Peugeot 306 serves as an example, with the wife of a young married-with-children family looks fondly at her husband's car-washing, after which the couple passionately make love.

FIGURE 1
Relationship and Design of the Four Types of Love and Loving Ads:
Sexual Content and Nature of Relationships as Differentiating Conditions

		The Degree of Sexual Content	
		High	Low or None
The Nature of Relationships	Romantic Relationship	**The passionate ad** Definition: Two actors in a sexual situation implying a romantic relationship Content: A just married scantily dressed couple passionately kissing. A pair of wedding rings is in one corner implying that the relationship is romantic.	**The platonic ad** Definition: Two actors in a neutral situation implying a romantic relationship Content: A close-up of a tastefully clothed, demure couple smiling. A pair of wedding rings is in one corner implying that the relationship is romantic.
	Parental Relationship	N/A	**The companionate ad** Definition: Two actors in a neutral situation implying a parental relationship Content: A father and son playing chess in a park.
	No Relationship	**The sexual ad** Definition: Two actors in a sexual manner without an implied relationship Content: A close-up of a nude couple in a sexually suggestive pose.	N/A

Companionate Love

Companionate love, commonly known as the warmth construct, is a pleasant emotion that can be experienced in various relationships without involving any sexual implications. MacDonald (1992) defined warmth as a positive emotion that evolved to facilitate cohesive family relationships and paternal investment in children. He considered warmth to be essential in parent-child relationships, and to a lesser extent, in relationships of friendship among peers. Aaker, Stayman, and Hagerty (1986) conceptually defined warmth as a positive, mild, volatile emotion, involving physiological arousal and precipitated by experiencing, directly or vicariously, a love, family, or friendship relationship. Time spent with other people, being reunited with close friends or relatives, being at a party with friends, or going out on a pleasant date are social contexts depicted in ads to generate warmth.

The possibility of sex is prohibited in non-romantic relationships, such as parental or fraternal, as a result of societal rules (Lazarus and Lazarus 1994, p. 114), and thus sexual implications are excluded from companionate love. Lazarus and Lazarus (1994, p. 109) considered that the absence of sexual interest in companionate love distinguishes companionate love from its romantic counterpart. They argue that erotic passion is missing in these variants of companionate love, whereas it holds center stage in romantic love (p.112). Shaver and Hazan (1988) state that parental love differs from romantic love in that sexual attraction and sexual behavior are part of romantic love, while sex is irrelevant to parental love.

METHOD

As important as love is in both consumers' lives and advertising, the lack of proper measurement for ad-evoked love makes difficult an assessment of the effectiveness of ads aiming at portraying love. Thus our understanding of the role of love plays in consumer research and advertising is deterred. To fill the gap, this study uses various subtypes of love to develop a reliable and valid measure, taking into account the content characteristics of loving ads.

The Ad-Evoked Love Scale

A pool of eighteen items was collected from a variety of sources to tap into the three basic components of ad-evoked love: platonic love, sex, and companionate love. The subscale of passionate love is achieved by summing the subscales of platonic love and sex.

Sources of the item collection contain measures of emotions in psychology, advertising, and consumption. Items obtained from advertising studies include the warm/tender cluster identified in Aaker, Stayman, and Vezina's (1988) feelings elicited by advertising, and the warm dimension of Edell and Burke's (1987) three-dimension ad feeling scales. Items collected from psychological studies include the love cluster in Shaver, Schwartz, Kirson, and O'Connor's (1987) prototype view for the psychology of emotion, and the pleasure and arousal factors of Russell and Mehrabian's (1977) three-factor theory of emotions. Items taken from consumption studies are Richins' (1997) romantic love and love consumption emotions.

The final 18 items that constitute the ad-evoked love scale and which were subjected to the subsequent empirical testing are: sexy, romantic, passionate, intimate, in love, affectionate, erotic, lustful, infatuated, sexually attractive, desired, sentimental, warmhearted, tender, warm, loving, caring, and companionate. Respondents were asked to indicate the intensity of the emotion they felt while exposed to the ad using a five-point scale ranging from "very slightly or not at all" to "extremely."

Stimuli

Four perfume print ads were developed to generate four subtypes of love using two dimensions derived from the previous discussion. The dimensions were the degree of sexual content and the nature of relationships. The four subtypes of love that were manipulated were consistent in format. The platonic loving ad has low sexual content in a romantic relationship, the passionate loving ad depicts high sexual content in a romantic relationship, the companionate loving ad pictures low sexual content in a parental relationship, and the sexual ad portrays high sexual content without a relationship (see Figure 1). The common elements for all ads are a dominant photo depicting the intended content characteristics of each type of love and two bottles of the advertised perfume in the lower part of the ad. For the romantic ads (the platonic and the passionate ads), a pair of wedding rings is in the upper corner of the ads to imply the couple being in a romantic relationship. The platonic ad has a close-up of a tastefully clothed, demure couple smiling. The sexual ad shows a close-up of a nude couple in a sexually suggestive pose. The passionate ad describes a just-married, scantily-dressed couple passionately kissing. The companionate ad depicts a father and son playing chess in a park.

Perfume was selected as the test product since it is a "feeling" product (Erevelles 1998) which often contains both loving and sexual materials. An English perfume brand "After Six," which is only available at UK specialty stores, was used for its low familiarity to the respondents, thus avoiding idiosyncratic reactions to a familiar brand.

Respondents

Respondents for the study were 215 undergraduate students from a variety of major fields in a California university, who took part in the study to obtain extra course credit. One hundred and eighteen were men and 97 were women, with a mean age of 22.82 (SD = 4.45). Each respondent received a color-printed magazine-like booklet, which contained the four focal ads, mock ads and questions exploring consumption behavior irrelevant to the current study. The order of the ads was counterbalanced and rotated to minimize order effects and carryover biases. The booklets were distributed in classrooms and respondents were instructed to read the booklet as if they were reading a magazine, and to answer the questions independently. The feelings of love generated by these ads were measured right after each ad exposure.

RESULTS

Exploratory Factor Analysis

Principal component exploratory factor analysis with varimax rotation, extracting a three-factor solution, was first used to examine the dimensionality of love generated by the four ads, as measured by the 18-item loving scale. The application of Cattell's scree test confirmed this three-factor solution because eigenvalues became homogeneous and were smaller than 1.0 after the third factor. The results confirmed the distinct nature of the platonic love, sex and companionate love components. The first companionate love factor loaded the seven items of warmhearted, warm, tender, caring, loving, sentimental, and companionate, accounting for 48.7% of the variance in ad-evoked love. The second sex factor loaded the six items of lustful, erotic, infatuated, sexual attraction, desired, and sexy, accounting for 28.9% of the variance. The third platonic love factor loaded the five items of romantic, in love, affectionate, intimate, and passionate, accounting for 5.6% of the variance.

Second-order Confirmatory Factor Analysis

A second-order confirmatory factor analysis (CFA) with a maximum likelihood fitting function was then specified to confirm the three-component solution obtained from the exploratory factor analysis and to take into account the hierarchical structure of ad-evoked love. This approach has the following two advantages. First, it provides a more rigorous check of the appropriateness of the ad-evoked love scale items to measure their corresponding latent loving constructs than its exploratory counterpart. Second, the second-order latent factor, love, can be specified to examine its effect on the first-order latent factors, platonic love, sex and companionate love, thus examining whether or not those components of love belong to the broad emotional category of love.

An iteration procedure was adopted to select the best scale items. To provide better discriminant validity for each first-order factor, scale items loaded heavily on more than one factor were dropped from the analysis. After this procedure, four items remained for each factor, which all demonstrated satisfactory reliability. Figure 2 represents the model. The single second-order factor is love (ξ_1) that directly influences the three first-order factors: platonic love (η_1), sex (η_2), and companionate love (η_3). These first-order factors have direct effects on their corresponding scale items. The Λ_y is 12 x 3, with one scale item per construct chosen to scale the latent first-order factors. Similarly, the first element in Γ scales the second-order factor love (ξ_1) to platonic love (η_1), with the remaining second-order factor loadings that are free. This procedure gives the first-order factors the same scale as the observed items, and the second-order factor the same scale as the first-order factors. The Ψ matrix provides the variance in the first-order factors not explained by the second-order factor.

Estimation

All first- and second-order factor loadings (Λ_y and Γ) are statistically significant and positive. The R^2_{yi}'s for the scale items range from .68 to .89, and the $R^2_{\eta i}$'s are 1.00 (fixed), .39, and .17, respectively. Though these are somewhat good, the chi-square estimate of 789.70 with 52 df is highly significant (p < .000). Moreover the other measures of overall fit suggest that some improvements could be made (e.g., RMSEA = .13). A screen of the modification indices of Λ_y's suggests that the first-order factor, platonic love (η_1), has a direct effect on the scale item 'desired,' and the first-order factor, sex (η_2), has a direct effect on the scale item 'intimate.' The two parameters are thus relaxed and the chi-square estimate is significantly improved to 382.92 with 50 df (p < .000). The RMSEA is at .088, NFI at .96, and CFI at .97, all three overall model fit indices suggested the appropriateness of the hypothesized model.

The composite reliability estimates for platonic love, sex, and companionate love were .921, .928, and .942, and the estimates of variance extracted were .717, .744, and .802, respectively, both indices suggesting satisfactory reliabilities and variance accounted for by those scale items (Bagozzi and Yi 1988).

Posteriori Manipulation Check

A posteriori manipulation check was conducted to examine whether there was a one-to-one correspondence between the ads'

FIGURE 2

Path Diagram and Solution for the Second-order Confirmatory Factor Analysis

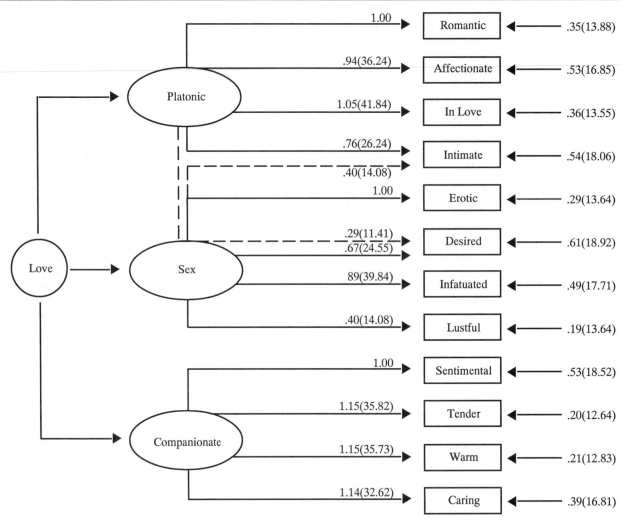

χ^2 (50df) = 382.92 (p=.000), RMSEA = .088, GFI = .93, AGFI = .89, NFI = .96, CFI = .97

Note: Entries in parentheses are t-values

content and the feelings of love generated by them. The check could not be made in advance due to the undetermined nature of scale items describing the specific type of love. By summing up the four items of each component of love, with passionate love further averaged from the platonic love and sex, the average scores were subjected to analyses of variances with posteriori Tukey-HSD tests. The mean levels of platonic love generated by platonic loving, passionate loving, and sexual ads were homogeneous, but were significantly higher than the companionate loving ad (3.23, 3.70, 3.00 versus 1.53), F = 183.001, *p* = .000, suggesting the distinctiveness of the companionate love from the romantic love. The sexual ad was rated as being sexier than the passionate, the platonic, and the companionate loving ads (3.38 versus 2.86, 1.89, 1.14), F = 214.081, *p* = .000. The mean levels of companionate love generated by the companionate, the passionate, and the platonic loving ads were no different (3.13, versus 3.02, 3.23), but were distinct from the sexual ad (2.11), F = 46.644, *p* = .000. This strengthens the view that the example of companionate love does not contain a sexual component. The passionate loving ad was higher on passionate loving than the platonic and the companionate loving ads (3.28 versus 2.56, 1.34), F = 213.968, *p* = .000, but it was as passionate

as the sexual ad (3.28 versus 3.19), confirming sex as their common component.

DISCUSSION

Conclusion

This study, reporting results using a second-order CFA analysis, developed a set of loving scales that represent the three major subtypes of ad-evoked love - platonic love, passionate love, and compassionate love - through the three basic components of love - platonic love, sex, and companionate love. The current ad-evoked love scales possess a higher degree of discriminant validity to determine which specific type of love is elicited by ads than previous ad feeling scales.

Measuring Romantic Love

The measurement of romantic love can be achieved through different combinations of the subscales of platonic love and sex. The four core items of romantic, in love, affectionate, and intimate, can each assess platonic love. The fifth item 'desired' is included to provide a complete measure. Summing the subscales of platonic

APPENDIX
The Ad-Evoked Love Scale

Platonic love (α = .921, .928*)
    Romantic (α = .82)
    Affectionate (α = .83)
    In love (α = .74)
    Intimate (α = .74)
    (Desired) (α = .72)
Sex (α = .928, .937)
    Erotic (α = .86)
    Desired (α = .72)
    Infatuated (α = .75)
    Lustful (α = .91)
    (Intimate) (α = .74)
Companionate love (α = .942)
    Sentimental (α = .68)
    Tender (α = .88)
    Warm (α = .88)
    Caring (α = .78)

*The second values in the parentheses are the composite reliability estimates taking into account the shared items.

---

love and sex yields the subscale of passionate love. These subscales are romantic, in love, affectionate, intimate, erotic, lustful, infatuated, and desired. The coefficient alpha for this 8-item set is satisfactory at .909. Compared with Richins' (1997) romantic love scale, this set of items has the advantage of being able to distinguish the two subtypes of romantic love, depending on whether or not the subscale of sex is included. Thus it provides a more specific measure for love to various loving advertising appeals. For example, the items of 'sexy' and 'passionate' used in Richins' (1997) romantic love scale might not be appropriate for measuring romantic appeals that do not involve explicit sexual implications. A typical example is the Taster's Choice ad series where a romance is developed without involving explicit sex or passion.

Measuring Companionate Love

To measure companionate love, the four items of sentimental, tender, warm, and caring are recommended. This companionate love scale set has an advantage over the warmth measure used in past advertising studies in that it is neither compounded with the higher order construct of love nor intertwined with the related but distinct construct of platonic love. Compared to the love subscale developed by Richins (1997), which includes items of loving, sentimental, and warm hearted, the current set does not involve the item of loving, an item that can be used to measure all love-related constructs and is thus lacking in discriminant validity. Compared with the warm/tender cluster identified by Aaker, Stayman, and Vezina (1988), this companionate loving scale provides a more specific measure to the construct of warmth by dropping the fringed items, such as sympathetic and empathetic; or the compounding items, such as love. Compared with the warm feelings obtained in Edell and Burke (1987) and Burke and Edell (1989), this scale distinguishes the emotion of companionate love from the arousal dimension of emotion (e.g., Russell and Mehrabian 1977) by dropping items such as calm and peaceful. It is also clarified by dropping cognitive-oriented items, such as contemplative and hopeful, thereby providing a more valid measure for the emotion of companionate love.

REFERENCES

Aaker, David, A. and Douglas M. Stayman (1989), "What Mediates the Emotional Responses to Advertising? The Case of Warmth," in *Cognitive and Affective Responses to Advertising*, eds. P. Cafferata and A. Tybout, Lexington, MA: Lexington Books, 287-303.

_____ and Richard Vezina (1988), "Identifying Feelings Elicited by Advertising," *Psychology & Marketing*, 5(Spring), 1-16.

_____ and Michael R. Hagerty (1986), "Warmth in Advertising: Measurement, Impact, and Sequence Effects," *Journal of Consumer Research*, 12(March), 365-381.

Bagozzi, Richard P. and Youjae Yi (1988), "On the Evaluation of Structural Equation Models," *Journal of the Academy of Marketing Science*, 16(1), 74-94.

Belch, George E. and Michael A. Belch (1998), *Advertising and Promotion: An Integrated Marketing Communication*, Boston, MA: Irwin/McGraw-Hill, 264-295.

Branden, Nathaniel (1988), "A Vision of Romantic Love," in *The Psychology of Love*, Robert J. Sternberg and Michael L. Barnes, eds., New Haven: Yale University Press, 218-231.

Burke, Marian Chapman and Julie A. Edell (1989), "The Impact of Feelings on Ad-Based Affect and Cognition," *Journal of Marketing Research*, 6(February), 69-83.

Cleland, Kim and Mark Gleason (1997), "AT&T Brand Revamp Gets First Support in New Ads," *Advertising Age*, March 3, 3, 37.

Edell, Julie A. and Marian Chapman Burke (1987), "The Power of Feelings in Understanding Advertising Effects," *Journal of Consumer Research*, 14(December), 421-433.

Erevelles, Sunil (1998), "The Role of Affect in Marketing," *Journal of Business Research*, 42, 199-215.

Hendrick, Susan S. and Clyde Hendrick (1992), *Romantic Love*, Newbury Park, CA: Sage.

Lazarus, Richard S. and Bernice N. Lazarus (1994), Passion and Reason: Making Sense of Our Emotions, New York, NY: Oxford University Press, 86-115.

MacDonald, Kevin (1992), "Warmth as a Developmental Construct: An Evolutionary Analysis," *Child Development*, 63(August), 753-773.

Richins, Marsha L. (1997), "Measuring Emotions in the Consumption Experience," *Journal of Consumer Research*, 24(September), 127-146.

Russell, James A. and Albert Mehrabian (1977), "Evidence for a Three-Factor Theory of Emotions," *Journal of Research in Personality*, 11, 273-294.

Severn, Jessica, George E. Belch and Michael A. Belch (1990), "The Effects of Sexual and Non-sexual Advertising Appeals and Information Level on Cognitive Processing and Communication Effectiveness," *Journal of Advertising*, 19(1), 14-22.

Shaver, Phillip R. and Cindy Hazan (1988), "A Biased Overview of the Study of Love," *Journal of Social and Personal Relationships*, 5, 473-501.

_____, Cindy Hazan and Donna Bradshaw (1988), "Love as Attachment: The Integration of Three Behavioral Systems," in *The Psychology of Love*, Robert J. Sternberg and Michael L. Barnes, eds., New Haven: Yale University Press, 68-99.

_____, Judith Schwartz, Donald Kirson and Cary O'Connor (1987), "Emotion Knowledge: Further Exploration of a Prototype Approach," *Journal of Personality and Social Psychology*, 52(6), 1061-1086.

Shimp, Terence A. (1997), *Advertising, Promotion, and Supplemental Aspects of Integrated Marketing Communication*, Orlando, FL: The Dryden Press.

Sternberg, Robert J. (1988), "Triangulating Love," in *The Psychology of Love*, Robert J. Sternberg and Michael L. Barnes, eds., New Haven: Yale University Press, 119-138.

Tompkins, Silvan S. (1984), "Affect Theory," in *Approaches to Emotion*, Klaus R. Scherer and Paul Ekman, eds., Hillsdale, NJ: Lawrence Erlbaum Associates, 163-195.

Consumers' Attitudinal Profiles: An Examination at the Congruence Between Cognitive, Affective and Conative Spaces

Jacques-Marie Aurifeille, The University of La Reunion
Fabrice Clerfeuille, University de Nantes
Pascale Quester, The University of Adelaide

INTRODUCTION

From its early presentation by Rosenberg and Hovland (1960), the three component view of attitudes has been the object of a prolific research, following two major directions. Some researchers have examined the question of whether these components are co-linear or autonomous, whilst others have debated whether attitudes result mainly from situational elements or from more durable consumer characteristics (Anand, Holbrook and Stephens 1988).

Researchers favouring the influence of situation conceptualise attitudes as resulting from situational variables such as involvement, purchase environment or product type (Park and Young 1985). For instance, the involvement profiles developed by Laurent and Kapferer (1985) correspond to ten possible combinations of cognitive (interest), affective (pleasure) and conative (probability of mistake, importance of consequences) factors.

Other researchers have suggested that attitudes are more permanent and based on consumers' style or profile. First introduced in marketing by Bieri (1961), cognitive styles have been the objects of many subsequent developments (Schaninger and Sciglimpaglia 1981; Alba and Hutchinson 1987, Bagozzi and Foxall 1996). In relation to attitudinal components, styles based on affective and cognitive elements have been categorised by Sojka and Giese (1997). In a 2-dimensional space (cognitive/affective) they identified four types of consumers. 'Thinking Processors' favour cognitive processes rather than affective ones whereas 'Feeling Processors' do the opposite.

Several reported studies have provided support for the interrelated nature of affective and cognitive attitudinal components (i.e. Breckler 1984, Breckler and Wiggins 1989 or Miniard and Barone 1997). The contribution of this study is its examination of the outcomes of such inter-relatedness. In particular we believe that both affective and cognitive components of attitudes contribute, with varying degrees of congruence, to an overall attitudinal space which may differ between individuals and/or product category. Furthermore, we believe that the conative component also influences this overall attitudinal space. Thus, whilst cognitive, affective and conative components of consumers' attitudes are a fundamental focus of much theoretical development in marketing research, this paper aims specifically at providing a new direction for their *empirical* examination. As a result, these concepts are defined in this study from an empirical perspective. Cognitive aspects of consumers' attitudes refer to their beliefs and knowledge about products as well as to their perceptions of differences between products (Cooper 1983). Affective aspects comprise the "emotions, moods, feelings and motives" that reflect the matching of consumers' motives with products (Lelkoff-Hagius and Mason 1993) and are more commonly measured via stated preferences (Creusen and Schoormans 1997). Conative aspects, on the other hand, relate to behavioural consequences and are more easily understood via intention to buy or actual purchase behaviour.

The autonomous nature of conative elements and the opportunity to combine affective and conative elements independently from the cognitive one have already been examined, particularly with respect to retailing. Hirschman and Holbrook (1992) introduced the concept of 'hedonic consumption' whereby the emotive stimulation derived from the act of purchase itself equals or exceeds that expected from the product consumption. Similar effects were found for 'purchase involvement' -as opposed to product involvement- (Ohanian and Tashchian 1992, Lockshin, McIntosh and Spawton 1998). In the case of this latter study, the particular purchase or usage situation of the product (wine), seems to add an affective component (pleasure to buy), to that resulting from the product consumption (pleasure to drink).

OBJECTIVES AND HYPOTHESES OF THE STUDY

Current research appears to favour the identification and segmentation of typical profiles whereby consumers' affective and cognitive predispositions are examined simultaneously (eg. Sojka and Giese's four classes 1997). This is also the approach adopted in this study where all three elements of attitudes (cognitive, affective and conative) are taken into account, using a quantitative process providing a more precise understanding of both conceptual and operational aspects of the problem.

Our objective is to demonstrate the existence of consumer segments based on attitudinal profiles and to test how such profiles can be related to consumer or product characteristics. The methodology used involves first the determination of a shared space between cognitive, affective and conative consumers' attitudinal structures using a non-parametric multi-dimensional analysis 'INDSCAL' (Caroll and Chang 1970), with the contribution of the dimensions of the shared attitude space to each of these structures reflecting the manner in which the structures combine to provide a profile. By shared space, we mean a reduced-size space that accurately reflects the cognitive, affective and conative structures.

Multi-dimensional scaling (MDS) enables the representation of differences between objects as Euclidean distance in a n-dimensions space. The algorithm on which it is based (Torgerson 1952) has since been extensively modified, for example to reflect the ordinal nature of the data (Young and Hamer 1987). An important adaptation of the initial MDS algorithm, INdividual Difference SCALing (INDSCAL), enables the identification of the space common to several dissimilarity matrices (Caroll and Chang 1970) and the estimation of the weight representing the degree to which a dimension of the common space contributes to the representation of the matrix.

In this study, INDSCAL is used to examine simultaneously for each consumer, three matrices representing respectively his or her cognitive, affective and conative predisposition towards a product category. Assuming that m_1, m_2 and m_3 represent the cognitive, affective and conative attitudinal matrices of a consumer, translated in a H-dimensional space, each matrix would be characterised by H parameters w_{mh} measuring the contribution of a dimension h to the representation of the matrix M in the shared space. Matrices would be found to be congruent when their w_{mh} parameters are highly correlated ie. when they share equally the dimensions of the common space. The congruence of a matrix with other matrices translated in the same space could then be measured by the correlation between the w_{mh} of the matrix and the average w_{mh} across all other matrices. This correlation coefficient, ranging from 0 (high correlation) to 1 (low correlation), is known as the 'weirdness

TABLE 1
Congruence and weights of three matrices in a 3-dimensional space of dimensions h_1, h_2 and h_3.

Matrix	Congruence	Weights w_{jh}		
		h_1	h_2	h_3
m_1	0	1	0	0
m_2	0	0	1	0
m_3	0	0	0	1

TABLE 2
Congruence and weights of three matrices in a 3-dimensional space of dimensions h_1, h_2 and h_3.

Matrix	Congruence	Weights w_{jh}		
		h_1	h_2	h_3
m_1	1	1/3	1/3	1/3
m_2	1	1/3	1/3	1/3
m_3	1	1/3	1/3	1/3

index' and is available in most statistical softwares allowing INDSCAL analysis (such as SPSS).

In this paper, the congruence of a matrix with the shared space is simply defined as (1–Weirdness index), and the consumer's *attitudinal profile* is the vector of the congruence values of his or her matrices. In this study, therefore, the attitudinal profile has always 3 values, corresponding to the cognitive, affective and conative matrices, even though the number of dimensions of the shared space may be less or more than 3. For example, a consumer whose weights are shown in Table 1 exhibits a totally non-congruent profile {0, 0, 0}, indicating a complete autonomy of the three attitudinal matrices and illustrating an extension of the cognitive/affective independence hypothesis (Zajonc 1968) to all three attitudinal components. Conversely, Table 2 shows a case where the consumer's three attitudinal matrices are perfectly congruent since each was equally reflected by the dimensions of their common space, hence creating a perfectly congruent profile {1, 1, 1}. Such co-linearity of the three attitudinal components is consistent with researchers who have argued in favour of hierarchical models. These two examples are represented in Figure 1, along with 3 other possible typical attitudinal profiles (congruent matrices are shown as belonging to the same rectangle).

The first profile shows the totally non-congruent example described in Table 1, whereas the second one illustrates the totally congruent example described in Table 2. Profile No 3 shows a consumer whose affective and conative components are congruent but autonomous from his or her cognitive component, consistent with Zajonc's view of the behavioural and the affective being linked independently from beliefs and knowledge which the consumer might have about the product. Profile No 4 is that of a consumer whose conative and cognitive components are congruent but autonomous from affective processes, consistent with the business-to-business paradigm where rational or collegial decision-making

is thought to preclude affective considerations (Brown and Brucker 1990). Finally, Profile No 5 represents a consumer whose conative element (intention to buy) is autonomous from both affective and cognitive components. Intuitively, such instances would seem more likely in the case of impulse purchases or stock-out situations (Vaughn 1980).

Clearly, however, observed attitudinal profiles would be less neatly defined than those 5 typical cases. Their identification and classification should rely on a segmentation process requiring that discrimination between observed profiles be achieved, using such operational variables as consumer demographics or product category. With this operational aim, and to illustrate how such variables could be associated practically with attitudinal profiles, several hypotheses were developed:

H1: A single reduced-size space can reflect consumers' cognitive, affective and conative attitude structures (matrices) towards a product.

H2: Attitudinal profiles vary according to some consumer characteristics (eg. demographics, loyalty, etc…)

H3: Attitudinal profiles vary by product category and/or brand

H1 will be tested by examining the adjustment indices of the INDSCAL solutions. Stress will be calculated according to Kruskal's formula (Kruskal 1964). H2 will be tested by comparing the average age, gender and brand loyalty across segments of attitudinal profiles, H2 being rejected if the corresponding F-tests indicate that no differences exist between profile clusters. H3 can be tested by analysing whether consumers are grouped in the same profile clusters when different Fast Moving Consumer Goods (FMCG) are considered, H3 being rejected if the corresponding Chi-Square test yields a less than .05 probability of no difference.

FIGURE 1
Five typical attitudinal profiles
(A=affective, B=conative (behavioural) and C=cognitive)

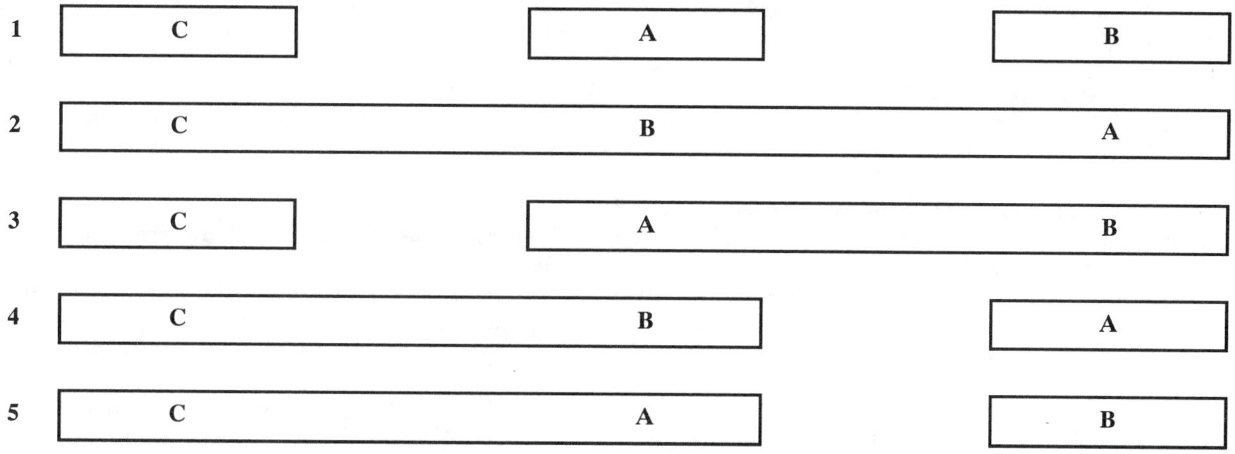

1	C	A	B

2	C	B	A

3	C	A	B

4	C	B	A

5	C	A	B

DATA COLLECTION METHOD

The choice of products for this study was driven by the need to examine product categories within which consumers would be familiar with many (10 or so) brands. This is the result of the positive degree of freedom constraint imposed by the need to extract a non-random space with a large enough number of dimensions. In line with previous work using MDS, our study was based on soft drinks and confectionary bars and relied on the use of a student sample (Green, Carmone and Smith 1989, Hoolbrook, Moore and Winer 1982). Several studies have demonstrated the importance of all three attitudinal components on the buyer behaviour relating to these products (Clayes et al. 1995, Vaughn 1980), and students represent a core target market for both products.

MDS is often used to measure brand perceptions when evaluative attributes are unclear or hard to quantify. Thus, our data collection involved measuring perceived brand differences using pair comparisons, the most respondent-friendly and reliable method for collecting such data (Whipple 1976). With this method, respondents appear to adopt different perspectives according to the pair of objects between which they are asked to estimate a difference (Malhotra, Jain and Pinson 1988). As a result, several latent contexts may underpin the dissimilarity space (Lehman 1971, Hustard, Mayer and Whipple 1975) corresponding for example to different purchase or consumption situations. Therefore, one can expect to find multi-dimensionality, not only in the cognitive element but also in the affective and conative ones, since both preference and inclination to buy may vary according to the context embedded in the particular pair of objects under consideration. Involvement profiles (Laurent and Kapferer 1985) are similarly linked to the concept of purchase situation. Their multi-dimensionality demonstrates the degree to which cognitive (or interest), affective (pleasure) and conative (probability of mistake) are combined differently according to the specific purchase situation faced by the consumer.

The questions used in this study were designed to measure the attitude components for each pair of 10 brands of soft drinks and each pair of 10 brands of confectionary bars. Cognitive structures were measured by asking respondents the differences they perceived for 10 brands of soft drinks and 10 brands of confectionary bars. For each pair of product in the same category, the following question was asked:

"Please note with a cross the degree of difference which you perceive between the two following products": (eg Coca Cola-Pepsi Cola)

Not at all
different:____: X :____:____:____:____:____: Completely
different

The affective structure was measured in such a way as to enable the researchers to test its dimensionality. In a similar study, Moore, Pessemier and Little (1979) had used the 'dollarmetrics' approach (Pessemier 1975). However this approach is unsuited for the inexpensive products used in this study. As a result, a two-step approach was adopted. First, consumers were asked to rank brands by order to preference. Based on this, pairs (A, B) were determined where A is preferred over B. Whilst preferences may also, in part, result from a cognitive process (Zajonc and Markus 1982, Miniard and Barone 1997), the INDSCAL design would indicate how the affective and cognitive structure are reflected along the dimensions of the common space. Hence, the following question was asked about each of the identified pairs of products:

"Please indicate with a cross to what extent you prefer A to B":

Very
Little: ____:____:____:____: X :____:____: Enormously

For the conative structure, purchase frequency was deemed a better indicator than purchase intentions because the products selected were in the low involvement/frequent purchase category. Therefore, for each pair (A,B) of products within the same category, the following question was asked:

"Please compare your usage frequency of brand A with your usage frequency of brand B and mark with a cross the corresponding answer":

A much less
often than B:___: X :___:___:___:___:___: A much
more often
than B

In order to test H2 and H3, other variables were also collected concerning consumers' age, gender and brand loyalty. Furthermore, questions were rotated to avoid any order effects and subsequent tests concerning the potential effect of question order showed that its contribution to explaining the results was negligible.

The sample comprised 150 consumers. In order to ensure that respondents with experience with the chosen product categories were selected, undergraduate and postgraduate students were used, with 75 males and 75 females aged between 19 and 48. The 10 brands used for each product category were selected on the basis of the top-of-the-mind awareness they achieved in preliminary research and included, for softdrinks: Canada Dry, Coca-Cola, Fanta, Gini, Orangina, Pepsi Cola, Ricles, Schweppes, Seven-up and Sprite and for confectionary bars: Bounty, Kinder, Kit Kat, Lion, Mars, Milky Way, Nuts, Snickers, Sundy and Twix. The total data base, therefore, consisted in 900 matrices (150 respondents x 3 matrices x 2 products).

METHOD OF ANALYSIS AND RESULTS

Hypothesis concerning a common space

To examine H1, that a common space existed between the three attitudinal component of any individual, it was first necessary to check that each of the component spaces had a structure. This was achieved by undertaking a MDS analysis for each of the 900 collected matrices. This analysis was undertaken in 4 dimensions, the larger dimensionality possible with a positive degree of freedom, given the number of products used in the study.

As noted previously, the stress function to minimise was that based on Kruskal formula. According to Kruskal, solutions providing a stress level inferior to .1 should be accepted. However, when the number of dimensions and objects is high, a lower level of stress might be expected. Indeed, Spence and Oglivie (1973) suggested that when undertaking a MDS analysis of 10 objects in 4 dimensions, the maximum level of stress allowing the rejection of the null hypothesis with a 95% confidence level is .07. This value was therefore retained in this study.

In order to avoid a degenerescence of the solution, the number of iterations was limited to 20 and the dissimilarity/distance diagrams (Green 1975) were systematically controlled. In total, only 3 matrices were rejected after this process, requiring the removal of the three corresponding respondents from the sample and leaving a total of 882 useful matrices (147x3x2) for further analysis. Thus, all matrices exhibited a non-random structure when represented in a reduced-size multi-dimensional space. This supports the hypothesis that consumers bring a multi-faceted perspective to pair evaluations and that they hold a multi-dimensional view of each attitudinal space.

The next step involved a direct examination of H1, that a common space exists between the three components of an individual's attitude. In order to perform this test, two distinct INDSCAL analyses were undertaken, one for each product category. The process is similar to the one described above except that the one-matrix approach of MDS is replaced by the three-matrices approach afforded by INDSCAL. Furthermore, in order to better represent the three initial spaces, the analysis was undertaken in 5 dimensions. The recommended maximum level of stress for analyses of this type is .07 (Spence and Oglivie 1973).

When compared with the previous analysis, INDSCAL generated higher levels of stress, indicating that, as expected, the differences in each matrix was less perfectly reflected in the common space. However, stress remained in a confidence interval (at 95%) of [.0377, .0393], well below the threshold of .07. Only 12 matrices exceeded marginally the .07 mark. However, considering

how close to the acceptable range they were, and to avoid removing 12 individuals, these were kept in the data set.

In summary, these results show that attitudinal components share a non-random reduced-size space which is both non-random and multi-dimensional. The existence of a common space (ie. a space of reasonable dimension reflecting accurately the non-random structures of the attitudinal components) enables us to propose a definition of *attitudinal profiles* comprising the congruence scores of the consumer's cognitive, affective and conative matrices within their common space.

Hypothesis relating to consumer characteristics and product influence

In order to examine H2 and H3, a cluster analysis was undertaken for each of the two product categories, using the k-means algorithm and the Euclidean distance criterion of Ward. The results of this analysis, for solutions comprising 2 to 6 clusters, are presented in Table 3. Internal validity was assessed using Biserial correlation (Milligan 1981) which varies between 1 (very efficient clustering) to -1 (very inefficient clustering). This measure was deemed the most reliable (Milligan 1981) and is equivalent to other commonly used indices (Klastorin 1983). Whether the means of congruence varied significantly between clusters was assessed using ANOVA which results are included in the column so-titled, indicating the proportion of variables for which the congruence means differed significantly between clusters (P<.05).

At the consumer's level, the INDSCAL analysis of the three matrices (cognitive, affective and conative) defines a common space reflecting the observed distances in the three matrices. Each matrix is characterised by a weight, one for each of the dimensions of the common space. The greater the weight of a matrix on one dimension, the more it determines this dimension. Two matrices of equal weights would therefore influence equally all dimensions, and be described as congruent. The congruence of a matrix can therefore be measured by comparing its weights to the average of the weights of the three matrices. The greater the difference (weirdness index) and the less congruent the matrix. Formally then, congruence was calculated by the correlation of the weights of one matrix with the average weights of all matrices.

For each product, the number of clusters and their respective size (number of individuals per cluster) provided some indication of the operational validity of the analysis. As Table 3 shows, the solutions with 2 or 3 clusters are better for soft drinks whereas the solution with 2 clusters is clearly superior for confectionary bars. In these solutions, a clear distinction is found between those individuals whose attitudinal components are strongly congruent and those whose attitudinal components exhibit little congruence. In the former group, all three components are restituted equally by the space dimensions, consistent with the hierarchical effect model whereby all three components interact in sequence. For example, in cluster 1 of the 3-clusters-solution for soft drinks, consumers are congruent (.863, .861, .862) whereas consumers in cluster 3 exhibit components that appear to contribute to different dimensions (.596, .450, .605). The same observation applies to confectionary bars. In general, clusters with individuals exhibiting more congruent profiles tended to be larger, suggesting the predominance of dependant effects models.

Partial congruence, where congruence of two of the three components is observed, was only found in higher number solutions. For example, in the 5-clusters solution for confectionary bars, cluster 3 is characterised by a clear autonomy of the affective component in relation to the cognitive and conative ones (.452 against .673 and .691), supporting the notion that the affective component is autonomous. In the same cluster solution (cluster 4),

TABLE 3
2-to 6-clusters solutions obtained: Soft drinks and Confectionnary bars

	SOFTDRINKS							CONFECTIONNARY BARS					
Numb clusters	Biserial Correl.	Anova	No	Cluster profile (ind. congruence)			Numb clusters	Biserial Correl.	Anova	No	Cluster profile (ind. congruence)		
				cog.	aff.	con.					cog.	aff.	con.
2	0.545	100%	89	.812	.814	.794	2	0.634	100%	103	.767	.781	.745
			58	.623	.559	.615				44	.565	.447	.561
3	0.547	100%	50	.863	.861	.862	3	0.572	100%	33	.862	.870	.852
			67	.707	.722	.673				78	.712	.728	.684
			30	.596	.447	.605				36	.553	.405	.554
4	0.517	100%	49	.866	.866	.858	4	0.57	100%	34	.858	.866	.853
			30	.743	.768	.589				71	.715	.741	.675
			45	.682	.654	.749				25	.655	.447	.676
			23	.564	.431	.561				17	.443	.401	.445
5	0.505	100%	40	.887	.879	.872	5	0.567	100%	31	.869	.872	.856
			43	.756	.748	.747				66	.727	.750	.699
			18	.700	.762	.528				22	.673	.452	.691
			28	.632	.589	.720				14	.559	.641	.523
			18	.561	.405	.535				14	.445	.332	.442
6	0.497	100%	40	.887	.879	.872	6	0.487	100%	31	.869	.872	.856
			41	.765	.745	.750				49	.722	.699	.734
			17	.703	.772	.528				26	.716	.806	.617
			21	.675	.504	.649				16	.676	.374	.644
			18	.582	.657	.726				15	.530	.581	.563
			10	.496	.357	.500				10	.407	.314	.408

cognitive and affective are little congruent (.559 and .523 respectively) while the affective component contributes to their respective dimensions (.641), suggesting an instance where purchase is autonomous from the perceptions of the product and where both are associated with a specific affective effect. As previously noted, simultaneous product and purchase involvements (Ohanian and Tashchian 1992, Lockshin, Macintosh and Spawton 1998) may characterise a type of festive consumption situation associated with chocolate products.

The internal and face validity of the profiles identified above must be associated with some operational validity in order to assist marketing decision making. In particular, H2 and H3 relate these profiles to consumer characteristics and to product category. Table 4 summarises the results obtained from those cluster analyses offering the best internal validity (similar results were achieved when examining higher-number cluster solutions). Only one significant relationship is revealed by this analysis, in the case of confectionary bars and only for gender, so that female respondents exhibited a more congruent attitudinal profile than men with respect to this product category. Thus, H2, strictly speaking, cannot be rejected.

The analysis summarised in Table 4 also suggests that attitudinal profiles vary according to product category. However, H3 can be tested more formally by comparing the clusters derived from the

TABLE 4
Significance between gender, age, loyalty and attitudinal profiles

P-values	Soft drinks	Confectionary bars
Gender	.574	.018
Age	.723	.714
Consumption	.234	.214
Global Model	.511	.048

TABLE 5
Discriminant analysis of brands, according to congruence scores

Brand pairs	Sig. (Lambda Wilks)	Standard Canonical Coefficients		
		Cognitive	Affective	Conative
Lion vs Snickers	.0067	.6940	.7740	-.2975
Bounty vs Snickers	.0254	.7727	.6260	-.2584
Snickers vs Mars	.0276	.8810	1.0032	-1.0224
Coca Cola vs Schweppes	.0473	.9648	-.9009	.5540

data concerning soft drinks and confectionary bars. A Chi-Square test indicated that consumers allocated to a cluster for one product would not be allocated to the same cluster for the other product, hence providing further support for H3. In other words, in explaining a given consumer's attitude towards two products, the cognitive, affective and conative components would play different parts.

Hypothesis concerning a relationship between brands and attitudinal profile

Once a relationship is established between product category and attitudinal profiles, a natural extension of this hypothesis involves examining whether such a relationship also exists with regards to brands. In order to answer this question, consumers' scores were examined to determine whether they allowed a discrimination amongst brands. Table 5 presents those brand pairs most clearly discriminated by the analysis.

As Table 5 shows, attitudinal profiles of consumers of one brand may differ markedly from that of consumers of another brand. For example, attitudinal profiles of Snickers' consumers (.62, .62, .62) are clearly less congruent than that of other brands' consumers (eg Bounty: .75, .74, .74). Likewise, Coca Cola consumers' attitudinal profiles (.70, .69, .68) are significantly less congruent than that of Schweppes consumers (.78, .77, .79).

Since a lack of congruence indicates that cognitive, affective and conative contribute to different dimensions, consumers of Snickers or Coca Cola may require a more varied mix, emphasising differently cognitive, affective and conative aspects, depending on their particular attitudinal profiles. For example, advertising messages may be included jointly in the communication strategy that appeal to cognition or to emotions while, at the same time, packaging and point-of-sale material may provide the conative element.

CONCLUSION

This study examined the issue of autonomy or congruence of the cognitive, affective and conative attitudinal structures by using a novel approach based on the concept of attitudinal profiles. We observed empirically that a consumer's cognitive, affective and conative structures were multi-dimensional and that they could be represented in a reduced-size common space. The restitution of these structures by the dimensions of the common space enabled the determination of attitudinal profiles which, when grouped into clusters, exhibited high internal validity and could be significantly related to some consumer and product characteristics.

A majority of consumers were found to be 'congruent', consistent with traditional views whereby cognitive, affective and conative predispositions all contribute similarly to overall attitudes. However, other consumers were identified who exhibited a much less congruent profile and whose attitudinal structures were more autonomous, consistent with more recent theories of attitude.

For marketing managers, these findings are interesting since attitudinal profiles may enable a segmentation of consumers that can be related to both personal and product characteristics. Furthermore, the relationship found to exist between attitude profiles and brands suggests that an attitudinal profile segmentation may assist in revisiting previous positioning strategies by differentiating the dimensions of the attitudinal space according to their restitution of consumers' cognitive, affective and conative structures. Thus, alternative persuasion strategies might be open to marketers who would be able to position their products in terms of cognitive, affective or conative elements as well as segment their consumers in terms of attitudinal profiles.

Of course, this exploratory research has a number of limitations. In particular, student samples are often suspect in research. However, given their competence and importance as a target market for both products used in this study, the use of a student sample appeared justifiable here.

Attitudinal profiles such as the ones identified here in the case of two product categories provide only a limited picture of what this approach might be able to do. Clearly, future research should explore further the potential contribution of this type of approach to the examination of consumers' attitudinal components. For instance, other consumer variables may provide useful descriptors of consumer segments based on attitudinal profiles. Whilst this study suggested only one discriminant factor (gender), it may well be that for other products, other operational variables such as income, education or household size could prove useful for marketers wanting to reach target consumers exhibiting a given attitudinal profile.

REFERENCES

Alba J. and Hutchinson J.W. (1987), "Dimensions of Consumer Expertise", *Journal of Consumer Research*, 13, 411-455.

Anand P., Holbrook M.B. and Stephens D. (1988) "The formation of affective judgements: the cognitive-affective model versus the independance hypothesis", *Journal of Consumer Research*, 15, 386-391.

Bagozzi R. P. and Foxall G.R. (1996) "Construct validation of a measure of adaptative-innovative cognitive styles in consumption", *International Journal of Market Research*, 13, 201-214.

Bieri J. (1961)"Cognitive Simplicity as a personality Variable in Cognitive and Preferential Behavior", In D.W. Fiske and S.R. Maddi eds, *Functions of Varied Experiences*, Homewood, Ill., The Dorsey Press, 355-379.

Breckler S.J. (1994) "Memory from the experience of donating blood:Just how bad was it?", *Journal of Basic and Applied Social Psychology*, 14(4), 467-488.

Breckler S.J. and Wiggins E.C. (1989), "Affect vs evaluation in the structure of attitudes", *Journal of Experimental Social Psychology*, 25(3), 253-271.

Brown H. and Brucker (1990)" Charting the Industrial Buying Stream", *Industrial Marketing Management*, 19, 55-61.

Caroll J.D, et J.J Chang (1970), "Analysis of individual differences in multidimensional scaling via an n-way generalization of " Eckart-Young " decomposition ", *Psychometrika*, 35, 238-319.

Claeys C., A. Swinnen, et P.V. Abeele (1995), "Consumer'means-end chains for "Think " and "Feel " products ", *International Journal in Marketing*, 12, 193-208.

Cooper L.G. (1983), "A Review of Multidimensionnal Scaling in Marketing Research ", *Applied Psychological Measurement*, 7, 427-450.

Creusen M.E.H., J.P.L. Schoormans (1997), "The nature of differences between similarity and preference judgements, a replication with extension ", *International Journal of Marketing Research*, 14, 81-87.

Green P.E. (1975) " On the Robustness of MultiDimensionnal Scaling Techniques", *Journal of Marketing Research*, 12, 73-81.

Green P.E., Carmone F.J., Smith S.M. (1989), *Multidimensional Scaling: concepts and Applications*, Allyn and Bacon, Boston.

Hirschman E.C. and Holbrook M.B. (1982), "Hedonic Consumption:emerging concepts, methods and propositions", *Journal of Marketing*, 46, 92-101.

Holbrook M.B., Moore W.L. et Winer R.S., "Constructing joint spaces from pick-any data: A new tool for consumer analysis, *Journal of Consumer Research*, 9, 99-105.

Hustard T.P, Mayer C.S. and Whipple T.W. (1975), "Consideration of Context differences in Product Evaluation and Market Segmentation", *Journal of the Academy of Marketing Science*, 3, 435-439.

Klastorin T.D. (1983), "Assessing Cluster Analysis results", *Journal of Marketing Research*, 20, 1, 92-98.

Kruskal J.B. (1964), " Multidimensional scaling by optimizing goodness of fit to a non-metric hypothesis", *Psychometrika*, 29, 1-27.

Laurent G. and Kapferer, J-N (1985) "Measuring Consumer Involvement Profiles", *Journal of Marketing Research*, 22, 41-53.

Lefkoff-Hagius R., C.H. Mason (1993), "Characteristics, beneficial, and image attributes in consumer judgements of similarity and preference ", *Journal of Consumer Research*, 20, 100-110.

Lehman D.R. (1971) "Television Show Preferences: Application of a Choice Model" *Journal of Marketing Research*, 8, 47-55.

Lockshin L.S., Macintosh G. et Spawton, T. (1998), "Using Product Brand and Purchasing Involvement for Retail Segmentation", *Journal of Retailing and Consumer Services*, 4, 1, 171-183.

Malhotra N.K., Jain A.K. and Pinson C. (1988), "The Robustness of MDS Configarations in the Case of Incomplete Data", *Journal of Marketing Research*, 25, 95-102.

Milligan G.W. (1981), "A Monte Carlo Study of Thirty internal validity criterion measures for cluster analysis", *Psychometrika*, 46, 2, 40-47.

Miniard P.W. and Barone M.J. (1997), "The Case for Noncognitive Determinants of Attitude: A Critique of Fishbein and Middlestadt", *Journal of Consumer Psychology*, 6(1), 39-44.

Moore W.L., Pessemier E.A. and Little T.E (1979), "Predicting Brand Purchase Behaviour: Marketing Application of the Schonemenn and Wang Unfolding Model" *Journal of Marketing Research*, 9, 206-210.

Ohanian, Roobina and Armen Tashchian, (1992), "Consumers' Shopping Effort and Evaluation of Store Image Attributes: The Roles of Purchasing Involvement and Recreational Shopping Interest," *Journal of Applied Business Research*, 8 (6), 40-49.

Park C.W. et M. Young (1985), " Consumer responses to television commercials: The impact of involvment and background music on brand attitude formation", *Journal of Marketing Research*, 2, 11-24.

Pessemier E.A. (1975)" Market Structure Analysis of New Product and Market Opportunity" *Journal of Contemporary Business*, 4, 35-67.

Rosenberg M.J. and Hovland L. (1960) *Attitude Organisation and Change: An Analysis of Consistency Among Attitude Components*, Yale University Press, New Haven.

Schaninger C.M. and Sciglimpaglia D. (1981) "The Infleunce of Cognitive Personality Traits and demographics on Consumer Information Acquisition", *Journal of Consumer Research*, 8, 208-216.

Sojka J.Z. et J.L. Giese (1997), "Thinking and/or Feeling: An Examination of Interaction Between Processing Styles ", *Advances in Consumer Research*, 24, 438-442.

Spence I. and Oglivie J.C. (1973) "A Table of Expected Stress Values from Random Rankings in Nonmetric Multidimensional Scaling", *Multivariate Behavioural Research*, 8, 551-558.

Torgerson W.S. (1952), " Multidimensional scaling: I. Theory and method ", *Psychometrika*, 17, 401-419.

Young F.W., R.M. Hamer (1987), *Multidimensional scaling: History, theory, and applications*. Hillsdale, N.J.: Lawrence Erlbaum Associates.

Vaughn R. (1980)," How Advertising Workds: A Planning Model", *Journal of Advertising Research*, 20, 27-33.

Whipple T.W. (1976), "Variation Among Multidimensional Scaling Solutions: An Examination of the Effect of Data Collection Differences", *Journal of Marketing Research*, 13, 98–103.

Zajonc R.B. (1968) "Attitudinal effects of mere exposure", *Journal of Personality and Social Psychology*, 9, 2(2), 1-28.

Zajonc, R.B. et H. Markus (1982), "Affective and Cognitive Factors in Preferences ", *Journal of Consumer Research"*, 9, 123-131.

Living with Contradictions: Representational Politics and Politics of Representation in Advertising

Ozlem Sandikci, Bilkent University

ABSTRACT

Drawing from postmodern art theory this study explores the notions of representational politics and politics of representation in advertising. The paper begins with a review of key concepts of postmodern aesthetics and practices, and discusses various postmodern representational strategies identified as a result of a critical visual analysis of a controversial advertising campaign of the Italian clothing company Diesel. The paper concludes with a discussion of the problems and possibilities inherent in postmodern representation in advertising, the importance of critical literacy in the reception of such advertisements, and future research venues.

"In contemporary capitalism, in the society of simulacrum, the market is 'behind' nothing, it is in everything."

Burgin (1986, p.174)

In recent years art theoretical approaches were introduced into the analysis of consumer culture (Ger 1999; Stern 1998; Witkowski 1999) and advertising (Kates and Shaw-Garlock 1999; Schroeder 1999; Scott 1992, 1994). In the consumption area, this stream of research is based on the premise that art expresses historical and cultural context and, hence, reveals social dynamics, including daily consumption practices. In advertising research, it is suggested that art theory can advance our understanding of how meaning is produced, constructed and understood within a given time period and social context. In one such application, for instance, Schroeder (1999) outlines various insights that can be gained from an analysis of the genre of Dutch art, which have markedly influenced the development of photography, and exert a strong influence on contemporary pictorial advertising conventions. Drawing from postmodern art theory, this exploratory study aims to contribute to this emerging field of inquiry by discussing various issues pertaining to the nature of representation in advertising through a case study of a highly controversial ad campaign of the Italian clothing company Diesel.

The paper begins with a review of the key concepts of postmodern aesthetics and, especially, its expression in photography, and argues that the critical discourses and practices that first arose as the symptoms of postmodernism in art are appropriated and reassumed for the use of capital itself. A Diesel advertising campaign is used as an illustration of this argument, and various postmodern representational strategies that are identified through a critical visual analysis are outlined. The paper concludes with a discussion of the problems and the possibilities inherent in postmodern representation in advertising, the role that critical literacy plays in reception of such advertising messages, and suggestions for future research.

POSTMODERN AESTHETICS, POLITICS AND COMMERCE

While there is no single definition of postmodernism and the term is used to describe multiple phenomena including a philosophy, an aesthetic sensibility, and a cultural condition, there is an overall consensus that the postmodern condition is related to dramatic changes in the material and cultural dimensions of life, resulting from immense advances in production, distribution, communication, and computer technologies (Baudrillard 1983; Harvey 1989; Jameson 1991; Lyotard 1984). In the cultural domain, discussions on postmodernism are centered around the issues of meaning and representation. Postmodern culture is characterized as a landscape saturated with hyperreal images and free-floating signifiers that proclaim the end of fixed, transcendental meanings and truth claims. The aesthetic sensibility emerging out of the postmodern condition is often viewed as related to the market place, and it is argued that postmodernism is the artform of consumer culture, the expression of a fragmented and aestheticized experience of everyday life in the late capitalist societies (Hassan 1985; Jameson 1991; Gitlin 1989; Lash 1990; McRobbie 1989).

As an aesthetic category postmodernism can be read as a breaking away from modernism. The modernist aesthetic can be interpreted in two ways. The formalist account (e.g., Greenberg [1939] 1986) conceptualizes modernism as the pursuit of 'purity'. That is, different art forms such as painting, sculpture, architecture exist as distinct mediums, and each has a specific code governing them. The critical account of modernism, including Cubism, Dada, the readymade and conceptual art, and Futurism, on the other hand, can be understood as an avant-garde critique of the former aesthetic conventions (Frisby 1986; Lash 1990). Whether formalist or critical, the dominant logic of modernism was to challenge the realist notion of representation as a transparent reflection of reality. For modernist, reality was no longer immediately apparent from surface appearances, and their goal was to capture, through formal experimentation, the essential truths hidden from immediate perception.

In contrast to modernist aspiration to reveal the essential truths of the world through appropriate aesthetic medium, postmodernism rejects the existence of such essential truths. In postmodernism, reality, whether it is represented transparently or abstractly, is viewed as a fiction, produced and sustained only by its cultural representation (Foster 1985). As Owens explains while "modernist theory presupposes that mimesis ... can be bracketed or suspended, and that the art object itself can be substituted (metaphorically) for its referent ... Postmodernism neither brackets nor suspends the referent but works to problematize the activity of reference" (1980, p.235). Furthermore, postmodern art, in contrast to modern art's search for purity, exists between and across forms, or in neglected forms like photography and video (Foster 1982). The postmodern artists manipulate old signs in a new logic: they are "not in search of sources or origins, but of structures of signification" (Crimp 1979, p.87). The transgression of aesthetic limits and the opening up of cultural codes through strategies such as appropriation, fragmentation, hybridization, repetition, pastiche, framing, and staging distinguish postmodern art from its modernist predecessors (Foster 1982; Gitlin 1989; Jameson 1991; Owens 1980).

Photography, which as a visual art form offers many insights into the understanding of advertising, has an important place within postmodernist art. The works of postmodern photographers highlight many of the issues related to the postmodern crisis of representation, and exhibit the divergences from the formal categories of modernist aesthetic. However, originally, photography came into existence as a major carrier and shaper of modernism (Nichols 1981). Given its technical ability to reproduce from actuality with more accuracy than any other form of representation, photography was seen as revelatory, bringing the hidden truths into the light of day. Thus, photography, itself a part of scientific and technological development, seemed to fit within the spirit of modernity, as well as offering realist possibilities for representing aspects of modern life (Wells 1997). The changes in cultural sphere accompanied by new image production and manipulation techniques including digital technology, brought into question the traditional conception of photography as a document of reality. The central emphasis in postmodernism on construction, the forging, staging and fabrication of images found a strong voice in postmodern photography which refused to take the world at face value and instead invite the spectator to actively read the construction and implicate questions of subjectivity and identity. The notion of construction entailed, first, the idea that art can intervene politically, and, second, the notion of deconstruction.

Indeed, initially, postmodern photography, such as the works of Cindy Sherman, Richard Prince, Sharon Levine and Barbara Kruger, was identified with a specially critical stance which was characterized by its dismantling of reified, idealist conceptions of modernist aesthetics, including subjectivity and aura, and its engagement with the simulacral (Crimp1979; Krauss 1985). These artists pillaged the mass media and advertising for its subject which is then "repositioned in ways that sought to denaturalize the conventions that encode the ideological and, in doing so, to make those very ideological contents available to scrutiny and contestation" (Solomon-Gadeau 1991, p.134). For instance, Richard Prince's rephotographs of the 'Marlbora Man' advertisements that appeared in the early years of the Reagan administration were a critique of the new conservative agenda. By recropping, rephotographing, and recontextualizing the image of the Marlboro men, Prince made visible the link between a mythical notion of masculinity and the prevailing political rhetoric.

Quickly, however, this critical agenda of postmodern photography disappeared, resulting in the domestication of the critical potential of photographic appropriation (Crimp 1983). According to Solomon-Gadeau "the assimilation of postmodernist strategies back into mass culture that had in part engendered them" had, on the one hand, rendered postmodern photography comprehensible and expanded its market, but, on the other hand, signalled "its near-total assimilation into those very discourses (advertising, fashion, media) it professed to critique" (1991, p.139). That is, although appropriation developed as a descriptive hallmark of postmodern culture, the critical function that it has been expected to perform had become increasingly difficult to maintain and justify once it was appropriated for commercial purposes. The disappearance of a critical motivation has resulted not only in a collapse of any solid distinction between art and advertising, but also the use of postmodern representational strategies in advertising has led to a set of ontological and ideological paradoxes that challenge the conventions of advertising as a commercial genre.

CASE STUDY: DIESEL FOR SUCCESSFUL LIVING

During 1990s a handful of companies have abandoned conventional advertising formats and executed ad campaigns that involved 'shocking' imagery and explicit political and social messages. Pioneering this move was the Italian clothing company, Benetton, whose advertisements included images of AIDS, environmental disasters, wars, and racism. This highly controversial representational strategy, which is referred to as the 'Benetton-Toscani' (Falk 1997) effect in contemporary advertising, was soon adopted by a number of companies, including Calvin Klein, Diesel and Death. In 1991 Diesel, another Italian clothing company, started its 'Successful Living' campaign, which, since then, mocked everything from American evangelism to Japanese consumerism, from sexual and racial stereotypes to materialism. The advertisements

used as exemplars in this study is part of the fall/winter 1997 campaign, and entails six different images, all shot in photojournalistic style in Pyongyang, North Korea by the photographer Peter Gehrke (see Exhibit for one execution). The ads feature various fictional 'Brand O' products and are intended to highlight, according to the company, "the insensitivity of large companies marketing products in poor countries without considering their audience" (Krol 1997, p.11). One advertisement, for example, promotes the 'Brand O Diet', and features waiflike Western models while the copy reads, "there is no limit how thin you can get". Another one shows a run-down neighbourhood where a poster hanged on the wall of a house promotes 'Brand O Tours' through a picture of a happy-looking Western couple and a copy that reads "escape now!". Set in a country where a million people are dying of starvation and poverty, the ironic attitude sets the tone of the entire campaign.

PARADOXES IN THE PARADISE: POSTMODERN STRATEGIES AND ADVERTISING PRACTICE

Advertising, given its commercial goal of creating a positive image for the brand, is, traditionally, guided by a representational strategy of showing the pleasurable, happy and idealistic experiences associated with the product. Advertising language is characterized by the hedonistic aspects of the good life and festive situations, and by the promises of prestige, self-esteem, luxury, good times, and work-free existence. As such, advertising is viewed as belonging to the realm of fantasy, fiction and 'unreality'.

The emphasis on fantasy is even more pronounced in the genre of fashion advertising, which is particularly concerned by showing what is dramatic, glamorous and exotic. In creating worlds of illusion, fashion photography has been influenced by other genres of photographic practice, and had close links with art photography. Early portrait photography was adopted by fashion photographers (Ewing 1991), and photographers such as Andre Barre, Irving Penn and Erwin Blumenfield have been influenced by Surrealism. Photojournalism and documentary photography in the 1930s also affected fashion imagery. Given this historical connection between fashion photography and art photography, it is not surprising to expect that postmodern aesthetics and photographic practices will be adapted by fashion photographers and used in fashion advertising. What is interesting, however, in this interaction is the resultant nature of the ad imagery, engendered largely by the postmodern problematic of representation, which is at once about politics, ethics and pedagogy.

A close reading of the Diesel advertisements from the perspective of postmodern theory reveals various representational strategies operating in these advertisements and help us better understand how they might function within the sign economy. Such an analysis, as outlined below, suggests that these advertisements cannot be understood only as functional tools within the utilitarian logic of classical economy. Rather, they operate as a representational system that introduces a radical challenge to the landscape of consumption, which is yet to be fully explored. As any representational system, they are embedded in power relations and are an integral part of social processes of differentiation, exclusion and incorporation.

Hybridity

One of the first things that one observes after viewing the Diesel ads is their hybrid structure that combines the conventions of advertising and the genre of documentary photography. Hybridization, the picking-and-mixing of styles and genres, is an important feature of postmodern art which eclectically combines

previously distinct conventions and art mediums. The appropriation and the recycling of texts, images and styles, and the forms of past and present aim to question and deconstruct the very representations they quote, in order to decenter the subject of such representations, and render cultural meanings ambiguous and indeterminate (Foster 1985).

Diesel advertisements use a photojournalistic approach that addresses consumers through stylized representation whose structuring principle is shock. In contrast to the glamour images that characterize much of fashion advertising, they place images of human suffering, poverty and misery. The disjuncture between subject matter and the motivation of the ad is a shock delivered to the advertising genre itself. The ads do not only blur the boundaries of advertising and documentary photography but also problematize the cultural codes that distinguish different forms. Within their discursive context, the distinction between 'documentary' and advertising disappears, while social problems become subordinated to the logic of commodity culture. What determines the effect of these images is a function of what has been appropriated and how it has been re-presented. The dramatic, almost violent quality of the images of Koreans, their poverty and suffering creates an element of nightmare that is attached to the erotic and ironic glitter of the commodity and the models that personify its glamour. While the documentary-like nature of the imagery appears to register the poverty and misery of the people featured in the ads and call attention to their problems, their ironic juxtaposition to the ads-within-ads negate the possibility of emergence of any 'true' social consciousness.

It is not only the blurring of the distinctions between the conventions of advertising and documentary photography that distinguishes these advertisements but the implosion of politics and commerce. Baudrillard (1983) uses the term 'implosion' to refer to erosion of boundaries and distinctions within culture that were previously differentiated by modernity, and argues that under the regime of simulation in contemporary Western societies the social and the cultural, and the public and private become indistinguishable. The sheer bulk of representations in film, television and advertising, not only threaten the integrity of private world, they actually abolish the distinction between the private and public spheres: the public possesses the private, the private encompasses the public. In contrast to the conventional indifference of advertising discourse to social and political problems, Diesel ads invades the personal world of consumption through the incorporation of political and social messages. However, the resultant is a blend of both the conflictual and the comic view of the third world subsumed under the logic of commodity consumption. While there is no necessary connection between the two texts (the First World and the Third World), what emerges is a perplexing hybrid that simultaneously acts as a tool to foster capitalist and consumerist ideology and a critique of the very same ideology.

Allegory

In two influential articles, art theorist Craig Owens makes a strong case for the close affiliation between postmodern artistic practices and allegory which, as a genre, allows proliferation of irony and parody through eclecticism (1980). When one narrative is read as covertly representing one or more other meanings, then it is described as being allegorical. Allegory was an important convention in reading and writing until the late eighteenth century, when it was increasingly diminished as outmoded. Owens argues that postmodern art exhibits a strong allegorical impulse because allegory is inherently appropriative, often chooses fragmentary and incomplete materials, and allows texts to be read through each other. Allegory does not restore an original meaning, it supplants an antecedent one, hence it is "consistently attracted to the fragmentary, the imperfect, the incomplete" and "only affirms its own arbitrariness and contingency (Owens 1980, p.70). Using works of artists such as Laurie Anderson, Robert Rauschenberg, Sherrie Levine and Robert Longo as exemplars, Owens points out to the existence of mutually incompatible and even antithetical meanings, and ambiguity in these texts that dissolve them into complicity, ambivalence, and deconstruction.

It is such an ambivalence that sets the tone of the Diesel advertisements and highlights the problem of representation's relation to the real. On the one hand, by appealing to photo-documentary style the ads stimulate a notion of 'realism'; on the other hand, the logic of commodity consumption and the stylized contrast between 'third world' misery and 'first world' joy constructs a spectacle that lands the ads into hyperreality. Suspended in a still picture, poverty, hunger and despair are transformed into a fascination of consumption. The images and the words are all double-coded. "Escape now!" for example one ad-within-ad reads, juxtaposing a happy and smiling Western couple under palm trees to malnourished, poor Koreans standing in despair in a torn-down neighborhood. Should one escape from the suffering and poverty of underdeveloped nations, from communism or from the greed and materialism of capitalism? Multiple, incompatible and even antithetical meanings can be activated in such a way that it is impossible to choose among them, and this works, more than anything, to problematize the act of reading. And, it is precisely this ambivalence that allows shock and violence to be transformed into an aesthetic spectacle.

Fragmentation

In discussions of postmodernism, fragmentation refers both to the end of grand narratives and universal truths (Lyotard 1984), and to the fragmentation of meaning and subjectivity due to constant and ever increasing exposure to a whirlpool of images (Baudrillard 1983; Jameson 1991). In postmodern works, fragmentation is used to emphasize that different realities coexist, collide, and interpenetrate (McHale 1987), and to call into question all the assumptions of fixed systems of representation (Foster 1982). Owens (1980) connects postmodernist fragmentation to poststructuralist decentering of language. Postmodern art, he suggests, not only stresses "ephemeral space and fragmentary images" but, more importantly, has an impulse "to upset stylistic norms, to redefine conceptual categories, and to challenge the modernist idea of symbolic totality" (Owens 1980, p.66). The sense of narrative in postmodern works is one of its simultaneous presence and absence, in which continuity exist only in the 'trace' of the fragment, as it moves from production to consumption.

Diesel ads simultaneously offer and defer a promise of meaning. They appear strangely incomplete, ironic and shocking fragments that both solicit and frustrate our desire to decipher. If by reading we mean extracting from a text a monolithic message, all attempts to decipher these ads fail. The absence of product related claims, the inclusion of socially and politically charged images, the mixing of the codes of different genres contradict with the expectations of an audience and challenge their interpretive assumptions about reading ads. The ambiguous, unconventional, and shocking nature of the ads encourages a polarization of opinions and multiplicity of

readings, and poses many challenging questions: What does the framing of third world misery as a pictorial spectacle aim to achieve? What alternative visions are suggested by these images? What meanings do these ads communicate about the Diesel brand? Not providing easy answers to these questions, they construct a pedagogical site that operates at the intersection of morality, identity and consumption.

DISCUSSION: ADVERTISING, CRITICAL LITERACY AND THE FUTURE

Culture is increasingly constituted by commerce, and the penetration of commodity culture into every facet of daily life has become the major axis of relations of exchange through which corporations actively produce new, increasingly effective forms of address and new sign values. Diesel, along with companies such as Benetton and Calvin Klein engages in a representational strategy that challenges both the conventions of advertising and the relation between consumption, identity and politics. What legitimizes advertising is its commercial logic embodied in its production and reception. Employment of a postmodern sensibility, as exemplified in these advertisements, points at a transformation in the nature of advertising: a new kind of advertising which is sceptical about the legitimizing discourse of advertising. We have, in other words, a form of advertising whose representational means embody a scepticism as to the commercial logic of advertising through incorporation of images and themes that are directly antithetical to advertising. The effects and possibilities of such a transformation, however, are highly debatable. It seems that any advertising set forth with internal critical intent is bound to be assimilated into its operational logic–selling commodities–and redistributed in the form of a style.

In his analysis of Benetton advertisements, Giroux argues that use of shocking and violent images of social and political events in advertising attempts to "redefine the link between commerce and politics by emphasizing both the politics of representation and the representation of politics" (1994, p.5). Clearly, these advertisements appropriate politics and, in this process, aim to position the brands they are promoting as socially and politically conscious. By employing highly shocking and capturing images, Diesel advertisements can achieve broader public recognition of the problems faced in North Korea and add a moral dimension to advertising by turning it into a platform to engage with problems that are traditionally excluded from the sphere of commerce. However, in this process politics becomes highly aestheticized and spectacularized, thus, being stripped away from its socio-cultural context. The ironic offering of commodity consumption, and capitalism at large, as a solution to the problems of poverty and hunger negates the ads' critical potential. As politics is defined largely through the consumption of images and products, social consciousness appears to be only about consumption, but not necessarily changing oppressive and unequal conditions of life and relations of power.

Implosion of politics and commerce also constructs such advertisements as a pedagogical site, in which knowledge is produced, values are articulated, identities are shaped and communities are formed. Because advertising is not conventionally associated with politics, such advertisements powerfully challenge our understanding of "who speaks under what conditions and under what authority" (Giroux 1991, p.4). Indeed, a common response to shock advertising[1] both at public and academic level, is the accusation

---

[1] Consider for example Benetton's recent 'Death Row' campaign and the criticism it received especially from those whose relatives were killed and those who are pro-death penalty.

that these companies are commercializing and trivializing political issues to promote sales of their brands and gain free publicity. From such a perspective, we can easily condemn these advertisements and distrust the sincerity of companies engaging in such advertising. Or alternatively without becoming overtly optimistic, we, as marketing scholars, can start exploring the ramifications of a postmodern sensibility in advertising, and the possibility of a new 'performative' function of advertising, one that reconciles capitalist aims and critical consciousness, however perplexing it may appear. It is true that spectacles do not invite situating information into a context, but rather create their own meaning systems and own versions of the social. However, these meaning systems may or may not exist in harmony with market ideologies, and by transforming advertising to a language of conflict instead of consensus and inciting debate and dialogue about social and political issues, such advertising may create almost a Habermasian public sphere (1989). Within such an expanded field of advertising, questions pertaining to the functioning and reading of such advertisements require a critical research agenda that is attentive to the dynamics of production and reception as well as to the politics of identity and consumption.

Representation is always contextual and the meanings produced are inseparable from the discursive and institutional structures that contain them as well as the interpretive strategies and options available to the audiences. Consumers produce rather than merely receive meanings, even though the range of reading practices are influenced and shaped by various social, economic and cultural forms of capital (Holt 1996). The advertisements by Diesel, Benetton and the like generate a polarization of opinions and employment of various types of cultural literacy and subcultural skills. Thus, empirical research is needed to find out how these advertisements are read by different groups of consumers, what brand images are formed and what consumption behaviors are motivated. Given that a uniform global culture is said to be formed especially within the young populace, cross-cultural studies are also needed to explore the nature of reception of such advertisements among countries who are at different stages of consumption culture.

From a social policy perspective, such advertisements highlight the importance of critical media and advertising literacy. The notion of critical media literacy points to the fact that representations are instrumental not only in producing meanings but also in constructing subjectivities (Giroux and McLaren 1991; McLaren 1988; McLaren and Hammer 1996). Critical media literacy emphasizes the spatial and temporal features of reception, the relations of power and the distribution of resources among recipients, the social institutions within which individuals appropriate mediated knowledges, the systematic asymmetries and differentials that characterize the contexts of reception, and see them as situated practices (Thompson 1990). Accordingly, future studies on critical advertising literacy need to explore how mediated messages are rejected or incorporated by individuals as well as how the appropriation of mediated messages shapes identities and creates virtual communities of consumers in the sense of 'neo-tribes' as suggested by Maffesoli (1996).

Representations are always produced within cultural limits and theoretical borders, and, hence, are implicated in particular economies of truth, value, power, and politics. Representations accompany, adapt to, and influence the nature of changes and trends in the capitalist economy. As Burgin argues "in contemporary capitalism, in the society of simulacrum, the market is 'behind' nothing, it in everything. It is thus that in a society where the commodification of art has progressed apace with the aestheticization of the commodity, there has evolved a universal rhetoric of the aesthetic in which commerce and inspiration, profit and poetry, may rapturously entwine" (1986, p.174). The consumer is never the consumer of just a commodity but equally of the commodity's text and ideology. As such, perhaps the highest challenge these advertisements pose is to consumer behavior researchers: how are we to engage with the representational politics in advertising and promote a critical research practice which is not only attentive to representational ideologies, institutional forms and social relationships, but also self-conscious about its own organizing principles, structuring codes and ethical/political standing?

REFERENCES

Baudrillard, Jean (1983), *Simulations*, New York: Semiotexte.

Burgin, Victor (1986), *The End of Art Theory*, Atlantic Highlights, NJ: Humanities Press.

Crimp, Douglas (1983), "Appropriating Appropriation," in *Image Scavengers*, Exhibition Catalogue, University of Pennsylvania, Institute of Contemporary Art, December 8, 1983–January 30, 1983, 27.

Crimp, Douglas (1979), "Pictures," *October*, 8, 75-88.

Ewing, William (1991), *The Idealizing Vision: The Art of Fashion Photography*, New York: Aperture.

Falk, Pasi (1997), "The Benetton-Toscani Effect: Taking the Limits of Conventional Advertising," in M. Nava, A. Blake, I. MacRury and B. Richards (eds.), Buy This Book: Studies in Advertising and Consumption, New York: Routledge.

Foster, Hall (1982), "Re: Post," *Parachute*, 26 (Spring), 11-15.

Foster, Hall (1985), *Recodings: Art, Spectacle, Cultural Politics*, Port Townsend, WA: Bay Press.

Frisby, David (1986), *Fragments of Modernity*, Cambridge: Polity Press.

Ger, Guliz (1999), "Art Consumption in Late Ming China, 1550-1644," in *Advances in Consumer Research*, eds. Eric J. Arnould and Linda M. Scott, Vol.26, Provo, UT: Association for Consumer Research, 640.

Giroux, Henry (1994), Disturbing Pleasures: Learning Popular Culture, New York: Routledge.

Giroux, Henry and Peter McLaren (1991), "Leon Golub's Radical Pessimism: Toward a Pedagogy of Representation," *Exposure*, 28(12), 18-33.

Gitlin, Tod (1989), "Postmodernism Defined At Last!," The Utne Reader, (July/August), 52-61.

Greenberg, Clement ([1939] 1986), "Avant-Garde and Kitsch," *The Collected Essays and Criticism*, Vol.1, ed. J. O'Brian, Chicago: University of Chicago Press.

Habermas, Jurgen (1989), *The Structural Transformation of the Public Sphere: An Inquiry Into A Category of Bourgeois Society,* trans. T. Burger and F. Lawrence, Cambridge, MA: MIT Press

Harvey, David (1989), *The Condition of Postmodernity*, Cambridge, MA: Blackwell.

Hassan, Ihab (1985), "The Culture of Postmodernism," *Theory, Culture and Society*, 2(3), 119-132.

Holt, Douglas B. (1998), "Does Cultural Capital Structure American Consumption," *Journal of Consumer Research*, 25(June), 1-25.

Jameson, Frederick (1991), *Postmodernism or, The Cultural Logic of Late Capitalism*, Durham: Duke University Press.

Kates, Steven M. and Glenda Shaw-Garlock (1999), "The Ever Entagling Web: A Study of Ideologies and Discourses in Advertising to Women," *Journal of Advertising*, 28(2), 33-49).

Krauss, Rosalind (1985), *The Originality of the Avant-Garde and Other Modernist Myths*, Cambridge: MIT Press.

Krol, Carol (1997), "Diesel Uncovers Fall Jeans Campaign," *Advertising Age*, November, 11.

Lash, Scott (1990), *Sociology of Postmodernism*, New York: Routledge.

Lyotard, Jean-Francois (1984), *The Postmodern Condition*, Minneapolis: University of Minnesota Press.

McCracken, Grant (1988), "Advertising: Meaning or Information?," in Advances in Consumer Research, eds. M. Walledorf and Paul Anderson, Vol.14, Provo, UT: Association for Consumer Research, 121-124.

Maffesoli, Michel (1996), *The Time of the Tribes: The Decline of Individualism in Mass Society,* Thousand Oaks, CA: Sage.

McHale, Brian (1987), *Postmodernist Fiction*, New York: Methuen.

McLaren, Peter (1988), "Critical Pedagogy and the Politics of Literacy," *Harvard Educational Review*, 58(2), 213-134.

McLaren, Peter and Rhonda Hammer (1996), "Media Knowledges, Warrior Citizenry, and Postmodern Literacies," in *Counternarratives: Cultural Studies and Critical Pedagogies in Postmodern Space*, eds., H. Giroux, C. Lankshear, P. McLaren, M. Peters, New York: Routledge, 81-115.

McRobbie, Angela (1989), "Postmodernism and Popular Culture," *Postmodernism*, ICA Documents-4, London: ICA Publications, 165-180

Nichols, Bill (1981), *Image and Ideology*, Bloomington: University of Indiana Press.

Owens, Craig (1980), "The Allegorical Impulse: Toward a Theory of Postmodernism," *October*, 12 (Spring) 67-86 and 13 (Summer) 59-80.

Schroeder, Jonathan E. (1999), "Consuming Representation: Insights from Dutch Art of the Golden Age," in *Advances in Consumer Research*, eds. Eric J. Arnould and Linda M. Scott, Vol.26, Provo, UT: Association for Consumer Research, 641-643.

Scott, Linda M. (1992), "Playing with Pictures: Postmodernism, Poststructuralism and Advertising Visuals," in *Advances in Consumer Research*, eds. J. F. Sherry and B. Sternthal, Vol.19, Provo, UT: Association for Consumer Research, 596-612.

Scott, Linda M. (1994), "Images in Advertising: The Need for A Theory of Visual Rhetoric," *Journal of Consumer Research*, 21(September), 252-273.

Solomon-Godeau, Abigail (1991), *Photography at the Dock*, Minneapolis: University of Minnesota Press.

Stern, Barbara (1998), *Representing Consumers: Voices, Views, and Visions*, New York: Routledge.

Thompson, John B. (1990), *Ideology and Modern Culture*, Stanford, CA: Stanford University Press.

Wells, Liz (1997), "On and Beyond the White Walls," in *Photography: A Critical Introduction*, ed. L. Wells, New York: Routledge, 199-248.

Witkowski, Terence H. (1999), "Painting the Domestication of Consumption in 19th Century America," in *Advances in Consumer Research*, eds. Eric J. Arnould and Linda M. Scott, Vol.26, Provo, UT: Association for Consumer Research, 644-651.

SPECIAL SESSION SUMMARY
Consumer Trust in an Internet Environment
Marlene Morris, Georgetown University

Although it has a long history of attention in management literature, the concept of trust has only in recent years become a common topic in consumer behavior literature. Despite its recent growth in use and popularity, the uncertainty that remains inherent in the emerging electronic consumer environment brings the issue of trust to the forefront of marketing research with many interesting implications for practice and theory alike. To this point, much of the research conducted in the area of consumer trust in Internet environments has dealt with the issues of privacy and security. The three studies in this session examined various additional aspects of trust as they pertain to electronic commerce–dimensions of consumer trust as well as antecedents and consequences of varying levels of consumer trust in Internet marketers.

The first paper, "Antecedents and Dimensions of Consumer Trust in Quality of Recommendations Made by Agents in an Online Shopping Environment," by Lerzan Aksoy and Paul Bloom (University of North Carolina at Chapel Hill), examined the antecedents, and dimensions of, consumer trust in the quality of recommendations made, across three popular types of agents. It was postulated that this trust is a multi-dimensional construct, which has separate antecedents. The impact of this trust on amount of information search, consideration set size and decision quality, was examined, over a variety of recommendation agent types. It was expected and found that the different dimensions of trust exert opposing effects on information search, consideration set size and decision quality and hence have a differential impact on consumer welfare, satisfaction, loyalty and retention.

The second paper, "None of Your Business: The Critical Role of Trust in Information-Driven Marketing Relationships," by Tiffany Barnett White (University of Illinois, Urbana-Champaign), investigated attempts by Internet marketers to build relationships with consumers by collecting personal information from them that will allow for provision of increasingly personalized services and products. This research measured consumers' willingness to reveal the personal information that is necessary for such relationship-building efforts to be successful, with a focus on the role that consumer trust plays in facilitating and hindering consumer disclosure in Internet environments. This investigation demonstrated that consumers with greater trust and familiarity with a given Internet provider are more willing than those with relatively lower trust to reveal financially risky personal information. However, these "high trust" consumers are less likely to reveal socially risky personal information.

Finally, the third paper, "The Effects of Individual Differences on Consumer Trust in Internet Marketers," by Marlene Morris (Georgetown University), addressed differences across individuals that are predicted to affect perceived reliability of information in on-line shopping environments as well as trust in the information and information-provider. Specifically, individuals' gender and ethnicity are found to affect trust and perceived likelihood of victimization at the hands of Internet retailers.

Taken together, along with stimulating discussion from the various session attendees, the papers in this session did help to further our understanding of the dimensions of consumer trust as it pertains to electronic commerce as well as some of the antecedents and consequences of varying levels of trust in Internet marketers, including customer retention and relationships. While many of the practical and theoretical marketing issues that are studied within the context of the Internet and electronic commerce mirror those that have been studied in traditional consumer environments, the importance of trust in this particular domain continues to present a unique issue for Internet marketers and researchers.

The Influence of Consumers' Price Expectations on Value Perception and Purchase Intention

Kyoung-Nan Kwon, University of Tennessee
David W. Schumann, University of Tennessee

Price promotion has become an integral part of American culture. In recent times marketers have been increasing the use of price promotion by strategically cutting budgets for traditional advertising. This has resulted in greater price/promotion sensitivity on the part of consumers (Mela, Gupta and Lehmann 1997). As consumers are more frequently exposed to price promotion, an interesting research question persists. How do consumers come to a conclusion regarding price and what is this conclusion based upon?

It is commonly known that consumers form their own price expectations based on pricing patterns they have observed over time (Jacob and Obermiller 1989,1990; Kalwani et al. 1990; Kalwani and Yim 1992; Krishna 1991, 1992, 1994; Mela and Urbany 1997; Winer 1986). Consumers appear to develop personal forecasting rules for price. Furthermore, a consumer's purchase decision may depend on what kind of price expectation exists. For example, if a promotion for a discounted price is run frequently, consumers may adjust to the lower price and may be adverse to paying the normal price when the promotion ceases. Moreover, when a shopper encounters a sales promotion, (s)he might not respond positively if (s)he has a specific anticipation of a further price drop. In this situation, the price discount may not increase actual purchases as intended. Consumers observe prices and obtain price information from various sources, from which they develop decision rules. Thus, the price expectation may alter the purchase behavior in either way, accelerating towards or deferring from the current purchase.

Over the past two decades there have been several studies that specifically explored the notion of consumer price expectation through modeling approaches (Helsen and Schmittlen 1992; Kalwani et al. 1990; Mayhew and Winer 1992; Winer 1986) or experiments (Jacobson and Obermiller 1989, 1990; Kalwani and Yim 1992; Krishna 1994). However, as these studies only examined purchase decision or actual response to sales, they have been limited in providing an adequate description of how the price expectation influences the current purchase decision. To date, there has been little direct examination of the role that expected future price plays in the current purchase decision. These researchers have called for further study of pricing that taps into the "forward looking" (Jacobson and Obermiller 1989, 1990) concept of expected price. That is, at the point-of-purchase, do consumers actively assess the gain or loss of buying a product, in part, based upon their expectation of the product's future price?

The study reported here explores the notion of 'forward looking' expected price, termed expected future price (EFP). We examine the impact of EFP on current purchase intention and the value perceptions, i.e., acquisition value and transaction value, as antecedents of the intention. This study also explores the impact of a potential moderating factor, the credibility of EFP information.

REVIEW OF LITERATURE

Consumer response to a price promotion depends on the evaluation of the promotion in light of the reception of benefit or utility associated with the purchase. This corresponds to the notion of "value." Understanding the value customers seek becomes the core within the pricing strategies of both manufacturers and retailers. Zeithaml (1988) defines perceived value as "the consumer's overall assessment of the utility of a product based on perceptions of what is received and what is given." Monroe (1990) views customer value as "a consequence of evaluating perceived quality and benefits in the product or service and perceived cost of acquiring and using them." As such, value is defined as the trade-off between benefits, i.e., the "get" component, and sacrifices, i.e., the "give" component (Woodruff and Gardial 1996).

Several researchers have argued that the total perceived value of a product being considered for purchase is further broken down into two categories: acquisition value and transaction value (Grewal, Monroe and Krishnan 1998; Lichtenstein, Netemeyer and Burton 1990; Monroe 1990; Monroe and Chapman 1987; Thaler 1983, 1985; Urbany et al. 1997). Acquisition value is the expected benefit to be gained from acquiring the product compared to the net cost of paying for it (Thaler 1985). It can be thought of as the difference between the price one would pay for acquiring a product of this quality and the current price. Transaction value comes from the feeling of having received a good bargain or deal, which is independent of quality consideration (Thaler 1983, 1985). Buyers are thought to experience pleasure from the fact they buy the product at a price less than the regular price, and/or less than the price of other similar products in the store (or another store). The total value received by the purchaser is thought to be the sum of acquisition value and transaction value, both of which are considered antecedents to actual purchase behavior.

This value perception comprised of acquisition and transactional value, is the output from evaluating the current deal against some standard or reference prices (Grewal, Monroe and Krishnan 1998; Monroe1990; Monroe and Chapman 1987; Thaler 1983, 1985; Zeithaml 1988). Consumers do not have an absolute response to pricing, rather their response is related to one or more reference prices. Although different terms are used to refer to reference price, e.g., fair price, reservation price, value equivalent price (Thaler 1983, 1985) and maximum acceptable price (Monroe 1990), the consensus is that consumers use various kinds of reference price as a standard to evaluate acquisition value and/or transaction value. Four judgmental theories from psychology can be used to explain the logic of reference price. These include prospect theory (Kahneman and Tversky 1979), mental accounting (Thaler 1985), adaptation level theory (Helson 1964), and assimilation-contrast theory (Sherif 1963). The first two suggest that consumers may perceive the current price/deal as a loss or a gain, relative to their reference price. The latter two would posit that a new price can be assimilated in order to update the reference price or it can be rejected, both situations affecting the reference price.

Although the notion of price expectation as another reference price has been introduced in the literature, e.g., expected future price (Winer 1986), last price paid, and going price (modal price from the buyer's historical experience - Morris and Morris 1990), the consumer's price expectation has not been a focal point of research. Among the few studies, there are several that have taken a modeling approach to estimate expected price. This modeling approach has employed various scanner data such as a brand's last period prices, frequency of promotion, and price trend (Kalwani et al. 1990; Helsen and Schmittlen 1992; Mayhew and Winer 1992; Winer 1986). The previous research generally suggests that a model incorporating the concept of price expectation provides better predictive power for brand choice and purchase decision. This result is attributed to the fact that sellers set price based on historical price levels and accordingly, consumers develop their expectations (Briesch et al. 1997). As such, the most often employed technique to operationalize expected price has been an estimation approach using scanner data.

However, this estimation method has a limitation in demonstrating how consumers' expectations of the future price actively influence current purchase behavior. This limitation was discussed by Jacobson and Obermiller (1989, 1990) as they introduced the conceptual difference between expected prices as backward-looking and forward-looking. The early studies conceptualized expected prices as if consumers were looking back at the past rather than looking forward to a future price. Thus research did not take into consideration the potential for a consumer's conscious and active anticipation of future price. A forward-looking expected price is part of the active price anticipation that derives its basis from 1) the buyer's knowledge about past prices, 2) current market prices, and 3) the expectation of future price. All three are important to consider in attempting to identify and understand the consumer's interpretation of the current deal. This paper presents a study that examines the role of the least explored of the three pricing considerations listed above, expected future price (EFP).

A few studies have employed the concept of EFP as the forward-looking strategy. Expected future price taps into what consumers think they will have to pay for a product in the future (Jacobson and Obermiller 1990; Kalwani and Yim 1992; Krishna 1994). These researchers conducted experiments and measured the concept of forward-looking expected price by asking subjects their expected price (Jacobson and Obermiller 1990; Kalwani and Yim 1992), and by providing information on future price deals. However, these studies only tested the impact of future expected price on the final purchase decision or brand choice, they did not provide insight into how this expectation influences the purchase decision.

RESEARCH OBJECTIVES AND HYPOTHESES

This study investigates the impact of consumers' expectation of future price (EFP) on the response to a discounted price promotion. The purpose of this study is threefold: 1) to examine the effect of consumers' EFP on current purchase intention and on the value perception as an antecedent of the intention, 2) to test the asymmetric nature of EFP in the situations where EFP is greater than, equal to, or less than a current discounted price, and 3) to explore the effect of credibility of EFP information as a possible moderating factor.

In this study, EFP is considered as it may relate to a current deal price (CDP). As such, there are three possibilities: 1) EFP is greater than CDP (EFP>CDP), where consumers' expectation of the future price exceeds the current price, 2) EFP is same as CDP (EFP=CDP), where no price change is expected in the future, and 3) EFP is less than CDP (EFP<CDP), where further price decrease is expected in the future. As suggested in the literature (Winer 1992), EFP may act as another reference point for price, with consumers using multiple reference points for a purchase decision. If EFP is used as another reference point, then when EFP>CDP, consumers are more likely to make an immediate purchase. Thus the present perceived value should be better, and purchase intention should be more likely, than when EFP=CDP or when EFP<CDP. Conversely, when EFP<CDP, the consumer has to weigh the fact that the future price will be less than what is being charged presently. In this case, the value perception and purchase intention are expected to be diminished compared to when EFP>CDP or when EFP=CDP. The following hypothesis is offered below.

Hypothesis 1. Those individuals who expect a future price decrease (EFP<CDP) are likely to perceive diminished acquisition and transaction value, and are less likely to purchase the product compared to those expecting no price change

(EFP=CDP) or those individuals who expect an increase in future price (EFP>CDP). Furthermore, those expecting no price change (EFP=CDP) are likely to perceive diminished acquisition and transaction value, and are less likely to purchase the product compared to those individuals expecting an increase in future price (EDP>CDP).

However, the magnitude of difference between EFP=CDP and EFP>CDP, and EFP=CDP and EFP<CDP, may not be symmetric. There are several studies that have explored an asymmetric response to price change. It is generally believed consumers respond to price increase more sensitively than price decrease. Uhl and Brown (1971) conducted a survey in which customers were asked to indicate how they would respond to price increases and decreases of 5%, 10% and 15%. The authors reported that customers were considerably more sensitive to price increases than to decreases.

Kalwani et al. (1990) tested the hypothesis of asymmetry in customer response to positive deviations (losses) and negative deviations (gain) of the retail price from the expected price. Customers were found to react more strongly to price losses than to price gains. Kalwani and Yim (1992) found that, compared to the effect of the presence of a promotional deal when one was not expected, the absence of a promotional deal when one was expected had a significant impact on consumer brand choice.

The literature suggests a consumer's response to price promotion may be asymmetric in a loss versus a gain, depending on one's expectations. Following Prospect Theory (Kahneman and Tversky 1979), if negative and positive deviations of the current deal price from the EFP are taken to represent perceived gains and losses, the response to a positive price deviation (loss) is likely to be stronger than the response to a negative price deviation (gain). Regarding the relationship between EFP and CDP, the following hypothesis is proposed:

Hypothesis 2. For perceived transaction value, perceived acquisition value, and purchase intention, the difference when expected future price is less than the current deal price (EFP<CDP and EFP=CDP) will be greater than the difference when the expected future price is more than the current deal price (EFP>CDP and EFP=CDP).

Intuitively it makes sense that the credibility of EFP information should serve as a moderating factor in the relationship between EFP and value perception/purchase intention. It is likely that the credibility of EFP information increases the current value perception and purchase intention when EFP>CDP. On the other hand, when EFP<CDP, the credibility will stimulate the consumer's loss perception regarding current price, and consequently it will likely lower the value perception and purchase intention. That is, when the EFP information is credible, the reliance on the EFP is greater, and the value perception and the current purchase intention will likely drop further. When EFP=CDP, customers expect no further price discount in the future, the information credibility may convince them that the current deal is as good as the future one, thus increasing the consumer's confidence. This confidence is expected to contribute to the perceptions of both acquisition and transaction value, and lead to greater likelihood of purchase.

Hypothesis 3. The credibility of EFP information will moderate the relationship between value perceptions/current purchase intention and EFP. Scores in the perception of acquisition value and transaction value and the current purchase intention are likely to be higher under the credible condition

FIGURE 1

Hypothesized Relationship of EFP and the Credibility of EFP Information As It Predicts Perceived Transaction / Acquisition Value, and Current Purchase Intention

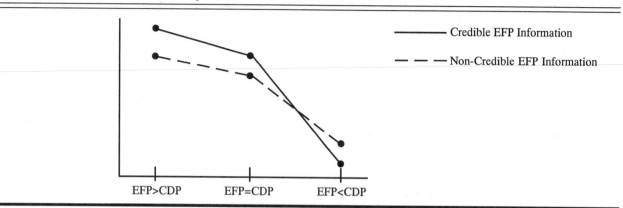

versus the non-credible condition when EFP is higher than the current deal price (EFP>CDP), or equal to the EFP price (EFP=CDP). The opposite is expected when expected future price is lower than current deal price (EFP<CDP).

The main effect predicted in H1, the asymmetric effect predicted in H2, and the moderating effect predicted in H3 are reflected in Figure 1 above.

METHODOLOGY

Study Design Manipulations

A 3 (EFP>CDP; EFP=CDP; EFP>CDP) x 2 (credible versus non-credible EFP information) between-subjects design was employed in this study. For the first factor, expected future price (EFP), brief summaries of fictitious magazine inserts were generated. Subjects were shown a magazine cover along with a page that included an insert with EFP information. The information reported that for this product class, expected future price would, in three months, be 15% less than today's regular price, 30% less than today's regular price, or 45% less than today's regular price. Subjects were also given information that stated, given this brand, exactly what this discount would mean in terms of savings or loss comparing CDP and EFP.

The second factor, the credibility of EFP information, was manipulated through the same magazine insert described above. Two magazines were employed: a popular computer magazine and a popular women's fashion magazine. For credible EFP information, the insert from the computer magazine contained the reported announcement of a future price change as stated by the CEO of the computer monitor company. The insert from the women's fashion magazine reported the result of a random survey on the perceived change of price for computer monitors. The survey reported in the fashion magazine was conducted at a department store in a metropolitan area with a sample size of fifteen department store shoppers (non-credible EFP information).

Procedures

A computer monitor was selected for the experiment because the product occasionally is marked down, so it would be realistic for expected future price to be considered in this high involvement context. A hypothetical brand of computer monitor was used to minimize the potential respondents' tendency to invoke an image or previous experience.

One hundred ninety-nine undergraduate students participated in the experiment. Participants were randomly assigned to one of the six conditions. After excluding 6 respondents who did not finish the questionnaire booklet and 13 respondents who did not correctly recall the price information provided, responses of one hundred eighty subjects were used in the analysis.

Respondents received a booklet containing all the experimental material. The first page contained the name and picture of the monitor marked "30% Off." In addition, the regular price of $875.99 was crossed out and the discounted price of $613.19 was underlined. On the lower half of the page, respondents were asked to imagine they were in the market for a new computer monitor, having typically purchased computer monitors separate from their basic computer. They were told that when they entered the store they would find a sale for the monitor marked down 30%. They were reminded of, and were referred to, a *Consumer Reports* test that rated this brand as one of the best choices within the $500-$1000 price range. They were told that they had set their personal budget around $800. On the second page the respondents were provided with a page out of *Consumer Reports* with a copy of a blown up, fictitious table comparing five different brands on some key attributes. The results of this table reflected that this brand was better than or equal to the other brands listed on the table. The attributes included price, overall score (Poor, Fair, Good, Very Good, Excellent), image quality, ease of use, viewable image size, and maximum resolution. The purpose of the information from *Consumer Reports* was to minimize the possible confounding effect of quality certainty on the value perceptions and purchase intention due to respondents' different quality perception. Urbany et al. (1997) reports the moderating effect of quality certainty in the relation of transaction value and purchase intention. The first two pages in the booklet were the same for everyone. The manipulation of EFP and the credibility of EFP information as previously described above, appeared on the third page. The remainder of the booklet contained the questionnaire.

Measures

Perceived transaction value and acquisition value were measured using twelve statements adapted from Grewal et al. (1998). Three items that supposedly measured transaction value and nine items that supposedly measured acquisition value were anchored at 9-points from "strongly disagree" to "strongly agree" (Grewal et al. employed 7-point scales). The sum of the scores on these items was used in the analysis. To measure purchase intention, two questions were used. One asked the likelihood of purchasing the monitor and it employed a 9-point scale anchored with "very unlikely" and "very likely." The other question asked their intention in terms of probability of purchase voiced in percentage (e.g., 70% likely). They were left a blank space to fill in the percentage. As the two questions used different scales, standardized scores of the two items were used for purchase intention. The sum standardized score was employed in the analysis.

RESULTS

Manipulation Check

A manipulation check was conducted to assess if the credibility of the EFP information was perceived significantly different between the kinds of information: the announcement of the corporate CEO of the brand under consideration cited in the computer magazine and the result of a small consumer survey reported in the woman's fashion magazine. The sum of three items (9-point semantic differential scales assessing dependability, reliability, and trustworthiness) were employed in the manipulation check of credibility. Those respondents who reviewed the computer magazine information perceived it as more credible (mean = 20.133) compared to those respondents who reviewed the study appearing in the women's fashion magazine (mean=11.011), $F(1,179) = 205.005$, $p = .000$. In addition, whether information from a particular magazine was perceived more credible by a specific gender due to the familiarity or the readership of the magazine (i.e., fashion magazines to females) was tested. For the both fashion and computer magazines, there were no significant gender differences found for information credibility.

Subjects were asked to answer a series of questions for the manipulation check of EFP. They were asked to recall CDP and EFP in the information they reviewed in the dollar term and percentage. If a respondent answered the questions correctly, (s)he had an idea how the price would change in relation with the current deal price. In order to assess the true consequences of EFP, it was mandatory that subjects understood all the pricing information provided. Among the total 199 subjects, 13 recalled information incorrectly and were excluded from the analyses.

Factor Analysis on Value Perceptions

A factor analysis was conducted on the 12 items purported by Grewal et al. (1998) to measure perceived transaction and acquisition value. The factor analysis revealed some overlap with Grewal et al., but also some differences. Two of the original three transaction value items loaded highly on one factor while the third item loaded poorly and was discarded ("Beyond the money I save, taking advantage of this price discount will give me a sense of joy."). Eight of the nine original acquisition value items loaded highly on one factor. The one poorly loading item ("Compared to the maximum price I would be willing to pay for this monitor, the discounted price conveys good value.") loaded highly on the transaction value factor. After considering the face validity of the item, it was decided to retain it under transaction value rather than acquisition value. Thus with the exception of this one item that loaded highly on transaction value and the discarded item, all of the remaining items from the Grewal et al. index loaded in a similar fashion in this study.

Results of MANOVA

A MANOVA with appropriate contrasts was conducted with the three dependent variables: perceived transaction value, perceived acquisition value and the current purchase intention. The

initial MANOVA included EFP, the credibility of EFP information and the interaction. The multivariate effect was significant for EFP (Wilks' Lambda = .882; $F(6) = 3.663$, $p = .002$) and for credibility (Wilks' Lambda = .948; $F(3) = 3.070$, $p = .029$). The multivariate interaction effect of EFP*Information Credibility was not significant. The multivariate main effect revealed that EFP influenced both perceived acquisition value, $F(2) = 3.900$, $p = .022$ and purchase intention, $F(2) = 6.697$, $p = .002$. It also appealed that Information Credibility affected current purchase intention, $F(1) = 6.638$, $p = .011$.

Hypothesis 1 predicts a main effect for EFP. The results of the MANOVA test provide support for the hypothesis for two of the three dependent variables. For perceived transaction value, planned contrasts tests revealed a significant difference between EFP=CDP and EFP<CDP ($p = .041$) (Please see Figure 2). However, there was no difference between EFP=CDP and EFP>CDP. The same difference was found for acquisition value ($p = .010$). Both perceived transaction value and acquisition value seemed to be significantly diminished when subjects expected a further price drop than when they expected no price change in the future. For purchase intention the significant drop in likelihood of purchase occurred between EFP>CDP and EFP=CDP ($p = .022$). In this case, while the slope continued downward as expected price decreased, there was no significant difference between EFP=CDP and EFP<CDP. Purchase intention appears likely to be greatest when one anticipates a future price increase than when one does not expect a change or expects a drop in price. Therefore the results of the MANOVA with contrasts tests partially support Hypothesis 1. The expectation of future price appears to have the potential to influence both perceived value and purchase intention.

The asymmetric effects for perceived transaction value, perceived acquisition value and purchase intention (Hypothesis 2) were examined using the results of the planned contrasts used in testing Hypothesis 1. For perceived transaction and acquisition value, it was found there was no difference between the first two levels (EFP>CDP and EFP=CDP), but a difference emerged between EFP=CDP and EFP<CDP (please refer to Figure 2). Therefore it is concluded that H2 has partial support. What emerged in the analysis of purchase intention was counter to what was predicted. In this case, the significance was found between EFP>CDP and EFP=CDP and not between EFP=CDP and EFP<CDP. Thus while some indication of the asymmetric effect exists for both the value perceptions and purchase intention, for the latter, the asymmetric effect is opposite to what was predicted.

Hypothesis 3 predicted the moderating effect of the EFP information credibility (as represented in Figure 1). Planned contrast tests showed that there were significant differences due to credibility under certain comparison conditions (see Table for means). For transaction value, when no price change was expected, the perception was marginally different between the two credibility levels; the perception of transaction value was somewhat greater when it was based on a credible EFP information ($p = .077$), while there was no difference found between the two credibility levels when further price decrease or increase were expected. There was no support for credibility serving as a moderator in the analysis of acquisition value (at all three EFP levels). However, further suggestion of the moderating influence of credibility did surface. The main effect difference found for Hypothesis 1 for both perceived acquisition and transaction value must be viewed in light of the further planned contrasts. For both measures of value, the main effect difference found between EFP=CDP and EFP<CDP was shown through planned contrasts tests to only exist under the high credible source conditions ($p = .008$). In addition, a significant difference in transaction value emerged between EFP>CDP and

FIGURE 2
Estimated Marginal Mean Differences in EFP Condition

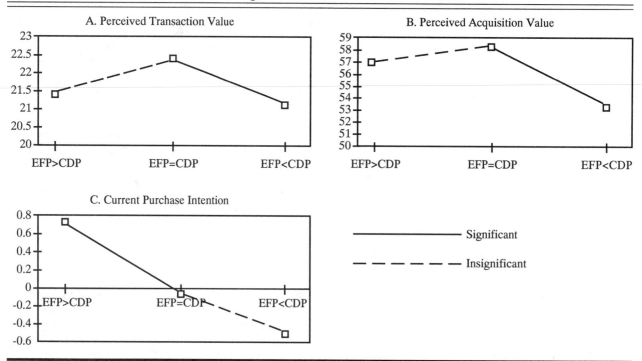

EFP=CDP ($p = .048$) under the high credibility source condition. Interestingly, this difference was in the opposite direction from what was hypothesized. No main effect for EFP was forthcoming when credibility of the source was low.

When the price expectation was based on the credible information, purchase intention was significantly less than when it was based on less credible information when EFP<CDP ($p = .013$), and marginally less when EFP=CDP ($p =.075$). The latter effect, EFP=CDP, was found to be in the opposite direction from what was hypothesized, with purchase more likely when the non-credible information was employed. No difference was found between the two credibility conditions when EFP>CDP. While Hypothesis 3 was not fully supported, the planned contrasts did reveal the potential for information credibility to play a moderating role. As in the value perception result, the main effect found in Hypothesis 1 was moderated by the credibility of the EFP information. The significant main effect found for the difference between EFP>CDP and EFP=CDP was present only under the high credibility conditions.

DISCUSSION

This study sought to consider the influence of expected future price on a current purchase decision. The results of the experiment presented here revealed support for the notion that expected future price does potentially influence perceived value as well as current purchase intention. Furthermore, the planned comparisons reflect the potential moderating role that EFP information credibility can play.

Transaction value can be thought of as a difference between the desired price to pay and the current price offered. It is very much related to how one feels about the deal. Is it a bargain or is it a "rip-off?" The results in this study provide both, support for the predictions, as well as some evidence counter to the predictions. In this study, it appears there is a significant drop in transaction value

from EFP=CDP to EFP<CDP. In addition, the credibility of information appeared to moderate the relationship. Under the low information credibility condition transaction value was the same across EFP conditions. However, when EFP=CDP, the high credibility condition respondents perceived significantly stronger transaction value than the low credibility respondents. It appears that, when no change in price is expected, the credible information encourages greater transaction value than does a less credible information. Respondents seem to attend to, and feel confident in credible information whereas this confidence seems to be missing with non-credible information. Thus, the confidence gained from credible information justifies the beliefs about the deal when EFP=CDP. Non-reliable information may undermine that confidence, thus reducing the value of transaction. The transaction value also appears to be reduced when highly credible information suggests that the future price will be higher (compared to when this source suggests that the future price will be the same). Perhaps in this case the credible information seems contrary to the industry norm. In the computer industry, it is the standard for hardware to decrease price significantly over time, not increase. This may have led to a strong degree of skepticism towards the source and the deal.

Acquisition value can be thought of as the difference between the price one would pay for acquiring a product of this quality and the current price offered (Thaler 1983, 1985). First, the same drop in future price reported for perceived transaction value was also found for perceived acquisition value, that is respondents recorded diminished transaction value from EFP=CDP to EFP<CDP. Respondents who were given information about the potential drop in prices rated acquisition value as significantly lower than when no expected drop in price was expected. It is important to note that this effect is moderated by the information credibility. This relationship only emerges for those who received the credible EFP information. With non-credible information, no difference exists between the perceived acquisition value for all three EFP conditions. Thus

TABLE 1
Estimated Marginal Means EFP by Information Credibility

	EFP>CDP	EFP=CDP	EFP<CDP
A. Perceived Transaction Value			
Credible Information	21.452 [a] ⟷	23.267 [b] ⟷	20.750 [a]
Non-Credible Information	21.400	21.607 [a]	21.400
B. Perceived Acquisition Value			
Credible Information	56.774	59.533 [b] ⟷	51.393 [a]
Non-Credible Information	57.667	56.429	54.933
C. Current Purchase Intention			
Credible Information	.677 [a] ⟷	-.447 [b]	-1.021 [b] ↕
Non-Credible Information	.729 [a]	.373 [a]	.129 [a]

Note: Superscripts with different letters are significantly different from each other, $p<.10$.
Connecting arrows represent significantly different conditions, $p<.05$.

when one is exposed to credible information promoting a decrease in future price, the value of acquiring the product in the future, may be higher in the consumer's mind than acquiring it under the present price offering.

Contrary to the results of transaction and acquisition values, respondents showed diminished purchase intention from EFP>CDP to EFP=CDP, while there is no significance found between EFP=CDP and EFP<CDP. The insignificant result may be related to the ecological issue of technology products.[1] A consumer may experience cognitive dissonance associated with buying an outdated monitor at a future time, if (s)he believes that a price drop is due to the introduction of a new improved model. In this case, the consumer may not postpone the purchase, even though further price decline is expected in the future.

The relationship of EFP to current purchase intention was also moderated by information credibility. While there were no differences for EFP under the low credibility conditions, purchase intention was affected under the high credibility conditions. As EFP went from greater than to equal to CDP, intention to purchase decreased significantly, but only when information credibility was high. However, while the difference in credibility was predicted at EFP<CDP, the expected effect did not emerge. Thus when EFP=CDP, the low credibility condition respondents voiced a higher likelihood to purchase than those respondents exposed to the high credibility information. Again, this was counter to the hypothesis offered and it is difficult to think about why this might have happened. Replicating this finding would be important and it is suggested that experimenters take cognitive response thought listings to better understand these potential differences.

The predicted asymmetric effect emerged for value perceptions but interestingly, not for purchase intention. In fact, Kalwani and his colleagues (1990, 1992) found an asymmetric effect for purchase decision in a similar direction to that hypothesized in this study. Thus, finding the opposite type of asymmetry in this study raises a question for future research. Again, employing cognitive response thought listings may shed light on the answer.

Future Research

The perception of acquisition value is the result of the quality perception of the product compared to a current price. Conceptually, the question why EFP as a reference price affects acquisition value in addition to transaction value raises. One of the possible explanations would be that, for example, transaction and acquisition values are not completely independent constructs, therefore the effect of EFP on transaction value might be carried over to the perception of acquisition value. This research question should be pursued by structural equation modeling.

REFERENCES

Brieschs, Richard A., Lakshman Krishnamurthi, Tridib Mazumdar and S. P. Raj (1997), "A Comparative Analysis of Reference Price Models," *Journal of Consumer Research*, 24 (September), 202-214.

Grewal, Dhruv, Kent B. Monroe and R. Krishnan (1998), "The Effect of Price-Comparison Advertising on Buyers' Perceptions of Acquisition Value, Transaction Value, and Behavioral Intentions," *Journal of Marketing*, 62 (April), 46-59.

Helsen, Kristiaan and David C. Schmittlein (1992), "How Does a Product Market's Typical Price-Promotion Pattern Affect the Timing of Households' Purchases? An Empirical Study Using UPC Scanner Data," *Journal of Retailing*, 68(3), 316-338.

Helson, Harry (1964), *Adaptation Level Theory*. New York: Harper And Row.

Jacobson, Robert and Carl Obermiller (1989), "The Formation of Reference Price," *Advances in Consumer Research*, 16, 234-240.

Jacobson, Robert and Carl Obermiller (1990), "The Formation of Expected Future Price: A Reference Price for Forward-Looking Consumers," *Journal of Consumer Research*, 16 (March), 420-432.

Kahneman, Daniel and Amos Tversky (1979), "Prospect Theory: An Analysis of Decision Under Risk," *Econometrica*, 47 (March), 263-91.

Kalwani, Manohar U. and Chi Kin Yim (1992), "Consumer Price and Promotion Expectations: An Experimental Study," *Journal of Marketing Research*, 29 (February), 90-100.

---

[1]The authors appreciate and agree with one of the reviewer's suggestion for the possible explanation why the insignificant result occurred.

Kalwani, Manohar U., Chi Kin Yim, Heikki J. Rinne and Toshi Sujita (1990), "A Price Expectation Model of Consumer Brand Choice," *Journal of Marketing Research*, 27 (August), 251-262.

Krishna, Aradhna (1991), "The Effect of Dealing Patterns on Consumer Perceptions of Deal Frequency and Willingness to Pay," *Journal of Marketing Research*, 28 (November), 441-451.

Krishna, Aradhna (1992), "The Normative Impact of Consumer Price Expectations for Multiple Brands on Consumer Purchase Behavior," *Marketing Science*, 11 (Summer), 266-286.

Krishna, Aradhna (1994), "The Effect of Deal Knowledge on Consumer Purchase Behavior," *Journal of Marketing Research*, 31 (February), 76-91.

Lichtenstein, Donald R., Richard G. Netemeyer and Scot Burton (1990), "Distinguishing Coupon Proneness from Value Consciousness: An Acquisition-Transaction Utility Theory Perspective," *Journal of Marketing*, 54 (July) 54-67.

Mayhew, Glenn E. and Russell S. Winer (1992), "An Empirical Analysis of Internal and External Reference Prices Using Scanner Data," *Journal of Consumer Research*, 19 (June), 62-70.

Mela, Carl F., Sunil Gupta and Donald R. Lehmann (1997), "The Long-Term Impact of Promotion and Advertising on Consumer Brand Choice," *Journal of Marketing Research*, 34 (May), 248-261.

Mela, Carl and Joe Urbany (1997), "Promotion Over Time: Exploring Expectations and Explanations," *Advances in Consumer Research*, 24, 529-535.

Monroe, Kent B. (1990), *Making Profitable Decisions*, New York: McGraw-Hill.

Monroe, Kent B. and Joseph D. Chapman (1987), "Framing Effects on Buyer's Subjective Product Evaluations," *Advances in Consumer Research*, 14, 193-197.

Morris, Michael H. and Gene Morris (1990), *Market-Oriented Pricing: Strategies for Management*. New York: Quorum Books.

Sherif, Carolyn W. (1963), "Social Categorization as a Function of Latitude of Acceptance and Series Range," *Journal of Abnormal Psychology*, 67 (August), 148-156.

Thaler, Richard (1983), "Transaction Utility Theory," *Advances in Consumer Research*, 10, 296-301.

Thaler, Richard (1985), "Mental Accounting and Consumer Choice," *Marketing Science*, 4 (Summer), 199-214.

Uhl, Hoseph N. and Harold L. Brown (1971), "Consumer Perception of Experimental Retail Food Price Changes," *Journal of Consumer Affairs*, 5 (Winter), 174-185.

Urbany, Joel E., William O. Bearden, Ajit Kaicker and Melinda Smith-de Borrero (1997), "Transaction Utility Effects When Quality is Uncertain," *Journal of the Academy of Marketing Science*, 25 (1), 45-55.

Winer, Russell S. (1986), "A Reference Price Model of Brand Choice for Frequently Purchased Products," *Journal of Consumer Research*, 13 (Spring), 250-256.

Woodruff, Robert B. and Sarah Fisher Gardial (1996), *Know Your Customer: New Approaches to Customer Value and Satisfaction*. Cambridge, MA: Blackwell.

Zeithaml, Valarie A. (1988), "Consumer Perceptions of Price, Quality, and Value: A Means-End Model and Synthesis of Evidence," *Journal of Marketing*, 52 (July), 2-22.

The Role of Selective Hypothesis Testing in the Overestimation of Price-Quality Correlation

Maria L. Cronley, Wright State University
James J. Kellaris, University of Cincinnati
Frank R. Kardes, University of Cincinnati
Steven S. Posavac, University of Rochester

ABSTRACT

When consumers expect to see a relationship between price and quality, they are likely to perceive a strong relationship even when the objective relationship is weak. The present experiment shows that price-quality correlation overestimation is reduced (but not eliminated) when a large amount of price-quality data is presented in a random order, provided that consumers are sufficiently motivated to process the data thoroughly due to a low need for cognitive closure (Kruglansi and Webster 1996) or a high need to evaluate (Jarvis and Petty 1996). These interactions are consistent with the implications of a selective hypothesis testing model of data-driven information processing (Sanbonmatsu, Posavac, Kardes, and Mantel 1998).

Price-Matching Refunds and Consumer Price Perceptions: Effect on Store Price Image and Processing of Price Information

Nicholas Lurie, University of North Carolina, Chapel Hill
Joydeep Srivastava, University of California, Berkeley

ABSTRACT

This paper examines how price-matching refund policies affect consumer perceptions and processing of product price information. Study 1 finds that price-matching policies affect perceptions of overall store prices only in the absence of other low-price cues. Study 2 finds that price-matching policies are effective when such policies accompany high, but not low, prices. Study 3 finds that price-matching policies change consumer estimates of lowest and expected market prices and that these estimates of market prices mediate price perceptions. Despite lowering store price perceptions, price-matching policies are not found to have a deleterious effect on quality perceptions.

Advances in Consumer Research
Volume 28, © 2001

Factors Affecting Consumer Choices Between Hedonic and Utilitarian Options

Ran Kivetz, Columbia University

Michal Strahilevitz, University of Arizona

This session consisted of three papers that took distinct approaches to examining how consumers choose between hedonic, luxury consumption and utilitarian, necessary consumption. Using diverse methodologies, such as laboratory experiments, field studies, process measures, and surveys, the papers shed new light on consumers' perceptions of and responses to a wide range of promotional tools, including coupons, free gifts, frequency programs, rebates, and sweepstakes. Each paper provided insights into underlying psychological mechanisms, such as justification (to the self and to others), accountability, guilt, mental accounting, and categorization.

The first paper by O'Curry and Strahilevitz examined the effects of the probability of receiving a chosen outcome and mode of acquisition (e.g., as a lottery prize or as a purchase) on choices between hedonic and utilitarian alternatives. The results suggest that the lower the probability of receiving the selected item, the more likely individuals will be to choose the more hedonic alternative in a choice set. Mode of acquisition was also found to affect preferences, even when probability of acquisition is held constant. The data suggests that hedonic options are more popular as prizes than as purchases, whereas utilitarian options appear to be more popular as purchases than as prizes. The mediating roles of anticipation of pleasure and accountability for frivolity were discussed.

The second paper by Kivetz and Simonson examined how consumers sometimes constrain their purchase and consumption of hedonic luxuries because such expenditures are difficult to justify and may evoke feelings of guilt. The authors proposed that the completion of a long effort stream may serve as a compelling reason for pleasurable consumption ("earning the right to indulge through hard work"). For example, consumers who participate in frequency (loyalty) programs are more likely to prefer luxury over necessity rewards when these rewards are contingent upon the completion of relatively effortful consumption requirements. On the other hand, consistent with the authors' theoretical framework, increasing the monetary costs of obtaining rewards shifts preferences away from pleasurable luxury rewards. These propositions were investigated and supported in a series of studies in which the amount and type of efforts were systematically manipulated and respondents' choices between hedonic and utilitarian rewards were observed. Potential rival accounts were discussed as well as different moderators of the effects of effort on reward preference.

The final paper by Chandon and Wansink pointed out that when selecting a reward for a sales promotion, marketers tend to rely on utilitarian incentives more often than on hedonic incentives. The authors argued that the effectiveness of a consumer incentive is ultimately determined by the utilitarian or hedonic nature of the benefits it delivers, and by the congruence these benefits have with the task, product, and decision-maker. Three compelling studies were presented that supported this benefit congruency hypothesis, demonstrating that hedonic incentives can, in fact, increase brand choice and improve brand image when they are targeted at hedonic products or consumers.

The session ended with an extremely insightful and thought provoking discussion by Drazen Prelec.

Qualitative Research Perspectives in Computer Mediated Environments

Hope Jensen Schau, Temple University
Mary Wolfinbarger, California State University, Long Beach
Albert Muniz, DePaul University

The objectives of this session were to investigate three diverse consumer behaviors in online environments: online shopping, development and enhancement of personal websites, and online user/brand communities. Each of the presentations employed or advocated a different type of qualitative research, and each unearthed some fundamental, but surprising insights based on their focus on consumer perceptions and experiences.

"Nibbling on the Net," by Mary Wolfinbarger and Mary C. Gilly (University of California, Irvine), was based on qualitative data about online shopping collected from online and offline focus groups. Online focus groups result in informants being able to participate in research in the comfort of their own homes, and within an interactive, familiar and sociable environment. The relative anonymity and almost instantaneous familiarity between participants of online focus groups results in a relatively intimate, disclosive environment. The authors find that goal-oriented shoppers quite strikingly report that they "nibble" at shopping sites, shopping in brief spurts, and making purchase decisions across multiple visits over time. While the majority of online shoppers are goal-oriented and not impulsive, some consumers engage in experiential buying behavior on the Internet, particularly at auction sites, while pursuing hobbies, and finding bargains.

In "Identity Hacking: Consumer Self-Expression in Personal Websites," Hope Schau examined the ways consumers use commercial brands and symbols to represent and communicate identities in two forms of CMEs: personal websites and electronic communities. Through adapting the ethnographic techniques of in-depth interviewing (eight informants face-to-face and electronically), naturalistic and participant observation in online communities inhabited by the informants, and socio-semiotics of informant sites, the study explores consumer self-expression strategies and manifestations. The interview methodology employed live feed of each creator's website(s) as elicitation devices akin to Heisley and Levy's autodriving techniques (1991). The findings based on this analysis reveal that personal website creators use CMEs as dynamic servicescapes, communication tools and entertainment. Most importantly, consumers intelligently and conspicuously employ brands in self-identification in their personal websites.

Thomas O'Guinn (Duke University) and Albert Muniz in, "Correlates of Brand Communal Affiliation Strength in High Technology Products," looked at online communities in a relatively new high-tech product category: personal digital assistants (PDAs). Still early in the product life cycle, a number of different operating systems (Palm, PocketPC, Epoch) are competing to become the standard. Each of these operating systems is the center of a brand community which utilizes usenet newsgroups as one forum for interacting. Grounding their research in the ample literature on community in both online and face-to-face realms, this paper examined strength of communal affiliation in these brand communities. The researchers sampled messages from one month's worth of posting to each group and coded them on the frequency of occurrence of a variety of community markers. Collectively, the members of these brand communities implicitly understood the importance and power of the community in this product category. Differences between the newsgroups suggest that communities

centering on newer brands operate differently than even those a few months older.

Qualitative methodologies are particularly important in the online environment, as CMEs are a relatively new phenomenon that is not presently well understood. Examining these emerging experiences requires a rich understanding of consumers and their behaviors online. To capture the strategies and meanings of consumer self-expression, brand communities and online shopping in CMEs, consumer researchers must modify their research methodologies. Qualitative research should be employed to overcome researchers' tendencies to rely too heavily on pre-existing "mirror" concepts and theories that will limit our thinking about computer mediated environments.

New Perspectives on Consumer Evaluations of Experiences that Extend Over Time: Empirical Regularities, Integration Rules and Formal Modeling

Gal Zauberman, The University of North Carolina at Chapel Hill

Research on hedonic evaluations of extended experiences has focused on the relationship between the patterns of experiences that extend over time and their corresponding overall hedonic evaluations. The general finding is that when consumers provide global evaluations of extended experiences, they appear to extract only a few key aspects of these sequences and use them to form overall evaluations of the sequence as a whole (e.g., trend, peak and end intensity). The purpose of this session was to present three lines of research that extend the current understanding of the way that consumers perceive sequences. Collectively, this session extend current knowledge in three ways: 1) examine sequential effects in greater detail and present novel empirical regularities; 2) demonstrate the rules consumers use when evaluating experiences over time, both for single and multiple experiences; and 3) present a formal model with a goal of accounting for multiple empirical regularities under a single framework.

The presentation by Rebecca Ratner, Deborah MacInnis and Allen Weiss focused on the way that people make decisions about how to sequence items within a collection (e.g., a set of poems, a sequence of songs on a CD). Previous research indicated that people prefer improving sequences that end on a "positive note." In this paper, the researchers presented evidence that, in addition to a strong end, people also prefer a strong beginning. The authors find that respondents' prototypical "ideal" pattern is to start with a favorite and end with a favorite. Whereas previous research focused on people's preference for a (relatively) favorable ending, one of the main points highlighted here was that consumers also want a favorable beginning.

The presentation by Gal Zauberman focused on the integration rules that consumers utilize to evaluate experiences that extend over time. A set of experiments illustrated two main points. First, the integration rules consumers use are highly context dependent and systematically vary as a function of their evaluation goal. Second, the evaluation of sequences is affected by the way the sequence is perceived, whether as a single unit or a combination of separate parts. A theory of how people evaluate extended experiences was proposed.

The presentation by Dan Ariely and Teck Ho focused on the importance of a formal model of the way consumers evaluate extended experiences. The authors presented a simple integration model that accounts for a wide range of stylized facts that have been identified in past research. In addition to accounting for the known results, their model also provides two new predictions, which are tested and verified in two experiments. The first prediction is that holding peak and end constant, consumers will prefer sequences that are characterized by greater improvement in the latter part of their experience. The second prediction is that breaks from the slope (first derivative) will decrease overall evaluation, even if they cause overall improvement in the intensity of the experience.

Collectively, the three papers suggest new directions for research on extended experiences. The first paper presented new insights about consumers' preferences for how to sequence events, including a comparison of the actual sequences marketers have used with the ideal sequences that consumers report that they would like to experience. The second paper demonstrated the context dependency of the integration rules and extends existing research

about single experiences to a focus on multiple experiences. The final paper presented a formal model as a simple, parsimonious way of understanding how consumers evaluate experiences that extend over time. Drazen Prelec, the discussant, outlined how the session's three papers inform and qualify the findings of previous research.

Consuming Identity: The Case of Scotland

Emma Combes, University of Strathclyde
Sally Hibbert, University of Strathclyde
Gillian Hogg, Glasgow Caledonian University
Richard Varey, University of Salford

ABSTRACT

The paper examines national identity in Scotland. The research explores how consumers perceive the symbols used to represent Scotland, how these symbols relate to their perceptions of contemporary Scottish identity and their responses to the use of these symbols to promote Scotland and Scottishness. A series of in-depth interviews revealed that national identity in Scotland was seen to be multidimensional. Activities associated with art and culture, as opposed to business and industry, were identified as primary characteristics of contemporary Scotland. The traditional symbols of Scottish identity (e.g. tartan and whiskey) remain dominant signifiers, however, and the problems of this are discussed.

INTRODUCTION

Recent research in consumer behaviour has demonstrated that individuals create, transform and maintain self-identity through the consumption of goods and services (see for example, Belk 1989; Schouten and Alexander 1995; Celsi et al 1993; Hill and Stamey 1990; Hogg and Michell 1996). Goods and services are recognised to embody signs and symbols that communicate meaning to other individuals and groups. It is emphasised in the literature that in defining identity there is interdependence between the individual and society (McCracken 1986, 1990). This interdependence of self and society is summed up by Berger (1966 p109): "one identifies oneself, as one is identified by others, by being located in a common world".

Our location within a common world relates to the notion that we live in communities. Community, as a number of authors point out, as been largely over looked in studies of consumption behaviour (see Muinz and O' Guinn 1999; Cova 1997; Mc Grath Sherry and Heisley 1993). The idea of communal consumption, however, is not new. Within specific communities or cultures, certain products or brands become ideologies of consumption (Hebidge 1979, Schouten and Alexander 1995). Unifying these activities is a set of common values that determine consumption patterns and are a direct reflection of the commitment of individuals to the ethos.

In this paper we are concerned with consumption and symbolism of national identity, focusing on the case of Scotland. Political Devolution in the UK in 1999, establishment of the Scottish Parliament and, particularly, the call for total political independence from the Scottish National Party has drawn attention to the importance of national identity within Scotland. The purpose of this research is to examine how individuals in Scotland perceive the symbols used to represent Scotland, how these symbols relate to their perception of contemporary Scottish identity and their response to the use of these symbols.

NATIONAL IDENTITY AND CONSUMPTION

National identity is the manifestation of the cultural tradition within which we are social actors comprising unity, position, reputation, stimulated and inhibited behaviour. In developing and maintaining a favourable self-defining social relationship (often subtle and unrecognised) with a controlling agent, we are able to construct a favourable self-image. This type of conformity facilitates the adoption of collective norms and values; identity provides the means by which individuals create and survive social change (McCracken 1990, Hogg and Michell 1996, Berger 1996).

The construct of a national identity is founded on the idea that the components that characterise a nation tie sub-cultures together within a national boundary. Keillor and Hult (1999) suggest that national identity has four components: cultural identity or a set of meanings that set it apart from other cultures; a belief structure facilitating cultural participation and solidarity; national heritage defined as a sense of the culture's unique history; and ethnocentrism, the way in which individuals or societies make judgements and attributions using their own cultural perspectives as baseline criteria. However, as Cooke and MacLean (1999) point out, in a post-modern society where social structures are rapidly changing, the politics of consumption are inextricably linked to expressions of identity. National identity is therefore an abstraction, an imagined communion (Anderson 1983) whereby individuals are united not by a geographical space but by a collective identity (Schlesinger 1991). Indeed, Bouchet (1995), following Despres (1975) argues that this identity can be self-ascribed and need not correspond to identities that others impose, with the most important criterion being that individuals want to belong to a group. National culture, or the signs and symbols of such identity are a way of constructing meanings that influence people's actions and conceptions of self (Hall 1992). Thus, social and cultural differences seem less significant than what is shared.

THE DERIVED SELF

The self is composed of multiple identities with associated loyalty to relationships of ethnic community, religion, locality, and nation or supra-nation (Smith, 1991). With some products, we develop a relationship such that they come to be important parts of our identity. Others cannot be so readily accommodated. These, if they are to be absorbed, require an exploration of identity – "the quest for outer difference becomes a quest for inner meaning" (Gabriel & Lang, 1995, p. 78). Consumption has become an opportunity to display one's identity – but is this creative opportunity or cultural determinism? For Belk (1988), certain objects are vital elements of our identity as if physical extensions of our bodies. These also act as filters to organise and interpret our social existence – each affects the whole psychic and social complex. As communicator, the consumer uses products as bridges to relate to other people. As identity-seeker, the consumer searches for a real self in consumed objects (see Gabriel & Lang, 1995).

Burke (1950) proposed three sources of identification. *Material identification* results from goods, possessions, things - I am like you because we own the same model of car or have the same taste in clothes, music, books, etc. *Idealistic identification* is based on shared ideas, attitudes, feelings, and values. We attend the same church or are members of the same political party, etc. *Formal identification* results from arrangement, form, or organisation of an event in which both participate.

Identification is the opposite of division. Tomlinson (1994) sees debate on consumerism as essentially about stages of cultural transformation – fundamental shifts in values – about confusions over class, regional, generational, and gender identities. Style, for example, is a visible manifestation of power relations, and a process of creating commodity images (c.f. 'imagination') for people to emulate and believe in. Identity is a 'symbol sphere' (Gerth and Mills, 1967) or zone of meaning (Heath, 1994) within the universe of discourse (of vocabularies, pronunciations, emblems, formulas, types of conversation). Langer (1967) has pointed out that a word, sound, mark, object, or event can be a symbol to a person, without that person's thinking consciously going from it to a meaning. Participation in constructing identity, knowledge, and meaning should be a matter of ensuring the survival of the communicating community (Deetz, 1992). Identity, as a sense of self, requires a sense of other ("other than me"). This in-out distinction (inclusive-exclusive) is inherently divisive (see Cohen 1994 for a full discussion of these issues).

Rapport, on the other hand, comes from a sense of shared social identities, which may be chosen or ascribed. Identification arises in an adopted social (relational) identity through association - how we are placed in relation to those around us. Cultural identity is a social construction that is 'given' to us. People's orientations to their institutional identities (employee, customer, consumer, supplier, etc.) are not exogenous and determining variables, but rather are accomplished in interaction (van Dijk, 1997). From this we conclude that identity is a cultural performance – identity is expressed through and within culture, by means of consumption. This performance, or discourse, is expressed through constructed meanings, evoking emotional responses from the community (Smith 1991). These are not, however, shared symbols that the entire population stands in identical relations, instead there is a need to articulate and define such symbols.

National identity is expressed through the institutions, both public and private associated with the country, events, symbols and ceremonies (Richards 1997) or, as Daniels (1993) suggests, 'legends and landscapes'. Smith (1991) details the promotion of national identity through flags, anthems, parades, coinage, war memorials, folklore, museums, popular heroes/heroines, national recreations, legal and educational procedures all of which can be translated into consumption activities to create a collective sense of belonging or purpose. These become the symbols of a national identity and the representation of the nation state in emotional form (Joy et al 1995).

COUNTRY OF ORIGIN

One of the institutional uses of symbols to represent a nation is evident when organisations attempt to identify goods and services with their country of origin (COO). COO has been widely studied as an influence on consumer behaviour, indeed Tan and Farley (1987) conclude that is it the "most researched international aspect of consumer behaviour" (p. 540). COO effects have been broadly described as "any influence, positive or negative, that the country of manufacture might have in consumer's choice processes or subsequent behaviour (Samiee 1987). According to Hong and Wyer (1989, 1990) consumers have well developed, frequently stereotypical, beliefs about countries and the types of products emanating from these countries which are used as cues to provide simplicity, coherence and predictability in complex decision settings (Taylor 1981). These cues are be used by consumers to imply quality, although research is inconsistent on the use of these cues by particular consumer groups. Within these studies the nationality of the consumer has been shown to affect the COO images of products both with regard to foreign products and 'home' products, although again these studies are inconsistent (see for example Reirson 1966a; Narayana 1981; Johansson et al 1985; Bruning 1997). Papadopoulos and Heslop (1993) suggest that the

whole notion of 'country of origin' is misleading and too narrow since it assumes a single place of origin for a product. He suggests a broader notion of product-country image to account for the fact it is the image of the country associated with the product that is relevant. As Han (1989) points out, the general image of a country is transferred to either a country's products or specific product categories – hence Japanese electronics were until recently associated with the efficiency of the Japanese economy.

If we consider the views of the inhabitants of a country, Bruning et al. (1991) and Bruning (1997) suggest that there is a 'national loyalty' effect, based on a fundamental predisposition of consumers towards ethnocentric attitudes. These are separate from stereotyping processes in that the values ascribed to the COO cue are based on an individual's group identity. Thus national loyalty in purchasing can be seen to be a development of Shimp and Sharma's 'consumer ethnocentrism' scale (CETSCALE) (Shimp and Sharma 1987). Bruning (1997) suggests that this national loyalty concept can be used to distinguish between consumers' response to promotional messages; individuals with a strong sense of national loyalty are likely to respond to "patriotic' messages or to exhibit more 'home country' bias because of the way that 'nation' fits with their sense of self – identity. What is not clear from these studies, however, is how consumers achieve this 'fit' and how consumers interpret the symbols of nation within their own identity. However, as Askegaard and Ger (1998) assert, product country images can not be taken at face value, but are inseparable from the myths they are inscribed in.

CONSUMING NATIONAL IDENTITY – SCOTLAND

In order to explore the issues of national identity in more depth we turn to the case of Scotland. Scotland is a part of the UK that has always promoted its separate identity and where the idea of a nation with its own cultural identity, belief structure, heritage and ethnocentrism has been strengthened by political Devolution. The meeting of Scotland's first parliament for 300 years in 1999 has led to resurgence in national identity. The historical background to the cultural ethnocentrism and belief structure within Scotland is complex and beyond the scope of this paper. Put simply, after the Treaty of Union in 1707 Scotland retained its own legal, educational, civil and health service systems that have served to reiterate its identity over the last three centuries. However, whilst Scotland and Scottishness has retained an image separate from Britain, there had been an increasing trend during the 1970's and 1980's towards downplaying the need for a separate Scottish identity. Scotland was increasingly viewed as a quaint, if wet, country characterised by thrift, tartan and dourness. In response to this image Scottish Enterprise and the Scottish Office set up a quango in 1994 to promote trade, tourism and culture within and out-with Scotland under the title *'Scotland the Brand'*.

The aim of 'Scotland the Brand' is to promote an image of Scotland that Scots can identify with and to promote Scottish identity to the rest of the world. The success of this initiative is difficult to evaluate as it is inseparable from the political and social change that has led to devolved government. One indicator that can be used to estimate the success of this initiative is the value that corporations within Scotland place on a Scottish identity. A number of high profile organisations have chosen to retain the 'Scottish' aspect of their identities, the sense of 'belonging' and homogeneity of a nation is therefore reinforced through its corporations. From a consumer perspective however, very little research considers how Scottish identity is viewed by consumers. The objectives of this research were to explore how individuals in Scotland perceive the symbols used to represent Scotland, how these symbols relate to their perception of contemporary Scottish identity and their response to the use of these symbols by institutions in Scotland.

RESEARCH METHOD

The research involved a series of depth interviews conducted with consumers visiting the McLellan Galleries *Architecture of Democracy* exhibition in Glasgow. Within this exhibition was a model of the new Scottish Parliament building, which provided the catalyst for discussing Scottish identity.

The sample of respondents were collected at the gallery was a convenience sample due to the nature of the data collection method of intercepting respondents within the public gallery environment, thus the interviews were relatively short, around 15 to 20 minutes. A total of 30 respondents were interviewed including 10 who described themselves as Scottish, 6 said there were English and 6 described themselves as British. The remaining 8 interviewees were from outside the UK. The labels that individuals chose for themselves are themselves interesting when discussing national identity given the "fuzziness" and ambiguity that characterises "Britishness" and its distinction from the English, Scottish and Welsh nations that it comprises (see Cohen, 1994). This range of respondents provided both internal and external perspectives on Scottish national identity. The interviews were taped and later transcribed.

RESULTS

In order to discuss the results of these interviews the following section is divided into three sections: firstly we consider respondents overall view of the current Scottish identity and the degree of inclusion/exclusion generated by this identity, secondly we consider the stereotypical images of Scotland and whether these reflect respondents views of Scotland, finally we examine contemporary Scotland the relationship between the images of Scotland and consumption of those images.

Scottish Identity

Overall, most respondents were positive about Scotland and Scottish identity. However, most views were hazy, referring to a general feel or atmosphere. One Canadian respondent made such a vague reference to this issue:

Yes - every time I'm over it looks like it's [Scotland] *making steps forward.*

However, some provided more specific views relating to this progress within contemporary Scottish identity. An English respondent stated:

I think Scottish identity is becoming better, in the same way as what's happening with Wales - this new cool identity about anywhere that's not England but in the UK. Young people seem to be moving out and going to Edinburgh University, Cardiff University, Glasgow University, Belfast University. They're all becoming very cool and popular. I think the film industry and all that seem to be doing a lot in that respect too.

Such a view seemed to highlight that the nature of any Scottish identity progression was based in the creative industries, Arts and culture, and that this theme was particularly related to issues concerning younger generations. Another (Scots) view highlighted this point by stating:

People talk about, um, all things like the fashion industry and the club industry and stuff is very big here [Glasgow] and art. I mean everyone I know from London have always wanted to come up here because of the whole art scene in Glasgow.

However, overall there was little mention of the modern telecommunications, electronics and general business sectors that 'Scotland the Brand' see as vibrant (but largely unrecognised) factors within the nation's contemporary identity although one British respondent stated:

I think Scotland is known for business and technology industry developments that it did not have, say, 20 years ago.

Overall these research results present a worrying picture for 'Scotland the Brand'. The organisation stresses the many revolutions taking place across varied political, culture, leisure and industry sectors within Scottish nationhood. Their research was particularly concerned with a contemporary Scottish business and industry identity that is not being communicated within a global context. It would be necessary for such a business identity to be clearly recognised and related to by a nation's consumers if it were to form a valid symbolic contribution to the overall national identity. If a nation's consumers do not interact with such identity aspects then they can not perform an effective symbolic function, and discordance could be experienced between the communicated symbolic identity and perception.

Stereotypical Scotland

The literature identified the Scottish media and film industries as generally upholding the stereotypical images and characteristics that research identified as damaging to contemporary Scotland. Such aspects as the Scottish music and club scene were identified by Bickett (1999) as upholding many regressive Scottish identity characteristics, particularly in such recent films as *Trainspotting* (1996). Of course, the recognition overall of a healthy and vibrant cultural scene cannot be condemned.

The suggestion of a prominent creative drive within current Scottish identity can obviously not overall be viewed as a negative factor. Indeed, a strong relationship can be uncovered between this theme and respondent views concerning Scotland's new political context. One of the most positive aspects to be related to the devolution of government was the idea that Scotland would now become accountable for its actions. Such factors of accountability it was suggested would contribute to a more positive and creative method of governing within Scotland. A Scottish respondent stated:

I think it will be a bit more creative now we're 'doing it ourselves'

Clearly there is a tendency to associate Scotland and Scottishness with stereotypical images. Asked to comment on the symbols associated with Scottish identity kilts and tartan were repeatedly mentioned by Scots,

Edinburgh is most guilty in putting forward that image of just tartan and Edinburgh rock. There's an awful lot more layers to Scotland and hundreds more cities that have got different and expressive things.

The overall impression gained from respondent views concerning Scottish identity within the contemporary context seemed to stress issues concerning creativity, multiple identities and a generally positive atmosphere surrounding current developments within the nation. In essence, Scotland is viewed to be a nation currently characterised by many dynamic entities.

When respondents were consulted concerning their views of Scottishness, an interesting and dominant theme concerning the stereotyped images was identified. Their stereotypical place was clearly recognised. Typical Scottish answers included:

I'm stumped! I suppose the things that normally come to mind are, kind of like, your kilts and tartan.... but to me that's not something I think of personally. That's not the sort of thing I equate with being Scottish.

To most respondents, images of Scottishness were inherent to their personal lives and experiences within the country, and often did not initially state the stereotyped images at all. This Scottish respondent stated

[Scottishness] is more to do with my upbringing and growing up in Scotland and the kind of influences of the actual physical area and my social background.

In this respect, such stereotypical images were seen as a distinct separate entity from contemporary Scotland. These findings uphold the dominant theories in the literature of Human, Richards, Barker and the corporate identity theorists. Respondents are seeing the stereotyped images as divorced from real life and their every day life as consumers, as such images are not the product of any interaction experienced between respondents and contemporary life in Scotland. Such images do not relate to the everyday experiences of individuals. Non Scots tended to share these same views, stressing the importance of life within Scotland as shaping their views of Scottish identity. Two English respondents, both having lived in Scotland for a while, stated:

Scots are seen as drunk and pennypinching in England, but I've not found that while living here
Well there's things its associated with [stereotypical images] but that is, you know, having since moved up here six years ago, that's obviously got nothing to do with it and with how I see Scottishness now.

With respondents clearly able to segregate Scottish stereotypical images from reality, the question is begged as to whether these images are seen as problematic to the current identity. To answer this question, respondents were asked how they viewed these images compared to contemporary Scottish identity.

The first purpose identified by respondents for such stereotypical images was as serving 'commercial' Scotland. Many talked negatively of the Scottish Tourism Industry and its usage of stereotyped Scottish images. Indeed, the concept of tourism within 'commercial Scotland' was seen as separate entity irrelevant to current Scottish identity – by Scots and non-Scots - with no potential to impact on it:

I think they [the images] should be used purely as marketing and tourism and things like that, and amongst ourselves we shouldn't conform to that, you know?

This theme also concurred with the idea that these images and icons were 'visual' and what people 'see' as opposed to life experiences and everyday happenings. Such arguments lend fur-

ther weight to the findings of Barker (1927) and Richards (1997) and Human (1999) that valid identity symbols and images are only created through people's interaction with and recognition of their current national identity. It is clearly concluded here that respondents do not relate to Scottish stereotyped images, as they are obviously not a 'real' occurrence within current Scottish life. However, this issue raises a problem in that the tourism industry is in fact of great relevance and value to Scotland's economy. 'Scotland the Brand' portrays the tourist industry as one of its key sector concerns within its objectives. These findings suggest that it is time for the Scottish tourist industry to find new icons of contemporary Scotland to incorporate into its strategy.

Images of the Scottish landscape were suggested by many as of value to Scottish contemporary identity and were often differentiated from other stereotyped Scottish images were viewed as in relation to respondents' real lives. The statement of one Scottish respondent sums up these views:

I suppose everyone thinks of Edinburgh Castle although I don't particularly identify with it. The landscape, hills and mountains and streams and heather and organic things like that are more in keeping with what I think of having to do with Scotland. Tartan, pipes and Edinburgh Castle are for the outsiders.

The value of historical aspects to contemporary identity was also stressed in the research findings. Another English respondent strongly upheld this view:

I don't think about modern day things because it's your history that makes your country what it is isn't it? I don't think you think particularly about the day to day things. It's what you know about a place, and that generally means your history.

The validity of this theme to contemporary Scottish identity could be explained by the fact that such a sense of history is central to providing an idea of the roots of the contemporary identity. A symbolic interaction between people and historical myths is thus created through this relationship. Such interaction is experienced with the landscape and rural images possibly because they are so physically prominent and shape so many peoples' professions, habitats and leisure activities. An Englsih respondent spoke of the eternal nature of historical and landscape related images:

I don't think these images are tired. Shortbread and whisky might fade as they are more kind of to do with business than cultural...... The historical has survived on its own. They appeal to older and younger generations, especially now.

If historical and landscape images are seen as so eternally valid, they could perhaps be seen as core traits (Huntington, 1997) that are unique to Scottish identity. The literature concerning the National Identity Framework can be related to this issue (Keillor and Hult, 1998). If the four identity dimensions are referred to, the National Heritage dimension could be seen as rated particularly highly for Scotland. This framework aims to identify factors that are most identified and related to by nation members, and are hence unique traits to that nation. However, this research identified historical and scenery issues as potentially detrimental to contemporary Scottish identity as they lent to the image of Scotland as an isolated island stuck in the past with no technological infrastructure.

Contemporary Scotland

When consumers were asked about the problem of 'fit' between stereotyped Scottish images and contemporary Scottish identity there appeared to be a general consensus. People identified that although the stereotyped images discussed so far had no relation to reality within the Scottish nation, they were not as such seen to present any serious problem to current national identity. However, although not discussed often, Scottish film was seen to promote certain negative 'personality' characteristics such as drunkenness and violence, thus upholding the media literature themes.

A point of contrast with regard to these themes is that the Scottish film industry was stated by some respondents as a vibrant and relevant element of the nation's current identity. If such negative national characteristics are promoted then by Scottish film, the need for the more positive national characteristics to find a symbolic form, as proposed by Scotland the Brand, is heightened. However, with reference to the literature review, some concern is presented relating to the emphasis on cultural aspects over contemporary industry sectors. This point relates to Khachaturian and Morganosky's (1990) findings that the image of a less industrialised country can lead to a decline in product quality image. If progress in Scotland is defined entirely in terms of culture, does that help the image of Scottish products.

Respondents in general seemed not see Scottish stereotyped images as a problem to contemporary Scottish identity. A theme which highlighted this point and was expressed by many respondents was the idea that any contrast present between contemporary identity and national stereotypes was the same as experienced by any other country. Thus, the situation did not make Scotland exceptional in any way. When asked what her views on Scottish stereotyped images were, an English respondent replied:

Those images are naff! But they're the same as fish and chips on Brighton pier – they don't mean anything.

It's an ignorance on other peoples behalf rather, rather than of Scotland, like anywhere. Scotland will always have these images though because, because of the countryside being so dramatic will evoke that type of feeling and the history.

What can be gathered from the respondent data overall was there was no need for Scottish stereotyped images to be eradicated. With historical and landscape images in particular, a strong degree of relevance to contemporary Scottish identity was stressed in many views, both by Scots and non-Scots. What can perhaps be linked to this theme is the identification by many respondents of Scotland as a dynamic nation with multiple identities. What is suggested by this factor is that the diversity of identities allows valid space for Scotland's stereotyped identity. The historic and landscape aspects can be seen as an inclusive part of the progressive nature of Scottish identity that respondents, as this study concluded earlier, seemed to relate to.

The contemporary Scottish identity was generally viewed to consist of developments that were the product of an inherently progressive and dynamic nature within that identity. This allows a place for Scotland's stereotyped images. The question can now be asked as to whether respondents saw the need for new identity symbols to be created for Scottish contemporary identity. If Scottish identity is constantly progressing, then the nation's consumers have to interact with that identity through relevant symbolic interpretations of it. The research findings were found to agree with this argument. As one Scottish respondent stated:

These [stereotypical] *images have a basis within history, but you need more modern ones to show Scotland has changed.*

Another Scots respondent commented:

You can learn from the past but must not hark back. I often feel as if nothing has happened since the '45. [the second Jacobite Rebellion , 1745]

The role of Scotland's past as continually providing the roots of a contemporary national identity is suggested in the last comment, as well as the recognition of the lack of contemporary symbols for Scotland as part of this progressive relationship. The fact that Scottish stereotyped images should overall take a low profile to these new symbolic interpretations was however the majority view, and summed up in the following comment by a Scot:

I don't think the Piper and kilts will ever be out of place. I think they have to fall at a lower level though. I hope other things become more prominent – I'm not sure what they would be!

What was clear from this study was that in terms of 'culture consumed' (Fuat Firat 1995) the stereotypical aspects of Scottish culture are actively and enthusiastically consumed by both Scots and non Scots alike. Scots in particular look forward to a future in which historical symbols are relevant but not dominant in defining identity.

CONCLUSIONS

The research reveals that consumer perceptions of contemporary Scotland reflect the multidimensionality of the nation's identity. Primary features with which the respondents identified related to recent developments in art and culture, whereas business and industry were seen to be less central to their conception of present day Scotland. Many of the stereotypical images and established symbols used to signify Scottishness, particularly those that have a heavy presence in tourist "hot spots" as souvenirs (e.g. tartan and whiskey), are not seen by consumers to represent reality of everyday life. There are, however, some images with which consumers identify more closely, such as the portrayal of the Scottish countryside. Despite lack of identification with traditional symbols of Scotland, the consumers recognised that the use of these symbols to communicate to external groups might be appropriate, depending on the group's motives for interacting with 'things Scottish'. This sentiment fails to acknowledge, however, the consequences of transmitting conflicting meanings about national identity and ideology (Schouten and Alexander, 1995).

Scotland's image is a commercial and economic matter and as such national identity is an important part of the economic development of the country (Patton, 1999). O'Shea (1999) points to a 'chicken and egg' situation where the value of the national image outside of Scotland lies to a large extent with the corporations who choose to promote themselves as Scottish. If these organisations retain the misty tartan image then Scotland will continue to be perceived as old-fashioned; if however Scottish companies are perceived to be modern, dynamic and innovative, the image of Scotland changes. Nationalism is a relatively recent phenomenon. The Church was replaced as the dominant cultural institution with the coming of the modern worldview. The Renaissance saw the ascent of nationalism. In more recent times still the corporation has become for most people the dominant institution (Deetz, 1992). Habermas (1975) shows how we have experienced a shift from social identity to individual identity due to economic changes in our (Western) society. In recent months we might be forgiven for thinking that nationalism is re-surging and that this is not necessarily beneficial.

REFERENCES

Allen, B J., Tompkins, P K. and Busemeyer, S. (1996) 'Organizational Communication', In Salwen, M B. and Stacks, D W. (eds.), *An Integrated Approach to Communication Theory and Research*, Mahwah, NJ.: Lawrence Erlbaum Associates, pp. 383-395.

Askegaard S and Ger G (1998) 'Product Country images : towards a contextualised approach' in *European Advances in Consumer Research* vol3, pg 50-58 ACR.

Berger P (1966) 'Identity as a Problem in the Sociology of Knowledge' *European Journal of Sociology* vol 7, pp105-115.

Birtchnell, J. (1993) *How Humans Relate: A New Interpersonal Theory*, Hove: Psychology Press.

Bouchet, D. (1995) "Marketing and the Redefinition of Ethnicity" in *Marketing in a Multicultural World*, J.A. Costa and G. Bamossy (eds.), Sage, California.

Burke, K. (1969) *A Rhetoric of Motives*, Berkeley, CA.: University of California Press.

Cheney, G. (1992) 'The Corporate Person (Re)Presents Itself', In Toth, E. and Heath, R L., *Rhetorical and Critical Approaches to Public Relations*, Mahwah, NJ.: Lawrence Erlbaum Associates.

Cohen, R. (1994) *Frontiers of Identity: The British and Others*, Longman, London.

Deetz, S A. (1992) *Democracy in an Age of Corporate Colonization: Developments in Communication and the Politics of Everyday Life*, Albany, NY.: State University of New York Press.

Despres, L.A. (1975) "Towards a Theory of Ethnic Phenomena" in L.A. Despres (ed.) *Ethnicity and Resource Competition in Plural Societies*, LaHaye-Paris, Mouton.

Dewey, J. (1916/1966) *Democracy and Education*, New York: The Free Press.

Dittmar H (1992) *The Social Psychology of Material Possessions* Harverster, Hemel Hempstead.

Fuat Firat A (1995) 'Consumer Culture or Culture Consumed' in *Marketing in a Multicultural World*, J.A. Costa and G. Bamossy (eds.), Sage, California.

Gerth, H H. and Mills, C W. (1967) 'Symbol Spheres in Society', In Matson, F W. and Montagu, A. (eds.), *The Human Dialogue: Perspectives on Communication*, New York: The Free Press, pp. 404-410.

Goodman, M B. (1998) *Corporate Communication for Executives*, Albany, NY.: State University of New York Press.

Goyder, M. (1998) *Living Tomorrow's Company*, Aldershot, Gower Publishing Company.

Habermas, J. (1975) *Legitimation Crisis*, Boston, MA.: Beacon Press.

Halal, W E. (1996) *The New Management: Democracy and Enterprise Are Transforming Organisations*, San Francisco, CA.: Berrett-Koehler Publishers, Inc.

Hampden-Turner, C. (1970) *Radical Man*, New York: Anchor Books.

Heath, R L. (1994) *Management of Corporate Communication: From Interpersonal Contacts to External Affairs*, Hillsdale, NJ.: Lawrence Erlbaum Associates.

Heath, R L. and Bryant, J. (1992) *Human Communication Theory and Research: Concepts, Contexts & Challenges*, Hillsdale, NJ.: Lawrence Erlbaum Associates.

Hogg, M., and Michell, P. (1996) 'Identity, Self and Consumption: A Conceptual Framework', *Journal of Marketing Management*, Vol. 12, pp. 629-644.

Jay, A. (1972) *Corporation Man*, London: Jonathan Cape.

Jackson, T. (1999) 'UK goes Cool on Britannia', *Financial Times*, 14/15 May.

Joy A, Hui M, Chankon K and Laroche M (1995) 'The Cultural Past in the Present: The Meaning of Home and Objects in the Homes of the Working Class Italian Immigrants in Montreal' in *Marketing in a Multicultural World*, J.A. Costa and G. Bamossy (eds.), Sage, California.

Keillor, B. and Hult, G T. (1999) 'A Five Country Study of National Identity: Implications for international marketing research and practice' *International Marketing Review*, Vol. 16, No. 1, pp. 65-82.

Kelman, H C. (1961) 'Processes of opinion change', *Public Opinion Quarterly*, Vol. 25, pp. 57-78.

Langer, S K. (1967) 'On a New Definition of "Symbol"', In Matson, F W. and Montagu, A. (eds.) (1967) *The Human Dialogue: Perspectives on Communication*, New York: The Free Press, pp. 548-554.

Leeds-Hurwitz, W. (ed.) (1995) *Social Approaches to Communication*, New York: Guilford Press.

Lewicki, R J. (1981) 'Organizational Seduction: Building Commitment to Organizations', *Organizational Dynamics*, Vol. 10, No. 2, pp. 5-21.

March, J G. and Simon, H A. (1958) *Organization*, New York: John Wiley & Sons.

McCracken G (1990) *Culture and Consumption* Indiana University Press, Indianapolis.

O'Shea, S. (1999) 'Scotland Rebranded', *Scotland on Sunday*, 16 May.

Papadopoulos N and Heslop L (1993) *Product Country Images : Impact and Role in International Marketing* New York: International Business Press.

Patton, L. (1999) 'How Other's See Us', *The Herald*, 17 May.

Schultz, M., Larsen, M H. and Hatch M J. (1999) 'The Expressive Organization: New Ways of Communicating the Organization', paper presented to the *3rd International Conference on Corporate Identity, Reputation, and Competitiveness*, San Juan, Puerto Rico, 7-9 January.

Tompkins, P K. and Cheney, G. (1985) 'Communication and unobtrusive control in contemporary organizations', In McPhee, R D. and Tompkins, P K. (eds.), *Organizational Communication: Traditional Themes and New Directions*, Beverley Hills, CA.: Sage Publications, pp. 123-146.

van Dijk, T A. (ed.) (1997) *Discourse as Social Interaction*, London: Sage Publications.

Varey, R J. (1997) 'Capitalist Society, Social Character, and Communication Attitude', paper presented as a seminar on "Communication for Communicators: A Possible New World", at the *'New World Strategies' International Conference of the International Association of Business Communicators*, Los Angeles, California, USA, June 1997.

Camp as Cultural Capital: Further Elaboration of a Consumption Taste

Steven M. Kates, Monash University

ABSTRACT

This article reports selected findings of an ethnographic study of gay men's consumption patterns. In particular, it elaborates upon the "homosexual sensibility" known as "camp." Herein, the author interprets various experiential aspects of camp consumption and then places camp, the institution, within a theoretical framework, arguing that it is usefully conceptualized as a specialized expression of "subcultural capital" and habitus development.

Traditionally, consumption has often been viewed as expressions of social organization, status or hierarchy (e.g., Simmel 1900; Veblen 1899). The work of Pierre Bourdieu, the French sociologist, is of considerable relevance and importance to this continuing stream of research (Bourdieu 1984). Over the past three decades, Bourdieu has pursued a continuing project exploring the various dimensions of social life. Drawing selectively and critically from Marx, Durkheim, and Weber, Bourdieu has developed an extensive and dense body of sociological work that broadly conceptualizes social organization as an arena of competition for economic and cultural resources (see Bourdieu 1984). His central research question concerns the ways that stratified systems and domination reproduce and persist (Swartz 1997). Most relevant to this article, consumption emerges as a key field–an arena in which people compete for various resources - in which tastes are enacted and social distinctions are made manifest and hierarchical structures systematically reproduced (see Holt 1998). Particularly, consumers are thought to possess various kinds and degrees of cultural capital–tastes, skills, knowledge, and abilities acquired through formal education, upbringing, work experience, and social interactions–that enables them to "properly" appreciate goods and services.

Bourdieu's work and that drawing from it provides the theoretical springboard for the present work. The purpose of this article is to explore the consumption sensibility known as "camp," the homosexual perspective or aesthetic (Sontag 1964). Although many cultural theorists have written about camp (Babuscio 1993; Bergman 1993; Bronski 1984; Newton 1993; Ross 1989; Sontag 1964), it has yet to be explored empirically. How do gay consumers experience campy objects and activities? The one exception is the study by Kates (1997), but this latter study, although presenting some of the lived experiential dimensions of camp consumption, does not adequately conceptualize it within a broader field of social and political relations. It is the objective of the present article to interpret various aspects of lived camp experience and to place camp, the cultural phenomenon, within a theoretical framework, arguing that it is usefully conceptualized as a specialized expression of cultural capital and gay men's habitus development. Such an endeavour adds to the consumer research discipline in the following manners. First, the empirical study of camp provides us with an understanding of one particular aspect of gay men's consumption, a relatively unknown area (Kates 1997). Second, a study of camp adds to a continuing stream of consumer research investigating the social patterning of consumption in postmodern conditions (e.g., Bourdieu 1984; Holt 1995, 1997, 1998). Finally, as part of the recent "postmodern project" in consumer research, this paper contributes to the critical excavation of the voices of previously silenced or stigmatized consumers. Overall, insights about camp contribute to our knowledge of culture and consumption in a complex, fragmented societal configuration characterized by a plurality of changing alignments, allegiances, and difference.

CONCEPTUAL BACKGROUND

What is camp?

The literature on camp suggests that it is a specific manner or style of consuming characterized by the ironic appreciation of excess, exaggeration, and flamboyance (privileging "style over substance"; see Sontag [1964]). In a sense, camp consumption is a cultural mode of interpretation or way of consuming (see Holt 1995) that "rummages" through the things, icons, and meanings of popular culture and ironically reworks them in a gay social context (Kates 1997; Newton 1993; Ross 1989). As Sontag (1964) suggests, camp consumption is usually associated with gay cultures that exist in large European, North American, and Australian urban spaces (Altman 1982; D'Emilio 1983). Recent conceptual work on camp converges on a number of salient points. First, camp is the aesthetic of the overblown, exaggerated, and ironic, as personified by garish, elaborately dressed and coiffed drag queens who perform in gay bars. But camp is not always the aesthetic of the extreme. Often (and perhaps most relevantly) the ineffable camp perspective playfully, subtly, gently, and ironically reworks the oppression experienced by gay men by re-inscribing everyday objects and shared social practices with different meanings.

Yet, from the perspective of consumer researchers, camp has yet to be conceptualized and studied empirically as a family of meanings or discourse that informs consumption *taste*, particularly given the renewed interest and work in this area (Bourdieu 1984; Holt 1997, 1998). For purposes herein, taste is usefully conceptualized as elaborated consumer preferences that serve to socially classify both self and other and have important implications for social stratification or hierarchy (Bourdieu 1984, p. 77; Holt 1997, 1998). Given the sociological orientation of this article, it is necessary to incorporate the insights of Pierre Bourdieu, a theorist who provides the necessary conceptual language and empirical insights to further our understanding of camp as a cultural mode of symbolic consumption.

Cultural Capital, Habitus, and Taste: A Brief Account of the Work of Pierre Bourdieu

For Bourdieu (1984), social reality is conceptualized as a struggle over key resources, and classes reproduce themselves within the context of this struggle. Particularly germane is the notion of "cultural capital," as distinguished from economic capital (money, property, and so on). Cultural capital is, in turn, internalized by the habitus, a "system of durable, transposable dispositions" (see Holt 1998, p. 431) that is developed through upbringing since childhood, education that stresses abstract reasoning and critical thinking skills, social interactions, and work experience in which these skills may be actively practised and enhanced. Another way of expressing this is that the habitus is the organizing set of principles–structured by past experience, yet also generative of inventive possibilities - for continued strategic practice. The habitus also internalizes classifications for good or bad, vulgar or refined, or cultured or uncouth. Hence, consumers gradually become predisposed to exercising consumption preferences characteristic of their class habitus and corresponding level of cultural capital (Bourdieu 1984; Holt 1998), demonstrating a systematic (and often subtle or unconscious) opposition or distaste for the preferences of other classes. It is the habitus that mediates between objective conditions of social existence (such as poverty) and the individual consumption practices that subsequently emerge (Bourdieu 1984). Further it is the habitus that "organizes how one classifies the universe of consumption objects to which one is exposed, constructing desire toward consecrated objects and disgust toward objects that are not valued in the field" (Holt 1998, p. 4). In other words, consumers routinely enact their tastes in everyday life, and by doing so, they classify self and other, implicitly indicating their level of cultural capital by the nuanced manners in which they consume. Differences in the standard of living between dominant and subordinate classes, as internalized by the habitus, are thought to produce a "basic opposition between the taste of luxury and the tastes of necessity" respectively (Bourdieu 1984, p. 183).

Although cultural capital broadly structures patterns of tastes for those possessing the lowest and highest levels of it (Holt 1998), many important questions still remain to be explored, given the complex North American social context of social mobility, fragmentation, and differentiation. Relatedly, Bourdieu has been criticized for the supposed "hyperdeterminism" of habitus (Swartz 1997). Defenders of Bourdieu are quick to note that the habitus is a *mediating*, not a determinative, construct. Hence, the habitus, and by implication, consumption practice, is open to subsequent modification, *particularly under different social contexts from which it was formed to begin with* (see Swartz 1997). I propose that gay subculture and "coming out of the closet" (i.e., a socialization process usually entailing the acceptance and disclosure of one's sexual orientation to others, the concurrent exploration of urban gay "ghettos," and the formation of social and sexual bonds with other gay men) does indeed constitute such a radically different social context. This claim is strongly supported by extensive historical and psychological literature in the gay and lesbian studies field (e.g., Altman 1982; Chauncey 1994; D'Emilio 1983). Further, gay men must negotiate between gay and heterosexual social worlds whilst engaging in socialization within the gay subculture (Kates 1997) and this phenomenon has implications for consumption tastes, the habitus, and cultural capital. As I illustrate below, camp consumption tastes are incorporated into participants' consumption practices, in most instances *regardless* of educational, class, or occupational background, for the social field of gay culture intersects with the habitus, with meaningful effects.

METHOD

This article reports selected findings from an ethnographic study of gay men's consumption patterns. In addition to participant observation of a gay and lesbian youth group and a gay men's professional organization over the course of a year and a half, forty-four gay men were formally interviewed (McCracken 1988). The men were identified through the gay and lesbian youth group and the gay men's social organization (The "Brotherhood"). From initial contacts, more men volunteered and the sample "snowballed" from there. Interviewing was conducted until redundancy of themes was identified (see Corbin and Strauss 1990; Glaser and Strauss 1967). It should also be noted that the audiotaped interviews were not transcribed until after all interviews were conducted. However, during the fieldwork, the researcher took copious notes during each interview, and these notes guided further questioning and investigation. The men were aged from 16 to 53 and although most were white, a concerted effort was made to include black, Asian, and First Nation participants. Further, and relevant to this report, informants' family backgrounds, education levels, and occupations were also discussed.

During the long interviews, a variety of topics were discussed including personal biographies, "coming out of the closet," and social activities. Further, many areas of consumption were discussed in depth: food, home décor, socializing, drinking, clothes, cultural products (theatre, film, art, reading, and other live performances), attending bars, travel, and advertising. Although the interviewer set the topics of interest (consumption and coming out, for example), interviews were semi-structured, allowing participants to set directions and express their own views and attitudes (see McCracken 1988). After the interviews were all completed, tapes were transcribed verbatim. The written interviews were read over several times in order to get a broad sense of the common themes grounded in the text (Glaser and Strauss 1967; Spiggle 1994). After that, themes were refined and related to each other conceptually and to relevant literature, a process called "tacking." It should be noted that the data resonated and "made sense" particularly well after a review of various sociological works of Pierre Bourdieu. Although the etic categories of cultural capital, habitus, and field (Bourdieu's main conceptual terms) do *not* derive directly from the interview data, painstaking attention was paid in the descriptions and interpretations below to show that the data meaningfully illustrates these etic categories (cf. Holt 1997, 1998; Thompson and Haytko 1997; Thompson and Hirschman 1995). The findings were interpreted with Bourdieu's framework deliberately in mind in order to elaborate on camp as a consumption sensibility that has significant implications for social hierarchy and classification, including some but excluding others, as accounted for below.

FINDINGS: UNPACKING CAMP

One of the purposes of this article is to illustrate the lived dimensions of camp consumption. In other words, in what ways do the study's participants consume in campy manner? How do they classify, evaluate and appreciate campy things, experiences and people (cf. Holt 1995; Kates 1997)? To do this, findings were organized and classified into three major headings for conceptual exposition and clarity: appreciation of objectified cultural capital, embodied cultural capital and gay diva worship, and camp as problematizing the social status quo.

"It's a Gay Thing–You wouldn't understand!" Appreciation of Objectified Camp

Some consumption objects such as feather boas or Aubrey Beardsley prints are considered campy due to their enduring association with gay or theatre subcultures (Kates 1997; Sinfield 1994; Sontag 1964) and serve as examples of objectified cultural capital. Yet, products have different meanings for different interpretive communities, given the complex fragmentation of society. Further, objects do not have any immanent meaning *per se*, but become meaningful only in practice and social context (see Holt 1997). It is more accurate to conceptualize camp consumption as a particular style of consuming or as consumption with a distinctive manner of expression. Hence, many object or constellations of objects can be campily consumed if the consumer has acquired the requisite skills and tastes.

Jordan's passage below illustrates one of the ways in which objectified camp taste is acquired in everyday or informal consumption experiences:

There's a joke that a friend of mine and I came up with when we went to the gay campground: "How can you tell it's a gay campground? Well, the bar's open 24 hours. There's an inground heated swimming pool. There's a barn that's converted into a dance club at night. And there's minigolf!" (laughs) [I: Did they have all those things?] They HAD all those things! But you pitched your tent, or you could rent an old trailer. You do the campfire thing. It's wood. It's huge. It's a huge property. [I: You talked about the campsite itself. And the in joke about gay men and camping. Can you explain the joke to me?] Okay. I think it's a lot to do with the fact that gay men are not necessarily seen as the types that will go out and rough it. In the brush, portaging through. A lot of the stereotype of gay men is that their very urban. I think a lot of the stereotype is that of gay men as very urban. And you find them in the cities, usually downtown in apartments, in condos and stuff like that. And that's a really big stereotype because as I said before, I get a lot of people at the youth group that I host from out of town, from like [a nearby town]. From way out in [the country] and out the other end too. So...the campground being characterized as gay plays on that stereotype of being very urban and in ground swimming pool at a campground?! A bar? You don't do your hoedowns, but you do your club music on Friday, Saturday nights with the DJ trucked up from [a nearby city]. Minigolf is a city type of thing and stuff like that. [I: Is there some truth in the stereotype? To a certain extent yes 'cause you do find a lot of the gay population concentrated in urban centres because that's where gay men and women tend to be...tend to congregate. Being able to go to the ghetto is you know, a self-empowering experience because when you're out alone in Holland's Landing or in Newmarket, you're alone. Yes, you have [straight] friends and stuff, but I don't honestly think it's the same. Being able to talk to your friends...your straight friends about your experiences as being able to talk to another gay person who has experienced or *gone through the exact same thing that you have or close to it.* But I think the campground plays on the stereotype of having the minigolf. Stuff like that, yeah. There is some truth to that, but I think you'll find that now, a lot of gay couples or a lot of gay groups of friends are venturing further outside of the community as a group as gay people. And so it's starting to come down, but...yeah, the stereotype is still there and I think that's why you could say Cedars is a gay campground other than, I don't know, the [other national] park isn't. (Jordan, 26, Eurasian, university degree, IT systems consultant)

For Jordan, a campground became a "camp"-ground when gay men consumed in it. The transmission of cultural consumption knowledge in the gay men's social *milieu* was very much like having an "in joke" explained and finally "getting the joke" on an ongoing basis, and then realizing that one is "in". In this regard, the stereotyped behaviors or images of camp taste and gay men as urban aesthetes serve as important guides or templates of acceptable styles and meanings of camp consumption. Gay men can then improvise and play in the spirit of the bricoleur, slyly undermining the seriousness of the elegance by applying an ironic sensibility. The other important social dynamic at play is that gay men are able to socialize on their own in conditions free of antigay violence or social disapproval in gay urban "ghettos" or campgrounds, as above. Such material conditions set the stage for an exclusive camp cultural sensibility to be apprehended, acquired, enjoyed, and expanded upon. When Jordan notes "you're alone," he is referring to the fact *that he was alone with other gay men,* and heterosexuals were systemically excluded from the festivities. Consumption practices then become part and parcel of a process of social differentiation and stratification (cf. Holt 1998).

Informants provided numerous examples of consumption situations in which their own consumption tastes are positively framed in contrast to those of heterosexual men (and a range of feelings of hostility, disgust, sympathy, or indulgent amusement are proffered toward the latter, their "vulgar" tastes and consumption

practices). In these instance and others, consumption tastes serve as valuable expressions of cultural capital. It is the *manner* of consumption that distinguishes gay men from others. Jordan and other informants link their use and appreciation of these products to a heightened, conscious sense of social affiliation with gay men, disaffiliation from allegedly unenlightened and vulgar straight men, and more liberated, progressive gender identities. It was often articulated in the interviews that due to their unthinking and *uncritical* adherence to outdated masculine conventions, heterosexual men are unable to consume in a refined manner that acknowledges and appreciates the finer, "classy" attributes of products. It is this belief and the ironic pleasure it afforded that served as a form of social distinction for gay informants. As some informants expressed it, "straights just don't get it!" Campy consumption, one type of the "taste of luxury," (Bourdieu 1984) was demarcated as the exclusive preserve of gay men–and some "enlightened," "gay positive," or "educated" straight men.

"It's the pictures that got small": Embodied Cultural Capital and Gay Diva Worship

One distinct aspect of gay men's consumer culture is "diva worship," the passionate and almost fetishistic devotion to female Hollywood stars such as Marilyn Monroe or Judy Garland or more recent celebrities such as Cher, Barbra Streisand, or Madonna (Ross 1989). During the fieldwork of this study, diva worship was observed in many social contexts: during drag shows in gay bars, references in casual conversation to the 1939 film, the Wizard of Oz, starring Judy Garland ("Something tells me we're not in Kansas anymore, Toto!"), posters of Madonna and Marilyn Monroe displayed publicly in shops, and the constant presence of Madonna in gay nightclubs. Diva worship has a long history in North American gay communities as well, as evinced by the presence of so many screaming, crying gay men during Judy Garland's last concerts in New York during the 1960's. Indeed, to ask if someone is "a friend of Dorothy's" is a covert manner of asking "are you gay?" What are we to make of this cultural particularity?

It should be emphasized that not all of the gay informants expressed a fondness or taste for diva worship, but all were aware of it. Antonio, in the following passage, reflects on the heavily gendered character of this consumption practice and recount a narrative common to informants and even cultural critique of camp:

I think that that gay men are attracted by...well, they're attracted by two things. Either, two extremes. Either extremely strong women or extremely weak women. On the strong end of the spectrum, you have Barbra Streisand. You have Cher, I suppose, to a degree. People who have come back or fought there way to the top, survivors, and also people who have the reputation of being nasty. People who step on other people to get there, you know, and then I guess, you know, they respect that kind of toughness. I don't know if Barbra Streisand is a nasty person, but she certainly has a very kind of, domineering trait, from what I hear. People like that. *On the other hand, you have someone like Judy Garland, just the opposite. You know, made a mess of her life, had no business sense whatsoever. People loved her because she was such a victim. This is a...she was a victim, in many ways. She wasn't a happy person. She was successful, but she had an unhappy life.* Alcohol, pills, these addictions that they had. (Antonio, WM, 38, university degree, interpreter, emphasis added)

As alluded to above, there are noteworthy aspects of diva worship that should be emphasized. First, diva worship is usually founded upon an appreciation of a cliched tragic narrative or myth, as exemplified by the aging star, Norma Desmond, in the film *Sunset Boulevard* ("I'm still big. It's the pictures that got small.") A person, despite the odds and personal tragedy, "makes it big," experiences a great public success usually in the entertainment world (the rise), and then, as a tragic victim of circumstances or personal demons, suffers calamitous misfortune and subsequently passes into obscurity (the fall). The second point to note is that these people are *invariably* glamorous women. Gay men, through camp consumption, identify gladly with the "plight" of the other gender!

The appreciation of divas consists of both experiential enjoyment and the more distanced, ironic camp sensibility. Although the songs of Garland or Streisand are enjoyed for their immediate pleasure and gratification, proper, "campy" consumption of a diva requires the knowledge of the tragic diva myth and the identification with a woman for her strong *and* weak personal characteristics. The drag queen or female star may appear exaggerated, over the top, and outrageous, but the consumption style employed by informants to appreciate her is actually rather subtle and intricate. It not only acknowledges the overblown aspects of the diva's appearance or personae, but also it plays with the "tragic narrative" of her life and evokes a level of identification with her suffering. At the same time, there is a *gentle* undercurrent of parody of that suffering, revealing its contrived character.

Gamson (1994), in his study of celebrity consumption, identifies five distinct styles with which consumers enjoy famous people. Although some consumers still take the notion of celebrity at face value and defend talent and accomplishments as the legitimate foundation of fame, many more consumers adopt a more "postmodern" strategy, enjoying the marketing artifice as part of the packaged personae. But diva worship may defy easy classification. Diva worship is a form of communal co-optation of mainstream cultural elements (cf. Kopytoff 1986; Miller 1987) wherein celebrities are re-inscribed with meanings local to gay culture (see Geertz 1983). The parody of diva worship lies in the incongruity and contradiction created by, for example, the juxtaposition of the wholesomeness of Dorothy (the main character of *The Wizard of Oz*) and its significations in gay men' lives–a "telltale" sign of same sex desire. This manifestation of camp brings delight in the privileged knowledge and unintended uses of divas by this particular interpretive community.

Most relevant to the social stratification argument (based on Bourdieu's work as outlined above) is that diva worship may constitute one of the most enduring and visible types of symbolic boundaries between the gay men's consumer subculture and mainstream heterosexual culture (see Holt 1997). As a distinct form of consumption practice, diva worship serves as a key basis for social affiliation with other gay men. The visible, garish, and "screaming" drag queen so often featured during telecasts of Lesbian and Gay Pride Day celebrations is a constant and potent reminder of the differences between the cultures, differences that reinforce the social boundaries. In recent practice, diva worship of Garland and older celebrities has transformed into admiration for contemporary figures such as Madonna, Cher, and Roseanne. Like the older celebrities, they are "strong" women who have coped with tragic circumstances (perhaps surviving as a successful woman in a patriarchal world can be painful enough). Yet, according to informant reports, these newer divas are considered more resilient and openly "gay positive," and subsequently, worthy of widespread adoration (cf. Gamson 1994). Perhaps most tellingly, some informants made derogatory comments about heterosexual's presumed ignorance of these diva's signifiance to gay culture and how the messages in their lives and works are "meant" for gay men. In such a manner, gay men lay claim to their celebrities and socially organize around their consumption.

Camp–But more so: Camp as Problematizing the Social Status Quo

One of the other discoveries about the lived experience of camp is that some of the informants were aware of the term itself and were able to relate it to sophisticated analyses of homophobic prejudice. Some of the informants explicitly "philosophised" about camp:

Camp to me means fun, it means experimentation with drag. It means role playing. Basically, it means a dark, twisted humour whether it's in a film or whether it's experimentation among friends, but it basically means letting down your guard and having fun, being with people, you can be open and honest and trustworthy with, and kind of experimenting with your own personal boundaries. So I think one of the reasons that gay people have picked up on camp is because...my God! With the way society has ostracized gayness and gays and lesbians in general, we've really had to dig deep right down to our souls and realize, what do we want out of life? What are our true beliefs? What is our purpose in this world? By camp or campiness, I find that we know what our boundaries are. We know when we can be vulnerable, and when we know when to hold back and through camp, we can share some humor and some closeness, and at the same time, laugh, have fun, I mean, this world, there's no reason for so much hatred and violence and negativity. [Something] seems to be camp because it's exaggerated. It doesn't need to be realistic. It needs to be testing the boundaries, so to speak, and by doing that, it become very camp. I find that camp is something that gay people understand a little bit better than straight people simply because, for some strange reason, well two reasons, actually. One I think it's really because we did have to get in touch with our emotions, so we can understand a little bit more where people are coming from when it is humor, when it's meant to be vulgar, when it's meant to make you laugh or make you cry. Or it's the double entendres, which brings us to the second point, which gay people have gone through life and got through mainstream using double entendre meanings, double entendre type...products and words and things like that. Like, if you were "a friend of Dorothy's," that meant that you were gay, so when it comes to camp, a lot of camp has to do with double entendres, so with gay people, Oh, my God! They love it, and if they don't get the joke, they want to get it, whereas with a lot of straight people, if they don't get the joke the first time, they may not want to know the answer, they don't question. "What do you mean? I don't get it!" They just accept it for what it is, just like in society, you suddenly become of a certain age, and you get married, and you go through the patterns of life because that's what's expected of you. You don't ever have to question your own life, your own thoughts and values and beliefs and all the rest, so therefore you never have any reason to doubt what's being presented to you. And with camp, that's exactly what it's doing is its giving you that other perception and it wants to do it in such a way that it's a pleasant experience if you allow it to be. (Russ, 29, WM, university degree and professional designation, management accountant)

Such thoughtful commentary reflects an awareness that exceeds the usual ironic perspective and knowledge of most informants; in effect, Russ' passage evinces a metadiscursive awareness of this knowledge and camp perspective of the world. This type of awareness is elucidated by Giddens' (1984) concept of the "double hermeneutic." Scholars study the emic understandings that consumers hold about their social worlds. Researchers then invent or elaborate upon (or, in the case of camp, even co-opt!) conceptual terms about the social world that frame their academic debates so they may develop systematic insights into the dynamics and structures of society. Some etic terms seep into everyday usage and popular speech ("deconstruction" is a good case in point), enriching the understandings of some educated consumers. "Camp" is both an academic, etic term used extensively by theorists in cultural and gay and lesbian studies and a culturally specific term commonly employed by gay men. For example, a group of gay men might agree to maintain "low camp" in a location populated by possibly hostile heterosexuals. What this means is that all flamboyant, feminine, colorful, and ironic expressions (such as "Oh Mary! Get that tacky ensemble *she's* wearing!") and/or gestures should be eliminated in order to "pass" as heterosexual, if temporarily.

Russ–in common with those informants with high cultural capital from upbringing, education, and professional backgrounds - demonstrates a penetrating social reflexivity about the complex social world that he negotiates daily. He has gained the sophisticated understanding that camp is a perspective of the social world (or an interpretive framework) particular to "out" gay men. Implicitly, Russ links a form of consumption (camp) to a form of social oppression (homophobia), and hence, his appreciation of a particular instance of camp consumption (the song "I'm too Sexy") allows him to problematize the "natural" givens in a field of pervasive social inequity.

Russ' passage also illustrates the critical, reflexive, and questioning orientation to the world so characteristic of camp–*and* of high cultural capital (see Bourdieu 1984; Gouldner 1979; Holt 1998). It should be noted that Russ' exposition is uncharacteristic of most informants due to its depth and critical disposition. Camp, as an interpretive framework, is best described as a presuppositional, taken-for-granted understanding or as a form of practical knowledge that remains unarticulated until realized in consumption contexts (Bourdieu 1984; Giddens 1984). Yet, systematic reading of the interview transcripts yielded an interesting insight. Almost all of the informants spoke of various funny, ironic, campy types of consumption experience (usually to do with drag, gender bending, or extremes of masculinity or femininity, or even food as illustrated above). In contrast, a substantial number of informants (approximately one quarter), in *addition* to recounting enjoyable camp experiences, were able to explicitly identify and define camp as a politicized way of looking at the world or as the gay sensibility that was "loose," "funny," "gay," or "critical." In short, they could "theorize" about it in a "pop psychology" manner. Importantly, these were the informants who had attended university, worked in professional occupations, and came from homes with educated parents. The difference between the two consumer interpretations is not a difference of kind, but of nuanced quality, characterized by the application of critical reflectivity, a key characteristic of humanistic education (Gouldner 1979). Yet, through the appreciation of camp experience, almost all of the informants demonstrate some conscious understanding of their "social situatedness" (i.e., how they are treated in relation to other groups and an abstracted heterosexual Other). And for a minority of them, this conscious understanding is inflected with an explicit, sophisticated analysis of how camp consumption relates to life possibilities, power, and social positioning (see Swartz 1979). Hence, for Russ, learning to "get the joke" of camp is a means of understanding self in relation to an occasionally hostile society and criticizing normative views on gender and sexuality as exclusive, unduly limiting, and unfair.

Among the other informants who offered thoughtful appraisals as camp and oppression was the consensus that camp sensibility offered a challenge to a particular aspect of the societal status quo. Corey, a law student with self-confessed Marxist sympathies, articulated a commonly held (and now, often challenged) stereotype about gay men–that they are most often "creative" and engaged in artistic occupations such as interior design, and act as fashion arbiters–but then used that observation to make a more penetrating insight. Like Russ, he linked an understanding of camp consumption to social oppression. But he specifically identifies the historically transgressive character of camp sensibility (Chauncey 1994; Sinfield 1994)—its subversive challenge to gendered conventions and to the very heart of the institution of gender itself.

CAMP CONSUMPTION AND SOCIAL ORGANIZATION

The central finding of this paper is that the gay informants–of diverse class, occupational, ethnic, and cultural backgrounds–acquired the appreciation of the camp "tastes of luxury" and the parody associated with it (cf. Bourdieu 1984; Holt 1997). Camp is, foremost, an orientation to the social world and a strategy that seeks to play, exaggerate, and gently satirize, exposing underlying assumptions. For example, the drag queen is an embodied form of camp that calls into questioned the "natural" quality of masculine and feminine gender roles, accomplished through inversion and outrageous hyperbole. Camp consumption entails the acquisition of not *the* aesthetic taste, but of a *particular* aesthetic taste with a rich history behind it (cf. Altman 1982; Bourdieu 1984; Chauncey 1994; Sinfield 1994). Camp is lively, funny, mocking, sometimes "bitchy," and assumes a self-referential pose to its own parody.

Camp may also be considered a democratic leveler in some ways. The informants came from a variety of class backgrounds and occupations. Yet, with some qualitative nuances, they were all able to appreciate the camp sensibility as embodied in drag, clothing, food, or décor. Yet, given Bourdieu's conceptualization of the habitus, this finding is somewhat problematic. How is the "taste of luxury" so widely disseminated? Cultural capital is, traditionally, embodied during consumers' upbringings and social interactions with family and peers. Through formal education and informal socialization, those who have higher levels of cultural capital develop a more critical, problematizing, and distanced appreciation of the world and an accompanying, metaphysical aesthetic taste (e.g., Holt 1998). Yet, it is recognized that the early development of the habitus does not necessarily preclude further development and change later in adulthood (Swartz 1997). Theoretically, camp consumption is used as a means to experiment with identity, finding one's social space in society. According to the findings of this study, once a gay male consumer develops an understanding of camp's multifaceted meanings, he can interact more freely with other gay men, ironically re-appropriating the dominant meanings of consumer culture to fit new social contexts. Through the appreciative lens of camp experience, almost all of the informants demonstrate some conscious understanding of their "social situatedness" (i.e., how they are treated in relation to other groups and an abstracted heterosexual Other). And for a minority of them, this conscious understanding is inflected with an explicit, sophisticated analysis of how camp consumption relates to life possibilities, power, and social positioning (see Swartz 1979). For instance, for Russ, learning to "get the joke" of camp is a means of understanding self in relation to an occasionally hostile society and criticizing normative views on gender and sexuality as exclusive, unduly limiting, and unfair.

All informants gave accounts of their "coming out" process, when they accepted that they were gay, disclosed it to others, and began exploring the gay urban subculture. Despite the individual and group differences of these narratives, there was one important commonality evinced among them: coming out required the explicit rejection of an old "way of thought" and even of an old way of life. Many informants reported that they painfully struggled with guilt, fear and shame, but eventually arrived at a kind of acceptance of a socially awkward sexual bias. Coming out also meant coming to terms with a new social reality. Marriage, children, and social connections with the family of origin were all recast in a new light. Yet, with some measure of self-acceptance came a qualitatively different way of looking at the social world. In the terms of the rhetoric of gay liberation that intertextually informed so many of informants' accounts, "gay is as good as straight!" Within periods ranging from months or years, informants learned to reassess their old beliefs about homosexuality and positively recast them. Sometimes, informants felt anger and rage at systemic inequalities. In almost all cases, informants developed a relatively more critical, penetrating orientation toward the naturalized givens of the social world. This critical mindset impacts the structure and contents of the habitus, albeit in subtly different ways. Hence, is contended that the struggle of the coming out process–and the new social interactions it entails–that underlies the complex camp sensibility learned by university professors and warehouse workers alike. The social implications of camp are of great interests to consumer researchers. Camp consumption is strategically employed by informants to legitimate and construct social differences with heterosexuals (cf. Bourdieu 1984) through a localized form of "subcultural capital." The data support the contention that camp includes some and excludes the many. The experience of camp is like being "let in on" an in-joke and enjoying the privilege of knowing what those excluded do not. But more seriously, camp tastes serve as a multifaceted basis for social stratification. Camp sensibility unites gay men, for example, by allowing them to denigrate the allegedly "low-class" tastes of heterosexuals. Cam (Asian male, 22), for example, in a rather exasperated tone noted that he "could not believe" that heterosexuals still did not know that the 1970's pop singer Sylvester was, in fact, a woman. In the micropolitics of everyday social interactions, such knowledge and distinctions have real, practical effects and serve to bring gay men together, united in pleasurable contempt. In so doing, camp tastes creates discursive and social distance between gay men and the abstracted (and denigrated) "mainstream" or "heterosexual" other.

REFERENCES

Babuscio, Jack (1993), "Camp and the Gay Sensibility," in *Camp Grounds: Style and Homosexuality*, ed., David Bergman. Amherst, MA: University of Massachusets Press.

Bergman, David (1993) , "Introduction," in *Camp Grounds: Style and Homosexuality*, ed., David Bergman. Amherst, MA: University of Massachusets Press.

Bourdieu, Pierre (1984), *Distinction: A Social Critique of the Judgment of Taste*. Cambridge, MA: Harvard University Press.

Bronski, Michael (1984), *Culture Clash: The Making of a Gay Sensibility*, Boston, MA: South End Press.

Cass, V.C. (1979), "Homosexual Identity Formation: A Theoretical Model," *Journal of Homosexuality*, 4, 3, 143-167.

Chauncey, George (1994), *Gay New York: Gender, Urban Culture, and the Making of The Gay Male World 1890-1940*. New York: Basic Books.

Corbin, Juliet and Anselm Strauss (1990), "Grounded Theory Research: Procedures, Canons, and Evaluative Criteria," *Qualitative Sociology*, v. 13, no. 1, 3-20.

D'Emilio, John (1983), *Sexual Politics, Sexual Communities: The Making of a Homosexual Minority in the United States 1940-1970*. Chicago: The University of Chicago Press.

Gamson, Joshua (1994), *Claims to Fame: Celebrity in Contemporary America*, Los Angeles: University of California Press.

Glaser, Barney G. and Anselm L. Strauss (1967), *The Discovery of Grounded Theory: Strategies for Qualitative Research*, New York: Aldine de Gruyter.

Gouldner, Alvin (1979), *The Future of the Intellectuals and the Rise of the New Class*, London: MacMillan.

Holt, Douglas B. (1995), "How Consumers Consume: A Typology of Consumption Practices," *Journal of Consumer Research*, 22 (1), 1-16.

Holt, Douglas B. (1997), "Poststructuralist Lifestyle Analysis: Conceptualizing the Social Patterning of Consumption in Postmodernity," *Journal of Consumer Research*, 23 (March), 326-350.

_____ (1998), "Does Cultural Capital Structure American Consumption?" *Journal of Consumer Research*, 25, 1, 1-25.

Kates, Steven M. (1997), "Sense vs. Sensibility: An Exploration of the Lived Experience Of Camp," in Advances in Consumer Research, v. 24, ed. Merrie Brucks and Deborah MacInnes, Provo: UT: Association for Consumer Research, 132-137.

McCracken, Grant (1988a), *The Long Interview*. Newbury Park: Sage Publications.

Miller, Daniel, (1987), *Material Culture and Mass Consumption*. Oxford: Basil Blackwell.

Minton, Henry L. and Gary J. McDonald (1984), "Homosexual Identity Formation as a Developmental Process", *Journal of Homosexuality*, 4(20), 91-103.

Newton, Esther (1993), "Role Models," in *Camp Grounds: Style and Homosexuality*, ed., David Bergman. Amherst, MA: University of Massachusets Press.

Ross, Andrew (1989), "Uses of Camp," in *No Respect: Intellectuals and Popular Culture*. New York: Routledge.

Simmel, Georg ([1904] 1957), "Fashion," *American Journal of Sociology*, 62 (May), 541-558.

Sinfield, Alan (1994), *The Wilde Century: Effeminacy, Oscar Wilde, and the Queer Movement*. New York: Columbia University Press.

Sontag, Susan, (1964), "Notes on Camp," (1964), in *Against Interpretation*. New York: Farrar, Straus, and Giroux.

Spiggle, S. (1994), "Analysis and Interpretation of Qualitative Data in Consumer Research, " *Journal of Consumer Research*, 21, 3, 491-503.

Strauss, Anselm, and Juliet Corbin (1994), "Grounded Theory Methodology," in *Handbook of Qualitative Research*, ed. Norman K. Denzin and Yvonna S. Lincoln. London: Sage, 273-285.

Swartz, David (1997), *Culture & Power: The Sociology of Pierre Bourdieu*, Chicago: University of Chicago Press.

Veblen, Thorstein ([1899] 1970), *The Theory of the Leisure Class*, London: Unwin.

Death Becomes Us:
Negotiating Consumer Identities through Funerary Products in Ghana

Sammy Bonsu, University of North Carolina, Greensboro

ABSTRACT

Death is an inevitable aspect of the consumer experience. In spite of this, consumer researchers have neglected the phenomenon in their studies. This paper reports a preliminary investigation into death ritual consumption and its use as a vehicle for the competitive expression of consumer identities. The study is set in Asante, Ghana in an effort to further broaden consumption research beyond the scope of western philosophical boundaries.

INTRODUCTION

As doctors, when they examine the state of a patient and recognize that death is at hand, pronounce: 'He is dying, he will not recover', so we must say from the moment a man is born: 'He will not recover.'" (St. Augustine, quoted in Sarpong 1974, p. 20)

As St. Augustine remarks, death is the only true guarantee for every person, an ubiquitous phenomenon that pervades all aspects of the lived consumer experience. Graveyards around the world are filling up quickly due in part to the graying of the American population, wars in the Balkans and parts of Africa, and HIV/AIDS epidemics. The importance of death rituals in the USA is reflected in the fact that related products constitute the 3rd largest expenditure for most Americans, after homes and automobiles (Lino 1990). In less affluent parts of the world, the importance of death extends far beyond monetary value of related expenditures. Among the Asante people of central Ghana, for instance, there is a belief in the existence of the Kingdom of the Dead (*Asamando*) and custom suggests that great attention be paid to the proper conduct of burials and funeral celebrations (Gyekye 1995). This often translates into elaborate death ritual consumer activities that require spending far in excess of the bereaved's means.

In spite of the global relevance of death ritual consumption, references to the phenomenon in consumer research are very rare. A literature search on the subject within the discipline yielded only a handful of scholarly work (e.g., Gabel, Mansfield and Westbrook 1996; Gentry, Kennedy, Paul and Hill 1995; Schwartz, Jolson and Lee 1986). The conspicuous absence of death related issues in marketing and consumer research is partly a result of social restrictions on the public space of death in western cultures (Aries 1974). The rarity of death product advertising and the absence of product sales outlets in high traffic areas provide marketplace evidence to this effect.

This "pornography of death", as Gorer (1955) puts it, is a result of consumers' inherent fear of death. Guided by this fear, consumers perceive death as an inevitable nuisance whose time for eradication has arrived (Baudrillard 1993; Harrington 1969). Consumer strategies towards this end include the creation of symbolic immortality modes such as shrines (Gentry et al 1995), electronic memorials (e.g., http://virtual-memorials.com) and cryonic suspension–the freezing of a corpse in liquid nitrogen with the hope of bringing it back to life one day (Brown 1997). In the course of rendering their deceased immortal, bereaved persons also seek to facilitate mobility towards their own social status and identity aspirations.

The primary purpose of this study was to seek preliminary insights into how consumers negotiate their social identities through consumption of death rituals. The study is premised on the view that culturally entrenched meanings of death inculcate "ideolog[ies] of consumption" in bereaved consumers across different cultures, thereby fostering social ideals that fuel the unending project of the consumer self (Giddens 1991; Thompson and Haytko 1997), albeit uniquely within each society. The study's primary objective was achieved through a careful reading of interview data gathered from bereaved consumers among the Asante people of central Ghana, a small country on the west coast of Africa. The Asante inhabit an area of Ghana, about one-third the size of England. They constitute the single largest ethnic group in Ghana, making up about 15% of the country's population. Scholarly dialogue on issues of consumption has often been restricted to the experiences of affluent societies. The choice of the Asante people for this study was, therefore, an effort to extend consumption research beyond the dominant western philosophical boundaries of thought in the discipline. It was also influenced in part by the openness in that culture about death-related issues and by the author's familiarity with the society.

Furthermore, the Asante [the term may be used to refer to the people, their location and culture] offer an interesting research site by reason of their infamy for the elaborate display of material wealth during death ceremonies (Arhin 1994, Rattray 1927). It is not uncommon for bereaved consumers to spend the equivalent of US$2000 on a casket alone. This is in spite of the fact that the society (as part of Ghana) has consistently ranked among the world's poorest (WDR 1980–1998), with a per capita annual GDP of about US$420. The context, thus, challenges the oft-assumed view that poverty leads to frugality and carefully considered product choices.

BACKGROUND

Bird (1980, p.19) defined ritual as culturally transmitted symbolic codes that are manifested in prescribed behavior forms used by individuals or groups to cope with the pressures of reality. Within the framework of this definition, rituals have symbolic expression, complexity and ambiguity (Bell 1997). These intangible aspects are objectified in the form of ritual artifacts, scripts and performances for a target audience, and are repeated as and when sanctioned by social authority (Rook 1986). Like other rituals, Asante death ceremonies exhibit these characteristics, including strongly scripted performances that follow a well-defined order of occurrence. However, as Bourdieu (1977) contends, ritual is not just about following scripts but is also about reshuffling the rules and other cultural categories to meet the needs of the relevant society in time and space. Bereaved persons in Asante are very much a part of this reshuffling as they symbolically consume the dead for social benefits.

Death ritual symbolism is global in nature and is exemplified in festivals such as the "day of the dead" in Mexico, the Festival of the Hungry Ghosts in China, and the "Obon" in Japan. These festivals are recognized by many as systems of activities to remember the dead and honor them appropriately for the sacrifices they made to ensure the way of life of the living. The festivals allow for a blurring of the line between death and life, and provide a symbolic melding of the communities of the dead and the living for the mutual benefit of both (Bell 1997). Death in Asante lends itself to such interpretation. The occasion is regarded as a time when deceased persons set out on a journey to a better world where their ancestors have already gone–a place where they must settle any account they have with those who have gone before them and to claim rewards for sacrifices made on earth (Sarpong 1974, p. 22). Death is,

TABLE 1

Pseudonym	Gender	Age	Occupation
Annoh	Male	33	Unemployed
Diana	Female	55	General Merchant
Manu	Female	36	Funeral Store Owner
Prempeh	Male	69	Retired Bureaucrat
Nana	Male	60	Traditional Leader
Pokuah	Female	31	School Teacher
Akyiaa	Female	57	Trader (wholesaler)
Donko	Male	—	Preferred not to say
Boafo	Male	72	Retired Farmer
Badu	Female	38	Bank Teller
Ofori	Male	58	Retired Banker

therefore, a necessary condition for continued growth into a New World. Communication between the living and the dead is maintained by way of prayer through a power structure whereby the living rely on the dead for protection and prosperity, among other things (Gyekye 1995; Kopytoff 1971).

According to Deighton (1992, p. 393), a performance is "a witnessed event, whose audience perceives it to happen in relation to an obligation, and who holds it to be standard". In this sense, death rituals are uniquely placed as performances because they represent a negative aspect of life that is forced on us by nature (Fulton 1994). Often, death ritual performances are scripted into mini parts such as wake keeping, funeral and burial–very much like 'acts' in a play. As much as one cannot make utter sense of Shakespeare's *Julius Caesar* by reading or watching only Act 1, so the various parts of death rituals do not make sense as independent "acts". Death ritual acts are necessarily stringed together, with each depending on the others for completeness of meaning.

To the extent that death rituals are performances that use products to enhance their ability to influence significant others, it is reasonable to accept Deighton's (1992, p. 362) argument that "performances, not products, are the most general objects of the verb "to consume"." Through death ritual performances, bereaved persons gain a range of socio-economic benefits (Arhin 1994) that are extended to the deceased by association (Grainger 1998). These intangible social resource exchanges during death rituals the symbolic use of the dead for purposes of identity enhancement for both the bereaved and the deceased (Baudrillard 1993; Kastenbaum, Peyton & Kastenbaum 1977). The current study sought to explore this process of identity negotiations.

METHODOLOGY

The discovery orientation of this study suggested the use of phenomenological hermeneutic analysis (Thompson 1997). Long open-ended interviews were conducted with eleven consumers who had been bereaved at least once in the past 5 years. Table 1 provides summary characteristics of the respondents. The main purpose of the interviews and their open-endedness was to allow respondents ample opportunity to express their broader views on the issues of death ritual consumption and their roles in shaping sociocultural dynamics (McCracken 1988). All interviews were conducted in the local language (Asante Twi) and were audiotaped.

In the course of data gathering, interview tapes were regularly reviewed in order to guide, but not restrict, the foci of future interviews (cf. Schouten 1991). This reading improved researcher familiarity with the data, facilitating "meaning discrimination" (Giorgi 1997, p. 246). In the hermeneutic tradition of constituting

lived experiences in a specific sociocultural context (Dilthey 1977), analysis started with a close reading of the verbatim transcripts in the local language. A contextualized analysis of interview data within the confines of the specific times and spaces that influence the death ritual consumption experience among the Asante was adopted. Consumption issues were summarized within the framework of the symbolic project of the self (cf. Cerulo 1997; Belk 1991; Giddens 1991; Wicklund and Gollwitzer 1982).

PRELIMINARY FINDINGS

As background to subsequent discussion, it is worth noting that all eleven respondents repeatedly expressed utmost concern for the remaking and preservation of a good image for the dead, especially when the person lived what would be described as a "good" life. "Good" and "bad" lives correspond to the two major categories of funerals in Asante, as determined by the perceived expense invested in the ceremony by the bereaved family and the number of people who attend (Sarpong 1974, p.29). Most people strive for the good funeral, which are manifested in the form of a large number of people attending, along with the careful selection and use of expensive consumer items that are imbued with symbolic expressions of wealth, social status and other markers of identity. The small number of participants and the perceived low quality of funeral artifacts used identify bad funerals. While good funerals enhance the social status of the deceased and the bereaved, bad ones have the opposite effect on the parties concerned.

As with many rituals, participants in Asante death ceremonies may have a temporary reprieve from some social norms (Gluckman 1963). For instance, social rules about frugality and wastage are suspended, allowing bereaved consumers to be excessively extravagant and to display their wealth (borrowed, earned or inherited) as expressions of their ideal social selves. Under normal circumstances, such action would be considered cause for alienation, but in the context of death rituals, the bereaved can glaringly engage in such behavior without the risk of social ostracism. Thus, there is ample opportunity for consumers to use death ritual artifacts and rituals as vehicles for remaking the identities of their deceased relatives, as well as their own.

Remaking the Identities of Deceased Consumers

One of the main uses of funerals among bereaved consumers in Asante is to develop a sense of personal identity for their dead by publicly presenting them in a manner consistent with societal expectations of an honorable and presentable funeral for colleagues of comparable social status. Through this process, bereaved consumers may on each funeral occasion renegotiate social identities through perceived contrast of their rituals to others in the defined social setting. Various bereaved consumers suggested how identity boundaries are defined in Asante death rituals and how they devise strategies to subtly extend these boundaries, as and when necessary, in efforts to present a positive public image of the deceased. (At the time of the interviews, US$1 was equal to C2500–the Ghanaian currency is called Cedi and denoted by C).

> *Diana*: ...he did not make any real contribution to the family and he has no friends who are willing to share in the overall costs of his funeral. In this case, for a person like that, the family has to be very modest in an effort to minimize the funeral costs...for us, our mother was the best thing that happened to us. She took very good care of us and so we cannot allow her to be placed in such a bad dwelling place. That is the house we are building for her and so we the children will take care of the casket at C500,000 or even C5 million. That is the way it is [*pauses*]. Perhaps you are in a family and you are lazy, you don't contribute in any way to the well being of members of the family. As soon as you drop dead, as soon as the head of the family is notified, he immediately sends someone to get a casket and perhaps, he will purchase one at C50,000, because if he gets himself into debt, he will be responsible. Funerary rites and products are for the glorification of the deceased. This is to indicate that the deceased lived a very reputable life on this earth, and so the funeral was very beautiful and his children have made sure to let people know, and to "lift his face".

Diana indicates her understanding of death ritual activities and related consumption choices as a function of the life that the deceased was perceived to have lived. She considers her mother to have lived a "good" life, and so she was willing to expend significant resources to give her mother a funeral that was consistent with the deceased's perceived social status. Her comments suggest that death provides occasions for the living to reflect on the quality of a deceased's life on earth. The outcome of this reflection influences the level of negotiations that is deemed necessary as the bereaved apply death products to represent the perceived social status of the deceased. Invitations are not necessary to attend a funeral in Asante. It stands to reason, then, that not all participants in a funeral would have personally known the person whose final rites they are attending. For such participants, the funeral becomes the main yardstick for assessing the deceased's social prominence. Offering expensive caskets and other symbols of wealth and power for funeral rituals become very important in this context.

While the deceased person's perceived social status in life may guide the nature of his/her funeral, bereaved families may exaggerate the deceased's social status through the use of consumer objects indicative of higher levels of status and identity. Strategies of this kind are expected to be most effective when the deceased was not known enough in the local community. This may be one of the reasons why Asantes may prefer that their funerals be held in their places of birth, even though they may not have grown up or even lived in that community (Arhin 1994). Even when members of a community have formed their opinions of a person prior to his/her death, the nature of consumption during the person's funeral may enhance the person's social status, as reflected in the following interview excerpt from a respondent talking about his brother.

> *Donko:* ...well, what do you do? Others may have written him off but he was one of us, my flesh and blood. I couldn't let him go in a disgraceful manner...that was why we did all we could to make sure that he got a decent funeral and burial. Later, a lot

of people came to tell us that we did well to "lift the face" of our prince. ...we had to make people aware of his sense of community, his life before he started drinking...there was a part of him that wasn't known.

Donko clearly recognizes the potential for remaking the identity of his deceased brother through funeral ritual consumption. In the course of the interview, he pointed to the fact that it was in his own interest as well as that of his deceased brother to make sure that people saw the other, more positive, side of the deceased. He indicated that while many may have counted him as a destitute, he believes they now think of him in a different light. By his own account, Donko successfully manipulated public opinion to enhance his deceased brother's image through the funeral. Granted that the deceased was notorious in the community and that many had formed their opinions of him prior to his death and expected a "bad" funeral for him, the social negotiations for remaking his identity were difficult. Donko summarily described his brother's funeral as one fit for a king. He noted that he pooled all his available resources towards this end and that was the only way he could erase the bad images that the society held about his brother.

In spite of the relaxation in social restrictions on extravagance during ritual activities, the rigorous pursuit of newer, positive identities through funerary products must be tempered with caution. Society still expects a reasonably level of modesty in the use/display of material wealth in Asante death rituals and so bereaved consumers in Asante may choose to indulge in the subtleties of those aspects of death ritual consumption that do not infringe on social rules regarding extravagance. For instance, the data suggest that bereaved Asante consumers associate the number of people at a funeral with high social status, probably because the "draw", symptomatic of spectacular consumption (Penaloza 1999), is indicative of the level of respect the deceased commanded in society. Because people attending funerals in Asante have to be offered drinks and sometimes food (Arhin 1994), a large number of participants may signify that large expenditures are associated with the funeral. This may explain Prempeh's clear preference for crowded funerals over economic gains in the following excerpt:

> When your loved one dies, you expect that people will attend the funeral. We are not as concerned with the money that is raised, ... We are more interested in the number of people who attend the funeral. I am not saying that we do not like the money, we do, absolutely. However, the people, people often say "the funeral came" [*literal translation meaning that there were too many people at the funeral*]. ...not enough standing room even. This is a more visible representation of the deceased's prominence in society. People can see without doubt that the person who has died was important and had a lot of respect in his community. And we like that. I pray and hope that I get such a good funeral when I go.

This perspective is important when viewed within the context that invitations to funerals are not necessary for attendance, and that on any Saturday (the usual day for Asante funerals), there are many funerals that are competing for community participation by way of attendance. The more people there are at one's funeral, the more social status is accorded the deceased. To gain the necessary competitive advantage towards this end, bereaved consumers may resort to mass media advertisement of the funeral arrangements. This effort is designed to appeal to the community orientation of Asante society in a subtle manner, and the ads are presented as if to inform and *not* to persuade (Lawuyi 1991).

The intense competition for funeral ritual participants on any given day has encouraged bereaved persons to adopt novel and foreign approaches to gaining the attention of their target audiences. Recent trends indicate the use of non-traditional methods such as serving of food to attract the poor masses and sending out funeral invitation cards. Some bemoan this increasingly popular trend, casting it in negative light.

Diana: … you see, those who need cards to invite people to funerals are those who do not attend funerals in the community. Which means if you specifically invite people, nobody will attend. Me, when my mother died, I can say that even today, some people meet me and ask how my mother is doing. When I tell them that she died a few years a go, they make funeral donations.
Interviewer: Oh, really?
Diana: Yes.…The old lady herself attended all relevant funerals. If you live in this city and you attend funerals, then invitation cards are not necessary. Because when I hear of your loss, when I meet you, I will tell you that so-and so's mother has died. The next Monday, I will come by and express my condolences. I will indicate that this person told me when I met her yesterday. ….You are always attending funeral and wishing people well and so if they see you at a social gathering they will inquire about you. So when your loved one dies, everyone wants to help you out.
I: *Wode woho gyigya*? [You make as many friends as possible now to get help in the future when you need it]
D: Exactly!

The respondent acknowledges the importance of radio and newspaper announcements but frowns on the use of funeral invitational cards for the same purpose. She suggests that the use of these cards is tantamount to telling the community that the deceased did not attend local funerals and, therefore, is not deserving of the support of others. She alludes to the transactional nature of funeral rituals where you give up some time and money now in exchange for future attendance of your family funerals. In short, she views people who use non-traditional forms of advertising to gain competitive advantage as cheaters who are trying to find ways of deriving benefits (large attendance at funerals and hence social status) that they do not deserve (because they did not attend funerals often).

While elaborate and expensive funerals may be the norm in negotiating social identities, there are instances where a bereaved family may opt to have no funeral for their deceased. This is often the case when the family believes that their deceased lived a life that was perceived to be socially unacceptable, and that the family would have tremendous difficulty in creating new identities for the deceased. Rather than expend economic and social resources to enhance the deceased's social status through elaborate funerals, the bereaved may decide to acknowledge the death through a visitation only. A reception is held where family members receive verbal condolences from sympathizers. Tradition mandates visitations as the main death ritual event when a woman loses a child for the first time (Sarpong 1974). When the ritual is applied in "regular" death situations, it is often as a way of sending a message about the deceased to the community.

Prempeh: Look, my own elder brother died, my mother's son *(with a notable change in his tone of voice and facial expression to indicate the closeness of the relationship)* but I did not organize a funeral for him. The head of the family and his children interceded on his behalf but I held my ground. To this

day, no funeral has been organized for him. I didn't want to be involved and without my involvement, I knew things would go wrong [pauses], and my reputation is at stake.

Prempeh went on to tell a story about how his brother took advantage of his generosity and exploited him. He also recounted various instances where he made significant sacrifices just to be able to support his brother and his nuclear family, only to be rewarded with conscious efforts on his brother's part to undermine him. The conspicuous absence of a funeral was to be a loud message to the community about the deceased's "bad" life. People who do not know the deceased may conclude that he was too horrible a person to be so despised by the family. By not publicly saying a final farewell to his brother, Prempeh communicated the low status of his brother to the community and suggested that he (Prempeh) was a person with character and integrity who did not want to be associated with his brother. The irony of this "deafening silence" that it has the potential to backfire into a devastating negative image for the bereaved, as was the case with the British royal family on rumors that Princess Diana wouldn't be granted a royal funeral (Adato 1997).

The foregoing seem to suggest that altruism is the major driving force behind bereaved consumers' decisions to offer elaborate funerals for their deceased. However, the data suggest that inasmuch as the image of the deceased is negotiated through expensive and socially symbolic consumer products, so the bereaved also seek identity enhancements through these products.

Remaking the Identities of Bereaved Consumers
The data indicates that bereaved consumers use stereotypical meanings of death ritual consumption objects as motifs in their own symbolic self-completion strategies (Wicklund and Gollwitzer 1982). Offering pump funerals for deceased persons may, in fact, be more for the living who apply such rituals as coping strategies (Grainger 1998; Parkes 1998). While pursuing the "good" funeral in honor of the deceased, the bereaved consciously incorporate consumption choices that move them closer to their own identity aspirations. For instance, in one 130-minute interview, the respondent made at least 12 references to the fact that he hopes that his relatives look at the good funerals he is organizing and later give him a similar farewell on his passing. This respondent is obviously using the funerals he arranges to express his death product preferences to the community. He is also communicating a conception of his own identity, as he believed it to be reflected in the death ritual choices he had organized for his "good" relatives. Other respondents related similar latent consumer motives in their interviews.

Annoh: The casket that he was displayed in, you have to see it to believe it. Knowing that children are the ones often responsible for purchasing caskets for their parents, this translated into significant praise and respect for the deceased and his children. It became the talk of the town. As soon as people left the funeral site, they were talking to each other about the funeral, the people and the casket, saying: "Did you see the casket that his children purchased for him to be buried in?" This is such good status for the children. In other instances where the children are afraid of incurring any debts, they will purchase a simple casket for your burial. People are going to talk about this too but in a negative way. Some will insult the eldest child thus: "when your mother died, we saw the awful casket in which she was buried".

Annoh reinforces the view that funeral rituals are for reshaping the identities of deceased persons while emphasizing the use of these rituals for negotiating the identities of the bereaved. Reflected in his comment is the social stigma associated with a bad funeral and how it may be taken out on the bereaved. Many respondents indicated that they would not lead any family activities where members were not willing to expend the necessary resources for an honorable funeral because "they didn't want any shame to come upon them". Towards this end, consumers purchase death products that are imbued with positive symbolic implications for their own social status.

Manu: Well, for example, our father, he took very good care of all his children. So when he died, we purchased a casket for about C2 million. We bought his suit from America, a very expensive, top quality suit to make him up for the public viewing, to show the kind of life that he led on earth and how much he took care of his children. Asante custom dictates that children buy their parents' caskets and so if you take good care of your children, they will purchase the best casket available for your burial and give you the best funeral that money can buy.

She goes on

If you do not buy a beautiful casket for your father's burial, people are going to talk ill of you, which means that the children themselves have no stature in the society. That is why normally, whether or not the children can afford it, they have to do the best they can to purchase a casket that is presentable to the society, for their dad [*Presentable here relates to the beauty/details of the casket, often indicative of the price paid for it. Caskets may range in price from C30,000–C20 million*]. That is why most people buy expensive and beautiful caskets. In fact, some people buy caskets on credit, that is the casket, some people buy on credit…. It all comes down to the fact that if you do not purchase a beautiful casket for your father, or your mother, people are going to look down on you and describe you as irresponsible members of society. That is why you couldn't buy a presentable casket and give them a good funeral. That is just the way it is.

Implicit in the above excerpt is the idea that the respondent and her siblings are respectable members of society because her father had taken very good care of them and they had reciprocated by way of the consumption objects used for his funeral. In a society where a person's worth is measured by the number of children he/she has and their stations in life, it is important for children to make conspicuous those items that represents the status levels they seek for their parents as they express their own successes in life. Manu indicates in her story the extent to which her father was a man of high repute and how she and her siblings represented that in his funeral. She uses her family's access to western cultural capital (American suit) to offer a glimpse of her and her siblings' life successes, and attributes this success to having had a good father. The American suit represents their identity in that it distinguishes them from others who would bury their dead in locally manufactured clothing. In essence, she is using the American suit on her dead father as an identity marker, communicating social status and her conception of herself and her family to the rest of society (cf Appiah 1992; Bourdieu 1984). Many other respondents made references to foreign cuisine, unique hearses and other imported items they have used in death rituals.

By going through such social negotiations process, Manu and others like her exhibit two consumption motives that have been described as consummatory and instrumental (Alderson 1957).

Consummatory motives underlie consumer behavior that is intrinsically rewarding while instrumental motives are seldom rewarding in themselves, but are necessary to achieve other goals. The data suggests that bereaved consumers may harbor both motives in the face of death. The bereaved's consummatory motives lead them to lavish final gifts on the deceased as a way to alleviate their guilt and other psychological costs and to reward the deceased through enhanced social status derived from the expensive funeral objects (Grainger 1998). This motive was evident in Manu's narrative. In addition, Manu's conspicuous display of her deceased father in an American suit reflects her instrumental motives by the use of her father as a symbolic vehicle towards her social status and identity aspirations. Thus, she engaged in a lavish and elaborate funeral as much for herself as for her deceased father.

Death related consumption are so important in shaping the social identities of the living that some consumers may resort to unorthodox approaches in efforts to be associated with these rituals. For instance, strangers to a family may offer to take financial and social responsibility for the death ritual of a person they never knew. This is similar to the culturally mediated global phenomenon that was Princess Diana's funeral, where complete strangers across the world organized real and virtual activities (vigils, parties and virtual funerals) for the Princess. However, in the case of the Asante, the strangers are consciously seeking to gain the relevant social and economic benefits from taking on such responsibility. Those who are wealthy and have need to redefine their identities may actively seek those who have limited resources to provide elaborate funerals for their relatives and provide the necessary resources for them. This market offering is often on condition that the person providing the funds is allowed to present himself as a relative of the deceased and to be recognized by the society as having provided the "fine things" used for the deceased's funeral.

Annoh:…These days, when someone dies, a complete stranger may offer to take full responsibility for the funeral and burial [*gesturing disgust at the practice, with his hands*].
Interviewer: What is wrong with that?
Annoh: All of these have to do with money and social status. When the person makes money [*from donations given by wellwishers*] he keeps it. All the praise and glory that comes with the funeral also go to him. In my village, we are taking steps to stop the funeral from becoming a commercial enterprise. They have just introduced a law that when somebody dies, those who live in the town contribute a maximum of C1000.

Under these circumstances, funerals and the potential identities associated with them are offered for sale on the open market to high bidding stranger. Mercantilism takes control of the social order and offers mutually beneficial options to all involved. The arrangement helps the truly bereaved as it enhances their social status while helping the sponsoring party by opening him up to the society at large as one who spares no expense to express love and respect for his deceased relatives. According to Annoh, although a family may not have money, they still want the best for their deceased but may be unwilling to sacrifice their current level of social status for financial ends. Thus, when they perceive an interested bidder as a potential liability in terms of reputation, they will not sell the funeral rights to that person. This development is obviously worrisome for the elders of the community, as evidenced by their efforts to reverse the trend. Still, one observes intangible consumer resource exchange in its truest form as part of the social negotiations that ultimately define the identity of the bereaved, derived from funeral product acquisition and consumption in the name of the deceased.

It stands to reason, then, that the identities of the bereaved and the deceased are interwoven in a manner that facilitates a direct relationship between the perceived social standing of the bereaved. The exaggerated identity profiles of deceased persons expressed through the material aspects of Asante death rituals underscore the extent to which communities of the living and the dead are melded together. Furthermore, good Asante people who die are believed to become ancestors in their New World while bad people are simply punished for all their irresponsible deeds. In the hierarchy of authority in that world, ancestors are next in line to the smaller deities who report directly to the Supreme Being (Gyekye 1995). A good life on earth, reflected in an accompanying elaborate funeral, indicates the deceased's ascendancy to a position of authority in the ancestral world. Ancestors are believed to be the makers of the bereaved's destinies, by virtue of their superior authority over the living. Treating them well on their deaths encourages them to be generous in their dealings with the living. By seeking and gaining enhanced social status for a deceased person, the bereaved may gain similar status by association to the deceased.

DISCUSSION–DEATH BECOMES US

Many a consumer researcher has argued that goods and services are means of social communication among people (e.g. Levy 1959; Mick 1986; Solomon 1983). Viewed within the contexts of ritual/symbolic consumption (Douglas and Isherwood 1979; Rook 1985; Schouten 1991), death rituals have significant meanings for the dead and the bereaved beyond functional utility. In fact, death rituals and the material things associated with them may procure a particularly strong social representation of identity, for both the bereaved and the deceased (Csikszentmihalyi and Rochberg-Halton 1981; Grainger 1998). This is facilitated by the fact that death provides the necessary quick and easy access to self-symbolizing for consumers pursuing symbolic self-completion (Wicklund and Gollwitzer 1982) through the frequency of death and the accompanying relaxation of social norms on death ritual occasions. Through this process, bereaved buyers of death products may employ the products' symbolic entitlements to redefine themselves…and that is how *Death Becomes the Consumer*.

For the Asante, death is a welcome inevitability that indicates regeneration of a life that continues in another form beyond death (Arhin 1994; Gyekye 1995). Efforts are made to preserve a positive identity for the deceased to facilitate progress in status for the bereaved (Lawuyi 1991). This is achieved through the use of consumer identity markers during death rituals. Death rituals and related products, therefore, are perceived and conceived as vehicles for the competitive expression of status and status aspirations for the living and the dead (Cannon 1989). While they may be performed under the guise of serving the dead only, death rituals and their associated symbolism are often opportunities for social advancement in which people may aspire to brief lives of further ostentation denied them in everyday life (Cannadine 1981).

From such a perspective, the dead serve as a basis for the living to engage in conspicuous consumption for purposes of enhanced self-image and social status towards their own self-completion projects. Expensive caskets, embalming and the public display of the corpse at its best, flowers and other items supposedly for the "dearly departed", thus, provide an extended self that enhances social status for the "immortal beloved" still walking the face of the earth. If this were not so, why would caskets be chosen for their superior padding as if comfort was of extreme importance to the corpse (cf. Metcalf and Huntington 1991)?

The increasing need for death products poses many challenges for the new millennium, which require significant research effort (Loewen Group 1997; Manus 1998; Spiegler 1995). This study is a step in the right direction as it offers preliminary insights into some of the ways that bereaved consumers symbolically consume the dead for purposes of social identity negotiations. However, the study is limited in that its general implications were derived from a small set of respondents. Additionally, the researcher's familiarity with the Asante culture may have biased some of the interpretations drawn. To address these limitations, further research efforts are needed to provide a greater understanding of consumer behavior in the context of death.

REFERENCES

Due to space requirements, a few citations were deliberately left out. Please contact author for full list of references.

Adato, Allison (1997), "Farewell to a Princess and to an Angel," *Life Magazine*, *20*(Nov.), 14.

Alderson, Wroe (1957), *Marketing Behavior and Executive Action: A Functionalist Approach to Marketing Theory*. Homewood, IL: Irwin.

Appiah, Kwame A. (1992), *In My Father's House: Africa in the Philosophy of Culture*. New York: Oxford University Press.

Arhin, Kwame (1994), "The Economic Implications of Transformations in Akan Funeral Rites," *Africa*, *64*(3), 307-322.

Aries, Philippe (1974), *Western Attitudes Towards Death: From the Middle Ages to the Present* (Patricia M. Ranum, Trans.). Baltimore: Johns Hopkins.

Baudrillard, Jean (1993), *Symbolic Exchange and Death* (Iain Grant, Trans.). Newbury Park: Sage.

Belk, Russell W. (1991), "Possessions and the Sense of Past", in *Highways and Buyways: Naturalisitc Research from the Consumer Behavior Odyssey,* ed. Russell W. Belk, Provo, UT: Association for Consumer Research, 114-130.

Bell, Catherine. (1997), *Ritual: Perspectives and Dimensions*. New York: Oxford Univ. Press

Bird, Frederick (1980), "The Contemporary Ritual Milieu", in *Rituals and Ceremony in Popular Culture,* ed. Ray. B. Browne, Bowling Green: Popular Press, 19-35.

Bourdieu, Pierre (1977), *Outline of a Theory of Practice* (Richard Nice, Trans.). Cambridge:

_____ (1984), *Distinction: A Social Critique of the Judgment of Taste* (Richard Nice, Trans.). Cambridge, MA: Harvard University Press.

Brown, Ed. (1997), "Would You Pay $125,000 to Get Frozen?", *Fortune*, Nov. 24, p 70,74.

Cannadine, David (1981), "War and Death, Grief and Mourning in Modern Britain", in *Mirrors of Mortality: Studies in the Social History of Death,* ed. Joachim Whaley, London: 187-242.

Cannon, Aubrey (1989), "The Historical Dimension in Mortuary Expression of Status and Sentiment," *Current Anthropology*, *30*(4), 437-458.

Cerulo, Karen A. (1997), "Identity Construction: New Issues, New Directions," *Annual Review of Sociology*, *23*, 385-409.

Csikszentmihalyi, Mihaly and Eugene Rochberg-Halton (1981), *The Meaning of Things: Domestic Symbols and the Self*. Cambridge: Cambridge University Press.

Deighton, John (1992), "The Consumption of Performance," *Journal of Consumer Research*, *19*(December), 362-372.

Dilthey, Wilhelm (1977), "The Understanding of Other Persons and their Expressions of Life", in *Descriptive Psychology and Historical Understanding,* eds. Richard M. Zaner & Kenneth L. Heiges, The Hague: Nijhoff, 121-145.

Douglas, Mary and Baron Isherwood (1981), *The World of Goods*. New York: Basic Books.

Fulton, Robert (1994), "The Funeral In Contemporary Society", in *Death and Identity,* eds. Robert Fulton & Robert Bendiksen, Philadelphia: The Charles Press, 288-312.

Gabel, Terence G., Phylis Mansfield and Kevin Westbrook (1996), "The Disposal of Consumers: An Exploratory Analysis of Death-Related Consumption," *Advances in Consumer Research*, *23*, 361-367.

Gentry, James W., Patricia F. Kennedy, Catherine Paul, and Ronald P. Hill (1995), "Family Transitions During Grief: Discontinuities in Household Consumption Patterns," *Journal of Business Research*, *34*(September), 67-79.

Giddens, Anthony (1991), *Modernity and Self-Identity: Self and Society in the Late Modern Age*. Cambridge, UK: Polity Press

Giorgi, Amedeo (1997), "The Theory, Practice, and Evaluation of the Phenomenological Method as a Qualitative Research Procedure," *Journal of Phenomenological Psychology*, *28* (Fall),

Gluckman, Max (1963), *Order and Rebellion in Tribal Africa*. New York: Free Press.

Goffman, Erving. (1963), *Stigma: Notes on the Management of Spoiled Identity*: Prentice Hall.

Gorer, Geoffrey (1955), "The Pornography of Death," *Encounter*, *5*, 49-53.

Grainger, Roger (1998), *The Social Symbolism of Grief and Mourning*. London: Jessica Kingsley

Gyekye, Kwame (1995), *An Essay on African Philosophical Thought*. (Revised ed.). Philadelphia: Temple University Press.

Harrington, Alan (1969), *The Immortalist: Approach to the Engineering of Man's Divinity*. New York: Random House.

Kastenbaum, R., Peyton, S., & Kastenbaum, B. (1977), "Sex Discrimination after Death," *Omega*, *7*, 351-359.

Kopytoff, Ivor (1971), "Ancestors As Elders in Africa," *Africa*, *41*(2), 129-142.

Lawuyi, Olatunde B. (1991), "The Social Marketing of Elites: The Advertised Self in Obituaries and Congratulations in Some Nigerian Dailies," *Africa*, *61*(2), 247-263.

Levy, Sidney J. (1959), "Symbols for Sale," *Harvard Business Review*, *37*(Jul-Aug), 117-124.

Lino, M. (1990), "The $3800 Funeral," *American Demographics*, *12*(July), 8.

Metcalf, Peter and Huntington, Richard (1991), *Celebrations of Death: Anthropology of Mortuary Practices*. New York: Cambridge University Press.

Rook, Dennis (1985), "The Ritual Dimension of Consumer Behavior," *Journal of Consumer Research*, *12*(December), 251-264.

Sarpong, Peter K. (1974), *Ghana in Retrospect*. Accra: Ghana Publishing Corporation.

Schouten, John W. (1991), "Selves in Transition: Symbolic Consumption in Personal Rites of Passage and Identity Reconstruction," *Journal of Consumer Research*, *17*(March), 412-425.

Schwartz, Martin L., Marvin A. Jolson, and Ronald H. Lee (1986), "The Marketing of Funeral Services," *Business Horizons* (March-April), 40-45.

Solomon, Michael. R. (1983), "The Role of Products as Social Stimuli: A Symbolic Interaction Perspective," *Journal of Consumer Research*, *10*(December), 319-329.

Thompson, Craig J. (1997), "Interpreting Consumers: A Hermeneutical Framework for Deriving Marketing Insights from the Texts of Consumer's Consumption Stories," *Journal of Marketing Research*, *34*(November), 438-455.

Wicklund, Robert A. and Peter M. Gollwitzer (1982), *Symbolic Self-Completion*. Hillsdale. NJ: LEA Publishers.

Tourism, Art Stars and Consumption: Wyland's Whales

Shay Sayre, California State University, Fullerton

"I have seen the future of public art. It swims. It smiles. It is the spirit of our times."
Steve Mannheimer, Indianapolis Star, 1997

ABSTRACT

Tourism, as a major industry in the U.S., has as its focus luring travelers to a location where their trips are consummated with purchases that commemorate and validate their visits. Characterized by Belk and Costa (1991) as "prestige-seeking through the collection of unique, exotic or unusual travel destinations and experiences," tourism fosters purchases of souvenirs. In tourist cultures, tourists experience an *exotopy*: leaving home, coming into contact with a cultural other, and returning home with some sign of gain [souvenir] reflecting the experience (Bakhtin 1981; Harkin 1995). Tourists' souvenir purchases memorialize and authenticate their experiences (Hahn 1990) in the form of displayed trophies. As part of their 'quest for the authentic' (Cohen 1990), travelers seek out locally produced arts and crafts.

Producers of these crafts strive to provide such an experience for tourists with localized art that is symbolic of both the traveler and the destination. Together, artist and traveler act as integral components of the emic sociology of tourism that includes perspectives of the various participants in the tourist situation. In situations where art production and sales functions exist, reciprocity between artist and patron is an important component of successful consumption activities (Pearce 1982).

Recently, massive cultural interaction has evolved tourism into a para-tourist phase (Wollen 1996) where artists, who began with local color motifs, have commodified their art for mass-market sales. A complex relationship exists between urban vernacular, tourist art and para-tourist gallery art that fosters 'art stars.'

This paper focuses on a single artist who has combined eclectic media with a growing consumer thirst for place souvenirs into a multi-million dollar business: Wyland of Laguna Beach, California. Wyland's art has become what Wollen calls a "hybrid aesthetic in which the new corporate forms of communication and display are constantly confronted by new vernacular forms of invention and expression" (1996). This research was conducted to answer the question, "What is the role of tourist art in the supermarket of travel?" By deconstructing Wyland, who has developed an ecology of whale-wall murals and figurative art, we may better understand the role of consumption in the tourist experience.

Attending Performing Arts: A Consumption System Model of Buying-Consuming Experiences

M.L. Caldwell, University of New South Wales
Arch Woodside, University of New South Wales

ABSTRACT

Consumers seek pleasurable experiences when attending performing arts. Yet no theory exists to explain and predict the buying-consuming experiences associated with this unique consumption activity. We apply "General Living Systems Theory" (GLST) to offer a systems-based model intended to be useful in this respect. Our work contributes to some important streams of research. For certain types of hedonic consumption, behaviour can only be understood in the light of the subtleties of consumer interpretation and the entire buying-consuming process. The suggested GLST paradigm attempts to go beyond choice to achieve an understanding of lived experiences within the realities perceived by consumers.

The Film Audience: Theater versus Video Consumers

Michael D. Basil, University of Lethbridge

ABSTRACT

Feature film producers maximize profits using a form of price discrimination called "windowing." Here, films are released to theaters before the video market. For a consumer, waiting for the video release offers a potential cost savings. This study makes use of Lifestyles data to model movie and video consumption. The results demonstrate that consumer choice is rational and generally compatible with the windowing model. Specifically, people with higher incomes see more movies in theaters. People from larger families see more videos. The desire to be the first to own a new product predicts the ratio of theater to video viewing.

Previous theorists have questioned what happens when a new product is introduced that threatens an established product (Carpenter & Nakamoto, 1989; 1990). In the specific domain of mass media, some research has examined what happened to newspapers when radio diffused to a majority of the population, and what happened to the film and radio industries with the diffusion of television (Dimmick, Patterson & Albarran, 1992; Levin, 1998). A similar situation can be seen today with the diffusion of videocassette players on motion pictures.

Immediately after the invention of home video recording devices in the 1970s, there was a period where the industry was unsure of what material would provide content for these machines (Sommer, 1980). At first, they were used by the industry to prerecord television programs for later broadcast. With the invention of the handy videocassette in the 1980s, taping television programs off the air appeared to be the main utility of this device (Anonymous, 1984; Hall, 1984; McLaughlin, 1987). In the 1980s, Sony's Beta and RCA's VHS represented two formats competing for dominance with this new media form (Gross, Brull & Grover, 1997). This period was quickly followed by the accumulation of major feature film titles for home viewing (Klopfstein, 1989, p. 31-32). With this focus, the VCR and video market began to take off (Caravatt, 1985; Sherrid, 1983). Retail outlets began to buy these releases and rent them to consumers (Keith, 1986).

With the diffusion of VCRs, film industry has taken several steps to protect their profits. The foremost of these is a specific form of price discrimination on the public's need to see the latest film. The theatrical release of feature films is later followed by release to videocassette, sometimes referred to as "windowing" (Owen & Wildman, 1992; Litman, 1999). Under this approach, a feature film is held in first-run theaters for several months before it is released on videotape, similar to what used to happen with second-and third run theaters. Some evidence suggests this is a useful strategy for maximizing profits (Owen & Wildman, 1992; Litman, 1999).

The question remains, however, of whether and how consumers adapt to this strategy. This paper will address this question from the perspective of the consumer. Specifically, to what extent is movie theater attendance distinctive from video consumption? What is the relationship between feature films and video consumption – that is, who consumes more movies and who consumes more videos?

THEORY

Some previous research has shown that people can and do substitute home videos for going out to see a film at the theater (Greenberg & Lin, 1989). Further, other research has shown that home videos can be seen by consumers as similar to the film viewing experience (Krugman, Shamp & Johnson, 1991). There-

fore, there appears to be the possibility of some substitution between these products.

There are, however, also reasons to believe that there are differences between seeing a film in a theater and seeing it on video. For one, the theater experience is often communal (Austin, 1989, p. 45). As such, it is often the excuse for a date with friends or romantic interests (DeSilva, 1999, p. 153-154). A second difference between film attendance and video is the cost of attending a movie. Film attendance is priced on a per-seat basis. Therefore, when a large group of people are interested in seeing a movie, the price rises quickly (DeSilva, 1999, p. 154). As the number of audience members increase, so does the cost of seeing a movie in a theater. In addition, babysitting, transportation, and food costs often increase, too.

So then, one might ask, why bother going out to the movies at all? When faced with this threat to their theater audience the film industry hit on an ingenious solution. Theories of price discrimination suggest that consumers often have different elasticities of demand. Managerial theories suggest the optimal profit maximization function occurs through the segmentation of consumers based on their willingness to pay (Owen & Wildman, 1992). In the case of films, the film industry tries to maintain its theater audience by making it the only route to see the latest film. Most typically, this occurs by not releasing a video version of a film for several months, most typically a period of 6 to 12 months.

We know that for a large number of consumers, there is a desire to be up-to-date, have the latest and newest gadget, or, in this case, see the latest movie. Previous research on the importance of this factor has shown that the desire to be up-to-date depends on a number of factors including personality characteristics of the adopter, interest in the product category, and "venturesomeness" [a construct speaking to people's willingness to take risks associated with buying the newest product] (Hoyer & Ridgway, 1984; Mitchell, 1994; Rogers, 1995). Therefore, it appears that an individual's desire to see the latest movie should be a predictor of his or her willingness to pay the premium associated with the price discrimination windowing practiced of the film industry.

HYPOTHESES

Research has shown that young people appear to be especially interested in films, both in terms of going to the theater (DeSilva, 1999) as well as being more likely to rent videos (Greenberg & Lin, 1989). In general, this appears to be due to an amalgam of factors— a greater value for entertainment (therefore interest in the product category), a greater likelihood of being single (and therefore only need to buy a single seat; DeSilva, 1999), and being more likely to live at home (therefore often have higher percentage of disposable income). In addition, however, younger people often see theater attendance as a venue for a seeing friends and dating (DeSilva, 1999, p. 153-154). Therefore, we predict that:

H1: Younger people will (a) attend more movies, (b) rent more videos, and (c) buy more videos. Further, given the desire for out-of-the-house activities, we predict that young people (d) will be more likely to see films in theaters than on video.

One of the largest predictors of movie attendance is age and income, with younger and affluent people seeing more films (DeSilva, 1999). In addition, people who are more affluent often

TABLE 1
New Movies

Definitely disagree	1486 (47.8%)
Generally disagree	708 (22.8%)
Moderately disagree	451 (14.5%)
Moderately agree	263 (8.5%)
Generally agree	113 (3.6%)
Definitely agree	88 (2.8%)
Mean	2.06

TABLE 2
Movie Viewing

Times last year	Attended a film	Rented a video	Bought a video
None	965 (31.1%)	1264 (41.4%)	931 (30.2%)
1-4 times	1051 (33.6%)	527 (17.1%)	932 (30.5%)
5-8 times	510 (16.3%)	455 (14.7%)	442 (14.5%)
9-11 times	265 (8.5%)	367 (11.9%)	226 (7.4%)
12-24 times	215 (6.9%)	414 (13.4%)	123 (4.0%)
25-51 times	68 (2.2%)	248 (8.0%)	45 (1.5%)
52 or more	29 (0.9%)	143 (4.6%)	23 (0.8%)
Mean	2.37	3.04	2.10

show a propensity for the latest product (Mitchell, 1994; Rogers, 1995). The cost of renting or purchasing videos, as well as the relative price discrimination for seeing the latest film becomes relatively less for people with larger incomes. Therefore, we predict that:

H2: Affluent people will (a) attend move movies, (b) rent more videos and (c) purchase more videos. Further, because the premium for theaters appears less imposing, we predict that more affluent people (d) will be more likely to see films in theaters than on video.

In addition to income, as the number of people in each household increases, the cost of attending a movie (on a per-seat basis) rises quickly based on the increasing number of seats that must be purchased as well as the cost of babysitting (DeSilva, 1999, p. 154). The cost of video, however, is on a per-day basis. Therefore, we predict that

H3: People from larger households will be (a) less likely to attend movies, but (b) more likely to rent and (c) more likely to purchase videos. Further, we predict that as household size increases, (d) people will be less likely to see films in theaters than on video.

Finally, Litman (1999, p. 74-75) predicts that classes of consumers can be identified for whom different elasticities exist. This leads us to predict that:

H4: People with more interest in newer products will (a) attend more movies and (b) rent fewer videos. Perhaps most critically, they will (c) see a higher proportion of films in theaters than on video.

Because the window for video purchases is between theater showing and average rental dates, no prediction is made with regard to purchasing videos.

METHODS

The data for this study were compiled from *DDB Needham's Lifestyle Survey*, a mail panel survey conducted in 1996. Quota sampling was used to generate a list of 5,000 people who were representative of all US adults. The sample was stratified (balanced) on age, gender, marital status, race/ethnicity, income, region, household size, and population density. This group of potential respondents was supplemented by a mailing to 420 households (210 low-income households and 210 minority households) to compensate for low response rates among African Americans, Hispanics, and people with low incomes.

Responses to the general *Lifestyle* survey mailing numbered 3,748 (75%). Responses to the supplemental mailing totaled 293 (70%). Thus, there were 4,041 respondents in 1996. Of these persons, 3,130 respondents also responded to a subsequent mailing (77%), and thus were included in this sample.

Measures

Demographics. A number of questions on the survey asked about demographics. This study examined the effects of age, gender, race, household income, and household size.

Importance of newness. One item asked for level of agreement with "I like to be the first to try a new product" on a 1-to-6 strongly disagree to strongly agree scale. In addition, a second item asked for level of agreement with "I like to be the first to see a new movie" on a 1-to-6 strongly disagree to strongly agree scale. The responses are shown in Table 1.

Film and video measures. Three items asked about film and video viewing. The first asked, "In the last year, how many times did you go to the movies?" Response categories were "None in the past year, 1-4 times, 5-8 times, 9-11 times, 12-24 times, 25-51 times, 52 or more times. The second question asked, "In the last year, how many times did you buy a movie on video cassette tape?" with the same response categories as item 1. The third question asked about rentals, "In the last year, how many times did you rent a movie on videocassette tape?" also with the same categories. These responses are show in Table 2.

RESULTS

One measure of the potential overlap between film and video audiences can be seen in responses to the question asking about people's interest in seeing the latest movie. The results suggest that only a minority of the public show a need to be the first to see a new release (15%). This suggests that people may be willing to wait for films to be released on videocassette, more evidence that there may not be a great distinction between film and video audiences.

A second measure of the possible distinctiveness of films versus videos is the correlation between these three forms of film viewing. The correlations between number of films attended with the number of videos rented and number of videos purchased are .278 and .138, respectively (both significant at $p < >001$). These correlations suggest that the number of movies attended shows a positive relationship with the number of videos rented, and, to a lesser extent, purchased. Therefore, people who see more movies are more likely to rent and buy movies on videocassette. This finding suggests that films are generally appealing to the same audience as videocassettes.

A third measure of the possible overlap between film and video audiences is to make use of a multiple regression to examine the factors determining film and video viewing, and compare across these two media. Four regressions were run – one for each media use measure and one for the ratio of film to videos.

The regression on movie attendance showed that women (*Beta* = .049, $p < .01$) and non-whites (*Beta* = .050, $p < .01$) attended more movies. Consistent with Hypothesis 1a, younger people attended more movies (*Beta* = -.191, $p < .001$). Consistent with Hypothesis 2a, people from households with higher incomes attended more movies (*Beta* = .201, $p < .001$). Consistent with Hypothesis 3a, people from larger households attended fewer movies (*Beta* = -.138, $p < .001$). After these variables were included, the importance of newness was included in the equation. This variable was a significant addition to the equation (*F* change [1,3029] = 35.7). As predicted in Hypothesis 4, the desire for new products showed a positive relationship with movie attendance (*Beta* = .138, $p < .001$).

The regression of video *rentals* showed, consistent with Hypothesis 1b, that younger people rented more videos (*Beta* = -.391, $p < .001$). Consistent with Hypothesis 2b, people from households with higher incomes (*Beta* = .109, $p < .001$) also rented more videos. Consistent with Hypotheses 3b, people from larger households rented more videos (*Beta* = .106, $p < .001$). Although not predicted, importance of newness showed a positive relationship with number of video rentals (*F* change [1,2984] = 30.8, *Beta* = .091, $p = .001$).

The regression of video purchases showed that women (*Beta* = .040, $p < .01$) purchased more videos. Consistent with Hypothesis 1c, younger people purchased more videos (*Beta* = -.141, $p < .001$). Contrary to Hypothesis 2c, people from households with higher incomes did not purchase more videos (*Beta* = .007, $p > .10$). Consistent with Hypothesis 3c, people from larger households purchased more videos (*Beta* = .142, $p < .001$). Although not predicted, importance of newness showed a positive relationship with number of videos purchased (*F* change [1,2984] = 10.8, *Beta* = .059, $p = .001$).

The fourth regression was run on the ratio of the number of movies attended to the number of videos rented or purchased (the larger the number, the higher the percentage of movies). This regression showed that non-whites were more likely to attend movies than were whites (*Beta* = .061, $p < .001$). After controlling for race, younger people were more likely than older people to see films in theaters (*Beta* = .153, $p < .001$). People from households with higher incomes were more likely to see films in theaters than were poorer people (*Beta* = .082, $p < .001$). People from larger households were *less* likely than people from smaller households to

see films in theaters (*Beta* = -.189, $p < .001$). After controlling for these factors, the importance of newness showed a positive relationship with seeing films in theaters (*F* change [1,2980] = 119, *Beta* = .192, $p = .001$).

CONCLUSIONS

These results are consistent with Hypotheses 1a, b, c, & d — that younger people attend more movies, rent move videos, and purchase more videos. Consistent with Hypothesis 2a, b, & d, more affluent people attend more movies and rent more videos. They did not, however, *purchase* more videos. Consistent with Hypothesis 3a, b, c, & d, household size does appear to be a significant determinant of whether one sees movies out or rents or purchases videos – with people from large households more likely to rent or buy videos. Finally, as predicted by Hypothesis 4a, the importance of newness is related to greater levels of movie attendance, but contrary to Hypothesis 4b, to *higher* levels of video rentals. The importance of newness was also shown to have a positive relationship with the number of videos purchased. Finally, consistent with Hypothesis 4c, people who have a higher interest in having the newest products consume a higher proportion of films in theaters than to films on video.

These results show that younger people and people that are more affluent consume more feature films. This finding is consistent with previous research on the movie audience (DeSilva, 1999). In addition, however, younger and more affluent people also buy and rent more videos (Greenberg & Lin, 1989). These results suggest that the most active film fans are more likely to consume feature films in both theaters and on video. For these audiences, entertainment appears to be desired, and entertainment appears to be entertainment, regardless of in which format it comes.

People with lower incomes and larger families are more likely to buy or rent a video than to see a film in a theater. This is consistent with the notion of increased cost of attending movies in terms of the number of admissions that must be purchased or in terms of other costs of seeing films in theaters (DeSilva, 1999, p. 154).

The results of this research, therefore, suggest that consumers are behaving rationally in response to the windowing model. Previous theory has suggested that the timing home video occurs immediately after theater exhibition, and the pricing is slightly lower than theater prices, and before pay-per-view, cable, network, and syndicated TV, respectively. These results suggest that consumers appear to operate consistently with that approach. That is, although there is a good level of overlap between film attendance and video rental and purchase, there are also differences between these windows with regard to a price discrimination model. Accordingly, some consumers appear to be using videocassette purchases and rentals to substitute for other, more expensive, exhibition windows (Litman, 1999). Our research suggests that the level of substitution can be predicted by knowing the consumer's age, level of income, number of people in their household and desire for new products. These findings generally suggest that the main criterion for price discrimination in the movie industry is people's desire to see the most recent release.

These results, then, suggest that videos may pose less of a cannibalization threat for first run theater audience than previously thought (Trachtenberg, 1985). It also suggests that the pricing of video releases may be set at a reasonable level to compensate film producers for the reduction in theater attendance (Owen & Wildman, 1992). Because consumers seem to be applying a rational criterion to the choice of seeing films in theaters or seeing them in video, especially when household size gets large, this may suggests that the VCR may be a larger threat to other per viewing pricing structures such as pay per view and premium cable systems (Gruen,

1985; McLaughlin, 1987; Spillman, 1984). Here, other factors such as the desire to see a specific movie, a monthly price versus per-movie price, "bundling" a number of movie channels, or niche-specializations such as exclusive movie rights movies may help to differentiate cable and video outlets for producers and audiences (Collette & Litman, 1997; Gruen, 1985).

It is still not clear, however, whether the positive relationship between seeing movies in theaters, renting videos, and buying videos is a generally positive or negative omen for the film industry. There are four possible scenarios. First, the video window may simply allow audiences to modify their film viewing in theaters for less expensive video window. To the extent that the film industry prices videos to cover the loss in film attendance (minus the lower cost of video distribution), there may be no loss in revenue (Owen & Wildman, 1992). Second, the video venue may allow easier access to feature films, and therefore generating an interest in films and creating a cohort of entertainment active film fans. This would be a positive outcome for the film industry. Third, consumers may have a given entertainment budget and simply allocate this to a variety of possible venues. As the number of film windows increase, people may allocate a constant share of their disposable incomes to selecting between these various outlets. This would be a neutral outcome for the film industry. A fourth possibility is that the increased options for seeing feature films may take away from other entertainment activities such as sports and music events. Further research at both the managerial and consumer levels will be necessary to understand which of these outcomes is occurring, or perhaps which occur under which situations.

REFERENCES

Anonymous (1984). Readers Use Full Range of TV Choices. *Nation's Business,* 72(9), 36.

Block, Alex Ben (1984). Priced to Sell? *Forbes,* 134(12), 41-42.

Caravatt, Paul J., Jr. (1985). Videocassettes explore the demographics. *American Demographics,* 7(12), 31-33, 41.

Carpenter, Gregory S. & Nakamoto, Kent (1989). Consumer preference formation and pioneering advantage. *Journal of Marketing Research,* 26, 285-289.

Carpenter, Gregory S. & Nakamoto, Kent (1990). Competitive market strategies for late entry into a market with a dominant brand. *Management Science, 36,* 1268-1278.

Collette, Larry, and Litman, Barry R. (1997). The peculiar economics of new broadcast network entry: The case of United Paramount and Warner Bros. *Journal of Media Economics,* 10 (4), 3-22.

DeSilva, Indra (1999). Consumer selection of motion pictures. In B. Litman (Ed.), *The motion picture mega industry.* Boston, MA: Allyn and Bacon (pp. 144-171).

Dimmick, John W., Patterson, Scott, and Albarran, Alan B. (1992). Competition between the cable and broadcast industries: A niche analysis. *Journal of Media Economics,* 5 (1, Spring), 13-30.

Fuller, Richard (1990). The Home Picture Show. *Philadelphia Magazine,* 81(2), 59-60.

Greenberg, B. S. & Lin, Carolyn (1989). Adolescents and the VCR boom: Old, new and nonusers. In M. Levy (Ed) *The VCR age* (pp. 73-91). Newbury Park, CA: Sage Publications.

Gross, Neil, Brull, Steven V., & Grover, Ronald (1997). Betamax Wars All Over Again? *Business Week,* 3546, 35-36.

Gruen, Erica (1985). VCRs Up! Cable Down? *Marketing & Media Decisions,* 20, 80-81.

Hall, Peter (1984). Home entertainment. *Financial World,* 153(18), 10-16.

Howard, Niles (1982). The drive for a VCR tax. *Dun's Business Month,* 120(3), 88-93.

Hoyer, Wayne D. & Ridgway, Nancy M. (1984). Variety seeking as an explanation for exploratory purchase behavior: A theoretical model. In Thomas C. Kinnear (ed.), *Advances in Consumer Research, 11,* 114-119. Provo, UT: Association for Consumer Research.

Keith, Bill (1986). Videotapes/programs a money-maker in Midwest drugstores. *Drug Topics,* 130(7), 80-81.

Klopfenstein, Bruce C. (1989). The diffusion of the VCR in the United States. In M. Levy (Ed), *The VCR age* (pp. 21-39). Newbury Park, CA: Sage Publications.

Krugman, Dean M., Shamp, Scott A., and Johnson, Keith F. (1991). Video movies at home: Are they viewed like film or like television? *Journalism and Mass Communication Quarterly,* 68, 120-130.

LaRose, Robert, and Atkin, David. (1991). Attributes of movie distribution channels and consumer choice. *Journal of Media Economics,* 4 (1, Spring), 3-17.

Levin, Gerald M (1998). Media and entertainment: Shaping the new millennium. *Executive Speeches,* 13(1), 28-31.

Litman, Barry R. (1999). *The motion picture mega industry.* Boston, MA: Allyn & Bacon.

MacEvoy, Bruce. (1994). Change leaders and the new media. *American Demographics,* 16(1), 30-56.

McLaughlin, Mark (1987). Cable TV uses pay-per-view to vie with VCRs. *New England Business,* 9(1), 48-49.

Mitchell, Susan (1994). Technophiles and technophobes. *American Demographics,* 16, 36-42.

Rogers, Everett M. (1995). *Diffusion of innovations (4th Ed).* New York: Free Press.

Sherrid, Pamela (1983). Beautiful Model Meets Sumo Wrestler. *Forbes,* 132(6), 38-40.

Sommer, Jeff (1980). VCR Yet to Record Expected Boom ... *Advertising Age,* 51(24), S 2,4,6.

Spillman, Susan (1984). Cable Sees Growing Threat from VCRs. *Advertising Age,* 55(22), 60.

Trachtenberg, Jeffrey A. (1985, Feb 25). Reel Dollars. *Forbes,* 135(4), 67.

The Act of Learning and the Acquisition of Knowledge

Anne L. Roggeveen, Columbia University

There has been a substantial amount of work on the effects of prior learning on various dependent variables such as product evaluations and choice (see, e.g., Bettman and Sujan 1987, Brucks 1985). However, as noted by Hutchinson and Alba (1991), in general, there has been little empirical effort devoted to how knowledge develops (see Huffman and Houston 1993 for an exception). This session aimed to stimulate interest in the areas of learning and the development of knowledge by focusing on recent empirical research in this area. It brought together three papers that examined how people learn.

Markman and Moreau presented a paper titled "Systematicity in Analogical Inference: Implications for the Marketing of New Products." Their research considered learning via systematic relation-based knowledge transfer. They demonstrated that when participants were able to construct relation-based mappings between a known product and an unfamiliar target, they were more likely to generate inferences based on shared-system facts about the target. These inferences then affected the construction of preferences for the new product. Thus, the relation among attributes drove learning and preference formation about a new product.

Broniarczyk and West presented a paper titled "Integrating Multiple Opinions: The Role of Aspiration Level, Prior Beliefs, and Critic Diagnosticity." Their research addressed learning in the context of consistency with prior beliefs and strength of data. Specifically, their work focused on the two-stage process of how individuals learn which critic opinion is personally most diagnostic and how individuals then utilize critic opinions in their own judgments. They found that critic disagreement in the data increased the salience of the dissenting critics and hence facilitated learning of their diagnosticity and hindered learning of the other critics. Consumer learning did not appear to be affected by prior beliefs but critic utilization was. Specifically, consumers utilized critic opinions in their own judgments if it was consistent with their prior critic beliefs and if they learned true critic diagnosticity due to disagreement in the data.

Roggeveen and Johar presented a paper titled "Integration of Market Research about Customers." Their work examined the impact of negative information on how people update and learn new information. Specifically, their work examined quantitative information and teased apart two aspects to negativity–meaning (e.g., higher launch cost than initial information) and change from a reference point (e.g., lower launch costs than initial information). Results found support for a "lower numbers" bias such that the classic negativity bias manifested for new information regardless of whether the new information implied good news (e.g., lower launch costs) or bad news (e.g., lower sales forecasts) for the company. The authors proposed a two-stage model of perceptual then conceptual encoding to explain these findings.

Steve Hoch acted as the discussion leader highlighting the interesting points from each paper and tying the three streams of work into the general topic of how people learn and update beliefs. The session concluded with an active discussion between session participants and members of the audience.

Consumer Psychological Attachment: Exploring Differences Across Customer Segments and Product Categories

Melissa Moore, Mississippi State University
S. Ratneshwar, University of Connecticut

ABSTRACT

How and why do consumers become psychologically attached and ultimately committed to firms? This topic is an important issue in relationship marketing but also one that raises important questions regarding consumer behavior. Recent research has shown that the structure of consumer psychological attachment entails four key dimensions (i.e., utilitarian, affective, symbolic, and obligatory). We focus here on how these four dimensions of psychological attachment are likely to vary across different customer segments (e.g., committed vs. transactional customers) *and* across different product categories (e.g., high vs. low involvement). We first briefly describe the consumer psychological attachment (CPA) model and then develop hypotheses regarding profile differences between customer segments on specific CPA dimensions for different types of product categories. We test these hypotheses using survey data from 142 adult female respondents. The results suggest that the various consumer psychological attachment dimensions play significantly different roles in distinguishing specific market segments and that these roles are contingent on the product category.

Us Versus Them: Oppositional Brand Loyalty and the Cola Wars

Albert M. Muniz, Jr., DePaul University
Lawrence O. Hamer, DePaul University

—I avoid Coke whenever possible - I'm more of a Pepsi kind of girl   from a message posted to Usenet

Brand loyalty refers to a consumer's attachment or devotion to a brand (Aaker 1991). Frequently investigated in terms response to brand marketing (Blackston 1995) or purchase behavior (Dyson, Faar and Hollis 1996), brand loyalty can actually encompass a great deal more (Fournier 1998(b); McAlexander and Schouten 1998). In fact, consumers can express their attachment and loyalty to a brand through a variety of thoughts and behaviors in a variety of settings. For example, consumers may express their loyalty in social settings by actively defending and promoting their brand as superior to a particular competitive offering.

It is relatively well-established that consumers derive meaning and identity from what and how they consume (Belk and Costa 1998; Celsi, Rose and Leigh 1993; Englis and Solomon 1995; Fournier 1998a; Schouten and McAlexander 1995). A more recently documented twist is that consumers may also define themselves in terms of what and how they *do not* consume (Englis and Solomon 1997; Fournier 1998(b); Hogg and Mitchell 1996; Hogg and Savolainen 1997; Wilk 1996). For example, Hogg and Savolainen (1997) found consumers use brand choices to mark both their inclusion and exclusion from various lifestyles. Essentially, consumers avoided those brands that they saw as defining membership in groups (yuppies) with which they did not identify. This suggests that a consumer's loyalty toward any particular brand may be embedded in a larger set of brand constellations (Solomon and Assael 1987) and anti-constellations (Hogg and Mitchell 1996). In other words, loyal users of a given brand may derive an important component of the meaning of the brand and their sense of self from their perceptions of competing brands, and may express their brand loyalty by playfully opposing those competing brands. This phenomenon is termed oppositional brand loyalty.

This paper presents findings on consumer oppositional brand loyalty behavior in a social environment, Usenet newsgroups. Analyzing consumer messages posted to multiple newsgroups, it documents the tendency of oppositional brand loyalty among consumers of soft drinks, particularly Coke and Pepsi. This opposition manifest itself in two ways. First, consumers of a particular product category define themselves by the brands they consume, as well as the brands they *do not* consume. Frequently these consumers would state the brands they actively avoided, as well as those that they sought. Second, these consumers express their opposition to these competing brands by initiating and participating in playful rivalries with consumers loyal to competing brands. These behaviors included insulting the competing brand and its consumers and challenging consumers of the other brand to defend their choice. During a one-month period of 1999, oppositional brand loyalty was evident in multiple Usenet newsgroups, devoted to a multitude of topics, all varying in their level of relevance to the product category of soft drinks.

Usenet, the Internet and the World Wide Web

The Internet[1] is a series of global computer networks. First started as a medium for information exchange among the U.S. Military, these networks rapidly grew to include universities and researchers working all around the globe. Despite its origins as a medium for information exchange, the most powerful impetus for the growth of this medium derived from its ability to allow for social interaction among a widely dispersed group of people (Jones 1995; Rheingold 1993). One of the most widely used components of the Internet are Usenet newsgroups. Participants in Usenet can share their thoughts, experiences and information with millions of others from around the world.

Usenet, a globally distributed conferencing and discussion system, is a network of 75,000 computers that allow participants to exchange messages on over 15,000 different topics (Mclaughlin, Osborne and Smith 1995; Whittaker, Terveen, Hill and Cherny 1998). Over 24 million users worldwide (www.dejanews.com) participate in Usenet through Internet connections provided by universities, libraries, government agencies, businesses and commercial Internet providers such as America Online, Compuserve and WebTV. Usenet is heavily trafficked with more than 250,000 articles being posted to it daily (www.deja.com). A survey conducted by Georgia Tech's Graphics, Visualization and Usability Center suggests that over forty-three percent of all Web users participate in Usenet newsgroups weekly (GVU WWW survey).

Usenet newsgroups function much like electronic bulletin boards. Each newsgroup is devoted to a particular topic ranging from very general (rec.audio - dealing with audio enthusiasts, hobbyists and recreationsists) to very specific (alt.politics.clinton - dealing with the policies and activities of President Bill Clinton). Participants post messages to these newsgroups, sending a message much like an email message, to that group. Posted messages are then distributed to other sites carrying that newsgroup and are made available to anyone accessing or subscribing to that newsgroup. Participants to these newsgroups can read and respond to any previously posted message or can initiate conversations on any topic relevant to the newsgroup's focus. Newsgroup reading software, widely available both as part of world wide web software (Netscape Navigator, Microsoft Internet Explorer) or as stand alone applications for Windows (Agent), Macintosh (InterNews) and UNIX based systems (Pine), allow the reader to sort messages by topic, sender or time/date sent. Many of these programs are available as free shareware.

METHOD

This research was ethnographic, naturalistic and observational (Adler and Adler 1994; Hammersley and Atkinson 1983). The content of consumer-generated documents (Lincoln and Guba 1985), posted to the public realm of Usenet newsgroups were analyzed (Hodder 1994). This approach has a benefit of capturing the way that consumers talk to one another about consuming brands. It observes the behavior and communications of consumers in a naturally occurring, social setting, one that is very similar in structure to conversational discourse (MacKinnon 1995). Moreover, this approach is consistent with methods applied in previous research on the dynamics of Usenet-based communication (MacKinnon 1995; Mclaughlin et al. 1995; Whittaker, Terveen, Hill and Cherny 1998). For example, McLaughlin et al. (1995) archived and analyzed several days of Usenet newsgroup data from five different newsgroups in order to develop a taxonomy of Usenet posting offenses (those that violated "netiquette" or acceptable

---

[1]The Internet, as it is being used here in its most generic sense, refers to all the components of the worldwide computer network with which it is commonly associated: the World Wide Web, Usenet, and Internet Relay Chat.

Usenet protocol) and the subsequent group-based regulation of those infractions.

Data for the current project were collected using an online archive of newsgroup postings. Dejanews (www.dejanews.com) is a World Wide Web-based archive of articles posted to over 15,000 Usenet newsgroups (dejanews FAQ). Each article or posting is indexed and stored allowing for intricate Boolean-logic searches on keywords (of any word in the posting), subject headings, forums (i.e., different newsgroups), authors and dates posted. For example, a search on "wind-up toys" messages posted to alt.toys.low-tech newsgroup would produce a list of all the messages posted to that newsgroup that contained the words "wind-up toys."

For the purposes of the present study, a keyword search was used, searching for the occurrence of two brand names across all Usenet newsgroups during a one-month period in 1999. A search was conducted looking for all the messages containing both the keywords "Coke" and "Pepsi," occurring between February 1, 1999 and February 28, 1999. Coke and Pepsi were chosen as they are two widely consumed brands with a history of a rivalry, particularly in the content of their advertising (Pendegrast 1993). It was assumed that the rivalry between these two brands could impact consumer communication regarding soft-drink preference. Extrapolating from the findings of Hogg and Savolainen (1997), it was reasoned that consumers of one brand (i.e., Coke) might define their brand choice largely in opposition to the other brand (i.e., Pepsi). This search yielded 1,253 different messages that contained both the word Coke and the word Pepsi. The search results were presented ranked according to confidence with the most relevant messages listed first.[2]

The first 1000 messages were downloaded and examined.[3] Not surprisingly, there was a lot of variation in how these two brand names were used in everyday communication. For example, a consumer might note in a somewhat detached manner that Coke and Pepsi both spent a lot of money on advertising. While interesting in their own right, such messages were not directly related to the focus of the study and were excluded from analysis. Messages in which one brand was pitted against another were downloaded and recorded for more detailed analysis. These included messages in which a posted message declared a consumer's soft-drink choice relative to the competition, debased a competing brand, or challenged users of another brand to defend their choice. In order to better understand the context in which these message appeared (Hodder 1994), prior and subsequent messages in that thread were also downloaded.[4] These threads occasionally extended beyond the one-month period specified in the initial search and sometimes originated as a discussion of an unrelated topic. This enabled each instance of oppositional brand loyalty to be understood in terms of the messages on that topic immediately preceding it and those responses that followed it.

The corpus of messages forming the data of this investigation were analyzed in a manner consistent with previous investigations of Usenet based communication (MacKinnon 1995; McLaughlin et al. 1995; Whittaker, Terveen, Hill and Cherny 1998). The messages were read during the initial downloading to confirm that the relevant processes were evident. Some very preliminary interpretations, as well as areas to examine, were recorded at this time. Messages with evidence of some form of oppositional brand loyalty were read and re-read several times, along with the messages providing the context in which they appeared. Categories of oppositional brand loyalty were created, based on the form and degree of the opposition to competing brands. All the differing instances of oppositional brand loyalty were categorized to provide a better understanding of the phenomenon.

FINDINGS

Oppositional brand loyalty was a spontaneous phenomenon evident in several different newsgroups. During a one-month period of 1999, oppositional brand loyalty behavior occurred independently in newsgroups devoted to a multitude of topics, all varying in their level of relevance to the product category of soft-drinks. Evidence of this behavior was found in fifty different newsgroups during February 1999. In some instances, several people would participate in these threads, in other cases only two or three. Table 1 provides a listing and brief content description of all the newsgroups in which evidence of oppositional brand loyalty behavior was found. These groups varied widely in both their topical focus and, more importantly, their relevance to the product category of soft drinks. For example, while the newsgroup alt.foods.cocacola (a discussion of all things Coke) is truly germane to the category of soft drinks, others such as alt.support.childfree (a support group for childless couples) and rec.sport.paintball (a discussion of the survival game paintball) are decidedly less relevant. Despite the varying relevance of the newsgroups, this behavior was remarkably consistent.

Oppositional brand loyalty manifest itself in two closely related ways. In the first, and more subtle way, consumers would define their product category preferences not only by what they did consume, but also by what they did not consume. This behavior included frequently stating their preferences in terms of the brand they did not consume. Such preferences would often take the form of lists of brands sought and avoided. In the second way, these consumers would state their opposition to the competing brand and initiate playful rivalries with users of the competing brand. This behavior included degrading the other brand and challenging the users of that brand to defend their choice. Frequently, these others users would defend their choices, leading to an extended brand choice debate. In many instances, the first behavior would precede the second. That is, in many newsgroups, what started as a simple stating of preferences and anti-preferences would escalate to a more unabashed opposition.[5] Both forms of oppositional brand loyalty

---

[2] Relevance is based on strength of match of keywords (dejanews FAQ). Thus, messages with two instances of both keywords would provide a stronger match than messages in which both keywords occurred only once.

[3] For the purposes of the present study, only messages written in English were analyzed.

[4] A thread refers to all the messages posted by different users with the same subject heading. It is proper netiquette to include the subject header of a previous message when responding to that message of commenting on the same topic (McLaughlin et al. 1995). Frequently, several messages are posted to a thread, most referencing those messages that preceded them. Thus, if someone posts a message on the best vacations they have taken, several other people might respond with their thoughts on their favorite vacations, producing a thread of several messages.

[5] A possible concern here is that such messages were posted by employees of the companies in question. While possible, it seems unlikely for two reasons. First, given the truly spontaneous nature of these messages, it seems unlikely that they were part of an orchestrated scheme. Many of these messages originated in discussions of unrelated topics. Second, and more importantly, the posting histories of all the participants quoted in this paper were investigated using the same archive from which the data used in this project were collected. Posting histories document all the newsgroups a particular author or email address have posted to. All of the participants cited in this paper posted to multiple newsgroups on a variety of topics beyond their choice of soft drink.

TABLE 1

Newsgroups Containing Oppositional Brand Loyalty Messages Between February 1 and February 28, 1999

Newsgroup	Description
alt.abuse.recovery	Helping victims of abuse to recover
alt.elvis.king	Fans of the late(?) king of rock and roll
alt.fan.mark-brian	The Mark & Brian radio program
alt.fan.mr.tribe	Fans of Mr. Tribe
alt.fan.phiberoptik	Fans of Phiberoptik
alt.fan.sailor-moon	Sailor Moon animation, manga, and merchandise
alt.fan.scream	Fans of the *Scream* movie series
alt.food.cocacola	Fans of the classis American softdrink
alt.games.kesmai-legends	Online multiplayer game Legends of Kesmai
alt.games.nintendo.pokemon	Nintendo Pokemon videogame
alt.gnashing-teeth	Angry sales people
alt.games.video.nintendo-64	Nintendo-64 videogame system
alt.gothic	The gothic movement: things mournful and dark
alt.kids-talk	A place for the pre-college set on the net
alt.music.no-doubt	The group No Doubt
alt.music.oasis	British group Oasis
alt.music.ska	Discussions of ska (skank) music, bands and suchlike
alt.religion.christian.boston.church	The International Churches of Christ
alt.religion.scientology	Church of Scientology
alt.smokers.cigars	Cigar Smokers
alt.sports.basketball.nba.boston-celtics	Boston Celtics NBA basketball
alt.support.childfree	Childless by choice support group
alt.support.srs	Support and information on sex reassignment
alt.teens.poetry.and.stuff	Teens sharing poetry and stuff
alt.tv.er	The tv show "E.R."
alt.tv.highlander	The Highlander tv show and related movies
borland.public.delphi.non-technical	Non-technical questions on Borland Delphi
comp.dsp	Digital Signal Processing using computers
comp.graphics	Computer graphics
comp.robotics.misc	All aspects of robots and their applications
misc.consumers.frugal-living	Practicing a frugal lifestyle
res.arts.movies.current-films	The latest movie releases
rec.arts.poem	For the posting of poems
rec.arts.tv.mst3k.misc	Fans of Mystery Science Theater 3000
rec.arts.sf.written.robert-jordan	Books by author Robert Jordan
rec.audio.high-end	High-end audio systems (Moderated)
rec.autos.makers.jeep+willys	Discussions on Jeep and Willys vehicles
rec.autos.sport.f1	Formula 1 motor racing (Moderated)
rec.autos.sport.nascar.moderated	NASCAR and Stockcar Racing (Moderated)
rec.food.cooking	Food, cooking, cookbooks and recipes
rec.heraldry	Discussion of coats of arms
rec.music.rem	The musical group R.E.M.
rec.music.tori-amos	Discussion of the female singer/songwriter Tori Amos
rec.roller-coaster	Roller coasters and other amusement park rides
rec.skydiving	Hobbyists interested in skydiving
rec.sport.football.college	US-style college football
rec.sport.paintball	Discussins all aspects of the survival game paintball
rec.sport.pro-wrestling	Discussion about professional wrestling
rec.sport.skating.ice.figure	Figure/artistic skating
rec.travel.cruises	Travel by cruise ship

selected descriptions courtesy of gopher://ftp.duke.edu/00/pub/newsgroups

are explored subsequently, as well as some other characteristics of this behavior.

There was a wide variety of ways in which these beverage brand choice conversations were started. For example, in the pokemon videogame group (alt.games.nintendo.pokemon), the conversation thread got started as participants were discussing aspects of the game. Apparently, one of the screens in this video game includes a giant bottle of Diet Coke in the background. A discussion of this screen image served as the basis for a discussion of soft-drink preferences. This discussion eventually progressed from soft-drink preferences to a prankish rivalry with the competing brands. In the rec.music.tori-amos newsgroup (devoted to fans of the singer Tori Amos), someone posted an informal questionnaire to the group, asking others to respond and tell a little about themselves. The form contained over fifty questions about, love, life, things spiritual and preferences for either Coke or Pepsi.

Subject: -O- Get to know me, get to know you
Date: 1999/02/06
Forum: rec.music.tori-amos
So anyway, one of my friends sent me this. She's always sending me these jokes, which gets really annoying, but this was cool. They're some pretty basic questions, but try to have fun with it. I'll start off, but you guys feel free to skip any you don't want to answer. I warn you though, it is kind of long. Enjoy!

NAME: Rojeania
BIRTH DATE: December 24, 1973
...
HOW MANY TIMES DO YOU WASH YOUR HAIR A DAY: Once
DO YOU CARE ABOUT THE WAY YOU LOOK: I do if I will be leaving my apartment.
DO YOU PREFER PEPSI OR COKE: Pepsi
DO YOU BELIEVE IN GHOSTS: Sure, why not?

Apparently, the author of the form felt that the choice of Pepsi versus Coke was revealing about the character of a person. Given that over two-hundred participants in the newsgroup completed the form, some supporting their choice with a sentence or two, it appears that others agreed that beverage preference was a non-insignificant descriptor of character. Similar forms using the Coke/Pepsi dichotomy as a descriptor variable were posted to alt.fan.scream (fans of the Scream series of movies), alt.gnashing-teeth (angry salespeople) and alt.kids-talk (a place for the pre-college set on the net). Such forms reveal that consumers of these brands do define themselves by what they do not consume, as well as what they do consume. Coke and Pepsi were recognized as being diametrically opposed.

In the rec.sport.football.college (devoted to discussing collegiate football teams), the brand choice debate was started with a rather simple message.

Subject: Pepsi or Coke
Date: 1999/01/22
Forum: rec.sport.football.college

I'm in the minority, but my taste buds are kinder to Pepsi than Coke. I'm taking votes here. So far it's Pepsi 1-0....

Fifteen other people participated directly in this thread, each posting their choice. Many provided a rational for their choice and kept cumulative score.

---

[6]As is custom in Usenet communications, an individual responding to a specific preceding message will quote all or part of that message in the text of the current message, typically including the name and email address of the original poster. Such quoted text is typically blocked with arrows (>) or colons (:). This habit is fortunate as it provides a glimpse of what prompted the message.

Frequently, as these soft-drink preference discussions progressed, the tendency toward rivalry would increase. One contributor might attempt to justify the choice of one brand over the other, prompting others to respond with their thoughts on why their brand choice was superior. Consider the following in which, the arrows (>) preceding the first six lines of text indicate that these lines are quoted from s previous message.[6]

Re: My Favorite Soda (TR Re: I've found paradise!!!)
Date: 1999/02/03
Forum: alt.support.childfree

On 3 Feb 1999 00:35:19 GMT, (Wallacd) wrote:
>I'm a Diet Coke junkie (I drink it for breakfast). I won't drink Diet Pepsi
>(swill) and I always ask in a restaurant if they serve Coke or Pepsi. If it's
>Pepsi, I order an ice tea.

I'm the same on the Coke vs. Pepsi thing, except I don't drink the diet varieties. If Pepsi's all they've got, I'll drink just about *anything* else (and yes, iced tea is way up on the list).

Pepsi has that additional aftertaste thing going on that I just don't like. Coke is more about straight-ahead sugary-ness. Mmmmm.

Elise

These statements extended beyond mere statements of choice to express the strength of their cola conviction and their rationale for the choice (in this case taste).

Sometimes the rationale for choice of one brand over the other would be tied into the topic of the newsgroup. For example, one participant in the paintball newsgroup claimed to like Coke better than Pepsi because Pepsi was anti-gun. Other times, the choice of the brand would be tied into lore or history about the brand, such as famous people who had used the brand. Consider the following example from an Elvis Preseley newsgroup.

Re: Jesse !
Date: 1999/02/08
Forum: alt.elvis.king

... Personally I like Pepsi better and so did Elvis.

This conversation thread started out as a discussion of singers that sounded like Elvis. One participant claimed that comparing Elvis with one of the other singers (Jimmy "ORION" Ellis), was like comparing Coke and Pepsi. This participant then noted what their preference was and then added that their preference was consistent with what the King preferred. Such a statement was probably intended to legitimatize their choice and underscore their allegiance to the brand.

As the discussion of beverage preferences and anti-preferences progressed, rivalries with the competing brand became more pronounced and involved. Fans of one brand would begin to direct insults toward the other brand and its devotes. These fans would then retaliate in kind. Consider the following exchange.

Re: [PW!][WG] Location: The Diet Coke Bottle From Hell: Evolved form.
Author: Elwen <unlisted@softhome.net>
Date: 1999/02/08
Forum: alt.games.nintendo.pokemon

|>*It is MY doing, and Adrian Tymes! Bow to diet coke!*
|>
|
|*I will not!*

Yeah. Diet Coke is icky.

Here, the message quotes two previous messages.[7] One telling others to bow to Diet Coke, the next stating that the individual would not and finally, the author's retort.   The first message, suggesting all others bow to Diet Coke was directed toward consumers of competing brands. The two subsequent messages were resistance to this suggestion. It is almost conversational in form and illustrates how participants typically built upon the comments of others.

Most of these exchanges had an almost ritualistic quality about them. The players all seemed to know the routine, and enjoyed participating in the fun. One possible interpretation of this is that the competitive relationship is an important part of the brand experience. These brands were defined, to no small extent, in the advertising and promotion as competing. Participating in such ritual most likely functioned to-reinforce these already well-established meanings (Douglas and Ishwerwood 1977). In addition, such interactions were a chance to engage other contributors of the newsgroup in conversation. Consider the next three messages. All three were taken from the same newsgroup, and the same thread or conversational topic. They are presented in the order in which they were posted. This last point is clear as the third message quotes the second, which quotes the first. Note that the conversation takes place within a discussion of doughnut shops. The first poster notes that the brand of beverage served there was the "best news" about the place.

Krispy Kreme Taste Test - Part 2
Date: 1999/01/31
Forum: alt.fan.mark-brian

**** IMHO ****
Krispy Kreme doughnuts are the BEST that I have ever had...

The best news is that they serve Pepsi, not that "Coke" stuff.

Re: Krispy Kreme Taste Test - Part 2
Date: 1999/02/01
Forum: alt.fan.mark-brian

>*The best news is that they serve Pepsi, not that "Coke" stuff.*

That's good news? (uh-oh I feel a Coke/Pepsi debate coming on).

Anyway, I prefer coffee with my doughnuts. (Preferably a Deidrichs).

:) Mike.

Re: Krispy Kreme Taste Test - Part 2
Date: 1999/02/01
Forum: alt.fan.mark-brian

>*That's good news? (uh-oh I feel a Coke/Pepsi debate coming on).*
>
>*Anyway, I prefer coffee with my doughnuts. (Preferably a Deidrichs).*
>
>*:) Mike.*

I, myself, like Pepsi. It's great for removing the rust off of my barbecue ;)

Bruce

Here it is evident that while recognizing and participating in these rivalries, most participants understood the playful nature in which they were enacted. Consider the last message above. It can be interpreted in one of two ways, both of which suggest an understanding of the game being played. In the first interpretation, the contributor could be jokingly deprecating the brand in the light-hearted spirit of the preceding messages. Instead of attacking the competing brands, he light-heatedly attacks his own brand of choice. In the second interpretation, the contributor could be a coke drinker masquerading as a Pepsi drinker with a backhanded compliment to Pepsi. Either interpretation suggests a fairly well-developed understanding of the rules of this exchange.

These rivalries and oppositional behaviors also occurred for other soft-drink brands, as well. In many cases, Dr. Pepper drinkers, 7-Up drinkers, as well as consumers of more regional brands would contribute to the thread.

Re: [PW!][WG] Location: The Diet Coke Bottle From Hell: Evolved form.
Date: 1999/02/14
Forum: alt.games.nintendo.pokemon

>*I refuse to bow to that weak and chemical-tasting rendition of the One True*
>*Coke!*

Ha! Your pitifull shrine to Coke is a minor setback to my leader's path for
Global Domination! Bow before the Great Dr. Pepper!!

In this case, a Dr. Pepper ensured that one of the smaller players in the beverage skirmish was represented.

In an interesting twist, sometimes, oppositional brand loyalty posts would contain elements of the advertising for the brand. These elements would be creatively employed to bolster the supporter's argument in favor of their brand. Consider the following.

Re: Pepsi or Coke
Date: 1999/02/21
Forum: rec.sport.football.college

> *I'm in the minority, but my taste buds are kinder to Pepsi than Coke. I'm*
> *taking votes here. So far it's Pepsi 1-0....*

---

[7]The | symbol next to the > indicates that the author is quoting a prior message that in turn quoted still another prior message. The text preceded by |> are from the original message, while the text preceded by | are from the response to that message being quoted.

Well, I'm a Coke person, and I must say that you can't beat the real thing!

Here a consumer justifies his choice of Coke by quoting part of that beverage's advertising (Coke frequently positioned itself as being "The Real Thing"). Another participant in this newsgroup responded to this message by noting that he preferred Coke, adding that he would "like to teach the world to post in perfect harmony." In so doing, he was paraphrasing an earlier Coke advertising campaign that sought to teach the world to *sing* in perfect harmony. This use of advertising in consumer conversation is consistent with those described by Alperstein (1989) in which consumers use the content of advertising in daily communication in a playful way.

These rivalry exchanges would end as the subject of the thread drifted or was dropped. Usenet messages in general appear to suffer from a form of message degradation or drift. Essentially, as more messages were posted to a particular subject thread, the topic would begin to vary from the original posting, much like a face-to-face conversation can stray from topic to topic. Oppositional brand loyalty threads, like most threads in Usenet, tended to drift or degrade into discussions of unrelated topics. Discussions of brand preference and rivalry threads eventually changed to discussions of other matters. For example, in the rec.sport.football.college newsgroup, an oppositional brand loyalty thread evolved into a lengthy discussion of great names for rock bands. These topics ended as quickly as they started. However, it should be noted, that topic drift was also responsible for starting several oppositional threads. Thus, in many cases these discussions also ended via the same process by which they started.

DISCUSSION

This paper presented data on consumer brand loyalty behavior in a social setting, Usenet newsgroups, during a one-month period of 1999. It demonstrates how consumers talk about brands and the consumption experiences that surround in everyday social settings. It also demonstrates that some consumers derive a part of the meaning of the brand and their identity from their opposition to competing brands. Some consumers of soft-drinks define themselves not only by the brands that they did consume, but also by the brands that they did not consume. In some cases, these consumers would extend this behavior and initiate rivalries with the users of competing brands.

This work has implications for our understanding of brand loyalty, and the ways in which brands connect consumers to one another. Oppositional brand loyalty is obviously related to brand loyalty and most likely has impact on brand equity at some level (Keller 1993), perhaps even for those who do not currently consume the brand. This last point is likely as such competitive brand skirmishes take place in settings visible to consumers of all brands. Thus, these interactions would serve to reinforce existing understandings of these brands. At the least, it suggests that associations for any one brand may be embedded in a larger set of brand constellations (Solomon and Assael 1987) as well as anti-constellations (Hogg and Mitchell 1996).

This work also ties in nicely with and contributes to work on brand communities (Fischer and Gainer 1996, Fournier 1998a, McAlexander and Schouten 1998; Muniz and O'Guinn 1995; Schouten and McAlexander 1995). Oppositional brand loyalty could be an example of a less-communal, socially-embedded brand behavior. This would suggest a continuum with the extreme cult-like community of Harley-Davidson riders documented by Schouten and McAlexander (1995) sitting at one end, less intense brand communities such as those described by Muniz and O'Guinn (1995) sitting closer to the middle, and oppositional brand loyalty at the other end.

REFERENCES

Aaker, David A. (1991), "What is Brand Equity," Managing Brand Equity, New York: The Free Press, 1-33.

Adler, Patricia A. and Peter Adler (1994), "Observational Techniques," in Norman K. Denzin and Yonna S. Lincoln (eds), Handbook of Qualitative Research, Thousand Oak, California: Sage, pages 377-392.

Alperstein, Neil M. (1989), "The Uses of Television Commercials in Reporting Everyday Events and Issues," *Journal of Popular Culture* 22 (2) 127-135.

Belk, Russell (19xx), "Possessions and the Extended Self," *Journal of Consumer Research*.

Belk, Russell W. and Janeen Arnold Costa (1998), "The Mountain Man Myth: A Contemporary Consuming Fantasy," *Journal of Consumer Research*, 25 (December), 218-240.

Blackston, Max (1995), "The Qualitative Dimension of Brand Equity, *Journal of Advertising Research*, 35 (4), RC2.

Celsi, Richard L., Randall L. Rose, and Thomas W. Leigh (1993), "An Exploration of High-Risk Leisure Consumption Through Skydiving," *Journal of Consumer Research*, 20 (June), 1-23.

Dejanews, FAQ: http://www.dejanews.com/help/faq.shtml#newsgroup

Douglas, Mary and Baron Isherwood (1977), The World of Goods, New York: Basic Books.

Dyson, Paul, Andy Farr, and Nigel S. Hollis (1996), "Understanding, Measuring, and Using Brand Equity," *Journal of Advertising Research*, 36 (6), 9-22.

Englis, Basil G. and Michael R. Solomon (1997), "To Be and Not to Be: Lifestyle Imagery, Reference Groups, and the Clustering of America," *Journal of Advertising*, 24 (Spring), 13-28.

Englis, Basil G. and Michael R. Solomon (1997), "I Am Not…, Therefore, I Am: The Role of Avoidance Products in Shaping Consumer Behavior," in Merrie Brucks and Deborah J. MacInnis (eds), Advances in Consumer Research, 24, Provo, UT: Association for Consumer Research.

Fischer, Eileen, Julia Bristor and Brenda Gainer (1996), "Creating or Escaping Community? An Exploratory Study of Internet Consumers's Behaviors," in K. P. Corfman and J. Lynch (Eds.), Advances in Consumer Research, Volume 23, Provo, UT: Association for Consumer Research, pages 178-182.

Fournier, Susan (1998a), "Consumers and Their Brands: Developing Relationship Theory in Consumer Research," *Journal of Consumer Research*, 24(4), 343-373.

Fournier, Susan (1998b), "Consumer Resistance: Societal Motivations, Consumer Manifestations, and Implications in the Marketing Domain," Special Session Summary in Joseph W. Alba and Wesley Hutchinson (eds), *Advances in Consumer Research*, 25, Provo, UT: Association for Consumer Research.

GVU WWW Survey, Georgia Tech, Graphics, Visualization and Usability Survey: http://www.gvu.gatech.edu/user_surveys/

Hammersley, Martyn and Paul Atkinson (1983), Ethnography: Principles in Practice, London: Routledge.

Hodder, Ian (1994), "The Interpretation of Documents and Material Culture," in Norman K. Denzin and Yonna S. Lincoln (eds), Handbook of Qualitative Research, Thousand Oak, California: Sage, pages 393-402.

Hogg, Margaret K. and Paul C. N. Mithcell (1996), "Exploring Anti-Constellations: Content and Consensus," presentation at Association for Consumer Research Annual Conference, Tuscon, AZ.

Hogg, Margaret K. and Maria Savolainen (1997), "The Role of Aversion in Product/Brand Choice," presentation at Association for Consumer Research Annual Conference, Denver, CO.

Jones, Steven G. (1995), "Understanding Community in the Information Age," in Steven G. Jones (ed.), Cybersociety: Computer-Mediated Communication and Community, Newbury Park: Sage,10-35.

Keller, Kevin Lane (1993), "Conceptualizing, Measuring, and Managing Customer-Based Brand Equity," *Journal of Marketing*, 57 (Janurary), 1-22.

Lincoln, Yvonna S. and Egon G. Guba (1985), Natrualistic Inquiry, Beverly Hills, CA: Sage.

MacKinnon, Richard C. (1995), Searching for Leviathan in Usenet, in Steven G. Jones (ed.), Cybersociety: Computer-Mediated Communication and Community, Newbury Park: Sage, 112-138.

McAlexander, James H. and John W. Schouten (1998), "Brandfests: Servicescpaes for the Cultivation of Brand Equity," in John F. Sherry, Jr. (ed), Servicescapes: The Concept of Place in Contemporary Markets, Chicago: NTC Business Books.

McLaughlin, Margaret L., Kerry K. Osborne and Christine B. Smith (1995), Standards of Conduct on Usenet, in Steven G. Jones (ed.), Cybersociety: Computer-Mediated Communication and Community, Newbury Park: Sage, 90-111.

Muniz, Albert M. and Thomas C. O'Guinn (1995), "Brand Community and the Sociology of Brands," paper presented to Association for Consumer Research Annual Conference.

Pendegrast, Mark (1993), For God, Country, and Coca-Cola: the Unauthorized History of the Great American Soft Drink and the Company that Makes It, New York: Charles Scribner and Sons.

Reference.com, Details About Usenet: http://www.reference.com/pn/help_1.0/sources.html#Usenet

Rheingold, Howard (1993), The Virtual Community: Home-steading on the Electronic Frontier, New York: Harper Collins.

Schouten, John W. And James McAlexander (1995), "Subcultures of Consumption: An Ethnography of the New Bikers," *Journal of Consumer Research*, Volume 22 (1), 43-61.

Solomon, Michael R. and Henry Assael (1987), "The Forest or the Trees?: A Gestalt Approach to Symbolic Consumption," in Jean Umiker-Sebeok (ed), Marketing and Semiotics: new Directions in the Study of Signs for Sale, Berlin: Mouton de Gruyter, 189-218.

Whittaker, Steve (stevew@research.att.com), Loren Terveen, Will Hill, and Lynn Cherny (1998), "The Dynamics of Mass Interaction," ACM Conference on Computer Supported Cooperative Work, http://www.acm.org/sigchi/cscw98/

Wilk, Richard (1996), "Leanirng to Not-Want Things," presentation at Association for Consumer Research Annual Conference, Tuscon, AZ.

Collecting Brand Loyalty: A Comparative Analysis of How Coca-Cola and Hallmark Use Collecting Behavior to Enhance Brand Loyalty

Jan S. Slater, Ohio University

ABSTRACT

Brand loyalty is a central construct to marketing. Keeping the consumer satisfied, and loyal enough to frequently purchase just one brand, is more difficult in today's marketplace than ever before. But today, major brands are experiencing heightened brand loyalty due to the growing popularity of the brand as a collectible.

Two of the most prominent brands to move into the collectible category in the last twenty years are Hallmark and Coca-Cola. This paper highlights these two brands as case studies in exploring the market of collectible brands and the loyal relationship that collectors have with the brands. The research posits some of the reasons companies such as Hallmark and Coca-Cola are attracted to the collectible marketplace, as well as explaining how brand loyalty is enhanced via the collectibles.

While brand loyalty is considered a central construct of marketing, keeping the consumer loyal to just one brand is more difficult in today's competitive and changing marketplace than ever before. In light of this consumer infidelity, companies are extending brands into lines of collectible merchandise such as Christmas ornaments, dolls, figurines, plush animals, glassware, etc. This merchandise not only heightens brand loyalty, it extends the brand message exposure. Today, this collecting activity has been prepackaged with manufacturing, marketing and distribution controlled by some of the most prominent Fortune 500 companies, as well as some of the most recognizable brands in the U.S.

This study will explore two of the most prominent brands to move into the collectible category - Coca-Cola and Hallmark. The focus of the paper is how the collecting behavior has enhanced brand loyalty among collectors. The paper will be divided into four sections. The first will explore what makes a brand collectible and how collectible brands differ from consumable brands. The second section will explain how these two case studies were researched and the data analyzed. An overview of both brands will be provided in section three and the loyal collector relationships with the brands will be discussed in section four.

The Case for Collectible Brands

Brands are most often thought of as products, products that are consumed or used. But recently, brands such as Planter's Peanuts, McDonald's, Hershey, Oreo, and Coca-Cola have been acquired for collection rather than consumption. This is not how marketers and researchers have traditionally perceived brands. Therefore, it becomes necessary to distinguish collecting from other related consumption processes.

Belk (1995 p. 67) has defined collecting as "the process of actively, selectively and passionately acquiring and possessing things removed from ordinary use and perceived as part of a set of non-identical objects or experiences." This definition is consistent with others (Alsop 1982; Muensterberger 1994) and helps distinguish collecting behavior from other consumption activities and patterns.

In the collecting form of consumption acquisition is the key. Collecting differs from most other types of consumption because it involves forming what is seen to be a set of things - the collection (Belk, Wallendorf, Sherry and Holbrook 1991). Also, the things comprising a collection are removed from ordinary use. For instance, a collection of salt and pepper shakers is not used at the dinner table, and a collection of postage stamps is not used for mailing letters. Therefore, collecting is non-utilitarian. It is however, a highly involving passionate consumption, rather than an uninvolving form of consumption such as buying a soft drink. As a result, collectors tend to feel attached to their collections in ways that may seem irrational if viewed in terms of the normal functions of consumption (Belk 1995). Belk (List 1991 p. 47) has called collecting "the distilled essence of consumption." Basically collectors are the ultimate consumers. But collectors of brands? Here's a look at the brand collectible market.

Brand collectibles are big business. Mattel currently manufactures a collectible line of Barbie® dolls, some in designer clothing such as Donna Karan, others as movie characters such as Scarlett O'Hara, as well as brands such as *Got Milk?* Barbie®, Harley-Davidson Barbie®, Coca-Cola Barbie® and The Gap Barbie®. Hallmark has a line of collectible Christmas ornaments, the *Keepsake Ornament* line. McDonald's is selling Ronald McDonald cookie jars on QVC and hand-beaded designer evening purses in the shapes of burgers and fries for $2,000 on Rodeo Drive. Franklin Mint has forged a partnership with a variety of corporate marketers to create collectible products for some of the top commercial brands. Coca-Cola, Walt Disney, Hallmark, Pillsbury, LifeSavers, Ralston Purina, McDonald's, Harley-Davidson and Campbell's Soup are just a few of the corporations that have signed agreements to tie their brands to collectible dolls, plates, sculptures and Christmas ornaments (Loro 1995). These mass-merchandising efforts have extended the individual brands by making them collectible. Companies are using marketing strategies to attract new collectors and increase purchase frequency among current collectors; two classic strategies for building a brand's business (Jones 1992).

When reviewing the collectible brands listed above, three similarities are immediately evident; 1) all are relatively old brands, ranging from 40 to over 100 years in production; 2) each brand is the leader in its product category, i.e. soft drinks, soup, entertainment, fast food, greeting cards, etc.; and 3) each brand is in a mature product category, meaning that there is little opportunity for extensive natural growth in U.S. markets. Large groups of consumers are not entering these categories; most people already use these established brands. Therefore, the only opportunity to grow the category, as well as the brands, is to increase purchase frequency among current users.

It is likely that these brands and many others have reached maximum market penetration, i.e. consumers already purchase the product and purchase frequency is saturated. If that is the case, the only means to grow the brand is a "defensive strategy," which advocates retaining existing users and maintaining their purchase frequency (Jones 1992). Collectible marketing may be viewed as a brand extension, which capitalizes on the added values of these brands and strengthens the relationship with consumers by making the brand collectible. Extending the brand, using the brand name on new products to enter new product categories, i.e. the collectible category, is a key ingredient in maximizing the value of the brand in terms of profit, as well as brand loyalty (Aaker 1991).

Retaining existing customers and keeping them brand loyal is more difficult today for many reasons. Product proliferation is a primary concern. It is not uncommon for current supermarkets to stock upwards of 20,000 products. In addition, more than 3,000 brands are introduced each year for supermarket distribution (Aaker 1991). According to MRI (1995) data, there are 93 cat-food brands, 80 different brands of soft drinks, 76 brands of beer, 73 brands of dog-food, 23 brands of toilet paper, 30 brands of margarine and 119 different brands of ready-to-eat cereal overflowing supermarket shelves. In addition to these nationally distributed brands, supermarkets have begun to add to the fray by developing their own brands of soft drinks, margarine, toilet paper, and cereal to compete with the national brands on the shelf. This saturation only provides more choices for the consumer and in some cases, more confusion. With this brand overload, coupled with the slowing growth of mature product categories, collectibles may be a strategy for brands to maintain existing users and a means to reinforce loyalty.

Obviously, collecting is a different type of consumption and the collector is a different type of consumer. The entry and growth of major brand manufacturers into the collecting market signals the need for exploration and is the focus of this study.

METHOD

Design of the Study

This research uses two collectible brands as case studies to understand the market of collectible brands and explore the loyalty factor of brand collectors. To this end, this case study was designed to explore the perspectives of both the company (the brand) and the collector (the consumer).

The case study has been described as a means for exploring an entity or phenomenon ("the case") bounded by time and activity (a process or event), wherein the researcher collects detailed information by using a variety of data collection procedures during a sustained period of time (Creswell 1994: Yin 1994). In order to provide a broader perspective of collectible brands, two brands - Coca-Cola and Hallmark - are used for this analysis. The multiple-case design is often preferred as it offers the opportunity for comparisons while providing greater understanding and more compelling data (Yin 1994; Stake 1995). The brands were chosen for a number of reasons. Both Hallmark and Coca-Cola are producing or licensing extensive lines of collectibles, both have active and large collector's clubs, and both have been in the collectible market for almost 20 years. Furthermore, both fit the profile of being market leaders and mature brands with significant added values. Profiles of both brands will be provided in a later section of the paper.

Data Collection & Analysis

Data was gathered via in-depth interviews with collectors and company personnel involved with the brand collectible. These interviews were conducted in either the collector's home or at a collector-only event, such as the annual Coca-Cola Collectors Club Convention or the Hallmark Artists on Tour event. The collectors interviewed were members of either the Coca-Cola or Hallmark Collectors Club. In all, twelve collectors were interviewed – six for each brand. There is no typical profile of a collector in terms of demographics. However, it should be reported that both male and female collectors were included, ages ranged from 25 to 79, race was predominantly white (two were African-American), and the interviewees had been collecting for an average of 6 years (the range was from 3 years to 30 years).

In addition, company press releases, advertisements, brochures, and correspondence to collectors were analyzed. In-depth interviews were also conducted with company officials, including Phil Mooney, archivist for The Coca-Cola Company and Linda Fewell, a marketing specialist for the Hallmark Keepsake Ornament Collectors Club. Finally, collecting industry experts and authors were consulted for input regarding this activity to provide triangulation.

As with any qualitative data, the process of analysis is to bring order, structure and meaning to the data collected. The strategies employed here reflect that belief (Glaser & Strauss 1967; Charmaz 1988; Bogdan and Biklen 1992). Coding was divided into the two-phase process described by Glaser & Strauss (1967), initial coding and focused coding. During the initial phase, more than 1000 pages of data were coded line by line with emerging ideas, topics, and themes coded as such during the process. The second phase of focused coding was more selective. Here the sets of codes were narrowed to build categories by continuously re-examining the data. Themes then became more defined and supportable via the data. As suggested by Strauss and Corbin (1990), this process of coding and recoding continued until it became apparent that all the incidents could be classified and the categories were saturated.

The analysis of the data suggests that the bond between brand collectors and the collectible brands extend beyond brand loyalty. To understand that bond, the next section profiles each brand and provides an explanation of the relationship collectors have forged with Hallmark and Coca-Cola.

COLLECTIBLE BRANDS

Collecting Coca-Cola: It's the Real Thing

The history of this American icon is a textbook case in building, managing and maintaining a brand. Since its beginning, Coca-Cola has built a powerful brand image, imbued with added values: the discriminating benefits that go beyond the functionality of a refreshing soft drink (Jones 1986). The brand is seen as traditional, patriotic, friendly, and American. Bill, a college math professor and a Coca-Cola collector for 30 years described the brand this way:

> Because it has been so ubiquitous for 110 years now – it's in everybody's past somewhere. Everybody has some story that has something to do with Coca-Cola. It has always been there. You put it together with Mom, apple pie, the American flag and Coca-Cola. Around the world – this is America. This is the symbol of America.

Although the brand dates back to the late 1880s, the basic brand proposition - Coca-Cola satisfies, Coca-Cola is a delightful, refreshing beverage - has remained virtually unchanged, as has the brand name and its distinctive logo. Early on, the company developed a strong franchise for the brand by creating a distinctive personality that appealed emotionally to consumers. In addition, the company has consistently supported the brand and its identity with powerful advertising messages and substantial investments to expose those messages.

The story behind Coca-Cola, a product that is 99 percent sugar and water, and its ascent to a $18 billion business marketed in 195 countries, is an American phenomenon. But what is as phenomenal is the Coca-Cola Collectors Club which boasts 7,500 members in 23 countries who collect Coca-Cola memorabilia from bottles and cans, to delivery uniforms and old advertisements, to vending machines and coolers. The club is independent of The Coca-Cola Company. It is completely governed and financially supported by its members. Carol, a medical technician and former president of a regional Coca-Cola Collectors Club describes the club's relationship with Coca-Cola:

The Coke collectors club is a very, very strong club. We have a very strong loyalty to the product. We have Coca-Cola employees come to our meetings and conventions and we feel we have a strong relationship with the company. But the club is for collectors, so it's run by those who collect.

Coca-Cola is not only the largest brand in the world; it is also the largest brand collectible in the world (Allen 1994). From the time the secret formula for Coca-Cola was introduced in 1886, The Coca-Cola Company has been producing a wide range of promotional materials to encourage the consumption of the drink. Long before today's mass media, The Coca-Cola Company used hundreds of promotional items to advertise and sell its product to the masses. These items range from utilitarian merchandising items such as bottles and coolers, to traditional and familiar advertising items such as signs and print advertisements; from point-of-purchase items such as trays and calendars, to complimentary novelties such as toys and bookmarks (Schaeffer and Bateman 1995). Today these items are considered antiques and are considered rare and extremely valuable. Coca-Cola calendars from 1891 and 1892 are valued at $10,000 or more (Petretti 1994). A 1903 metal sign was recently sold at auction for $12,000.

These items form the basis for today's collections of Coca-Cola memorabilia. Part of the charm for the collector is that the original purpose of these items was to promote the sale of Coca-Cola, not to be collected. This is the attraction for Bill and his companion Randy:

The new stuff is made-to- order collectibles. They are strictly manufactured to be collected. The old stuff was not. That's the appeal to us. This is something that the company thought so little of – it literally cost pennies to make. The company knew a different one was coming out next year and the next year, so they just threw things away. These items weren't meant to be saved. And that makes it much more interesting than to collect things that were meant to be saved.

Unlike other collectibles that are somewhat one-dimensional (e.g. Hallmark Christmas ornaments, salt and pepper shakers, stamps, etc.), Coca-Cola collectibles literally span the full range of artifacts manufactured to merchandise and advertise consumer products since the 1880s. These include fans, chewing gum, pocket mirrors, pocket knives, wallets, cuff links, thimbles, pins, clocks, ashtrays, pens and match books and even match safes; a long but not exhaustive list. The considerable interest in collecting older Coca-Cola memorabilia has created a secondary level of new collectibles manufactured strictly to be collected. This new line of products, such as polar bear ornaments, glassware, trays, posters, kitchen-ware, etc., has been developed to feed the appetite people have for collecting Coca-Cola.

Today, more than 250 companies worldwide are issued licenses to manufacture over 10,000 different products bearing the Coca-Cola trademark. More than 50 million Coca-Cola items were sold in 1997 in various mass-merchandising retail outlets, as well as in the Coca-Cola Catalog and Coca-Cola's own retail outlets in Atlanta, New York City and Las Vegas. The Coca-Cola Company receives annual licensing fees from the manufacturers of the collectibles as well as an estimated 8 to 10 percent of the manufacturer's gross sales value, according to archivist Phil Mooney. So, while Coca-Cola's core business remains soft drinks, the income generated from collectibles and the added value the collectibles provide, add to Coca-Cola's bottom line while enhancing brand loyalty.

Hallmark Collecting: When You Care Enough

According to independent research provided to Hallmark, "When You Care Enough to Send the Very Best" is one of the most trusted and believed slogans in America because it associates the product with the experience of Hallmark. Not only has the advertising slogan "When You Care Enough" been in use for more than 50 years, it is the philosophy of the Hallmark company as well. Founder Joyce C. Hall wrote, "while we thought we had only established a good advertising slogan, we soon found out we had made a business commitment. The slogan constantly puts pressure on us to make Hallmark 'the very best' " (Hall 1979).

Hallmark Cards, Inc. claims to be "the world's largest manufacturer of greeting cards and other personal expression products" (Hallmark Press Release 1995). This line of products includes cards, gift-wrap and stationary items. In 1973, the company was looking to expand its product line, while staying within the guidelines of manufacturing what they do best, "personal expression" items (Fewell 1995). It was the annual Hallmark employee gift to founder Joyce C. Hall that marked the company's entry into the ornament line. The tradition of crafting a special greeting card for Hall began in 1938. Each year the card became more sophisticated, until 1966, when the card became a Christmas tree. This tradition continued until Hall's death in 1982. It was these immense, ornate, theme-designed trees that provided the idea, as well as some of the designs for Hallmark's Keepsake line of Christmas ornaments. The first offering included six decorated balls and 12 yarn figures as Christmas decorations. Today, Hallmark manufactures over 250 different ornaments per year under the Hallmark Keepsake Ornament umbrella. Clara, a great-grandmother and avid Christmas ornament collector, is proud to own every ornament that Hallmark has ever made. That would total more than 6,000 ornaments.

These ornaments are great. They're really something different and I like something different. I try to get things that will excite me. Little round balls are not for me. Anybody can have those.

According to industry experts, ornament collecting has grown quickly since Hallmark's introduction into the marketplace (Unity 1997). Total annual sales volume of the ornament industry was $2.4 billion for 1996, an increase of 25% over 1995. More than 22 million households collect Christmas ornaments and it is estimated that 75% of those households collect Hallmark Keepsake Ornaments (Unity 1997).

Because of this interest in collecting, the company launched the Hallmark Keepsake Ornament Collector's Club in 1987, which is now the largest collector's club in the nation, with a membership of more than 350,000. It is one of the few, if not the only, club that is completely managed and maintained by the manufacturing company. Most clubs are volunteer organizations with little or no company involvement, such as The Coca-Cola Collectors Club.

In addition, there are approximately 300 local clubs nationwide, sponsored by local Hallmark retailers. According to Hallmark research, joining the national club is the first step. A recent buyer's study conducted by Hallmark showed that a non-collector purchases one to three ornaments per year. A person begins to call himself/herself a "collector" when purchasing grows to 13 ornaments a year. Buying jumps to an average of 40 ornaments per year when the collector joins the national club and doubles to 80 per year when the collector joins a local club. Therefore, club membership does indeed increase purchasing. Estimating national membership fees, event fees, event purchasing and annual collector purchasing, the Hallmark Collector's Club generates $128 million annually.[1]

Hallmark's marketing strategy, including products, events and communications to collectors, all serve to enhance a strong brand association with this special group of consumers. This translates into the retention of a consumer/collector over a long period of time and this relationship provides Hallmark a competitive advantage in the marketplace.

THE RELATIONSHIP WITH HALLMARK AND COCA-COLA

As stated earlier, the purpose of this research was to explore the market of collectible brands and understand the relationship between the collector and the collectible brand. The following discussion highlights the collecting behavior as it relates to brand loyalty.

Collecting Strategies

As defined by Aaker (1991), brand extensions use the brand name to enter new product classes. Naturally, a key element in a successful brand extension is a strong brand. Both Hallmark and Coca-Cola capitalized on that brand strength to expand into the collectibles product category. Hallmark did so intentionally. It wanted to expand the product line in the early 70s, and decided ornaments were a good "fit." About the same time, Coca-Cola realized that the marketplace was littered with unlicensed Coca-Cola merchandise and people couldn't get enough of it. Coca-Cola capitalized on the situation and developed a licensing program that allowed them to control and profit from collectibles. Whether opportunistic or intentional, there is little doubt that collectibles extend the brands and these extensions are profitable.

Although Hallmark would not release ornament sales figures, it was estimated that the membership and purchasing power of the club add more than $117 million to the company's bottom line. This income is just from collectors. Hallmark's research revealed that non-collectors purchase one to three ornaments per year and collectors, who are not yet club members, purchase 13 ornaments a year. Using Hallmark's data on the number of households who collect Hallmark ornaments, this estimated purchasing power generates approximately $1.4 billion in ornament sales from non-club members alone.[2] If this is true, the sale of ornaments would account for almost half of Hallmark's $3.6 billion in overall sales.

Coca-Cola has licensing agreements with over 125 companies in the U.S. alone. The licensing fees generate more than $20 million. In addition, Coca-Cola receives a royalty based on sales of licensed merchandise, estimated between 8%-10% of the sale of each item. For example, when Coca-Cola teamed with Mattel to create a collectible vintage Coca-Cola Barbie™, Mattel paid a licensing fee as well as providing Coca-Cola 8% of the sales of the doll. Ten thousand dolls were sold for $130 each, garnering Coca-Cola more than $104,000. It is estimated that the other three dolls in the series will generate even more sales, making Coca-Cola Barbie™ worth half a million dollars. And that's just one licensed product; Coca-Cola licenses hundreds more.

Two key elements in brand growth are penetration and purchase frequency (Jones 1992). Penetration refers to the number of people who buy the brand and purchase frequency is obviously how many times they buy. Penetration must come first. Once the consumer has tried the brand, the next step is to get them to repurchase and eventually buy more.

This same strategy is apparent in the collectibles market - first, get the person to buy a collectible, and then get them hooked by buying more. People start collecting for various reasons. Clara, a

Hallmark collector who owns every ornament the company has made, connected an ornament with the memory of her husband. A metal serving tray intrigued Bill and Randy, who are credited with the largest private collection of Coca-Cola. Pete, who houses his Coca-Cola collection in three garages, bought a knife. Nora, who owns 3,000 ornaments, was buying gifts for her children and Luann, whose collection of ornaments tops 5,000, received a Hallmark ornament as a gift. Something internal, a desire, a want, a need drive the first purchase. But the next purchase and the next purchase can be driven by something internal as well as external. Pete, a collector for almost 25 years, is still uncertain about what attracted him:

> I bought a Coca-Cola pocketknife for $3. I don't know why. I didn't carry a pocketknife. I'd never owned a pocketknife. And I didn't even drink Coca-Cola. But something about that knife interested me and I bought it. Then I began to buy a bit more. By the fall of 1975, I had 20 or 30 different Coca-Cola things, but I didn't consider myself a collector. Then I read about a group of collectors getting together and decided to go. It was the first Coca-Cola collection I had seen. I was like a kid in a candy store. It really got my adrenaline going and I was hooked.

The internal drive is what Muensterberger (1994) titles "replenishment." There is no rational need for anyone to have 200,000 Christmas ornaments, when the average Christmas tree holds perhaps 100; or a need to have 60 metal serving trays that are never used to serve anything. It is an emotional need that causes the collector to be in a "constant replenishment" mode. The need, according to Muensterberger (1994) and Belk et al. (1991), can vary from one of excitement, approval, acceptance, security, control, power, comfort, or escape. These emotional needs are fulfilled through the collecting of Hallmark ornaments or Coca-Cola metal trays. As these needs surface, replenishment is necessary. Muensterberger (1994 p. 16) relates it to the recurring state of hunger; "regardless of how often and how much one ingests, within a few hours hunger returns and one must eat again." So it is with collectors. According to many of the collectors interviewed, they call it the "collector's mentality." Bob, a Pentagon employee and former president of the national Coca-Cola Collectors Club describes his mentality:

> I grew up with Coke and I always liked it and always wanted a Coke machine. I had a pinball machine and a jukebox in the basement when I was in high school, and I thought a Coke machine would be neat alongside of them. My girlfriend – she's my wife now – bought me a Coke thermometer because we couldn't find a Coke machine. Then a few months later we

---

[1]Based on membership fees of $20 for 300,000 members; ten special collector events, sold out @ 2,000 for $10 registration each; purchasing 2,000 special event ornaments at all ten events at $60 each; and the average collector spending $400 annually.

[2]Hallmark estimates that of the 22 million households who collect ornaments, half of those collect Hallmark ornaments. Deducting club membership from that figure, it is estimated that non-member collectors total 10.7 million households. Hallmark's research estimates that non-members who collect buy, on average, 13 ornaments per year. The average Hallmark ornament costs $10, therefore the spending would approximate to be $130 annually. Multiplied by the 10.7 million households, the non-member collectors generate $1.4 billion in ornament sales.

found a Coke machine. When we bought it, the guy threw in a Coke sign to sweeten the deal. We thought that sign was pretty neat, so we just started picking things up. It's just snowballed from there into two houses full of Coca-Cola memorabilia.

As Ted, who referred to himself as a novice collector of only 5 years admitted, "It's like a mistress, or a habit like drugs. Every so often, you have to have a fix."

Using this theory as a means of understanding the motivations of collectors is beyond the scope of this particular study. But it is important in understanding how Coca-Cola and Hallmark capitalize on the "collector's mentality" in marketing strategies and use these strategies to enhance brand loyalty.

Marketing strategies

If Muensterberger (1994) is correct that the collector needs repeated nourishment, then there is a need for a constant new supply of collectibles. Both Hallmark and Coca-Cola excel at this strategy, although in different ways.

Hallmark issues approximately 250 new ornaments each year. That fact alone offers the collector several opportunities to "replenish." But Hallmark spreads out the purchase opportunity for several months, so the collector doesn't overdose. In February, the collector begins the process with the *Dream Book,* a brochure/catalog showing the current years selection, by making a list of what to buy. Luann and her Aunt Nora both collect. Their activity begins when the *Dream Book* arrives.

We get the book and look through it and discuss it. Generally – we're on the phone saying – look at page 32 and yea, did you see the one on page… We go back and forth about what we like, what we don't. I mean this isn't a spur of the moment decision. We study this book. We make a list of "really like," "really want," "gotta have." Then we wait for the premiere and we go together and buy the "gotta haves."

In March, the collector can pre-order ornaments from the *Dream Book.* In July, almost two-thirds of the ornaments are in the Hallmark stores for purchase. By August and September, the collector can attend special collector's events and purchase exclusive items. In November, the last group of ornaments arrive in stores just before Thanksgiving. Then, there's Christmas, when an ornament might be received as a gift, and the after-Christmas sale, where they can pick up the leftovers. The following year, the cycle begins again with a new batch of ornaments. Hallmark is in constant communication with the collector via newsletters, POP displays, web-sites and events, with information on when the ornaments will arrive, who made the ornaments, and what other collectors are doing.

While Coca-Cola has no control over the antique memorabilia that exists in the marketplace, they do perpetuate the collector's mentality in marketing the new Coca-Cola collectible merchandise. As stated earlier, Coca-Cola licenses the logo to more than 250 manufacturers of various products. There is no shortage of new Coca-Cola collectibles in the marketplace. Many of the manufacturers sell to mass merchandisers such as Wal-Mart, Target, Hills, K-Mart, and Kohl's. In addition, some manufacturers such as Franklin Mint and Cavanaugh Productions have exclusive rights to certain products and sell directly to the collector. Other items are made exclusively for the Coca-Cola Collectible Hour on QVC every other month, or for sale only in Coca-Cola retail outlets or through the Coca-Cola catalog. For instance, the

Coca-Cola Barbie™ was only sold in the Coca-Cola Fifth Avenue Store in New York, the World of Coca-Cola in Atlanta, and through a special mail order from Mattel. The 10,000 limited-edition doll sold out in two weeks.

There is an abundance of Coca-Cola collectibles in the marketplace to keep collectors satisfied. However, unlike Hallmark, Coca-Cola is not in constant contact with its collectors. Coca-Cola doesn't inform collectors as to what merchandise is available. Most often, the collectors hear about new products as well as old merchandise from fellow collectors. This is one of the fundamental differences in the structure of the two collector's clubs, which ultimately create very different brand relationships.

Beyond Brand Loyalty

These brand collectors are brand loyal. They are drinking Coca-Cola, talking about Coca-Cola, reading about Coca-Cola, buying Coca-Cola, displaying Coca-Cola, selling Coca-Cola, investing in Coca-Cola. Coca-Cola is a part of their lives. They are immersed in the brand. The same is true with Hallmark, to an extent. The collectors are definitely brand loyal, buying Christmas ornaments, as well as cards, wrapping paper, etc. However, collecting Hallmark Keepsake Ornaments has some built in seasonality. Therefore, the immersion is not constant. Hallmark is trying to make it a twelve month activity by introducing the *Dream Book* in February, allowing pre-orders, and unveiling the ornaments in July. But basically, the collecting events and purchasing occurs during the six months prior to Christmas. Coca-Cola collectors are in the hunt year-round.

The Coca-Cola Collectors Club and the Hallmark Keepsake Collector's Club perpetuate the collecting behavior, but because the two clubs vary in structure, they vary in influence regarding the collector's relationship with the brand. Here's a comparison of the two organizations.

Hallmark

The Hallmark Keepsake Collector's Club is company-driven. Hallmark started the club, markets the club, and basically controls the club and reaps the profits the club generates. Furthermore, the collectors are dependent on the company for replenishment each year.

The Hallmark model is to put the collector closer to the brand using events, exclusive products and communication tactics. Rewards are offered for joining or renewing memberships. Exclusive products are offered at member-only events. Ornament artists are the focus of special events where collectors can collect autographs of those who designed the collectible ornament. And the magic of the ornament is enhanced by Hallmark sharing information about how it is made and what is being planned for next year. Finally, Hallmark infuses its correspondence with the emotionally charged references to tradition, holidays, family and the "Hallmark experience," which embodies the company's image. This tone infiltrates all communication efforts, whether it is mass-media advertising, the *Dream Book*, the guide to starting a collection, or the quarterly newsletter; the purpose is to create an emotional attachment to this emotionally-driven product and brand. All the while, Hallmark is driving the collectors to buy what it provides. The collectors in turn are obedient.

It is no surprise that this emotional attachment creates a strong brand relationship. But this relationship goes beyond brand loyalty; it's brand intimacy. These collectors are more than just loyal, they are faithful, devoted, obedient, and steadfast. They love Hallmark, they love the ornaments. Marie, a long-time Hallmark collector, spoke of the company as likeable, warm, friendly, comfortable to be with – almost like a companion. "I like Hallmark," she said. "They make me feel important." Nora speaks of Hallmark with even more emotion:

> I love Hallmark. Hallmark is like fireplaces, a cup of tea, sit around with scrapbooks, that kind of nostalgia. It feels like – pull up a chair, have a bite to eat – even if it's peanut butter and jelly, we'll sit around the table and talk.

When Clara discusses her collection, she speaks of her ornaments in a very personal way. The collection is the outcome of a tragic personal loss and she states that her first purchase "connected spiritually to my husband." By using the activity as a means of emotional and spiritual comfort, the body of what she has collected is no doubt strengthened. Now the collecting activity and the collection have become her life. In the interview, she sounds like a spokesperson for Hallmark and she interchanges collecting jargon with discussions of her family. She often refers to her grandchildren as a collection and her son as a limited edition (she has only one son). With the recent birth of her first great-grandchild, she boasts about a "first in the series" addition to the collection. When asked about her Hallmark ornaments she claims, "My favorite ornament is every ornament I have. My ornaments are truly like my children. There's not a one that I want to do without."

To these collectors, Hallmark is like a lover; dating, seducing, and tying the knot on an enduring and dependent relationship. As Fournier and Yao (1997 p. 462) suggest, this relationship is similar to the "marriage metaphor assumed in traditional loyalty definitions." However, these Hallmark loyalists have a passion and emotion about that brand that provides an intimacy with the brand. While Fournier and Yao (1997) report that both relationships are indeed possible with one brand, what may be occurring in the case of Hallmark is a progression of the relationship – intimacy and then marriage.

The process of dating is very similar to how Hallmark attracts and hooks collectors. First, the introduction. The consumer is already a Hallmark customer, although not a member of the collector's club. Throughout the retail environment many opportunities exist to introduce the consumer to the club. The ornaments are meticulously displayed in the store, membership kits are available, the *Dream Book* displays all the ornaments and touts the benefits of collecting, and the *Get Hooked on Collecting* book can get you started.

Next, the seduction. The key here is finding something in common and Hallmark has no problem with getting the conversation started with 250 ornaments; one of them has to spark an interest. Hallmark has done the research. The ornament line consists of some of the most popular cartoon characters, movie stars, and sports heroes, while using brands, hobbies, religion and family themes to attract a broad collector base. Certainly, something catches the eye - the holiday Barbie™, the Coca-Cola Santa, the Star Trek ships, the rocking horse, the teddy bear, the Christmas stamp, the car, the angel. The seduction occurs when the membership dues are paid.

At that point, the courtship begins. The brand and the collector become more intimate through the constant correspondence venues, love letters of a sort. The brand reassures the collector that it is trustworthy, comforting, warm, caring and steadfast. The collector becomes more familiar and comfortable with the brand, leading to more involvement. Here, the brand arranges dates in public places, such as the ornament premiere at the local Hallmark store. This allows the collector to relax in an informal, yet familiar setting and to meet some of the brand's

friends. Gradually, the dates move to exclusive events outside the retail environment, and as more friends are made, the comfort level and the intimacy increases.

Eventually, the collector is hooked. They fall in love with Hallmark and believe the brand is important in their life. Hallmark is everything desired in a brand or a spouse. Hallmark is always interested, doesn't take the collector for granted, is a good communicator and an even better listener. Hallmark and the collector are married, the ornaments are their children. They live happily-ever-after in the Land of Hallmark.

Coca-Cola

Whereas Hallmark's club is company driven, Coca-Cola's club is collector driven. Since its inception in 1975, the club has been organized and managed by collectors. This is a much different scenario than Hallmark's control model. Here, the Coca-Cola Collectors Club is controlled and supported by the collectors. They have created a volunteer structure that allows for elected representatives from various regions, as well as elected officials and board members. No one appoints officers, candidates campaign for the offices and ask for the votes of fellow collectors. These volunteers publish a monthly newsletter, plan and coordinate the annual national convention, create retail opportunities, and develop collectible merchandise. The company doesn't sponsor any event, doesn't provide any underwriting, nor does it have any input in the planning. It is the collector's convention. As former Coca-Cola CEO Roberto Goizueta explained, "The brand does not belong to us. We're just the custodians" (personal conversation, Phil Mooney April 3, 1997).

Indeed this is about brand ownership. Coca-Cola collectors feel they own the brand. Every Coca-Cola collector interviewed here only drinks Coca-Cola. Pete has been known to walk out of a restaurant that offers Pepsi instead of Coke. Somewhat jokingly, he contends that his 1993 multiple by-pass heart surgery was caused by "someone slipping me a Pepsi. That would do it."

These collectors not only use the brand, they live with it everyday. Pete not only has three garages full of his collection, his house is decorated with Coca-Cola items. Guests eat on Coca-Cola dishes and drink out of Coca-Cola glasses. Cold Coca-Colas are kept in a Coca-Cola refrigerator behind a Coca-Cola bar. His license plates tout Coke and his phone number is 558-COKE. But his prized possession is his parrot, Cokey, whom Pete has taught to say "Drink Coca-Cola" over and over again. Bill and Randy's Victorian house is decorated with more than 20,000 pieces of Coca-Cola memorabilia.

These collectors work tirelessly to protect the brand, market the brand and advertise the brand. They invest in the brand by buying stock (all of them are stockholders). They are the voice of the brand. When New Coke was introduced, the company became concerned about the collectors. Club members voiced opinions forcefully to the company, but not to the press. However, the company knew the press would arrive at the annual collectors club convention and was fearful that an even greater backlash of bad publicity would emerge from this large group of loyalists. When the company decided to reintroduce Classic Coke, the first delivery truck was sent to Dallas to deliver the Real Thing to the collectors convention.

The collectors believe they are part of the history of the brand. Allan, an active collector since the early 70s, claims the Coca-Cola pieces are a "work of art. It's no different from viewing paintings in a museum. This is history. It is beautiful artwork. It is Americana in its purest form." Because they collect historical pieces, their knowledge about the brand is unparalleled. In fact, it is a common belief among collectors that they know more about the brand than the people working at Coca-Cola. Bill and Randy's collection is often acknowledged to be more extensive and complete than the company's archives. Phil Mooney, Coca-Cola archivist says, "Bill and Randy have found out things that we didn't even know. What they do is of extreme quality."

Coca-Cola collectors drive the company to produce collectibles. They are vocal, through the club, the convention, the newsletter and through their purchasing, as to what they want from the company, and perhaps more importantly, what they don't want. Collectors shared concerns regarding saturation of the marketplace with new Coca-Cola items that were not necessarily collectible. These included the products that were produced in mass quantities and sold by mass-merchandisers with no limitations. From these conversations, the Coca-Cola Barbie™ emerged as one of the few limited-edition collectibles licensed by the company in recent years. This is not to say that Coca-Cola allows the collectors to determine what is licensed. That is certainly not the case. However, it is important to note that the company does listen to the collectors. As Phil Mooney claims, "These are a powerful group of consumers."

Belk et al. (1991) posits collecting celebrates ownership. The acquisition and possessive nature of the collector makes brand ownership possible. The collection is mine, the brand is mine. The collectors invest enormous amounts of time and resources in the collecting activity and maintenance of the collection, just like the owner of a business.

These collectors are not only masters of the brand, they are highly visible in the marketplace, making the brand more visible as well. Coca-Cola collectors are written about in antique and travel magazines, newspaper articles, collecting magazines and newsletters. They often appear on television programs that spotlight collectors and collections, including QVC and the Home Shopping Network. Collector conventions and local club activities are covered by the local media, while collectors are often invited to special events sponsored by The Coca-Cola Company, such as anniversary parties and retail store openings. As Bill states, "We're good fodder for the press. We don't bad mouth the company." Each collector is considered a specialist of his/her own collection, affording each one the opportunity of being an authority on Coca-Cola. Many collectors are considered experts in Coca-Cola collectibles. Their advice and insights are sought after by other Coca-Cola collectors, the collecting industry, the media and even The Coca-Cola Company. Carol claims, "Having people such as Bill and Randy look at your pieces or at your collection, in some way validates the collection."

They write articles and books, conduct lectures and workshops, lending much visibility to the brand and establishing enormous credibility as a spokesperson for the brand. Much like an owner. Coca-Cola is theirs. They possess it. They possess the collectible, they possess the brand. According to Coca-Cola archivist Phil Mooney, "These collectors are very, very brand loyal. No other brand has this kind of loyalty. These people not only consume the product, they acquire it, save it, and totally immerse themselves in the brand. These collectors are Coca-Cola."

CONCLUSION

There is no question that brands are under siege. Supermarkets house more than 20,000 products; hypermarkets stock more than 30,000. Product proliferation, product parity, price-conscious consumers, mature product categories and saturated markets make it very difficult for old brands as well as new brands to survive

in the marketplace. Brand loyalty has become brand infidelity. Mature brands, such as Coca-Cola and Hallmark have adopted the brand collectible strategy as a means of retaining a core base of devoted consumers.

Both Hallmark and Coca-Cola have contact with these collectors beyond the retail shelf. By extending the brand as a collectible, Coca-Cola and Hallmark have created a multiple contact marketing environment. According to Larry Light, a branding expert, this type of environment positions the brand as a "trustmark" instead of a trademark, and that becomes the point of differentiating the brand in the marketplace (Matthews 1995). Therefore, Coca-Cola isn't just a big company that manufactures a refreshing soft drink. It becomes a prized possession. The Hallmark Keepsake Ornament is not simply a resin decoration for the Christmas tree. It is an intimate part of life. Light (1996) suggests that brands, such as Hallmark and Coca-Cola are moving from a "transaction mentality" (sell the product off the shelf), to a "relationship mentality" (building an affinity to the brand that is positive and long lasting). Brand loyalty as defined by Light, is "a positive, suitable, mutually beneficial relationship" between the consumer and the brand (Matthews 1995 p. B4). In the case of Hallmark and Coca-Cola collectibles, the relationship is beyond loyalty, it is one of intimacy and ownership.

REFERENCES

Aaker, David A. (1991), *Managing Brand Equity*, New York: The Free Press.

Allen, Frederick (1994), Secret *Formula*, New York: Harper Collins Publishers.

Alsop, Joseph (1982), *The Rare Art Traditions: the History of Art Collecting and its Linked Phenomena Wherever These Have Appeared*, New York: Harper & Row.

Belk Russell W. (1982). "Acquiring, Possessing, and Collecting: Fundamental Processes in Consumer Behavior," in *Marketing Theory: Philosophy of Science Perspectives*, eds. R.F. Bush and S.D. Hunt, Chicago: American Marketing Association, 185-190.

Belk, Russell W. (1995), *Collecting in a Consumer Society*, New York: Routledge.

Belk, Russell W., Melanie Wallendorf, John Sherry, and Morris B. Holbrook (1991), "Collecting in a Consumer Culture," in *Highways and Buyways: Naturalistic Research from The Consumer Behavior Odyssey*, ed. R.W. Belk, Provo, Utah: Association for Consumer Research, 178-215.

Bogdan, Robert C. and Sari K. Biklen (1992), Qualitative *Research for Education*, Boston: Allyn and Bacon.

Charmaz, Kathy (1988), "The Grounded Theory Method: an Explication and Interpretation," in *Contemporary Field Research*, ed. R. Emerson, Prospect Heights, IL: Waveland Press, 109 -126.

Creswell, John W. (1994), Research *Design: Qualitative and Quantitative Approaches,* Thousand Oaks, CA: Sage Publications.

Fewell, Linda (1995), Personal conversation with Hallmark marketing specialist, September 16, 1995.

Fournier, Susan and Julie L. Yao (1997), "Reviving Brand Loyalty: A Reconceptualization Within the Framework of Consumer-Brand Relationships," *International Journal of Research in Marketing*, 14, 451-472.

Glaser, Barney G. and Anselm L. Strauss (1967), The *Discovery of Grounded Theory,* Chicago: Aldine.

Hall, Joyce C. (1979), When *You Care Enough*, Kansas City, MO: Hallmark Cards, Inc.

Hallmark Press Release, July 1, 1995.

Jones, John P. (1986), What's *in a Name? Advertising and the Concept of Brands*, New York: Lexington Books.

Jones, John P. (1992*), How Much is Enough: Getting the Most from Your Advertising Dollar,* New York: Lexington Books.

Light, Larry (1996), The *Fourth Wave: Brand Loyalty.* New York: American Association of Advertising Agencies.

List, S.K. (1991), "More Than Fun and Games," *American Demographics* (August), 44- 47.

Loro, Laura. (1995), "Nostalgia for Sale at Franklin Mint," *Advertising Age*, May 15, 33.

Matthews, Ryan (1995), "Branding the Store," Progressive *Grocer*, 74, November B4.

Mediamark Research, Inc. Spring 1995.

Mooney, Phil (1997), personal conversation with Coca-Cola archivist, April 3, 1997.

Muensterberger, Werner (1994), *Collecting, an Unruly Passion: Psychological Perspectives*, Princeton, NJ: Princeton University Press.

Petretti, Allan (1994), Coca-*Cola Collectibles Price Guide*, 9th Ed. Hackensack: Nostalgia Publications.

Schaeffer, Randy and Bill Bateman (1995), Coca-*Cola: A Collector's Guide*, London: Quintet Books.

Stake, Robert E. (1995), The *Art of Case Study Research*, Thousand Oaks, CA: Sage Publications.

Strauss, Anselm L. and Juliet Corbin (1990), Basics *of Qualitative Research*, Newbury Park, CA: Sage Publications.

Unity Marketing (1997), *Annual Collectible Industry Research*.

Yin, Robert K. (1994), Case *Study Research*, Thousand Oaks, CA: Sage Publications.

The Impact of Mixed Consumption Emotions on Relationship Quality

Julie A. Ruth, Rutgers University
Frédéric F. Brunel, Boston University
Cele C. Otnes, Rutgers University

ABSTRACT

Although emotions experienced by relationship partners pervade their exchange processes, the impact of emotions in contexts of consumption exchanges has not received a great deal of research attention. This study addresses this gap by focusing on the relationship outcomes associated with one aspect of emotional experience–consumer ambivalence, or the co-occurrence or sequential experience of mixed positive and/or negative emotions in one consumption episode. For this investigation, the context of gift receipt is used because it is highly relational and emotion-laden. Content analysis and analysis of variance procedures are used to assess the impact of such emotions on perceptions of relationship outcomes. The results demonstrate that rather than the overall amount of emotions, it is the balance or mix of positive and negative emotions that is strongly associated with perceptions of relationship outcomes. It also appears that emotional coping processes may exist to allow individuals to realize an overall neutral or positive assessment of the relationship, even if negative emotions are experienced. These results have important theoretical and practical implications for the study of marketing relationships of all types.

Disentangling Regret from Expectancy-Disconfirmation

Lisa J. Abendroth, Boston University

ABSTRACT

Expectancy-disconfirmation has long been the dominant paradigm in satisfaction research. However, recent research suggests that multiple comparison standards may influence consumer satisfaction (Oliver, 1997, Fournier and Mick, 1999). One alternative comparison referent is the outcome of the unchosen product or service. When the chosen alternative is seen as inferior to a foregone alternative and the consumer experiences self-blame, the resulting emotion is regret (Sugden, 1985). Regret has been found to detrimentally affect consumer satisfaction (Inman, Dyer, and Jia, 1997; Taylor 1997) and reduce repurchase intent (Inman and Zeelenberg, 1998; Zeelenberg and Pieters, 1999).

The goal of this research is to disentangle regret from expectancy-disconfirmation by examining the unique and combined effects from using performance expectations and/or a preferred, foregone alternative for comparison. Effects on perceptions, emotions, and post-purchase behaviors are examined in turn following a brief description of the methods.

In this experiment, 129 participants chose between 2 cordless phones knowing that they might receive the phone they selected. In order to tease apart the effects of expectancy-disconfirmation and regret, participants then received Consumer Reports information containing 2 key manipulations. The chosen alternative either met expectations (rated as "very good") or performed below expectations (rated as "good"), while the foregone alternative was either unknown (not rated) or known to be better (rated as "excellent"). This outcome information was manipulated between subjects along with a manipulation of processing measures, which were either asked pre- and post-outcome or post-outcome only.

Perceived Performance and Decision Quality. Although the perceived difference in performance between the chosen and foregone alternatives is the main driver of regret, I examined the individual ratings of the chosen and foregone alternatives and later computed the magnitude of the counterfactual comparison. There were two key findings. First, the results indicated that negative expectancy-disconfirmation caused a reevaluation of an <u>unknown</u>, foregone alternative. When the chosen alternative's outcome was below expectation, the foregone alternative was perceived to perform below expectation as well, which is consistent with anchoring and adjustment. However, the reevaluation also led the foregone alternative to be perceived as slightly better than the chosen alternative, which is consistent with counterfactual thinking. Second, the results suggested that the precursor to regret–knowing the foregone alternative was better–caused the chosen alternative to be rated worse relative to expectations, even when it's outcome was described as very good (meeting expectations).

Self-blame should stem from the perceived quality of the decision–the source of the wrong choice. When the foregone alternative was described as better, decision quality (process and reasons) should be perceived in hindsight to be poor, and the results showed a pre- to post-outcome decline in decision quality. However, the negativity associated with a below expectations outcome should also trigger attributional processes (Weiner, 1985) that cause perceived decision quality to decline. This was also found to be the case. The shifts in perceived performance and decision quality based on outcome information are important, as they are the key components of regret.

Affective Responses. Regret should be greater when the foregone alternative is known to be better, which it was. More interesting is the magnitude of regret when the foregone alternative's performance was unknown. Given that negative expectancy-disconfirmation caused the foregone alternative to be reevaluated as better than the chosen alternative and perceptions of decision quality to decline, then regret should have increased when the chosen alternative performed below expectations, which it did. However, when the chosen alternative performed below expectations, providing information that the foregone alternative was better did not further increase regret. The conclusion from this is that expectancy-disconfirmation alone, through its effect on perceived performance and decision quality, can trigger the same level of regret as information that the foregone alternative is better.

Satisfaction should decrease when the chosen alternative performs below expectation (Oliver, 1997) or when the foregone alternative is known to be better (Inman et al., 1997). Not only were both effects significant, but the magnitude of decrease was the same. However, their combined effect (chosen below expectations and foregone known to be better) was no different than either effect alone.

Looking at the relationship between the regret and its determinants, regression results showed that expectancy-disconfirmation, counterfactual comparison (the difference in perceived performance between the chosen and foregone alternatives), and decision quality were all significant predictors of regret. In addition, building on earlier research which showed that regret decreases satisfaction (Inman et al., 1997; Taylor 1997), mediation analyses found that regret only partially mediated the effects of expectancy-disconfirmation and counterfactual comparison on satisfaction, although it fully mediated the effect of decision quality on satisfaction.

Post-Purchase Behavior. Brand switching should increase when the chosen alternative performs below expectations as well as when the foregone alternative is known to be better. Although both effects were significant, the magnitude of the effect from information about the foregone alternative was much greater. Loyalty, a factor of positive word of mouth and repurchase intent, was also affected by both manipulations as predicted. More interesting results were found in the regression and mediation analyses. Brand switching and loyalty were both affected by counterfactual comparison and satisfaction, with the latter mediating the effects from regret. However, expectancy-disconfirmation had no effect on switching behavior, but had a large effect on loyalty. These results are significant for two reasons. First, they show that post-purchase behaviors are affected by both cognitive and emotional factors, and second, that different referents for comparison have different effects on post-purchase behaviors, even if they have the same effect on satisfaction.

REFERENCES

Fournier, S. and D. G. Mick (1999), "Rediscovering Satisfaction," *Journal of Marketing, pp. 5-23.*

Inman, J.J., S.S. Dyer, and J. Jia (1997), "A Generalized Utility Model of Disappointment and Regret Effects on Post-Choice Valuation," *Marketing Science,* v. 16, pp. 97-111.

Inman, J.J., and M. Zeelenberg (1998), "'Oh Wow, I Could've Had a V8!': The Role of Regret in Consumer Choice," Working Paper, University of Wisconsin-Madison, Madison, WI.

Oliver, R.L. (1997), *Satisfaction: A Behavioral Perspective on the Consumer,* Boston, MA: Irwin McGraw-Hill.

Sugden, R. (1985), "Regret, Recrimination, and Rationality," *Theory and Decision,* v. 19, pp. 77-99.

Taylor, K.A. (1997), "A Regret Theory Approach to Assessing Consumer Satisfaction," *Marketing Letters,* v. 8, pp. 229-238.

Weiner, B. (1985), "'Spontaneous' causal thinking," *Psychological Bulletin,* v. 97, pp. 74-84.

Zeelenberg, M., and R.G.M. Pieters (1999), "Comparing service delivery to what might have been: Behavioral responses to regret and disappointment in services," *Journal of Service Research,* v. 2, pp. 86-97.

Consumer Vengeance: Getting Even at the Expense of Getting a Good Deal

Nada Nasr Bechwati, University of Illinois, Urbana-Champaign
Maureen Morrin, University of Pittsburgh

ABSTRACT

This paper introduces the concept of *consumer vengeance*. Consumer vengeance is conceptualized as the desire of decision makers to "get even" with an entity, such as a firm, in response to a perceived wrongdoing. A theoretical framework is proposed for understanding variables that influence the extent to which consumer vengeance is felt and the conditions under which one acts on such feelings. The results of two experiments, in purchasing and voting contexts, are reported. These studies examine how feelings of consumer vengeance impact the choice process in competitive contexts, and whether, given sufficient feelings of vengeance, such choices can result in suboptimal decisions. We also examine conditions under which consumers might choose *not* to act on their feelings of vengeance. Implications of the research are discussed.

When Technology Meets the Consumer: An Integrative Approach Towards the Understanding of Technological Innovations

Paschalina (Lilia) Ziamou, Baruch College, The City University of New York

SESSION OVERVIEW

In the last decade, rapid and radical technological developments have spurred the emergence of technological innovations. Although a growing stream of research has argued that high-technology markets have unique implications for consumer decision-making, most of our understanding of consumer behavior is 'technology neutral' (Glazer 1995). In recent years, there is a steadily growing stream of consumer technology research (e.g., Deighton 1996; Hoffman and Novak 1996; Mick and Fournier 1998; Venkatesh 1996, 2000; Ziamou 1998). However, to the best of our knowledge, previous research has not investigated consumer behavior for 'Smart Products'–i.e., product and service offerings that adapt or respond to changes in their environment as they interact with consumers (Glazer 1999).

This session represents the confluence of a variety of research perspectives. It brings together researchers with different skills and expertise from both academia and industry and offers an integrative approach towards the understanding of emerging technological innovations.

PRESENTATION SUMMARIES

"Challenges and Issues in the Application of Living Space Model for Home-Based Information Technology"
Alladi Venkatesh, University of California, Irvine
Wai On Lee, Microsoft Corporation

This paper reports on a field study of introducing Internet terminals into the home. This study revealed that the acceptance of an Internet terminal such as the WebTV set-top box is dependent upon the existing social, physical, and technological spaces of the home, their interaction with each other, and their interaction with the external world. Analysis of the findings showed how the new technology changes the dynamics and the relationships in and between these spaces and how the home in turn reconstructs itself as part of the process of appropriation. Analysis of the findings also suggests that theoretical conceptualization of the uptake of technologies in the home needs to consider not only the spaces within the home but also the larger social space in which the home is embedded. The authors conclude by drawing out some near term implications for the design of Internet terminals in the context of the home.

"Estimating the Market Potential of a New Service Category"
John Rotondo, AT&T Laboratories–Research
Gary Rozal, AT&T Laboratories
Mani Subramaniam, AT&T Laboratories–Research

This paper proposes a new methodology for assessing the market potential of a new service category. Estimating new product or service demand continues to be a central and challenging problem in marketing science. The problem is exacerbated when the product or service is radically new and does not clearly belong to an existing category. This is often the case for technology-based products and services. The authors present a new theory and accompanying experimental procedures for estimating new service demand. Prospects and problems in extending the methodology beyond services to products are also discussed.

"Households and the Networked Home"
Erik Kruse, Ericsson, Consumer Lab

This paper focuses on the use of ethnographic and qualitative methodologies in the design and development of radically new technological innovations. One of the major challenges for technology companies developing truly novel product concepts is to understand consumers' unarticulated needs and incorporate 'the voice of the consumer' into the new product design and development process. This paper presents specific product prototypes and user interaction scenarios and describes how the new product development team at Ericsson used ethnographic and qualitative methodologies for identifying implicit user needs for radical technological innovations to reduce the probability of product failure for such innovations.

Discussion
Rashi Glazer, University of California, Berkeley

The discussion leader highlighted the importance of integrating quantitative and qualitative data when investigating consumers' interaction with technology. The presentations were linked to existing research on innovation adoption (e.g., Rogers 1983). Next, the discussion leader presented a framework to guide future consumer research technological innovations. The framework pointed to four general factors that are likely to facilitate or inhibit the adoption of 'smart' products: (1) convenience (i.e., one-stop shopping), (2) participation (i.e., individuals and firms together design product/service offerings), (3) anticipation, (4) balance between the individual and the group (i.e., private vs. public).

Judgment Correction: Antecedents, Consequences, and Explanations

Prashant Malaviya, INSEAD

Judgment correction refers to the process by which people change prior judgments to incorporate new information. The success of several marketing actions, such as re-positioning and erasing effects of negative publicity, hinges on consumers correcting prior judgments. Consumers could also initiate judgment correction of their own accord because they became aware of a bias in prior judgments, or they might engage in correction when confronted with new, may be inconsistent, information. While a mountain of research has examined how judgments are formed, less attention has been paid to judgment correction (Johar and Simmons, 2000). Thus, for both practical and theoretical reasons, the issue of judgment correction should be of interest to consumer researchers.

The first presentation, by Wegener, briefly reviewed the bias correction literature and offered evidence in support of the Flexible-Correction Model (FCM; Wegener and Petty 1997). A key feature of this model is that people correct prior judgments by invoking their "naïve theories" about how their judgments became biased (in the consumer psychology context, this could be the notion of a "schemer schema"; Friestad and Wright, 1994). Another feature of the FCM is that, unlike other accounts of correction, which hold that correction attempts lead to contrast effects, the FCM predicts that correction could result in both assimilation and contrast outcomes. Another key postulate of the FCM is that correction is a resource demanding task, which is dependent on the respondent's motivation and ability to engage in bias correction.

The second presentation, by Johar and Sengupta, examined correction processes when consumers encounter new information that is inconsistent with their prior attitudes. This research examined conditions in which inconsistent information would lead to attitude correction and the effect of such correction on attitude strength, which is an important predictor of subsequent behavior. Findings suggested that correction could result in attitudes that are either stronger or weaker than prior attitudes, depending on whether the correction process (i.e., the resolution of inconsistent information) was successful or not.

Building on theorizing presented by Gilbert (1991), in the third presentation, Jung, Malaviya and Sternthal examined how negated product attributes (such as "not difficult to use") are processed. The findings suggest that the processing of negated information involves two steps: first, people elaborate on the affirmative message ("difficult to use") and then correct it to incorporate the negation ("not"). This process is resource demanding and produces the interesting outcome that when adequate cognitive resources are available product judgments reflect the negation, but when only moderate resources are available judgments are the opposite of what is implied by the message, presumably due to a failure to incorporate the negation.

The discussion leader of the session, Brendl, raised important issues about judgment correction that need additional research. One observation was that while the FCM assumes awareness of the bias to be a pre-condition for correction to occur, it might be possible that under some conditions correction occurs without such awareness (e.g., Schwarz and Clore 1983). Another issue was raised about the outcome of judgment correction, where it was suggested that correction could either result in the "overwriting" of the prior judgment, or lead to the formation of a second, new judgment (e.g., Wilson, Lindsey and Schooler 2000).

REFERENCES

Friestad, M and P. Wright (1994), "The Persuasion Knowledge Model: How People Cope with Persuasion Attempts," *Journal of Consumer Research*, 21 (1), 1-31.

Gilbert, D. T. (1991), "How Mental Systems Believe," *American Psychologist*, 46(2), 107-119.

Johar, G. V. and C. J. Simmons (2000), "The Use of Concurrent Disclosures to Correct Invalid Inferences," *Journal of Consumer Research*, 26(4), 307-322.

Schwarz, N., and Clore, G. L. (1983), "Mood, misattribution, and judgments of well-being: Informative and directive functions of affective states," *Journal of Personality and Social Psychology*, 45(3), 513-523.

Wegener, D. M. and R. E. Petty (1997), "The flexible correction model: The role of naive theories of bias in bias correction," in M. P. Zanna (Ed.), *Advances In Experimental Social Psychology*, 29, 141-208, Mahwah, NJ: Erlbaum.

Wilson, T. D., Lindsey, S., and Schooler, T. Y. (2000), "A model of dual attitudes," *Psychological Review*, 107(1), 101-126.

ABSTRACTS

"On the Use of Naive Theories to Remove or Avoid Bias: The Flexible Correction Model"

Duane T. Wegener, Purdue University
Please refer to full text included in this publication.

"Updating Attitudes: Effects of Structural Inconsistencies on Attitude Strength"

Gita Venkataramani Johar and Jaideep Sengupta

The entire set of responses that is associated with an attitude object is referred to as its internal structure. Previous research has found that inconsistency in structural elements (e.g., evaluative-cognitive inconsistency) leads to lower attitude strength, as manifested in lowered attitude accessibility (Bargh et al. 1992) and attitude-behavior link (e.g., Chaiken, Pomerantz, and Giner-Sorolla 1995; Norman 1975; Rosenberg 1960). Notably, these findings all relate the *holding* of inconsistent attitudes to attitude strength. However, research on the immediate consequences of *incorporating* inconsistencies is sparse. The present research aims to fill this gap in the literature by examining how the incorporation of inconsistencies affects the strength of the corrected, or updated, attitude.

Intuitively, it appears that incorporating inconsistencies should yield strength results similar to those produced by holding inconsistencies–i.e., a lowering of attitude strength–because of the response competition between inconsistent attitudinal elements. On the other hand, the introduction of inconsistencies may sometimes result in activation and elaboration of existing links, increasing the strength of the corrected attitude. Thus, it seems possible that the incorporation of inconsistent information in an existing attitude structure can lead to both strengthening and weakening effects. The current research seeks to isolate both of these effects. Because these two opposing consequences can potentially mask each other, we examine a context which is conducive to documenting a pure strengthening effect (i.e., one where rehearsal of existing links occurs, but not creation of a competing link), and also a context which enables us to isolate a pure weakening effect (i.e., a context in which a competing link is set up, but no activation of existing links occurs).

One particularly interesting context that is conducive to studying the strengthening effect is that of attitude dissimulation–i.e., lying about one's true attitude. People often lie about their attitudes in their daily lives (e.g., white lies, lying for social desirability reasons).

Lying about existing attitudes represents a particularly suitable context for studying the strengthening effects of inconsistency incorporation because, while such dissimulation involves the rehearsal of existing links, it may not result in the creation of an actual link between the attitude object and the "false" attitude. Based on this reasoning, the first two studies of the current research use the dissimulation context (lying about product attitudes) to seek to provide process evidence for the hypothesis that inconsistency incorporation produces strengthening via activation of existing links. Such evidence is provided in two different ways. First, we examine the moderating effects of initial attitude strength on the strengthening impact of repeated dissimulation about product attitudes. For both strongly held and weakly held product attitudes, participants in our experiments were repeatedly asked to either express the opposite of their true attitudes (dissimulation) or their true attitudes (truthful expression). The effects of these manipulations were compared to a control, wherein participants did not express any attitudes. Each successive dissimulation trial should involve activation and elaboration of the true attitude, which is highly accessible on exposure to the attitude object, for strong attitudes. Such repeated activation and elaboration is less likely for weak attitudes. Thus, repeated dissimulation and repeated truthful expression (compared to the control) should result in equivalent amounts of attitude strengthening for strong attitudes but not weak attitudes (cf. Maio and Olson 1995). Support for this hypothesis–which relies on the premise that dissimulation leads to strengthening only to the extent to which it involves activation of existing links–is obtained in both our experiments, using two related measures of attitude strength–attitude accessibility and the attitude-behavior link. Further support for our hypothesized process comes from our finding that the difference between strong and weak attitudes disappears if participants are forced to activate the true attitude on each dissimulation trial.

Experiment 3 investigates a context that allows for a demonstration of the weakening effects of inconsistency incorporation. While evaluating a new product, people may first be exposed to only positive information about the product (e.g., through advertising). Later, they may also be exposed to negative product information, from sources such as word-of-mouth, independent consumer agencies, etc. Such a scenario is likely to create attitudinal ambivalence, and result in a weakening effect (as compared to a condition in which the subsequent evaluative information is also positively valenced) because of response competition between the inconsistent elements in the attitude structure. Apart from proposing that inconsistent information in such a context should lead to greater ambivalence (and weakening) than consistent information, we also investigate a boundary condition for this effect–information accessibility. We hypothesize that exposure to inconsistent information is likely to result in a process of elaborative reconciliation when earlier information is more accessible (vs. less accessible). Such elaboration will prevent a weakening effect, and can in fact produce a strengthening effect (as compared to a condition where only consistent information is provided). However, if earlier information is not accessible at the time of exposure to the inconsistent information, elaboration is less likely to occur. In such a case, a weakening effect (as compared to the consistent information condition) should be observed because of heightened attitude ambiva-

lence. Results from a 2 (Accessibility of initial information: high/low) * 2 (Valence of later information: consistent/inconsistent) study, with the attitude-behavior link as the indicator of attitude strength, are strongly supportive of our predictions.

In sum, our research investigates the corrective impact of incorporating inconsistent links, in terms of its effects on attitude strength. Apart from providing some interesting insights into the specific contexts studied (e.g., the effects of dissimulation), these findings further our understanding of the relationship between attitude structure and attitude strength. In particular, we provide support for the processes that underlie opposing effects of inconsistency incorporation. If such incorporation leads to a rehearsal of existing links, a strengthening effect is likely to be obtained; however, in the absence of such rehearsal, the creation of an inconsistent link in the attitude structure should yield a weakening effect.

REFERENCES

Bargh, John A., Shelly Chaiken, Rajen Govender and Felicia Pratto (1992), "The Generality of the Automatic Attitude Activation Effect," *Journal of Personality and Social Psychology*, 62, 893-912.

Chaiken, Shelly, Eva M. Pomerantz, and Roger Giner-Sorolla (1995), "Structural Consistency and Attitude Strength," in Richard E. Petty and Jon A. Krosnick (eds.), *Attitude Strength: Antecedents and Consequences*, 387-412, Mahwah, NJ: Lawrence Erlbaum.

Maio, Gregory R. and James M. Olson (1995), "The Effect of Attitude Dissimulation on Attitude Accessibility," *Social Cognition*, 13(2), 127-144.

Norman, R. (1975), "Affective-Cognitive Consistency, Attitudes, Conformity and Behavior," *Journal of Personality and Social Psychology*, 32, 83-91.

Rosenberg, Milton J. (1960), "Cognitive Reorganization in Response to the Hypnotic Reversal of Attitudinal Affect," *Journal of Personality*, 28, 39-63.

"The Processing Of Negated Product Attributes: Evidence for a Two-step Correction Process"

Susan Jung, Prashant Malaviya and Brian Sternthal

In this paper we examine how consumers process negated product attribute information. For example, the attribute "not difficult to use" is a negated form of presenting the affirmative "easy to use". While on the surface both forms of presentation appear to convey the same information, research in semiotics suggests that affirmation and negation communicate distinct meanings (Pinson 1998). In psychology, research indicates that when people are offered possible gains versus non-losses, they invoke different goals (Higgins 1997), experience different affective reactions (Brendl, Higgins and Lemm 1995), differ in their recall and judgment (Tykocinski, Higgins and Chaiken 1994), and form different preferences and choices (Tversky and Kahneman 1981). These findings highlight that negated and affirmative presentation of information differ in how people process them and integrate them into judgment.

Although most advertising copy employs the affirmative form of presentation, advertisers sometimes present negated information about the brand. Negated attributes are included in so called "two-sided" advertising messages, when advertisers acknowledge some apparent product weakness, which of course is overshadowed by the positive features of the product that are the focus of the advertising message. Negated attributes are also included in some forms of comparative advertising. Finally, negated attributes are sometimes included in advertising copy to establish a departure from the past to communicate a point of difference (e.g., "not your father's Oldsmobile"). Thus, advertising messages often speak about something that the product will "not" deliver, presumably because the benefit from the product is obtained only when the particular attribute is absent. How do message recipients process negated product information and form judgments of the product?

Theorizing proposed by Gilbert (1991) seems appropriate for understanding how people process a negated message. According to this thesis, processing of negated information ("not difficult to use") follows a *two-step* process. Message recipients first encode the affirmation ("difficult") and then correct this initial encoding to incorporate the negation ("not"). In contrast, information that is presented with affirmation ("easy to use") would require only one step to process.

An implication of a two-step process is that under conditions of resource constraint, such as when there are distractions to message processing, elaboration of a negated ad message could breakdown at either of the two stages of processing. Under some conditions resources might be so limited that the threshold for processing even the affirmative portion of the information is not crossed and consequently, no aspect of the negated product attribute would be processed. In this situation, the negated product attribute should have no impact on the product's judgment.

In other conditions where more moderate levels of resources become available (e.g., fewer distractions are present during message processing), message recipients might be able to process the affirmative portion of the message, although the available resources might not be adequate for the next step of correcting for and incorporating the negation. Such processing would produce different judgment outcomes. Specifically, if the available resources are sufficient to process affirmation ("difficult") but not for correcting negation ("not"), judgments should be the opposite of what is implied by the message content.

Finally, in yet other conditions the available resources could be adequate to process the entire message, including the negation of the product attribute. In such conditions, which may arise under minimal distractions to message processing, the available resources might be sufficient for processing the affirmative information, as well as for correcting for negation. In these circumstances, product judgments should follow the implication of the message content ("not difficult to use").

The two-step model could be contrasted to a *one-step* model of processing negated information. Such a model would be based on the assumption that negation is processed simultaneously with affirmation, such that the part-phrase "not difficult" is processed together, rather than as two separate words or meanings (McKoon and Ratcliff 1989). This one-step model would also predict that negation requires more cognitive resources to process than affirmation, because compared to the phrase "easy to use", "not difficult to use" requires that we elaborate on more words and meanings.

Although both one-step and two-step models would predict that negation requires more resources to process than affirmation, depending on which model operates, different outcomes would be anticipated. A one-step model would be implicated if under conditions of minimal resource constraint the negated product attribute has an impact on product judgments, but under more severe constraints it does not have an effect. In contrast, a two-step model would predict that depending on the severity of resource constraint, three outcomes are possible: no effect of negated attribute, an effect that is opposite to the message content, or an effect that is consistent with the message claims.

We test these ideas in a study in which respondents were required to read an advertisement for toothpaste and later answer some questions related to the product. One attribute included in the ad was presented in a negated form ("not difficult to use dispenser"). All other attributes (ten in all) were kept constant across conditions. The focal dependent variable was product evaluation. Respondents were exposed to the target ad under conditions that varied in the extent of resource constraint for processing the information presented in the target advertisement. This was done so that predictions pertaining to the one- and two-factor account of the processing of negated information could be tested. These resource constraints were either naturally occurring individual differences ("need for cognition"), or were induced by experimental manipulations ("distraction" by misleading respondents about whether they would be asked to judge the target product or a competing brand; and "involvement" by asking respondents to assume either that they were evaluating the product to buy it for themselves or for someone else).

Consistent with Gilbert's theorizing, results of this study offer support for the notion that processing of negated information follows a two-step process. Specifically, product judgments revealed three effects. In some conditions, the negated attribute had no effect on judgments, suggesting that respondents did not elaborate on this information. This outcome was observed for respondents who indicated low need for cognition. In other conditions, product judgments were just the opposite of what the message content implied, suggesting that respondents had failed to incorporate the negation in the message. This outcome was observed for respondents classified as high in need for cognition, but who were distracted and did not have high motivation to elaborate on the message. Finally, in some conditions, product judgments followed the intent of the message, suggesting that respondents had successfully processed the negated attribute. This outcome was observed for respondents high in need for cognition, and who were either not distracted or had a high degree of motivation to process the message. This pattern of outcomes is consistent with the notion that negated product attributes are processed in two steps: elaboration of affirmation, followed by correction for negation.

REFERENCES

Brendl, C.M., E. T. Higgins, and K. M. Lemm (1995), "Sensitivity to Varying Gains and Losses: The Role of Self-Discrepancy and Event Framing," *Journal of Personality and Social Psychology*, 69(6), 1028-1051.

Gilbert, D. T. (1991), "How Mental Systems Believe," *American Psychologist*, 46(2), 107-119.

Higgins, E. T. (1997), "Beyond Pleasure and Pain," *American Psychologist*, 52(12), 1280-1300.

McKoon, G. and R. Ratcliff (1989), "Assessing the Occurrence of Elaborative Inferences with Recognition: Compatibility Checking versus Compound Cue Theory," *Journal of Memory and Language*, 28, 547-563.

Pinson, C. (1998), "Semiotics of Marketing," *Concise Encyclopedia of Pragmatics*, ed. J. L. Mey, London: Pergamon Press, 538-544.

Tversky, A. and Kahneman, D. (1981), "The Framing of Decisions and the Psychology of Choice," *Science*, 211, 453-458.

Tykocinski, O., E. T. Higgins and S. Chaiken (1994), "Message Framing, Self-Discrepancies, and Yielding to Persuasive Messages: The Motivational Significance of Psychological Situations," *Personality and Social Psychology Bulletin*, 20, 107-115.

Discussion Leader
C. Miguel Brendl, INSEAD

On the Use of Naive Theories of Bias to Remove or Avoid Bias: The Flexible Correction Model

Duane T. Wegener, Purdue University
Richard E. Petty, Ohio State University

ABSTRACT

In recent years, much attention in social psychology has focused on avoidance or removal of bias. The Flexible Correction Model (FCM; Wegener and Petty, 1997) conceptualizes such attempts as guided by individuals' naive theories of bias (i.e., individuals' beliefs and perceptions regarding the direction and magnitude of potential biases relevant to a given judgment). This paper introduces the core of the FCM, differentiates it from past models of bias correction, presents empirical support for theory-based correction, and addresses recent alternative explanations for FCM studies.

Over the years, a number of potential "biases" have been studied in consumer settings. For example, attributes of products have been assimilated to the qualities of previous information encountered prior to the ad (e.g., Yi, 1990), evaluations of products have been influenced by the emotional qualities of programs in which ads occur (e.g., Gardner, 1985; Petty, Schumann, Richman, and Strathman, 1993), and evaluations have also been influenced by perceptions of the ad itself aside from perceptions of product attributes (Brown and Stayman, 1992). Many of these "biases" occur with little or no awareness on the part of consumers. What happens, however, if people realize that one or more of these biasing factors might be influencing their perceptions of products? In many settings within and outside consumer behavior, people might go out of their way to avoid "bias." Sometimes this might occur because of external influences, as when people are explicitly warned not to use particular information (e.g., when judges instruct juries to disregard inadmissible evidence, see Fleming, Wegener, and Petty, 1999; Wegener, Kerr, Fleming, and Petty, in press). At other times, people might attempt to "correct" for bias without being asked to do so (e.g., because of a salient bias or personal concerns about bias, DeSteno, Petty, Wegener, and Rucker, 2000; Dunton and Fazio, 1997). In the current paper, we discuss the Flexible Correction Model (FCM; Wegener and Petty, 1997) as a general model of bias correction. The FCM relies on peoples' use of their own perceptions of the bias at work in a given judgment setting, and this role for theories of bias makes the resultant corrections more flexible than in previous theories.

THEORETICAL BACKDROP

When we began work on the FCM in 1991, few models of bias correction existed. The most well-developed of these models were in the priming and categorization literatures. Taken together, these models might be called "partialling" models. The first of these, the set-reset approach, was introduced by Martin (1986). Consistent with the traditional priming stimuli, Martin (1986) began by assuming that representations of a target might include both positive and negative elements. When a concept or reaction is primed (e.g., by unscrambling sentences containing the concept), there is some overlap between reactions to the prime and reactions to the target (called "setting"). "Setting" results in an "assimilation" bias in judgment with perceptions of the target being more similar to the primes than when no primes have been encountered. However, if social perceivers identify some of their reactions as being due to the primes rather than the target (e.g., when the priming procedure was

recent and blatant, Martin, 1986), they attempt to "partial out" the reactions to the primes (called "resetting"). "Resetting" reduces the number of prime-consistent reactions attributed to the target, which can reduce the assimilative bias or remove the assimilative bias. Also, if the social perceiver mistakenly identifies true reactions to the target (i.e., elements present in the initial target representation) as being reactions to the context (i.e., the primes), "resetting" can produce a contrast effect–with reactions to the target being less like the context than if no context had been encountered. For a schematic representation of "setting" and "resetting" and more thorough discussion, see Wegener and Petty (1997; cf., Martin, Seta, and Crelia, 1990).

Schwarz and Bless (1992) developed a similar model referred to as the "inclusion-exclusion" model. Like Martin's (1986) concept of "setting," "inclusion" of information in a target representation is expected to result in assimilation (with judgments of the target being more similar to the included information than when that information is not encountered). Also, like "resetting," "exclusion" (subtraction) of information from one's representation of the target is expected to lessen the impact of information that could have been "included" in the representation. Exclusion can lessen assimilation or even create contrast, assuming that the excluded information is sufficiently extreme to shift the reaction to the target. In addition, excluded information can create this contrast due to the exclusion itself (as in "resetting") or because the excluded information is used to define the scale anchor or to set up a standard of comparison (see Schwarz and Bless, 1992, for additional discussion).

These "partialling" theories have both been viewed as correction models by regarding the exclusion and resetting processes as correcting for the overlap between the representation of the target and the context experience or information. The models share a great deal, including the assumption that assimilation is the "default" bias, and that corrections lessen this assimilation and can even lead to contrast. Because both models equate partialling or subtraction with higher levels of cognitive effort, these models couple judgmental outcome (i.e., assimilation versus contrast) with levels of effortful processing. For example, Schwarz and Bless (1992) noted that "the emergence of contrast effects requires extra processing steps, and more effort, than the emergence of assimilation effects" (p. 240). That is, the set-reset and inclusion-exclusion models equate assimilation with "uncorrected" and lower effort default outcomes and contrast with more effortful "corrected" outcomes (see Wegener and Petty, 1997, for additional discussion).

A number of potential biases in consumer settings have been thought similar to this "overlap" view of bias, and efforts to avoid such bias have fit reasonably well with partialling models of bias correction. For example, Meyers-Levy and Sternthal (1993) reasoned that information about previous businesses occupying the same building as a current restaurant might influence perceptions of the current restaurant. Moreover, Meyers-Levy and Sternthal reasoned that information about a different class of business (i.e., a previous clothing store) would be viewed as information that should not be used in evaluating the current restaurant (i.e., that people might correct for effects of such information). Results were generally consistent with these notions and with a "partialling" view of the corrections. That is, when the previous business was a restaurant (and influences might be viewed as appropriate), assimilation to the valence of the previous restaurant was found. However, when the previous business was a clothing store (and influences might be viewed as inappropriate), contrast was found among research participants disposed toward putting high levels of effort into information processing. Assimilation was found for participants disposed toward cognitive simplification. More recently, Meyers-Levy and Tybout (1997) used blatant primes similar to Martin (1986)–brief positive or negative news stories–and argued that cognitive resources of the type studied by Martin et al. (1990) have separate effects at encoding of product information and at the time of product judgment.

Despite many reasonable predictions and effects that have come out of this approach, it seemed to us that there are significant limitations to the partialling views of correction when thinking about developing a general bias correction theory. For example, assimilation might not be the only type of "uncorrected" effect, even when contextual stimuli are capable of activating relevant concepts. For example, Herr (1986) found that extreme exemplars associated with hostility (e.g., Adolf Hitler) made an ambiguous target person seem less hostile (a contrast effect; see also Herr, Sherman, and Fazio, 1983; Wegener, Petty, and Dunn, 1998). As noted by Petty and Wegener (1993), such effects need not rely on "corrective" exclusion or resetting but could be "uncorrected" biases and could be based on comparisons with an extreme anchor or standard (see Moskowitz and Skurnik, 1999; Stapel, Koomen, and Velthuijsen, 1998). If contrast is a possible default or "uncorrected" bias, then the partialling models are ill-equipped to serve as general correction theories (because they only deal with corrections for assimilative biases– "setting" or "inclusion;" see Petty and Wegener, 1993; Wegener and Petty, 1997).

As a result, Wegener and Petty (1997; see also Petty and Wegener, 1993; Wegener and Petty, 1995; Wegener et al. 1998) developed the FCM as a more general model of bias correction. The FCM holds that corrections are aimed at removing (avoiding) the bias that social perceivers believe are associated with the factor(s) at hand. Consider, for example, a situation in which a person realizes that his or her views of a political candidate might be unduly influenced by a particular political advertisement. The direction of the perceived bias should influence corrections that are made. That is, if the perceiver believes that the bias is to make the candidate seem negative because the ad categorizes him or her with a disliked politician (e.g., a politician rocked by recent scandal), the perceiver would likely adjust assessments of the target to be more positive. If the perceiver believes that the bias is to make the politician seem better than usual, because he or she is clearly not as bad as the scandalized politician and might be contrasted with him or her, the perceiver would adjust assessments of the target politician to be more negative. The perceived magnitude of the bias should also matter. If the perceiver believes there is a small bias, he or she would adjust assessments of the true qualities of the target less than if he or she believes that there is a large bias.

THE FLEXIBLE CORRECTION MODEL

The first four postulates of the FCM have guided much of the initial work on the model, and those postulates can be summarized as follows (see Wegener and Petty, 1997, for more detail and discussion).

1. Across situations and perceivers, there is variation in uncorrected effects.
2. Efforts at correction depend on motivation and ability to A) identify potential biases and B) to correct for those biases.

3. Identification of bias and bias correction itself are guided by naive theories of bias held and/or generated by the social perceiver.

A few comments serve to differentiate the FCM from the previous "partialling" models. Whereas the partialling models deal with "default" assimilative biases, the FCM assumes that people and situations differ in the extent to which the uncorrected effect is assimilative, nonexistent, or contrastive. For example, some people might interpret information about a target using an accessible construct, but others might spontaneously compare the target with a well-known exemplar available in the same setting. One situation might provide a universally salient exemplar against which targets are contrasted, whereas the same situation absent that salient exemplar might dispose most social perceivers toward interpreting target information in a context-consistent way. Whatever the source(s) of variation might be, the FCM acknowledges this variability and separates it from the processes of correction. That is, a given correction might operate similarly even if instigated across differing magnitudes or directions of "uncorrected" bias (see later examples of empirical studies). This can be compared with the partialling model assumptions of default assimilation and amount of correction (and the size of the default bias) being proportional to the amount of overlap between reactions to the context and to the target.

Many factors could influence motivation or ability to engage in corrections. Some motivations are quite global, such as motivations to engage in thoughtful activities (e.g., need for cognition, Cacioppo and Petty, 1982). Others might relate more specifically to a particular bias, such as motivation to avoid "prejudiced" responses (e.g., Dunton and Fazio, 1997), and many such motivations could be enhanced or diminished by situations themselves (e.g., presence or absence of a television program that discusses racial bias in legal settings). From the FCM point of view, people could also identify a bias but be unmotivated to correct for it because the bias is viewed as legitimate or even necessary (Petty, Wegener, and Fleming, 1996; see Wegener and Petty, 1995, 1997).

When people identify potential bias and are motivated and able to engage in corrections, they attempt to adjust target assessments in a direction opposite to the perceived bias and in a magnitude commensurate with the perceived size of the bias. Therefore, corrections can go in different directions or in different amounts, depending on perceptions of the bias at work. Of course, this corrective attempt does not take place in a vacuum. That is, available information (in memory or in the judgment setting) might often be consulted in the process of correcting. Part of the theory-guided correction is likely to include seeking of information (in memory or the environment) that might support these "corrected" assessments. If no such supporting information can be found, this might be one factor that could undermine theory-based correction. Also, some efforts at correction might involve information seeking and scrutiny to a greater extent than other corrections (see Wegener and Petty, 1997).

We assume that corrective processes often ensue when people become aware of a potential bias (and are motivated and able to engage in corrections).[1] Therefore, corrections for bias need not

---

[1] This does not mean that perceivers must be able to consciously report correction processes they undertake, though people might often be able to report their perceptions of bias associated with a given context and target. Some studies that ask participants whether or not a context affected them face the ambiguity that a person might report a lack of a biasing effect because of corrections rather than because of a lack of perception of potential bias.

occur only after reacting to the target. People might also anticipate a bias and attempt to avoid it (see Wegener and Petty, 1997; Wilson, Houston, and Meyers, 1998). Before people have a great deal of experience with a given type of bias, corrections would likely depend on some level of conscious awareness of the potential bias. However, with more experience of the bias and related corrections, less conscious awareness might be sufficient for instigating the corrections (and the correction itself might become routinized; Wegener and Petty, 1997). Even if awareness of the bias is quite conscious, the whole of the correction process would not generally be consciously reportable (consistent with Nisbett and Wilson, 1977). For example, people might often be unable to report which theory(ies) were used, even if the content of the relevant theory(ies) is "explicit" (see Wegener and Petty, 1998).

INITIAL EVIDENCE

One clear comparison between the FCM and the previous partialling models concerns the FCM's assertion that people can make theory-based corrections for perceived contrastive bias (i.e., where the target is viewed as less similar to the context that when no context has been encountered). Obviously, a correction for contrast shifts judgments to be more like the context than when no correction occurs. Therefore, correction for contrast is in a direction opposite to the partialling of overlap between reactions to contextual stimuli and representations of targets. In a typical correction-for-contrast study, extreme exemplars are rated on some dimension, followed by ratings of more moderate targets either immediately or after an instruction not to let ratings of the contextual stimuli influence perceptions of the targets. Such instructions maximize the likelihood that correction will occur, but they do not specify whether people should be correcting in one direction or another. If corrections are guided by theories of bias (pretested prior to the study as being beliefs in contrast bias), then corrections should make assessments of targets more like assessments of the contextual stimuli. If, however, corrections consist of partialling for potential overlap between reactions to contexts and reactions to targets, then corrections should either leave target assessments unchanged (if no overlap is perceived) or should make target assessments less like the context (if overlap is perceived and removed).

Wegener et al. (1998) conducted one such study using stimuli similar to those used by Herr (1986). That is, Wegener et al. asked research participants to rate three violent people (e.g., Josef Stalin, Adolf Hitler, Saddam Hussein) or three non-violent people (e.g., Gandhi, the Pope, Jesus) and then to rate George Foreman and Arnold Schwarzenegger (either with or without a correction instruction). Both Foreman (an active boxer, but also an active product endorser at the time of the study) and Schwarzenegger (an actor in many violent movies, but also the spouse of Maria Shriver and a representative for the Presidential Physical Fitness program) were relatively ambiguous with respect to hostility. Therefore, it seemed that people might believe there is some overlap between the context and target people. However, pretests had shown that people believed the violent context (contemplating Stalin) would make the targets seem *less* violent than usual and that the nonviolent context (contemplating Jesus) would make the targets seem *more* violent than usual (i.e., perceived contrast).

Consistent with the Herr (1986) result noted earlier, participants rated the targets as less violent when they followed the violent rather than nonviolent context people (a contrast effect), so research participants happened to be directionally correct in their beliefs about bias. Presumably because they used these beliefs when asked to correct, however, the correction instruction led target ratings to become *more like* the context than when no correction instruction

was given (e.g., targets were viewed as more violent when providing corrected rather than uncorrected ratings after contemplating Hitler—consistent with adjustments for the perceived contrastive bias; see also Wegener and Petty, 1995; Stapel, Martin, and Schwarz, 1998). This correction was in a direction opposite to corrections that would have occurred if people correct by partialling out overlap between context and target.

In the Wegener et al. (1998) violence-rating experiment, opposite corrections (some more violent, some less violent) occurred when opposite theories (one suggesting too little perceived violence, the other suggesting too much perceived violence) were associated with two different contexts (see also Wegener et al., 1998, Study 1). Opposing corrections have also been associated with opposing theories about the impact of the same context on different targets (i.e., attractive models making average women appear less attractive, but making endorsed products appear more desirable, Wegener and Petty, 1995, Studies 2 and 3).[2] Different people can also hold opposing theories about the impact of the same context on the same targets (Wegener and Petty, 1995, Study 4). Moreover, people who perceive greater bias have been found to correct to a greater extent than people who perceive less bias (Wegener and Petty, 1995, Study 4), and corrections consistent with naive theories of bias have been found when only subtle instructions are used (Petty and Wegener, 1993) and when no correction instructions are present (DeSteno et al. 2000; Fleming et al. 1999).

In addition to evidence supporting theory-based correction, the importance of motivation and ability to identify bias has also gained support. For example, DeSteno et al. (2000) found people high in need for cognition assimilating judgments to experienced emotion when the bias was difficult to identify (e.g., because a separate-study paradigm was used and no manipulation checks on emotion occurred prior to target judgments), but found people high in need for cognition contrasting judgments to emotion when the bias was easy to identify (because an emotion manipulation check immediately preceded target judgments). Also, Stapel, Martin, and Schwarz (1998), used a more "conditional" correction instruction than in the original research (to correct only if a bias was detected) and found that participants were more likely to correct if the bias itself was blatant rather than subtle. Of course, this is entirely consistent with the FCM.[3] The extent to which the biasing factor is blatant versus subtle should influence ability to detect the bias. Also, different correction instructions could influence motivation to search for bias and could affect the thresholds used in identifying a reaction as being "biased."

---

[2]To the extent that theories of bias are generally beliefs in assimilative biases in the contexts where partialling models have been studied (e.g., see Petty and Wegener, 1993), the FCM is also capable of accounting for such corrections for perceived assimilation.

[3]Stapel, Martin, and Schwarz (1998) seemed to agree with the FCM that likelihood of identifying a bias moderated the likelihood of theory-based corrections (p. 805), but believed that corrections following blatant instructions were based on the uncorrected judgments themselves rather than associated theories of bias (p. 803; the "valence-switching" alternative discussed in the next section). This approach has difficulty accounting for existing FCM research (see next section), and theories of bias provide a more parsimonious explanation. Rather than referring to different processes depending on whether participants detect bias on their own or are directed to it, it seems quite possible that theory-based corrections took place in both cases.

RECENTLY GENERATED ALTERNATIVES TO THEORY-BASED CORRECTION

Over the years, a number of potential alternative explanations of correction studies have been generated (either in print or in less formal discussions).

Discounting or recomputation.

One such alternative likens correction to processes in which people are hypothesized to set aside an unwanted response, ignore the biasing factor, and provide an independent response based on alternative inputs. For example, Schwarz and Clore (1983) proposed that people can discount their mood as an input to life satisfaction judgments if attention is brought to a cause of that mood (e.g., the weather or an unusual experimental chamber).[4] In such circumstances, people are supposed to compute satisfaction judgments based on inputs other than current feelings (e.g., satisfaction with work, with one's spouse, etc.). Similar processes have been hypothesized for avoidance of category-based responses in impression formation, where people have been characterized as replacing the category-based reaction with piecemeal integration (attribute-by-attribute analysis) of individuating information about the target (e.g., Fiske and Neuberg, 1990). In most correction studies (and discounting or recomputation studies), the alternative inputs or individuating information would be the same across conditions because the information about the target is the same. Therefore, recomputation hypotheses would be for such processes to reduce or eliminate biases, not to reverse them. As we have seen in a number of correction studies, however, corrections often result in "overcorrections" wherein biases opposite to the suspected bias are created. For example, in one study (Petty, Wegener, and White, 1998), people who corrected for possible source effects on their judgments were more influenced by a dislikable than a likable source (see also DeSteno et al. 2000; Martin et al. 1990; Wegener and Petty, 1995; Wegener et al. 1998). Therefore, although discounting or recomputation might sometimes occur, this type of process does not seem to be a likely alternative explanation of many correction studies.

Valence-switching strategy.

Another alternative to theory-based corrections is that correction instructions (especially blatant instructions) make people provide a rating of a different valence from their initial reactions (Stapel, Martin, and Schwarz, 1998). Though not originally designed to address this explanation, a number of existing FCM studies are not very consistent with this alternative. In particular, a number of studies have found that respondents engage in different corrections consistent with differing theories of bias even when they give the same uncorrected ratings. For example, Wegener et al. (1998, Study 1) asked participants to rate the size of ambiguous animals after either a set of extremely large or moderately large animals (cf. Herr et al. 1983). Unexpectedly, there was no effect of context on people's uncorrected ratings of targets. However, pretests had shown that people believed that the two contexts would have opposite uncorrected effects (that the extremely large context would make people view the ambiguous targets as relatively small, but the moderately large context would make people view the ambiguous targets as relatively large). If the valence-switching alternative is correct, correction instructions would lead to similar

corrections for each context (because the uncorrected reactions were the same across conditions). In contrast, theory-based corrections should push ratings in opposite directions. The results showed opposite corrections, with target judgments significantly higher following the correction instruction when the context was extremely large rather than moderately large; see Wegener et al. 1998).

Theory-based responding.

Another existing study addresses not only the valence-switching alternative, but also confronts another possibility: theory-based responding. That is, one might wonder whether participants in the studies described earlier have initial reactions to targets and then correct those assessments. An alternative would be that theories themselves suggest an appropriate response and that initial reactions are cast aside (similar to a portion of the discounting alternative). Yet, if corrections occur for perceived rather than for actual bias (and we have seen corrections consistent with theories of bias even when no bias actually exists in uncorrected settings), it would seem possible that similar corrections could take place regardless of whether an initial bias exists or not. If people have these initial reactions, and these initial reactions constitute a starting point from which corrections occur, then the same corrections could result in different final judgments when initial reactions differ.

Petty, Wegener, and White (1998) conducted an FCM-based study that addresses this possibility. The study was initially predicated on the idea that the amount of effort given to a persuasion task can vary, regardless of whether or not corrections occur in that setting (see FCM Postulate 6, Wegener and Petty, 1997). That is, one way to conceptualize the persuasion domain is to partition the literature into situations in which bias is not salient (where traditional models such as the Elaboration Likelihood Model, Petty and Cacioppo, 1986, organize that work) and in which bias is salient (where models such as the FCM might be brought to bear; see Wegener and Petty, in press, for a discussion of this partitioning in the context of mood effects on judgment). This partitioning does not attempt to change current conceptualizations of persuasion (such as the ELM). Rather, it notes that issues of potential bias correction have largely been ignored in previous work on persuasion.

Half of the Petty et al. participants engaged in a replication of many past studies of attitude change. Participants encountered either a likeable or dislikeable communicator presenting a persuasive message under either low- or high-processing conditions (a combination of high relevance and low distraction in high-processing conditions and low relevance and high distraction in low-processing conditions). Results for these conditions replicated past findings, with greater impact of source likeability under low- rather than high- processing conditions (cf. Chaiken, 1980). When participants were asked not to let any nonmessage factors influence their perceptions of the proposed policy, however, people who encountered the message under low-processing conditions were no longer influenced by source likeability. However, the same corrections occurred for people who encountered the message under high-processing conditions (where no impact of source likeability had occurred in uncorrected settings). This created the opposite bias whereby people provided more favorable ratings of the policy when it was presented by the dislikeable rather than the likeable source. Such a result suggests that people "started" with initial reactions because the same size and direction of correction led to different final judgments for people who had different initial (uncorrected) reactions (based on high versus low processing effort). Therefore, this initial work suggests that people take their current reactions into account during the correction process, rather

---

[4]Interestingly, this discounting of mood was supposed to be most likely for negative rather than positive moods (but see Gorn, Goldberg, and Basu, 1993).

than simply providing responses that are directly called for by the theories themselves. This result also addresses the earlier valence-switching alternative because different corrections occurred for the different sources even though uncorrected reactions were the same across sources in high-processing conditions. Finally, the FCM approach and the Petty et al. (1998) results also suggest that social perceivers can exert a great deal of effort attempting to seek "correct" assessments of a target without necessarily also being concerned about avoiding bias. In other words, seeking "correctness" does not necessarily imply avoiding "bias."

Therefore, it seems that observed effects of correction instructions have been quite consistent with the theory-based corrections hypothesized by the FCM but have been somewhat at odds with past theories (i.e., the partialling approaches) and with recent alternatives.

CONCLUSIONS AND FUTURE DIRECTIONS

By conceptualizing corrections as driven by naive theories of bias, the FCM goes beyond past partialling views that were developed within the longstanding priming/construct accessibility tradition. One important way in which the FCM goes beyond these perspectives is by uncoupling judgment outcomes (i.e., assimilation versus contrast) from categories of judgment process (i.e., "corrected" versus "uncorrected;" "effortful" versus "noneffortful"). According to the FCM, assimilation or contrast can be relatively effortful or effortless and can be either "corrected" or "uncorrected" outcomes (Petty and Wegener, 1993; Wegener and Petty, 1995, 1997). These and other flexibilities inherent in the model open up a wide variety of potentially interesting and useful research directions (see also Wegener and Petty, 1997; Wegener et al., 1998).

Although this paper focuses on outlining the model and the existing support for it, there are substantial portions of the model that have not yet been thoroughly addressed. That is, the model postulates that use of a theory of bias in correction depends on accessibility of the theory, applicability of the theory, and utility of the theory in serving the perceiver's judgment goals. The model also specifies that there can be variation in cognitive effort involved in both uncorrected and corrected judgments. Finally, similar to some dual-process theories in social psychology, such as the Elaboration Likelihood Model (Petty & Cacioppo, 1986; Petty & Wegener, 1999), the FCM specifies that increases in effort and elaboration involved in correction increases the likelihood of that corrected perception persisting over time, resisting future attempts at change, and influencing future thoughts and behavior. That is, although correction is often an additional step beyond uncorrected assessments, the amount of effort in that correction can vary and so can the consequences of that correction (see Wegener and Petty, 1997; Wegener, Dunn, and Tokusato, in press, for additional discussion).[5] It is our hope that the FCM serves to spark interest in widely applicable models that accentuate commonalities in process across research domains. We believe that such models hold great promise for integrating work in social psychology, consumer behavior, and related domains, and we look forward to similar future developments and integration.

---

[5]Though corrections might generally require more effort than lack of corrections, this does not mean that "corrected" assessments should necessarily persist over time or resist changes more than "uncorrected" assessments (see Wegener, Dunn, and Tokusato, in press; see Petty and Wegener, 1998, for similar comments regarding comparison of changed and unchanged attitudes; see also Priester, Wegener, Fabrigar, and Petty, 1999).

REFERENCES

Brown, Steven P. and Douglas M. Stayman (1992), "Antecedents and Consequences of Attitude Toward the Ad: A Meta-analysis," *Journal of Consumer Research*, 19 (June), 34-51.

Cacioppo, John T. and Richard E. Petty (1982), "The need for cognition," *Journal of Personality and Social Psychology*, 42 (January), 116-131.

Chaiken, Shelly (1980), "Heuristic Versus Systematic Information Processing and the Use of Source Versus Message Cues in Persuasion," *Journal of Personality and Social Psychology*, 39 (November), 752-756.

DeSteno, David, Richard E. Petty, Duane T. Wegener, and Derek Rucker (2000), "Beyond Valence in the Perception of Likelihood: the Role of Emotion Specificity," *Journal of Personality and Social Psychology*, 78 (March), 397-416.

Dunton, Bridget C. and Russell H. Fazio (1997), "An Individual Difference Measure of Motivation to Control Prejudiced Reactions," *Personality and Social Psychology Bulletin*, 23 (March), 316-326.

Fiske, Susan T. and Steven L. Neuberg (1990), "A Continuum of Impression Formation, from Category-based to Individuating Processes: Influences of Information and Motivation on Attention and Interpretation," In *Advances in experimental social psychology*, Vol. 23, ed. Mark P. Zanna, New York: Academic Press, 1-74.

Fleming, Monique, Duane T. Wegener, and Richard E. Petty (1999), "Procedural and Legal Motivations to Correct for Perceived Judicial Biases," *Journal of Experimental Social Psychology*, 35 (March), 186-203.

Gardner, Meryl P. (1985), "Mood States and Consumer Behavior: A Critical Review," *Journal of Consumer Research*, 12 (December), 281-300.

Gorn, Gerald J., Marvin E. Goldberg, and Kunal Basu (1993), "Mood, Awareness, and Product Evaluation," *Journal of Consumer Psychology*, 2 (3), 237-256.

Herr, Paul M. (1986), "Consequences of Priming: Judgment and Behavior," *Journal of Personality and Social Psychology*, 51 (December), 1106-1115.

Herr, Paul M., Steven J. Sherman, and Russell H. Fazio (1983), "On the Consequences of Priming: Assimilation and Contrast Effects," *Journal of Experimental Social Psychology*, 19 (May), 323-340.

Martin, Leonard L. (1986), "Set/reset: Use and Disuse of Concepts in Impression Formation," *Journal of Personality and Social Psychology*, 51 (September), 493-504.

Martin, Leonard L., John J. Seta, and Richard A. Crelia (1990), "Assimilation and Contrast as a Function of People's Willingness and Ability to Expend Effort in Forming an Impression," *Journal of Personality and Social Psychology*, 59 (July), 27-37.

Moskowitz, Gordon B., and Ian W. Skurnik (1999), "Contrast Effects as Determined by the Type of Prime: Trait Versus Exemplar Primes Initiate Processing Strategies That Differ in How Accessible Constructs Are Used," *Journal of Personality and Social Psychology*, 76 (June), 911-927.

Meyers-Levy, Joan and Brian Sternthal (1993), "A Two-Factor Explanation of Assimilation and Contrast Effects," *Journal of Marketing Research*, 30 (August), 359-368.

Meyers-Levy, Joan and Alice M. Tybout (1997), "Context Effects at Encoding and Judgment in Consumption Settings: The Role of Cognitive Resources," *Journal of Consumer Research*, 24 (June), 1-14.

Nisbett, Richard E., and Timothy D. Wilson (1977), "Telling More than We Can Know: Verbal Reports on Mental Processes," *Psychological Review*, 84 (March), 231-259.

Petty, Richard E., and John T. Cacioppo (1986), *Communication and Persuasion: Central and Peripheral Routes to Attitude Change*, New York: Springer-Verlag.

Petty, Richard E., David Schumann, Steven Richman, and Alan Strathman (1993), "Positive Mood and Persuasion: Different Roles for Affect under High and Low Elaboration Conditions," *Journal of Personality and Social Psychology*, 64 (January), 5-20.

Petty, Richard E., and Duane T. Wegener (1993), "Flexible Correction Processes in Social Judgment: Correcting for Context-induced Contrast," *Journal of Experimental Social Psychology*, 29 (March), 137-165.

Petty, Richard E., and Duane T. Wegener (1998), "Attitude Change: Multiple Roles for Persuasion Variables," in *the Handbook of Social Psychology (4th ed.)*, Vol. 1, ed. Daniel Gilbert et al., New York: McGraw-Hill, 323-390.

Petty, Richard E., and Duane T. Wegener (1999), "The Elaboration Likelihood Model: Current Status and Controversies," in *Dual Process Theories in Social Psychology*, eds. Shelly Chaiken and Yaacov Trope, New York: Guilford Press, 41-72.

Petty, Richard E., Duane T. Wegener, and Monique A. Fleming (1996), "Flexible Correction Processes: Perceived Legitimacy of Bias and Bias Correction," Sturbridge, MA: *Society for Experimental Social Psychology* annual meeting (October).

Petty, Richard E., Duane T. Wegener, and Paul White (1998), "Flexible Correction Processes in Social Judgment: Implications for Persuasion," *Social Cognition*, 16 (Spring), 93- 113.

Priester, Joseph R., Richard E. Petty, Duane T. Wegener, and Leandre R. Fabrigar (1999), "Examining the Psychological Processes Underlying the Sleeper Effect: the Elaboration Likelihood Model Explanation," *Media Psychology*, 1 (1), 27-48.

Schwarz, Norbert and Herbert Bless (1992), "Constructing Reality and its Alternatives: an Inclusion/exclusion Model of Assimilation and Contrast Effects in Social Judgment," in *The Construction of Social Judgments*, eds. Leonard L. Martin and Abraham Tesser, Hillsdale, NJ: Erlbaum, 217-245.

Schwarz, Norbert and Gerald L. Clore (1983), "Mood, Misattribution, and Judgments of Well-being: Informative and Directive Functions of Affective States," *Journal of Personality and Social Psychology*, 45 (September), 513-523.

Stapel, Diederik A., Willem Koomen, and Aart S. Velthuijsen (1998), "Assimilation or Contrast?: Comparison Relevance, Distinctness, and the Impact of the Accessible Information on Consumer Judgments," *Journal of Consumer Psychology,* 7 (1), 1-24.

Stapel, Diederik A., Leonard L. Martin, and Norbert Schwarz (1998), "The Smell of Bias: What Instigates Correction Processes in Social Judgments?," *Personality and Social Psychology Bulletin*, 24 (August), 797-806.

Wegener, Duane T., Meghan Dunn, and Danny Tokusato (in press), "The Flexible Correction Model: Phenomenology and the Use of Naive Theories in Avoiding or Removing Bias," in *Cognitive Social Psychology: On the Tenure and Future of Social Cognition*, ed. Gordon B. Moskowitz, Mahwah, NJ: Erlbaum.

Wegener, Duane T., Norbert Kerr, Monique A. Fleming, and Richard E. Petty (in press), "Flexible Corrections of Juror Judgments: Implications for Jury Instructions," *Psychology, Public Policy, and Law*.

Wegener, Duane T., and Richard E. Petty (1995), "Flexible Correction Processes in Social Judgment: the Role of Naive Theories in Corrections for Perceived Bias," *Journal of Personality and Social Psychology*, 68 (January), 36-51.

Wegener, Duane T., and Richard E. Petty (1997), "The Flexible Correction Model: the Role of Naive Theories of Bias in Bias Correction," in *Advances in Experimental Social Psychology*, Vol. 29, ed. Mark P. Zanna, Mahwah, NJ: Erlbaum, 141-208.

Wegener, Duane T., and Richard E. Petty (1998), "The Naive Scientist Revisited: Naive Theories and Social Judgment," *Social Cognition*, 16 (Spring), 1-7.

Wegener, Duane T., and Richard E. Petty (in press), "Understanding Effects of Mood Through the Elaboration Likelihood and Flexible Correction Models," in *Theories of Mood and Cognition: A User's Handbook*, eds. Leonard Martin and Gerald Clore, Mahwah, NJ: Erlbaum.

Wegener, Duane T., Richard E. Petty, and Meghan Dunn (1998), "The Metacognition of Bias Correction: Naive Theories of Bias and the Flexible Correction Model," in *Metacognition: Cognitive and Social Dimensions*, ed. Vincent Yzerbyt et al., London: Sage, 202-227.

Wilson, Timothy D., Christopher E. Houston, and Jonathan M. Meyers (1998), "Choose Your Poison: Effects of Lay Beliefs about Mental Processes on Attitude Change," *Social Cognition*, 16 (Spring), 114-132.

Yi, Youjae (1990), "The Effects of Contextual Priming in Print Advertisements," *Journal of Consumer Research*, 17 (September), 215-222.

Rituals Three Gifts and Why Consumer Researchers Should Care
Eric J. Arnould, University of Nebraska

SESSION OVERVIEW

"If we set out to catalog all the functions that rituals serve, taking into account every sort of culture and all variety of social circumstances, we should no doubt find that the tasks of ritual are numberless. I shall not, therefore, attempt a catalog of functions but instead propose that there are three major gifts that rituals bestow upon society....I shall call them order, community, and transformation" (Driver 1998, 132). Following Driver, the three presentations in this session set out to focus on the three gifts that ritual provides to society and to underscore why marketers should care about ritual. While the idea of consumer ritual was introduced into the consumer research paradigm over 15 years ago (Rook 1985), the topic has languished. Only limited and disconnected empirical studies have been reported (e.g., Escalas 1993; Holt 1992; Stamps and Arnould 1998; Wallendorf and Arnould 1991). It may be that this relative neglect is traceable to the failure of researchers to show the relevance of consumer ritual to marketers. This session will correct this problem.

As Driver and indeed other specialists in ritual studies have argued (Grimes 1996), ritual delivers three gifts to society, community, order and transformation. To achieve these effects, ritual always manipulates objects and symbols. The objects and symbols that people manipulate allow them to give form to ritual experience and to associate an emergent shared emotion (what anthropologists term "liminality"), with these experiences (Douglas 1971). Subsequently, this shared emotion develops motivational force that may shape purchase and consumption decisions and behaviors. In taking ritual action, people in Western consumer societies naturally have recourse to consumer goods, the ready-to-hand material of consumer culture. Rituals play a role germane to the one Douglas and Isherwood (1979) ascribed to goods in their ability to stabilize culture categories. However, goods, especially mass-marketed consumer goods do not provide a simple catalogue of cultural categories. Performances, especially ritual performances are required to activate object meanings pertinent to social life. Marketers typically use marketing communications to initiate this effect. Consumers develop their own rituals. But without ritual, the categories are at best merely potential, the objects inert.

Each paper presented in this session emphasizes one of the three ritual gifts to society detailing the creative interplay between consumer agency, culture, and market driven signs and objects.

"Inheritance Ritual and the Creation of Order"
Eric Arnould and Linda Price, University of Nebraska

In the service of the theme of the role of ritual in creating order, this presentation makes a few points about ritual in American families. In particular we draw attention to the longing for ritual, the behavioral latitude that ritual can absorb, and the characteristic bricolage through which people compose ritualized activity. Finally, we identify an emergent social structure for ritual action that is disparate from the usual groups examined in ritual studies.

Order is perhaps the most obvious of ritual's functions, and for many persons the entire value of ritual activity is that it brings order and solace. Order is bestowed not only as a sense of organization, form or regularity, but also as an imperative or directive (Rappaport 1979). Order viewed as an imperative or directive is described in our discussion of ritual longings.

Individuals evince a longing for ritual that enables them to link their own lived experience to imagined communities past and future and which will anchor their behavior in cultural continuities. Participation in ritualized preparation of home-made foods, many of which are inherited traditions is one mechanism people use to do this. For others, ritualized activities—behaviors and story-telling—emerge around objects inherited from departed loved ones. For many persons the value of ritual activity is that by anchoring behavior in cultural continuity, it brings order and solace. Through ritual, order is bestowed as an imperative (Rappaport 1979).

We show that consumers' ritual longings are not amorphous. They are translated into a modest number of motives and actions that enlist tradition while providing scope for personal agency. We present evidence that our informants' strategies of ritualization serve them pretty well. These small rituals certainly persist. Small rituals are a means of preserving and producing decommodified material culture and meanings. Through inheritance rituals consumers create, reinforce, and negotiate order in household relationships, and assert the little traditions of the household and family. Ritualization enables people to solidify cultural categories for action and interpretation, and thereby create temporary orders of facticity.

Classic accounts of American kinship are virtually silent on the subject of ritual actions related to inheritance. Our research identifies cherished possessions that carry meanings particular to individual family groups. Through inheritance rituals, our informants speak and act in a subjunctive mode, that is, in ways that privilege a future molded in tradition. Our data shows how rituals that collect around particular cherished possessions constitute meaningful, elective descent groups for particular families. Their behavior suggests that they believe that traditions, including those constructed today, can endure indefinitely. We suggest that marketers may find fruitful opportunities in providing goods and services that enable consumers to construct effective inheritance rituals.

"The Ritual Creation of Consumption Communities"
Cara Okleshen, University of Georgia and Sanford Grossbart, University of Nebraska

This paper emphasizes a second social gift of ritual—community. Rituals are bearers of communitas, which is a spirit of unity and mutual belonging. Rituals are informed both by a greater than usual sense of order and by a heightened sense of freedom and possibility that releases feelings of love and participation (Driver 1998, p. 164). The context for the second paper is the Winnebago-Itasca Travelers group, the nation's largest marketer managed customer community. The authors show not only how ritual activity unites people emotionally but also the significance of community to strategic marketer outcomes. While the first paper draws on depth interviews across a number of studies, this paper uses quantitative and qualitative methodologies to link communitas, ritual activity and marketing outcomes.

The study creates a framework for understanding the character and effects of brand-focused customer communities in terms of participation at ritualized group events, the community sentiments such events evoke and the interconnectedness of community micro-structure they help to create. Customer communities form around shared experiences and values including lifestyle related events and

Advances in Consumer Research
Volume 28, © 2001

activities. This study focuses on the customer community associated with the Winnebago-Itasca Travelers group, the largest (over 17,000 members) marketer supported brand community in the US. Sharing of meals, stories, tours, and the repetition of participation in the brandfest (Schouten and McAlexander 1998), in this case the Winnebago-Itasca Travelers annual rally, builds a liminal community. Participation in this liminal community is characterized by a sense of interdependence, density, and "localness." The emergent WIT community is built from an interconnected structure of relationships & sentiments. One important emotion that emerges from customer participation in brandfests is communitas, a short-lived but transcendent emotional sense of oneness with others. The experience of communitas in the context of the brandfest also leads to more enduring affective relationships including a sense of belonging and shared identity, consciousness of kind, and group member attachment.

The authors emphasize the playful and imaginative interplay between communitas, social structure, and ritual activity (Turner 1969). And they emphasize that the effects of ritual may not be uniform across participants.

Participation in ritualized group events is also positively related to a relationship with the brand. And this relationship with the brand is positively linked to repurchase, positive word-of-mouth and willingness to pay more for the brand.

"Rituals of Giving, Destruction and Decoration: Transformational Consumption at Burning Man"
Robert V. Kozinets, Northwestern University

This presentation focuses on the transformational power of consumption rituals as discovered through a consumer ethnography of the Burning Man project in 1999 (and 2000). The Burning Man project is a utopian celebration and art festival held for one week every year in Nevada's barren Black Rock Desert. The event attracted over twenty-three thousand people in 1999. For its one week, Burning Man becomes a place where consumption of incredible diversity and intensity is celebrated. Along with the most official "rules" that this anarchic organization can marshal, the performance of ritualized acts are key elements used by Burning Man participants to psychically distance consumption at the festival from the everyday and to re-enchant it into a transformational experience. This presentation will focus on three types of transformational consumption ritual used at Burning Man –gift-giving, burning, and body decoration– and will utilize an anthropological lens to examine each of them.

The first transformational consumption ritual is used to decouple everyday consumption from the capitalist economy in which (for the mainly American group of participants at the event) it is normatively situated. Capitalism is suspended as monetary exchange is forbidden by the "no vending" rule; the economy becomes based primarily on gifts (and to a lesser extent barter). At Burning Man 1999, a variety of gifts were ritually given away, including ice cream bars, water, admission to rave and other dance clubs, free food, sunscreen, massages and alcohol. Burning Man's gifting society resembles one of continuous potlatch, an informed altruism (common in nomadic and desert societies) where each person gives to one another. Potlatch is a Chinook word meaning "a gift." The terms refer to a category of ceremonial events during which culture members enhance their rank through the provision of elaborate feasts and gifts. Some people would give away to such a great extent (their homes, spouse and land) that they were left utterly poor. Others would destroy goods (often through burning), in order to seek to outdo a rival. In Rosman and Rubel's (1971) thorough examination of the potlatch phenomenon, they describe

them as transformative occasions, as *rites de passages* (see Van Gennep [1909] 1960) in the life of individuals and, more importantly, in the progression of the social structure. Occurring at "critical junctures" of social structural succession, such as funerals, or change of rank or status (e.g., marriage), potlatches "serve to reaffirm the new arrangement of the [social] structure" (Rossman and Rubel, 1971, p. 203).

Distinct from the traditional potlatch ceremony, Burning Man's ritual gift-giving is a communal norm and not an act performed by wealthy individuals seeking social status or collective favor. While the competitive extremes are not as obvious, the practice of ritual destruction and the notion of change and rites of passage seem to accord well with the ethos of Burning Man. Seeking social change, rather than stability, the Burning Man event encourages its participants to adopt a new social attitude in which learning to gift-giving becomes the norm. In the new social order of Burning Man, old status standings are replaced by conspicuous acts of giving, and destruction (which are gifts to the community of a fiery spectacle).

Burning Man's "No Spectators" rule seeks to foster a participative culture of grass roots entertainment and outlandish "theme camps" such as the quasi-parodic religious camps "Papal Indulgence," "The Temple of Atonement," "Transcendental Realm" and "the Sacred Disorder of the Enigmata." In line with the atonement themes of these religion quasi-parodies, there is a vast variety of burning rituals aimed at ritual purification. These rituals reach their culmination at the end of the weeklong event when the forty-five foot tall neon-and-wood effigy of "the Man," located at the center of the vast campground, is set ablaze to wild cheering, dancing and general celebration. Afterwards, many other works of art are also burned by festival participants. The burning of the Man is intended as a purgative cleansing ritual with strong Judeo-Christian overtones, in which people psychically heap influences that they wish to remove from their lives (for instance, encumbrances, habits, past relationships, sins, compulsions) onto the figure of the Man. This transference of negative forces is also performed in a variety of other rituals, such as ritual burnings, ecstatic dance, acting or exhibition and confession.

Finally, through costuming, exhibitionism and body decoration, many participants express the Burning Man rule "Give of Yourself." The intense freedom and live-and-let-live ethos of the event sponsor an environment in which nudity, body decoration, and costuming lend the event a carnivalesque, Mardi-Gras-in-the-desert feel. However, nudity and body decoration (body painting and covering with glitter were two popular forms of this at Burning Man 1999) can also be seen as a form of gift-giving, in which knowledge of a normally very intimate possession (one's naked body) is openly bestowed upon community members. This openness and gift-giving is further reinforced by the willingness of most participants to pose for pictures (some of these pictures end up as gifts to the entire world posted on public web-sites). A form of sexual transgression appears to be at play here, as the natural, sexual body is revealed for the enjoyment and admiration of self and others. Body decoration and costuming are transformational rituals that enact a distinct change in appearance, allowing participants to transcend their everyday appearance and identity. Animal appearances are "tried on," as people draw tiger, zebra and other types of stripes and spots on their bodies and genitals. Gender reversals are frequent, particularly among men who wear female garb and wrap feather boas around their necks. Another very common form of body decoration is "tribal" (pre-Western) in appearance, with the nude body being painted a dark color such as green, black or blue, or being caked in mud. Each of these consumption rituals uniquely combines the thing consumed with the self, combining thing/other and body into an extraordinary consumption experience. They also contribute strongly to the sense of extraordinary, magical place –a sense of liminality in which boundaries can be breached and desired self-transformations can occur (Turner 1967).

In summary, participants employ consumption rituals of gift-giving, burning, and decoration in order to distance Burning Man-related consumption from everyday consumption. These actions sacralize Burning Man as a liminal location in which the magical, mystical spells of transformation can be successfully cast. Through consumption rituals, participants seek to open "primitive" doors in their own, and other's psyches, allowing ancient and meaningful senses and feelings to emerge (see Torgovnick 1997). In a liminal space, they work and play with their identities. Hastened by the burning, cleansed by the fire, joined by the gift, ritually exposed, they consume community and consume themselves.

REFERENCES

Douglas, Mary (1971), *Purity and Danger*, New York: Praeger.

Douglas, Mary and Baron Isherwood (1979), *The World of Goods*, New York: W. W. Norton.

Driver, Tom F. (1998), *Liberating Rites*, Boulder, CO: Westview Press.

Escalas, Jennifer (1993), "The Consumption of Insignificant Rituals: A Look at Debutante Balls," *Advances in Consumer Research*, Vol. 20, Leigh McAlister and Michael L. Rothschild, eds., Provo, UT: Association for Consumer Research, 709-716.

Grimes, Ronald L., ed., (1996) *Readings in Ritual Studies*, Upper Saddle River, NJ: Prentice Hall.

Holt, Douglas B. (1992), "Examining the Descriptive Value of 'Ritual' in Consumer Behavior: A View from the Field," *Advances in Consumer Research*, vol. 19, John F. Sherry, Jr. and Brian Sternthal, eds., Provo, UT: Association for Consumer Research, 213-218.

Rappaport, Roy A. (1979), *Ecology, Meaning, and Religion*, Berkeley, CA: North Atlantic Books.

Rook, Dennis (1985), "The Ritual Dimension of Consumer Behavior," *Journal of Consumer Research*, 13 (December), 251-264.

Rosman, Abraham and Paula G. Rubel (1971), Feasting with Mine Enemy: Rank and Exchange Among Northwest Coast Societies, Prospect Heights, IL: Waveland.

Schouten, John (1991), "Selves in Transition: Symbolic Consumption in Personal Rites of Passage and Identity Reconstruction," *Journal of Consumer Research*, 17 (March), 412-425.

Schouten, John and James McAlexander (1995), "Subcultures of Consumption: An Ethnography of the New Bikers," *Journal of Consumer Research*, 22 (June), 43-61.

Stamps, Miriam B. and Eric J. Arnould (1998), "The Florida Classic: Performing African American Community," *Advances in Consumer Research*, Vol. 25, Joseph W. Alba and Wesley Hutchinson, eds., Provo, UT: Association for Consumer Research,

Torgovnick, Marianna (1997), Primitive Passions: Men, Women, and the Quest for Ecstasy, New York: Knopf.

Turner, Victor (1967), *The Forest of Symbols: Aspects of Ndembu Ritual*, Ithaca and London: Cornell University.

_____ (1969), *The Ritual Process: Structure and Anti-Structure*, Baltimore, MD: Penguin Books.

Van Gennep, Arnold ([1909] 1960), *The Rites of Passage*, Chicago: University of Chicago.

Wallendorf, Melanie and Eric J. Arnould (1991), "'We Gather Together': The Consumption Rituals of Thanksgiving Day," *Journal of Consumer Research*, 18 (June), 13-31.

Interactions Between Positive and Negative Affect in Consumer Behavior: How Consumers Respond to Mixed Emotional Experiences

Patti Williams, Wharton
Loraine Lau, UCLA

Individuals are often faced with multiple and conflicting emotions that arise during their consumer-related experiences. However, existing consumer and psychological research has focused mostly on single discrete emotions or single valenced experiences, and more specifically, how they impact consumer satisfaction (e.g., Westbrook and Oliver 1991), advertising response (e.g., Batra and Ray 1987; Edell and Burke 1987, 1989; Stuart, Shimp and Engel 1987), attitude formation and change (e.g., Cacciopo and Petty 1989), memory (e.g., Bower 1981; Isen 1987), decision making and other behaviors such as compulsion, impulsive, complaining, risk-seeking, and variety-seeking (e.g., Luce 1998; Rook 1987; Nyer 1996; Raj and Pham 1999; Kahn and Isen 1993). Surprisingly little theoretical work has been done to advance our knowledge about the practical complexity of most emotional experiences and the effects this complexity has on consumer behavior. Indeed there is a need for theoretical models that outline how consumers process, maintain, and integrate competing emotional experiences, and this session aimed to shed some initial light onto this important yet largely neglected area of research. While the three papers presented in this session were all concerned with understanding consumer responses to their conflicted experiences, each paper explored not only a unique set of questions but also different kinds of mixed emotional experiences.

Lau examined consumers' overall retrospective evaluations of four unique sequences or patterns of mixed emotional experiences, all of which contained positive, negative and neutral affective outcomes. Results from three experiments suggest that when consumers view the sources of these affect outcomes as similar, overall retrospective evaluations should be influenced by the pattern characteristics, Final Trend, which reflects either improvement or decline, and End, which reflects the magnitude of the affective outcome occurring last. In contrast, when the sources of affect outcomes are viewed as dissimilar, then overall retrospective evaluations are influenced by how close in proximity the positive and negative affective outcomes arise. Specifically, when experiential patterns reflect positive and negative outcomes arise closely together, favorable overall retrospective evaluations tend to result. Research in hedonic psychology and that in renewable resources were used as bases to support these two sets of findings. Finally, thought protocols suggest that overall retrospective evaluations may be driven by the degree to which individuals elaborate on the positive versus negative aspects of the mixed affective experience.

In contrast to Lau's focus on sequential mixed emotional experiences, Williams' emphasis was on simultaneous mixed emotions. Specifically, she examined differences in the propensity to experience mixed emotions and evaluations of mixed emotional stimuli, based upon individual differences in tolerance for duality. The results of four experiments show that individuals with a low propensity to accept duality (e.g., Anglo-American individuals, younger individuals) have less favorable attitudes toward mixed emotional appeals relative to those with a higher propensity to accept duality (e.g., Asian-American individuals, older individuals). Across all experiments, the relationship between the stimuli and the attitude is mediated by heightened feelings of discomfort. The process that underlies these persuasion effects was discussed, and limiting conditions of the basic finding were identified.

Finally, a surprise to us all (J), Ariely presented his work with Wertenboch on procrastination. A set of studies investigated how sophisticated people are in dealing with their own procrastination behavior in effortful tasks in which the cost of procrastination is performance deterioration. Findings indicate that people are willing to self-impose meaningful (i.e., costly) deadlines to overcome procrastination, these self-imposed deadlines work as an effective mechanism in improving task performance, and finally, self-imposed deadlines are not as effective as some externally imposed deadlines in improving task performance. That is, people are sophisticated enough to recognize their own tendencies to procrastinate, but if left to their own devices they solve this self-control problem only partially.

Aimee Drolet provided a synthesis of the three papers and highlighted their distinct contributions, as well as the contribution of the session as a whole, in the light of additional work in psychology and consumer behavior that focuses on mixed emotional experiences. Specifically, the work presented focuses on the complex nature of consumer's emotional experiences and suggests that individuals frequently try to cope with and balance such duality of emotional experience, though they are not always successful in doing so. In addition, the research presented suggests that consumers can adopt more cognitive, rational methods for dealing with emotional conflict (Lau, Ariely) as well as more emotional ones (Williams).

Creating Effective Name Translations for Global Brands

Shi Zhang, University of California, Los Angeles
Bernd Schmitt, Columbia University

ABSTRACT

Past research on brand naming has focused almost exclusively on English name creation and has made little progress toward a conceptual understanding of brand name translations. We develop a framework for the creation of local names for global brands. Using Chinese as the local language to translate U.S. brands either phonetically (i.e., by sound) or phono-semantically (i.e., by sound plus meaning association), in two experiments we show that consumer evaluation of phonetic vs. phono-semantic names requires an analysis of the processing and mental representation of language and writing systems as well as a consideration of contextual factors.

Contextual Communication Styles and their Effect on Visual Imagery in Print Advertising:
A Cross-Cultural Study

Michael A. Callow, Morgan State University
Leon G. Schiffman, Baruch College

ABSTRACT

Although visual images are becoming increasingly popular in global advertising, very little is known about the effect that cultural differences have on processing these types of messages. This paper examines the roles of cultural context and visual complexity in the interpretation and evaluation of standardized visual print advertisements among consumers from America, Spain, and the Philippines. The results of our study suggest that consumers from high-context cultures tend to interpret images at a greater symbolic level than consumers from low-context cultures. Additionally, complex visual images were viewed as more affective and simple images were seen as more informative, regardless of context.

Advances in Consumer Research
Volume 28, © 2001

Examining the Deleterious Effects of Advertising Repetition in a Competitive Environment

Sharmistha Law, University of Toronto at Scarborough

ABSTRACT

The most ubiquitous practice in advertising is repetition. The goal is to create memory and help readers learn about the product. Are there circumstances where repetition has unwanted effects? Two studies reported here examined the unwanted effects of advertising repetition when similar claims are simultaneously repeated by different brands. Study 1 showed that increased repetition in a competitive environment leads to substantial increases in both accurate brand-claim associations as well as false brand-claim endorsements. These repetition induced advantages and disadvantages was found to persist over time. Study 2 found that encoding instructions that initiate the binding of claims with a brand name mitigates this deleterious effect of ad repetition. This research indicates that negative consequences of repetition warrant further attention.

Lattice Analysis: An Approach for Studying the Dual Containment Structures of Consumption Phenomena

Stephen Brownstein, Arizona State University
James Ward, Arizona State University
Peter Reingen, Arizona State University
Ajay Sirsi, York University

ABSTRACT

Consumer researchers have had a long fascination with the complex interrelations of the forces producing consumption behavior, but have struggled with a limited set of graph analytic tools for visualizing the interrelations of different types of phenomena (e.g., social relations, beliefs, consumption preferences). The purpose of this paper is to introduce lattice analysis as a method for revealing and visualizing the dual containment structures of unlike and complexly ordered phenomena.

Consider a set of individuals who are members of a group involved in a subcultural belief system that motivates them to consume (or avoid consuming) a set of products. At least three sets– the sets of people, beliefs, and products–interact in creating behavior. For example, expertise in the belief system is likely to vary. Cultural participants who are more deeply embedded in the belief system are likely to behave differently and have different cultural roles than those less embedded. Furthermore, the belief system is likely to vary in its relevance to products. The intersection of beliefs and chains of beliefs with products is likely to influence their categorization, meaning, and consumption. Thus, the structures of people, beliefs, and products are embedded intricately in one another. Understanding how the orders of people, beliefs, and products relate to one another in a way that at once captures the intimate idiographic detail of single linkages between a particular person, belief, and/or product, and at the same time reveals the overall gestalt of linkages across sets seems crucial for a deeper understanding of consumption behavior.

In this paper we employ lattice analysis as a method for revealing and visualizing such linkages. Lattice analysis applies rigorously developed mathematical theorems to construct graphs that reveal the dual ordering of two-mode binary data. Dual mode binary data are represented in a table where the rows and columns represent different phenomena (e.g., actors in the rows and beliefs in the column) rather than the same phenomena (e.g., actors by actors in social network analysis or beliefs by beliefs in cognitive network analysis). Lattices summarize complex dual orderings in a single easily grasped picture that is capable of revealing overall patterns in a data set that might otherwise not be discerned.

The ability of lattice analysis to reveal the dual ordering of different types of phenomena and the relevance of these dual orders for understanding consumer motivation is illustrated using data from a study of animal rights activists. Beginning with data on the participants' food avoidances, their beliefs about these food avoidances, and their social relations we examine three types of lattices: participants-by-beliefs lattices, beliefs-by-foods avoidance lattices, and participants-by-cliques membership lattices.

These three types of lattices each summarized the complex relations between two different orders of phenomena into a single diagram that revealed interrelations that might have otherwise been difficult to discern. The lattice diagrams of beliefs by participants for honey and beef provided, at a single glance, pictures of the distribution of motivating beliefs across participants, their implicational structure, and the cognitive containment structure relating the individuals. These diagrams produced immediate insight into which beliefs were more structurally central in the subculture for motivating product avoidance, and which individuals were likely to supply the cognitive motives for avoidance to others through their deep embedding in the belief system. The participants-by-cliques lattice provided additional insight into how these expert participants bound together the many cliques within the group through their embeddedness in the social structure, and, thus, how they were in positions of both cognitive and social dominance. Finally, the food avoidances-by-beliefs lattices provided insight into the degree to which foods were central to or perhaps good exemplars of the belief system, prompting speculation about the role of ideologies in categorization processes.

The paper concludes by noting that lattice analysis may be productive of insight in any circumstance where the consumer researcher is interested in the patterning of the interrelations of two phenomena.

Advances in Consumer Research
Volume 28, © 2001

Involved with What? The Impact of Heterogeneity in Goal Hierarchies on High Enduring Involvement

Glenn L. Christensen, The Pennsylvania State University
Jerry C. Olson, The Pennsylvania State University

ABSTRACT

We view goal hierarchies as the foundational structure supporting and focusing a consumer's product involvement. As the underlying consumption goals change, the locus of their perceptions of personal relevance change as well. To demonstrate the feasibility of this view, we selected a group of highly-involved mountain bikers and assessed their goal hierarchies with regard to the sport. We found that over time and with greater experience, consumers' goals change and this in turn changes the focus of their involvement with the product.

Ad Cognitions in Television Ad Processing: The Expectation-Motivation-Matching Model (E3M)

Mark Peterson, University of Texas at Arlington
Naresh Malhotra, Georgia Tech

ABSTRACT

In the Expectation-Motivation-Matching Model (E3M), the authors propose a conceptualization of ad processing including antecedents of ad cognitions–1) product interest, and 2) schemas for ads of a product category. Such schemas include expectations for ad themes to be used, and expectations for feelings to be experienced during television ad viewing. The E3M also includes a richer operationalization of ad cognitions using the constructs of 1) motivations and 2) the matching of the ad with viewer expectations for television ads of the product category. The E3M receives empirical support through large-scale ad pre-testing and structural equation modeling.

Advances in Consumer Research
Volume 28, © 2001

Consumer Perceptions of Product Parity in E-Commerce Markets: The Effect of Search Set Size on Parity Judgments and Choice Satisfaction

Stacy Wood, University of South Carolina
Scott Swain, University of South Carolina
J. Daniel Wadden, University of South Carolina

ABSTRACT

The ease of navigation afforded by e-commerce threatens to remove many of the consumer search costs that some retailers rely upon to create or enhance product differentiation and exposes consumers to more products within the scope of a typical search period than ever before. The existence of (and the ability to reasonably search) a greatly-expanded universe of options may impact consumers' perceptions of product category parity and consumption emotions such as choice confidence and satisfaction. The effect of parity judgments and choice satisfaction on issues of price sensitivity and channel adoption, respectively, render this an important issue. We investigate this domain via multiple methodologies. Findings suggest that e-retailers may have little to fear, and even much to gain, from the effects of larger search sets on consumers.

Advances in Consumer Research
Volume 28, © 2001

Type of Information Processing in Judging Utilitarian and Expressive Product Attributes

Marielle Creusen, Delft University of Technology
Jan Schoormans, Delft University of Technology

ABSTRACT

In an experimental study, the well-known but not often vali-dated notions are confirmed that consumers judge utilitarian prod-uct attributes with the use of analytic information processing and expressive product attributes with the use of holistic information processing. Furthermore, we make an addition to this framework. In some cases, utilitarian attributes are judged on the basis of the overall appearance of a product, with the use of holistic information processing. We found indication that this happens more often for consumers with a relatively low level of product knowledge.

Customization Decisions: The Roles of Assortment and Consideration

John Godek, University of Michigan
J. Frank Yates, University of Michigan
Seigyoung Auh, Symmetrics Marketing Corporation

ABSTRACT

Customization has become increasingly popular as a strategy to attract and retain customers. Even so, little definitive research has examined the effect of customization on consumers and their decision making. Marketers have assumed that customization is virtually guaranteed to improve upon non-customization under all conditions. There are reasons to suspect, however, that there might be specifiable conditions under which customization actually does worse than non-customization. Both managerial practice and previous research suggest that the increased decisional control afforded by customization should benefit consumers by giving them a product that better matches their preferences while simultaneously making them feel more in control of the purchase decision. However, because customized products are often compared and selected on an attribute by attribute basis rather than on an whole product basis, in addition to the effects of matching preferences and increasing control on consumers' evaluations, consumers may also experience effects associated with perceptions of less assortment as well as consider fewer alternatives prior to making a selection. The current research compares the effects of customization and non-customization decisions on consumer' judgment and decision making. Controlling for availability of alternatives, we hypothesized that customization decisions will lead to perceptions of less assortment as well as fewer alternatives considered, and that these effects in turn would offset some or all of the benefits derived from matching preferences and increasing decisional control. Two studies testing these predictions were conducted, with results indicating, contrary to managerial practice, that customization performs poorly when compared to a non-customization strategy.

Realer than Real: Retail Hyperreality and the Encoding of "Authentic" Cultural Symbolism

Michael R. Solomon, Auburn University

Many retail settings, from the Rainforest Café to Disney's EPCOT Center, are engineered to allow consumers to vicariously experience some other place, time or reality. In this context, Baudrillard's notions of simulacra and hyperreality meet the everyday reality of marketing and retailing activities. These establishments cleverly blend traditional hospitality services, merchandising opportunities and carefully calculated design to offer "one-stop shopping" for those wishing to experience a foreign culture. For many consumers, these artificial *qua* real environments may literally constitute their sole contact with that culture. Indeed, the ability of clever marketers to create sanitized reproductions of "authentic" cultural experiences may result in the ironic outcome that consumers prefer the simulation to the actual experience.

The first paper: *But is it True Blue Mate? Cross-Cultural Perceptions of Authenticity* by Ronald Groves, Michael Solomon and Natalie Quilty focuses on encoding strategies utilized by The Outback Steakhouse chain to evoke Australian culture. Australian students reacted to photographs taken at an Outback restaurant in Alabama. They then created their own collages of an "authentic" Australian steakhouse. These were shown to both Australian and American students who were asked to comment on the authenticity of these Australian images. The findings of these cross-cultural interpretations on authenticity suggest that during the consumption of a host culture (in this case, literally including its food and drink), outgroup members ironically prefer the idealized prototypes to "the real thing."

The second paper by Patrick Hetzel was entitled *Authenticity in Public Settings: A Socio-Semiotic Analysis of Two Parisian Department Stores.* He uses a socio-semiotic approach on two very different Parisian department stores in order to show that "Le Bon Marche" created in 1852 on one hand and "Les Galeries Lafayette" on the other hand convey a sense of "authenticity" which is very different. This paper emphasizes that the aesthetic reference to "authenticity" is a multi-dimensional concept.

The final paper, *Le Parc Disney: Creating an "Authentic" American Experience* by Gary Bamossy and Janeen Arnold Costa focuses on efforts by the French theme park to offer an "authentic" American experience. Based upon stereotypical images of America in the 1950s - 1960s, the created hyperreality ignores social issues relevant to that place and time. Moreover, Europeans consume the American images uncritically, as intended. Here, America is the "exotic other" in the context of a sanitized hyperreality that provides entertainment, "fun" and a liminal experience.

The specific encoding strategies used to physically represent a culture are important both in terms of their marketing and consumer socialization value. How do managers and designers decide what design elements—such as the generous use of icons and artwork stereotypically associated with the culture—will capture the vicarious cultural experience? How do consumers use this information to form inferences about other countries and peoples? As we witness the increased "Disneyfication" of popular culture, to what extent does vicarious consumption of culture provided by commercial entities supplant "the real thing?"

Le Parc Disney: Creating an "Authentic" American Experience

Janeen Arnold Costa, University of Utah
Gary J. Bamossy, University of Utah and Vrije Universiteit, Amsterdam

INTRODUCTION

Le Parc Disney is located approximately one hour by car or train from the center of Paris. Originally named "EuroDisney," the financing and ownership of the amusement park was restructured in the mid 1990s to include greater French and European control and influence. However, despite minor alterations, the space itself has remained largely unchanged in structure and intent.

The organization of Disney spaces has been influenced by the values of Walt Disney, the founder and great innovator of the original Disney concepts and Theme Parks. American Disney executives viewed Disney parks as ideally free from any sort of controversy, and as such, alcoholic beverages were not part of the park's offerings. On the European continent, beer and wine are an integral part of meals and, indeed, of everyday life, and such a ban was culturally inappropriate. In order to adapt to European culinary habits, as well as to create a center for food, drink and entertainment to serve the captive audience of the theme park, a separate space was created, which is external to the gated and pay-for-entrance Disney Park area.

Originally entitled "Streets of America," more recent names of this space include "Rhythm of America," located within "Disney Village." While some of the specific retail and entertainment outlets have changed over the last decade, the reference to "American" streets or music remains. Located between the park hotels (themselves themed American spaces) and the gated park proper, The Rhythm of America area provides eating and drinking opportunities, retail, and entertainment spaces, all based upon stereotypical American themes. We contend that the design, signage, merchandising, fare and general products and services offered here create an "authentic" American space in the eyes of the typical European consumer.

THEORETICAL CONCERNS

Assessing "Authenticity"

"Authenticity" is a problematic concept, reflecting the extreme complexity of interacting phenomena involving cultural contact, issues of identity, appropriation and commodification, and dialectical tensions of tradition and change, as well as self and cultural Other. For purposes of simplifying the data and analysis presented here, we have chosen to focus on "authenticity" as defined and described within the literature concerning "primitive art." Within this context, discussion of "authenticity" has generated clear delineation and application, while simultaneously precipitating substantial debate that helps us to understand the factors and parameters relevant to the discussion.

In the early part of the twentieth century, the market for art from "primitive" societies was substantial. At the same time, the societies from which such art had originally derived were changing, often partly in response to the market for art. As "marketizing" economies in terms of both production and consumption came into being in places formerly characterized by subsistence orientation, art collectors of the "developed" world became concerned with the impact of such changes on the artists and art of the "developing" countries. In particular, art connoisseurs became wary of the "mass-produced" art that began to appear in the marketplace, and they felt

compelled to differentiate between such objects and those individualized, unique pieces for which they could charge a premium price or place on display in appropriate venues.

In 1935, curators at the Museum of Modern Art (MoMA) in New York City produced an exhibit entitled "African Negro Art." The contents of the accompanying exhibit catalogue firmly established the reputation of the author, James Johnson Sweeney, as an authority on the definition and evaluation of "authenticity." Sweeney's pronouncements became entrenched over the ensuing decades, pervading curators' and collectors' appraisals until the present day. A half century later, Sweeney's work was revisited at MoMA, this time in the context of an exhibit concerning "primitivism" in the twentieth century. The author of *this* catalogue, William Rubin, problematizes Sweeney's conceptualization of authenticity but fails to provide a viable alternative. In the end, like Sweeney, Rubin indicates:

> An authentic object is one created by an artist for his own people and used for traditional purposes. Thus, works made by African or oceanic artists for sale to outsiders such as sailors, colonials, or ethnologists would be defined as inauthentic. The problem begins when and if a question can be raised–because of the alteration of tribal life under the pressure of modern technology or Western social, political, and religious forms— as to the continuing integrity of the tradition itself (1984, p. 76; see Errington 1998 for detailed discussion)

Thus, "authentic" art has been judged on the basis of production by an artist and in a manner deemed to be "untouched" by both time and the marketplace itself. This definition has thereby excluded the multiple copies of similar, although often handmade, which have appeared in local marketplaces for sale to tourists or traders. The definition has further precluded innovations on the part of artists, as well as any alterations deemed to be a response to market demand in terms of style or form, not to mention quantity!

Clearly, the attribution of "authentic" as applied to art of the cultural Other is problematic. It implies notions of knowledge hierarchy both within Western society and vis-à-vis non-Western societies, and it invokes primitivism (Torgovnick 1990) and images of Rousseau's "noble savage" (1762). As we attempt to understand "authenticity" in marketing and consumption contexts beyond so-called "primitive art," the difficulties increase. Nevertheless, it is apparent that marketers attempt to impart–and consumers often ascribe—an aura of "authenticity" to given products. We propose, therefore, that elements of the definition developed within the art world may be useful in understanding "authenticity" in the context of the marketing and consumption of other products as well.

Sweeney's and Rubin's definition and assessment of "authenticity" is based upon an invocation of timelessness and isolation from the market. It may be difficult to understand how either factor can be achieved today, particularly 'market isolation' within the marketplace itself! We contend, however, that both the marketer and the consumer engage in acts of imagination and 'suspension of disbelief' to attain a context in which some or all of a product offering can be seen as "authentic." This attribution of "authenticity" in a fantasy context illustrates the dialectical tensions between present and past, between real and unreal, between self and cultural/temporal Other, and between consumer and marketer.[1]

We do not mean to imply that "authenticity" beyond the product category of primitive art can only exist in a fantasy setting. On the contrary, inherent in consumers' attribution of authenticity to a given product is the emphasis on originality, appropriate production and use of the product, assessment of "fit" between the product and the time and place of its perceived origin. These elements can and do fit numerous consumption venues and experiences beyond both the museum and fantasy milieus. Replicas of home furnishings from earlier historic periods or from other countries are marketed as "authentic reproductions," for example, in an apparent oxymoron that nevertheless holds meaning for the consumer. Similarly, despite the romantic primitivism asserted by Sweeney regarding authenticity in "primitive" art, tourists themselves ascribe authenticity to mass-produced, miniaturized, or stylistic conglomerate versions of souvenirs from non-Western societies.

Who, then, decides upon "authenticity" as a product trait? In several of our research projects over the last decade, we have attempted to ascertain the source and context of ascribed "authenticity" in various product categories. It has become clear that "authenticity" varies according to several factors, including place, time, intended use of the product, basis for knowledge, product type, and the person assessing the characteristic. For example, in our research on museum gift shops, we found that curators, managers, museum directors, and customers from different societies bequeathed the coveted assessment of "authentic" in different ways and to varying extent according to their own purposes and knowledge (Costa and Bamossy 1995). In tourism, one tourist may assess a product as "authentic," while another may disagree (see various essays in Phillips and Steiner 1999 for details). Even in the case of "primitive art," a product category that we have found to be foundational for defining authenticity, collectors, designers and curators may offer opposing opinions (see Errington 1998). In the end, within the context of consumer behavior, we believe it is most appropriate to view "authenticity" from the perspective of the consumer. However, in order to attain a full understanding of the consumer's apperception of "authenticity," the intentions and efforts of the marketer vis-à-vis the consumer should be assessed. Marketing strategies, particularly in product design and merchandising, but also in advertising and other promotional tactics, may provide valuable cues to the consumer as she/he evaluates "authenticity." On the other hand, in some circumstances marketing may actually have little to do with consumers' determination that a product is "authentic;" such a situation, in and of itself, would also enlighten us as to the parameters and process involved in the consumers' judgment of "authenticity."

---

[1] Some theorists would refer to this as part of the "postmodern" condition. While we would agree that the particular example we will describe here, *Le Parc Disney* and its Disney Village, fits the description of postmodernity, we prefer to develop a framework for "authenticity" that is less ethnocentric than that which we believe characterizes some of the literature on postmodernism. In particular, we believe that the accentuation on choice, celebratory populism, and the emphases on pastiche and bricolage are all reflective of Western post-industrial society and consumption and do not apply in the same way or to the same extent to much of the rest of the world. Therefore, we eschew the reference to postmodernism for our purposes here, despite its apparent applicability to the specific instance that we apply to exemplify consumption and perception of the "authentic."

Consumer Space: Theming

The issue of "authenticity" arises in multiple product categories. It is, however, more prevalent in the "contact zone," where people or products from two or more cultures, societies, or countries interact (Pratt 1992). Furthermore, as discussed above with reference to Sweeney, Rubin and the definition of "authenticity" in "primitive" art, temporal distance and dimensions can be important in the assignation of "authenticity." Similarly, in themed places, cultural/geographic space and time are often created to give the consumer the illusion of consuming Otherness. Thus, because themed environments often emphasize Other space as well as temporal difference, the issue of "authenticity" may arise. This is ironically the case, even though the themed spaces themselves are *created*, a situation that would seem to be inimical to assignation of "authenticity." From the perspective of both marketers and consumers, however, the overall artifice of the created space seems to have little relevance to assessment of "authenticity," as we shall see.

According to Gottdiener (1998), theming of retail establishments is increasing. Greater competition and the resultant need for managers/owners to create a space that is distinctive in the minds of the consumer is one factor in the expanding use of themed environments. Gottdiener also suggests, however, that consumer desire, the creation and experience of fantasy, and the overwhelming influence of popular culture and the media are notable factors in this trend. For example, Gottdiener points to the "...creation of image-driven, themed environments that are attractions themselves but also contain outlets for the sale of commodities...this commercial universe melds seamlessly with the mediascape of popular culture programming on TV and in magazines, advertising, Hollywood films, and the rock music industry" (1998, p. 51). Thus, the development and consumption of themed environments is part of an overall consumption 'scape that derives from, ad fits well with, the media-filled experience of everyday life, at least in Western and other post-industrial societies. At the same time, however, the consumer is aware of the fantasy creation, and we argue that the consumer typically apprehends these spaces, their origins, references and messages in the manner in which they were created. In that context, the "authenticity" of the space is viewed uncritically, perhaps even with celebratory applause at the clever and appropriate creation of a themed environment designed for play.

SETTING AND METHOD

While this paper is largely conceptual, we collected data specific to this project for the purpose of understanding themed spaces. Within that context, the issues of authenticity and representation became salient over time. In addition, touristic and playful consumption experiences also became relevant foci for our investigation. Thus, while we were originally interested in themed environments and in culturally-based products, several of the important conceptual themes emerged during our investigation.

Both authors visited *Le Parc Disney* separately and together over a period of eight years. During the original visit, we interviewed (what was then) Eurodisney's manager of "The Streets of America." At that time and in subsequent visits, we engaged in informal interviewing, participant-observation, and the collection of visual data. As mentioned above, restructuring of Eurodisney led to retitling the park as *Le Parc Disney*; Streets of America became "Disney Village," with certain parts referred to as "The Rhythm of America." Some of the retail outlets and space changed during the interim, while others remained largely intact. The overarching theme of "America" endures.

After initial exposure to the retail venues in this space, we researched the European historical experience concerning several of the American motifs; some of this research was developed and published elsewhere (cf Bamossy, Hogg, and Askegaard, 2001). While much of our knowledge concerning the issue of authenticity had already been refined as other research projects on tourism, the museum, and the American West matured, we nevertheless returned to relevant literature on this and other theoretical concepts significant to the project. Thus, we continually engaged in tacking between research projects, collected data, historical information, and relevant theory.

In the following sections, we describe the space as "thickly" as possible (Geertz 1972) in order to provide for both reader experience and transferability (Erlandson et al 1993). As is evident from the description of data collection, we also utilized researcher, data, and method triangulation.

DISNEY VILLAGE, RHYTHM OF AMERICA, AND STREETS OF AMERICA

As indicated above, *Le Parc Disney* is located approximately one hour by car or train from Paris, France. The train is used by visitors staying in Paris or by Parisian residents who are coming to the park in greater numbers since the financial restructuring that added a larger percentage of French ownership and control. Since the park is isolated from local villages and metropolitan Paris, it has been developed as a resort destination, complete with numerous hotels, eating and drinking establishments, and entertainment venues in addition to the amusement park. While the hotels themselves are themed as American spots (Newport, New York, etc), offering architecture, interior design, retail establishments and products appropriate to and representative of these American places, we chose to focus our research on the strip of eating, drinking, entertainment, and retail outlets that is located between the hotels and the amusement park. As indicated, once referred to as "Streets of America," it is now part of "Disney Village" and "Rhythm of America." Since its inception, park managers have continually visited and re-visited the question as to whether or not to make this section of the resort into a gated area for which an entrance fee would be charged.

The visitor enters Disney Village either from the hotel area or from a large open area that separates the Village from the amusement park. From this direction, the first images confronting the visitor are of the Buffalo Bill's Wild West Show on the far right, Planet Hollywood just to the left of that, and, across the pedestrian corridor to the left, Annette's Diner. Alternatively, entering from the hotel section, the visitor first sees the Key West restaurant with a shark suspended from a large hook, as if just caught and in the process of being weighed. A small lagoon with small radio-controlled boats serves to further indicate the maritime character of this first establishment. Seats decorated in red and white stripes with stars flank the corridor. As the visitor navigates the crowded aisle, a gaze upward reveals larger-than-life human statues suspended from large steel structures. On each side of the pedestrian mall, retail outlets offering Disney and Mattel products, food from various American cities, and entertainment showcasing American cultural icons beckon the customer.

Various stereotypical and/or nostalgic American themes are played out in Disney Village. Images of the American West are evident throughout the site. At one entrance, the visitor is confronted with a marquis topped with statues of Buffalo Bill and Sitting Bull that marks the entrance to a large theatre. Here, the turn-of-the-century Buffalo Bill's Wild West Show is re-enacted twice each evening, complete with warring cowboys and "Indians," horses, cavalry rescuing damsels in distress as their stagecoach is attacked, bison pawing and rolling in the dust and dirt, settings that attempt to capture the sunrise and stone of a Western desert, not to mention actors playing the part of Buffalo Bill, Annie Oakley, and Sitting Bull. Further down the retail strip is another Western venue, a trading post, offering such products as child-sized bows, arrows, guns, tomahawks and hatchets, Western-styled clothing, old-fashioned candy, canned tobacco products and buffalo meat, as well as a very expensive line of cowboy boots. The remarkable merchandising includes the front half of a red cadillac apparently crashing through the wall, with large bull horns extending from the grille, the use of old wood reminiscent of Western saloons, and a portrait of Ronald Reagan in one of his acting roles as sheriff of an old Western town! In the pedestrian corridor outside the trading post, a large, lanky cowboy leans casually back against the immense steel structure supporting his huge torso in mid-air, words "thank you, ma'am!" seemingly poised on his lips, his hand raised to tip his hat. Close to the trading post is Billy Bob's saloon, fronted by a smiling cowboy complete with lit cigarette, rumpled cowboy hat and cowboy boots; both the saloon and the cowboy are outlined in red, white and blue neon. In front of the tavern is a separate marquis, this time boasting a Country Western singer strumming his guitar, with the name of the band that will provide that evening's entertainment on signage reminiscent of an American movie house. Inside Billy Bob's, a "barn-dance" layout allows spectators on the balconies to look down upon the wooden dance floor below. The saloon's walls are adorned with photos of "good ol' boy" Country and Western singers from the USA, while the tables, chairs, and bar replicate the imagined furnishings of saloon in the old West. Finally, decorating a sign external to Disney Village and marking its entrance, is the image of a Native American Indian, dressed in "traditional" clothing replete with feathered headdress and a loincloth and leggings, bent over, apparently dancing to a rhythmic beat and carring a bow and arrow. Below the dancing Indian, the "Arizona Frontier Motel" is pictured, with a stylized American Indian representation of the sun, indicating "Sun and Sand" in the blue sky above the restaurant, while sagebrush fill a rocky desert landscape to the side.

Overlapping with the theme of the American West is the image of Hollywood. This is perhaps most apparent in the recently added Planet Hollywood restaurant and bar, the entrance to which is again lined with photos of "classic" Hollywood icons, particularly those from the 1950s and 1960s. Another bar, situated half-way down the corridor is named "Rock 'N Roll America" and is again lit with neon, this time in the likeness of Elvis playing a guitar, glittering lights once more beckoning the consumer. Yet the influence of Hollywood is obvious throughout Disney Village, as evidenced by the polysemic Ronald Reagan portrait, but also in the 1950's themed spaces and the restaurants that recreate Florida and California scenes so unmistakably derived from television and movie programs from the Hollywood entertainment scene.

Annette's diner, including the design of the space in front of the restaurant itself, is clearly evocative of 1950s and early 1960s America, particularly as represented in "Beach Blanket" movies starring Annette Funicello, (a Disney product). Decorated in shades of pink with turquoise accents, neon and chrome, waitresses in tight pants and short aprons skate to each table. A curving bar, again reminiscent of 1950s drug stores serving milk shakes and sodas, flows along one edge of the restaurant. Outside, a large statue of a buxom waitress, wearing skates, a short-sleeved shirt and form-fitting pants in red, white and blue carries a tray balanced in one hand, suggestive of "Dairy Queen" or "A&W Root Beer" drive-ins. An original 1950s pink Cadillac, its length and fins startling in their dimensions, and two smaller American sportscars from the same period complete the impression of a drive-in eating experience in the United States (a rare and relatively recent type of establishment in Europe, primarily in the form of American-based franchises such as McDonald's). A short distance down the pedestrian corridor, another pair of statues soars in the air above consumers strolling up and down Disney Village. Placed to tie together Annette's and the nightclubs and bars, a young man, haircut, sideburns, jeans and shirt indicative of the 1950s or of Country Western music, swings a young woman clad in a flowing turquoise skirt, pink bobby socks and pony tail, into the air. Musical notes surround the couple, who appear to be caught up in a wild, swirling motion, evoking a feeling of the "jitterbug" in process. Finally, it is worth noting that two other restaurants in the area, "Key West" and "Los Angeles" are designed in ways that represent these American places in the 1950s or early 1960s, rather than the 1980s-90s when Disney Village was built. They evoke a sense of nostalgia and simplicity, again perhaps deriving from Hollywood images of these vacation spots.

The use of vehicles to adorn the space in front of Annette's is representative of another stereotypical image associated with the United States: Cars! Europeans continue to be astounded at the size of American cars, even the smaller sportscars positioned outside Annette's. As indicated, the front portion of a large 1950s red Cadillac appears to burst through the wall of one retail outlet, seemingly flying through the air above the head of the customer, and festooned with the horns of an American Longhorn steer. The open trunk of the same car is placed below, filled with merchandise. Decorating stores in the original "Streets of America," cars were used to represent other famous American cities. For example, a 1950s black-and-white San Francisco Police Department (SFPD) car carried merchandise in one outlet, while a yellow-and-black New York City "Checker Cab" again burst through a brick wall in another spot. A sign exterior to Disney Village, beckoning consumers to enter the space, portrays a blue, white and chrome Harley Davidson with saddle bags.

A final American motif clearly represented in Disney Village is sports. Here, representation emphasizes the American sport of football, played exclusively in the United States, but merchandising and additional images pertain to other sports activities as well. For example, a large florescent "sign" in the middle of the pedestrian corridor portrays a footbal player, rushing forward with the ball in hand, lights streaming behind him to give the impression of speed and strength. Near the status is the "Sports Bar," not only serving American style food but evocatively designed true to its namesake, brown wood and brass, television cameras suspended throughout the bar showing sports matches, with photos and statues of various American sports heroes, and pennants and trophies festooning the walls. The Disney product outlets that feature sports gear also display various Disney characters in sports outfits, while the customer aisles are designed to resemble a running track. Most interestingly, on one of our visits we noted the external signage to this retail outlet, portraying what we interpreted as a quintessential American approach to competition in the sports world. The marquis announces "Tonight: World Championship! Mickey Mouse versus The Bad Guys."

This concludes our description of Disney Village. While more detail could be provided and some areas are not described fully, space limitations are a consideration. Readers who are interested in reviewing the visual representations described in this paper can refer to the *Center for Consumer Culture* website (go to: http://c3.business.utah.edu/ and then go to Scholarly Connections and click on "Working Papers"). We turn now to further interpretation and analysis of the themes and motifs represented in this themed consumer environment.

DISCUSSION AND CONCLUSION

According to the Disney manager of this retail space adjacent to the park itself, Disney set out to create a "fun space" in Disney Village (personal interview, 1993). As indicated, these "American" venues for food, alcohol and entertainment include the Sports Bar,

Billy Bob's Western Saloon, Rock 'N Roll America, Annette's Diner, restaurants based on re-creating 1950s and 60s versions of Key West, Los Angeles and New York Deli locations, Planet Hollywood, and, of course, Buffalo Bill's Wild West Show. A Mattel store, Hollywood Pictures, Mickey Mouse sports shop, Disney products store, the Western Trading Post, and the Planet Hollywood Merchandise Store all feature products of America and of Disney. Although a store was added in the late 1990s which features products of Paris, this is the only retail outlet in the entire space with no Disney or American products.

The overall design of the space is based upon stereotypical and uncritical images of the United States, focused primarily upon the American West or America of the 1950s and 1960s. Hollywood versions of famous places in America, as well as Hollywood film and television stars pervade the created environments. The music form unique to America, Country/Western, is well-represented, as is rock-and-roll, particularly those versions which were globally influential, such as the music of Elvis Presley, said to have inspired the 1960s music revolutions in Europe. Hollywood images of "cowboys and Indians" play out in live entertainment as well as pictures and tangible products for sale. But these again are primarily images from American film or likeness presumed to be "authentic" to the original foray of American cowboys onto the European continent with Buffalo Bill's Wild West Show. Romanticized images of American sports and of America in the 1950s are also prevalent.

Thus, Disney has carefully designed and constructed a "fun space" that is a sanitized, idealized, "unreal" representation of America. Issues of ethnic diversity, gender-based conflict, the Cold War, and exploitation of and discrimination against Native America Indians are all ignored here, for example. Instead, the symbols of the '50s and '60s are presented as fun, hyperreal, authentic, "other," and *"American"* in the "best sense" of what that American era signified.

Our research suggests that Europeans consume the presented image of America in the intended, non-critical fashion. In essence, Europe's appetite for "authentic America" is based upon an "exotic other" that never existed in the hyperreal, sanitized form presented at Disney Village. The original Buffalo Bill's Wild West Show that toured throughout Europe in the 1890s is reproduced here, complete with its romanticizing of the cowboy and cavalry as heroes and Indians as spiritual yet wild, untamed savages. American film stars are consumed as they are portrayed—glamorous, romantic and sexual. American sports heroes are presented as successful, competitive icons of prowess and athleticism. Europeans eat in establishments that seem to re-create the most exciting and pleasurable locations of an America caught up in post-World War II prosperity.

It is important to remember that, while the 1950s and 1960s were periods of intense conflict in Europe because of the Cold War, Western Europeans generally believe the United States served Europe heroically through the Marshall Plan and the Berlin airlift. Europeans saw the American 1950s President, Eisenhower, as a "wholesome" president, a general who had helped save Europe in World War II. Then, Kennedy was elected in the early 60s, a charismatic and cosmopolitan figure devoted to defending the world, including Europe, against communism, and founding the American "Camelot."

Thus, we would suggest that, while European criticism of cultural hegemony in the form of "Americanization" has pervaded the continent in the last two or more decades, most of this condemnation is directed toward the transfer of cultural symbols of the 1980s and 1990s. On the other hand, the symbols of America in the 1950s and 1960s as accepted as fun, hyperreal and entertaining in the best sense of what that America era signified.

Returning to the issue of authenticity and themed environments, Disney designed this space to portray representations of America developed specifically for the purpose of entertainment, fun, and liminality. They chose eras and motifs that are not only stereotypically American for European consumers but are also removed from the present-day conflicts. Thus, the themed environment represents to Europeans an America that is temporally, geographically and culturally Other. In that context, Europeans have found it possible to proclaim the images as "authentic" representations. A close analysis of this consideration, however, reveals that consumers "suspend disbelief" in their assessment of "authenticity" in this situation. They "know" that some of the items used to create the themed environment are "real," while others are replicas or synthetic products utilized in the creation of a space that is evocative of "authenticity." As such, our data from *Le Parc Disney*, Disney's Village supports a contention that consumers' assessment of "authenticity" is context-dependent and involves issues of time and space. Furthermore, there is a clear dialectical interaction here between what the marketer intends and what the consumer is willing to experience. Thus, a joint production of marketer-consumer involvement ensues, both partners engaging in fantasy construction and consumption, with resulting judgment of "authenticity" as the outcome.

REFERENCES

Bamossy, Gary J., Margaret Hogg, and Soren Askegaard, (2001) "Europeans' Imaginations of the American West" working paper, David Eccles School of Business, University of Utah, Salt Lake City, UT. 84112.

Costa, Janeen Arnold and Gary J. Bamossy (1995), "Culture and the 'Marketing of Culture:' The Museum Retail Context," *Marketing in a Multicultural World: Ethnicity, Nationalism and Cultural Identity*, Janeen Arnold Costa and Gary J. Bamossy, eds., Newbury Park, CA: Sage Publications, Inc., 299-328.

Erlandson, David A. et al. (1993), *Doing Naturalistic Inquiry*, Newbury Park, CA: Sage Publications, Inc.

Errington, Shelly (1998), *The Death Of Authentic Primitive Art*, Berkeley and Los Angeles, CA: University of California Press.

Geertz, Clifford (1973), *The Interpretation of Cultures*, New York, NY: Basic Books.

Gottdiener, M. (1998), "The Semiotics of Consumer Spaces: The Growing Importance of Themed Environments," *ServiceScapes: The Concept of Place in Contemporary Markets*, John F. Sherry, Jr., ed., Chicago, IL: American Marketing Association and NTC/Contemporary Publishing Company.

Phillips, Ruth B. and Christopher Steiner, eds. (1999), *Unpacking Culture: Art and Commodity in Colonial and Postcolonial Worlds,* Berkeley and Los Angeles, CA: University of California Press.

Pratt, Mary Louise (1992), *Imperial Eyes: Travel Writing and Transculturation,* New York, NY: Routledge.

Rousseau, Jean Jacques (1762), *Du Contrat Social*, Amsterdam: M.M.Rey.

Sweeney, James Johnson, ed. (1935), *African Negro Art*, New York, NY: Museum of Modern Art.

Torgovnick, Marianna (1990), *Gone Primitive: Savage Intellects, Modern Lives*, Chicago: University of Chicago Press.

Rubin, William, ed. (1984), *"Primitivism" in 20th Century Art*, New York, NY: Museum of Modern Art.

Do Consumers' Genes Influence Their Behavior? Findings on Novelty Seeking and Compulsive Consumption

Elizabeth C. Hirschman, Rutgers University
Barbara B. Stern, Rutgers University

INTRODUCTION

Throughout its history, consumer research has progressed by unpacking a series of "black boxes"; that is, by delving into those aspects of consumption that once had appeared impenetrably complex. The present paper examines one of the last remaining such frontiers—consumers' genetic heritage, believed by many researchers in neuropsychology to account for approximately half of the variance in human behavior (see e.g. Bouchard 1994; Bouchard et al 1990a,b; Copeland and Hamer 1998; Kagan 1994; Wright 1998). The debate within the social sciences as to whether nature (i.e., genetics) or nurture (i.e., cultural influences) is the predominant cause of human behavior has recently been reignited by a series of studies indicating the large and direct role genetic heritage plays in the lives of individuals (Wright 1998; Zuckerman 1995).

Our intent is to review critically the burgeoning literature in neuropsychology and relate it to two important aspects of consumer behavior (1) the exploratory activities of novelty seeking, innovativeness and sensation seeking and (2) impulsive and compulsive consumption. As we shall show, these two aspects of consumption appear to be the result of the same underlying genetic structure. Our paper develops a longitudinal model of the development of these two characteristics and shows how they are additionally linked to Attention Deficit Hyperactivity Disorder and High Risk Leisure Consumption.

MEASURING GENETIC INFLUENCE

At the present time, most genetic research on human behavior employs the theory and method of *quantitative genetics*. Quantitative genetics is capable of identifying genetic influence even when multiple genes and significant environmental effects are present (Plomin 1991). This method determines the *sum* of hereditable genetic influence on a given human trait, regardless of the genetic interactions or the number of genes influencing the behavior. Several behaviors related to consumption have been found to be substantially shaped by genetics.

For example, studies of twins have found estimated genetic influence to range from .52 for general intelligence (i.e., cognitive ability) to .28 for the personality traits of agreeableness and conscientiousness. Studies have also provided evidence as regards the influence of family socialization on behavior. For example, for the five primary personality traits of extraversion, agreeableness, conscientiousness, neuroticism and openness, *genetic hereditabilities* were estimated at .36, .28, .28, .31, and .46 respectively, while the *common environmental* component was found to be .00, .09, .04, .05 and .05 for the same five dimensions (Loehlin 1992). Thus, shared home environment appears to have little effect on most human (and presumably, consumer) behaviors (Bouchard 1994).

Molecular Genetics. Increasingly, genetics researchers are supplementing large-scale quantitative studies of general genetic hereditability with more precise, finely tuned studies aimed at identifying the genes or gene systems responsible for observed genetic differences in behavior.

Genetic linkage studies attempt to identify defects in a single gene which cause particular abnormalities. Disorders such as Huntington's disease result from just such a single-gene defect and carriers may be identified by testing (Plomin, Owen and McGuffin 1994). Single-gene defects have also been implicated in bipolar disorder (manic-depression), but results are not yet conclusive (Wahlsten 1999). However, many traits relevant to consumer behavior are not linked to a single gene, but rather to several genes, each of which may play a role in the behavior (Plomin, Owen and McGuffin 1994). Indeed, many consumer behavior disorders are now viewed by geneticists as normally distributed traits that most persons will exhibit in moderation, while a few will exhibit at extreme levels. For example, impulse buying and drug addiction are now believed to result from extreme manifestations of normally distributed pleasure seeking traits (McGue and Bouchard 1998). Genes that contribute to the genetic variance in these behavioral traits are termed *quantitative trait loci* (QTL)[1] (Wahlsten 1999). QTL studies search for particular versions of a gene (termed alleles) that are differentially associated with a given trait (Wahlsten 1999). For example, certain alleles of two neurotransmitter genes have been found associated with impulse purchasing and drug addiction, along with several other forms of compulsive consumption. This phenomenon is also termed *allelic association* and *linkage disequilibrium* (Ball *et al* 1997; Plomin, Owen, & McGuffin 1994).

BRAIN CHEMISTRY AND NEUROTRANSMITTERS

From a consumer behavior standpoint, probably the most important site of genetic influence is in the brain. The human brain is a highly complex organ composed of approximately 100 billion neurons, a specialized class of cells anatomically and chemically designed for intercellular communication (Barondes 1993; Carlson 1995). Neurons come in diverse shapes and sizes, making possible numerous patterns of interaction. The basic shapes and branching patterns of neurons and the selection of the partners with which they form synapses are largely determined by the genes that control nervous system structure (Cooper, Bloom and Roth 1991). This is the mechanism by which genetics influences consumer behavior (see e.g., Kolb and Whishaw 1995, 1998).

Neurotransmitters

The complexity of interneuronal transmission is increased dramatically by the existence of many different neurotransmitters, each having distinctive chemical properties. Several are amino acids, including glutamate, the primary excitatory neurotransmitter, and glycine and GABA, the major inhibitory (i.e., retarding) neurotransmitters. Others are monoamine derivatives of amino acids, including dopamine, norepinephrine, and epinephrine, collectively called the catecholamines, which originate from the protein tyrosine. A fourth neurotransmitter, serotonin, is derived from tryptophan. These four *monoamines* are of great importance to consumer behavior as they are believed to influence one's emotional state, as well as experiences of fear and pleasure (see e.g. Carlson 1995). Another group of substances involved in synaptic communication is the *neuropeptides*. Among the most significant of these for consumer behavior are the *endorphins*, which play a

---

[1] An earlier term for QTL was *polygenic*, meaning that many genes contributed to the observed traits.

Advances in Consumer Research
Volume 28, © 2001

role in pain perception. Their actions are mimicked by some widely abused drugs, such as morphine and heroin (see Carlson 1995).

When neurotransmitters are released into the synaptic cleft, they create their effects by binding to receptors on the postsynaptic neuron. To stop this action, the neurotransmitter must be removed from the receptors, either by chemical degradation (decomposition) of the neurotransmitters or by pumping the neurotransmitter molecules back to the neuronal terminal that released them. The catecholamines and serotonin are removed by the latter process, which is termed *reuptake* (see e.g. Barondes 1993). Several recent anti-depressant drugs (e.g., Prozac, Zoloft) inhibit this reuptake process in order to elevate the mood of depressed persons (see e.g., Zuckerman 1994,1995).

Brain Plasticity and Gene Expression

Brain structure can adapt as a result of experience over the consumer's lifetime (Kolb and Whishaw 1995). It is believed that experience leads to the observed brain structural differences by altering *gene expression*; this is the degree to which a given gene is able to act upon the physical aspects of the individual. As Kolb and Whishaw (1998) observe, "there is ample evidence that the expression of genes in the mature brain is influenced by environmental and behavioral events...Gene expression thus provides a mechanism whereby [neuronal] cells can synthesize new proteins needed to form more synapses...[Neuronal] activity initiated by experience or behavior could therefore increase the activity of genetic mechanisms responsible for dendritic and synaptic growth and, ultimately, behavioral change (p. 60)."

Although each of us is born with a full set of genes, not all are operative at any one time (Tully 1997). Some genes are activated only at specific stages of the life span, while others may became inactivated over time (Pederson et al 1992). Environmental influences, such as those studied by consumer researchers[2] vary throughout the life span. If only a single set of genes operates throughout one's development, while environmental effects are accumulated over time, we would expect to see a *decrease* in the hereditability of behavioral traits over one's life. However, contrary to this "accumulated environment" thesis, many significant behaviors have been found to exhibit *increased hereditabilty* (i.e., genetic influence) as one ages, up to at least mid-life (see e.g. Pederson et al 1992). For example, general cognitive ability has been found to be 80% genetically determined at age 65, while it is about 50% genetically determined in adolescence (Pederson et al 1992).

How does this contrary result come about? As Plomin and Bergeman (1991, p. 373) state, "In the traditional stimulus-response model, the environment is independent of the organism. It is something imposed on the organism from the outside...This view allows no role for DNA, because the organism has [no control over] the environment that impinges on it." What this simple S→R model overlooks, Plomin and Bergeman note, is that an organism–guided by its genetics–can *actively manipulate its environment*, making the environment more compatible with its inborn traits and tendencies

(Scarr 1992, 1997). Thus, over time the environment surrounding the organism becomes more genetically determined, rather than the organism becoming more environmentally determined (Scarr and McCartney 1983; McGue et al 1993).

Researchers have identified three distinct types of interactions that can occur between an individual's genetic structure and the environment:

(1) *Passive interaction* occurs when children inherit from their parents a family environment that is linked to their familial genetic propensities. (For example, intelligent parents may provide more books for their intelligent child). Thus, high cognitive ability in the parents and child is not caused by the presence of books, rather the presence of books is caused by genetically high cognitive ability in the parents and child.

(2) *Reactive interaction* refers to the experiences of children resulting from others' reactions to their genetic propensities. For example, a child whose anti-social behavior is caused by hereditary factors may cause others (e.g., parents, teachers) to treat him/her negatively, thus further exacerbating the anti-social trait.

(3) *Active interaction* occurs when people select, modify or create experiences as a result of their hereditary traits (Plomin 1995). For example, a novelty-seeking consumer may surround him/her self with new, interesting products.

With this background, we now turn to two consumer behavior applications: novelty seeking and impulsive/compulsive consumption. As we shall see, these two disparate areas of consumption are not only genetically influenced, but also integrally linked.

NOVELTY SEEKING, INNOVATIVENESS AND SENSATION SEEKING

Although *novelty seeking* (Hirschman 1981), *sensation seeking* (Raju 1980, Zuckerman 1983, 1994, 1995) and *innovativeness* (Rogers 1995) have long been topics of interest to consumer researchers, it is only within the past few years that a possible genetic and neuropsychological basis for this behavioral pattern has been discovered. All three of these consumer behavior traits are characterized by high levels of *exploratory behavior* (i.e., venturesomeness) in hopes of finding potentially rewarding stimuli (Cloninger 1987; Zuckerman 1983, 1994, 1995). Cloninger *et al* (1993, 1996) proposed that individual variations in innovativeness, sensation seeking and novelty seeking are mediated by genetic variability in the transmission of the neurotranmitter, dopamine.

Thus, it was empirically encouraging when a 1996 study, (Ebstein *et al*) reported that high scores on the Cloninger Novelty Seeking Scale[3] "are significantly associated with...the 7-repeat allele in the locus for the D4 dopamine receptor gene (D4DR)" (p. 78), a finding that "provides the first replicated association between a specific genetic locus involved in neurotransmission and a normal personality trait (p. 78).[4]" Insofar as the 7-repeat allele has a longer

---

[2]For example, the relationship between conformist tendencies and dysfunctional consumer behaviors such as alcohol consumption and drug addiction (Rose, Bearden, and Teel 1992) has been studied primarily among young people-high school and college students. Although this relationship was found to be robust across adolescence and young adulthood, the absence of longitudinal studies does not allow for possible developmental variations in comorbidity.

[3]Individuals who score higher on Cloninger's TPQ Novelty Seeking scale are impulsive, exploratory, excitable, quick-tempered and extravagant, whereas those who score lower are characterized by being cautious, rigid, stoic, slow-tempered, and frugal (Cloninger 1987, et al 1996, 1993; Plomin et al 1994).

[4]Not all studies have replicated this finding, see e.g., Chang et al 1997.

string of proteins that can serve as binding sites for the dopamine neurotransmitter, consumers carrying this allele exhibit a different pattern of dopamine reception than do other consumers. This variation in dopamine utilization causes them to exhibit novelty seeking behavior, likely as a means to generate additional internal production of dopamine, which serves as a chemical 'reward' by stimulating pleasure-responding areas of the brain. Indeed, novelty seekers experience "exhilaration or excitement in response to novel stimuli" (Benjamin et al 1996); thus, the discovery of a novel product would stimulate a pleasurable response in a novelty seeking/ innovative consumer. The broad heritability of novelty seeking has been found to be 41% in twin studies, hence there is ample room for genetic causation.

In addition to the D4DR allele already discussed, a second dopamine receptor gene has also been found related to innovativeness, novelty seeking and sensation seeking. The A-1 allele of the DRD2 dopamine receptor gene has also been linked to these exploratory traits (McGue and Bouchard 1998). This allele causes fewer than normal dopamine receptor sites to be present in the brain. In order to stimulate additional dopamine production, the individual seeks out new and exciting experiences, which then create a sense of pleasure due to the enhanced levels of dopamine. Thus, consumer innovators are stimulated, in part, by their genes to seek out new products.

Research on the dopamine receptor genes has opened up an additional avenue of research with direct relevance to consumer behavior–that of the origins of compulsive consumption.

IMPULSIVE AND COMPULSIVE CONSUMPTION

Impulsive Consumption. Since Rook's work in the mid-1980's (Rook 1987), impulsive consumption has been of interest to consumer researchers. Impulse purchasing appears to be a widespread phenomenon in America, with an average of 38 percent of adults in national surveys conducted between 1975 and 1992 responding affirmatively to the statement, "I am an impulse buyer" (DDB Needham Annual Lifestyle Survey,1974-1993). In recent research, impulse buying has been defined as "a consumer's tendency to buy spontaneously, unreflectively, immediately and kinetically...their thinking is likely to be relatively unreflective, prompted by physical proximity to a desired product, dominated by emotional attraction to it, and absorbed by the promise of immediate gratification (Rook and Fisher 1995 p. 306)". This response pattern bears much in common with Cloninger's definition of novelty seeking. And there is yet another related behavioral pattern, as well. Ratey and Johnson (1997) suggest that a large proportion of impulse purchasing is due to mild to moderate adult levels of Attention Deficit Hyperactivity Disorder (ADHD), which is highly hereditary (60%), (McGue and Bouchard 1998). As adults, persons exhibiting Attention Deficit Hyperactivity Disorder are impulsive in their behavior and easily distractible by external stimuli. ADHD is caused by *slower* than average metabolism in the frontal lobes of the brain, the region responsible for controlling attention and motor behaviors, as well as impulses. Persons with ADHD metabolize glucose at a rate 10 to 12 percent below average; this low rate of metabolism makes it difficult for them to control their behavioral impulses and easily distractable by nearby stimuli, such as a varied array of products (Cook et al 1995).

The below average frontal lobe activity in ADHD accounts for the ability of stimulant medications such as Ritalin and Dexedrine to *reduce* impulsivity. Once metabolism is increased to normal levels via stimulants, the frontal lobes are able to exert control over behavior. Significantly, the chemical mechanism through which this is accomplished is an increase in the levels of the neurotransmitters dopamine and norepinephrine (Ratey and Johnson 1997).

Consumers with ADHD also exhibit a strong tendency to utilize cocaine, caffeine and nicotine (i.e., cigarettes), because these stimulant drugs act to increase dopamine and norepinephrine levels (Volkow et al 1993). Ratey and Johnson (1997) point out that "Adults with frank cases of ADHD are notorious risk-takers; they are attracted to any situation that shocks the brain (p. 196)". Thus, it is likely that at least a portion of the high-risk leisure consumption described by Celsi, Rose and Leigh (1993)–as well as novelty seeking, sensation seeking and innovativeness—is attributable to ADHD. If this reasoning is correct, we would anticipate a positive correlation among ingestion of central nervous system stimulants (cocaine, tobacco, caffeine), impulsive purchasing, novelty seeking, and high-risk leisure consumption, as all are linked to consumers' efforts to increase frontal lobe activation by enhancing dopamine and norepinephrine levels. And indeed, in recent genetic linkage studies this connection has been found (Battaglia et al 1996).

This constellation appears to be traceable, in part, to the neurological effects of the designated alleles in the D4DR and D2DR dopamine receptor genes. Alleles of these genes, which result in reduced numbers of dopamine receptors in the consumer's brain, leave him/her in a *reward deficient state* (Blum et al 1995, 1996); to compensate for this, these consumers may engage in stimulating, high risk activities, seek out new and different products, purchase on impulse and ingest legal and/or illegal stimulants (e.g. cocaine, caffeine, nicotine, chocolate).

These genetically dopamine-deficient consumers also typically experience feelings of anger, aggressiveness, hyperactivity, irritability or defiant behavior when/if their dopamine levels fall. To remedy these unpleasant feelings, they usually seek out stimulation and/or ingest substances which will alleviate their emotional distress. Thus, Blum and his colleagues (Blum et al 1996; Blum, Briggs and Trachtenberg 1989; Blum and Kozlowski 1990; Blum and Noble 1994; Blum et al 1990) proposed that genetic dopamine deficiencies are responsible, in part, for a host of compulsive consumption disorders, ranging from drug abuse to obesity to compulsive purchasing. The next section discusses the empirical evidence supporting their proposal.

Compulsive Consumption.

Research from the late 1980's and early 1990's has suggested that the phenomenon of *compulsive consumption* is generalized across several domains, including drug abuse (Hirschman 1992), compulsive purchasing (O'Guinn and Faber 1989), binge eating (Braun, Sunday and Halmi 1994; Castonguay, Eldredge and Agras 1995; Faber, Christenson, Zwaan and Mitchell 1995), alcoholism (Blum and Noble 1994), kleptomania (Marlatt et al 1988), and bulimia (Krahn 1991). For a given consumer, various forms of compulsive consumption may occur simultaneously or may be manifest in a serial fashion.

Since 1970 a series of studies (Blum, Briggs and Trachtenberg 1989; Blum and Noble 1994; Blum et al 1996; Comings et al 1991; Lawford et al 1995; Noble et al 1991) has confirmed that a very high proportion of severe alcoholics carry the A-1 allele of the D2DR gene. This allele is relatively common, appearing in 20% to 25% of the general population (Ratey and Johnson 1997). However, genetic linkage research has found that this same allele is *disproportionately present* in persons having a variety of compulsive consumer behaviors. For example, it is found in 51% of cocaine addicts and in 80% of persons addicted to cocaine who also exhibit other forms of substance abuse (Comings et al 1994). Further, among compulsive eaters, the allele is found 50 percent of the time, (Bouchard 1995) and rises to 87% when the compulsive eater is also a substance abuser (Blum et al 1996). Among pathological gamblers, the allele's presence is 51%; among those pathological gamblers who are also substance abusers, the rate rises to 80% (Blaszczynski, Wilson and McGonaghy 1986). In general, the *more severe the addictive behavior, the greater the likelihood that the consumer carries the A-1 D2DR allele* (Comings et al 1996a, b, c).

Additional research (Copeland and Hamer 1998) revealed that this same allele was often present in persons exhibiting Obsessive-Compulsive Disorder (OCD). This was a theoretically satisfying finding, because addictive behaviors share an underlying compulsive quality (see O'Guinn and Faber 1989). Further, recent research has indicated that the D4DR allele found associated with novelty seeking is *also* present in some alcohol and heroin dependency (Sander et al 1997; Muramtsu et al 1996; Li et al 1997). Recall that this allele, like D2DR, is believed to be a genetic source of lowered dopamine synthesis in the brain.

These findings are of great importance to consumer behavior because staggering numbers of consumers are estimated to use illicit drugs on a monthly basis, likely in an effort to alter their deficient dopamine levels. According to Nash (1997), in a given month 200,000 consumers use heroin, 800,000 use amphetamines, 1.5 million use crack/cocaine, 10 million use marijuana, 11 million will become drunk on alcohol, 61 million acquire nicotine via cigarettes, over 130 million consume caffeine, and millions more overeat[5] buy compulsively or engage in pathological levels of gambling. The empirical data suggest that these consumers are bound together by a common genetic bond—possession of the D2DR and/or the D4DR allele, as well as others as yet unidentified, in a QTL system (see e.g., Black 1996, Black et al 1998).

Thus, the research conducted within neuropsychology leads us to reformulate our views of both innovativeness/novelty seeking and compulsive consumption. At a biological level, these two distinct forms of consumer behavior appear to be integrally related. Both appear genetically tied to below normal levels of dopamine which lead to higher levels of environmental scanning for stimulation, above average environmental distractibility (due to lowered ability to remain internally focused, i.e., ADHD) and a lack of impulse control.

Copeland and Hamer (1998, pp 30-32) describe aspects of this systematic linkage in their description of Novelty Seeking behavior:

High novelty seekers find pleasure in *varied*, *new*, and *intense* experiences. They are not necessarily fond of risk, but they are willing to take risks for the reward of the new sensation...
Although novelty seeking is a single temperamental trait, it can be expressed in many different ways. *Physical thrill seeking* includes the desire to participate in dangerous sports such as mountain climbing, surfing, or skydiving. *Experience seeking* [refers to the fact that] novel stimuli can be mental or social. New sensations can be found through the mind and senses, such as through avant-garde music and art, exotic travel, or counter-culture experiences. High scorers get excited about new ideas; they are unconventional or innovative. *Disinhibition* and *impulsiveness* are the final dimensions of novelty seeking and are the most important to the real-life problems of drinking, drug use, risky sex, and gambling.

[Novelty Seekers] cannot control their impulses. [They] live at the edge.

The research reviewed can be summarized by the relationships depicted in Figure 1. A complex QTL system of interrelating genes is the origin of novelty seeking behavior. Thus far, two members of this QTL system, specific D2DR and D4DR alleles, have been identified, but many more are likely operant. These are currently being searched for using genetic linkage techniques (see eg. Gelernter et al 1997; Kidd 1996). During early childhood, and continuing into adulthood, consumers carrying this Novelty Seeking QTL system will exhibit not only heightened levels of exploratory behavior (i.e., novelty seeking, sensation seeking, innovativeness, variety seeking, etc.), but will also typically be characterized by Attention Deficit/Hyperactivity Disorder.

By adolescence, these consumers will be engaging in various forms of *compulsive consumption* (likely mediated by social norms, Rook and Fisher 1995), as well as impulse purchasing, innovativeness and 'high risk' leisure consumption activities. As adults these same consumers will migrate into relatively stable patterns of impulsive, compulsive, innovative and excitatory consumption, consistent with their genetic heritage. (Recall the extensive findings that genetic influence *increases* through mid-life). Thus, genetics research provides us with an answer to a question we have never been able to satisfy before regarding innovativeness, impulse purchasing and compulsive consumption: Why do some, but not all, consumers manifest these behaviors excessively? The answer suggested by the present empirical evidence is that the consumers who do exhibit these behaviors in an extreme fashion are those whose genetic structure impels them to do so.

Some Consumer Welfare Issues

The fact that consumption phenomena such as impulsive purchasing, substance abuse, novelty seeking, and high risk leisure activities are genetically influenced confronts us with the need to rethink our notions regarding free will and consumer behavior. Virtually all consumer behavior models have been premised upon the assumption of free will; that is, that persons are born into the world with the primary responsibility for their consumption decisions, and that they possess the ability to reason and to choose in a rational fashion. Indeed, perhaps the most influential theory of consumer behavior, Bettman's information processing model (1979), assumed the primacy of rational cognitive processes controlling consumer choice. Although this framework has been substantially modified in recent years to accommodate emotional factors (Bettman, Luce and Payne 1998), the discovery of specific alleles associated with novelty seeking and compulsive consumption–as well as the documented hereditability of general cognitive ability and common disorders such as ADHD and obesity—challenge the notion that all consumers are able to control their actions and choices. Clearly, we do not all start at the same genetic base-line for consumer behavior, do not all have the same cognitive or emotional structures to guide our decisions, and do not all have the same predispositions for constructing preferences and comparing alternatives.

Given that our heredity will affect our behaviors within and upon the consumption environment, how are we to deal with those whose genotypic endowment encourages impulsive or compulsive behaviors? Should those consumers bearing, say, D2DR A-1 alleles be freed from the responsibility for their impulsive actions if they go on a shopping binge? Schwartz and his colleagues (Schwartz et al 1996; 1997) have recently presented very encouraging results in their work with persons having obsessive-compulsive disorder (OCD), which is associated with the same genetic pattern

---

[5]Some obese consumers eat large quantities of carbohydrates (termed 'carbohydrate craving') in order to boost their dopamine levels. In the digestive system, carbohydrates are transformed to glucose, which stimulates dopamine production.

FIGURE 1
A Longitudinal Model of Genetic Influence on Novelty Seeking and Compulsive Consumption

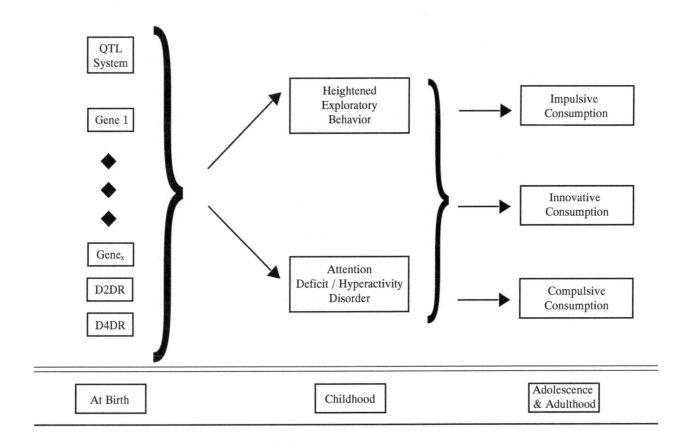

TABLE 1
Hereditability of Five Personality Traits

	Heritability (additive)
Extraversion	.36
Neuroticism	.31
Agreeableness	.28
Conscientiousness	.28
Openness to experience	.46

Derived from Loehlin (1992)

Definitions

Extraversion: Individual is outgoing, decisive, persuasive and enjoys leadership roles

Neuroticism: Individual is emotionally unstable, nervous and prone to worry

Conscientiousness: Individual is planful, organized, responsible, practical and dependable

Agreeableness: Individual is sympathetic, warm, kind, good natured and will not take advantage of others.

Openness: Individual is insightful, curious, original, imaginative, and open to novel experiences and stimuli (Bouchard 1994)

underlying novelty seeking and impulsive purchasing. OCD responds not only to medication (Prozac), but also to cognitive treatment as well. Schwartz has found that once OCD patients are made aware of the genetic/structural anomolies associated with their condition, they often can utilize behavior modification therapy to overcome or at least control the disorder. Most significantly, the treatment, which consists of both cognitive and behavioral exercises, has been shown to alter metabolic activity in the key brain structures believed responsible for the disorder. In essence, as Schwartz *et al* (1997) note, consumers can use their *minds* to change their *brains*. Thus, consumers are not hopelessly bound by their genetic traits.

Yet, as Schwartz et al (1996; 1997) also found, not all OCD sufferers were able to fully eradicate their compulsions. It appears that while the mind can help the brain deal with its predispositions, it cannot always overcome them. This confronts consumers with the responsibility for learning as much as possible about their inborn tendencies. This need not involve direct biological testing, as reliable survey instruments are available (Bucholz et al 1994). Knowledge of one's innate behavioral predispositions can be used auspiciously to help guide one's life. With such awareness each of us can best develop our strengths and best control our weaknesses, as consumers and as human beings.

REFERENCES

Ball, David, Linzy Hill, Bernard Freeman and Robert Plomin, (1997), "The Serotonin Transporter Gene and Peer-Rated Neuroticism", *Cognitive Neuroscience and Neuropsychology,* Vol. 8, #5, March, 1301-1304.

Barondes, Samuel H., (1993), *Molecules and Mental Illness,* New York: Scientific American Library.

Battaglia, Marco, Thomas R. Przybeck, Laura Bellodi and Robert Cloninger, (1996), "Temperament Dimensions Explain the Comorbidity of Psychiatric Disorders", *Comprehensive Psychiatry,* July-August, Vol 37, #4, 292-298.

Bettman, James R. (1979), *An Information Processing Theory of Consumer Choice,* Redding, MASS: Addison-Wesley.

Bettman, James R., Mary Frances Luce and John W. Payne (1998), "Constructive Consumer Choice Processes," *Journal of Consumer Research,* Vo. 25, December 187-217.

Benjamin, J., L. Li, C. Patterson, B.D. Greenberg, D.L. Murphy, and D.H. Hamer. (1996). "Population and Familial Association Between the D4 Dopamine Receptor Gene and Measures of Novelty Seeking." *Nature Genetics* 12, 81-4.

Black, D.W.: (1996) "Compulsive Buying: a Review. *Journal of Clinical Psychiatry*: 57 (suppl 8): 50-55.

_____, Susan Repertinger, Gary R. Gaffney and Janelle Gabel (1998), "Family History and Psychiatric Comorbidity in Persons With Compulsive Buying', *American Journal of Psychiatry,* 155, 7, July, 960-963.

Blaszczynski, A.P., A.C. Wilson, and N. McGonaghy. (1986). "Sensation Seeking and Pathological Gambling." *British Journal of Addiction* 81, 113-7.

Blum, K., E.R. Braverman, R.G. Wood, J. Gill, C. Li, T.J.H. Chen, M. Taub, S.T. Montgomery, J.G. Cull and P.J. Sheridan (1996). "Increased prevalence of the *Taq 1* allele of the dopamine receptor gene (DRD2) in obesity with comorbid substance use disorder: preliminary findings". *Phamacogenetics,* 8, 191-196.

Blum, Kenneth, Robert C. Wood and Peter Sheridan, (1995), "The D2 Dopamine Receptor Gene as a Predictor of Compulsive Disease", *Functional Neurology,* 10, 1, 37-44.

Blum, K. A.H. Briggs and M.C. Trachtenberg (1989). Ethanol ingestive behavior as a function of central neurotransmission. *Experiential* 46:444-452.

Blum, K., and G.P. Kozlowski 1990. Ethanol and neuromodulator interactions: a cascade model of reward. *Progress in Alcohol Research* 2:131-149.

Blum, K. and E.P. Noble (1994). The sobering D2 story. *Science* 265:1346-1347.

Blum, K., E.P. Noble, P.J. Sheridan (1993), "Genetic Predisposition in Alcoholism: Association of the D2 Dopamine Receptor With Severe Alcoholics", *Alcohol, Vol 10,* 59-67.

Blum, K., E.P. Noble, P.J. Sheridan, A. Montgomery, T. Ritchie, P. Jagadeeswaran, H. Nogami, A. H. Briggs and J.B. Cohn (1990). Allelic association of human dopamine D2 receptor gene in alcoholism. *Journal of the American Medical Association* 263:2055-2060.

Bouchard, T. J., Jr., D. T. Lykken, M. McGue, N.OL. Segal, and A. Tellegen. (1990a) "Sources of Human Psychological Differences: The Minnesota Study of Twins Reared Apart." *Science* 250, 223-8.

Bouchard, R.J., N.L. Segal and D.T. Lyklan (1990b), "Genetic and environmental Influences on Special Mental Abilities in a Sample of Twins Reared Apart", *Acta. Genet. Medi. Gemellol,* 193-198.

_____, and"Genes, Environment, and Personality." (1994) *Science* 264, 1700-1.

Bouchard, C. (1995). Genetics of obesity: An update on molecular markers. *International Journal of Obesity* 19 (Supplement3): S10-S13.

Braun D.L., S.R., Sunday, K.A. Halmi. (1994). Psychiatric comorbidity in patients with eating disorders. *Psychological Medicine* 24:859-67.

Bucholz, K.K., R. Cadoret, C.R. Cloninger, S.H. Dinwiddle, and M.A. Schuckit, (1994), "A New Semi-Structured Psychiatric Interview for Use in Genetic Linkage Studies", *Journal of Studies on Alcohol,* Vol. 55, 2, March, 149-158.

Carlson, Neil R. (1995) *Foundations of Physiological Psychology.* 3rd ed. Boston: Allyn and Bacon.

Castonguay, L.G., K.L. Eldredge, and W.S.Agras. (1995). "Binge eating disorder: current state and future directions." *Clinical Psychological Review* 15:865-90.

Celsi, Richard L., Randall L. Rose and Thomas W. Leigh (1993), 'An Exploration of High Risk Leisure Consumption Through Skydiving.' *Journal of Consumer Research,* Vol. 20, June, 1-23.

Chang, F., H. Ko, R. Lu, A.J. Pakstis, and K.K. Kidd,1997. "The Dopamine D4 Receptor Gene (DRD4) is Not Associated With Alcoholism in Three Taiwanese Populations: Six Polymorphisms Tested Separately and as Haplotypes." *Biological Psychiatry* 41:394-405.

Cloninger, C.R. (1987) "A Systematic Method for Clinical Description and Classification of Personality Variants." *Archives of General Psychiatry* 44, 573-88.

_____, D.M. Svrakic, and T. R. Przybeck. (1993) "A Psychobiological Model of Temperament and Character." *Archives of General Psychiatry* 50, 975-90.

_____, Rolf Adofsson, and Nenad M. Svrakic. (1996) "Mapping Genes for Human Personality." *Nature Genetics* 12, 3-4.

Comings, D.E., B.G. Comings, D. Muhleman, G. Deitz, B. Shahbahrami, D. Tast, E. Knell, P. Kocsis, R. Baumgarten, B.W. Kovacs, D.L. Levy, M. Smith, J. M. Kane, J.A. Lieberman, D.N. Klein, J. MacMurray, J. Tosk, J. Sverd, R. Gysin and S. Flanagan (1991). "The dopamine D2 receptor locus as a modifying gene in neuropsychiatric disorders." *Journal of the American Medical Association* 266:1793-1800.

Comings, D.E., L. Ferry, S. Bradshaw-Robinson, R. Burchette, C. Chiu and D. Muhleman (1996). "The dopamine D2 receptor (DRD2) gene: A genetic risk factor in smoking." *Pharmacogenetics.* 8. 65-73.

Comings, D.E., D. Muhleman, C. Ahn, R. Gysin and S.D. Flanagan (1994). The dopamine D2 receptor gene: a genetic risk factor in substance abuse. *Drug and Alcohol Dependence* 34:175-180.

Cook, E.H., M.A. Stein, M.D. Drajowsi, W. Cox, D.M. Olkon, J.E. Kieffer and B.L. Leventhal (1995). "Association of attention-deficit disorder and the dopamine transporter gene." *American Journal of Human Genetics* 56:993-998.

Cooper, Jack R., Floyd E. Bloom, and Robert H. Roth. (1991) *The Biochemical Basis of Neuropharmacology.* 6th edition. New York: Oxford University Press.

Copeland, Peter and Hamer, Dean. (1998) *Living With Our Genes,* Doubleday.

Ebstein R. P. (1996). "Dopamine D4 receptor (D4DR) axon III polymorphism associated with the human personality trait of novelty seeking." *Nature Genetics* 12:78-80.

Faber, R.J., G.A.Christenson, M. de Zwaan, and J. Mitchell (1995). "Two forms of compulsive consumption: Comorbidity of compulsive buying and binge eating." *Journal of Consumer Research,* 22, 296-304.

Gelernter, J., Kranzler, H., Coccaro, E., Siever, L., New, A., Mulgrew, C.L., (1997). "D4 Dopamine-Receptor (DRD4) alleles and Novelty Seeking in Substance-Dependent, Personality-Disorder, and Control Subjects. *American Journal of Human Genetics.* 61:1144-52.

Hirschman, Elizabeth C. (1992), 'The Consciousness of Addiction: Toward a General Theory of Compulsive Consumption'. *Journal of Consumer Research,* 19 (September), 155-179.

_____ (1981), "Innovativeness, Novelty Seeking and Consumer Creativity", *Journal of Consumer Research,* December.

Kagan, Jerome. (1994). *Galen's Prophecy.* Basic Books.

Kidd, K.K., A.J. Pakstis, C.M. Castiglione, J.R. Kidd, and W.C. Speed et al. (1996). "DRD2 Halotypes Containing the TaqI A1 Allele: Implications for Alcoholism Research. *Alcohol Clinical Experimental Research.* 20:697-705.

Kolb, Bryan and Ian Whishaw, (1998), "Brain Plasticity and Behavior", in *Annual Review of Psychology,* 49, 43-64.

_____, (1995). *Brain Plasticity and Behavior.* Mahwah, NJ: Erlbaum.

Krahn, D. (1991). The Relationship of Eating Disorders and Substance Abuse. *Journal of Studies on Alcohol* 3:239-253.

Lawford, B. R., R. M. Young, J. Rowell, J. Qualichefski, B. H. Fletcher, K. Syndulko, T. Ritchie and E.P. Noble. (1995). Bromocriptine in the treatment of alcoholics with the D2 dopamine receptor A1 allele. *Nature Medicine* 1: 337-341.

Li, T. *et. al.* (1997), "Association Analysis of the Dopamine D4 exon III VNTR and Heroin Abuse in Chinese Subjects", *Molecular Psychiatry,* 2, 413-416.

Loehlin, J.C., (1992), *Genes and Environment in Personality Development,* Newbury Park, CA: Sage.

Marlatt, G. Alan, John S. Baer, Dennis M. Donovan, and Daniel R. Kivlahan (1988), 'Addictive Behaviors: Etiology and Treatment'. *Annual Review of Psychology,* 39, 223-252.

McGue, M. and Thomas J. Bouchard (1998), "Human Behavioral Genetics", *Annual Review of Neuroscience.* P. 1-24.

McGue, M., T.J. Bouchard, W.G. Iacono, and D.T. Lykken (1993), "Behavioral Genetics of Cognitive Ability: A Live Span Perspective. In Robert Plomin and Gerald E. McClearn, (eds), *Nature, Nurture and Psychology,* American Psychological Association., Washington, D.C., 59-76.

Muramatsu, T. *et. al.* (1996), "Association Between Alcoholism and the Dopamine D4 Receptor Gene", *Journal of Medical Genetics,* 33, 113-115.

Nash, Madeline, (1997), "Addicted", *Time,* May 5, 69-76.

Noble, E.P., K. Blum, M.E. Khalsa, T. Ritchie, A. Montgomery, P.J. Sheridan. (1991). Allelic association of the D2 dopamine receptor gene with receptor binding characteristics in alcoholism. *Archives of General Psychiatry* 48:648-654.

O'Guinn, Thomas C. and Ronald J. Faber (1989), "Compulsive Buying: APhenomenological Exploration." *Journal of Consumer Research,* 16 (September), 147-157.

Pedersen, N.L., R. Plomin, J.R. Nesselroade, and G.E. McClearn, (1992), "A Quantitative Genetic Analysis of Cognitive Abilities During the Second Half of the Life Span", *Psychological Science,* Vol. 3, #6, November, 346-353.

Plomin, Robert (1991), "The Role of Inheritance in Behavior", *Science,* Vol. 248, April 13, 183-188.

Plomin, Robert, Michael J. Owen, and Peter McGuffin. (1994) "The Genetic Basis of Complex Human Behaviors." *Science* 264, 1733-9.

Plomin, Robert, (1995), "Genetics and Children's Experiences in the Family", *Journal of Child Psychology and Psychiatry,* Vol. 36, 1, January, 33-68.

Raju, P.S. (1980), 'Optimum Stimulation Level: It's Relationship to Personality, Demographics and Exploratory Behavior'. *Journal of Consumer Research,* 7 (December), 272-282.

Ratey, John J. And Catherine Johnson, (1997), *Shadow Syndromes,* New York: Pantheon Books.

Rogers, Everett M. (1995) *Diffusion of Innovation,* Fourth Ed. New York: Free Press.

Rook, D. W., and R.J. Fisher, (1995), Normative Influences on Impulsive Buying. *Journal of Consumer Research,* 22, 296-304.

Rook, Dennis (1987), 'The Buying Impulse'. *Journal of Consumer Research,* 14 (September), 189-199.

Rose, Randall L., William O. Bearden, and Jesse E. Teel (1992), "An Attributional Analysis of Resistance to Group Pressure Regarding Illicit Drug and Alcohol Consumption," Journal of Consumer Research, 19, (June), 1-13.

Sander, T., H. Harms, P. Dufeu, S. Kuhn, H. Rommelspacher, and L.G. Schmidt, (1997). "Dopamine D4 receptor exon III alleles and variation of novelty seeking in alcoholics." *American Journal of Medicine Genetics and Neuropsychiatric Genetics,* 74: 483-87.

Scarr, Sandra (1997), "Behavior Genetic and Socialization Theories of Intelligence: Truce and Reconciliation" in R.J. Sternerg, E.L. Grigorenko (eds.) *Intelligence, Heredity and Environment.* New York, Cambridge University Press. 3-41.

_____ (1992), "Developmental Theories For the 1990's: Development and Individual Differences: *Child Development,* 63, 1-19.

_____ and K. McCartney (1983), "How People Make Their Own Environments: A Theory of Genotype Environment Effects", *Child Development,* 54, 424-435.

Schwartz, Jeffrey M., (1997), "Cognitive Behavioral Self-Treatment for OCD Systematically alters Cerebral metabolism", in E. Hollander and D.J. Stein (eds.), *Obsessive Compulsive Disorders: Diagnosis, Etiology and Treatment.* Marcel Dekker, New York.

_____ et al. (1996), "Systematic Changes in Cerebral Glucose Metabolic Rate after Successful Behavior Modification Treatment of Obsessive-Compulsive Disorder", *Archives of General Psychiatry,* 53, (February), 109-113.

Tully, T. (1997) "Regulation of Gene Expression and its Role in Long-Term Memory and Synaptic Plasticity." *Proceedings of the National Academy of Science.* USA 94:4239-41.

Volkow, N.D., J.S. Fowler, G. J. Wang, R. Hitzemann, J. Logan, D. Schlyer, S. Dewey and A.P. Wolf. (1993). "Decreased dopamine D2 receptor availability is associated with reduced frontal metabolism in cocaine abusers." *Synapse* 14:169-177.

Wahlsten, D. (1999), "Single-Gene Influences on Brain and Behavior", *Annual Review of Psychology*, 50: 599-624.

Wright, William. (1998) *Born That Way*. Knopf.

Zuckerman, Marvin. (1995) "Good and Bad Humors: The Biochemical Basis of Personality and Its Disorders." *Psychological Science* 6, 325-33.

_____ (1994) *"Behavioral Expressions and Biosocial Bases of Sensation Seeking*. Cambridge: Cambridge University Press.

Pleasures of Different Intensity Levels: Properties of Their Online Hedonic Ratings and Their Impact on Consumption Behavior

Jordan L. Le Bel, Concordia University
Laurette Dubé, McGill University

ABSTRACT

The study reported in this paper focused on sensory pleasures of different intensity at the onset of a consumption episode. The objective was to model the pattern of change, as the episode unfolded, in online hedonic ratings (pleasure and desire to consume next unit) and to study the relationship between initial pleasure intensity and amount consumed. Twenty-two adults (14 women, 8 men) participated and consumed three different flavors of dark chocolate selected on an idiosyncratic basis to induce sensory pleasures of a broad range of intensity. The three chocolates were consumed in three separate test sessions following an identical procedure. Results suggest two important properties of online hedonic ratings: (1) moment-to-moment pattern of change reflects a Markov property, (2) increases in initial pleasure intensity are associated with diminishing marginal hedonic responses overall (observed for both pleasure and desire). Initial pleasure intensity was positively related to the amount consumed, but not by as large a quantity as might be expected. Theoretical and managerial implications are discussed.

The Role of Customers' Arousal for Retail Stores – Results from An Experimental Pilot Study Using Electrodermal Activity as Indicator

Andrea Groeppel-Klein, European University Viadrina
Dorothea Baun, European University Viadrina

ABSTRACT

As reported in different empirical studies based on insights of environmental psychology, visual merchandising and interior design of store environments must evoke an optimum level of customers' arousal. However, valid verbal measurement of arousal is difficult to determine: Traditional interviews are mostly done after the shopping trip through a store or a particular part of the store so that customers have to *remember* their emotions. That means using self-reporting methods only allow to measure activation and/or emotions with a time-lag. Moreover, the validity of verbal scales that are intended to measure a psychophysiological response must be called into question. Conversely, electrodermal activity (EDA) is considered to be a valid and also very sensitive indicator that clearly responds to the smallest variation in arousal. Latest technical development offer larger storage capacity, thus allowing telemetric measurement of electrodermal activity which in turn makes field experiments in retail stores possible.

The present paper delivers insights on arousal theory and presents empirical results from a pilot study using EDA to measure arousal. An experiment comparing two retail stores with different environmental settings was conducted.

SHOPPING ENVIRONMENT AND AROUSAL

Fierce competition and saturated markets in retail business make it more and more important for retailers to gain competitive advantage over rivals in order to attract and keep customers. The store atmosphere is playing a major role in this context.

An activating store atmosphere is necessary to evoke positive feelings and approach behavior. However, high orientation pleasantness is necessary, otherwise the store atmosphere is perceived as cluttered and chaotic by the consumers and negative emotions and avoidance are the result.

Environmental psychology is a special field of psychology modeling the influence of diverse environments (e.g. buildings, rooms, landscapes, or other environments of human beings) on emotion and behavior (Mehrabian 1978, 1976). We can gain knowledge from both cognitive and affective approaches of environmental psychology on how store environments affect consumers' arousal and emotions during their shopping trips. However, as we shall see later, empirical findings so far have not brought out clear results on how arousal and shopping behavior are related. This might at least partly be due to the measurement method.

COGNITIVE APPROACHES OF ENVIRONMENTAL PSYCHOLOGY AND CONSUMERS' AROUSAL

The central question of cognitive approaches to environmental psychology concern the ability of individuals to perceive, realize and remember environments. Findings of brain research, perception theory and gestalt theory can help explain the memory representation of spatial information, the so called "mental maps" (Ittelson 1977, Russell and Ward 1982, Golledge 1987).

Several empirical studies of store environments (e.g. Sommer and Aitkens 1982, Grossbart and Rammohan 1981, Bost 1987) give evidence of a significant correlation between the existence of store maps (knowledge about the location of specific products, service centers, escalators, cashier's zone, etc.) and sentiments regarding shopping convenience. Grossbart and Rammohan draw the conclusion that retailers should study the imparting of verbal and non-verbal information in order to improve the internal maps of consumers. Such "landmarks" can be provided by "merchandising themes" (products that are usually used together are presented side by side in the store and decorated as taken from life), visually striking elements, and clearly separated aisles and product display zones.

Consequently, in order to best achieve orientation pleasantness in retail stores, a most favorable level in stimulation is recommended: a clear and simple structure which is cognitively "relaxing" on the one hand, but highly activating key objects that help to form mental store maps on the other hand (Groeppel 1991, Groeppel-Klein 1998b, Flicker and Speer 1990, Wener 1985).

EMOTIONAL APPROACHES OF ENVIRONMENTAL PSYCHOLOGY AND AROUSAL

Using the Stimulus-Organism-Response (S-O-R) model as theoretic basis, Mehrabian and Russell (1974) developed an emotion dominated model of environmental psychology. Various stimuli (e.g. colors, music, shapes) engender primary emotional responses, which provoke reactions to that environment.

Mehrabian and Russell (1974) characterize an environment by the "information rate", defined as the novelty (the unexpected, surprising, unfamiliar in an environment) and the complexity (the number of elements, motions or changes in the setting) of an environment. The more varied, novel, surprising and animating the environment, the higher is the information rate. Environmental stimuli generate primary emotional reactions of three fundamental dimensions - pleasure, arousal, and dominance. According to Mehrabian and Russell (1974) arousal states the active, excited, stimulated, fidget feeling. "Pleasure" means an individual is joyful and in a good mood. "Dominance" states that you "feel unrestricted or free to act in a variety of ways" (Mehrabian and Russell 1974, p. 19). The response variable can turn out into "approach behavior" (an individual reacts positively to an environment) and "avoidance behavior" (characterized by an aversion to the environment).

The environmental psychology model of Mehrabian and Russell (see figure 1) has been used as theoretical framework for several empirical investigations on point-of-sale (PoS) environments.

Donovan and Rossiter (1982) were the first researchers to apply this model to retail stores. They investigated emotional states produced from three different store environments. For the reaction variable they gathered data on test subjects' stated behavioral intention (approach – avoidance) by asking for the time people had stayed in the store, the probability that they would spend more money than planned in that particular store, and the likelihood that they would return. Donovan and Rossiter's findings revealed that both, arousal and pleasure perceived in *pleasant* store environments determine the following:

· shopping enjoyment
· time spent in the store for browsing and exploring
· willingness to talk to sales personnel

FIGURE 1
Studies at the PoS based on the Mehrabian and Russell Model

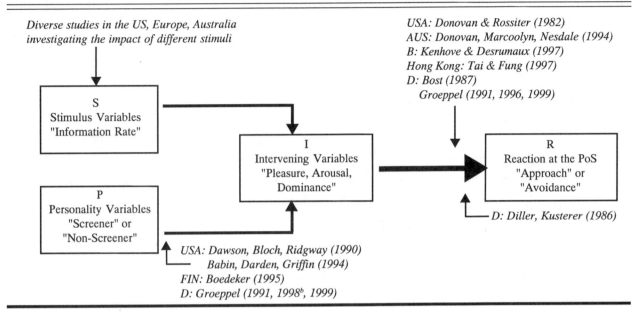

· tendency to spend more money than originally planned
· probability to return to the store

For neutral or unpleasant stores regression coefficients between arousal and the response variables did not turn out to be significant.

In a second study Donovan, Rossiter, Marcoolyn, and Nesdale (1994) extended the study of Donovan and Rossiter from 1982. Basically, the same methodology was applied[1]. However, only respondents who were not familiar with the store environment were interviewed. Instead of the wide range of stores considered in the first study, only discount department stores were employed in the second study. Pre-measures of reaction variables (estimated spending and time to be spent in the store) were compared to post measures. Arousal and pleasure was measured "during" the shopping experience. "During" here means that the test subjects were interviewed after they had spent five minutes shopping in the store.

The results of this second study show again that the variable "pleasure" predicts the response variables "intended shopping behavior" and also the actual shopping behavior. Contrary to the first study, arousal did not show significant positive effect on the response variables in pleasant store environments. The prediction for unpleasant stores (higher arousal will reduce spending) was found to be significant contrary to results of the first study.

Donovan, Rossiter, Marcoolyn, and Nesdale (1994) wonder whether the differences between the results of the first and the second study might be due to the minor changes in the experimental design. Yet, the verbal scale might also be a reason for distortion. The authors report that for some customers it had been difficult to relate items like "aroused-unaroused", "jittery-dull", and "frenzied-sluggish" to their experienced feelings. Another problem might be that in the 1994 study as well as in the previous study, the item "relaxed" was applied to measure both, the pleasure and the arousal variable.

Flicker and Speer (1990) employed a renovated store as the experimental store and another, not renovated store as the control store for their study. They used the same scale for arousal and pleasure as Donovan and Rossiter did for their study in 1982. No significant relation was found between arousal and the response

variables (avoidance – attraction; intended – actual behavior), neither for the control store nor for the experimental store.

Van Kenhove and Desrumaux (1997) also tested the Mehrabian-Russell model on behalf of pleasure-arousal and impacts on approach and avoidance behavior in seven large retail stores (clothing, furniture, and garden centers) in Belgium. Subjects not familiar with the stores were interviewed five minutes after entering the store. Van Kenhove and Desrumaux applied Donovan and Rossiter's original scales on pleasure, arousal, approach and avoidance behavior, translated into Dutch. These researchers found a clear importance of arousal for all three behavioral variables. However, exploratory and maximum likelihood confirmatory factor analysis revealed that a large number of the original items from the pleasure/arousal-scale are not good indicators to measure pleasure and arousal. Van Kenhove and Desrumaux come to the conclusion "that careful inspection of the items selected to test the pleasure/arousal approach-avoidance relationship is needed" (p. 364). Nevertheless, these researchers summarize that this relationship could be of high interest for retailers.

Investigations of Groeppel-Klein (Groeppel-Klein, 1998a, 1997) in Germany revealed, that a store atmosphere that evokes pleasure, a relaxed mood state, and dominance results in a positive value-for-money assessment, and a positive attitude towards the interior design. Also, the duration of staying in the store is extended and consumers rate their intention to come back with a higher probability. Thus, the interior design on the one hand needs to bring about arousal, but on the other hand it shall not exceed an optimum level resulting in a frantic mood.

SUMMARY AND RESEARCH QUESTIONS

Summarizing the results of these studies one can conclude that the variable "arousal" plays a major role. Thus, the "right mix of stimulus factors" is crucial for retailers. Yet, the question arises whether the items of the arousal scale are good indicators. In all

---

[1] In the second study the variable "dominance" was not examined because it had not shown significant difference in the first study.

FIGURE 2
Three Dimensional Model on Arousal

Arousal System	Physiological Reaction (example)	Behavior and experience (example)
System 1: (General activation, RF)	Desynchronisaton of EEG Tonic change in vegetative nerve system	Being alert General activation
System 2: (Affect Arousal, basically emotional component of arousal)	Spontaneous electrodermal frequency (tonic) Phasic cardiovascular change	Behavioral inhibition Negative emotions
System 3: (Preparatory Activation basically motivational component of arousal)	Tonic cardiovascular change Electrodermal response (phasic)	Activation of behavior Positive emotions

Source: Own illustration in accordance with Boucsein 1997

studies mentioned, verbal scales were used to indicate arousal. Are the differences between the results of the studies at least partly due to the applied scales?

The most important question is how to measure the arousal evoked from a specific environmental setting with a higher validity than verbal scales, to determine:

· whether arousal influences emotional states (that means emotions play a mediating role for the response variables) and
· whether there is a difference between consumer behavior in higher and in lower arousing store environments.

A look from a psychophysiological perspective on the construct "arousal" and the association with emotional constructs such as "pleasure" leads to the conclusion that verbal scales might not be an appropriate way to measure arousal.

A PSYCHOPHYSIOLOGICAL PERSPECTIVE: INSIGHTS FROM AROUSAL THEORY

Unidimensional concepts of arousal theory describe the Reticular Activating System ([RAS], which comprises the sensoric inflow, the Reticular Formation [RF], as well as cortical, hypothalamic, and thalamic areas) as the fundamental component for the formation of arousal (Boucsein 1992, 1997). The RF is a complex network of fibers and cell bodies in the core of the brain stem. It is involved in the filtering process of sensory information from the central nervous system (e.g. from visual, haptic, acoustic stimulation). According to these theories, all sensory and motor nerve fibers can enhance general arousal of the RF via collaterals. The RF in turn can indistinctly activate large parts of the central nervous system, generating general activity and reactivity. Thus, an increase of inner or outer stimuli might lead to a higher activation and attention, whereas habituation to these stimuli lead to de-activation and tiredness (Boucsein 1997).

The unidimensional approach would suggest correlation between diverse physical outcomes of arousal such as heart rate, blood pressure, EEG (Electroencephalogram), or EDA (electrodermal activity). Since empirical findings were not consistent with this unidimensional approach, recent efforts yielded towards a more complex arousal theory (Eysenck 1982, Le Doux 1996). Boucsein (1997, 1991), for example, presented a three-dimensional theoretical framework based on neurophysiological insights on arousal and information processing (see figure 2). The model also considers the dependency between arousal and emotion / motivation as well as the effects on central and peripheral psychophysiological parameters. In this model, the first dimension is in accordance with the concept of the unidimensional approach. That means the RF forms the physiological basis of this dimension. EEG (Electroencephalogram) can serve as an indicator. Results from the first dimension are perceived as general activation with a vigilant feeling and an alert state of mind. The second dimension, the "affect-arousal"-system, comprises primarily emotional components of arousal. Headed by the Amygdala, attention, orienting reflex and overall behavior is enhanced via hypothalamic reactions. The physiological outcome results in phasic cardiovascular (heart rate) and/or tonic electrodermal variations. When it comes to behavior and perception, processes of this second dimension lead to defense and negative emotions. Attention that turns into an orienting reflex may also directly impinge on the third system. This so-called "preparatory activation"-system is basically encompassing motivational aspects of arousal. Expectations are transformed into a ready state for reaction. This part of the system interacts especially with motor and pre-motor activation of behavior, and with positive emotion. Phasic electrodermal amplitude, for example, can serve as an indicator.

For marketing purpose, and especially when testing the impact of in-store stimuli on customers' arousal and behavior tendency, the "preparatory activation"-system and in part the "affect-arousal"-system (here especially attention and orienting reflex) are of major relevance (Groeppel-Klein 2000, Boucsein 1997).

Arousal is definitely considered as being fundamental to behavior that is related to emotions (Bagozzi, Gopinath and Nyer 1999) and, as previously shown, arousal plays a major role for customers' interaction with the store environment. Yet, despite diverse methods applied in order to measure arousal, the variable is extremely difficult to indicate in a valid manner. Among the applied methods are verbal scales like the PAD-scale (Donovan and Rossiter 1982), non-verbal scales (e.g. color- and pattern-scale, Meyer-Hentschel 1983), and self-reporting methods. The PAD-scale has been discussed above. The color- and the pattern-scale of Meyer-Hentschel has not yet been implemented often enough to support valid conclusions. Responses from self-reporting methods often suffer from distortion (Vitouch 1997). Another way to approach arousal – but in fact rather measuring emotion – is the observation of non-verbal communication, especially facial features e.g. via FAST[2] (Ekman, Friesen, and Tomkins 1971) or FACS[3] (Ekman and Friesen 1978, Bekmeier 1989) or the use of picture scales that represent specific emotional states (Groeppel and Bloch, 1990).

In contrast to these methods, psychophysiological measures such as heart rate, EEG and EDA are the most valid indicators, since willingly influencing test results is almost impossible.

Electrodermal activity in general "is regarded as a sensitive and valid indicator for the lower arousal range, reflecting small, mostly cognitively conditioned variations in arousal." (Boucsein 1992, p. 263). Contrary to the heart rate, the EDR points to even the very smallest psychological change (Boucsein 1992). It is thus delivering the most sensitive indicator of arousal that might potentially be relevant to behavior. EDR can therefore deliver a valuable contribution to further research on the consumers' arousal induced shopping behavior.

ELECTRODERMAL ACTIVITY AS PSYCHO-PHYSIOLOGICAL INDICATOR FOR AROUSAL

The human skin basically consists of two layers, the dermis and the epidermis. The epidermis is located at the surface and consists of epithelial tissue. This layer is more callous, the closer to the surface. The comparatively thicker and deeper lying dermis consists of taut, fibrous connective tissue. Underneath the dermis lies the subcutis, which contains the secretory part of the sweat glands, fatty tissue, and vessels that supply the body surface (Boucsein 1992).

The epidermis is of great importance to EDA. Although it becomes dryer towards its outside layer as the regularly arranged cells become less tightly packed, there is a permanent insensible perspiration from the dermis via the epidermis even while no sweat gland activity occurs. This hydration depends on external and internal factors and leads to good electric conductivity of the skin, thus making it possible to measure it by means of two electrodes attached to the skin. The conductivity of the skin is then transmitted to the computer by means of an amplifier. The conductivity of the skin is primarily responsible for *tonic* EDA, while active membrane processes following upon a nerve impulse bring about *phasic* EDA which turns into electrodermal reactivity (Boucsein 1992). Following the three dimensional model of Boucsein (1997), phasic electrodermal reactivity (EDR) is the most crucial indicator for research concerning arousal at the point-of-sale.

Basically EDA can be measured via endosomatic or exosomatic recording. While endosomatic recording does not use any external voltage to measure potential differences on the skin, exosomatic recording uses either direct current (DC) or alternating current (AC). Exosomatic recording with direct current is most frequently used to measure either skin conductance (SC, measured in μS[4]) or skin resistance (SR, measured in kW[5]). Each of these methods measures both, skin conductance / resistance *level* (tonic arousal) as well as skin conductance / resistance *reactivity* (phasic arousal) from the EDA-signal (Boucsein 1992).

For practicability and safety reasons for test subjects, exosomatic recording must strongly be recommended for in-store investigations since endosomatic recording requires one of the electrodes being placed in an "inactive" site on the skin that has been pretreated (so called "skin-drilling"). For exosomatic measurement both electrodes are simply attached to the left palm of

right-handed test persons or vice versa for left-handers. (For a detailed description of recording sites see Boucsein 1992).

EXPERIMENTAL DESIGN

The following empirical investigation was conducted in November 1999 and was intended to deliver a first experience in recording EDA at the point-of-sale. A questionnaire was applied in addition for control reasons. Testing the influence of different stimuli settings on arousal was of major interest.

The investigation was conducted in the fruit and vegetable department of two Austrian grocery stores. Both stores belong to the same retail chain and are located in a distance of a ten minutes walk from another. The management of that retail chain pursues different marketing strategies with both stores. For "Store 1" (opened at the beginning of 1999) insights from environmental psychology have been considered. Here, fruits and vegetables are presented in large-scale on broad and deep carriers and are arranged according to colors. Exotic fruits, fresh herbs and flowers are used as eye-catchers. Part of the products are presented on sort of an "island" in the middle. The whole store is spacious and high-ceilinged, and has bright electric light. In our investigation we treat this store as the experimental store. In "Store 2", our control store that was opened in 1974, the same assortment of fruits and vegetables are offered. Quality and prices are exactly equal. However, insights from environmental psychology have not been considered for the store decoration. The light appears less bright. Shelves are put along side the wall and display tables are arranged in a row in the middle of a long and narrow aisle. Contrary to "Store 1", an extraordinary product presentation (for example, by an arrangement according to colors) was not applied.

We hypothesize that the "Store 1" that is decorated according to the principles of environmental psychology would evoke higher arousal than the ordinary "Store 2". That is, customers of "Store 1" would be more highly aroused during shopping than customers of "Store 2".

In the experimental store 15 test persons were asked to do their ordinary shopping in the vegetable department while EDA[6] was registered. In the control store we collected EDA data from 12 test persons. Test customers were asked to participate right after entering the store. The two electrodes were attached to the palm of those who agreed. Both, the EDA apparel and the telemetric device were either laid in the trolley or put in the test subject's pocket. The data was transmitted via the telemetric device to the computer that was installed at the end of the fruit and vegetable department for online registration. From that part of the store, we also observed the participants. In both stores the fruit and vegetable section is the first part of the store the test subjects walked through. Before they went on to another part of the store, electrodes were detached and

---

[2] FAST = Facial Affect Scoring Technique

[3] FACS = Facial Acting Coding System

[4] μS = mikrosiemens. Siemens is the unit to measure conductance between two objects.

[5] kW = kiloohm. Ohm is the unit to measure resistance between two objects.

[6] For registration we chose an exosomatic approach applying DC (0.4V) and measuring skin conductance. The technical equipment runs with a 12 bit A/D (analog to digital) converter. We used two Ag/AgCl electrodes filled with a 0.5% NaCl electrode creme. Electrodes were attached to the left palm of right-handers and vice versa. The apparel allows telemetric online registration and is thus suitable for studies at the point-of-sale.

TABLE 1

items	store	mean (for illustration)	n	mean rank	Mann -Whitney	Monte Carlo Sig.
total amplitude	experimental	12.753	15	17.07	44.000	.024
	control	6.752	12	10.17		
frequency	experimental	84.73	15	17.20	42.000	.016
	control	47.25	12	10.00		
total amplitude/ min.	experimental	5.790	15	14.60	81.000	.679
	control	3.340	12	13.25		
duration of stay	experimental	13,142.33	15	17.73	34.000	.005
	control	7,547.88	12	9.33		

TABLE 2

items		Total amplitude	frequency	total amplitude per min
DES-dim. joy: "glad" (n=27)	Pearson Corr. (2-tailed Sig.)	.464 (.015)	.420 (.029)	.322 (.101)
Information rate: "varied" (n=27)	Pearson Corr. (2-tailed Sig.)	.381 (.050)	.333 (.089)	.402 (.038)

registration stopped. Each individual was then asked to answer a standardized questionnaire. The questionnaire was the same for both stores.

RESULTS FROM EDA MEASUREMENT

Concerning socio-demographic data, no significant differences were found between the two samples concerning age, education, number of persons living in the same household, income and sex.

Prior to statistical evaluation from EDA, parameters have to be extracted from recordings. In order to gain valid parameters, we first excluded all artifacts[7] from the recorded curves. Also the first part of the curves were not rated up to the point where the test subjects were used to the electrodes and their curve showed a consistent level.

For phasic EDA, the amplitude is the most frequently used parameter in order to describe each single reaction (Boucsein 1992; Cacioppo, Marshall-Goodell, and Gormezano 1983). For the calculation of the amplitude, an amplitude criterion needs to be defined: that is, the minimum an amplitude has to show in order to be evaluated as a "true" reaction to a stimulus. The amplitude might otherwise be due to a recording artifact derived from the frequency noise of the direct current (Boucsein 1992). Although signal-to-voice ratio of the applied apparel would allow an amplitude criterion of 0.01μS, we decided to apply 0.05μS in accordance with recommendations in the literature (Venables and Christie 1980).

Basically, there are two ways to evaluate overlapping amplitudes: (1) The amplitude of the second reaction is measured from its peak to the extrapolated recovery line of the preceding amplitude; (2) evaluating the second amplitude from its own baseline regardless of the recovery time of the preceding amplitude. The latter method is considered to be standard and sufficient (Boucsein 1992) and was thus preferred in order to gain the amplitudes for our statistical evaluation.

With this paper we want to focus the impact of stimuli in the store environment on arousal. Therefore, when measuring arousal at the point-of-sale, we have two problems to deal with: (1) The test person is not exposed to a single stimuli but to the overall appearance of the store; (2) He/she can look at and approach whatever

attracts attention for as long as he/she wants to. That means there is no fixed time a certain stimuli is presented. The first problem is similar to lab-examinations of TV-commercials. We therefore referred to Steiger (1988), who suggests to sum up the amplitudes per person recorded over the total length of the commercial (receiving the total amplitude). When summing up the amplitudes of the test persons produced over their controlled shopping time, we in fact found significant difference in total amplitudes for the two stores by means of a Mann-Whitney U Test[8] (see Table 1). This means that the *experimental store* evokes a *higher arousal* than the *control store*.

If each skin conductance response demonstrates special attention of the individual towards an object of its environment, the frequency of responses becomes relevant. Thus, Steiger (1988) also suggests evaluating the frequency of skin conductance responses. Our data shows significantly higher frequency in the response rate of test persons in the experimental store compared to those in the control store. This indicates that the environment of the experimental store provides more information that has potential to attract enough attention to be cognitively processed.

Yet, the second problem mentioned above (different duration of exposure to stimuli) is not solved with these parameters. If a pleasing store atmosphere also leads to a longer duration of stay, there should be a significant difference between both stores concerning this variable. We compared the duration of shopping in the fruit and vegetable section, which is equivalent to the duration of recording and is given on a 1/100-second index base. The mean

---

[7] Among the most frequently detected artifacts during our measurements were for example turning the trolley too rapidly by using the hand connected to the electrodes, "struggling" to tear off one of the plastic bags for fruits and vegetables, any kind of pressure upon electrodes, or change in intimacy of contact between electrode and skin. In some cases also speech activity occurred and was excluded as artifact. For a detailed description of physiologically produced artifacts see Boucsein (1992).

[8] Mann-Whitney U was chosen to replace Independent Samples T-Test for the small samples here are not fulfilling the Normal Distribution assumption.

TABLE 3

items	store	mean (for illustration)	n	mean rank	Mann - Whitney	Monte Carlo Sig.
"irresistible"	experimental	2.94	16	18.50	64.000	.042
	control	2.07	14	12.07		
"caught my eye"	experimental	4.00	16	16.53	47.500	.039
	control	2.73	11	10.32		
DES-dim. surprise	experimental	2.25	16	19.38	66.000	.021
"astonished"	control	1.53	15	12.40		
DES-dim. joy	experimental	2.75	16	19.25	68.000	.028
"happy"	control	1.93	15	12.53		
DES-dim. surprise	experimental	2.00	16	19.06	71.000	.021
"amazed"	control	1.13	15	12.73		

TABLE 4

Items	store	mean (for illustration)	n	mean rank	Mann -Whitney	Monte Carlo Sig.
Orientation	experimental	4.24	17	16.24	123.000	.861
pleasantness	control	4.40	15	16.80		
"clear structure"	experimental	4.47	17	16.76	123.000	.872
	control	4.40	15	16.20		
"fair prices"	experimental	3.63	16	14.44	95.000	.301
	control	3.87	15	17.67		
"prices are	experimental	4.18	17	14.62	95.500	.203
all right"	control	4.33	15	18.63		

TABLE 5

items	store	mean	n	Signif. F	Homogeneous subgroups
"I will return"	experimental	4.68	37	0.030	no
	control	4.14	36		
"I will recommend"	experimental	4.68	37	0.008	no
	control	3.97	36		
estimated amount	experimental	öS 357.94	36	0.031	no
spent previously	control	öS 226.21	34		

length of stay is 13,142.33 sec. in "Store 1" and 7,547.83 sec. in "Store 2". The assumption turned out to be true as the Mann-Whitney U Test showed.

Concerning the time problem, one can argue that there should also be a difference in total arousal in a given period of time (arousal per minute). Comparing test subjects' total amplitude per minute between both stores, the results point into the right direction; however the difference is not significant.

Considering these outcomes, it is fair to assume that once a product is discovered, it evokes higher arousal in "Store 1" than in "Store 2". Compared to the control store, more objects are discovered in the experimental store and the customer stays longer in the fruit and vegetable department. In other words, the experimental store has a higher arousing overall store atmosphere.

RESULTS FROM THE QUESTIONNAIRE

Basically, EDA measures arousal, but the perceived emotion (cognitively interpreted arousal) that is derived from arousal cannot be indicated from any EDA parameter. We therefore used verbal scales with items on the overall store perception and emotions. In order to measure whether the perceived emotions were

more or less positive, we used a German version of Izard's (1994) positive dimensions of the Differential Emotions Scale (DES). The dimensions are "interest", "surprise", and "joy". For the total sample, both, the total amplitude and the frequency show significant correlation, but only with the item "glad" of the dimension "joy". Another scale on the overall appearance of the store that has been used in several previous studies in order to measure the information rate (Groeppel 1991, 1992) shows significant correlation between the item "varied" and the total amplitude, as well as with the amplitude per minute. There is also correlation on the 90% level between the item "varied" and the frequency of electrodermal response (see table 2).

On a five point disagreement-agreement scale products appeared more "irresistible" to test subjects in the experimental store than in the control store. A product they had picked had more often "suddenly caught their eye". Also test subjects in "Store 1" were significantly more "astonished", "happy", and "amazed" when discovering a chosen product compared to those in "Store 2".

The results of the DES-items and of the items "irresistible" as well as "caught my eye" can lead to the conclusion that a higher arousing store environment can also lead to a higher rate of unplanned and impulse purchases. Results are also in line with the above stated outcome from the frequency index.

CONTROL VARIABLES

From the cognitive approach of environmental psychology we learn that the perceived orientation pleasantness is an important variable. A store with many activating stimuli designed to serve as "landmarks" for cognitive maps should not be perceived as cluttered or chaotic. Therefore, we also measured orientation pleasantness. In addition we controlled the perceived price image of the two stores in order to check whether a store with a pleasant atmosphere and decoration is perceived as more expensive. This would lead to a boomerang for the retailer.

Table 4 shows that concerning the orientation pleasantness and the price image there is no significant difference between the two stores.

In addition, we took a larger sample size in order to control response variables. This sample also included all test persons who had been shopping with the EDA apparatus. The results from a Oneway ANOVA show significant differences in the intention variables "I will return to the shop", "I will recommend the store to others" as well as in the estimated amount spent during the last shopping trip in that particular store (see table 5).

One can summarize that optimum arousal evoked at the point-of-sale can improve the overall perception of the store, lead to a better information processing, extend the duration of stay and thus eventually enhance purchases.

CONCLUSION

The results show that recording EDA at the point-of-sale is a practicable way to measure arousal in a valid manner. The findings confirm hypotheses from environmental psychology and our hypothesis which postulates that the experimental store represents the higher arousing store environment. EDA can thus be a future research method in order to work out visual merchandising themes that evoke an optimum of arousal. EDA recording can also be applied to explore arousal and orienting reflexes derived from different environmental stimuli settings and the arousal potential of elements designed to be visually striking. Verbal scales that indicate arousal can also be validated. Furthermore, EDA records arousal evoked at the point of sale *simultaneously* to the perception of stimuli *during* shopping.

However, EDA recording has also limitations, especially concerning the time that is needed in order to collect satisfying sample sizes. Not every consumer is willing to be "connected" to electrodes. Also, as long as a computerized artifact detection is not possible, artifact detection needs to be done manually by screening each single curve. Another restriction is the fact that EDA cannot reveal whether an arousing situation was perceived with positive or with negative emotions, whether a situation was rather pleasing or unpleasing. Verbal control of perceived emotions by a standardized questionnaire is therefore necessary.

Further discussion is needed with respect to suitable parameters calculated from the EDA curves when data is collected at the point of sale.

Larger research samples may reveal the actual role of arousal for shopping behavior. What is the optimum information rate of a store environment, which stimuli can actually serve as eye catchers and which others are more suitable for relaxation in order to prevent a frantic mood? Despite the limitations, EDA seems to be a promising method in order to do further research on these and other open questions related to store environments.

REFERENCES

Babin, Barry J., William R. Darden, and Mitch Griffin (1994), "Work and/or Fun: Measuring Hedonic and Utilitarian Shopping Value," *Journal of Consumer Research*, Vol. 10, March, 644-656.

Bagozzi, Richard P., Mahesh Gopinath, and Prashanth U. Nyer (1999), "The Role of Emotions in Marketing," *Journal of the Academy of Marketing Science*, 27, Spring 1999, 184-206.

Bekmeier, Sigrid (1989), *Nonverbale Kommunikation in der Fernsehwerbung*, Heidelberg: Physica.

Boedeker, Mika (1995), Optimum Stimulation Level and Recreational Shopping Tendency," *European Advances in Consumer Research*, Vol. 2, ed. Fleming Hansen, Provo, UT: Association for Consumer Research, 372-380.

Bost, Erhard (1987), *Ladenatmosphaere und Konsumentenvarhalten*, Heidelberg: Physica.

Boucsein, Wolfram (1997), "Aktivierung," *Handbuch Arbeitswissenschaft*, eds. Luczak, Holger and Walter Volpert, Stuttgart: Schaeffer-Poeschel, 309-312.

Boucsein, Wolfram (1992), *Electrodermal Activity*. New York, London: Plenum Press.

Cacioppo, John T., Berverly S. Marshall-Goodell, and Isidore Gormezano (1983), "Social psychology: Bioelectrical Measurement, Experimental Control, and Analog-to-Digital Data Aquisition," *Social Psychology,* ed. John T. Cacioppo, Richard E. Petty, and David Shapiro, New York: Guilford Press, 666-690.

Dawson, A., P. H. Bloch, and N. M. Ridgway (1990), Shopping Motives, Emotional States, and Retail Outcomes," *Journal of Retailing*, Vol. 66, 4, 408-427.

Donovan, Robert J., John R. Rossiter, Gilian Marcoolyn, and Andrew Nesdale (1994), "Store Atmosphere and Purchasing Behavior," *Journal of Retailing*, Vol. 70, 3, 283-294.

Donovan, Robert J. and John R. Rossiter (1982), "Store Atmosphere: An Environmental Psychology Approach," *Journal of Retailing*, Vol. 28, 1, Spring 1982, 34-57.

Doux Le, Joseph (1996), *The Emotional Brain: The Mysterious Underpinnings of Emotional Life*, New York: Simon & Schuster.

Ekman, Paul and Wallace V. Friesen (1978), *Facial Action Coding System (FACS): A Technique for the Measurement of Facial Actions*, Palo Alto, CA: Consulting Psychologists Press.

Ekman, Paul, Wallace V. Friesen, and Silvan S. Tomkins (1971), "Facial Affect Scoring Technique: A First Validity Study," *Semiotica*, Vol. 3, 1, 37-58.

Eysenck, Michael W. (1982), *Attention and Arousal*, Berlin: Springer.

Flicker, Marcia H. and William C. Speer (1990), "Emotional Responses to Store Layout and Design: An Experimental Approach," *Enhancing Knowledge Development in Marketing*, eds. Parasuraman, A., 1990 AMA Educators' Proceedings, Vol. 1, Chicago, IL: AMA, 1-5.

Golledge, Reginald G. (1987), "Environmental Cognition", *Handbook of Environmental Psychology*, Vol. I, eds. Daniel Stokols and Irvin Altman, New York: Wiley, 131-174.

Groeppel-Klein, Andrea (2000), "Aktivierung," *Vahlens Großes Marketing-Lexikon*, ed. Hermann Diller, Muenchen: Vahlen (upcoming soon).

Groeppel-Klein, Andrea (1999), "The Impact of Shopping Motives on Store Assessment," paper presented at the ACR European Summer Conference in June 24-26, 1999, Paris, France.

Groeppel-Klein, Andrea (1998a), *Wettbewerbsstrategien im Einzelhandel – Chancen und Risiken von Preisfuehrerschaft und Differenzierung*, Wiesbaden: Gabler.

Groeppel-Klein, Andrea (1998b), "Findings of Environmental Psychology for Differentiation Strategies in International Retailing," *Contemporary Developments in Marketing*, ed. An International Publication of the Scientific Committee of the Montpellier Graduate School of Management, Paris: ESKA.

Groeppel-Klein, Andrea (1997), "The Influence of the Dominance Perceived at the Point-of-Sale on the Price-Assessment," *European Advances in Consumer Research*, Vol. 3, eds. Englis, Basil G. und Anna Olofsson, Provo, UT: Association for Consumer Research, 304-311.

Groeppel, Andrea (1996), Preiswuerdigkeitsimages und Differenzierungsstrategien – Der Einfluss der am Point-of-Sale empfundenen Dominanz auf die Preisbeurteilung, *Handelsforschung 1996/97*, ed. Volker Trommsdorff, Berlin: Gabler, 297-315.

Groeppel, Andrea (1992), "Erlebnishandel und Verbundpraesentation", *Thexis*, 4, September, 16-21.

Groeppel, Andrea (1991), *Erlebnisstrategien im Einzelhandel*, Heidelberg: Physika.

Groeppel, Andrea and Brian Bloch (1990), "An Investigation of Experience-Orientated Consumers in Retailing," *The International Review of Retail, Distribution and Consumer Research*, October 1990, 101-118.

Grossbart, Sanford L. and Balusu Rammohan (1981), "Cognitive Maps and Shopping Convenience," *Advances in Consumer Research*, Vol. 8, ed. K. B. Monroe, Ann Arbor, 128-133.

Ittelson, William H. (1977), *Einfuehrung in die Umweltpsychologie*, Stuttgart: Klett-Cotta.

Izard, Carroll E., 1994, *Die Emotionen des Menschen. Eine Einfuehrung in die Grundlagen der Emotionspsychologie*, 3rd ed., Weinheim: Beltz.

Kenhoven Van, Patrick and Patrick Desrumaux (1997), "The relationship between emotional states and approach or avoidance responses in a retail environment," *The International Review of Retail, Distribution and Consumer Research*, 7:4, October 1997, 351-368.

Mehrabian, Albert (1978), *Raeume des Alltags oder wie die Umwelt unser Verhalten bestimmt*, Frankfurt am Main, New York: Campus.

Mehrabian, Albert (1976), Public Places and Private Spaces. The Psychology of Work, Play, and Living Environments, New York: Basic Books.

Mehrabian, Albert and James A. Russell (1974), *An Approach to Environmental Psychology*, Cambridge, MA: MIT.

Meyer-Hentschel, Gundolf (1983), *Aktivierungswirkung von Anzeigen*, Wuerzburg, Wien: Physica.

Russell, James A. and M. Ward (1982), "Environmental Psychology," *Annual Review of Psychology*, 651-688.

Sommer, Robert and Susan Aitkens (1982), "Mental Mapping of Two Supermarkets," *Journal of Consumer Research*, Vol. 9, September 1982, 211-215.

Steiger, Andreas (1988), *Computergestuetzte Aktivierungsmessung in der Marketing-forschung*, Frankfurt am Main, Bern, New York, Paris: Peter Lang.

Tai, Susan H. C. and Agnes M. C. Fung (1997), "Application of an environmental psychology model to in-store buying behaviour," *The International Review of Retail, Distribution and Consumer Research* 7:4, October 1997, 311-337.

Venables, Peter H. and M. J. Christie (1980), Electrodermal activity, ed. Irene Martin and Peter H. Venables, Techniques in psychophysiology, New York: Wiley, 3-67.

Vitouch, Peter (1997), "Psychophysiological Methods in Media Research," *New Horizons in Media Psychology*, eds. Peter Winterhoff-Spurk and Tom H. A. van der Voort, Opladen: Westdeutscher Verlag.

Wener, Richard (1985), "The Environmental Psychology of the Service Encounter," *The Service Encounter*, eds. John A. Czepiel, Michael R. Solomon, and Carol F. Surprenant, Lexington, MA: Lexington Books, 101-112.

Defending Against Consumerism: An Emergent Typology of Purchase Restraint Strategies

Omar Shehryar, University of Missouri-Columbia
Timothy D. Landry, University of Missouri-Columbia
Todd J. Arnold, University of Missouri-Columbia

ABSTRACT

The lack of consumption restraint, indicative of consumerism, is causing concern among media members, policy makers and academics alike. Past research, however, has looked at consumer self-control only in cases of compulsive consumption and impulse driven purchases. The present study looks at strategies used by consumers who actively contemplate their buying decision in non-impulse situations and yet restrain from purchasing. Based on a content analysis of qualitative responses, an emergent typology of purchase restraint strategies is presented.

"The world is too much with us; late and soon,
Getting and spending, we lay waste our powers:
Little we see in Nature that is ours;
We have given our hearts away, a sordid boon!"
  -William Wordsworth, *The World is Too Much With Us*

INTRODUCTION

The causes and effects of consumerism—a preoccupation with the purchase of consumer goods—continue to receive substantial attention in both the mass media and in the academic press (e.g., Dollars and Sense 1999; Grossman, Cogan and Lui 2000; Rindfleisch, Burroughs and Denton 1997). At the consumer level, the lack of consumption restraint, indicative of consumerism, may result in feelings of guilt, anxiety, frustration and loss of control, financial hardships, and domestic dissension (O'Guinn and Faber 1989; Rook 1987). The broader socio-economic consequences associated with unrestrained consumption, it has been argued, include massive consumer debt, global resource depletion, and increasing environmental problems (Business Week 1999; World Futures 1999). Consumer researchers are not alone in viewing consumerism as the economically and morally debilitating pervasiveness of consumption. Other social scientists have defined consumerism in the same light in their critiques of consumption (Borgmann 2000; Schor 1998; Wuthnow 1996). Some even frame Western culture's obsession with "getting and spending" as religion; consumption is argued to be central in directing human lives through dictating daily activities and long term life goals—though often to the detriment of the individual and society (cf. Barber 1995).

Thus, understanding how individual consumers restrain their consumption activities is warranted. Past research on purchase restraint, however, has only looked at cases of compulsive consumption and impulse driven purchases. This research adds to that literature by exploring how consumers exhibit purchase restraint in situations involving substantial cognition about the purchase decision. While understanding this phenomenon is important in its own right, this research should provide guidance for counseling consumers on developing specific strategies to defend against their own consumerism.

BACKGROUND

While some have associated cultural shifts over the last quarter century with deleterious changes in consumer buying behavior (Meninger 1973; Wood 1998), others contend that the "excessiveness of the eighties" is being followed by a societal sensitivity toward consumerism's negative consequences (Tapscott 1998).

Certainly, society is increasingly exposed to arguments against consumerism (Grossman et al. 2000). To illustrate, the 1992 United Nations "Earth Summit" in Rio de Janeiro was widely publicized in its attempt to make the world more aware of the problems and potential solutions related to consumerism. Society's focus on consumerism, however, is largely unparalleled in the consumer behavior literature. Despite calls for better understanding of the means for moderating consumption (e.g., Borgmann 2000), few frameworks have been developed to address consumerism.

The phenomenon investigated here is different from the phenomena of restraint from compulsive consumption or impulse buying (e.g., Rook 1987; O'Guinn and Faber, 1989). Where those studies address purchase processes driven largely by habit or through spontaneous urges, the research presented here focuses on purchases involving substantial problem solving. Such a distinction between purchase types is supported in current conceptualizations of consumer problem solving in which purchases are categorized by the extent to which cognition is involved (Schiffman and Kanuk 2000).

Additionally, the research presented here differs by focusing specifically on purchase restraint for products perceived by the consumer as pleasurable and desired but not "necessary". While typical motivational models of purchase behavior fail to distinguish between wants and needs, a distinction between the two, even if defined by the individual consumer, is critical in addressing consumerism. Evidence that consumers do make such a distinction is implied in sociological commentary about the increasing consumer sensitivity to the perils of consumerism (Grossman et al. 2000; Tapscott 1998). Conceptually, the distinction between need and want is implied in viewing consumerism as excess consumption over what is needed for subsistence (cf. Borgmann 2000).

To better understand consumption restraint, as investigated in this study, useful similarities with the research on compulsive consumption and impulse purchasing will be exploited (Bellenger, Robertson and Hirschman, 1978; Hirschman 1992; Rook, 1987; Rook and Hoch 1985). For example, each has focused on explaining the consumption behaviors relating to product purchase and, further, has provided guidance for developing categories of purchase restraint. Moreover, extant research has relied heavily on theories from psychology (e.g., delay of gratification) that may apply to understanding the phenomenon of interest in this study.

Rook (1987) acknowledges that a lack of conceptual frameworks for exploring consumption restraint has limited the understanding of purchase behavior, and certainly no frameworks exist for specifically exploring the type of purchase restraint examined in this study. For example, a framework for understanding consumer restraint behavior *relating to impulse purchases* was offered by Hoch and Loewenstein (1991), but it was not validated by actual consumer responses and does not fit the phenomenon explored here. As such, the past research related to consumption restraint is a rich literature that can be *contrasted* with this study's findings but does not offer a conceptual framework for exploring the uniqueness of the phenomenon under investigation.

In sum, this study explores how consumers exhibit restraint from purchases that entail substantial cognition and involve a judgment of product necessity. To develop the conceptual framework (i.e., a typology of consumers' self-control strategies), quali-

TABLE 1
Emerging Categories and Classification of Responses

Strategy	No. of Responses	% of Total Responses
Need Re-Assessment	30	16%
Choice Re-Assessment	30	16%
Reprioritization	24	12.8%
Delay	32	17.2%
Time Binding	52	27.8%
Others	19	10.2%

tative data was collected from consumers to understand how they overcome purchase desires. The results of our study show that consumers employ several strategies to delay purchases. Many of these help clarify the self-control categories conjectured in related streams of research (i.e., impulse purchases; Hoch and Loewenstein 1991) and several are unique to more cognitive purchases. Again, these results not only provide a first step in achieving a better understanding of consumer self-control strategies but may also be useful in helping consumers avoid the negative consequences of consumerism.

THE STUDY

Purchase restraint was investigated through an open-ended questionnaire. This method of investigation is justified for the following reasons. First, as a social psychological phenomenon, delay of gratification, from which much of the extant theory on restraint is drawn, is a self-attributed need that derives from deep-seated personal and cultural values (McClelland 1989). That is, purchase restraint is reflective of an individual's conscious determination of product need influenced by societal values. Because purchase restraint is determined at a conscious level, the examination of personal accounts and behaviors through self-report is an appropriate means of investigating the phenomenon (Geen 1995). Second, the use of open-ended questions allows for content analysis of the data (Strauss and Corbin 1990). Content analysis allows for data to be broken down into discrete parts, examined closely, and compared for similarities and differences. Thus, comparisons across similar phenomena are less biased than would be the case if an extant framework were applied to the new phenomenon. It is through this process that Strauss and Corbin (1990, p. 62) note, "one's own and others' assumptions about phenomena are questioned or explored, leading to new discoveries". Thus, the use of open-ended questions allows for the development of purchase restraint categories that have not surfaced in previous research and affords systematic comparison of purchase restraint strategies across studies of similar phenomena (e.g., impulsive purchasing; Hoch and Loewenstein 1991).

Instrument and Sample

The data reported here were collected using a questionnaire that asked respondents open-ended questions about their purchase restraint behaviors. The first question asked the consumer to identify the thought process that allowed them to delay the purchase of a specific product they had previously identified as something they 1) actively contemplated purchasing, 2) could afford, and 3) wanted but did not consider a necessity. The specific recall technique used in this study has been used in other qualitative studies to elicit more accurate responses of the recalled event (e.g., "critical incidents"; Bitner, Booms and Mohr 1994). Next, consumers were asked about what other "tactics" or "strategies" they had employed to delay the purchase of a product. Approximately one-quarter of a page was allocated as response space for each

question. Respondents were encouraged to provide complete and detailed answers to the questions using the full space provided.

The questionnaires were completed using a self-report approach. Usable responses were collected from all subjects in a sample of 56 undergraduate and graduate respondents (21 males and 35 females). The sample's social status was generally representative of the lower middle to upper middle class groups in a mid-Western college town.

Data Analysis

Respondents' written responses were analyzed using content analytic procedures. This is an appropriate method for categorizing qualitative responses to open-ended questions (Kassarjian 1977; Strauss and Corbin 1990). Initially, a detailed analysis of each sentence included in a respondent's answer was conducted to determine the central idea brought out by the sentence. Each sentence was then labeled to represent a general action or thought. These labels were then grouped based upon the similarity of actions or thoughts to arrive at overarching categories that explained the same or similar purchase restraint techniques.

Category Reliability

Based upon the above procedure, six coding categories were defined for third party analysis of respondent's descriptions of their purchase restraint behaviors (Kassarjian 1977). Explicit written definitions of each category were provided to trained judges. The two judges (both doctoral students) conducted a content analysis, where consumer responses were coded based upon the described categories. Following this, some category definitions were revised. No coding categories had to be discarded due to the judges' inability to reach a reasonable level of reliability.

Interjudge Reliability

The content analysis involved a judgment of a total of 187 separate responses. There were 17 inter-judge disagreements. This resulted in an overall inter-judge reliability of 90.9 percent, which conforms to conventional acceptance criteria (Kassarjian 1977). Coding disagreements tended to cluster around the more abstract categories (i.e., "other"). All disagreements between judges were discussed and resolved by the authors, and the reported research results reflect a 100 percent resolution.

FINDINGS

The above analysis revealed six distinct strategies that consumers employ to restrain from purchase. These strategies differ from those previously proposed in related research (i.e., impulse purchases; Hoch and Loewenstein 1991). This is not surprising in that Hoch and Loewenstein (1991, p. 493) focused upon time-inconsistent choice where, "… a purchase choice would not have been made if it had been contemplated from a removed, dispassionate perspective". In contrast, this study focuses specifically upon consumer purchases that are actively contemplated. Therefore, certain categories of purchase restraint unique to the impulsiveness phenomenon (e.g., not bringing a credit card to the store or avoiding shopping centers altogether) did not emerge from our data.

Respondents' anecdotes provide the clearest picture of typical non-impulse consumer restraint techniques. Therefore, each of the following emergent strategies will be illustrated through the use of specific responses. Before presenting the categories, it should be noted that not every respondent used all six strategies. Table 1 highlights, however, that each of the categories was adequately represented across the responses.

NEED REASSESSMENT

Need reassessment refers to the strategy where consumers' internal dialogue urged a reappraisal of the basic need. The reappraisal did not reflect negatively on the product to be purchased or any other marketplace factors such as price, quality or variety but was purely a self-instruction to review the necessity of the given purchase. The following examples illustrate this strategy:

- I did not purchase the camera because I knew that I would not use it that often.
- I'm not sure why I wanted the watch. I didn't purchase it because I certainly didn't need it.
- I wanted to play hockey but I didn't have the skates. I asked myself, how important is playing hockey?

CHOICE REASSESSMENT

In contrast with need assessment, choice reassessment occurs when the decision not to purchase is deferred by either berating the available choice or by enhancing the value of a present possession for which the prospective choice will serve as a substitute. These two tactics were seen as complementary and responses often contained both elements when mentioning the use of this strategy. Examples of each include:

- I didn't buy the new CD because I thought I might get sick of the song fast. My favorite song was already being played on the radio quite often and I wasn't sure I would enjoy the CD as a whole. *(Berating Available Choice)*
- Is my old car really so bad that I need to get a new one? *(Enhancing Value of Present Possession)*
- My old CD player worked fine, and the new one would probably not sound much different. *(Both elements)*

RE-PRIORITIZATION OF NEED

Instead of reassessing the basic need, consumers may defer a purchase decision regarding a particular product by lowering its priority in their "shopping list". Thus, consumers may restrain themselves from buying a product by reminding themselves of other things they can buy instead. Contrary to need re-assessment the basic need is not being questioned. It is only the urgency of the need that is being contemplated which leads to the deferral of the purchase. The reprioritization of needs does not reflect affordability concerns on the part of the consumers since respondents were told specifically that they should only consider forgone purchases situations where they had the money to buy a product, yet decided not to purchase. Examples of re-prioritization include:

- I had a lot of other things I wanted to buy which made more sense than a new coat.
- Before purchasing I think of something I might need even more.

- I said to myself, there is something more practical I could use this money for.

TIME BINDING

A decision to delay choice has been conceptualized as postponement or time binding (Jones and Gerard 1967; Hoch and Loewenstein 1991). The distinction between the two, however, is unclear. Postponement has been defined as a delay tactic characterized by further information seeking, whereas time-binding has been defined as delay focusing on the positive benefits of the deferral (Jones and Gerard1967; Hoch and Lowenstein 1991). Although past research does not define these categories as mutually exclusive, through our data it became clear that there does exist a difference between two types of "postponement".

Thus, time binding is conceptualized here as a purchase postponement wherein purchase consideration is re-activated only by an external trigger. Three such triggers consistently emerged. First, consumers may wait for a sale even though they are able to buy a product at its current price. Secondly, consumers may defer purchase until more products are made available. Finally, consumers may wait for a technological advance that will make present choices obsolete. Examples for each include:

(Sale)
- I waited to purchase the minidisk player because I knew the price would go down.
- I'll wait to buy books because I know they will go on sale.

(More Products)
- I didn't want to purchase the camera at the time because I was sure that other products would be introduced later.
- I waited to buy the car because I know the more I save the better the car I can get.

(Technological Advances)
- I'm hesitant to buy stereos because I know that certain features will soon be outdated by technological advances.
- I waited to purchase a VCR because I knew the technology was getting better (DVD players).

DELAY

It is suggested here that delay is a strategy that is not contingent on the occurrence of a future trigger. Rather delay is characterized by a postponement of purchase where reconsideration is dependent upon actions controllable by the consumer. For example, delay occurs when consumers feel that they need to continue searching for products. Similarly, delay occurs when consumers feel that they should seek out the expertise of a peer or family member before the purchase. The conceptual differences between delay and time binding are important as each may differentially impact the effectiveness of purchase restraint. Examples of delay include:

(Search)
- I waited to buy because I would like to see all the different products.
- I didn't purchase the rock shocks (shock absorbers for mountain bike) because I really wanted to look at other brands.

(Seeking Expertise)
- I didn't want to buy the outfit right away because I thought I should probably have someone come see it on me to make sure it looked good.
- Before I buy I like to talk to people who already own the product or who have conducted a search.

OTHER

Other strategies used by respondents did not appear consistently enough to warrant a separate category. However, each of these is conceptually important and thus needs to be discussed. These strategies were merged into the 'other' category. Responses depicting three distinct types of tactics were obtained.

The Slippery Slope:

This tactic was used by consumers to remind themselves that the purchase of a particular product would lead to further purchases and was tantamount to going down a slippery slope of unrestrained buying behavior. Examples of the slippery slope include:

- I didn't buy the CD player for my car because I knew I would spend even more money on CD's.
- I didn't buy the TV because such a purchase would require more purchases, like a VCR.

Anticipated Gifts:

Some respondents mentioned that they delay purchases by hoping that a family member might give them the same product as a gift on a special occasion. Such anticipations help consumers restrain purchase behavior. Examples of responses depicting this tactic are as follows:

- I waited to see if my parents would give me the cell phone as a gift.
- I didn't buy the running shoes because I was hoping my mom would buy them for me for my birthday.

Guilt:

Respondents mentioned that they felt guilty when committing excesses in purchasing. Other researchers have also associated psychic costs with excesses in purchases (O'Guinn and Faber 1989; Hoch and Loewenstein 1991). Our data supports the use of this tactic. The following responses provide examples of the use of this strategy by respondents.

- I didn't buy the CD because I felt that I had already bought too many.
- I could not justify having two leather jackets.

DISCUSSION

Past research suggests that impulse purchases arise from sudden and unexpected urges to buy (O'Guinn and Faber, 1989; Rook, 1987). While frameworks for restraint from those types of purchases have been offered, they are yet to be verified (e.g., Hoch and Loewenstein 1991). In the Hoch and Loewenstein (1991) conceptualization of restraint from impulsive purchases, restraint categories have been discussed as contributing to either increasing willpower or decreasing product desire. Our findings, however, are more generalizable to the many purchases that are not based on resisting a spontaneous urge but on rethinking if a purchase is necessary. Such deliberation does not readily fit into the willpower/desire model. Thus, this research makes a contribution by identifying purchase restraint strategies that are associated with more traditional consumer behavior models of rational and reasoned action. Moreover, by collecting and analyzing qualitative data we point to possible shortcomings in the unverified related conceptualizations of consumption restraint.

Additionally, this study highlights an important difference in two types of purchase postponement tactics: delay and time binding. These tactics, now conceptually distinct, are important in that one type may be substantially more successful than the other.

Empirical validation of this idea is warranted as it appears that postponement based on an external "trigger" (i.e., time binding) may allow the consumer to temporarily step out of the purchase process and better defend against the desire to purchase. Viewed in terms of purchase involvement, time binding may allow the consumer to become situationally un-involved (cf. Bloch and Richins 1983) until the external trigger is activated (e.g., a new, improved line of products becomes available).

A surprising finding was that people apparently engage in re-prioritization of needs even for purchases that are affordable. The generality of this finding needs verification. It could be that our sample was susceptible to monetary considerations due to their demographic profile. Or, it may be that consumers do, in fact, re-order their purchases as a conscious attempt to distance them from a particular purchase that is viewed as a non-necessity.

Interestingly, anticipation of gifts as a purchase restraint behavior was mentioned in several responses. To the best of our knowledge, this strategy is unique to purchase restraint involving substantial cognition having never before appeared in the purchase restraint literature. It is fair to say that this finding is not particular to our set of respondents since gift giving is not restricted to parents and children but is also common between spouses, and friends among others.

Finally, unlike the restraint literature dealing with compulsive consumption or impulse buying, our typology reveals that consumers may engage in at least one of two distinct approaches to re-evaluating need: reconsidering basic needs and reappraising the value of the particular purchase. Additionally, it was found that devaluing a given purchase is often accompanied by revaluing an existing product. Empirical work is needed to understand the impact that these strategies, either considered individually or in combination, have on actual purchase restraint.

FUTURE RESEARCH

While this study was not intended as a review of the delay of gratification research, that research stream points to other considerations that could be included in a purchase restraint study such as socio-economic status variables like education (Wood, 1998), as well as personality variables like aggressiveness, intelligence and ego-resilience (Funder and Block 1990; Funder, Block and Block 1980; Kruger et al. 1996). While such individual differences have been proposed as difficult for a consumer to overcome, other research supports the view that using cognitive restructuring techniques people can be taught to restrain from instant gratification (Nisan and Koriat 1984; Moore, Mischel and Zeiss 1977). Using the typology proposed here, similar contentions for purchase restraint could be explored empirically. Thus, validating the typology of strategies used by consumers to restrain from "cognitive" purchasing not only broadens the theoretical perspective on purchase restraint but also may help in developing consumer counseling about purchase restraint. To illustrate, credit counseling typically offers little psychological counseling but focuses heavily on debt consolidation (as such counseling is often provided by credit bureaus whose motives may be less than forthright). We hope this research serves as the basis for developing real strategies for consumption restraint.

Finally, other researchers have sought to explain consumers' increased interest in products in terms of a materialistic mindset (e.g., Belk, 1985; Richins and Dawson 1992; Rindfleisch, Burroughs and Denton 1997). The relation between consumerism and materialism, however, is complex and largely unexplored. Broadly, as society acknowledges that excesses are undesired (Tapscott 1998), consumers may choose to purchase products that are better aligned with needs and not with desires. In the strictest sense, these consumers remain materialistic as their possessions, albeit the bare necessities, define their success (Richins and Dawson 1992). In this case, however, "success" is redefined in terms of more restrained consumption. More philosophical and sociological inquiry is needed to better understand the complexities between materialism and consumerism.

REFERENCES

Barber, Benjamin R. (1995), *Jihad vs. McWorld*, New York: Times Books, 1995

Belk, Russel W. (1985), "Materialism: Trait Aspects of Living in the Material World," *Journal of Consumer Research*, Vol. 12 (December), 265-280.

Bellenger, Danny, D. H. Robertson and Elizabeth C. Hirschman (1978), "Impulse Buying Varies by Product," *Journal of Advertising Research*, 18 (December), 15-18.

Bitner, Mary Jo, Bernard H. Booms and J. Mohr (1994), "Critical Service Encounters: The Employee's Viewpoint," *Journal of Marketing*, Vol. 58 (October), 96-106.

Bloch, Peter H. and Marsha L. Richins (1983), "A Theoretical Model for the Study of Product Importance Perceptions," *Journal of Marketing*, Vol. 47 (Summer), 59-81.

Borgmann, Albert (2000), "The Moral Complexion of Consumption," *Journal of Consumer Research*, 26 (4), 418-422.

Business Week, November 1, 1999, p. 4041.

Dollars and Sense, July-August, 1999, p24 (5).

Funder, David C. and Jack Block (1990), "The Role of Ego-Control, Ego-Resiliency, and IQ in Delay of Gratification in Adolescence," *Journal of Personality and Social Psychology*, Vol. 57 (6), December, 1041-1050.

_____ , Jeanne H. Block and Jack Block (1983), "Delay of Gratification: Some Longitudinal Personality Correlates," *Journal of Personality and Social Psychology*, Vol. 44 (6), June, 1198-1213.

Geen, Russel (1995), *Human Motivation: A Social Psychological Approach,* Pacific Grove, CA: Brooks/Cole.

Grossman, David, John J. Cogan, and Mei-Hui-Lui (2000), "Citizenship: The Democratic Imagination in Global/Local Context," *Social Education*, 64, 48 – 52.

Hirschman, Elizabeth C. (1992), "The Consciousness of Addiction: Toward a General Theory of Compulsive Consumption," *Journal of Consumer Research*, Vol. 19 (Sep), 155-179.

Hoch, Stephen J. and George F. Loewenstein (1991), "Time-inconsistent Preferences and Consumer Self-Control," *Journal of Consumer Research*, Vol. 17 (March), 492-507.

Jones, Edward and Harold B. Gerard (1967), *Foundations of Social Psychology*, New York: Wiley.

Kassarjian, Harold H. (1977), "Content Analysis in Consumer Research," *Journal of Consumer Research*, Vol. 4 (1), 8-17.

Krueger, Robert F., Avshalom Caspi, Terrie E. Moffitt, Jennifer White, and Magda Stouthamer-Loeber (1996), "Delay of Gratification, Psychopathology, and Personality: Is Low Self-Control Specific to Externalizing Problems?" *Journal of Personality*, Vol. 64 (1) March, 107-129.

McClelland, David C. (1989), "Motivational Factors in Health and Disease," *American Psychologist*. Vol 44 (4), 675-683.

Meninger, Karl (1973), *Whatever Became of Sin?*, New York: NY American Library.

Moore, Bert, Walter Mischel, and Antonette Zeiss (1976), "Comparative Effects of the Reward Stimulus and its Cognitive Representation in Voluntary Delay," *Journal of Personality and Social Psychology*, Vol. 34 (3), September, 419-424.

Nisan, Mordecai and Asher Koriat (1984), "The Effect of Cognitive Restructuring on Delay of Gratification," *Child Development*, Vol. 55 (2) April, 492-503.

O'Guinn, Thomas and Ronald J. Faber (1989), "Compulsive Buying: A Phenomenological Exploration," *Journal of Consumer Research*, Vol. 16 (September), 147-157.

Richins, Marsha L. and Scott Dawson (1992), "A Consumer Values Orientation for Materialism and Its Measurement: Scale Development and Validation," *Journal of Consumer Research*, Vol. 19 (3), 303-316.

Rindfleisch, Aric, James E. Burroughs and Frank Denton (1997), "Family Structure, Materialism, and Compulsive Consumption," *Journal of Consumer Research*, Vol. 23 (4), 312-326.

Rook, Dennis and Stephen J. Hoch (1985), "Consuming Impulses," in *Advances in Consumer Research*, Vol. 12 eds. Morris B. Holbrook and Elizabeth C. Hirschman, Provo, UT: Association for Consumer Research, 23-27.

_____ (1987), "The Buying Impulse," *Journal of Consumer Research*, Vol. 14 (September), 189-199.

Schiffman, Leog G. and Leslie L. Kanuk (2000), *Consumer Behavior*, Seventh Edition: Prentice Hall.

Schor, Juliet B. (1998), *The Overspent American*, New York: Basic.

Strauss, Anselm L. and Juliet M. Corbin (1990), *Basics of Qualitative Research: Grounded Theory Procedures and Techniques*, Newbury Park, California: Sage Publications

Tapscott, Don (1998), *Growing Up Digital: The Rise of the Net Generation*, NY: McGraw Hill.

Wood, Michael (1998), "Socio-economic Status, Delay of Gratification, and Impulse Buying," *Journal of Economic Psychology*, Vol. 19, 295-320.

World Futures, December 1999, p. 377

Wuthnow, Robert (1996), *Poor Richard's Principle*, Princeton, NJ: Princeton University Press.

Letting Go: The Process and Meaning of Dispossession in the Lives of Consumers

Catherine A. Roster, University of Missouri

ABSTRACT

The disposition of possessions involves more than the act of disposal. It is a process, one that facilitates the physical and psychological severance of an object from its possessor. While the act accomplishes final physical severance from the good, its meaning to consumers and the psychological process that enables it is more aptly described as that of "dis*possession*." This paper presents findings from depth interviews with 21 consumers that suggest stages in this process. Furthermore, findings reveal that consumers voluntarily dispose of possessions with special meanings, which serves to heighten the relevance of this final stage of the consumption experience.

INTRODUCTION

Possessions are valued for the meanings they embody, the instrumentalities they provide, and the contributions they make to our well being. Periodically, however, we discover that circumstances surrounding us have changed and that perhaps even we ourselves have changed. Furthermore, rapid change is a pervasive characteristic of contemporary North America, creating constant flux in the culturally constituted world (McCracken 1986). As a result of these dynamic influences, the meanings associated with our possessions may then change in tandem as we contemplate the culminating impact such developments have had upon our lives. Research exploring changes in possession meaning has suggested that when objects inhibit developmental goals (Csikszentmihalyi and Rochberg-Halton 1981), fall prey to disuse and neglect (Belk 1988; Belk, Wallendorf, and Sherry 1989; LaBranche 1973), or fail to represent images of current or future selves (Kleine, Kleine, and Allen 1995; Pavia 1993), such objects may become candidates for disposal.

Despite numerous calls for research, disposition has received only scant attention from consumer researchers. Perhaps one reason the topic has failed to attract a concerted research effort is that it appears at first glance to be a relatively mundane, thoughtless act of little importance to consumers. Early researchers viewed disposition narrowly as actions toward an object taken by an owner following a decision to get rid of something (Burke, Conn, and Lutz 1978; Debell and Dardis 1979; Jacoby, Berning, and Dietvorst 1977). Yet at the same time, consumer researchers have long recognized emotionally laden meanings lurking behind even the most seemingly ordinary household objects (e.g., Csikszentmihalyi and Rochberg-Halton 1981; Dichter 1964).

Possessions become imbued with our sense of self as meanings are cultivated by simply knowing objects are available for our use and can enhance our "doing and being" (Belk 1988). Lingering emotional ties to highly cathectic objects may take years to dissipate and may never entirely disappear. Special possessions are often harbored long past their period of immediate relevance in our lives for they enable us to relive important memories and feel connected to significant people and places from our past. These issues prompted Young and Wallendorf (1989) to adopt a broad definition of disposition as "the process of detachment from self."

Disposition *is* a process. It entails a process of detaching from and ultimately severing the relationship between the possessor and a possession. Although various taxonomies of disposition behaviors (e.g., Jacoby et al. 1977; Young and Wallendorf 1989) have been advanced, the emotional and psychological process of dispo-sition has not been fully explored or articulated. This paper presents an overview of findings obtained through depth interviews with 21 informants who were actively involved in disposition activities. The objective of this study was to explore behaviors and associated meanings accompanying the disposition of consumer goods. The emic perspectives offered by informants provide the basis for the model (see Figure 1) of the psychological process to be introduced and discussed in this paper. These findings suggest that while the final act may be one of disposition, its meaning and the psychological process enabling severance of the relationship between a consumer and a possession is more aptly described as that of "dis*possession*."

METHOD

In-depth interviews averaging an hour in length were conducted with 21 consumers, 16 females and five males, who had recently disposed of personal possessions including such items as clothing, furniture, toys, appliances, and various other household goods. The age of informants ranged from 22 to 75. Purposive sampling guided the selection of informants for the study. Informants were identified through advertisements for garage sales, moving sales, estate sales, and from referrals. Although in all cases informants were selling goods, they had also engaged in numerous other methods of disposal, such as throwing items away, giving items away to friends or family members, and donating goods to charities or other organizations.

Sampling criteria required that (1) the informant was the owner or co-owner of the goods, (2) the decision to dispose was voluntary, and (3) no more than two weeks had passed following an act of disposition. Diversity in sampling also sought to maximize situational influences, taking into consideration the number and type of objects being disposed of, as well as circumstances surrounding the actions (e.g., life transitions, moving, "downsizing," remodeling projects, "spring cleaning," etc.). This simultaneously influenced the emotional significance of actions and their impact on the owner. For instance, for some informants, the process involved little more than cleaning out a garage or storage room. For others, especially those conducting estate sales, the process marked the disposition of nearly all their accumulated life possessions.

A semi-structured interview guide was used to probe domains of inquiry. Topics included: 1) the owner's past "history" with a particular object, including any memories or symbolic meanings associated with the object; 2) why particular objects were being disposed of; 3) actions accompanying the disposition of goods; and 4) any emotions, positive or negative, associated with the disposition of particular goods and the process as a whole. The audiotaped interviews were later transcribed to produce approximately 225 pages of verbatim data. The constant comparative method (Glaser and Strauss 1967) and grounded theory techniques described by Strauss and Corbin (1990) guided data collection and analysis. Process analysis explored the consequences of action/ interaction sequences and the implications of these for future actions or outcomes (Strauss and Corbin 1990).

FINDINGS

Strauss and Corbin (1990) note that sometimes the analysis of a single word or phrase can increase theoretical sensitivity and

FIGURE 1

The Psychological Process of Dispossession

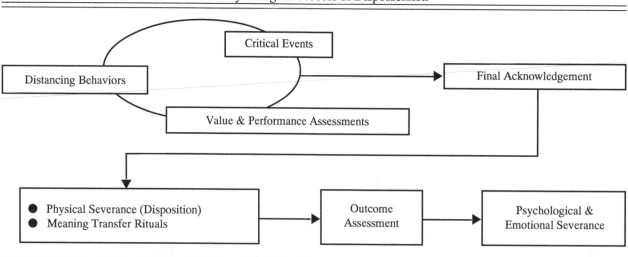

"open up" the data to deeper levels of analysis. This can be achieved by concentrating on possible meanings underlying a single word or other "indigenous concepts" (Patton 1990) voiced repeatedly by a number of informants. During data analysis, it was observed that two such terms, "finally" and "letting go," were voiced repeatedly by a number of informants. Both terms suggested that informants did indeed view disposition as a process, and that it was, at least in some cases, an emotional process.

Figure 1 represents the psychological process of dispossession that emerged from the etic interpretation of informants' emic descriptions. Some caveats are important to note. First, consumers dispose of goods daily, often in a fairly routinized manner. The nature and meaning of a product can dramatically influence consumers' emotional involvement with the dispossession process. Therefore, it is not necessary for the process to entail all of the stages depicted in Figure 1. Second, the temporal span associated with any of these stages or the process as a whole can vary widely, from seconds to years. A consumer might spend months deliberating whether or not it is time to upgrade their computer, but require only minutes to assess and acknowledge it is time to throw away a worn-out pair of gloves. Third, the initial starting point and directionality of the flow of events can be blurred. Consumers may enter into the process as a result of a culmination of factors and only then reflect on past incidences that initiated the process. Also, consumers may retreat to previous stages if they experience conflict or uncertainty at any point.

Space limitations preclude presentation of the multitude of verbatim data across a variety of situational contexts and types of possessions that provide the basis and support for the model in Figure 1. Disposition is most complex, both cognitively and emotionally, when objects are imbued with symbolic and meaningful associations to self. Thus, the verbatim data presented here will highlight these types of possessions in order to illustrate more fully the psychological and emotional process depicted in Figure 1. While only a few such examples can be provided in any detail, the interpretation is supported by the recurrence of behavioral patterns and emergent themes across numerous informants. These themes are best described as "tensions" created by the juxtaposition of conflicting needs and desires that arise during the course of the dispossession process.

Detachment

On the basis of their research, Young and Wallendorf conclude that "disposition is a process rather than a discrete event," but note that "it is impossible to pinpoint the moment when emotional or physical detachment occurs" (1989, p. 34). Findings from this study support the conclusions reached by these authors, and further illuminate factors that instigate and perpetuate the sometimes slow and insidious process of physical and emotional detachment from a possession. Three factors, 1) distancing behaviors, 2) "critical events," and 3) ongoing value and performance assessments, surfaced as primary indicators that the process of physical and emotional detachment between an owner and a possession was underway.

Several behaviors served to distance an object spatially from the owner. These included continued storage without use or clear intent toward future use, neglect, concealment, and hierarchical downgrades in terms of the object's centrality or functional role in the informant's life. Through such behaviors, possessions migrated further and further away from the innermost walls of the sanctuary of the home as it embodied self to extremities that while still encompassing self, were more centrifugal (McCracken 1989). Possessions that later became candidates for disposal had frequently been packed away for years in closets, attics, sheds, garages, and other storage areas. Storage separated these goods from those possessing more immediate relevance in informants' lives, but kept them close should a need or desire for them arise. For instance, one informant, Jane (WF 49), described the objects in her storage room this way:

> I don't know what else is in there. To tell you the truth, some are items, some household items, [things] that we just chose not to put out in this house that we have moved around with us from place to place because we think we will someday use them. But we probably never will! They're still back in storage, just in case. In the holding mode!

A related distancing behavior was concealment or hiding of undesirable or disliked possessions. These objects, many of which were unwanted gifts, were relegated to less trafficked areas of the home so as to minimize contact. For instance, Shelly (WF 39) described her efforts to conceal from view an "atrocious" 3-D picture of a deer that her mother-in-law had given her and her husband this way:

> I hate it! I've never seen anything so ugly! We've moved it from room to room, but always put it in an inconspicuous place. We finally hung it up in the basement.

Despite their dislike for these objects, informants were reluctant to part with unwanted gifts for fear the giver would discover the repudiation. For example, Tom and Kathy were frustrated by a large flower arrangement their daughter had given them. Tom (WM 65) provided the following account of their efforts to avoid appearing ungrateful:

> It was big and just too much for us. We had it everywhere trying to make it fit and finally put it in the spare bedroom. But every time she'd come over, we'd run and put it out, sit them out where she could see them!

A second factor that fostered growing detachment between owner and object was "critical events." Critical events represented occurrences or changes in circumstances that served to alter the relationship between owner and object by provoking feelings of dissatisfaction or a heightened sense of awareness that a product no longer represented relevant aspects of self. Major life transitions such as moving, a change in employment status, changes in health status, or changes in the composition of the family unit (c.f., McAlexander 1991; Pavia 1993; Young 1991) often provoked fundamental shifts in the owner-object relationship. However, critical events also included occurrences of a more innocuous nature, such as performance deficiencies, changes in fashion or stylistic preferences, or replacement purchases that relegated the incumbent good to a secondary role such as that of a "back up." Regardless of how far-reaching their impact, critical events created chasms in the owner's relationship with an object that cultivated emotional detachment.

Ongoing value and performance assessments emerged as the third factor signaling growing detachment. From time to time, and often following a critical event, informants described assessments in which the value of the object, whether financial, utilitarian, symbolic, or any combination of these, was compared to the costs of continuing to retain the object in their possession. As long as the accumulation of goods did not present problems or impose costs associated with moving them, storing them, or otherwise continuing to maintain them, informants often seemed content to ignore unwanted, infrequently used, or forgotten possessions. However, when costs outweighed benefits, objects became candidates for disposal.

The primary theme to emerge from informants' emic descriptions of the detachment process was an underlying tension expressed as ambivalence. Informants were reluctant to part with objects they might later need and possessions that represented interpersonal ties or affiliations to others. Yet, at the same time, the effort and costs of trying to accommodate these objects became increasingly unjustifiable. For instance, Stan (WM 38) and his wife LeAnn disposed of many things during the move to their new home. "Anything we questioned, we put in a box in the garage," Stan explained. But pointing to the stacks of boxes still lining his garage, he lamented, "as you can see, there's a lot of stuff we can't let go of!" In the following excerpt, 22-year old Edward describes his feelings of ambivalence as he searched through belongings prior to his and his mother's moving sale:

> Every once in awhile you come across something which is kind of sentimental to you and you have to decide if it's worth keeping and lugging around for 20 more years. I found some stuff that would be neat to look at when I'm 40, but do I want to keep it for 18 years in a box? So that was kinda tough but for the most part, it was fairly simple. If you don't use it and don't want it, either sell it or get rid of it.

Importantly, distancing behaviors, critical events, and value assessments in and of themselves did not inevitably lead to the final act of disposition. It was only following the acknowledgement of changes and the resulting impact on their lives that informants began to actively engage in actions that would culminate in the final severance of their relationship with these objects. Rhonda (WF 44), for example, though remarried, had found it difficult to go through her deceased husband's clothing, choosing instead to keep them in storage. In this excerpt from the interview with her, Rhonda expresses how the passage of time and the culmination of many critical events led her to decide it was time to take actions she had put off:

> For a long time, I wouldn't get rid of anything. It's just now that I'm able to part with all of it. It's like, well, now that they're leaving [her parents] and going to another part of the world, and my brother-in-law is thinking about moving, I started thinking it was time for me to put my house together, get rid of all this stuff. Like my previous husband's clothes. I've been married again now for 23 years and it's just time to let go. Both my sons have moved out, one's at college now, and my other son, he's finding his way. So, I'm clearing out all this stuff that I just hung onto and hung onto.

Acknowledgement of change, whether change within themselves, change in the family, social, or cultural environment, or change in general life circumstances, prompted informants to take actions that would ultimately dissolve their relationship with possessions that no longer had a place in their lives. Sometimes reluctantly, but often with conviction, informants acknowledged that it was time to let go of the past and the things that embodied past selves.

Severence

By engaging in the act of disposition, informants relinquished possession of the object, abdicated responsibility and control over it, and symbolically severed emotional and psychological ties associated with ownership of the object. For some informants, severance was a form of release, as it was for Stan, who proclaimed, "I'm like, 'good riddance!' It was nice knowing you—goodbye!" For others, severance meant saying a final "goodbye" to memories of loved ones. For example, in the following excerpt, Delores (WF 69) describes her feelings about selling an old coffeepot that reminded her of her deceased brother:

> I've had it in sales several times before, and I think I purposefully didn't try to sell it because of the associations, the jokes my brother and I always made about it. It was always kind of the white elephant of the sale. I kind of hated to see it go. When it finally sold yesterday, it was sad.

To prepare for severance, informants engaged in divestment rituals such as those described by McCracken (1986), including cleaning objects to rid them of "contamination" and restoring them to their natural or neutral state. Divestment rituals erased personal

428 / Letting Go: The Process and Meaning of Dispossession in the Lives of Consumers

meanings associated with objects to prepare them for transition to another owner. Once emptied of these meanings and symbolic properties, it was easier for informants to dispose of the object. However, an underlying tension to emerge during interviews with informants as they described the physical severance process was a simultaneous need to also protect the physical or symbolic properties of the good as ownership passed to another. This theme of "safe passage" reflected informants' desire to dispose of the item in a manner that would reassure value was retained and that the new owner acknowledged and appreciated sources of value, including sources of value that were private or symbolic in nature (Richins 1994).

For possessions being sold "in the profane world of commerce" (Belk et al. 1989), especially those with symbolic value, informants described two strategies to accomplish safe passage. The first was employing pricing barriers. By imposing "higher than market" or nonnegotiable prices on the sale of the item, informants gained reassurance that a possession would not pass easily to the new owner without some appreciation of its value. For instance, Carol (WF 46) was reluctant to sell a favorite old sweater she had once worn in a family photograph. "I put $5 on it," she said, "because I didn't think anyone would pay that for it and if not, it's worth more to me to keep it." In another example, a sign advertising the sale of a piano at Edward and his mother's sale stated firmly that there would be "no negotiations on the price." Later in the interview, Edward offered that the piano had sentimental value as well, because it was "the piano my brother and I took lessons on when we were young." Edward went on to add: "She [his mother] actually made the comment to me last night that she wants to make sure she sells it to someone who will really use it and take care of it."

A second strategy for assuring safe passage to emerge was that of "storytelling." Informants often described relaying the history of the object to a new owner as they were giving it away or selling it. Reliving these memories and telling stories about the object's past seemed to help them relinquish lingering emotional ties. New owners in turn often relayed their own plans for the object, which further reassured informants of the "safe passage" of once-treasured possessions and the retention and appreciation of its value. Carol offered the following observation:

It's fun to hear the stories of what they're going to do with things as well as to tell your own. There's sentimental value attached to some of these items, and so you tell the story as they're buying it, reliving that, and then kind of letting it go.

Roberta (WF 57) likewise admitted that she told the "history" of furniture and clothing to buyers. She reflected on why she felt a need to do this in the following excerpt:

I told probably more than they cared about! But that makes it easier somehow, to tell people about the things when they buy it. It just seemed important to me, even if it wasn't important to them.

One particularly poignant illustration of the importance of storytelling was told by one informant, Juanita (WF 72) who threw away, gave away, or sold most of her own possessions and those she had inherited from her mother when she decided to "move to town" at her son's urgings. "If I couldn't picture it in my new little apartment I didn't keep it," explained Juanita. One very important item she could not "picture" was the flag that had been on her father's casket. Her decision to sell it in the estate sale was

wrenching, but the following description of this item's safe passage vividly illustrates how crucial these exchanges between buyer and seller often were to the transfer of meaning during physical severance:

It was my dad's, he fought in WWI, the flag that had been placed on his casket when he died in 1941. I had kept it all these years in storage. But I was thinking about the senior apartments, and thinking, what am I going to do with this? So, I finally decided to put it in the sale. And some man bought it, and he came back in [the house] and told me that he was going to take it someplace in Florida. There was a museum there, he said, where they just had flags of veterans, and it would be in a glass case. He got all the information about when my dad was in the service and all, and he said it would have a plaque. That was hard, but it turned out really good, and it made me feel better.

Belk et al. (1989) previously observed that the "never sell" rule applies nearly universally to objects regarded as "sacred." Informants in the present study did appear to be willing to sell possessions that if not sacred, were at least "special." However, through pricing strategies and storytelling, they imposed particular conditions on the sale to reassure them of the object's safe passage and continued separation from the profane. When such reassurance could not be provided, informants sometimes abandoned plans to dispose of the object. The following account offered by Bonnie (WF 62), concerning the sale of a treasured shell collection she had brought with her from the Philippines, reflects both strategies and illustrates how conflict at any stage of the disposition process can result in a return to previous stages:

Bonnie: This lady picked it up to take it, and I said, "what are you going to do with that?" She said, "well, I'm going to put them in my garden." And I said, "no, I don't want it to go to do that." I wanted it to go to a teacher who would take it to school and show it to students. I didn't have a price marked on it, and when she told me what she was going to do with it, I told her it was $20. I just made up some number.
Interviewer: What if she had said, "ok, $20?"
Bonnie: She could have had it. But not at a cheap price. I didn't think she would buy it at $20, and she didn't. After she left, I pulled it out of the sale. There's this emotional attachment to things that you want something you have treasured to be used by someone else in some fashion other than just trash.

Through the final act of disposition, informants physically severed their relationship with an object. The process of making this severance was aided by meaning transfer rituals, both those that erased meaning and associations as well as those that assured some meanings would be retained with the product. These meanings were often public meanings or sources of value related to the good's economic or exchange value. However, for many objects imbued with sentimental meaning, informants also sought to protect sources of private value rooted in the owner's history with the good (Richins 1994), which seemed to facilitate the impending psychological severance to follow.

Outcome Assessment and Psychological Severance

Following disposal, informants frequently reflected on their decisions, the outcomes both financially and psychologically, and the overall impact of severing their relationships with possessions. For most informants, this assessment elicited positive emotions, feelings of release from obligations to possessions that tied them down, and a newfound awareness of opportunities more suitable to their current situation (Pavia 1993). Informants described a sense of "regained control" over their environment and a sense of emotional closure to the past. Even Juanita, who had disposed of so many of her possessions, described her feelings of relief and renewal in this excerpt from her interview:

Relief! Definitely, that was it, relief! I knew it was going to be hard. But after you get rid of everything that hurts so bad to get rid of, you just feel better. I won't have to go through that again. I had dreaded it, but it's past me now. It wasn't really anything traumatic, but then again, it was. I've lived here 52 years and the kids were raised here too. So, it just hurts. But it's a new beginning.

Although most informants expressed positive feelings, others reported negative feelings of regret and a sense of loss following the disposition of special possessions. Jane (WF 49), for instance, still regrets the circumstances surrounding the sale of her grandmother's dishes. She relived her emotions in the following story recounted during the interview with her:

I sold candy dishes and things that had been my grandmother's. And I knew they didn't cost very much, I mean, I'm not saying they were worth $50 or anything like that. But they were Depression glass, and they were hers, and I put them out there [in the sale] for 75 cents. Well, the first person that came through picked up every single one of them. And I thought, "I am so stupid!" It was *hard* for me to do that, they were *worth* something, and now they're gone! What was I thinking! They were my grandmother's!

The assessment process appeared to provide a sense of psychological and emotional closure to the act of physically severing ties to a possession once owned. Although the feelings accompanying physical severance were predominately positive, negative affect such as that experienced by Jane continued to haunt informants and appeared to exert influence on future acts of disposition undertaken by these consumers. A special possession might be gone, even voluntarily, but its meaning, the impact of its loss, and the circumstances and personal responsibility surrounding the loss were not always easily forgotten or reconcilable.

DISCUSSION: THE MEANING OF DISPOSITION REVISITED

It is important for consumer researchers to understand not only how relationships with possessions are cultivated through consumption experiences, but also how these relationships are severed through the act of disposition. At first glance, it would seem contradictory that consumers would voluntarily choose to discard possessions imbued with special meanings. Indeed, the "willingness to discard" possessions, and particularly the decision to dispose of them in the "profane world of commerce," have been treated as criteria that separate "sacred" goods from ordinary or "profane" commodities (Belk et al. 1989). Clearly, many of the goods disposed in this context were devoid of meaning and were frequently characterized by informants as useless "junk" that they were glad to be rid of. However, the conflicting emotions that accompanied decisions to part with many possessions that, at least at one time, had embodied very special meanings and ties to self identity would suggest that the demarcation point between "sacred" and "profane" involves a subtle continuum of meaning.

Coming to terms with this distinction, in fact, may very well be a primary function of behaviors that facilitate the process of dispossession. The frequency with which informants referred to the process as that of "letting go" and the thick descriptions that accompanied their interpretations of the event serve to emphasize that it was not merely the object they were "letting go" of, but more importantly, those aspects of self embodied in possessions. The chronology of events surrounding the act suggest that oftentimes, it is prefaced by a series of stages that reflect these changes in self and signal the forthcoming demise of the relationship. Predisposition behaviors represent growing detachment from an object, but at the same time, make possible a "cooling off" period (McCracken 1988) that enables individuals to deal with feelings of ambivalence and obligation. Disposition rituals and actions enable the physical severance of control over a possession, and if appropriately matched to the possession's importance in a consumer's life, facilitate psychological severance. Furthermore, if outcomes are deemed appropriate, these previous actions lead to a much-needed sense of psychological reassurance that provides a sense of closure once the relationship is finally terminated once and for all.

Thus, it appears useful to distinguish the "act of disposition" from the "process of dispossession." The act of disposition signifies the final physical and perhaps legal severance of control over a possession. On the other hand, dispossession represents the broader psychological process through which a person comes to feel physically or emotionally detached and separated from a possession within their control. Dispossession includes instances of detachment and physical severance that may occur while an object is still within a person's control, as well as psychological severance following the loss of control over a possession.

Viewed in this manner, what it means to dispose of something implies the *opposite* of what it means to possess something. A voluminous stream of research has addressed the meaning of possession. Belk asserts that possessions become part of the extended self in that they "contribute to our capabilities for doing and being" (1988, p. 145). Furby likewise concludes that a defining characteristic of possessions are that they "appear to be seen as a means to an end—they allow one to do what one wants" (1978, p. 312). Furby (1978) summarizes her research on possession meaning by noting that the two most frequently mentioned features of possession are (1) use of the object and (2) the right to control use.

In summary, through the voluntary act of disposition, a person abdicates responsibility for and control over the object, forfeits any current or future capabilities or benefits continued possession of the object may afford, and severs any ties that were represented through symbolic aspects of ownership and consumption. If a consumer feels encumbered by continued responsibility for an object, fails to appreciate value associated with any current or future benefits represented by continued ownership, or no longer feels psychologically or emotionally bound by symbolic aspects of ownership, disposition may indeed be an unemotional action that arises from recognition of these factors. However, conflicts present in any or all of the above meanings of possession may present complexities, contribute to emotional distress, or create psychological tension that serves to prolong the process of dispossession and may intensify the impact of psychological severance.

CONCLUSION

The dispossession process highlights the inextricable and dynamic interplay between development of self and material possessions. Objects assume self cathectic properties and alternatively become "not me possessions" as the self continually meta-morphoses through critical events, some of which systematically arise as consumers transition from one life stage to another or go about goal-directed activities, and others that evolve much more slowly and less obviously (Ball and Tasaki 1992; Kleine et al. 1995; Young 1991). As Ball and Tasaki (1992) have noted, it may be more difficult to capture the significance of minor events, such as critical comments of others, performance successes and failures over time, and diminishing returns to self-esteem that accumulate over long periods of time and culminate in the conclusion that a possession is no longer "me."

In conclusion, by examining dispossession as a process, such subtle nuances will not remain hidden behind the seemingly mundane and uneventful act of disposition. Nevertheless, it is perhaps the psychological impact that is imparted by the final severance of the relationship between an object and its possessor through the act of disposition that captures the true meaning and richness of this final stage of consumption in the lives of consumers.

REFERENCES

Ball, A. Dwayne and Lori H. Tasaki (1992), "The Role and Measurement of Attachment in Consumer Behavior," *Journal of Consumer Psychology,* 1 (2), 155-172.

Belk, Russell W. (1988), "Possessions and the Extended Self," *Journal of Consumer Research,* 15 (September), 139-168.

_____, Melanie Wallendorf, and John F. Sherry (1989), "The Sacred and the Profane in Consumer Behavior: Theodicy on the Odyssey," *Journal of Consumer Research,* 16 (June), 1-38.

Burke, Marian, W. David Conn, and Richard J. Lutz (1978), "Using Psychographic Variables to Investigate Product Disposition Behaviors," in *Proceedings of the AMA Educators' Conference,* ed. Subhash C. Jain, Chicago, IL: American Marketing Association, 321-326.

Csikszentmihalyi, Mihaly and Eugene Rochberg-Halton (1981), *The Meaning of Things: Domestic Symbols and the Self,* Cambridge, MA: Cambridge University Press.

DeBell, Margaret and Rachel Dardis (1979), "Extending Product Life: Technology Isn't the Only Issue," in *Advances in Consumer Research,* Vol 6, ed. William L. Wilkie, Ann Arbor, MI: Association for Consumer Research, 381-385.

Dichter, Ernest (1964), *The Handbook of Consumer Motivations: The Psychology of the World of Objects,* New York: McGraw-Hill.

Furby, Lita (1978), "Possessions: Toward a Theory of Their Meaning and Function throughout the Life Cycle," in *Life-Span Development and Behavior,* Vol. 1, ed. Paul B. Baltes, New York: Academic Press, 297-336.

Glaser, Bernard and Anselm Strauss (1967), *The Discovery of Grounded Theory,* Chicago: Aldine.

Jacoby, Jacob, Carol K. Berning, and Thomas F. Dietvorst (1977), "What About Disposition?," *Journal of Marketing,* 41 (April), 22-28.

Kleine, Susan Schultz, Robert E. Kleine, and Chris T. Allen (1995), "How is a Possession "Me" or "Not Me"?: Characterizing Types and an Antecedent of Material Possession Attachment," *Journal of Consumer Research,* 22 (December), 327-343.

LaBranche, Anthony (1973), "Neglected and Unused Things: Narrative Encounter," *Review of Existential Psychology and Psychiatry,* 12 (2), 163-168.

McAlexander, James H. (1991), "Divorce, the Disposition of the Relationship, and Everything," in *Advances in Consumer Research,* Vol. 18, ed. Rebecca H. Holman and Michael R. Solomon, Provo, UT: Association of Consumer Research, 43-48.

McCracken, Grant (1986), "Culture and Consumption: A Theoretical Account of the Structure and Movement of the Cultural Meaning of Consumer Goods," *Journal of Consumer Research,* 13 (June), 71-84.

_____ (1988), *Culture and Consumption: New Approaches to the Symbolic Character of Consumer Goods and Activities,* Bloomington, IN: Indiana University Press.

_____ (1989), "Homeyness: A Cultural Account of One Constellation of Consumer Goods and Meanings," in *Interpretive Consumer Research,* Provo, UT: Association of Consumer Research, 168-182.

Pavia, Teresa (1993), Dispossession and Perceptions of Self in Late Stage HIV Infection," in *Advances in Consumer Research,* Vol. 20, ed. Leigh McAlister and Michael L. Rothschild, Provo UT: Association of Consumer Research, 425-428.

Patton, Michael Quinn (1990), *Qualitative Evaluation and Research Methods,* Newbury Park, CA: Sage.

Richins, Marsha L. (1994), "Valuing Things: The Public and Private Meanings of Possessions," *Journal of Consumer Research,* 21 (December), 504-521.

Strauss, Anselm and Juliet Corbin (1990), *Basics of Qualitative Research: Grounded Theory Procedures and Techniques,* Newbury Park, CA: Sage Publications.

Young, Melissa Martin (1991), "Disposition of Possessions During Role Transitions,". in *Advances in Consumer Research,* Vol. 18, ed. Rebecca H. Holman and Michael R. Solomon, Provo, UT: Association of Consumer Research, 33-39.

_____ and Melanie Wallendorf (1989), "Ashes to Ashes, Dust to Dust: Conceptualizing Consumer Disposition of Possessions," in *Proceedings of the AMA Winter Educator's Conference,* ed. Terry L. Childers et al., Chicago, IL: American Marketing Association, 33-39.

Moral Orientation: Its Relation to Product Involvement and Consumption

Hyokjin Kwak, University of Georgia
George M. Zinkhan,University of Georgia
Warren A. French, University of Georgia

ABSTRACT

Moral orientation is investigated with respect to its relation to consumers' purchases of and involvement with products of questionable social value. At the same time, impulsive and compulsive buying tendencies as well as the trait of materialism are tested for their possible relations to moral orientation. Following a pretest, four product categories (i.e., tobacco, drugs, alcohol, pornography) are identified as being socially harmful. In the main study, we find that consumers who follow a pattern of rule-driven moral reasoning are less likely to consume socially harmful products.

INTRODUCTION

Product consumption is a normal part of most people's lives. For some people, purchasing becomes a life unto itself and addictive. Compulsive buying, impulsive buying, and to some extent, a materialistic drive, are such examples. Thus, consumer researchers attentive to these behaviors have refined related concepts, explained the origins and causes of these addictive behaviors and assessed their personal and social effects (Belk 1985; Faber 1992; Faber and O'Guinn 1989; Hanley and Wilhelm 1992)

One topic that has received scant attention in this area is the moral reasoning process associated with the buying process. Compulsive buyers realize that their behavior can cause interpersonal problems, social problems and domestic tensions; yet, since they cannot control their urge to buy, these individuals attempt to conceal the evidence of their abnormal behavior in order to avoid conflict with social expectations (or rules) (Faber and O'Guinn 1992). One major theme of the present study is to shed light on behavior-driven consumers' (i.e., compulsive buyers) ethical standards. Just how vulnerable are compulsive buyers to marketing efforts if their buying is negatively associated with a certain decision-making process (e.g., rule-oriented moral reasoning)?

Also worth investigation is consumers' ethical consideration of socially undesirable products. For example, we supposedly react positively toward socially "good" products and services (e.g., charitable giving and recycled products) and negatively toward socially harmful products (e.g., drugs, pornographies). For some consumers, such socially stigmatized products and services are viewed as just part of a shopping list that they purchase from. We do not know much about this specific domain of products or the moral orientation of the people who purchase them.

The major purpose of the paper is two-fold: a) to investigate the relationship between two types of moral orientation (i.e., act vs. rule) and the involvement and consumption of socially harmful products (e.g., drugs, alcoholic beverages) and b) to explore the role of impulsive buying tendencies, compulsive buying tendencies, and materialism. In the following section, we discuss some psychological and philosophical aspects associated with moral orientation.

CONCEPTUAL BACKGROUND

For the last two decades attempts to link consumer behavior with morality may have been influenced as much by the availability of measurement instruments as by the articulation of theory. The prevailing instrument of moral choice has been the Defining Issues Test (DIT), which is grounded in moral development theory. This theory, first gaining notoriety with Piaget (Piaget 1950; Piaget 1952; Piaget 1965) and later popularized by Kohlberg (1969), entails the use of a lengthy interview process to obtain projectable results.

Searching for efficiency in moral measurement, Rest (1979) synthesized major findings within Kohlberg's database into an objective test called the DIT. The instrument has been widely used, although it, like Kohlberg's interview results, shows only modest predictive validity. The DIT's roots, though, come from developmental psychology with its strong body of theoretical as well as empirical research.

The cognitive moral development approach of Piaget, Kohlberg and Rest appears to be grounded primarily on the concept of justice. Newer approaches to ethical decisions, under the label of sociomoral development (Kurtines and Gewirtz 1987), incorporate the notion of an ethics of care as postulated by Gilligan (1982) along with justice. To establish the link between moral developmental psychology and the traditional moral classification schemes employed in the philosophical study of ethics Colby et al. (1980) matched both the modal and value elements uncovered in moral development interviews to the taxonomy used in philosophy. This paper reports on an effort to revert back to the traditional philosophical orientation to investigate possible links between ethical orientation and consumer behavior.

The primary distinction among philosophical theories of morality relates to the two components constituting the traditional definition of ethics. Under that definition, those components are "moral principles" directed at enhancing "societal well-being." Those who stress principles are labeled deontologists. The origin of that term comes from the Greek word, "deontos," meaning obligation. Those who stress societal well-being pay attention to the rationale behind an act, and are labeled teleologists. The derivation of that term comes from the word "telos," translated as purpose.

The secondary distinction among moral theories is one that concentrates on acts versus rules. According to Frankena, this is a meaningful distinction since he identifies both act deontologists and act teleologists as well as rule deontologists and rule teleologists. It is this secondary distinction that will be treated as a potential explanatory variable in the research reported here. Here, we first discuss these two moral reasoning patterns (i.e., act vs. rule) and, then, apply them to consumption phenomena. Finally, several research questions are provided.

Act Orientation vs. Rule Orientation

Act-Oriented Moral Reasoning. Act theories maintain that moral judgments are particularistic rather than generalizable. Those influenced by an act orientation in market behavior intuitively seem prone to adopt a teleological orientation in their decisions. This emphasis on the intended consequences of their decisions would be reflected in their weighing of alternatives. Frankena's description of this orientation (1973, p. 35) is depicted by the decision criterion of an act utilitarian in the question: "What effect will *my* doing *this* act in *this* situation have on the general balance of good over evil?"

Frankena, though, claims that is difficult to do without rules, for no other reason than our lack of time to judge each situation anew. An act-deontologist, as contrasted to an act-teleologist, might answer that past experiences are not totally discounted in the moral decision making process but provide loose "rules of thumb" when evaluating responsibilities in new situations. But, those loose rules are no more than secondary considerations in the decision making process. It is one's personal experiential and, perhaps, intuitive sense of right or wrong that influences one's moral decision in any given situation. Among the philosophers who advocated an act or particularistic approach to moral decisions are Carritt (1928) a deontologist, Bentham (1962) a utilitarian, and Fletcher (1966) who founded the school labeled "situation ethics."

Those who make moral decisions based on the intended results of their acts fall under Trompenaars' (Trompenaars and Hampden-Turner 1998) classification of particularists. Particularists pay less attention to what they consider to be abstract social codes and more attention to the circumstances surrounding an act. The continuity of relationships and the effects of one's decision on others weight heavily in a particularist's judgments of right and wrong. For particularists, linear logic takes a secondary position to the humanitarian effects of one's actions. Changes in context dramatically affect particularists' perceived obligations. Treating each case based on its merits attains fairness for them. The trustworthy person in the particularist view is one who honors changing mutualities.

Rule-Oriented Moral Reasoning. While an act orientation to morality is widely recognized in the ethics literature, most ethical work appears to center on rules related to moral goals or activities. Those rules, often internalized and not necessarily vocalized, exist to both guide and limit behavior. The etemological root of the word morality is the Latin word for custom. Customs are culturally defined. Rules are created to give a semblance of order to the community. They serve to promote and maximize the commonweal within the proximate community.

Berkeley (1965) justified a rule approach to morality by pointing out the problems with making act specific decisions. Rules preclude mistakes made in an act by act approach — mistakes caused by ignorance, emotion and lack of time spent in deliberation. On the positive side, rules are said to embody communal standards of right and wrong. Philosophers who advocated a rule or universalistic approach to moral decisions are deontologists such as Kant (1963), utilitarians like Mill (1951) and those who bridge both deontology and teleology like Ross (Ross 1930).

Trompenaars (1998) claims that a rule-based orientation is equivalent to a universalist orientation; "The universalist approach is roughly: What is good and right can be defined and always applies" (Trompenaars and Hampden-Turner 1998, p 8). In purchase situations, according to universalists, it is not relationships but rules that provide the focal point for some people's behavior. This approach to decision making tends to be rational, if somewhat impersonal. Rules provide one commonality that bridges the deontological - teleological chasm since both rule deontologists and rule utilitarians would fall under the universalism classification. That commonality, simplistically put, is that the purchases of universalists or rule driven consumers are made with due deliberation. Consistency is their watchword to the point that marketplace relationships could possible be viewed as informal contracts entailing reciprocal responsibilities.

Application to Consumer Behavior

O'Guinn and Faber (1989) defined compulsive buying as "chronic, repetitive purchasing that becomes a primary response to negative events or feeling. The activity, while perhaps providing short-term rewards, becomes very difficult to stop and ultimately results in harmful consequences" (p. 155). With easier access to malls, a sea of products available, and little or no social stigma attached to constant shopping (which formerly had been consid-

ered as an indication of moral or spiritual decay, e.g., Hirschman [1992]), compulsive shoppers encounter temptations daily.

Currently, compulsions are considered repetitive behaviors and irresistible desires which occur in response to obsessions, and which are generated against one's will (Yaryura-Tobias and Neziroglu 1997). The notion of the existence of "will" in compulsive buying is important to understand compulsive buying behavior. Consumers who have compulsive buying tendencies might engage in uncontrollable purchases with a self-cognition that they can rationalize. Compulsive buying also can be socially unacceptable or punishable since the behavior often generates financial and interpersonal difficulties (Faber and O'Guinn 1992; Krueger 1988). If this is the case, consumers might have some degree of cognitive ability to identify such societal sanctions or disapprobation.

From a cognitive view of attitudinal and behavioral change, Fishbein's theory of reasoned action (Ajzen and Fishbein 1977) can be viewed as an alternative approach to look at consumers' moral reasoning behind their additive purchase patterns. The theory focuses on the role of consumers' subjective norms in predicting consumers' buying intention followed by their actual buying behavior. For Fishbein, the concept of subjective norms is defined along two dimensions: a) the accumulation of beliefs and b) the individual's desires and motivations to comply with social beliefs. These dimensions seem to apply to compulsive buyers as well. As mentioned above, compulsive and impulsive buyers may think that their excessive and repetitive buying behavior will be condemned by a social referent. Thus, compulsive and impulsive buying behavior have been typically associated with post-purchase feelings of shame and guilt, financial and interpersonal problems, and to an increased susceptibility to social influence (d'Astous, Maltais, and Roberge 1990; Rook 1985).

However, the degree of cognitive moral reasoning or willingness to accept social norms behind these two types of buying behaviors might be lower than in a "normal" consumer group. For example, using cross-cultural data from the US and Korea, Kwak (2000) investigates the role of social norms on compulsive and impulsive buying. The author concludes that subjective norms do not play an important role in either of the cases. Thus, the compulsive and impulsive consumers' low cognitive moral reasoning for social acceptance may play a consequential role in their purchase behavior.

The issue of materialism is pervasive as the role of marketing's social responsibility grows in significance. Thus, academic research studying the impact of materialism has become of greater interest to those in marketing and consumer research (Belk 1985; Richins and Dawson 1992). The main issue underpinning materialism lies in its societal significance. A materialistic view may increase a society's economic wealth and material acquisitions. However, materialism may also have negative effect on the quality of life. For example, materialism has been significantly related to family disruption (Rindfleisch, Burroughs, and Denton 1997).

Materialism involves the importance attached to worldly possessions (Belk 1985; Richins and Dawson 1992). For a materialist, possessions are central to life in that s/he feels that increased consumption enhance satisfaction with quality of life. However, materialism may become problematic when the physical goal of consumption overwhelms all other goals of self and interactive development (Belk 1985). Researchers have raised questions about ethical issues related to consumers' materialistic value. For example, Belk (1985) relates greater materialism to an inevitable loss of a sense of community, which might in turn make people less sensitive to those behaviors that might negatively affect others.

Muncy and Eastman (1998) argue that materialistic consumers are more likely to have lower ethical standards than are the

FIGURE 1: PILOT STUDY
Products and Services Perceived As Socially Good and Bad

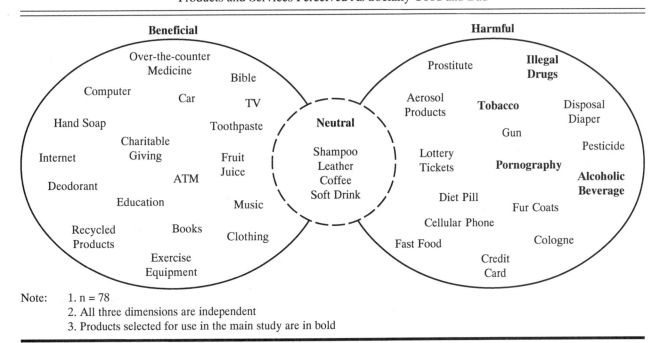

Note:
1. n = 78
2. All three dimensions are independent
3. Products selected for use in the main study are in bold

counterpart group. That is, consumers who are more materialistic show less concern for ethical issues. Compulsive and impulsive buying behaviors are the byproduct derived from a materialistic society (Faber and O'Guinn 1992; Rindfleisch, Burroughs, and Denton 1997; Rook and Fisher 1995).

Consumers who demonstrate compulsive and impulsive buying tendencies may be more likely to engage in other addictive consumption behaviors at the same time. For instance, compulsive buyers are frequently caught up in an irresistible pursuit of buying things in order to release them from an internally unstable status, to alleviate their discomfort and feelings of self-loathing. They may also turn to binge eating, illegal drugs, or alcoholic products. However, the short-term gratifications derived from compulsive buying never satisfy the internal emptiness; therefore, compulsive buyers increasingly search for more powerful reinforcers. These carryover effects are frequently noted; for instance, most alcoholics smoke, and heroin users are also likely to use a wide variety of drugs including alcohol (Winger, Hofmann, and Woods 1992). Given these behaviors and the above discussion about consumers' two different moral reasoning patterns — act orientation vs. rule orientation, we generate the following four research questions:

RESEARCH QUESTIONS

R1: Consumer involvement with socially harmful products (e.g., drugs, alcoholic beverages) will be positively associated with consumers' act-oriented moral reasoning, but will be negatively linked to consumers' rule-oriented moral reasoning.

R2: Consumers' frequent consumption of socially harmful products (e.g., drugs, alcoholic beverages) will be positively associated with consumers' act-oriented moral reasoning, but will be negatively linked to consumers' rule-oriented moral reasoning.

R3: Consumers' behavior-driven personalities (i.e., impulsive buying tendencies, compulsive buying tendencies, materialism) will be positively associated with consum-

ers' act-oriented moral reasoning, but will be negatively linked to consumers' rule-oriented moral reasoning.

R4: Behavior-driven personalities (i.e., impulsive buying tendencies, compulsive buying tendencies, materialism) will be related to positive involvement with socially harmful products (e.g., drugs, alcoholic beverages) and will be positively associated with frequent consumption for socially harmful products (e.g., drugs, alcoholic beverages).

METHOD
Pilot Study

Before investigating our main research themes, a pilot study was conducted to identify and verify some possible products that are perceived to be socially harmful. A questionnaire was administered to undergraduate business students at a large state university. Respondents were asked to list products or services that they perceive to be socially bad and good.

There were 78 responses for the pilot study—male (55%) and female (45%). Major products and services identified as socially good and bad are presented in Figure 2. It is interesting to note that some products are considered neutral (e.g., shampoo, leather, coffee, soft drink). For our main study, we selected four products that are socially undesirable: a) tobacco, b) drugs, c) alcoholic beverage, and c) pornographic material. These products were identified by more than 50 respondents as socially bad products. A graphical presentation of consumers' perceived socially good and bad products/services is shown in Figure 1.

Sample

Having identified socially harmful products, a second survey was conducted to explore our main research questions. This survey included some scales to measure consumers' attitudes, behaviors, personality traits (e.g., impulsive buying tendencies), and moral reasoning orientation (i.e., rule orientation and act orientation) Measures are geared to the four specific products (i.e., tobacco, illegal drugs, alcohol, and pornographic material). Respondents were undergraduate business students who were given a credit for participating in the survey. After eliminating some responses because of missing information, there were 76 responses available for the main analysis. The sample consists of 36 males (47%) and 40 females (53%). More than 97% of respondents come from the 20 to 24-year-old age group.

Measures

Attitudinal and Behavioral Measures. In order to measure consumers' degree of involvement with the socially harmful products, Zaichkowsky's revised Personal Involvement Inventory (Zaichkowsky 1985; Zaichkowsky 1994) was employed. The scale consists of 10 semantic differential items with 7 points (e.g., unimportant/important, worthless/valuable) to assess consumers' perceived relevance of the object based on inherent needs, values, and interests. One example question reads: "To me pornographic material is." Acceptable reliability estimates are obtained for the four products: .97 for tobacco, .96 for drug, .96 for alcohol, and .96 for pornographic. Higher scores of the scale represent higher involvement with the products.

Consumers' behavior regarding the four products was measured using a single item. For example, "Approximately, how often did you purchase an alcoholic beverage in the last one month?" As anticipated, a only small portion of respondents report that they purchase pornographic materials (4%), whereas a considerable number of respondents purchased tobacco (41%), illegal drugs (17%), and alcohol beverages (85%).

Personality Traits. Faber and O'Guinn's (1992) seven-item Diagnostic Screener for Compulsive Buying (CB) which is a Likert-type scale with 5 points (strongly disagree/strongly agree and never/very often) was adopted to measure consumers' compulsive buying tendency. This scale shows appropriate reliability (Cronbach's alpha of .80). Consumers' impulsive buying tendency (IB) is measured via Rook and Fisher's (1995) 9-item scale. This Likert-type scale is anchored by 5-point intervals with two bipolar words (strongly disagree/strongly agree). An acceptable reliability estimate is obtained (Cronbach's alpha of .93). Higher values in the two scales indicate higher levels of compulsive buying tendencies and buying impulsiveness.

Finally, consumers' materialism (MT) is measured using Richins and Dawson's (1992) material value scale. The measure employs a five-point Likert-type scale with eighteen items. The scale has three dimensions: possession centrality, possession as the pursuit of happiness, and possession-defined success. The reliability of the scale is appropriate with Cronbach's alpha of .84. Higher scores for the scale represent a higher emphasis on materialism.

Moral Orientation. We adopted Boyce and Jensen's (1978) Moral Content Test (MCT) to measure consumers' moral orientation. Although MCT is based on Kohlberg's theory and Rest's methodology, it is not considered a measure of moral development. The MCT is an objective recognition test that is concerned with how individuals choose different statements representing different moral orientations.

There are five stories and ten statements about each story that require respondents' moral judgment skills. In order to complete the test, respondents rate the importance of each statement relevant to a decision on a five point Likert-type scale and rank the four statements that they believe are most important. Evaluation of an individual MCT results in a number of scores, including "Rule Orientation" and "Act Orientation." Rule Orientation is calculated based on the percentage score for the following collapsed categories: hedonistic rule utilitarianism, non-hedonistic rule utilitarian-

ism, and rule deontology. Consumers' act orientation (in their moral reasoning) is measured by using the percentage score of the three categories: hedonistic act utilitarianism, non-hedonistic act utilitarianism, and act deontology. A high score on a either of these two scales represents higher emphasis on either rule orientation or act orientation.

Looking at the relationship between them assesses validity of the two measures. As expected, we find a strong negative correlation between the two constructs (r=-.824, p<.01). It is interesting to note that 66 percent of our respondents score more than 50 out of 100 in the act-orientation scale, indicating highly act oriented, whereas only 21 percent of them have scores of 50 out of 100 in rule-orientation moral reasoning, representing highly rule oriented.

ANALYSIS AND RESULTS

Moral Reasoning and Socially Undesirable Products (R1 and R2)

A series of correlation analyses were conducted to examine the effects of consumers' moral reasoning and attitudinal and behavioral issues dealing with socially "bad" products. As expected, the results suggest that higher involvement with some socially harmful products (i.e., drugs, alcoholic beverages, pornography) are negatively related consumers' rule-oriented moral reasoning (RO): $r_{drug+RO}$=-.240, p<.01; $r_{alcohol+RO}$=-.223, p<.01; $r_{pornographic+RO}$=-.240, p<.05. We also find that higher involvement with drugs is positively associated with their act-oriented moral reasoning (AO): $r_{drug+AO}$=.206, p<.01.

We find some evidence that purchasing of, in addition to involvement with, some of socially harmful products is related to moral orientation. That is, the results suggests that buying drugs is not only negatively associated with consumers' rule-oriented moral reasoning (r=-.230, p<.01), but also positively linked to consumers' act-oriented way of moral reasoning (r=.243, p<.01). Therefore, some portion of R1 and R2 are supported. Summarized correlation analysis is shown in Table 1.

Moral Reasoning and Personality Traits (R3 and R4)

We anticipated that behavior-driven personality traits such as consumers' buying impulsiveness, compulsive buying tendencies, and materialistic consumption are associated with a certain type of moral reasoning. Here, we find that consumers' rule-oriented moral reasoning is negatively linked to their impulse to buy (r=-.186, p<.05) and materialism (r=-.304, p<.01). We don't find any relationships between consumers' act-oriented moral reasoning and their consumption-related personality variables.

In addition to exploring the relationship between consumers' moral reasoning and personality traits, the results also show that higher involvement with socially harmful products is associated with the personality variables. That is, personal involvement with drugs is positively related with buying impulsiveness (r=215, p<.05), compulsive buying tendencies (r=.236, p<.01), and materialism (r=.263, p<.01). Higher involvement is also positively linked to compulsive buying tendencies (r=.199, p<.05). Regarding behavioral components, frequent buying of tobacco and alcoholic beverage is positively associated with impulsive buying ($r_{IB+Tobacco}$=.313, p<.01; $r_{IB+Alcohol}$=.332, p<.01) and compulsive buying tendencies ($r_{CB+Tobacco}$=.290, p<.01; $r_{CB+Alcohol}$=.249, p<.01). Interestingly, materialism is positively related with purchasing pornographic materials (r=.213, p<.05). Thus, Research Questions 3 and 4 are partially supported. Again, all the results are presented in Table 1.

TABLE 1
Hypothesized Correlations

	Moral Reasoning		Personality Traits		
	Rule Orientation	Act Orientation	Impulsive Buying	Compulsive Buying	Materialism
Involvement with					
Tobacco	.168	-.160	.314*	.199**	.107
Drug	-.240*	.206**	.182	.146	.002
Alcohol	-.223*	.142	.215**	.236*	.263*
Pornographic	-.210**	.126	-.022	-.108	-.015
Buying					
Tobacco	-.011	-.021	.313*	.290*	.068
Drug	-.230*	.243*	.009	.103	.044
Alcohol	-.138	.104	.332*	.249*	.102
Pornographic	-.001	-.046	.028	.016	.213**
Personality Traits					
Impulsive Buying	-.186**	.143			
Compulsive Buying	-.129	.101			
Materialism	-.304*	.179			

Note: * significant at p<.01, one-tailed test
** Significant at p<.05, one-tailed test
n=76

DISCUSSION

Consumer moral orientation is associated with consumers' motivation to consume socially harmful products. Via our two exploratory studies, we find some important issues surrounding consumers' style of moral reasoning — act orientation and rule orientation. We find that tobacco, drugs, alcohol, and pornography are perceived as socially "bad" products. Next, we investigated the associations between consumers' product involvement, behavioral components, and personality traits and their attached moral reasoning patterns.

As anticipated, those who show rule-driven moral reasoning are less likely to be involved with socially harmful products (i.e., drugs, alcohol beverages, pornographic materials). Such a negative feeling toward socially harmful products seems to dampen consumers' consumption of such products. For instance, our respondents with rule orientation are found to be less likely to engage in buying drugs. As expected, we find a positive relationship between consumers' act orientation and their involvement with socially undesirable products. For instance, act-oriented moral reasoning is found to be positively associated with consumers' involvement with drugs. As is traditional in consumer behavior literature, this favorable attitude toward drug products serves to enhance purchase behavior. In other words, the results suggest that purchasing drugs is positively related with consumers' act-driven moral reasoning.

In general, impulsive buying and compulsive buying are unplanned behaviors. These buying patterns often carry emotional and psychological decision making that might provide consumers with a temporary power to avoid some possible social inhibitions. For instance, established social norms might discourage consumers from having favorable attitudes toward alcoholic beverages or tobacco products and even purchasing them due to their harmful effects on public health and public at large. However, as we find that those who have impulsive buying tendencies are likely to have negative rule-oriented moral reasoning, this is not the case for some consumers. Those who have impulsive and compulsive buying tendencies (and materialistic propensities) are likely to be consumers of some socially harmful products (i.e., tobacco. Illegal drugs, alcoholic beverages).

According to the study conducted by the Substance Abuse and Mental Health Services Administration, it is estimated that illicit drug-use treatment cost $7.6 billion and alcohol abuse treatment cost $5 billion in 1996 (Peterson, Balasubramanian, and Bronnenberg 1997). Use of socially harmful products (e.g., drugs, alcohol) can produce negative outcomes for the public at large. Thus, it is important to learn more about the circumstances that lead to the abuse of such products.

A Freudian approach argues that the moral constraints of the super ego control a compulsive and impulsive personality. Public policy makers, thus, may want to facilitate educational functions in marketing activities from a long-term perspective. For instance, requirement of tell-tale tags in socially harmful products can be a useful start to reduce act-driven consumers' consumption on these product categories.

Compulsive and impulsive consumers, however, may not be prone to read descriptions/warnings, especially at the point of purchase. Other sensory stimuli may be needed to discourage purchases. It will take an imaginative mind to create aural and visual stimuli to impede what tend to be the emotion-based purchases of act-oriented decision makers.

Limitations of the present study arise from the characteristics of our sample (e.g., small number of respondents, use of students even though they are at an age which lends to susceptibility to persuasion). Future studies may want to use a larger sample from a general consumer group to look at the broad effects of moral standards. Here, we provide an initial step for understanding consumer motivations related to the consumption of socially harmful products.

REFERENCES

Ajzen, Icek, and Martin Fishbein (1977), "Attitude-Behavior Relations: A Theoretical Analysis and Review of Empirical Research," *Psychological Bulletin*, 84(3), 888-918.

Belk, Russell W. (1985), "Materialism: Trait Aspects of Living in the Material World," *Journal of Consumer Research*, 12(December), 265-280.

Bentham, J. (1962), "An Introduction to the Principles of Morals and Legislation," in *The works of Jeremy Bentham*, ed. J. Bowring, New York, NY: Russell and Russell

Berkeley, G. (1965), "Berkeley's Philosophical Writings ed. D. A. Armstrong, New York, NY: Collier Books

Boyce, William D., and Larry Cyril Jensen (1978), *Moral Reasoning*, Lincoln, Nebraska: University of Nebraska Press.

Carritt, E. F. (1928), *That Theory of Morals*, London: Oxford University Press.

Colby, A., Jr. Gibbs, L. Kohlberg, B. Speicher - Dubin, and D. Candee (1980), *The measurement of Moral Judgment*, Cambridge, MA: Center for Moral Education - Harvard University.

d'Astous, Alain, Julie Maltais, and Caroline Roberge (1990), "Compulsive Buying Tendencies of Adolescent Consumers," in *Advances in Consumer Research*, Vol. 17, eds. Marvin E. Goldberg and Gerald Gorn and Richard W. Pollay, Provo, UT: Association for Consumer Research, 306-312.

Faber, Ronald J. (1992), "Money Changes Everything," *American Behavioral Scientist*, 35(6), 809-819.

Faber, Ronald J., and Thomas C. O'Guinn (1989), "Classifying Compulsive Consumers: Advances in the Development of a Diagnostic Tool," in *Advances in Consumer Research*, Vol. 16, ed. Thomas Srull, Provo, UT: Association for Consumer Research, 738-744.

Faber, Ronald J., and Thomas C. O'Guinn (1992), "A Clinical Screener for Compulsive Buying," *Journal of Consumer Research*, 19(December), 459-469.

Fletcher, J. (1966), *Situation Ethics*, Philadelphia: Westminister Press.

Frankena, W. K. (1973), *Ethics* (Vol. 2nd), Englewood Cliffs, NJ: Prentice-Hall, Inc.

Gelligan, Carol (1982), *In a Different Voice: Psychological Theory and Women's Development*, Cambridge, MA: Harvard University Press.

Hanley, Alice, and Mari S. Wilhelm (1992), "Compulsive Buying: An Exploration into Self-Esteem and Money Attitudes," *Journal of Economic Psychology*, 13, 5-18.

Hirschman, Elizabeth C. (1992), "The Consciousness of Addiction: Toward a General Theory of Compulsive Consumption," *Journal of Consumer Research*, 19(September), 155-179.

Kant, I. (1963), *Lecture in Ethics* (Louis Infeld, Trans.), New York: Harper and Row.

Kohlberg, Lawrence (1969), "Stage and Sequence: The Cognitive-Developmental Approach to Socialization," in *Handbook of Socialization: Theory, Research and Social Issues*, ed. D. G. Goslin, New York, NY: Holt, Rinehart and Row, 347-480.

Krueger, David W. (1988), "On Compulsive Shopping and Spending: A Psychodynamic Inquiry," *American Journal of Psychotherapy*, 42(4), 574-584.

Kurtines, William, and Jacob Gewirtz (1987), *Moral Development Through Social Interaction*, New York, NY: John Wiley and Sons.

Kwak, Hyokjin (2000), "Compulsive Consumers in the US and Korea," *Journalism and Mass Communication Abstracts*, 37, forthcoming.

Mill, J. S. (1951), *Utilitarianism, Liberty and Representative Government*, New York, NY: E. P. Dutton.

Muncy, James A., and Jacqueline K. Eastman (1998), "Materialism and Consumer Ethics: An Exploratory Study," *Journal of Business Ethics*, 17(2), 137-145.

O'Guinn, Thomas C., and Ronald J. Faber (1989), "Compulsive Buying: A Phenomenological Exploration," *Journal of Consumer Research*, 16(September), 147-157.

Peterson, Robert A., Sridhar Balasubramanian, and Bart J. Bronnenberg (1997), "Exploring the Implications of the Internet for Consumer Marketing," *Journal of the Academy of Marketing Science*, 25(4), 329-346.

Piaget, Jean (1950), *Psychology of Intelligence*, New York, NY: Harcourt.

Piaget, Jean (1952), *The Origins of Intelligence in Children*, New York, NY: International Universities Press.

Piaget, Jean (1965), *The Moral Judgment of the Child*, New York, NY: Free Press.

Rest, James R. (1979), *Deveopment in Judging Moral Issues*, Minneapolis, MN: The University of Minnesota.

Richins, Marsha L., and Scott Dawson (1992), "A Consumer Values Orientation for Materialism and Its Measurement: Scale Development and Validation," *Journal of Consumer Research*, 19(December), 303-316.

Rindfleisch, Aric, James E. Burroughs, and Frank Denton (1997), "Family Structure, Materialism, and Compulsive Consumption," *Journal of Consumer Research*, 23(March), 312-325.

Rook, Dennis W. (1985), "The Ritual Dimension of Consumer Behavior," *Journal of Consumer Behavior*, 12(December), 251-264.

Rook, Dennis W., and Robert J. Fisher (1995), "Normative Influences on Impulsive Buying Behavior," *Journal of Consumer Research*, 22(December), 305-313.

Trompenaars, F., and C. Hampden-Turner (1998), *Riding the Waves of Culture* (Vol. 2nd), London: McGraw-Hill.

Yaryura-Tobias, Jose A., and Fugen A. Neziroglu (1997), *Obesessive-Compulsive Disorder Spectrum: Pathogenesis, Diagnosis, and Treatment*, Washington, DC: American Psychiatric Press, Inc.

Zaichkowsky, Judith Lynne (1985), "Measuring Involvement Construct," *Journal of Consumer Research*, 12(December), 341-352.

Zaichkowsky, Judith Lynne (1994), "The Personal Involvement Inventory: Reduction, Revision, and Application to Advertising," *Journal of Advertising*, 23(4), 59-70.

Discrete Emotions and Coping Strategies: Implications for Persuasion, Behavior, and Public Policy

Mary Frances Luce, University of Pennsylvania

SESSION OVERVIEW

This special session investigated the impact of different negative emotions in a variety of consumption situations. Although, in recent years there has been an increasing attention to the impact of arousal and affect on consumer behavior, very little research has addressed how distinct negative emotions differentially impact behaviors. This session investigated a variety of negative emotions (fear, disappointment, anger, guilt, etc.) and their impact on how consumers' cope in stressful purchase situations, respond to persuasion, as well as the differential impact of these distinct emotions on purchase intentions and behaviors.

"How Consumers Cope with Negative Emotions"
Sunghwan Yi and Hans Baumgartner, Penn State University

In the first presentation, Sunghwan Yi and Hans Baumgartner investigated a broad range of negative emotions associated with stressful purchase-related situations. Although coping has been a key construct in recent psychological research on emotions, little research is available on how consumers deal with stressful emotional experiences. This multi-stage study first examined the range of strategies consumers use to cope with negative emotions and stressful events. The study constructed a scale of consumer coping strategies, and identified eight distinct types of coping strategies, such as planful problem-solving, seeking social support, confrontive coping, acceptance, positive reinterpretation, self control, mental distancing, and behavioral distancing. It then looked for systematic links between specific coping strategies and six different negative emotions, such as anxiety/worry, disappointment, regret, sadness, guilt, and anger. Finally, it investigated how the use of particular coping strategies improves or deteriorates a person's subsequent emotional state. The study has implications for researchers interested in the psychological processes associated with different negative emotions, and it focuses attention on how consumers cope with stressful events and how the use of different coping strategies influences the evolution of emotional experiences.

"Differentiated Fear Appeals"
Kirsten Grasshoff and Mita Sujan, Penn State University

In the second presentation, Kirsten Grasshoff and Mita Sujan examined the impact of differentiated fear appeals on persuasion. This study examined four differentiated emotions (fear alone vs. fear coupled with guilt, challenge or hope) and their impact on cognitions, coping strategies, persuasion and behaviors with respect to receiving a vaccination. The results indicated that the appraisal of personal accountability, rather than valence, is important for persuasion. Thus, guilt (negative) and challenge (positive), both of which are high in accountability, enhance persuasion relative to the two low accountability emotions, fear (negative) and hope (positive). More importantly, actual behaviors (getting vaccinated) are consistent with these appraisal differences. These findings have relevance for both academics and practitioners interested in how discrete emotions impact persuasion and behaviors.

"Emotional Antecedents of Protection Motivation"
Punam Anand Keller, Ardis Olson, and Deborah Shields, Dartmouth College and Dartmouth Hitchcock Medical Center

In the final presentation, Punam Keller, Ardis Olson, and Deborah Shields investigated the practical implications of two negative emotions, fear and dejection, in terms of multiple preventative behaviors in such domains as solar protection, nutrition, exercise and bike helmet usage. This study extends current emotion research and health behavior models by conceptually and empirically supporting the role of negative emotions in health cognitions and preventative behaviors. The results indicated that dejection and fear increase vulnerability, and dejection reduces responsiveness to the appeal and also dampens self-efficacy. Furthermore, dejection reduces preventative behavior, whereas fear increases preventative behavior. These findings have implications for researchers, practitioners and public policy makers interested in understanding the link between emotions, cognition and preventative behavior.

Discussion
Julie Edell, Duke University

The discussion leader summarized the presentations and linked how emotions, similar and different across the three studies, had similar versus distinct impact on the range of dependent measures studied by either drawing consumers towards certain (positive) behaviors and coping or by pushing them towards more negative responses. The format was then opened to address questions from the audience. Three presentations share a rising interest in the role of coping in consumer emotional processes: how consumers deal with their emotions and the behaviors they thus enact.

Recalling Events: Examples as Cues in Behavioral Questions

Carolyn Simmons, University of Virginia
Joan Phillips, University of Notre Dame
Barbara Bickart, Rutgers-Camden

ABSTRACT

We examine how examples in survey questions affect recall of events. Building on the part-set cuing literature, we propose that examples increase recall when they cue low-accessibility subcategories of events, but decrease recall when they cue high-accessibility subcategories. Further, cuing with examples rather than subcategory names may in some situations clarify questions and reduce non-useable open-ended responses. A pilot study piggy-backed on a survey of Medicaid recipients confirms many of our predictions. Future work will incorporate validation measures (precluded by our piggy-backed pilot), including pretests of subcategory accessibility and objective measures of recall accuracy.

Sponsorship and Congruity Theory: A Theoretical Framework for Explaining Consumer Attitude and Recall of Event Sponsorship

Emma Jagre, University of Canterbury
John J. Watson, University of Canterbury
John G. Watson, Saint Bonaventure University

ABSTRACT

Sponsorship as a marketing communication tool has increased remarkably over the past two decades. Drawing from research in social psychology, a conceptual framework which affords a clearer understanding of the appropriate sponsoring of events when objectives are to improve consumer attitudes and increase recall is developed. The framework suggests that companies sponsoring events that provide a moderately inconsistent "fit" to their company will be viewed more favorably by consumers.

INTRODUCTION

Corporate sponsorship as a promotional activity has increased remarkably over the past two decades and has been acknowledged as an increasingly important element of the communication strategy used by marketing-driven corporations in order to reach their customers. In 1996 sponsorship expenditure reached $13.5 billion worldwide (Sandler and Shani 1998) and is expected to reach $19 billion in 1999, making sponsorship the fastest growing area of promotion (Taylor 1999; Ukman 1995). Notably, more companies are involved in sponsoring leisure activities such as sports and music, while fewer are involved in the science, education, culture and charities (Klincewicz 1998). For example, in 1996, North American businesses spent 66% of the total sponsorship dollars on the sponsorship of sports alone (Meenaghan 1998b).

Sponsorship has come to be viewed as a cost-effective alternative promotion strategy with an ability to transcend national and cultural barriers (Meenaghan 1998b). Additional reasons for the growth in sponsorship of leisure activities is the greater media coverage of these events combined with the rising cost of media advertising and increasing public indifference to conventional forms of communications (Meenaghan 1991b; Sandler and Shani 1998). Sponsorship involves two main activities: 1) an exchange between a sponsor and a sponsoree whereby the latter receives a fee and the former obtains the right to associate itself with the activity sponsored and 2) the marketing of the association by the sponsor (Cornwell and Maignan 1998). Sponsorship may be defined as investments in causes or events to support corporate or marketing objectives (Gardner and Shuman 1998, p. 44). The objectives primarily concern increasing awareness, enhancing image, improving goodwill, improving profitability and reaching otherwise unreachable customers, although sales objectives are sometimes specified and achieved (Hoek, Gendall, and West 1990; Meenaghan 1998b; Ukman 1996).

Consumer awareness of sponsorship status has been measured by the ability to both recognize and recall sponsors of an event (Sandler and Shani 1989), but the sponsorship literature has been limited in assessing its effectiveness in reaching this objective. The studies that have been conducted on consumers' recall of sponsors have not had encouraging results, and many sponsors have been unsuccessful in creating awareness (Cornwell and Maignan 1998; Crimmins and Horn 1996; Sandler and Shani 1998). For example, D'Alessandro (1998) reports that 55% of the respondents in one study correctly identified Reebok as an Olympic sponsor at the Atlanta Games, but 70% thought non-sponsor Nike was in fact a sponsor. Explanations for these results include the large amount of clutter, ambush marketing, and confusion which is due to the many layers of sponsorship within events (Meenaghan 1998a).

Despite the allocation of resources to sponsorship, a recent review of the literature reported that the processes underlying sponsor identification are poorly understood and that scholars have not adopted any specific theoretical framework guiding investigations of consumers' memory, recall, and attitude toward sponsorship (Cornwell and Maignan 1998; Johar and Pham 1999). An additional issue in the sponsorship literature concerns the importance of "fit" among the sponsoring company, the event, and the company's target audience when trying to reach sponsorship objectives (Kate 1995; Sandler and Shani 1998; Taylor 1999). Some researchers espouse ideas that are in direct contrast to the findings reported in cognitive psychology of memory.

For the purposes of this paper, we will attempt to answer two questions:

1. Can the congruity perspective developed in social psychology be applied to sponsorship in the development of a conceptual framework of "fit"?
2. Can the congruity perspective help explain and predict the right "fit" between sponsor and event when the goal is to reach objectives such as increased awareness and enhancement of image?

In order to answer these questions, we will first provide a brief synthesis of congruity theory and how it has been applied to *person memory* and attitude formation in social psychology. Next, we will examine how the theory has been applied to consumer behavior and advertising, as well as how it can be applied to sponsorship. Propositions which focus on the perception of fit between the companies sponsoring events and the actual events being sponsored, and the subsequent effects these relationships have on viewer recall and attitudes are then put forward. The final section concludes with a discussion of theoretical and managerial implications of the proposed framework.

CONGRUITY THEORY IN PSYCHOLOGY

Congruity (congruence) theory has been applied in social psychology to the investigations of memory as well as for explaining attitude formation. According to the principle of cognitive consistency, people value harmony among their thoughts, feelings, and behaviors, and they are motivated to maintain uniformity among these elements (Solomon 1996). Researchers conducting studies on incongruity have used a variety of terminologies interchangeably such as congruent/incongruent, expected/unexpected, and consistent/inconsistent (Heckler and Childers 1992).

The congruity model was originally formulated as a specific explanation for the attitude change that occurs when a *source* is connected to a particular *attitude object*. The statements that sources make about objects are associative when the statement implies a positive connection and dissociative when the statement implies a denial of a connection. The third element of congruity theory is the *evaluation* placed on both the source and the object by

Advances in Consumer Research
Volume 28, © 2001

FIGURE 1
Possible Outcomes of Congruity and Incongruity in Terms of Values and Affective Intensity

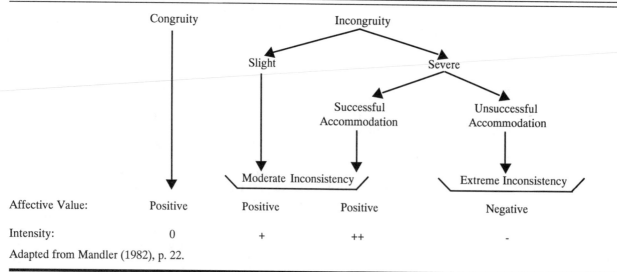

Adapted from Mandler (1982), p. 22.

the person whose attitude is being considered (Shaver 1987). The theory predicts that the value of the more negatively valued element will rise when linked to a positively valued one (Solomon 1996).

Memory

Congruity theory also suggests that the storage in memory and retrieval of information is influenced by prior expectations. A major aim of social psychologists has been to investigate the ways "expectancy-driven" processing influences social memory. These studies have investigated how social expectations influence when and how behavioral and trait information that is congruent or incongruent with expectations about persons or groups is stored in and retrieved from long-term memory (Stangor and McMillan 1992). Stangor and McMillan (1992) reported the most recent review of the social developmental literatures of schema-based expectancy theory of memory for expectancy-congruent and expectancy-incongruent memory. Schemas are "representations of experiences that guide action, perception and thought. These are developed as a function of the frequency of encounters with relevant instantiations where new encounters are evaluated against existing schemas" (Mandler 1982, p. 3).

Some studies in social cognition have found that generally congruent information is remembered better than information incongruent or irrelevant with existing schema. Yet other studies have found that incongruent information is better remembered; Stangor and McMillan (1992) conducted a meta-analysis of models from social psychology with competing predictions of how social memory will be influenced by social expectations. The results of this meta-analysis indicated that memory is better for expectancy-incongruent than expectancy-congruent information on recall and recognition measures (Stangor and McMillan 1992). Thus, the theoretical framework we outline is based on the notion that expectancy-incongruent information leads to better recall and recognition.

Attitudes

Attitudes have been defined as relatively stable opinions containing a cognitive element and an emotional element (Wade and Tavris 1996). Consideration has also been given in social psychology to the question of whether or not schemas elicit affect.

Fiske (1982) suggested that if an item is congruent with an existing schema, it will receive the affect linked to that schema. Fiske also proposed that with irrelevant or incongruent items, where a match does not occur, this transfer of affect to the item does not take place.

Madler (1982) expanded the concept by including elaboration as a moderating variable when examining how congruity is linked to affect. He further supported the concept proposed in the associative network model, that congruent relationships are not very noteworthy and therefore do not prompt extensive elaboration or get deeply processed. Consequently, Mandler (1982) proposed that the thoughts generated after elaboration in the congruent condition are favorable because people like objects that conform to their expectations and allow predictability. He added that these thoughts are typically mild rather than extreme.

Mandler (1982) also argued that whether an evaluation of an inconsistent relationship is relatively more favorable or more unfavorable is a function of how readily the processor can satisfactorily resolve the incongruity. Positive valuation and affect is enhanced when the increased elaboration leads to resolution of the incongruity. These resolutions occur for congruity, as well as for moderate incongruity, but not for extreme incongruity. These proposed relationships are depicted in Figure 1 and will be applied to sponsorship. Extreme incongruity is defined as incongruity that requires extensive elaboration that cannot be resolved and thus leads to frustration which elicits more negative evaluations. In contrast, moderate incongruities are regarded as "interesting and positively valued" (Mandler 1982, p. 22), thereby leading to more positive affect than elicited by either extreme incongruity or congruity, toward which response will only be mild.

Congruity Theory and Consumer Behavior

Consumer researchers have focused on building a theoretical understanding of the processes involved in consumers' comprehension and memory of ads (Heckler and Childers 1992), while advertising practitioners have been applying this knowledge so creative efforts can be optimized (Ogilvy 1983). Practitioners hope to increase the amount of attention given to an advertisement and hence, the degree to which the information being presented is processed (Heckler and Childers 1992). In support of the theories developed in social psychology, results of incongruity research applied to consumer behavior demonstrate that when information is somehow incongruent with prior expectations, individuals will engage in more effortful or elaborative processing which resulted in superior recall and recognition (Heckler and Childers 1982; Myers-Levy and Tybout 1989; Wansink and Ray 1996).

Attitude. Within consumer behavior, attitudes have been defined as individuals' internal evaluations of objects such as brands, products or companies where affect refers to the way people feel about an object (Mitchell and Olson 1981; Solomon 1996). Meyers-Levy and Tybout (1989) examined how the presentations of congruent versus incongruent information about soft drinks affected the development of attitudes toward those products. Their experiments provided support for Mandler's (1982) hypotheses that schema congruity influences evaluations and that moderate schema incongruity enhances evaluations. Moderate schema incongruity led to more favorable evaluations than either schema congruity or extreme schema incongruity. Also in support for Mandler's hypotheses, Wansink and Ray (1996) found that when the goal of advertising strategies is to increase usage frequency, the greater cognitive effort required for processing extremely incongruent information leads to unfavorable attitudes toward the source when incongruity remained unresolved.

Congruity has also been applied to advertising and consumer behavior when addressing how attitudes are affected when a person, such as a celebrity, is linked to an object, such as a brand or company (Solomon 1996). The central tenet of the celebrity-endorser advertising stream has been that the use of celebrities is a way to cut through the clutter of commercials and gain consumers' attention. Celebrities are also used to transfer the endorser's positive attributes, such as physical attractiveness and trustworthiness, to the product they endorse (O'Mahone and Meenaghan 1997/1998; Walker, Lanmeyer, and Langmeyer 1993). The simple presence of a celebrity increases the odds for higher recall, but does so because of an effect on attention, not brand linkage (Lukeman 1991). In this research stream, arguments are supportive of the need for congruence between the celebrity and the product in order for the message to be perceived as credible and believable. For example, celebrities who endorse beauty products are typically perceived as attractive in order for the message to be believable and lead to favorable product attitudes. Likewise, for a message to be perceived as credible, celebrities that endorse technical products must be perceived as having expertise with the products they endorse in order to create favorable product attitudes (Kamins 1990; Kamins and Gupta 1994; Lukeman 1991; O'Mahone and Meenaghan 1997/1998; Walker, Lanmeyer, and Langmeyer 1993). In sum, these findings (with respect to the transfer of affect) are inconsistent with the theories of incongruity in social psychology.

Congruity Theory and Sponsorship

While practitioners in the area of consumer research have focused on building a theoretical understanding of the process involved in consumers' comprehension and memory of ads, there is a lack of such a theoretical framework in the sponsorship literature with regard to both memory and attitudes toward companies sponsoring events.

Although the expectancy-congruent and expectancy-incongruent memory models in social psychology were developed to explain encoding, storage, and retrieval for person perception, they have been applied successfully to advertising and consumer behavior for explaining both recall and attitude formation. Thus, these models may be equally applicable to building a theoretical understanding with regard to sponsorship. Although the results of the congruity research applied to celebrity endorser advertising have

not supported the relationships between incongruity and affect, we will argue that when developing this conceptual framework the findings related to celebrity endorser advertising are probably not generalizable to sponsorship.

Sponsor-Event "Fit" as Consistent or Inconsistent

It is clear that the sponsorship literature is lacking a conceptual framework that adequately explains "fit" relationships among a sponsoring company, an event, and a company's target audience (D'Alessandro 1998; Kate 1995; Taylor 1999). As no clear definition of "fit" has been proposed in the sponsorship literature, scholars discussing fit actually do not distinguish between two different types of fit. Some scholars have highlighted the ability of sponsorship to target a wide and/or specific range of audiences and the relationships between the characteristics of events and the demographics, lifestyle, and AIO (activities, interests, and opinions) of the attendees or viewers (Cornwell and Maignan 1998; Nicholls, Roslow, and Laskey 1994). This is the first type of fit, and it occurs when the sponsoring company's target audience attends the event; it is the fit between the audience and the company's customers of interest. The second fit is between the sponsoring company's brand, product or service, and its perceived closeness with an event, based on consumers' perceptions and expectations. This fit is referred to as fit between the sponsor and the event and is the type of fit of interest to us.

A limited amount of research has focused on the compatibility and congruence between the attributes of the sponsor and the sponsored event in order to maximize the communication potential (Ferrnand and Pages 1996; Gwinner 1997; Martin 1994). These studies have proposed that the process of a positive image transfer from an event to the sponsoring company is similar to the process of meaning transfer from celebrity-endorsers to the products they endorse. The focus of these studies has been to establish that there exist multiple aspects within the image of sports. However, these research streams have not assessed this impact on reaching communication objectives.

The question of fit or congruence between the sponsor and the event is a very new area of research and only two studies, Johar and Pham (1999) and McDaniel (1999) have addressed the effects of congruence on recall and attitudes by empirical testing. McDaniel (1999) used a schema-based approach to examine the brand/sport matchups effect on attitudes toward the sponsoring brand as a persuasive influence. He suggested that the theory of meaning transfer in celebrity-endorser advertising may be applicable to sponsorship, but he did not focus on whether the brand-event relationships were consistent or inconsistent; he only focused on the attributes of sporting events, such as whether the sport is perceived as negative or positive. However, McDaniel (1999) found no support for his propositions that brands sponsoring more negatively perceived sports such as bowling would have significantly lower post-test attitudes toward the brand than brands sponsoring more positively perceived sports such as hockey or an Olympic team. Such a finding leads to questions about whether celebrity-endorser advertising is actually generalizable to event marketing. While celebrity-endorser advertising is concerned with the transfer of specific attributes such as attractiveness and credibility, event marketing is more concerned with the transfer of the general positive valence the audience has for the event as a whole. In addition, celebrity-endorser advertising is likely to be more effective for new products or ones with low awareness and when specific attributes such as attractiveness and credibility are of great importance for the persuasiveness of the message (Howard and Crompton 1995).

FIGURE 2
Conceptual Model of the Effects of FIT Between Sponsor and Event

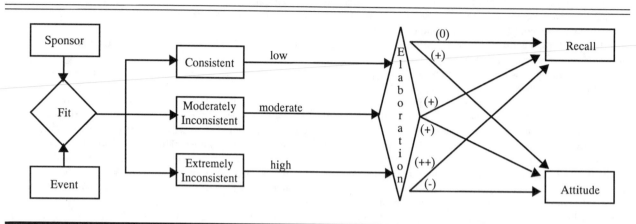

FIGURE 3
Example of Fit in Terms of Affective Intensity and Recall When Nike Sponsors Various Events

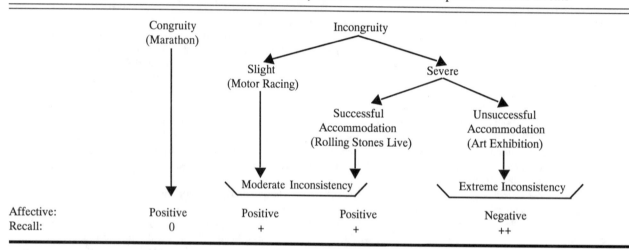

The second study of fit between sponsor and event was conducted by Johar and Pham (1999). They investigated how the brand-event relatedness relationship operates in sponsor identification. Johar and Pham (1999) proposed that "in sponsor identification tasks, consumers rely on the semantic overlap between features of the event and those of potential sponsors" (p. 300), and as a consequence, sponsor identification is biased toward brands that are semantically related to an event. Their study provides additional support for what is established within social psychology of memory, that when assessing recognition, subjects make response biases toward expectancy-congruent information due to subjects engaging in guessing strategies (Stangor and McMillan 1992). However, Johar and Pham failed to discuss some of their more intriguing findings, such as the fact that 91.5% of the unrelated sponsors compared to 60.5% of the related sponsors were recalled. Obviously, such a result is contrary to hypotheses of relatedness but supports the argument that unrelated or inconsistent fit results in higher recall.

To assess how to most effectively invest sponsorship resources in event marketing when the objectives are to increase awareness and enhance image, we have developed a conceptual framework that incorporates the contributions of the incongruity research developed in social psychology. Figure 2 depicts our proposed framework. In the following section, we will describe this framework by presenting three types of sponsor-event relationships with respect to consistency or fit. We will then put forward proposals concerning each relationship's relative effectiveness in reaching the objectives of recall and enhanced attitudes toward the sponsoring company.

Sponsor Event Fit as Consistent, Extremely Inconsistent, and Moderately Inconsistent

Schemas were discussed previously with regard to social psychology and can also be applied to event sponsorship. New encounters, such as new sponsors of events, are evaluated against existing schemas of events, acquired through experience from attending them in person and/or viewing them on television where the interaction between an event and a schema determines the perception of new relationships. These schemas might also contain product categories that are typically part of fans' event experience (McDaniel 1999). When new information is received, individuals will tend to use existing schemas to process the relevance or congruence of this new information (i.e., fit with existing schema).

Incongruity refers to the extent that structural correspondence is achieved between entire configuration of attribute relations associated with the sponsor and the event and the configuration of attribute relations associated with the sponsor and the event and the configuration specified by the existing schema (Meyers-Levy and Tybout 1989). An inconsistent fit between a sponsor company and an event can be operationalized by the degree to which the relationship is perceived to be incongruent with viewer expectations and pre-existing knowledge structures associated with the theme (Heckler and Childers 1992). Thus, a fit between an event and a sponsor is expected when an individual's knowledge of the sponsor's functional similarity or image-related similarity with the event is consistent, but not expected when the relationship is inconsistent with existing knowledge structures and schema.

An example of sponsorship fit that is "expected and consistent" would be Adidas sponsoring a sporting event or Montana wine sponsoring a wine and food festival. An "unexpected and inconsistent" fit would be the Bank of America sponsoring a sporting event or Nike sponsoring a wine and food festival. Figure 3 depicts examples of these different types of relationships for Nike.

In practice, the (in)congruity between a sponsor and its associated event may lie between the extremes of a perfect match or mismatch. The distinction between moderate and extreme incongruity can be operationalized by the ease with which anomalies can be resolved (Mandler 1982). As noted above, research has reported that information which is incongruent with prior expectations will result in individuals engaging in more effortful or elaborative processing resulting in superior recall (Heckler and Childers 1992; Mandler 1982; Meyers-Levy and Tybout 1989; Wansink and Ray 1996). In the situation of a consistent fit between sponsor and event, viewers should not engage in elaborate processing. On the other hand, extreme incongruity between sponsor and event should result in the audience getting surprised due to the unexpectancy of the relationship, which in turn would result in the largest amount of elaboration and processing. Whether a fit is congruent, moderately incongruent, or extremely incongruent can only be determined from the viewpoint of the audience's expectations. As each sponsor-event relationship will be processed and elaborated upon to different extents, it is these differences in processing that would lead to differences in recall and attitude (Wansink and Ray 1996).

Awareness and Recall

As mentioned earlier, one of the main objectives of companies engaging in sponsorship is to increase awareness. Awareness is created as events, and consequently corporate sponsors, intrude on the consciousness of event audiences (Meenaghan 1998a). In general, memory measures in social psychology have either been based on recognition or on recall paradigms (Stangor and McMillan 1992). Recognition measures assess the ability of the individual to identify whether previously presented information has been seen before or not. One danger with this measure of memory is that it is easily contaminated by response biases; individuals are more likely to guess that an item that is congruent with an expectation rather than an item which is incongruent with that expectation (Stangor and McMillan 1992). In the second memory measure, that of free recall, subjects are asked to list the information that comes to mind, requiring subjects to retrieve the item from memory.

The results of the meta-analysis of social psychology showed that overall, memory was better for expectancy-incongruent than for expectancy-congruent information on recall and recognition measures (Stangor and McMillan 1992). Taking into account the vast amount of support this framework has received in advertising

and consumer behavior may make it equally applicable to the development of propositions in the area of sponsorship.

Audiences that attend events will have expectancies of the type of companies that usually sponsor these events. Such expectations will be based on experience. Presented with a new sponsor that does not fit into the present schema is likely to result in increased elaboration and processing as the novelty of the incongruency increases arousal (Mandler 1982). This more effortful, elaborative processing should result in superior recall (Graesser 1981; Hastie 1980; Heckler and Childer 1992; Srull 1981). During sponsor-event relationships that are characterized by extreme incongruity (low fit), the novelty of the new relationship will result in the largest increase of elaboration and result in the greatest increase of recall of the sponsor. For this reason, extremely inconsistent relationships between sponsor and event should result in the most extensive elaboration, leading to the most superior recall of the actual sponsor. The opposite should hold when the sponsor and event relationship is completely congruent (high fit). Consequently, the following propositions are made:

P1: Companies that sponsor events which are *extremely inconsistent* with viewer expectations (low fit) will have significantly higher recall rates than companies that sponsor events that are either completely consistent (high fit) or moderately consistent (moderate fit) with viewer expectations.

P2: Companies that sponsor events that are *completely consistent* with viewer expectations (high fit) will have significantly lower recall rates than companies that sponsor events that are either extremely inconsistent (low fit) or moderately inconsistent (moderate fit).

Attitude

Another objective for companies engaging in sponsorship is to increase the company's image or consumer attitudes toward the company (McDaniel and Kinney 1998; Howard and Crompton 1995). Attitudes may be considered relatively stable and enduring predispositions to behave and should be useful predictors of consumers' behavior toward products and services (Mitchell and Olson 1981). Enhanced sponsor image derives from the fact that the association of the sponsor with the event results in a rub off or transfer of values from the event to the sponsor (Meenaghan 1983). When evaluating the effect of consistency between a sponsor and an event, most research indicates that a completely consistent fit leads to a transfer of affect from the event to the sponsor which does not occur under conditions of extreme incongruity. However, Mandler (1982) proposed that as congruent relationships between sponsor and the event are not very note-worthy, the thoughts that are generated are likely to be favorable but typically mild rather than extreme.

Applying this rationale to sponsorship would suggest that an extremely inconsistent fit between a sponsoring company and an event would increase elaboration to such an extent that it would lead to difficulty in resolving the incongruity. In turn, consumers' frustration would increase and when it was not possible to resolve the incongruity, consumers would generate unfavorable thoughts of the relationship and have negative attitudes toward the sponsor (Mandler 1982; Wansink and Ray 1996). However, when Mandler's (1982) idea of moderate incongruity is introduced, the incongruity may be regarded as interesting and positively valued, thereby leading to more positive affect than ones elicited by either extreme incongruity or complete congruity. It may therefore be proposed that:

P3:   Companies that sponsor events which are *extremely inconsistent* with viewer expectations (low fit) will produce lower attitude ratings from consumers and lead to less favorable sponsor evaluations than companies that sponsor events that are either completely consistent (high fit) or moderately consistent (moderate fit) with viewer expectations.

P4:   Companies that sponsor events which are *moderately inconsistent* with viewer expectations (moderate fit) will produce significantly higher attitude ratings from consumers and lead to more favorable sponsor evaluations than companies that sponsor events that are either completely consistent (high fit) or extremely inconsistent (low fit).

CONCLUSION

This paper has set forward a number of research propositions that are consistent with our proposed conceptual model. Obviously, the propositions are in need of empirical validation. The biggest challenge in the empirical testing of these propositions will likely be the measurement development of the "fit" construct. Consequently, managers considering sponsorship would benefit from the development of a scale measuring degrees of "fit" for guiding choice of sponsor-event relationships.

The process underlying sponsor identification is poorly understood and scholars have not adopted a conceptual framework that can guide research concerned with recall and attitude toward sponsors. Practitioners have assumed for example, that sponsoring events consistent with a product or company will increase awareness and result in positive attitudes toward the sponsor. To date, there is little evidence that supports this argument. As was articulated in the paper, the tendency to sponsor events that provide a consistent "fit" with a company may not in fact result in significant levels of awareness and may not be an effective way to enhance the company's image.

REFERENCES

Cornwell, T. Bettina and Isabelle Maignan (1998), "An International Review of Sponsorship Research," *Journal of Advertising*, 27(1), 1-21.

Crimmins, James and Martin Horn (1996), "Sponsorship: From Management Ego Trip to Marketing Success," *Journal of Advertising Research*, 36(4), 11-21.

D'Alessandro, David (1998), "Event Marketing: Winners, Losers, and Chumps," *Vital Speeches of the Day*, 64(10), 296-301.

Fiske, Susan T. (1982), "Schema-Triggered Affect: Applications to Social Perception," in the *17th Annual Carnegie Symposium on Cognition*, eds. Margaret S. Clark and Susan T. Fiske, Hillside, NJ: Erlbaum, 55-78.

Gardner, Meryl P. and Philip Shuman (1998), "Sponsorship and Small Business," *Journal of Small Business Management*, 26(4), 44-52.

Graesser, A.C. (1981), *Prose Comprehension: Beyond the Word*, New York: Springer.

Gwinner, Kevin (1997), "A Model of Image Creation and Image Transfer in Event Sponsorship," *International Marketing Review*, 14(3), 145-158.

Hastie, Reid and P. Kumar (1979), "Person Memory: Personality Traits as Organizing Principles in Memory for Behaviors," *Journal of Personality and Social Psychology*, 37, 25-38.

Hastie, Reid (1980), "Memory for Behavioral Information that Confirms or Contradicts a Personality Impression," *Person Memory: The Cognitive Basis of Social Perception*, R. Hastie et al., eds., Hillsdale, NJ: Lawrence Erlbaum Associates, 155-177.

Heckler, Susan E. and Terry L. Childers (1992), "The Role of Expectancy and Relevancy in Memory for Verbal and Visual Information: What is Incongruency?" *Journal of Consumer Research*, 18(March), 475-491.

Hoek, Janet A., Philip J. Gendall, and Rohan D. West (1990), "The Role of Sponsorship in Marketing Planning Selected New Zealand Companies," *New Zealand Journal of Business*, 12, 87-95.

Houston, Michael J., Terry L. Childers, and Susan E. Heckler (1987), "Picture-Word Consistency and the Elaborative Processing of Advertisements," *Journal of Marketing Research*, 24(December), 359-369.

Howard, Dennis R. and John L. Crompton (1995), *Financing Sport*, Morgantown: Fitness Information Technology Inc.

Johar, Gita V. and Michael T. Pham (1999), "Relatedness, Prominence, and Constructive Sponsorship Identification," *Journal of Marketing Research*, 36(August), 299-312.

Kamins, Michael. A. (1990), "An Investigation into the Matchup Hypothesis in Celebrity Advertising: When Beauty is Only Skin Deep," *Journal of Advertising*, 19, 4-13.

Kamins, Michael. A. and Kamal Gupta (1994), "Congruence Between Spokesperson and Product Type: A Matchup Hypothesis Perspective," *Psychology and Marketing*, 11(6), 569-586.

Kate, Nancy T. (1995), "And Now, a Word from Our Sponsors," *American Demographics*, (June), 46-52.

Klincewicz, Krzysztof (1998), "Ethical Aspects of Sponsorship," *Journal of Business Ethics*, 17, 1103-1110.

Lukeman, Gerald (1991), "Analysis Shows New Way to Think About TV Recall Scores," *Marketing News*, 25(8), 24.

Mandler, George (1982), "The Structure of Value: Accounting for Taste," in the *17th Annual Carnegie Symposium on Cognition*, Margaret S. Clark and Susan T. Fiske, eds., Hillsdales, NJ: Erlbaum, 3-36.

Martin, James H. (1994), "Using a Perceptual Map of the Consumer's Sport Schema to Help Make Sponsorship Decisions," *Sport Marketing Quarterly*, 3(3), 27-33.

McDaniel, Stephen R. (1999), "An Investigation of Match-up Effects in Sport Sponsorship Advertising: The Implications of Consumer Advertising Schemas," *Psychology and Marketing*, 16(2), 163-184.

McDaniel, Stephen R. and Lance Kinney (1998), "The Implications of Recency and Gender Effects in Consumer Response to Ambush Marketing," *Psychology and Marketing*, 15(4), 385-403.

Meenaghan, Tony (1983), "Commercial Sponsorship," *European Journal of Marketing*, 17(2), 5-73.

Meenaghan, Tony (1991a), "Sponsorship: Legitimising the Medium," *European Journal of Marketing*, 25(11), 5-10.

Meenaghan, Tony (1991b), "The Role of Sponsorship in the Marketing Communications Mix," *International Journal of Advertising*, 10(1), 35-47.

Meenaghan, Tony (1996/1997), "Ambush Marketing, A Threat to Corporate Sponsorship," *Sloan Management Review*, 38(1), 103-113.

Meenaghan, Tony (1998a), "Ambush Marketing: Corporate Strategy and Consumer Reaction," *Psychology and Marketing*, 15(4), 305-322.

Meenaghan, Tony (1998b), "Current Developments and Future Directions in Sponsorship," *International Journal of Advertising*, 17(1), 3-28.

Meyers-Levy, Joan and Alice M. Tybout (1989), "Schema Congruity as a Basis for Product Evaluation," *Journal of Consumer Research*, 16(June), 39-54.

Mitchell, Andrew A. and Jerry C. Olson (1981), "Are Product Attribute Beliefs the Only Mediator of Advertising Effects on Brand Attitude?" *Journal of Marketing Research*, 18(August), 318-330.

Neisser, U. (1976), *Cognition and Reality*, New York: Plentum Press.

Nicholls, J.A.F, Sydney Roslow, and Henry A. Laskey (1994), "Sports Event Sponsorship for Brand Promotion," *Journal of Applied Business Research*, 10(4), 35-40.

Ogilvy, David (1983), *Ogilvy on Advertising*, New York: Crown.

Sandler, Dennis M. and David Shani (1989), "Olympic Sponsorship vs. Ambush Marketing: Who Gets the Gold?" *Journal of Advertising Research*, (August/September), 9-14.

Sandler, Dennis M. and David Shani (1998), "Ambush Marketing: Is Confusion To Blame for the Flickering Fame?" *Psychology and Marketing*, 15(4).

Shaver, Kelly G. (1987), *Principles Social Psychology*, 3rd ed., Hillsdale, NJ: Lawrence Erlbaum Associates.

Solomon, Michael (1996), *Consumer Behavior*, New Jersey: Prentice Hall, Inc.

Srull, Thomas K. (1981), "Person Memory: Some Tests of Associative Storage and Retrieval Models," *Journal of Experimental Psychology: Human Learning and Memory*, 7(6), 440-463.

Stangor, Charles and David McMillan (1992), "Memory for Expectancy-Congruent and Expectancy-Incongruent Information: A Review of the Social and Social Developmental Literatures," *Psychological Bulletin*, 3(1), 42-61.

Taylor, Tim (1999), "Audience Information the Key to Sports Marketers," *Marketing News*, 33(2), 10.

Ukman, L. (1995), *The IEG's Complete Guide to Sponsorship: Everything You Need to Know About Sports, Arts, Events, Entertainment, and Cause Marketing*, Chicago, IL: IEG, Inc.

Ukman, L. (1996), "Evaluating ROI of a Sponsorship Program," *Marketing News*, 30(18), 5-14.

Wade, Carole and Carol Tavris (1996), *Psychology*, 4th ed., New York: HarperCollins College Publishers, Inc.

Walker, Mary, Lynn Lanmeyer, and Daniel Langmeyer (1993), "Commentary: Celebrity Endorsers—Do You Get What You Pay For?" *Journal of Product and Brand Management*, 2(3), 36-43.

Wansink, Brian and Michael L. Ray (1996), "Advertising Strategies to Increase Usage Frequency," *Journal of Marketing*, 60(1), 31-46.

Cultural Models as Meaning Makers: An Empirical Exploration of Consumer Interpretations of Marketing Communications

Torsten Ringberg, Penn State University

ABSTRACT

This study investigates how internalized cultural models guide consumer interpretations of marketing messages. First I briefly explain how the epistemological positions of four dominant paradigms—cognitivism, structuralism, postmodernism, and post-structuralism—create contradictory understandings of how consumers go about making sense of marketing messages. Second, I introduce a pilot study of (1) the interpretive strategies used by individuals to interpret advertisements and (2) how internalized cultural models influence these interpretive strategies. Third, I introduce an integrative conceptual framework that shows how, when, and why cultural models affect consumers' understanding of the embedded meaning in marketing messages.

The Role of Attributions in Evaluating Exchange Relationships

Michael Tsiros, University of Miami
Vitas Mittal, University of Pittsburgh

ABSTRACT

The paper examines how the locus and stability of a cause influence the level of satisfaction and the future of the exchange relationship for both positive and negative outcomes. Several hypotheses are derived from the literature and tested in two studies– an experiment and a field study. Stability influences commitment levels when the experienced outcome is positive whereas locus influences commitment levels when the experienced outcome is negative. In addition, the future of a relationship is influenced differentially by locus and stability depending on the valence of the outcome.

Attention Grabbers: An Exploration of the Automatic Categorization of Advertisement Headlines

Jesper Nielsen, University of North Carolina at Chapel Hill
Charlotte Mason, University of North Carolina at Chapel Hill

ABSTRACT

The research presented here draws on previous research in preattentive processing and automaticity and investigates new ways for marketers to elicit attention to their advertisements. The study finds support for the hypothesis that advertising headlines located in the periphery are semantically processed prior to conscious attention and that these headlines are able to initiate automatic categorization that leads to differential shifts in attention. Using Signal Detection Theory measures and a second study, we were able to eliminate alternative explanations such as differential memorability of individual words employed, differential decay in memory of the two types of stimuli, and response bias.

College Students' Attributions of Responsibility For a Drunk Driving Accident

M. Elizabeth Blair, Ohio University
Eva Hyatt, Appalachian State University

ABSTRACT

After reviewing the current research on alcohol and US college students, this study examines the amount of blame placed on various participants in a hypothetical drunk-driving accident (the student who was driving, the beer manufacturer, the driver's friends who celebrated the student's birthday with him/her, and the bar where the party occurred). The influence situation and level of company ethics were manipulated to produce several scenarios. Results indicate that in general, student subjects are reluctant to blame the bar or manufacturer, but place the bulk of blame on the birthday friend who drank too much and then had the accident, regardless of the situation. The vast majority of student subjects felt that the birthday friend should have seen what was coming. It appears that college students know not to drink irresponsibly and realize the potential consequences, but neglect to behave responsibly nonetheless.

Strategic Framing: The Art and Science of Influencing Others

Rebecca W. Hamilton, University of Maryland

This session examined framing as a persuasion tactic that people use strategically when communicating with others. The first paper, presented by Tom Nelson, began by distinguishing framing from more traditional forms of persuasion. While traditional definitions of persuasion suppose that beliefs change when individuals are given *new* information, framing causes individuals to weight the information they already have differently. The next two papers examined the strategic behavior of "naïve" people–those without formal training in persuasion tactics–in negotiations and group decision making. Rick Larrick discussed the effectiveness of naïve bargainers in choosing the frames that are most beneficial for them. Rebecca Hamilton presented experimental evidence suggesting that people may intuitively influence others' choices by defining the context in which alternatives are evaluated.

"Issue Framing, Value Tradeoffs, and Political Choice"
Thomas E. Nelson, Ohio State University

Tom Nelson, from the Political Science department at Ohio State University, suggested that framing analysis appeals as much to scholars studying political choice as it does to those studying consumer choice. Political actors and institutions, from candidates for office to the news media, frame issues of public concern, with implications for public opinion and policy choice. His research examines how issue frames influence the tradeoffs citizens make between competing social values. He contrasted this mechanism for opinion change with other plausible psychological processes, such as belief revision and cognitive accessibility, and he described three specific framing strategies that affect citizens' resolution of value conflict: issue categorization, value ranking, and institutional goal assignment.

"On Choosing Frames and Being Framed in Bargaining"
Richard P. Larrick, University of Chicago
Sally Blount, University of Chicago

An abundance of research shows that people's choices are influenced by how decisions are framed. This research asked two new questions: Can self-interested parties use framing to influence social interactions? How do recipients of influence attempts react to "being framed?" The authors addressed these questions using a simple bargaining task known as the ultimatum game. Across four studies and three framing effects, they found that bargainers are poor at choosing the frame most advantageous to them. Rick Larrick discussed the motivational and cognitive reasons for these shortcomings, and concluded by reviewing on-going research on how people react to "being framed" in bargaining.

"Why Do People Suggest What They Don't Want? Using Menus to Influence Others' Choices"
Rebecca W. Hamilton, University of Maryland

Why would people suggest alternatives to others that they don't want them to choose? Constructing comparisons for others can draw out tradeoffs among alternatives or create contrasts that influence others' choices. Because the contrasts and tradeoffs inherent in a menu can systematically affect others' choices, the person suggesting alternatives for a choice has substantial power to shape the decision process and the outcome. Rebecca Hamilton

discussed four studies that tested subjects' knowledge of these strategies, their willingness to use them for real group choices, and the effectiveness of these strategies given others' beliefs about the manner in which the menu was constructed.

Online Shopping Environments: Empowered Consumers or Browsers Beware?

Gerald Häubl, University of Alberta

Against the background of the rapid growth of electronic commerce and, more specifically, consumer online shopping, it becomes increasingly important to develop an understanding of how consumers process product information and make purchase decisions in electronic environments. Two important characteristics of artificial marketplaces are that they allow for a high degree of personalization of information and that they greatly facilitate stimulus-based, as opposed to memory-based, decision making. While these and other properties of electronic shopping environments may be highly beneficial to shoppers in some respects, they also provide new possibilities for influencing consumers' preferences and, ultimately, their purchasing decisions.

The focus of this special session was on the question of how susceptible consumers' shopping behavior in digital marketplaces is to being influenced in a significant way by characteristics of the information environment, in particular characteristics that can be very easily manipulated by vendors. The paper by *Häubl and Murray* examines this question in the context of electronic recommendation agents, and shows that the mere inclusion of selected attributes in the calibration and sorting algorithm of such agents can alter consumers' preferences and that this preference-construction effect may persist even beyond agent-assisted shopping encounters. The paper by *Mandel and Johnson* investigates the idea that Web page backgrounds may change preferences by influencing attribute importance through associative priming, and provides empirical evidence that this type of priming effect may occur in digital environments. Finally, the paper by *Häubl and Popkowski Leszczyc* examines the effects of different characteristics of Internet auctions that are under the vendor's control on important auction outcomes, and shows that bidders tend to discount some unambiguously relevant pieces of information while unduly relying on certain types of irrelevant information.

The papers that were presented in this session are complementary in that each of them approaches an important mechanism by which consumers' shopping behavior in digital marketplaces may be influenced. Taken together, the three papers enhance our understanding of human decision making in electronic environments which, given the rapid growth of electronic commerce and online shopping, is becoming an increasingly important area of consumer research.

"Preference Construction and Persistence in Artificial Marketplaces: The Role of Electronic Recommendation Agents"

Gerald Häubl, University of Alberta
Kyle B. Murray, University of Alberta

The objective of this paper is to examine the role of electronic recommendation agents in connection with the construction of preferences by decision makers in online shopping environments. Following Häubl and Trifts (2000), an electronic recommendation agent is conceptualized as a software tool that (1) calibrates a model of the preference of a consumer based on his/her input and (2) uses this model to make personalized product recommendations (in the form of a sorted list) in a decision task based on its understanding of the consumer's preference structure.

Interactive artificial marketplaces allow for the unbundling of product information from the actual products. In such electronic environments, the constraints of physical space no longer govern the organization of information (Johnson, Lohse, and Mandel 1999). In addition, online shopping represents a retail format that dramatically increases the potential for consumers to make choices within highly interactive environments (Alba, Lynch, Weitz, Janiszewski, Lutz, Sawyer, and Wood 1997). Therefore, it is important to obtain a better understanding of how consumers process product information and make purchase decisions in artificial marketplaces that are effectively unconstrained in their presentation of information.

The interactive nature of artificial marketplaces allows for highly customized and personalized information environments. Johnson et al. (1999) argue that "because the decision environment can actually influence how ... preferences are constructed, it can influence what is chosen" and that "if, in fact, such manipulation can be 'customized' at the individual level, the potential for influencing choice is very significant" (p. 20).

A recommendation agent is an example of a tool that can personalize and customize information at the individual level. Evidence from Häubl and Trifts (2000) suggests that consumers tend to rely on such an agent to help them reduce their search costs and to improve their decision quality. Given this reliance on a recommendation agent to assist or even lead in the customization of the shopping environment, and the impact the environment can have on preference construction, it is particularly interesting to examine the potential influence that a recommendation agent can have on preferential choice processes.

Along these lines, we propose that a recommendation agent that considers only a subset of the attributes that are relevant in a particular product category and choice situation may induce a preference-construction effect that is reflected in a change of the relative importance that consumers attach to different attributes. Specifically, our key hypothesis is that, everything else being equal, the mere inclusion of an attribute in a recommendation agent will render this attribute more prominent in consumers' purchase decisions. The results of Experiment 1 provide support for the existence of this *mere-inclusion* effect in an agent-assisted shopping task.

Furthermore, we suggest three possible explanations of the mere-inclusion effect; it might be: (1) a direct consequence of the format of information presentation, (2) the result of feature-based priming, or (3) a reflection of decision makers inferences about relative attribute importance. These alternative explanations are investigated in Experiment 2. The results suggest that this type of preference construction is due primarily to consumers' inferences about attribute importance. We also find that the mere-inclusion effect persists beyond the agent-assisted shopping experience and into subsequent preferential choice tasks in which no recommendation agent is available.

REFERENCES

Alba, Joseph, John Lynch, Barton Weitz, Chris Janiszewski, Richard Lutz, Alan Sawyer, and Stacey Wood (1997), "Interactive Home Shopping: Consumer, Retailer, and Manufacturer Incentives to Participate in Electronic Marketplaces," *Journal of Marketing*, 61 (July), 38-53.

Häubl, Gerald and Valerie Trifts (2000), "Consumer Decision Making in Online Shopping Environments: The Effects of Interactive Decision Aids," *Marketing Science*, 19, 1, in print.

Johnson, Eric J., Gerald L. Lohse, and Naomi Mandel (1999), "Designing Marketplaces of the Artificial: Four Approaches to Understanding Consumer Behavior in Electronic Environments," working paper, Columbia University.

"Can Web Pages Change Choices? Priming, Search and the Construction of Preferences"

Naomi Mandel, Arizona State University
Eric J. Johnson, Columbia University

This paper examines the idea that Web page design can change preferences by influencing attribute importance. Specifically, preference construction (Payne, Bettman and Johnson, 1993) may be influenced by Web page backgrounds through associative priming, which occurs when a person retrieves an item from long-term memory and activation spreads automatically to other related items in memory (Herr 1989). When a subject looks at a Web page, he or she may experience this priming from stimuli such as the page's background pictures or color, which may affect the subject's judgments about the product's attributes and whether to buy the product.

Most importantly, this paper explores the nature of priming effects on information search, and examines the possibility that priming changes external search as well as internal retrieval. If we believe that priming works by increasing the accessibility of product related information, we might suggest that its effects are primarily limited to memory-based choice. However, it is possible that priming leads to differences in search, thereby impacting stimulus-based search as well. In addition, experts and novices may differ on the richness of their internal representation of products, which may produce differences in the mechanism of priming.

Experiment 1 showed that visual stimuli can manipulate salient features. For example, subjects who were shown car descriptions after reading an introduction with a red flaming background rated safety significantly more important in automobile purchasing than did those who saw a green background with pennies. Experiment 2 replicated these results with a large sample, and also studied differences in the decision making process. The priming affected the order in which subjects examined attribute information, which in turn influenced their choices. Experiment 3 found that priming affected the choices of both experts and novices, but through different mechanisms. Novices spent an increased amount of time looking at information about the attribute on which they were primed, affecting their subsequent choices. However, for experts, information search did not mediate the effect of priming on choice.

REFERENCES

Herr, Paul M. (1989), "Priming Price: Prior Knowledge and Context Effects," *Journal of Consumer Research*, 16, 67-75.

Payne, John W., James R. Bettman, and Eric J. Johnson (1993), *The Adaptive Decision Maker*, Cambridge: Cambridge University Press.

"Going, Going, Gone–Determinants of Bidding Behavior and Selling Prices in Internet Auctions"

Gerald Häubl, University of Alberta
Peter T. L. Popkowski Leszczyc, University of Alberta

Due to the rapidly increasing prevalence of Internet auctions, particularly person-to-person auctions, as a selling format, developing an enhanced understanding of individuals' bidding behavior in such auctions is critically important. While there has been a considerable amount of mostly theoretical research on auctions in economics (e.g., Milgrom and Weber 1982), the psychological aspects of bidding in auctions have received very little attention in the literature to date. This paper investigates the effects of several characteristics of Internet auctions on two important auction outcomes, (1) the number of bidders and (2) selling prices. The focus is on auction characteristics that are under the control of the vendor. The primary objective of this work is to examine whether individuals' bidding behavior in Internet auctions reflects some of the context-induced biases that have been observed either in the context of fixed-price marketplaces or in laboratory studies of consumers' value judgments. The paper is based on two controlled field experiments involving sets of real-world public auctions conducted on a large Internet auction site using ascending-bid auctions with predetermined end times.

Experiment 1 focuses on the effects of specifying a *fixed price component* (e.g., a shipping-and-handling charge), as well as of the magnitude of such a component, on bidding behavior and auction prices. From a consumer-behavior standpoint, it is important to understand how consumers process information about such fixed price components in the context of Internet auctions. Classical economic theory predicts that consumers take fixed price components into account perfectly when expressing their willingness to pay for a product in the form of a maximum bid in an auction. Thus, market demand should be invariant to the magnitude of the fixed price component, and the total price paid by the winner of an auction (i.e., the sum of the fixed price component and the winning bid) should be unaffected by the magnitude of this fixed charge.

Recent work by Morwitz, Greenleaf, and Johnson (1998) suggests that the mere partitioning of a given total price may decrease consumers' recalled total costs and increase demand relative to an all-inclusive price. These authors proposed cost-benefit trade-offs in connection with the processing of information and anchoring-and-adjustment processes of information integration as potential explanations of why consumers might react more favorably to a partitioned than to a combined price. Since merely altering the presentation of a full price through different types of partitioned pricing may affect market demand for a product, it is of interest to examine whether a similar phenomenon can be observed in the context of Internet auctions that involve fixed charges. Based on the work by Morwitz et al. (1998), we predict that, when constructing their willingness to pay for a given product, bidders in Internet auctions will fail to fully take into account a fixed component of the product's price.

The magnitude of fixed price components was varied systematically in a controlled field experiment that involved auctions of sets of collectable postage stamps. The results suggest that, as predicted, the fixed price component has a significant effect on the total selling price such that the latter increases as the magnitude of the fixed price component increases. The results of Experiment 1 suggest that bidders in real-world Internet auctions fail to fully take into account a fixed price component. Everything else being equal, consumers buying in online auctions tend to pay more for a given product when a fixed price component is included, and this effect increases as the magnitude of the fixed component increases.

Experiment 2 examines the effects of providing different types of *external reference-price information* on bidding behavior and selling prices in auctions. While there is ample evidence suggesting that external reference prices affect consumer purchase decision making in fixed-price markets (e.g., Mayhew and Winer 1992), their role in the context of auctions has not been explored to date.

One important price-related piece of information that may be part of the stimulus environment of an Internet auction is the seller-specified reserve price. Potential bidders may use the reserve price as a cue when making inferences about a product's value to them. That is, a reserve price may serve as a signal for value. Therefore, we predict that seller-specified reserve prices have a positive effect on bidders' willingness to pay for a product, and that higher reserve prices will lead to higher selling prices in auctions. At the same time, however, an increase in reserve price will also lead to a decrease in the number of bidders. The latter may, in turn, have a negative effect on selling prices. Therefore, reserve prices should have a dual effect on selling prices in Internet auctions. First, higher reserve prices are expected to have a direct positive effect on selling prices through their role as a signal for product value. Second, they should have an indirect negative effect on selling prices that is mediated by a reduction in the number of bidders.

The magnitude of the signaling effect of seller-specified reserve prices should be positively related to the amount of ambiguity that bidders perceive with respect to the value of a product to them. That is, consumers will rely more heavily on reserve price as a cue for value when their ability to assess the subjective utility of a product is poor. One way of reducing the ambiguity about a product's value is to provide potential bidders with an external reference price that is not under the complete control of the seller. Catalog values or other published types of price information may be used for this purpose. We expect that the availability of such an objective piece of reference-price information will reduce the signaling effect of reserve prices.

As in Experiment 1, a controlled field experiment using real-world auctions of stamps was conducted to test our hypotheses regarding the effects of external reference prices on auction outcomes. The magnitude of seller-specified reserve prices and the availability of objective reference-price information were varied systematically. As predicted, the inclusion (and increasing magnitude) of a reserve price reduces the number of bidders. In addition, consistent with our hypothesis, selling price increases as reserve price increases. Finally, the positive effect of reserve price on selling price may be diminished by the availability of an objective reference price.

This paper represents a first effort aimed at developing an understanding of consumers' bidding behavior in person-to-person auctions on the Internet. The results of two controlled field experiments suggest that individuals who place bids in real-world Internet auctions are subject to seemingly irrational biases–they tend to discount some unambiguously relevant pieces of information while unduly relying on certain types of unimportant, and possibly irrelevant, information. These findings demonstrate that bidders' valuations of products may be affected by characteristics of Internet auctions that can be specified by the seller in a largely arbitrary fashion, such as fixed price components and reserve prices. This suggests that auction markets on the Internet should not be uncritically classified as highly efficient. From a consumer-welfare standpoint, the findings reported here lead us to conclude that the potential for systematically manipulating consumer bidding behavior in Internet auctions appears to be large.

REFERENCES

Mayhew, Glenn E. and Russell S. Winer (1992), "An Empirical Analysis of Internal and External Reference Prices Using Scanner Data," *Journal of Marketing Research*, Vol. 19. (June), 62-70.

Milgrom, Paul and Robert J. Weber (1982), "A Theory of Auctions and Competitive Bidding," *Econometrica*, Vol. 50, No. 5, 1089-1122.

Morwitz, Vicki G, Eric A. Greenleaf, and Eric J. Johnson (1998), "Divide and Prosper: Consumers' Reactions to Partitioned Prices," *Journal of Marketing Research*, Vol. XXXV (November), 453-63.

Author Index